READINGS IN NATURAL LANGUAGE PROCESSING

edited by

Barbara J. Grosz
(SRI International)

Karen Sparck Jones
(University of Cambridge, Computer Laboratory)

Bonnie Lynn Webber
(University of Pennsylvania)

MORGAN KAUFMANN PUBLISHERS, INC.

95 FIRST STREET, LOS ALTOS, CALIFORNIA 94022

Editor and President   *Michael B. Morgan*
Permissions and Coordinating Editor   *Jennifer Ballentine*
Production Manager   *Mary Borchers*
Cover Designer   *Beverly Kennon-Kelley*
Typesetting   *Shirley Tucker and Valerie Brewster*
Production Assistants   *Debra Kern and Lisa de Beauclair*

Library of Congress Cataloging-in-Publication Data
Readings in natural language processing.
Bibliography: p.
Includes index.
1. Linguistics—Data processing.   I. Grosz,
Barbara J.   II. Sparck Jones, Karen, 1935–
III. Webber, Bonnie Lynn.
P98.R43   1986   410'.028'5   86-18488
ISBN 0-934613-11-7

Morgan Kaufmann Publishers, Inc.
95 First Street, Los Altos, California 94022
© 1986 by Morgan Kaufmann Publishers, Inc.
All rights reserved.
Printed in the United States of America

90 89 88 87 86   5 4 3 2 1

CONTENTS

CONTENTS

ACKNOWLEDGMENTS

The editors would like to offer the following transcontinental and transatlantic thanks: to Doug Appelt and Martha Pollack for their help with the index; to Bran Boguraev, Phil Cohen, Bob Moore, Ray Perrault, Fernando Pereira, Martha Pollack, and Steve Pulman for their advice on papers; to Roger Needham for moral support; to Ira Winston for rescuing us from a *Murphy's Law* disk crash on the day the manuscript had to go to the publisher; to David Cebula for his help in mastering KERMIT; and to all our computer networks without which, in spite of their failings, our distributed deliberating, editing, and commiserating could not have been done.

The editors would also like to thank the authors and publishers for their permission to reprint the articles in this volume:

C. R. Perrault, "On the Mathematical Properties of Linguistic Theories," *Computational Linguistics* 10, 1984, 165–176. Copyright © 1984, Association for Computational Linguistics. All rights reserved. Used by permission of ACL and the author. Copies of the publication from which this material is derived can be obtained from Dr. Donald E. Walker (ACL), Bell Communications Research, 445 South Street, Morristown, NJ 07924, USA.

A. Kuno and A. Oettinger, "Multiple Path Syntactic Analyzer," *Information Processing-62*, 1963, 306–312. *Proceedings of the ISIP Congress* 1962, C. M. Popplewell, ed., Amsterdam: North-Holland Publishing Company, 1962. Copyright © 1962, North-Holland Publishing Company. All rights reserved. Reprinted by permission of North-Holland and the authors.

J. Earley, "An Efficient Context-Free Parsing Algorithm," *CACM* 13(2), 1970, 94–102. Copyright © 1970, Association for Computing Machinery, Inc. All rights reserved. Reprinted by permission of ACM.

M. Kay, "Algorithm Schemata and Data Structures in Syntactic Processing," *CSL-80-12*, October 1980. Copyright © 1980, Xerox Corporation. All rights reserved. Reprinted courtesy of Xerox PARC and the author.

W. A. Woods, "Transition Network Grammars for Natural Language Analysis," *CACM* 3(10), 1970, 591–606. Copyright © 1970, Association for Computing Machinery, Inc. All rights reserved. Reprinted by permission of ACM and the author.

M. Marcus, "A Computational Account of Some Constraints on Language," *Theoretical Issues in Natural Language Processing-2*, D. Waltz, ed., 236–246, Urbana-Champaign: Association for Computational Linguistics, 1978. Copyright © 1978, Association for Computational Linguistics. All rights reserved. Used by permission of ACL and the author.

F. Pereira and D. Warren, "Definite Clause Grammars for Language Analysis," *Artificial Intelligence* 13, 1980, 231–278. Copyright © 1980, North-Holland Publishing Company. All rights reserved. Reprinted by permission of North-Holland and the authors.

M. Kay, "Parsing in Functional Unification Grammar," *Natural Language Parsing*, D. R. Dowty, L. Kartunnen, and A. Zwicky, eds., 251–278, Cambridge, England: Cambridge University Press, 1982. Copyright © 1982, Cambridge University Press. All rights reserved. Reprinted by permission of Cambridge University Press and the author.

J. Robinson, "DIAGRAM: A Grammar for Dialogues," *CACM* 25(1), 1982, 27–47. Copyright © 1982, Association for Computing Machinery, Inc. All rights reserved. Reprinted by permission of ACM and the author.

D. McDermott, "Tarskian Semantics, or No Notation Without Denotation!," *Cognitive Science* 2(3),

INTRODUCTION

Aim

The aim of these Readings is to bring together key papers in the field of automatic natural language processing (NLP) to provide an introduction and reference collection for students and researchers. For which students and researchers? We see at least three groups benefiting from this source book in NLP. First and most obviously, students and researchers already committed to NLP can benefit: for them, it puts into their hands many articles that have heretofore only appeared in technical journals, conference proceedings, and other books with limited availability. And, as we are all well aware, such volumes have a habit of disappearing from one's own shelves, as well as from library shelves, just when one needs them most.

But we also see this collection benefiting students and researchers in Artificial Intelligence (AI): for one, many of the problems confronting NLP come down to three of the central issues in AI—that is, representation, reasoning, and recognition. It should be a challenge to AI researchers to confront these problems and develop solutions that are not only elegant of themselves but are also applicable to NLP. Secondly, as AI attempts to give a computational account of those aspects of behavior we call intelligent, communicative behavior is firmly within its purview, and understanding the use of natural language is crucial to understanding communication. In this regard, this collection presents a rich array of approaches taken by the study of natural language communication. Thirdly, much of the world's knowledge has been set down in natural language: if it is to be of use to artificially intelligent entities, it must be converted to forms that such entities can absorb and manipulate. Thus from a practical point of view, AI students and researchers can benefit from an awareness of the field of NLP, as this collection provides.

Finally, we see students and researchers in linguistics benefiting from this collection: showing them the range of directions that processing accounts of language behavior (parsing, semantic interpretation, discourse-based interpretion, language generation, etc.) have taken and what these accounts are able to offer. More and more, processing notions are being integrated into linguists' vocabularies, and this collection presents both background and current information that can be of use to linguists in their own research.

Theoretical issues

The challenge of NLP is that a text is much less ambiguous to its audience than its parts are. Unambiguous wholes are built from elements that may be lexically, structurally, or referentially ambiguous. Therefore, a natural language processor has to resolve ambiguity, applying context to select from the possibilities allowed by the lexicon, grammar, and other processor components. This is hard because the discourse context that constrains the interpretation of text is also specified in large part by that text. Knowledge of the extralinguistic context makes ambiguity resolution easier but does not get rid of the problem. Ambiguity has to be resolved so the communicative functions of texts, like "requesting" and "informing," can be achieved, and larger-scale language-dependent tasks, like translation, can be carried out. These functions or tasks refer to the real world and are motivated by the need for action in that world, so the representation of text meaning has to serve the manipulation of knowledge about the world.

Ambiguity is most obviously an issue in natural language interpretation, but it is equally a concern of natural language generation. Language production requires not merely that the output utterances express the intended concepts, but that it does this effectively and unambiguously.

Thus for both interpretation and generation, a language processing system has to identify and characterize such things as word senses, message structure, and intended referents; and it has to determine the explicit and implicit meanings, and direct and indirect functions, of the individual utterance and the larger discourse. For this it requires a lexicon, a grammar, and an encoding of semantic, discourse, and pragmatic constraints, as well as processors to apply them to interpret or generate sentences and to determine and organize discourse. Additional processors embody knowledge about the referential and communicative properties of language and comprise many complex subprocesses, for example, for handling focus of attention, extracting presuppositions, or maintaining coherence. The language system must have access to knowledge about the world, both general and particular, including knowledge about the discourse participants and also about nonlinguistic tasks to which the system may be directed. It must have a meaning representation language for providing discourse representations capable of mediating communications between linguistic and nonlinguistic processes.

Architectural issues

Primary issues in NLP include characterizing the capabilities that various components of a language processing system should have, what form they should take, what part they play in processing, and how they should be organized to ensure that they play their parts effectively (i.e., what the system architecture should be). For example, what sort of grammar should be used with what parsing strategy, and what kind of lexical sense definition is appropriate, complemented by what set of pragmatic concepts and rules and what world knowledge representation schemes. These questions refer both to the substance of a language processor and, more abstractly, to the formalisms in which data and procedures are expressed. Underlying these issues are more general ones about the relative scope of linguistic and nonlinguistic system constituents. NLP, because of its manifest human connection, also raises issues about the kinds of models sought, giving particular emphasis to the general issue of the status of computational models in AI.

Structure

The papers we have assembled fall naturally into six groups dealing respectively with parsing and grammars, semantic interpretation, discourse interpretation (covering, for example, anaphor resolution), language actions and the intentions underlying them, language generation, and systems (notably interface systems). These chapter headings should be treated broadly and should not be taken to imply either that we are adopting a particular position about the way processing, and particularly input processing, should be done, or that problems and solutions assigned to one category have no relevance elsewhere. Many individual papers, placed in their most appropriate categories, also contribute to other areas. Since integrating different subprocesses is a major challenge for NLP, we regard the systems chapter as particularly important in marking significant contributions in this area, as well as more generally illustrating the development and current state of system building research.

Scope

Our main criterion for selecting papers was the manifest importance of their problem analyses or solution proposals to the topics discussed earlier. Within these topics, we have tried to cover a broad range of approaches to NLP. However, there are some conspicuous absences: for example, the treatment of "ill-formed" input, and tasks, such as translation, for which no key papers were offered. This does not imply we think these areas are unimportant. In some cases, like that of ill-formed input, the area is one of current activity that cannot be evaluated yet.

Our particular emphasis has been on computational language processing. The result is an absence of papers in subjects that are clearly relevant to NLP, linguistics and logic for example, but are not themselves language processing. We have not tried to include any linking papers even from the nearest parts of these areas, for instance ones on grammatical formalisms, since our space restrictions would have made the selection too arbitrary. But we think it important to note the relevance to language processing of the very substantial work being done in linguistic theory and especially grammar theory, in pragmatic and sociolinguistics, in formal language theory and logic, and in knowledge representation and inference, and to emphasize that this work can and should be brought to bear on NLP research. It is also necessary to draw attention to the value of the descriptive linguistic material available in conventional grammars and dictionaries.

We have also excluded papers in speech processing, primarily because it is a very large area but also because computational approaches to speech and language processing have been largely disjoint. And, though speech is currently an area of activity and great practical importance, very little speech processing work has yet made serious use of syntactic or higher levels of linguistic information or of extensive information on these levels, with the particularly strong requirements for an effective system architecture and process control that this implies.

The number of papers we could include in these Readings was necessarily very limited. We have included references to other particularly relevant items in the chapter introductions but have not attempted a comprehensive bibliography.

The historical context

NLP has a long and honorable history. The Dartmouth Conference on Artificial Intelligence, widely taken as the effective starting point for AI research, was held in 1956—so was the Second International Conference on Mechanical Translation. There is a widespread belief that AI-oriented NLP research began in the late sixties, and an equally widespread myth that the early workers on machine translation were all crooks or bozos. Both belief and myth are ill-founded. We had hoped to include more historical material, both to set later research in its developmental context by showing how early some ideas were put forward and to indicate the intrinsic interest and continuing relevance of some of the ideas put forward. However, it turned out to be impossible to provide a useful historical section, partly through pressure on space and partly because many early publications are now opaque and inadequate. We have included a key early syntactic paper by Kuno and Oettinger [17], (see Chapter 1), and a significant early system paper describing the BASEBALL system [11], (see Chapter 6), but we were unable to obtain a useful paper on the semantic research (focused on lexical disambiguation and using semantic primitives defined via a thesaurus as the basic interpretive apparatus,) of the Cambridge Language Research Unit [19], though this was the beginning of a continuing tradition.

Since we have necessarily been so selective, it should be noted here for the historical record that AI-flavor systems involving NLP built in the early sixties included, as well as Green et al's BASEBALL [11], Lindsay's SAD SAM [18], Bobrow's STUDENT [4], and Raphael's SIR [24]—the latter two found in [20]. The machine translation work itself led to a good deal of work on grammars and parsing, including the Harvard project [17,22], Hays' [13] and Robinson's [25] work at Rand, Harman's research [12], and Petrick's transformational effort [21], as well as Yngve's complementary work on generation [34] and Darlington's interpretation into logical form [8], and to the formulation of processing theories like Yngve's Depth Hypothesis [33]. Semantic case frames and networks figured in Ceccato's translation research [6]. (The bibliography following this Introduction lists additional historical references, including both important individual items and some collections and surveys.)

Setting aside political ramifications, the early machine translation work was in fact very valuable in focusing attention on the serious problems of dealing with unrestricted text in weakly circumscribed domains [1, 5]. The language processing research of the late sixties and early seventies followed the BASEBALL-type model, and in comparison with translation work, compensated for the convenience of domain restrictions by more concern with the requirements for explicit meaning representations and language-driven reasoning demanded by their tasks [26, 29, 30]. Woods' Airlines Guide query system [32], LUNAR, SHRDLU and, in a different style, MARGIE mark this phase, as the relevant papers in this collection show (see Chapter 2). Other papers in these Readings illustrate the subsequent development of NLP research. Broadly speaking, it focused first on the sentence, alone or in its immediate context, and on determining a sentence's literal meaning. The latter relied heavily on systems being limited to specific domains and relatively straightforward tasks. (That is, if you didn't let semantics get messy, any old hack seemed to work.) The results of this research are now being developed and applied in commercial systems, notably for database query. The sublanguage approach was also applied in the relatively limited amount of work done on longer texts, for example at New York University [15]. The relative tractability of syntax, and the large amount of work put into it by the linguistics community, made for useful progress and consolidation in the development of computational grammars and parsers, which can now be exploited as tools. During the seventies, the main focus of attention was on interpretation rather than generation. In the early part of the decade, attention was also on syntax-driven processing (though this was somewhat weakened by the use of semantic grammars), and on sequential rather than conjunctive architectures. There were exceptions to this dominent paradigm, most notably the work of Schank's group at Yale (see Chapter 2).

Starting in the late seventies, more attention was paid to semantic questions, though primarily in relation to expression structure rather than word sense; to discourse phenomena and such requirements as those for focusing and anaphor determination mechanisms; to the role of communicative goals and plans and their associated speech acts in language use; and to the problem-solving application of language for complex consultation and instruction tasks calling for the recognition and characterization of the user's mental state in terms of beliefs, task goals and plans, etc. At the same time, building interfaces for more demanding purposes than database query, or systems for such purposes as message processing, has called for more extensive world knowledge and a better integration of linguistic and nonlinguistic processing.

The state of the art

The current state of the art is characterized by, on the one hand, research effort devoted to the problems of discourse interpretation and generation, with the emphasis on above-sentence connectivity and communicative function, methods of integrating linguistic and nonlinguistic knowledge, and the provision of formalisms rich and powerful enough to express the heterogenous and complicated information all this requires. Language processing on the other, practical, hand is characterized by confident (sometimes overconfident) system building for restricted applications, including database query, message handling, and translation, typically on a fairly eclectic basis, and with some measure of success. However it is normally hard, if not impossible, to scale current systems up, either to widen the scope of their original task or to apply them to a new, more exigent task, as shown by the difficulty of extrapolating from a database to an expert system interface. Bringing principled theoretical approaches to bear effectively on practical, and hence usually idiosyncratic, applications remains a challenge. More importantly, there are crucial activities in language processing, like word sense determination or continuous summarizing, where little, if any, material progress has been made.

Briefly, the state of the art is one in which:

- enough has been learned about parsing and syntax for these to be textbook matters, and for there to be several large computational grammars.

- some semantic techniques have been proven useful in specific cases, though effective and comprehensive approaches have still to be demonstrated, indeed devised.

- discourse interpretation has had some valuable initial work done on it, as have language actions and intentions, but much more needs to be done on these and on how ways of handling them are to be combined with other system processes.

- a beginning has been made on generation not narrowly constrained by prior interpretation, but work is needed on the interplay between the conceptual and the linguistic elements in longer and freer text generation and between large and small scale discourse structure.

- as the systems chapter shows, those aspects of natural language *understanding* research ready for development primarily consist of being able to deal with literal meaning and direct function in a limited and well-defined task and domain context.

There has been some progress, but little in relation to what is wanted. We nevertheless believe the more recent papers in this collection show ways forward.

References

[1] Bar-Hillel, Y., A Demonstration of the Nonfeasibility of Fully Automatic High Quality Translation. In Alt, F. L. (editor), *Advances in Computers*, pages 158–163. Academic Press, New York, 1960, Reprinted in Bar-Hillel, "Language and Information," 1964.

[2] Bely, N., Borillo, A., Virbel, J. and Siot-Decauville, N., *Procedures d'Analyse Semantique Appliquees a la Documentation Scientifique*, Gauthier-Villars, Paris, 1970.

[3] Bobrow, D. G., Syntactic Theory in Computer Implementations. In Borko, H. (editor), *Automated Language Processing*, pages 215–251. Wiley, New York, 1967.

[4] Bobrow, D. G., Natural Language Input for a Computer Problem-Solving System. In Minsky, M. (editor), *Semantic Information Processing*, pages 135–215. MIT Press, Cambridge MA, 1968.

[5] Booth, A. D. (editor), *Machine Translation*, North-Holland, Amsterdam, 1967.

[6] Ceccato, S., Automatic Translation of Languages, *Information Storage and Retrieval* 2:105–158, 1964. See also Ceccato in Booth.

[7] Craig, J. A., Berezner, S. C., Carney, H. C. and Longyear, C. R., Deacon: Direct English Access and Control. In *AFIPS Conference Proceedings*, pages 365–380, 1966.

[8] Darlington, J. L., Machine Methods for Proving Logical Arguments Expressed in English, *Mechanical Translation* 8(3/4):41–67, 1965.

[9] Dewar, H., Bratley, P. and Thorne, J. P., A Program for the Syntactic Analysis of English Sentences, *Communications of the ACM* 12:476–479, 1969.

[10] Feigenbaum, E. and Feldman, J. (editor)., *Computers and Thought*, McGraw-Hill, New York, 1963.

[11] Green, B. F., Wolf, A. K., Chomsky, C. and Laughery, K., BASEBALL: An Automatic Question Answerer. In Feigenbaum, E. and Feldman, J. (editor), *Computers and Thought*, pages 207–216. McGraw-Hill, New York, 1963. Reproduced in this collection.

[12] Harman, G. H., Generative Grammars Without Transformation Rules, *Language* 39:597–616, 1963.

[13] Hays, D. G., Dependency Theory: A Formalism and Some Observations, *Language* 40:511–525, 1964.

[14] Hays, D. G. (editor), *Readings in Automatic Language Processing,* American Elsevier, New York, 1966.

[15] Hirschman, L., Grishman, R., and Sager, N., From Text to Structured Information—Automatic Processing of Medical Reports. In *Proceedings of the 1976 NCC,* pages 267–275. National Computer Conference, 1976.

[16] Klein, S., Automatic Paraphrasing in Essay Format, *Mechanical Translation* 8(3/4):68–83, 1965.

[17] Kuno, S. and Oettinger, A. G., Multiple-Path Syntactic Analyser. In Popplewell, C.M. (editor), *Information Processing 62,* pages 306–312. North-Holland, Amsterdam, 1963. Reproduced in this collection; see also Kuno in Hays.

[18] Lindsay, R. K., Inferential Memory as the Basis of Machines which Understand Language. In Feigenbaum, E. and Feldman, J. (editor), *Computers and Thought,* pages 217–233. McGraw-Hill, New York, 1963.

[19] Masterman, M., Needham, R. M., Sparck Jones, K. and Mayoh, B. *Agricola Incurvo Terram Dimovit Aratro,* Technical Report, Cambridge Language Research Unit, Cambridge, England, November, 1957. Reprinted, with a new introduction by K. Sparck Jones, Computer Laboratory, University of Cambridge, 1986.

[20] Minsky, M. (editor), *Semantic Information Processing,* MIT Press, Cambridge MA, 1968.

[21] Petrick, S. R., *A Recognition Procedure for Transformational Grammars,* PhD thesis, Massachusetts Institute of Technology, 1965.

[22] Plath, W. J., Multiple-Path Analysis and Automatic Translation. In Booth, A.D. (editor), *Machine Translation,* pages 267–315. North-Holland, Amsterdam, 1967.

[23] Quillian, M. R., Semantic Memory. In Minsky, M. (editor), *Semantic Information Processing,* pages 227–270.

MIT Press, Cambridge MA, 1968.

[24] Raphael, B., SIR: Semantic Information Retrieval. In Minsky, M. (editor), *Semantic Information Processing,* pages 33–145. MIT Press, Cambridge MA, 1968.

[25] Robinson, J. J. and Marks, S., *PARSE: A System for Automatic Analysis of English Text,* Technical Report, The Rand Corporation, Santa Monica CA, September, 1965. Two parts, AD 621 310 and 311.

[26] Rustin, R. (editor), *Natural Language Processing,* Algorithmics Press, New York, 1973, Courant Computer Science Symposium 8.

[27] Salton, G., *Automatic Information Organization and Retrieval,* McGraw-Hill, New York, 1968. See also Salton in Hays.

[28] Simmons, R. F., Klein, S. and McConlogue, K. L., Indexing and Dependency Logic for Answering English Questions, *American Documentation* 15:196–204, 1964.

[29] Simmons, R. F., Answering English Questions by Computer: A Survey, *Communications of the ACM* 8:53–70, 1965. Also reported in H. Borko (ed), "Automated Language Processing," 1967.

[30] Simmons, R. F., Natural Language Question-Answering Systems: 1969, *Communications of the ACM* 13:15–30, 1970.

[31] Weizenbaum, J., ELIZA—A Computer Program for the Study of Natural Language Communication Between Man and Machine, *Communications of the ACM* 10:36–43, 1966.

[32] Woods, W. A., Procedural Semantics for a Question Answering Machine. In *1968 AFIPS Conference Proceedings,* 33:457–471, 1968.

[33] Yngve, V. H., The Depth Hypothesis. In *Proceedings of Symposia in Applied Mathematics,* pages 130–138. American Mathematical Society, Providence RI, 1961.

[34] Yngve, V. H., Random Generation of English Sentences. In *Proceedings of the 1961 International Conference on Machine Translation of Languages and Applied Language Analysis,* pages 65–80. Her Majesty's Stationery Office, London, 1962.

I. SYNTACTIC MODELS

The oldest and most well-developed area of NLP is that concerned with the syntax of natural languages—how it is that the words in a sentence group into phrases[1] and phrases into larger phrases. Research in this area is concerned with two different (but obviously related) notions: *grammars* and *parsing algorithms.*

A *grammar* is a finite specification of a possibly infinite language that captures its regularities. (Any NL is most certainly infinite.) A grammar can be used in generating the sentences of the language; it can also be used to determine whether a given string belongs to the language and if so, to determine its structure according to the grammar. Phrase structure grammars, often used in NLP systems, are collections of rules that specify how individual phrases can be expanded into their constituent subphrases. In many cases, the phrase structure rules are augmented in various ways (see *Pereira and Warren* and *Robinson,* this chapter). Other types of grammars that have been used for NLs include transformational grammars [5], systemic grammars [9] and tree adjunction grammars [10].

Parsing algorithms specify how to apply a grammar to a sequence of words to produce a structured representation, or *parse tree.*[2] A *parser* comprises a grammar and a parsing algorithm, although in several NLP systems, the "parser" sometimes also includes a separate or integrated process that produces a representation of the meaning of the input utterance.[3]

Work on syntactic models for NLP systems has drawn on results from both linguistic theory (e.g., formalisms that can be used to characterize the grammatical strings of a NL) and computer science (e.g., results in formal language theory, parsing, and compiling). Both endeavors share (in addition to a common ancestor in the Chomsky hierarchy [4]) concern with generative power. However, whereas linguistic theory has been motivated by issues such as language universals, (formal) learnability, psychological reality and simplicity, parsing and compiler theory have been more concerned with efficiency and control of search. Research on parsers for NLP systems has typically focused on the concerns of the latter more than of the former, with additional concern with coverage (the range of constructions that are handled).

The literature on syntactic models is vast, and we have been able to include in this collection only a small sample of the work that has been done. An excellent discussion of syntactic issues from a computational perspective is provided in [20]. We have included a paper on mathematical properties of linguistic formalisms (*Perrault*), one on a large grammar

---

[1]Syntax broadly construed also includes issues of word structure, or *morphology,* but we have not included any papers on that topic here. Winograd's text [20] provides a simple algorithm; one of the most sophisticated treatments is that of Koskenniemi [12].

[2]If the algorithm just checks whether or not a string belongs to the language generated by the grammar and does not assign it any structure, it is usually called a "recognition algorithm."

[3]Some of these NLP systems never actually construct a parse tree: they may do a complete parsing of the string according to a grammar, but integrate semantic processing in such a way as to produce only a representation of the meaning of the input [14] or they may use grammatical information only minimally to identify phrases and rely almost solely on semantic processing to put the phrases (or their interpretations) together (see *Schank* and *Wilks,* Chapter 2).

(*Robinson*), three that describe particular techniques for efficient parsing of context-free languages (*Kuno and Oettinger, Earley, Kay*), and four that describe different architectures used in NLP systems (*Woods, Marcus, Kay, Pereira and Warren*).

We have focused on parsers for context-free (CF) languages for three reasons. First, they are widely studied and understood and hence have an array of efficient algorithms. Secondly, many of the grammars used for NLP systems are CF. Thirdly, even where the grammars are not CF (e.g., where CF rules have been augmented with additional conditions), parsers for them can be based on techniques for efficient CF parsing, though with various adaptations and extensions. While it has long been conjectured that NLs are not CF, it is only recently that solid arguments to this effect have been advanced [17, 6], and these arguments have centered on constructions not handled in any NLP system thus far.

The papers in this chapter are almost entirely concerned with grammars and parsing algorithms for English. This focus on English has been true of (formal) linguistic theory as well. While there are both theoretical and practical reasons for investigating other NLs, computationally oriented work on these has so far been less extensive.

On the Mathematical Properties of Linguistic Formalisms

Perrault's paper provides a survey of the mathematical properties of several of the most well-known linguistic formalisms: transformational grammar, lexical-functional grammar, generalized phrase structure grammar, and tree adjunction grammar. As well as providing excellent pointers into the literature on issues of complexity and generative capacity, this paper provides an interesting perspective on the significance of such results and suggests a range of issues that should be considered (but typically are not) when comparing formalisms with respect to computational use.

Multiple Path Syntactic Analyzer

As mentioned above, parsing algorithms for CF grammars have played an important role in syntactic models for NLP systems. Because of the inherent ambiguity of NLs, control issues of top-down (expectation-driven) versus bottom-up (data-driven) parsing, lookahead, and backtracking have been major concerns in adapting parsing algorithms for use in NLP systems.

This paper describes the top-down parsing algorithm used by Kuno and Oettinger in the Harvard Syntactic Analyzer. We have included it here not only for historical reasons, but also because it reports on the first use of a well-formed substring table (WFST), which was later used in Wood's ATN parser (see *Woods*, this chapter). A WFST is a record of all complete constituents that have been found thus far and is a way of preventing a top-down parser from looking for and finding the same constituent multiple times.

An Efficient Context-Free Parsing Algorithm

Earley's paper describes an algorithm (commonly referred to as the *Early algorithm*) that combines both top-down and bottom-up processing, called here "prediction" and "scanning," respectively. It also provides for k-symbol lookahead, although it is most efficient when k = 1. In addition to presenting the parsing algorithm,[4] the paper reports both on time and space bounds for the algorithm and on empirical results in using it. This algorithm is a classic departure point for parsing algorithms used in many NLP systems.

Algorithm Schemata and Data Structures in Syntactic Processing

Kay's paper provides an overall framework in which to examine parsing strategies for CF grammars. It discusses these from the vantage points both of psychological models and of computer systems (as well as commenting on the relationship between the two). We have included it, however, because it contains an extensive and clear explanation of the *chart* data structure and its use in eliminating redundant parsing of constituents of ambiguous sentences. The chart is an extension of the WFST (see *Kuno and Oettinger*, this chapter) that has been incorporated in a large number of parsing algorithms for NL. (It is used for the same purpose as the parsing matrix in Earley's algorithm; see *Earley*, this chapter.)

Transition Network Grammars for Natural Language Analysis

Woods' paper describes one of the first substantial parsers for non-CF languages for NLP. *Augmented transition networks* (ATNs) are an extension of recursive transition networks (RTNs) which recognize exactly the class of CF languages. Unlike RTNs, ATNs have *registers* that can be used for storing partial parse trees or flagging features, and *conditions*

---

[4]A recognition algorithm is given first. The section "Practical Use" describes the augmentations needed to produce a parser.

that typically test registers to determine whether a given arc should be taken. These extensions enable ATN grammars to generate all recursively enumerable sets, thereby making them equal in capacity to transformational grammar (TG). In fact, ATNs were developed in the framework of TG, as a computationally efficient way to recover the base structure of a sentence (for input to subsequent semantic processing) without having to find the appropriate sequence of reverse transformations.

Parsers for ATN grammars are primarily top-down processors, though practical implementations incorporate substantial lookahead in the form of word (WRD) tests on the arcs. A great deal of effort has gone into efficient implementation of ATN parsers, including work on compiling the parser and grammar into a LISP program and on identifying mutually exclusive sets of arcs [3].[5]

ATNs have been incorporated in a large number of NLP systems; they have been used as the basis of "semantic-grammar" systems (see *Hendrix et al.* and *Burton and Brown,* Chapter 6) as well as for more general grammars of English. ATNs have proved to be a convenient means for specifying large grammars [1]. A good overview of ATNs and their use in specifying grammars appears in [2].

DIAGRAM: A Grammar for Dialogues

Augmented phrase structure grammars (APSGs) provide an alternative way of moving from simple CF grammars to ones sufficiently powerful for specifying a NL. Like ATNs, they have been used to write large grammars for NLP systems. Robinson's DIAGRAM (described here) is one such effort, and the grammar developed for the Linguistic String Project [15] is another. DIAGRAM grew out of a grammar developed for the SRI speech understanding system [18] and has subsequently been incorporated into several NLP systems, most recently TEAM (see *Martin, Appelt and Pereira,* Chapter 6).

An extensive grammar is a crucial component of any robust NLP system, because it prescribes the range of constructions the system can handle. A major contribution of this paper is the discussion of various major design decisions. The construction of large grammars remains difficult because of the complexity of interactions among rules as the grammar increases. It is an art as much as a science. Robinson's paper thus provides important insight

for anyone designing a large grammar, even one based on a different formalism.

A Computational Account of Some Constraints on Language

Marcus' paper describes a radically different approach to dealing with local ambiguity.[6] Marcus rejects the backtracking control strategy that ATNs use to cope with local ambiguity and instead proposes a mechanism that operates "strictly deterministically." The "Determinism Hypothesis" underlying the paper claims that NLs can be parsed without either backtracking or pseudo-parallelism, and that all structures created by the parser are permanent. Although no formal results have been published, the basic Marcus parser appears to accept CF languages. Note however that the parser performs recognition in linear time (i.e., the strings it accepts are linear-time parseable).

Marcus' parser uses two data structures: an active node stack and a three-cell constituent buffer. The buffer provides lookahead for the parser. Although it is severely limited in size (a limitation that is crucial to the determinism hypothesis), each cell of the buffer is permitted to hold a single grammatical constituent of any type and size. The extension of lookahead from words (individual symbols) to constituents is an important contribution of Marcus' work.

In addition to describing the basic mechanisms of the parser, the paper discusses how the parser and the determinism hypothesis on which it is founded explain two constraints on NLs proposed by Chomsky. The book based on Marcus' dissertation [13] contains more detail on both the parser and its relevance to current linguistic theory.

Definite Clause Grammars for Language Analysis

Pereira and Warren describe a formalism for defining grammars, based on a restricted form of first-order logic, namely *definite* (or, Horn) clause logic. This is the same subclass of logic treated in the programming language PROLOG because of its available efficient proof procedures. Grammar rules in a *Definite Clause Grammar* (DCG) are written as logical formulas. The process of recognizing whether a string belongs to the language of the DCG then becomes equivalent to proving a theorem in the logic.

---

[5]These latter are called "Group Arcs": if one arc in a group can be traversed successfully, it blocks the others from being tried if the parser subsequently backtracks to that point.

[6]A sentence is locally ambiguous if one cannot decide unequivocably at a particular point how the input at that point should be analyzed, but information in the remainder of the sentence will resolve this ambiguity. In contrast, a sentence is globally ambiguous when the complete sentence actually has multiple readings.

Additional arguments to predicates (corresponding to nonterminals in the grammar) are used both to build parse structures and to provide for testing contextual features such as number agreement. DCGs, like ATNs and APSGs, are an extension of CFGs: in DCGs, logical variables perform the work of registers in ATNs, and goal constructs accomplish the work of tests and actions on arcs.

DCGs can be implemented directly in PROLOG, and a number of NLP systems have been written based on them [19, 7]. These systems use (1) unification to pass around information and to build structures and (2) PROLOG's built-in backtracking mechanism to handle ambiguity.

The paper provides a comparison of DCGs with ATNs (see *Woods*, this chapter), including a discussion of how to translate an ATN grammar into a DCG. Pereira and Warren argue for DCGs as a formalism on a number of grounds, including the inherently execution-related features of an ATN grammar (which a grammar writer must be aware of) versus a DCT's clear separation of its declarative and procedural aspects

Unification Grammar

The idea of using unification as the main operation in parsing actually predates DCGs and other logic grammars. Kay's paper describes one of the earliest proposed formalisms, functional unification grammar (FUG). The formalism was called simply "unification grammar" in Kay's earlier papers; the newer name both makes clear the distinction from other formalisms that use unification and the importance Kay attributes to the functions that various language constructs can serve. Although the current paper describes methods for parsing using FUG, the formalism was designed to be neutral with respect to generation versus parsing and has been applied to both (see *Appelt, McKeown*, Chapter 5, for its application to NL generation).

A number of unification-based formalisms developed in the last several years build on FUG. This includes work both within the formal linguistic tradition (most notably LFG [11] and versions of GPSG [8]) and in computational linguistics (PATR [16]).

References

[1] Bates, M. and Bobrow, R. J., A transportable natural language interface. In *Proc. of 6th Ann. Int'l SIGIR Conf. on Research and Development in Information Retrieval*, ACM, 1983.

[2] Bates, M., The Theory and Practice of Augmented Transition Network Grammars. In Bolc, L. (editor), *Natural Language Communication with Computers*, Springer-Verlag, 1978.

[3] Burton, R. R. and Woods, W. A., A Compiling System for Augmented Transition Networks. In *COLING 76. Int'l Conf. on Comp. Ling.*, 6th, Ottawa, 1976.

[4] Chomsky, N., Three models for the description of language, *IEEE Trans. on Information Theory* 2:113–124, 1956.

[5] Chomsky, N., *Aspects of the Theory of Syntax*, MIT Press, Cambridge MA, 1965.

[6] Culy, C. D., The complexity of the vocabulary of Bambara, *Linguistics and Philosophy* 8:345–51, 1985.

[7] Dahl, V., Un systeme deductif d'interrogation de banques de donnees en espagnol, November, 1977.

[8] Gazdar, G., Klein, E., Pullum, G. K., and Sag, I., *Generalized Phrase Structure Grammar*, Blackwell, 1985.

[9] Halliday, M. A. K., Notes on Transitivity and Theme in English, *Journal of Linguistics* 3,4:199–244, 179–215, 1967.

[10] Joshi, A. K., Tree adjoining grammars: How much context-sensitivity is required to provide reasonable structural descriptions? In Dowty, D., Karttunen, L., Zwicky, A. (editors), *Natural Language Processing: Psycholinguistics, Computational and Theoretical Properties*, pages 206–250. Cambridge University Press, Cambridge, 1985.

[11] Kaplan, R. and Bresnan, J., Lexical-functional grammar: a formal system for grammatical representation. In Bresnan, J. (editor), *The Mental Representation of Grammatical Relations*, pages 173–281. MIT Press, Cambridge MA, 1982.

[12] Koskenniemi, K., *Two-level Model for Morphological Analysis*, PhD thesis, Univ. of Helsinki, 1983.

[13] Marcus, M. P., *A Theory of Syntactic Recognition for Natural Language*, MIT Press, Cambridge, MA, 1980.

[14] Pulman, S. G., A Parser That Doesn't. In *Proceedings of the Second European Conference of the ACL*, pages 128–135, 1985.

[15] Sager, N., *Natural Language Information Processing*, Addison Wesley, New York, 1981.

[16] Shieber, S. M., The design of a computer language for linguistic information. In *Proc of Int'l Conf. on Comp. Ling.*, 10th, pages 362–66. COLING, 1985.

[17] Shieber, S. M., Evidence against the context-freeness of natural language, *Linguistics and Philosophy* 8:333–43, 1985.

[18] Walker, D., *Understanding Spoken Language*, Elsevier North-Holland, New York, 1978.

[19] Warren, D. H. D. and Pereira, F. C. N., An efficient easily adaptable system for interpreting natural language queries. *AJCL* 8(3–4):110–22, 1982.

[20] Winograd, T., *Language as a cognitive process. Volume 1: Syntax*, Addison Wesley, Reading, MA, 1983.

On the Mathematical Properties of Linguistic Theories[1]

C. Raymond Perrault

Artificial Intelligence Center
SRI International
Menlo Park, CA 94025
and
Center for the Study of Language and Information
Stanford University

Metatheoretical findings regarding the decidability, generative capacity, and recognition complexity of several syntactic theories are surveyed. These include context-free, transformational, lexical-functional, generalized phrase structure, tree adjunct, and stratificational grammars. The paper concludes with a discussion of the implications of these results with respect to linguistic theory.

1. Introduction

The development of new formalisms for expressing linguistic theories has been accompanied, at least since Chomsky and Miller's early work on context-free languages, by the study of their metatheory. In particular, numerous results on the decidability, generative capacity, and, more recently, the recognition complexity of these formalisms have been published (and rumored!). This paper surveys some of these results and discusses their significance for linguistic theory. However, we will avoid entirely the issue of whether one theory is more descriptively adequate than another. We will consider context-free, transformational, lexical-functional, generalized phrase structure, tree adjunct, and stratificational grammars.[2]

Although this paper focuses on metatheoretic results as arbiters among theories as models of human linguistic capacities, they may have other uses as well. Complexity results could be utilized for making decisions about the implementation of parsers as components of computer-based language-understanding systems. However, as Stanley Peters has pointed out, no one should underestimate the pleasure to be derived from ferreting out these results![3]

2. Preliminary Definitions

We assume that the reader is familiar with the basic definitions of regular, context-free (CF), context-sensitive (CS), recursive, and recursively enumerable (r.e.) languages, as well as with their acceptors (see Hopcroft and Ullman 1979). We will be much concerned with the problem of recognizing whether a string is contained in a given language (the **recognition problem**) and with that of

[1] This research was sponsored in part by the National Science and Engineering Research Council of Canada under Grant A9285. It was made possible in part by a gift from the Systems Development Foundation. An earlier version of this paper appeared in the *Proceedings of the 21st Annual Meeting of the Association for Computational Linguistics*, Cambridge, MA, June 1983.

I would like to thank Bob Berwick, Alex Borgida, Jim Hoover, Aravind Joshi, Lauri Karttunen, Fernando Pereira, Stanley Peters, Peter Sells, Hans Uszkoreit, and the referees for their suggestions.

[2] Although we will not examine them here, formal studies of other syntactic theories have been undertaken: e.g. Warren (1979) for Montague's PTQ (1973). Pereira and Shieber (1984) use techniques from the denotational semantics of programming languages to investigate the feature systems of several unification-based theories.

[3] It may be worth pointing out that the introduction of formal argumentation in linguistics has not always been beneficial. Some pseudoformal arguments against rival theories were unquestionably accepted by an audience that did not always have the mathematical sophistication to be critical. For example, Postal's claim (1964b) that two-level stratificational grammars generated only context-free languages was based on an imprecise definition by its proponents, as well as by the failure to see that among the more precise definitions were many very powerful ones.

generating one (or all) derivations of the string (the **parsing problem**).

Some elementary definitions from complexity theory may be useful. Further details may be found in Aho et al. (1974). Complexity theory is the study of the resources required by algorithms, usually space and time. Let $f(x)$ be a function, say, the recognition function for a language L. The most interesting results we could obtain regarding f would be a lower bound on the resources needed to compute f on a machine of a given architecture, say, a von Neumann computer or a parallel array of neurons. These results over whole classes of machines are very difficult to obtain, and none of any significance exist for parsing problems.

Restricting ourselves to a specific machine model and an algorithm M for f, we can ask about the **cost** (e.g., in time or space) $c(x)$ of executing M on a specific input x. Typically, c is too fine-grained to be useful: what one studies instead is a function c_w whose argument is an integer n denoting the size of the input to M, and which gives some measure of the cost of processing inputs of length n. Complexity theorists have been most interested in the **asymptotic** behaviour of c_w, i.e., the behaviour of c_w as n gets large.

If one is interested in upper bounds on the behaviour of M, one usually defines $c_w(n)$ as the maximum of $c(x)$ over all inputs x of size n. This is called the **worst-case complexity function** for M. Other definitions are possible: for example, one can define the **expected complexity function** $c_e(n)$ for M as the average of $c(x)$ over all inputs of length n. c_e might be more useful than c_w if one had an idea as to the distribution of possible inputs to M. Not only are realistic distributions rarely available, but the introduction of probabilistic considerations makes the study of expected complexity technically more difficult than that of worst-case complexity. For a given problem, expected and worst-case measures may be quite different.[4]

It is quite difficult to get detailed descriptions of c_w; for many purposes, however, a cruder estimate is sufficient. The next abstraction involves ".lumping". classes of c_w functions into simpler ones that demonstrate their asymptotic behaviour more clearly and are easier to manipulate. This is the purpose of O-notation (read "big-oh notation"). Let $f(n)$ and $g(n)$ be two functions. Function f is said to be $O(g)$ if a constant multiple of g is an upper bound for f, for all but a finite number of values of n. More precisely, f is $O(g)$ if there is are constants K and n_0 such that for all $n > n_0$, $f(n) < K * g(n)$.

Given an algorithm M, we will say that M is $TIME(g)$ or, equivalently, that its worst-case time complexity is $O(g)$ if the worst-case time cost function $c_w(n)$ for M is $O(g)$.[5] This merely says that almost all inputs to M of size n can be processed in time at most a constant times $g(n)$. It does *not* say that all inputs require $g(n)$ time, or Ruzzo machine that implements f. Also, if two algorithms A_1 and A_2 are available for a function f, and if their worst-case complexity can be given respectively as $O(g_1)$ and

$O(g_2)$, and $g_1 \leq g_2$, it may still be true that for a large number of cases (maybe even all those likely to be encountered in practice), A_2 will be the preferable algorithm simply because the constant K_1 for g_1 may be much larger than is K_2 for g_2. A parsing-related example is given in Section 3.

In examining known results pertaining to the recognition complexity of various theories, it is useful to consider how robust they are in the face of changes in the machine model from which they were derived. These models can be divided into two classes: sequential and parallel. Sequential models (Aho et al. 1974) include the familiar single- and multitape Turing machines (TM) as well as random-access machines (RAM) and random-access stored-program machines (RASP). A RAM is like a TM except that its working memory is random-access rather than sequential. A RASP is like a RAM but stores its program in its memory. Of all these models, the RASP is most like a von Neumann computer.

All these sequential models can simulate one another in ways that do not require great changes in time complexity. For example, a k-tape Turing Machine that runs in time $O(t)$ can be simulated by a RAM in time $O(t \log t)$, conversely, a RAM running in $O(t)$ can be simulated by a k-tape TM in time $O(t^2)$.. In fact, all the familiar sequential models are **polynomially related:** they can simulate one another with at most a polynomial loss in efficiency.[6] Thus, if a syntactic model is known to have a difficult recognition problem when implemented on one sequential model, execution of an equivalent algorithm on another sequential machine will not be much easier.

Transforming a sequential algorithm to one on a parallel machine with a fixed number K of processors provides at most a factor K improvement in speed. More interesting results are obtained when the number of processors is allowed to grow with the size of the problem, e.g., with the length of the string to be parsed. These processors can be viewed as connected together in a circuit, with inputs entering at one end and outputs being produced at the other. The *depth* of the circuit, or the maximum number of processors that data must be passed through from input to output, corresponds to the parallel *time* required to complete the computation. A problem that has a solution on a *sequential* machine in polynomial time and in space s will have a solution on a *parallel* machine with a polynomial number of processors and circuit depth (and hence parallel time) $O(s^2)$. This means that algorithms with sequential solutions requiring small space (such as deterministic CSLs) have fast parallel solutions.

---

[4] Hoare's Quicksort algorithm, for example, has expected time complexity of $O(n \log n)$ and worst-case complexity of $O(n^2)$, using notation defined in the next paragraph.

[5] Similarly, let M be $SPACE(g)$ if the worst-case space complexity of M is $O(g)$.

[6] RAMs and RASPs are allowed to store arbitrarily large numbers in their registers. These results assume that the cost of performing elementary operations on those numbers is proportional to their length, i.e. to their logarithm.

For a comprehensive survey of parallel computation, see Cook (1981).

3. Context-Free Languages

Recognition techniques for context-free languages are well known (Aho and Ullman 1972). The so-called CKY or "dynamic programming" method is attributed by Hays (1962) to J. Cocke; it was discovered independently by Kasami (1965) and Younger (1967), who showed it to be $O(n^3)$. It requires the grammar to be in Chomsky Normal Form, and putting an arbitrary grammar in CNF may square its size. Berwick and Weinberg (1982) point out that, since the complexity of parsing algorithms is generally at least linearly dependent on the size of the grammar, this requirement may make CKY less than optimal for parsing short sentences.

Earley's algorithm recognizes strings in arbitrary CFGs in time $O(n^3)$ and space $O(n^2)$, and in time $O(n^2)$ for unambiguous CFGs. Graham, Harrison, and Ruzzo (1980) offer an algorithm that unifies CKY and Earley's algorithm (1970), and discuss implementation details.

Valiant (1975) showed how to interpret the CKY algorithm as the finding of the transitive closure of a matrix and thus reduced CF recognition to matrix multiplication, for which subcubic algorithms exist. Because of the enormous constants of proportionality associated with this method, it is not likely to be of much practical use, either an implementation method or as a "psychologically realistic" model.

Ruzzo (1979) has shown how CFLs can be recognized by Boolean circuits of depth $O(\log(n)^2)$, and therefore that parallel recognition can be accomplished in time $O(\log(n)^2)$. The required circuit size is polynomial in n.

So as not to be mystified by the *upper bounds* on CF recognition, it is useful to remember that no known CFL requires more than linear time, nor is there even a nonconstructive proof of the existence of such a language.

This is also a good place to recall the difference between recognition and parsing: if parsing requires that distinct structures be produced for all parses, it will be $TIME(2^n)$, since in some grammars sentences of length n may have 2^n parses (Church and Patil 1982). For an empirical comparison of various parsing methods, see Slocum (1981).

4. Transformational Grammar

From its earliest days, discussions of transformational grammar (TG) have included consideration of matters computational.

Peters and Ritchie (1973a) provided some the first nontrivial results regarding the generative power of TGs. Their model reflects the *Aspects* version quite faithfully, including transformations that move and add constituents, and delete them subject to recoverability. All transformations are obligatory, and applied cyclically from the bottom up. They show that every r.e. set can be generated by applying a set of transformations to a context-sensitive base. The proof is quite simple: the right-hand sides of the type-0 rules that generate the r.e. set are padded with a new "blank" symbol to make them at least as long as their left-hand sides. Rules are added to allow the blank symbols to commute with all others. These context-sensitive rules are then used as the base of a TG whose only transformation deletes the blank symbols.

Thus, if the transformational formalism itself is supposed to *characterize* the grammatical strings of possible natural languages, then the only languages being excluded by the formalism are those that are not enumerable under any model of computation. The characterization assumption is further discussed in Section 9.

At the expense of a considerably more intricate argument, the previous result can be strengthened (Peters and Ritchie 1971) to show that every r.e. set can be generated by a context-free based TG, as long as a **filter** – an intersection with a regular set – can be applied to the phrase-markers produced by the transformations. In fact, the base grammar can be *independent* of the language being generated. The proof involves the simulation of a TM by a TG. The transformations first generate an "input tape" for the TM being simulated, then apply the TM productions, one per cycle of the grammar. The filter ensures that the base grammar will generate just as many S nodes as necessary to generate the input string and do the simulation. In this case too, if the transformational formalism is supposed to characterize the possible natural languages, the **universal base hypothesis** (Peters and Ritchie 1969), according to which all natural languages can be generated from the same base grammar, is empirically vacuous: *any* recursively enumerable language can.

Following Peters and Ritchie's work, several attempts were made to find a restricted form of the transformational model that is descriptively adequate, yet whose generated languages are recursive (see, for example, LaPointe 1977). Since a key part of the proof in Peters and Ritchie (1971) involves the user of a filter on the final derivation trees, Peters and Ritchie (1973c) examined the consequences of forbidding final filtering. They show that, if S is the recursive symbol in the CF base, the generated language L is *predictably enumerable* and *exponentially bounded*. A language L is **predictably enumerable** if there is an "easily" computable function $t(n)$ that gives an upper bound on the number of tape squares needed by its enumerating TM to enumerate the first n elements of L. L is **exponentially bounded** if there is a constant K such that, for every string x in L, there is another string x' in L whose length is at most K times the length of x.

The class of nonfiltering languages is quite unusual, including all the CFLs (obviously), but also properly intersecting the CSLs, the recursive languages, and the r.e. languages.

The source of nonrecursivity in transformationally generated languages is that transformations can delete large parts of the tree, thus producing surface trees that are arbitrarily smaller than the deep structure trees they were derived from. This is what Chomsky's "recoverability of deletions" condition was meant to avoid. In his thesis, Petrick (1965) defines the following condition on transformational derivations: a derivation satisfies the terminal-length-increasing condition if the length of the yield of any subtree u, resulting from the application of the transformational cycle to a subtree t, is greater than the length of the yield of any subtree u' resulting from the application of the cycle to a subtree t' of t.

Petrick shows that, if all recursion in the base grammar "passes through S" and all derivations satisfy the **terminal-length-increasing** condition, then the generated language is recursive. Using a slightly more restricted model of transformations Rounds (1973) strengthens this result by showing that the resulting languages are in fact context-sensitive.

In an unpublished paper, Myhill shows that, if Petrick's condition is weakened to terminal-length-nondecreasing, the resulting languages can be recognized in space that is at most *exponential* in the length of the input. This implies that recognition can be done in at most double-exponential time, but Rounds (1975) proves that not only can recognition be done in *exponential time*, but that every language recognizable in exponential time can be generated by a TG satisfying the terminal-length-nondecreasing condition and recoverability of deletions.

This is a very strong result, because of the closure properties of the class of exponential-time languages. To see why this is so requires a few more definitions.

Let **P** be the class of all languages that can be recognized in polynomial time on a deterministic TM, and **NP** the class of all languages that can be recognized in polynomial time on a nondeterministic TM. **P** is obviously contained in **NP**, but the converse is not known, although there is much evidence that it is false.

There is a class of problems, the so-called **NP-complete** problems, which are in NP and "as difficult" as any other problems in NP in the following sense: if any of them could be shown to be in P, all the problems in NP would also be in P. One way to show that a language L is NP-complete is to show that L is in NP and that every other language L_0 in NP can be **polynomially transformed** into L, − i.e., that there is a deterministic TM, operating in polynomial time, that will transform an input w to L into an input w_0 to L_0 such that w is in L if and only if w_0 is in L_0. In practice, to show that a language is NP-complete, one shows that it is in NP and that some already known NP-complete language can be polynomially transformed into it.

All the known NP-complete languages can be recognized in exponential time on a deterministic machine, and none have been shown to be recognizable in less than exponential time. Thus, since the restricted transformational languages of Rounds *characterize* the exponential languages, if all of them were to be in P, P would be equal to NP. Putting it another way, if P is not equal

to NP, some transformational languages (even those satisfying the terminal-length-nonincreasing condition) have no "tractable" (i.e., polynomial-time) recognition procedures on any deterministic TM. It should be noted that this result also holds for all the other known sequential models of computation, as they are all polynomially related, and even for parallel machines with as many as a polynomial number of processors.

All the results outlined so far in this section are inspired by the model of transformational grammar presented in *Aspects*. More recent versions of the theory are substantially different, primarily in that most of the constructions handled in terms of deletions from the base trees are now handled using traces (i.e., constituents with no lexical material) indexed to other constituents. In his contribution to this issue (p. 189), Berwick presents a formalization of the theory of Government and Binding (GB) and some of its consequences. The formalization is unusual in that it reduces grammaticality to well-formedness conditions on what he calls annotated surface structures. From these conditions, two results follow. One is that for every GB grammar G there is a constant K such that for every string w in $L(G)$ and for every annotated surface structure s whose yield is w, the number of nodes in s is bounded by $K*length(w)$. This, of course, ensures that the $L(G)$ is recursive. The second result is that GB languages all have the linear growth or arithmetic growth property: for every sufficiently long string w in a GB language L there is another string w' in L which is at most K symbols shorter than w.

A few comments about Berwick's formalization and results are in order. To begin with, the formalization is clearly a quite radical simplification of current practice among GB practitioners, as it does not reflect D-structure, LF, or PF, nor case theory, the theta-criterion, and control theory. Thus, in its current form, the formalization does not include the machinery necessary to account for passives and raising. It also assumes that *X*-bar theory limits the base to trees generated by CFGs with no useless nonterminals and no cycles, except presumably through the S and NP nodes. This excludes accounts of stacked adjectives, as in *the white speckled shaggy Pekingese*, and of stacked relative clauses.

We suspect that most of these features could be added to the formalization without affecting either result, and that it is extremely useful to have even a first approximation of one to work with. Although Berwick is mute on the subject, we conjecture that recognition in the model he gives can be done in polynomial time. What is less clear is what will happen to recognition complexity under models that include the other constraints.

Berwick's result about the linear growth property has no immediate functional consequence for complexity or even for weak generative capacity. It is presented as a property that natural languages seem to have and thus that should be predicted by the linguistic model.

5. Lexical-Functional Grammar

In part, transformational grammar seeks to account for a range of constraints or dependencies within sentences. Of particular interest are subcategorization, predicate-argument dependencies, and long-distance dependencies, such as *wh*-movement. Several recent theories suggest different ways of accounting for these dependencies, but without making use of transformations. We examine three of these in the next several sections: lexical-functional grammar, generalized phrase structure grammar, and tree adjunct grammar.

In the lexical-functional grammar (LFG) of Kaplan and Bresnan (1982), two levels of syntactic structure are postulated: constituent and functional. All the work done previously by transformations is instead encoded both in the lexicon and in links established between nodes in the constituent and functional structures.

The languages generated by LFGs, or LFLs, are CSLs and properly include the CFLs (Kaplan and Bresnan 1982). Berwick (1982) shows that a set of strings whose recognition problem is known to be NP-complete, namely, the set of satisfiable Boolean formulas, is an LFL. Therefore, as was the case for Rounds's restricted class of TGs, if P is not equal to NP, then some languages generated by LFGs do not have polynomial-time recognition algorithms. Indeed only the "basic" parts of the LFG mechanism are necessary to the reduction. This includes mechanisms necessary for feature agreement, for forcing verbs to take certain cases, and for allowing lexical ambiguity. Thus, no simple change in the formalism is likely to avoid the combinatorial consequences of the full mechanism. It should be noted that the c-structures and f-structures necessary to make satisfiable Boolean formulas into an LFL are not much larger than the strings themselves; the complexity comes in finding the assignment of truth-values to the variables. In his paper in this issue (p. 189), Berwick argues that the complexity of LFLs stems from their ability to unify trees of arbitrary size, and that such a mechanism does not exist in GB. However, the recognition complexity of GB languages, as formalized in Berwick (1984) or in more "faithful" models, remains open, and may arise from other constraints.

Both Berwick and Roach have examined the relation between LFG and the class of languages generated by **indexed grammars** (Aho 1968), a class known to be a proper subset of the CSLs, but including some NP-complete languages (Rounds 1973). They claim (personal communication) that the indexed languages are a proper subset of the LFLs.

6. Generalized Phrase Structure Grammar

In a series of papers, Gerald Gazdar and his colleagues (1982) have argued for a joint account of syntax and semantics that is like LFG in eschewing the use of transformations, but unlike it in positing only one level of syntactic description. The syntactic apparatus is based on a nonstandard interpretation of phrase-structure rules and on the use of metarules. The formal consequences of both these devices have been investigated.

6.1. Node admissibility

There are two ways of interpreting the function of CF rules. The first, and most common, is to treat them as rules for *rewriting strings*. Derivation trees can then be seen as canonical representatives of classes of derivations producing the same string, differing only in the order in which the same productions are applied.

The second interpretation of CF rules is as *constraints* on derivation trees: a legal derivation tree is one in which each node is "admitted" by a rule, i.e., each node dominates a sequence of nodes in a manner sanctioned by a rule. For CF rules, the two interpretations obviously generate the same strings and the same set of trees.

Following a suggestion of McCawley's, Peters and Ritchie (1973b) showed that, if one considered context-sensitive rules from the node-admissibility point of view, the languages defined were still CF. Thus, for example, the use of CS rules in the base to impose subcategorization restrictions does not increase the weak generative capacity of the base component. (For some different restrictions of context-sensitive rules that guarantee that only CFLs will be generated, see Baker (1972).)

Rounds (1970b) gives a simpler proof of Peters and Ritchie's node admissibility result, using the techniques from tree-automata theory, a generalization to trees of finite state automata theory for strings. Just as a finite-state automaton (FSA) **accepts** a string by reading it one character at a time, changing its state at each transition, a finite-state tree automaton (FSTA) traverses trees, propagating states. The **top-down FSTA** "attaches" a starting state (from a finite set) to the root of the tree. Transitions are allowed by productions of the form

$$(q, a, n) => (q_1,...,q_n)$$

such that if state q is being applied to a node labeled a and dominating n descendants, then state q_i should be applied to its ith descendant. Acceptance occurs if all leaves of the tree end up labeled with states in the accepting subset. The **bottom-up FSTA** is similar: starting states are attached to the leaves of the tree and the productions are of the form

$$(a, n, (q_1,..., q_n) => q)$$

indicating that, if a node labeled a dominates n descendants, each labeled with states q_1 to q_n, then node a gets labeled with state q. Acceptance occurs when the root is labeled by a state from the subset of accepting states.

As is the case with FSAs, FSTAs of both varieties can be either deterministic or nondeterministic. A set of trees is said to be **recognizable** if it is accepted by a nondeterministic bottom-up FSTA. Once again, as with FSAs, any set of trees accepted by a nondeterministic bottom-up FSTA is accepted by a deterministic bottom-up FSTA, but the result does not hold for top-down

FSTA, even though the recognizable sets are exactly the languages recognized by nondeterministic top-down FSTAs.

A set of trees is **local** if it is the set of derivation trees of a CF grammar. Clearly, every local set is recognizable by a one-state bottom-up FSTA that checks at each node to verify that it satisfies a CF production. Furthermore, the **yield** of a recognizable set of trees (the set of strings it generates) is CF. Not all recognizable sets are local: an example is the set of trees that satisfies the constraints of X-bar theory and the θ-criterion. However, they can all be mapped into local sets by a simple homomorphic mapping.[7] Rounds's proof (1970a) that CS rules under node admissibility generate only CFLs involves showing that the set of trees accepted by the rules is recognizable – i.e., that there is a nondeterministic bottom-up FSTA that can check at each node that some node admissibility condition holds there. This requires confirming that the "strictly context-free" part of the rule holds and that a proper analysis of the tree passing through the node satisfies the "context-sensitive" part of the rule.

Joshi and Levy (1977) strengthened Peters and Ritchie's result by showing that the node admissibility conditions could also include arbitrary Boolean combinations of **dominance** conditions: a node could specify a bounded set of labels that must occur either immediately above it along a path to the root, or immediately below it on a path to the frontier.

In general, the CF grammars constructed in the proof of weak equivalence to the CS grammars under node admissibility are much larger than the original, and not useful for practical recognition. Joshi, Levy, and Yueh (1981), however, show how Earley's algorithm can be extended to a parser that uses the local constraints directly.

6.2. Metarules

The second important mechanism used by Gazdar (1982) is **metarules,** or rules that apply to rules to produce other rules. Using standard notation for CF rules, one example of a metarule that could replace the *Apects* transformation known as "particle movement" is

$$V \rightarrow V\ N\ Pt\ X\ \Longrightarrow V \rightarrow V\ Pt\ N[\text{-}PRO]\ X$$

The symbol X here behaves like variables in structural analyses of *Aspects* transformations. If such variables are restricted to being used as *abbreviations*, that is, if they are allowed to range only from a *finite* subset of strings over the vocabulary, then closing the grammar under the metarules produces only a finite set of derived rules; and thus the generative power of the formalism is not increased. If, on the other hand, X is allowed to range over strings of *unbounded length*, as are the **essential variables** of transformational theory, then the consequences are less clear. It is well known, for example, that, if the

right-hand sides of phrase structure rules are allowed to be arbitrary regular expressions, the generated languages are still context-free. Might something like this not be happening with essential variables in metarules? It turns out that such is not the case.

The formal consequences of the presence of essential variables in metarules depend on the presence of another device, the so-called **phantom categories.** It may be convenient in formulating metarules to allow, in the left-hand sides of rules, occurrences of syntactic categories that are never introduced by the grammar, i.e., that never appear in the right-hand sides of rules. In standard CFLs, these are called *useless categories;* rules containing them can simply be dropped, with no change in weak generative capacity. Not so with metarules: it is possible for metarules to be used to rewrite rules containing phantom categories into rules without them. Such a device was proposed at one time as a way to implement passives in the GPSG framework.

Uszkoreit and Peters (1983) have shown that essential variables in metarules are powerful devices indeed: CF grammars with metarules that use at most one essential variable and allow phantom categories can generate all recursively enumerable sets. Even if phantom categories are banned, some nonrecursive sets can be generated as long as the use of at least one essential variable is allowed.

Two constraints on metarules have been proposed to restrict the generative capacity of metarule systems. Gazdar (1982) has suggested replacing essential variables by abbreviative ones, i.e. variables that can only range over a finite set of (predetermined) alternatives. Shieber et al. (1983) argue that a generalization is lost in so doing, in the sense that the class of instantiations of the variable must be defined by extension rather than by intension. Given the alternative, this seems a small price to pay.

The other constraint, suggested by Gazdar and Pullum (1982), is *finite closure* of the metarule derivation process: no metarule is allowed to apply more than once in the derivation of a rule. Shieber et al. (1983) present several examples, namely the treatment of discontinuous noun phrases in Walpiri, adverb distribution in German, and causatives in Japanese, that cannot be handled under the finite closure constraint.

It should be noted that other ways of using one grammar to generate the rules of another have been proposed. VanWijngaarden (1969), for example, presented a scheme in which one grammar's *sentences* are the *rules* of another. Greibach (1974) gives some of its properties.

7. Tree Adjunct Grammar

The tree adjunct grammars (TAG) of Joshi and his colleagues (1982, 1984) provide a different way of accounting for syntactic dependencies. A TAG consists of two finite sets of finite trees, the **centre** trees and the **adjunct** trees.

---

[7] This mapping is a bottom-up finite-state tree transducer that simply labels each node with the state the recognizing bottom-up FSTA would have been in at that node.

The centre trees correspond to the surface structures of the "kernel" sentences of the languages. The root of the adjunct trees is labelled with a nonterminal symbol that also appears exactly once on the frontier of the tree. All other frontier nodes are labelled with terminal symbols. Derivations in TAGs are defined by repeated application of the **adjunction operation.** If *c* is a centre tree containing an occurrence of a nonterminal *A*, and *a* is an adjunct tree whose root (and one node *n* on the frontier) is labelled *A*, then the adjunction of *a* to *c* is performed by "detaching" from *c* the subtree *t* rooted at *A*, attaching *a* in its place, and reattaching *t* at node *n*. Adjunction may then be seen as a tree analogue of a context-free derivation for strings (Rounds 1970a). The string languages obtained by taking the yields of the tree languages generated by TAGs are called **tree adjunct languages** (TAL).

In TAGs, all long-distance dependencies are the result of adjunctions separating nodes that at one point in the derivation were "close". Both crossing and noncrossing dependencies can be represented (Joshi 1983)). The formal properties of TALs are fully discussed by Joshi, Levy, and Takahashi (1975); Joshi and Levy (1982); and Yokomori and Joshi (to appear). Of particular interest are the following.

TALs properly contain the CFLs and are properly contained in the indexed languages, which in turn are properly contained in the CSLs. Although the indexed languages contain NP-complete languages, TALs are much better behaved: Joshi and Yokomori report (personal communication) an $O(n^4)$ recognition algorithm and conjecture that an $O(n^3)$ bound may be possible.

8. Stratificational Grammar

The constituent and functional structures of LFG, the metarules of GPSG, the constraints on deep and surface structures in TG, and the two-level grammars of van Wijngaarden are all different ways in which syntactic constraints can be distributed across more than one structure. The Stratificational Grammar (SG) of Lamb and Gleason (Lamb 1966, Gleason 1964) is yet another.

SG postulates the existence of several coupled components, known as **strata;** phonology, morphology, syntax, and semology are examples of linguistic strata. Each stratum specifies a set of correct structures, and an utterance has a representative structure at each stratum. The strata are linearly ordered and constrained by a **realization** relation.

Following Gleason's model, Borgida (1983) defines the realization relation so that it couples the application of specific pairs of *productions* (or sequences of productions) in the different grammars. Note that this is a generalization of the pairing of syntactic and semantic rules suggested by Montague, for example.

With any derivation in a rewrite grammar, one can associate a string of the productions used in the derivation. If a canonical order is imposed on the derivations – for example, that the leftmost nonterminal must be the next one to be expanded – a unique string of productions can be associated with each derivation tree. A **two-level stratificational grammar** consists of two rewrite grammars G_1 and G_2, called **tactics,** with sets of productions P_1 and P_2, respectively, and a realization relation R, which is a finite set of pairs, each consisting of a string of productions of P_1 and a string of productions of P_2. A derivation D_1 in G_1 is **realized** by a derivation D_2 in G_2 if the strings of productions s_1 and s_2 associated with D_1 and D_2 can be decomposed into substrings $s_1=u_1..u_n$ and $s_2=v_1...v_n$, respectively, such that $R(u_i, v_i)$, for all *i* from 1 to *n*. The language generated by a two-level SG is the set of string generated derivations in G_2 that realize derivations in G_1.extended to more than two **strata.**

Because the realization relation binds *derivations,* it is the strong generative capacity of the tactics that determines the languages generated. Borgida (1983) studied the languages of two-level SGs as the strong generative capacity of the tactics is systematically varied. Some of his results are unexpected. All r.e. languages can be generated by two-level SGs with CF tactics. On the other hand, if the upper tactics are restricted to being right-recursive, only CFLs can be generated, even with type 0 lower tactics. If the grammars are restricted to have no length-decreasing rules, the languages describable by SGs lie in the class of *quasi-real time languages,* defined as recognizable by nondeterministic TMs in linear time.

The principal feature of SGs that accounts for high generative power is the presence of left recursion in the tactics: to escape from the regular languages, one needs left recursion on at least one stratum; to escape context-free languages, two non-right-recursive strata are needed. These results apply to SGs with arbitrary number of strata.

9. Seeking Significance

How, then, can metatheoretical results be useful in selecting among syntactic theories? The obvious route, of course, is to claim that the computationally most restrictive theory is preferable. However, this comparison is useful only if the theories to be compared rest on a number of shared assumptions and observations concerning the scope of the syntax, the computational properties of the human processor and the relation between the processor and the syntactic theory.

In this section, we first briefly consider the assumption of common syntactic coverage and the computational consequences of theory decomposition. We then ask how metatheoretical results can be used first as lower bounds and then as upper bounds on acceptable theories.

9.1. Coverage

Competing linguistic theories must obviously agree on the burden of their respective syntactic components. We consider here one example of a constraint for which two analyses have been presented, one purportedly completely syntactic, and the other partly semantic. The problem at hand is the distribution of the so-called *polarity-sensitive* items, such as *any* and the metaphorical sense of *lift a finger*. Simply put, these terms need to appear within the scope of a **polarity reverser,** such as *not*, or *rarely*. The question is: how are scope and polarity reverser defined? In Linebarger's syntactic analysis (1980), the scope relation is defined on the logical forms of the government and binding theory (GB):

> An item is in the immediate scope of NOT if (1) it occurs only in the proposition which is the entire scope of NOT and (2) within the proposition there are no logical elements intervening between it and NOT.

In this analysis, *scope* and *intervening* must be defined configurationally, and one assumes that *logical element* is defined in the lexicon. Note that *not* is the only lexical element that can be a license. Linebarger assumes that

> all other cases are, strictly speaking, ill formed and salvaged only by the availability of an implicature which can be formalized to contain the polarity items in the appropriate relation to NOT. (Ladusaw 1983)

Ladusaw's analysis (1979), within the framework of Montague grammar, is in three parts:

1. A negative polarity item will be acceptable only if it is in the scope of a polarity-reversing expression.
2. For any two expressions α and β, constituents of a sentence S, α is in the scope of β with respect to a composition structure of S, S', iff the interpretation of α is used in the formulation of the argument of β's interpretation in S'.
3. An expression D is a polarity reverser with respect to an interpretation function ϕ if and only if, for all expressions X and Y,[8]

$$\phi(X) \subseteq \phi(Y) => \phi(d(Y)) \subseteq \phi(d(X))$$

In (1), "acceptable" is predicated of negative polarity items; these are clearly parts of surface structures, and thus syntactic objects. The condition on acceptability is in terms of *scope* and *polarity-reversing expression*. In (3), *polarity reverser* is applied to syntactic objects and defined in terms of their denotations. In (2) α *is in the scope of β*. is defined again of syntactic objects α and β, but in terms of the function that interprets the structure they occur in, not of their denotations. So the condition applies to syntactic structures, but is defined in terms of the denotations of parts of that structure and in terms of the interpretation function itself. Although it would be satisfying to do so, there appears to be no natural way to recast Ladusaw's constraint as one that is fully semantic, namely, by making the interpretation function partial (i.e., in a way that allows *John knows anything* to be grammatical but uninterpretable) because the definition of scope is in terms of the interpretation function, not the denotations themselves. We seem condemned to straddle the fence on this one.

Thus we have here one theory that deals, completely within the syntactic domain, only with the license *not*, and another that accounts for a much broader range of

licenses by imposing on syntactic structures conditions defined in terms of their interpretations and of the interpretation function itself. They are computationally incomparable.

We close this section with an aside on the separation of constraints. Constraint separation can occur in two ways. In the case of polarity-sensitive items, it takes place across the syntax-semantics boundary. In several *syntactic* theories, such as GB and LFG, it can also occur within the syntactic theory itself: grammaticality in LFG, for example, is defined in terms of the existence of pairs of appropriately related constituent and functional structures.

In general, the class resulting from the intersection of the separated classes will be at least as large as either of them: e.g., the intersection of two CFLs is not always a CFL. More interesting is the fact that separation sometimes has beneficial computational effects. Consider, for example, the constraint in many programming languages that variables can only occur in the scope of a declaration for them. This constraint cannot be imposed by a CFG but can be by an indexed grammar, at the cost of a dramatic increase in recognition complexity. In practice, however, the requirement is simply not checked by the parser, which only recognizes CFLs. The declaration conditions are checked separately by a process that traverses the parse tree. In this case, the overall recognition complexity remains some low-order polynomial. It is not clear to me whether one wants to consider the declaration requirement syntactic or not. The point is that, in this case, the "unified account" is more general, and computationally more onerous, than the modular one. Some arguments of this kind can be found in Berwick and Weinberg (1982).

9.2. Metatheoretical results as lower bounds

The first use of formal results is to argue that a theory should be rejected if it is insufficiently powerful to account for observed constraints. Chomsky used this strategy initially against finite-state grammars[9] and then against CFGs. It obviously first requires extracting from empirical observation (and decisions about idealization) what the minimal generative capacity and recognition complexity of actual languages are. Several arguments have been made against the weak generative adequacy of CFGs. The best known of these are Bar-Hillel's claim (1961) based on the occurrence of *respectively* and Postal's (1964a) on nominalization in Mohawk. Higginbotham (1984) claims non-context-freeness for English

---

[8] Following Fauconnier, Ladusaw's denotation functions take as their values sets, ordered as usual. Sentences, for example, get as denotations the set of all worlds in which they are true.

[9] There has always been interest in finite-state grammars to account for some perceptual constraints on sentence recognition, such as the difficulty of center-embedded sentences – e.g., "The rat that the cat that the dog chase ate died" (Langendoen 1975, Church 1981, Langendoen and Langsam 1984). They have also provided useful models in morphology (Kay 1983, Koskenniemi 1983) and phonology (Church 1983),

on the basis of sentences containing *such that*. Postal and Langendoen (this issue, p. 177) do so with cases of sluicing. Pullum and Gazdar (1982) (convincingly, I believe) refute the first two cases by claiming that the constraints on which they are based do not in fact hold. Similarly, Pullum (this issue, p. 182) argues against Postal and Langendoen, and against Higginbotham, again on the basis of the linguistic facts. Pullum and Gazdar also consider the case of verb and noun-phrase ordering in Dutch; although they show that no evidence has been given suggesting that the weak generative capacity of Dutch is greater than context-free, the phrase structure trees generated by their fragment are not obviously adequate for a compositional semantic analysis. This point is also made by Bresnan et al. (1982).

The most convincing evidence so far against the weak context-freeness of natural languages comes from Swiss-German. Shieber (1984) shows that, like Dutch, Swiss-German allows cross-serial order in subordinate clauses but also requires that objects be marked for case, as in German. Given that the verb *hälfed* 'help' takes a dative object while *aastriiche* 'paint' and *lönd* 'let' take accusative objects, we get the following subordinate clauses, which can be made into complete sentences by prefixing them with *Jan säit das* 'Jan says that'.

> ... mer em Hans es huus hälfed aastriiche
> ... we Hans-DAT the house-ACC helped paint
> ... we helped Hans paint the house
>
> ... *me em Hans es huus lönd aastriiche
> ... we Hans-DAT the house-ACC let paint
> ... we let Hans paint the house
>
> ... mer d'chind em Hans es huus lönd hälfed aastriiche
> ... we the children-ACC Hans-DAT the house-ACC let help paint
> ... we let the children help Hans paint the house
>
> ... *mer d'chind de Hans es huus lönd hälfed aastriiche
> ... we the children-ACC Hans-ACC the house-ACC let help paint
> ... we let the children help Hans paint the house

The proof that Swiss-German (SG) is not context-free is classic: intersect SG with the following regular language:

> Jan säit das mer (d'chind)*(em Hans)*
> es huus händ wele (laa)*(hälfe)* aastriche.

With some care, Shieber argues from the data that *SG* ∩ *L* is the language

> Jan säit das mer (d'chind)^m (em Hans)^m
> es huus händ wele (laa)^m (hälfe)^m aastriche.

which is not context-free. Since context-free languages are closed under intersection with regular languages, Swiss-German is not context-free either.

Hintikka (1977) claims that English is not recursive, let alone context-free, based on the distribution of the words *any* and *every*. His account of why *John knows everything* is grammatical while *John knows anything* is not, is that *any* can appear only in contexts where replacing it with *every* changes the meaning. If equivalence of meaning is taken to be logical equivalence, this means that grammaticality is dependent on the determination of equivalence of logical formulas, an undecidable problem.

Several responses could be made to Hintikka's claim. One is to argue, as did Ladusaw (1979), that the constraint is semantic, not syntactic. Another route, followed by Chomsky (1980), is to claim that a simpler solution is available, namely, one that replaces logical equivalence with syntactic identity of some kind of logical form. This is the basis for Linebarger's analysis.

9.3. Metatheoretical results as upper bounds

In the preceding section, we discussed ways in which formal results about syntactic theories can be used against them on the grounds that they show them to be insufficiently powerful to account for the observed data. Now, given a theory that is powerful enough, can its formal properties be used against it on the basis that it fails to *exclude* impossible languages?

The classic case of an argument of this form is Peters and Ritchie's argument against the TG model, discussed in Section 4.

More generally, the premises are the following:

1. The possible languages are decidable.
2. The correct syntactic theory must generate exactly the possible languages.
3. The correct syntactic theory is T.
4. The class of languages C generated by T is a priori too large to be the class of possible languages.

One conclusion from this argument is that theory T is incorrect, i.e., that assumption (3) fails. Chomsky rejects assumption (1) instead, insisting that the possible languages are those that can be *learned*.[10]

Although Chomsky also claims that the class of possible languages is *finite*,[11] the crucial concern here is that, finite or not, the class of possible languages could contain languages that are not recursive, or even not recursively enumerable. For example, let *L* be a non-recursive language and *L'* its complement (also non-recursive). Let *s* be some string of L and *s'* some string of *L'*. The procedure by which the subject chooses *L* if *s* is encountered before *s'* and *L'* otherwise will learn one of *L* or *L'*.

---

[10] Learning algorithms can be compared along several dimensions. For a mathematical framework for learnability theory, see Osherson et al. (1983).

[11] Actually, finiteness is claimed for the class of core grammars, from which the possible languages are assumed to be derived. Core languages and possible languages would be the same only "under idealized conditions that are never realized in fact in the real world of heterogeneous speech communities. . . . Each actual 'language' will incorporate a periphery of borrowings, historical residues, inventions, and so on, which we can hardly expect to — and indeed would not want to — incorporate within a principled theory of UG." (Chomsky 1981: 8)

Chomsky (1980) argues convincingly that there is no case for natural languages being necessarily recursive. Nevertheless, languages might just *happen* to be recursive. Putnam (1961) gives three reasons he claims "point in this direction":

1. "Speakers can presumably classify sentences as acceptable or unacceptable, deviant or nondeviant, et cetera, without reliance on extra-linguistic contexts. There are of course exceptions to this rule...",
2. Grammaticality judgments can be made for nonsense sentences,
3. Grammars can be learned.

The first reason is most puzzling. The reference to "extra-linguistic context" is irrelevant; without it, reason (1) seems to be asserting that acceptability can be decided except where it cannot be. With respect to the second reason, the fact that grammaticality judgments could be made for *some* nonsense sentences in no way affects the question of whether they can be made for all *grammatical* sentences. Finally, languages could be learnable without being recursive, as it is possible that all the rules that need to be acquired could be on the basis of sentences for which the recognition procedure succeeds.

Peters and Ritchie (1973a) contains a suggestive but hardly conclusive case for contingent recursivity:

1. Every TG has an exponentially bounded cycling function, and thus generates only recursive languages,
2. Every natural language has a descriptively adequate TG, and
3. The complexity of languages investigated so far is typical of the class.

If learnability rather than recognizability is the defining characteristic of possible languages, no claim refuting a theory on the grounds that it allows difficult languages will bear any weight, unless it can also be shown that possible languages are in fact easier to recognize than the recognizability theory predicts them to be. However, our everyday experience with language understanding leads us to think that syntactic recognition is a computationally efficient process – an observation, of course, that is the basis for Marcus's claim (1980) that a large part of it can be done in linear time, if not in real time. How are we to reconcile this with the $O(g)$-results we have for most theories, where g is at least quadratic?[12]

These intuitive conclusions are based on observations (1) of "everyday" sentences, (2) where some nonsyntactic processing is done in parallel, (3) by the human processor. Each of these points is important.

Although recognition may appear to be done in real time for most sentences encountered day to day, the O-results are asymptotic worst-case measures. It is therefore essential to obtain measures of recognition times for a variety of strings of words, whether sentences or not, and especially see if there are short, difficult ones. There are at least two cases of interest here. The first is that of garden-path sentences such as *The horse raced past the barn fell* and *Have the students who failed the exam take the supplementary,* which are globally unambiguous but locally ambiguous. These appear to be psychologically difficult. Another case is that of sentences that, in most grammars, are ambiguous because of attachment choices, such as those discussed by Church and Patil (1982). Finding one parse of these sentences is easy, but finding them all may be exponentially difficult. Psychological measures show these sentences *not* to be difficult, suggesting that not all parses are constructed·or that they can all be examined in parallel.

O-results depend on some underlying machine model, and most of the results known for language recognition have been obtained on RAMs. Can implementation changes improve things on relevant range? As mentioned above, the sequential models are all polynomially related, and no problem not having a polynomial time solution on a sequential machine is likely to have one on a parallel machine limited to at most a polynomial number of processors, at least if P is not equal to NP.

Both these results restrict the improvement one can obtain by changing implementation, but are of little use in comparing algorithms of low complexity. Berwick and Weinberg (1982) give examples of how algorithms of low complexity may have different implementations differing by large constant factors. In particular, changes in the form of the grammar and in its representation may have this effect.

It is well-known that implementation of machines with infinite storage on finite devices leads to a change in specification. A context-free parser implemented on a machine with finite memory will have a bounded stack and therefore recognize only finite-state languages. The language recognized by the implemented machine could therefore be recognized by another machine in linear time. Although one would rarely use this strategy as a design principle, a variant of it is more plausible: use a restriction of the general method for a subset of the inputs and revert to the general method when the special case fails. Marcus's parser (1980) with its bounded look-ahead is a good example. Sentences parsable within the allowed look-ahead have "quick" parses, but some grammatical sentences, such as "garden path" sentences cannot be recognized without an extension to the mechanism that would distort the complexity measures. A consequence of the possibility of implementation of this character is that observations of their operation ought to show "discontinuities" in the processing time, depending on whether an input is in or out of the restricted subset.

---

[12] It has already been pointed out that $O(g)$ results are upper bounds, and showing that a recognition problem, for example, is $O(g)$ does not mean that, for any language, it is necessary to reach the upper-bound. Better upper-bounds can be achieved by tighter proofs, not just by better algorithms.

There is obviously much more of this story to be told. Allow me to speculate as to how it might go. We may end up with a space of linguistic theories, differing in the idealization of the data they assume, in the way they decompose constraints, and in the procedural specifications they postulate. I take it that two theories may differ in that the second simply provides more detail than the first as to how constraints specified by the first are to be used. Our observations, in particular our measurements of necessary resources, are drawn from the "ultimate implementation", but this does not mean that the "ultimately low-level theory" is necessarily the most informative, or that less procedural theories are not useful stepping stones to more procedural ones.

It is also not clear that theories of different computational power may not be useful as descriptions of different parts of the syntactic apparatus. For example, it may be easier to learn statements of constraints within the framework of a general machine. The constraints once learned might then be subjected to transformation to produce more efficient special-purpose processors also imposing resource limitations.

Whatever we decide to make of existing formal results, it is clear that continuing contact with the complexity community is important. The driving problems there are the $P = NP$ question, the determination of lower bounds, the study of time-space tradeoffs, and the complexity of parallel computations. We still have some methodological house-cleaning to do, but I don't see how we can avoid being affected by the outcome of their investigations.

References

Aho, A.V. 1968 Indexed Grammars: An Extension of the Context-Free Grammars. *JACM* 15: 647-671.

Aho, A.V.; Hopcroft, J.E.; and Ullman, J.D. 1974 *The Design and Analysis of Computer Algorithms*. Addison-Wesley, Reading, Massachusetts.

Aho, A.V. and Ullman, J.D. 1972 *The Theory of Parsing, Translation, and Compiling*. Prentice Hall, Englewood Cliffs, New Jersey.

Baker, B.S. 1972 Arbitrary Grammars Generating Context-Free Languages. Center for Research in Computing Technology, Harvard University.

Bar-Hillel, Y.; Perlis, M.; and Shamir, E. 1961 On Formal Properties of Simple Phrase Structure Grammars. *Z. Phonetik, Sprach. Komm.* 14: 143-172.

Berwick, R.C. and Weinberg, A. 1982 Parsing Efficiency, Computational Complexity, and the Evaluation of Grammatical Theories. *Linguistic Inquiry* 13: 165-191.

Berwick, R.C. 1982 Computational Complexity and Lexical Functional Grammar. *American Journal of Computational Linguistics* 8(3-4): 97-109.

Berwick, R.C. 1984 Strong Generative Capacity, Weak Generative Capacity and Modern Linguistic Theories. *CL* 10(3-4):, 189-203.

Borgida, A.T. 1983 Some Formal Results about Stratificational Grammars and their Relevance to Linguistics. *Math. Sys. Th.* 16: 29-56.

Bresnan, J.; Kaplan, R.M.; Peters, P.S.; and Zaenen, A. 1982 Cross-serial Dependencies in Dutch. *Ling. Inq.* 13.

Chomsky, N. 1980 *Rules and Representations*. Columbia University Press, New York, New York.

Chomsky, N. 1981 *Lectures on Government and Binding: the Pisa Lectures*. Foris Publications Holland, Dordrecht.

Church, K. 1981 On Memory Limitations in Natural Language Processing. Master Th., M.I.T.

Church, K. 1983 A Finite-State Parser for Use in Speech Recognition. *Proceedings of 21st Annual Meeting of the ACL*. Cambridge, Massachusetts: 91-97.

Church, K. and Patil, R. 1982 Coping with Syntactic Ambiguity or How to Put the Block on the Table. *American Journal of Computational Linguistics* 8(3-4): 139-149.

Cook, S.A. 1981 Towards a Complexity Theory of Synchronous Parallel Computation. *L'Enseignement Mathématique* 27: 99-124.

Earley, J. 1970 An Efficient Context-Free Parsing Algorithm. *Communications of ACM* 13: 94-102.

Gazdar, G. 1982 Phrase Structure Grammar. In Jacobson, P. and Pullum, G., Eds., *The Nature of Syntactic Representation*. Reidel, Dordrecht.

Gazdar, G. and Pullum, G. 1982 Generalized Phrase Structure Grammar: A Theoretical Synopsis. Indiana Univ. Linguistic Club.

Gleason, H.A. Jr. 1964 The Organization of Language: a Stratificational View. In *Monograph Series on Language and Linguistics, no. 21*. Georgetown University Press, Washington.

Graham, S.L.; Harrison, M.A.; and Ruzzo, W.L. 1980 An Improved Context-Free Recognizer. *ACM Trans. on Prog. Lang. and Systems* 2: 415-462.

Greibach, S.A. 1974 Some Restrictions on W-Grammars. Int. J. of Comp. and Info. Sc. 3: 415-462.

Hays, D.G. 1962 *Automatic Language Data Processing*. Prentice Hall, Englewood Cliffs, New Jersey.

Higginbotham, J. 1984 English Is Not a Context-Free Language. *Ling. Inq.* 15: 225-234.

Hintikka, J.K.K. 1977 Quantifiers in Natural Language: Some Logical Problems. II. *Linguistics and Philosophy* 2: 153-172.

Hopcroft, J.E. and Ullman, J. 1979 *Introduction to Automata Theory, Languages and Computation*. Addison Wesley, Reading, Massachusetts.

Joshi, A.K. 1983 Factoring Recursion and Dependencies: an Aspect of Tree Adjoining Grammars and a Comparison of Some Formal Properties of TAGs. *Proceedings of 21st Annual Meeting of the ACL*. Cambridge, Massachusetts: 7-15.

Joshi, A.K. 1984 How Much Context-Sensitivity Is Required to Provide Reasonable Structual Descriptions: Tree Adjoining Grammars. In *Natural Language Processing: Psycholinguistic, Computational and Theoretical Properties*. Cambridge University Press, New York, New York.

Joshi, A.K. and Levy, L.S. 1977 Constraints on Structural Descriptions: Local Transformation. *SIAM J. on Computing* 6: 272-284.

Joshi, A.K. and Levy, L.S. 1982 Phrase Structure Trees Bear More Fruit than You Would Have Thought. *American Journal of Computational Linguistics* 8(1): 1-11.

Joshi, A.K.; Levy, L.S.; and Takahashi, M. 1975 Tree Adjunct Grammars. *J. Comp. and Sys. Sc.* 10: 136-163.

Joshi, A.K.; Levy, L.S.; and Yueh, K. 1980 Local Constraints on Programming Languages, Part 1: Syntax. *Th. Comp. Sc.* 12: 265-290.

Kaplan R. and Bresnan, J. 1982 Lexical-Functional Grammar: a Formal System for Grammatical Representation. In Bresnan, J., Ed., *The Mental Representation of Grammatical Relations*. MIT Press, Cambridge, Massachusetts: 173-281.

Kasami, T. 1965 An Efficient Recognition and Syntax Algorithm for Context-Free Languages. AF-CRL-65-758, Air Force Cambridge Research Laboratory, Bedford, Massachusetts.

Kay, M. 1983 When Meta-Rules Are Not Meta-Rules. In Sparck-Jones, K. and Wilks, Y., Eds., *Automatic Natural Language Parsing*. John Wiley, New York.

Koskenniemi, K. 1983 Two-Level Model for Morphological Analysis. Ph.D. Th., Univ. of Helsinki.

Ladusaw, W. 1979 Polarity Sensitivity as Inherent Scope Relations. Ph.D. Th., University of Texas at Austin.

Ladusaw, W. 1983 Logical Forms and Conditions on Grammaticality. *Ling. and Phil.* 6: 373-392.

Lamb, S. 1966 *Outline of Stratificational Grammar*. Georgetown University Press, Washington, DC.

Langendoen, D.T. 1975 Finite-State Parsing of Phrase-Structure Languages and the Status of Readjustment Rules in Grammar. *Ling. Inq.* 6(4): 533-554.

Langendoen, D.T. and Langsam, Y. 1984 The Representation of Constituent Structures for Finite-State Parsing. *Proceedings of COLING-84.* Stanford, California: 24-27.

LaPointe, S. 1977 Recursiveness and Deletion. *Ling. Anal.* 3: 227-265.

Linebarger, M. 1980 The Grammar of Negative Polarity. Ph.D. Th., MIT.

Marcus, M.P. 1980 *A Theory of Syntactic Recognition for Natural Language.* MIT Press, Cambridge, Massachusetts.

Montague, R. 1973 The Proper Treatment of Quantification in Ordinary English. In Hintikka, J.K.K.; Moravcsik, J.; and Suppes, P., Eds., *Approaches to Natural Language: Proceedings of the 1970 Stanford Workshop on Grammar and Semantics.* Reidel, Dordrecht: 221-242.

Osherson, D.N.; Stob, M.; and Weinstein, S. 1983 Formal Theories of Language Acquisition: Practical and Theoretical Perspectives. *Proceedings of IJCAI-83:* 566-572.

Pereira, F.C.N. and Shieber, S. 1984 The Semantics of Grammar Formalisms Seen as Computer Languages. *Proceedings of COLING-84:* 123-129.

Peters, P.S. and Ritchie, R.W. 1969 A Note on the Universal Base Hypothesis. *Ling. and Phil.* 5: 150-152.

Peters, P.S. and Ritchie, R.W. 1971 On Restricting the Base Component of Transformational Grammars. *Inf. and Control* 18: 483-501.

Peters, P.S. and Ritchie, R.W. 1973a On the Generative Power of Transformational Grammars. *Inf. Sc.* 6: 49-83.

Peters, P.S. and Ritchie, R.W. 1973b Context-Sensitive Immediate Constituent Analysis – Context-Free Languages. *Math. Sys. Theory* 6: 324-333.

Peters, P.S. and Ritchie, R.W. 1973c Non-Filtering and Local Filtering Grammars. In Hintikka, J.K.K.; Moravcsik, J.; and Suppes, P., Eds., *Approaches to Natural Language.* Reidel, Dordrecht: 180-194.

Petrick, S.R. 1965 Recognition Procedure for Transformational Grammars. Ph.D. Th., MIT.

Postal, P.M. 1964a Limitations of phrase-structure grammars. In *The Structure of Language: Readings in the Philosophy of Language.* Prentice Hall, Englewood Cliffs, New Jersey: 137-151.

Postal, P.M. 1964b Constituent Structure: A Study of Contemporary Models of Syntactic Structure. *Int. J. of Amer. Ling.* 3.

Postal, P.M. and Langendoen, D.T. 1984 English and the Class of Context-Free Languages. *CL* 10(3-4): 177-181.

Pullum, G.K. 1984 On Two Recent Attempts to Show that English Is Not a CFL. *CL* 10(3-4): 182-186.

Pullum, G.K. and Gazdar, G. 1982 Natural and Context-Free Languages. *Ling. and Phil.* 4: 471-504.

Putnam, H. 1961 Some Issues in the Theory of Grammar. *Proceedings, American Math. Soc.*

Rounds, W.C. 1970a Mappings and Grammars on Trees. *Math. Sys. Th.* 4(3): 257-287.

Rounds, W.C. 1970b Tree-Oriented Proofs of Some Theorems on Context-Free and Indexed Languages. *Second Symp. on Th. Comp. Sc., ACM:* 109-116.

Rounds, W.C. 1973 Complexity of Recognition in Intermediate-Level Languages. *Symp. on Sw. & Aut. Th., IEEE:* 145-158.

Rounds, W.C. 1975 A Grammatical Characterization of Exponential-Time Language. *Symp. on Found. of Comp. Sc., IEEE:* 135-143.

Ruzzo, W.L. 1979 Uniform Circuit Complexity. *Proceedings of 20th Annual ACM Symp. on Found. of Comp. Sc.:* 312-318.

Shieber, S.M. 1984 Evidence Against the Context-Freeness of Natural Language. TN-330, SRI International, Menlo Park, California. To appear in *Linguistics and Philosophy.*

Shieber, S.M.; Stucky, S.U.; Uszkoreit, H.; and Robinson, J.J. 1983 Formal Constraints on Metarules. *Proceedings of 21st Annual Meeting of the ACL.* Cambridge, Massachusetts: 22-27.

Slocum, J. 1981 A Practical Comparison of Parsing Strategies. *Proceedings of the 19th Annual Meeting of the ACL.* Stanford, California: 1-6.

Uszkoreit, H. and Peters, P.S. 1983 Essential Variables in Metarules. Technical Note 305, SRI International, Menlo Park, California.

Valiant, L. 1975 General Context-Free Recognition in Less Than Cubic Time. *J. Comp. and Sys. Sc.* 10: 308-315.

Van Wijngaarden, A. 1969 Report on the Algorithmic Language ALGOL 68. *Numerische Mathematik* 14: 79-218.

Warren, D.S. 1979 Syntax and Semantics of Parsing: An Application to Montague Grammar. Ph.D. Th., University of Michigan.

Yokomori, T. and Joshi, A.K. to appear Semi-linearity, Parikh-boundedness and Tree Adjunct Languages. *Inf. Pr. Letters.*

Younger, D.H. 1967 Recognition and Parsing of Context-Free Languages in Time n^3. *Inf. and Control* 14: 189-208.

MULTIPLE-PATH SYNTACTIC ANALYZER *

S. KUNO AND A. G. OETTINGER

Harvard Computation Laboratory, Cambridge, Mass., USA

1. INTRODUCTION

The method of predictive syntactic analysis [1-4] aims at obtaining a single most probable description of the structure of an input sentence in a single left-to-right scan through the sentence. The computer program uses a storage area called the *prediction pool*. At any intermediate point in the analysis of a sentence, the prediction pool contains a single set of *predictions*, generated by the processing of the preceding words, that may be fulfilled by the remaining words. The prediction pool is similar to a pushdown store in that the prediction fulfilled and discarded is usually among the topmost in the pool, and in that the newly generated predictions are placed above the remaining predictions.

Experiments on Russian and English texts have demonstrated the capability of predictive analysis for handling complex sentence structures including many levels of subordination or coordination, but the results have been disappointing for the following reasons:

1. There are many syntactically ambiguous sentences in natural texts. Provision for determining all legitimate alternative syntactic structures is therefore essential from both the theoretical and the practical points of view. Neither estimates of the reliability of syntactic analysis, nor significant attacks on the problems of choosing the semantically correct structures, are possible without such provisions. A storage area termed *hindsight* has been provided in predictive analysis programs in the hope of enabling at least local alternative parsings, but practical use of this facility now appears inordinately difficult.

2. When a single-path analysis comes to a dead end, determining which of the previous branch points was the cause of the failure poses serious problems.

3. Owing to the lack of an effective method for distinguishing paths which have already been followed from those which have not, it has not been possible to try different paths in a systematic loop-free sequence.

A new method has been developed for extending the predictive approach by including effective and economical provisions for multiple analyses of syntactically ambiguous sentences. The prediction pool for this method is of variable size, consisting of one or more *subpools*, each of which contains a set of predictions

corresponding to a path that may lead to an acceptable structure for the complete sentence. Each subpool is a pushdown store in the strict sense; that is, only the topmost prediction in each subpool is tested against the next word of the sentence.

After the $(k-1)$st word in a sentence has been processed, the prediction pool contains a subpool for each sentence structure compatible with the first $(k-1)$ words. The topmost prediction of each subpool is then tested against all the homographs of the k-th word. By a simple process of grammar table look-up, each allowable combination of a prediction and a homograph is associated with new predictions which replace the topmost prediction of the appropriate subpool. Subpools for which no allowable combination exists are discarded. The subpools resulting from this process are used in turn for the processing of the $(k+1)$st word. After the processing of the last word of a sentence, only those subpools which have no predictions remaining are retained in the prediction pool. By tracing back the paths that have yielded these subpools, the alternative acceptable syntactic structures of the sentence are obtained.

2. DICTIONARY AND SYNTACTIC WORD CLASSES

Each word of an input sentence is looked up in a dictionary and is coded for membership in all the syntactic word classes to which it belongs. For example, the input English sentence THEY ARE FLYING PLANES. will be coded as shown in table 1. Punctuation marks are treated like words in the ordinary sense.

3. GRAMMAR TABLE

A grammar table is a rectangular array defining the *grammatical matching function G* of a language whose syntax is described in terms of a set of predictions P, a set of syntactic word classes S, and a set of syntactic role indicators R. Each prediction stands for a certain syntactic structure recognized in the language. To each ordered argument pair (P_i, S_j), G assigns a set, possibly empty, of ordered pairs

$$G(P_i, S_j) = \{[(p_1{}^1, p_1{}^2, \ldots, p_1{}^{m_1}), (r_1)],$$

$$[(p_2{}^1, p_2{}^2, \ldots, p_2{}^{m_2}), (r_2)], \ldots, [(p_q{}^1, p_q{}^2, \ldots, p_q{}^{m_q}), (r_q)]\},$$

where $p_k{}^l \in P$ and $r_k \in R$ $(k = 1, 2, \ldots, q; l = 1, 2, \ldots, m)$.

Each element of $G(P_i, S_j)$ corresponds to a set of structures that may follow when the syntactic structure represented by the given prediction P_i is initiated by

* This work has been supported in part by the National Science Foundation.

a word belonging to class S_j. Whenever P_i and S_j are grammatically incompatible, $G(P_i, S_j) = \Phi$, the empty

defined as a couple $[(P_i, S_j), g_k(P_i, S_j)]$, where

$$g_k(P_i, S_j) \in G(P_i, S_j).*$$

Table 1. Sample from an English Dictionary.

English Word	Class Code	Comments (not stored in machine)
THEY	PRN	personal pronoun in the nominative case
ARE	BE1	finite complete intransitive verb, as in "They *are* in the sky." (A prepositional phrase, according to the present grammar, is considered to be adverbial, and cannot fulfill the role of a complement or object of a verb.)
	BE2	finite copula, as in "They *are* students." and "They *are* good."
	BE3	finite auxiliary verb for the progressive form, passive voice, and be-to form, as in "They *are* coming.", "They *are* seen.", and "They *are* to come here."
FLYING	RI1	present participle of complete intransitive verb, as in "They are *flying* to Boston" and "It is a *flying* plane."
	RT1	present participle of single-object transitive verb, as in "He is *flying* a plane."
	GI1	gerund of complete intransitive verb, as in "*Flying* is pleasant."
	GT1	gerund of single-object transitive verb, as in "*Flying* a plane is pleasant."
PLANES	NOU	noun, as in "They are *planes*."
	VI1	finite complete intransitive verb, as in "The glider *planes*."
	VT1	finite single-object transitive verb, as in "He *planes* the surface of the board."
	PRD	period as end of sentence punctuation

set. Each couple $[(P_i, S_j), G(P_i, S_j)]$ in G is a *rule* of the grammar. A rule subsumes as many *subrules* as there are members of $G(P_i, S_j)$, each subrule being

In the present English grammar, the rule for $(P_i, S_j) = $ (SENTENCE, PRN) (PRN = personal pronoun in the nominative case) consists of the subrules shown in table 2. The vertical lines in $g_k(P_i, S_j)$ denote the boundaries of predictions; the slashes in the English examples denote the boundaries of the corresponding structures. The prediction which comes last in a subrule is the first to be tested, hence the subrules should be read from right to left. The syntactic role indicator r is SUBJECT OF PREDICATE VERB OF DECLARATIVE SENTENCE for the first five subrules, and SUBJECT OF PARTICIPIAL PHRASE for the last three subrules.

In practice, rules are stored sequentially in machine memory in the alphabetic order of their argument pairs, those pairs for which $G(P_i, S_j) = \Phi$ being omitted. The present experimental grammar has approximately 3400 subrules.

4. Analysis of a Sentence

The procedure for analysing a sentence will be explained in this section using THEY ARE FLYING PLANES. as an example. At the beginning of the analysis of the sentence, the prediction of SENTENCE is stored in the prediction pool. Next, this prediction is paired with the syntactic word class (PRN) of the first word (THEY) to form an argument which, when looked up in the grammar table, yields the eight sets of predictions and syntactic role indicators shown in table 2; these new predictions then replace the initial prediction of SENTENCE. The prediction pool now contains eight subpools each of which corresponds to a different way, recognized by the present grammar, of terminating the sentence initiated by PRN.

The analysis proceeds to the second word, and the three syntactic word classes (BE1, BE2, BE3) assigned to ARE are coupled with the topmost prediction of each of the eight subpools in the prediction pool. The resulting arguments are

---

* This characterization of the grammatical matching function is due to Warren Plath.

Table 2. The Subrules of G (Sentence, PRN).

g_1(SENTENCE, PRN) = | PERIOD | PREDICATE (as in " / They / go / .")

g_2 = | PERIOD | PREDICATE | ADJECTIVE CLAUSE (as in " / We / who are ready to die / salute you / .")

g_3 = | PERIOD | PREDICATE | COMMA | ADJECTIVE PHRASE | COMMA (as in "/ They / , / knowing the truth / , / came to the right conclusion / .")

g_4 = | PERIOD | PREDICATE | COMMA | SUBJECT PHRASE | COMMA (as in " / We/ , / the people of the United States / , / love peace / .")

g_5 = | PERIOD | PREDICATE | SUBJECT PHRASE | AND-OR (as in " / They / and / John / came / .")

g_6 = | SENTENCE | COMMA | PARTICIPLE (as in " / They / having done the right thing / , / we can trust them.")

g_7 = | SENTENCE | COMMA | PARTICIPLE | SUBJECT PHRASE | AND-OR (as in " / They / and / John / having done the right thing / , / we can trust them.")

g_8 = | SENTENCE | COMMA | PARTICIPLE | COMMA | SUBJECT PHRASE | COMMA (as in " / They / , / the Russians / , / having said no / , / we took a decisive step.")

(PREDICATE, BE1), (PREDICATE, BE2), (PREDICATE, BE3); (ADJECTIVE CLAUSE, BE1), . . . ; (COMMA, BE1) . . . ; (COMMA, BE1), . . . ; (AND-OR, BE1), . . . ; (PARTICIPLE, BE1), . . . ; (AND-OR, BE1), . . . ; (COMMA, BE1), ...

Each of these 24 arguments is looked up in the grammar table, but only (PREDICATE, BE1), (PREDICATE, BE2) and (PREDICATE, BE3) yield non-empty $G(P_i, S_j)$. All the subpools stored in the prediction pool—except that with PREDICATE as the topmost prediction—are discarded, since the predictions in them cannot be fulfilled by the sentence in question.

The subrules for (PREDICATE, BE1), (PREDICATE, BE2) and (PREDICATE, BE3) are shown in table 3. All of these subrules have PREDICATE VERB as their syntactic role indicator.

Now, the new predictions given by these grammar subrules replace the topmost prediction (PREDICATE) of the subpool which orginally contained | PERIOD | PREDICATE. Twelve new subpools, all of which have the prediction of PERIOD as the bottom prediction, are generated and stored in the prediction pool. These subpools in turn are used for the processing of the next word, FLYING, and so on.

The current grammar yields three analyses for THEY ARE FLYING PLANES. The first in table 4 shows the syntactic structure of the sentence applicable when THEY refers to planes. The second shows the syntactic structure of the sentence acceptable when THEY refers to people. Analysis No. 03 is semantically absurd, but it reflects the structure of a sentence such as "The facts are smoking kills.", which is not semantically absurd. The same three analyses would be obtained for "The facts are smoking kills.", but only one would be semantically correct for this sentence.

The analyses obtained for THEY ARE FLYING PLANES. can be limited to the two syntactically and

semantically acceptable ones simply by deleting the subrule pertaining to

g_4(PREDICATE, BE2) = | DECLARATIVE CLAUSE.

However, the semantically correct analysis of "The facts are smoking kills." would thereby be lost, leaving only two unacceptable analyses. The easy way out of this particular dilemma would be to rule out "The facts are smoking kills." as ill-formed and accept only "The facts are: smoking kills.". The problem is, however, a more general one to which the solution must be sought, not within the presently defined precincts of syntax but in the shadowy realm of semantics. A set of multiple analyses provides, for the first time, a firm base from which to start such an exploration.

The same grammar produced two analyses for IT HAS ALREADY BEEN MENTIONED THAT A RESPONSE MAY BE LEARNED BY THE MACHINE IF ENCOURAGED BY THE EXPERIMENTER. Analysis No. 01 (table 5) shows the structure of the sentence in which IT is a *temporary* subject without normal pronominal reference and in which THAT introduces the *real* subject noun clause. This analysis corresponds to the way in which the sentence is generally understood. Analysis No. 02 (table 6) shows the structure of the sentence in which THAT introduces an adverbial clause, with IT referring to something mentioned before. The syntactic structure reflected in the analysis corresponds to the structure of such semantically similar but more normal expressions as "It has already been mentioned so that a response may be learned by the machine . . ." or "It has already been mentioned lest a response may inadvertently be learned by the machine . . ."

The second analysis is due to subrules pertaining to adverbial "that"-clauses as in "We eat that we may live." or "It has been kept polished that it may glitter forever." One solution is to keep the syntactic classifi-

Table 3.   The Subrules of G (Predicate, BEi).

g_1(PREDICATE, BE1) = | ADVERBIAL PHRASE (as in "They are / *in the sky* / .")

g_2 = | PREDICATE | AND-OR-COMMA | ADVERBIAL PHRASE (as in "They are / *in the sky* / *and* / *are over us* / .")

g_1(PREDICATE, BE2) = | NOUN COMPLEMENT (as in "They are / *students* / .")

g_2 = | ADJECTIVE COMPLEMENT (as in "They are / *good* / .")

g_3 = | NOUN CLAUSE (as in "The fact is / *that it smells* / .")

g_4 = | DECLARATIVE CLAUSE (as in "The fact is / *it smells* / .")

g_5 = | PREDICATE | AND-OR-COMMA | NOUN COMPLEMENT (as in "You are / *a student* / *and* / *are a scholar* / .")

g_6 = | PREDICATE | AND-OR-COMMA | ADJECTIVE COMPLEMENT (as in "They are / *diligent* / *and* / *are working every day* / .")

g_1(PREDICATE, BE3) = | PARTICIPLE (as in "They are / *coming* / ." and "They are / *seen* / ."

g_2 = | INFINITIVE (as in "They are / *to come* / .")

g_3 = | PREDICATE | AND-OR-COMMA | PARTICIPLE (as in "They are / *coming* / *and* / *are staying here* / ." and "They are / *seen* / *and* / *are heard* / .")

g_4 = | PREDICATE | AND-OR-COMMA | INFINITIVE (as in "They are / *to come* / *and* / *are to stay here* / .")

Table 4. Analyzed Sentence

ANALYSIS NO. 01

ENGLISH	SWC	SYNTACTIC ROLE	CLAUSE LEVEL	PREDICTION		PARTIAL INTERPRETATION OF PREDICTION CODES
THEY	PERSONAL PRN NOM	SUBJECT OF PREDICATE VERB	DECLARATIVE SENT	SEX	SENTENCE	
ARE	BE2-COPULA	PREDICATE VERB	DECLARATIVE SENT	VBX	PD	PREDICATE
FLYING	PRESENT P OF VII	COMPLEMENT OF PREDICATE VERB	DECLARATIVE SENT	N3A	PD	NOUN COMPLEMENT (A)
PLANES	NOUN 1	COMPLEMENT OF PREDICATE VERB	DECLARATIVE SENT	N6A	PD	NOUN COMPLEMENT (B)
.	PERIOD	END OF SENTENCE	END OF SENTENCE		PD	

ANALYSIS NO. 02

ENGLISH	SWC	SYNTACTIC ROLE	CLAUSE LEVEL	PREDICTION		PARTIAL INTERPRETATION OF PREDICTION CODES
THEY	PERSONAL PRN NOM	SUBJECT OF PREDICATE VERB	DECLARATIVE SENT	SEX	SENTENCE	
ARE	BE3-AUXILIARY	PREDICATE VERB	DECLARATIVE SENT	VBX	PD	PREDICATE
FLYING	PRESENT P OF VTI	PREDICATE VERB	DECLARATIVE SENT	PAA	PD	PARTICIPLE
PLANES	NOUN 1	OBJECT OF PREDICATE VERB	DECLARATIVE SENT	N2A	PD	OBJECT PHRASE (A)
.	PERIOD	END OF SENTENCE	END OF SENTENCE		PD	

ANALYSIS NO. 03

ENGLISH	SWC	SYNTACTIC ROLE	CLAUSE LEVEL	PREDICTION		PARTIAL INTERPRETATION OF PREDICTION CODES
THEY	PERSONAL PRN NOM	SUBJECT OF PREDICATE VERB	DECLARATIVE SENT	SEX	SENTENCE	
ARE	BE2-COPULA	GERUND-SUBJECT	DECLARATIVE SENT	VBX	PD	PREDICATE
FLYING	GERUND OF VII	PREDICATE VERB	COMPLEMENT CLAUSE	SGE	PD	DECLARATIVE CLAUSE
PLANES	COMPLETE VI	PREDICATE VERB	COMPLEMENT CLAUSE	VBE	PD	PREDICATE
.	PERIOD	END OF SENTENCE	END OF SENTENCE		PD	

Table 5. Analyzed Sentence

ANALYSIS NO. 01

ENGLISH	SWC	SYNTACTIC ROLE	CLAUSE LEVEL	PREDICTION		PARTIAL INTERPRETATION OF PREDICTION CODES
IT	TEMPORARY SUBJECT	TEMPORARY SUBJECT	DECLARATIVE SENT	SEX	SENTENCE	
HAS	HAVE3-TENSE AUX	PREDICATE VERB	DECLARATIVE SENT	VBX	PD	PREDICATE
ALREADY	ADVERB 1	ADVERB	DECLARATIVE SENT	PFA	PD	
BEEN	PAST P OF BE3	PREDICATE VERB	DECLARATIVE SENT	PFA	PD	
MENTIONED	PAST P OF VTI	PREDICATE VERB	DECLARATIVE SENT	PPA	PD	
THAT	NOUN CONJUNCTION	CONJUNCTION	SUBJECT CLAUSE	NCC	PD	NOUN CLAUSE
A	ADJECTIVE 3	SUBJECT OF PREDICATE VERB	SUBJECT CLAUSE	NCC	PD	NOUN CLAUSE
RESPONSE	NOUN 1	SUBJECT OF PREDICATE VERB	SUBJECT CLAUSE	NCC	N4A	NOUN CLAUSE
MAY	AUXILIARY VERB	PREDICATE VERB	SUBJECT CLAUSE	NCC	PD	NOUN CLAUSE
BE	INFINITE BE3	PREDICATE VERB	SUBJECT CLAUSE	SGC	PD	DECLARATIVE CLAUSE
LEARNED	PAST P OF VTI	PREDICATE VERB	SUBJECT CLAUSE	VBC	PD	PREDICATE
BY	PREPOSITION	PREPOSITION	SUBJECT CLAUSE	BVA	PD	PREDICATE
THE	ADJECTIVE 3	OBJECT OF PREPOSITION	SUBJECT CLAUSE	PAA	PD	NON-FINITE VERB
MACHINE	NOUN 1	OBJECT OF PREPOSITION	SUBJECT CLAUSE		PD	PARTICIPLE
IF	ADVERB CONJUNCT	CONJUNCTION	ADVERBIAL CLAUSE	N2G	PD	OBJECT PHRASE (A)
ENCOURAGED	PAST P OF VTI	PARTICIPIAL VERB	ADVERBIAL CLAUSE	N5G	PD	OBJECT PHRASE (B)
BY	PREPOSITION	PREPOSITION	ADVERBIAL CLAUSE	PAC	PD	PARTICIPLE
THE	ADJECTIVE 3	OBJECT OF PREPOSITION	ADVERBIAL CLAUSE	N2G	PD	OBJECT PHRASE (A)
EXPERIMENTER	NOUN 1	OBJECT OF PREPOSITION	ADVERBIAL CLAUSE	N5G	PD	OBJECT PHRASE (B)
.	PERIOD	END OF SENTENCE	END OF SENTENCE		PD	SUBJECT PHRASE (B)

Table 6. Analyzed Sentence (continued)

ANALYSIS NO. 02

ENGLISH	SWC	SYNTACTIC ROLE	CLAUSE LEVEL	PREDICTION		PARTIAL INTERPRETATION OF PREDICTION CODES
IT	INDEFINITE PRN	SUBJECT OF PREDICATE VERB	DECLARATIVE SENT	SEX	SENTENCE	
HAS	HAVE3-TENSE AUX	PREDICATE VERB	DECLARATIVE SENT	VBX	PD	PREDICATE
ALREADY	ADVERB 1	ADVERB	DECLARATIVE SENT	PFA	PD	PAST PART. PERFECT
BEEN	PAST P OF BE3	PREDICATE VERB	DECLARATIVE SENT	PFA	PD	PAST PART. PERFECT
MENTIONED	PAST P OF VTI	PREDICATE VERB	DECLARATIVE SENT	PPA	PD	PAST PART. PASSIVE
THAT	ADVERB CONJUNCT	CONJUNCTION	ADVERBIAL CLAUSE	SGG	PD	DECLARATIVE CLAUSE
A	ADJECTIVE 3	SUBJECT OF PREDICATE VERB	ADVERBIAL CLAUSE	VBG	N4A	PREDICATE
RESPONSE	NOUN 1	SUBJECT OF PREDICATE VERB	ADVERBIAL CLAUSE	VBG	PD	PREDICATE
MAY	AUXILIARY VERB	PREDICATE VERB	ADVERBIAL CLAUSE	BVA	PD	NON-FINITE VERB
BE	INFINITE BE3	PREDICATE VERB	ADVERBIAL CLAUSE	PAA	PD	PARTICIPLE
LEARNED	PAST P OF VTI	PREDICATE VERB	ADVERBIAL CLAUSE		PD	
BY	PREPOSITION	PREPOSITION	ADVERBIAL CLAUSE	N2G	PD	OBJECT PHRASE (A)
THE	ADJECTIVE 3	OBJECT OF PREPOSITION	ADVERBIAL CLAUSE	N5G	PD	OBJECT PHRASE (B)
MACHINE	NOUN 1	OBJECT OF PREPOSITION	ADVERBIAL CLAUSE		PD	
IF	ADVERB CONJUNCT	CONJUNCTION	ADVERBIAL CLAUSE		PD	
ENCOURAGED	PAST P OF VTI	PARTICIPIAL VERB	ADVERBIAL CLAUSE	PAC	PD	PARTICIPLE
BY	PREPOSITION	PREPOSITION	ADVERBIAL CLAUSE	N2G	PD	OBJECT PHRASE (A)
THE	ADJECTIVE 3	OBJECT OF PREPOSITION	ADVERBIAL CLAUSE	N5G	PD	OBJECT PHRASE (B)
EXPERIMENTER	NOUN 1	OBJECT OF PREPOSITION	ADVERBIAL CLAUSE		PD	
.	PERIOD	END OF SENTENCE	END OF SENTENCE		PD	SUBJECT PHRASE (B)

cation of words simple and the grammar rules general and to tolerate getting Analysis No. 02 for "It has already been mentioned that a response may be learned . . ." and Analysis No. 01 for "It has been kept polished that it may glitter forever." Another approach is to make the syntactic classification of words more detailed, and the grammar rules more complicated, so that a *real* subject noun clause introduced by "that" is admitted only when it is preceded by "it" plus special verbs and adjectives ("*It is known* that the number is greater than zero."; "*It is clear* that there is no solution to the question.") and so that an adverbial clause introduced by "that" is admitted only in other cases. Further theoretical and empirical studies are necessary to determine which choice to make for any given purpose.

The column headed PREDICTION in tables 5 and 6 shows the status of a prediction subpool before the processing of the word in the same row. Whenever PD (PERIOD prediction) appears alone in that column, the word in the preceding row is the last of a well-formed substring of the sentence. Thus the sentence could have been terminated with a period in any position marked by a slash: IT HAS ALREADY BEEN MENTIONED / THAT A RESPONSE MAY BE LEARNED / BY THE MACHINE / IF ENCOURAGED / BY THE EXPERIMENTER.

5. PROGRAM

The analysis program for an IBM 7090 was written to follow only one path at a time, so that all data transfers and table references required in the course of analysis might be effected entirely within the core memory (32 000 words).

A path is determined in part by the choice of a single homograph S_{β_k} for each word position k ($k = 1, 2, \ldots, n$), where n is the number of words in a sentence. If the kth position has α_k homographs $S_{\beta_k}(\beta_k = 1, 2, \ldots, \alpha_k)$, then the total number of distinct selections is

$$N = \prod_{k=1}^{n} \alpha_k.$$

These N selections are effectively enumerated by means of a variable radix representation in which the kth digit β_k is initially set to 1 for all k; then β_n is incremented by unity until $\beta_n = \alpha_n + 1$, following which β_n is reset to 1 and β_{n-1} is increased by a unit carry, and so on in the usual way until $\beta_k = \alpha_k$ for all k.

Let p_k be a subpool in the prediction pool following the analysis of the kth word, and P_{ik} the topmost prediction in p_k. The number of paths from word k to the homograph $S_{\beta_{k+1}}$ due to p_k is then equal to the number γ_k of subrules

$$[(P_{ik}, S_{\beta_{k+1}}), g_{l_k}(P_{ik}, S_{\beta_{k+1}})] \quad (l_k = 1, \ldots, \gamma_k).$$

A single path from k to $k + 1$ is thus determined by fixing β_{k+1} and l_k. When

$$g_{l_k}(P_{ik}, S_{\beta_{k+1}})$$

replaces P_{ik} at the top of p_k, a new subpool p_{k+1} and a

corresponding $P_{i,k+1}$ are obtained, and the single path may, if possible, be extended to $k + 2$.

The extension will not be possible if either

$$k + 2 = n + 1 \text{ or } G(P_{i,k+1}, S_{\beta_{k+2}}) = \Phi.$$

In the former case, a path has been found through the sentence which, if p_{k+1} is empty, corresponds to an acceptable analysis. In the latter case, the path has no continuation to and through $S_{\beta_{k+2}}$; hence β_{k+2} is incremented. If $\beta_{k+2} + 1 = \alpha_{k+2} + 1$, extension of the path from k to $k + 1$ and on to $k + 2$ is ruled out completely and hence a new path from k to $k + 1$, determined by $l_k + 1$, is tried; β_{k+1} is reset to 1. Similarly, if $k + 2 = n + 1$, the path from k to $k + 1$ determined by $l_k + 1$ is checked. In either case, when $l_k + 1 = \gamma_k + 1$, the paths from k to $S_{\beta_{k+2}}$ have been exhausted, β_{k+1} is incremented, a new γ_k is provided, and l_k is reset to 1. If $\beta_{k+1} + 1 = \alpha_{k+1} + 1$, then β_{k+1} is set to 1 and a new path from $k - 1$ to k is tried, providing a new P_{ik}. The process terminates when $l_k = \gamma_k$, and $\beta_k = \alpha_k$ for all k.

Thus, branchings caused by homography (membership of a given word form in more than one syntactic word class) and by multiple functions of a given word class (more than one subrule in a grammar rule) are followed in a systematic loop-free sequence in which any given partial path is never followed more than once. The amount of core storage required in the course of analysing a sentence is proportional to n.

6. MINIMIZING THE NUMBER OF PATHS TO BE FOLLOWED

It was originally feared that the number of different paths to be taken, and hence the processing time, would grow exponentially with n, and make the method impractical. The programming technique of section 5 has, however, proved to be a very effective means of discarding irrelevant paths: if no path is open to S_{β_k} because $G(P_{i,k-1}, S_{\beta_k}) = \Phi$, then at least $\prod_{k+1}^{n} \alpha_i$ path continuations are eliminated at one stroke.

Several other techniques have been developed that eliminate additional irrelevant paths without destroying any paths which may yield acceptable analyses.

7. RUNNING TIME

The analysis of THEY ARE FLYING PLANES. on an IBM 7090 took less than one second. The analysis of IT HAS ALREADY BEEN MENTIONED THAT A RESPONSE MAY BE LEARNED BY THE MACHINE IF ENCOURAGED BY THE EXPERIMENTER. took approximately one minute. Twelve minutes were needed for the analysis of the 35-word sentence: A SHEAR STRESS APPLIED DURING THE RECOVERY HAD NO EFFECT ON THE AMOUNT OF RECOVERY, IF THE STRESS WAS LESS THAN THE INSTANTANEOUS YIELD POINT, IRRESPECTIVE OF THE DIRECTION OF THE STRESS.

The time necessary for the analysis of a sentence is not directly proportional to the length of the sentence, since it strongly depends on the nature of the sequence of homograph sets that are assigned to the words in the sentence.

8.   CONCLUSION

A program for multiple-path syntactic analysis of English has been written for both the Univac I and the IBM 7090 and tested on a variety of sentences. Experiments so far have yielded satisfactory results, and have given hints as to what should be done toward improving the definitions of word classes and of grammar rules and toward further reducing running time.

The application of the system to the analysis of Russian is now being studied, and it is expected that the basic principles of the method offer a convenient framework for the development of more powerful syntactic analyzers for both English and Russian. Since arbitrary sets of homographs can be assigned to one or more word positions, the system is also an experimental tool for the study of distributional and generative grammars.

9.   ACKNOWLEDGEMENTS

The authors are indebted to R. Thorpe, D. Isenberg, and W. Bossert for their programming of the multiple-path English syntactic analyzer on the IBM 7090.

10.   REFERENCES

1) Alt, F. L. and I. Rhodes: *Recognition of Clauses and Phrases in Machine Translation of Languages.* Proc. of the First International Conference on Machine Translation of Languages and Applied Language Analysis, NPL 1961. (to appear).
2) Oettinger, A. G.: *Automatic Syntactic Analysis and the Pushdown Store.* Proc. of Symposia in App. Math., Amer. Math. Soc. **12** (1961).
3) Rhodes, I.: *A New Approach to the Mechanical Translation of Russian.* NBS Report No. 6295 (1959).
4) Sherry, M.: *Comprehensive Report on Predictive Syntactic Analysis.* Mathematical Linguistics and Automatic Translation, Report No. NSF-7, Section I, Harvard Computation Laboratory (1961).

ABSTRACTS

Multiple analyses of syntactically ambiguous sentences have, for the first time, been effectively and economically realized, by a new extension of the method of predictive syntactic analysis. Branchings caused by homography (membership of a given word form in more than one syntactic word class), and by multiple functions of a given word class, are followed in a systematic loop-free sequence in which each partial path is traversed once only. Different paths that reach the last word in a sentence correspond to different acceptable syntactic structures of the sentence.

The prediction pool for this method is a pushdown store in the strict sense; the topmost prediction in the pool is matched against the class of the next word form of the sentence by look-up in an internally stored table of grammar rules, whose content may be varied at will without affecting the program for the analysis algorithm.

Satisfactory results have been obtained with programs for the analysis of English. The basic principles of the new method offer a convenient framework for the development of powerful techniques for the syntactic analysis, not only of English but also of Russian. The availability of alternative acceptable syntactic structures clarifies some of the issues lumped under the heading of *semantic ambiguity*.

Благодаря усовершенствованию метода предварительного синтаксического анализа впервые удалось осуществить анализ синтаксически многозначных предложений действительно эффективным и экономичным способом. Ветвления, обусловливаемые омонимикой (принадлежность одинаковых по форме слов к различным классам) или выполнением словами одного класса различных функций в предложении, осуществляется при помощи систематической линейной последовательности, каждый участок которой проходится только один раз. Различные пути, приводящие к последнему слову, соответствуют различным возможным синтаксическим структурам предложения.

При применяемом методе накопление информации по предварительному анализу выполняется, строго говоря, в форме последовательного накопления (последнее введенное в ячейки сведение выдается первым); верхнее из предварительно накопленных в ячейке сведений объединяется с данными класса следующего слова и отыскивается по заранее введенной в память машины таблице грамматических правил, содержание которой может меняться по желанию; такие изменения содержания таблицы не требуют изменений алгорифма программы.

Анализ английских текстов по рассматриваемой программе дал удовлетворительные результаты. Основные принципы данного метода являются доступным вспомогательным средством развития действенных технических приемов анализа как английских, так и русских текстов. Возможность получения разнообразных вариантов синтаксических структур способствует выяснению некоторых проблем объединяемых общим понятием "семантической многозначности".

Les différentes analyses de phrases syntaxiquement ambigues ont été effectivement et économiquement obtenues pour le première fois, par un développement nouveau de la méthode de l'analyse syntaxique prédictive. Les chemins multiples causés par les homographies (appartenance d'un mot donné à plus d'une classe syntaxique) et par les fonctions multiples d'un mot de classe déterminée, sont parcourus par un procédé séquentiel systématique par lequel chaque chemin partiel n'est traversé qu'une seule fois. Les chemins qui aboutissent au dernier mot de la phrase correspondent à différentes structures syntaxiques acceptables pour la phrase.

Dans cette méthode, la liste des prédictions est une *pushdown store* au sens strict; la prédiction immédiatement accessible dans cette liste est comparée à la classe de la forme suivante de la phrase, par la consultation d'une table grammaticale placée en mémoire interne et dont le contenu peut varier à volonté sans modification du programme d'analyse. Des programmes d'analyse de l'anglais ont fourni des résultats satisfaisants. Les principes de cette nouvelle méthode fournissent un cadre pratique au développement de techniques puissantes pouvant servir non seulement à l'analyse de l'Anglais mais aussi à celle du Russe. Le fait de disposer de l'ensemble de toutes les structures possibles éclaire certains faits rassemblés sous l'étiquette *ambiguïté sémantique.*

Die Analyse von syntaktisch mehrdeutigen Sätzen ist erstmalig durch eine Erweiterung der Methode der voraussagenden Syntax-Analyse auf eine wirkungsvolle und ökonomische Weise verwirklicht worden. Die Verzweigungen, welche durch Homonyme (Zugehörigkeit einer Wortform zu mehreren syntaktischen Wortklassen) oder durch mehrere Funktionen einer Wortklasse im Satz entstehen, werden in einer systematischen schleifenfreien Reihenfolge behandelt, in der jeder Teilweg nur einmal durchlaufen wird. Verschiedene Wege, die das letzte Wort erreichen, entsprechen verschiedenen möglichen syntaktischen Strukturen des Satzes.
Bei dieser Methode ist der Voraussagespeicher im genauen Sinne ein Stapelspeicher (letzte Eingabe ergibt erste Ausgabe); die oberste Voraussage des Stapels wird mit der Klasse des nächsten Wortes zusammengefasst und in einer intern gespeicherten Tabelle von grammatischen Regeln aufgesucht, deren Inhalt nach Belieben verändert werden kann, ohne dass das Programm für den Algorithmus der Analyse verändert wird.
Die Programme für die Analyse von englischen Sätzen haben zufriedenstellende Ergebnisse geliefert. Die Grundlagen dieser neuen Methode bilden ein einfaches Hilfsmittel für die Entwicklung von wirkungsvollen Techniken für die Analyse von sowohl englischer als auch russischer Syntax. Die Möglichkeit, mehrere Alternativen für die syntaktischen Strukturen zu erhalten, klärt einige der Fragen, die sich unter dem Begriff der „semantischen Mehrdeutigkeit" verbergen.

Por primera vez se han realizado, de forma efectiva y económica, el análisis multiple de sentencias sintácticas ambiguas por una nueva extensión del método de análisis sintáctico predictivo. Las ramas causadas por la homografía (cuando una forma de palabra dada es miembro de mas de una clase sintáctica) y por las funciones multiples de una clase de palabra dada son seguidas en una secuencia sistemática y sin lazos, en la que cada trayectoria parcial se atraviesa solamente una vez. Las trayectorias diferentes que alcanzan la última palabra de una sentencia corresponden a estructuras sintácticas diferentes y aceptables, de la sentencia.

El conjunto de predicciones por este metodo es un *pushdown store* en el sentido estricto; la predicción a la cabeza del conjunto se acopla de acuerdo con las formas de la clase de la próxima palabra de la sentencia, por medio de una consulta a una tabla de reglas gramaticales que se encuentra en una memoria interna, cuyo contenido puede ser cambiado a voluntad, sin afectar el programa del algoritmo para el análisis.

Se han obtenido resultados satisfactorios con programas para el análisis del inglés. Los principios basicos del nuevo método ofrecen un sistema adecuado para el desarrollo de fecundas técnicas para el análisis sintáctico, no, solamente del inglés, sino tambien del ruso. La posibilidad de estructuras sintácticas, alternativas, aceptables aclara algunos de los problemas agrupados bajo el encabezamiento de *ambiguedad secántica.*

An Efficient Context-Free Parsing Algorithm

Jay Earley

University of California, * *Berkeley, California*

A parsing algorithm which seems to be the most efficient general context-free algorithm known is described. It is similar to both Knuth's LR(k) algorithm and the familiar top-down algorithm. It has a time bound proportional to n^3 (where n is the length of the string being parsed) in general; it has an n^2 bound for unambiguous grammars; and it runs in linear time on a large class of grammars, which seems to include most practical context-free programming language grammars. In an empirical comparison it appears to be superior to the top-down and bottom-up algorithms studied by Griffiths and Petrick.

KEY WORDS AND PHRASES: syntax analysis, parsing, context-free grammar, compilers, computational complexity

CR CATEGORIES: 4.12, 5.22, 5.23

1. Introduction

Context-free grammars (BNF grammars) have been used extensively for describing the syntax of programming languages and natural languages. Parsing algorithms for context-free grammars consequently play a large role in the implementation of compilers and interpreters for pro-

* Computer Science Department. This work was partially supported by the Office of Naval Research under Contract No. NONR3656(23) with the Computer Center, University of California, Berkeley, and by the Advanced Research Projects Agency of the Office of the Secretary of Defense (F44620-67-C-0058), monitored by the Air Force Office of Scientific Research.

gramming languages and of programs which "understand" or translate natural languages.

Numerous parsing algorithms have been developed. Some are general, in the sense that they can handle all context-free grammars, while others can handle only subclasses of grammars. The latter, restricted algorithms tend to be much more efficient. The algorithm described here seems to be the most efficient of the general algorithms, and also it can handle a larger class of grammars in linear time than most of the restricted algorithms. We back up these claims of efficiency with both a formal investigation and an empirical comparison.

This paper is based on the author's 1968 report [1] where many of the points studied here appear in much greater detail. In Section 2 the terminology used in this paper is defined. In Section 3 the algorithm is described informally and in Section 4 it is described precisely. Section 5 is a study of the formal efficiency properties of the algorithm and may be skipped by those not interested in this aspect. Section 6 has the empirical comparison and in Section 7 the practical use of the algorithm is discussed.

2. Terminology

A *language* is a set of strings over a finite set of symbols. We call these *terminal* symbols and represent them by lowercase letters: a, b, c. We use a *context-free grammar* as a formal device for specifying which strings are in the set. This grammar uses another set of symbols, the *nonterminals*, which we can think of as syntactic classes. We use capitals for nonterminals: A, B, C. Strings of either terminals or nonterminals are represented by Greek letters: α, β, γ. The empty string is λ. α^k represents

$$\overset{k \text{ times}}{\overbrace{\alpha \cdots \alpha}}.$$

$|\alpha|$ is the number of symbols in α. There is a finite set of productions or rewriting rules of the form $A \rightarrow \alpha$. The nonterminal which stands for "sentence" is called the root R of the grammar. The productions with a particular non-terminal D on their left sides are called the *alternatives* of D. Hereafter we use grammar to mean context-free grammar.

We will work with this example grammar of simple arithmetic expressions, grammar AE:

$$E \rightarrow T$$
$$E \rightarrow E + T$$
$$T \rightarrow P$$
$$T \rightarrow T * P$$
$$P \rightarrow a$$

The terminal symbols are $\{a, +, *\}$, the nonterminals are $\{E, T, P\}$, and the root is E.

Most of the rest of the definitions are understood to be with respect to a particular grammar G. We write $\alpha \Rightarrow \beta$ if $\exists \gamma, \delta, \eta$, A such that $\alpha = \gamma A \delta$ and $\beta = \gamma \eta \delta$ and $A \rightarrow \eta$ is a production. We write $\alpha \overset{*}{\Rightarrow} \beta$ (β is *derived* from α) if $\exists$ strings $\alpha_0, \alpha_1, \cdots, \alpha_m$ $(m \geq 0)$ such that

$$\alpha = \alpha_0 \Rightarrow \alpha_1 \Rightarrow \cdots \Rightarrow \alpha_m = \beta.$$

The sequence $\alpha_0, \cdots, \alpha_m$ is called a derivation (of β from α).

A *sentential form* is a string α such that the root $R \overset{*}{\Rightarrow} \alpha$. A *sentence* is a sentential form consisting entirely of terminal symbols. The *language defined by a grammar* $L(G)$ is the set of its sentences. We may represent any sentential form in at least one way as a *derivation tree* (or *parse tree*) reflecting the steps made in deriving it (though not the order of the steps). For example, in grammar AE, either derivation

$$E \Rightarrow E + T \Rightarrow T + T \Rightarrow T + P \Rightarrow T * P + P$$

or

$$E \Rightarrow E + T \Rightarrow E + P \Rightarrow T + P \Rightarrow T * P + P$$

is represented by

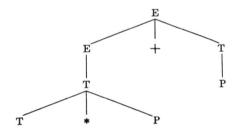

The *degree of ambiguity* of a sentence is the number of its distinct derivation trees. A sentence is *unambiguous* if it has degree 1 of ambiguity. A grammar is *unambiguous* if each of its sentences is unambiguous. A grammar has *bounded ambiguity* if there is a bound b on the degree of ambiguity of any sentence of the grammar. A grammar is *reduced* if every nonterminal appears in some derivation of some sentence.

A *recognizer* is an algorithm which takes as input a string and either *accepts* or *rejects* it depending on whether or not the string is a sentence of the grammar. A *parser* is a recognizer which also outputs the set of all legal derivation trees for the string.

3. Informal Explanation

The following is an informal description of the algorithm as a recognizer: It scans an input string $X_1 \cdots X_n$ from left to right looking ahead some fixed number k of symbols. As each symbol X_i is scanned, a set of states S_i is constructed which represents the condition of the recognition process at that point in the scan. Each state in the set represents (1) a production such that we are currently scanning a portion of the input string which is derived from its right side, (2) a point in that production which shows how much of the production's right side we have recognized so far, (3) a pointer back to the position in the input string at which we began to look for that instance of the production, and (4) a k-symbol string which is a syntactically allowed successor to that instance of the production. This quadruple is represented here as a production, with a dot in it, followed by an integer and a string.

For example, if we are recognizing $a * a$ with respect to grammar AE and we have scanned the first a, we would be in the state set S_1 consisting of the following states (excluding the k-symbol strings):

$P \rightarrow a.$	0
$T \rightarrow P.$	0
$T \rightarrow T. * P$	0
$E \rightarrow T.$	0
$E \rightarrow E. + T$	0

Each state represents a possible parse for the beginning of the string, given that only the $a \cdot$ has been seen.[1] All the states have 0 as a pointer, since all the productions represented must have begun at the beginning of the string.

There will be one such state set for each position in the string. To aid in recognition, we place $k + 1$ right terminators " $\dashv$ " (a symbol which does not appear elsewhere in the grammar) at the right end of the input string.

To begin the algorithm, we put the single state

$$\phi \rightarrow .R \dashv \quad \dashv^k \quad 0$$

into state set S_0, where R is the root of the grammar and where ϕ is a new nonterminal.

In general, we operate on a state set S_i as follows: we process the states in the set in order, performing one of three operations on each one depending on the form of the state. These operations may add more states to S_i and may also put states in a new state set S_{i+1}. We describe these three operations by example.

In grammar AE, with $k = 1$, S_0 starts as the single state

$$\phi \rightarrow .E \dashv \quad \dashv \quad 0 \qquad (1)$$

The *predictor* operation is applicable to a state when there is a nonterminal to the right of the dot. It causes us to add one new state to S_i for each alternative of that nonterminal. We put the dot at the beginning of the production in each new state, since we have not scanned any of its symbols yet. The pointer is set to i, since the state was created in S_i. Thus the predictor adds to S_i all productions which might generate substrings beginning at X_{i+1}.

In our example, we add to S_0

$$E \to .E+T \quad \dashv \quad 0 \qquad (2)$$

$$E \to .T \quad \dashv \quad 0 \qquad (3)$$

The k-symbol look-ahead string is $\dashv$, since it is after E in the original state. We must now process these two states. The predictor is also applicable to them. Operating on (2), it produces

$$E \to .E+T \quad + \quad 0 \qquad (4)$$

$$E \to .T \quad + \quad 0 \qquad (5)$$

with a look-ahead symbol $+$ because it appears after E in (2). Operating on (3), it produces

$$T \to .T*P \quad \dashv \quad 0$$

$$T \to .P \quad \dashv \quad 0$$

Here the look-ahead symbol is $\dashv$ because T is last in the production and $\dashv$ is its look-ahead symbol. Now, the predictor, operating on (4) produces (4) and (5) again, but they are already in S_0, so we do nothing. From (5) it produces

$$T \to .T*P \quad + \quad 0$$

$$T \to .P \quad + \quad 0$$

The rest of S_0 is

$$T \to .T*P \quad * \quad 0$$

$$T \to .P \quad * \quad 0$$

$$P \to .a \quad \dashv \quad 0$$

$$P \to .a \quad + \quad 0$$

$$P \to .a \quad * \quad 0$$

The predictor is not applicable to any of the last three states. Instead the *scanner* is, because it is applicable just in case there is a terminal to the right of the dot. The scanner compares that symbol with X_{i+1}, and if they match, it adds the state to S_{i+1}, with the dot moved over one in the state to indicate that that terminal symbol has been scanned.

If $X_1 = a$, then S_1 is

$$P \to a. \quad \dashv \quad 0$$

$$P \to a. \quad + \quad 0 \qquad (6)$$

$$P \to a. \quad * \quad 0$$

these states being added by the scanner.

If we finish processing S_i and S_{i+1} remains empty, an error has occurred in the input string. Otherwise, we start to process S_{i+1}.

The third operation, the *completer*, is applicable to a state if its dot is at the end of its production. Thus the completer is applicable to each of these states in S_1. It compares the look-ahead string with $X_{i+1} \cdots X_{i+k}$. If they match, it goes back to the state set indicated by the pointer, in this case S_0, and adds all states from S_0 which have P to the right of the dot. It moves the dot over P in these states. Intuitively, S_0 is the state set we were in when we went looking for that P. We have now found it, so we go back to all the states in S_0 which caused us to look for a P, and we move the dot over the P in these states to show that it has been successfully scanned.

If $X_2 = +$, then the completer applied to (6) causes us to add to S_1

$$T \to P. \quad \dashv \quad 0$$

$$T \to P. \quad + \quad 0$$

$$T \to P. \quad * \quad 0$$

Applying the completer to the second of these produces

$$E \to T. \quad \dashv \quad 0$$

$$E \to T. \quad + \quad 0$$

$$T \to T.*P \quad \dashv \quad 0$$

$$T \to T.*P \quad + \quad 0$$

$$T \to T.*P \quad * \quad 0$$

and finally, from the second of these, we get

$$\phi \to E. \dashv \quad \dashv \quad 0$$

$$E \to E.+T \quad \dashv \quad 0$$

$$E \to E.+T \quad + \quad 0$$

The scanner then adds to S_2

$$E \to E+.T \quad \dashv \quad 0$$

$$E \to E+.T \quad + \quad 0$$

If the algorithm ever produces an S_{i+1} consisting of the single state

$$\phi \to E \dashv. \quad \dashv \quad 0$$

then we have correctly scanned an E and the $\dashv$, so we are finished with the string, and it is a sentence of the grammar.

A complete run of the algorithm on grammar AE is given in Figure 1. In this example, we have written as one all the states in a state set which differ only in their look-ahead string. (Thus "$\dashv+*$" as a look-ahead string stands for three states, with "$\dashv$", "$+$", and "$*$" as their respective look-ahead strings.)

The technique of using state sets and the look-ahead are derived from Knuth's work on LR(k) grammars [2]. In fact our algorithm bears a close relationship to Knuth's algorithm on LR(k) grammars except for the fact that

GRAMMAR AE

root: E → T | E+T   input string = a+a*a
      T → P | T*P
      P → a

$k = 1$

S_0	φ → .E⊣	⊣	0		S_3	P → a.	⊣+*	2
(X_1=a)	E → .E+T	⊣+	0			T → P.	⊣+*	2
	E → .T	⊣+	0			E → E+T.	⊣+	0
	T → .T*P	⊣+*	0			T → T.*P	⊣+*	2
	T → .P	⊣+*	0		S_4	T → T*.P	⊣+*	2
	P → .a	⊣+*	0		(X_5=a)	P → .a	⊣+*	4
S_1	P → a.	⊣+*	0					
(X_2=+)	T → P.	⊣+*	0		S_5	P → a.	⊣+*	4
	E → T.	⊣+	0		(X_6=⊣)	T → T*P.	⊣+*	2
	T → T.*P	⊣+*	0			E → E+T.	⊣+	0
	φ → E.⊣	⊣	0			T → T.*P	⊣+*	2
	E → E.+T	⊣+	0			φ → E.⊣	⊣	0
S_2	E → E+.T	⊣+	0			E → E.+T	⊣+	0
(X_3=a)	T → .T*P	⊣+*	2					
	T → .P	⊣+*	2		S_6	φ → E⊣.	⊣	0
	P → .a	⊣+*	2					

FIG. 1

he uses a stack rather than pointers to keep track of what to do after a parsing decision is made.

Note also that, although it did not develop this way, our algorithm is in effect a top-down parser [3] in which we carry along all possible parses simultaneously in such a way that we can often combine like subparses. This cuts down on duplication of effort and also avoids the left-recursion problem. (A straightforward top-down parser may go into an infinite loop on grammars containing left-recursion, i.e. $A \rightarrow A\beta$.)

4. The Recognizer

The following is a precise description of the recognition algorithm for input string $X_1 \cdots X_n$ and grammar G.

NOTATION. Number the productions of grammar G arbitrarily $1, \cdots, d - 1$, where each production is of the form

$$D_p \rightarrow C_{p1} \cdots C_{p\bar{p}} \qquad (1 \leq p \leq d - 1)$$

where $\bar{p}$ is the number of symbols on the right-hand side of the pth production. Add a 0th production

$$D_0 \rightarrow R \dashv$$

where R is the root of G, and $\dashv$ is a new terminal symbol.

Definition. A *state* is a quadruple $\langle p, j, f, \alpha \rangle$ where $p, j,$ and f are integers $(0 \leq p \leq d - 1)$ $(0 \leq j \leq \bar{p})$ $(0 \leq f \leq n + 1)$ and α is a string consisting of k terminal symbols. *state set* is an ordered set of states. A *final state* is one in which $j = \bar{p}$. We *add* a state to a state set by putting it last in the ordered set *unless it is already a member.*

Definition. $H_k(\gamma) = \{\alpha \,|\, \alpha$ is terminal, $|\alpha| = k$, and $\exists \beta$ such that $\gamma \overset{*}{\Rightarrow} \alpha\beta\}$.

$H_k(\gamma)$ is the set of all k-symbol terminal strings which begin some string derived from γ. This is used in forming the look-ahead string for the states.

THE RECOGNIZER. This is a function of three arguments REC(G, $X_1 \cdots X_n$, k) computed as follows:

Let $X_{n+i} = \dashv$ $(1 \leq i \leq k + 1)$.
Let S_i be empty $(0 \leq i \leq n + 1)$.
Add $\langle 0,0,0,\dashv^k \rangle$ to S_0.

For $i \leftarrow 0$ step 1 until n do
Begin
  Process the states of S_i in order, performing one of the following three operations on each state $s = \langle p, j, f, \alpha \rangle$.
  (1) Predictor: If s is nonfinal and $C_{p(j+1)}$ is a nonterminal, then for each q such that $C_{p(j+1)} = D_q$, and for each $\beta \in H_k(C_{p(j+2)} \cdots C_{p\bar{p}}\alpha)$ add $\langle q, 0, i, \beta \rangle$ to S_i.
  (2) Completer: If s is final and $\alpha = X_{i+1} \cdots X_{i+k}$, then for each $\langle q,l,g,\beta \rangle \in S_f$ (after all states have been added to S_f) such that $C_{q(l+1)} = D_p$, add $\langle q,l+1, g, \beta \rangle$ to S_i.
  (3) Scanner: If s is nonfinal and $C_{p(j+1)}$ is terminal, then if $C_{p(j+1)} = X_{i+1}$, add $\langle p, j+1, f, \alpha \rangle$ to S_{i+1}.
  If S_{i+1} is empty, return rejection.
  If $i = n$ and $S_{i+1} = \{\langle 0,2,0,\dashv \rangle\}$, return acceptance.
End

Notice that the ordering imposed on state sets is not important to their meaning but is simply a device which allows their members to be processed correctly by the algorithm. Also note that i cannot become greater than n without either acceptance or rejection occurring because of the fact that $\dashv$ appears only in production zero. This does not really represent a complete description of the algorithm until we describe in detail how all these operations are implemented on a machine. The following description assumes a knowledge of basic list processing techniques.

Implementation

(1) For each nonterminal, we keep a linked list of its alternatives, for use in prediction.

(2) The states in a state set are kept in a linked list so they can be processed in order.

(3) In addition, as each state set S_i is constructed, we put entries into a vector of size i. The fth entry in this vector $(0 \leq f \leq i)$ is a pointer to a list of all states in S_i with pointer f, i.e. states of the form $\langle p, j, f, \alpha \rangle \in S_i$ for some p, j, α. Thus, to test if a state $\langle p, j, f, \alpha \rangle$ has already been added to S_i, we search through the list pointed to by the fth entry in this vector. (This takes an amount of time independent of f.) The vector and lists can be discarded after S_i is constructed.

(4) For the use of the completer, we also keep, for each state set S_i and nonterminal N, a list of all states $\langle p, j, f, \alpha \rangle \in S_i$ such that $C_{p(j+1)} = N$.

(5) If the grammar contains null productions ($A \rightarrow \lambda$), we cannot implement the completer in a straightforward way. When performing the completer on a null state ($A \rightarrow \cdot\ \alpha\ i$) we want to add to S_i each state in S_i with A to the right of the dot. But one of these may not have been added to S_i yet. So we must note this and check for it when we add more states to S_i.

The above implementation description is not meant to be the only way or the best way to implement the algorithm. It is merely a method which does allow the algorithm to achieve the time and space bounds which we quote in Section 5.

The correctness of this recognizer has been proved in [1]. It requires no restrictions of any kind on the context-free grammar to be successful.

5. Time and Space Bounds

To develop some idea of the efficiency of the algorithm, we can use a formal model of a computer and measure the time as the number of primitive steps executed by this model and the space as the number of storage locations used. We use a random access model (described in the Appendix) because we feel that this model represents most accurately the properties of real computers which are relevant to syntax analysis.

We are interested in upper bounds on the time (and less important the space) as a function of n (the length of the input string) for various classes of context-free grammars. Specifically, an n^2 algorithm for a subclass A of grammars means that there is some number C (which may depend on the size of the grammar, but not on n), such that Cn^2 is an upper bound on the number of primitive steps required to parse any string of length n with respect to a grammar in class A.

THE GENERAL CASE. Our algorithm is an n^3 recognizer in general. The reasons for this are:

(a) The number of states in any state set S_i is proportional to i ($\sim i$) because the ranges of the p, j, and α components of a state are bounded, while only the f component depends on i, and it is bounded by n.

(b) The scanner and predictor operations each execute a bounded number of steps per state in any state set. So the total time for processing the states in S_i plus the scanner and predictor operations is $\sim i$.

(c) The completer executes $\sim i$ steps for each state it processes in the worst case because it may have to add $\sim f$ states for S_f, the state set pointed back to. So it takes $\sim i^2$ steps in S_i.

(d) Summing from $i = 0, \cdots, n + 1$ gives $\sim n^3$ steps.

This bound holds even if the look-ahead feature is not used (by setting $k = 0$). The bound is no better than that obtained by Younger [4] for Cocke's algorithm [5], but our algorithm is better for two reasons. Ours does not require the grammar to be put into any special form (Cocke's required normal form), and ours actually does better than n^3 on most grammars, as we shall show (Cocke's always requires n^3). Furthermore, although Younger's n^3 result is obtained on a Turing machine, his algorithm is in no way made faster by putting it on a random access machine.

UNAMBIGUOUS GRAMMARS. The completer is the only operation which forces us to use i^2 steps for each state set we process, making the whole thing n^3. So the question is, in what cases does this operation involve only i steps instead of i^2? If we examine the state set S_i after the completer has been applied to it, there are at most proportional to i states in it. So unless some of them were added in more

than one way (this can happen; that's why we must test for the existence of a state before we add it to a state set) then it took at most $\sim i$ steps to do the operation.

In the case that the grammar is unambiguous and reduced, we can show that each such state gets added in only one way. Assume that the state $\langle q, j+1, f, \alpha \rangle$ is added to S_i in two different ways by the completer. Then we have

$$s_1 = \langle p_1, \bar{p}_1, f_1, X_{i+1} \cdots X_{i+k} \rangle \in S_i,$$

$$s_2 = \langle p_2, \bar{p}_2, f_2, X_{i+1} \cdots X_{i+k} \rangle \in S_i,$$

$$\langle q, j, f, \alpha \rangle \in S_{f_1} \quad \text{and} \quad S_{f_2}, \quad D_{p_1} = C_{q(j+1)} = D_{p_2}$$

and either $p_1 \neq p_2$ or $f_1 \neq f_2$, for otherwise s_1 and s_2 would be the same state.

So we have

$$X_1 \cdots X_f C_{q1} \cdots C_{q(j+1)} \overset{*}{\Rightarrow} X_1 \cdots X_{f_1} C_{p_1 1} \cdots C_{p_1 \bar{p}_1}$$
$$\overset{*}{\Rightarrow} X_1 \cdots X_i$$

and

$$X_1 \cdots X_f C_{q1} \cdots C_{q(j+1)} \overset{*}{\Rightarrow} X_1 \cdots X_{f_2} C_{p_2 1} \cdots C_{p_2 \bar{p}_2}$$
$$\overset{*}{\Rightarrow} X_1 \cdots X_i$$

and since $p_1 = p_2$ and $f_1 = f_2$ cannot both be true, the above two derivations of $X_1 \cdots X_i$ are represented by different derivation trees. Therefore since the grammar is reduced, every nonterminal generates some terminal string, and so there exists an ambiguous sentence $X_1 \cdots X_i \alpha$ for some α.

So if the grammar is unambiguous, the completer executes $\sim i$ steps per state set and the time is bounded by n^2. Notice that the time is also n^2 for grammars with bounded ambiguity since each state can then be added by the completer only a bounded number of times. In [1] we show that the time is n^2 for an even larger class of grammars, and thereby also obtain Younger's n^2 results for linear and metalinear grammars [6].

Kasami [7] has also obtained independently the result for unambiguous grammars, but his algorithm (which is a modification of Cocke's) has the disadvantage that it requires the grammar in normal form. His algorithm, like ours, achieves its time bound on a random access machine only.

LINEAR TIME. We now characterize the class of grammars which the algorithm will do in time n. We notice that for some grammars the number of states in a state set can grow indefinitely with the length of the string being recognized. For some others there is a fixed bound on the size of any state set. We call the latter grammars *bounded state grammars*. They can be done by the algorithm in time n for the following reason. Let b be the bound on the number of states in any state set. Then the processing of the states in a state set together with the scanner and predictor requires $\sim b$ steps, and the completer requires $\sim b^2$ steps. Summing over all the state sets gives us $\sim b^2 n$ or $\sim n$ steps.

So the class of time n grammars for our algorithm includes the bounded state grammars, but it actually includes more. We now examine how this class of grammars compares with those that can be done in linear time by other algorithms. Most of the previously mentioned "restricted" algorithms work on some subclass of grammars which they can do in time n, and we will henceforth call them *time n* algorithms. Knuth's LR(k) algorithm [2] works on a class of grammars which includes those of just about all the others, so his will be a good one for comparison if we expect to do well.

It turns out that almost all LR(k) grammars are bounded state (except for certain right recursive grammars). And even though some LR(k) grammars may not be bounded state, all of them can be done in time n by our algorithm if a look-ahead of k or greater is used. In fact any finite union of LR(k) grammars (obtained by combining the grammars in a straightforward way in order to generate the union of the languages) is a time n grammar for our algorithm given the proper look-ahead. (This is proved in [1].)

It is here that the look-ahead feature of the algorithm is most obviously useful. We can obtain the n^3 and n^2 results without it, but we cannot do all LR(k) grammars in time n without it. In addition, a look-ahead of $k = 1$ is a good practical device for cutting down on a lot of extraneous processing with many common grammars.

The time n grammars for our algorithm, then, include bounded state grammars, finite unions of LR(k) grammars, and others. They include many grammars which are ambiguous, and some with unbounded degree of ambiguity, but unfortunately there are also unambiguous grammars which require time n^2.

The following examples illustrate some of the ideas in this section. Grammar UBDA (Figure 2) actually re-requires time proportional to n^3. Notice that state

$$A \to AA. \quad \dashv x \quad 0^2$$

gets added twice by the completer. This is signified by the superscript on the 0. One can tell by the looks of the superscripts on states

$$A \to AA. \quad \dashv x \quad 2$$

$$A \to AA. \quad \dashv x \quad 1^2$$

$$A \to AA. \quad \dashv x \quad 0^3$$

in S_4 that there are $\sim i$ states, each of which is added $\sim i$ times, in $\sim n$ state sets, producing the n^3 behavior.

Grammar BK (Figure 3) has unbounded ambiguity, but it is a time n grammar, and in fact it is bounded state. This can be seen because all the state sets after S_1 are the same size. Grammar PAL (Figure 4) is an unambiguous grammar which requires time n^2. S_i and S_{i+1} each have $i + 4$ states in them, up to and including S_n, so the total number of states is $\sim n^2$.

SPACE. Since the space is taken up by $\sim n$ state sets, each containing $\sim n$ states, the space bound is n^2 in general. This is comparable to Cocke's and Kasami's algorithms, which also require n^2. However, it has the advantage over Cocke's in that the n^2 is only an upper bound for ours, while his requires n^2 all the time.

GRAMMAR UBDA

root: $A \to x \mid AA$ sentences: x^n $(n \geq 1)$

REC(UBDA, x^4, 1)

S_0	$\phi \to .A\dashv$	$\dashv$	0
	$A \to .x$	$\dashv x$	0
	$A \to .AA$	$\dashv x$	0
S_1	$A \to x.$	$\dashv x$	0
	$\phi \to A.\dashv$	$\dashv$	0
	$A \to A.A$	$\dashv x$	0
	$A \to .x$	$\dashv x$	1
	$A \to .AA$	$\dashv x$	1
S_2	$A \to x.$	$\dashv x$	1
	$A \to AA.$	$\dashv x$	0
	$A \to A.A$	$\dashv x$	1
	$\phi \to A.\dashv$	$\dashv$	0
	$A \to A.A$	$\dashv x$	0
	$A \to .x$	$\dashv x$	2
	$A \to .AA$	$\dashv x$	2

$\dot{S_3}$	$A \to x.$	$\dashv x$	2
	$A \to AA.$	$\dashv x$	1
	$A \to AA.$	$\dashv x$	0^2
	$A \to A.A$	$\dashv x$	2
	$A \to A.A$	$\dashv x$	1
	$\phi \to A.\dashv$	$\dashv$	0
	$A \to A.A$	$\dashv x$	0
	$A \to .x$	$\dashv x$	3
	$A \to .AA$	$\dashv x$	3
S_4	$A \to x.$	$\dashv x$	3
	$A \to AA.$	$\dashv x$	2
	$A \to AA.$	$\dashv x$	1^2
	$A \to AA.$	$\dashv x$	0^3
	$A \to A.A$	$\dashv x$	3
	$A \to A.A$	$\dashv x$	2
	$A \to A.A$	$\dashv x$	1
	$\phi \to A.\dashv$	$\dashv$	0
	$A \to A.A$	$\dashv x$	0
	$A \to .x$	$\dashv x$	4
	$A \to .AA$	$\dashv x$	4
S_5	$\phi \to A\dashv.$	$\dashv$	0

Fig. 2

GRAMMAR BK

root: $K \to \mid KJ$ sentences: x^n $(n \geq 0)$
   $J \to F \mid I$
   $F \to x$
   $I \to x$

REC(BK, x^n, 1)

S_0	$\phi \to .K\dashv$	$\dashv$	0
	$K \to .$	$\dashv x$	0
	$K \to .KJ$	$\dashv x$	0
	$\phi \to K.\dashv$	$\dashv$	0
	$K \to K.J$	$\dashv x$	0
	$J \to .F$	$\dashv x$	0
	$J \to .I$	$\dashv x$	0
	$F \to .x$	$\dashv x$	0
	$I \to .x$	$\dashv x$	0
S_1	$F \to x.$	$\dashv x$	0
	$I \to x.$	$\dashv x$	0
	$J \to F.$	$\dashv x$	0
	$J \to I.$	$\dashv x$	0
	$K \to KJ.$	$\dashv x$	0^2
	$K \to K.J$	$\dashv x$	0
	$\phi \to K.\dashv$	$\dashv$	0
	$J \to .F$	$\dashv x$	1
	$J \to .I$	$\dashv x$	1
	$F \to .x$	$\dashv x$	1
	$I \to .x$	$\dashv x$	1

S_i	$(2 \leq i \leq n)$		
	$F \to x.$	$\dashv x$	$i - 1$
	$F \to x.$	$\dashv x$	$i - 1$
	$J \to F.$	$\dashv x$	$i - 1$
	$J \to I.$	$\dashv x$	$i - 1$
	$K \to KJ.$	$\dashv x$	0^2
	$K \to K.J$	$\dashv x$	0
	$\phi \to K.\dashv$	$\dashv$	0
	$J \to .F$	$\dashv x$	i
	$J \to .I$	$\dashv x$	i
	$F \to .x$	$\dashv x$	i
	$I \to .x$	$\dashv x$	i
S_{n+1}			
	$\phi \to K\dashv.$	$\dashv$	0

Fig. 3

```
                    GRAMMAR PAL

A → x | xAx          sentences:  xⁿ (n ≧ 1, n odd)
                     REC(PAL, x⁵, 0):

S₀  φ → .A⊣     0      S₄  A → xAx.     1
    A → .x       0          A → x.        3
    A → .xAx     0          A → x.Ax      3
S₁  A → x.       0          A → xA.x      0
    A → x.Ax     0          A → xA.x      2
    φ → A.⊣      0          A → .x        4
    A → .x       1          A → .xAx      4
    A → .xAx     1      S₅  A → xAx.     0
S₂  A → x.       1          A → xAx.      2
    A → x.Ax     1          A → x.        4
    A → xA.x     0          A → x.Ax      4
    A → .x       2          φ → A.⊣       0
    A → .xAx     2          A → xA.x      1
S₃  A → xAx.     0          A → xA.x      3
    A → x.        2          A → .x        5
    A → x.Ax     2          A → xAx.      5
    φ → A.⊣      0      S₆  φ → A⊣ .      0
    A → xA.x     1
    A → .x       3
    A → .xAx     3

                    Fɪɢ. 4
```

```
   G1          G2          G3          G4
root:        root:       root:       root:
  S → Ab       S → aB      S → ab | aSb   S → AB
  A → a | Ab   B → aB | b              A → a | Ab
                                       B → bc | bB | Bd

Gram- Sen-
mar  tence   TD        STD       BU        SBU       Ours
G1   abⁿ   (n²+7n    (n²+7n    9n+5      9n+5      4n+7
            +2)/2     +2)/2
G2   aⁿb   3n+2      2n+2      11·2ⁿ+7   4n+4      4n+4
G3   aⁿbⁿ  5n−1      5n−1      11·2ⁿ⁻¹−5 6n        6n+4
G4   abⁿcd ∼2ⁿ⁺⁶    ∼2ⁿ⁺²    ∼2ⁿ⁺⁶    (n³+21n²+46n  18n+8
                                         +15)/3
```

Fɪɢ. 5

```
        PROPOSITIONAL CALCULUS GRAMMAR
        root:  F → C | S | P | U
               C → U ⊃ U
               U → (F) | ∼U | L
               L → L' | p | q | r
               S → U ∨ S | U ∨ U
               P → U ∧ P | U ∧ U

      Sentence            Length  PA   SBU  Ours
p                           1     14   18   28
(p∧q)∨r∨p∨q'                 5     89   56   68
(p'∧q)∨r∨p∨q'               13    232  185  148
p⊃((q⊃∼(r'∨(p∧q))           26    712  277  277
   ⊃ (q'∨r)
∼(∼p'∧(q∨r)∧p')             17   1955  223  141
((p∧q)∨(q∧r)∨(r∧p'))        38   2040  562  399
   ⊃∼((p'∨q')∧(r'∨p))
```

Fɪɢ. 6

6. Empirical Results

We have programmed the algorithm and tested it against the top-down and bottom-up parsers evaluated by Griffiths and Petrick [8]. These are the oldest of the context-free parsers, and they depend heavily on backtracking. Perhaps because of this, their upper bounds for time are exponential (C^n for some constant C). However, they also can do well on some grammars, and both have been used in numerous compiler-compilers, so it will be interesting to compare our algorithm with them.

The Griffiths and Petrick data is not in terms of actual running times but in terms of "primitive operations." They have expressed their algorithms as sets of nondeterministic rewriting rules for a Turing-machine-like device. Each application of one of these is a primitive operation. We have chosen as our primitive operation the act of adding a state to a state set (or attempting to add one which is already there). We feel that this is comparable to their primitive operation because both are in some sense the most complex operation performed by the algorithm whose complexity is independent of the size of the grammar or input string.

We compare the algorithms on seven different grammars. Two of their examples were not used because the exact grammar was not given. For the first four, Griffiths and Petrick were able to find closed-form expressions for their results, so we did also (Figure 5). BU and TD are the bottom-up and top-down algorithms respectively and SBU and STD are their selective versions. It is obvious from these results that SBU is by far the best of the other algorithms, and the rest of their data bears this out. There-

```
              GRAMMAR GRE
        root:  X → a | Xb | Ya
               Y → e | YdY

   Sentence      Length   PA      SBU     Ours
ededea             6       35       52      33
ededeab⁴          10       75       92      45
ededeab¹⁰         16       99      152      63
ededeab²⁰⁰       206      859     2052     633
(ed)⁴eabb         12      617      526      79
(ed)⁷eabb         18    24352    16336     194
(ed)⁸eabb         20    86139    54660     251
```

Fɪɢ. 7

```
              GRAMMAR NSE
        root:  S → AB
               A → a | SC
               B → b | DB
               C → c
               D → d

   Sentence           Length   SBU    Ours
adbcddb                  7       43     44
ad³bcbcd³bcd⁴b          18      111    108
adbcd²bcd⁵bcd³b         19      117    114
ad¹⁸b                  20      120    123
a(bc)³d³(bcd)²dbcd⁴b    24      150    141
a(bcd)²dbcd³bcb         16      100     95
```

Fɪɢ. 8

fore we compare our algorithm with SBU only. We used our algorithm with $k = 0$. The two are comparable on G1, G2, G3, the simple grammars, but on G4, which is very ambiguous, ours is clearly superior—n to n^3.

For the next three grammars we present only the raw data (Figures 6–8). The data for our algorithm was obtained by programming it and having the program compute the number of primitive operations it performed. We have also included the data from [8] on PA, the predictive analyzer, which is a modified top-down algorithm. On the propositional calculus grammar, PA seems to be running in time n^2, while both SBU and ours run in time n, with ours a little faster. Grammar GRE produces two kinds of behavior. All three algorithms go up linearly with the number of "b"'s, with SBU using a considerably higher constant coefficient. However, PA and SBU go up exponentially with the number of "ed"'s, while ours goes up as the square. Grammar NSE is quite simple, and each algorithm takes time n with the same coefficient.

So we conclude that our algorithm is clearly superior to the backtracking algorithms. It performs as well as the best of them on all seven grammars and is substantially faster on some.

There are at least four distinct general context-free algorithms besides ours—TD, BU, Kasami's n^2, and Cocke's n^3. We have shown so far that our algorithm achieves time bounds which are as good as those of any of these algorithms, or better. However, we are also interested in how our algorithm compares with these algorithms in a practical sense, not just at an upper bound.

We have just presented some empirical results in this section which indicate that our algorithm is better than TD and BU. Furthermore, our algorithm must be superior to Cocke's since his always achieves its upper bound of n^3. This leaves Kasami's. His algorithm [7] is actually described as an algorithm for unambiguous grammars, but it can easily be extended to a general algorithm. In this form we suspect that it will have an n^3 bound in general and will be n^2 as often as ours. We are aware of no results about the class of grammars that it can parse in time n.

7.   The Practical Use of the Algorithm

In this section we discuss the question, in what areas and in what form can the algorithm best be put to use?

THE FORM.   Before we can do much with it, we must make the recognizer into a parser. This is done by altering the recognizer so that it builds a parse tree as it does the recognition process. Each time we perform the completer operation adding a state $E \rightarrow \alpha D . \beta$ g (ignoring look-ahead) we construct a pointer from the instance of D in that state to the state $D \rightarrow \gamma$. f which caused us to do the operation. This indicates that D was parsed as γ. In case D is ambiguous there will be a set of pointers from it, one for each completer operation which caused $E \rightarrow \alpha D . \beta$ g to be added to the particular state set. Each symbol in γ will also have pointers from it (unless it is terminal), and so on, thus representing the derivation tree for D.

In this way, when we reach the terminating state $\phi \rightarrow R \dashv . 0$ we will have the parse tree for the sentence hanging from R if it is unambiguous, and otherwise we will have a factored representation of all possible parse trees. In [1] a precise description of this process is given.

The time bounds for the parser are the same as those of the recognizer, while the space bound goes up to n^3 in general in order to store the parse trees.

We recommend using consistently a look-ahead of $k = 1$. In fact it would probably be most efficient to implement the algorithm to do just a look-ahead of 1. To implement the full look-ahead for any k would be more costly in programming effort and less efficient overall since so few programming languages need the extra look-ahead. Most programming languages use only a one character context to disambiguate their constructs, and if two characters are needed in some cases, our algorithm has the nice property that it will not fail, it may just take a little longer.

Our algorithm has the useful property that it can be modified to handle an extension of context-free grammars which makes use of the Kleene star notation. In this notation: $A \rightarrow \{BC\} * D$ means A may be rewritten as an arbitrary number (including 0) of BC's followed by a D. It generates a language equivalent to that generated by $A \rightarrow D \,|\, BCA$. However, the parse structure given to the language is different in the two grammars:

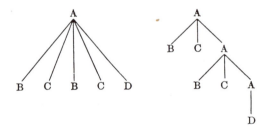

Structures like that on the left cannot be obtained using context-free grammars at all, so this extension is useful. The modification to our algorithm which implements it involves two additional operations:

(1) Any state of the form

$$A \rightarrow \alpha . \{\beta\} * \gamma \quad f$$

is replaced by

$$A \rightarrow \alpha \{ . \beta\} * \gamma \quad f$$
$$A \rightarrow \alpha \{\beta\} * . \gamma \quad f$$

indicating that β may be present or absent.

(2) Any state of the form

$$A \rightarrow \alpha \{\beta . \} * \gamma \quad f$$

is replaced by

$$A \rightarrow \alpha \{ . \beta\} * \gamma \quad f$$
$$A \rightarrow \alpha \{\beta\} * . \gamma \quad f$$

indicating the β may be repeated or not.

THE USE. The algorithm will probably be most useful in natural language processing systems where the full power of context-free grammars is used. It should also be useful in compiler writing systems and extendible languages. In most compiler writing systems and extendible languages, the programmer is allowed to express the syntax (or the syntax extension) of his language in something like BNF, and the system uses a parser to analyze subsequent programs in this language. Programming language grammars tend to lie in a restricted subset of context-free grammars which can be processed efficiently, yet some compiler writing systems in fact use general parsers, so ours may be of use here. In addition to its efficiency properties, ours has the advantage that it accepts the grammar in the form in which it is written, so that semantic routines can be associated with productions without fear that the parser will not reflect the original structure of the grammar.

Our algorithm will not compete so favorably with the time n algorithms, however. Certainly ours will do in time n any grammar that a time n parser can do at all, but this does not take into account the constant coefficient of n. Most of the time n algorithms really consist of a two-fold process. First they compile from an acceptable grammar a parser for that particular grammar, and then the grammar may be discarded and the compiled parser used directly to analyze strings. This allows the time n algorithms to incorporate much specialized information into the compiled parser, thus reducing the coefficient of n to something quite small—probably an order of magnitude less than that of our algorithm.

Consequently we have developed a compilation process for our algorithm which works only on time n grammars and reduces our coefficient to approximately the same order of magnitude as those of the time n parsers. This may make our algorithm competitive with them, but we have not implemented and tested it, so this is speculation. Some sort of efficient time n parser for a larger class of grammars is needed, however, because most restricted parsers suffer from the problem that the grammar one naturally writes for many programming languages is not acceptable to them, and much fiddling must be done with the grammar to get it accepted. Knuth's algorithm is an exception to this, but it has the problem that the size of the compiled parser is much too great for reasonable programming language grammars (see [1, p. 129]). Unfortunately, our compiled algorithm, since it is similar to Knuth's, may also have these problems.

8. Conclusion

In conclusion let us emphasize that our algorithm not only matches or surpasses the best previous results for times n^3 (Younger), n^2 (Kasami) and n (Knuth), but it does this with one single algorithm which does not have specified to it the class of grammars it is operating on and does not require the grammar in any special form. In other words, Knuth's algorithm works only on LR(k)

grammars and Kasami's (at least in his paper) only on unambiguous ones, but ours works on them all and seems to do about as well as other algorithms automatically.

Appendix

RANDOM ACCESS MACHINE. This model has an unbounded number of registers (counters), each of which may contain any nonnegative integer. These registers are named (addressed) by successive nonnegative integers. The primitive operations which are allowed on these registers are as follows:

(1) Store 0 or the contents of one register into another.
(2) Test the contents of one register against 0 or against the contents of another register for equality.
(3) Add 1 or subtract 1 from the contents of a register (taking $0 - 1 = 0$).
(4) Add the contents of one register to another.

The control for this model is a normal finite state device. The most important property of this machine is that in the above four operations, the register R to be operated on may be specified in two ways:

(1) R is the register whose address is n (register n).
(2) R is the register whose address is the contents of register n.

This second mode (sometimes called indirect addressing) plus primitive operation 4 (used for array accessing) gives our model the random access property. The time is measured by the number of primitive operations performed, and the space is measured by the number of registers used in any of these operations.

Acknowledgments. I am deeply indebted to Robert Floyd for his guidance in this research. I also benefited from discussions with Albert Meyer, Rudolph Krutar, and James Gray, and from detailed criticisms by the referees.

RECEIVED FEBRUARY, 1969; REVISED JUNE, 1969

REFERENCES

1. EARLEY, J. An efficient context-free parsing algorithm. Ph.D. Thesis, Comput. Sci. Dept., Carnegie-Mellon U., Pittsburgh, Pa., 1968.
2. KNUTH, D. E. On the translation of languages from left to right. *Information and Control 8* (1965), 607–639.
3. FLOYD, R. W. The syntax of programming languages—a survey. *IEEE Trans. EC-13*, 4 (Aug. 1964).
4. YOUNGER, D. H. Recognition and parsing of context-free languages in time n^3. *Information and Control 10* (1967), 189–208.
5. HAYS, D. Automatic language-data processing. In *Computer Applications in the Behavioral Sciences*, H. Borko (Ed.) Prentice Hall, Englewood Cliffs, N.J., 1962.
6. YOUNGER, D. H. Context-free language processing in time n^3. General Electric R & D Center, Schenectady, N.Y., 1966.
7. KASAMI, T., AND TORII, K. A syntax-analysis procedure for unambiguous context-free grammars. *J. ACM 16*, 3 (July 1969), 423–431.
8. GRIFFITHS, T., AND PETRICK, S. On the relative efficiencies of context-free grammar recognizers. *Comm. ACM 8*, 5 (May 1965), 289–300.
9. FELDMAN, J., AND GRIES, D. Translator writing systems. *Comm. ACM 11*, 2 (Feb. 1968), 77–113.

Algorithm Schemata and Data Structures in Syntactic Processing

by Martin Kay

CSL-80-12   October 1980

Abstract: The space in which models of human parsing strategy are to be sought is large. This paper is an exploration of that space, attempting to show what its dimensions are and what some of the choices are that the psycholinguist must face. Such an exploration as this may provide some protection against the common tendency to let some choices go by default.

A notion of *configuration tables* is used to locate algorithms on two dimensions according as (1) they work top-down or bottom-up, and (2) they are directed or undirected. The algorithms occupying a particular place in this two dimensional space constitute an *algorithm schema*. The notion of a *chart* is used to show how to limit the amount of work a parser must do by ensuring that nothing is done more than once. Finally, the notion of an *agenda* is introduced to show how a rich variety of psychological strategies can be combined in a principled way with a given algorithm schema to yield an algorithm.

A version of this paper will appear in the proceedings of the *Nobel Symposium on Text Processing*, Gothenburg, 1980.

CR Categories: 3.42, 3.36, 3.65, 5.23

Key words and phrases: Natural Language, Psycholinguistics, Parsing, Syntax.

XEROX

PALO ALTO RESEARCH CENTER
3333 Coyote Hill Road / Palo Alto / California 94304

1. INTRODUCTION

Interest in context-free grammars and associated parsing techniques has recently been rekindled among theoretical linguists and psycholinguists. A number of reasons for this suggest themselves. Chomsky's program for linguistics values a grammar more highly the more constrained the theoretical framework in which it is written. It is only by assuming that the human linguistic faculty is specialized for a narrow class of languages that we may hope to explain the prodigious feats of language learning accomplished by even the dullest of children in their first six years. So goes the argument. Generally, the most desirable constraints have been held to be those that place a theory low on the scale of weak generative power. In other words, the larger the class of languages that a theory cannot characterize at all—provided this class contains no natural languages—the better the theory.[1] However, determined attempts to modify tranformational grammar so as to reduce its weak generative power in a reasonably motivated manner have been largely unsuccessful. The overall theory remains relatively unconstrained. Bids for explanatory adequacy on its behalf continue to be based almost entirely on lists of *constraints*. These are more or less arbitrary from the point of view of the theory, and appended to it as riders and footnotes.

At the same time, it came to be recognized that the so called *proofs* made by early generative grammarians of the proposition that natural languages are not context free had been accepted far too eagerly (see, for example, Gazdar 1979a and 1979b). Context-free grammars occupy a low position in the hierarchy of weak generative power and they have the additional advantages of conceptual simplicity and susceptibility to algorithmic treatment. This last is not, of course, a requirement for a theory of linguistic competence but, *ceteris paribus*, a competence theory that also makes claims about the nature of linguistic performance is to be preferred.

Bresnan (1978) and others have pointed out that much of the machinery of transformations was not only unnecessary but also inappropriate even for such established and apparently natural uses as passivization. Bresnan proposed eliminating large numbers of transformational rules in favor of much weaker lexical redundancy rules. The only transformations that would remain according to this proposal would be *unbounded-movement* rules, such as topicalization and relativation, or possibly just a single *WH-movement* rule. With so much of the burden removed from it, the idea of eliminating the heavy machinery of transformations altogether becomes increasingly attractive.

At the same time, various new theories of grammar have been developed by computational linguists. While often not strictly context free, their grammars were of a sufficiently similar kind to be processed by minor variants of context-free algorithms. A sadly neglected early contribution to this line of development was that of Gilbert Harman (1963) whose theory made use of phrase-marker trees with complex symbols at the nodes and conventions by which features of dominating nodes were

---

[1]This is not an accurate characterization of Chomsky's own current view.

inherited by their descendents. Far more influential were the Augmented Transition Network (ATN) grammars of Woods and Kaplan (1971). These are not equivalent to context-free grammars but, like Harman's scheme, they arise by making relatively minor changes to the basic context-free formalism, mainly in the direction of permitting operations on complex symbols. Fairly straightforward and easily understood processing strategies can be used. Because of their susceptibility to algorithmic treatment, the ATN grammars have been proposed as a theory of linguistic performance (see, for example Kaplan (1972 and 1978), Wanner, Kaplan and Shiner (1975) and Wanner and Maratsos (1978).

A psychological model of sentence production or comprehension based on context-free grammar or a related formalism will seek to make predictions about the computational resources required for these activities. It must therefore be related to specific computational strategies. However, the number of parsing and generation algorithms available is large and there is no reason to suppose that it will not grow indefinitely. It seems, therefore, that a psycholinguist interested in syntax must conduct his investigations in a very large space having as three of its dimensions the linguistic theory, the particular language description within that theory, and the processing algorithms. In principle, at least, he may look to theoretical linguists for some guidance in exploring the first two of these dimensions. He should expect to receive some assistance with the third from computer scientists in general and computational linguists in particular. For the most part, however, very little such assistance has been forthcoming. I think there are two reasons for this.

First, most work by computer scientists, for example that quoted in Kimball (1973), has been done with a view to the formalization of programming languages and the automatic analysis of programs written in them. The first requirement of a programming language is that it should not admit syntactic, or indeed any other, ambiguities. Furthermore, the languages are usually designed so as to make it possible for a parser to make local choices on the basis of strictly limited contexts. As a result, the parsing algorithms that have been explored have been of a highly specialized kind, by no means appropriate for application to natural languages.

Second, computer scientists and computational linguists have usually approached questions of syntactic processing as engineers in search of algorithms that would achieve processing economies of one kind or another. While it is true that this line of attack could, in principle, produce plausible psychological models, there is no *a priori* reason to suppose that an investigation guided entirely by questions of efficiency on existing computers will ever lead in this direction. Griffiths and Petrick (1965) provided a useful classification of existing parsing algorithms and restatements of canonical members of each class in an ingenious form designed to highlight their salient features and to provide some basis for comparison, mostly from the point of view of computational efficiency.

If, as I shall argue at the end of this paper, the notion of an algorithm as normally conceived is an inappropriate component of a model of linguistic performance, then a great deal of groundwork must still be laid before any substantial results in the psycholinguistic investigation of syntax can be expected. In some respects, my aim in this paper will be similar to that of Griffiths and Petrick (1965) in that I shall attempt to provide a conceptual vantage point from which to view a variety of different processing strategies and to assess the properties that distinguish them. I shall also discuss canonical representations of classes of algorithms. However, unlike Griffiths and Petrick, I shall not attempt to remove the mechanisms for achieving nondeterminism from the representations. In fact, I hold nondeterminism to be the crucial dimension along which systems that countenance ambiguity must be judged. Accordingly, there will be three major sections to the paper.

In the section 2, I shall review the principal classes of syntactic processing method that have been proposed[2] While it is true that my main concern will be with parsing, I shall begin with some consideration of sentence generation. I do this mainly to introduce some basic notions and to show that it is all of a piece with parsing when viewed from an appropriate vantage point. I shall concentrate heavily on those properties of a syntactic processor that guarantee that it will do everything that must be done when processing a sentence, leaving until later the question of how to avoid duplication of effort. Following a practice that has become common, especially in the psychological literature, I shall assume a fairly general back-up strategy to provide for non-determinism. To achieve a representation of classes of processing strategies, suppressing unnecessary detail, I shall make use of what I call *algorithm schemata* which differ from algorithms as usually conceived in that the sequence of events is not always uniquely specified, though the function eventually computed is.

Section 3 will be devoted to showing the error of so cavalier an approach to ambiguity and non-determinism. I shall show that it is not sufficient to simply assume some unspecified backup strategy and that, when this problem is given a central position in the assessment of processing techique, a different picture of the problem emerges. In particular, judgments of the probable computational costs of this or that strategy or grammatical device must be made afresh in the light of processing models that take nondeterminism seriously. The properties of a syntactic processor that enable it to avoid unnecessary computation steps will be a major concern in this section.

In section 4, I shall briefly consider how the algorithm schemata of the first two sections relate to specific algorithms and processing strategies. I shall urge the adoption of an algorithm schema, rather than any specific algorithm, in the construction of computer programs and psychological models of syntactic processing. The schema can be simulated by a particular algorithm, but this higher-order algorithm will have various properties that recommend it over the more well known first-order algorithms.

2. CONFIGURATION TABLES AND ALGORITHM SCHEMATA

For expository purposes, context-free grammars are usually described in terms of a *top-down*

---

[2] I shall not consider predictive analysis which, while it can be assimilated to the framework to be developed, requires grammars to be cast in a special form, thereby raising problems that are beyond the scope of this paper.

sentence-production process in which rules are applied to *derivation strings* to produce new derivation strings. The sequence of derivation strings involved is a *derivation* of the sentence. The process starts with a special derivation string consisting of just the initial symbol of the grammar. A derivation string to which no further rules can be applied is a *sentence*.

If it is required to obtain structures for the strings produced, one of a variety of modified versions of the basic procedure must be used. Suppose, for example, that syntactic structures, whether partial or complete, are represented by labeled bracketings, or *phrase markers*, $[\beta_1 \ldots \beta_k]_\alpha$ in which α is a non-terminal symbol and the β_i $(1 \leq i \leq k)$ are either terminal symbols or other labeled bracketings. Partial structures will contain subexpressions of the form $[?]_\alpha$, called *open boxes*, to indicate nonterminals whose substructure has yet to be developed. Given a symbol α, it will sometimes be convenient in the discussion that follows to use $\mathcal{F}(\alpha)$ to refer to the open box $[?]_\alpha$ in case α is non-terminal, and otherwise to α itself.

The production process starts with the expression $[?]_S$ on the first line of the derivation. A new line is derived from an old one by applying the *transition rule* (1):

(1) Select one open box $[?]_\alpha$ on the line and a rule $\alpha \rightarrow \beta_1 \ldots \beta_k$ from the grammar. Create a new configuration replacing the open box with $[\mathcal{F}(\beta_1) \ldots \mathcal{F}(\beta_k)]_\alpha$

Given the grammar shown in (2), such a *structural derivation* for the sentence *radio broadcasts pay* is shown in (3).

(2)

1.	S $\rightarrow$	NP VP
2.	NP $\rightarrow$	A N
3.	NP $\rightarrow$	N
4.	VP $\rightarrow$	V NP
5.	VP $\rightarrow$	V
6.	A $\rightarrow$	pay, radio, ...
7.	N $\rightarrow$	broadcasts, pay, radio, ...
8.	V $\rightarrow$	broadcasts, pay, radio, ...

Each line in (3) shows, in the *Rule* column, the number of the grammar rule by which it was obtained and, in the *Parent* column, the number of the line giving the immediately preceding state of the process. In this case, the entry in the *Parent* column always refers to the immediately preceding line. This will not be true of the tables we shall consider later.

(3)

#	Parent	Rule	Configuration
1	0		$[?]_S$
2	1	1	$[[?]_{NP}[?]_{VP}]_S$
3	2	2	$[[[?]_A[?]_N]_{NP}[?]_{VP}]_S$
4	3	6	$[[[radio]_A[?]_N]_{NP}[?]_{VP}]_S$
5	4	7	$[[[radio]_A[broadcasts]_N]_{NP}[?]_{VP}]_S$
6	5	5	$[[[radio]_A[broadcasts]_N]_{NP}[[?]_V]_{VP}]_S$
7	6	8	$[[[radio]_A[broadcasts]_N]_{NP}[[pay]_V]_{VP}]_S$

(4)

#	Par.	R	Configuration
1	0		$[?]_S$
2	1	1	$[[?]_{NP}[?]_{VP}]_S$
3	2	2	$[[[?]_A[?]_N]_{NP}[?]_{VP}]_S$
4	2	3	$[[[?]_N]_{NP}[?]_{VP}]_S$
5	3	6	$[[[pay]_A[?]_N]_{NP}{}^{VP?}]_S$
6	3	6	$[[[radio]_A[?]_N]_{NP}[?]_{VP}]_S$
7	4	7	$[[[broadcasts]_N]_{NP}[?]_{VP}]_S$
8	4	7	$[[[pay]_N]_{NP}[?]_{VP}]_S$
9	4	7	$[[[radio]_N]_{NP}[?]_{VP}]_S$
10	3	6	$[[[pay]_A[broadcasts]_N]_{NP}[?]_{VP}]_S$
11	3	6	$[[[pay]_A[pay]_N]_{NP}[?]_{VP}]_S$
12	3	6	$[[[pay]_A[radio]_N]_{NP}[?]_{VP}]_S$
13	7	4	$[[[broadcasts]_N]_{NP}[[?]_V[?]_{NP}]_{VP}]_S$
14	7	5	$[[[broadcasts]_N]_{NP}[[?]_V]_{VP}]_S$
15	8	4	$[[[pay]_N]_{NP}[[?]_V[?]_{NP}]_{VP}]_{S'}$
16	8	5	$[[[pay]_N]_{NP}[[?]_V]_{VP}]_S$
17	9	4	$[[[radio]_N]_{NP}[[?]_V[?]_{NP}]_{VP}]_S$
18	9	5	$[[[radio]_N]_{NP}[[?]_V]_{VP}]_S$
19	10	4	$[[[pay]_A[broadcasts]_N]_{NP}[[?]_V[?]_{NP}]_{VP}]_S$
20	10	5	$[[[pay]_A[broadcasts]_N]_{NP}[[?]_V]_{VP}]_S$
21	11	4	$[[[pay]_A[pay]_N]_{NP}[[?]_V[?]_{NP}]_{VP}]_S$
22	11	5	$[[[pay]_A[pay]_N]_{NP}[[?]_V]_{VP}]_S$
23	12	4	$[[[pay]_A[radio]_N]_{NP}[[?]_V[?]_{NP}]_{VP}]_S$
24	12	5	$[[[pay]_A[radio]_N]_{NP}[[?]_V]_{VP}]_S$
25	13	8	$[[[broadcasts]_N]_{NP}[[broadcasts]_V[?]_{NP}]_{VP}]_S$
26	13	8	$[[[broadcasts]_N]_{NP}[[pay]_V[?]_{NP}]_{VP}]_S$
27	13	8	$[[[broadcasts]_N]_{NP}[[radio]_V[?]_{NP}]_{VP}]_S$
28	14	8	$[[[broadcasts]_N]_{NP}[[broadcasts]_V]_{VP}]_S$
29	14	8	$[[[broadcasts]_N]_{NP}[[pay]_V]_{VP}]_S$
30	14	8	$[[[broadcasts]_N]_{NP}[[radio]_V]_{VP}]_S$

The derivation process just described is not an algorithm in the strict sense of the word because it does not specifiy the sequence of steps to be followed exactly. Rather it is an *algorithm schema*. The transition rule (1) does not specify which open box should be chosen or which of the rules expanding α is to be applied. However, all algorithms derived from this schema by determining these choices generate the same sentences, though possibly with different derivations.

Suppose that the transition rule (1) is revised to read:

(5) Select one open box $[?]_\alpha$ on the line. For *each* rule $\alpha \rightarrow \beta_1 \ldots \beta_k$ in the grammar, create a new configuration, replacing the open box $[?]_\alpha$ with $[\mathcal{F}(\beta_1) \ldots \mathcal{F}(\beta_k)]_\alpha$

The result is an algorithm schema for producing all the sentences in the language of the grammar and the process will clearly terminate only in the degenerate case of a grammar like (2) that generates a finite language. The first thirty lines of a table generated according to this schema from the grammar (2) is shown in (4).

(3) and (4) are simple cases of *configuration tables*. Each line in such a table is a complete record

of the *state* of a process at a particular moment. In other words, each line either represents a final state in the process or contains all the information necessary to take the next step. The outputs of the computation chronicled in a configuration table are typically configurations that have a certain syntactic property. In the case of structural derivations like (3) and (4), a line containing no open boxes is part of the output. Generally speaking, several different steps can be taken independently from a given state, as in (4), and in these cases, the process as a whole is said to be *non-deterministic*. It is therefore no longer the case that each rule in a configuration table is derived from the one above it and for this reason a *Parent* column is printed in each table. It is there entirely for expository purposes, as is the *Rule* column, and plays no role in the algorithm. All the processes I shall examine below are non-deterministic.

It is also generally true that configuration tables belong to equivalence classes the members of each of which show the computation of a single function of the same inputs. There are two reasons for this. First, while all lines with a given parent must follow the parent line, the transition rules impose no constraint on the way they are ordered relative to one another. Second, the transition rules in accordance with which the process passes from state to state may be underdetermined, as in the case of the standard sentence-production derivations with which we started. (1) specifies that an open box is to be replaced by a new subexpression, but the choice of the open box to replace is open. There is an implicit claim that the results will be the same whichever choice is made.

Bottom-up Production

Sentence production can also be described in terms of *bottom-up* operations on *coverings*. A covering is simply a sequence of phrases made up of the words in the string. So, for example, the sentence *I know the girl he married* has one covering consisting of a pronoun, a verb, and a noun phrase, and another consisting of a pronoun, a verb, two noun phrases, and another verb. It also has others. More precisely, a covering of a string is a sequence of phrase markers the labels on whose terminal nodes, when concatenated in the order of the sequence, constitute the string. It will usually be implicit that the coverings we are considering are constructed according to the rules of a particular grammar. The string of symbols obtained by reading off the root labels from a covering is a *root string* so that the two coverings of the sentence *I know the girl he married* just mentioned correspond to the root strings *PRON V NP* and *PRON V NP NP V*. Clearly every derivation string relative to a grammar is the root string for some covering, but covering strings are not necessarily also derivation strings. For example, *I know the girl he married* can be seen as the concatenation of the sentence *I know* and the topicalized sentence *the girl he married*. Accordingly, it has a covering whose root string is *S S* even though this would presumably not be a line in its derivation by any reasonable grammar. Similarly, relative to the grammar (2), the sentence *radio broadcasts pay*

Algorithm Schemata and Data Structures in Syntactic Processing

(6)

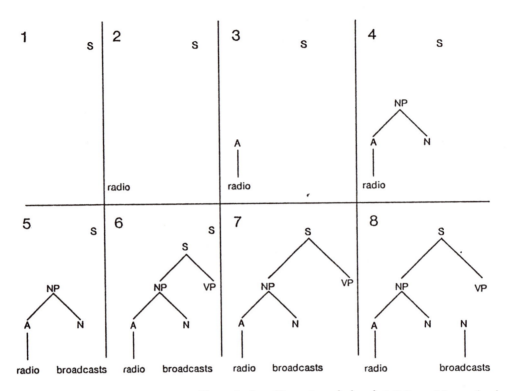

has a covering consisting of a sentence ($[[[\mathrm{radio}]_N]_{NP}[[\mathrm{broadcasts}]_V]_{VP}]_S$) followed by verb phrase ($[[\mathrm{pay}]_V]_{VP}$), but no derivation *S VP*.

If the root string of a covering relative to a given grammar contains a substring that matches the right-hand side of a rule, a new covering relative to that grammar can be produced by replacing the corresponding subsequence of trees with a single tree whose root is labeled with the symbol on the left-hand side of the rule and whose immediate descendants are that subsequence of trees. The new covering is a *reduction* of the original one. Consider the sentence *I know the girl he married* once more. As we saw, an intuitively reasonable grammar would give it a covering with the root string *PRON V NP NP V*. Assuming a rule that rewrites *VP*'s as *V*'s, *PRON V NP NP VP* and *PRON VP NP NP V* are both reductions of this. Assuming another rule that expands *S* into *NP NP V*, the first of these has the further reduction *PRON V S*. The bottom-up procedure aims to produce a string from which a root string consisting of the initial symbol of the grammar can be obtained by a series of reductions.

A fairly straightforward method of bottom-up generation makes use of a *reachability* table which shows, for every non-terminal symbol α in a grammar, the set $\mathcal{R}(\alpha)$ of terminal and non-terminal symbols each of which can be the first element in a string dominated by α. The reachability table for the grammar in (2) is as follows:

(7)

α	$\mathcal{R}(\alpha)$
S	NP, A, N, broadcasts, pay, radio
NP	A, N, broadcasts, pay, radio
VP	V, broadcasts, pay, radio
A	pay, radio, ...
N	broadcasts, pay, radio, ...
V	broadcasts, pay, radio, ...

The overall goal is to construct a sentence and accordingly the initial configuration consists of the open box $[?]_S$. Whereas in (3) and (4), a configuration is a single phrase marker, we shall henceforth be working with configurations that are sequences of *terms* each of which is a phrase marker. A term that contains at least one open box will be called *active*; others are *inactive*. The interpretation is as follows: the part of the sequence to the right of a given term shows the current state of progress towards filling the first open box in that term. So, for example, in the sequence $[?]_S[?]_{NP}[radio]_N$, the noun *radio* will fill the open box in the noun phrase, either alone or with other material yet to be obtained, and that will go towards filling the sentence. Thus, a well formed configuration can contain at most one inactive term which must be in the final position.

The sequence of terms that make up a configuration are portions of a single tree structure that will eventually be constructed. The top node first term in a configuration will become the root of the final tree. Nonterminal symbols in a term that have no structure below them are the open boxes. Terms that contain open boxes are "looking for" other terms to dominate and they are therefore said to be *active*. If one term precedes another in a configuration, the latter will eventually come to be dominated by one such nonterminal in the former, that is, it will "fill the open box". (6) gives a graphic representation of the first eight configurations in the table (9). Notice that lines 5 and 6 in (9) each contain three terms and that squares 5 and 6 in (6) each contain three disconnected subtrees. Left-to-right ordering in the table corresponds to top-to-bottom ordering in the diagrams. The aim of the procedure will always be to conflate pairs of adjacent subtrees, building new structure below the upper one or above the lower one when necessary.

Suppose $[?]_\alpha$ is the first open box of the last term in the configuration. Using the reachability table, a terminal t is chosen that could be initial in a phrase of type α. If the grammar contains the rule $\alpha \rightarrow t$, then t can simply be used to fill the open box. In other words, a new configuration is created replacing the last two terms by $[t]_\alpha$ (See, for example, lines 3, 8, and 11 in (9)). Otherwise, a rule of the form $\beta \rightarrow \gamma_1 \ldots \gamma_k$ is found in the grammar, such that β can be initial in a phrase of type α and $\gamma_1 = t$. t is replaced as the last term in the configuration by $[\mathcal{F}(\gamma_1) \ldots \mathcal{F}(\gamma_k)]_\beta$. A rule of the required form must exist, given the way the terminal was chosen using the reachability table. If the term contains other open boxes, new terminals are chosen and the process repeats until they are all full. If the last term in a configuration contains no open boxes, it is inactive and is treated as though it were the most recently chosen terminal. The aim now becomes that of incorporating this term in the one that immediately precedes it in the configuration.

In summary, the process is governed by three transition rules:

(8) 1. Append a terminal symbol: If the last term in the configuration is active, let $[?]_\alpha$ be the first open box it contains. Select a terminal $t \in \mathcal{R}(\alpha)$ and create a new configuration by appending t to the current one.

2. Find a dominating non-terminal: If the last term is inactive, consider two adjacent terms g_i and g_{i+1}, of the current configuration. If g_{i+1} is of category α (i.e. it consists of the terminal α or an expression of the form $[\ldots]_\alpha$) and $[?]_\beta$ is the first open box in g_i, for each rule $\gamma \to \delta_1 \ldots \delta_n$ such that $\gamma = \beta$ or $\gamma \in \mathcal{R}(\beta)$ and $\alpha = \delta_1$, create a new configuration replacing g_{i+1} with $[g_{i+1} \; \mathcal{F}(\delta_2) \ldots \mathcal{F}(\delta_n)]_\gamma$.

3. Incorporate completed subgoal: If the last term is inactive, consider two adjacent terms g_i and g_{i+1}, of the current configuration. If g_{i+1} is of category α and the first open box in g_i is $[?]_\alpha$, replace that open box with g_{i+1} and delete g_{i+1} from the configuration.

Rule 1 can apply only in circumstances in which rules 2 and 3 do not. Rules 2 and 3, however, do not exclude one another and, when both apply to the same configuration, the values chosen for i must be the same. The reason is easy to see. The application of each destroys the conditions of applicability of the other so that, if both lines of attack are to be explored, the rules must be applied simultaneously. In the examples in this paper, i is systematically chosen to be as large as possible. One result of this, which will be of interest in the next section, is that rules 2 and 3 will invariably be applied to a pair of terms the first of which is active, as the rules require, and the second of which is inactive. But if rules 2 or 3 can be applied in more than one place, that is, for more than one value of i, then only one is chosen and the choice is arbitrary. This is because applications of the rules to different terms is independent. To see that this is true, consider three adjacent terms $\ldots t_i \; t_{i+1} \; t_{i+2} \ldots$ of a configuration and suppose that transition rule 2 applies to both pairs $< t_i, t_{i+1} >$ and $< t_{i+1}, t_{i+2} >$. If it is applied to the first pair, t_{i+1} will be replaced by a new term u of the form $[t_{i+1}]_\alpha$, for some α. Since t_{i+1} is the first term dominated by α in u, the first open box in u is the same as the first open box in t_{i+1}. Applying rule 2 to the pair $< u, t_{i+2} >$ will therefore be the same as applying it to $< t_{i+1}, t_{i+2} >$. Suppose, on the other hand, that rule 2 is applied first to $< t_{i+1}, t_{i+2} >$. In this case, t_{i+1} is unchanged and application to the first pair is therefore unaffected. An exactly parallel argument applies to rule 3 and to combinations of the two.

(9) is a configuration table showing how these transition rules can be used to generate the sentence *radio broadcasts pay*, in one of its syntactic readings, using the grammar (2). The column headed *T. R.* gives the number of the transition rule employed.

2. Configuration Tables and Algorithm Schemata

(9)

#	T. R.	Par.	R	Configuration
1				$[?]_S$
2	1	1		$[?]_S\text{radio}$
3	2	2	6	$[?]_S[\text{radio}]_A$
4	2	3	2	$[?]_S[[\text{radio}]_A[?]_N]_{NP}$
5	1	4		$[?]_S[[\text{radio}]_A[?]_N]_{NP}\text{broadcasts}$
6	2	5	1	$[?]_S[[[\text{radio}]_A[?]_N]_{NP}[?]_{VP}]_S\text{broadcasts}$
7	3	6		$[[[\text{radio}]_A[?]_N]_{NP}[?]_{VP}]_S\text{broadcasts}$
8	2	7	7	$[[[\text{radio}]_A[?]_N]_{NP}[?]_{VP}]_S[\text{broadcasts}]_N$
9	3	8		$[[[\text{radio}]_A[\text{broadcasts}]_N]_{NP}[?]_{VP}]_S$
10	1	9		$[[[\text{radio}]_A[\text{broadcasts}]_N]_{NP}[?]_{VP}]_S\text{pay}$
11	2	10	8	$[[[\text{radio}]_A[\text{broadcasts}]_N]_{NP}[?]_{VP}]_S[\text{pay}]_V$
12	2	11	5	$[[[\text{radio}]_A[\text{broadcasts}]_N]_{NP}[?]_{VP}]_S[[\text{pay}]_V]_{VP}$
13	3	12		$[[[\text{radio}]_A[\text{broadcasts}]_N]_{NP}[[\text{pay}]_V]_{VP}]_S$

Bottom-up Parsing

Bottom-up sentence production is something of a *tour de force*. It is essentially a procedure of *synthesis by analysis*—a parsing procedure in which the string is constructed so as to ensure that the first hypothesis made about its structure at each step turns out right. The fully fledged parsing procedure can be derived from that just given with very few modifications. This time, however, the process is non-deterministic because it must countenance ambiguities.

I shall follow the usual practice in discussing parsing procedures of assuming that the terminals have been looked up in the lexicon in a previous step so that the data consists not of a string of terminals but a string of alternative lexical entries each of which is a family of degenerate phrase markers of the form $[t]_\alpha$, where t is a terminal and α a *pre-terminal* symbol. After lexical lookup, the sentence *radio broadcasts pay* takes on essentially the following form.

$$\begin{Bmatrix}[\text{radio}]_A\\ [\text{radio}]_N\\ [\text{radio}]_V\end{Bmatrix}\quad \begin{Bmatrix}[\text{broadcasts}]_V\\ [\text{broadcasts}]_N\end{Bmatrix}\quad \begin{Bmatrix}[\text{pay}]_A\\ [\text{pay}]_N\\ [\text{pay}]_V\end{Bmatrix}$$

Only the first two transition rules of the production procedure in (8) require modification. They must now read:

(10) 1. **Append a terminal symbol:** If the last goal in the list is active, let $[?]_\alpha$ be the first open box that it contains. For each lexical entry $[w_i]_\beta$ of the next word in the string, w_i, such that $\beta = \alpha$ or $\beta \in R(\alpha)$ create a new line in the table in which the open box is replaced by $[w_i]_\beta$.

   2. **Find a dominating non-terminal:** Consider two adjacent terms g_i and g_{i+1}, of the current configuration. If g_{i+1} is of category α and $[?]_\beta$ is the first open box in g_i, then for all rules $\gamma \to \delta_1 \ldots \delta_n$ such that $\gamma = \beta$ or $\gamma \in R(\beta)$, and $\alpha = \delta_1$, replace g_{i+1} with $[g_{i+1}\ \mathcal{F}(\delta_2) \ldots \mathcal{F}(\delta_n)]_\gamma$.

(11)

#	T.R.	Pos.	Par.	R	Configuration
1		0	0		$[?]_S$
2	1	1	1		$[?]_S[radio]_A$
3	1	1	1		$[?]_S[radio]_N$
4	2	1	2	2	$[?]_S[[radio]_A[?]_N]_{NP}$
5	2	1	3	3	$[?]_S[[radio]_N]_{NP}$
6	1	2	4		$[?]_S[[radio]_A[?]_N]_{NP}[broadcasts]_N$
7	2	1	5	1	$[?]_S[[[radio]_N]_{NP}[?]_{VP}]_S$
8	3	2	6		$[?]_S[[radio]_A[broadcasts]_N]_{NP}$
9	1	2	7		$[?]_S[[[radio]_N]_{NP}[?]_{VP}]_S[broadcasts]_V$
10	2	2	8	1	$[?]_S[[[radio]_A[broadcasts]_N]_{NP}[?]_{VP}]_S$
11	2	2	9	4	$[?]_S[[[radio]_N]_{NP}[?]_{VP}]_S[[broadcasts]_V[?]_{NP}]_{VP}$
12	2	2	9	5	$[?]_S[[[radio]_N]_{NP}[?]_{VP}]_S[[broadcasts]_V]_{VP}$
13	1	3	10		$[?]_S[[[radio]_A[broadcasts]_N]_{NP}[?]_{VP}]_S[pay]_V$
14	1	3	11		$[?]_S[[[radio]_N]_{NP}[?]_{VP}]_S[[broadcasts]_V[?]_{NP}]_{VP}[pay]_A$
15	1	3	11		$[?]_S[[[radio]_N]_{NP}[?]_{VP}]_S[[broadcasts]_V[?]_{NP}]_{VP}[pay]_N$
16	3	2	12		$[?]_S[[[radio]_N]_{NP}[[broadcasts]_V]_{VP}]_S$
17	2	3	13	4	$[?]_S[[[radio]_A[broadcasts]_N]_{NP}[?]_{VP}]_S[[pay]_V[?]_{NP}]_{VP}$
18	2	3	13	5	$[?]_S[[[radio]_A[broadcasts]_N]_{NP}[?]_{VP}]_S[[pay]_V]_{VP}$
19	2	3	14	2	$[?]_S[[[radio]_N]_{NP}[?]_{VP}]_S[[broadcasts]_V[?]_{NP}]_{VP}[[pay]_A[?]_N]_{NP}$
20	2	3	15	3	$[?]_S[[[radio]_N]_{NP}[?]_{VP}]_S[[broadcasts]_V[?]_{NP}]_{VP}[[pay]_N]_{NP}$
21	3	2	16		$[[[radio]_N]_{NP}[[broadcasts]_V]_{VP}]_S$
22	3	3	18		$[?]_S[[[radio]_A[broadcasts]_N]_{NP}[[pay]_V]_{VP}]_S$
23	3	3	20		$[?]_S[[[radio]_N]_{NP}[?]_{VP}]_S[[broadcasts]_V[[pay]_N]_{NP}]_{VP}$
24	3	3	22		$[[[radio]_A[broadcasts]_N]_{NP}[[pay]_V]_{VP}]_S$
25	3	3	23		$[?]_S[[[radio]_N]_{NP}[[broadcasts]_V[[pay]_N]_{NP}]_{VP}]_S$
26	3	3	25		$[[[radio]_N]_{NP}[[broadcasts]_V[[pay]_N]_{NP}]_{VP}]_S$

Rule 1 adds a terminal—or more strictly, a preterminal—to the end of a configuration whose current last term contains open boxes, that is, that represents a subtree with nonterminal symbols that dominate no substructure. The only lexical interpretations of the terminal that need be considered are those that can be dominated by the first nonterminal in the subtree that is still in need of substructure. Rule 2 builds some additional structure on top of the lower of a pair of adjacent subtrees with a view to eventually conflating them (by rule 3).

Complete analyses appear in the table as lines that contain no active terms. (11) is a configuration table showing the analysis of the sentence *radio broadcasts pay* using the grammar in (2). The entries in the Pos. column show the serial number of the last terminal considered. Where transition rule 1 has been applied, the number of the relevant grammar rule is also given.

In transition rule 2, rules of grammar are chosen in accordance with two criteria: (i) The symbol on the left-hand side of the rule must be reachable from the symbol beneath which it is eventually to be inserted ($\gamma = \beta$ or $\gamma \in \mathcal{R}(\beta)$) and (ii) the first symbol on the right-hand side of the rule must match a particular symbol already established in the configuration ($\alpha = \delta_1$). It is the second of these criteria that is characterisitic of a bottom-up process since it ensures that new non-terminals are introduced only when at least one branch connecting them to a terminal symbol has already been constructed. The first criterion characterizes the process as *directed* and it serves only to prevent the creation of certain phrases for which there is known to be no place in a higher-level structure. This process is also directed to the extent that transition rule 1 requires the terminal selected to be in the reachability set of a particular non-terminal symbol $\beta = \alpha$ or $\beta \in \mathcal{R}(\alpha)$). The *undirected* process that results from removing these conditions, though less efficient, is not only viable, but represents the type of bottom-up procedure that has most often been proposed. The complete set of transition rules for an undirected bottom-up parser would be as in (12):

(12) 1. **Append a terminal symbol:** If the last term in the configuration is active and there remain terminals in the string to be considered, create a new configuration for each lexical alternative of the next one and append it to the end of the configuration.

2. **Find a dominating non-terminal:** If the last term is inactive and g_i is of category α and a term of the current configuration, other than the last, then for all rules $\gamma \to \delta_1 \ldots \delta_n$ such that $\alpha = \delta_1$, replace g_i with $[g_i \; \mathcal{F}(\delta_2) \ldots \mathcal{F}(\delta_n)]_\gamma$. This operation is inhibited if the sum of terminals and open boxes in a new configuration would be greater than the number of words in the string being analyzed.

3. **Incorporate completed subgoal:** If the last term is inactive, consider two adjacent terms g_i and g_{i+1}, of the current configuration. If g_{i+1} is of category α and the first open box in g_i is $[?]_\alpha$, replace that open box with g_{i+1} and delete g_{i+1} from the list.

The modification to rule 2 that inhibits the production of configurations with more open boxes than can be filled by the remainder of the string under analysis is called the *shaper* test and is due to Kuno and Oettinger (1964). It is needed here to ensure that the process will terminate even if the grammar contains *left-recursive* groups of rules. A rule of the form $\alpha \to \alpha \ldots$ constitutes such a group by itself. In general, a left-recursive group is of the form

$$\alpha_1 \to \alpha_2 \ldots$$
$$\alpha_2 \to \alpha_3 \ldots$$
$$. \to .$$
$$. \to .$$
$$. \to .$$
$$\alpha_i \to \alpha_1 \ldots$$

Top-down strategies are notoriously unstable in the presence of such rules unless restrained by something like the shaper test. We make the usual assumption that the grammar contains no cyclic sets of nonbranching rules, that is, there are no sets of the form:

$$
\begin{aligned}
\alpha_1 &\rightarrow \alpha_2 \\
\alpha_2 &\rightarrow \alpha_3 \\
. &\rightarrow . \\
. &\rightarrow . \\
. &\rightarrow . \\
\alpha_i &\rightarrow \alpha_1
\end{aligned}
$$
s

The initial configuration consisting of the single term $[?]_S$ can be usefully eliminated from the configuration table for undirected bottom-up parsing provided that a configuration is entered in the table for each lexical entry of the first item in the string before the process begins. The complete configuration table for *radio broadcasts pay* using grammar (2) contains 72 configurations. A more modest example appears later in the paper at (25).

Top-down Parsing

We come finally to top-down parsing which is illustrated, in its directed variety, in (15). As before, the initial configuration is $[?]_S$. The transition rules are the same as in (10) except for the second which now reads as follows:

(13) 2. **Find a dominating non-terminal:** If the last term is inactive, consider two adjacent terms g_i and g_{i+1}, of the current configuration. If g_{i+1} is of category α and $[?]_\beta$ is the first open box in g_i, then for all rules $\beta \rightarrow \gamma_1 \ldots \gamma_n$ such that $\alpha = \gamma_1$ or $\alpha \in \mathcal{R}(\gamma_1)$, replace the first open box $[?]_\beta$ in g_i with $[g_{i+1} \; \mathcal{F}(\gamma_2) \ldots \mathcal{F}(\gamma_n)]_\beta$. As before, the operation is inhibited if the sum of terminals and open boxes in a new configuration would be greater than the number of words in the string being analyzed.

An undirected top-down parser differs in that the selection of the grammar rule to be applied does not make use of the reachability table. The appropriate transition rule is:

(14) 2. **Find a dominating non-terminal:** If the last term is inactive and g_i is a term in the current configuration and $[?]_\beta$ is the first open box that it contains, then for all rules $\beta \rightarrow \gamma_1 \ldots \gamma_n$, replace the open box $[?]_\beta$ with $[\mathcal{F}(\gamma_2) \ldots \mathcal{F}(\gamma_n)]_\beta$. The operation is inhibited if the sum of terminals and open boxes in a new configuration would be greater than the number of words in the string being analyzed.

Rule-Selection Tables

When expressed in terms of configuration tables, the differences between bottom-up and top-down parsing appear quite small. In (11), the transition from line 2 to line 4 uses rule 2 because the terminal at the end of the configuration on line 2 is of category A and rule 2 permits this to be

(15)

#	T.R.	Pos.	Par.	R	Configuration
1		0	0		$[?]_S$
2	1	1	1		$[?]_S[radio]_A$
3	1	1	1		$[?]_S[radio]_N$
4	2	1	2	1	$[[?]_{NP}[?]_{VP}]_S[radio]_A$
5	2	1	3	1	$[[?]_{NP}[?]_{VP}]_S[radio]_N$
6	2	1	4	2	$[[[?]_A[?]_N]_{NP}[?]_{VP}]_S[radio]_A$
7	2	1	5	3	$[[[?]_N]_{NP}[?]_{VP}]_S[radio]_N$
8	3	1	6		$[[[radio]_A[?]_N]_{NP}[?]_{VP}]_S$
9	3	1	7		$[[[radio]_N]_{NP}[?]_{VP}]_S$
10	1	2	8		$[[[radio]_A[?]_N]_{NP}[?]_{VP}]_S[broadcasts]_N$
11	1	2	9		$[[[radio]_N]_{NP}[?]_{VP}]_S[broadcasts]_V$
12	3	2	10		$[[[radio]_A[broadcasts]_N]_{NP}[?]_{VP}]_S$
13	2	2	11	4	$[[[radio]_N]_{NP}[[?]_V[?]_{NP}]_{VP}]_S[broadcasts]_V$
14	2	2	11	5	$[[[radio]_N]_{NP}[[?]_V]_{VP}]_S[broadcasts]_V$
15	1	3	12		$[[[radio]_A[broadcasts]_N]_{NP}[?]_{VP}]_S[pay]_V$
16	3	2	13		$[[[radio]_N]_{NP}[[broadcasts]_V[?]_{NP}]_{VP}]_S$
17	3	2	14		$[[[radio]_N]_{NP}[[broadcasts]_V]_{VP}]_S$
18	2	3	15	5	$[[[radio]_A[broadcasts]_N]_{NP}[[?]_V]_{VP}]_S[pay]_V$
19	1	3	16		$[[[radio]_N]_{NP}[[broadcasts]_V[?]_{NP}]_{VP}]_S[pay]_A$
20	1	3	16		$[[[radio]_N]_{NP}[[broadcasts]_V[?]_{NP}]_{VP}]_S[pay]_N$
21	3	3	18		$[[[radio]_A[broadcasts]_N]_{NP}[[pay]_V]_{VP}]_S$
22	2	3	20	3	$[[[radio]_N]_{NP}[[broadcasts]_V[[?]_N]_{NP}]_{VP}]_S[pay]_N$
23	3	3	22		$[[[radio]_N]_{NP}[[broadcasts]_V[[pay]_N]_{NP}]_{VP}]_S$

immediately incorporated in a higher-level phrase, namely an NP. The reachability table guarantees that there is a place for this at the beginning of a sentence. A top-down strategy applies a rule that expands the symbol S, secure in the knowledge that the first symbol on the right-hand side of that rule can have an adjective on its left-most branch. Notice, however, that the only difference between the two strategies resides in the way the rules are chosen and not in any other detail of how the configuration table develops. A single set of transition rules could be written for both kinds of procedure if it were made to depend on a *Rule-Selection Table* instead of a reachability table.

A Rule-Selection Table is an $m \times n$ array, where m is the number of non-terminal symbols in the grammar that are not pre-terminals and n is the total number of non-terminals. The cell $S_{\alpha,\beta}$ of a rule-selection table S contains the list of grammar rules to be used in transition rule 2 when α is the *upper* symbol and β is the *lower*. In other words, α is the label of the first open box in a term and the immediately following term in the configuration is $\mathcal{F}(\beta)$. For a top-down procedure, these rules will all be of the form $\alpha \rightarrow \gamma_1 \ldots \gamma_n$. If the procedure is undirected, all rules whose left-hand symbol is α will be on the list. If it is directed, the list will contain only those for which $\beta = \gamma_1$ or $\beta \in \mathcal{R}(\gamma_1)$. (16) is a rule-selection table specifying a directed top-down procedure for grammar (2). The directed top-down procedure would have 2,3 in place of 2 in the NP row. The table for an undirected top-down procedure has the same value in every non-null cell of a given row. Conversely, the table for an undirected bottom-up procedure procedure has the same value in every non-null cell of a given column. For a bottom-up procedure, the rules will all be of the form

$\gamma \to \delta_1 \ldots \delta_n$ where $\delta_1 = \beta$. In the directed case, only rules for which $\gamma = \alpha$ or $\gamma \in \mathcal{R}(\alpha_1)$ will be included.

(16)

	S	NP	VP	Λ	N	V
S		1		1	1	
NP				2	3	
VP						4,5
Λ						
N						
V						

We can now write a general set of transition rules that implements whatever strategy the rule-selection table provided to it dictates:

(17) 1. **Append a terminal symbol:** If the last term in the· configuration is active, let $[?]_\alpha$ be the first of them. If there remain terminals in the string to be considered, then for each lexical alternative of the next terminal $[t]_\beta$ such that $\beta \in \mathcal{R}(\alpha)$ that can be on a left branch of α, create a new configuration by appending $[t]_\beta$ to the end of the current one.

   2. **Find a dominating non-terminal:** If the last term is inactive, consider two adjacent terms g_i and g_{i+1}, of the current configuration. If $g_{i+1} = \mathcal{F}(\alpha)$ and $[?]_\beta$ is the first open box in g_i, for each rule $\gamma \to \delta_1 \ldots \delta_n$ in $S_{\beta,\alpha}$, create a new configuration introducing $[\mathcal{F}(\delta_1) \ldots \mathcal{F}(\delta_n)]_\gamma$ between g_i and g_{i+1}.

   3. **Incorporate completed subgoal:** If the last term is inactive, consider two adjacent terms g_i and g_{i+1}, of the current configuration. If $g_{i+1} = \mathcal{F}(\alpha)$ and the first open box in g_i is $[?]_\alpha$, replace that open box with g_{i+1} and delete g_{i+1} from the list.

A word of explanation is in order about the second of these transition rules which, unlike corresponding transition rules in previous schemes, is formulated so as to introduce a new term that does not replace any existing ones. In the top-down scheme, it was possible to eliminate an open box in this step because the rules were chosen precisely to provide contents for such a box. In the bottom-up scheme, an existing item could be incorporated into the newly introduced structure because the structures were chosen with a view to making that possible. However, the rules supplied by the rule-selection table may be such as to allow neither possibility. We therefore leave the incorporation of existing material to a later application of rule 3. An alternative solution would have been to recognize three cases of rule 2 according as (i) $\beta = \gamma$, (ii) $\alpha = \delta_1$ but $\beta \neq \gamma$, or (ii) neither of the above. Clearly, it would also be possible to give special treatment to the case in which $\beta = \gamma$ and $\alpha = \delta_1$ for, under these circumstances both g_i and g_{i+1} could be incorporated in the new structure. The solution I have adopted, while it makes for more lines in the configuration table, is the simplest. More important, we shall see that it leads to important generalizations in the next section.

(18)

	S	NP	VP	A	N	V
S		1		2	1	
NP				2	3	
VP						4,5
A						
N						
V						

By now it should be clear that the distinction between top-down and bottom-up procedures is not primary. Rule tables can generally be assembled in a large number of ways only some of which correspond to either top-down or bottom-up procedures. Perhaps these procedures should be characterized as *middle-out*. (18) is a trivial example, based on (2). According to this table, sentences beginning with N will be analyzed by a procedure whose first move is top-down, whereas the analysis of those beginning with A will begin bottom-up.

The conditions under which a rule-selection table properly represents a given grammar are quite straightforward. Clearly, the rules in the cell $S_{\alpha,\beta}$ must be chosen from the set $\mathcal{G}_{\alpha,\beta} = \{\gamma \to \delta_1 \ldots \delta_n \mid \gamma \in \mathcal{R}(\alpha) \; . \; \beta \in \mathcal{R}(\delta_1)\}$. In other words, the symbol on the left-hand side of each rule must be reachable from the upper symbol and the lower symbol must be reachable from the first symbol on the right-hand side of the rule. Suppose now that $\mathcal{G}_{\alpha,\beta}$ contains the pair

(19)
$$\kappa \to \lambda_1 \ldots \lambda_m$$
$$\mu \to \nu_1 \ldots \nu_n$$

and that

(20)
$$\mu \in \mathcal{R}(\lambda_1)$$

Only one member of the pair must be included in $\mathcal{R}_{\alpha,\beta}$ because leaving both in the set will give rise to redundancies in the analysis process. To see that this is true, it is sufficient to consider how they would apply to a configuration of the form

$$\ldots [?]_\alpha \; \mathcal{F}(\beta) \ldots$$

Clearly two new configurations would be produced as follows:

(21)
$$\ldots [?]_\kappa \; [[?]_{\lambda_1} \; \mathcal{F}(\lambda_2) \ldots \mathcal{F}(\lambda_m)]_\kappa \; \mathcal{F}(\beta) \ldots$$

(22)
$$\ldots [?]_\alpha \; []_\mu \mathcal{F}(\nu_1) \ldots \mathcal{F}(\nu_n) \; \mathcal{F}(\beta) \ldots$$

but, since $\mu \in \mathcal{R}(\lambda_1)$, (22) must also arise, directly or indirectly from (21).

Proper values for $S_{\alpha,\beta}$ are therefore those that are derived from $\mathcal{G}_{\alpha,\beta}$ by deleting one member of any pair of rules standing in the relation (19) and (20) and continuing to do this until no such pairs remain. The table corresponding to a bottom-up strategy is arrived at by systematically removing the rule corresponding to the first member of the pair in (19) and the top-down strategy, by removing the second member.

The Efficiency Question

It is often supposed that the most efficient parsers use top-down methods. So long as the discussion is confined to undirected strategies, there is doubtless some broad statistical validity to the claim though it is easy to construct grammars and strings that falsify it in general. The intuition on which it is based is presumably this: The undirected bottom-up strategy has the property that every substring that can be construed as a phrase is identified as such, completely without regard to context. So, for example, the last two words of *radio broadcasts pay* would appear in several lines of the configuration table as a sentence. This does not happen when a top-down procedure is used. In this case, a phrase is sought only when a string of symbols could occur to its right—though possibly not the one actually there—that would complete a sentence containing that phrase. In other words, the search for a phrase of a given category at a given place in the string is undertaken by a top-down parser only if such a phrase could be combined with phrases already found into a legal structure for a sentence beginning with the words of the string under analysis up to the current point. On the other hand, an undirected top-down parser can postulate phrases, and phrases within those phrases, that cannot accomodate even the very next word to be examined. For example, a more ample grammar than (1) would provide for sentences beginning with infinitives, gerunds, and topicalized prepositional phrases, and a top-down parser would attempt all these expansions of the initial $[?]_S$ even though no sentence beginning with phrases of these types could also begin with the word *radio*.

Stronger claims can be made for directed strategies. A situation that favors one or the other kind of undirected parsing method favors all directed methods as against them. Consider, as in transition rule 2, an adjacent pair of items, g_i and g_{i+1} in a configuration, g_i being active with $[?]_\alpha$ as its first open box and g_{i+1} being inactive and of category β. The top-down strategy is to fill the open box in g_i with a string of new open boxes and to continue doing this until the first member of the most recently introduced string is $[?]_\beta$. The number of steps in this process is determined by the grammar and the shaper test together, if the rules involved contain no cycles, and otherwise by the shaper test alone. In any case, once it is set in motion, it takes no further cognizance of the symbols in the string. Thus, if the rules involved do contain cycles or the operation takes place in the early part of a long string, a long train of events may take place without reference to the string being analyzed. Ignoring possible interventions by the shaper, rules of the form $\gamma \to \beta \ldots$ must be applied at least once during the processing, given that β is the category of the next terminal, for this is precisely what the reachability table (or the rule-selection table) guarantees to parsers employing directed methods. Let us call these *bottom* rules because they complete the bottom end of a left branching path from the upper symbol, α, to the lower symbol, β.

Under the same initial conditions, a bottom-up procedure starts by applying the bottom rules against the possibility that the same left branching path can be constructed in the reverse order. If successful, this process will finish by applying *top* rules of the form $\alpha \rightarrow \ldots$. But it may not be successful, and therein lies the crucial difference. The left branch will not necessarily be constructed by the bottom-up procedure because the next rule applied after the bottom rule will be the next one in this sequence only if the bottom rule is nonbranching. Otherwise, the second symbol on its right-hand side becomes a new upper symbol whose corresponding lower symbol is the next terminal in the string. In general, the next upward step in the construction of a left branch will be taken only when the most recent symbol has been established at the root of a complete phrase, without open boxes. For every new rule application—every invocation of transition rule 2—made in the bottom-up process, a corresponding application of the same rule, with a view to establishing a phrase at the same place in the overall structure, will be made by the top-down process. The reverse, however, is not true.

Suppose, for example, that the string to be analyzed is *alpha beta gamma delta*, the words belonging to the categories A, B, C, and D respectively. The input to the parser will therefore be $[\text{alpha}]_A [\text{beta}]_B [\text{gamma}]_C [\text{delta}]_D$. Let the grammar be as in (23).

(23)
                                 1. $S \rightarrow P\ D$
                                   2. $P \rightarrow Q\ C$
                                   3. $Q \rightarrow A\ B$

The string has one structure which is readily discovered by all the methods we have discussed with about equal ease. Now consider what happens if the category of the second word is changed so that the string is no longer accepted by the grammar. The first symbol continues to be reachable from the initial symbol of the grammar, S. The top-down strategy proposes rule 2 because the first symbol in the string is also reachable from Q. Then rule 3 is invoked. Its first symbol matches, the second one fails to match, and the process comes to an end, two rules having been considered. The bottom-up strategy calls for rule 3 to be the first one considered. Its first symbol matches the first item in the string, but the second one fails, bringing the whole process to an end after only one rule has been considered. The example could have been constructed so as to make the chain of rules needlessly invoked in the top-down procedure of any desired length.

Contrary to intuitions deriving from better understood undirected methods, it is therefore possible to assert that bottom-up directed methods are superior to all others within this framework. This is falsified only in situations where short sentences must be parsed using grammars with long rules for these are the cases where the functional load born by the shaper is high. Under these circumstances, the shaper may be in a position to curtail the construction of a left branch before the bottom rule is applied often enough to recommend the top-down method. This argument in favor of directed bottom-up parsing methods does not rest on an analysis of the worst case that can arise because, as far as is known, the methods discussed here cannot be distinguished in that way. The claim is to the effect that such differences in performance as do arise will invariably favor the directed bottom-up technique. *Pace* the use of the shaper, no case can be constructed in which, say, directed top-down parsing fares better.

3. THE CHART

In the last section, our aim was to abstract from a large class of syntactic-processing algorithms those properties of them that ensure that all the processing is done that has to be. We now turn to the problem of eliminating unnecessary repetition of parts of the computation. By far the major part of this repetition comes from a phenomenon that the simple example used was carefully designed to avoid. The phenomenon is this: if a particular initial segment of a long string is analyzable as a phrase of a given type, but in more than one way, then any computation aimed at recognizing phrases in the remainder of the string will be repeated once for each analysis. This is because no mechanism has been provided for recognizing when the phrases required to advance a particular configuration already exist in another.

Consider the sentence *Failing students looked hard.* The first two words can be construed as a noun phrase in two ways meaning approximately *students that fail* and *the failing of students.* Likewise, the second pair of words can be construed as a verb phrase in two ways with the meanings *looked intently* and *looked difficult to do.* These constructions are provided for in the grammar (24). According to this grammar, therefore, the sentence has four structures, each construction of the subject being combinable with each construction of the predicate. But, whereas the parsing strategies so far examined would discover each construction of the subject only once, they would reanalyze the predicate independently for each of these.

(24)
1. S → NP VP
2. NP → A N
3. NP → PRP N
4. VP → V A
5. VP → V AV
6. A → failing, hard, ...
7. PRP → failing, ...
8. N → students, ...
9. V → looked, ...
10. AV → hard, ...

(25) shows the analysis by the undirected bottom-up strategy. The two constructions of the subject are established in lines 7 and 8. A following verb phrase is postulated for each construction

of the subjects in lines 9 and 10 and the verb *looked* is adjoined to each of these configurations in lines 11 and 12. Each of these configurations has two offspring corresponding to the two constructions of the predicate that will eventually be found. From this point on, four lines of development are pursued independently to the final results in lines 29 through 32. Lines 17, 19, 21, and 23 are derived from their parent lines by exactly parallel moves. Those terms that serve to differentiate these lines, but which are not affected by the operation, are therefore brought forward unchanged to lines 22 and 24. These unchanged terms are, in an important sense, *equivalent*, and the new terms introduced are equivalent to one another in the same sense. In this section, I shall first explicate this notion of equivalence and then propose a new data structure, called a *chart*, a kind of well-formed substring table,[3] to replace configuration tables. A chart admits only one member of an equivalence class of terms and, when transitions rules are defined on it corresponding to those defined for configuration

(25)

#	T.R.	Pos.	Par.	R	Configuration
1		1	0		$[\text{failing}]_A$
2		1	0		$[\text{failing}]_{PRP}$
3	2	1	1	2	$[[\text{failing}]_A[?]_N]_{NP}$
4	2	1	2	3	$[[\text{failing}]_{PRP}[?]_N]_{NP}$
5	1	2	3		$[[\text{failing}]_A[?]_N]_{NP}[\text{students}]_N$
6	1	2	4		$[[\text{failing}]_{PRP}[?]_N]_{NP}[\text{students}]_N$
7	3	2	5		$[[\text{failing}]_A[\text{students}]_N]_{NP}$
8	3	2	6		$[[\text{failing}]_{PRP}[\text{students}]_N]_{NP}$
9	2	2	7	1	$[[[\text{failing}]_A[\text{students}]_N]_{NP}[?]_{VP}]_S$
10	2	2	8	1	$[[[\text{failing}]_{PRP}[\text{students}]_N]_{NP}[?]_{VP}]_S$
11	1	3	9		$[[[\text{failing}]_A[\text{students}]_N]_{NP}[?]_{VP}]_S[\text{looked}]_V$
12	1	3	10		$[[[\text{failing}]_{PRP}[\text{students}]_N]_{NP}[?]_{VP}]_S[\text{looked}]_V$
13	2	3	11	4	$[[[\text{failing}]_A[\text{students}]_N]_{NP}[?]_{VP}]_S[[\text{looked}]_V[?]_A]_{VP}$
14	2	3	11	5	$[[[\text{failing}]_A[\text{students}]_N]_{NP}[?]_{VP}]_S[[\text{looked}]_V[?]_{AV}]_{VP}$
15	2	3	12	4	$[[[\text{failing}]_{PRP}[\text{students}]_N]_{NP}[?]_{VP}]_S[[\text{looked}]_V[?]_A]_{VP}$
16	2	3	12	5	$[[[\text{failing}]_{PRP}[\text{students}]_N]_{NP}[?]_{VP}]_S[[\text{looked}]_V[?]_{AV}]_{VP}$
17	1	4	13		$[[[\text{failing}]_A[\text{students}]_N]_{NP}[?]_{VP}]_S[[\text{looked}]_V[?]_A]_{VP}[\text{hard}]_A$
18	1	4	13		$[[[\text{failing}]_A[\text{students}]_N]_{NP}[?]_{VP}]_S[[\text{looked}]_V[?]_A]_{VP}[\text{hard}]_{AV}$
19	1	4	14		$[[[\text{failing}]_A[\text{students}]_N]_{NP}[?]_{VP}]_S[[\text{looked}]_V[?]_{AV}]_{VP}[\text{hard}]_A$
20	1	4	14		$[[[\text{failing}]_A[\text{students}]_N]_{NP}[?]_{VP}]_S[[\text{looked}]_V[?]_{AV}]_{VP}[\text{hard}]_{AV}$
21	1	4	15		$[[[\text{failing}]_{PRP}[\text{students}]_N]_{NP}[?]_{VP}]_S[[\text{looked}]_V[?]_A]_{VP}[\text{hard}]_A$
22	1	4	15		$[[[\text{failing}]_{PRP}[\text{students}]_N]_{NP}[?]_{VP}]_S[[\text{looked}]_V[?]_A]_{VP}[\text{hard}]_{AV}$
23	1	4	16		$[[[\text{failing}]_{PRP}[\text{students}]_N]_{NP}[?]_{VP}]_S[[\text{looked}]_V[?]_{AV}]_{VP}[\text{hard}]_A$
24	1	4	16		$[[[\text{failing}]_{PRP}[\text{students}]_N]_{NP}[?]_{VP}]_S[[\text{looked}]_V[?]_{AV}]_{VP}[\text{hard}]_{AV}$
25	3	4	17		$[[[\text{failing}]_A[\text{students}]_N]_{NP}[?]_{VP}]_S[[\text{looked}]_V[\text{hard}]_A]_{VP}$
26	3	4	20		$[[[\text{failing}]_A[\text{students}]_N]_{NP}[?]_{VP}]_S[[\text{looked}]_V[\text{hard}]_{AV}]_{VP}$
27	3	4	21		$[[[\text{failing}]_{PRP}[\text{students}]_N]_{NP}[?]_{VP}]_S[[\text{looked}]_V[\text{hard}]_A]_{VP}$
28	3	4	24		$[[[\text{failing}]_{PRP}[\text{students}]_N]_{NP}[?]_{VP}]_S[[\text{looked}]_V[\text{hard}]_{AV}]_{VP}$
29	3	4	25		$[[[\text{failing}]_A[\text{students}]_N]_{NP}[[\text{looked}]_V[\text{hard}]_A]_{VP}]_S$
30	3	4	26		$[[[\text{failing}]_A[\text{students}]_N]_{NP}[[\text{looked}]_V[\text{hard}]_{AV}]_{VP}]_S$
31	3	4	27		$[[[\text{failing}]_{PRP}[\text{students}]_N]_{NP}[[\text{looked}]_V[\text{hard}]_A]_{VP}]_S$
32	3	4	28		$[[[\text{failing}]_{PRP}[\text{students}]_N]_{NP}[[\text{looked}]_V[\text{hard}]_{AV}]_{VP}]_S$

[3]See Kuno (1965).

(26)

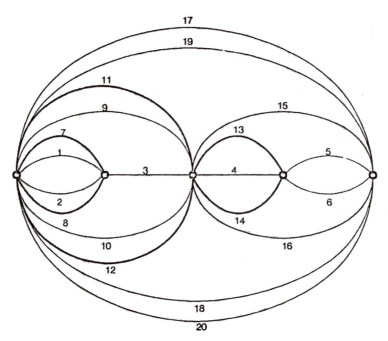

(27)

#	Locus	Length	Term
1	0	1	[failing]$_A$
2	0	1	[failing]$_{PRP}$
3	1	1	[students]$_N$
4	2	1	[looked]$_V$
5	3	1	[hard]$_A$
6	3	1	[hard]$_{AV}$
7	0	1	[[failing]$_A$[?]$_N$]$_{NP}$
8	0	1	[[failing]$_{PRP}$[?]$_N$]$_{NP}$
9	0	2	[[failing]$_A$[students]$_N$]$_{NP}$
10	0	2	[[failing]$_{PRP}$[students]$_N$]$_{NP}$
11	0	2	[[[failing]$_A$[students]$_N$]$_{NP}$[?]$_{VP}$]$_S$
12	0	2	[[[failing]$_{PRP}$[students]$_N$]$_{NP}$[?]$_{VP}$]$_S$
13	2	1	[[looked]$_V$[?]$_{AV}$]$_{VP}$
14	2	1	[[looked]$_V$[?]$_A$]$_{VP}$
15	2	2	[[looked]$_V$[hard]$_{AV}$]$_{VP}$
16	2	2	[[looked]$_V$[hard]$_A$]$_{VP}$
17	0	3	[[[failing]$_A$[students]$_N$]$_{NP}$[[[looked]$_V$[hard]$_{AV}$]$_{VP}$]$_{VP}$]$_S$
18	0	3	[[[failing]$_{PRP}$[students]$_N$]$_{NP}$[[[looked]$_V$[hard]$_{AV}$]$_{VP}$]$_{VP}$]$_S$
19	0	3	[[[failing]$_A$[students]$_N$]$_{NP}$[[[looked]$_V$[hard]$_A$]$_{VP}$]$_{VP}$]$_S$
20	0	3	[[[failing]$_{PRP}$[students]$_N$]$_{NP}$[[[looked]$_V$[hard]$_A$]$_{VP}$]$_{VP}$]$_S$

tables in the last section, redundant operations are therefore naturally eliminated.

Undirected Parsing

In what follows, I shall describe two ways of representing in a chart the data that a parsing procedure operates on, one appropriate to undirected and the other to directed parsing. This section is devoted to the first of these. I shall first provide fairly direct translations into the new formalism of the undirected strategies described in the last section. I shall then go on to consider the case in which the grammar is represented as a rule-selection table so that the top-down and bottom-up cases will not have to be distinguished. Of course, the information contained in a rule selection table is largely degenerate in the undirected case. However, we shall see that a nondegenerate table—one designed for a directed procedure—can be combined with chart operations appropriate to undirected processing. The result is a *partially directed* strategy which is not only viable but, in some ways, attractive. If a degenerate rule-selection table—one intended for undirected parsing—is used with chart operations appropriate to directed parsing, the result is simply an inefficient version of undirected parsing with no redeeming features.

I shall refer to the number of terminal symbols represented in a term as the *length* of that term. Open boxes do not count as terminals so that, for example, $[?]_{NP}$ and $[[?]_{Adj}[?]_N]_{NP}$ both have lengths of 0; $[[radio]_{Adj}[?]_N]_{NP}$ has length 1, and $[[radio]_{Adj}[broadcasts]_N]_{NP}$ has length 2. The length of a sequence or a configuration will be the sum of the lengths of the terms in it. The *locus* of a term in a configuration is simply the sum of the lengths of the terms that precede it in the configuration. Intuitively, the locus captures the notion of position in the sentence; two terms have the same locus if they follow the same sequence of words. The first term in a configuration has a locus of 0.

The undirected processing strategies we have considered have the property that the only terms that need be considered when creating a new term with a given locus are exisiting terms with the same or greater loci. This is trivially true of undirected top-down strategies because all constructed terms—that is, all non-terminals—have locus 0. Configurations are of three types: (i) Those consisting of a single inactive term, (ii) Those consisting of a sequence of active terms, and (iii) Those consisting of a sequence of active terms followed by a single inactive term. Now, a crucial fact about a configuration table arising from an undirected procedure is that the configurations making it up are just those that can be constructed from the terms in it, and their loci, subject to the constraints just mentioned. In other words, the set of entries in a configuration table can be generated knowing only the set of different terms that it contains and the loci of each.

Table (25) is a configuration table showing the analysis of *failing students looked hard* by the undirected bottom-up method and grammar (24). A corresponding chart is given at (27). It contains all the terms in (25), and gives the locus and length of each. Now, (27) contains 8 inactive terms with locus 0, two terminals from the initial string, two noun phrases, one for each interpretation of the subject of the sentence, and four different analyses of the complete sentence. These contribute 8 configurations to (25). 8 different sequences of active terms can be constructed such that the first one has locus 0, four with one member and four with two. 16 sequences can be constructed from active terms followed by a single inactive term. The unambiguous terminals *students* and *looked* are each final members of two of these as are the two verb phrases representing alternative structures of the predicate. Each of the two lexical entries for *hard* is the final member of four sequences. The resulting 32 sequences are precisely the ones that make up the configuration table (25). For undirected strategies, then, a pair of similar terms are equivalent for present purposes if they have the same locus. Table (27) contains only one representative of each equivalence class.

A natural way to represent a chart is as a directed graph. The graph for a sentence of n words has $n + 1$ vertices. Terms label edges, and all the terms with a given locus label edges incident from the vertex for that locus. An edge is said to be active or inactive depending on the status of the term that labels it. A term with locus i and length j is incident to the vertex for locus $i + j$. (26) is the graph corresponding to the table (27). The active edges are shown as thicker lines. Arrowheads are not used in the diagrams in this paper because all edges are either oriented from left to right, or loop back to the same vertex.

It remains to restate the transitions rules for undirected parsing so that they apply to a chart instead of a configuration table. The new set of transition rules need have no member corresponding to rule 1 in the old sets. The chart must contain an entry for each lexical entry of each word in the string being analyzed and the locus of each of these is determined simply by the position in the string of the word. Each of these is the sole member of an equivalence class and they can simply be entered in the chart before the analysis proper begins. In (27), they are lines 1 through 6.

For bottom-up parsing, rule 1 of the new set, corresponding to the old rule 2, is:

(28) 1. **Find a dominating non-terminal:** Let e_i be an inactive edge of category α incident from a vertex v. For all rules of the form $\beta \rightarrow \gamma_1 \ldots \gamma_n$ in the grammar such that $\gamma_1 = \alpha$, introduce a new edge e_i with the term $[\alpha \ [?]_{\gamma_2} \ldots [?]_{\gamma_n}]_\beta$, incident from and to v, provided there is no such edge in the chart already.

The replacement for Rule 3 must be constrained to apply at only one place in a configuration in the same way. Rule 2 in the new system is thus:

(29) 2. **Incorporate completed subgoal:** Let e_a and e_i be adjacent active and inactive edge. e_a is incident from vertex v and e_i is incident to vertex w. Let $[?]_\alpha$ be the first open box in e_a. If e_i is of category α, create a new edge between v and w whose term is that of e_a with the first open box replaced by the term of e_{i+1}.

Both these rules are applied to all qualifying edges or pairs of edges, including any that arise as a result of applying these rules. All but the initial six entries in (25) will be seen to be generable by these rules and, as we have seen, (25) contains the same information as (27). Unnecessary steps

(30)

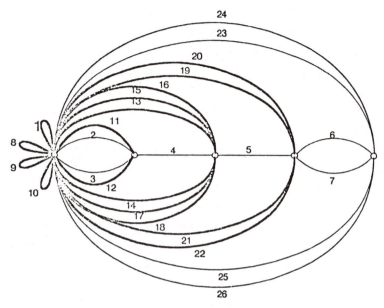

(31)

#	Locus	Length	Term
1	0	0	$[?]_S$
2	0	1	$[failing]_A$
3	0	1	$[failing]_{PRP}$
4	1	1	$[students]_N$
5	2	1	$[looked]_V$
6	3	1	$[hard]_A$
7	3	1	$[hard]_A$
8	0	0	$[[?]_{NP}[?]_{VP}]_S$
9	0	0	$[[[?]_A[?]_N]_{NP}[?]_{VP}]_S$
10	0	0	$[[[?]_{PRP}[?]_N]_{NP}[?]_{VP}]_S$
11	0	1	$[[[failing]_A[?]_N]_{NP}]_S$
12	0	1	$[[[failing]_{PRP}[?]_N]_{NP}]_S$
13	0	2	$[[[failing]_A[students]_N]_{NP}[?]_{VP}]_S$
14	0	2	$[[[failing]_{PRP}[students]_N]_{NP}[?]_{VP}]_S$
15	0	2	$[[[failing]_A[students]_N]_{NP}[[?]_V[?]_A]_{VP}]_S$
16	0	2	$[[[failing]_A[students]_N]_{NP}[[?]_V]_{AV}]_{VP}]_S$
17	0	2	$[[[failing]_{PRP}[students]_N]_{NP}[[?]_V[?]_A]_{VP}]_S$
18	0	2	$[[[failing]_{PRP}[students]_N]_{NP}[[?]_V]_{AV}]_{VP}]_S$
19	0	3	$[[[failing]_A[students]_N]_{NP}[[looked]_V[?]_A]_{VP}]_S$
20	0	3	$[[[failing]_A[students]_N]_{NP}[[looked]_V]_{AV}]_{VP}]_S$
21	0	3	$[[[failing]_{PRP}[students]_N]_{NP}[[looked]_V[?]_A]_{VP}]_S$
22	0	3	$[[[failing]_{PRP}[students]_N]_{NP}[[looked]_V]_{AV}]_{VP}]_S$
23	0	4	$[[[failing]_A[students]_N]_{NP}[[looked]_V[hard]_A]_{VP}]_S$
24	0	4	$[[[failing]_A[students]_N]_{NP}[[looked]_V[hard]_{AV}]_{VP}]_S$
25	0	4	$[[[failing]_{PRP}[students]_N]_{NP}[[looked]_V[hard]_A]_{VP}]_S$
26	0	4	$[[[failing]_{PRP}[students]_N]_{NP}[[looked]_V[hard]_{AV}]_{VP}]_S$

in the computations have, however, been eliminated because each locus-term pair is computed only once.

Rule 1 for top-down parsing is:

(32)   1.   Find a dominating non-terminal: Let e_a be an active edge whose first open box is $[?]_\alpha$, incident to a vertex v. For all rules of the form $\alpha \to \beta_1 \ldots \beta_n$ in the grammar introduce a new edge incident from and to v whose term is the term of e_a with the first open box replaced by $[[?]_{\beta_1} \ldots [?]_{\beta_n}]_\alpha$, provided there is no such edge in the chart already.

(30) and (31) show charts generated by this method for the same example. I have already remarked that all terms in a top-down configuration table have locus zero. If the transition rules are translated directly, as I have just done, the chart therefore offers little advantage. The reason for this is that, when the transition rule (32) is applied, the new phrase marker is created which fills an open box in a structure with locus 0. In the bottom-up case, the newly introduced phrase marker was not immediately engulfed by a higher structure; in fact it engulfed a lower one and the result could have any locus. The decision to write this transition rule so as to amalgamate the new phrase marker into an existing term is made in the interests of efficiency. As we saw, the procedure that makes use of a rule-selection table inserts a new term into the sequence, leaving it to a later application of the old rule 3 to perform the amalgamation. However, it now appears that the minor logical confusion that comes from confounding the functions of the two transition rules leads to considerable inefficiencies in the chart method.

The procedure that uses a rule-selection table must apply to an adjacent pair of edges, the first active and the second inactive in spite of the fact that the active edge influences the result only in top-down methods and the inactive edge only in bottom-up methods. By excluding pairs both of which are active we implement the policy established previously of applying rule 1 only to one pair of terms in a configuration. For this method, the required rule is given in (33) and (34) and (35) repeat the example with this method.

(33)   1.   Find a dominating non-terminal: Let e_a and e_i be adjacent active and inactive edges, e_a being incident from v and e_i being incident to w. Let $[?]_\alpha$ be the first open box in e_a and let β be the category of e_i. For all rules $\gamma \to \delta_1 \ldots \delta_n$ in $S_{\alpha,\beta}$, introduce a new edge between v and w and with the term $[[?]_{\delta_1} \ldots [?]_{\delta_n}]_\gamma$, provided there is no such edge in the chart already.

Examination of (34) is instructive. All applications of transition rule 1 cause a term of length 0 to be introduced and these are recognizable in the graph as active edges that are incident to and from the same vertex. Other edges are either initial lexical edges or arise from applications of rule 2. For this particular example, it is not necessary to state whether the rule-selection table used corresponds to a top-down or a bottom-up strategy because the results are the same in both cases. This, however, is an artefact of the trivial grammar used. The chart does, however, accord equal advantages to both methods both here and in general. Furthermore, nothing turns on whether a

(34)

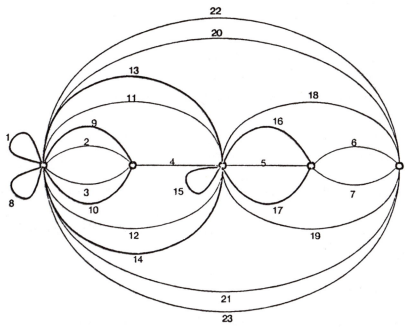

(35)

#	Locus	Length	Term
1	0	0	$[?]_S$
2	0	1	$[failing]_A$
3	0	1	$[failing]_{PRP}$
4	1	1	$[students]_N$
5	2	1	$[looked]_V$
6	3	1	$[hard]_A$
7	3	1	$[hard]_{AV}$
8	0	0	$[?]_{NP}$
9	0	1	$[[failing]_A[?]_N]_{NP}$
10	0	1	$[[failing]_{PRP}[?]_N]_{NP}$
11	0	2	$[[failing]_A[students]_N]_{NP}$
12	0	2	$[[failing]_{PRP}[students]_N]_{NP}$
13	0	2	$[[[failing]_A[students]_N]_{NP}[?]_{VP}]_S$
14	0	2	$[[[failing]_{PRP}[students]_N]_{NP}[?]_{VP}]_S$
15	2	1	$[?]_{VP}$
16	2	1	$[[looked]_V[?]_{AV}]_{VP}$
17	2	1	$[[looked]_V[?]_A]_{VP}$
18	2	2	$[[looked]_V[hard]_{AV}]_{VP}$
19	2	2	$[[looked]_V[hard]_A]_{VP}$
20	0	3	$[[[failing]_A[students]_N]_{NP}[[[looked]_V[hard]_{AV}]_{VP}]_{VP}]_S$
21	0	3	$[[[failing]_{PRP}[students]_N]_{NP}[[[looked]_V[hard]_{AV}]_{VP}]_{VP}]_S$
22	0	3	$[[[failing]_A[students]_N]_{NP}[[[looked]_V[hard]_A]_{VP}]_{VP}]_S$
23	0	3	$[[[failing]_{PRP}[students]_N]_{NP}[[[looked]_V[hard]_A]_{VP}]_{VP}]_S$

rule-selection table is in fact used; the crucial requirement is that the functions of the two transition rules should remain dissociated.

There is one respect in which the chart procedures using a rule-selection table fails to reflect the top-down parsing strategy accurately. This arises when there are sets of left-recursive rules. Careful examination of the transition rules shows that the phrases will not be built in a strictly top-to-bottom order in this case but that the phrases constructed in the bottom cycle of such a set of rules will be produced first. The topmost member of the set of phrases will then serve as a terminal and the cycle will repeat. This happens because the zero-length edge introduced by transition rule 2 for each rule in the set is the same each time; it incorporates nothing from the edges on the basis of which it was introduced. There will be only one such edge for each rule in the left-recursive set regardless of how many cycles of the set take place at a given point in the analysis. The only move open, once such an edge has been established is therefore to pursue the downward path. One consequence of this is that the shaper test is no longer required because the deviation from the top-down strategy occurs in just such a way as to break the vicious cycle.

Directed Parsing

Representing the state of a parsing device by means of a chart can bring the same advantages to directed as to undirected parsing. However, the chart must be used differently because the equivalence classes of terms that are of interest now are not simply those that have the same locus. The point is best illustrated by a string with more than one left branching structure. Consider the sentence *Can openers work* which, punctuation aside, can be read as an assertion about can openers or a question about openers. The first word presumably has two lexical entries, one as a modal verb, and the other as a noun. In its capacity as a modal, we may assume it can be an auxiliary and, as a noun, it can become a noun phrase. I shall refrain from attempting to write explicit context-free rules for the relevant parts of English grammar. Relations between concision and verisimilitude have already been sufficiently strained in this paper.

Using a reachability, or rule-selection, table, the parser posits an initial noun phrase on the basis of the first noun and an auxiliary on the basis of the modal. Four questions now arise: (i) Can the modal begin an auxiliary? (ii) Can the noun begin a noun phrase? (iii) Can the modal begin a noun phrase? and (iv) Can the noun begin an auxiliary? But clearly only the first two of these are proper questions to be considered as part of a directed strategy. Now, it is true that a number of questions that an undirected parser would have to consider are avoided. An undirected top-down parser would, for example establish hypotheses—configurations—that could only be born out if the first word was a determiner, an infinitive or, indeed, any category that can begin a sentence. Each of these would be eventually ruled out when neither lexical entry for the first word matched them. Similarly, an undirected bottom-up parser, observing that *can* can be a main verb, would go on to discover that *can openers* is a verb phrase.

The reason that two irrelevant questions arise is that the chart puts all terms with a given locus on the same footing. In the purportedly directed procedure we are now investigating, grammar rules will therefore be applied to all terms with a given locus provided the reachability table sanctions their application to any term with that locus. As more phrases are formed, more unnecessary work is done. Later in the analysis, it will emerge that the first two words, *can openers* constitute a noun phrase and, at that point, the question of whether this could be initial in an auxiliary will be considered. In short, a procedure that uses a reachability, or rule-selection, table together with the chart-management regime just decribed, is only partially directed.

I shall now show that the chart representation can easily be made to support fully directed context-free parsers. The crucial observation has just been made, namely that terms with the same locus do not constitute the interesting equivalence classes for directed processing. Each class must now contain terms at a given locus and with a given category. But, the full generality of the chart representation will be preserved only if there continues to be a vertex corresponding to each locus. This is the vertex to which terms whose successors have that locus will be incident. For ease of reference, I shall call these *locus vertices*. Those from which edges representing terms of a certain category are incident will be called *term vertices*. Two kinds of edge will also be required. The *term edges*, familiar from the last section, will always be incident from *term vertices*. Inactive term edges will be incident to locus vertices and active term edges to term vertices. The term vertices for a given locus will be accessible from the corresponding locus vertex by following a *category edge* whose label, instead of being a term, will simply be the category characteristic of the term vertex in question.

Each lexical entry for a string to be parsed is represented in the new chart by a pair consisting of a category edge followed by a term edge. The category edges for the i-th word are incident from locus vertex i. If α is a category of the i-th word, a category edge will be constructed from the locus edge i to the term vertex $i : \alpha$, and from there a term edge, labeled with the lexical entry, will be constructed to the locus vertex $i + 1$. Suppose now that an arbitrary inactive term is to be entered into the chart at locus L. Let its length be ℓ, and its category α. The edge that it labels will be incident from the term vertex $L : \alpha$, and to the locus vertex $L + \ell$. If vertex $L : \alpha$ did not previously exist, it would be necessary, at the same time, to create a category edge giving access to that vertex from the locus vertex L.

The parsing procedure starts when an active edge labeled with the open box $[?]_S$ is entered into the chart, incident from and to the locus vertex 0. From this point on, the process is governed by (36).

(36) 1.   **Find a dominating non-terminal:** Let e_a be an active edge incident from vertex v to the vertex w, and e_i an inactive edge of category ϵ incident from w. Let L be the locus of w or, more strictly, of the edges incident from w. (If e_i is a category edge, ϵ is its label and L is the name of the vertex w; if e_i is a term edge, its label is of the form $[\ldots]_\epsilon$ and the

(37)

#	Left	Right	Term
1	0	0:A	A
2	0:A	1	[failing]$_A$
3	0	0:PRP	PRP
4	0:PRP	1	[failing]$_{PRP}$
5	1	1:N	N
6	1:N	2	[students]$_N$
7	2	2:V	V
8	2:V	3	[looked]$_V$
9	3	3:A	A
10	3:A	4	[hard]$_A$
11	3	3:AV	AV
12	3:AV	4	[hard]$_{AV}$
13	0	0:S	S
14	0:S	0:A	[?]$_S$
15	0:S	0:PRP	[?]$_S$
16	0	0:NP	NP
17	0:S	0:NP	[[?]$_{NP}$[?]$_{VP}$]$_S$
18	0:NP	0:A	[[?]$_A$[?]$_N$]$_{NP}$
19	0:NP	0:PRP	[[?]$_{PRP}$[?]$_N$]$_{NP}$
20	0:NP	1	[[failing]$_A$[?]$_N$]$_{NP}$
21	0:NP	1	[[failing]$_{PRP}$[?]$_N$]$_{NP}$
22	0:NP	1:N	[[failing]$_A$[?]$_N$]$_{NP}$
23	0:NP	1:N	[[failing]$_{PRP}$[?]$_N$]$_{NP}$
24	0:NP	2	[[failing]$_A$[students]$_N$]$_{NP}$
25	0:NP	2	[[failing]$_{PRP}$[students]$_N$]$_{NP}$
26	0:S	2	[[[[failing]$_A$[students]$_N$]$_{NP}$]$_{NP}$[?]$_{VP}$]$_S$
27	0:S	2	[[[[failing]$_{PRP}$[students]$_N$]$_{NP}$]$_{NP}$[?]$_{VP}$]$_S$
28	0:S	2:VP	[[[[failing]$_A$[students]$_N$]$_{NP}$]$_{NP}$[?]$_{VP}$]$_S$
29	2:VP	2:V	[[?]$_V$[?]$_A$]$_{VP}$
30	0:S	2:VP	[[[[failing]$_{PRP}$[students]$_N$]$_{NP}$]$_{NP}$[?]$_{VP}$]$_S$
31	2:VP	2:V	[[?]$_V$[?]$_{AV}$]$_{VP}$
32	2:VP	3	[[looked]$_V$[?]$_A$]$_{VP}$
33	2:VP	3	[[looked]$_V$[?]$_{AV}$]$_{VP}$
34	2:VP	3:A	[[looked]$_V$[?]$_A$]$_{VP}$
35	2:VP	3:AV	[[looked]$_V$[?]$_{AV}$]$_{VP}$
36	2:VP	4	[[looked]$_V$[hard]$_A$]$_{VP}$
37	2:VP	4	[[looked]$_V$[hard]$_{AV}$]$_{VP}$
38	0:S	4	[[[[failing]$_A$[students]$_N$]$_{NP}$[[looked]$_V$[hard]$_A$]$_{VP}$]$_S$
39	0:S	4	[[[[failing]$_A$[students]$_N$]$_{NP}$[[looked]$_V$[hard]$_{AV}$]$_{VP}$]$_S$
40	0:S	4	[[[[failing]$_{PRP}$[students]$_N$]$_{NP}$[[looked]$_V$[hard]$_A$]$_{VP}$]$_S$
41	0:S	4	[[[[failing]$_{PRP}$[students]$_N$]$_{NP}$[[looked]$_V$[hard]$_{AV}$]$_{VP}$]$_S$

label of w is $L : \epsilon$). Let the term of e_a be of category α and its first open box be $[?]_\beta$. For each rule $\gamma \to \delta_1 \ldots \delta_n \in \mathcal{R}_{\beta,\epsilon}$, create whatever is not already present in the chart of the following structure: (i) the term vertex $L : \gamma$, (ii) a term edge with the same label as e_a from v to $L : \gamma$, (iii) a term edge labeled $[\mathcal{F}(\delta_1) \ldots \mathcal{F}(\delta_n)]_\gamma$ from $L : \gamma$ to $L : \epsilon$, and (iv) a category edge labeled γ from w to $L : \gamma$.

2. **Extend Active Edge:** Let e_a be an active edge incident from vertex v to the locus vertex

L, and e_i a category edge labeled α incident from L to $L : \alpha$. If $[?]_\alpha$ is the first open box in e_a, create a new edge whose term is the same as that of e_a from v to $L : \alpha$.

3. **Incorporate completed subgoal:** Let e_a be an active edge incident from vertex v to the term vertex $L : \alpha$, and e_i a term edge of category α incident from $L : \alpha$ to x. If $[?]_\alpha$ is the first open box in e_a, create a new edge whose term is that of e_a with the first open box replaced by the label of e_i incident from v and to x.

(38) and (37) show the results of analyzing *failing students looked hard* using the grammar at (24) and the directed bottom-up method. Each transition rule operates on a pair consisting of an active edge and an immediately following inactive edge and, wherever a rule is applicable to such a pair, it must be applied before the process is complete. A measure of the amount of work done by the procedure at each vertex is therefore given by the product of the number of active edges incident to it and the number of inactive vertices incident from it. The sum of these measures for this example is 24. The comparable result for (34) and (35), the undirected counterpart of this procedure is 28. The small difference in the results is due mainly to the triviality of the example. Directed methods,

(38)

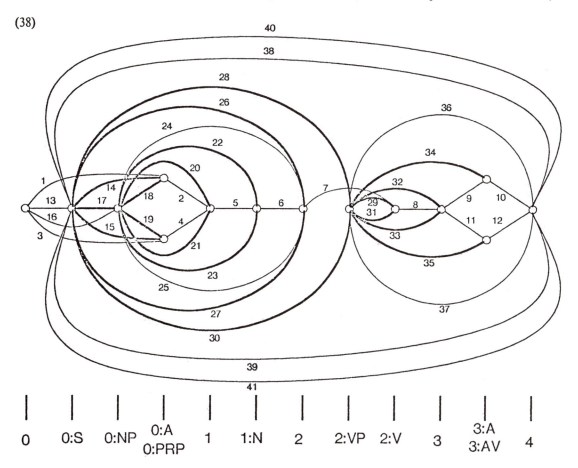

0	0:S	0:NP	0:A 0:PRP	1	1:N	2	2:VP	2:V	3	3:A 3:AV	4

Algorithm Schemata and Data Structures in Syntactic Processing

and particularly directed bottom-up methods, come into their own in the face of structures with long left branches.

I believe that the superiority of directed bottom-up parsing methods have not been generally appreciated. However, I also believe that they may not always be appropriate or that the advantages that they offer over simpler undirected methods may not be enough to recommend them in all circumstances. One argument for simpler techniques is based on the presumed nature of natural languages. The number of categories that linguists have thought it right to use in their grammars has usually been very small[4] and the left branches that are constructed without repeating symbols are very short so that, empirically, the advantages of the directed schemes are minimal.

The value of the information in the reachability or rule-selection tables is further debased if rules are stored as transition networks. This method of representing rules has the advantage of conflating subsequences of symbols that occur in more than one rule. In particular, if the right-hand sides of a pair of rules have a common initial substring, then any work that a parser does comparing these symbols against a string contributes to the matching of both rules. However, such a pair of rules may well have different symbols on the left-hand side so that there is no reason to suppose that they would be called upon under similar circumstances by a directed parser.

Finally, as I pointed out at the outset, the current interest in context-free processing techniques is due in part to the fact that they can often be applied to grammatical formalisms that are not strictly context free, for example, various formalisms involving complex symbols. Under these circumstances, the appropriateness of directed processing methods is governed in large measure by whether it is easy, or indeed possible, to construct reachability tables or rule-selection tables within these formalisms.

4. The Agenda

An algorithm schema becomes an algorithm when all the choices that must be made in executing it are determined. The indeterminacy arises because the transition rules we have considered call for some action to be taken whenever an edge of a certain kind is created or, more importantly, whenever a pair consisiting of an active edge followed by an inactive edge comes into being. The actions that take place under these circumstances can easily give rise to new instances of the same kinds of circumstance. In other words, each step in the process can produce the conditions for more than one subsequent step. Clearly, entering one new edge into a chart can increase by an arbitrary amount the number of active-inactive pairs that there are. It is therefore a fundamental feature of parsing that the material to be processed is amassed, during certain phases of the enterprise, faster than it can be treated.

[4]Gazdar (1979a and 1979b) are notable exceptions to this.

A classical response to this problem is through recursion. Suppose there is a procedure whose job is to add new edges to the chart and then to rehearse the new situations thus created to which transition rules must be applied. It applies the rules, calling itself recursively to add new edges as necessary. In general, some number of edges or pairs of edges will be waiting for treatment by transition rules. The queue is maintained by the recursion mechanism. What results is a so-called *depth first* algorithm in which the most recently proposed task is always the next one to be carried out. In parsing, the result is that one, essentially arbitrary, hypothesis about the grammatical structure of the string at hand is pursued relentlessly until it either succeeds or can be pursued no further.

Another technique which preserves the conceptual clarity and operational simplicity of the chart involves a list of *tasks* called an *agenda* and a policy for managing it. A task is simply an edge, or pair of edges—whatever the transition rules require. Whenever new edges are added to the chart, any new tasks that can be created as a result, are added to the agenda. If they are always added to the front of the agenda and are also removed from the front of the agenda for execution, the same depth-first strategy just described results. If they are added to one end of the agenda, but removed from the other, so that the agenda serves as a queue in the usual sense, the result is a *breadth-first* strategy in which, roughly speaking, equal time is given to each currently open hypothesis. Work on a given hypothesis is resumed only when those corresponding to all others have been cycled through.

The agenda, like the other data structures I have proposed, has the appeal of leaving as many options as possible open. Observe that, if the aim of the parsing exercise is to discover all the structures of a potentially ambiguous string of symbols, tasks can be removed from the agenda in any order whatsoever, in as nearly a random way as can be contrived, without influencing the results eventually arrived at or the time taken to reach them. All the tasks must be done and the cost of executing a given task is not affected by the others on the agenda. If, on the other hand, some significance is attached to the order in which solutions are arrived at, then the policies governing the management of the chart become crucially important. Suppose one holds, for example, that the grammar that represents a person's linguistic competence assigns some number of interpretations to a string but that only certain of these will be recognized under conditions of actual performance. Presumably such facts would be explained by positing a specific parsing algorithm or the agenda-management policy that gives rise to that algorithm.

Before pursuing this line too far, we shall do well to assess what the true value of an algorithm as opposed to an algorithm schema actually is. The important fact is that computers, as they exist today, are algorithmic machines *par excellence*. They require algorithms to direct their operations and they are, in principle, able to execute all algorithms indifferently. But machines can be envisaged, and some are being built, which force some reassessment of the notion of an algorithm in the direction suggested in this paper. The main reason for requiring that the order of events be exactly specified is that the computer can do only one thing at once and everything turns on knowing what that shall be. If a machine were able to do more than one thing at once and, if the outstanding tasks were independent of one another, then a number of them could be under way at any moment and no importance would attach to whether one was finished before or after another. Such a machine might be thought of as having a number of work stations at each of which tasks of the same kind could be done. But some could be faster and some slower; some work stations could be removed from service and others introduced without influencing the outcome. The interest of all this for present purposes has nothing to do with possible future directions in computer science but simply with the very real possibility that algorithms, narrowly construed, are not necessarily what is required as mental models. Indeed, the proposition that the brain is patterned after the computer that we know today is, *prima facie*, implausible.

On the other hand, a standard computer can be set to predict something of the behavior of mental models which countenance the simultaneous execution of several tasks. For example, suppose it was proposed that syntactic tasks all took unit time and that some fixed number, say k, of them could be in process at any time. A computer model of this behavior would maintain a main agenda and a secondary agenda. Tasks would be taken from the secondary agenda in any convenient order for execution and, as new tasks were produced, they would be appended to the main agenda. When the secondary agenda was exhausted, k tasks would be chosen from the main agenda according to a policy laid down as part of the model and transferred to the secondary agenda. If the main agenda only contained k or less tasks, they would all be transferred. The model would predict that the time taken to analyze a string would be proportional, not to the number of tasks executed, but to the number of times the secondary agenda was replenished from the main agenda. The explanatory power of a model which specifies more is surely greater than one that specifies less, but this is not to say that a model is to be preferred that makes von Neuman seem to have invented the brain.

Psychological experiments aimed at obtaining data about syntactic processing strategies are carefully designed to control for any possible intrusion by other mental processes, particularly semantic effects. It seems reasonable and, indeed, it is often observed, that the syntactic reading that first suggests itself to a subject is conditioned by previous context, the meanings of the words involved, and such like. A psychological model must eventually explain this behavior as well as what happens when these effects are, to the extent possible, avoided. A model that took the form of an algorithm, in the narrow sense, would be poorly placed to do this. In fact, the advocate of such a model would be forced into the position that the strategies used in controlled psychological experiments were unrelated to those used in understanding sentences in context. A model based on the agenda can associate priorities with tasks in more or less complex ways and can thus ascribe the variation observed in experimental results to a variety of sources. The simpler experiments reveal what the priorities are when there is little or no semantic contribution but, when the time comes to give an account of that contribution, the work will center on how the priorities are computed and not on designing a completely new algorithm.

An objection that might be raised against a psychological model based on charts and agendas is that it assumes that the result of every intermediate result involved in the overall computation is remembered and equally accessible at any later time. Indeed, the conceptual clarity of this way of doing things comes largely from the fact that there are almost no state variables in the abstract machine. The quantities that such variables would contain in other processors here become permanent parts of a data structure. This argument would be persuasive against a proposal that charts and agendas as described here be accorded the status of a psychological model. But that would be an absurd proposal. High on the long list of additions that would have to be made to it before it could fill that role would be a model of short term memory that would have a notion of time and of the intervals of time during which particular parts of each data structure were accessible. But the notion of time would not be taken over uncritically from the instruction counter of the computer. In short, what I have presented here is what I claimed it would be, namely a framework within which parsers, conceptual and actual, can be designed and constructed. The choices that it invites the designer to make are choices that are motivated by inherent properties of the problem of syntactic processing and not by more or less irrelevant considerations from automata theory and electrical engineering.

REFERENCES

1. Bresnan, J. (1978) "A Realistic Transformational Grammar" in M. Halle, J. Bresnan and G. A. Miller (eds.) *Linguistic Theory and Psychological Reality.* MIT Press.

2. Frazier, L. (1978) "On comprehending sentences: syntactic parsing strategies". Unpublished doctoral dissertation, University of Connecticut.

3. Frazier, L. and J. D. Fodor (1978), "The sausage machine: a new two-stage parsing model", *Cognition 6*, 291-325.

4. Gazdar, G. (1979a), "English as a context-free language", University of Sussex, Mimeo.

5. Gazdar, G. (1979b), "Constituent structures", University of Sussex, Mimeo.

6. Griffiths, T. V. and S. R. Petrick (1965), "On the relative efficiencies of context-free grammar recognizers", *CACM 8, 5*, 289-300.

7. Harman, G. H. (1963), "Generative grammars without transformation rules: a defense of phrase structure", *Language* 39, 4, pp. 597-616.

8. Kaplan, R. M. (1972), "Augmented transition networks as psychological models of sentence comprehension", *Artificial Intelligence, 3*, 77-100.

9. Kaplan, R. M. (1978) "Computational resources and linguistic theory", *TINLAP 2*.

10. Kay, M. (1977) "Moprphological and syntactic analysis" in A. Zampolli (ed.), *Syntactic Structures Processing.* North Holland.

11. Kimball, J. (1973) "Seven principles of surface structure parsing in natural language". *Cognition 2*, 15-47.

12. Kuno, S. and A. Oetinger (1962), "A multiple path syntactic analyzer". *Information Processing 62.* North Holland.

13. Kuno, S. (1965) "The predictive analyzer and a path elimination technique. *CACM, 8,* 453-462

14. Marcus, M. P. (1978) "A theory of syntactic recognition for natural language", Unpublished doctoral dissertation, MIT.

15. Woods, W. A. and R. M. Kaplan (1971), "The lunar sciences natural language information system", Bolt, Beraneck and Newman.

16. Wanner, E., R. Kaplan and S. Shiner (1975) 'Garden paths in relative clauses". Unpublished Paper. Harvard University.

17. Wanner, E. and M. Maratsos (1978) "An ATN approach to comprehension". in M. Halle, J. Bresnan and G. A. Miller (eds.) *Linguistic Theory and Psychological Reality.* MIT Press.

Transition Network Grammars for Natural Language Analysis

W. A. Woods
Harvard University, Cambridge, Massachusetts

The use of augmented transition network grammars for the analysis of natural language sentences is described. Structure-building actions associated with the arcs of the grammar network allow for the reordering, restructuring, and copying of constituents necessary to produce deep-structure representations of the type normally obtained from a transformational analysis, and conditions on the arcs allow for a powerful selectivity which can rule out meaningless analyses and take advantage of semantic information to guide the parsing. The advantages of this model for natural language analysis are discussed in detail and illustrated by examples. An implementation of an experimental parsing system for transition network grammars is briefly described.

KEY WORDS AND PHRASES: computational linguistics, grammars, grammar models, linguistics, natural language analysis, parsing, semantic interpretation, transition network grammars, transformational grammars
CR CATEGORIES: 3.42, 4.12

1. Motivation

One of the early models for natural language grammars was the finite state transition graph. This model consists of a network of nodes and directed arcs connecting them, where the nodes correspond to states in a finite state machine and the arcs represent transitions from state to state. Each arc is labeled with a symbol whose input can cause a transition from the state at the tail of the arc to the state at its head. This model has the attractive feature that the sequences of words which make up a sentence can be read off directly by following the paths through the grammar from the initial state to some final state. Unfortunately, the model is grossly inadequate for the representation of natural language grammars due to its failure to capture many of their regularities. A most notable inadequacy is the absence of a pushdown mechanism that permits one to suspend the processing of a constituent at a given level while using the same grammar to process an embedded constituent.

Suppose, however, that one added the mechanism of recursion directly to the transition graph model by fiat.

The research reported here was supported in part by NSF grant GS-2301.

That is, suppose one took a collection of transition graphs each with a name, and permitted as labels on the arcs not only terminal symbols but also nonterminal symbols naming complex constructions which must be present in order for the transition to be followed. The determination of whether such a construction was in fact present in a sentence would be done by a "subroutine call" to another transition graph (or the same one). The resulting model of grammar, which we will call a *recursive transition network*, is equivalent in generative power to that of a context-free grammar or pushdown store automaton, but as we will show, allows for greater efficiency of expression, more efficient parsing algorithms, and natural extension by "augmentation" to more powerful models which allow various degrees of context dependence and more flexible structure-building during parsing. We argue in fact that an "augmented" recursive transition network is capable of performing the equivalent of transformational recognition (cf. Chomsky [6, 7]) without the necessity of a separate inverse transformational component, and that this parsing can be done in an amount of time which is comparable to that of predictive context-free recognition.

2. Recursive Transition Networks

A *recursive transition network* is a directed graph with labeled states and arcs, a distinguished state called the start state, and a distinguished set of states called final states. It looks essentially like a nondeterministic finite state transition diagram except that the labels on the arcs may be state names as well as terminal symbols. The interpretation of an arc with a state name as its label is that the state at the end of the arc will be saved on a pushdown store and the control will jump (without advancing the input tape) to the state that is the arc label. When a final state is encountered, then the pushdown store may be "popped" by transferring control to the state which is named on the top of the stack and removing that entry from the stack. An attempt to pop an empty stack when the last input character has just been processed is the criterion for acceptance of an input string. The state names that can appear on arcs in this model are essentially the names of constructions that may be found as "phrases" of the input tape. The effect of a state-labeled arc is that the transition that it represents may take place if a construction of the indicated type is found as a "phrase" at the appropriate point in the input string.

Figure 1 gives an example of a recursive transition network for a small subset of English. It accepts such sentences as "John washed the car" and "Did the red barn collapse?" It is easy to visualize the range of acceptable sentences from inspection of the transition network. To recognize the sentence "Did the red barn collapse?" the network is started in state S. The first transition is the aux transition

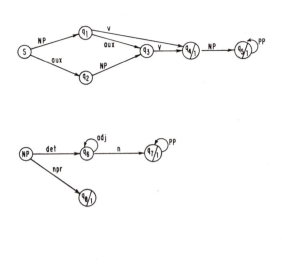

FIG. 1. A sample transition network. S is the start state. q_4, q_5, q_7, q_8, and q_{10} are the final states.

to state q_2 permitted by the auxilliary "did". From state q_2 we see that we can get to state q_3 if the next "thing" in the input string is an NP. To ascertain if this is the case, we call the state NP. From state NP we can follow the arc labeled det to state q_6 because of the determiner "the". From here, the adjective "red" causes a loop which returns to state q_6, and the subsequent noun "barn" causes a transition to state q_7. Since state q_7 is a final state, it is possible to "pop up" from the NP computation and continue the computation of the top level S beginning in state q_3 which is at the end of the NP arc. From q_3 the verb "collapse" permits a transition to the state q_4, and since this state is final and "collapse" is the last word in the string, the string is accepted as a sentence.

In the above example, there is only one accepting path through the network—i.e. the sentence is unambiguous with respect to the grammar. It is an inherent feature of natural language, however, that except for contrived subsets of the language there will be ambiguous sentences which have several distinct analysis paths through the transition network. The transition network model therefore is fundamentally a nondeterministic mechanism, and any parsing algorithm for transition network grammars must be capable of following any and all analysis paths for any given sentence.

The fact that the recursive transition network is equivalent to a pushdown store automaton is not difficult to establish. Every recursive transition network is essentially a pushdown store automaton whose stack vocabulary is a subset of its state set. The converse fact that every pushdown store automaton has an equivalent transition net could be established directly, but can be more simply

established by noting that every pushdown store automaton has an equivalent context-free grammar which has an equivalent recursive transition net.

3. Augmented Transition Networks

It is well known (cf. Chomsky [6]) that the strict context-free grammar model is not an adequate mechanism for characterizing the subtleties of natural languages. Many of the conditions which must be satisfied by well-formed English sentences require some degree of agreement between different parts of the sentence which may or may not be adjacent (indeed which may be separated by a theoretically unbounded number of intervening words). Context-sensitive grammars could take care of the weak generation of many of these constructions, but only at the cost of losing the linguistic significance of the "phrase structure" assigned by the grammar (cf. Postal [27]). Moreover, the unaided context-free grammar model is unable to show the systematic relationship that exists between a declarative sentence and its corresponding question form, between an active sentence and its passive, etc. Chomsky's theory of transformational grammar [7], with its distinction between the surface structure of a sentence and its deep structure, answers these objections but falls victim to inadequacies of its own (cf. Schwarcz [28] or McCawley [21]). In this section we describe a model of grammar based on the notion of a recursive transition network which is capable of performing the equivalent of transformational recognition without the need for a separate transformational component and which meets some of the objections that have been raised against the traditional model of transformational grammar.

The basic recursive transition network model as we have described it is weakly equivalent to the context-free grammar model and differs in strong equivalence only in its ability to characterize unbounded branching, as in structures of the form:

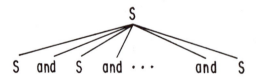

The major features which a transformational grammar adds to those of the context-free grammar are the abilities to move fragments of the sentence structure around (so that their positions in the deep structure are different from those in the surface structure), to copy and delete fragments of sentence structure, and to make its actions on constituents generally dependent on the contexts in which those constituents occur. We can add equivalent facilities to the transition network model by adding to each arc of the transition network an arbitrary condition which must be satisfied in order for the arc to be followed, and a set of structure building actions to be executed if the arc is followed. We call this version of the model an *augmented transition network*.

The augmented transition network builds up a partial structural description of the sentence as it proceeds from state to state through the network. The pieces of this partial description are held in *registers* which can contain any rooted tree or list of rooted trees and which are automatically pushed down when a recursive application of the transition network is called for and restored when the lower level (recursive) computation is completed. The structure-building actions on the arcs specify changes in the contents of these registers in terms of their previous contents, the contents of other registers, the current input symbol, and/or the result of lower level computations. In addition to holding pieces of substructure that will eventually be incorporated into a larger structure, the registers may also be used to hold flags or other indicators to be interrogated by conditions on the arcs.

Each final state of the augmented network has associated with it one or more conditions which must be satisfied in order for that state to cause a "pop". Paired with each of these conditions is a function which computes the value to be returned by the computation. A distinguished register, *, (which usually contains the current input word when a word is being scanned) is set to the result of the lower level computation when the network returns to an arc which has called for a recursive computation. Thus the register * in every case contains a representation of the "thing" (word or phrase) which caused a transition.

3.1. Representation of Augmented Networks.   To make the discussion of augmented transition networks more concrete, we give in Figure 2 a specification of a language in which an augmented transition network can be represented. The specification is given in the form of an extended context-free grammar in which a vertical bar separates alternative ways of forming a construction and the Kleene star operator (*) is used as a superscript to indicate arbitrarily repeatable constituents. The nonterminal symbols of the grammar consist of English

⟨transition network⟩ → (⟨arc set⟩⟨arc set⟩*)
⟨arc set⟩ → (⟨state⟩⟨arc⟩*)
⟨arc⟩ → (CAT ⟨category name⟩⟨test⟩⟨action⟩* ⟨term act⟩)|
        (PUSH ⟨state⟩⟨test⟩⟨action⟩* ⟨term act⟩)|
        (TST ⟨arbitrary label⟩⟨test⟩⟨action⟩* ⟨term act⟩)|
        (POP ⟨form⟩⟨test⟩)
⟨action⟩ → (SETR ⟨register⟩⟨form⟩)|
          (SENDR ⟨register⟩⟨form⟩)|
          (LIFTR ⟨register⟩⟨form⟩)
⟨term act⟩ → (TO ⟨state⟩)|
            (JUMP ⟨state⟩)
⟨form⟩ → (GETR ⟨register⟩)|
        *|
        (GETF ⟨feature⟩)|
        (BUILDQ ⟨fragment⟩⟨register⟩*)|
        (LIST ⟨form⟩*)|
        (APPEND ⟨form⟩⟨form⟩)|
        (QUOTE ⟨arbitrary structure⟩)

Fig. 2. Specification of a language for representing augmented transition networks

descriptions enclosed in angle brackets, and all other symbols except the vertical bar and the superscript * are terminal symbols (including the parentheses, which indicate list structure). The * which occurs as an alternative right-hand side for the rule for the construction ⟨form⟩, however, is a terminal symbol and is not to be confused with the superscript *'s which indicate repeatable constituents. The first line of the figure says that a transition network is represented by a left parenthesis, followed by an arc set, followed by any number of arc sets (zero or more), followed by a right parenthesis. An arc set, in turn, consists of a left parenthesis, followed by a state name, followed by any number of arcs, followed by a right parenthesis, and an arc can be any one of the four forms indicated in the third rule of the grammar. The remaining rules are interpreted in a similar fashion. Nonterminals whose expansions are not given in Figure 2 have names which should be self-explanatory.

The expressions generated as transition networks by the grammar of Figure 2 are in the form of parenthesized list structures, where a list of the elements A, B, C, and D is represented by the expression (A B C D). The transition network is represented as a list of arc sets, each of which is itself a list whose first element is a state name and whose remaining elements are arcs leaving that state. The arcs also are represented as lists, possible forms of which are indicated in the figure. (The conditions and functions associated with final states are represented as (pseudo) "arcs" with no actions and no destination.) The first element of each arc is a word which names the type of the arc, and the third element is an arbitrary test which must be satisfied in order for the arc to be followed. The CAT arc is an arc which can be followed if the current input symbol is a member of the lexical category named on the arc (and if the test is satisfied), while the PUSH arc is an arc which causes a pushdown to the state indicated. The TST arc is an arc which permits an arbitrary test to determine whether an arc is to be followed. In all three of these arcs, the actions on the arc are the structure-building actions, and the terminal action specifies the state to which control is passed as a result of the transition. The two possible terminal actions, TO and JUMP, indicate whether the input pointer is to be advanced or not advanced, respectively—that is, whether the next state is to scan the next input word or whether it is to continue to scan the same word. The POP arc is a dummy arc which indicates under what conditions the state is to be considered a final state, and the form to be returned as the value of the computation if the POP alternative is chosen. (One advantage of representing this information as a dummy arc is the ability to order the choice of popping with respect to the other arcs which leave the state.)

The actions and the *forms* which occur in the network are represented in "Cambridge Polish" notation, a notation in which a function call is represented as a parenthesized list whose first element is the name of the function and whose remaining elements are its arguments. The three actions indicated in Figure 2 cause the contents of the indicated register to be set equal to the value of the indicated *form*. SETR causes this to be done at the current level of computation in the network, while SENDR causes it to be done at the next lower level of embedding (used to send information down to a lower level computation) and LIFTR causes it to be done at the next higher level computation (used to return additional information to higher level computations).

The *forms* as well as the conditions (*tests*) of the transition network may be arbitrary functions of the register contents, represented in some functional specification language such as LISP (McCarthy et al. [20]), a list processing programming language based on Church's lambda calculus and written in Cambridge Polish notation. The seven types of forms listed in Figure 2 are a basic set which is sufficient to illustrate the major features of the augmented transition network model. GETR is a function whose value is the contents of the indicated register, * is a form whose value is usually the current input word, and GETF is a function which determines the value of a specified feature for the current input word. (In the actions which occur on a PUSH arc, * has the value of the lower level computation which permitted the PUSH transition.)

BUILDQ is a useful structure-building form which takes a list structure representing a fragment of a parse tree with specially marked nodes and returns as its value the result of replacing those specially marked nodes with the contents of indicated registers.[1] Specifically, for each occurrence of the symbol + in the list structure given as its first argument, BUILDQ substitutes the contents of one of the listed registers (the first register replacing the first + sign, the second register the second +, etc.). In addition, BUILDQ replaces occurrences of the symbol * in the fragment with the value of the form *.

The remaining three forms are basic structure-building forms (out of which any BUILDQ can be duplicated) which respectively make a list of the values of the listed arguments, append two lists together to make a single list, and produce as value the (unevaluated) argument form. An illustrative fragment of an augmented transition network is given in Figure 3. In Section 3.2 the operation of

this network is described and some of the features of the augmented transition network model are discussed.

3.2. An Illustrative Example. Figure 3 gives a fragment of an augmented transition network represented in the language of Figure 2. This fragment is an augmentation of the portion of the transition network of Figure 1 which consists of the states S/, Q1, Q2, Q3, Q4, and Q5. The augmented network builds a structural representation in which the first constituent of a sentence is a *type* (either DCL or Q) which indicates whether the sentence is de-

```
(S/ (PUSH NP/ T
        (SETR SUBJ *)
        (SETR TYPE (QUOTE DCL))
        (TO Q1))
    (CAT AUX T
        (SETR AUX *)
        (SETR TYPE (QUOTE Q))
        (TO Q2)))
(Q1 (CAT V T
        (SETR AUX NIL)
        (SETR V *)
        (TO Q4))
    (CAT AUX T
        (SETR AUX *)
        (TO Q3)))
(Q2 (PUSH NP/ T
        (SETR SUBJ *)
        (TO Q3)))
(Q3 (CAT V T
        (SETR V *)
        (TO Q4)))
(Q4 (POP (BUILDQ (S+++(VP+)) TYPE SUBJ AUX V) T)
    (PUSH NP/ T
        (SETR VP (BUILDQ (VP (V+) *) V))
        (TO Q5)))
(Q5 (POP (BUILDQ (S++++) TYPE SUBJ AUX VP) T)
    (PUSH PP/ T
        (SETR VP (APPEND (GETR VP) (LIST *)))
        (TO Q5)))
```

Fig. 3. An illustrative fragment of an augmented transition network

---

[1] The BUILDQ function which is implemented in the experimental parsing system (See Section 10) is considerably more versatile than the version described here. Likewise, the implemented parser contains additional formats for arcs as well as other extensions to the language specified here. There has been no attempt to define a basic irredundant set of primitive conditions, actions, and forms, but rather an effort has been made to allow flexibility for adding "natural" primitives which facilitate the writing of compact grammars. For this reason, the set of possible conditions, actions, and forms has been left open-ended to allow for experimental determination of useful primitives. However, the arc formats and actions described here, together with arbitrary LISP expressions for conditions and *forms*, provides a model which is equivalent in power to a Turing machine and therefore complete in a theoretical sense.

clarative or interrogative, the second constituent is the subject noun phrase, the third is an auxilliary (or NIL if there is no auxilliary), and the fourth is the verb phrase constituent. This representation is produced regardless of the order in which the subject noun phrase and the auxilliary occur in the sentence. The network also produces a representation of a verb phrase constituent even though there is no pushdown in the network corresponding to a verb phrase. It will be helpful, both for the understanding of the notation and for the understanding of the operation of the augmented network, to follow through an example at this point using the network fragment of Figure 3.

Before proceeding to work an example, however, it is necessary to explain the representation of the parse trees which is used by the network fragment. The parse trees are represented in a parenthesized notation in which the representation of a node consists of a list whose first element is the name of the node and whose remaining elements are the representations of the constituents of that node.

For example, the parse tree

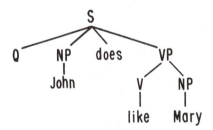

would be represented in this notation by the expression:

(S (NP John) (VP (V likes) (NP Mary))

This representation can also be viewed as a labeled bracketing of the sentence in which a left bracket for a phrase of type X is represented by a left parenthesis followed by an X, and the matching right bracket is simply a right parenthesis.

Let us now consider the operation of the augmented network fragment of Figure 3 for the input sentence "Does John like Mary?"

1. We begin the process in state S/ scanning the first word of the sentence, "does". Since this word is an auxiliary, its dictionary entry would mark it as a member of the category AUX and therefore (since its arbitrary condition T is the universally true condition) the arc (CAT AUX T ⋯) can be followed. (The other arc which pushes down to look for a noun phrase will not be successful.) In following this arc, we execute the actions: (SETR AUX *), which puts the current word "does" into a register named AUX, (SETR TYPE (QUOTE Q)), which puts the symbol "Q" into a register named TYPE, and (TO Q2), which causes the network to enter state Q2 scanning the next word of the sentence "John".

2. State Q2 has only one arc leaving it, which is a push to state NP/. The push will be successful and will return a representation of the structure of the noun phrase which will then become the value of the special register *. We will assume that the representation returned is the expression "(NP John)". Now, having recognized a construction of type NP, we proceed to perform the actions on the arc. The action (SETR SUBJ *) causes the value "(NP John)" to be placed in the register SUBJ, and the action (TO Q3) causes us to enter the state Q3 scanning the next word "like". The register contents at this point are:

TYPE: Q
AUX: does
SUBJ: (NP John)

3. From state Q3, the verb "like" allows a transition to state Q4, setting the contents of a register V to the value "like" in the process, and the input pointer is advanced to scan the word "Mary".

4. Q4, being a final state could choose to "POP", indicating that the string that has been processed so far is a complete sentence (according to the grammar of Figure 1); however, since this is not the end of the sentence, this alternative is not successful. However, the state also has an arc which pushes down to state NP/, and this alternative will succeed, returning the value "(NP Mary)". The action (SETR VP (BUILDQ (VP (V +) *) V)) will now take the structure fragment "(VP (V +) *)" and substitute the current value of * for the occurrence of * in the fragment and replace the occurrence of + with the contents of the indicated register V. The resulting structure, "(VP (V like) (NP Mary))" will be placed in the register VP, and the action (TO Q5) causes a transition to state Q5 scanning beyond the end of the input string. The register contents at this point are:

TYPE: Q
AUX: does
SUBJ: (NP John)
V: like
VP: (VP (V like) (NP Mary)).

5. We are now scanning the end of the sentence, and since Q5 is a final state (i.e. it has a "POP" arc) and the condition T is satisfied, the sentence is accepted. The form "(BUILDQ (S + + + +) TYPE SUBJ AUX VP)" specifies the value to be returned as the analysis of the sentence. The value is obtained by substituting the contents of the registers TYPE, SUBJ, AUX, and VP for the successive instances of the symbol "+" in the fragment "(S + + + +)" to give the final sentence analysis

(S Q (NP John) does (VP (V like) (NP Mary))),

which represents the parse tree:

In ordinary context-free recognition, the structural descriptions of sentences are more or less direct representations of the flow of control of the parser as it analyzes the sentence. The structural descriptions assigned by the structure building rules of an augmented transition network, as we can see from the example, are comparatively independent of the flow of control of the algorithm. This is not to say that they are not determined by the flow of control of the parser, for this they surely are; rather we mean to point out that they are not isomorphic to the flow of control as in the usual context-free recognition algorithms. It is possible for a constituent that is found in the course of analysis to appear in the final structural description several times or not at all, and its location may be entirely different from that in which it was found in the surface structure. In addition, the structural description assigned to a constituent at one point during the analysis may be changed or transformed before that structure is incorporated into the final structural description of the sentence as a whole. These facilities, plus the ability to test arbitrary conditions, allow the equivalent of a transformational deep structure to be constructed while the parser is performing transitions that are isomorphic to the surface structure of a sentence.

4. Transformational Recognition

The usual model of transformational grammar is a generative model consisting of a context-free (base) grammar and a set of transformational rules which map syntax trees into new (derived) syntax trees. The generation of a sentence with such a grammar consists of first constructing a deep structure using the base component grammar and then transforming this deep structure into a surface structure by successive applications of transformations. The terminal nodes (or leaves) of the surface structure tree give the final form of the sentence. This model of transformational grammar is totally oriented toward the generation of sentences rather than their analysis, and although there is clearly an algorithm for the use of such a grammar to analyze a sentence—namely the procedure of "analysis by synthesis" (Matthews [23])—this algorithm is so inefficient as to be out of the question for any practical application. (The analysis by synthesis method consists of applying the rules in the "forward" (generative) direction in all possible ways to generate all of the possible sentences of the language while looking to see if the sentence which you are trying to analyze turns up in the list.)

Two attempts to formulate more practical algorithms for transformational recognition (Petrick [26] and Mitre [24]) resulted in algorithms which were either too time consuming for the analysis of large numbers of sentences or else lacking in formal completeness. Both of these algorithms attempt to analyze sentences by applying the transformations in reverse, a procedure which is far less straightforward than it sounds. The difficulty with simply performing the transformations in reverse is twofold. First, the transformations operate on tree structures and produce tree structures as their values. In the forward direction, they begin with the deep structure tree and end with the surface structure tree. To reverse this process, it is first necessary to obtain a surface structure tree for the input sentence. However, there is no component in the transformational model which characterizes the possible surface structures (their only characterization is implicit in the changes which can be made in the deep structures by means of the transformations). Both the Mitre and the Petrick analysis procedures solve this problem by constructing an "augmented grammar" which consists of the rules of the original base component grammar plus additional rules which characterize the structures that can be added by transformations. In the Mitre procedure, this "surface grammar" is constructed by hand and no formal procedure is available for constructing it from the original transformational grammar. In the Petrick procedure, there is a formal procedure for obtaining an augmented grammar but it will not necessarily terminate unless the length of the possible input sentences is first circumscribed. When sentences longer than the chosen length are encountered, more augmented grammar rules must be generated.

In the Mitre procedure, the augmented grammar is used to assign a complete "tentative" surface structure which is then subjected to inverse transformations. In the Petrick procedure, inverse transformations are applied to partially built up surface structures and the processes of applying transformations and building structure are interwoven. In both systems, the inverse transformations may or may not produce a legitimate deep structure. If they do, the sentence is accepted, but if they do not, the tentative surface structure was spurious and is rejected. There is no way to construct a context-free surface grammar which will assign all and only legitimate surface structures. One must settle for one which will assign all legitimate surface structures plus additional spurious ones. Moreover, the only way to tell the two apart is to perform the inverse transformations and check the resulting "tentative" deep structures.

A second difficulty with the Petrick algorithm is the combinatorial explosion of the number of possible inverse transformation sequences that can be applied to a given surface structure tree. Although many of the transformations when applied in the forward direction are obligatory so that only one possible action can be taken, almost all of the inverse transformations are optional. The reason for this is that even though a given structure looks like it could have been produced by a given forward transformation so that the inverse transformation can be performed, there is no guarantee that the same structure could not have arisen in a transformational derivation in some other way. Therefore both the alternative of applying the inverse transformation and that of not applying it must be tried whenever an inverse transformation can apply. The number of active paths can grow exponentially with the number of transformations applied. Moreover, the forward transformations usually do not specify much information about the structure which results from applying the transformation (even though the linguist may know a good deal about what the resulting structure must be like). For this reason, the inverse transformations are not as selective as their forward counterparts and many more spurious applications of transformations are allowed. That is, whereas most forward sequences of transformations will lead to successful surface structures, most inverse sequences will not lead to legitimate deep structures, and a large amount of wasted effort is therefore expended on dead-end paths. The Mitre parser avoids the nondeterminism of the inverse transformational process by constructing a deterministic set of inverse transformational rules ad hoc to a particular grammar. This method, however, is not guaranteed to produce all legitimate deep structures of a sentence, and there is no formal procedure for constructing the necessary set of inverse transformations.

5. Augmented Transition Networks for Transformational Recognition

In 1965 Kuno [18] suggested that it should be possible to augment the surface structure grammar of a transformational grammar in such a way that it "remembered" the equivalent deep structure constructions and could build the deep structure of the sentence while doing the surface structure parsing—without the necessity of a separate inverse transformational component. The model which he proposed at that time, however, was not adequate to deal with some of the more powerful transformational mechanisms such as the extraposition of a constituent from an arbitrarily deep embedding. The augmented transition network, on the other hand, provides a model which is capable of doing everything that a transformational grammar can do and is therefore a realization of part of the Kuno prediction. It remains to be seen whether a completely mechanical procedure can be developed to take a transformational grammar in the usual formalism and translate it into an equivalent augmented transition network. I conjecture, however, that such is the case.

Even if such a mechanical procedure is available, it may still be more appropriate to use the transition network model directly for the original linguistic research and grammar development. The reasons for this are several. First, the transition network that could be developed by a mechanical procedure from a traditional transformational grammar could not be expected to be as efficient as that which could be designed by hand. Moreover, the transition network model provides a mechanism which satisfies some of the objections which have been raised by linguists against the transformational grammar as a linguistic model (such as its incompatibility with many psycholinguistic facts which we know to characterize human language performance).

A third reason for preferring the transition network model to the usual formulation of transformational grammar is the power which it contains in its arbitrary conditions and its structure building actions. The model is equivalent to a Turing machine in power, and yet the actions which it performs are "natural" ones for the analysis of language. Most linguistic research in the structure of language and mechanisms of grammar has attempted deliberately to build models which do not have the power of a Turing machine but which make the strongest possible

hypotheses about language mechanisms by proposing the least powerful mechanism that can do the job. As a result of this approach, many variations of the transformational grammar model have been proposed with different basic repertoires of transformational mechanisms. Some have cyclic transformation rules, others do not; some have a distinct "post cycle" that operates after all of the cyclic rules have been applied. There are various types of conditions that may be asked: some models have double structural descriptions, some have ordered rules, some have obligatory rules, some have blocking rules, etc. In short, there is not a single transformational grammar model, there are many models which are more or less incomparable. If one such model can handle some features of language and another can handle different features, there is no systematic procedure for incorporating them both into a single model. In the augmented transition network model, the possibility exists of adding to the model whatever facility is needed and seems natural to do the job. One can add a new mechanism by simply inventing a new basic predicate to use in conditions or a new function to use in the structure-building rules. It is still possible to make strong hypotheses about the types of conditions and actions that are required, but when one finds that he needs to accomplish a given task for which his basic model has no "natural" mechanism, there is no problem extending the augmented transition network model to include it. This requires only the relaxation of the restrictions on the types of conditions and actions, and no reformulation of the basic model.

6. Previous Transition Network Models

The basic idea of the recursive transition network—that of merging the right-hand sides of context-free grammar rules which have the same left-hand side into a single transition diagram that merges the common parts of the different rules—has been known to the designers of syntax-directed compilers and artificial programming languages at least since 1963 when it was described in a paper by Melvin Conway [8]. The concern of that time, however, was not with the full generality of the nondeterministic mechanism, but rather with a set of sufficient conditions that would guarantee the diagram to be deterministic. Conway describes a rudimentary form of action associated with the arcs of his transition diagram, but these actions are limited to output commands which write information into a separate output stream that serves as input to the code-generation component. (The model is very close to the usual model of a finite state transducer with the exception of the additional recursion capability.) There is no analog to the holding of temporary pieces of information in registers, or the subsequent use of such information in conditions on the arcs.

More recently, two natural language parsing systems

based on a form of recursive transition network have been described in the literature. Thorne, Bratley, and Dewar [29] describe a procedure for natural language analysis based on a "finite state transition network" (which is applied recursively), and Bobrow and Fraser [1] describe a system which is "an elaboration of the procedure described by Thorne, Bratley, and Dewar." Although these systems bear considerable similarity to the one we have described, they differ from it in a number of important respects which we will describe shortly. Let us first, however, briefly describe the two systems.

6.1. THE THORNE SYSTEM. The Thorne system [29] assigns a representation of syntactic structure which attempts to represent simultaneously the deep structure and the surface structure of a sentence. Constructions are listed in the order in which they are found in the surface structure, with their deep structure functions indicated by labeling. Inversions in word order are indicated by marking the structures which are found "out of place" (i.e. in positions other than their deep structure positions) without moving them from their surface structure positions, and later in the string the position where they would have occurred in the deep structure is indicated by the appropriate deep structure function label followed by an asterisk. (They do not describe a procedure for constituents which are found in the surface structure to the right of their deep structure positions. Apparently their grammar does not deal with such constructions.)

Thorne views his grammar as a form of transformational grammar whose base component is a finite state grammar and permits recursion to take place only via transformations. According to Thorne, the majority of transformation rules can be viewed as "meta rules" in the sense that "they operate on other rules to produce derived rules rather than operating on structural descriptions to produce new structural descriptions." He uses an augmented transition network containing both the original deep structure rules plus these derived rules as the grammar table to drive his parsing algorithm, but is not able to handle the word order inversion transformations and the conjunction transformations in this way. Instead, he implements these features as exceptions embedded in his parsing program.

6.2. THE SYSTEM OF BOBROW AND FRASER. Bobrow and Fraser [1] describe a parsing system which is an elaboration of the Thorne parser. Like the Thorne parsings, the general form of their analysis "resembles the surface structure analysis of the sentence, with added indications of moved constituents and where they are located in deep structure." This grammar model is also a form of augmented transition network, whose actions include setting flags and function labels and whose conditions include testing previously set flags. Unlike the Thorne system, however, Bobrow's system provides a facility for transferring information back to some previously analyzed constituent. In general, the conditions on an arc can be arbitrary LISP functions (the system is programmed in LISP), and the actions for transferring information can be arbitrary LISP functions. The conditions and actions actually implemented in the system, however, are limited to flag testing and to transferring new deep structure function labels back into previously recognized structures.

According to Bobrow[2] the major differences between his system and that of Thorne are the use of symbolic flag names (instead of bit positions), a facility for mnemonic state names, the ability to transfer information back to previously analyzed constituents, and a facility for active feature values in the dictionary (these are actually routines which are stored in the dictionary entry for the word rather than merely activated by features stored in the dictionary).

6.3. COMPARISON WITH THE PRESENT MODEL. In comparing the augmented transition network model described in this paper with the systems of Bobrow and Fraser [1] and of Thorne et al. [29], there are two domains of comparison which must be distinguished: the formal description of the model and the implementation of the parsing system. One of the major differences between this parsing system and those of Bobrow and Thorne is the degree to which such a distinction is made. In [29] Thorne does not describe the augmented transition network model which is used except to point out that the grammar table used by the parsing program "has the form of a finite state network or directed graph—a form appropriate for the representation of a regular grammar." The transition network model is apparently formalized only in the form in which it actually occurs in the parsing program (which is not described). The conditions on the arcs seem to be limited to tests of agreement of features associated with lexical items and constituents, and the actions are limited to recording the current constituent in the output representation, labeling constituents, or inserting dummy nodes and markers. The mechanisms for word order inversion and conjunction are not represented in the network but are "incorporated into the program."

The Bobrow and Fraser paper [1] improves considerably on the power of the basic transition network model used by Thorne et al. It adds the facility for arbitrary conditions and actions on the arcs, thus increasing the power of the model to that of a Turing machine. In this system as in Thorne's, however, there is no distinction between the model and the implementation. Although the conditions and actions are arbitrary as far as the implementation is concerned, there is no separate formal model which characterizes the data structures on which they operate. That is, in order to add such an arbitrary condition, one would have to know how the LISP implementation of the parsing algorithm works and where and how its intermediate results are stored. The range of conditions and actions available without such information—i.e. the condition and action subroutines actually provided in the implementation—consists of setting and testing flags and transmitting func-

---

[2] Personal communication.

tion labels back into previously analyzed constituents. In both Bobrow's and Thorne's systems the actual representation of constituent structure is isomorphic to the recursive structure of the analysis as determined by the history of recursive applications of the transition network, and it is produced automatically by the parsing algorithm.

The augmented transition network, as we have defined it, provides a formalized transition network model with the power of a Turing machine *independent of the implementation*. The model explicitly provides for the isolation of various partial results in named registers and allows arbitrary conditions and actions *which apply to the contents of these registers*. Thus it is not necessary for a grammar writer to know details of the actual implementation of the parsing algorithm in order to take advantage of the facility for arbitrary conditions and actions.[3] The building of the constituent structure is not performed automatically by the parsing algorithm in this model, but must instead be specified by explicit structure-building rules. The result of this feature is that the structures assigned to the sentence no longer need to be isomorphic to the recursion history of the analysis, but are free to move constituents around in the representation. Thus the representation produced by the parser may be a true deep structure representation of the type assigned by the more customary transformational grammar models (or it could also be a surface structure representation, a dual-purpose representation as in the Thorne and Bobrow systems, or any of a number of other representations such as dependency representations). The explicit structure-building actions on the arcs together with the use of registers to hold pieces of sentence structure (whose function and location may not yet have been determined) provides an extremely flexible and efficient facility for moving constituents around in their deep structure representations and changing the interpretation of constituents as the course of an analysis proceeds. It is even possible to build structures with several levels of nesting while remaining at a single level of the transition network, and conversely to go through several levels of recursion of the network while building a structure which has only one level. No facility like this is present in either the Thorne or the Bobrow systems.

Another feature of the augmented transition network model presented here which distinguishes it from the Thorne and Bobrow systems is the language for the specification of the transition network grammar. This language is designed to be convenient and natural for the grammar designer rather than for the machine or for a computer programmer. It is possible in a few pages to completely specify the possible syntactic forms for the representation

of an augmented transition network. Each arc is represented by a mnemonic name of the type of arc, the arc label, an arbitrary condition, and a list of actions to be executed if the arc is followed. The condition and actions are represented as expressions in Cambridge Polish notation with mnemonic function names, and care has been exercised to provide a basic repertoire of such functions which is "natural" to the task of natural language analysis. One of the goals of the experimental transition network parsing system which I have implemented is to evolve such a set of natural operations through experience writing grammars for it, and many of the basic operations described in this paper are the result of such evolution. One of the unique characteristics of the augmented transition network model is the facility to allow for evolution of this type.

7. Advantages of the Augmented Transition Network Model

The augmented transition network model of grammar has many advantages as a model for natural language, some of which carry over to models of programming languages as well. In this section we review and summarize some of the major features of the transition network model which make it an attractive model for natural language.

7.1. Perspicuity. Context-free grammars have been immensely successful (or at least popular) as models for natural language in spite of formal inadequacies of the model for handling some of the features that occur in existing natural languages. They maintain a degree of "perspicuousness" since the constituents which make up a construction of a given type can be read off directly from the context-free rule. That is, by looking at a rule of a context-free grammar, the consequences of that rule for the types of constructions that are permitted are immediately apparent. The pushdown store automaton, on the other hand, although equivalent to the context-free grammar in generative power does not maintain this perspicuousness. It is not surprising, therefore, that linguists in the process of constructing grammars for natural language have worked with the context-free grammar formalism and not directly with pushdown store automata even though the pushdown store automaton, through its finite state control mechanism, allows for some economies of representation and for greater efficiency in resulting parsing algorithms.

The theory of transformational grammar proposed by Chomsky [6] is one of the most powerful tools for describing the sentences that are possible in a natural language and the relationships that hold among them, but this theory as it is currently formalized (to the limited extent to which it is formalized) loses the perspicuousness of the context-free grammar. It is not possible in this model to look at a single rule and be immediately aware of its consequences for the types of construction that are possible. The effect of a given rule is intimately bound up with its

---

[3] In the experimental parsing system which has been implemented, there is sometimes an advantage to using conditions or actions which apply to features of the implementation that are not in the formal model. Actions of this sort are considered to be *extensions* to the basic model, and the features of the implementation which allow them to be added easily are largely features of the BBN LISP system [2] in which the system is written.

interrelation to other rules, and in fragments of transformational grammars for real languages it may require an extremely complex analysis to determine the effect and purpose of any given rule. The augmented transition network provides the power of a transformational grammar but maintains much of the perspicuousness of the context-free grammar model. If the transition network model were implemented on a computer with a graphics facility for displaying the network, it would be one of the most perspicuous (as well as powerful) grammar models available.

7.2. GENERATIVE POWER.   Even without the conditions and actions on the arcs, the recursive transition network model has greater strong generative power than the ordinary context-free grammar. This is due to its ability to characterize constructions which have an unbounded number of immediate constituents. Ordinary context-free grammars cannot characterize trees with unbounded branching without assuming an infinite set of rules. Another way of looking at the recursive transition network model is that it is a finite representation of a context-free grammar with a possibly infinite (but regular) set of rules. When conditions and actions are added to the arcs, the model attains the power of a Turing machine, although the basic operations which it performs are "natural" ones for language analysis. Using these conditions and actions, the model is capable of performing the equivalent of transformational analysis without the need for a separate transformational component.

Another attractive feature of the augmented transition network model is the fact that one does not seem to have to sacrifice efficiency to obtain power. In the progression from context-free grammars to context-sensitive grammars to transformational grammars, the time required for the corresponding recognition algorithms increases enormously. The transition network model, however, while achieving all the power of a transformational grammar, does so without apparently requiring much more time than is required for predictive context-free recognition. (This is illustrated to some extent by the example in Section 8.)

An additional advantage of the augmented transition network model over the transformational grammar model is that it is much closer to a dual model than the transformational grammar. That is, although we have described it as a recognition or analysis model which *analyzes* sentences, there is no real restriction against running the model in a generative mode to *produce* or *generate* sentences. The only change in operation that would be required is that conditions which look ahead in the sentence would have to be interpreted in the generation algorithm as decisions to be made which, if chosen, will impose constraints on the generation of subsequent portions of the sentence. The transformational grammar model, on the other hand, is almost exclusively a generative model. The analysis problem for the transformational grammar is so extremely complicated that no reasonably efficient recognition algorithm for transformational grammar has yet been found.

7.3. EFFICIENCY OF REPRESENTATION.   A major advantage of the transition network model over the usual context-free grammar model is the ability to merge the common parts of many context-free rules, thus allowing greater efficiency of representation. For example, the single regular-expression rule S → (Q) (NEG) NP VP replaces the four rules:

$$S \rightarrow NP\ VP$$
$$S \rightarrow Q\ NP\ VP$$
$$S \rightarrow NEG\ NP\ VP$$
$$S \rightarrow Q\ NEG\ NP\ VP$$

in the usual context-free notation. The transition network model can frequently achieve even greater efficiency through merging because of the absence of the linearity constraints that are present in the regular expression notation.

The merging of redundant parts of rules not only permits a more compact representation but also eliminates the necessity of redundant processing when doing the parsing. That is, by reducing the size of the grammar representation, one also reduces the number of tests which need to be performed during the parsing. In effect, one is taking advantage of the fact that whether or not a rule is successful in the ordinary context-free grammar model, information is frequently gained in the process of matching it (or attempting to match it) which has implications for the success or failure of later rules. Thus, when two rules have common parts, the matching of the first has already performed some of the tests required for the matching of the second. By merging the common parts, one is able to take advantage of this information to eliminate the redundant processing in the matching of the second rule.

In addition to the direct merging of common parts of different rules when constructing a transition network model, the *augmented* transition network, through its use of flags, allows for the merging of *similar* parts of the network by recording information in registers and interrogating it with conditions on the arcs. Thus it is possible to store in registers some of the information that would otherwise be implicitly remembered by the state of the network and to merge states whose transitions are similar except for conditions on the contents of registers. For example, consider two states whose transitions are alike except that one is "remembering" that a negative particle has already been found in the sentence, while the other permits a transition which will accept a negative particle. These two states can be merged by setting a flag to indicate the presence of a prior negative particle and placing a condition on the arc which accepts the negative particle to block it if the negative flag is set.

The process of merging similar parts of the network through the use of flags, while producing a more compact representation, does not result in an improvement in processing time and usually requires slightly more time. The reason for this is the increased time required to test the conditions and the presence of additional arcs which must be processed even though the conditions will prevent them from being followed. In the absurd extreme, it is possible to reduce any transition network to a one-state network by using a flag for each arc and placing conditions on the arcs which forbid them to be followed unless one of the flags for a possible immediately preceding arc has been set. The obvious inefficiency here is that at every step it would be necessary to consider each arc of the network and apply a complicated test to determine whether the arc can be followed. There is thus a trade-off between the compactness of the representation which can be gained by the use of flags and the increase in processing time which may result. This seems to be just one more example of the ubiquitous space-time trade-off that occurs for almost any computer programming problem.

In many cases, the use of registers to hold pieces of an analysis provides automatic flags, so that it is not necessary to set up special registers to remember such information. For example, the presence of a previous negative particle in a sentence can be indicated by the nonemptiness of a NEG register which contains the particle. Similarly, the presence of an auxilliary verb is indicated by the non-emptiness of an AUX register which contains the auxilliary verb.

7.4. CAPTURING REGULARITIES. One of the linguistic goals of a grammar for a natural language is that the grammar capture the *regularities* of the language. That is, if there is a regular process that operates in a number of environments, the grammar should embody that process in a single mechanism or rule and not in a number of independent copies of the same process for each of the different contexts in which it occurs. A simple example of this principle is the representation of the prepositional phrase as a constituent of a sentence because the construction consisting of a preposition followed by a noun phrase occurs often in English sentences in many different environments. Thus the model which did not treat prepositional phrases as constituents would be failing to capture a generality. This principle is a variation of the *economy principle*, which says that the best grammar is that which can characterize the language in the fewest number of symbols. A grammar which made essentially independent copies of the same information would be wasting symbols in its description of the language, and that model which merged these multiple copies into a single one would be a better grammar because it used fewer symbols. Thus the economy principle tends to favor grammars which capture regularities.

The transition network model, with the augmentation of arbitrary conditions on the arcs and the use of registers to contain flags and partial constructions, provides a mechanism for recognizing and capturing regularities. Whenever the grammar contains two or more subgraphs of any size which are essentially copies of each other, it is a symptom of a regularity that is being missed. That is, there are two essentially identical parts of the grammar which differ only in that the finite state control part of the machine is remembering some piece of information, but otherwise the

operation of the two parts of the graph are identical. To capture this generality, it is sufficient to explicitly store the distinguishing piece of information in a register (e.g. by a flag) and use only a single copy of the subgraph.

7.5. EFFICIENCY OF OPERATION. In addition to the efficiency of operation which results from the merging of common parts of different rules, the transition network model provides a number of other advantages for efficient operation. One of these is the ability to postpone decisions by reworking the network. A great inefficiency of many grammars for natural language is the procedure whereby the grammar "guesses" some basic feature of a construction too early in the process of recognizing it—for example, guessing whether a sentence is active or passive before the processing of the sentence has begun. This results in the parser having to follow several alternatives until that point in the sentence where enough information is present to rule out the erroneous guesses. A much more desirable approach is to leave the decision unmade until a point in the construction is reached where the necessary information is present to make the decision. The transition network model allows one to take this approach.

By using standard finite state machine optimization techniques (see Woods [32]) it is possible to "optimize" the transition network by making it deterministic except for the pushdown operations (where nondeterminism can be reduced but not necessarily eliminated). That is, if several arcs with the same label leave some state, a modified network can be constructed which has at most one arc with a given label leaving any given state. This results in an improvement in operation efficiency because of the reduced number of active configurations which need to be followed during the parsing. The deterministic network keeps identical looking analyses merged until that point at which they are no longer identical, thus postponing the decision as to which path it is on until the first point where the two paths differ, at which point the input symbol usually determines the correct path. The augmented transition network may not permit the completely automatic optimization which the unaugmented model permits, but it is still possible to adopt the general approach of reducing the number of active configurations by reducing the nondeterminism of the network, thus postponing decisions until the point in the input string where they make a difference. The holding of pieces of the analysis in registers until their appropriate function is determined allows one to wait until such decisions have been made before building the syntactic representation, which may depend on the decision. This facility allows one to postpone decisions even when building deep structure representations of the type assigned by a transformational grammar.

The necessity of following several active configurations during parsing is a result of the potential ambiguity of natural language. The source of this ambiguity lies in the recursion operation of the network, since without recursion the network would be a finite state machine and could be made completely deterministic. We show elsewhere [32] that it is possible to eliminate much of the recursion from a transition network (in fact we can eliminate all of the recursion except for that induced by self-embedding symbols), thus reducing still further the number of active configurations which need to be followed. In the augmented network model, one seems in practice to be able to use conditions on the arcs to determine uniquely when to push down for a recursion, leaving only the action of popping up as the source of ambiguity and the cause for multiple active configurations. The use of appropriate conditions (including semantic ones) on the POP arcs of the network allows one to reduce this ambiguity still further.

One of the most interesting features of the use of registers in the augmented transition network is the ability to make tentative decisions about the sentence structure and then change one's mind later in the sentence without backtracking. For example, when one is at the point in parsing a sentence where he is expecting a verb and he encounters the verb "be," he can tentatively assign it as the main verb by putting it in the main verb register. If he then encounters a second verb indicating that the "be" was not the main verb but an auxilliary helping verb, then the verb "be" can be moved from the main verb register into an auxilliary verb register and the new main verb put in its place. This technique, like the others, tends to reduce the number of active configurations which need to be followed during the parsing. In Section 8 we give an example which provides a number of illustrations of this technique of making tentative decisions and then changing them.

7.6. Flexibility for Experimentation. Perhaps one of the most important advantages of the augmented transition network model is the flexibility that the model provides for experimental linguistic research. The open-ended set of basic operations which can be used on the arcs allows for the development of a fundamental set of "natural" operations for natural language analysis through experience obtained while writing grammars. A powerful BUILDQ function was developed in this way and has proven extremely useful in practice. The use of the hold list and the virtual transitions in Section 8 is another example of the evolution of a special "natural" operation to meet a need.

A second area of experimentation that is facilitated by the transition network model is the investigation of different types of structural representations. The explicit structure-building actions on the arcs of the network allow one to experiment with different syntactic representations such as dependency grammars, tagmemic formulas, or Fillmore's case grammar [11]. It should even be possible to produce some types of semantic representation by means of the structure-building actions on the arcs.

Finally, it is possible to use the conditions on the arcs to experiment with various types of semantic conditions for guiding the parsing and reducing the number of "meaningless" syntactic analyses that are produced. Within the framework of the augmented transition network one can

begin to take advantage of much of the extra-syntactic information which human beings seems to have available during parsing. Many good ideas in this area have gone untried for want of a formalism which could accommodate them.

8. A Second Example

In this section we give an example that illustrates some of the advantages of the augmented transition network which we have been discussing—especially the facilities for making tentative decisions that are changed as the

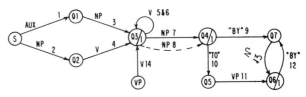

Fig. 4(a). A partial transition network—pictorial representation with numbered arcs

Q3:
    Condition: (INTRANS (GETR V))
    Form: (BUILDQ (S++(TNS+) (VP (V+))) TYPE SUBJ TNS V)
Q4 and Q6:
    Condition: T
    Form: (BUILDQ (S++(TNS+) (VP (V+)+)) TYPE SUBJ TNS V OBJ)

Fig. 4(b). A partial transition network—conditions and forms for final states

	Conditions	Actions
1.	T	(SETR V *)
		(SETR TNS (GETF TENSE))
		(SETR TYPE (QUOTE Q))
2.	T	(SETR SUBJ *)
		(SETR TYPE (QUOTE DCL))
3.	T	(SETR SUBJ *)
4.	T	(SETR V *)
		(SETR TNS (GETF TENSE))
5.	(AND (GETF PPRT)	(HOLD (GETR SUBJ))
	(EQ (GETR V)	(SETR SUBJ (BUILDQ
	(QUOTE BE)))	(NP (PRO SOMEONE))))
		(SETR AGFLAG T)
		(SETR V *)
6.	(AND (GETF PPRT)	(SETR TNS (APPEND
	(EQ (GETR V)	(GETR TNS)
	(QUOTE HAVE)))	(QUOTE PERFECT)))
		(SETR V *)
7.	(TRANS (GETR V))	(SETR OBJ *)
8.	(TRANS (GETR V))	(SETR OBJ *)
9.	(GETR AGFLAG)	(SETR AGFLAG NIL)
10.	(S-TRANS (GETR V))	(SENDR SUBJ (GETR OBJ))
		(SENDR TNS (GETR TNS))
		(SENDR TYPE (QUOTE DCL))
11.	T	(SETR OBJ *)
12.	(GETR AGFLAG)	(SETR AGFLAG NIL)
13.	T	(SETR SUBJ *)
14.	(GETF UNTENSED)	(SETR V *)

Fig. 4(c). A partial transition network—conditions and actions on arcs

parsing proceeds. Figure 4 gives a fragment of a transition network which characterizes the behavior of the auxiliary verbs "be" and "have" in indicating the passive construction and the perfect tense. We will consider the analysis provided by this sample network for the sentence "John was believed to have been shot"—a sentence with a fairly complex syntactic structure. In doing so, we will see that the augmented transition network clearly characterizes the changing expectations as it proceeds through the analysis, and that it does this without the necessity of backtracking or pursuing different alternatives.

Figure 4 is divided into three parts: (a) a pictorial representation of the network with numbered arcs, (b) a description of the conditions and forms associated with the final states, and (c) a list of the conditions and actions associated with the arcs of the network. In Figure 4(a), the pictorial representation, S, NP, and VP are nonterminal symbols; AUX and V are lexical category names; and the arcs labeled "TO" and "BY" are to be followed only if the input word is "to" or "by" respectively. The dotted arc with label NP is a special kind of "virtual" arc which can be followed if a noun phrase has been placed on a special "hold list" by a previous HOLD command. It removes the item from the hold list when it uses it. The hold list is a feature of the experimental parsing system which provides a natural facility for dealing with constituents that are found out of place and must be inserted in their proper location before the analysis can be complete. The items placed on the hold list are marked with the level at which they were placed on the list, and the algorithm is prevented from popping up from that level until the item has been "used" by a virtual transition at that level or some deeper level.

Final states are represented in Figure 4(a) by the diagonal slash and the subscript 1, a notation which is common in the representation of finite state automata. The conditions necessary for popping up from a final state and the expression which determines the value to be returned are indicated Figure 4(b). The parenthesized representation of tree structure is the same as that used in Section 3.2. Conditions TRANS and INTRANS test whether a verb is transitive or intransitive, respectively, and the condition S-TRANS tests for verbs like "believe" and "want", which can each take an embedded nominalized sentence as its "object". Features PPRT and UNTENSED, respectively, mark the past participle form and the standard untensed form of a verb.

We begin the analysis of the sentence "John was believed to have been shot" in state S, scanning the first word of the sentence "John". Since "John" is a proper noun, the pushdown for a noun phrase on arc 2 will be successful, and the actions for that arc will be executed placing the noun phrase (NP (NPR JOHN)) in the subject register SUBJ and recording the fact that the sentence is declarative by placing DCL in the TYPE register. The second word of the sentence "was" allows the transition of arc 4 to be followed, setting the verb register V to the standard form of

the verb "BE" and recording the tense of the sentence in the register TNS. The register contents at this point correspond to the tentative decision that "be" is the main verb of the sentence, and a subsequent noun phrase or adjective (not shown in the sample network) would continue this decision unchanged.

In state Q3, the input of the past participle "believed" tells us that the sentence is in the passive and that the verb "be" is merely an auxilliary verb indicating the passive. Specifically, arc 5 is followed because the input word is a past participle form of a verb and the current content of the verb register is the verb "be". This arc revises the tentative decisions by holding the old tentative subject on the special hold list, setting up a new tentative subject (the indefinite someone), and setting the flag AGFLAG which indicates that a subsequent agent introduced by the preposition "by" may specify the subject. The main verb is now changed from "be" to "believe" and the network returns to state Q3 scanning the word "to". The register contents at this point are:

SUBJ: (NP (PRO SOMEONE))
TYPE: DCL
V: BELIEVE
TNS: PAST
AGFLAG: T

and the noun phrase (NP (NPR JOHN)) is being held on the hold list.

None of the arcs leaving state Q3 is satisfied by the input word "to". However, the presence of the noun phrase "John" on the hold list allows the virtual transition of arc 8 to take place just as if this noun phrase had been found at this point in the sentence. (The transition is permitted because the verb "believe" is marked as being transitive.) The effect is to tentatively assign the noun phrase (NP (NPR JOHN)) as the object of the verb "believe". If this were the end of the sentence and we chose to pop up from the resulting state Q4, then we would have the correct analysis "someone believed John".

The input of the word "to" to state Q4 tells us that the "object" of the verb "believe" is not merely the noun phrase "John" but is a nominalized sentence with "John" as its tentative subject. The effect of arcs 10 and 11 is to send down the necessary information to an embedded calculation which will complete the embedded clause and return the result as the object of the verb "believe". Arc 10 prepares to send down the noun phrase (NP (NPR JOHN)) as the embedded subject, the tense PAST, and the type DCL. Arc 11 then pushes down to state VP scanning the word "have".

At this point, we find ourselves in an embedded computation with the register contents:

SUBJ: (NP (NPR JOHN))
TYPE: DCL
TNS: PAST

Arc 14 permits a transition if the current input is a verb

in its standard untensed, undeclined form, i.e. one cannot say "John was believed to *has* been shot." Since "have" is such a form, the transition is permitted and the main verb of the embedded sentence is tentatively set to "have" as would befit the sentence "John was believed to have money."

The subsequent past participle "been" following the verb "have" causes transition 6, which detects the fact that the embedded sentence is in the perfect tense (the effect of the auxilliary "have") and adopts the new tentative verb "be" as would befit the sentence "John was believed to have been a druggist." The register contents for the embedded computation at this point are:

SUBJ:	(NP (NPR JOHN))
TYPE:	DCL
TNS:	PAST PERFECT
V:	BE

Once again in state Q3, the input of the past participle "shot" with a tentative verb "be" in the verb register indicates that the sentence is in the passive, and transition 5 puts the noun phrase (NP (NPR JOHN)) on the hold list and sets up the indefinite subject (NP (PRO SOMEONE)). Although we are now at the end of the sentence, both the presence of the noun phrase on the hold list and the fact that the verb "shoot" is transitive prevent the algorithm from popping up. Instead, the virtual transition of arc 8 is followed, assigning the noun phrase "John" as the object of the verb "shoot". The register contents for the embedded computation at this point are:

SUBJ:	(NP (PRO SOMEONE))
TYPE:	DCL
TNS:	PAST PERFECT
V:	SHOOT
AGFLAG:	T
OBJ:	(NP (NPR JOHN))

At this point, we are at the end of the sentence in the final state Q4, with an empty hold list so that the embedded computation can return control to the higher level computation which called it. The value returned, as specified by the form associated with the state Q4, is

(S DCL (NP (PRO SOMEONE)) (TNS PAST PERFECT)
    (VP (V SHOOT) (NP (NPR JOHN))))

corresponding to the tree:

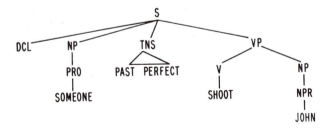

The higher level computation continues with the actions on arc 11, setting the OBJ register to the result of the

embedded computation. Since the higher level computation is also in a final state, Q6, the sentence is accepted, and the structure assigned to it (as specified by the form associated with state Q6) is:

(S DCL (NP (PRO SOMEONE)) (TNS PAST) (VP (V BELIEVE)
    (S DCL (NP (PRO SOMEONE)) (TNS PAST PERFECT)
        (VP (V SHOOT) (NP (NPR JOHN))))))

which in tree form is represented as:

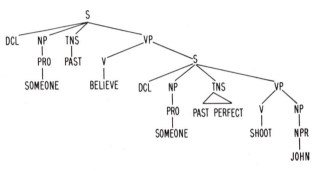

This structure can be paraphrased "Someone believed that someone had shot John." If the sentence had been followed by the phrase "by Harry" there would have been two possible interpretations depending on whether the additional phrase were accepted by the embedded computation or the top level computation. Either case would have resulted in replacing one of the indefinite subjects SOMEONE with the definite subject "Harry". The structure produced in one case would be paraphrased "Someone believed that Harry had shot John", while the other would be "Harry believed that someone had shot John."

9. Parsing with Transition Network Grammars

Since the unaugmented transition network grammar model is actually a mere permutation of the elements of a pushdown store automaton, a number of existing parsing algorithms for context-free grammars apply more or less directly to the transition network model. The basic top-down and bottom-up parsing strategies have their analog for recursive transition networks, and the opposing strategies for dealing with ambiguous sentences—following all of the analyses "in parallel" or following one analysis at a time (saving information at the choice points)—are both applicable to this type of model. In particular, one of the most powerful and efficient parsers for context-free grammars that has yet been discovered, the Earley recognition algorithm [9, 10], can be adapted with minor modification to use transition network grammars, and indeed an improvement in operating efficiency can accrue from doing so.

The Earley Algorithm, by following all analyses in parallel in a particularly careful way, obtains a representation of all the parses of a string with respect to a context-free grammar in an amount of time which can be bounded by Kn^3, where n is the length of the string and K is a constant depending only on the grammar and not on the input string. Moreover, for certain subclasses of context-free grammars, the time required can be shown to lie within smaller bounds—n^2 for linear grammars and others, and n for $LR(k)$ (Knuth [17]) grammars with lookahead k (and others). Many of these results have been obtained by other algorithms which capitalize on special features of different classes of grammars [15, 16, 33], but the Earley algorithm is the only such algorithm which works for any given context-free grammar (with no restriction to special forms, absence of left-recursion, etc.) within the n^3 bound, and furthermore, it *automatically* achieves the smaller bounds for the special case grammars without having to be told that the grammar falls within a special category (i.e. it does not invoke special techniques for these cases).

We give elsewhere (Woods [32]) a modified version of the Earley algorithm which can be used to parse sentences with respect to an (unaugmented) transition network grammar within the same time bounds, and we show there that a number of mechanical "optimization" techniques can be applied to a transition network grammar to reduce the constant of proportionality in the time bound.

The parsing problem for *augmented* transition networks using the Earley algorithm is somewhat more complicated due to the carrying of information in registers and the use of explicit structure-building actions. The potential for transitions which are conditional on the contents of registers makes it difficult to determine when configurations are "equivalent" and can be merged for further processing, and the use of registers and explicit structure-building actions complicates the task of choosing a suitable representation for the merged configurations. It is relatively straightforward to extend the Earley algorithm to overcome these difficulties, but since the n^3 time bound depends critically on the merging of equivalent configurations and a fixed bound on the amount of time to process each transition from a (merged) state, it is not clear what the bounds on the resulting algorithm will be.

If we distinguish between "flag" registers which can contain only "flags" chosen from a finite vocabulary and "content" registers which can hold arbitrary structure, and if we restrict the conditions and actions on the arcs so that: (1) the conditions can refer only to flag registers and symbols in the input string (e.g. for lookahead); (2) the conditions and actions themselves require a bounded amount of time; and (3) there is only one content register, which can be added to at the ends or built upon by means of the BUILDQ function but which cannot be "looked into", then we can build a version of the Earley recognition algorithm which will operate within the general n^3 time bound (and smaller n^2 or n bounds in special cases). However, if we relax these conditions appreciably, an increase in the time bound is inevitable—e.g. a condition or an action can itself require more than n^3 steps.

9.1. THE CASE FOR SERIES PARSING. For many applications of natural language analysis it is not necessary (or even desirable) to obtain a representation of all of the possible parsings of the input sentence. In applications where natural language is to be used as a medium of communication between a man and a machine, it is more important to select the "most likely" parsing in a given context and to do this as soon as possible. There will undoubtedly be cases where there are several "equally likely" parsings or where the "most likely" parsing turns out not to be the "correct" one (i.e. the one intended by the speaker); hence a nondeterministic algorithm is still required and a facility for eventually discovering any particular parsing is necessary. What is not necessary is a parallel approach which spends time discovering all of the analyses at once. In such an application a series approach (with an appropriate mechanism for selecting which analysis to follow first) has more to offer than a parallel approach since in most cases it will simply avoid following up the other alternatives. An appropriate record can be kept (if desired) of the analyses of well-formed substrings discovered by previous alternatives (in order to eliminate repetitive analysis of the same substring), but the savings in parse time for such an approach does not always justify the storage required to store all of the partial substring analyses.

The success of the series approach described above depends, of course, on the existence of a mechanism for selection of the semantically "most likely" parsing to be followed first. The augmented transition network grammar provides several such mechanisms. First, by ordering the arcs which leave the states of the network, it is possible to impose a corresponding ordering on the analyses which result. The grammar designer can thus adjust this ordering in an attempt to maximize the "a priori likelihood" (dependent only on the structure of the sentence as seen by the grammar, but not on other factors) that the first analysis chosen will be the correct one. Furthermore, by replicating some arcs with different conditions, it is possible to make this ordering dependent on particular features of the sentence being processed—in particular it can be made dependent on semantic features of the words involved in the sentence. Two additional features for selecting "most likely" analyses have been added to the model in the implemented experimental parsing system— a special "weight" register which contains an estimate of the "likelihood" of the current analysis (which can be used to suspend unlikely looking paths in favor of more likely ones) and a selective modifier-placement facility which uses semantic information to determine the "most likely" governing construction for modifiers in the sentence.

10. Implementation

An experimental parsing system based on the ideas presented here has been implemented in BBN LISP on the SDS 940 time-sharing systems at Harvard University and at Bolt, Beranek & Newman, Inc., and is being used for a number of experiments in grammar development and parsing strategies for natural language analysis. The objectives of this implementation have been the provision of a flexible tool for experimentation and evolution, and for this reason the system has been constructed in a modular fashion which lends itself to evolution and extension without major changes to the overall system structure. The system has already undergone several cycles of evolution with a number of new features being developed in this way, and more are expected as the research continues.

The implemented system contains a general facility for semantic interpretation (described in Woods [30, 31]), and a major motivation for the implementation is to explore the interaction between the syntactic and semantic aspects of the process of sentence "understanding". Special emphasis has been placed on the use of semantic information to guide the parsing, the minimization of the number of blind-alley analysis paths which need to be followed, and the ordering of analyses of sentences in terms of some measure of "likelihood". Experiments to date include a selective modifier placement facility using semantic information, several approaches to the problems of conjunction (including conjoined sentence fragments), and a facility for lexical and morphological analysis. Several different grammars have been developed and tested on the system, and a variety of English constructions and parsing strategies have been and are being explored. A report of the details of this implementation and of the experiments which are being performed with it is in preparation.

RECEIVED MAY 1970

REFERENCES

1. BOBROW, D. G., AND FRASER, J. B. An augmented state transition network analysis procedure. Proc. Internat. Joint Conf. on Artificial Intelligence, Washington, D.C., 1969, pp. 557–567.
2. BOBROW, D. G., MURPHY, D., AND TEITELMAN, W. *BBN LISP System*. Bolt, Beranek and Newman Inc., Cambridge, Mass., 1968.
3. BOOK, R., EVEN, S., GREIBACH, S., AND OTT, G. Ambiguity in graphs and expressions. Mimeo. rep., Aiken Computat. Lab., Harvard U., Cambridge, Mass., 1969. *IEEE Trans Comp* (to appear).
4. CHEATHAM, T. E., AND SATTLEY, K. Syntax-directed compiling. Proc. AFIPS 1964 Spring Joint Comput. Conf., Vol. 25, Spartan Books, New York, pp. 31–57.
5. CHOMSKY, N. Formal properties of grammars. In *Handbook of Mathematical Psychology, Vol. 2*, R. D. Luce, R. R. Bush, and E. Galanter (Eds.). Wiley, New York, 1963.
6. ——. A transformational approach to syntax. In *The Structure of Language*, J. A. Fodor, and J. J. Katz (Eds.), Prentice-Hall, Englewood Cliffs, N. J., 1964.
7. ——. *Aspects of the Theory of Syntax*. MIT Press, Cambridge, Mass., 1965.
8. CONWAY, M. E. Design of a separable transition-diagram compiler. *Comm. ACM 6*, 7 (July 1963), 396–408.
9. EARLEY, J. An efficient context-free parsing algorithm. Ph.D.th. Dep. Computer Sci., Carnegie-Mellon U., Pittsburgh, Pa., 1968.
10. EARLEY, J. An efficient context-free parsing algorithm. *Comm. ACM 13*, 2, (Feb. 1970), 94–102.
11. FILLMORE, C. J. The case for case. In *Universals in Linguistic Theory*, E. Bach, and R. Harms (Eds.), Holt, Rinehart and Winston, New York, 1968.
12. GINSBURG, S. *The Mathematical Theory of Context-Free Languages*. McGraw-Hill, New York, 1966.
13. GREIBACH, SHEILA A. A simple proof of the standard-form theorem for context-free grammars. In Mathematical linguistics and automatic translation, Rep. NSF-18, Comput. Lab., Harvard U., Cambridge, Mass., 1967.
14. HERRINGER, J., WEILER, M., AND HURD, E. The immediate constituent analyzer. In Rep. NSF-17, Aiken Comput. Lab., Harvard U., Cambridge, Mass., 1966.
15. KASAMI, T. An efficient recognition and syntax-analysis algorithm for context-free languages. Sci. Rep. AFCRL-65-558, Air Force Cambridge Res. Lab., Bedford, Mass., 1965.
16. KASAMI, T. A note on computing time for recognition of languages generated by linear grammars. *Inform. Contr.*, 10 (1964), 209–214.
17. KNUTH, D. E. On the translation of languages from left to right. *Inf. Contr. 8* (1965), 607–639.
18. KUNO, S. "A system for transformational analysis. In Rep. NSF-15, Comput. Lab. Harvard U., Cambridge, Mass, 1965.
19. —— AND OETTINGER, A. G. Multiple path syntactic analyzer. In *Information Processing 1962*, North-Holland Publishing Co., Amsterdam, 1963.
20. MCCARTHY, J., ET AL. LISP 1.5 programmer's manual. MIT Comput. Center, Cambridge, Mass., 1962.
21. MCCAWLEY, J. D. Meaning and the description of languages. In *Kotoba No Ucho*, TEC Co. Ltd., Tokyo, 1968.
22. MCNAUGHTON, R. F., AND YAMADA, H. Regular expressions and state graphs for automata. *IRE Trans. EC-9* (Mar. 1960), 39–47.
23. MATTHEWS, G. H. Analysis by synthesis of natural languages. *Proc. 1961 Internat. Conf. on Machine Translation and Applied Language Analysis*. Her Majesty's Stationery Office, London, 1962.
24. MITRE. English preprocessor manual, Rep. SR-132, The Mitre Corp., Bedford, Mass., 1964.
25. OTT, G., AND FEINSTEIN, N. H. Design of sequential machines from their regular expressions," *J. ACM 8*, 4 (Oct. 1961), 585–600.
26. PETRICK, S. R. A recognition procedure for transformational grammars. Ph.D. th., Dep. Modern Languages, MIT, Cambridge, Mass., 1965.
27. POSTAL, P. M. Limitations of phrase structure grammars. In *The Structure of Language*, J. A. Fodor and J. J. Katz (Eds.), Prentice-Hall, Englewood Cliffs, N.J., 1964.
28. SCHWARCZ, R. M. Steps toward a model of linguistic performance: A preliminary sketch. *Mechanical Translation 10* (1967), 39–52.
29. THORNE, J., BRATLEY, P., AND DEWAR, H. The syntactic analysis of English by machine. In *Machine Intelligence 3* D. Michie (Ed.), American Elsevier, New York, 1968.
30. WOODS, W. A. Semantics for a question-answering system. Ph.D. th., Rep NSF-19, Aiken Comput. Lab., Harvard U., Cambridge, Mass., 1967.
31. ——. Procedural semantics for a question-answering machine. Proc. AFIPS 1968 Fall Joint Comput. Conf., Vol. 33, Pt. 1, MDI Publications, Wayne, Pa., pp. 457–471.
32. ——. Augmented transition networks for natural language analysis. Rep. CS-1, Comput. Lab., Harvard U., Cambridge, Mass., 1969.
33. YOUNGER, D. H. Context free language processing in time n^3. G. E. Res. and Devel. Center, Schenectady, N.Y., 1966.

A Computational Account of Some Constraints on Language

Mitchell Marcus
MIT Artificial Intelligence Laboratory

In a series of papers over the last several years, Noam Chomsky has argued for several specific properties of language which he claims are universal to all human languages [Chomsky 73, 75, 76]. These properties, which form one of the cornerstones of his current linguistic theory, are embodied in a set of constraints on language, a set of restrictions on the operation of rules of grammar.

This paper will outline two arguments presented at length in [Marcus 77] demonstrating that important sub-cases of two of these constraints, the Subjacency Principle and the Specified Subject Constraint, fall out naturally from the structure of a grammar interpreter called PARSIFAL, whose structure is in turn based upon the hypothesis that a natural language parser needn't simulate a nondeterministic machine. This "Determinism Hypothesis" claims that natural language can be parsed by a computationally simple mechanism that uses neither backtracking nor pseudo-parallelism, and in which all grammatical structure created by the parser is "indelible" in that it must all be output as part of the structural analysis of the parser's input. Once built, no grammatical structure can be discarded or altered in the course of the parsing process.

In particular, this paper will show that the structure of the grammar interpreter constrains its operation in such a way that, by and large, grammar rules cannot parse sentences which violate either the Specified Subject Constraint or the Subjacency Principle. The component of the grammar interpreter upon which this result principally depends is motivated by the Determinism Hypothesis; this result thus provides indirect evidence for the hypothesis. This result also depends upon the use within a computational framework of the closely related notions of *annotated surface structure* and *trace theory*, which also derive from Chomsky's recent work.

(It should be noted that these constraints are far from universally accepted. They are currently the source of much controversy; for various critiques of Chomsky's position see [Postal 74; Bresnan 76]. However, what is presented below does not argue for these constraints, *per se*, but rather provides a different sort of explanation, based on a processing model, of why the sorts of sentences which these constraints forbid are bad. While the exact formulation of these constraints is controversial, the fact that some set of constraints is needed to account for this range of data is generally agreed upon by most generative grammarians. The account which I will present below *is* crucially linked to Chomsky's, however, in that trace theory is at the heart of this account.)

Because of space limitations, this paper deals only with those grammatical processes characterized by the competence rule "MOVE NP"; the constraints imposed by the grammar interpreter upon those processes characterized by the rule "MOVE WH-phrase" are discussed at length in [Marcus 77] where I show that the behavior characterized by Ross's Complex NP Constraint [Ross 67] itself follows directly from the structure of the grammar interpreter for rather different reasons than the behavior considered in this section. Also because of space limitations, I will not attempt to show that the two constraints I will deal with here *necessarily* follow from the grammar interpreter, but rather only that they *naturally* follow from the interpreter, in particular from a simple, natural formulation of a rule for passivization which itself depends heavily upon the structure of the interpreter. Again, necessity is argued for in detail in [Marcus 77].

This paper will first outline the structure of the grammar interpreter, then present the PASSIVE rule, and then finally show how Chomsky's constraints "fall out" of the formulation of PASSIVE.

Before proceeding with the body of this paper, two other important properties of the parser should be mentioned which will not be discussed here. Both are discussed at length in [Marcus 77]; the first is sketched as well in [Marcus 78]:

1) Simple rules of grammar can by written for this interpreter which elegantly capture the significant generalizations behind not only passivization, but also such constructions as *yes/no* questions, imperatives, and sentences with existential *there*. These rules are reminiscent of the sorts of rules proposed within the framework of the theory of generative grammar, despite the fact that the rules presented here must recover underlying structure given only the terminal string of the surface form of the sentence.

2) The grammar interpreter provides a simple explanation for the difficulty caused by "garden path" sentences, such as "The cotton clothing is made of grows in Mississippi." Rules can be written for this interpreter to

resolve local structural ambiguities which might seem to require nondeterministic parsing; the power of such rules, however, depends upon a parameter of the mechanism. Most structural ambiguities can be resolved, given an appropriate setting of this parameter, but those which typically cause garden paths cannot.

The Structure of PARSIFAL

PARSIFAL maintains two major data structures: a pushdown stack of incomplete constituents called *the active node stack*, and a small three-place *constituent buffer* which contains constituents which are complete, but whose higher level grammatical function is as yet uncertain.

Figure 1 below shows a snapshot of the parser's data structures taken while parsing the sentence "John should have scheduled the meeting.". Note that the active node stack in shown growing *downward*, so that the structure of the stack reflects the structure of the emerging parse tree. At the bottom of the stack is an auxiliary node labelled with the features *modal, past*, etc., which has as a daughter the modal "should". Above the bottom of the stack is an S node with an NP as a daughter, dominating the word "John". There are two words in the buffer, the verb "have" in the first buffer cell and the word "scheduled" in the second. The two words "the meeting" have not yet come to the attention of the parser. (The structures of form "(PARSE-AUX CPOOL)" and the like will be explained below.)

The Active Node Stack
    S1 (S DECL MAJOR S) / (PARSE-AUX CPOOL)
        NP : (John)
        AUX1 (MODAL PAST VSPL AUX) / (BUILD-AUX)
            MODAL : (should)

The Buffer
1 :   WORD3 (*HAVE VERB TNSLESS AUXVERB PRES
            V-3S) : (have)
2 :   WORD4 (*SCHEDULE COMP-OBJ VERB INF-OBJ
            V-3S ED=EN EN PART PAST ED) : (scheduled)

Yet unseen words: the meeting .

Figure 1 - PARSIFAL's two major data structures.

The constituent buffer is the heart of the grammar interpreter; it is the central feature that distinguishes this parser from all others. The words that make up the parser's input first come to its attention when they appear at the end of this buffer after morphological analysis. Triggered by the words at the beginning of the buffer, the parser may decide to create a new grammatical constituent, create a new node at the bottom of the active node stack, and then begin to attach the constituents in the buffer to it. After this new constituent is completed, the parser will then pop the new constituent from the active node stack; if the grammatical role of this larger structure is as yet undetermined, the parser will insert it into the first cell of the buffer. The parser is free to examine the constituents in the buffer, to act upon them, and to otherwise use the buffer as a workspace.

While the buffer allows the parser to examine some of the context surrounding a given constituent, it does not allow arbitrary look-ahead. The length of the buffer is strictly limited; in the version of the parser presented here, the buffer has only three cells. (The buffer must be extended to five cells to allow the parser to build NPs in a manner which is transparent to the "clause level" grammar rules which will be presented in this paper. This extended parser still has a window of only three cells, but the effective start of the buffer can be changed through an "attention shifting mechanism" whenever the parser is building an NP. In effect, this extended parser has two "logical" buffers of length three, one for NPs and another for clauses, with these two buffers implemented by allowing an overlap in one larger buffer. For details, see [Marcus 77].)

Note that each of the three cells in the buffer can hold a *grammatical constituent* of any type, where a constituent is any tree that the parser has constructed under a single root node. The size of the structure underneath the node is immaterial; both "that" and "that the big green cookie monster's toe got stubbed" are perfectly good constituents once the parser has constructed a subordinate clause from the latter phrase.

The constituent buffer and the active node stack are acted upon by a grammar which is made up of pattern/action rules; this grammar can be viewed as an augmented form of Newell and Simon's production systems [Newell & Simon 72]. Each rule is made up of a pattern, which is matched against some subset of the constituents of the buffer and the accessible nodes in the active node stack (about which more will be said below), and an action, a sequence of operations which acts on these constituents. Each rule is assigned a numerical *priority*, which the grammar interpreter uses to arbitrate simultaneous matches.

The grammar as a whole is structured into *rule packets*, clumps of grammar rules which can be activated and deactivated as a group; the grammar interpreter only attempts to match rules in packets that have been activated by the grammar. Any grammar rule can activate a packet by associating that packet with the constituent at the bottom of the active node stack. As long as that node is at the bottom of the stack, the packets associated with it are active; when that node is pushed into the stack, the packets remain associated with it, but become active again only when that node reaches the bottom of the stack. For example, in figure 1 above, the packet BUILD-AUX is associated with the bottom of the stack, and is thus active, while the packet PARSE-AUX is associated with the S node above the auxiliary.

The grammar rules themselves are written in a language called PIDGIN, an English-like formal language that is translated into LISP by a simple grammar translator based on the notion of top-down operator precedence [Pratt 73]. This use of pseudo-English is similar to the use of pseudo-English in the grammar for Sager's STRING parser [Sager 73]. Figure 2 below gives a schematic overview of the organization of the grammar, and exhibits some of the rules that make up the packet PARSE-AUX.

A few comments on the grammar notation itself are

in order. The general form of each grammar rule is:

{Rule <name> priority: <priority> in <packet>
<pattern> --> <action>}

Each pattern is of the form :

[<description of 1st buffer constituent>] [<2nd>]
[<3rd>]

The symbol "=", used only in pattern descriptions, is to be read as "has the feature(s)". Features of the form "*<word>" mean "has the root <word>", e.g. "*have" means "has the root "have"". The tokens "1st", "2nd", "3rd" and "C" (or "c") refer to the constituents in the 1st, 2nd, and 3rd buffer positions and the current active node (i.e. the bottom of the stack), respectively. The PIDGIN code of the rule patterns should otherwise be fairly self-explanatory.

Priority	Pattern Description of:				Action
	1st	2nd	3rd	The Stack	
				PACKET1	
5:	[ ]	[ ]	[ ]		--> ACTION1
10:	[ ]			[ ]	--> ACTION2
10:	[ ]	[ ]	[ ]	[ ]	--> ACTION3
				PACKET2	
10:	[ ]	[ ]			--> ACTION4
15:	[ ]			[ ]	--> ACTION5

(a) - The structure of the grammar.

{RULE START-AUX PRIORITY: 10. IN PARSE-AUX
[=verb] -->
Create a new aux node.
Label C with the meet of the features of 1st and pres,
        past, future, tnsless.
Activate build-aux.}

{RULE TO-INFINITIVE PRIORITY: 10. IN PARSE-AUX
[=*to, auxverb] [=tnsless] -->
Label a new aux node inf.
Attach 1st to C as to.
Activate build-aux.}

(b) - Some grammar rules that initiate auxiliaries.

Figure 2

The parser (i.e. the grammar interpreter interpreting some grammar) operates by attaching constituents which are in the buffer to the constituent at the bottom of the stack; functionally, a constituent is in the stack when the parser is attempting to find its daughters, and in the buffer when the parser is attempting to find its mother. Once a constituent in the buffer has been attached, the grammar interpreter will automatically remove it from the buffer, filling in the gap by shifting to the left the constituents formerly to its right. When the parser has completed the constituent at the bottom of the stack, it pops that constituent from the active node stack; the constituent either remains attached to its parent, if it was attached to some larger constituent when it was created, or else it falls into the first cell of the constituent buffer,

shifting the buffer to the right to create a gap (and causing an error if the buffer was already full). If the constituents in the buffer provide sufficient evidence that a constituent of a given type should be initiated, a new node of that type can be created and pushed onto the stack; this new node can also be attached to the node at the bottom of the stack before the stack is pushed, if the grammatical function of the new constituent is clear when it is created.

This structure is motivated by several properties which, as is argued in [Marcus 77], any "non-nondeterministic" grammar interpreter must embody. These principles, and their embodiment in PARSIFAL, are as follows:

1) *A deterministic parser must be at least partially data driven.* A grammar for PARSIFAL is made up of pattern/action rules which are triggered when constituents which fulfill specific descriptions appear in the buffer.

2) *A deterministic parser must be able to reflect expectations that follow from the partial structures built up during the parsing process.* Packets of rules can be activated and deactivated by grammar rules to reflect the properties of the constituents in the active node stack.

3) *A deterministic parser must have some sort of constrained look-ahead facility.* PARSIFAL's buffer provides this constrained look-ahead. Because the buffer can hold several constituents, a grammar rule can examine the context that follows the first constituent in the buffer before deciding what grammatical role it fills in a higher level structure. The key idea is that the size of the buffer can be sharply constrained if each location in the buffer can hold a single complete constituent, regardless of that constituent's size. *It must be stressed that this look-ahead ability must be constrained in some manner, as it is here by limiting the length of the buffer; otherwise the "determinism" claim is vacuous.*

The General Grammatical Framework - Traces

The form of the structures that the current grammar builds is based on the notion of *Annotated Surface Structure*. This term has been used in two different senses by Winograd [Winograd 71] and Chomsky [Chomsky 73]; the usage of the term here can be thought of as a synthesis of the two concepts. Following Winograd, this term will be used to refer to a notion of surface structure *annotated by the addition of a set of features* to each node in a parse tree. Following Chomsky, the term will be used to refer to a notion of surface structure annotated by the addition of an element called *trace* to indicate the "underlying position" of "shifted" NPs.

In current linguistic theory, a trace is essentially a "phonologically null" NP in the surface structure representation of a sentence that has no daughters but is "bound" to the NP that filled that position at some level of underlying structure. In a sense, a trace can be viewed as a "dummy" NP that serves as a placeholder for the NP that earlier filled that position; in the same sense, the trace's binding can be viewed as simply a pointer to that NP. It should be stressed at the outset, however, that a trace is indistinguishable from a normal NP in terms of normal grammatical processes; a trace *is* an NP, even though it is an NP that dominates no lexical material.

There are several reasons for choosing a properly annotated surface structure as a primary output representation for syntactic analysis. While a deeper analysis is needed to recover the predicate/argument structure of a sentence (either in terms of Fillmore case relations [Fillmore 68] or Gruber/Jackendoff "thematic relations" [Gruber 65; Jackendoff 72]), phenomena such as focus, theme, pronominal reference, scope of quantification, and the like can be recovered only from the surface structure of a sentence. By means of proper annotation, it is possible to encode in the surface structure the "deep" syntactic information necessary to recover underlying predicate/argument relations, and thus to encode in the same formalism both deep syntactic relations and the surface order needed for pronominal reference and the other phenomena listed above.

Some examples of the use of trace are given in Figure 3 immediately below.

(1a) What did John give to Sue?
(1b) What did John give *t* to Sue?
      |_____|
(1c) John gave *what* to Sue.

(2a) The meeting was scheduled for Wednesday.
(2b) The meeting was scheduled *t* for Wednesday.
      |_____|
(2c) ∇ scheduled a *meeting* for Wednesday.

(3a) John was believed to be happy.
(3b) John was believed [ₛ *t* to be happy].
     |_____|

Figure 3 — Some examples of the use of trace.

One use of trace is to indicate the underlying position of the wh-head of a question or relative clause. Thus, the structure built by the parser for 3.1a would include the trace shown in 3.1b, with the trace's binding shown by the line under the sentence. The position of the trace indicates that 3.1a has an underlying structure analogous to the overt surface structure of 3.1c.

Another use of trace is to indicate the underlying position of the surface subject of a passivized clause. For example, 3.2a will be parsed into a structure that includes a trace as shown as 3.2b; this trace indicates that the subject of the passive has the underlying position shown in 3.2c. The symbol "∇" signifies the fact that the subject position of (2c) is filled by an NP that dominates no lexical structure. (Following Chomsky, I assume that a passive sentence in fact has *no underlying subject*, that an agentive "by NP" prepositional phrase originates as such in underlying structure.) The trace in (3b) indicates that the phrase "to be happy", which the brackets show is really an embedded clause, has an underlying subject which is identical with the surface subject of the matrix S, the

clause that dominates the embedded complement. Note that what is conceptually the underlying subject of the embedded clause has been passivized into subject position of the matrix S, a phenomenon commonly called "raising". The analysis of this phenomenon assumed here derives from [Chomsky 73]; it is an alternative to the classic analysis which involves "raising" the subject of the embedded clause into object position of the matrix S before passivization (for details of this later analysis see [Postal 74]).

The Passive Rule

In this section and the next, I will briefly sketch a solution to the phenomena of passivization and "raising" in the context of a grammar for PARSIFAL. This section will present the Passive rule; the next section will show how this rule, without alteration, handles the "raising" cases.

Let us begin with the parser in the state shown in figure 4 below, in the midst of parsing 3.2a above. The analysis process for the sentence prior to this point is essentially parallel to the analysis of any simple declarative with one exception: the rule PASSIVE-AUX in packet BUILD-AUX has decoded the passive morphology in the auxiliary and given the auxiliary the feature *passive* (although this feature is not visible in figure 4). At the point we begin our example, the packet SUBJ-VERB is active.

The Active Node Stack (1. deep)
S21 (S DECL MAJOR) / (SS-FINAL)
          NP : (The meeting)
          AUX : (was)
          VP : ↓
C: VP17 (VP) / (SUBJ-VERB)
          VERB : (scheduled)

The Buffer
1 :   PP14 (PP) : (for Wednesday)
2 :   WORD162 (*. FINALPUNC PUNC) : (.)

Figure 4 - Partial analysis of a passive sentence: after the verb has been attached.

The packet SUBJ-VERB contains, among other rules, the rule PASSIVE, shown in figure 5 below. The pattern of this rule is fulfilled if the auxiliary of the S node dominating the current active node (which will always be a VP node if packet SUBJ-VERB is active) has the feature *passive*, and the S node has not yet been labelled *np-preposed*. (The notation "** C" indicates that this rule matches against the two accessible nodes in the stack, not against the contents of the buffer.) The action of the rule PASSIVE simply creates a trace, sets the binding of the trace to the subject of the dominating S node, and then drops the new trace into the buffer.

```
{RULE PASSIVE IN SUBJ-VERB
[** c; the aux of the s above c is passive;
        the s above c is not np-preposed] -->
Label the s above c np-preposed.
Create a new np node labelled trace.
Set the binding of c to the np of the s above c.
Drop c.}
```

Figure 5 - Six lines of code captures np-preposing.

The state of the parser after this rule has been executed, with the parser previously in the state in figure 4 above, is shown in figure 6 below. S21 is now labelled with the feature *np-preposed*, and there is a trace, NP53, in the first buffer position. NP53, as a trace, has no daughters, but is bound to the subject of S21.

```
        The Active Node Stack ( 1. deep)
        S21 (NP-PREPOSED S DECL MAJOR) / (SS-FINAL)
                NP : (The meeting)
                AUX : (was)
                VP : ↓
C:      VP17 (VP) / (SUBJ-VERB)
                VERB : (scheduled)

        The Buffer
1 :     NP53 (NP TRACE) : bound to: (The meeting)
2 :     PP14 (PP) : (for Wednesday)
3 :     WORD162 (*. FINALPUNC PUNC) : (.)
```

Figure 6 - After PASSIVE has been executed.

Now rules will run which will activate the two packets SS-VP and INF-COMP, given that the verb of VP17 is "schedule". These two packets contain rules for parsing simple objects of non-embedded Ss, and infinitive complements, respectively. Two such rules, each of which utilize an NP immediately following a verb, are given in figure 7 below. The rule OBJECTS, in packet SS-VP, picks up an NP after the verb and attaches it to the VP node as a simple object. The rule INF-S-START1, in packet INF-COMP, triggers when an NP is followed by "to" and a tenseless verb; it initiates an infinitive complement and attaches the NP as its subject. (An example of such a sentence is "We wanted John to give a seminar next week".) The rule INF-S-START1 must have a higher priority than OBJECTS because the pattern of OBJECTS is fulfilled by any situation that fulfills the pattern of INF-S-START1; if both rules are in active packets and match, the higher priority of INF-S-START1 will cause it to be run instead of OBJECTS.

```
{RULE OBJECTS PRIORITY: 10 IN SS-VP
[=np] -->
Attach 1st to c as np.}

{RULE INF-S-START1 PRIORITY: 5. IN INF-COMP
[=np] [=*to,auxverb] [=tnsless] -->
Label a new s node sec, inf-s.
Attach 1st to c as np.
Activate parse-aux.}
```

Figure 7 - Two rules which utilize an NP following a verb.

While there is not space to continue the example here in detail, note that the rule OBJECTS will trigger with the parser in the state shown in figure 6 above, and will attach NP53 as the object of the verb "schedule. OBJECTS is thus totally indifferent both to the fact that NP53 was not a regular NP, but rather a trace, and the fact that NP53 did not originate in the input string, but was placed into the buffer by grammatical processes. Whether or not this rule is executed is absolutely unaffected by differences between an active sentence and its passive form; the analysis process for either is identical as of this point in the parsing process. Thus, the analysis process will be exactly parallel in both cases after the PASSIVE rule has been executed. (I remind the reader that the analysis of passive assumed above, following Chomsky, does *not* assume a process of "agent deletion", "subject postposing" or the like.)

Passives in Embedded Complements - "Raising"

The reader may have wondered why PASSIVE drops the trace it creates into the buffer rather than immediately attaching the new trace to the VP node. As we will see below, such a formulation of PASSIVE also correctly analyzes passives like 3.3a above which involve "raising", but with no additional complexity added to the grammar, correctly capturing an important generalization about English. To show the range of the generalization, the example which we will investigate in this section, sentence (1) in figure 8 below, is yet a level more complex than 3.3a above; its analysis is shown schematically in 8.2. In this example there are two traces: the first, the subject of the embedded clause, is bound to the subject of the major clause, the second, the object of the embedded S, is bound to the first trace, and is thus ultimately bound to the subject of the higher S as well. Thus the underlying position of the NP "the meeting" can be viewed as being the object position of the embedded S, as shown in 8.3.

(1) The meeting was believed to have been scheduled for Wednesday.
(2) The meeting was believed [$_S$ *t* to have been scheduled *t* for Wednesday]
(3) ▽ believed [$_S$ ▽ to have scheduled *the meeting* for Wednesday].

Figure 8 - This example shows simple passive and raising.

We begin our example, once again, right after "believed" has been attached to VP20, the current active node, as shown in figure 9 below. Note that the AUX node has been labelled *passive*, although this feature is not shown here.

The Active Node Stack (1. deep)
S22 (S DECL MAJOR) / (SS-FINAL)
NP : (The meeting)
AUX : (was)
VP : ↓
C: VP20 (VP) / (SUBJ-VERB)
VERB : (believed)

The Buffer
1 :   WORD166 (*TO PREP AUXVERB) : (to)
2 :   WORD167 (*HAVE VERB TNSLESS AUXVERB
PRES ...) : (have)

Figure 9 - After the verb has been attached.

The packet SUBJ-VERB is now active; the PASSIVE rule, contained in this packet now matches and is executed. This rule, as stated above, creates a trace, binds it to the subject of the current clause, and drops the trace into the first cell in the buffer. The resulting state is shown in figure 10 below.

The Active Node Stack (1. deep)
S22 (NP-PREPOSED S DECL MAJOR) / (SS-FINAL)
NP : (The meeting)
AUX : (was)
VP : ↓
C: VP20 (VP) / (SUBJ-VERB)
VERB : (believed)

The Buffer
1 :   NP55 (NP TRACE) : bound to: (The meeting)
2 :   WORD166 (*TO PREP AUXVERB) : (to)
3 :   WORD167 (*HAVE VERB TNSLESS AUXVERB
PRES ...) : (have)

Yet unseen words: been scheduled for Wednesday .

Figure 10 - After PASSIVE has been executed.

Again, rules will now be executed which will activate the packet SS-VP (which contains the rule OBJECTS) and, since "believe" takes infinitive complements, the packet INF-COMP (which contains INF-S-START1), among others. (These rules will also deactivate the packet SUBJ-VERB.) Now the patterns of OBJECTS and INF-S-START1 will both match, and INF-S-START1, shown above in figure 7, will be executed by the interpreter since it has the higher priority. (Note once again that a trace is a perfectly normal NP from the point view of the pattern matching process.) This rule now creates a new S node labelled infinitive and attaches the trace NP55 to the new infinitive as its subject. The resulting state is shown in figure 11 below.

The Active Node Stack (2. deep)
S22 (NP-PREPOSED S DECL MAJOR) / (SS-FINAL)
NP : (The meeting)
AUX : (was)
VP : ↓
VP20 (VP) / (SS-VP THAT-COMP INF-COMP)
VERB : (believed)
C: S23 (SEC INF-S S) / (PARSE-AUX)
NP : bound to: (The meeting)

The Buffer
1 :   WORD166 (*TO PREP AUXVERB) : (to)
2 :   WORD167 (*HAVE VERB TNSLESS AUXVERB
PRES ...) : (have)

Yet unseen words: been scheduled for Wednesday .

Figure 11 - After INF-S-START1 has been executed.

We are now well on our way to the desired analysis. An embedded infinitive has been initiated, and a trace bound to the subject of the dominating S has been attached as its subject, although no rule has explicitly "lowered" the trace from one clause into the other.

The parser will now proceed exactly as in the previous example. It will build the auxiliary, attach it, and attach the verb "scheduled" to a new VP node. Once again PASSIVE will match and be executed, creating a trace, binding it to the subject of the clause (in this case itself a trace), and dropping the new trace into the buffer. Again the rule OBJECTS will attach the trace NP57 as the object of VP21, and the parse will then be completed by grammatical processes which will not be discussed here. An edited form of the tree structure which results is shown in figure 12 below. A trace is indicated in this tree by giving the terminal string of its ultimate binding in parentheses.

(NP-PREPOSED S DECL MAJOR)
  NP: (MODIBLE NP DEF DET NP)
      The meeting
  AUX: (PASSIVE PAST V13S AUX)
      was
  VP: (VP)
    VERB: believed
    NP: (NP COMP)
      S: (NP-PREPOSED SEC INF-S S)
        NP: (NP TRACE) (bound* to: The meeting)
        AUX: (PASSIVE PERF INF AUX)
            to have been
        VP: (VP)
          VERB: scheduled
          NP: (NP TRACE) (bound* to: The meeting)
          PP: (PP)
            PREP: for
            NP: (NP TIME DOW)
                Wednesday

Figure 12 - The final tree structure.

This example demonstrates that the simple formulation of the PASSIVE rule presented above, interacting with other simply formulated grammatical rules for parsing objects and initiating embedded infinitives, allows a trace to be attached either as the object of a verb or as the subject of an embedded infinitive, whichever is the appropriate analysis for a given grammatical situation. Because the PASSIVE rule is formulated in such a way that it drops the trace it creates into the buffer, later rules, already formulated to trigger on an NP in the buffer, will analyze sentences with NP-preposing exactly the same as those without a preposed subject. Thus, we see that the availability of the buffer mechanism is crucial to capturing this generalization; such a generalization can only be stated by a parser with a mechanism much like the buffer used here.

The Grammar Interpreter and Chomsky's Constraints

Before turning now to a sketch of a computational account of Chomsky's constraints, there are several important limitations of this work which must be enumerated.

First of all, while two of Chomsky's constraints seem to fall out of the grammar interpreter, there seems to be no apparent account of a third, the Propositional Island Constraint, in terms of this mechanism.

Second, Chomsky's formulation of these constraints is intended to apply to all rules of grammar, both syntactic rules (i.e. transformations) and those rules of semantic interpretation which Chomsky calls "rules of construal", a set of shallow semantic rules which govern anaphoric processes [Chomsky 77]. The discussion here will only touch on purely syntactic phenomena; the question of how rules of semantic interpretation can be meshed with the framework presented in this document has yet to be investigated.

Third, the arguments presented below deal only with English, and in fact depend strongly upon several facts about English syntax, most crucially upon the fact that English is subject-initial. Whether these arguments can be successfully extended to other language types is an open question, and to this extent this work must be considered exploratory.

And finally, I will not show that these constraints must be true *without exception*; as we will see, there are various situations in which the constraints imposed by the grammar interpreter can be circumvented. Most of these situations, though, will be shown to demand much more complex grammar formulations than those typically needed in the grammar so far constructed. This is quite in keeping with the suggestion made by Chomsky [Chomsky 77] that the constraints are not necessarily without exception, but rather that exceptions will be "highly marked" and therefore will count heavily against any grammar that includes them.

The Specified Subject Constraint

The Specified Subject Constraint (SSC), stated informally, says that no rule may involve two constituents that are Dominated by different cyclic nodes unless the lower of the two is the subject of an S or NP. Thus, no rule may involve constituents X and Y in the structure shown in figure 13 below, if α and β are cyclic nodes and Z is the subject of α, Z distinct from X.

$$[_{\beta}...Y...[_{\alpha} Z...X...]...Y...]$$

Figure 13 - SSC:
No rule can involve X and Y in this structure.

The SSC explains why the surface subject position of verbs like "seems" and "is certain" which have no underlying subject can be filled only by the subject and not the object of the embedded S: The rule "MOVE NP" is free to shift any NP into the empty subject position, but is constrained by the SSC so that the object of the embedded S cannot be moved out of that clause. This explains why (a) in figure 14 below, but not 14b, can be derived from 14c; the derivation of 14b from 14c would violate the SSC.

(a) John seems to like Mary.
(b) *Mary seems John to like.
(c) ∇ seems [$_S$ John to like Mary]

Figure 14 - Some examples illustrating the SSC.

In essence, then, the Specified Subject Constraint constrains the rule "MOVE NP" in such a way that only the subject of a clause can be moved out of that clause into a position in a higher S. Thus, if a trace in an annotated surface structure is bound to an NP Dominated by a higher S, that trace must fill the subject position of the lower clause.

In the remainder of this section I will show that the grammar interpreter constrains grammatical processes in such a way that annotated surface structures constructed by the grammar interpreter will have this same property, given the formulation of the PASSIVE rule presented above. In terms of the parsing process, this means that if a trace is "lowered" from one clause to another as a result of a "MOVE NP"-type operation during the parsing process, then it will be attached as the subject of the second clause. To be more precise, if a trace is attached so that it is Dominated by some S node S1, and the trace is bound to an NP Dominated by some other S node S2, then that trace will necessarily be attached so that it fills the subject position of S1. This is depicted in figure 15 below.

The Active Node Stack
.....
S2 ... / ...
...
NP2
...
C: S1 ... / ...
NP: NP1 (NP TRACE) : bound to NP2

Figure 15 - NP1 must be attached as the subject of S1 since it is bound to an NP Dominated by a higher S.

Looking back at the complex passive example involving "raising" presented above, we see that the parsing process results in a structure exactly like that shown above. The original point of the example, of course, was that the rather simple PASSIVE rule handles this case without the need for some mechanism to explicitly lower the NP. The PASSIVE rule captures this generalization by dropping the trace it creates into the buffer (after appropriately binding the trace), thus allowing other rules written to handle normal NPs (e.g. OBJECTS and INF-S-START1) to correctly place the trace.

This statement of PASSIVE does more, however, than simply capture a generalization about a specific construction. As I will argue in detail below, the behavior specified by both the Specified Subject Constraint and Subjacency follows almost immediately from this formulation. In [Marcus 77], I argue that this formulation of PASSIVE is the only simple, non-*ad hoc*, formulation of this rule possible, and that all other rules characterized by the competence rule "MOVE NP" must operate similarly; here, however, I will only show that these constraints follow naturally from this formulation of PASSIVE, leaving the question of necessity aside. I will also assume one additional constraint below, the *Left-to-Right Constraint*, which will be briefly motivated later in this paper as a natural condition on the formulation of a grammar for this mechanism.

> The Left-to-Right Constraint: the constituents in the buffer are (almost always) attached to higher level constituents in left-to-right order, i.e. the first constituent in the buffer is (almost always) attached before the second constituent.

I will now show that a trace created by PASSIVE which is bound to an NP in one clause can only serve as the subject of a clause dominated by that first clause.

Given the formulation of PASSIVE, a trace can be "lowered" into one clause from another only by the indirect route of dropping it into the buffer before the subordinate clause node is created, which is exactly how the PASSIVE rule operates. This means that the ordering of the operations is crucially: 1) create a trace and drop it into the buffer, 2) create a subordinate S node, 3) attach the trace to the newly created S node. The key point is that at the time that the subordinate clause node is created and becomes the current active node, the trace must be sitting in the buffer, filling one of the three buffer positions. Thus, the parser will be in the state shown in figure 16 below, with the trace, in fact, most likely in the first buffer position.

The Active Node Stack
    .....
C: S123 (S SEC ...) / ...

The Buffer
    ...
    NP123 (NP TRACE) : bound to NP in S above S123
    ...

Figure 16 - Parser state after embedded S created.

Now, given the L-to-R Constraint, a trace which is in the buffer at the time that an embedded S node is first created must be one of the first several constituents attached to the S node or its daughter nodes. From the structure of English, we know that the leftmost three constituents of an embedded S node, ignoring topicalized constituents, must either be

COMP NP AUX
or
NP AUX [$_{VP}$ VERB ...].

(The COMP node will dominate flags like "that" or "for" that mark the beginning of a complement clause.) But then, if a trace, itself an NP, is one of the first several constituents attached to an embedded clause, the only position it can fill will be the subject of the clause, exactly the empirical consequence of Chomsky's Specified Subject Constraint in such cases as explained above.

The L-to-R Constraint

Let us now return to the motivation for the L-to-R Constraint. Again, I will not attempt to prove that this constraint must be true, but merely to show why it is plausible.

Empirically, the Left-to-Right Constraint seems to hold for the most part; for the grammar of English discussed in this paper, and, it would seem, for any grammar of English that attempts to capture the same range of generalizations as this grammar, the constituents in the buffer are utilized in left-to-right order, with a small range of exceptions. This usage is clearly not enforced by the grammar interpreter as presently implemented; it is quite possible to write a set of grammar rules that specifically ignores a constituent in the buffer until some arbitrary point in the clause, though such a set of rules would be highly *ad hoc*. However, there rarely seems to be a need to remove other than the first constituent in the buffer.

The one exception to the L-to-R Constraint seems to be that a constituent C_i may be attached before the constituent to its left, C_{i-1}, if C_i does not appear in surface structure in its underlying position (or, if one prefers, in its unmarked position) and if its removal from the buffer reestablishes the unmarked order of the remaining constituents, as in the case of the AUX-INVERSION rule discussed earlier in this paper. To capture this notion, the L-to-R Constraint can be restated as follows: All constituents must be attached to higher level constituents according to the left-to-right order of constituents in the unmarked case of that constituent's structure.

This reformulation is interesting in that it would be a natural consequence of the operation of the grammar interpreter if packets were associated with the phrase structure rules of an explicit "base component", and these rules were used as templates to build up the structure assigned by the grammar interpreter. A packet of grammar rules would then be explicitly associated with each symbol on the right hand side of each phrase structure rule. A constituent of a given type would then be constructed by activating the packets associated with each node type of the appropriate phrase structure rule in left-to-right order. Since these base rules would reflect the unmarked l-to-r order of constituents, the constraint suggested here would then simply fall out of the interpreter mechanism.

Subjacency

Before turning to the Subjacency Principle, a few auxiliary technical terms need to be defined: If we can trace a path up the tree from a given node X to a given node Y, then we say *X is dominated by Y*, or equivalently, *Y dominates X*. If Y dominates X, and no other nodes intervene (i.e. X is a daughter of Y), then *Y immediately (or directly) dominates X*. [Akmajian & Heny 75]. One non-standard definition will prove useful: I will say that if Y dominates X, and Y is a cyclic node, i.e. an S or NP node, and there is no other cyclic node Z such that Y dominates Z and Z dominates X (i.e. there is no intervening cyclic node Z between Y and X) then *Y Dominates X*.

The principle of Subjacency, informally stated, says that no rule can involve constituents that are separated by more than one cyclic node. Let us say that a node X *is subjacent to* a node Y if there is at most one cyclic node, i.e. at most one NP or S node, between the cyclic node that Dominates Y and the node X. Given this definition, the Subjacency principle says that no rule can involve constituents that are not subjacent.

The Subjacency principle implies that movement rules are constrained so that they can move a constituent only into positions that the constituent was subjacent to, i.e. only within the clause (or NP) in which it originates, or into the clause (or NP) that Dominates that clause (...). This means that if α, β, and ϵ in figure 17 are cyclic nodes, no rule can move a constituent from position X to either of the positions Y, where $[_\gamma...X...]$ is distinct from $[_\gamma X]$.

$$[_\epsilon...Y...[_\beta...[_\gamma...X...]...]...Y...]$$

Figure 17 - Subjacency:
No rule can involve X and Y in this structure.

Subjacency implies that if a constituent is to be "lifted" up more than one level in constituent structure, this operation must be done by repeated operations. Thus, to use one of Chomsky's examples, the sentence given in figure 18a, with a deep structure analogous to 18b, must be derived as follows (assuming that "is certain", like "seems", has no subject in underlying structure): The deep structure must first undergo a movement operation that results in a structure analogous to 18c, and then another movement operation that results in 18d, each of these movements leaving a trace as shown. That 18c is in fact an intermediate structure is supported by the existence of sentences such as 18e, which purportedly result when the ∇ in the matrix S is replaced by the lexical item "it", and the embedded S is tensed rather than infinitival. The structure given in 18f is ruled out as a possible annotated surface structure, because the single trace could only be left if the NP "John" was moved in one fell swoop from its underlying position to its position in surface structure, which would violate Subjacency.

(a) John seems to be certain to win.
(b) ∇ seems $[_S \nabla$ to be certain $[_S$ John to win$]]$
(c) ∇ seems $[_S$ John to be certain $[_S t$ to win$]]$
(d) John seems $[_S t$ to be certain $[_S t$ to win$]]$
(e) It seems that John is certain to win.
(f) John seems $[_S \nabla$ to be certain $[_S t$ to win$]]$

Figure 18 - An example demonstrating Subjacency.

Having stated Subjacency in terms of the abstract competence theory of generative grammar, I now will show that a parsing correlate of Subjacency follows from the structure of the grammar interpreter. Specifically, I will show that there are only limited cases in which a trace generated by a "MOVE-NP" process can be "lowered" more than one clause, i.e. that a trace created and bound while any given S is current must almost always be attached either to that S or to an S which is Dominated by that S.

Let us begin by examining what it would mean to lower a trace more than one clause. Given that a trace can only be "lowered" by dropping it into the buffer and then creating a subordinate S node, as discussed above, lowering a trace more than one clause necessarily implies the following sequence of events, depicted in figure 19 below: First, a trace NP1 must (a) be created with some S node, S1, as the current S, (b) bound to some NP Dominated by that S and then (c) dropped into the buffer. By definition, it will be inserted into the first cell in the buffer. (This is shown in figure 19a) Then a second S, S2, must be created, supplanting S1 as the current S, and then yet a third S, S3, must be created, becoming the current S. During all these steps, the trace NP1 remains sitting in the buffer. Finally, NP1 is attached under S3 (fig. 19b). By the Specified Subject Constraint, NP1 must then attach to S3 as its subject.

The Active Node Stack

.....
C: S1 ... / ...

The Buffer
1st: NP1 (NP TRACE) : bound to NP Dominated by S1
...

(a) - NP1 is dropped into the buffer
while S1 is the current S.

The Active Node Stack

.....
S1 ... / ...
S2 ... / ...
C: S3 ... / ...
NP1 (NP TRACE) : bound to NP Dominated by S1

(b) - After S2 and S3 are created,
NP1 is attached to S3 as its subject (by the SSC).

Figure 19 - Lowering a trace more than 1 clause

But this sequence of events is highly unlikely. The essence of the argument is this:

Nothing in the buffer can change between the time that S2 is created and S3 is created if NP1 remains in the buffer. NP1, like any other node that is dropped from the active node stack into the buffer, is inserted into the first buffer position. But then, by the L-to-R Constraint, nothing to the right of NP1 can be attached to a higher level constituent until NP1 is attached. (One can show that it is most unlikely that any constituents will enter to the left of NP1 after it is dropped into the buffer, but I will suppress this detail here; the full argument is included in [Marcus 77].)

But if the contents of the buffer do not change between the creation of S2 and S3, then what can possibly motivate the creation of both S2 and S3? The contents of the buffer must necessarily provide clear evidence that both of these clauses are present, since, by the Determinism Hypothesis, the parser must be correct if it initiates a constituent. Thus, the same three constituents in the buffer must provide convincing evidence not only for the creation of S2 but also for S3. Furthermore, if NP1 is to become the subject of S3, and if S2 Dominates S3, then it would seem that the constituents that follow NP1 in the buffer must also be constituents of S3, since S3 must be completed before it is dropped from the active node stack and constituents can then be attached to S2. But then S2 must be created *entirely* on the basis of evidence provided by the constituents of another clause (unless S3 has less than three constituents). Thus, it would seem that the contents of the buffer cannot provide evidence for the presence of both clauses unless the presence of S3, by itself, is enough to provide confirming evidence for the presence of S2. This would be the case only if there were, say, a clausal construction that could only appear (perhaps in a particular environment) as the initial constituent of a higher clause. In this case, if there are such constructions, a violation of Subjacency should be possible.

With the one exception just mentioned, there is no motivation for creating two clauses in such a situation, and thus the initiation of only one such clause can be motivated. But if only one clause is initiated before NP1 is attached, then NP1 must be attached to this clause, and this clause is necessarily subjacent to the clause which Dominates the NP to which it is bound. Thus, the grammar interpreter will behave as if it enforces the Subjacency Constraint.

As a concluding point, it is worthy of note that while the grammar interpreter appears to behave exactly as if it were constrained by the Subjacency principle, it is in fact constrained by a version of the Clausemate Constraint! (The Clausemate Constraint, long tacitly assumed by linguists but first explicitly stated, I believe, by Postal [Postal 64], states that a transformation can only involve constituents that are Dominated by the same cyclic node. This constraint is at the heart of Postal's attack on the constraints that are discussed above and his argument for a "raising" analysis.) The grammar interpreter, as was stated above, limits grammar rules from examining any node in the active node stack higher than the current cyclic node, which is to say that it can only examine clausemates. The trick is that a trace is created and bound while it is a "clausemate" of the NP to which it is bound in that the current cyclic node at that time is the node to which that NP is attached. The trace is then dropped into the buffer and another S node is created, thereby destroying the clausemate relationship. The trace is then attached to this new S node. Thus, in a sense, the trace *is* lowered from one clause to another. The crucial point is that while this lowering goes on as a result of the operation of the grammar interpreter, it is only implicitly lowered in that 1) the trace was never *attached* to the higher S and 2) it is *not* dropped into the buffer because of any realization that it must be "lowered"; in fact it may end up attached as a clausemate of the NP to which it is bound - as the passive examples

presented earlier make clear. The trace is simply dropped into the buffer because its grammatical function is not clear, and the creation of the second S follows from other independently motivated grammatical processes. From the point of view of this processing theory, we can have our cake and eat it too; to the extent that it makes sense to map results from the realm of processing into the realm of competence, in a sense *both* the clausemate/"raising" and the Subjacency positions are correct.

Evidence for the Determinism Hypothesis

In closing, I would like to show that the properties of the grammar interpreter crucial to capturing the behavior of Chomsky's constraints were originally motivated by the Determinism Hypothesis, and thus, to some extent, the Determinism Hypothesis explains Chomsky's constraints.

The strongest form of such an argument, of course, would be to show that (a) either (i) the grammar interpreter accounts for *all* of Chomsky's constraints in a manner which is conclusively universal or (ii) the constraints that it will not account for are wrong and that (b) the properties of the grammar interpreter which were crucial for this proof were *forced* by the Determinism Hypothesis. If such an argument could be made, it would show that the Determinism Hypothesis provides a natural processing account of the linguistic data characterized by Chomsky's constraints, giving strong confirmation to the Determinism Hypothesis.

I have shown none of the above, and thus my claims must be proportionately more modest. I have argued only that important sub-cases of Chomsky's constraints follow from the grammar interpreter, and while I can show that the Determinism Hypothesis strongly *motivates* the mechanisms from which these arguments follow, I cannot show necessity. The extent to which this argument provides evidence for the Determinism Hypothesis must thus be left to the reader; no objective measure exists for such matters.

The ability to drop a trace into the buffer is at the heart of the arguments presented here for Subjacency and the SSC as consequences of the functioning of the grammar interpreter; this is the central operation upon which the above arguments are based. But the buffer itself, and the fact that a constituent can be dropped into the buffer if its grammatical function is uncertain, are directly motivated by the Determinism Hypothesis. Given this, it is fair to claim that if Chomsky's constraints follow from the operation of the grammar interpreter, then they are strongly linked to the Determinism Hypothesis. If Chomsky's constraints are in fact true, then the arguments presented in this paper provide solid evidence in support of the Determinism Hypothesis.

Acknowledgments

This paper summarizes one result presented in my Ph.D. thesis; I would like to express my gratitude to the many people who contributed to the technical content of that work: Jon Allen, my thesis advisor, to whom I owe a special debt of thanks, Ira Goldstein, Seymour Papert, Bill

Martin, Bob Moore, Chuck Rieger, Mike Genesereth, Gerry Sussman, Mike Brady, Craig Thiersch, Beth Levin, Candy Bullwinkle, Kurt VanLehn, Dave McDonald, and Chuck Rich.

This paper describes research done at the Artificial Intelligence Laboratory of the Massachusetts Institute of Technology. Support for the laboratory's artificial intelligence research is provided in part by the Advanced Research Projects Agency of the Department of Defence under Office of Naval Research Contract N00014-75-C-0643.

BIBLIOGRAPHY

Akmajian, A. and F. Heny [1975] *An Introduction to the Principles of Transformational Syntax*, MIT Press, Cambridge, Mass.

Bresnan, J. W. [1976] "Evidence for a Theory of Unbounded Transformations", *Linguistic Analysis* 2:353.

Chomsky, N. [1973] "Conditions on Transformations", in S. Anderson and P. Kiparsky, eds., *A Festschrift for Morris Halle*, Holt, Rinehart and Winston, N.Y.

Chomsky, N. [1975] *Reflections on Language*, Pantheon, N.Y.

Chomsky, N. [1976] "Conditions on Rules of Grammar", *Linguistic Analysis* 2:303.

Chomsky, N. [1977] "On Wh-Movement", in A. Akmajian, P. Culicover, and T. Wasow, eds., *Formal Syntax*, Academic Press, N.Y.

Fillmore, C. J. [1968] "The Case for Case" in *Universals in Linguistic Theory*, E. Bach and R. T. Harms, eds., Holt, Rinehart, and Winston, N.Y.

Gruber, J. S. [1965] *Studies in Lexical Relations*, unpublished Ph.D. thesis, MIT.

Jackendoff, R. S. [1972] *Semantic Interpretation in Generative Grammar*, MIT Press, Cambridge, Mass.

Marcus, M. P. [1977] *A Theory of Syntactic Recognition for Natural Language*, unpublished Ph.D. thesis, MIT.

Marcus, M. P. [1978] "Capturing Linguistic Generalizations in a Parser for English", in the proceedings of *The 2nd National Conference of the Canadian Society for Computational Studies of Intelligence*, Toronto, Canada.

Newell, A. and H.A. Simon [1972] *Human Problem Solving*, Prentice-Hall, Englewood Cliffs, N.J.

Postal, P. M. [1974] *On Raising*, MIT Press, Cambridge, Mass.

Pratt, V. R. [1973] "Top-Down Operator Precedence", in the proceedings of *The SIGACT/SIGPLAN Symposium on Principles of Programming Languages*, Boston, Mass.

Sager, N. [1973] "The String Parser for Scientific Literature", in [Rustin 73].

Winograd, T. [1971] *Procedures as a Representation for Data in a Computer Program for Understanding Natural Language*, Project MAC-TR 84, MIT, Cambridge, Mass.

Woods, W. A. [1970] "Transition Network Grammars for Natural Language Analysis", *Communications of the ACM* 13:591.

Definite Clause Grammars for Language Analysis—A Survey of the Formalism and a Comparison with Augmented Transition Networks

Fernando C. N. Pereira and David H. D. Warren
Department of Artificial Intelligence, University of Edinburgh

Recommended by Daniel G. Bobrow and Richard Burton

ABSTRACT

A clear and powerful formalism for describing languages, both natural and artificial, follows from a method for expressing grammars in logic due to Colmerauer and Kowalski. This formalism, which is a natural extension of context-free grammars, we call "definite clause grammars" (DCGs).

A DCG provides not only a description of a language, but also an effective means for analysing strings of that language, since the DCG, as it stands, is an executable program of the programming language Prolog. Using a standard Prolog compiler, the DCG can be compiled into efficient code, making it feasible to implement practical language analysers directly as DCGs.

This paper compares DCGs with the successful and widely used augmented transition network (ATN) formalism, and indicates how ATNs can be translated into DCGs. It is argued that DCGs can be at least as efficient as ATNs, whilst the DCG formalism is clearer, more concise and in practice more powerful.

1. Introduction

The aims of this paper are:

(1) to give an introduction to "definite clause grammars" (DCGs)—a formalism, originally described by Colmerauer (1975), in which grammars are expressed as clauses of first-order predicate logic, providing a natural generalisation of context-free grammars;

(2) to explain how DCGs constitute effective programs of the programming language Prolog, and how they can thereby be used to implement practical systems for language analysis;

(3) to compare DCGs with the augmented transition network (ATN) formalism, and to show how an ATN can be translated into a DCG. It is NOT our intention to propose any definite solutions to the many unsolved linguistic problems of particular languages such as English; we describe only how DCGs *can* be used, not how they *should* be used. We take an informal approach wherever possible. We start by reviewing some basic concepts, making clear our terminology in the process.

The usual way one attempts to make precise the definition of a **language**, whether it is a natural language or a programming language, is through a collection of **rules** called a **grammar**. (Following normal usage, we restrict the term "grammar" to language definitions of this kind.) The rules of a grammar define which strings of words or symbols are valid **sentences** of the language. In addition, the grammar generally gives some kind of **analysis** of the sentence, into a **structure** which makes its meaning more explicit.

A fundamental class of grammar is the **context-free grammar** (CFG), familiar to the computing community in the notation of "BNF" (Backus–Naur form). In CFGs, the words, or basic symbols, of the language are identified by **terminal** symbols, while categories of **phrases** of the language are identified by **non-terminal** symbols. Each rule of a CFG expresses a possible form for a non-terminal, as a sequence of terminals and non-terminals. The analysis of a string according to a CFG is a **parse tree**, showing the constituent phrases of the string and their hierarchical relationships.

An important idea, due to Colmerauer and Kowalski (cf. Kowalski, 1974b; Colmerauer, 1975), is to translate the special purpose formalism of CFGs into a general purpose one, namely first-order predicate logic. They devised a particular method (having its origins in Colmerauer's (1970) Q-systems) for expressing context-free rules as logic statements of a restricted kind, known as **definite clauses** or "Horn clauses". The problem of recognising, or **parsing**, a string of a language is then transformed into the problem of proving that a certain theorem follows from the definite clause axioms which describe the language.

These ideas might only have been of theoretical interest. However, at the same time, Colmerauer and Kowalski originated a more far-reaching idea. This was that a collection of definite clauses can be considered to be a **program** (see Kowalski (1974a, 1974b); van Emden (1975).) It turns out that automatic deduction can exhibit all the characteristics we associate with effective computation, provided the deduction is pursued in a suitably goal-directed way.

A practical realisation of this concept of "programming in logic" was developed by Colmerauer and his colleagues in the form of the programming language Prolog. (See Roussel (1975), Pereira et al. (1978).) Prolog is based on a very simple but efficient proof procedure. Several implementations of the language have been completed, and these implementations have shown that Prolog can be as efficient as conventional high-level programming languages, cf. Warren et al. (1977). Prolog has been successfully used to write large-scale programs for a number of

Artificial Intelligence 13 (1980), 231–278

useful applications, including algebraic "symbol crunching" (Bergman and Kanoui, 1975), architectural design (Markusz, 1977), drug design (Darvas et al., 1977) and compiler implementation (Warren, 1977a, 1977b).

Now if a CFG is expressed in definite clauses according to the Colmerauer–Kowalski method, and executed as a Prolog program, the program behaves as an efficient top-down parser for the language the CFG describes.[1] This fact becomes particularly significant when coupled with another discovery—that the technique for translating CFGs into definite clauses has a simple generalisation, resulting in a formalism far more powerful than CFGs, but equally amenable to execution by Prolog. This formalism—the main subject of our paper—we call **definite clause grammars** (DCGs). DCGs are a special case of Colmerauer's (1975) "metamorphosis grammars", which are for Chomsky type-0 grammars what DCGs are for CFGs. Although metamorphosis grammars can be translated into definite clauses, the correspondence is not nearly so direct as that for DCGs.

DCGs are a natural extension of CFGs. As such, DCGs inherit the properties which make CFGs so important for language theory: the possible forms for the sentences of a language are described in a clear and modular way; it is possible to represent the recursive embedding of phrases which is characteristic of almost all interesting languages; there is an established body of results on CFGs which is very useful in designing parsing algorithms.

Now it is well known that CFGs are not fully adequate for describing natural language, nor even many programming languages. DCGs overcome this inadequacy by extending CFGs in three important ways.

Firstly, DCGs provide for context-dependency in a grammar, so that the permissible forms for a phrase may depend on the context in which that phrase occurs in the string. Secondly, DCGs allow arbitrary tree structures to be built in the course of the parsing, in a way that is not constrained by the recursive structure of the grammar; such tree structures can provide a representation of the "meaning" of the string. Thirdly, DCGs allow extra conditions to be included in the grammar rules; these conditions make the course of the parsing depend on auxiliary computations, up to an unlimited extent.

DCGs, as implemented via Prolog, have been used to write a number of practical systems for language analysis, e.g. for natural language question answering (Dahl, 1977), and in compiler implementation (Warren, 1977).

DCGs bear some similarities to other formalisms known to computer scientists, notably the "van Wijngaarden grammars" used in the Algol-68 Report (van Wijngaarden, 1974), and the "affix grammars" which Koster (1971) took as the basis for the compiler definition language CDL. Like a van Wijngaarden grammar, a DCG can be viewed as a grammar consisting of an infinite number of context-free rules. Like an affix grammar, a DCG extends a CFG by augmenting non-terminals with arguments. However the three formalisms have significant

[1] The efficiency of the parser also depends on a "suitable" choice of CFG to describe the language.

differences; it seems fair to say that both van Wijngaarden grammars and affix grammars can be viewed as special cases of DCGs.

In this paper we shall be specifically concerned with comparing DCGs with a formalism which at first sight is less obviously similar, namely "augmented transition networks" (ATNs). ATNs were introduced by Woods (1970) as a powerful and practical formalism for natural language analysis. They have been used to implement a number of working natural language systems (Woods et al., 1972, 1976; Bates, 1975; Burton, 1976), and some efficient implementations of the formalism have been developed (Burton and Woods, 1976; Finin and Hadden, 1977). For the reader not familiar with ATNs, we recommend Bates (1978) as a clear and thorough introduction.

We have chosen ATNs for comparison because they are widely known, because they are often considered to represent the "state of the art" in formalisms for practical natural language analysis, and because some of the most interesting natural language systems have been written within the ATN formalism. We shall argue that DCGs can be at least as efficient as ATNs, whilst the DCG formalism is clearer, more concise and in practice more powerful.

The paper begins with a concise introduction to logic as a programming language and to Prolog. We recommend the reader to skim through this section and refer back to it later. The next section explains in detail the basic DCG formalism. This is followed by an account, for the ATN-minded reader, of how ATNs can be translated into DCGs. Finally we give a detailed discussion of the advantages of DCGs relative to ATNs, and conclude with a summary of why we think DCGs represent a significant advance. The appendices contain a full example of the translation of an ATN into a DCG, and also some DCG performance data obtained using our DECsystem-10 implementation of Prolog.

Note that, in describing various formalisms, we shall often use bold-face symbols as meta- or syntactic variables. These symbols are NOT part of the formalism under discussion, but are a device which helps to make our description of the formalism shorter and more precise.

2. Logic as a Programming Language—The Definite Clause Subset

In this section, we define the syntax and semantics of a certain subset of logic ("definite clauses"), which amounts essentially to a dropping of disjunction ("or") from the logic, and we indicate how this subset forms the basis of the practical programming language known as Prolog. Definite clauses have also been called "Horn clauses" or "regular clauses", but we prefer the name coined by van Emden (1975), since it gives at least some indication of their nature. We describe the definite clause subset from a conventional programming standpoint, using the notation and terminology of Prolog.

2.1. Syntax, terminology and informal semantics

2.1.1. Terms

The data objects of the language are called **terms**. A term is either a **constant**, a **variable** or a **compound term**.

The constants include **integers** such as:

0 1 999

and **atoms** such as:

a void = : = 'Algol-68' []

The symbol for an atom can be any sequence of characters, which in general must be written in quotes unless there is no possibility of confusion with other symbols (such as variables, integers). As in conventional programming languages, constants denote definite elementary objects.

Variables will be distinguished by an initial capital letter, e.g.

X Value A A1

A variable should be thought of as standing for some particular but unidentified object. Note that a variable is not simply a storage location which can be assigned to, as in most programming languages; rather it is a local name for some data object, cf. the variable of pure Lisp and identity declarations in Algol-68.

The structured data objects of the language are the compound terms. A compound term comprises a **functor** (called the **principal** functor of the term) and a sequence of one or more terms called **arguments**. A functor is characterised by its **name**, which is an atom, and its **arity** or number of arguments. For example the compound term whose functor is named 'point' of arity 3, with arguments X, Y and Z, is written:

point(X,Y,Z)

One may think of a functor as a record type and the arguments of a compound term as the fields of a record. Compound terms are usefully pictured as trees. For example, the term:

s(np(john),vp(v(likes),np(mary)))

would be pictured as the structure:

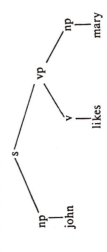

Sometimes it is convenient to write a compound term using an optional infix notation, e.g.

X+Y (P;Q) X<Y

instead of:

+(X,Y) ;(P,Q) <(X,Y)

Note that we consider an atom to be a functor of arity 0.

An important class of data structures are the **lists**. A list either is the atom:

[]

representing the empty list, or is a compound term with functor ' · ' and two arguments which are respectively the head and tail of the list. Thus a list of the first three natural numbers is the structure:

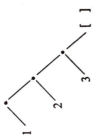

This would be written in standard syntax as:

· (1, · (2, · (3,[])))

but we shall write it, using a special list notation, as:

[1,2,3]

Our notation when the tail of a list is a variable is exemplified by:

[X | L] [a,b | L]

representing respectively:

2.1.2. Clauses

A fundamental unit of a logic program is the **goal** or **procedure call**. Examples are:

gives(tom,apple,teacher) reverse([1,2,3],L) X<Y

A goal is merely a special kind of term, distinguished only by the context in which it appears in the program. The (principal) functor of a goal is called a **predicate**. It corresponds roughly to a procedure name in a conventional programming language.

A logic **program** consists simply of a sequence of statements called **clauses**. A clause comprises a **head** and a **body**. The head either consists of a single goal or is empty. The body consists of a sequence of zero or more goals (i.e., it too may be empty).

If neither the head nor the body of the clause is empty, we call it a **non-unit clause**, and write it in the form:

P :- Q, R, S.

where **P** is the head goal and **Q**, **R** and **S** are the goals which make up the body. We can read such a clause either declaratively as:

"**P** is true if **Q** and **R** and **S** are true."

or **procedurally** as:

"To satisfy goal **P**, satisfy goals **Q**, **R** and **S**."

If the body of the clause is empty, we call it a **unit clause**, and write it in the form:

P.

where **P** is the head goal. We interpret this declaratively as:

"**P** is true."

and procedurally as:

"Goal **P** is satisfied."

Finally, if the head of the clause is empty, we call the clause a **question** and write it in the form:

?- P, Q.

where **P** and **Q** are the goals of the body. Such a question is read declaratively as:

"Are **P** and **Q** true?"

and procedurally as:

"Satisfy goals **P** and **Q**."

Clauses generally contain variables. Note that variables in different clauses are completely independent, even if they have the same name – i.e., the "lexical scope" of a variable is limited to a single clause. Each distinct variable in a clause should be interpreted as standing for an arbitrary value. To illustrate this, we give some examples of clauses containing variables, with possible declarative and procedural readings:

(1)   employed(X) :- employs(Y,X).
"For any X and Y, X is employed if Y employs X."
"To find whether X is employed, find a Y that employs X."

(2)   derivative(X,X,1).
"For any X, the derivative of X with respect to X is 1."
"The goal of finding a derivative for the expression X with respect to X itself is satisfied by the result 1."

(3)   ?- ungulate(X), aquatic(X).
"Is it true of any X, that X is an ungulate and X is aquatic?"
"Find an X which is both an ungulate and aquatic."

In a logic program, the **procedure** for a particular predicate is the sequence of clauses in the program whose head goals have that predicate as principal functor. For example, the procedure for a ternary predicate 'concatenate' might well consist of the two clauses:

concatenate([X | L1],L2,[X | L3]) :- concatenate(L1,L2,L3).
concatenate([],L,L).

where 'concatenate(L1,L2,L3)' means "the list L1 concatenated with the list L2 is the list L3".

As we have seen, the goals in the body of a clause are linked by the operator ',', which can be interpreted as conjunction ("and"). For convenience, we sometimes also use an operator ';' standing for disjunction ("or"). (The precedence of ';' is such that it dominates ',' but is dominated by ':-'). An example is the clause:

grandfather(X,Z) :-
(mother(X,Y); father(X,Y)), father(Y,Z).

which can be read as:

"For any X, Y and Z,
X has Z as a grandfather if
either the mother of X is Y or the father of X is Y,
and the father of Y is Z."

Such uses of disjunction can always be eliminated by defining an extra predicate — for instance the previous example is equivalent to:

grandfather(X,Z) :- parent(X,Y), father(Y,Z).
parent(X,Y) :- mother(X,Y).
parent(X,Y) :- father(X,Y).

— and so disjunction will not be mentioned further in the following, more formal, description of the semantics of clauses.

2.2. Declarative and procedural semantics

The semantics of definite clauses should be fairly clear from the informal interpretations already given. However, it is useful to have a precise definition. The

declarative semantics of definite clauses tells us which goals can be considered true according to a given program, and is defined recursively as follows.

A goal is **true** if it is the head of some clause instance and each of the goals (if any) in the body of that clause instance is true, where an **instance** of a clause (or term) is obtained, by substituting, for each of zero or more of its variables, a new term for all occurrences of the variable.

For example, if a program contains the preceding procedure for 'concatenate', than the declarative semantics tells us that:

concatenate([a],[b],[a,b])

is true, because this goal is the head of a certain instance of the first clause for 'concatenate', namely,

concatenate([a],[b],[a,b]) :- concatenate([],[b],[b])

and we know that the only goal in the body of this clause instance is true, since it is an instance of the unit clause which is the second clause for 'concatenate'.

Note that the declarative semantics makes no reference to the sequencing of goals within the body of a clause, nor to the sequencing of clauses within a program. This sequencing information is, however, very relevant for the **procedural semantics** which Prolog gives to definite clauses. The procedural semantics defines exactly how the Prolog system will execute a goal, and the sequencing information is the means by which the Prolog programmer directs the system to execute his program in a sensible way. The effect of executing a goal is to enumerate, one by one, its true instances. Here then is an informal definition of the procedural semantics.

To **execute** a goal, the system searches for the first clause whose head **matches** or **unifies** with the goal. The **unification** process (Robinson, 1965) finds the most general common instance of the two terms, which is unique if it exists. If a match is found, the matching clause instance is then **activated** by executing in turn, from left to right, each of the goals (if any) in its body. If at any time the system fails to find a match for a goal, it **backtracks**, i.e., it rejects the most recently activated clause, undoing any substitutions made by the match with the head of the clause. Next it reconsiders the original goal which activated the rejected clause, and tries to find a subsequent clause which also matches the goal.

For example, let us consider the question:

?- concatenate(X,Y,[a,b])

which can be read declaratively as:

"Are there lists X and Y which when concatenated yield the list [a,b]?"

If we execute the goal expressed in this question, we find that it matches the head of the first clause for 'concatenate', with X instantiated to [a | X1]. The new variable X1 is constrained by the new goal (or recursive procedure call) which is produced:

concatenate(X1,Y,[b])

Again this goal matches the head the first clause, instantiating X1 to [b | X2], and yielding the new goal:

concatenate(X2,Y,[])

Now this goal will only match the second clause, instantiating both X2 and Y to []. Since there are no further goals to be executed, we have a solution:

X = [a,b]
Y = []

i.e., a true instance of the original goal is:

concatenate([a,b],[],[a,b])

If we reject this solution, backtracking will generate the further solutions:

X = [a]   Y = [b]
X = []   Y = [a,b]

in that order, by re-matching, against the second clause for 'concatenate', goals already solved once using the first clause.

2.3. Notable features of logic programs

The simplicity of the syntax and semantics of logic programs conceals a number of notable features not found in conventional programming languages. These are discussed in Warren et al. (1977). Here we list briefly those features which are especially relevant to grammar writing.

(1) Pattern matching (unification) replaces the conventional use of selector and constructor functions for operating on structured data.

(2) The arguments of a procedure can serve, not only for it to receive one or more values as input, but also for it to return one or more values as output. Procedures can thus be "multi-output" as well as "multi-input".

(3) The input and output arguments of a procedure do not have to be distinguished in advance, but may vary from one call to another. Procedures can thus be "multi-purpose".

(4) Procedures may generate (via backtracking, in the case of Prolog) a set of alternative results. Such procedures are called "non-determinate". Backtracking amounts to a high-level form of iteration.

(5) Procedures may return "incomplete" results, i.e. the term or terms returned as the result of a procedure may contain variables, which are only filled in later, by calls to other procedures. The effect is similar to the use of assignment in a conventional language to fill in fields of a data structure. Note, however, that

there may be many occurrences of an uninstantiated variable, and that all of these get filled in simultaneously (in a single step) when the variable is finally instantiated. Note also that when two variables are unified together, they become identified as one. The effect is as though an invisible pointer, or reference, linked one variable to the other. We refer to these related phenomena as the "logical variable".

(6) "Program" and "data" are identical in form. A procedure consisting solely of unit clauses is closer to an array, or table of data, in a conventional language.

3. How to Write Grammars in Logic

In this section we describe the formalism of definite clause grammars. The basic idea has been discussed by Kowalski (1974b) and Colmerauer (1975) has given a fully formal treatment.

3.1. Expressing context-free grammars in definite clauses

To describe how grammars can be expressed in logic, we begin by considering context-free grammars (CFGs). For these, we use the following notation, which will prove convenient later.

Each rule has the form:

$$nt \rightarrow body.$$

where **nt** is a **non-terminal symbol** and **body** is a sequence of one or more items separated by commas. Each item is either a non-terminal symbol or a sequence of **terminal symbols**. The meaning of the rule is that **body** is a possible form for a phrase of type **nt**. A non-terminal symbol is written as a Prolog atom, while a sequence of terminals is written as a Prolog list, where a terminal may be any Prolog term. The null string is written as the empty list '[]'. As in the syntax of clauses, this basic notation is extended by allowing alternatives to appear in **body**. Alternative sequences of symbols are separated by semi-colons, with parentheses where necessary.

We now show a simple CFG to illustrate the notation. The grammar covers sentences such as "John loves Mary" and "Every man that lives loves a woman":

```
sentence → noun_phrase, verb_phrase.
noun_phrase → determiner, noun, rel_clause.
noun_phrase → name.
verb_phrase → trans_verb, noun_phrase.
verb_phrase → intrans_verb.
rel_clause → [that], verb_phrase.
rel_clause → [].
determiner → [every].
determiner → [a].
noun → [man].
noun → [woman].
name → [john].
name → [mary].
trans_verb → [loves].
intrans_verb → [lives].
```

We regard each rule of a CFG as "syntactic sugar" for a definite clause of logic. To get the translation, we associate with each non-terminal a 2-place predicate (having the same name). The arguments of the predicate represent the beginning and end points in the string of a phrase for that non-terminal. The first seven rules in the example translate into:

```
sentence(S0,S) :- noun_phrase(S0,S1), verb_phrase(S1,S).
noun_phrase(S0,S) :- determiner(S0,S1), noun(S1,S2), rel_clause(S2,S).
noun_phrase(S0,S) :- name(S0,S).
verb_phrase(S0,S) :- trans_verb(S0,S1), noun_phrase(S1,S).
verb_phrase(S0,S) :- intrans_verb(S0,S).
rel_clause(S0,S) :- connects(S0,that,S1), verb_phrase(S1,S).
rel_clause(S,S).
```

We can read the first clause as "a sentence extends from S0 to S if there is a noun phrase from S0 to S1 and a verb phrase from S1 to S"; we can read the last clause as "a relative clause extends from S to S", i.e., "a relative clause may be empty".

To represent terminal symbols in rules, we use a 3-place predicate, 'connects', where 'connects(S1,T,S2)' means "terminal symbol T lies between points S1 and S2 in the string". Thus the remaining rules translate into:

```
determiner(S0,S) :- connects(S0,every,S).
determiner(S0,S) :- connects(S0,a,S).
noun(S0,S) :- connects(S0,man,S).
noun(S0,S) :- connects(S0,woman,S).
name(S0,S) :- connects(S0,john,S).
name(S0,S) :- connects(S0,mary,S).
trans_verb(S0,S) :- connects(S0,loves,S).
intrans_verb(S0,S) :- connects(S0,lives,S).
```

The first clause, for instance, reads "there is a determiner from S0 to S if the word "every" lies between S0 and S".

Now, to represent a particular sentence to be recognised, say:

```
Every man that lives loves Mary .
  1    2    3    4     5    6   7
```

we tag the sentence with integers as shown, and translate it into the following set of unit clauses:

connects(1,every,2).
connects(2,man,3).
connects(3,that,4).
connects(4,lives,5).
connects(5,loves,6).
connects(6,mary,7).

Then to determine whether that sentence is grammatical, we try to prove the goal:

?- sentence(1,7).

The proof procedure used determines the parsing strategy, cf. Kowalski (1974b). This will be discussed further in Section 3.4 with particular reference to the Prolog proof procedure.

We may now notice that the representation of a context-free grammar by clauses is *data-independent*, in the sense that the actual representation of the string to be parsed is not "known" by the clauses—only the predicate 'connects' and the goal to be proved take it into account. If we tag a point in a string, not by an integer, but instead by the list of symbols occurring after that point in the string, it is no longer necessary to provide a separate 'connects' clause for each symbol in the string. Instead we can *define* the 'connects' predicate in a single, general clause:

connects([W | S],W,S).

which can be read as "The string position labelled by the list with head W and tail S is connected by symbol W to the string position labelled S". The goal of proving the original sentence grammatical is now expressed as:

?- sentence([every,man,that,lives,loves,mary],[]).

Depending on the proof procedure, one representation or the other may be preferred, for efficiency reasons. In the case of Prolog, the proofs with the two representations will be essentially the same, with integer tags substituted by final segments of the input string.

Note that in cases where the second representation is used, it is possible to execute, or "preprocess", all the calls to 'connects' at "compile-time", thereby dispensing with any need to refer to the predicate at "run-time". For example, preprocessing in this way the clause:

rel_clause(S0,S) :- connects(S0,that,S1), verb_phrase(S1,S).

we get:

rel_clause([that | S1],S) :- verb_phrase(S1,S).

Note that in Colmerauer (1975), grammar rules are directly identified with definite clauses of this preprocessed form, and there is therefore no mention of the 'connects' predicate.

The foregoing discussion allows us to identify context-free rules with definite clauses of a certain form. A context-free grammar is thus identified with a set of such clauses.

3.2. Definite clause grammars

We now generalise context-free grammars, in a way that will maintain the correspondence with definite clauses, to obtain the formalism of definite clause grammars.

3.2.1. *Notation*

The notation for DCGs extends our notation for context-free grammars in the following way:

(1) **Non-terminals** are allowed to be compound terms in addition to the simple atoms allowed in the context-free case, e.g.

np(X,S) sentence(S)

(2) In the right-hand side of a rule, in addition to non-terminals and lists of terminals, there may also be sequences of **procedure calls**, written within the brackets '{' and '}'. These are used to express extra conditions which must be satisfied for the rule to be valid, e.g.,

noun(N) → [W], {rootform(W,N), is_noun(N)}.

The last example can be read as "a phrase identified as the noun N may consist of the single word W, where N is the root form of W and N is a noun".

Non-terminals, terminals and procedure calls in the right-hand side of a rule will be referred to collectively as **goals**.

3.2.2. *The meaning of the DCG notation as definite clauses*

A rule of a DCG is again no more than "syntactic sugar" for a certain kind of definite clause. Terminal symbols are translated exactly as before; a non-terminal of arity N translates into an N + 2 place predicate (having the same name), whose first N arguments are those explicit in the non-terminal and whose last two arguments are as in the translation of a context-free non-terminal; procedure calls in the right-hand side of a rule are simply translated as themselves. For example, the rule:

noun(N) → [W], {rootform(W,N), is_noun(N)}

represents the clause:

noun(N,S0,S) :- connects(S0,W,S), rootform(W,N), is_noun(N).

3.3. The use of definite clause grammars

We now discuss how the DCG formalism provides for three important mechanisms in language analysis, namely the building of structures (such as parse trees), the imposing of extra conditions on the constituents of a phrase, and a general treatment of context dependency.

3.3.1. Building structures

The extra arguments of non-terminals provide the means of building structure in grammar rules. As non-terminals are "expanded", by matching against grammar rules, structures are progressively built up in the course of the unification process.

Here we just present a simple example. The context-free grammar of Section 3.1 is modified to produce explicitly for each phrase an interpretation which is simply its parse tree. We also take the opportunity of introducing a more compact, and (as we shall see later) more efficient, way of representing the dictionary, i.e., the rules defining those non-terminals which correspond to word classes (or parts of speech). In general, instead of having a rule of the form:

category(arguments) → [word].

for each word in the class category, we write a general rule:

category(arguments) → [W], {cat(W, arguments)}.

and define a "dictionary procedure" cat consisting of clauses of the form:

cat(word, arguments).

for each word in category.

The rules for the modified example are:

sentence(s(NP,VP)) → noun_phrase(NP), verb_phrase(VP).
noun_phrase(np(Det,Noun,Rel)) → determiner(Det), noun(Noun), rel_clause(Rel).
noun_phrase(np(Name)) → name(Name).
verb_phrase(vp(TV,NP)) → trans_verb(TV), noun_phrase(NP).
verb_phrase(vp(IV)) → intrans_verb(IV).
rel_clause(rel(that,VP)) → [that], verb_phrase(VP).
rel_clause(rel(nil)) → [].

determiner(det(W)) → [W], {is_determiner(W)}.
noun(n(W)) → [W], {is_noun(W)}.
name(name(W)) → [W], {is_name(W)}.
trans_verb(tv(W)) → [W], {is_trans(W)}.
intrans_verb(iv(W)) → [W], {is_intrans(W)}.

We read an augmented non-terminal such as 'noun-phrase(NP)' as "a noun phrase with interpretation NP". Thus the first rule is read as "A sentence with interpretation s(NP,VP) may consist of a noun phrase with interpretation NP followed by a verb phrase with interpretation VP". Examples of clauses from the associated dictionary are:

is_determiner(every).
is_noun(man).
is_name(mary).
is_trans(loves).
is_intrans(lives).

The analysis of the sentence "Every man loves Mary" with these rules produces the following parse tree:

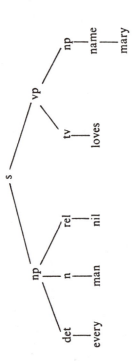

i.e., it follows from the declarative semantics of definite clauses that:

sentence(theta,[every,man,loves,mary],[])

is a true term, where **theta** is the term depicted above.

3.3.2. Extra conditions

The use of explicit procedure calls in the body of a rule to restrict the constituents accepted, is illustrated by the following rule:

date(D,M) → month(M), [D], {integer(D), 0 < D, D < 32}.

We can read this rule as "A phrase representing the date day D of month M may be written as a phrase representing the month M followed by a symbol D, where D is an integer greater than 0 and less than 32".

3.3.3. Context dependency

The arguments of non-terminals in a DCG can be used not only to build structures but also to carry and test contextual information. For instance, we can modify the example of Section 3.3.1 to handle the "number" agreement (singular or plural) required between certain determiners, nouns and verbs. The modified grammar will accept sentences such as "Every man loves some girl" and "All men like girls", but will reject an ungrammatical sentence such as "All men that lives love a woman". To handle the number agreement, certain non-terminals will have an extra argument which can take the values 'singular' or 'plural'; the dictionary predicates will have the "number" argument and also an argument to return the root form of a word. The modified rules are:

sentence(s(NP,VP)) →
    noun_phrase(N,NP), verb_phrase(N,VP).
noun_phrase(N, np(Det,Noun,Rel)) →
    determiner(N,Det), noun(N,Noun), rel_clause(N,Rel).

noun_phrase(singular, np(Name)) → name(Name).
verb_phrase(N, vp(TV,NP)) →
    trans_verb(N,TV), noun_phrase(N1,NP).
verb_phrase(N, vp(IV)) → intrans_verb(N,IV).
rel_clause(N, rel(that,VP)) → [that], verb_phrase(N,VP).
rel_clause(N, rel(nil)) → [].

determiner(N, det(W)) → [W], {is_determiner(W,N)}.
determiner(plural, det(nil)) → [].
noun(N, n(Root)) → [W], {is_noun(W,N,Root)}.
name(name(W)) → [W], {is_name(W)}.
trans_verb(N, tv(Root)) → [W], {is_trans(W,N,Root)}.
intrans_verb(N, iv(Root)) → [W], {is_intrans(W,N,Root)}.

Examples of clauses from the associated dictionary are:

is_determiner(every,singular).
is_determiner(all,plural).
is-noun(man,singular,man).
is_noun(men,plural,man).
is_name(mary).
is_trans(likes,singular,like).
is_trans(like,plural,like).
is_intrans(live,plural,live).

3.4. How DCGs are executed by Prolog

So far, we have been discussing DCGs from a *declarative* point of view. To understand a DCG, this is perfectly adequate—for since the DCG is no more than a set of definite clauses, its meaning is independent of any execution mechanism. However, as we have already noted, each proof procedure for definite clauses corresponds to a different parsing strategy for DCGs. We now discuss what this means in the case of the Prolog proof procedure.

From the procedural semantics of Prolog, it follows that, to parse a sentence, the grammar rules are used top-down, one at a time, and that goals in a rule are executed from left to right (i.e. the sentence is parsed from left to right). If there are alternative rules at any point, backtracking will eventually return to them. It is up to the grammar writer to formulate the grammar in such a way that the same work is not repeated unnecessarily on different backtracking alternatives. In practice this is not too difficult for languages intended to be read from left to right, although it often makes the grammar less readable than it would otherwise have been. All the work of the analysis is done by the same uniform mechanism (the Prolog proof procedure) and, in current Prolog implementations, the back-tracking is performed very efficiently.

To show how Prolog executes a DCG, and in particular the backtracking and the pattern matching, we will now describe the main steps in parsing the "garden path" sentence:

That man that whistles tunes pianos .
 1   2   3   4   5   6   7

according to the DCG in the previous section, with a dictionary including the following clauses:

is_determiner(that,singular).
is_noun(man,singular,man).
is_noun(men,plural,man).
is_noun(pianos, plural,piano).
is_noun(tunes,plural,tune).
is_trans(whistles,singular,whistle).
is_trans(tunes,singular,tune).
is_intrans(whistles,singular,whistle).

For greater readability, we will here write Prolog goals coming from DCG non-terminals or terminals in the form:

symbol from **point1** to **point2**

where **symbol** is a non-terminal or list of terminals and **point1**, **point2** are positions in the input string, as labelled above.
The initial goal is:

sentence(S)   from 1 to 7

This matches the single rule for 'sentence', creating the instantiation:

S = s(NP,VP).

and the goals:

noun_phrase(N,NP)   from 1 to P1,
verb_phrase(N,VP)   from P1 to 7,

Prolog next matches the first of those goals against the first rule for 'noun_phrase', producing the instantiation:

NP = np(Det,Noun,Rel).

and the goals:

determiner(N,Det)   from 1 to P2,
noun(N,Noun)   from P2 to P3,
rel_clause(N,Rel)   from P3 to P1,

Now the first of these goals expands into two subgoals:

[W] from 1 to P2
is_determiner(W,N)

both of which succeed immediately, since the word at position 1 in the string is "that" and because the dictionary contains the clause:

    is_determiner(that,singular).

The solution to the 'determiner' goal is therefore:

    determiner(singular, det(that)) from 1 to 2

Prolog now proceeds to the goal for 'noun', which is currently instantiated to:

    noun(singular,Noun) from 2 to P3

This succeeds in a manner similar to the goal for 'determiner', with solution:

    noun(singular, n(man)) from 2 to 3

Note that, had the word at position 2 been "men" instead of "man", the goal would not have succeeded, since no match would be found for the intermediate subgoal:

    is_noun(men,singular,Root)

Prolog now proceeds to match the 'rel_clause' goal against the first rule for 'rel_clause' yielding the new goals:

    [that]   from 3 to P4,
    verb_phrase(singular,VP1)   from P4 to P1,

The first of these goals succeeds trivially, with:

    P4 = 4

and the second matches the first rule for 'verb_phrase', producing the subgoals:

    trans_verb(singular,TV)   from 4 to P5,
    noun_phrase(M,NP1)   from P5 to P1,

Both subgoals eventually succeed, with solutions:

    trans_verb(singular, tv(whistle))   from 4 to 5
    noun_phrase(plural,
      np(det(nil),n(tune),rel(nil)))   from 5 to 6

where the second solution is obtained via a match against the first rule for 'noun_phrase'.

We have now obtained a solution to the original 'noun_phrase' goal, corresponding to the phrase "that man that whistles tunes". The next goal to be executed, which comes from the original activation of the rule for 'sentence', is:

    verb_phrase(singular,VP)   from 6 to 7.

(Now remember that the word at position 6 is "pianos"). Matching this goal against the first rule for 'verb_phrase' leads to the goal:

    trans_verb(singular,TV1)   from 6 to P6,

which cannot succeed, because "pianos" is not a 'trans_verb'. In the same way, the second rule for 'verb_phrase' fails, because "pianos" is not an 'intrans_verb'. At this point, Prolog backtracks to the most recent goal for which there is still an alternative rule available, namely:

    noun_phrase(M,NP1)   from 5 to P1

This goal is now matched against the second rule for 'noun_phrase', leading to the goal:

    name(Name)   from 5 to P1

which fails because the word at position 5, "tunes", is not a 'name'. Backtracking again, the most recent choice is the use of the first rule for 'verb_phrase' to match the goal:

    verb_phrase(singular,VP1)   from 4 to P1

So, this goal is now matched against the second rule for 'verb_phrase', producing eventually the solution:

    verb_phrase(singular, iv(whistle))   from 4 to 5

We have now found a second solution to the original 'noun_phrase' goal, corresponding to the phrase "that man that whistles". The only goal still pending is the second goal from the original activation of the rule for 'sentence'. This goal is currently instantiated to:

    verb_phrase(singular,VP)   from 5 to 7.

Execution of the goal this time succeeds, producing the result:

    verb_phrase(singular, vp(tv(tune),np(det(nil),n(piano),rel(nil)))   from 5 to 7

thus completing the parsing. Putting together the various instantiations, we obtain, as result S, the structure depicted below:

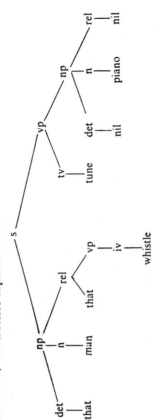

3.5. The role of the logical variable in DCGs

The feature of logic programs which we have called the "logical variable" makes DCGs a very powerful formalism for implementing practical language analysers.

chosen to illustrate how naturally and concisely one can express complex structure building in a DCG. We leave to the reader the detailed analysis of the example.

The DCG is again an extension of our original context-free example. It formalises the mapping between English and formulae of classical logic which is usually outlined in introductory logic textbooks. For example, the term constructed as the representation of the sentence:

Every man that lives loves a woman.

will be:

$$all(X) : (man(X) \ \& \ lives(X) \Rightarrow exists(Y) : (woman(Y) \ \& \ loves(X,Y)))$$

(where ':', '&' and '⇒' are binary functors written as infix operators). Notice how different the structure of this term is from that of the corresponding parse tree, i.e., compare:

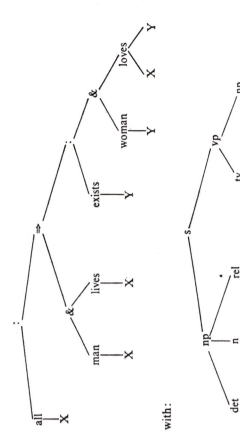

with:

The DCG follows. To avoid details not essential to the purpose of the example, we have not introduced auxiliary predicates for the dictionary.

sentence(P) → noun_phrase(X,P1,P), verb_phrase(X,P1).

noun_phrase(X,P1,P) →
    determiner(X,P2,P1,P), noun(X,P3), rel_clause(X,P3,P2).
noun_phrase(X,P,P) → name(X).

Structures can be built piecemeal, leaving unspecified parts as variables. The structure can be passed around, and be completed as the parsing proceeds. When the fragments needed are available, the "holes" in the structure represented by variables are filled by unification. Thus it is easy to build terms with structures which do not parallel the parse tree. We illustrate this first with a very simple example, and then in the following section give a much deeper example.

For the first example, we want to recognise sentences comprising a verb 'precedes' or 'follows', and names of months, e.g., "May follows April". The interpretation given to a sentence of this type will be a term of the form "before(M1,M2)". For instance, the interpretation of "May follows April" will be "before(april,may)". The context-free grammar for this example is given by the rules:

sentence → month,verb,month.

verb → [precedes].
verb → [follows].

month → [january].
month → [february].
    etc.

To construct the required interpretation, we give the non-terminals extra arguments as follows:

sentence(S) → month(M1),verb(M1,M2,S),month(M2).

verb(M1,M2,before(M1,M2)) → [precedes].
verb(M1,M2,before(M2,M1)) → [follows].

month(january) → [january].
month(february) → [february].
    etc.

We read the non-terminal 'verb(M1,M2,S)' as "a verb whose interpretation, in the context of a subject M1 and object M2, is S".

Notice that, in general, it is not necessary that the first two arguments of 'verb' be known when the proof procedure builds the third argument during the execution of a rule for 'verb'. That is, the relationship between the arguments of a non-terminal is defined independently of any particular order of executing the rules.

Running the example with Prolog, the parsing proceeds from left to right, so in the first rule, the structure S is built before one of its components, M2, is known. This component gets filled in later during the parsing of the rest of the sentence. Note that it is cumbersome and less natural to postpone the building of the structure S until M2 is known, i.e., until the end of the rule for 'sentence', since the form of S depends crucially on the nature of the verb.

3.6. A more sophisticated example

The more sophisticated example of the logical variable in this section has been

4. How to Translate ATNs into DCGs

The purpose of this section is to explain to the ATN-minded reader how an ATN can be translated into a DCG describing the same language and producing the same analysis in essentially the same way. We do not attempt to give a definitive algorithm, as there is always room for ingenuity in producing a good DCG translation. Rather, we indicate the basic ideas underlying the translation process. We take (Bates, 1978) as the definitive reference on ATNs.

4.1. Decomposing the network

A **simple** transition network, i.e., a network without cycles and with a single start and end node, can be directly translated as follows:

(1) the simple network corresponds to a non-terminal;

(2) each distinct path from the start node to the end node translates into a distinct rule for that non-terminal;

(3) the body of each rule is a translation, in order, of the arcs which make up the corresponding path.

Now in general a network has cycles. But it is clear that any network is equivalent to a set of simple networks connected by PUSHes and POPs, what we shall call a **decomposition**. To illustrate all this, we now show how an *unaugmented* transition

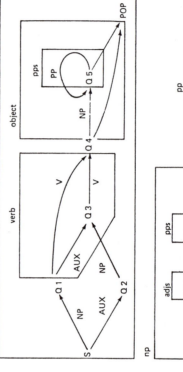
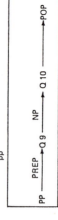
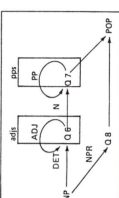

Fig. 1.

verb_phrase(X,P) → trans_verb(X,Y,P1), noun_phrase(Y,P1,P).
verb_phrase(X,P) → intrans_verb(X,P).

rel_clause(X,P1,P1 & P2) → [that], verb_phrase(X,P2).
rel_clause(X,P,P) → [].

determiner(X,P1,P2, all(X) : (P1 ⇒ P2)) → [every].
determiner(X,P1,P2, exists(X) : (P1 & P2)) → [a].

noun(X, man(X)) → [man].
noun(X, woman(X)) → [woman].

name(john) → [john].

trans_verb(X,Y, loves(X,Y)) → [loves].
intrans_verb(X, lives(X)) → [lives].

Each non-terminal has one or more arguments. The last argument gives the interpretation of the corresponding phrase. This interpretation in general depends on other items, as specified by the preceding arguments of the non-terminal. For example, the word "loves" has the interpretation 'loves(X,Y)', which depends on individuals X and Y. A more complex case is the word "every", which has the interpretation:

all(X) : (P1 ⇒ P2)

in the context of two properties P1 and P2 of an individual X. (The property P1 will correspond to the rest of the noun phrase containing the word "every", and the property P2 will come from the rest of the sentence). Observe that the non-terminal for a noun phrase takes the form 'noun_phrase(X,P1,P)', i.e., the interpretation P of the noun phrase will depend on a property P1 of an individual X. This is because in general a noun phrase contains a determiner such as "every". For example, the interpretation of the noun phrase "every man" will be:

all(X) : man(X) ⇒ P1.

The second rule for 'noun_phrase' tells us the interpretation of a noun phrase which consists solely of a name, or "proper noun", e.g., "John". We see that this interpretation, in the context of a property P of some individual X, is simply P itself, provided the individual X is that named by the proper noun (e.g., 'john').

The reader familiar with Montague's (1973) work, will note the similarity of this analysis to Montague's treatment.

Executing this DCG with Prolog brings into play the full power of the logical variable. For the order in which phrases are parsed is such that some parts of the translation of a phrase are not available when that translation is built. For example the interpretation P of a sentence is produced by its subject noun phrase, and, naturally, this interpretation P will also depend on the (as yet unknown) interpretation of the verb phrase which completes the sentence. Such unknown items are left as variables to be filled in later.

adjs → adj, adjs.
adjs → [].
pps → pp, pps.
pps → [].
pp → prep, np.

Note that the V arc from Q3 to Q4 has been translated into two separate occurrences of 'v', in the second and fourth rules.

Not all decompositions lead to equally concise translations. In general, a more concise translation is obtained if each simple network obeys a **minimality constraint**, that the different paths through the network only meet at the start and end nodes. The decomposition shown above roughly accords with this principle.

4.2. Translating the arcs

We will assume that the Lisp test in an arc is translated into a goal, **test**, and the Lisp actions into a sequence of goals, **actions**. Each arc type is then translated as follows in the body of a rule:

```
(CAT category ...)      [W], {test, category(W), actions},
(WRD word ...)          [word], {test, actions},
(MEM list ...)          [W], {test, in(W,list), actions},
(TST ...)               [W], {test, actions},
(JUMP ...)              {test, actions},
(PUSH subnetwork ...)   {test}, subnetwork, {actions},
(POP ...)               {test, actions}.
```

Of course, in cases where the original test or actions are empty, the corresponding goals can be completely omitted from the DCG version. The predicate 'in(X,L)' tests whether X is a member of the list L. Note that these translations are incomplete, as no attention is paid to argument passing in PUSH arcs (SENDRs) and return values in POP arcs. This will be discussed later.

The VIR arc and its associated HOLD action do not have a straightforward translation, and their special-purpose effect must be achieved in DCGs with some of the general purpose mechanisms available. The chief purpose of HOLD and VIR is to handle what transformational grammarians call **constituent extraposition**, that is the phenomenon where a constituent occurs in the "surface" sentence outside the phrase to which it belongs in the "deep structure". A general and powerful means for treating constituent extraposition is provided by an extension of DCGs, called "extraposition grammars" (Pereira, 1979). However, an alternative solution is available in DCGs, through the use of extra arguments to carry the extraposed constituents. A technique directly analogous to this second approach is discussed by Woods (1973) to avoid VIR/HOLD in ATNs, and has been used in situations where parsing cannot proceed from left to right (Bates, 1975; Woods et al., 1976). We shall therefore not go into further detail.

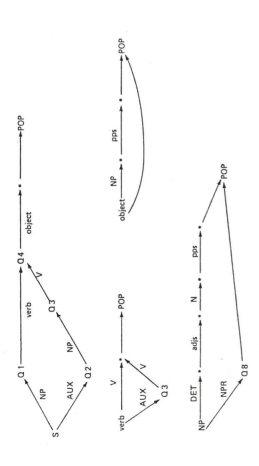
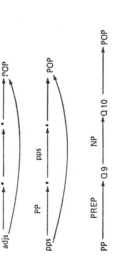

FIG. 2.

network (taken from Woods (1970)) translates into a DCG which is simply a CFG. The network is shown in Fig. 1, where the boxes identify a decomposition into the simple networks of Fig. 2 (where anonymous nodes are labelled by '*'). These in turn translate into the following rules:

s → np, verb, object.
s → aux, np, v, object.

verb → v.
verb → aux, v.

object → np, pps.
object → [].

np → det, adjs, n, pps.
np → npr.

4.3. Treatment of registers, tests and actions

All tests and actions on an arc act upon values kept in **registers**. Now the concept of a register, i.e. a named updatable location where a value can be assigned to or retrieved from, does not exist in logic programming — instead **values** are passed or built in **variables**, where a variable is a local name for a value used in a particular clause, rather than an assignable location. The effects achieved in ATNs using registers are obtained in DCGs through the use of variables. The values of the variables get filled in by the pattern matching which takes place when a goal or non-terminal is executed. Therefore, non-terminals in the translation of an ATN must be augmented with extra arguments, to make use of the pattern matching.

Each non-terminal has at least one argument, which represents the structure returned by the corresponding simple network. This is usually written as the last argument of that non-terminal, and we shall always follow this convention.

For each register of a simple network which is set by a SENDR in some PUSH for that network, there must be a further ("input") argument in the non-terminal representing that network. In the same way, each value sent back to the calling network by a LIFTR in the called network corresponds to an ("output") argument in the non-terminal for the called network.

The case of PUSH arcs which were not in the original network, but which arise from its decomposition, is treated as if there were a SENDR for each original network register used in the simple network PUSHed for, and a LIFTR for each original network register which is changed in the invoked network. (And, in the case of a subnetwork introduced by the decomposition, there need be no argument for a return value.)

For a simple network, each register used in a path from the start node to a POP arc is translated into as many variables as the register takes different values in that path. (Usually we name these variables with variants of the name of the corresponding register.)

The value returned at the POP exit of a path in a simple network is just filled into the return value argument of the head of the rule for that path.

BUILDQs are translated in a straightforward and much simpler fashion as terms containing variables corresponding to register values.

The foregoing discussion is better illustrated by a small example. This example is a simplification of the network in Appendix 1 (taken from Woods, 1970). The network covers simple declarative sentences in active and passive form. We depict the network with the arcs labelled by integers, followed by the details of each arc:

```
1: (PUSH NP T
    (SETR SUBJ *))
2: (CAT V T
    (SETR V *))
3: (CAT V (AND (GETF * PPRT)
    (EQ (GETR V) (QUOTE BE)))
    (SETR OBJ (GETR SUBJ))
    (SETR SUBJ (BUILDQ (NP (PRO (SOMEONE))))
    (SETR V *)
    (SETR AGFLAG T))
4: (PUSH NP T
    (SETR OBJ *))
5: (WRD BY (GETR AGFLAG))
6: (POP (BUILDQ (S + (VP (V+) +))
                SUBJ V OBJ)
    T)
7: (PUSH NP T
    (SETR SUBJ *))
8: (POP (BUILDQ (S + (VP (V+) +))
                SUBJ V OBJ)
    T)
```

The context-free rules corresponding to a decomposition of the network are as follows (where 'aN' stands for the translation of arc N):

s → a1,a2,rest_verb,agent.

rest_verb → a3.
rest_verb → a4.

agent → a5,a7.
agent → [].

We now add arguments to the non-terminals in these rules in the way described above, and insert the translation of tests and actions. Tests and actions will be translated whenever possible via by pattern matching in the head of a rule, rather than by actual goals in the body of a rule. The dictionary predicate 'v' resulting from the CAT arcs has two extra arguments, to return the root form of the verb and the tense feature to be used in the GETF test in arc 3. Here are the augmented rules:

s(R) →
    np(Subj0),
    [V], { v(V,V0,Tense) },
    rest_verb(Subj0,V0,Subj1,V1,Obj,Agflag),
    agent(Subj1,V1,Obj,Agflag,R).

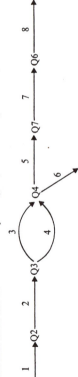

```
rest_verb(Subj0,be, np(pro(someone)),V1,Subj0,t) →
  [V], { v(V,V1,pprt) }.
rest_verb(Subj,V,Subj,V,Obj,f) → np(Obj).
agent(Subj0,V,Obj,t, s(Subj1,vp(v(V),Obj)) ) →
  [by],
  np(Subj1).
agent(Subj,V,Obj,Agflag, s(Subj,vp(v(V),Obj)) ) → [].
```

5. The Advantages of DCGs

Woods (1970) discusses the advantages of the ATN formalism under six headings covering, in our view, just five essentially distinct criteria:

Woods's headings	essential criteria
1. Perspicuity	1. Perspicuity
2. Generative Power	2. Power and Generality
3. Efficiency of Representation	3. Conciseness
4. Capturing Regularities	ditto
5. Efficiency of Operation	4. Efficiency
6. Flexibility for Experimentation	5. Flexibility

We argue that, on each of these criteria, and on one extra criterion of our own (6. Suitability for Theoretical Work), DCGs rate at least as highly as ATNs, and that in several respects DCGs represent a significant advance.

5.1. Perspicuity

Practical systems for natural language analysis are necessarily large and complex, and, for the time being at least, writing them is very much an experimental activity. Therefore perspicuity—desirable in any formalism—is particularly important here. The subjective quality of being easy to understand takes on a more objective form—how much real time and effort does it take to modify and extend the system?

Perspicuity is the area where we think DCGs show the most marked improvement over ATNs.

The main reason is that DCGs can be understood in a way which is qualitatively different from the way one understands an ATN. Like an ATN, a DCG can be understood as a *machine* for analysing a particular language. However, unlike an ATN, a DCG can also be understood as a *description* of a language. DCGs share this property with CFGs. As Woods puts it (referring to CFGs), "by looking at a rule, the consequences of that rule for the types of construction that are permitted are immediately apparent".

This can be accounted for informally by noting that it is a straightforward mechanical process to translate each rule of a DCG (or CFG) into a statement of ordinary English, given a glossary of all the symbols (i.e., functors) used in the grammar. The resulting English statements describe what forms are permissible for the phrases which make up the object language in question. We have given examples of this informal translation in our discussion of DCGs. Note that a DCG is unlikely to be readily comprehensible without such a glossary, or some equivalent explanation of the meaning of each symbol and the purpose of its arguments. However, a good choice of names for functors and variables can do much to suggest the intended interpretation.

The immediacy of the relationship between a DCG and the language it describes can also be given a completely formal explication in terms of the declarative semantics of definite clauses. We have previously discussed how a DCG can be identified with a set of definite clauses. The declarative semantics allows us to further identify this set of definite clauses with a (probably infinite) set of "true terms". Each one of these true terms specifies that a certain phrase of the object language occurs between certain points in a certain string. The set of true terms as a whole amounts to an enumeration of all possible occurrences of all possible phrases of the object language. Note that nowhere does this explication involve any notion of *executing* a DCG.

An ATN shares none of the foregoing properties of a DCG. To explain formally how an ATN defines a language seems necessarily to involve the notion of how an ATN is executed. Certainly this is the way ATNs are always explained informally in the literature—see for instance Bates (1978), Section 2, and contrast this with the way we introduce DCGs. Conceptually at least, an ATN is no more than a particular mechanism for parsing a language top-down, left-to-right, and the sequencing imposed by this parsing strategy is implicit in the way registers are operated on. Although it is possible (with ingenuity) to produce other kinds of parsers for ATNs, this requires a re-interpretation of the meaning of arc actions, and necessitates restrictions on register usage.

Bates (1978), in her introduction, claims that "one does not need to know how to program a computer in order to write or use an ATN". However, from the outset, her account of ATNs uses such computing jargon as "pushing the current computation onto a stack". Now although it might be possible to explain the PUSH arc in other terms to non-programmers, it is hard to see how the function of ATN registers could be explained other than by going into some basic computing concepts. Thus, despite Bates's claims to the contrary, it does seem that a knowledge of conventional programming is necessary to properly understand an ATN, whereas the declarative semantics of a DCG is genuinely independent of any notions specific to computing.

However, what we have been discussing so far is not the only aspect in which DCGs are clearer than ATNs. Even without their capability to be understood as language descriptions, and viewed simply as machines, DCGs are in many ways more perspicuous than ATNs.

One of the main reasons for this is that DCGs are more **modular**. The machinery of a DCG is made up of small components (clauses) which communicate only through explicitly passed arguments. There are no global variables—the scope of each variable is limited to a single clause. As a result, the behaviour of each clause in a DCG can be understood independently of any other. In an ATN, on the other hand, the smallest unit which can be isolated in this way is a subnetwork (i.e. a part of the network not connected to the rest except via PUSHes and POPs). No smaller unit can be isolated, since the scope of a register is an entire subnetwork. Now in practice (e.g. LUNAR), subnetworks tend to be very large, and contain too great a mass of detail to be readily assimilated in one piece.

A second factor making DCGs easier to understand is that there is no assignment, i.e. the value of a variable, once fixed, cannot change. No assignment means no side effects, and therefore no possibility of the various sources of confusion which stem from unforseen side effects. Happily, most ATNs actually published only use assignment in a restrained way, and are therefore relatively easy both to understand and to translate into a DCG. In effect, DCGs enforce (and extend) this good practice. It is also worth noting that the ATN writer would lose nothing (in terms of efficiency) by adopting a "single assignment" policy in the style of a DCG. For, given the way ATN register assignment has actually been implemented, it is just as efficient to assign each new value to a fresh register as to update the values of registers already assigned.

Another important feature of DCGs, which helps to make them much more readable than ATNs, is the use of pattern matching in place of explicit tests and BUILDQs. Pattern matching enables what are basically the same underlying operations to be specified in a more concise and "visual" way.

A further point contributing to the clarity of DCGs is that they consist of a single uniform formalism of maximum simplicity. In contrast, ATNs are a more elaborate mixture of two formalisms—transition networks and Lisp. Generally speaking, it does not make for easy comprehension to have a superabundance of ways of saying the same thing, as is the case in ATNs.

5.2. Power and generality

One judges the "power and generality" of a formalism by considering what can, and cannot, be expressed in the formalism—in both a theoretical and a practical sense.

Theoretically, both ATNs and DCGs have the power of a Turing machine, and in that sense are as general as can be. (The adequacy of definite clauses for programming any computable task, without "coding" of the data, is proved by Andreka and Nemeti (1976).)

Of more interest is the question of what tasks can *usefully* be programmed in the two systems. In this context, one of the key features of DCGs is that they provide an essentially more powerful mechanism for building structures than is available in ATNs.

In an ATN, it is impracticable to build structures which do not closely mirror the recursive analysis of the string produced by the PUSH/POP mechanism. This is because a POP arc can only return a single structure, and all of the subcomponents of this structure must be known at the time of the POP. In a DCG, on the other hand, a non-terminal may return more than one structure as its result, and these structures may contain variables which only later get a value. Thus the structure(s) generated in a DCG as the result of the analysis of a phrase may depend on items in the sentence which are **outside** the phrase concerned, and which may not yet have been encountered in the parsing. A good illustration of why this greater generality is useful is provided by the "Sophisticated Example" of Section 3.6.

To simulate such use of the "logical variable" in an ATN, one might be tempted to modify a previously generated structure using **rplaca** and **rplacd**. However, in current ATN implementations at least, this would produce an unwanted side effect on alternative branches of the parser's search space. The other way out would be to use a function such as **substitute**, which involves copying all the structure "above" the point to be modified. However the cost of this copying is likely to be unacceptable in practice.

DCGs are more general than ATNs in that they can be used in a wider variety of ways. This characteristic follows from the fundamental difference between DCGs and ATNs discussed under "Perspicuity", namely that an ATN is a particular machine for parsing a language top-down left-to-right, whereas a DCG is primarily a language description, neutral towards implementation. As a result, a DCG can be executed in a variety of different ways.

For example, Woods (1970) has discussed the question of whether ATNs can be used for *generation* as well as for recognition, i.e. given a "deep-structure", to generate the corresponding surface string(s), instead of the usual inverse process. Now to use an ATN for generation would involve substantial changes in interpretation of the operations labelling the arcs, and the feasibility of this reinterpretation is questionable, particularly if arbitrary Lisp code is involved in arc actions.

In contrast, it is perfectly feasible to program a generation process as a DCG without any change whatsoever to the DCG *formalism*. Moreover, the same proof procedure (e.g., in particular, Prolog) can be adequate for implementing both generation and recognition processes. It is even possible to use the same DCG for both kinds of task, although this will only be practicable in certain cases, and then only with careful design.

A generation problem is specified by presenting an initial goal of the form:

?- sentence(**structure**,S,[]).

where **structure** is a term representing a deep-structure. The result will be to instantiate S to a list representing the surface form of **structure**. Compare this with the usual recognition problem, which is specified in the form:

?- sentence(T,**string**,[]).

where **string** is a list representing the initial surface string, and T becomes instantiated to a corresponding deep structure.

If a DCG is to be used for generation, the only clause for the 'connects' predicate should be:

connects([W | S],W,S).

(and, as described earlier, all calls to 'connects' may be preprocessed away prior to execution). For an example of a generation task programmed as a DCG and executed by Prolog, see Chapter 4 of Colmerauer (1975).

We have been discussing an example of DCG generality where DCGs are used to formalise two quite different kinds of task—generation as well as recognition—using the same proof procedure, Prolog. Another case of DCG generality is that a variety of different processes for solving a given task (such as recognition) can be obtained from the same DCG, by applying different proof procedures to it. Thus the top-down left-to-right parsing entailed by using Prolog is by no means the only way to execute a DCG. Other proof procedures would give different parsing mechanisms (e.g., breadth-first, bottom-up). In particular, Earley's (1970) parsing algorithm can be generalised to give a complete proof procedure for definite clauses (Warren, 1975). Note, however, that a DCG which is efficient for execution by one proof procedure will not necessarily be efficient for another.

A final point concerning the generality of DCGs is that they are not in principle restricted to input consisting of a simple string of atomic symbols. The symbols can be generalised to arbitrary tree structures (possibly with variables) and, more interestingly, instead of a simple list of symbols one can have a "chart" (Kaplan, 1973) catering for alternatives in the input. For example, if part of the input string is:

```
... definite clause grammar ...
      1       2      3
                             4
```

and the lexical items 'definite', 'clause', 'grammar', 'definite_clause', and 'definite_clause_grammar' are in the dictionary, the following clauses for the 'connects' predicate would represent the possible lexical interpretations:

connects(1, definite, 2).
connects(1, definite_clause, 3).
connects(1, definite_clause_grammar, 4).
connects(2, clause, 3).
connects(3, grammar, 4).

5.3. Conciseness

In his discussion of "Efficiency of Representation" and "Capturing Regularities", Woods is really concerned with the conciseness of a formalism. This criterion is aptly summed up in his "economy principle"—that the best grammar is that which can characterise a language in the least number of symbols.

If, according to this principle, one compares the *textual* forms of equivalent ATNs and DCGs (counting each identifier as one symbol, and discounting punctuation symbols such as brackets and commas), one generally finds that DCGs are significantly smaller. Typically, the DCG is only around half the size of the ATN.

DCGs are more concise than ATNs for the same reasons that logic programs are in general more concise than programs in conventional languages. The main factor is the use of pattern matching instead of explicit operations for setting and testing registers and building structures.

As has been seen, DCGs are a natural generalisation of context-free grammars. Woods (1970) states that "a major advantage of the transition network model over the usual context-free grammar model is the ability to merge the common parts of many context-free rules, thus allowing greater efficiency of representation". Here Woods is claiming an advantage for the ATN formalism over CFGs, and his subsequent argument to support the claim clearly also applies when comparing ATNs with DCGs. However, we do not think that Woods's argument is correct. The ability to merge the common parts of many context-free rules is not unique to transition networks, but can be achieved without even going beyond the formalism of context-free rules. For example, the sample grammar which Woods uses to illustrate his argument:

s → np,vp.
s → q,np,vp.
s → neg,np,vp.
s → q,neg,np,vp.

is better re-expressed as:

s → q,s1.
s → s1.

s1 → neg,s2.
s1 → s2.

s2 → np,vp.

and this is not so very different from (and in fact it is far more concise than) the *textual* form of the transition network:

Q
S —→ S1 ⇄ S2 —NP→ S3 —VP→ S4
      NEG

i.e.,

```
(S
    (PUSH Q T (TO S1))
    (JUMP S1 T))
(S1
    (PUSH NEG T (TO S2))
    (JUMP S2 T))
(S2
    (PUSH NP T (TO S3)))
(S3
    (PUSH VP T (TO S4)))
(S4
    (POP NIL T))
```

If one allows, as we do, alternatives to be given in a rule, then the grammar reduces to a single rule, very close to the original regular expression:

$$s \rightarrow (q;[]),(neg;[]),np,vp.$$

Woods makes much of the ability in ATNs to merge similar parts of a network by recording and testing extra information in registers. There is a direct counterpart of this in DCGs, where similar rules can be coalesced by attaching extra arguments to non-terminals. Whereas Woods seems to favour such merging for ATNs, we think it encourages an intricate and low-level style of language description. Moreover it does not necessarily produce a more concise result. In the case of ATNs, for example, information which was previously explicit in the network is now encoded in Lisp as more complex tests and actions.

The modularity of DCGs encourages the grammar writer to keep separate what are conceptually distinct parts of the grammar, and not to indulge in merging of parts which are superficially similar.

5.4. Efficiency

The operational efficiency of a formalism for language analysis is a matter of crucial importance for applications, such as LUNAR, intended to be genuinely useful. Hence we discuss efficiency at length in this section.

First, let us recall that executing a DCG with Prolog gives a parsing mechanism which can be described as "top-down, left-to-right, depth-first (i.e. one alternative at a time)". Now this is precisely the parsing mechanism used in the majority of ATN applications. Moreover, it is the required mode of operation for recent ATN implementations (Burton and Woods, 1976; Finin and Hadden, 1977) which *compile* the ATN into low-level code (using Lisp as an intermediary). Accordingly, we shall restrict our discussion of efficiency to Prolog implementations of DCGs and to such comparable ATN implementations.

A key property of DCGs, as regards their efficiency, is that a DCG is expressed directly in a general purpose programming language, Prolog. Apart from optional "syntactic sugar", a DCG *is* a Prolog program. DCGs do not need a special interpreter or compiler. To discuss DCG efficiency, therefore, is to discuss Prolog efficiency.

Now Warren, Pereira and Pereira (1977) have described how Prolog can be compiled directly into efficient machine code. They put forward simple reasons why one might expect the speed of the code produced to be comparable with that for more conventional high-level languages, such as Lisp, and argue in particular that pattern matching encourages a better implementation of operations on structured data than the conventional use of selector and constructor functions (such as **car, cdr** and **cons**). A practical implementation exists for the DECsystem-10 machine and actual timing data (Warren, 1977a) supports these conclusions. On the basis of this evidence, one can therefore say that a DCG is expressed directly in a general purpose programming language which has an efficiency comparable with Lisp.

An ATN, on the other hand, needs a special interpreter or compiler. Since the ATN formalism relies so heavily on Lisp constructions for expressing tests etc., it is difficult to imagine an ATN compiler which did not generate Lisp code as an intermediary. Therefore it is probably fair to say that ATN efficiency is limited by, and necessarily somewhat inferior to, the efficiency of Lisp for writing grammars.

A disadvantage of ATNs, or at least of the implementations described, is that the system does not have immediate access to the value of a register—the GETR function has to search down an association list of register-value pairs. In Prolog implementations, on the other hand, each variable's value is stored at a known location. This is achieved without any overheads of copying information into or out of variable value cells at procedure call and exit (as happens, for example, in "shallow binding" implementations of Lisp).

The only significant overhead of this kind in Prolog is attributable to its non-determinacy. In certain circumstances when instantiating a variable, the variable's address is remembered on a push-down list, so that the variable can be reset to "uninstantiated" on backtracking. In the DECsystem-10 implementation, these operations are implemented very efficiently at the machine-code level, and only account for a small proportion of the time spent in a typical Prolog computation. Note that the non-determinacy of ATNs has to be achieved using what facilities are provided by the higher level language Lisp, which, unlike Prolog, does not itself incorporate any machinery for non-determinate computation.

A discussion in Warren et al. (1977) attributes much of Prolog's surprisingly competitive speed, compared with Lisp, to the use of "structure sharing" (Boyer and Moore, 1972; Warren, 1977a) to build new data structures. The argument applies a fortiori if we compare with the structure building operations of ATNs. Essentially structure sharing enables arbitrarily large data structures to be constructed with virtually no time cost. Constructing the new object merely involves bringing together two pointers. One is a pointer to a "skeleton" structure, created at compile-time, which corresponds to a term of the source program. The other pointer is to an already existing vector of value cells, called a "frame", which contains the values of variables occurring in the skeleton.

Now compare this one trivial operation with what is involved in the BUILDQ of ATNs. There, space for the new structure has to be allocated from Lisp's "heap" storage (and ultimately garbage-collected), and all the information corresponding to the skeleton structure and the values of its variables has to be copied over into the newly allocated space. It is interesting to note a comment by Woods (1973, p. 133), which, while acknowledging the inefficiencies of register access in ATNs, appears to foresee the advantages of structure sharing: "if the structure returned by the POP arc were merely the list of register contents themselves, then the process of searching for registers by names could be almost totally eliminated".

A feature of the DECsystem-10 Prolog implementation which can make a very significant contribution to the speed of operation of a DCG is the automatic indexing provided for the clauses of each predicate (Warren et al., 1977; Warren, 1977a). When trying to execute a goal, the relevant clauses from the corresponding predicate are accessed through a hash table keyed on the principal functor of the first argument of the goal. In suitable circumstances, the indexing provides for the immediate selection of an appropriate grammar rule from amongst a set of alternatives. This is instead of having to try all the alternatives one by one. A comparable facility does not appear to be available in ATN implementations. Incidentally, the same indexing makes it practicable to implement "dictionary" predicates as sets of unit clauses (cf. many of our examples), since the indexing ensures that the time to look up an individual word in the dictionary is (generally speaking) independent of the number of words in the dictionary.

To recapitulate, we have described a number of aspects in which (compiled) Prolog implementations of DCGs might be expected to be more efficient than current (compiled) ATN implementations:

(1) Compilation of a DCG is only a one stage process, and does not involve an intermediate high level language (Lisp).

(2) Access to variable values is immediate and the overheads attributable to non-determinacy are minimal.

(3) Structure building is done "on the fly", by "structure sharing", at almost no extra cost.

(4) Automatic indexing provides for the immediate selection of appropriate alternatives in the grammar.

Above all, a DCG is merely a particular kind of program in an efficient and general purpose programming language, whereas an ATN is a special purpose formalism.

The decisive test of efficiency is, of course, to compare actual performance data. For the comparison to be meaningful, one must compare equivalent grammars, expressed in equivalent ways, building equivalent structures. The difficulty here is that none of the ATNs for which times have been quoted in the literature has actually been listed in full detail, and these ATNs are in any case unnecessarily big for the purpose simply of making an exact comparison with an equivalent DCG.

Our experience with DCGs, which probably applies equally to ATNs, is that the speed of a grammar depends predominantly on whether the grammar writer chooses to aim at efficiency, or at maximal conciseness and simplicity. The physical size of the grammar (number of rules, or arcs, say) is not, alone, a reliable indicator of the likely parsing times.

In Appendix 2, we give some timing figures for a DCG translation of an early specimen ATN, given by Woods (1970), and also data for a DCG of some complexity covering a sizable subset of English. For what it is worth, bearing in mind our previous remarks: this latter DCG running on a DEC KI10 takes approximately 8 msec. per word to parse an English sentence, while figures quoted for a compiled version of LUNAR on a KA10 (generally reckoned to be only half as fast as a KI10) are of the order of 34 msec. per word on superficially similar sentences.

5.5. Flexibility

In providing a framework for language analysis, a formalism should not be so restrictive that it prevents experimentation with new and diverging ideas. Necessary flexibility of this kind is available in ATNs by virtue of the open-ended use which can be made of Lisp—to build diverse structures, to express special conditions on arcs, etc.

In an exactly analogous way, DCGs have access to the full power of the definite clause subset of logic as a general purpose programming language. As in ATNs, there is wide scope for building different kinds of structures to represent the result of the analysis. Also, by using explicit calls to separately defined procedures, one may easily incorporate into the grammar arbitrarily complex tests, and these tests may depend on auxiliary information passed as extra arguments to non-terminals. As mentioned previously, within the basic DCG formalism one can simulate the effects of special purpose ATN facilities such as the "hold list".

The DCG formalism is more flexible than ATNs in that, as previously discussed, it is in no way tied to a particular parsing or execution mechanism (although the style in which the grammar is written will usually be optimised towards some particular parsing mechanism). Thus writing a grammar as a DCG makes it much easier to experiment with radically different parsing strategies, such as were tried out in the BBN Speech Understanding System (Woods et al., 1976).

5.6. Suitability for theoretical work

In this section we argue that, unlike ATNs, DCGs can also be a useful formalism for theoretical studies of language, and that, as a consequence, they potentially provide a bridge between the work of theoretical linguists and philosophers, such as Chomsky and Montague, and the work of those, such as Woods, concerned with engineering practical natural language systems. To fully justify these claims would call for another paper, so here we merely outline the key points of the argument.

The theorists have (properly) concentrated on describing *what* natural language is, in a clear and elegant way. In this context, details of *how* natural language is actually recognised or generated need not be relevant, and indeed should probably not be allowed to obscure the language definition. This concern with the "what" rather than the "how" of language analysis is reflected in the kinds of formalism developed by the theorists. At the time ATNs were developed, it was not clear how such formalisms could be used as a basis for practical systems to actually carry out language analysis, and the need to achieve workable systems necessitated the more machine-oriented formalism of ATNs.

In consequence, the ATN formalism is fundamentally different from any used in theoretical work. As has already been discussed under "Perspicuity", an ATN is a description of a *process* for recognising a language, rather than a description of the language itself. A symptom of the ATN's process orientation is the use of the assignment operation—a concept virtually unknown outside computing, and one which does not naturally enter into formal descriptions in mathematics or other fields. For these reasons, the ATN formalism is not really suitable for theoretical purposes (except in so far as it is more precise than other semi-formal methods for describing language).

Because of this major difference between the ATN formalism and those normally used by theorists, it has been difficult for the ATN writer to draw directly on theoretical work, and difficult for the outsider to relate what is going on inside an ATN with the kind of language analysis proposed by theorists.

In the years since ATNs were developed, the discovery that logic can be used as a programming language has given us a formalism, DCGs, which can serve both as a description of a language, and, by virtue of the procedural interpretation of logic, as a description of a process for analysing that language. For practical purposes, DCGs, while being less overtly machine-oriented than ATNs, can nevertheless be implemented as efficiently and are a powerful tool for implementing working natural language systems. Furthermore, DCGs seem eminently suitable as a formalism for theoretical work—they are a natural and sufficiently powerful generalisation of CFGs, and they have a clear declarative semantics independent of any execution mechanism. Unlike ATNs, DCGs do not incorporate the concept of assignment.

Indeed it could be argued that DCGs are more suitable as a formalism for theoretical purposes than those in current use. It appears that current theoretical formalisms are either less powerful than DCGs, or else, through being biased towards the process of language generation, incorporate unnecessary notions of execution order.

6. Conclusion

On both practical and philosophical grounds, we believe DCGs represent a significant advance over ATNs.

Considered as practical tools for implementing language analysers, DCGs are in a real sense more powerful than ATNs, since, in a DCG, the structure returned from the analysis of a phrase may depend on items which have not yet been encountered in the course of parsing the sentence. Such use of the power of the "logical variable" is well illustrated by the "Sophisticated Example" of Section 3.6, which we do not believe can be directly mimicked in an ATN.

Also on the practical side, the greater clarity and modularity of DCGs is a vital aid in the actual development of systems of the size and complexity necessary for real natural language analysis. Because the DCG consists of small independent rules with a declarative reading, it is much easier to extend the system with new linguistic constructions, or to modify the kind of structures which are built. Our own experience of just these kinds of problems came from adapting a natural language system written by Veronica Dahl (cf. Appendix 2). The modifications involved substituting English for Spanish as the discourse language, and completely changing the domain of discourse. We found it quite straightforward to make these substantial alterations, and doubt whether this would have been so, had the system not been implemented as a DCG.

Finally, on the philosophical side, DCGs are significant because they potentially provide a common formalism for theoretical work and for writing efficient natural language systems. Note that we are NOT claiming that a DCG formulated as a clear theoretical description of a language is likely to be suitable for execution as a practical language analyser. We have argued only that a common formalism is feasible for both. Normally a substantial transformation would be necessary to turn a DCG conceived as a theoretical description of a language into a practical implementation. It is an interesting problem for future research to see whether such transformations can be performed systematically, possibly by generalising known results on parsing with context-free grammars.

Appendix 1. A Full Example

The ATN from Woods (1970), as amended in Burton and Woods (1976), is listed here, together with a DCG translation of a slightly modified network. The modifications were mainly to prevent the acceptance of ungrammatical sequences of verbs at node Q3/ of the original ATN.

After the DCG proper, there is listed an extract from the dictionary of the DCG; just one clause for each predicate is illustrated. Because of the indexing provided

```
(Q2/
 (CAT V T
  (SETR V *)
  (SETR TNS (LIST (GETF * TENSE)))
  (TO Q3/)))
(Q3/
 (CAT V (AND (GETF * PPRT)
             (EQ (GETR V)
                 (QUOTE BE)))
  (HOLD (GETR SUBJ))
  (SETR SUBJ (BUILDQ (NP (PRO SOMEONE))))
  (SETR AGFLAG T)
  (SETR V *)
  (TO Q3/))
 (CAT V (AND (GETF * PPRT)
             (EQ (GETR V)
                 (QUOTE HAVE)))
  (SETR TNS (APPEND   (GETR TNS)
                      (QUOTE (PERFECT))))
  (SETR V *)
  (TO Q3/))
 (PUSH NP/ (TRANS (GETR V))
  (SETR OBJ *)
  (TO Q4/))
 (VIR NP (TRANS (GETR V))
  (SETR OBJ *)
  (TO Q4/))
 (POP (BUILDQ (S + + (TNS +) (VP (V +)))
              TYPE SUBJ TNS V)
  (INTRANS (GETR V))))
(Q4/
 (WRD BY (GETR AGFLAG)
  (SETR AGFLAG NIL)
  (TO Q7/))
 (WRD TO (S-TRANS (GETR V))
  (TO Q5/))
 (POP (BUILDQ (S + + (TNS +) (VP (V +) +))
              TYPE SUBJ TNS V OBJ)
  T))
(Q5/
 (PUSH VP/ T
  (SENDR SUBJ (GETR OBJ))
```

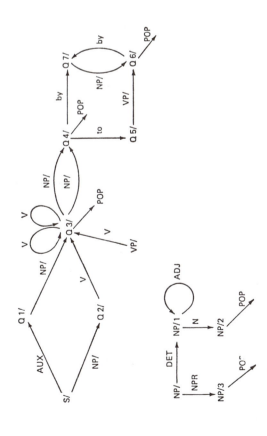

FIG. 3. Diagram of the ATN.

by the DECsystem-10 Prolog implementation, the speed of operation of the DCG is not affected by the size of the dictionary (i.e., by the number of clauses provided for each predicate).

Note the mutually exclusive nature of the three rules for the non-terminal 'complement' in the DCG proper. The Prolog indexing also serves to automatically select the correct alternative from among these three rules.

Listing of the ATN

```
(S/
 (CAT AUX T
  (SETR V *)
  (SETR TNS (LIST (GETF * TENSE)))
  (SETRQ TYPE Q)
  (TO Q1/))
 (PUSH NP/ T
  (SETR SUBJ *)
  (SETRQ TYPE DCL)
  (TO Q2/)))
(Q1/
 (PUSH NP/ T
  (SETR SUBJ *)
  (TO Q3/)))
```

The DCG Proper

```
sentence(S) →
    [W], {aux_verb(W,Verb,Tense)},
    noun_phrase(G_Subj),
    rest_sentence(q,G_Subj,Verb,Tense,S).

sentence(S) →
    noun_phrase(G_Subj),
    [W], {verb(W,Verb,Tense)},
    rest_sentence(dcl,G_Subj,Verb,Tense,S).

rest_sentence(Type,G_Subj,Verb,Tense,
              s(Type,L_Subj,tns(Tense1),VP) ) →
    rest_verb(Verb,Tense,Verb1,Tense1),
    {verbtype(Verb1,VType)},
    complement(VType,Verb1,G_Subj,L_Subj,VP).

rest_verb(have,Tense,Verb,(Tense,perfect)) →
    [W], {past_participle(W,Verb)}.
rest_verb(Verb,Tense,Verb,Tense) → [].

complement(copula,be,Obj,Subj, vp(v(Verb),Obj1) ) →
    [W], {past_participle(W,Verb), transitive(Verb)},
    rest_object(Obj,Verb,Obj1),
    agent(Subj).

complement(transitive,Verb,Subj,Subj, vp(v(Verb),Obj1) ) →
    noun_phrase(Obj),
    rest_object(Obj,Verb,Obj1).
complement(intransitive,Verb,Subj,Subj, vp(v(Verb)) ) → [].

rest_object(Obj,Verb,S) →
    {s_transitive(Verb)},
    [to,Verb1], {infinitive(Verb1)},
    rest_sentence(dcl,Obj,Verb1,present,S).
rest_object(Obj,Verb,Obj) → [].

agent(Subj) → [by], noun_phrase(Subj).
agent(np(pro(someone))) → [].

noun_phrase(np(Det,adj(Adjs),n(Noun))) →
    [Det], {determiner(Det)},
    adjectives(Adjs),
    [Noun], {noun(Noun)}.
noun_phrase(np(npr(PN))) → [PN], {proper_noun(PN)}.

adjectives([Adj | Adjs]) →
    [Adj], {adjective(Adj)},
    adjectives(Adjs).
adjectives([]) → [].
```

```
        (SENDR TNS (GETR TNS))
        (SENDRQ TYPE DCL)
        (SETR OBJ *)
        (TO Q6)))
(Q6/
   (WRD BY (GETR AGFLAG)
        (SETR AGFLAG NIL)
        (TO Q7/))
   (POP (BUILDQ (S + + (TNS +) (VP (V +) +))
                 TYPE SUBJ TNS V OBJ)
        T))
(Q7/
   (PUSH NP/ T
        (SETR SUBJ *)
        (TO Q6/)))
(VP/
   (CAT V (GETF * UNTENSED)
        (SETR V *)
        (TO Q3/)))
(NP/
   (CAT DET T
        (SETR DET *)
        (TO NP/1))
   (CAT NPR T
        (SETR NPR *)
        (TO NP/3)))
(NP/1
   (CAT ADJ T
        (ADDL ADJS *)
        (TO NP/1))
   (CAT N T
        (SETR N *)
        (TO NP/2)))
(NP/2
   (POP (BUILDQ (NP (DET +) (ADJ +) (N +))
                 DET ADJS N)
        T))
(NP/3
   (POP (BUILDQ (NP (NPR +))
                 NPR)
        T))
```

Extract from the Dictionary of the DCG

```
aux_verb(W,V,T) :- verb(W,V,T),auxiliary(V).
auxiliary(be).
verb(is,be,present).
proper_noun(john).
determiner(the).
adjective(nice).
noun(book).
verbtype(be,copula).
verbtype(V,transitive) :- transitive(V).
verbtype(V,intransitive) :- intransitive(V).
transitive(shoot).
intransitive(sleep).
s_transitive(believe).
infinitive(be).
past_participle(been,be).
```

Appendix 2. Performance Data

The DCG timing data which follows is for compiled code produced by the DECsystem-10 Prolog implementation, running on a KI-10 processor. We list the CPU times in milliseconds, averaged over 100 tests for examples in Part 1, and over 10 tests for examples in Part 2.

Part 1

The DCG is that listed in Appendix 1. For each example, there is listed the time to obtain the first parse, followed by the time to exhaust all parses and the total number of parses. For reference, the parse tree(s) obtained are also listed in selected cases.

Observe that in those cases where there is a unique parse, the overhead of going on to seek alternative parses is very low. This is a result of the efficient implementation of backtracking, and of the generally highly determinate nature of this particular grammar for top-down, left-to-right parsing.

(1)   fred shot john—3 words
3.0 msec.   3.2 msec.   1 parse
s(dcl,np(npr(fred)),tns(past),vp(v(shoot),np(npr(john))))

(2)   mary was liked by john—5 words
3.9 msec.   4.1 msec.   1 parse

(3)   fred told mary to shoot john—6 words
5.1 msec.   5.7 msec.   1 parse

(4)   john was believed to have been shot by fred—9 words
5.7 msec.   8.3 msec.   2 parses
s(dcl,np(pro(someone)),tns(past),vp(v(believe,s(dcl,np(npr(fred)),
tns((present,perfect)),vp(v(shoot),np(npr(john)))))))
s(dcl,np(npr(fred)),tns(past),vp(v(believe),s(dcl,np(pro(someone)),
tns((present,perfect)),vp(v(shoot),np(npr(john)))))))

(5)   was dave believed to have told mary to tell fred to buy the book by john—16 words
9.6 msec.   12.1 msec.   1 parse

Part 2

Here we attempt to offer some kind of a comparison with the only available published ATN timing data. We list five examples taken from Burton (1976) of sentences with their CPU times for parsing by the compiled LUNAR system running on a DEC KA-10 processor. Each of these examples is followed, for comparison, by a superficially similar sentence accepted by a DCG based on the parsing component of a natural language question-answering system written by Veronica Dahl (1977). This system treats a sizable subset of natural language, approaching in scale that of LUNAR.

All times are to obtain the first parse only. One structure produced as the result of the DCG analysis is listed for reference. Note particularly that the DEC KI-10 processor used for the DCG times is generally reckoned to be nearly twice as fast as a KA-10.

(1)   Give me all analyses of S10046.
245 msec.
What are the files of David?
78 msec.

(2)   How many breccias contain olivine?
175 msec.
How many files date from Monday?
39 msec.
how_many(X:[] & file,
and(and(pr(file(X)),and(true,true)),
pr(dateof(X,[monday]))))

(4)   List modal plag analysis for lunar samples that contain olivine.
265 msec.
Which people are owners of small files that date from Monday?
98 msec.

(5) What is the average composition of olivine?
275 msec.

What is the size of PLC?
40 msec.

(7) How many breccias do not contain Europium?
240 msec.

How many files do not date from Friday?
38 msec.

ACKNOWLEDGEMENTS

We would like to thank all the people who read drafts of this paper, and particularly Chris Mellish, William Woods, Alan Bundy and the referees for their detailed comments and suggestions. The paper was written while Pereira was supported by a British Council Fellowship and Warren by a British Science Research Council Grant (BRG/9445.5).

REFERENCES

Andreka, H. and Nemeti, I. (1976), The generalised completeness of Horn predicate-logic as a programming language, Dept. of AI Research Report 21, Edinburgh (March 1976).

Bates, M. (1975), Syntactic analysis in a speech understanding system, BBN Report 3116 (August 1975).

Bates, M. (1978), The theory and practice of augmented transition networks, in: L. Bolc (Ed.), *Natural Language Communication with Computers* (Springer, Berlin, May 1978).

Bergman, M. and Kanoui, H. (1975), Sycophante: système de calcul formel et d'intégration symbolique sur l'ordinateur, Groupe d'Intelligence Artificielle, Université de Marseille-Luminy (October 1975).

Boyer, R. S. and Moore, J. S. (1972), The sharing of structure in theorem proving programs, in: Meltzer and Michie (Eds.), *Machine Intelligence 7*, (Edinburgh, 1972).

Burton, R. R. (1976), Semantic grammar: an engineering technique for construction of natural language understanding systems, BBN Report 3453 (December 1976).

Burton, R. R. and Woods, W. A. (1976), A compiling system for augmented transition networks, Preprints of COLING-76, Ottawa (June 1976).

Colmerauer, A. (1970), Les systèmes-Q ou un formalisme pour analyser et synthétiser des phrases sur ordinateur, Internal publication no. 43, Départment d'Informatique, Université de Montreal, Canada (September 1970).

Colmerauer, A. (1975), Les grammaires de metamorphose, Groupe d'Intelligence Artificielle, Université de Marseille-Luminy (November 1975). Appears as "Metamorphosis Grammars" in: L. Bolc (Ed.), *Natural Language Communication with Computers*, (Springer, Berlin, May 1978).

Colmerauer, A. (1977), An interesting natural language subset, Groupe d'Intelligence Artificielle, Université de Marseille-Luminy (October 1977).

Dahl, V. (1977), Un systeme déductif d'interrogation de banques de données en Espagnol, Groupe d'Intelligence Artificielle, Université de Marseille-Luminy (November 1977).

Darvas, F., Futo, I. and Szeredi, P. (1977), Logic based program system for predicting drug interactions, *Int. J. Biomedical Comput.* (1977).

Earley, J. (1970), An efficient context-free parsing algorithm, *C. ACM* **13** (February 1970).

van Emden, M. H. (1975), Programming with resolution logic, Report CS-75-30, Dept. of Computer Science, University of Waterloo, Canada (November 1975).

Finin, T. and Hadden, G. (1977), Augmenting ATNs, *Proc. 5th IJCAI, MIT*, Cambridge, MA (August 1977).

Kaplan, R. M. (1973), A general syntactic processor, in: Randall Rustin (Ed.), *Natural Language Processing* (1973).

Koster, C. H. A. (1971), Affix grammars, in: J. E. L. Peck (Ed.), *Algol-68 Implementation* (North Holland, Amsterdam, 1971).

Kowalski, R. A. (1974a), Predicate logic as programming language, *Proc. IFIP 74*, Stockholm (1974).

Kowalski, R. A. (1974b), Logic for problem solving, DCL Memo 75, Dept. of AI, Edinburgh (March 1974). (To be published by North-Holland, Amsterdam as part of a book of the same title.)

Markusz, Z. (1977), Designing variants of flats, *Proc. IFIP Conf.* (1977).

Montague, R. (1973), The proper treatment of quantification in ordinary English, in: R. M. Thomason (Ed.), *Formal Philosophy* (Yale University Press: 1974).

Pereira, F. (1979), Extraposition grammars, Working Paper No. 59, Dept. of AI, University of Edinburgh (June 1979).

Pereira, L., Pereira, F. and Warren, D. (1978), User's guide to DECsystem-10 Prolog, Div. de Informatica, LNEC, Lisbon and Dept. of AI, University of Edinburgh (September 1978).

Robinson, J. A. (1965), A machine-oriented logic based on the resolution principle, *J. ACM* **12** (1965).

Roussel, P. (1975), Prolog: manuel de référence et d'utilisation, Groupe d'Intelligence Artificielle, Université de Marseille-Luminy (September 1975).

Warren, D. H. D. (1975), Implementation of an efficient predicate logic interpreter based on Earley deduction, Research proposal to the Science Research Council, Dept. of AI, University of Edinburgh (1975).

Warren, D. H. D. (1977a), Implementing Prolog—compiling predicate logic programs, Dept. of AI Research Reports 39 and 40, University of Edinburgh (May 1977).

Warren, D. H. D. (1977b), Logic programming and compiler writing, Dept. of AI Research Report 44, University of Edinburgh (September 1977). To appear in *Software Practice and Experience*.

Warren, D. H. D., Pereira, L. M. and Pereira, F. C. N. (1977), Prolog—the language and its implementation compared with Lisp, Proc. ACM Symposium on AI and Programming Languages, *SIGPLAN/SIGART Newsletter* (Rochester NY, August 1977).

van Wijngaarden, A. (Ed.) (1974), Revised Report on the Algorithmic Language Algol-68 (Springer, Berlin, 1976).

Woods, W. A. (1970), Transition network grammars for natural language analysis, *C. ACM* **13** (October 1970).

Woods, W. A. (1973), An experimental parsing system for transition network grammars, in: Randall Rustin (Ed.), *Natural Language Processing* (1973).

Woods, W. A., Kaplan, R. M. and Nash-Webber, B. (1972), The lunar sciences natural language information system: final report, BBN Report 2378 (June 1972).

Woods, W. A. et al. (1976), Speech understanding systems: final report, BBN Report 3438 (December 1976).

Parsing in functional unification grammar

MARTIN KAY

Language is a system for encoding and transmitting ideas. A theory that seeks to explain linguistic phenomena in terms of this fact is a *functional* theory. One that does not miss the point. In particular, a theory that shows how the sentences of a language are all generable by rules of a particular formal system, however restricted that system may be, does not explain anything. It may be suggestive, to be sure, because it may point to the existence of an encoding device whose structure that formal system reflects. But, if it points to no such device, it simply constitutes a gratuitous and wholly unwelcome addition to the set of phenomena to be explained.

A formal system that is decorated with informal footnotes and amendments explains even less. If I ask why some phenomenon, say relativization from within the subject of a sentence, does not take place in English and am told that it is because it does not take place in any language, I go away justifiably more perplexed than I came. The theory that attempts to explain things in this way is not functional. It tells me only that the source of my perplexity is more widespread than I had thought. The putative explanation makes no reference to the only assertion that is sufficiently self-evident to provide a basis for linguistic theory, namely that language is a system for encoding and transmitting ideas.

But, surely there is more to functionalism than this. To fill their role as systems for encoding and transmitting ideas, languages must first be learnable. Learnability is a functional property and language learning needs to be explained. But what is involved here is a derivative notion of function. A satisfactory linguistic theory will at least make it plausible that children could learn to use language as a system for encoding and transmitting ideas. It will *not* show how a child might learn to distinguish sentences from nonsentences, a skill with little survival value and one for which evolution probably furnished no special equipment.

It follows that any reasonable linguistic theory will be functional. To use the word to characterize one particular theory, as I shall shortly do, must therefore be accounted pretentious. However, while it is true that the label has been used before, it is manifestly untrue that linguistic theories have typically been functional. Just recently, there has been a partial and grudging retreat from the view that to formalize is to explain. This has not been because of any widespread realization of the essential vacuity of purely formal explanations, but for two other reasons. The first is the failure of the formalists to produce workable criteria on which to distinguish competing theories, and the second is the apparent impossibility of constructing theories whose most cogent remarks are made within the formalism rather than in footnotes and amendments. The search for sources of constraint to impose on formal grammar has led to an uneasy alliance with the psychologists and a belated rekindling of interest in parsing and other performance issues (for some discussion, see Gazdar, 1982; Kaplan, 1972, 1973, 1978; Kay, 1973, 1977, 1979).

My aim in this polemic is not to belittle the value of formalisms. Without them linguistics, like most other scientific enterprises, would be impotent. It is only to discredit them as an ultimate basis for the explanation of the contingent matters that are the stuff of science. What I shall describe under the banner of functional unification grammar is indeed a formalism, but one that has been designed to accommodate functionally revealing, and therefore explanatorily satisfying, grammars.

7.1. Functional unification grammar

A functionally adequate grammar must either be a particular transducer, or some kind of data structure that more general kinds of transducer – generators and parsers – can interpret. It must show not only what strings can be associated with what meanings, but how a given meaning can be expressed and a given utterance understood. Furthermore, it cannot take logic as the measure of meaning, abjuring any responsibility for distinctions that are not readily reflected in the predicate calculus. The semantic side of the transducer must traffic in quantifiers and connectives, to be sure, but also in topic and emphasis and given and new. Functional grammar will, therefore, at the very least, adopt some form of *functional* sentence perspective.

In practice, I take it that the factors that govern the production of a sentence typically come from a great variety of different sources, logical, textual, interpersonal, and so forth. In general, each of these, taken by itself, underdetermines what comes out. When they jointly overdetermine it, there must be priorities enabling a choice to be made among the demands of the different sources. When they jointly underdetermine the outcome, the theory must provide defaults and unmarked cases. The point is that we must be prepared to take seriously the claim that language in

independent transducer becomes the embodiment of a theory of perform-ance. But there is no reason to suppose that the same transducer should be reversible, taking responsibility for both generation and parsing. While the strongest hypothesis would indeed provide only one device, a more conservative position would separate these functions. This paper takes the conservative position. Given that generation and parsing are done by different transducers, a strong hypothesis would have both transducers interpret the same grammar; a more conservative position would associate a different formalism with each transducer and provide some mechanism for ensuring that the same facts were represented in each. This paper takes the conservative position. Specifically, the position is that the generator operates directly on the canonical form of the grammar – the competence grammar – and that the parser operates on a translation of this grammar into a different formalism. This paper will concentrate on how this translation is actually carried out; it will, in short, be about machine translation between grammatical formalisms.

The kind of translation to be explored here is known in computer sci-ence as *compilation*, and the computer program that does it is called a *compiler*. Typically, compilers are used to translate programs from so-called *high-level* programming like FORTRAN or ALGOL, into the *low-level* languages that directly control computers. But, compilers have also proved very useful in other situations.

Whatever the specific application, the term ''compilation'' almost al-ways refers to a process that translates a text produced by a human into a text that is functionally equivalent, but not intended for human con-sumption. There are at least two reasons for doing this. One is that those properties of a language that make for perspicuity and ease of expression are very different from those that make for simple, cheap, reliable com-puting. Put simply, computers are not easy to talk to and it is sometimes easier to use an interpreter. It is economical and efficient for man and machine to talk different languages and to interact through an interme-diary. The second reason has to do with flexibility and is therefore also economic. By compilation, the programming enterprise is kept, in large measure, independent of particular machines. Through different compil-ers, programs can be made to run on a variety of computers, existing or yet to be invented. All in all, compilers facilitate the business of writing programs for computers to execute. The kind of compiler to be described here confers practical benefits on the linguist by facilitating the business of obtaining parsing grammars. It does this by making the enterprise es-sentially indistinguishable from writing competence grammars.

It is possible to say things in the native language of a computer that never should be said, because they are either redundant or meaningless. Adding zero to a number, or calculating a value that is never used, is

general, and individual utterances in particular, fill many different *func-tions* and that these all affect the theory, even at the syntactic level.

I have outlined a broad program for linguistic theory, and the possibility of carrying it through rests on our being able to design clean, simple formalisms. This applies to the formal descriptions by which words, phrases, sentences, grammars, and languages are known and also to the operations that the theory allows to be performed on these descriptions.

Much of the character of the theory I shall outline comes from the set-theoretic properties that are imputed to descriptions of all kinds in every-day life. These properties do not, in fact, carry over to the descriptions provided for in most linguistic formalisms. In this theory, there is no limit on how detailed a description can be and no requirement that everything in it should serve some grammatical end. Generally speaking, to add more detail to a description is to narrow the class of objects described, and to remove material from a description is to widen its coverage. In fact, de-scriptions and the sets of things they refer to are mathematical duals of one another with respect to the operations of set theory. In other words, the intersection of a pair of descriptions describes the union of the sets of objects that they describe separately and the union of a pair of de-scriptions describes the intersection of the corresponding pairs of sets. These are properties we are entitled to look for in anything to which the term ''description'' is seriously applied.

Descriptions are sets of *descriptors* and prominent among the kinds of object that go to make up the sets are pairs consisting of an attribute, like *number*, with an associated value, like *singular*. An important subclass of attributes consists of grammatical *functions* like *Subject, Modifier,* and *Connective*.

The claim that this theory makes on the word ''functional'' in its title is therefore supported in three ways. First, it gives primary status to those aspects of language that have often been called functional; logical aspects are not privileged. Second, it describes linguistic structures in terms of the function that a part fills in a whole, rather than in terms of parts of speech and ordering relations. Third, and most important for this paper, it requires its grammars to *function*; that is, they must support the practical enterprises of language generation and analysis.

7.1.1. Compilation

The view that a grammar is a data structure that can be interpreted by one or more transducers has some attractions over the one that would have it actually be a transducer. On the one hand, while the grammar itself remains the proper repository of linguistic knowledge, and the for-malism, an encapsulation of formal linguistic universals, the language-

An attribute is a *symbol*, that is, a string of letters. A value is either a symbol or another FD. The equal sign, "=", is used to separate an attribute from its value so that, in α = β, α is the attribute and β the value. Thus, for example, (1) might be an FD, albeit a simple one, of the sentence *He saw her.*

$$
(1) \quad
\begin{bmatrix}
\text{CAT} & = & \text{S} \\[4pt]
\text{SUBJ} & = &
\begin{bmatrix}
\text{CAT} & = & \text{PRON} \\
\text{GENDER} & = & \text{MASC} \\
\text{CASE} & = & \text{NOM} \\
\text{NUMBER} & = & \text{SING} \\
\text{PERSON} & = & 3
\end{bmatrix} \\[24pt]
\text{DOBJ} & = &
\begin{bmatrix}
\text{CAT} & = & \text{PRON} \\
\text{GENDER} & = & \text{FEM} \\
\text{CASE} & = & \text{ACC} \\
\text{NUMBER} & = & \text{SING} \\
\text{PERSON} & = & 3
\end{bmatrix} \\[24pt]
\text{VERB} & = & \text{SEE} \\
\text{TENSE} & = & \text{PAST} \\
\text{VOICE} & = & \text{ACTIVE}
\end{bmatrix}
$$

$$
(2) \quad
\begin{bmatrix}
\text{CAT} & = & \text{S} \\[4pt]
\text{PROT} & = &
\begin{bmatrix}
\text{CAT} & = & \text{PRON} \\
\text{GENDER} & = & \text{MASC} \\
\text{NUMBER} & = & \text{SING} \\
\text{PERSON} & = & 3
\end{bmatrix} \\[20pt]
\text{GOAL} & = &
\begin{bmatrix}
\text{CAT} & = & \text{PRON} \\
\text{GENDER} & = & \text{FEM} \\
\text{NUMBER} & = & \text{SING} \\
\text{PERSON} & = & 3
\end{bmatrix} \\[20pt]
\text{VERB} & = & \text{SEE} \\
\text{TENSE} & = & \text{PAST}
\end{bmatrix}
$$

If the values of SUBJ and DOBJ are reversed in (1), and the value of VOICE changed to PASSIVE, it becomes an FD for the sentence *She was seen by him.* However, in both this and the original sentence, *he* is the protagonist (PROT), or logical subject, and *she* the goal (GOAL) of the action, or logical direct object. In other words, both sentences are equally well described by (2). In the sense of transformational grammar (2) shows a *deeper* struc-

redundant and therefore wasteful. Attempting to divide a number by zero makes no sense and an endless cycle of operations prevents a result ever being reached. These things can almost always be assumed to be errors on the part of the programmer. Some of these errors are difficult or impossible to detect simply by inspecting the program and emerge only in the course of the actual computation. But some errors can be dealt with by simply not providing any way of committing them in the higher-level language. Thus, an expression $n/0$, meaning the result of dividing n by 0, would be deemed outside the language, and the compiler would not be able to translate a program that contained it. The general point is this: compiling can confer additional benefits when it is used to translate one language into a *subset* of another. In the case of programming languages, the idea is to exclude from the subset useless constructions.

This benefit is easy to appreciate in the linguistic case. As I have said, competence grammars are written in a formal language designed to enshrine restrictions that have been found characteristic of the human linguistic faculty, in short, linguistic universals. The guarantee that performance grammars reflect these same universals can be provided by embedding them in the language of those grammars. But it can also be provided by deriving the performance grammars from the competence grammars by means of a process that is guaranteed to preserve all important properties. The language of the performance grammar is relatively unconstrained and would allow the expression of theoretically unmotivated things, but the translation procedure ensures that only a properly motivated subset is used. This strategy clearly makes for a stronger theory by positing a close connection between competence and performance. It has the added advantage of freeing the designer of the performance formalism of any concern for matters already accounted for in the competence system.

7.1.2. *Attributes and values*

As I have already pointed out, functional unification grammar knows things by their *functional descriptions*, (FDs). A *simple* FD is a set of *descriptors* and a descriptor is a *constituent set*, a *pattern*, or an attribute with an associated value. I shall come to the form and function of constituent sets and patterns shortly. For the moment, we consider only attribute-value pairs.

The list of descriptors that make up an FD is written in square brackets, no significance attaching to the order. The attributes in an FD must be distinct from one another so that if an FD *F* contains the attribute *a*, it is always possible to use the phrase "the *a* of *F*" to refer unambiguously to a value.

$\cdots a_{k-1}\rangle$. It can be read as *The a_k of the a_{k-1} $\cdots$ of the*

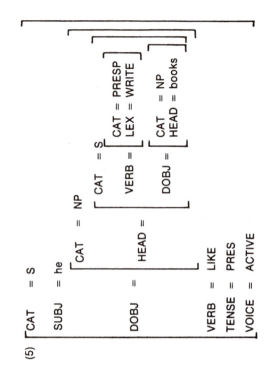

(4)
$$\begin{bmatrix} \text{CAT} & = & \text{S} \\ \text{SUBJ} & = & \text{he} \\ \text{DOBJ} & = & \begin{bmatrix} \text{CAT} & = & \text{NP} \\ \text{HEAD} & = & \text{books} \\ \text{MOD} & = & \begin{bmatrix} \text{CAT} & = & \text{PRESP} \\ \text{LEX} & = & \text{WRITE} \end{bmatrix} \end{bmatrix} \\ \text{VERB} & = & \text{LIKE} \\ \text{TENSE} & = & \text{PRES} \\ \text{VOICE} & = & \text{ACTIVE} \end{bmatrix}$$

(5)
$$\begin{bmatrix} \text{CAT} & = & \text{S} \\ \text{SUBJ} & = & \text{he} \\ \text{DOBJ} & = & \text{HEAD} = \begin{bmatrix} \text{CAT} = \text{NP} \\ \begin{bmatrix} \text{CAT} & = & \text{S} \\ \text{VERB} & = & \begin{bmatrix} \text{CAT} = \text{PRESP} \\ \text{LEX} = \text{WRITE} \end{bmatrix} \\ \text{DOBJ} & = & \begin{bmatrix} \text{CAT} = \text{NP} \\ \text{HEAD} = \text{books} \end{bmatrix} \end{bmatrix} \end{bmatrix} \\ \text{VERB} & = & \text{LIKE} \\ \text{TENSE} & = & \text{PRES} \\ \text{VOICE} & = & \text{ACTIVE} \end{bmatrix}$$

(3)
$$\begin{bmatrix} \text{CAT} & = & \text{S} \\ \text{SUBJ} = \text{PROT} & = & \begin{bmatrix} \text{CAT} & = & \text{PRON} \\ \text{GENDER} & = & \text{MASC} \\ \text{CASE} & = & \text{NOM} \\ \text{NUMBER} & = & \text{SING} \\ \text{PERSON} & = & 3 \end{bmatrix} \\ \text{DOBJ} = \text{GOAL} & = & \begin{bmatrix} \text{CAT} & = & \text{PRON} \\ \text{GENDER} & = & \text{FEM} \\ \text{CASE} & = & \text{ACC} \\ \text{NUMBER} & = & \text{SING} \\ \text{PERSON} & = & 3 \end{bmatrix} \\ \text{VERB} & = & \text{SEE} \\ \text{TENSE} & = & \text{PAST} \\ \text{VOICE} & = & \text{ACTIVE} \end{bmatrix}$$

ture than (1). However, in functional unification grammar, if a given linguistic entity has two different FDs, a single FD containing the information in both can be constructed by the process of *unification*, which we shall examine in detail shortly. The FD (3) results from unifying (1) and (2).

A pair of FDs is said to be *incompatible* if they have a common attribute with different symbols, or incompatible FDs, as values. Grammatically ambiguous sentences have two or more incompatible FDs. Thus, for example, the sentence *He likes writing books* might be described by (4) or (5). Incompatible simple FDs $F_1 \cdots F_k$ can be combined into a single *complex* FD $\{F_1 \cdots F_k\}$ which describes the union of the sets of objects that its components describe. The notation allows common parts of components to be factored in the obvious way, so that (6) describes all those objects that are described by *either* (4) or (5).

The use of braces to indicate alternation between incompatible FDs or sub-FDs provides a compact way of describing large classes of disparate objects. In fact, as we shall see, given a few extra conventions, it makes it possible to claim that the grammar of a language is nothing more than a single complex FD.

7.1.3. Unification

A string of atoms enclosed in angle brackets constitutes a *path* and there is at least one that identifies every value in an FD. The path $\langle a_1 a_2 \cdots a_k \rangle$ identifies the value of the attribute a_k in the FD that is the value of $\langle a_1 a_2$

(8)
$$\begin{bmatrix} \text{CAT} & = & \text{S} \\ \text{SUBJ} = \text{PROT} & = & \begin{bmatrix} \text{CAT} & = & \text{PRON} \\ \text{GENDER} & = & \text{MASC} \\ \text{CASE} & = & \text{NOM} \\ \text{NUMBER} & = & \text{SING} \\ \text{PERSON} & = & 3 \end{bmatrix} \\ \text{DOBJ} = \text{GOAL} & = & \begin{bmatrix} \text{CAT} & = & \text{PRON} \\ \text{GENDER} & = & \text{FEM} \\ \text{CASE} & = & \text{ACC} \\ \text{NUMBER} & = & \text{SING} \\ \text{PERSON} & = & 3 \end{bmatrix} \\ \text{VERB} & = & \begin{bmatrix} \text{CAT} & = & \text{VERB} \\ \text{WORD} & = & \text{SEE} \end{bmatrix} \\ \text{TENSE} & = & \text{PAST} \\ \text{VOICE} & = & \text{ACTIVE} \\ \text{ASPECT} & = & \begin{bmatrix} \text{PERFECT} & = & + \\ \text{PROGRESSIVE} & = & - \end{bmatrix} \end{bmatrix}$$

theoretic operations. Specifically, the union of a pair of FDs is not, in general, a well-formed FD. The requirement that a given attribute appear only once in an FD implies a similar constraint on the set of features corresponding to an FD. A path must uniquely identify a value. But, if the FD F_1 has the basic feature $\langle \alpha \rangle = x$ and the FD F_2 has the basic feature $\langle \alpha \rangle = y$, then either $x = y$ or F_1 and F_2 are incompatible and their union is not a well-formed FD. So, for example, if F_1 describes a sentence with a singular subject and F_2 describes a sentence with a plural subject, then $S_1 \cup S_2$, where S_1 and S_2 are the corresponding sets of basic features, is not well formed because it would contain $\langle$SUBJ NUMBER$\rangle$ = SINGULAR and $\langle$SUBJ NUMBER$\rangle$ = PLURAL.

When two or more simple FDs are compatible, they can be combined into one simple FD describing those things that they both describe, by the process of unification. Unification is the same as set union except that it yields the null set when applied to incompatible arguments. The "=" sign is used for unification, so that $\alpha = \beta$ denotes the result of unifying α and β. Examples (10)–(12) show the results of unification in some simple cases.

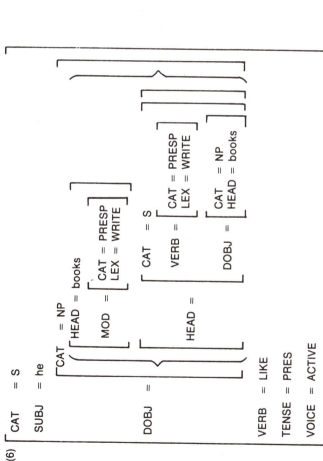

(6)

a_1. Paths are always interpreted as beginning in the largest FD that encloses them. Attributes are otherwise taken as belonging to the smallest enclosing FD. Accordingly,

(7) $[A = [B = \langle C \rangle = X]] = \begin{bmatrix} A = [B = X] \\ C = \langle A\ B \rangle \end{bmatrix}$

A pair consisting of a path in an FD and the value that the path leads to is a *feature* of the object described. If the value is a symbol, the pair is a *basic feature* of the FD. Any FD can be represented as a list of basic features. For example, (8) can be represented by the list (9).

It is in the nature of FDs that they blur the usual distinction between features and structures. Example (8) shows FDs embedded in other FDs, thus stressing their structural properties. Rewriting (8) as (9) stresses the componential nature of FDs.

It is the possibility of viewing FDs as unstructured sets of features that makes them subject to the standard operations of set theory. However, it is also a crucial property of FDs that they are not *closed* under set-

The result of unifying a pair of complex FDs is, in general, a complex FD with one term for each compatible pair of terms in the original FDs. Thus $\{a_1 \cdots a_n\} = \{b_1 \cdots b_m\}$ becomes an FD of the form $\{c_1 \cdots c_k\}$ in which each c_h $(1 \le h \le k)$ is the result of unifying a compatible pair $a_i = b_j$ $(1 \le i \le m, 1 \le j \le n)$. This is exemplified in (13).

(9)

$$
\begin{aligned}
\langle \text{CAT} \rangle &= \text{S} \\
\langle \text{SUBJ CAT} \rangle &= \text{PRON} \\
\langle \text{SUBJ GENDER} \rangle &= \text{MASC} \\
\langle \text{SUBJ CASE} \rangle &= \text{NOM} \\
\langle \text{SUBJ NUMBER} \rangle &= \text{SING} \\
\langle \text{SUBJ PERSON} \rangle &= 3 \\
\langle \text{PROT CAT} \rangle &= \text{PRON} \\
\langle \text{PROT GENDER} \rangle &= \text{MASC} \\
\langle \text{PROT CASE} \rangle &= \text{NOM} \\
\langle \text{PROT NUMBER} \rangle &= \text{SING} \\
\langle \text{PROT PERSON} \rangle &= 3 \\
\langle \text{OBJ CAT} \rangle &= \text{PRON} \\
\langle \text{OBJ GENDER} \rangle &= \text{FEM} \\
\langle \text{OBJ CASE} \rangle &= \text{ACC} \\
\langle \text{OBJ NUMBER} \rangle &= \text{SING} \\
\langle \text{OBJ PERSON} \rangle &= 3 \\
\langle \text{GOAL CAT} \rangle &= \text{PRON} \\
\langle \text{GOAL GENDER} \rangle &= \text{FEM} \\
\langle \text{GOAL CASE} \rangle &= \text{FEM} \\
\langle \text{GOAL NUMBER} \rangle &= \text{SING} \\
\langle \text{GOAL PERSON} \rangle &= 3 \\
\langle \text{VERB CAT} \rangle &= \text{VERB} \\
\langle \text{VERB WORD} \rangle &= \text{SEE} \\
\langle \text{TENSE} \rangle &= \text{PAST} \\
\langle \text{VOICE} \rangle &= \text{ACTIVE} \\
\langle \text{ASPECT PERFECT} \rangle &= + \\
\langle \text{ASPECT PROGRESSIVE} \rangle &= -
\end{aligned}
$$

(10)
$$
\begin{bmatrix} \text{CAT} & = \text{VERB} \\ \text{LEX} & = \text{RUN} \\ \text{TENSE} & = \text{PRES} \end{bmatrix}
=
\begin{bmatrix} \text{CAT} & = \text{VERB} \\ \text{NUM} & = \text{SING} \\ \text{PERS} & = 3 \end{bmatrix}
\rightarrow
\begin{bmatrix} \text{CAT} & = \text{VERB} \\ \text{LEX} & = \text{RUN} \\ \text{TENSE} & = \text{PRES} \\ \text{NUM} & = \text{SING} \\ \text{PERS} & = 3 \end{bmatrix}
$$

(11)
$$
\begin{bmatrix} \text{CAT} & = \text{VERB} \\ \text{LEX} & = \text{RUN} \\ \text{TENSE} & = \text{PRES} \end{bmatrix}
=
\begin{bmatrix} \text{CAT} & = \text{VERB} \\ \text{TENSE} & = \text{PAST} \\ \text{PERS} & = 3 \end{bmatrix}
\rightarrow \text{NIL}
$$

(12)
$$
\begin{bmatrix} \text{CAT} & = \text{PP} \\ \text{HEAD} & = \begin{bmatrix} \text{PREP} = \text{MIT} \\ \text{CASE} = \text{DAT} \end{bmatrix} \end{bmatrix}
=
\begin{bmatrix} \text{CAT} & = \text{PP} \\ \text{HEAD} & = \begin{bmatrix} \text{CAT} = \text{NP} \\ \text{CASE} = \langle \text{CASE} \rangle \end{bmatrix} \end{bmatrix}
\rightarrow
\begin{bmatrix} \text{CAT} & = \text{PP} \\ \text{PREP} & = \text{MIT} \\ \text{CASE} & = \text{DAT} \\ \text{HEAD} & = \begin{bmatrix} \text{CAT} = \text{NP} \\ \text{CASE} = \langle \text{CASE} \rangle \end{bmatrix} \end{bmatrix}
$$

(13)
$$\left.\begin{matrix} \begin{bmatrix} \text{TENSE} = \text{PRES} \\ \text{FORM} = \text{is} \end{bmatrix} \\ \begin{bmatrix} \text{TENSE} = \text{PAST} \\ \text{FORM} = \text{was} \end{bmatrix} \end{matrix}\right\} = \begin{bmatrix} \text{CAT} = \text{VERB} \\ \text{TENSE} = \text{PAST} \end{bmatrix} \Rightarrow \begin{bmatrix} \text{CAT} = \text{VERB} \\ \text{TENSE} = \text{PAST} \\ \text{FORM} = \text{was} \end{bmatrix}$$

(14)
$$\begin{bmatrix} \text{C-set} & = & (\text{SUBJ VERB OBJ}) \\ \text{Pattern} & = & (\text{SUBJ VERB OBJ}) \\ \text{CAT} & = & \text{S} \\ \text{SUBJ} = \text{PROT} & = & \begin{bmatrix} \text{CAT} = \text{PRON} \\ \text{GENDER} = \text{MASC} \\ \text{CASE} = \text{NOM} \\ \text{NUMBER} = \text{SING} \\ \text{PERSON} = 3 \end{bmatrix} \\ \text{DOBJ} = \text{GOAL} & = & \begin{bmatrix} \text{CAT} = \text{PRON} \\ \text{GENDER} = \text{FEM} \\ \text{CASE} = \text{ACC} \\ \text{NUMBER} = \text{SING} \\ \text{PERSON} = 3 \end{bmatrix} \\ \text{VERB} & = & \begin{bmatrix} \text{CAT} = \text{VERB} \\ \text{WORD} = \text{SEE} \end{bmatrix} \\ \text{TENSE} & = & \text{PAST} \\ \text{VOICE} & = & \text{ACTIVE} \\ \text{ASPECT} & = & \begin{bmatrix} \text{PERFECT} = + \\ \text{PROGRESSIVE} = - \end{bmatrix} \end{bmatrix}$$

Unification is the fundamental operation underlying the analysis and synthesis of sentences using functional unification grammar.

It is important to understand the difference between saying that a pair of FDs are *equal* and saying that they are *unified*. Clearly, when a pair of FDs has been unified, they are equal; the inverse is not generally true. To say that a pair of FDs A and B are unified is to say that A and B are *two names for one and the same description*. Consequently, if A is unified with C, the effect is to unify A, B, and C. On the other hand, if A and B, though possibly equal, are not unified, then unifying A and C does not affect B and, indeed, if A and C are not equal, a result of the unification will be to make A and B different. A crucial consequence of this is that the result of unifying various pair of FDs is independent of the order in which the operations are carried out. This, in its turn, makes for a loose coupling between the grammatical formalism as a whole and the algorithms that use it.

7.1.4. Patterns and constituent sets

We come now to the question of recursion in the grammar and how constituency is represented. I have already remarked that functional unification grammar deliberately blurs the distinction between structures and sets of features. It is clear from the examples we have considered so far that some parts of the FD of a phrase typically belong to the phrase as a whole, whereas others belong to its constituents. For example, in (8), the value of SUBJ is the FD of a constituent of the sentence, whereas the value of ASPECT is not. The purpose of constituent sets and patterns is to identify constituents and to state constraints on the order of their occurrence. Example (14) is a version of (8) that specifies the order. (SUBJ VERB DOBJ) is a pattern stating that the values of the attributes SUBJ, VERB, and DOBJ are FDs of constituents and that they occur in that order. As the example illustrates, patterns appear in FDs as the values of attributes. In general, the value is a list of patterns, and not just one as in (14). The attribute *pattern* is distinguished, its value being the one used to determine the order of the immediate constituents of the item being described. The attribute *C-set* is also distinguished, its value being a single list of paths identifying the immediate constituents of the current item, but imposing no order on them. Here, as elsewhere in the formalism, one-step paths can be, and usually are, written without enclosing angle-brackets. The patterns are templates that the string of immediate constituents must match. Each pattern is a list whose members can be

1. *A path.* The path may have as its value
    a. *An FD.* As in the case of the constituent set, the FD describes a constituent.
    b. *A pattern.* The pattern is inserted into the current one at this point.
2. *A string of dots.* This matches any number of constituents.
3. *The symbol #.* This matches any one constituent.
4. *An FD.* This will match any constituent whose description is unifiable with it. The unification is made with a *copy* of the FD in the pattern, rather than with the FD itself, because the intention is to impute its properties to the constituent, but not to unify all the constituents that match this part of the pattern.
5. *An expression of the form* (* *fd*), *where fd is an FD.* This matches zero or more constituents, provided they can all be unified with a copy of *fd*.

The ordering constraints in (14) could have been represented by many other sets of patterns, for example, those in (15).

(15) (SUBJ VERB ···) (··· VERB DOBJ)
      (SUBJ ··· DOBJ) (··· VERB ···)
      (··· SUBJ ··· DOBJ) (# VERB ···)
      (··· SUBJ ··· VERB ··· DOBJ)
      (··· SUBJ ··· VERB ···) (··· DOBJ)

The pattern (16) requires exactly one constituent to have the property [TRACE = NP]; all others must have the property [TRACE = NONE].

(16) ((* [TRACE = NONE]) [TRACE = NP] (* [TRACE = NONE]))

Clearly, patterns, like attribute-value pairs, can be incompatible thus preventing the unification of FDs. This is the case in examples in (17).

(17) (··· SUBJ ··· VERB ···) (··· VERB ··· SUBJ ···)
      (# SUBJ ···) (SUBJ ···)
      (··· SUBJ VERB ···) (··· SUBJ DOBJ ···)

The last of these could be a compatible pair just in case VERB and DOBJ were unified, but the names suggest that the first would have the feature [CAT = VERB] and the other [CAT = NP], ruling out this possibility.

The value of the *C-set* attribute covers all constituents. If two FDs are unified, and both have *C-set* attributes, the *C-set* attribute of the result is the intersection of these. If a member of the pair has no such attribute, the value is taken from the other member. In other words, the universal set of constituents can be written by simply omitting the attribute altogether. If there are constituents, but no patterns, then there are no constraints on the order in which the constituents can occur. If there are patterns, then each of the constituents must be assimilated to all of them.

7.1.5. Grammar

A functional unification grammar is a single FD. A sentence is well formed if a constituent-structure tree can be assigned to it each of whose nodes is labeled with an FD that is compatible with the grammar. The immediate descendents of each node must be properly specified by constituent-sets and patterns.

Generally speaking, grammars will take the form of alternations, each clause of which describes a major category; that is, they will have the form exhibited in (18).

(18) [CAT = c_1 ...]
      [CAT = c_2 ...]
      [CAT = c_3 ...]
      ⋮

Example (19) shows a simple grammar, corresponding to a context-free grammar containing the single rule (20).

(19) [CAT = S
        SUBJ = [CAT = NP]
        [SCOMP = NONE]
        [(··· SCOMP)
         [SCOMP = [CAT = S]]
        (SUBJ VERB ···)
        [CAT = NP]
        [CAT = VERB]]

(20) S → NP VERB (S)

FD (19) describes *either* sentences *or* verbs *or* noun phrases. Nothing is said about the constituency of the verbs or noun phrases described – they are treated as terminal constituents. The sentences have either two or three constituents depending on the choice made in the embedded alternation. All constituents must match the FD (19). Since the first constituent has the feature [CAT = NP], it can only match the second term in the main alternation. Likewise, the second constituent can only match the third term. If there is a third constituent, it must match the first term in the alternation, because it has the feature [CAT = s]. It must therefore also have two or three constituents also described by (19). If (19) consisted only of the first term in the outer alternation, it would have a null extension because the first term, for example, would be required to have the incompatible features [CAT = NP] and [CAT = s]. On the other hand, if the inner alternation were replaced by its second term, so that [SCOMP = NONE] were no longer an option, then the FD would correspond to the rule (21), whose derivations do not terminate.

(21) S → NP VERB S

7.2. The parser

7.2.1. *The General Syntactic Processor*

As I said at the outset, the transducer that is used for generating sentences operates on grammars in essentially the form in which they have been given here. The process is quite straightforward. The input is an FD that constitutes the specification of a sentence to be uttered. The more detail it contains, the more closely it constrains the sentence that will be produced. The transducer attempts to unify this FD with the grammar. If this cannot be done – that is, if it produces a null result because of incompatibilities between the two descriptions – there is no sentence in the language that meets the specification. If the unification is successful, the result will, in general, be to add detail to the FD originally provided. If the FD that results from this step has a constituent set, the process is repeated, unifying each constituent in turn with the grammar. A constituent that has no constituents of its own is a terminal that must match some entry in the lexicon.

Parsing is by no means so straightforward. Grammars, as I have characterized them, do not, for example, enable one to discern, in any immediate way, what properties the first or last word of a sentence might have. It is mainly for this reason that a compiler is required to convert the grammar into a new form. Compilation will result in a set of *procedures*, or miniature programs, designed to be embedded in a general parsing program that will call upon it at the appropriate time.

The general program, a version of the *General Syntactic Processor*, has been described in several places. The basic idea on which it is based is this. There are two principal data structures, the *chart*, and the *agenda*. The chart is a directed graph each of whose edges maps onto a substring of the sentence being analyzed. The chart therefore contains a vertex for each of the possible end points of such substrings, $k + 1$ vertices for a sentence of k words. Vertices are directed from left to right. The only loops that can occur consist of single edges incident from and to the same vertex.

Each word in the sentence to be parsed is represented by an edge labeled with an FD obtained by looking that word up in the lexicon. If the word is ambiguous, that is, if it has more than one FD, it is represented by more than one edge. All the edges for the ith word clearly go from vertex $i - 1$ to vertex i. As the parser identifies higher order constituents, edges with the appropriate FDs are added to the chart. A particular analysis is complete when an edge is added from the first to the last vertex and labeled with a suitable FD, say one with the feature [CAT = s].

The edges just alluded to are all *inactive*; they represent words and phrases. *Active* edges each represent a step in the recognition process. Suppose a phrase with c constituents is recognized. Since the only knowledge the parser has of words and phrases is recorded in the chart, it must be the case that the constituent edges are entered in the chart before the process of recognizing the phrase is complete, though the recognition process can clearly get underway before they are all there. If the phrase begins at vertex v_i, the chart will contain c vertices (possibly among others) beginning at v_i, each ending at a vertex where one of the constituents ends. The one that ends where the final constituent ends is the one that represents the phrase itself. That one is inactive. The remainder are *active*

edges and each records what is known about a phrase when only the first of so many of its constituents have been seen, and also what action must be taken to incorporate the next constituent to the right. The label on an active edge therefore has two parts, an FD describing what is known about the putative phrase, and a *procedure* that will carry the recognition of the phrase one step further forward. It is these procedures that constitute the parsing grammar and that the compiler is responsible for constructing.

Parsing proceeds in a series of steps in each of which the procedure on an active edge is applied to a pair of FDs, one coming from that same active edge, and the other from an inactive edge that leaves the vertex where the active edge ends. In other words, if a and i are an active and an inactive edge respectively, a being incident to the vertex that i is incident from, the step consists in evaluating $P_a(f_a, f_i)$, where f_a and f_i are the FDs on a and i, and P_a is the procedure. The step is successful if f_i meets the the requirements that P_a makes of it, one of which is to unify it with the value of some path in a copy of f_a. This copy then becomes part of the label on a new edge beginning where f_a begins and ending where f_i ends. The requirements imposed on f_i, the path in the copy of f_a with which it is unified, and the procedure to be incorporated in the label of the new edge, are all built in to P_a. The last step completes the recognition of a phrase, and the new edge that is produced is inactive and therefore has no procedure in its label.

This process is carried out for every pair consisting of an active followed by an inactive edge that comes to be part of the chart. Each successful step leads to the introduction of one new edge, but this edge may result in several new pairs. Each new pair produced therefore becomes a new item on the agenda which serves as a queue of pairs waiting to be processed.

The initial step in the recognition of a phrase is one in which the active member of the pair is incident from and to the same vertex – the same vertex from which the inactive edge is also incident. This is reasonable because active edges are like a snapshot of the process of recognizing a phrase when it is still incomplete. The initial active edge is therefore a snapshot of the process before any work has been done. These edges constitute the only cycles in the chart. Their labels clearly contain a process, but no FD. The question that remains to be answered is how these initial active edges find their way into the chart.

Suppose the first step in the recognition of all phrases, of whatever type, is carried out by a single procedure. I leave open, for the moment, the question of whether this is true of the output of the functional grammar compiler. This process will be the only one that is ever found in the label of initial, looping, active edges. If a looping edge is introduced at every vertex in the chart labeled with this process, then the strategy I have outlined will clearly cause all substrings of the string that are phrases to be analyzed as such, and all the analyses of the string as a whole will be among them. This technique corresponds to what is sometimes called undirected, bottom-up parsing.[1] If there is a number of different processes that can begin the recognition of a phrase, then a loop must be introduced for each of them at each vertex. Undirected top-down parsing is modeled by a strategy in which the only loops introduced initially are at the first vertex and the procedures in their labels are those that can initiate the search for a sentence. Others are introduced as follows: when the FD that a given procedure is looking for on an inactive edge corresponds to a phrase rather than a lexical item, and there is no loop at the relevant vertex that would initiate the search for a phrase of the required type, one is created.

7.2.2. The parsing grammar

The parsing grammar, as we have seen, takes the form of a set of procedures, each of which operates on a pair of FDs. One of these FDs, the *matrix FD*, is a partial description of a phrase, and the other, the *constituent FD*, is as complete a description as the parser will ever have of a candidate for inclusion as constituent of that phrase. There may be various ways in which the constituent FD can be incorporated. Suppose, for example, that the matrix is a partial FD of a noun phrase and that it already contains the description of a determiner. Suppose, further, that the edge representing the determiner ends where the current active edge ends. The current procedure will therefore be a specialist in noun-phrase constituents that follow initial determiners. Offered a constituent FD that describes an adjective, it will incorporate it into the matrix FD as a modifier and create a new active edge whose label may contain itself – on the theory that what can follow a determiner can also follow a determiner and an adjective. But, if the constituent FD describes a noun, that must be incorporated into the matrix as its head. At least two new edges will be produced in this case, an inactive edge representing a complete noun phrase and an active edge labeled with a procedure that specializes in incorporating prepositional phrases and relative clauses.

We have seen that the process of recognizing a phrase is initiated by an active edge that loops back to its starting vertex, and which has a null FD in its label. For the case of functional grammar, all such loops will be labeled with the same procedure, one capable of recognizing initial members of all constituents and building a matrix FD that incorporates them appropriately. Thus, for example, if this procedure is given a constituent FD that is a determiner description, it will put a new active edge

in the chart whose FD is a partial NP description incorporating that determiner FD.

The picture that emerges, then, is of a network of procedures, akin in many ways to an augmented transition network (ATN) (Wood, 1969). The initial procedure corresponds to the initial state and, in general, there is an arc connecting a procedure to the procedures that it introduces. The arc that is followed in a particular case depends on the properties that the procedure finds in the constituent FD it is applied to.

Consider the situation that obtains in a simple English sentence in the active voice after a noun phrase, a verb, and a second noun phrase have been seen. Three different grammar procedures are involved in getting this far. Let us now consider what would face a fourth procedure. If the verb is of the appropriate kind, the question of whether the second noun phrase is the direct or the indirect object is still open. If the current constituent FD is a noun phrase, then one possible way to continue the analysis will accept that noun phrase as the direct object and the preceding one as the indirect object. But, regardless of what the constituent FD is, another possibility that must be explored is that the preceding noun phrase was in fact the direct object. Let us assume that what can follow is the same in both cases; in ATN terms, a transition is made to the same state. A grammar procedure that does this is given below in (22).

```
(22)  [1]   (PROG ((OLDMATRIX MATRIX)
      [2]          S1)
      [3]     (SELECTQ (PATH 4 CAT)
      [4]         (NP)
      [5]         (NIL (SETQ S1 T))
      [6]         (GO L1))
      [7]     (AND S1 (NEWPATH 4 CAT
                               (QUOTE NP)))
      [8]     (ASSIGN 3 IOBJ)
      [9]     (ASSIGN 4 DOBJ)
      [10]    (TO S/DOBJ))
      [11]
      [12] L1 (SETQ MATRIX OLDMATRIX)
      [13]    (ASSIGN 3 DOBJ)
      [14]    (TO S/DOBJ))
      [15] OUT)
```

The procedure is written in Interlisp, a general programming language, but only a very small subset of the language is used, and the salient points about the example will be readily understood with the help of the following remarks. The major idiosyncrasy of the language for present expository purposes is that the name of a function or procedure, instead of being written before a parenthesized list of arguments, is written as the first item within the parentheses. So what would normally be written as $F(x)$ is written as (F x).

The heart of the procedure is in lines 3 through 6, which constitute a call on the function SELECTQ. SELECTQ examines the value of the CAT attribute of the constituent FD, as specified by the first argument (PATH 4 CAT). This returns the value of the (CAT) path of the fourth, that is, the current constituent.[2] The SELECTQ function can have any number of arguments, and the remaining ones give the action to be taken for various values of the first one. All but the last give the action for specific values, or sets of values, and the last says what is to be done in all other cases. In (22), the specific values are NP (line 4), and NIL (line 5). The nonspecific case is given in line 6: (GO L1). Now let us examine these cases more closely.

The last case is the most straightforward. If the value of the constituent FD has some value other than NP, or NIL for its CAT attribute, then it must describe something other than a noun phrase. NP is the value it would have if it did describe a noun phrase, and NIL is a purely conventional value that the procedure finds when the attribute is absent altogether. The only other possibility is that the attribute has some other substantive value, like VP. If this happens, the instruction (GO L1) is executed, causing processing to resume at line 12. The first thing that is done here, (SETQ MATRIX OLDMATRIX), is of minor interest, and we will return to it shortly. After this, only two instructions remain, on lines 13 and 14. The effect of the first of these, (ASSIGN 3 DOBJ), is to unify the description of the third constituent of the phrase – the noun phrase immediately preceding the phrase that this procedure examines – with the value of the path DOBJ. In short, it implements the hypothesis that that constituent was the direct object. The instruction (TO S/DOBJ), intentionally reminiscent of the language of ATNs, causes a new active edge to be created, labeled with the procedure S/DOBJ.

In the remaining cases, the constituent either has, or could be given, the feature [CAT = NP]. These are the cases in which the current constituent could be the direct, and the preceding constituent the indirect, object. However, if the value of the CAT attribute of the current constituent is NIL, it must be assigned the value NP before the hypothesis is acted upon and the procedure sets the local variable S1 to T (Interlisp's own name for "true") in line 5 to remind it to do this. It is actually done in by the instructions on lines 7 and 8; if S1 has a nonnull value, the instruction (NEWPATH 4 CAT) (QUOTE NP)) is carried out, causing NP to become the new value of the CAT attribute of the constituent FD. Setting and testing the local variable S1 is an efficiency measure, enabling the cost of the NEWPATH operation to be avoided when the required value is already in place.

The instructions on lines 9 and 10 are similar to the one on line 13. They cause the third and fourth constituents to be assigned the functions IOBJ and DOBJ, respectively. (TO S/DOBJ) then causes a new active edge to be created as before. The procedure then goes on to do what it would

have done in the default case described above. But it must first restore the FDs to the condition they were in when the procedure was entered, and this is the purpose of the instruction (SETQ MATRIX OLDMATRIX) on line 12.[3] The original matrix FD was preserved as the value of the temporary variable OLDMATRIX in line 1 and the constituent FD is embedded in the same data structure by a subterfuge that is best left unexamined.

If, in the case we have just examined, the grammar made no provision for constituents following the direct object, the instruction (TO S/DOBJ) appearing on lines 11 and 14 would have been replaced by (DONE). This has the effect of creating an inactive edge labeled with the current matrix FD. More realistically, the procedure should probably have both instructions in both places, on the theory that material can follow the direct object, but it is optional.

Before going on to discuss how procedures of this kind can be compiled from functional grammars, a few words are in order on why procedures like (22) have the particular structure they have. Why, in particular, is the local variable S1 used in the way it is rather than simply embedding the (NEWPATH 4 CAT) (QUOTE NP)) in the (SELECTQ) instruction? The example at (23) will help make this clear. The procedure succeeds, and a transition to the state NEXT is made, just in case the current constituent has the features [CAT = NP] and [ANIMATE = NONE]. If attribute CAT in the constituent FD has the value NIL, then as we have seen, the function NEWPATH must be called to assign the value NP to this attribute. However, there is no point in doing this if the other requirements of the constituent are not also met. Accordingly, in this case, the procedure verifies the feature [ANIMATE = NONE] before making any reassignments of values.

```
(23)  [1]   (PROG ((OLDMATRIX MATRIX)
      [2]          S2 S1)
      [3]      (SELECTQ (PATH 1 CAT)
      [4]         (NP)
      [5]         (NIL (SETQ S1 T)
      [6]            (GO OUT))
      [7]         (SELECTQ (PATH 1 ANIMATE)
      [8]            (NONE)
      [9]            (NIL (SETQ S2 T)
      [10]              (GO OUT))
      [11]            (AND S2 (NEWPATH 1 ANIMATE)
      [12]                     (QUOTE NONE)))
      [13]            (AND S1 (NEWPATH 1 CAT)
      [14]                     (QUOTE NP)))
      [15]       (TO NEXT)
      [16] OUT)
```

A second point that may require clarification involves instructions like (ASSIGN 3 DOBJ), which can cause the assignment of constituents other than the current one to grammatical functions – attributes – in the matrix FD. In principle, all such assignments could be made when the constituent in question is current, in which case no special instruction would be required and it would not be necessary to use numbers to identify particular constituents. These devices are the cost of some considerable gains in efficiency. A situation that illustrates this is now classic in discussions of ATN grammars. Suppose that the first noun phrase in a sentence is to be assigned to the SUBJ attribute if the sentence is active, and to the DOBJ attribute if it is passive. The voice is not known at the time the noun phrase is encountered what the voice of the sentence is. A perfectly viable solution to the problem this raises is to make both assignments, in different active edges, and to unify the corresponding value with that of the VOICE attribute. When the voice is eventually determined, only the active edge with the proper assignment for the first noun phrase will be able to continue. But, in the meantime, parallel computations will have been pursued redundantly. The numbers that appear in the ASSIGN instructions serve as a temporary label and enable us to defer the decision as to the proper role for a constituent.

7.3. The compiler

The compiler has two major sections. The first part is a straightforward application of the generation program to put the grammar, effectively, into disjunctive normal form. The second is concerned with actually building the procedures.

A grammar is a complex FD, typically involving a great many alternations. As with any algebraic formula involving *and* and *or*, it can be restructured so as to bring all the alternations to the top level. In other words, if F is a grammar, or indeed any complex FD, it is always possible to recast it in the form $F_1 \lor F_2 \cdots F_n$, where the F_i ($1 \le i \le n$) each contain no alternations. This remains true even when account is taken of the alternations implicit in patterns, for if the patterns in an FD do not impose a unique ordering on the constituents, then each allowable order is a different alternative.

Now, the process of generation from a particular FD, f, effectively selects those members of $F_1 \cdots F_n$ that can be unified with f, and then repeats this procedure recursively for each constituent. But F is, in general, a conjunct containing some atomic terms and some alternations. Ignoring patterns for the moment, the procedure is as follows:

1. Unify the atomic terms of F with f. If this fails, the procedure as a whole fails. Some number of alternations now remain to be considered. In other words, that part of F that remains to be unified with f is an expression F' of the form $(a_{1,1} \lor a_{1,2} \cdots a_{1,k_1}) \land (a_{2,1} \lor a_{2,2} \cdots a_{2,k_2}) \cdots (a_{n,1} \lor a_{n,2} \cdots a_{n,k_n})$.

2. Rewrite as an alternation by *multiplying out* the terms of an arbitrary alternation in F', say the first one. This gives an expression F'' of the form $(a_{1,1} \land (a_{2,1} \lor a_{2,2} \cdots a_{2,k_2}) \land (a_{n,1} \lor a_{n,2} \cdots a_{n,k_n})) \lor (a_{1,2} \land (a_{2,1} \lor a_{2,2} \cdots a_{2,k_2}) \land (a_{n,1} \lor a_{n,2} \cdots a_{n,k_n})) \cdots (a_{1,k_1} \land (a_{2,1} \lor a_{2,2} \cdots a_{2,k_2}) \land (a_{n,1} \lor a_{n,2} \cdots a_{n,k_n}))$.

3. Apply the whole procedure (steps 1–3) separately to each conjunct in F''.

If f is null, then there are no constraints on what is generated and the effect is to enumerate all the sentences in the language, a process that presumably only terminates in trivial cases. Unconstrained generation does terminate, however, if it is applied only to a single level in the constituency hierarchy and, indeed, the effect is to generate precisely the disjunctive normal form of the grammar required by the compiler.

It remains to spell out the alternatives that are implicit in the patterns. This is quite straightforward and can be done in a separate part of the procedure applied to each of the FDs that the foregoing procedure delivers. The basic idea is to generate all permutations of the constituent set of the FD and to eliminate those that do not match all the patterns. This process, like the one just described, can be considerably streamlined. Permutations are generated in an analog of alphabetical order, so that all those that share a given prefix are produced together. But, if any such prefix itself violates the requirements of the patterns, the process is truncated and the corresponding suffixes are not generated for them.

The result of this phase of the compilation is a list of simple FDs, containing no alternations, and having either no pattern, or a single pattern that specifies the order of constituents uniquely. Those that have no pattern become lexical entries and they are of no further interest to the compiler. It seems likely that realistic grammars will give rise to lists which, though quite long, are entirely manageable. If a little care is exercised and list-processing techniques are used in a thoroughgoing manner, a great deal of structure turns out to be shared among members of the list.

When FDs are simplified in this way, an analogy between them and phrase structure rules begins to emerge. In fact, a simple FD F of this kind could readily be recast in the form $F \to F_1 \cdots F_k$ where $F_1 \cdots F_k$ are the subdescriptions identified by the terms in the pattern taken in the order given there. The analogy is not complete because the items that make up the right-hand side of such a rule cannot be matched directly against the left-hand sides of other rules. A rule of this kind can be used to expand a given item, not if its left-hand side is that item, but if it can be *unified* with it.

The second phase of the compiler centers around a procedure which, given a list of simple FDs, and an integer n, attempts to find an attribute, or path, on the basis of which the *n*th constituent of those FDs can be distinguished. In the general case, the result of this process is (1) a path *A*, (2) a set of values for *A*, each associated with the subset of the list of FDs whose *n*th constituent has that value of *A*, and (3) a residual subset of the list consisting of FDs whose *n*th constituent has no value for the attribute *A*. The procedure attempts to find a path that minimizes the size of the largest of these sets. The residual set cannot be distinguished from the other sets on the basis of the chosen path; in other words, for each member *R* of the residual set, a new member can be added to each of the other sets by adding a path with the appropriate value to a copy of *R*. The same procedure is applied to each of the resulting sets, with the same constituent number, until the resulting sets cannot be discriminated further. The overall result of this is to construct a discrimination tree that can be applied to an FD to determine in which of the members of the list it could be incorporated as the *n*th constituent.

The discrimination procedure also has the responsibility of detecting features that are shared by all the FDs in the list provided to it. For this purpose, it examines the whole FD and not just the *n*th constituent. Clearly, if the list is the result of a previous discrimination step, there will always be at least one such feature, namely the path and value on the basis of which that previous discrimination was made. The discrimination procedure thus collects almost all the information required to construct a grammar procedure. All that is lacking is information about the other procedures that a given one must nominate to label active chart edges that it produces. This in its turn is bound up with the problem reducing equivalent pairs of procedures to one. Before going on to these problems, we shall do well to examine one further example of a grammar procedure to see how the operation of the discrimination process is reflected in its structure.

The procedure below, (24), shows the reflexes of all the important parts of the procedure. It is apparent that two sets of FDs have been discriminated on the basis that the discriminating path was CAT. If the value of the path is VERB, a further discrimination is made on the basis of the TRANSITIVE attribute of the third constituent. If the constituent is a transitive verb, the next active arc will be labeled with the procedure V-TRANS, and if intransitive with V-INTRANS. If the category is AUX, the next procedure will be AUX-STATE. This discrimination is reflected in lines 5–23. Lines 3 and 4 reflect the fact that all the FDs involved have the subject in first position, and that subject is singular. The instruction (OR (UNIFY (SUBJ) (1)) (GO OUT)), for example, say that either the value of the subject attribute can be unified with the first constituent or the procedure terminates without further ado.

```
(24)   [1]   (PROG ((OLDFEATURES FEATURES)
       [2]          S1 S2)
       [3]       (OR (UNIFY (SUBJ) (1)) (GO OUT))
       [4]       (OR (UNIFY SING (SUBJ NUM)) (GO OUT))
       [5]       (SELECTQ (PATH (3 CAT))
       [6]           (VERB (GO L2))
       [7]           (AUX (GO L1))
       [8]           (NIL (SETQ S1 T))
       [9]           (GO OUT))
       [10]      (NEWPATH 3 CAT (QUOTE VERB))
       [11] L2   (SELECTQ (PATH (3 TRANSITIVE))
       [12]          (PLUS (GO L4))
       [13]          (MINUS (GO L3))
       [14]          (NIL (SETQ S2 T))
       [15]          (GO OUT))
       [16]      (NEWPATH 3 TRANSITIVE (QUOTE PLUS))
       [17] L4   (TO V-TRANS)
       [18]      (SETQ FEATURES OLDFEATURES)
       [19]      (AND S2 (NEWPATH 3 TRANSITIVE (QUOTE MINUS))
       [20] L3   (TO V-INTRANS)
       [21]      (OR S1 (GO OUT))
       [22]      (NEWPATH 3 CAT (QUOTE AUX))
       [23] L1   (TO AUX-STATE)
       [24] OUT)
```

It remains to discuss how a procedure is put in touch with its successor procedures. In the examples I have shown, instructions like (TO V-IN-TRANS), provide more or less mnemonic names for the procedures that will be used to label new active edges, but, in doing so, I was exercising expository license. When the time comes to insert a name like this into the procedure, the discrimination process is invoked recursively to compile the procedure in question. Having done this, it compares the result with a list of previously compiled procedures. If, as frequently happens, it finds that the same procedure has been compiled before, it uses the old name and throws away the result of the compilation just completed; otherwise it assigns a new name. The effect of this is to substantially reduce the total number of procedures required. In ATN terms, the effect is to conflate similar tails of the transition networks. If this technique were not used, the network would in fact have the form of a tree.

7.4. Conclusion

The compilation scheme just outlined is based on the view, expressed at the outset, that the competence grammar is written in a formalism with theoretical status. This is the seat of linguistic universals. Since the parsing grammar is tightly coupled to this by the compiler, the language that it is written in is of only minor theoretical interest. The obvious choice

Kay, Martin. 1973. The mind system. In: Rustin (ed.), *Natural language processing*. Englewood Cliffs, N.J.: Prentice-Hall.
1977. Morphological and syntactic analysis. In: A. Zampolli (ed.). *Syntactic structures processing*. Amsterdam: North Holland.
1979. Functional grammar. *Proceedings of the Fifth Annual Meeting of the Berkeley Linguistic Society*.
1980. Algorithm schemata and data structures in syntactic processing. CSL-80-12 Xerox Palo Alto Research Center.
Woods, William A. 1969. Transition network grammars for natural language analysis. *Communications of the Association for Computing Machinery* 13:591–602.

is therefore a standard programming language. It is not only relatively straightforward to compile the grammar into such a language, as I hope to have shown, but the result can then be further compiled into the language of a particular computer. The result is therefore an exceedingly efficient parser. But there is a concomitant inefficiency in the research cycle involved in developing the grammar. This comes from the fact that the compilation itself is a long and very time-consuming enterprise.

Two things can be said to mitigate this to some extent. First, the parsing and generation grammars do indeed describe exactly the same languages, so that much of the work involved in testing prototype grammars can be done with a generator that works directly and efficiently off the competence grammar. The second point is this: it is not in fact necessary to compile the whole grammar in order to obtain an entirely satisfactory parser. Suppose, for example, that every constituent is known to have a value for the attribute CAT. Some such assumption is almost always in order. Suppose, further, that a parsing grammar is compiled ignoring completely all other attributes; in other words, the compiler behaves as though any attribute-value pair in the grammar that did not mention CAT was not there at all. The resulting set of parsing procedures clearly recognizes at least all the sentences of the language intended, though possibly others in addition. However, the results of the parsing process can be unified with the original grammar to eliminate false analyses.

Notes

1. See Kay (1980) for a fuller discussion of these terms.
2. The functions PATH, NEWPATH, and ASSIGN all take an indefinite number of arguments which, since the functions are all FEXPRS, are unevaluated. The first argument is a constituent number and the remainder constitute a path.
3. Argumentative LISP programmers may find this construction unconvincing on the grounds that OLDMATRIX in fact preserves only a pointer to the data structure and not the data structure itself. They should subside, however, on hearing that the data structure is an association list and the only changes made to it involve CONSing new material on the beginning, thus masking old versions.

References

Gazdar, Gerald. 1982. Phrase structure grammar, In: Pauline Jacobson and Geoffrey K. Pullum (eds.), *The nature of syntactic processing*. Dordrecht, Holland: D. Reidel, pp. 131–86.
Kaplan, Ronald M. 1972. Augmented transition networks as psychological models of sentence comprehension. *Artificial Intelligence* 3:77–100.
1973. A General Syntactic Processor. In: Rustin (ed.). *Natural language processing*. Englewood Cliffs, N.J.: Prentice-Hall.
1978. Computational resources and linguistic theory. *Theoretical Issues in Natural Language Processing* 2.

Artificial Intelligence
and Language Processing

Christine Montgomery*
Editor

DIAGRAM:
A Grammar for Dialogues

Jane J. Robinson
SRI International

An explanatory overview is given of DIAGRAM, a large and complex grammar used in an artificial intelligence system for interpreting English dialogue. DIAGRAM is an augmented phrase-structure grammar with rule procedures that allow phrases to inherit attributes from their constituents and to acquire attributes from the larger phrases in which they themselves are constituents. These attributes are used to set context-sensitive constraints on the acceptance of an analysis. Constraints can be imposed by conditions on dominance as well as by conditions on constituency. Rule procedures can also assign scores to an analysis to rate it as probable or unlikely. Less likely analyses can be ignored by the procedures that interpret the utterance. For every expression it analyzes, DIAGRAM provides an annotated description of the structure. The annotations supply important information for other parts of the system that interpret the expression in the context of a dialogue.

Major design decisions are explained and illustrated. Some contrasts with transformational grammars are pointed out and problems that motivate a plan to use metarules in the future are discussed. (Metarules derive new rules from a set of base rules to achieve the kind of generality previously captured by transformational grammars but without having to perform transformations on syntactic analyses.)

CR Categories and Subject Descriptors: I.2.7 [**Artificial Intelligence**]: Natural Language Processing—*language parsing and understanding*; J.5 [**Arts and the Humanities**]—*language translation, linguistics.*

General Term: Languages

Additional Key Words and Phrases: phrase-structure grammar, transformations, dialogue, augmented rules, annotations, attribute inheritance, contextual constraints, likelihoods, metarules

---

This work was supported in part by the National Science Foundation under Grant MCS76-22004 and in part by the Defense Advanced Research Projects Agency under Contract N00039-79-C-0118 with the Naval Electronic Systems Command.

* Former Editor of Artificial Intelligence and Language Processing of which David L. Waltz is the current editor.

Author's present address: J. J. Robinson, Artificial Intelligence Center, SRI International, 333 Ravenswood Ave., Menlo Park, CA 94025.

1. Introduction

> All grammars leak.
> —Edward Sapir, *Language*, 1921.

DIAGRAM is a grammar used in an artificial intelligence system for interpreting dialogue. The system is a tool for ongoing research to find what structures and processes are necessary for dialogue interpretation. A basic premise is that dialogue participants interpret each other's expressions by taking into account not only the truth-conditional meanings of what is said, but also each other's intentions, goals, plans, beliefs, states of knowledge, and focus of attention as inferred from text and context [20]. DIAGRAM is an English grammar, not of the whole of English, of course, but of a substantial subset of it. It analyzes not only all the basic kinds of phrases but complex ones as well. It is extendible in a principled way independently of a particular domain of application. The following list is a sampling of the kinds of syntactic constructions that are successfully analyzed at present:

Her uncle gave the girl several books.
She was given more difficult books by her uncle.
Which ones did he give her?
I saw many more books than she did.
Two of them were by her uncle.
Do it quickly but be careful!
Be careful not to break the vase when you put it down.
Tell me what he told you.
Don't tell me any more about it!
There are some men here from the city.
The vase could easily break, if you aren't careful.
You could break this vase with that hammer.
They found her gone.
On arriving, we had something to eat.
Have there been many people who tried it?
Didn't those people want him to try to do it?
Is this any harder for him to do than that was?
Who wrote it?
By whom was it written?
Who was it written by?
What could he have been doing there?
Why did you want John to attach it?
Why do you think he wanted to go?
What did they tell you Mary said John tried to do?
How many more of them do you want him to have?

All grammars leak. No grammar for a reasonably extensive subset of English can claim to provide *all* and *only* the correct analyses for the sentences for which it is applicable. What is claimed is that every structurally distinct semantic interpretation of the sentences shown receives a corresponding, structurally distinct, syntactic analysis. A simple example may make the point. Consider the sentence: She was given more difficult books by her uncle. The sentence contains two syntactically ambiguous phrases: either the books were more difficult or there were more books and either the books were "by" her uncle or the giving was "by" her uncle. These two ambiguities combine to produce four different analyses of the sentence. (There is an additional lexical semantic ambiguity, since "by" has both a locative and an agentive sense.)

DIAGRAM successfully provides the four appropriate syntactic analyses. Figure 1 shows relevant parts of three of the four analyses and their corresponding interpretations. The fourth, in which the books were more difficult and were given by her uncle, is left as an exercise for the reader.

For this sentence and many others like it, DIAGRAM provides all and only the syntactic analyses that correspond to semantic ambiguities not arising from lexical ambiguity. However, for some sentences there will be incorrect analyses along with correct ones. The reasons for this are relatively well understood and are described later, together with methods for eliminating or controlling multiple analyses without losing correct ones.

DIAGRAM's rules have been written to capture the insightful generalizations about language that appear in the literature of theoretical linguistics. They also have been written with a constant awareness of the functional roles that syntactic phenomena play in communication. As a result, DIAGRAM contains some nonstandard definitions of syntactic categories and constituent boundaries along with much that is widely accepted. These definitions are explained, but not always justified. "Justifying" implies that the rules are superior to any currently conceivable alternatives, but DIAGRAM will continue to be revised as better ways are found to accommodate the tension between the requirements for capturing linguistic generalizations and for designing rules suitable for processing and interpreting interactive dialogues. Consequently, we describe an intermediate stage that is interesting because it incorporates the results of experience with other formulations of rules and procedures and because its unresolved problems establish a direction for significant future research and revision.

The next section presents an overview of DIAGRAM as a component in a larger system for analyzing and interpreting utterances in dialogues. This is followed in Sec. 3 by a detailed explication, beginning with a characterization of the category S (the category of independent sentences) and the subtypes of S, before describing, in Sec. 4, the categories of words and phrases that are the constituents of S. By starting from the top down in the order of description, a sense of the whole is conveyed first so that light can be shed on how constituent parts function with respect to that whole. Indeed, the description is as much in terms of functions as in terms of syntactic categories. Section 4 discusses the relationships of syntactic functions to syntactic categories. Section 5 presents current plans for revisions and the motives for them.[1]

---

[1] "Function," here, is to be understood in two senses: the sense in which a phrase is capable of serving a purpose in discourse and the sense in which it serves one of the traditional syntactic functions such as subject, predicate, object, and modifier. Context should make clear which is meant.

Fig. 1. (a) In this analysis the books are more difficult (i.e., harder to read) and they are (written) by her uncle. (b) In this analysis the difficult books were by her uncle and they were many. (c) In this analysis the giving was done by her uncle and the difficult books were many.

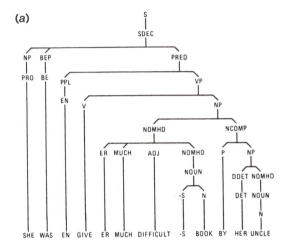

(a)

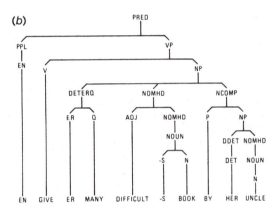

(b)

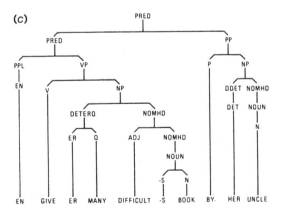

(c)

2. What DIAGRAM Does and How It Does It

DIAGRAM is a phrase-structure grammar whose context-free rules are augmented by procedures that increase its descriptive power and give it limited context-sensitive capabilities. There has been a resurgence of interest in phrase-structure grammars with various augmentations as alternatives to transformational grammars, and although little has been published so far, substantive work is beginning to surface. An extended comparison of the emerging grammatical formalisms with DIAGRAM's rules and procedures is perhaps premature and certainly beyond the scope of this paper, but some points of comparison are noted throughout, particularly in the final section.[2]

For every expression it defines (or accepts) as syntactically well-formed, DIAGRAM provides an annotated description that makes explicit the structural relations holding among its words and phrases. It identifies the syntactic categories of each word and phrase and specifies properties that each contributes to the whole expression or that each acquires as a result of its relationship to the whole. For example, applied to the analysis of

The fish are in the river

DIAGRAM will not only label "the fish" as a noun phrase but also as definitely determined, plural, and the subject of the sentence. Note that the last two properties are not inherent to "the fish" in isolation, but are resultant properties of its use in the whole expression. (Compare "John caught the fish," where the syntactic number is indeterminate for "fish.")

All these properties provide important pieces of information for the other parts of the system that interpret the phrase when it is used in ongoing discourse. From the fact that the noun phrase is plural, it follows that more than one of a set of discrete entities are being referred to. From the fact that it is definitely determined, one can infer that the speaker assumes the entities to be already identified or readily identifiable by the hearer. From the fact that "the fish" is the subject, one can infer that the focus of attention of the speaker is on the fish rather than on the river or on other elements in the context of the discourse. (Compare "The river contains many fish.")

2.1. Rules and Procedures

Appendix A contains a few of the rules and a sample lexicon. Here we are concerned with the formal properties of DIAGRAM rather than with details of its format.

The rules are augmented by procedures that constrain the application of a rule, add information to the structure created by the rule, and assign one or more interpretations to the resulting enriched structural analysis. These procedures apply at different points during processing.

---

[2] A very useful comparison of some of these alternatives appears in Joshi and Levy [13], but this remains in manuscript form as of this writing. Another grammatical model, only briefly mentioned there, is the Lexical–Functional Grammar proposed by Kaplan and Bresnan [14], whose formalism for representing predicate-argument structures invites comparison with the procedures used in DIAGRAM and in the semantic component of the system in which DIAGRAM is used.

One, called a *constructor*, applies immediately as the constituents of a phrase are being assembled. After the entire utterance has been analyzed, a second procedure, called a *translator*, is applied. The following simplified example should clarify the interactions of the constituent-structure statements with the constructors and translators.

Rule SBE   SDEC = NP BE ADJP;

Constructor:
(1) If NP and BE do not agree in syntactic number, then REJECT the analysis.
(2) If either BE contains "not" or NP directly dominates a determiner phrase containing "no," then SDEC is negative; else it is affirmative.

Translator:
(1) If the syntactic number of NP is null (undefined), then set it equal to the syntactic number of BE.
(2) Set NP as subject of SDEC.
(3) Set ADJP as predicate of SDEC.
(4) Combine the semantics of ADJP with the semantics of NP.

The constituent structure portion states that a declarative sentence can be composed of a noun phrase followed by an auxiliary BE phrase followed by a predicate adjective phrase, as in "the fish are very big."

Within the constructor, the first (sub)procedure accepts or rejects a string of constituents according to the results of a number-agreement test. This prevents the rule from applying to "the girls was very tall" in the course of analyzing "the father of the girls was very tall." The second procedure sets the value of an attribute for the dominating SDEC node created by the rule. Notice that the constructor has access to information about the words in the constituents. It can "look down" the parse tree, so to speak, in making decisions about acceptance and in setting attributes. The translator has similar capabilities, but it is also allowed to "reach down" the tree and set attributes on the constituents, thus resolving ambiguities not hitherto resolved and adding other information that cannot be determined without knowing the context in which a phrase is embedded. Thus, in the example, "the fish" acquires attributes of number and subject status. Constructors can also make semantic tests to decide whether constituents obey local selectional restrictions, that is, whether or not they are semantically as well as syntactically compatible.

The translator procedure for a rule derives one or more semantic interpretations of the phrase built by the rule. In doing so, the procedure can access all the attributes whose values have been set by translators of rules that have constructed the larger phrases in which the phrase to be interpreted forms a part. If the SDEC constructed by applying the rule in (1) is embedded in another SDEC, for instance, the translator for the embedding rule will add that information. This is necessary, since the independent sentence, "the fish are in the river," will be interpreted as an assertion about the world, but if it is embedded as part of a sentence beginning with "it is doubtful that . . ." or "I see that . . . ," its interpretations will be very different.

A third procedure, called an *integrator*, which we will only mention here, is more domain-dependent than the other procedures. (The separation of integrators from other procedures makes the grammar easier to adapt to new domains without extensive revision.) The integrator for a rule has access to facts about the world, or to a database, and can render decisions about the pragmatic well-formedness or appropriateness of a semantic interpretation.

The capability to apply tests at any of three points during the analysis of a sentence—during application of the constructor, or the translator, or the integrator procedures—raises theoretical and practical questions concerning processing. The major question is this: When should semantic and pragmatic criteria be invoked to avoid false parsing paths? The question involves matters of computational efficiency and of psycholinguistic processing, on the assumption that people store a certain amount of incoming text before they process it for meaning. We speculate that experiments with computational efficiency using DIAGRAM or some other sufficiently large grammar, may help us understand psycholinguistic phenomena and vice versa.

In brief, the procedures of constructors and translators provide the overall system with the capability for context-sensitive intensional interpretations and integrators provide the interface for extensional interpretations.

2.2. Attributes and Factors

Attributes that are set and tested by rule procedures are divided into two types: general and specific. Specific attributes are associated with specific categories of words and phrases and are often introduced in the lexical entries of words and inherited by the phrases in which the words are constituents. Others are introduced in the rule procedures themselves. One very important attribute, that of syntactic number, is introduced by both means. Syntactic number is primarily an attribute of the category NOUN and most NOUNs are formed by a rule that optionally combines a noun stem N with the plural suffix "-s". If the suffix is present, the value of the attribute is "plural" (PL); otherwise it is "singular" (SG). However, some words that do not combine with the suffix are inherently plural; e.g., "people." Such words are entered into the lexicon as members of the category NOUN with the value PL for the attribute @ NBR. The ambiguous word "fish" is also a NOUN, but it has no attribute for syntactic number. The tests for number agreement accept null values (meaning that the attribute is undefined) as agreeing with any value, so that the NP "the fish," which has not inherited an attribute of number from its NOUN constituent, agrees with either a singular or plural auxiliary.[3]

Among the general attributes referenced and used in the procedures is one called @ SPELLING. @ SPELLING is an attribute of every word in the lexicon and its value is the literal form of the word. This attribute is referenced in rules that attach particles and inseparable prepositions (Ps) as constituents of the inner core of verb phrases. For example, the lexical entry for "give" will list the form UP as a possible value for the attribute @ PARTICLE, and the rules (Rules VP1 and VP2) that analyze the phrases "give up the book" and "give it up" will test for agreement of the @ SPELLING attribute of the preposition "up" with the forms listed as possible particles for the verb "give." The @ SPELLING attribute is also used to check other "function" words and affixes.

Every phrase also has as attributes the categories of its immediate constituents, which can be referenced to any desired depth in the procedures that constrain the application of a rule. For example, noun phrases may contain modifying phrases that follow the central core (NOMHD) of the NP. Such modifying phrases belong to the category NCOMP, and NPs that contain them as immediate constituents will have an attribute @ NCOMP with the value T, meaning that the constituent is present. The NCOMP itself may have a prepositional phrase constituent, in which case it has the attribute @ PP.

DIAGRAM makes frequent use of such general attributes in the subprocedures called *factors* that are used to assign likelihood scores to syntactic or semantic analyses. Instead of simply accepting or rejecting an analysis, a rule can accept it with some assessment of the probability of its correctness. For example, the probability that a prepositional phrase is part of a nominal modifier NCOMP rather than a verbal modifier may depend on what the preposition is (i.e., how it is spelled), and on whether numerous other modifiers have already been added to NCOMP. Factors can specify the probabilities and attach scores to phrases that meet their specifications. Then when several possibilities for attaching the prepositional phrase result in multiple analyses of a sentence, the analyses can be ordered according to their likelihood by combining the judgments of the various factors for the various combinations. Less likely combinations can subsequently be ignored by semantic and pragmatic interpreters.[4]

To give a simple example, consider the use of factors in assessing the probability that a prepositional phrase is part of an NCOMP. A factor in the appropriate rule NCOMP4 stipulates that the probability is low (UNLIKELY) if the NCOMP already has a relative clause constituent, SREL. The designation for the attribute is (@ SREL NCOMP) and its value is T, meaning "true" or "present" for NCOMP modifiers like "that I saw" in

the man that I saw.

---

[3] Some of the syntactic categories assigned by DIAGRAM to words and phrases are listed in Appendix B. Appendix C lists some of the principal syntactic attributes associated with specific categories.

[4] Methods for combining scores derived from factors and ordering multiple analyses are described in Paxton [18, pp. 66–71].

In analyzing the larger phrase

> the man that I saw with the telescope

DIAGRAM currently assigns a higher score to the analysis in which "with the telescope" is part of the SREL "that I saw with the telescope," but will allow the alternative analysis in which "with the telescope" independently modifies "man."

It is worth noting that factors can be changed to adjust the analyses to particular styles and discourse domains without rewriting the grammar.

3. Sentence Categories and Structures

3.1. Major Sentence Types

We begin an account of the grammar itself with an explication of DIAGRAM's characterization of the category S, the category of independent sentences. Sentences, viewed functionally, perform many different tasks. Among other things, they encode propositional content that makes claims about the way the world is; they arrange that content so it meshes with what the speaker assumes the hearer knows and is currently attending to; and they express the speaker's attitudes toward the content and toward the hearer. The same propositional content may be encoded with different words in different syntactic structures. The differences reflect the influence of the other functions the sentence serves when it is used. Consequently, devising a grammar for recognizing and making explicit the significant variations in the syntactic structures of sentences and other phrases is a complicated affair. Decisions as to how some string of words should be structured and categorized in order to simplify the problem of interpreting them in a consistent and general way need to be guided by considerations of their communicative functions. These considerations should be kept in mind as part of the background in which various decisions about how to analyze English sentences were embodied in DIAGRAM.

Sentences are traditionally classified according to their modalities as imperative and indicative. Indicatives are subclassified as declarative and interrogative; interrogatives are further subclassified into two types according to whether the truth of a total proposition is being questioned or whether some argument of a proposition is marked as unknown. These two types of interrogatives are sometimes called Yes/No (or polar) questions and WH-questions.

This hierarchical concept is not preserved overtly in DIAGRAM. All of the distinctions are treated as equally important and although the special relatedness of WH-questions to Yes/No questions is implicitly recognized in the constituent structure assigned to the WH-questions (see Sec. 3.1.1.), DIAGRAM explicitly distinguishes four basic sentence types. These are given the mnemonic category names:

SIMP	imperative sentence
SDEC	declarative sentence
SQ	propositional interrogative
SWHQ	argument interrogative

The syntactic basis for this treatment is that each type has a distinctive initial category. SIMPs lack an initial NP; they typically begin with an uninflected auxiliary DO or BE or with an uninflected form of a verb. SDECs typically begin with a noun phrase that functions as the subject of the sentence. SQs begin with an auxiliary followed by an NP. SWHQs begin with a noun phrase marked by the presence of a WH-word (how, who, what, which, where, when, whose) in initial position or by an initial prepositional phrase with such a noun phrase as its object.[5] Examples are

SIMP	Put the apples in the basket.
	Don't drop them.
SDEC	He put the apples in the basket.
	They are there now.
	There are several of them.
SQ	Did he put them in the basket?
	Are they in the basket or in the sack?
	Are there more than two there?
SWHQ	How many apples did he put there?
	Which basket did he put them in?
	How many of them are there?

The differences in the types of messages each class of sentence is suited to convey are also equally important, conceptually. SIMP represents a directive speech act in which, to use Searle's terms [22], the direction of fit of the propositional content is from word to world; that is, the speaker asks the hearer to perform some action (putting apples in a basket) that will bring about a state of affairs in the world that realizes (makes true) the propositional content expressed in the words (the hearer has "put the apples in the basket"). For SDEC, the direction of fit is from world to word; that is, the speaker asserts that the propositional content expressed in the words is true ("they are there now"). SQ is a request for the hearer to judge whether the words fit the world and tell the speaker if the propositional content is true (if "he" did indeed put "them" in the basket). SWHQ presupposes the truth of some propositional content but requests the hearer to supply a missing argument or quantifier. Extending Searle's terminology somewhat, we can say that WH-interrogatives (SWHQs) presuppose speaker and hearer agree that the words of the propositional content fit the world—the apples are in some basket—but that the speaker is missing a piece of the content that the hearer is requested to supply ("which basket").

Although the four sentence types are distinguished by their initial constituents, all can be analyzed in terms of three basic functions: a subject, a predicate, and an

---

[5] WH-questions can also include sentences with a noninitial WH-marked phrase, as in "He put them where?" DIAGRAM does not accept this kind of sentence, but extending it to do so should pose no major problems.

indicator of mood. In most sentences, these functions are served by overtly present constituents. For example,

subject	mood	predicate
They	were	going there
That	is	a big bird
Your home	is	very beautiful
The cake	must be	in the oven

Under special circumstances, there may be no constituent to represent the mood; for example, in "they go here," where the sentence is affirmative, not interrogative, the predicate is a verb, the subject is plural, and there is no auxiliary to indicate perfective or progressive aspect. Of course, imperatives lack subjects. Nevertheless, the association of constituent phrases with these functions is strong. In general, subjects are NPs, mood is indicated by various positions of auxiliary phrases, and predicates are phrases headed by one of the four major parts of speech, VPs, NPs, ADJPs, or PPs.

Transformational grammars capture these generalizations by setting up canonical underlying forms of sentences in which each function is represented by an appropriate constituent category, arranged in declarative order. If we were writing such a grammar, we might represent the rules for S in a single schema like

$$S = NP \; AUX \; \{VP \, / \, NP \, / \, ADJP \, / \, PP\}$$

and subsequently derive our four subtypes from the canonical forms by moving and deleting constituents to form interrogatives and imperatives. Although it employs some local string transformations on the sentences presented to it for parsing, DIAGRAM represents the various sentence types separately. Imperatives, for instance, are not derived from some appropriately restricted canonical form by deleting an initial NP realized as "you." They are analyzed directly by a rule (see Appendix B, Rule SIMP.) Some relevant facts needed for interpreting imperatives are that the subject is not overtly expressed but is understood to be the hearer; that the mood is indicated by the absence of subject, tense, and aspect; and that the predicating expression directs the hearer to perform some action to make the world fit the words. These facts are represented in the rule's translator, which assigns semantic interpretations to the syntactic analysis the rule provides for strings it accepts. This approach achieves the same effect as that achieved by formulating an imperative "transformation" that is constrained to operate on just those "underlying" canonical forms that obey the restrictions on realizing the subject as "you," omitting tense and aspect markers, and confining the predicates to certain semantic subclasses.

Nevertheless, we feel that there is some loss of generality in writing so many separate rules that have so many elements in common, and we are therefore exploring the possibility of deriving some rules from other rules. (See Paxton [18, pp. 258–260] and Gazdar [6].) This approach to achieving generality promises to avoid inefficiencies in the traditional transformational approach that requires first building and then transforming

syntactic tree structures, some of which may have elaborate and redundant substructures that are not only moved around, but are subsequently deleted.

To sum up at this point, DIAGRAM does not derive sentences from underlying canonical syntactic forms but directly defines four basic kinds of sentences. The syntactic bases for classification are the presence or absence of subjects, of tense and aspect auxiliaries, of a specially marked WH-phrase, and their structural arrangements with respect to each other when present. The classification is expressed in the first sentence rule, S0, which defines the root category of independent sentences as any of four types, with or without certain marks of punctuation.[6]

Rule S0 S = {SDEC / SIMP / SQ / SWHQ} (ENDPUNCT);

3.1.1. The Two Interrogatives

Mention has been made of an implicit recognition of the special relatedness of the two types of interrogatives, SQ and SWHQ. The recognition is implied by the analysis of SWHQs as containing SQ constituents in all cases except those in which the questioned argument is the subject of the sentence. The latter cases are handled by a distinct rule.

The rules defining SWHQs are

SWH1   SWHQ = { WHNP / WHPP / WHADJP } SQ
SWH2   SWHQ = WHNP (AUX) { VP / BE PRED }

Examples are

WHNP[Which boat]	SQ[did you buy]	[Rule SWH1]
WHPP[From whom]	SQ[did you buy it]	[Rule SWH1]
WHADJP[How wide]	SQ[is it]	[Rule SWH1]
WHNP[Who]	SQ[did you buy it from]	[Rule SWH1]

but

Who bought it	(No embedded SQ)	[Rule SWH2]

When the SWHQ contains an embedded SQ, the initial WH-marked constituent also "stands for" (in some sense) a constituent that is lacking in the SQ. In other words, an embedded SQ is always semantically incomplete or underspecified. When the missing constituent is an obligatory object of a verb or preposition, the SQ is syntactically incomplete too; that is, it is not a well-formed independent sentence. Such syntactically incomplete SQs are exemplified in the SWHQ examples above by "did you buy" and "did you buy it from." This type of incompleteness is also present in relative clauses, and a discussion of its theoretical and practical implications for the analysis and interpretation of embedded SQs is deferred to the treatment of relatives and WH-questions in Sec. 3.4.

---

[6] Braces enclose a list of alternatives, separated by a "/". Parentheses enclose (a list of) optional elements.

3.1.2. Sentence Types and the Packaging of Information

Since the sentences analyzed by DIAGRAM are assumed to be utterances in a dialogue, it may be of interest to consider briefly how the information structures of sentences are related to their syntactic analysis. The preceding description of WH-interrogatives provides examples.

For SWHQs that embed SQs, the SQs contain the propositional material that is presupposed, that is, the information that is ostensibly "given" or "already activated" [3] and that is shared by both speaker and hearer. For the other SWHQs, the presupposed material is in the auxiliary and predicating constituents. Thus, "which boat did you buy" presupposes "you bought a boat," and "who bought it" presupposes "someone bought it." In both cases, the initial WH-marked constituent contains a pointer to the kind of information the speaker lacks and assumes that the hearer can supply. In declarative sentences, on the other hand, the initial constituent usually points to or contains the already activated, shared information, and the remainder adds the information the speaker assumes is not already activated and shared by the hearer. The most striking exception to this generalization occurs when the declarative is an answer to a WH-interrogative in which the subject is the WH-marked constituent. For example, in the first of the following exchanges, the declarative answer to the question packages the new information in the subject constituent, "John," which is likely to be stressed, and the already activated information is in the predicate that follows.

Who bought the boat?
John bought it.   (The subject is "new" information.)
What did John buy?
He bought a *boat*.   (The object is "new" information.)

This is just what we would expect from the way the preceding question serves to reverse the order in which given and new information is packaged. In the second example, the declarative answer contains a constituent in its predicate that is lacking in the predicate of the embedded SQ of the SWHQ, a constituent that also contains the kind of information indicated by the WH-marked initial constituent of the interrogative. As we might expect, therefore, the predicate of the second declarative answer contains the new information, which is also likely to be stressed in speaking.

These considerations of how information is packaged become important in designing computer systems for interacting with human users. For instance, it is important that mistaken presuppositions be corrected and that new information be appropriately related to already activated information. Otherwise, there is risk of misunderstanding or incoherence. The risk cannot be avoided if only the propositional content of sentences is considered; the syntactic packaging must be related to the propositional content in analyzable ways.[7]

---

[7] For a fuller discussion, see Hobbs and Robinson [10].

3.2. Subtypes of the Basic Types of Sentences
3.2.1. The BE/DO Dichotomy

Each of the four basic sentence types is divided into two classes according to whether or not an auxiliary BE is required. Only sentences with verb phrase predicates can occur without any member of the BE paradigm. Such sentences require a form of DO if they are interrogatives or if they are negated or emphatic; otherwise, they may omit an auxiliary constituent entirely, except for the suffix "−s" marking present tense in sentences with third person singular subjects. Examples of the first class are "it *is* here" and "it could *be* a bear." Examples of the second class are "they go," "they *did*n't go," and "he goe*s*."

The rule schema for imperatives, shown below in simplified form, reveals the differences in the two subtypes. Rule SIMP1 allows an imperative with a VP predicate to occur without any auxiliary. When an auxiliary is present, it is the infinitive form of DO. An imperative with a non-VP predicate requires the infinitive form BE, but occurs with an infinitive DO in emphatic and negated forms.[8]

Rule SIMP1   SIMP = ("DO" (NOT)) { "BE" PRED / VP }

Examples are

Don't be an idiot	Don't try
Do be careful	Do try
Be here by noon	Try again

Only a relatively small number of non-VP predicates are semantically appropriate as imperatives. Intuitively, the DO auxiliary and verbs are both associated semantically with actions while BE is associated semantically with states, as are adjectives, nouns (static objects), and prepositions. Only those states that are conceived of as requiring an act of will to maintain can appropriately be expressed with non-VP predicates in imperatives.

Except for imperatives, sentences that *require* a BE form in the auxiliary cannot also occur with a form of DO in the auxiliary. For example, *"He doesn't be an idiot" is not well-formed in modern English. DIAGRAM emphasizes the distinction by defining separate rules for the two subtypes of SDEC, although they could be represented in a single rule schema with some complication of the constructor and translator procedures. The two constituent structure statements are

Rule SD1   SDEC = NP (AUX) VP
Rule SB1   SDEC = NP (AUX) BE PRED

---

[8] Quotation marks around an item mean that the item is interpreted literally; otherwise, it is interpreted as the name of a syntactic category. Some categories (e.g., NOT, OF) may contain only one or two members, however. DO and BE are categories of the auxiliary forms, including inflected forms such as "did" and "is." Instead of quoting "DO" and "BE," it would be possible to name the categories and then reject all inflected forms by performing a test in the translator for the rule, but this would clearly be inefficient.

3.2.2. *Existential Sentences*

Sentences requiring a form of BE in the auxiliary have a special subtype that is also distinguished in DIAGRAM. These are the existential sentences like "there is someone here," "are there any more oranges in that basket," and "how many are there." The rules defining existential declaratives and interrogatives form a separate set, in which "there" is explicitly quoted as a constituent. Thus

Rule STHERE1

SDEC = "THERE" (AUX) BE (NP {ING (VP / "BE" PRED) / PRED})

Examples are

There could be two.
There is a man being held prisoner.
There is a man running away.
There are some oranges on the table.

Rule STHEREQ1

SQ = BE "THERE" (NP {ING (VP / "BE" PRED) / PRED})

Examples are

Are there?
Are there any going?
Are there any more here?
Are there some oranges left?

Separating the rules for existential sentences from the others allows much more economical treatment of certain special syntactic constraints. For example, unlike the other declaratives, number agreement in existential declaratives holds between the auxiliary and the NP that follows it, rather than the one that precedes it. Compare "this is a group" / "these are a group" / "there is a group." Also, the NP is typically indefinite rather than definite and this fact can easily be stated in the constructors for the rules. Moreover, the NP is always a referring expression unless the sentence contains a negation, whereas in typical declaratives, the NP immediately following the auxiliary is a predicating expression. (Compare "he is a man" versus "a man is here.")

These special syntactic and semantic facts stem from the special function that existential sentences perform in discourses. Some sentences in a discourse are analyzable as containing both 'old' (or 'given') information and 'new' information, but in existential sentences, all the information is presented to the hearer as 'new.' They are introductory sentences, quite literally, serving to introduce new objects into the domain of the discourse and focus the hearer's attention on them [8, 9]. This is true even when the NP is definite. For example, "There's the book by Chomsky" (with the existential reading for "there") is appropriate only if there has been some previous denial or questioning of the existence of certain kinds of objects, as in "there aren't any good books on syntax." In this case, the previous speaker is *reminded* rather than *introduced* to the object (Chomsky's book), but in any case, that object is newly introduced into the *discourse*.

It is fairly common to overlook the special discourse functions of sentences when devising grammars. Appeals are frequently made to the principle that one should try to 'capture' generalizations when arguing for one syntactic analysis over another. On such grounds, many linguists have claimed that existential "there" is to be categorized as NP and existential sentences are to be defined by the same constituent structure rules that define the other sentence types. However, I know of only one property of the existential "there" that it shares with NPs, and that is its ability to function as the subject of a sentence.[9] But to say that "there" is the subject is to describe its syntactic function rather than its syntactic category. To claim that it is an NP is to ignore the fact that it cannot appear as a predicate nominal nor as the object of a preposition. If it is categorized as NP, this means that every occurrence of "there" in a nonsubject position will have to be checked for in the rules for phrases with NP constituents. Otherwise, semantic filters must reject inappropriate analyses that will be produced, for example, by parsing sentences like "John is there" with the same rules that parse "John is a linguist."

In arguing against syntactic overgeneralization, I am not claiming that the current rules for generating existential sentences are sufficiently general. DIAGRAM does not provide analyses for certain embeddings of existentials such as "there appear to be many oranges on that table," although it handles "it appears that there are many oranges on that table" and "many oranges appear to be on that table."

3.3. Sentence Conjunction, Modification, and Embedding

Larger sentences can be created by conjoining sentences or by modifying or embedding them.

DIAGRAM's rules for conjoining should be taken primarily as experimental placeholders, awaiting the time when linguistic theory yields more insight into the nature of conjunction and the constraints to be obeyed. Currently, Rules SX1 and SX2 define sentence conjunction and accept sentences like

I went there but he wasn't there.   [Rule SX1]
He came, he saw, and he conquered.
                              [Rule SX1 followed by Rule SX2]

These rules do not cover sentences like "He came, he saw, he conquered." Also, DIAGRAM does not have rules capable of accepting sentences involving 'gapping,' like

John gave but would have preferred to sell Mary a book

where the sequence "Mary a book" is not a single constituent, but rather two constituents, serving as indirect and direct objects of both "gave" and "sell." The main problem with DIAGRAM's conjoining rules, how-

---

[9] That it does have this property is shown by its behavior in tags, where "there are some men here, aren't there" is comparable to "John is here, isn't he." This syntactic behavior is plausibly described by saying that the subject of the sentence is reduplicated in the tag.

ever, is not their failure to analyze some legitimate sentences. It is the problem that all syntax-based conjoining rules are prone to introduce: they assign too many structures. Attempts to constrain such rules syntactically will usually bar them from recognizing some legitimate structures.

The necessary constraints undoubtedly involve some notion of semantic parallelism. Meanwhile, DIAGRAM's conjoining rules for sentences are loosely constrained not to conjoin imperatives with nonimperatives. The constraint, which appears in the constructors, rejects the parsing of sentences like

> I like to jog, swim and play tennis

as the conjunction of a declarative "I like to jog" with an imperative interpretation of "swim and play tennis." However, it also rejects one possible correct parsing of the ambiguous sentence:

> I like her but don't tell her that.

Sentence modification poses less severe problems. Rules SX3 and SX4 analyze sentences like

At midnight, satisfied, he left.
> [Rule SX4 followed by Rule SX3]

After they arrived, he left.
> [Rule SX3]

However, modifiers that follow the sentences they modify are attached as parts of the predicates of the four basic sentence types, rather than as modifiers of the S that dominates them. That is, in

> He left after they arrived

the phrase "after they arrived" is analyzed as part of the verb phrase. (See Rule VP9.) This attachment is theoretically justifiable, if one considers that Rules SX3 and SX4 define structures in which the modifiers have been fronted from a normally following position, analogously to the fronted object noun phrase "that man" in "that man I don't like." Even so, the rules for sentence modification will not at present allow a sentence modifier to modify jointly all sentence constituents of a conjoined sentence. For example, in parsing

> He arrived and she left at two o'clock

the modifier "at two o'clock" is attached only to the second SDEC of the conjoined pair. One remedy would be to add the rule

$$S = S (",") PP$$

which is symmetrical to Rule SX3, but to do so would increase the already large number of parsings due to trailing prepositional phrases. For this reason, adding such a rule has been postponed, pending a more satisfactory solution to the general problems of conjunction.

In DIAGRAM, the root category of independent sentences S, may be conjoined with other Ss or it may be modified. When it is conjoined or modified, it is embedded in a higher S, as in the structures S[PP S] and S[S CONJ S]. This self-embedding differs, however, from the embeddings in which sentences are constituents of phrases of a different, nonsentential category. In DIAGRAM, the root category S is embedded only as an immediate constituent of a higher S, and SQ, as we have seen, is an immediate constituent of some SWHQs. The only sentence type to be embedded as an immediate constituent of nonsentential phrase category is the declarative type, SDEC. Languages achieve great complexity of expression in large part through providing for this latter kind of embedding of sentences inside nonsentential phrases.

Various rules define phrases in which SDEC is a constituent. It occurs as a complement of a verb phrase, as an object of a preposition, as a constituent in the complement of a comparative phrase, and as a constituent of a relative clause modifier in a noun phrase, as in

[SDEC]	embedding rule
I saw (that) SDEC[he had arrived].	[Rule VP3]
After SDEC[he had arrived], they left.	[Rule PP1]
It is wider than SDEC[it is high].	[Rule THANCOMP]
He is as tall as SDEC[she is].	[Rule ASCOMP]
I saw the boat SDEC[you bought].	[Rule SREL1]

Recall that SWHQs cannot be embedded except as immediate constituents of the root category S. Therefore, the expression "who just came in," in "I recognize the person who just came in" is analyzed as a distinct relative clause type and not as an embedding of SWHQ, although it would be so analyzed in isolation. (Compare Rules SREL1 and SREL2 in Appendix B.) Like the sentence types SIMP and SQ, SWHQ is, in general, disqualified on both syntactic and semantic grounds from being a constituent of relative clauses. That is, *"the man go home" (with "go home" as SIMP), *"the man did you see him," *"the man to whom did you give it," and *"the man which man came" are all ill-formed. Only those SWHQs that have "who" or "which" as subjects have the right shape, so to speak, to be relative clauses, as in "who just came in" or "(the thing) which fell." But this seems as fortuitous as the fact that the string "open the door" could be analyzed as an imperative and then combined with the plural NP, "they," to form the declarative "they open the door." It seems more general, therefore, to exclude all SWHQs from relative clause constituency and to account for those SRELs in which the subject of the embedded clause is "who" or "which" by means of a separate rule, SREL2.

In addition to the SDEC sentence type that can occur as an embedded constituent of a matrix sentence, certain sentencelike phrases also occur as constituents of complex expressions. These include infinitive phrases and gerunds, like

> for John to have been going there yesterday

and

> John's having been going there yesterday

which resemble embedded declaratives in having subjects, predicates, and aspectual auxiliaries, but which do not contain any finite (tensed or modal) auxiliary or verb forms. They may also lack subjects, as in "to have gone there." One way of recognizing the similarities while acknowledging the differences is to say that infinitives and gerunds, like some embedded declaratives, may have the same propositional content as an independent sentence but that a propositional commitment is lacking. Compare, for example, the difference between the nonfinite phrases exemplified above with "John could have been going there yesterday," uttered as an independent sentence. Both the gerund and the infinitive can be embedded in contexts that relate them to reality in different ways, as in

> For John to have gone there was impossible.
> John's going there was impossible.
>
> For John to have gone there was regrettable.
> John's going there was regrettable.

The possibility of John's going is denied in the first two examples; in the second two, its occurrence is presupposed. Embedded declaratives behave similarly, as shown by

> It is impossible that John could have gone there.
> It is surprising that John could have gone there.

3.4. Relatives and WH-Questions

The SDECs embedded in relative clauses and the SQs embedded in SWHQs have a common feature in that they contain 'holes'; that is, some normally present constituent is missing. In

I saw the boat you bought

the SDEC "you bought" is incomplete; the transitive verb "bought" lacks an object. The missing object is supplied by a constituent outside the SDEC; namely, by the nominal "the boat," which is a constituent of the NP in which the SDEC is embedded. Similarly, the SQ "did you buy it from" in "who did you buy it from," lacks the NP object of the preposition "from," which is supplied by the WHNP of the embedding matrix sentence. Holes occur in other phrasal categories as well. The problem of specifying where holes may occur and where the constituent can be found that provides the missing content is complicated because holes can occur at arbitrary depths and distances from the constituents that fill the semantic gaps. In addition to the examples above, in which the holes are in the next level of embedding, we also have

> I saw the boat that Mary told me John claimed it was not likely that you were going to buy (   ).

and

> Who(m) did they think it was possible for you to manage to buy it from (   ) if you needed it?

In other words, a phrase with a hole in it may depend on an arbitrarily distant constituent for its syntactic and semantic well-formedness.

The constituent-structure statements in DIAGRAM currently allow many constituents to be optional even in contexts where they may in fact be obligatory. The semantic interpretation procedures in the constructors and translators have the task of locating constituents that can fill holes in the interpretations of incomplete phrases or, in case of failure to find such constituents, to reject the analysis. This works tolerably well, but throws unwarranted burdens on semantic analysis. A current project is to adapt the formalism in which DIAGRAM's rules are written so that it is easy to define and apply something like Gazdar's linking rules or a hold mechanism. This will allow the rules to distinguish between constituents that are always optional and those that can be omitted only in case a linking rule is applicable to them or a suitable constituent is contained in the hold register. Some constructions, however, will probably be handled by special mechanisms in the parser; most likely, they will be those involving conjunction. Meanwhile, many of the restrictions found in the constructors of the present rules are motivated by the need to reduce the burden on semantics and to eliminate unwarranted parsings by syntactic means before trying to interpret the results.

4. Constituents of Sentences

There are three important decisions that a grammarian has to make in proposing rules for analyzing sentences. They are (1) what the ultimate unanalyzed constituents, the basic elements, are; (2) how the elements in the sentence are grouped into phrases (where the boundaries are); (3) what the categories are. The decisions are not independent of one another, and all are influenced by knowledge of the grammatical and communicative functions that are conceptually associated with a phrase of a given category. In this section, some of the problems and issues that arose in making these decisions in DIAGRAM are explored, focusing on the relationship of categories to the syntactic functions of predication and modification.

4.1. Words and Basic Elements

It is customary to think of sentences as ultimately decomposed into words and of phrases as sequences of words. It is also customary to think of words as appearing only in a lexicon where they are assigned to word-class categories and of phrases as built out of word-class and phrase categories by rules that contain only categories and not actual word forms. These concepts are valid only as generalizations and none holds in a precise way in DIAGRAM.

Some categories (e.g., N, V, ADJ, P) appear in the lexicon, are never defined by rules, and consist mostly of single words (technically 'word stems'). These are sometimes referred to as 'lexical' or 'word' categories. But some words (e.g., "of") and parts of words (e.g., the plural suffix "—s") appear in rules. Word sequences like "out of" can appear in the lexicon and be assigned to the same lexical category as that of a single word like "from." A single word may be assigned by the lexicon to a category that is also defined by the rules. For example, "John" is assigned to the category of noun phrases (NP). In addition, an idiom like "kick the bucket" may appear as a multiword lexical entry, assigned to the category VP that is also defined by rule. However, any category in DIAGRAM that is designatd as XP, where X ranges over various word categories, is a "phrasal" category, and there will be one or more rules defining it. Some reasons for these treatments of words, affixes, and phrases should become clear from the following description of the analysis of sentence constituents.

The sentences DIAGRAM analyzes have had suffixes stripped from inflected words like "bolts," "bolted," "running," and "taken." The suffixes are transposed to precede their stems, thus: "-s bolt," "-ed bolt," "-ing run," "-en take." (Reasons for preposing the suffixes appear shortly.) The uninflected forms appear in the lexicon, where they are assigned to the appropriate categories. It is not necessary, however, to enter "bolts," "bolting," and "bolted," since these words are defined by rule. A single rule statement suffices to combine any member of the class N with a plural suffix, allowing the meaning of the combination to be computed as the meaning of the N plus the meaning of plurality by the semantic interpretation procedures. The lexicon also supplies regular forms for irregularly inflected words like "children," which is given as "child -s," and "took," which is given as "take -ed."

Affix stripping is a common practice in lexicography, and the economies it offers are obvious. DIAGRAM extends the practice to irregular forms. Only inflectional suffixes are stripped. Derivational suffixes, which may effect major changes in the category of the base to which they are attached, are untouched, so that "civil" (ADJ), "civilize" (V), and "civilization" (N), for example, will have individual entries. Derived words not only differ in category from their bases; the meaning of a word composed of a base combined with a derivational suffix cannot be regularly stated as a composite of the meanings of the base and the suffix, whereas the meaning of a base and an inflectional suffix can. A noun stem N plus the plural suffix regularly produces a NOUN meaning "more than one N," whereas the relationship of the meaning of "civilization" to the base "civil" is less straightforward.

The participle suffix PPL is a borderline case. It is regularly suffixed to verb stems preceded by the auxiliary HAVE, to mark the perfective aspect as in "they have broken it." In this use, it is inflectional. Suffixed to transitive Vs, however, it can arguably be said to change the category of the stem from V to ADJ. Thus "broken," unlike "break," can modify a noun ("the broken vase," but not * "the break vase"), and can itself be modified by words like "very" and "completely" and the prefix

"un-," which typically associate with adjectives. Compare "completely broken" and "unbroken" with "completely happy" and "unhappy." Moreover, as a predicate, "broken" requires a form of BE in the auxiliary and does not occur with a form of "do." Compare "it is broken" and "is it broken" with "they break it" and "do they break it," as well as with the intransitive sense of "break" in "it breaks" and "it did break."

Much of what has just been said of the suffix PPL applies also to the suffix ING, with added complications. Parallel to "the broken vase," there is "the breaking vase," though not * "the completely breaking vase." In addition, Vs suffixed with ING occupy syntactic positions and serve syntactic functions associated with NPs, as in "the singing was excellent but the dancing was poor." In spite of the shifts in syntactic function, and possibly in syntactic category, however, the meanings of the stem Vs appear to remain constant. It is this constancy of meaning that DIAGRAM seeks to preserve by stripping the two participial suffixes from verb stems.

4.2. Constituents

4.2.1. Suffixes and the Auxiliary Constituent

Decomposing words with inflectional suffixes has consequences for DIAGRAM's definitions of the immediate constituents of phrases. One reason for preposing inflectional suffixes is to regularize the form of the whole phrase in which the stem is an immediate constituent and to provide a constant interpretation. Consider the sentences

			NP	AUX	VP
He	gives	her a book.	[He	-s	give her a book]
He is	giving	her a book.	[He	is -ing	give her a book]
He has	given	her a book.	[He	-s have -en	give her a book]
He	gave	her a book.	[He	-ed	give her a book]
He may give	her a book.	[He	may	give her a book]

The VP "give her a book" remains constant in DIAGRAM's analyses of the three different sentences. The difference in meaning is ascribed to the differences in the auxiliary constituents.

Notice that in this analysis the entire auxiliary, including tense and aspectual affixes, is an immediate constituent of the sentence rather than of the verb phrase. Functionally, the sentence is represented as composed of three constituents, with the subject NP and the predicate VP representing the timeless or neutral propositional content, while the auxiliary represents the speaker's attitude or perspective. It indicates whether the propositional content is considered to hold in the past or the present or in some possible world and whether it is considered to be ongoing or completed.

DIAGRAM's treatment of the form and meaning of auxiliaries and of their syntactic place in the sentence resembles that of Langacker [16], although independently conceived. Both treatments differ strongly from those in which suffixes are not stripped or preposed and in which modals, HAVE, and BE are categorized as verbs that accept VPs as complements. Compare Jackendoff [11] and Gazdar et al. [7]. Whether or not DIA-GRAM's current treatment of auxiliaries and its use of "affix hopping" can be claimed to represent some kind of psychological reality or to result in computational efficiencies in processing dialogue remains moot.[10]

4.2.2. The Passive Constituent

DIAGRAM's analysis of suffixes and V stems also affects its analysis of the regularities in form and meaning that appear in active–passive sentences. DIAGRAM's input for two passive sentences with "give" as predicate are

| She is given a book. | [she | is | -en | give a book] |
| A book is given her. | [a book | is | -en | give her |] |

During analysis of these sentences, "give a book" and "give her" will be parsed as VPs by the same rule (Rule VP1) that applies to the active versions in the preceding examples. The constituent structures to which the rule applies include a single V, a V followed by an object NP, and a V followed by two object NPs. Only those Vs whose attributes qualify them to take two object NPs will be recognized as predicates of well-formed active declaratives like "he gives her a book." As previously mentioned, DIAGRAM accepts such Vs as sole constituents of VPs when they occur without an obligatory object to permit recognition of sentences like "what did he give" or "what did he give her." When a verb like "give" is parsed with its two object NPs to form a VP, the constructor procedure of Rule VP1 simply checks for the appropriate attributes, named DIROBJ and INDI-ROBJ, whose values are either T for "present" or null. Here we are interested in the cases in which "give" occurs with only one or with none of its object NPs. In those cases, the procedure marks the resulting VP as lacking its full complement by setting the attribute DIROBJ of the V as an attribute of the VP. (In other words, the VP inherits the attribute of its 'head' V.) Subsequently, a rule PRED1 applies when such a VP is preceded by the participle PPL. The relevant parts of Rule PRED1 state the possible constituents of PRED and the conditions on well-formedness; thus

PRED 1   PRED {ADJP/NP/PP/PPL VP}

Constructor:
  (Informally) If VP is a constituent of PRED, then VP must have the attribute DIROBJ and cannot have a prepositional phrase (PP) constituent.

In this manner, the passive construction joins the categories of NP, ADJP, and PP as a member of the inclusive category PRED, which is essentially "stative"

in contrast to the predicates formed with active verbs.[11] However, it is easy to distinguish subcategories of PREDs on the basis of the categories of its constituents because DIAGRAM's formalism assigns, to each phrase analyzed by a rule, a set of attributes whose names are categories of its immediate constituents. A PRED formed with PPL and VP will have the attributes PPL and VP that can be tested for when their presence or absence is relevant.

4.3. The Major Categories

The phrases that are the major constituents of sentences are extensions of the four word catgories, noun (N), verb (V), adjective (ADJ), and preposition (P). These categories contain the words in a dictionary. In particular, they include the so-called content words—words that in some intuitive sense denote entities, actions, processes, qualities, and spatial and temporal properties.

With the possible exception of the prepositions, these are large classes that can easily grow when the introduction of new objects and activities into a culture creates the need for new words for talking about them. They contrast with 'function' words, whose semantic content is very difficult to specify. The word "of" is an example. Although customarily classed as a preposition, "of" is strikingly different from words like "in," "over," "with," etc. In effect, it is treated as an inflectional prefix of the NP rather than as a preposition. The infinitival "to," as in "he wants to go" is another example. In contrast to the directional preposition "to" in "he came to the office," it carries no semantic information. "Of" and infinitival "to" are not assigned to categories in DIA-GRAM; like some affixes, they are cited directly in the rules.

As their names indicate, the categories NP, VP, ADJP, and PP are regarded as phrasal extensions of the categories of the content words. Intuitively, each XP contains a word of category X that is the nucleus or *head* of the phrase.[12] In

those very young children requiring an escort

the head is clearly the noun "children." Most other phrases within the NP are said to 'depend on' or 'modify' the head. These latter terms are not well-defined and not matched in any simple way with syntactic categories. "Very young" (ADJP) and "requiring an escort" (ING VP) are modifiers, limiting the range of denotation of the head noun. In general, there is a tendency to call

---

[10] It should be noted also that the advantages of simplicity of statement afforded by this affix 'hopping' are more easily achieved for some affixes than for others. Transposing the plural suffix to precede a noun does not prefix it to the entire phrase headed by the noun and does not lead to the simplifying statements possible for the analysis of VP constituents. Although nouns and verbs are often homographic in English, it may still be practical to strip the homographic suffix "-s" from the category V and not from the category N.

[11] Another rule, Rule PRED2, analyzes prepositional phrase attachments to PREDs. The whole question of the treatment of the active–passive relationship raises many issues beyond the scope of this paper, issues that are also being vigorously raised in revisions of the theory of transformational grammar; e.g., by Bresnan [2] and Wasow [24]. We are examining them and exploring alternative ways of associating information about logical forms or predicate-argument structures with variations in syntactic arrangements of subjects, objects, and prepositional phrase complements.

[12] Compare discussions of the X-bar theory in the theory of transformational grammar in Robinson [19] and Jackendoff [12] and the references contained therein.

modifiers that follow a head 'complements'; however, the following modifiers or complements of VPs and PPs, which are typically NPs, are usually called 'objects.'

Function words are seldom classed with modifiers. They are variously called 'specifiers,' 'determiners,' or 'complementizers.' For example, "these" and "those" are not modifiers like "young," but belong to a small, closed class of function words labeled DDET in DIAGRAM. Elliptical headless NPs like "those requiring an escort" are possible when a function word specific to NPs is an initial constituent. Their full interpretation, of course, requires discourse context.

The foregoing description should provide a basis for understanding the interactions of the rules with the lexicon and with each other. Explication of a specific rule will further illustrate the principles involved.

4.3.1. A Rule for the Analysis of NP

The rule given below, analyzes noun phrases like "water," "boys," "the boy," "younger children than that," "those very young children requiring an escort," "those boys whom I had expected to see," "every school boy on our block who has been driven to school by his parents." It will reject as ill-formed *"many water," *"much boy," *"a boys," *"two boys than that," and *"those children who has been driven to school." It will mark as UNLIKELY an NP consisting solely of a singular count noun like "boy," "bolt," etc., as in "I saw boy," but allow it, in case no better analysis can be found. The judgments of likelihood are partly, perhaps even largely, intuitive and subject to alteration in different discourse environments, for example, in an environment where the participants use a "telegraphic" style and omit function words like "the."

```
NP1RULE   NP = (D={A / DDET / DETQ}) NOMHD (NCOMP)
              (where D is a cover symbol for various determiners)
CONSTRUCTOR (PROGN (COND
                  ((@ D)
      1.    [COND
              ((MASS? D)
                (OR (MASS? NOMHD)
                    (F.REJECT (QUOTE F.MASS]
      2.    [COND
              ((MASS? NOMHD)
               (OR (NOT (@ A))
                   (F.REJECT (QUOTE F.MASS]
      3.    [COND
              (((@ NCOMP)
                (SET NBR(@INTERSECT NBR D NOMHD NCOMP)))
               (T (SET NBR (@INTERSECT NBR D NOMHD]
      4.    ((AND (SG? NOMHD)
                  (NOT MASS? NOMHD)))
             (@FACTOR (QUOTE F.NODET)
                     UNLIKELY))
      5.    (((@ NCOMP)
             (SET NBR (@INTERSECT NBR NCOMP NOMHD)))
      6.    (T (@FROM NOMHD NBR)))
      7.    [AND (@ THANCOMP NCOMP)
                (OR (@ THANCOMP NOMHD)
                    F.REJECT (QUOTE F.THANC]
      8.    (@FROM NOMHD TYPE)))
```

The first line specifies a possible constituent structure for a well-formed NP as consisting of a nucleus containing a head noun (NOMHD). The nucleus is optionally preceded by a determiner (D) consisting of the word "a" or a definite determiner (DDET) like "the" or "those" or a determiner of a different type (DETQ) like "much" or "many." It is optionally followed by a complement (NCOMP).

The constructor contains several statements, numbered here for ease of reference, including statements of conditions that must be met for well-formedness. The first two require that if there is a determiner, it must agree with the NOMHD constituent with respect to the property MASS. This condition rejects combinations of a determiner like "much" with a count noun like "child."

Statements 3 and 5 require agreement in syntactic number (NBR) of all constituents and also assign the value of the property NBR to the NP on the basis of the values for the constituents. Statement 6 assigns the value of NBR from the NOMHD constituent when it is the sole constituent. Statement 4 rates as UNLIKELY the probability that an NP will lack a determiner if its head noun is a singular count noun like "child," a rating that will affect the score of any analysis containing such an NP. Statement 7 rejects as ill-formed such sequences as "two boys than that," although "taller boys than that" is acceptable. Statement 8 assigns to the analyzed NP the value COUNT or MASS for the attribute TYPE from the value assigned to the NOMHD constituent.

Other NP rules analyze elliptical NPs like "those

requiring an escort," comparative NPs like "more tall boys than that" and "as many more tall boys than that as there are girls," and several other types.

4.4. Syntactic Functions
4.4.1. Predication and Modification

The NP rules analyze phrases that can function as subjects of sentences and objects in VPs and PPs. They can also function as predicates; i.e., as members of the category PRED. In

Children are sleeping

the NP "children" functions as sentential subject. In

Those boys are children

"children" functions as a sentential predicate applied to the subject NP "those boys" in stating that they are members of the set of children. In

Those boys are the children of my friend

the NP "the children of my friend" is the predicate applied to "those boys" in stating that they are identical to the set of children of the speaker's friend.

We have already shown how DIAGRAM relates the major phrasal categories to the function of predication, making an important distinction between VP predication and predication by other categories. Because VPs can function as predicates without any accompanying auxiliary constituent, the term 'predicate' is sometimes taken to be commensurate with 'verb.' This usage mixes two levels of description of sentences, the categorical and the functional. Moreover, within the categorical level, it obscures the distinction between lexical heads of phrases (V) and phrases (VP). One consequence of such usage appears in the proposal that prepositions may be indistinguishable from verbs at some abstract level of description [1]. On similar grounds, Ross [21] has argued that adjectives, verbs, and nouns have deep similarities that outweigh their superficial differences. The mixed properties of passive constructions heighten the confusion.

The same kind of confusion shows up with respect to 'modifier,' which tends to be equated with 'adjective' and applied to any word that modifies a noun in prenominal position. However, three of the four major word categories appear in the function of prenominal modifier, as in

a *stormy* sea	(ADJ)
a *storm* coat	(N)
a *threatening* sea	(ING V)

All major phrasal categories, including prepositional phrases, occur in postnominal modifiers or complements, as in

a woman *of courage*	(OF NP)
a book *on the table*	(PP)
the cat *lying on the mat*	(VP)
diamonds *as big as your thumb*	(ADJP)

4.4.2. The Shifting of Categories

The pervasiveness of the association of particular categories with particular functions and notions ("a noun is the name of a person, place, or thing"; "adjectives modify nouns") is so notable that it cannot be ignored. Tesniere's notion of *translation* affords an interesting way of thinking about the interactions of syntactic categories with various functions of the kinds exemplified above.[13] Both function words and derivational affixes are considered to be *translatives* that serve to shift ("translate") a governor from one category to another, whenever it and the group of words it governs serve one of the functions of the category to which it is shifted. At first glance, these words and affixes would appear to be like the derivational suffixes that change the categories of word bases, previously exemplified in "civil," "civilize," and "civilization." The similarity is significant, but so are the differences. Translatives include words as well as affixes and they can shift the category of a phrase.[14] In constituent structure terminology, one would say that translatives are immediate constituents of *phrases*, even when they form parts of words.

There is a clear example of such a phenomenon in English. In NPs like "the mayor of Boston's hat," the constituent "the mayor of Boston's" is properly analyzed as having two subconstituents, "the mayor of Boston" and "-'s." In effect, the NP "the mayor of Boston" is now a determiner (DDET) of the larger NP of which it is a part. One could say that it had been "translated" from an NP to serve the function of a determiner by combining with the suffix. One of DIAGRAM's rules for analyzing determiner phrases could be so interpreted, namely, Rule DDET2, whose constituent-structure statement is

DDET2   DDET = NP "GEN"

where "GEN" is the lexical replacement for the genitive suffix.

It is customary to analyze preposed genitives in English in this fashion. DIAGRAM's extension of the concept to passive constructions in Rule PRED1 (*infra*) is not customary, but the extension seems quite natural.

5. Planned Revisions

It is relevant to consider how far one might want to push the process of category changing by translatives in

---

[13] Tesniere's syntactic theories, first published posthumously in 1959 [23], center around the concept of the head of a phrase, which he calls a 'governor.' Governors are content words, categorized (roughly speaking) as nouns, verbs, adjectives, and adverbs. In analyzing a sentence, other words are attached to governors as 'dependents' (hence the name 'dependency theory'). Each category of governors has a typical set of syntactic functions. Verbs function as predicates, and they alone can occur as independent governors of an entire sentence. Nouns function as subjects and objects, adjectives as modifiers of nouns, and adverbs as modifiers of adjectives and verbs.

[14] Although he often speaks as if only the governor were involved, Tesniere is specific on this point: "C'est le mot ou le groupe de mots resultant de la translation" [23, p. 367].

order to capture generalizations about the syntactic distributions and syntactic functions of phrases headed by lexical categories, and what constraints one would want to impose on its use. We propose to explore this issue in the future. Specifically, it is interesting to test the consequences of treating the auxiliary BE as a translative for NP, ADJP, and PP predicates, converting them to VP. This would seem to be a reasonable alternative to a more customary concept of copular BE as a 'main verb.' At present, BE is always an auxiliary but it is not a translative.

Another issue is the use of syntactic redundancy rules or *metarules* to capture generalizations and reduce the number of statements in the rule procedures. As mentioned in Sec. 3.1, there is a loss in efficiency along with a loss in generalization when separate rules are written that require duplicating much of the constructor and translator procedures. The duplication of tests for number agreement of subject NP and AUX or VP is a case in point. A single metarule modifying all the S-rules to add agreement tests could capture a significant generalization about English. The current metalanguage in which DIAGRAM is written already provides functions for such an operation on rule and category definitions before compilation (see Paxton [18, especially pp. 256–268.])The functions can also be used to derive new constituent-structure rules from a set of basic rules. One program for deriving constituent structure rules from other rules has already been implemented by Konolige [16] and its results are being studied.

The most promising as well as the most challenging uses of metarules are related to the problem of holes or traces, noted in Sec. 3.4. It was pointed out there that holes could be arbitrarily far from the constituents that filled them semantically, as in "I say the boat that Mary told me John claimed it was not likely that you were going to buy (   )."

In a transformational analysis, the holes are conceived of as originally occupied by constituents that were moved by transformations to an initial position or deleted when they were coreferential with some other constituent. The moved elements, according to the theory, leave a trace in their original positions, which is interpreted as a variable bound by the moved element or by the coreferential constituent. For example, "the man I saw" is represented with a trace as

$$NP[\text{the man } SDEC[\text{I saw } t]]$$

where t is 'bound' by "the man" [5].

Gazdar [6] has recently proposed a nontransformational analysis that accounts for the same phenomena. His method is to derive, from the basic rules, a finite set of rules, each dominating one empty node; i.e., a hole. In addition, the grammar will have a set of 'linking' rules for eliminating the derived nodes in an analysis by (in effect) 'canceling' them with the appropriate constituent that occurs elsewhere.

A more familiar alternative in computational linguistics and artificial intelligence systems is to use 'hold' registers to store constituents that may be needed to complete a phrase with a hole in it. The grammar might then define the syntactic sites at which the contents of a hold register could be 'emptied,' and a sentence could be accepted as syntactically well-formed only if nothing remained in the register at the end of an analysis. Woods [25] appears to have been the first to use a hold register for such a purpose in parsing natural language, but the tests for well-formedness were semantic rather than syntactic. Paxton [18] has proposed a combination of redundancy rules with null rules to derive SWHQs with holes in the appropriate places and a common procedure to establish the connection between the fronted WH-phrase and a corresponding null phrase, using a hold mechanism. Other alternatives have recently been advanced as well, some involving special parsing mechanisms rather than rules.[15]

A problem is always incurred when extending the rules to cover more expressions, whether by writing new rules explicitly or by deriving them from old rules. DIAGRAM is now a large, complex, and coherent English grammar. Introducing new rules almost inevitably has a perturbing effect as they interact with the old rules in unforeseen ways. These perturbations are worth studying for the light they shed on the English language, or more precisely, on a grammarian's intuitions about the English language.

Appendix A

Sample Lexicon and Rules

Sample Lexical Entries

(If a word W1 has the attribute LIKE with a word W2 as value, then word W1 has the same attributes as word W2 except for those specifically assigned to W1.)

Words for N

(APPRENTICE	(TYPE COUNT)
	(GENDER M F))
(BOY	(TYPE COUNT)
	(GENDER M))
(FISH	(TYPE MASS))
(FOOT	(TYPE COUNT))
(GIRL	(TYPE COUNT)
	(GENDER F))
(MAN	(LIKE BOY)
(THING	(TYPE COUNT))
(WATER	(TYPE MASS))
(WOMAN	(LIKE GIRL))

Irregular Forms in N

(FEET	(FOOT -S))
(MEN	(MAN -S))
(WOMEN	(WOMAN-S))

---

[15] Several proposals were discussed at length at a workshop on nontransformational theories of syntax, held at Stanford University, January 1980, sponsored by the Sloan Foundation.

Words in NOMHD
(FISH   (TYPE COUNT)
(PEOPLE   (TYPE CONT)
                             (NBR PL))
(U.S.   (NBR SG)
                             (PROPN T))

Words in NP
(JOHN   (NBR SG)
                             (DEF T)
                             (GENDER M)
                             (PROPN T))
(MARY   (LIKE JOHN)
                             (GENDER F)
((NEW YORK)   (NBR SG)
                             (TYPE COUNT)
                             (PROPN T))

Words for V
(ASSEMBLE   (DIROBJ T))
(BREAK   (DIROBJ T)
                             (PARTICLE UP OUT OFF))
                             (PPL EN)
(BUY   (DIROBJ T)
                             (INDIROBJ T)
                             (DIRECTION FOR FROM BY))
(FIND   (ADJOBJ T)
                             (DIROBJ T)
                             (INDIROBJ T)
                             (INFOBJ T)
                             INCGCOMP T)
                             (SOBJ T)
                             (DIRECTION FOR BY)
                             (PARTICLE OUT))

(FINISH   (INGCOMP T)
                             (LIKE ASSEMBLE)
(GO   (PPL EN))
(GIVE   (LIKE BUY)
                             (DIRECTION TO BY)
                             (PARTICLE UP)
                             (PPL EN))
(LOOK   (DIROBJ T)
                             (INSEPARABLE INTO)
                             (ADJOBJ T)
                             (PARTICLE UP)
(TRY   (INFOBJ T)
(WANT   (DIROBJ T)
                             (INFOBJ T))

Irregular Forms in V
(BOUGHT   (BUY ED))
(BROKE   (BREAK ED))
(GAVE   (GIVE ED))
(GONE   (GO EN))
(WENT   (GO ED))

Words for Q
(FEW   (LIKE MANY))
(LITTLE   (LIKE MUCH))
(MANY   (TYPE CONT)
                             (NBR PL))
(MUCH   (TYPE MASS)
                             (NBR SG))

Irregular Forms in Q
(MORE   (1 (MANY ER)))
(MORE   (2 (MUCH ER)))

Examples of Rules

(SD1   SDEC = NP (ADV) (AUXD) VP;
        CONSTRUCTOR [PROGN   (COND
                              [(@ AUXD)
                              (OR (AGREE·NBR NP AUXD)
                                  (F.REJECT (QUOTE R.NBRSD1]
                              (T (OR (NEQ (@ NBR NP)
                                          (QUOTE SG))
                                  (F.REJECT (QUOTE F.NBR)))
                              (@SET TENSE (QUOTE PRESENT]
        TRANSLATOR (PROGN   (@SET   ROLE (QUOTE SUBJECT)
                             NP)
                             (@SET   SEMANTICS (COMBINE   (@ SEMANTICS VP)
                                                           (@ SEMANTICS NP))

(VP1   VP = V (NP1 ({NP2 / P}));
        CONSTRUCTOR (PROG   ((PARTICLE (@ DIAMOND.SPELLING P)))
                             (COND
                             [(@ NP1)
                             (OR (@DIROBJ V)
                             (F.REJECT (QUOTE F.DIROBJ)))
                             (COND
                             [(@ NP2)
                               (OR (@ INDIROBJ V)
                                   (F.REJECT (QUOTE F.INDIROBJ))))
                             ((@ P)
                               (OR (FMEMB PARTICLE (@ PARTICLE V))
                                   (F.REJECT (QUOTE F.PARTICLE)))
                               (AND (@ PRO NP1)
                                   (@FACTOR (QUOTE F.PARTICLE)
                                            LIKELY))
                             (COND
                               ((@ NCOMP NP1)
                               (OR (@ NP NCOMP NP1)
                                   (@FACTOR (QUOTE F.PARTICLE)
                                            UNLIKELY))

```
                                    (AND (@ NCOMP NP NCOMP NP1)
                                         (@FACTOR (QUOTE F.PARTICLE)
                                                  UNLIKELY)
                                    (T (@SET BAREV T)
                                       (@FROM V DIRECTION DIROBJ))))
        TRANSLATOR (PROGN    [COND
                                    (((@ NP)
                                      (@SET ROLE (QUOTE DIROBJ)
                                            NP2)
                                      (@SET ROLE (QUOTE INDIROBJ)
                                            NP1)
                                      (@SET SEMANTICS (COMBINE
                                            (@ SEMANTICS V)
                                            (@ SEMANTICS NP2)
                                            (@ SEMANTICS NP1))))
                                     (T (AND (@ NP1)
                                             (OR (@ INDIROBJ V)
                                                 (@SET ROLE (QUOTE DIROBJ)
                                                       NP1)
                                     (@SET SEMANTICS (COMBINE(@ SEMANTICS V)
                                                     (@ SEMANTICS NP1))))
```

Appendix B

Word and Phrase Categories and Constituent Structure Rules

Phrase categories are followed by the constituent structure rules that analyze them. Rule names are distinguished from category names by numerical identifiers.

ADJ		Adjective Stems
		big, difficult, allowable, frequent, careful, quick, great, tall, short, far, near, close, operational, necessary, possible.
		(Some, but not all adjectives can be inflected "-er" or combined with "as," "more," "too" in comparisons of degree.)
ADJCOMP		Adjective Complements
		for him, to go there (as in difficult for him to go there; too heavy for me): that he went (as in possible that he went).
	ADJCOMP1	ADJCOMP = (ENOUGH) (FOR NP) (INFINITIVE)
	ADJCOMP2	ADJCOMP = "THAT" SDEC
ADJP		Adjective Phrases
		too big, more difficult than that, allowable for him to go there, largest, as ready to go as he is, possible to do, necessary that it is done.
	ADJP1	ADJP = ({(QPP) QDET / TDET}) ADJ (ADJCOMP)
	ADJP2	ADJP = (DETQ) ("NO") ER ("MUCH") ADJP (THANCOMP (ADJCOMP))
	ADJP 4	ADJP = AS ADJP (ASCOMP)
	ADJP6	ADJP = EST ("MUCH") ADJ (ADJCOMP)
ASCOMP		Adjective Complements for Equality Comparisons
		as that, as he appears to be.
	ASCOMP1	ASCOMP = AS {NP / SDEC}
ADV		Adverbs
		frequently, soon, carefully, quickly, often, necessarily, possibly.
		(Words formed from adjectives by adding the suffix "-ly" or that occupy the same syntactic positions as words so formed.)
ADVP		Adverb Phrases
		as frequently as that, too often, more carefully than John did it, most rapidly, after he came, when he is here, if they come.
	ADVP1	ADVP = ((PQQ) QDET) ADV
	ADVP2	ADVP = (DETQ) ER ("MUC") ADV (THANCOMP)
	ADVP7	ADVP = {P / "IF"} {SDEC / {PPL / ING} VP}
AUX		Auxiliary Phrases
		couldn't have been -ing, has, is, -ed, -s.
		(May consist of a single suffix.)
	AUX1	AUX = (MODALP) (HAVEP PPL) (BEP ING)
AUXD		DO-type Auxiliary Phrases
		could have -en, did, -ed.
		(See also DO and DOP.)

AUXD1	AUXD = C = {AUX / DOP}
DDET	**Definite Determiner Phrases** the, the many, all, all five, those, this, these two, the next man's.
DDET1	DDET = ((NOT) "ALL") DET ({NUMBER / QPP})
DDET2	DDET = NP "GEN"
DETERQ	**Compared Determiner Phrases** more, that much more, too many more. (See also DETQ.)
DETERQ1	DETERQ = (DETQ) ER Q
DETQ	**Determiner/Quantifier Phrases** many, much, too many, any, any two, two, no two, some, most. (Indefinite determiners, including indefinite quantifiers. See also categories Q, QDET, QPP.)
DETQ1	DETQ = (C={TDET / QDET / A}) Q (QPP)
INFINITIVE	Infinitive Phrases to have gone, to be informed, not to have realized, to have been very careful about that.
INFINITIVE1	INFINITIVE = (NOT) TO (HAVEP PPL) (BEP1 ING) {VP / BEP2 (PRED)}
INFINITREL	Nonfinite Relative Clause to whom to give it, for you to do, being attached (as in the man to whom to give it; the thing for you to do; the part being attached.)
INFINREL1	INFINITREL = {({FOR NP / P RELPRO}) INFINITIVE / ING ("BE" PPL) VP}
MODALP	Modal Auxiliary Phrases
MODALP1	MODALP = MODAL (NOT) Z(ADV)
N	Noun Stems man, woman, box, foot, inch, water, length, U.S., United States, time, doctor.
NCOMP	Noun-Phrase Complements of tea, on the corner, for you to do, that I saw. (Modifying phases that follow a head nominal or NOMHD.)
NCOMP1	NCOMP = {OF / P} NP
NCOMP2	NCOMP = {INFINITREL / SREL / ADJP / THANCOMP}
NCOMP4	NCOMP = NCOMP PP
NHD	Prenoun Modifier Heads twenty-one gun, three mile, stone (as in twenty-one gun salute, three mile swim, stone house; NHDs are constituents of compound nominals in which a noun stem (N) modifies a noun.)
NOMHD	Nominal Heads very big task, broken vases, running streams, more difficult task, fish, cats, people. (Constituents of NPs, containing the head noun and prenominal modifiers, but not determiners or quantifiers of the NP.)
NOMHD1	NOMHD = NOUN ({(",") "AND" / ","} NOMHD)
NOMHD2	NOMHD = {(QDET) ADJ / {ING / PPL} V} NOMHD
NOMHD3	NOMHD = (QPP) ER ("MUC") ADJ NOMHD
NOUN	Nouns (N stems with or without a fronted plural affix; e.g., cat, -s cat, -s child (children), fish. May be premodified by NHD or NOMHD, as in cat foot containers. Unlike Ns, NOUNS have an attribute of syntactic number, SG or PL, unless they are ambiguous with respect to number.)
NOUN1	NOUN = ("-S) N
NOUN2	NOUN = NHD NOUN
NP	Noun Phrases water, cats, very big cats that lie on mats, the length of that board, a length of two feet, as big a box as you could carry, two of them, more ships, a more difficult task than that, what he did, he, her, the best ones, the best I could find, his having gone there yesterday, those, those few, some, all of them that are here, John, Mary, September. (The most complicated category in the grammar.)
NP1	NP = (D={A / DDET / DETQ}) NOMHD (NCOMP)
NP2	NP = D={A / DDET / DETQ} (NCOMP)
NP3	NP = DETERQ (NOMHD) (NCOMP)
NP6	NP = DDET EST ("MUC") ADJ (NOMHD) (NCOMP)
NP8	NP = AS QPP ({OF NP / NOMHD}) (ASCOMP)
NP9	NP = AS ((QPP) ER ("MUCH")) ADJ (OF) NP (THANCOMP) (ASCOMP)
P	Prepositions, Particles, Subordinating Conjunctions at, in, on, before, after, by, to, for, with. (Does not include "of." Ps may occur as intransitives or particles, as in break up the pavement; or as transitives with NP objects, as in: in the box. Combined with sentences and verb phrases, however, they become "translatives," and the resultant phrase is ADVP.)
PP	Prepositional Phrases on it, after that, there (i.e., at that place).
PP1	PP = P (NP)

PRED		Predicate Phrases (no VP)
		(NPs, as in that is *a boy*; ADJPs, as in that could have been *very heavy*; PPs, as in that wasn't *in the box when I left*; passives, as in that was *attached to it yesterday*.)
	PRED1	PRED = {ADJP / NP / PP / PPL VP}
	PRED10	PRED = PRED (",") {PP / ADVP}
Q		Indefinite Quantifiers (nonstandard)
		(A small set of words, including only many, much, few, little. For other words usually called quantifiers, see DETQ and DDET. DETQs may have Q as sole constituents.)
QPP		Q phrases
		much, too much, too many, too few, little.
	QPP1	QPP = (QDET) Q (QPP)
S		Sentences
		(Independent sentences of various subtypes. Includes complex and compound sentences.)
	S0	S = C={SIMP / SDEC / SQ / SWHQ} (ENDPUNCT)
	SX1	S = CONJ S
	SX2	S = S1 (MIDPUNCT) S2
	SX3	S = {PP / ADVP} (",") S
	SX4	S = {PPL / ING} VP "," S
SDEC		Declarative Sentences
		they went there; they might have been going there then; it could be difficult; he is here; that is the book; there are some apples in that basket.
	SB1	SDEC = NP (AUX) (ADV1) BEP (ADV2) (PRED)
	SD1	SDEC = NP (ADV) (AUXD) VP
	STHERE1	SDEC = "THERE (AUX) BEP NP
		({ING {VP / "BE" PRED1} / PRED2 / SREL})
SIMP		Imperative Sentences
		Put them on the table; don't go; be careful; don't be difficult!
	SIMP1	SIMP = ("DO" (NOT)) {"BE" PRED / VP A}
SQ		Yes/No Interrogatives
		Is he going; could he have been going; did he go; is it here now; are there any more; was it hard to do?
	SBQ1	SQ = BEP NP ((ADV) (ING "BE") PRED)
	SBQ2	SQ = MODALP NP (ADV) PPL "BE" ((ING "BE") PRED)
	SBQ3	SQ = HAVEP NP (ADV) PPL "BE" ((ING"BE") PRED)
	SDQ1	SQ = DOP NP (ADV) VP
	SDQ2	SQ = MODALP NP (ADV) (HAVEP PPL) (BEP ING) VP
	SDQ3	SQ = BEP NP (NOT) ING VP
	STHEREQ1	SQ = BEP "THERE" (NP)
		({ING {"BE" PRED1 / VP} / PRED 2 / SREL})
	STHEREQ2	SQ = (MODALP "THERE" (NOT) (HAVEP PPL) BEP (NP)
		({ING {"BE" PRED1 / VP} / PRED 2 / SREL})
	STHEREQ3	SQ = HAVEP "THERE" PPL "BE" (NP)
		({ING {"BE" PRED1 / VP} / PRED2 / SREL})
SREL		Relative Clauses
		who went there yesterday; to whom he gave it; that was there; you saw yesterday; that you saw yesterday; that he attached it to; on which he placed it.
	SREL1	SREL = RELPRO {(AUX) BEP PRED / (AUXD) VP}
	SREL2	SREL = ((P) RELPRO) SDEC
SWHQ		WH-Questions
		who is it; who could it have been; what did he do; what could he have done; where did they go; on which table is it; which table is it on?
	SWH1	SWHQ = {WHNP / WHPP / WHADJP} SQ
	SWH2	SWHQ = WHNP (AUXD) VP
	SWH3	SWHQ = WHNP (AUX) BEP (PRED)
V		Verb Stems
		go, move, do, have, give, arrive, attach, see, seem, break, take, tell, say, know, think, want, try, tend.
VP		Verb Phrases
		go there in September, move it from here to there, arrive, seem difficult, give her a book, give a book to her, tell him that it is here, want to go, tend to be careful, look at it, look up a book, look it up, look into it, saw him leave, saw him leaving.
		(Verb stems combined with following objects, particles, prepositions, and prepositional phrase modifiers.)
	VP1	VP = V (NP1 ({NP2 / P}))
	VP2	VP = V P (NP)
	VP3	VP = V (NP) ("THAT") SDEC
	VP4	VP = V (NP) INFINITIVE
	VP5	VP = V (NP) {PPL VP / ADJP}
	VP7	VP = V (NP) (ING) {VP / BE PRED}
	VP8	VP = V (NP) {WHPP / WHNP / WHADJP} {SDEC / INFINITIVE}

VP9	VP = VP (",") [PP / INFINITIVE / ADVP}
WHADJP	Interrogative Adjective Phrases
	how big, how much bigger than that, how much more difficult to do.
WHADJP1	WHADJP = HOW ADJP
WHDET	Interrogative Determiners
	how much, how many more, whose, which man's.
WHDET1	WHDET = HOW Q1 (QPP) (ER Q2)
WHDET2	WHDET = WHNP "GEN"
WHNP	Interrogative NPs
	how many more women, how much water, whose book.
WHNP1	WHNP = WHDET (NUMBER) (NOMHD) (NCOMP)
WHPP	Interrogative PPs
	where, when, at what time, in which box, from where.
WHPP1	WHPP = {P WHNP / C={TO / FROM} "WHERE"}

Appendix C

Attributes

The major specific attributes that currently affect DIAGRAM's syntactic analysis of a phrase are listed below, grouped with the relevant categories. The name of the attribute is followed by a list of the values it may assume. Where values are not listed, the attribute is binary; it is either present or absent, and if present, its value is T.

Attributes of S

STYPE: (SIMP, SDEC, SQ, SWHQ). Sentence type; affects coordination.

CONJUNCT: Contains a conjunction; affects coordination.

Attributes of AUX, AUXD, BE, BEP, DO, DOP, HAVE, HAVEP

TENSE: (PAST, PRESENT) Marked as finite; cannot combine with preceding auxiliaries.

NBR: (SG, PL) Number agreement feature.

INFINITIVE: May be nonfinite; compare may have gone, they have gone.

Attributes of N, NOMHD, NP, PRO, WHNP

TYPE: (COUNT, MASS)

NBR: (SG, PL) Syntactic number: singular or plural. Used heavily in number-agreement tests.

NOMCASE: Is marked as nominative pronoun; e.g., he (compare him). Cannot be an object of V or P.

PROPN: Is a proper name; does not accept full range of determiners and complements of NPs, e.g., *every Missisipi.

Attributes of V and VP

VPPL: (EN, ED). Form of participial ending; e.g., taken, waited.

DIROBJ: Accepts a direct object; e.g., assemble it.

INDIROBJ: Accepts an indirect object; e.g., give them something.

INFOBJ: Accepts an infinitive object; e.g., want John to go.

SOBJ: Accepts an S object; e.g., said that he would go.

INGCOMP: Accepts gerundive complement; e.g., saw her leaving.

PPLCOMP: Accepts a participial complement; e.g., found her gone.

PARTICLE: Accepts any member of a list of Ps as a particle; e.g., give up, give away, give it up, give up something.

INSEPARABLE: Accepts any member of a list of Ps as an inseparable preposition; e.g., look into.

BAREV: Is a VP with no objects or complements. Affects ability to modify nominals or functions as a passive predicate PRED.

Attributes of ADJ, ADJP

SOBJ: Accepts an S complement; e.g., possible that he went.

ACOMP: Has a complement (of any type).

ERCOMP: Accepts a comparative complement; e.g., heavier than that.

Attributes of P, PP

INGCOMP: Accepts a participial complement to form an ADVP; e.g., on going there.

SCOMP: Accepts S complement to form an adverbial ADVP; e.g., after he left.

BAREPREP: A PP consisting only of P. May be a stranded preposition or a particle. Cannot modify a nominal; e.g., gave the book up.

Attributes of Minor Categories

The minor categories have some attributes of nominals and adjectivals, including TYPE, NBR, and THANCOMP.

Received 4/80; revised 5/81; accepted 6/81

References
1. Becker, A.L., and Arms, D.G. Prepositions as predicates. In *Papers from the 5th Regional Meeting of the Chicago Linguistic Society*, Univ. Chicago, Chicago, IL., April 18–19, 1969.
2. Bresnan, J. A realistic transformational grammar. In *Linguistic Theory and Psychological Reality*, Halle, M., Bresnan, J., and Miller, G.A. (Eds.) MIT Press, Cambridge, MA., 1978.
3. Chafe, W.L. Givenness, contrastiveness, definiteness, subjects, topics, and point of view. In *Subject and Topic*, C.N. Li (Ed.) Academic Press, New York, 1976.
4. Culicover, P.W., Wasow, T., and Akmajian, A. (Eds.) *Formal Syntax*. Academic Press, New York, 1977.
5. Dresher, B.E., and Hornstein, N. Trace theory and NP movement rules. *Linguistic Inquiry 10* (Winter 1979) 65–82.

6. Gazdar, G. English as a context-free language. Manuscript, April 1979.

7. Gazdar, G., Pullum, G.K., and Sag, I. A context-free phrase-structure grammar for the English auxiliary system. To appear.

8. Grosz, B. Focusing and description in natural language dialogues. In *Elements of Discourse Understanding*, A.K. Joshi et al. (Eds.) Cambridge Univ. Press, Cambridge, England, 1980.

9. Grosz, B., and Hendrix, G. A computational perspective on indefinite reference. Tech. Note 181, SRI International, Menlo Park, CA., 1980.

10. Hobbs, J., and Robinson, J. Why ask. *Discourse Processes 2*, 4 (Oct.–Dec. 1979) 311–318.

11. Jackendoff, R. Constraints on phrase-structure rules. In Culicover, P.W., Wasow, T., and Akmajian, A. (Eds.), *Formal Syntax*, Academic Press, New York, 1977, 249–283.

12. Jackendoff, R. *X-Bar Syntax: A Study of Phrase Structure.* MIT Press, Cambridge, MA, 1977.

13. Joshi, A.K., and Levy, L.S. Phrase structure trees bear more fruit than you would have thought. A revised and expanded version of a paper presented at the 18th Annual Meeting of the Association for Computational Linguistics, Univ. of Pennsylvania, Philadelphia, June 1980.

14. Kaplan, R.M., and Bresnan, J.W. Lexical-functional grammar: A formal system for grammatical representation. To appear in J.W. Bresnan (Ed.), *The Mental Representation of Grammatical Relations.* MIT Press, Cambridge, MA, 1980.

15. Konolige, K. Capturing linguistic generalizations with metarules in an annotated phrase—structure grammars. In Proceedings of the 18th Annual Meeting of the Association for Computing Linguistics, University of Pennsylvania, Philadelphia, June 1980.

16. Langacker, R.W. The form and meaning of the English auxiliary. *Language 54* (Dec. 1978), 853–882.

17. Paxton, W.H. The language definition system. In *Understanding Spoken Language*, D.E. Walker (Ed.) North-Holland, New York, 1978.

18. Paxton, W.H. A framework for speech understanding. Ph.D. dissertation, Stanford Univ., Stanford, CA, June 1977.

19. Robinson, J. Dependency structures and transformational rules. *Language 46* (June 1970), 259–285.

20. Robinson, A. Interpreting natural-language utterances in dialogs about tasks. Tech. Note 210, SRI International, Menlo Park, CA, March 15, 1980. (To appear.)

21. Ross, J.R. Adjectives as noun phrases. In *Modern Studies in English*, D.A. Reibel and S.A. Schane (Eds.) Prentice-Hall, Englewood Cliffs, NJ, 1969.

22. Searle, J.R. A classification of illocutionary acts. In *Proc. Texas Conf. Performatives, Presuppositions and Implicatures*, Center for Applied Linguistics, Arlington, VA, 1977.

23. Tesniere, L. *Elements de Syntaxe Structurale*, 2nd ed. Editions Klincksieck, Paris, France, 1976.

24. Wasow, T. Remarks on processing, constraints, and the lexicon. Presented at *Theoretical Issues in Natural Language Processing—2 (TINLAP—2)*, University of Illinois at Urbana-Champaign, July 25–27, 1978.

25. Woods, W.A., Transition network grammars for natural language analysis. *Comm. ACM 13*, 10 (Oct. 1970), 591–606.

II. SEMANTIC INTERPRETATION

Traditionally, semantics is taken as mapping from language to the world or to a model that corresponds to a real or imaginary world. NLP systems, nevertheless, cannot do this mapping directly: they need to first *represent* the meaning of an utterance, where that representation can then be interpreted in the world or the model. Many people claim that one cannot, in general, even compute the meaning representation of an utterance directly: one needs at least one intermediate level of representation, which takes account of only the utterance itself and not, for example, of the speaker's intention in uttering it. Thus *semantic interpretation* differs from semantics, in being the process of mapping NL utterances (or their syntactic analyses) onto some *representation* of meaning or intermediate analysis. (Note the inherent bias of the label "semantic interpretation" towards NL understanding. More will be said about packing meaning into utterances in Chapter 5, on NL generation.)

Before discussing semantic interpretation further, it is useful to clarify what we mean by three different terms: *domain, context,* and *task. Domain* is that piece of the world (real or imaginary) that the system knows about. The system may know general things about its domain (e.g., what kinds of objects particular words denote, what kinds of things relations hold between), as well as particular facts that are true (such as the particular properties of specific objects). The former is related to what has been called in knowledge representation circles the system's *terminological knowledge,* the latter, to its *assertional knowledge* [19].[1] The *context* of an utterance is determined by a combination of the previous utterances in the discourse, the location in space and time of the utterance, and the beliefs, desires, and intentions (both private and shared) of the discourse participants. (In systems with graphic displays, the display may also play a part in the context [17].) A system's *task* [13] is the service it offers a user (e.g., retrieving and organizing data from a database, answering questions, providing consultative or decision-support services, indexing or abstracting documents, translating texts, etc.). Thus *domain* is associated with systems and the kinds of texts they can understand. *Context* is associated with utterances and how, for example, referring expressions are understood. And *task* is associated with systems and users, and hence, what a user is trying to do with his or her utterances.

The full meaning representation of an utterance reflects all aspects of domain, context, and task, and can be interpreted directly in the world or model the system is connected to. The full meaning representation of an utterance reflects its lexical semantics, the particular entities denoted by its referring expressions, the arguments of its relations, additional relations that underlie those specified explicitly in the utterance, and also the speaker's intention in producing the utterance. While decisions about some of these features can be made locally, based simply on syntactic and lexical semantic knowledge, other decisions may require (1) information from the discourse, (2) particular factual or commonsense knowledge of the world or model, or (3) knowledge about the speaker's intentions.

One important question to ask about a given semantic interpretation process is whether it has

---

[1]The system's domain knowledge may also include beliefs about what is generally, if not always, true in the domain—e.g., commonsense knowledge and default knowledge. Such knowledge has not yet been treated as either terminological or assertional.

complete responsibility for computing the full meaning representation of an utterance or is only responsible for computing an intermediate representation. That is, do other processes with access to information about the discourse, the task, and the domain take this intermediate representation and compute a representation of the full meaning of the utterance?

A primary problem here, noted in the general Introduction, is that NL utterances, by themselves, may be both ambiguous and underdetermined in ways that cannot be resolved locally. They can be *ambiguous* with respect to three different things: they can be structurally ambiguous (that is, the same phrase or clause can be analysed in different ways into constituents and relations among those constituents), they can be lexically ambiguous (that is, even in one domain, words and phrases can convey more than one sense), and they can contain scope ambiguities (that is, there may be more than one way of reading which predicates, operators, and descriptions fall within the scope of negatives like "not," quantifiers like "every," "all," and "most," conjunctions and disjunctions ("and" and "or"), and intensional operators like "claim," "believe," "seek," etc.).

In addition, an utterance can be *underdetermined* with respect to information that has not been specified explicitly—for example, with respect to particular predicate arguments or specific relationships between events or objects. Examples of the first type include the (edible) object implicit in the utterance "John eats at 7 p.m. every day" and the instrument implicit in the utterance "John hit Mary" (i.e., he hit her with something, probably his hand). Examples of the second type include an "eating" relation that probably underlies the utterance "I like apples" (i.e., "I like to eat apples") or a "doing harm" relation that probably underlies "I fear alligators" (i.e., "I fear alligators doing something to harm me").

Given the ambiguity and underdetermination of NL utterances and given that resolving them may require information that is not local to the utterance, if a particular semantic interpretation process computes an intermediate representation (often called a *logical form* or LF), this intermediate representation may itself be ambiguous and/or underdetermined in various ways. The particular ways vary with the approaches of different researchers.

Of the articles included in this section, two discuss general issues in semantic interpretation (*McDermott; Moore*), while the others focus on particular systems. The approaches to semantic interpretation discussed here differ among themselves in

their answers to the following questions:

- Is the output of semantic interpretation an intermediate representation or a representation of the full meaning of the utterance?

- If an intermediate representation is produced, which, if any, aspects of the expression are ambiguous or underdetermined with respect to the full meaning of the utterance? How have the other aspects been resolved? Does the semantic interpretation process operate on the utterance itself (i.e., the surface string) or does it make use of its syntactic analysis? If the latter, does it operate on a single complete analysis, a set of alternative analyses, or a sequence of partial hypotheses?

- What aspects of meaning are made explicit in the meaning representation (e.g., individual entities, sets of entities, stuff, events, actions, intensional contexts, etc.)? That is, what kinds of things are significant in the system's world or model?

There are several related topics not covered in this section. We have not included papers on semantics *per se*—that is, on the problem of mapping from a meaning representation onto the world or a model of the world (but see [1, 9, 18] for three current theories of semantics). Also absent are papers on the interpretation of metaphoric language, where the meaning of words is extended beyond the lexicon in creative, though still regular, ways (see [2]). Finally, we have not included papers on the interpretation of noun-noun compounds—on discovering the implicit semantic relations between the components and hence, what the compound as a whole means (see [3, 8]).

There are several papers in other chapters that touch on issues of semantic interpretation. In Chapter 6, *Hendrix et al.* and *Burton and Brown* discuss semantic grammars, a method of mapping surface strings directly to a meaning representation, while *Cullingford* gives further examples of conceptual dependency (CD) formalism in use. In Chapter 1, by *Pereira and Warren* demonstrates a way of computing a logical form representation during syntactic analysis, using a PROLOG-based grammar formalism.

Tarskian Semantics, or No Notation Without Denotation

McDermott's brief essay on representation formalisms makes the important point that any such formalism that claims to be useful for representing knowledge (or, as here, the full meaning of an utterance) must itself have a systematic semantics. That is, if there is no systematic way of interpreting an expression of the formalism in some appropriate world or model and no systematic way of inferring the consequences of particular expressions with respect to a set of inference rules, one has no way of knowing what one is saying or whether it is what one wants to say. McDermott applies his criterion equally to the meaning representation formalisms of NLP (illustrating it with an example from Schank's Conceptual Dependency representation, see this chapter) and to the rule formalisms of production systems, both of which are meant to yield unambiguous expressions. Notice that this criterion would not apply to expressions in an intermediate representation, which may be ambiguous with respect to the full meaning of an utterance (see *Schubert and Pelletier,* this chapter).

Language and Memory

This article describes not only Schank's approach to semantic interpretation, but the development of his whole theory of language understanding and the reasoning it requires. In doing this, the article provides a motivation for Conceptual Dependency (CD)—the full meaning representation formalism that utterances are mapped into in this theory.

One feature of the full meaning representation of an utterance that has received particular attention in the CD approach is that of revealing things that have not been made explicit in the surface form of the utterance. As noted earlier, these can be of at least two types: (1) additional roles (usually belonging to verbs) that must be filled and (2) additional relations that intuitively seem to underlie those specified explicitly in the utterance. In a CD representation of an utterance, these roles, their fillers, and these relations are filled in through the system's knowledge of lexical semantics (i.e., how words map onto CD structures) and rules/heuristics it has been given for inferring what is (or is likely to be) true in the domain. CD's representation of surface verbs in terms of more primitive concepts simplifies the specification of these roles and relations.

One advantage of the CD approach is that any two sentences that share all or part of their meaning, regardless of their syntactic or lexical form, will have the same CD representation (or will share CD substructures[2]). Problems with CD include its lack of a clear semantics (see *McDermott* this chapter), and its conflation of necessary inferences with likely infer-

ences in fleshing out the full meaning of an utterance. The latter admit the possibility that the CD representation of an utterance will just be wrong. The mapping to CD is done directly from the surface form of the utterance, relying heavily on expectations raised by verbs about the realization of their arguments and minimally on syntactic analysis. For further information on CD and its expectation-driven approach to semantic interpretation, the reader is referred to [14, 15, 16].

An Intelligent Analyzer and Understander of English

Wilks' concern is with automatic translation. The semantic interpreter he describes is used for mapping utterances in one NL (the source language) to an unambiguous form (i.e., with word senses disambiguated, pronouns resolved, implicit information made explicit) that could then be mapped accurately into another NL (the target language).

In Wilks' system of "Preference Semantics" (PS), each sense of a word has an associated, structured semantic formula. These formulas contain such information as (1) the general category under which the word sense belongs, (2) the general categories of each of its arguments, if any, and (3) additional constraints on those arguments, if any, as to how they relate to the given word sense. During the semantic interpretation of an utterance, formulas for its word senses are bound together into "templates" to represent the meaning of the utterance and are also used to guide the interpretation process. As in the CD approach, Wilks' PS interpreter maps from utterances directly into templates, with syntax playing only a minor role.

One problem Wilks discusses is that of resolving word sense ambiguities. The semantic formulas used in PS not only characterize a particular word sense but also the preferred concepts associated with it. The semantic interpreter thus simultaneously chooses (1) word senses (formulas) for the words in an utterance and (2) a way of fitting them together that best satisfies the preferences in the chosen set of formulas. In this way, word sense disambiguation is simultaneous with interpretation. Wilks uses a similar preference-based method for resolving pronouns.

---

[2]Recall that one motivation for Transformational Grammar was the desire to ascribe to sentences with different surface syntactic forms the same logical form representation. This is not so different.

PS shares some of the advantages and disadvantages of CD. On the plus side, it addresses important problems of representing and trying to recognize word senses. On the other hand, the template representations themselves lack a semantics, and the mapping process, by ignoring syntactic structure, is *ad hoc* and prone to error.

Semantics and Quantification in Natural Language Question Answering

LUNAR was the seminal NL question-answering system developed by Woods and his colleagues at Bolt, Beranek and Newman. Semantic interpretation in LUNAR was notable for its attention to quantifiers and its innovative procedural semantics.

LUNAR represented the full meaning of an utterance to the system using an extended notational variant of the first-order predicate calculus, with designators, functions, predicates, quantifiers and variables, and also commands. Expressions in this formalism were then interpreted in LUNAR's domain model (a large database of analyses of lunar rock samples returned by the Apollo 10 mission) through a well-defined *procedural semantics.* Each designator in the representation corresponded to an entity or set of entities in the database; each predicate had a procedure for determining its truth, given values for its arguments; each function had a procedure for computing its value, given particular arguments; and each quantified proposition had a routine for instantiating and testing it appropriately against the database.

Input to LUNAR's semantic interpreter was a complete parse tree, and interpretation was done compositionally—that is, the meaning of any subtree was a systematic function of the meaning assigned to its branches. If the parse tree could not be interpreted, the parse was rejected and the parser recalled to backtrack and compute another alternative. If information needed for a complete representation was missing, it was supplied by default by the semantic intepreter. (For example, if simply "analyses" of some sample were requested, they were assumed by default to be "overall analyses"—that is, not specific to one phase of the sample—and to be analyses for the ten major elements.) Particular attention was paid to the interpretation of quantifiers to make sure they were assigned proper scope. If the parse tree was ambiguous with respect to word sense or quantifier scope, the semantic interpreter would produce a set of all possible interpretations. It was intended that another module (or the

user) would be able to choose among these alternatives, but this was not pursued.

A Procedural Model of Language Understanding

SHRDLU was the well-known system developed by Winograd that answered questions and responded to commands concerning its domain of toy blocks. SHRDLU was notable for the scope of linguistic and conversational phenomena it dealt with and for the level of performance it was able to demonstrate. This achievement was due in part to its meaning representation formalism and its incremental interpretation process. To SHRDLU, the meaning of an utterance was an unambiguous expression in MicroPlanner, a logic-based programming language that was a precursor of PROLOG. Thus the meaning representation of an utterance was an expression that had, as in LUNAR, a well-defined procedural interpretation (procedural semantics).

SHRDLU constructed the meaning representation of an utterance incrementally, using both syntactic hypotheses about the utterance proposed by the parser and lexical-semantic information associated with each word in the utterance. In SHRDLU, each word was defined as a program that would be called at an appropriate point in syntactic analysis (i.e., when a constituent was proposed), as the system attempted to determine whether the constituent was meaningful. These definition programs were able to do arbitrary computations on the current constituent hypothesis and the current state of the domain and were involved in such diverse tasks as resolving word sense ambiguities and determining the appropriate context-dependent referents (if any) of definite noun phrases. (The latter was done by the program associated with the word "the.")

Semantic Aspects of Translation

Hendrix's semantic interpreter was designed to be a part of a speech understanding system, rather than a system for understanding written text. As such, it had to deal with an additional source of ambiguity—the ambiguity of the acoustic wave form itself and its segmentation into a sequence of English words. One notable feature of Hendrix's interpreter was the way it implemented its meaning representation formalism, a way that allowed efficient encoding of alternative, competing hypotheses about the sequence of words, their syntactic analysis and their interpretation. The expressive power of the formalism was similar to that of LUNAR, containing first-order predicates, quantifiers, and the standard sort of individuals. It differed from LUNAR in that the meaning representation of an utterance was explicitly tied to the system's domain model, and its interpretation (not discussed here) was nonprocedural [6].

As in LUNAR, attention was paid to quantifiers and correctly determining their scope. Unlike LUNAR though, the system assigned scope to quantifiers during a postprocessing phase of interpretation, rather than during its regular bottom-up interpretation of the utterance's syntactic structure. This allowed scope decisions to be based on the entire utterance and its context.

Problems in Logical Form

Moore addresses problems here of representing the literal meaning of utterances. He argues strongly for such an intermediate level of representation, distinct from a representation of its full meaning (which Moore calls its "intended meaning"), based on the seeming open-endedness of the problem inferring a speaker's intention and on the explanatory value of literal meaning as a component of intended meaning. Moore acknowledges that all aspects of context may be required to resolve ambiguities in an utterance, but unlike *Schubert and Pelletier* (see below), he argues for mapping an ambiguous utterance into a set of distinct unambiguous representations, each corresponding to a different literal reading.

While the meaning representation formalisms used in LUNAR, SHRDLU, and Hendrix's systems were based on logic, the range of concept types they address was limited by their task (and the need to have a working system). Moore spends most of his paper discussing the representation of other important concept types expressible in NL, that had not, at the time of writing, received significant consideration by NL or knowledge representation researchers. These concepts include events, actions, and processes; time and space; collective entities and stuff; and propositional attitudes and modality.[3] All of these concept types have subsequently received great attention from researchers in both communities, but so far there has been no concensus regarding the proper treatment of any of them.

From English to Logic

One reason for presenting Schubert and Pelletier's article after Moore's is their treatment of propositional attitudes and modality. The article as a whole describes a method for mapping from a NL utterance to an unambiguous representation of its context-sensitive meaning, using an ambiguous logical form (LF) representation as an intermediate step. This paper describes that latter representation and its systematic computation.

Schubert and Pelletier adopt the rule-by-rule approach to semantic interpretation presented by Montague in [11] (as in other research, including [4]). The grammar formalism to which they link their interpretation rules is Gazdar's Generalized Phrase Structure Grammar (GPSG) [5]. Previously, Gazdar had shown that a GPSG can be annotated with rules for translating utterances to expressions in Montague's Intensional Logic (IL) [12]. Schubert and Pelletier depart from Gazdar in using a conventional logical language for both LF and their full meaning representation rather than IL.[4] In fact, one notable feature of this paper is Schubert and Pelletier's arguments in favor of conventional logics over ILs as the interpreted form of NL utterances. (An alternative view, which attempts to make sense of Montague's IL by relating it to procedural semantics, appears in [7].)

Schubert and Pelletier's LF expressions may be ambiguous, since there is no way, based on local information alone, of disambiguating lexical items, quantifier scope, and the scope of connectives. In the approach presented here, LFs produced by a rule-by-rule coordinated parsing/intepretation process are subsequently postprocessed into an unambiguous meaning representation, drawing on both the system's domain knowledge and information about the context to resolve vague or ambiguous predicates into precise ones, to resolve referring expressions, and to determine the scope of quantifiers and connectives.

Note that the expressive power of even their ambiguous LF representation exceeds that of Woods' and of Hendrix's full meaning representation formalisms. This is because the latter were applied to simple

---

[3]It is not that these concept types were not needed, but rather, in the few places they were needed, a limited *ad hoc* treatment was sufficient. For example, LUNAR finessed the concept of stuff, with an *ad hoc* treatment of the chemical elements as proper names (rigid designators). SHRDLU finessed events with an *ad hoc* treatment in terms of subgoals it tried to achieve in "proving" a MicroPlanner form.

[4]Conventional logics are first-order logics, augmented with a lambda operator, propositional and perhaps other nonextensional propositional operators, and perhaps even some second-order predicates. They do not include intensional and extensional operators, nor do they have a nonintuitive interpretation of, for example, noun phrases as property sets and verb phrases as sets of property sets.

database question/answering and did not require the kinds of propositional attitudes and modalities that Moore discusses in his paper and that Schubert and Pelletier provide for here.

A New Semantic Computation While Parsing

As noted earlier, the full meaning representation of an utterance may display aspects of meaning that have not been realized explicitly in its surface form. Deriving these aspects may require inferences of various types. Weischedel's work addresses two classes of limited inferences, called *entailment* and *presupposition*, which are shown here to be relatively inexpensive to compute. Weischedel further limits his consideration to those entailments and presuppositions keyed by lexical items and grammatical constructs alone, to avoid some of the difficult problems. (See [10] for a discussion of the debate over presupposition and entailment waged in linguistics.)

Broadly speaking, A entails B if B is a logical consequence of A. Also speaking broadly, A presupposes B if B is a precondition for A's being judgable as either true or false. For example, the utterance "John managed to stop" entails "John stopped" and presupposes "John tried to stop." Whether a potential presupposition of an utterance (computed on the basis of its lexical items and syntactic structure) is taken to be an actual presupposition of that utterance depends on context. For example, if it is already established in the context that John didn't even try to stop, the utterance "John didn't manage to stop" will not have the above presupposition.

The entailments and presuppositions of an utterance are part of its full meaning, even though they are not explicit in its surface form. However, rather than using a general purpose inference engine to compute them, Weischedel shows how those that are associated with particular lexical items and syntactic structures can be computed during the parsing process. He hypothesizes, but does not discuss, a second process that can verify whether potential presuppositions are consistent with the current context. Those that are not are discarded, and those that are are taken as actual presuppositions.

The contribution of Weischedel's work is in giving a systematic way of computing these two narrow but important classes of inferences.

References

[1]   Barwise, J. and Perry, J., *Situations and Attitudes.* MIT Press, Cambridge MA, 1983.

[2]   Carbonell, J., Metaphor: An Inescapable Phenomenon in Natural Language Comprehension. In Lehnert, W. and Ringle, M. (editors), *Knowledge Representation for Language Processing Systems.* Erlbaum, New Jersey, 1982.

[3]   Finin, T., Constraining the Interpretation of Nominal Compounds in a Limited Context. In Grishman, R. and Kittredge, R. (editors), *Analyzing Language in Restricted Domains.* Erlbaum, New Jersey, 1985.

[4]   Friedman, J. and Warren, D. S., A Parsing Method for Montague Grammars, *Linguistics and Philosophy* 2:347–372, 1978.

[5]   Gazdar, G., Phrase Structure Grammar. In Jacobson, P. and Pullum, G. (editors), *The Nature of Syntactic Representation.* D. Reidel, Dordrecht, 1981.

[6]   Hendrix, G., Encoding Knowledge in Partitioned Networks. In Findler, N. V. (editor), *Associative Networks: Representation and Use of Knowledge by Computers.* Academic Press, New York, 1979.

[7]   Hobbs, J. and Rosenschein, S., Making Computational Sense of Montague's Intensional Logic, *Artificial Intelligence* 9:287–306, 1978.

[8]   Jones, K. Sparck, Compound Noun Interpretation Problems. In *Computer Speech Processing*, Fallfide, F. and Woods, W. (editors), Prentice-Hall, New Jersey, 1985.

[9]   Kamp, H., A Theory of Truth and Semantic Representation. In Groenendijk, J., et al. (editors), *Formal Methods in the Study of Language,* pages 277–322. Mathematisch Centrum, Amsterdam, 1981.

[10]   Levinson, S.C., *Pragmatics,* Cambridge University Press, Cambridge, 1983.

[11]   Montague, R., English as a Formal Language. In Thomason, R. (editor), *Formal Philosophy: Selected Papers of Richard Montague.* Yale University Press, New Haven CT, 1974.

[12]   Montague, R., The Proper Treatment of Quantification in Ordinary English. In Thomason, R., (editor), *Formal Philosophy: Selected Papers of Richard Montague.* Yale University Press, New Haven CT, 1974.

[13]   Perrault, C.R. and Grosz, B.J., Natural Language Interfaces. In *Annual Review of Computer Science 1986*, pages 47–82. Annual Reviews, Inc., Palo Alto CA, 1986.

[14]   Riesbeck, C. and Schank, R., Comprehension by Computer: Expectation-Based Analysis of Sentences in Context. In Levelt, W.J.M. and Flores d'Arcais, G.B. (editors), *Studies in the Perception of Language.* John Wiley and Sons, Ltd., Chichester, England, 1979.

[15]   Schank, R., Inference and Paraphrase, *JACM* 22:309–328, 1975.

[16]   Schank, R., *Conceptual Information Processing,* North Holland, Amsterdam, 1976.

[17]   Sidner, C., What the Speaker Means: The Recognition of Speakers' Plans in Discourse, *Comp. and Maths with Appls.* 9(1):71–82, 1983.

[18]   Thomason, R. (ed.), *Formal Philosophy: Selected Papers of Richard Montague,* Yale University Press, New Haven CT, 1974.

[19]   Vilain, M., The Restricted Language Architecture of a Hybrid Representation System. In *Proc. of the 9th Int'l Meeting,* pages 547–551. Int'l Joint Conf. on Artificial Intelligence, Los Angeles CA, August, 1985.

Tarskian Semantics, or No Notation Without Denotation!

DREW MCDERMOTT
Yale University

Tarskian semantics is called "Tarskian" for historical reasons (Tarski, 1936). A more descriptive name would be "systematic denotational semantics," or SD for short. The method is called "denotational" because it specified the meanings of a notation in terms of what its expressions denote. The method is called "systematic" in hopes that the rules that assign meaning are precise enough to support statements and occasionally proofs of interesting properties of the notation.

In a typical predicate calculus, we assign to primitive symbols denotations which consist of objects, functions, or predicates. Then the meanings of more complex expressions are defined by rules which define their meanings in terms of the meanings of their parts. For sentences in such a language, this amounts to specifying the conditions which make any given sentence *true*. That is, the meaning of a sentence is a specification of what would make it denote T and what would make it denote NIL. This specification may thus be thought of as a generalization of an ordinary LISP predicate definition.

For example, we may assign to the predicate symbol PTRANS a predicate which is true only if its first argument has ever caused its second argument to be physically transferred from its third argument to its fourth argument. Then the denotation of (ACTOR x ⇔ PTRANS OBJ y FROM u TO v) should be T just if the denotation of x has ever transferred the denotation of y from the denotation of u to the denotation of v. (This is a long-winded way of writing a typical semantic rule, which maps the syntax of an expression into a denotation systematically. Syntax is not an issue in this paper, but notice that the use of SD does not commit us to any syntax in particular, so long as it is precise.) It is clear that the first argument of the denotation of PTRANS should be an animate agent; its second, a physical object; its third and fourth, places. If we wish to be precise, we must somehow forbid incongruous types to appear in these places, or go on to specify what the denotation (ACTOR x ⇔ PTRANS OBJ y FROM u TO v) is when x, y, u, or v is incongruous.

So far this may seem very fluffy stuff. What have we gained by (apparently) just repeating in the semantic domain what is fairly obvious in the first place? Mainly we have gained a certain *commitment*. By actually pinning ourselves down, for example, to the requirement that a PTRANS expression signifies

that a transfer *ever* occurred, we are in a position to pass judgment on the truth of certain inferences, and on systems which license them

The real power of this method appears when we embed the notation in an inference system of some kind. For example, say we require the inference rule, "If (ACTOR x ⇔ PTRANS OBJ y FROM u TO v), then infer (ACTOR y IS (LOC VAL v))." (Where is IS-LOC-VAL construct is to mean that x has at some time been at v.) Given an SD interpretation of this notation, we can ask, Is this rule *sound?* That is, is it true that if x ever transfers y to v, y will at some time have been at v? The answer is clearly yes. On the other hand, consider the rule, "If (ACTOR y IS (LOC VAL vl)) and (NOT (EQUAL vl v)) and (NOT (ACTOR x ⇔ PTRANS OBJ y TO v)) then (NOT (ACTOR y IS (LOC VAL v)))." If our intent is to capture the idea that nothing moves without a PTRANS, we have failed, since, by the interpretation we are building, there is no time relation between the hypothesized PTRANS and the statement (NOT (ACTOR y IS (LOC VAL v))). The rule for NOT will map (NOT p) into T just in case p is mapped into NIL, but this will happen only if the denotation of y has never been and never will be at the place denoted by v. So the rule says, "If y has been some place besides v, and some agent x has never transferred y to v, then y has never been at v." This rule is simply false. Of course, this one test does not mean there is no way to express what we want in this language, but it means the obvious way will not work. (And it provides a strong intuitive argument that this particular language requires extension to be able to denote particular times and events, and quantifications over them.)

Sometimes the precise study of semantics does enable us to make generalizations about everything statable or derivable in an inference system. In particular, we would like to know when a system allows us to infer too little or too much. The Holy Grail of this study is a theorem to the effect that, given an intuitively appealing assignment of meanings to the expressions of a system, its inference rules entitles us to infer exactly the true sentences (those with value T), no more and no less. Such a result is called a *completeness theorem*. Often we have to settle for less, and prove only that the inferences allowed by the system are true. This is a proof of *soundness* and *consistency*.

Even when a system is too complex or evolving too fast for these proofs to be available, the application of SD in an informal way can still be valuable. Here the method suggests a strong self-discipline to be applied in considering adding a rule or predicate symbol to the system. This discipline amounts to asking, Does this new construct denote something we can pin down? Is a proposed rule *true?* If we cannot answer this question, we have no way of foreseeing all the interactions of new constructs with old. Even if we must persist in adding a new rule "blindly," this attitude warns us to be on our guard.

This advice may seem vacuous, but it has application to real AI systems. For example, it puts a heavy burden on designers of production systems.

These are systems of rules of the form "condition → action," where the condition is to match some memory structure and prescribe an action which changes that structure. If the conditions can be given a precise semantics, and if the actions are always of the form, "infer p," we can give an obvious denotational semantics to the rules, and there will be no loose ends. (MYCIN (Shortliffe, 1976) is like this, more or less.) Unfortunately, these restrictions are not met by many such systems. This means that there is no way to say whether a particular rule is sound, without studying the entire system of which it is a part (and even then it is not clear what sort of statement we would like to make about it).

Consider the AMORD system of de Kleer, Doyle, Steele, and Sussman (1977). This is for the most part a very well-disciplined production system where the rules can be given an SD semantics. Its rules are used uniformly as "forward deduction" rules: a → b is used just to infer b after a has been inferred (Notice that heretofore I have not mentioned inference procedure; in practice one must distinguish between all inferences that are *allowed* and the subset that a particular procedure actually *does*.) What if we want to use the same abstract rule to try to prove a as a subgoal of trying to prove b? We can write this as "b ← a." and define "back-arrow" thus:

$$(q \leftarrow p) \rightarrow ((show\ q) \rightarrow (show\ p))$$

That is, "From q ← p, infer that if it is inferred that q is a goal, infer that p is a goal." Both of these symbols, → and SHOW, are defined by the user, not the system. SHOW can be used to define other goal-oriented constructs. For example, when the goal of proving a conjunction comes up, it is handled by a rule like this (don't worry too much about understanding it):

```
(show (p & q))
→ { (show p)
(p → { (show q)
(q → (p & q))}}]
```

which means, apparently, "If you wish to show p & q, then you wish to show p, and if p is concluded, you then wish to show q; if p and q are concluded, you may then infer p & q." I say "apparently" because we have not really given a meaning to SHOW, and hence are in no position to judge the soundness of the conjunction rule. You might think (SHOW p) means, "The system is currently interested in the truth of p," but what does (SHOW (ON X BLOCK1)) mean, when X is a variable? Is X to be thought of as universally quantified? That is, is the system, for all X, interested in the truth of (ON X BLOCK1)? This seems doubtful. For instance, if AMORD were to be used as an insurance-company data base, we might have a rule:

```
(show (health john-doe x))
→ (do (cancel-policy john-doe))
```

meaning, apparently, "If someone is interested in John Doe's health, cancel his policy." (Perverse, but not inconceivable for an insurance company.). But then assertion of (SHOW (HEALTH Z BAD)). meaning, "I am interested in whose health is bad," will trigger the rule and cause John's policy to be cancelled. This is not just unfair, it is unsound.

This does not mean AMORD is worthless. It just means it is unanalyzable at a crucial point. Most of the time the semantics of the system is well-behaved: in fact, it uses a version of the well-understood resolution rule of inference. But there are times when the only thing between the system's user and nonsense is caution on the part of the user not to push the SHOW symbol too far. (Not that he knows how far that is.)

Other examples abound. Any system which consists of undisciplined LISP programs is resting on rules whose soundness (and meaning) are in doubt. A system like KRL (Bobrow & Winograd, 1977), which consists of a splendid edifice of notation with no denotation, is a castle in air. Who can say whether two KRL expressions conflict, for instance? Similar criticisms can be made of KRL's cousins, the semantic networks (see Woods, 1975).

I realize that some AI people are liable to resist these ideas stubbornly. They are likely to ask why we should bother with the immediate goal that an inference system be sound, since in the long run the only criterion for such a system is whether it "works." Further, since inference procedures for practical reasons, are bound, to be incomplete with respect to their host inference systems, why insist that the host systems be complete semantically?

The answer is this: It is not just important that a system be correct; it is also crucial that it be understood. Granted that a practical system will be incomplete, we should be able to say in what ways it is incomplete, and why. (For this reason, in the long run, the study of the complexity of inference procedures will be as important as the study of the semantics of inference systems.) After all, a practical program will never be "finished"; it would be nice to know that whatever fragment of one exists will maintain its integrity as new rules are added or new applications are made of old rules. We would like our programs to be "additive," that is, to be able to assimilate new, correct rules from experts without destroying the correctness of old ones. (At least we would like. as in the MYCIN system, for the correctness of old rules to depend on criteria explicit enough for the system to maintain them (Davis, 1976).)

It would perhaps be surprising for an outsider to learn that computer scientists, in spite of the fact that they study purely formal objects like programs and data structures, have a pronounced "anti-formalist" streak. This arose initially from the painful discovery that even the most formal objects have to be debugged. In AI, it comes from our early experience that only trivia could be formalized. Impressive AI programs have been too complex. However, we should not let this stop us. It may be true that formal theories must always remain the study of ideal cases. This has been true in physics, without causing it any harm. (It is difficult to see how physics could have progressed without the ideal gas.) It is also true that formal inquiry will always depend on an influx of good ideas and urgent requirements from the empirical exploration of practical programs. Large practical programs are, however, likely to collapse under their own weight without a good foundation. The structure of programs like AMORD and MYCIN seems to me revealing; they consist of a secure semantic base and patchwork in the poorly understood areas. They work, but, more important, experience with them tells us how to fill in the gaps, so that the next wave of programs can go forward.

Let me now deal with a few more specific objections to "Tarskian semantics." First, there is the objection that, "People do not carry Tarskian semantics around in their heads, so Tarskian semantics is of no concern to AI researchers interested in the way people do things." The premise here is true, the conclusion false. Even the wildest denotationalist has not claimed that semantics should be located "in the head" of a robot. The semantics is for our use, as a tool in analyzing knowledge representations. Of course, if our goal is to duplicate the human representational system, it is not enough to be systematic; we must also be accurate.

The objection has been made that denotational semantics cannot be the semantics of natural language in all its glory. This may or may not be true (if "denotational" is construed broadly), but has nothing to do with its use as a semantics of internal knowledge structures.

One weakness of systematic denotational semantics as developed so far is that it has been mainly a tool of philosophers and logicians, whose goals are rather different from ours. Much of what they have done is of no interest to us, and questions of burning importance to AI they have left untouched. For example, it is characteristic of all logical systems that adding new axioms to a system leaves all old inferences valid. This property is called "monotonicity" (by Minsky, 1974). There is no way to say, for instance. "If you have car keys and gasoline (or money), and there is no information ruling it out, you may use your car to go distances up to a few hundred miles." (Then the required inference may be blocked by the addition of the axiom. "Someone has stolen your tires.") However, this is no objection to denotational semantics as such, but raises the technical problem *within* denotational semantics of representing" ... is not ruled out." Much progress has already been made on the practical side of developing programs that can handle constructions like this, but the underlying theory needs work.

There is another area in which most (but by no means all) logicians' results have been inadequate. I said earlier that the denotation of a proposition was always T or NIL. This is called *extensional* semantics, and is standard for mathematical applications. If our language includes a predicate like "BELIEVES," this is inadequate. Consider a proposition like (BELIEVES MARY (FAT JOHN)). Clearly, the truth value of this proposition does not depend at all on the truth value of (FAT JOHN). So, if the denotation of a formula is to depend only on the denotations of its parts, formulas will have to denote more abstract entities, and have truth values only indirectly. This is the object of *intensional* semantics (Bressan, 1972).

Systematic semantics is a method for solving representational problems, not a catalogue of solutions. We still do not know how to represent time, space, creation and destruction of individuals, knowledge, individuals made out of liquids (Hayes, 1974), and procedures. We will make faster progress on these problems if we keep semantics in mind.

ACKNOWLEDGMENTS

I wish to thank David Barstow. Eugene Charniak. and Patrick Hayes for ideas and criticism. (I haven't bothered to repeat many complementary remarks on semantics made by Hayes (1977).)

REFERENCES

Bobrow. D. & Winograd. T. An overview of KRL. a knowledge representation language. *Cognitive Science*, 1977. *1*, 3.

Bressan. A. *A general interpreted modal calculus.* New Haven: Yale Univ. Press. 1972.

Davis. R. Applications of meta level knowledge to the construction. maintenance and use of large knowledge bases. Stanford AI Laboratory Memo 283. Palo Alto. California. 1976.

Hayes. P. J. Some problems and non-problems in representation theory. *Proc. AISB.* 1974. *I*, 63.

de Kleer. J. Doyle. J.. Steele. G. L. & Sussman. G. J. Explicit control of reasoning. MIT AI Laboratory Cambridge. Mass. 1977 Memo. 427. Also in Proceedings of the conference on AI and Programming Languages. Rochester. New York.

Minsky. M. A framework for representing knowledge. MIT AI Memo 306. Cambridge. Mass.. 1974.

Shortliffe. E. H. *Computer-based medical consultations: MYCIN.* New York: American Elsevier. 1976.

Tarski. A. Der Wahrheitsbegriff in den formalisierten Sprachen. *Studia Philos,* 1936. *I.* 261.

Woods. W. What's in a link? In D. G. Bobrow & A. Collins (Eds.). *Representation and understanding.* New York: Academic Press. 1975.

Language and Memory*

ROGER C. SCHANK
Yale University

This paper outlines some of the issues and basic philosophy that have guided my work and that of my students in the last ten years. It describes the progression of conceptual representational theories developed during that time, as well as some of the research models built to implement those theories. The paper concludes with a discussion of my most recent work in the area of modelling memory. It presents a theory of MOPs (Memory Organization Packets), which serve as both processors and organizers of information in memory. This enables effective categorization of experiences in episodic memory, which in turn enables better predictive understanding of new experiences.

PREFACE

As an undergraduate, I naturally developed a simultaneous interest in the problem of cognition and its computer simulation. I also had a strong interest in language. Attempting to combine these three interests led me to the conclusion that there existed no academic discipline that could comfortably accommodate my interests. Linguists were not seriously interested in cognition. Psychologists were, but did not take seriously the idea of a computer program as the embodiment of a theory. Computer Science was still nascent and in many ways resistant to the "mushiness" of Artificial Intelligence (AI). Where AI did exist, concern with people as opposed to machines was frequently lacking.

In the last few years the situation in all three fields has begun to change. In AI, cognitive concerns have not only been accepted but are considered to be of prime importance. Many linguists have abandoned their overriding concern with syntax for a more balanced view of language phenomena. Psychologists are learning how to build computer models themselves and have begun to run experiments to test hypotheses taken directly from work in AI.

What we are seeing is the beginning of Cognitive Science.

INTRODUCTION

In this paper I will attempt to outline some of the issues and basic philosophy that have guided my work and that of my students in the last ten years. I will end by outlining some of the problems that I am currently working on in the area of the modelling of memory.

My initial research focused on the representation of meaning as it would be used for the generation of natural language sentences. I believed (and still do believe) that because people could easily translate from one language to another and, in a sense, think in neither, there must be available to the mind an interlingual, i.e., language-free, representation of meaning. I was very interested in the problem of mechanical translation of language and hoped that any representation I developed would be useful for solving that problem. Since I was looking for this interlingual representation based upon the assumption that people actually thought with such a thing, I developed an intense interest in making any representation I came up with as psychologically correct as possible. Unfortunately, psychologists were at this point very concerned with phenomena that could shed light on the validity of transformational grammars (e.g., Fodor et al., 1966; Mehler, 1963). This work did not provide much in the way of evidence one way or the other for the things I was interested in, so, since I was not trained to do experiments myself, I had only my intuitions to rely on for psychological evidence.

I began to think about the problem of representing meaning; but, since my guiding interest at the time was mechanical translation, I was particularly interested in the computational properties of any representation that I came up with. I was especially concerned with the question of how a meaning representation could be of use in the generation of natural language sentences and in the parsing of natural language sentences.

The first representation that I developed looked a lot like English words with arrows connecting them. The arrows were taken from dependency theory, which had been written about by Hays (1964) and used quite a bit by Klein (1965) and, to some extent, Lamb (1964). My contribution, as I saw it at that time, was to make the representation more conceptual.

The main claim that Conceptual Dependency made at that time (Schank, 1969) had nothing to do with the primitives with which the work has been primarily associated in recent times. Conceptual Dependency theory claimed that there was a predetermined set of possible relationships that made up an interlingual meaning structure. These relationships (or conceptual rules as I termed

*I would like to thank the following people for their help both in the writing of and the information of ideas in this paper: Wendy Lehnert, Christopher Riesbeck, Robert Abelson, Michael Lebowitz, Janet Kolodner, Mark Burstein, Lawrence Birnbaum, and Margot Flowers. I would also like to thank Donald Norman for his help in editing a previous version of this paper. This work was supported in part by the Advanced Research Projects Agency of the Department of Defense, monitored by the Office of Naval Research under contract N00014-75-C-1111.

them) could be used either to predict conceptual items that were implicit in a sentence or, coupled with syntactic rules, to inform a parser what was missing from a meaning and where it might be found in a sentence (Schank & Tesler, 1969). In generation, these rules could be used as the basis for generating meanings from which sentences could be formed. This changed generation to a process that was more realistic than one beginning with $S = NP + VP$ (Schank, 1968).

The key issue from my point of view, then—and my philosophy has not changed on this—was the creation of expectations about what slots needed to be filled in a conceptualization and the embodiment of those expectations to guide both parsing and generation. If information about the properties of a coherent meaning structure is available to parsers and generators, there seems no reason not to use it. Folk wisdom decided that I "didn't believe in syntax" because I pointed out the necessity of using meaning information to drive the parser. But, the only way to write such a parser is to use meaning-driven rules which have their basis in syntactic information about the input sentence. This is what we tried to do (Schank et al., 1973). The basic idea of slot filling and top down expectations drives our work today (Carbonell, 1979; DeJong, 1979; Gershman 1979; Riesbeck & Schank, 1976; Wilensky, 1978). The notion of scripts (Schank & Abelson, 1977), and to some extent frames (Minsky, 1975), uses this same basic philosophy.

As we began to work on building programs that mapped English into and out of Conceptual Dependency, we ran into a problem with ambiguous sentences whose resolution depended on world knowledge considerations. Prior to this time parsers were purely syntactic, so no good solution had been found for this problem.

As an example of the kind of issue I was concerned about at that time, consider the following sentences:

I hit Fred on the nose.
I hit Fred in the park.

In order to parse these sentences correctly it was necessary to know where a person can be located. Here, "correctly" depended on what had to be represented in CD. There was a locative relationship for entire conceptualizations and a "part of" relationship for objects, and either could be expressed in English with a locative prepositional phrase. To solve this problem I used the conceptual semantics I had invented for generation. [These were simple world knowledge rules that were tied to each CD conceptual rule (Schank, 1968). Thus the conceptual rule that actors can act would be modified by lists of what could do what according to semantic categories, such as "animals can eat," "planes can fly," and so on.] The rules that mapped from syntactic relationships to conceptual ones checked for acceptability according to the conceptual semantics each time a mapping was attempted.

Gradually, it became clear that the final parse of most sentences into Conceptual Dependency wound up adding information that was not in the original sentence explicitly. This took our work out of the domain of linguistics, since we had gone beyond language phenomena. This work was Cognitive Science, but since that field didn't then exist, a good home became a nontrivial problem.

CONCEPTUAL REPRESENTATIONS

In 1970 we started to make our representations more conceptual (Schank et al., 1970) than they had been. Until this point our supposedly language-free representations had a great deal of language in them. Our representation seemed to require us to put in a great deal more than was in the surface or deep structure representation of the sentence in order to make conceptual sense. There did not seem to be any way to avoid this introduction of elements that were not present in the utterance initially if we were to represent the meaning of what had been said. Examining our representations, we began the search for some regularities in the representation that would give us a more canonical form. What we had until that point was so free form that we could create anything at any time. This did not seem very sensible. In particular, there was a problem of determining which sense of the various multiple-sense verbs we had at any given time. We could not just continue writing "have" with subscripts to differentiate "have a soda" from "have ten dollars" from "have cancer." There had to be some underlying basic forms. Was "understand1" equal to "see3"? Which sense was more basic? And, more important, how many senses of a word would there turn out to be and what would their intersections be? In the case of partial overlap of senses, there was a definite problem with the subscript method.

As a side issue at this time, we attempted to clean up the mess in which we had left our representation of prepositions. We had been using an arrow to mean any prepositional relationship, in the faith that higher level processes that used our representations would figure out the true relationship that held between an action and its associated objects. We tried to think about what kinds of prepositional relationships there were.

We had already dealt adequately for our purposes with locations and "part of" relationships (Schank, 1969). Aside from these two classes of prepositions we found that there were only three kinds of prepositional relationships: instrumental, directional, and recipient. These relationships described the way an action could relate to an object in an event regardless of what preposition was being used. Since we were describing relationships and not prepositions, we realized that English could be considered to have a kind of null preposition denoting objective relationships. However, this objective relationship was not any less of a relationship between action and object than the others. We knew that Fillmore (1968) had said similar things about syntactic relationships in

English, so we christened our relationships "conceptual cases." The differences between the two systems were a lot greater than their names suggested and in retrospect this was probably a poor choice of names. [See Schank (1972) for a discussion of those differences.]

This new system of cases had immediate ramifications throughout our entire representation system. For example, we had previously represented "I want money" as:

```
        I<==>want
           ↑
           |        to
money <==>go    <_|
```

However, adding a recipient to this representation caused us to come up with the following representation:

```
          I<==>want
             ↑
Someone <=>  ??    O     R I---->I
                   <--money<---I
                   |----<someone
```

that is, we knew that we had a Recipient here and it had to be "I." Similarly there had to be an Object because what else could "money" be? It did not seem like an actor. The actor was unknown, but we knew he was the same person as the donor of the recipient case. Of course, the above diagram had a glaring hole. What was the action? Still this representation seemed to make a lot more sense than the first one where money was an actor doing the action "go."

What was needed at this point was a name for our unknown action, and since it obviously involved a kind of transfer of the money, we called it "trans." "Trans" helped us with other problems as well. It solved the partial overlap problem in the meaning of words such as "give," "take," "buy," and "sell." Furthermore, it eliminated the need for elaborate meaning transfer rules of the kind Katz (1967) had been proposing for mapping words like "buy" into "sell." We began to wonder what other actions like "trans" were around.

We began at this point to look more closely at the concept of an action. We attempted to classify the verbs we had been using according to the cases they took and the properties of their objects. This left us with S(tate)-ACTS, P(hysical)-ACTs, E(motional)-ACTs, and so on (Schank et al., 1970). Using this classification for verbs, we could now predict the missing cases that were implicit and that thus had to be inferred. We continued to look for effective groupings that would facilitate inference. Thus, although we did not actually set out to discover primitives, the considerations that we had in representation issues forced us to come up with some workable classification of actions that fit within our framework.

Inference was not yet a major issue in this regard, but other problems forced us to focus on it. For example, consider the sentence "I fear bears" and our proposed representation of it at that time:

```
I<=>fear
      ↑
bears<=>harm<---I
```

In the same paper where we were wrestling with the issue of representation of actions (Schank et al., 1970), we also introduced an idea we called "associative storage of concepts." In order to adequately represent sentences of the above type, it was necessary to have available a conceptualization that could serve as the object of the verb "fear." (At this point we viewed such a verb as a kind of stative ACT. We later realized such states were not ACTs but states of objects.) Obviously this conceptualization had to have in it both "bears" and "I" as part of the object of "fear." Here again we were faced with the question of what was the ACT? The answer we chose was an ACT called "harm." As we were not particularly interested in primitives, this should not seem strange. The focus of our interest was: how were we going to find the concept "harm" to add to our representation?

We tried using "associative storage of concepts." What we meant by this was that there had to be some connection between fear and bears that would allow us to infer "harm" as the missing ACT. Quillian (1966) had used the idea of a linked network of concepts that could be searched from two paths in order to find their shortest intersection. This idea had been used for disambiguation, but it now seemed that it could be extended for use here as well.

However, that seemed like a lot of work for so little. When we looked at other examples of the phenomenon we were trying to account for, an easier solution presented itself. For example, the sentence "I like books" clearly needed something about "I read books" inside the conceptualization that represented its meaning. It was obvious that this could be done simply by listing "books" in the dictionary as a "READ object." If we had an empty slot requiring an ACT, and an object of "book," we would simply infer "read." This depended on treating "like" as a state and not an ACT, of course.

This did not solve the problem when the object was not the source of the inference, however. A functional object like a "book" could well be listed as a "READ object," but what were we to do when "bears" or "Nixon" was the object of a stative ACT? Since these objects were not functional in the same way, it seemed that the missing ACT would have to be supplied as a part of the meaning of the word "fear." Here again we had, without quite intending to, decomposed the meaning of a word (fear) into more basic elements (fear plus expected harm). The reason for this was again attributable to the requirements we had placed on CD with respect to what slots there were in a conceptualization and how they were to be filled. So, we were left at this point with a representation like:

```
I fear Nixon
I <=> fear
          ↑
Nixon <=> do
        <=>|||
something <=> harm ———I
```

Thus at this point we were now freely adding to our representation concepts that were not present in the English sentence in the first place and, perhaps more importantly, concepts that were only probably part of the meaning. These were the first explicit inferences that we had.

INTENTIONS, BELIEFS, AND MEMORY

We began to focus on the problem of inferencing intentions (Schank, 1971). We got into this problem because of a peculiar use of language that we happened to come across, which we realized was crucial for a reasonable understanding system to handle. The example was:

Q: Do you want a piece of chocolate?
A: I just had an ice cream cone.

Clearly, it is necessary to understand the answer given here as meaning "no." In attempting to figure out how to do this, we realized that it was necessary to fill out the structure of the conceptualizations underlying both sentences so that a match could be made from the answer to the question. To do this required inferences that were different from the "fill in the ACT" ones we had been working on. Thus we needed a structure like:

want → trans → eat → satisfied

To get this structure we had to postulate that when a "trans" was present, the object of the "trans" might enable an actor to perform the usual functional ACT done to this object. That is, a paraphrase of this question might be: "Do you want me to 'trans' you an object which is edible so you can eat it so that it will make you feel some feeling (full, happy, etc.)?" The answer would then be: "I already have that feeling because I just did an action that resulted in that feeling." To do all this required a new set of resultative and enabling inferences, and caused us to begin to focus on the question of what kinds of inferences there were and where they came from.

One of the first issues, however, was the potential use of such inferences. Since we were primarily concerned with parsing at this stage, we focused initially on the issue of what expectations existed in processing that came from places other than the CD or syntactic expectations themselves.

We looked at an example of a conversation where a person, in a fit of anger at his wife, asks his friend for a knife and, when he is refused it, says:

I think I ought to . . . .

The question we asked was: What different kinds of things do you expect at this point? We isolated the following (Schank, 1971):

1. sentential — a verb is coming
2. conceptual — an entire conceptualization is coming
3. contextual — "ought to have fish" is excluded by the fighting context—something violent is expected
4. conversational — inference about the reason the person is talking—why talk about your future violence unless you want someone to stop it?
5. memory — what kind of person is John? should we take his anger seriously?
6. cultural — what happens in situations of this sort? memory structure inferences are used

These questions started us looking seriously at what else was going on in understanding besides parsing. Clearly we needed a memory full of facts about the world to do any sensible understanding. At this point our focus began to change. The issues of representation and parsing still existed of course, but memory, belief and inference were obviously at least as crucial.

Hemphill (1975) began to work on identifying how parsing was influenced by beliefs implicitly referred to in a text. I concentrated my efforts on representation; in particular, it was necessary, in order to handle the above example, to postulate a set of beliefs that could account for our expectations about an actor's behavior. To understand that John was not likely to want to sit down now and be friendly in the above example, we needed to know that when you are angry you do not like to be with the people you are angry with. This was represented as:

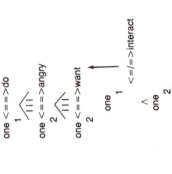

Beliefs of this sort were useful for predicting the future actions of an actor. Adding beliefs to the representation changed the idea of inference from that of simply additional information that would help in the parsing of a sentence. It suggested instead that we had to concentrate on problems having to do with the representation of information in memory and with the overall integration of incoming data with a given memory model. It thus became clear that natural language processing was a bit of a misnomer for our enterprise. What we were doing was not essentially different from what Colby (1967) or Abelson and Carroll (1965) were doing. That is, we had to deal with the problem of belief systems in general. But added to that was the problem of representation of meaning, knowledge, and memory.

The integration of all these problems caused us to deal with sentences whose meaning was a product of the combination of all these issues. For example, "He acts like Harry" means different things if Harry is a cat, a child, or an aged man. What is the correct representation for the meaning of such a sentence? Clearly it cannot be determined in any way apart from the memory structures its meaning relies on. Similarly, the sentence "He is dog-like in his devotion" means nothing if there is no belief available in memory about the devotion (or lack of it) of dogs.

We thus began to work on issues of memory and belief. But, in order to do this, we needed an adequate language for encoding beliefs and memory in general.

We returned to attempting to make the CD representations that we were using more rigorous so that we could better establish what was within the domain of a system like CD and what was outside of it. To do this, we considered the nature of the ACTs we had been using. At that point we had been using "trans" and a hodgepodge of others that suited us. To remedy this situation we looked at the mental verbs which we had, to this point, virtually ignored.

The significance of the primitive ACTs for us was that we could now be sure that we had a given agreed-upon representation for most of the sentences we were dealing with. This made our system usable by the large group of students who were beginning to concern themselves with programming systems that could communicate with each other. Further, we now knew what was in the bounds of the theory and what was not. We knew that to do the kind of work we were interested in, a canonical form was necessary. We were not as concerned with the ultimate correctness of that system as we were with its usability. No other canonical form existed, and transformational deep structure representations and predicate calculus, which were the major well-known alternatives, neither adequately represented meaning nor were in any sense canonical. The most important part of the primitives of CD for us was that they facilitated our getting on to the more interesting problems at hand. They did this because they gave us a language in which to describe those problems.

ORGANIZING INFERENCES

Eventually we began to realize that the most important problem in natural language processing was inference. The single most important fact about the primitive ACTs was that they helped to organize the inference problem (Schank, 1973). No primitive ACT meant anything in the system at all, other than the conceptualizations that might come to exist as inferences from it. Primitive ACTs served to organize the inference process, thus giving us a starting point from which to attack the problem.

We began to concern ourselves therefore with two principle kinds of inference: results from ACTs and enablements for ACTs. Then, having exhausted the inferences derivable from the ACTs themselves, we began to attempt to categorize the kinds of inferences that needed to be made in general. In Schank and Rieger (1974) we delimited 12 kinds of inference. Using these ideas, Rieger, Riesbeck, Goldman, and I began to design a computer implementation of these ideas in 1972 which resulted in the MARGIE system (Schank et al., 1973). During the implementation of these ideas our views on parsing, generation, and inference were altered by the task of attempting to specify precise algorithms for these processes. Rieger created a new classification of inferences based on his experiences with MARGIE (Rieger, 1975).

CAUSALITY

At this point we began to take seriously the problem of codifying the kinds of causal relations that there were. This work was crucial to the inference problem since we had come to believe that the major inferences were (forward) consequences and (backward) reasons. Thus the primary task of the inference process was to fill in causal chains. We identified four kinds of causal links: RESULT, REASON, INITIATE, and ENABLE. RESULT and ENABLE were the forward and backward causal rules for physical ACTs, and REASON and INITIATE were the forward and backward links for mental ACTs. We also added the rule that ACTs could only result in states and only states could enable ACTs. This had the consequence of making our causal chains, and thus our CD representations, both very precise and very cumbersome. The precision was of course important for any canonical form, but the cumbersomeness was obviously a problem that needed to be dealt with.

One of the advantages of all the detail necessary to connect all possible causal relations, aside from those already mentioned is that it provided a facility for tying together sentences in a text. Thus, a paragraph will frequently consist of a series of conceptualizations that can be related by their implicit causal connections.

THE REPRESENTATION OF TEXT

We began, therefore, to work on the problem of representing text. This was, after all, the major issue all along. We were not particularly interested in isolated sentences out of context. Dealing only with isolated sentences was probably the root of many of the problems involved with the theories proposed by transformationalists and computational linguists. People do not understand sentences in a null context. Why then did our theories try to deal with sentences out of context? The answer was obviously that this was thought to be a simplification that would facilitate research. But the problem was really significantly changed by this supposed simplification. Certainly parsing sentences in context is a more reasonable problem with respect to word sense disambiguation than is parsing out of context.

We had never dealt with texts of more than one sentence before because we just did not know how to represent them. Now, with the idea of causal chains, we could tie together texts in terms of their causal relations. Such causal chaining, when applied to real texts (Schank, 1975), helped to explain certain memory results (particularly those of Bartlett, 1932). Now we had a theory that said that a crucial piece of information had many causal connections and an irrelevant piece of information had no causal consequences.

The work on causal connectedness gave us a theory that was helpful in explaining problems of forgetting and remembering, and also helped tie together text. However, it could not explain how to tie together texts whose parts were not relatable by chains of results and enablements; something else was needed for those situations.

The something else was obvious once we thought about it. The answer was scripts. That is, scripts are really just prepackaged sequences of causal chains. Some causal chains are used so often that we do not spell out enough of their details for an understander to make the connections directly. Scripts are a kind of key to connecting events together that do not connect by their superficial features but rather by the remembrance of their having been connected before. The prototypical script we chose to examine described what goes on in a restaurant. In a story involving the setting of a restaurant, we cannot infer the causal connection to either ordering or paying from hearing simply that someone has entered a restaurant. However, speakers assume that you know this connection and they do not bother to mention it. There is a causal chain there, but inferring it bit by bit is impossible, which makes scripts necessary.

HIGHER LEVEL KNOWLEDGE STRUCTURES

We set about testing our assumptions about how scripts would facilitate the processing of connected text by building SAM (Script Applier Mechanism, described in Cullingford, 1978). While we worked on SAM we began to wonder about where scripts came from. In thinking about this we came up with the idea that plans gave rise to scripts and that goals gave rise to plans (Schank & Abelson, 1975). Meehan (1976) began to develop a story generator that served as a vehicle for developing our ideas about plans and goals. Wilensky (1978) developed a program to understand stories by tracking goals and plans. All this

work is adequately described in Schank and Abelson (1977), so we will not deal with it here.

OUR PRESENT VIEW

The last four years have found us developing the system of plans, goals, themes, and scripts for use in understanding systems. This work produced many working systems (Carbonell, 1979; Cullingford, 1978; DeJong, 1979; Wilensky, 1978) and has greatly broadened our ideas about inference. We now believe the following:

There are a great many possible levels of description. Each of these levels is characterized by its own system of primitives and conceptual relationships. [For example, we have recently introduced a set of "basic social acts" (Schank & Carbonell, 1979) to account for actions that have societal consequences] inferences occur at each of these levels. Thus, for every set of primitives there exists a set of inferences that applies to it. Some of these levels have been described in Schank and Abelson (1977) and will not be dealt with in any detail here. We currently make use of the following kinds of inferences.

Micro-CD

All events in a story can be connected at a level where each event is connected to the events that follow from it, and to the states which enable it. This produces a very detailed causal chain made up of the events and states that were actually mentioned in the text as well as those that had to be inferred in order to complete the chain. The causal chain made by the low level expression of facts is one part of understanding. Thus, in order to read a magazine, you must: ATRANS it; OPEN it; ATTEND to it; and MTRANS from it. When any one of these events is discerned, the others must be inferred.

Macro-CD

Another type of causal chain exists at the macro-CD level. There, events connect to other states and events in the same way as they did at the micro-CD level, but the level of description is different. Thus, going to Boston enables eating in a Boston restaurant at the macro-CD level; but, at the micro-CD level, the locations would have to be further specified, such that going to Boston results in being in Boston which enables beginning to look for and go to a restaurant. This latter level of description can regress in infinite detail where, for example, walking is enabled by putting one foot in front of the other. The level of detail of inferences is extremely important and is dependent on the purposes the understander has in mind.

In the magazine situation mentioned above, Micro-CD is concerned with opening the magazine, holding it, turning the pages, etc. Each of those ACTs also uses causal chains but at a much more detailed level. Macro-CD simply involves having a magazine, which enables reading it. Neither one of these levels of description is more correct than the other.

For causal chaining, then, the needed inference types are:

> What Enables
> What Results
> What are Reasons
> What Initiates

These apply at both the macro level and the micro level.

Filling in Missing Information

For every object and person we hear about we are always tracking where they are, the state they are in, what they know and believe, and how they feel. All these inferences are possibly appropriate at any given time. Thus, other kinds of inference types that are necessary are:

> Locational specifications
> Object specifications
> Emotional specifications
> Belief specifications

Scripts

Inferring the presence of scripts and the unstated parts of scripts is an important part of the understanding process. The following kinds of inference are significant:

> Filling in missing causal chains in a script
> Inferring what script is being used
> Inferring what unstated script was used instrumentally

Thus, when we hear that "John robbed the liquor store," it is appropriate to ask how he got there, how he got in, where he got his weapon, and so on. Such inquiries area part of the inference process, since it is only by knowing what we do not know that we can seek to infer it.

One of the main problems with regard to inferences about scripts is the question of why a script is being pursued. This leads to the problem of inferring plans.

Plans

For any given event, it is often important to know the motivations and intentions of the actors in that event. This means knowing the plans being pursued by an actor. Thus it is necessary to make the following kinds of inferences:

> Inferring the plan being used
> Why was a particular plan chosen?
> Inferring facts about an actor given his choice of plans
> Inferring other plans an actor is likely to pursue to get his goal
> Predictive inferences about future plans
> What goal is he operating under?

This last inference leads to another class of information that spawns new inferences.

Goals

Detecting the presence of a goal causes the following goal-based inferences to be made:

> Why was this goal chosen?
> What might it be in conflict with?
> Can it be subsumed?
> Given this goal, what other goals can we infer?
> Under what circumstances will it be abandoned?

Actually these inference types represent only the tip of the numerous kinds of goal-based inferences that have been isolated by Wilensky (1978) and Carbonell (1978).

Since goals are dominated by higher level structures which we call themes, detecting what theme is present and making the appropriate inferences is also necessary.

Themes

The theme-based inferences include finding out:

> What kinds of goals is an actor likely to pursue?
> What themes are likely to coexist with the given one?
> Are there any conflicts in themes?
> How might theme conflicts that are detected be resolved?
> Where did a given theme come from?

HOW INFERENCES LOOK TO US NOW

Our current work has led us to believe there are, in general, six kinds of inferences. These inference types apply at all the levels of analysis we have worked on so far (i.e., scripts, goals, plans, themes, and some others):

1. *Specification*: Given a piece of an event, what else can be specified about the rest of the pieces?

Schorr (1978) have already served to bolster the relationship between our group and cognitive psychology.

We now turn to where we are today. The mood in psychology has changed considerably since our early work. Psychologists have made various attempts to test experimentally some of the ideas that we have developed. As Cognitive Science develops, researchers whose original interests were in AI will have to take account of experimental results in their programs if they believe they are developing cognitive models. Of course, not all experiments necessarily reveal God's truth, but some undoubtedly will produce results that should cause Cognitive Scientists with computational orientation to alter their theories and thus their programs.

Our work on scripts has caused many people to use such notions for both programs and experiments. One piece of work in psychology that relates to scripts is that of Bower, Black, and Turner (1979). In addition to showing that script-like considerations are relevant in story understanding, one of the most valuable things to come out of that work was a problem it presented to us. Recognition confusions were found by Bower et al. to occur between stories about visits to the dentist and visits to the doctor. In no intuitive sense can this result be called surprising, since most people have experienced such confusions. But what accounts for it? Should we posit a ''visit to a health care professional'' script to explain it? Such a script is beyond our initial conception of what a script was, because it was not specific enough. We had always believed that scripts were rooted in actual experiences rather than in abstractions and generalizations from experiences.

The right question to ask at this point is: What phenomena are scripts supposed to explain? Previously we had used scripts, plans, etc., as data structures in terms of which we could make the right inferences to create connected causal chains. But we also always believed that scripts were more than just useful data structures. Scripts ought to tell us something about memory as well as processing. In Schank and Abelson (1977) we claimed that final memory representations for stories involving scripts would use the packaged scripts as the basis for those representations. For example, we would remember the RESTAURANT script (denoted $RESTAURANT) only and could ''recall'' INGEST by recognizing that INGESTING was a normal occurrence in $RESTAURANT. This is easily accomplished by saving the particular values of variables assigned to each script in a story. Under this view we remember only the salient new information and do not pay attention to the old stereotyped information. $RESTAURANT (lobster, John, Lundy's) should be enough to regenerate a rather dull story.

Our problem here, however, is not the final form of the story, but the initial form and level of the information that we use in understanding the story in the first place. If we used $DENTIST to interpret a relevant story, why should the remembrance of the story get confused with one that used $DOCTOR? If we used $HEALTHCAREVISIT, are we saying that there is no possibility of confus-

2. *Motivation:* Why did an event happen? Why this event and not another? What did the actor believe he was doing?
3. *Enablement:* What was necessary for the event to occur?
4. *Results:* What are the results or effects of this event?
5. *Structure:* What higher level structure does this fit into?
6. *Other Events:* What other events are known to occur with this event? What could not have happened if this event happened?

Scripts, plans, and so on fit in as events in the above description. Thus we can ask for *Specification, Motivation, Enablement, Results, Structure and Other Events* for a script, a plan, a goal, a theme, or probably any other higher level structure we are likely to invent.

Inference, then, is the fitting of new information into a context that explains it and predicts other facts that follow from it. Since these explanations can occur at many levels, inference is a very complex problem and one we expect to continue working on in an attempt to find out how people understand and how computers could understand.

THE CURRENT SITUATION

Our work started out as a linguistic theory, albeit one with a computer-based bias. Some linguists have explicitly rejected it as a possible linguistic theory (see, for example, Dresher & Hornstein, 1976). In one sense they are right. The phenomena we have become interested in over the years are not particularly phenomena of language per se; rather they are phenomena having to do with the processing of language in general and the issue of the representation of knowledge in particular.

At the same time that *our* work was going on, the field of Artificial Intelligence had been evolving too. When I first arrived at the Stanford AI lab, the major issues in AI were theorem proving, game playing, and vision. Natural language was not considered to be a serious part of AI until Winograd (1972) presented the AI community with SHRDLU. This work contributed substantially to the evolution of AI. The major concern of AI would now seem to be the issue of the representation of knowledge, which of course makes the work in natural language processing quite central.

In the future I expect that many of the relevant fields will begin to become less separate. AI must come to terms with the fact that it is concerned with many issues that are also of interest to philosophers. I hope that the cooperation here will be of more use than was the head-butting that has gone on between AI people and linguists. (Recently this too has changed, however, as the more liberal forces in linguistics have become both stronger and more interested in AI.) Also, the interaction between psychologists and AI people hopefully will continue to flourish. The works of Bower, Black, and Turner (1979) and Smith, Adams, and

ing a dentist story with a visit to an account's office? If we use $OFFICEVISIT, for what kind of entity is that? Do we really have information stored at that level to help us understand stories? If we do, then understanding such a story becomes much more complex than we had initially imagined. We cannot get away with simply applying scripts. Rather we will have to consult many levels of information at once.

Why would we store new inputs about dentists in terms of a structure which might confuse it with a visit to an accountants? It seems unreasonable on the surface unless we simply do not have a dentist script available at all. Is it possible that there is no dentist script?

Why haven't we run headlong into this problem before? The answer is, I think, that whereas psychologists worry about recognition confusions in due course, as a part of their natural interest in memory, people working in AI never really concern themselves with memory at all. We have not been in the habit of actually remembering very much at all in our programs, so the issue has not really come up. Once the issue has been raised, however, it seems obvious that what we posit as a processing structure is likely to be a memory structure as well, and this has profound implications for what we do.

LEVELS OF MEMORY

The problem that we must deal with is the question of the kinds of knowledge available to an understander. Every theory of processing must also be a theory of memory. To put this another way, if psychologists show that recognition confusions occur between two entities in memory, this would have to be taken as evidence against a theory that said those two entities existed and were proceeded entirely separately.

Thus, in order to address the question of what kinds of processing structures people have, we should investigate the kinds of things people are capable of remembering (and confusing). We have to become a special kind of psychologist—one who has available to him computer and thought experiments, in addition to more standard methods.

To begin our discussion about memory, it seems clear that there are many types of memory. The first we shall discuss is Event Memory.

Event Memory (EM)

One thing that people remember is a particular experience, often in some detail. So, we postulate a level of memory that contains specific remembrances of particular situations—*Event Memory*. Examples of Event Memory include all the details of "going to Dr. Smith's dental office last Tuesday and getting your tooth pulled" and "forgetting your dental appointment and having them call you up and charge you for it." Events are remembered as they happened, but not for long. After a while, the less salient aspects of an event fade away (e.g., where you got the phone call or why you forgot your appointment). What is left are Generalized Events plus the unusual or interesting parts of the original event from Event Memory.

Generalized Event Memory (GEM)

A *Generalized Event* is a collocation of events whose common features have been abstracted. This is where general information about situations that have been experienced numerous times is held. Particular experiences are initially a part of Event Memory. However, when such particular experiences refer to a common generalized event, that generalized event is brought in to help in the processing of the new input. Once the connection between an event and the generalized event that it references is established, the event itself is liable to gradually fade away leaving only the pointer to the generalized event and the salient features of the event not dominated by the generalized event.

Situational Memory (SM)

Memory for generalized events relies in a similar way upon what we shall call *Situational Memory*. Situational Memory contains information about specific situations in general. Thus while information about dentists resides in GEM, Situational Memory contains more general information. "Going to a health professional's office" or "getting a health problem taken care of" rely on knowledge about such instances in general. SM contains the kind of knowledge we have about waiting rooms and other things that doctors and dentists share.

In the understanding process, information found in Situational Memory is used to provide the overall context for a situation. When we go to a dentist's office and something happens there (e.g., you are overcharged), the specifics of the dental part of the experience are unimportant in the same way that what telephone you were using is unimportant in the event given as an example for Event Memory above. Situational Memory serves as a repository for relevant contextual knowledge as well as the final storage place for the relevant parts of new events in memory; thus it contains relevant contexts and the rules and standard experiences associated with a given situation in general.

Intentional Memory (IM)

The next level of memory experience is *Intentional Memory*. Experiences are encoded in Intentional Memory in terms of the generalizations relevant behind the information encoded in Situational Memory. Information encoded in Intentional Memory would include that relevant to "getting any problem taken care of by a societal organization." What resides here are the rules for getting people to do things for you and other plan-like information. But the decomposition can go on as before. Thus, specific events would lose the particulars that were best encoded at other levels on their way up to the Intentional level.

People often cannot recall the full details of a situation they are trying to remember. Often they can recall just their goals and the resolution of those goals. The specifics of the situation are often more elusive to recall. This suggests that events can be decomposed into the pieces having to do with their intentional basis and these intentions can then serve as the organizational focus where the relevant parts of such experiences can be found.

THE PLACE FOR SCRIPTS IN THE ORGANIZATION OF MEMORY

Where do scripts fit into this partitioning of memory? In particular, what is the dentist script and where can it be found in memory? The answer is that there is no dentist script in memory at all, at least not in the form of a list of events of the kind we have previously postulated. A more reasonable organization of memory would allow for the following kinds of information:

EM   Particular dental visits are stored in event memory (EM). These visits decay over time and thus are not likely to last in EM for a very long time. Rather, what will remain are particularly unusual, important, painful, or otherwise notable visits or parts of visits. These particulars are stored at the EM level.

GEM   At the level of General Event Memory (GEM), we find the information we have learned about dental visits in general that is applicable only to dental visits. Thus, "sitting in the waiting room" is not stored at the GEM level. The reason it is not stored at that level is clear; the lack of economy of storage would be fearsome. We know a great deal about office waiting rooms that has little to do with whether or not they were part of a dentist's office. In addition, any abstraction and generalization mechanism that we posit is likely to be so powerful that it would not be likely to stop operating at any given level. Thus if commonalities between DENTIST and DOCTOR are brought to its attention, it would *naturally* produce this result.

What is particular to a dentist's office is, perhaps, the X-ray machine, or the dental chair, or the kind of light that is present, and so on. These items are not scriptal in nature. Rather, they are just pieces of information about dental offices that are stored as part of what we know about them. For example, one might expect to find a giant toothbrush in a dentist's office. Such information is stored at the GEM level. However, it is also available from the EM level in terms of those particular experiences that can be remembered at that level of detail. (Such memories fade fast, however.) That is, to answer questions about dental offices, there is nothing to prevent us from consulting our knowledge of dental offices in general (GEM) or of particular prior experiences (EM) to the extent that they still can be found.

So where is the dentist script? So far it has not surfaced. The next two levels complete the framework for allowing *dynamic creation of the pieces of the dental script that are applicable in a given situation for use on demand.* The dentist script itself does not actually exist in memory in one precompiled chunk. Rather, it, or more likely its needed subparts, can be constructed as needed. The economy of such a scheme is very important. Moreover, the memory use and probable psychological sensibility of such a solution is highly significant. Now we will consider how that might work.

SM   In Situational Memory (SM) resides information about a situation in general. Here is where we find the kind of knowledge that would include facts such as "nurses wear white uniforms," "doctors frequently have many rooms so that they can work on lots of patients at once," "there are history charts that must be selected and updated by women in white outfits who might not actually be nurses," etc. We also find information about situations in general. This includes information such as the flow of events in an office, for example. Thus, the bare bones of the dentist script and, most importantly, many other scripts are found in SM. Here we have information such as: "If you need help you can go to the office of a professional who gives that help. You may have to wait for that help for a while in a waiting room. You may report your problem to an underling of the professional's. You will get a bill for services, etc."

IM   Intentional Memory contains more goal-based memories. Trips, romances, improving one's health, and other general contexts whose immediate goals are known are IM structures. Intentional Memories organize inputs according to their reason for existence. As a consequence of this, memory confusions at the IM level involve different situations whose intentions are the same.

According to this view of the information in memory, then, scripts do not exist as extant memory structures. Script-like structures (corresponding to what we have called scenes or even parts of scenes) are constructed from higher-level general structures *as needed* by consulting rules about the particular situation from the three other levels.

The words "as needed" are very important. Why bring an entire script in while processing if it will not be used? Since scripts are being constructed rather than being pulled in whole from memory, only the parts that there is reason to believe will be used (based upon the input text) need to be brought in.

As for retrieval and storage of the incoming information, new stories are available at the EM level for only a very short time. In the course of processing an initial input, pointers are created that preclude the necessity of storing all the details. These pointers are not to the dentist script, but to the relevant subscenes that are to be found at the various memory levels. Thus, something that happens in the waiting room is stored with a pointer to the waiting room scene. However, and this is the main point, the waiting room scene came from knowledge about waiting rooms that was only picked up for the occasion from the highest level (IM). Thus, it was not connected to any dentist script initially, and whatever has happened in the waiting room, unless it was of particular interest, will be stored at the IM level, virtually disassociated from the dentist sequence. Under this scheme, recognition confusions will occur among various waiting room scenes with regard to the question of the original overall situation of which they were a part. The only time when it will be clearly remembered which waiting room scene belongs to which story will be when the continuity is provided between scenes by the story itself. For example, if something special happens in the waiting room scene that affects later scenes, the connection would be a causal link and such connections should be more easily remembered.

MEMORY FOR DENTIST INFORMATION

To see how what we have outlined would work, it is perhaps useful to look at a diagram of the structure of memory for a story (shown at the EM level) involving a dentist:

```
IM    HEALTHPROBLEM
         FIND PROFESSIONAL + MAKE CONTRACT
         + PROFOFFICEVISIT

SM    GO TO OFFICE + WAITING ROOM + ENTER INNER OFFICE
      + HELP + LEAVE + BILLSENT

GEM   Dentist visits include:
         getting teeth cleaned—dentist puts
             funny tooth paste on teeth
             turns on machine
         etc.
         getting teeth drilled
             D does x-ray
             D gives shot of novocain
             D drills
         etc.
      also:  Dentists fill the health care professional role in
             HEALTHCAREVISIT

EM    The time I went to the dentist last week:
         I drove to the dentist.
         I read Newsweek. There were holes in all the pictures.
         I entered.
         He cleaned my teeth.
         He poked me in the eye with his drill.
         I yelled at him.
         He didn't charge me.
```

The events in EM are remembered in terms of the highest level memory structures that were activated.

After some time, decay sets in and allows the magazine reading to be stored as part of the WAITING ROOM scene of PROFOFFVISIT. It thus gets disassociated from the rest of the event. Similarly, the "eye poking" gets stored under HELP and is thus disconnected from the magazine experience. But, since HELP is filled by specific Dentist information from GEM, it is remembered as part of a Dentist experience whereas the magazine experience can get completely confused with any other situation in which one might read a magazine.

The main point is that memory breaks down its new information into appropriately interesting pieces and stores those pieces in the context to which they are relevant, i.e., the context which originally recognized them and explained them.

MEMORY ORGANIZATION PACKETS (MOPs)

What we have been addressing here is the overall question of how information is organized in memory. The old issue of semantic memory versus episodic memory and the newer issue of what kinds of memory structures are available are the key elements with respect to memory organization. To summarize so far: we are saying that scripts are not data structures that are available in one piece in some part of memory. Rather, script application is a reconstructive process. We build pieces of scripts as we need them from our store of knowledge to help us interpret what we hear. Thus the next key question is: What is the organization of the knowledge store? This is another way of asking the question: What kinds of knowledge do we have and how is that knowledge represented and used in the understanding process?

There are thus two relevant questions to ask of memory: First, how does any given experience get stored so that it will provide a capability for understanding new experiences in terms of it? And second, why do recognition confusions occur at all?

Situational level memory structures help us understand the experiences we have. They do this by generating parts of scripts. But, in addition, they tend to enable recognition confusions in two ways: First, since new events are understood by using these structures to interpret them, a connection is established between the new event as entered in EM and the memory structure that was used to interpret that event. This connection is established by means of two different kinds of pointers. The first, a *processing pointer*, connects the memory structure with the new event in order to help in the processing of that event. The second, a *memory pointer*, is established because the memory structure is itself affected by the new event. We call memory structures at the SM level Memory Organization Packets or MOPs. MOPs both organize episodic memories and help to process new inputs; that is, they are the means by which an appropriate episode in memory can be accessed for aid in processing a new input. At the basis of a MOP at the SM level is an abstraction of a mass of input events that have been mushed together in memory. A MOP is a collocation of all the events that have come to be stored under it. Thus, memory pointers must be established from a relevant MOP to the detailed event which that MOP is helping to process at the EM level.

Of these two pointers, only the memory pointer needs to last very long. When the processing is finished, the processing pointer is easily forgotten since it can always be regenerated as needed. The memory pointer stays but decays over time. Details that are insignificant in the EM event are forgotten. Significant or interesting details are remembered by virtue of there being more than one memory pointer available; that is, if more than one pointer has been established. The number of the possibly relevant structures at these levels may be high since a new event may call many kinds of structures in to help interpret it during processing. For every structure that is called in during processing, a memory pointer is established. The combination of what these pointers point to is what remains of the event at the EM level of memory.

Thus, since each new piece of information is stored in terms of the high level structure that was needed to interpret it, two kinds of confusions occur. Connections between items in the same episode that are interpreted by different high-level structures will tend to break down. A waiting room scene will tend to disconnect from the dentist script of which it was a part because it was interpreted by a different MOP (one having to do with office visits perhaps) than other parts of the story.

The second kind of confusion will occur within a script. When a high level structure is deemed relevant, all inputs are interpreted in terms of the norm. This causes small details not normally part of a script to get lost and normalized. Normalization does not occur for very interesting or weird deviations from a script. The reason for this has to do with the answer to the first question above.

REMINDING

Sometimes during the processing of new inputs an interesting phenomenon occurs: You are reminded of a previous experience that is somehow similar to the new input currently being processed. Such reminding experiences are not random. Rather they are dependent upon the very nature of the understanding and memory processes we have outlined.

The answer to the question of why one experience reminds you of another is of primary importance to any theory of human understanding and memory. If people are reminded of things during the natural course of a conversation, or while reading, or when seeing something, then this tells us something of great importance about the understanding process. It tells us that a particular memory piece—that is, a specific memory—has been excited or "seen" during the natural course of processing the new input. We can then ask two important questions:

1. Why did processing naturally pass through this piece of memory? That is, what is there about the processing of new information that requires a particular related piece of information to be noticed?

2. How did such a mechanism as reminding develop? Why is this phenomenon available consciously when so many other processing phenomena are not?

We can begin to attempt to answer these questions by considering the kinds of reminding experiences that people have. For example, there is a restaurant in Boston where you pay first, then eat, called Legal Seafood. Going to another such restaurant, and saying, "This restaurant reminds me of Legal Seafood," would of course be quite natural. According to our view of memory, the restaurant script is merely a first approximation of where search should begin for the most appropriate memory structure to be used in processing a new input. Thus, initial access of the restaurant script merely serves to begin our search for the high-level structure that will be used to understand this new experience. Accessing the restaurant script just means finding a relevant entry point to memory. We have, rather than a discrete set of such high-level structures, a potentially infinite set. There is not one restaurant script but thousands. The various refinements on restaurants all serve as nodes in memory that help to reconstruct a needed high level structure. By saying to ourselves, "Gee, you pay first here," we have caused our minds to traverse a particular path within the information organized by restaurants in order to complete our search for the highest level structure (i.e., the structure that explains the most information). At the end of that path is Legal Seafood, so reminding occurs.

More important than reminding, however, is that all the predictions from that previous experience are now available to help interpret the new input. Such predictions function no differently if the new input calls up a once-seen prior relevant experience or a multitude of experiences expressed in terms of high-level generalizations such as "the restaurant script."

The logical consequence of all this is that there is a potentially infinite set of such structures and that most people's sets would be extremely large and idiosyncratic. For example, an expert at chess would be able to recognize "famous games" or positions that have been seen before. Such recognition depends on the use of a high-level structure in the first place of the kind we have been discussing that would have been part of the understanding process. That is, during understanding, we are constantly seeking the highest level of analysis we can get. This works for understanding chess as well as for anything else. Former chess understandings are stored at particular subparts of the appropriate knowledge structures.

UNDERSTANDING

We can now reevaluate what it means to understand. When we enter Burger King, having before been to McDonald's but never having been to Burger King, we are confronted with a new situation which we must attempt to "understand."

We can say that a person has understood such an experience (i.e., he understands Burger King in the sense of being able to operate in it) when he says, "Oh, I see, Burger King is just like McDonald's."

To put this another way, we might expect that at some point during his Burger King trip he might be "reminded" of McDonald's. The point I want to make is that understanding means being reminded of the closest prior experienced phenomenon and being able to use the expectations generated by that reminding. When we are reminded of some event or experience in the course of undergoing a different experience, this reminding behavior is not random. We are reminded of this experience because the structures we are using to process this new experience are the same structures we are using to organize memory. Thus, we cannot help but pass through the old memories while processing a new input. There are an extremely large number of such high level memory structures. Finding the right one of these, (that is, the one that is most relevant to the experience at hand) is what we mean by understanding.

Is it any wonder that we are reminded of similar events? Since memory and processing structures are the same, sitting right at the very spot needed will be the experience most like the current one.

But all experiences are not identical to all others. A key issue then is the creation of new structures. This is done in terms of the old ones. To return to our fast food example, when Burger King reminds you of McDonald's, what you are doing goes as follows: "Ah yes, Burger King is just like McDonald's except the waitresses wear red and yellow and you can have it your way." A new discrimination on the net that contains McDonald's is then made, creating a node in which Burger King is a high-level structure that shares most, but not all, of its properties with the old McDonald's node. The differences are significant in that they themselves may form the basis of reminding experiences.

In this view, then, understanding is finding the closest higher-level structure available to explain an input and creating a new memory node for that input that is IN TERMS OF the old node's closely related higher-level structure. Understanding is a process that has its basis in memory, particularly memory for closely related experiences accessible through reminding and expressible through analogy.

MEMORY DISCRIMINATIONS

Now the question is: How do we go about finding what is stored in memory? If there are "have it your way" discriminations, in what way could they be used? The answer clearly depends on effective initial categorization of the input.

Memory is highly idiosyncratic. One person's organization is not another's. How people categorize experiences initially is how they remember them later. If Burger King is seen as an instance of McDonald's, it will be stored in terms of whatever discriminations the understander noticed as relevant at that time. However, it is possible for a person to make multiple discriminations as well as multiple categorizations. Thus, a person can see Burger King as "something tasteless that kids love," a "place where you can have it your way." Each of these is used as a path by which Burger King can be accessed. A fight with one's child in a Burger King might be stored solely as an instance of a child fight, or as a fight in a restaurant, or as a fight in a Burger King. If the latter categorization were used, fights with a child in McDonald's might not be noticed. Thus, an intelligent understander stores his experiences as high up and as generally as possible so as to be able to learn from them, i.e., so as to make them available for use as often as possible or in as many situations as possible.

One question often asked of these ideas is: "Why, when you enter a restaurant, are you not reminded of all restaurants, or even reminded of that particular restaurant?" I believe the answer to both questions is that you most certainly are. When you enter Naples (a Yale hangout) you are reminded of Naples. You then use that reminding as the source of predictions about what will happen next; that is, you use the most particular script available to help you process what you are experiencing. When Naples reminds you of Naples, you do not experience the same sensation of reminding for an obvious reason. The more appropriate a reminding experience is, the less it seems like reminding. But reminding is simply the bringing to mind of highly relevant memories to help in the processing of new inputs. To say or to feel upon entering a new restaurant that "this place reminds me of a restaurant" is rather absurd, but remind you it does. If this were not the case, how would you know that it was a restaurant? Thus, reminding is not just a rather interesting phenomenon that I have been seeking to explain. Reminding, in a very serious sense, is the most significant memory phenomenon that there is to explain.

WHAT MEMORY LOOKS LIKE INSIDE

We are now ready to take a look at a specific proposal for handling memory (and handling scripts in particular) in order to account for the issues we have been discussing. For old times' sake, we will again use restaurants. The difference between what we have said in the past and our new view has to do with how restaurant experiences are organized in memory. Consider two restaurant experiences that are virtually identical except for what was ordered. The chance for confusion in memory here is enormous. Which waitress (if there were two different ones in the same restaurant) served which food might be confused, for example. Such confusions are not accounted for by our original conception of scripts where each story, including information about the waitress and the food eaten, is uniquely stored with its own copy of the script.

trodden script. This experience is now used, just as any script is used, to predict what will happen next.

Thus, deep down inside the guts of a script, we find all the pointers to every specific memory experience we have had that has been organized in terms of that script and that has not been obliterated by multiple identical experiences. Thus script application is embellished by going down paths which the script itself organizes, that contain all prior deviant (that is, not completely standard) experiences. These experiences are functionally identical to scripts and thus are an integral part of the application process. This can occur within any script-piece at all.

As an example of all this, consider Figure 1, a picture of a possible set of memory experiences tied to, or organized by, the restaurant script.

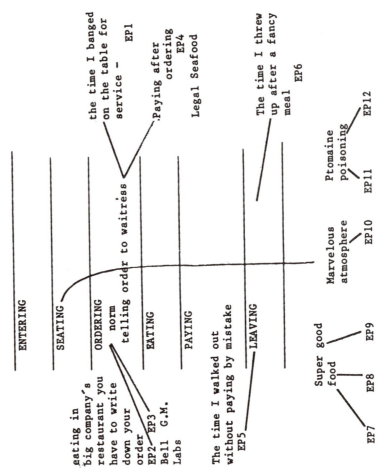

Figure 1.

SCRIPT EMBELLISHMENT

Scripts are formed for actual use by building them up from scenes. However, in building up a script we are also allowing for the possibility of memory experiences being allowed to generalize and be stored at the high-level structure that best explains them. This causes the script that was temporarily built up for processing purposes only to be broken down again, thus causing memory confusions and a certain lack of connectivity between the scenes of a story as it is stored in memory.

Recall that our purpose is to integrate the structures of processing with those of memory. We desire to have episodes stored in such a way that each one of them can serve as a kind of script itself; that is, we want predictions to be available from *all* prior experiences, not just from those we have labelled officially as "scripts" or "script pieces." After all, people make predictions about what will happen next from past experiences. Are scripts the only kind of past experience that aids processing by making predictions and filling in causal chain inferences? Obviously this cannot be. A person who has experienced something only once will expect his second time around to conform to the initial experience and will be "surprised" in some sense every time the second experience does not conform to the first.

This is how scripts get put together in the first place: first one experience, then another on top of it, strengthening those areas of agreement and beginning to solidify a script. But obviously there are times when "new" experiences for which there is one or no prior experience can occur in the middle of an old, well-understood experience. Thus, when you go to Legal Seafood, you modify your restaurant script so as to indicate that the PAYING scene has been placed immediately after the ORDERING scene in memory. What I want to propose is that what is happening here is *not* the creation of a new part or "track" in a script. I see very little evidence for tracks at all. Rather, the entire memory experience is being stored under this PAYING interruption or abnormality following the ORDERING scene.

Two kinds of reminding exercises are accounted for by this. First, any other script readjustment occurring after ORDERING might remind one of Legal Seafood. Second, a new placement of the PAYING scene in the restaurant script might be expected to remind one of Legal Seafood. This reminding would occur as a result of having categorized Legal Seafood as weird with respect to PAYING. So, when PAYING is placed in a new spot, the Legal Seafood experience is brought in because it is hanging off a "PAYING reassignment" discrimination.

Now what does this reminding buy you? The reminding actually causes the whole rest of the reminded experience to be brought into memory at this point just as would happen with any new experience not accounted for by a well-

From this diagram we can see that the ultimate purpose of scripts is as organizers of information in memory. The restaurant script that we have used in the past is no more than the standard default path, or basic organizing principle, that serves as the backbone for all remembered restaurant experiences that have been stored as restaurant experiences. Thus, we are saying that every deviation from the standard script is stored as a modification of the particular scene in which the deviation occurred.

So, one experience in Legal Seafood causes a deviation (these were previously referred to as being on the "weird list" in Schank & Abelson, 1977) in the ordering scene. This deviation serves as both the beginning of a reminding experience and the start of the script application process. As we have been saying, storage and processing must be taken care of by the same mechanism in order to get natural reminding to take place. In addition, the scheme that I am proposing allows for the use of all prior experiences in the interpretation of new experiences rather than a reliance on only standard normalized experiences (i.e., what we have previously called scripts).

If the new experience does have a counterpart, i.e., if similar deviations have been met before, *at some point* these experiences are collected together to form a scriptal subscene whose predictions are disembodied from actual episodes like the higher-level script itself. When enough of these are encountered, a new subscene is created that will *not* cause one to be reminded of the particular experiences that caused the creation of this subscene. As this subscene is created, all pointers to the relevant episodes that helped to create that subscene are erased, although other pointers not a part of this subscene but pointing to the same episode would still exist.

Memory collects similar experiences from which to make predictions; these are of general utility above some threshold of a number of prior experiences. Below that threshold, remindings of prior experiences serve as the source of relevant experiences. Thus uniqueness of experience, or, more accurately, unique classifications of experience, serve as a rich source of understandings about new experiences.

In the process of script embellishment via deviant paths we access entire episodes, many of which may have next to nothing to do with the story currently being processed. It is important to be able to separate the relevant from the irrelevant. On the other hand, it is hard not to be reminded of the parts of that experience that are connected to the scene that you have been reminded of. This is one aspect of *intelligence* that comes into play here. The discrimination of those experiences that are relevant for prediction and those that are irrelevant is one of the most formidable tasks facing an understander. *Such discriminations must be done at processing time since one cannot know beforehand where relevant similarities might lie for future inputs.* Thus, a very important part of understanding is the analysis of what is happening to you now with respect to the issue of how relevant newly encountered events might be for predictive purposes

to handle future inputs. The collocation of arguments and "paying right after ordering" is not a useful category for experience-based prediction. Clearly we are not born knowing such things. What form such knowledge takes and how we go about acquiring it is, it seems to me, one of the very big issues for the future.

HIGH-LEVEL MEMORY STRUCTURES

The key point in the issue of what is and what is not a script has to do with where we expect information to be found in memory. From the point of view of processing it makes sense to talk about having a restaurant script available. We have shown that such scripts will facilitate the processing of stories; but just because an entity exists as a chunk that has been prestored in memory. It is quite plausible that such entities are constructed on demand from information that is stored directly in memory. The key question before us, then, is whether scripts and other high level structures have only a processing role, or whether they are also memory pieces, useful for storage of information that has previously been processed using those high level structures. That is, are high level structures solely processing devices or are they also memory devices?

If the chunks we have been calling scripts are not solely processing devices, the demands on them change. Just as we would not expect that a sensibly organized memory would have the fact that George Washington was the first President stored in fifteen different places, we would not expect that "you eat when you are hungry," or "you order after reading a menu," or "if you don't pay your dentist bill you can be sued" to be stored in fifteen different places either.

Once the requirement that you have to find *one and only one* place to store general information comes into play, the question of where that information is stored becomes extremely important. To decide that question, notions such as scripts must be tightened up considerably so that general information shared by any two scripts is held outside them in some other memory store. To do this requires ascertaining what it might mean for two scripts to share the same information, and finding out when such sharing is "realized" by memory and when it is not.

The Creation of MOPs

When a child discovers that its personal restaurant script is also shared by other people, he or she can resort to a new method of storage of restaurant information: a standardized restaurant script with certain personal markings that store idiosyncratic points in view; that is, the child can begin to organize experiences in terms that separate out what is unique and what is shared by the culture. For example, adults know that getting in a car is not part of the restaurant script, but this may be a very salient feature of the child's personal restaurant script. It is very important for the child to separate the car experience from the restaurant experience. The child must learn to reorganize memory according to cultural norms.

This reorganization of stored information can continue indefinitely. New experiences are constantly being reorganized on the basis of similar experiences and cultural norms. The abstraction and generalization process is thus a fundamental part of adult understanding. When you go to the dentist for the first time, everything in that experience is stored as one chunk. Repeated experiences with the same dentist, other dentists, and vicarious experiences of others serve to reorganize the original information in terms of what is peculiar to your dentist, yourself in dental offices, dentists in general, and so on. This reorganization process never stops. When similarities between doctors and dentists are seen, a further reorganization can be made in terms of health care professionals. When doctors' and lawyers' similarities are extracted, yet another organization storage point emerges. The key to understanding is the continual creation of *Memory Organization Packets* (MOPs), which record the essential parts of the similarities in experience of different episodes.

The purpose of a MOP is to provide expectations that enable the prediction of future events on the basis of previously encountered, structurally similar events. These predictions can be at any level of generality or specificity. Thus, such predictions can come from nearly identical or quite different contexts or domains, since a context or domain can be described at many different levels of generality. The creation of a suitable MOP provides a class of predictions organized around the common theme of that MOP. The more MOPs that are available for processing a given input, the more predictions will be available to help in understanding that input. The ability of MOPs to make useful predictions in situations for which there is no direct experience but for which there are relevant analogous experiences is crucial to our ability to understand.

Seen this way, a MOP is a kind of high-level script. The restaurant script is itself a kind of MOP, but it is also related to many different and more general MOPs. There is a MOP about social situations, a MOP about requesting service from people whose profession is that service, and a MOP about business contracts—to name three that are relevant to restaurants.

Viewed as a whole, then, memory is a morass of MOP strands, each connected at the base to the relevant abstractions and generalizations that are the base of the MOP. At the end of each strand are particular experiences (i.e., individual episodes) or groups of experiences (i.e., scripts).

Using MOPs

Consider the information relevant in a visit to a doctor's office. At least five MOPs are relevant to the construction of the processing structures necessary for understanding a doctor's office visit. They are: PROFOFFVISIT; CONTRACT; FIND SERVICE PROFESSIONAL; USE SERVICE; and FIX PROBLEM.

As we will see, these five MOPs overlap quite a bit. There is nothing wrong with that; indeed it should be expected that any memory theory would propose overlapping structures since they are the source of both memory confusions and the making of useful generalizations across domains.

When a script is available it can be used without really looking at a MOP. However, because storage of information needs to be economical, we would not expect what is best stored in a MOP to be found in a script as well. Thus, the doctor script would not have the doctor suing the patient for nonpayment of the bill directly in it. Neither would the bill itself be in the domain of the doctor script. Each of those is best stored as part of a MOP for a CONTRACT, with strands pointing to the doctor script. A doctor visit is perhaps not best viewed as a contract, but it is one nonetheless, and the CONTRACT MOP must help to construct what we can sloppily call the DOCTOR ''script'' that might actually be useful in processing.

It is important to mention that $DOCTOR is connected to the CONTRACT MOP by a strand of the MOP, but that $DOCTOR does not contain that strand, i.e., it does not contain information about payment other than the presence of that MOP strand. Thus, $DOCTOR is smaller than is obvious at first glance, since we have essentially taken the paying scene out of the script. The actual DOCTOR script that exists in memory contains only the doctor-specific parts of the doctor experience.

Thus, waiting room information is not part of $DOCTOR; waiting rooms are part of PROFOFFICEVISITS, which are also MOPs. But PROFOFFICEVISITS are different from CONTRACTs, which are different from HUNGER and PROFSERVICE. Each of these are MOPs, but they represent different kinds of MOPs. PROFOFFICEVISIT has a strong structure that it imposes on any situation to which it is applied. This structure is in essence a kind of search procedure that helps one sort through the strands in a MOP.

MOPs are memory organization packets. Thus PROFOFFICEVISIT will grab up particular experiences and store them. An experience in a waiting room of an office will get disembodied from the rest of the visit. What happens in the waiting room will be stored with the PROFOFFVISIT MOP, but the actual consultation with the doctor or lawyer will be stored with a different MOP.

WAITINGROOM is a content strand of the PROFOFFVISIT MOP. That is, it has a great deal of information attached to it, such as what a waiting room looks like, what is in it, what happens there, and so on. The HELP strand, on the other hand, is entirely empty. It is a kind of place holder, the only content of which is what is connected temporarily to it on either side. This is where $DOCTOR or $DENTIST comes in. Under this view, scripts are very particular structures about a situation that can fill in an empty strand in a MOP. Actually, these scripts are strands of different MOPs. Thus, just as WAITINGROOM is a contentful strand of the PROFOFFVISIT MOP, so DENTIST is a contentful strand of the HEALTHCARE MOP.

Processing Using MOPs

Memory Organization Packets serve as the basis of memory and of processing. In order to understand an input it is necessary to find in memory the structure or particular episode most like the new input. Reminding is one way of telling that such things are happening.

Processing an input means finding a relevant memory piece. When such a piece is found, expectations are created that some from all the pieces to which the initial memory piece is connected. Thus, when we receive an input, we look for a relevant MOP. Upon finding this MOP, we create expectations at every level to which that MOP is naturally connected. Expectations from scripts that have been activated create demands for certain conceptualizations. Expectations are simultaneously generated from the relevant script that filled the slots of the MOPs.

To illustrate how some of this works, consider a story beginning "My drain pipe was overflowing." Now for our purposes the point is not whether this is the first line of the story or not; rather, it is important that this simply be an input to a cognitive system. The fact that you might hear such a thing in everyday conversation is important also. The questions we need to address are:

1. What comes to mind upon hearing such a sentence?
2. What structures are being activated in memory that cause such things to come to mind?
3. What state is the mind in after having received this input?

At Yale in recent years and among researchers in general who are concerned with scripts or schemata, it has seemed plausible to answer these questions with something called the "plumber script." Such a script implies that any body of knowledge can be a script. Clearly a body of knowledge about plumbing can be assembled from the various corners of memory in which it resides in order to create such an entity as a plumber script. One issue is whether such an entity preexists in memory or is constructed, and, if the latter is true, then the real issue is "constructed from what pieces by what method?" A second issue is where are our episodic memories to be found that will help us respond to what we have heard? It seems unlikely that every experience we have had with plumbers is organized by $PLUMBER. Clearly a great many memory structures are likely to be active.

Thus far we have taken the position that to have precompiled chunks of memory such as a plumber script is unrealistic, particularly when we consider facts of memory such as recognition confusions, memory searches, and forgetting based upon the breaking up of an experience into chunks. A great deal of information can be retrieved about plumbers (e.g., what a plumber is likely to wear, the estimated size of the bill, etc.) that is in no sense a part of the script, so it seems safe to say that some reconstruction is going on, or at least that various pieces of memory are being searched when an input is being processed. In our discussion we will assume that there is no plumber script in anything but the simplest of all forms, and that the main problem in responding to an input such as

There are also a great many other relevant structures. Some are relevant because MOPs can themselves be strands of other MOPs. There is a *twining* mechanism that can cause strands from many MOPs to fill the same empty strands in another MOP. In the end, then, what we are doing is constructing a DOCTOR superscript (shown at the bottom line of Figure 2). This superscript is constructed for use as needed by taking the strands of relevant MOPs and ordering them by time and enablement conditions. Often multiple strands account for one scene in a superscript. Below, the DELIVER strand of CONTRACT as well as the HELP strand of HEALTHCARE and the SERVICE strand of PROFFVISIT all relate to $DOCTOR. That is, they each explain to some extent the role that the doctor is playing.

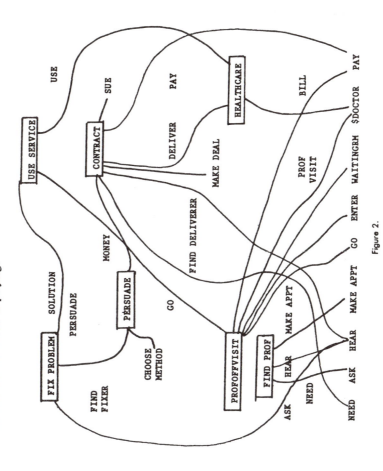

Figure 2.

Taking a look at Figure 2 for the construction of the doctor superscript, we see that a MOP has one clear characteristic: It organizes a class of information by the creation of sequences of slots that can be filled by various structures. In essence, the true differentiation of the kinds of MOPs that exist depends on the types of entities that can fill the slots in the MOP.

the one above is the accessing of the memory structures relevant to the creation of the plumber superscript.

What kind of high level structures might be relevant to "My drain pipe is overflowing"? Clearly at least the following information is relevant: Drains must be understood to be part of sinks in houses, thus determining the general location of the item in question. Such information is part of the meaning of "drain." It is unlikely that there would be a "drain MOP" available with that information in it. The existence of such a MOP implies that memories about drains are organized together in one place. This seems unlikely; however, there is nothing immutable about what can be a MOP. Different individuals with different levels of expertise are likely to have different needs in memory organization.

"Drain" points to information about bathrooms and kitchens, etc. Such information is stored in what Minsky (1975) refers to as a "room frame." These frames contain primarily visual information rather than episodic information (although again the latter is possible). The visual information attached to the room frame here is helpful for understanding future inputs such as: "To fix it I sat on the toilet," or "The overflow ruined $20 worth of cleanser stored underneath." Such statements would be quite impossible to understand without these active and ready frames. But such frames are not MOPs, they are, just, upon occasion, used by MOPs.

One way they are used by MOPs here is that, since these rooms are parts of houses, the combination of the implicit house and the possessive "my" causes information about HOMEOWNERSHIP to be activated. HOMEOWNERSHIP has information in it derived from preservation goals (P-GOALS; see Schank & Abelson, 1977) and, among other things, points to the FIX-PROBLEM MOP.

Of course people have drains in places they rent as well. This possibility is activated in the absence of knowledge to the contrary by activating D-AGENCY (Schank & Abelson, 1977). D-AGENCY points to knowledge about AGENCY relationships (which is what "landlords" are) so that HOMEOWNERSHIP can still be used although it would be mediated by D-AGENCY.

Until we see "overflowing" we do not really know what is being told to us. But, after we have seen it, a great many structures must become active. First, the conceptualization that is to be constructed here contains empty CD slots for what object is being PROPEL-ed (which comes from "overflow") and to where. The OBJECT defaults to "water" by consulting the "normal contents" part of the conceptual dictionary item for "drain." The "TO" slot is filled by consulting the relevant frames, in this case the candidates being "in house," "on floor," or "on carpet."

The activation of FIXPROBLEM causes an attempt at the creation of a solution. FIXPROBLEM has as its strands FINDFIXER, PERSUADE, and SOLUTION. Each of these, it turns out, is a possible topic of conversation where the first input is our above sentence. Thus we might hear:

1. I know a good plumber.

2. My, that's going to cost a lot of money.
3. Have you tried Drain-Fixing Drano?

The fact that all these are quite possible as responses here is an important indication that all these structures are active in the mind of the understander of these sentences. To test further the validity of the active high-level structures in this way, consider other possible responses based on the other ones given above:

1. That sink of yours has been rotten for ages.
2. I told you not to get such an old house.
3. Boy, isn't it a pain to own a house?

Each of these is perfectly plausible as a response. We attribute this to the fact that some high-level memory structure would have to have been activated by the input. What other kinds of statements might be acceptable here? Some candidates are:

4. Oh, isn't that awful.
5. Did you have to stay home from work?
6. Water can be awfully damaging.
7. Do you know how to fix it?
8. Would you like to borrow my Stilson wrench?
9. And with your mother coming to visit, too!
10. This has certainly been a bad month for you, hasn't it?

Assuming that these too are all legitimate, what structures do they come from? The ultimate questions here are what kinds of MOPs are there and how many of them are likely to be active at any given time? It seems plausible that the following high-level structures are likely to be active during the processing of our input sentence:

JOB: FAMILY RELATIONS
HOMEOWNERSHIP

FIX PROBLEM; PERSUADE
USE SERVICE

PROF HOME VISIT
FAMILY VISIT TO HOME
FIND PROFESSIONAL
MAKE CONTRACT

$PLUMBER

Are all these structures MOPs? Returning to our definition of a MOP, we can see that some of them clearly are and some of them fall into a rather grey area. Recall that a MOP is an organizer of information that can be used to create a superscript. Recall further that MOPs serve to organize terminal scenes that have within them a backbone of a sequence of events that are episodes from memory organized in terms of that backbone. These terminal scenes are either script-like (in which case they contain deviations from the normal flow of the script encoded as actual memories) or else they are locative in nature (in which case they contain actual episodes that are organized in a nonevent-based manner, possibly visually). Thus, a MOP is an organizer of terminal scenes or actual memory episodes. By this analysis, PROF HOME VISIT, FAMILY VISIT TO HOME, FIND PROFESSIONAL, and MAKE CONTRACT are all MOPs. They each organize terminal scenes such as PAY, PHONING FOR AN APPOINTMENT, FAMILY DINNER and so on. As we have said these terminal scenes are whether actual memories are to be found.

FIX PROBLEM, PERSUADE, and USE SERVICE are meta-MOPs; that is, they do not have memories in them directly. Rather, they are structures that serve to organize MOPs.

This leaves us with JOB, FAMILY RELATIONS, and HOMEOWNERSHIP as active knowledge structures that do not fit in with our previously established definition of MOPs and the structures that both organize and are organized by MOPs. What then are these structures and how do they differ from MOPs?

The first thing to notice about these labels is that we have a great deal of information about them in our memories. In fact, we have so much information and it is of such great importance to us (i.e., it concerns our high-level goals) that to begin to think that we can break such structures down into MOPs that organize terminal scenes is absurd. There is, for example, a JOB MOP that contains scenes about applying for jobs, getting paid, terminating employment, and so on. But there is a great deal more information about one's job or knowledge of jobs in general that could not be neatly contained in the JOB MOP. The point here is that such information is at a higher level than that of MOPs. We cannot begin to talk about that information here, since it is extremely complex, but later on we shall have a bit more to say about the role of the structures that are at a higher level than MOPs.

The MOPs that we have specified and the other high-level structures that we have not specified relate for this story as shown in Figure 3.

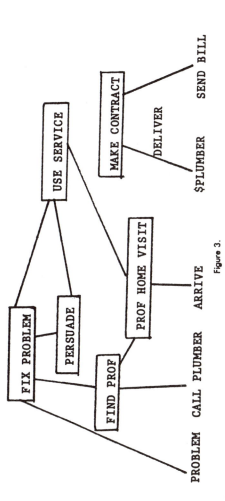

Figure 3.

All of the MOPs mentioned here are capable of making useful predictions about what is going on in this situation. The big questions, then, are exactly when such predictions are made, how they are called into play in processing, and where they come from.

MOPs REVIEWED

A MOP is a packet of knowledge that can be called into play for initial processing and memory storage. Thus, a MOP is a bundle of memories organized around a particular subject that can be brought in to aid in the processing of new inputs. All the subjects that we have considered so far have been events. Thus, MOPs are used insofar as we have described them for understanding and storing event-based information. The criteria we have been using for determining what can be a MOP has depended on the following questions:

1. Why is the information contained in that MOP contained there and not anywhere else?
2. How can we search that MOP?
3. What is the output (i.e., what is at the end of the strands) of that MOP?
4. How is that MOP known to be relevant and subsequently accessed?
5. What kind of processing help (i.e., what predictions are made) is available from having accessed that MOP?

First Conclusion

There are several technical conclusions we can make from what we have said here. In the next section I shall make some more general conclusions.

First, we are now in a position to see what a script really is. Scripts are a particular kind of MOP which we might call subMOPs. They are subject to temporal precedence search, produce Conceptual Dependencies, and contain memories—so they are obviously MOPs. But they are very particular. MOPs tend to organize information in general about an area and thus at one level of suborganization are methods of filling the various strands of the MOP. Scripts are standardized memory chunks that are particular methods of filling one or more strands in a MOP.

A second technical issue revolves around the kind of thing that is going on with respect to high-level structures in memory. We can see that there are basically three overall kinds of memory events: those that are classified uniquely, those that are mushed into a MOP for retrieval through that MOP, and those that have recurred so frequently that a MOP would be useless for aid in retrieval of these events.

Events that are uniquely classified can be retrieved by a variety of aids. For example, sometimes a particular word can have an episode attached to it in memory if that word is strongly identified with only one event. Such attachments can be made off of particular concepts as well. Such concepts are not MOPs, but they can and do have unique memories stored as a part of them.

At the other extreme, we have events that occur so frequently that they cannot be recalled at all. These would originally be grouped as MOPs, but a tremendous number of events can overwhelm a MOP and thus make that MOP effectively useless as a memory organizer. For example, "toothbrushing experiences" are likely to have been grouped as a MOP at one time, but eventually that MOP gets to be useless for retrieval.

A MOP, then, is in between these two extremes. A MOP must organize information in such a way as to provide useful processing structures (i.e., predictions) off the backbone or temporal precedences of the MOP and still have pointers to unique episodes that have been classified in terms of that MOP. As those unique episodes begin to get mushed with other episodes, they cease to be unique and become MOPs themselves. As those new MOPs begin to grow they develop pointers to unique episodes that they organize. But, if they grow too big, they lose their power as memory aids and become merely subMOPs, or scripts with no memory capabilities (what we had previously referred to as Instrumental Scripts in Schank & Abelson, 1977).

Second Conclusion

This paper has taken us through a number of issues in the area of the representation of language and memory. There seem to be two points worth mentioning—one theoretical and one methodological.

The theory I have been trying to build here is an attempt to account for the facts of memory to the extent that they are available. In order to do natural language understanding effectively (whether by humans or machine) it is necessary to have as part of the working apparatus of such a system as episodic memory. Scripts and other higher-level knowledge structures are not simply static data structures in such a memory. Rather, they are active processors as well as the organizers of memory. Processing and storage devices must be the same in order to account for the phenomenon of reminding. In order to account for the fact that reminding and recognition confusions in memory both can be disembodied from large notions of a script to much smaller pieces, it was necessary to restructure our notion of a script to be much more particular. Full blown scripts of the kind SAM used would have to be reconstructed by memory. This reconstruction implies a subsequent decomposition. Thus, we can expect pieces of stories or experiences to be stored in different parts of memory, commonly breaking the link between them. The advantage of this setup is to more effectively understand the world around us. This more effective understanding manifests itself in better predictions about what will happen in particular, well-constructed experiences that have been built up over time. But these predictions are only as good as the initial categorizations of the world that we make. Thus, an

effective categorization of new experience is the major problem for an understander as well as the major research problem facing those of us who work on understanding.

The negative effect of this breaking up of experience in order to make more effective predictions about the world is imperfect memory. People have imperfect memories because they are looking to make generalizations about experience that will serve as a source of useful predictions in understanding. That imperfect memory is a by-product of predictive understanding capabilities is a very important point for those of us working in computer modelling. I do not believe that there is any other alternative available to us in building intelligent machines other than modelling people. People's supposed imperfections are there for a reason. It may be possible that in the distant future we will build machines that improve upon what people can do; but machines will have to equal people first, *and I mean equal very very literally.*

This brings me to my methodological point. It is absolutely crucial that AI researchers and psychologists, as well as cognitively oriented linguists, begin to work together on the issues facing us. To pretend that we are interested in different things is folly—we are all working on the nature of the mind. The fact that we bring different tools to bear on this subject is terrific. So much the better for getting potentially different results and thus learning from each other. The field of Cognitive Science can have its computer modellers, its experimentalists, its field workers, and so on. When we stop arguing (and reporting on) methodology and begin to listen to what we have to say to each other, Cognitive Science will really begin to exist.

REFERENCES

Abelson, R. P., & Carroll, J. Computer simulation of individual belief systems. *American Behavioral Science*, 1965, 8,

Bartlett, R. *Remembering: A study in experimental and social psychology*. London: Cambridge University Press, 1932.

Bower, G. H., Black, J. B., & Turner, T. J. Scripts in text comprehension and memory. *Cognitive Psychology*, 1979, *I*, 177–220.

Carbonell, J. G. *Subjective understanding: Computer models of belief systems*. Ph.D. Thesis, Yale University, Computer Science Dept., Research Report 150, 1979.

Colby, K. M. Computer simulation of change in personal belief systems. *Behavioral Science*, 1967, *3*, 248–258.

Cullingford, R. E. *Script application: Computer understanding of newspaper stories*. Ph.D. Thesis, Yale University, Computer Science Dept., Research Report 116, 1978.

DeJong, G. F. *Skimming stories in real time: An experiment in integrated understanding*. Ph.D. Thesis, Yale University, Computer Science Dept., Research Report 158, 1979.

Dresher, B. E., & Hornstein, N. On some supposed contribution of artificial intelligence to the scientific study of language. *Cognition*, 1976, *4*, 321–398.

Fillmore, C. The case for case. In E. Bach & R. Harms (Eds.), *Universals in linguistic theory*. New York: Holt, Rinehart and Winston, 1968.

Fodor, J. A., Jenkins, J. J., & Saporta, S. Some tests of implications from transformation grammar. Unpublished study cited in R. Brown & R. J. Hernstein, *Psychology*. Boston: Little, Brown and Co., 1966.

Gershman, A. V. *Knowledge-based parsing*. Ph.D. Thesis, Yale University, Computer Science Dept., Research Report 156, 1979.

Hays, D. G. Dependency theory: A formalism and some observations. *Language*, 1964, 40, 511–525.

Hemphill, L. G. A conceptual approach to automated language understanding and belief structures. Stanford University, Computer Science Dept., AI Memo AIM-273, 1975.

Katz, J. Recent issues in semantic theory. *Foundations of Language*, 1967, 3.

Klein, S. Control of style with a generative grammar. *Language*, 1965, 41.

Lamb, S. M. On alternation, transformation, realization, and stratification. *Monograph Series on Languages and Linguistics*, 1964, 17, 105–122.

Meehan, J. *The metanovel: writing stories by computer*. Ph.D. Thesis, Yale University, Computer Science Dept., Research Report 74, 1976.

Mehler, J. Some effects of grammatical transformations on the recall of English sentences. *Journal of Verbal Learning and Verbal Behavior*, 1963, 2, 346-351.

Minsky, M. A framework for representing knowledge. In P. H. Winston (Ed.), *The psychology of computer vision*. New York: McGraw-Hill, 1975.

Quillian, R. *Semantic memory*. Cambridge, Mass.: Bolt, Beranek and Newman, 1966.

Rieger, C. Conceptual memory. In R. C. Schank (Ed.), *Conceptual information processing*. Amsterdam: North Holland, 1975.

Riesbeck, C. K. & Schank, R. C. Comprehension by computer: Expectation-based analysis of sentences in context. Yale University, Computer Science Dept., Research Report 78, 1976. Also in W. J. M. Levelt and G. B. Flores d'Arcais (Eds.), *Studies in the Perception of Language*. Chichester, England: John Wiley & Sons, Ltd., 1979.

Schank, R. C. A notion of linguistic concept. Stanford University, Computer Science Dept., A.I. Memo 75, 1968.

Schank, R. C. Outline of a conceptual semantics for computer generation of coherent discourse. *Mathematical Biosciences*, 1969, 5, 93-119.

Schank, R. C. Finding the conceptual content and intention in an utterance in natural language conversation. *Proceedings of the Second International Joint Conference on Artificial Intelligence*. London, England, 1971.

Schank, R. C. Conceptual dependency: A theory of natural language understanding. *Cognitive Psychology*, 1972, 3, 552-631.

Schank, R. C. Identification of conceptualizations underlying natural language. In R. C. Schank & K. Colby (Eds.), *Computer Models of Thought and Language*. San Francisco: W. H. Freeman, 1973.

Schank, R. C. *Conceptual Information Processing*. Amsterdam: North Holland, 1975.

Schank, R. C., & Abelson, R. P. Scripts, plans, and knowledge. *Proceedings of the Fourth International Joint Conference on Artificial Intelligence*. Tbilisi, USSR, 1975.

Schank, R. C., & Abelson, R. P. *Scripts, plans, goals, and understanding*. Hillsdale, N.J.: Lawrence Erlbaum, 1977.

Schank, R. C., & Carbonell, J. G. Re: The Gettysberg Address: Representing social and political acts. In N. Findler (Ed.), *Associative networks: Representation and use of knowledge by computers*. New York: Academic Press, 1979. Also Yale University, Computer Science Dept., Research Report 127, 1978.

Schank, R. C., & Rieger, C. Inference and the computer understanding of natural language. *Artificial Intelligence*, 1974, 5, 373-412.

Schank, R. C., & Tesler, L. A conceptual parser for natural language. *Proceedings of the International Joint Conference on Artificial Intelligence*. Washington, D.C., 1969.

Schank, R. C., Goldman, N., Rieger, C., & Riesbeck, C. MARGIE: Memory, analysis, response generation and inference in English. *Proceedings of the Third International Joint Conference on Artificial Intelligence*. Stanford, California, 1973.

Schank, R. C., Lebowitz, M., & Birnbaum, L. Integrated partial parsing. Yale University, Computer Science Dept., Research Report 143, 1978.

Schank, R. C., Tesler, L., & Weber, S. SPINOZA: Conceptual case-based natural language analysis. Stanford University, Computer Science Dept., A.I. Memo AIM-109, 1970.

Smith, E. E., Adams, N., & Schorr, D. Fact retrieval and the paradox of interference. *Cognitive Psychology*, 1978, 10, 438-464.

Wilensky, R. *Understanding goal-based stories*. Ph.D. Thesis. Yale University, Computer Science Dept., Research Report 140, 1978.

Winograd, T. *Understanding natural language*. New York: Academic Press, 1972.

Information Retrieval   C.A. Montgomery
and Language Processing   Editor

An Intelligent Analyzer and Understander of English

Yorick Wilks
Artificial Intelligence Project
Stanford University

The paper describes a working analysis and generation program for natural language, which handles paragraph length input. Its core is a system of preferential choice between deep semantic patterns, based on what we call "semantic density." The system is contrasted: (1) with syntax oriented linguistic approaches, and (2) with theorem proving approaches to the understanding problem.
Key Words and Phrases: artificial intelligence, computational linguistics, template, paraplate, stereotype, machine translation, understanding, natural language processing, semantic preference, semantic density
CR Categories: 3. 36, 3.42, 3.63

Introduction

After the unhappy conclusions of most early attempts at machine translation, some justification is required for presenting it again as a reasonable computational task. Minsky [4], among others, argued that there could be no machine translation without a system that, in an adequate sense, understood what it was trying to translate. The meaning structures and inference forms that constitute the present system are intended as an understanding system in the required sense, and as such, justify a new attack on an old but important problem.

Machine translation is an important practical task; furthermore, it has a certain theoretical significance for a model of language understanding. For it provides a

This work has been supported under Advanced Research Projects Agency Contract #457. Author's address: Instituto per gli Studi Semantici e Cognitivi, 6976 Castagnola, Villa Heleneum, Switzerland.

clear test of the rightness or wrongness of a proposed system for representing meaning, since the output in a second language can be assessed by people unfamiliar with the internal formalism and methods employed. Few other settings for a theory of language analysis leave room for such objective tests. Dialog systems are notoriously difficult to assess; and command systems are restricted to worlds in which commands are relevant, e.g. those of physical objects and the directions for picking them up, which domain excludes the world of real nonimperative discourse about such subjects as friendship, the United Nations, and the problems of juvenile delinquency. On the other hand, conventional systems of linguistics produce only complex representations that can be disputed only on internal grounds. They are never used to produce objective, discussable output, like a sentence in another language that would test the adequacy of the whole representation.

It should be added here that although the present system is cast in the role of a machine translation system, the popular forms of example to test "understanding"— i.e. finding the correct reference of a pronoun on the basis of knowledge of and inferences about the real world—can all be reconstructed within it, as will be shown.

Since the early machine translation work there has been a considerable development in formal linguistics, in particular, the creation of the school of transformational grammatical analysis. This form of analysis of natural language has little relation to the work described here, and for three reasons.

Firstly, Transformational Grammar was set up to be quite independent of all considerations of meaning, context, and inference, which constitutes something of a disqualification for the present task, namely understanding language. Consider such an even apparently structural-grammatical matter as the ambiguity of prepositions; "out of," for example, is highly ambiguous, which can be seen from any reflection on such sentences as: I live out of town. I hit her out of anger. I threw the ball out of the window. The statue is made out of marble. An objective measure of the ambiguity is that the occurrences of "out of" in those sentences would be translated into French in three different ways. Yet, even in such a basic structural area, Transformational Grammar makes no suggestions whatever as to how the choice should be made. Whereas in the Preference Semantics system, described below, the choice is made in a simple and natural manner. Such defects as this have been to some extent remedied in a recent development of the Transformational Grammar system, Generative

Semantics. However, for our purposes Generative Semantics, like Transformational Grammar, suffers from the other two defects below.

Secondly, it is a matter of practical experience, that Transformational Grammar systems have been extremely resistant to computational application. This practical difficulty is in part due to theoretical difficulties concerning the definition and computability of Transformational Grammar systems.

Thirdly, Transformational Grammar and Generative Semantics systems suffer one overwhelming defect, from the point of view of understanding natural language. Both have a "derivational paradigm," which is to say, both envisage a system which constructs a derivation by running from an initial symbol to a language sentence. Such derivations have the function of either accepting a sentence or rejecting it because no such derivation can "reach" the sentence from the starting symbol. Thus all sentences are sorted into two groups by such systems—the acceptable and the unacceptable—and by doing this they claim to define the notion of an "acceptable," "meaningful," or "grammatical" sentence.

One can see how far such a task is from the one of understanding language, for sorting in this way is exactly what human beings do not do when they hear a sentence. They endeavor to interpret it, changing their rules if necessary as they do so. Yet, within the Transformational Grammar and Generative Semantics derivational paradigm, it makes no sense to talk of changing the rules and trying another set, even though that is just what any "intelligent" understanding system must do. For example, most conventional grammatical systems are armed with some rule equivalent to "only animate things perform tasks of acertain class," which compels them to reject such perfectly comprehensible utterances as those which speak of the wind opening doors and cars drinking gas. (It is unimportant here whether any particular system employs such a particular rule. The point here is a general one about behavior in the face of rule failure.) Only an "intelligent" system, outside the derivational paradigm and able to reconsider its own steps, can overcome this defect. The limitations of Transformational Grammar and Generative Semantics systems, from the point of view of this project, have been discussed in detail in [12 and 13].

The proper comparisons for the present work are with systems of analysis orginating from within either artificial intelligence or computational linguistics, none of which (except the work of Woods [17]) owes any strong debt to the Transformational Grammar tradition all of which, in differing degrees, make the concept of meaning representation central, such as the work of Simmons [11], Winograd [16], Schank [8], and Sandewall [7].

Some points of difference between these systems and Preference Semantics may be mentioned briefly.

(i) **Preference Semantics** is very much oriented toward processing realistic text sentences of some complexity and of up to 20 to 30 words long. This difference of emphasis, and the sentence fragmentation and large-scale conceptual linkages its implementation requires, distinguishes Preference Semantics from all the approaches mentioned.

(ii) Preference Semantics copes with the words of a normal vocabulary, and with many senses of them, rather than with single senses of simple object words and actions. It is not wholly clear that the methods of [16] could, even in principle, be extended in that way.

(iii) Preference Semantics contains no conventional grammar for analysis or generation: its task is performed by a strong semantics. This contrasts with Winograd's use of a linguistic grammar and simple marker system, and to some extent with Simmons' use of case grammar.

(iv) Preference Semantics does not take theorem proving techniques, of whichever major type, to be the core manipulations for an understanding system, but rather sees them as techniques to be brought in where appropriate. In this respect it differs most strongly from Sandewall, whose work assumes some form of theorem prover of a resolution type, into which his predicate calculus representations of natural language sentences can be plugged. Preference Semantics also differs here from Winograd, whose PLANNER-based system is far more oriented to the proving of truths than the Preference Semantics system described below. Another major difference between Preference Semantics and these two other systems is that Preference Semantics inference rules operate on higher level items, structures of semantic concepts and cases representing whole sentences and paragraphs of text, rather than on items at the level of text words and facts (or predicates and features that replace such items one to one in grammatically parsed structures). The latter approach leads to an enormous multiplication of axioms/inference rules, with all the subsequent difficulty of searching among them.

Nothing here, of course, denies the need for knowledge of the physical world, and inferences based upon it, for understanding and translation. What is being argued for here is nondeductive, common sense inference expressed in a formalism that is a natural extension of the meaning representation itself.

A simple case will establish the need for such inference: consider the sentence "The soldiers fired at the women, and we saw several of them fall." That sentence will be taken to mean that the women fell, so that when, in analyzing the sentence, the question arises of whether "them" refers to "soldiers" or "women" (a choice which will result in a differently gendered pronoun in French), we will have to be able to infer that things fired at often fall, or at least are much more likely to fall than things doing the firing. Hence there must be access to inferential information here, above and beyond the meanings of the constituent words, from which we could infer that hurt beings tend to fall down.

The deductive approaches mentioned claim to tackle

just such examples, of course, but in this paper we will argue for a different approach to them, which we shall call common sense inference rules. These are expressions of "partial information" (in McCarthy's phrase): generalizations, like the one above about hurt things tending to fall down, which (a) are not invariably true and (b) tend to be of a very high degree of generality indeed. It is part of the case being made here that the importance of such apparently obvious truths in natural language understanding is considerable, but also easy to overlook.

A System of Semantics Based Language Analysis

A fragmented text is to be represented by an interlingual structure, called a *Semantic Block*, which consists of *templates* bound together by *paraplates* and *common sense inferences*. These three items consist of *formulas* (and predicates and functions ranging over them and subformulas), which in turn consist of *elements*.

Some of these semantic items represent text items in a fairly straightforward way as follows:

Items in semantic representation	Corresponding text items
formula	English word sense
template	English clause or simple sentence
semantic block	English paragraph or text

Paraplates and common sense inferences, as we shall see, serve to bind templates together in the semantic block. Semantic elements correspond to nothing in a text, but are the primitives out of which *all* the above complex items are made up.

Semantic Elements

Elements are 70 primitive semantic units used to express the semantic entities, states, qualities, and actions about which humans speak and write. The elements fall into five classes, which can be illustrated as follows (elements in uppercase, and the approximate concept expressed in lowercase):

(a) Entities: MAN (human being), STUFF (substances), SIGN (verbal and written symbols), THING (physical object), PART (parts of things), FOLK (human groups), ACT (acts), STATE (states of existence), BEAST (animals), etc.
(b) Actions: FORCE (compels), CAUSE (causes to happen), FLOW (moving as liquids do), PICK (choosing), BE (exists), etc.
(c) Type indicators: KIND (being a quality), HOW (being a type of action), etc.
(d) Sorts: CONT (being a container), GOOD (being morally acceptable), THRU (being an aperture), etc.
(e) Cases: TO (direction), SOUR (source), GOAL (goal or end), LOCA (location), SUBJ (actor or agent), OBJE (patient of action), IN (containment), POSS (possessed by), etc.

In addition to these primitive elements, there are *class* elements whose names begin with an asterisk, such as *ANI for the class of animate elements MAN, BEAST,

and FOLK; *HUM for human elements MAN and FOLK; *PHYSOB, which denotes the class of elements containing MAN, THING, etc., but not, of course, STUFF. There are also action class elements such as *DO.

The elements are not to be thought of as denotative, even of intensional entities, but as the elements of a micro-language in which more complex concepts are expressed. Thus their justification is wholly in terms of their use to construct semantic *formulas*.

Semantic Formulas

Formulas are constructed from elements and right and left brackets. They express the senses of English words; one formula to each sense. The formulas are binarily bracketed lists of whatever depth is necessary to express the word sense. Their most important element is always their rightmost, which is called the *head* of the formula, and it expresses the most general category under which the word sense in question falls. However, an element that is used as a head can function within formulas as well. So, for example, CAUSE is the head of the formula for the action sense of "drink" and it may be thought of as a "causing action," but CAUSE can also occur within the formula for a word sense, as it does, for example, within the formula for the action sense of "box," which can be paraphrased in English as "striking a human with the goal of *causing* him pain."

It will help in understanding the formulas to realize that there are conventional two-element subformulas, such as (FLOW STUFF) for liquidity, to avoid the introduction of new primitives. Another such is (THRU PART) to indicate an aperture. Formulas can be thought of, and written out, as binary trees of semantic primitives. In that form they are not unlike the lexical decomposition trees of Lakoff and McCawley. Here is a selection of formulas that will be needed in later examples. In each case I give the formulas as a tree of subformulas, with the head as the rightmost element, then as a table of subformulas, and lastly as a paraphrase in English. The formulas are for the English words "drink" (as an action), "grasp" (as a *physical* action), "fire at." I also give, in a less extended range of forms, the formulas for "policeman," "big," "interrogates," "crook" as a human being and as a physical object, and "singing" as an activity.

Nothing at all depends on these particular codings. What is at issue here is the claim that codings of this degree of complexity, and containing at least this much semantic information, are necessary for doing any interesting degree of linguistic analysis.

"drink" (action) → ((*ANI SUBJ) (((FLOW STUFF) OBJE)
((SELF IN)(((*ANI (THRU PART)) TO) (BE CAUSE)))))

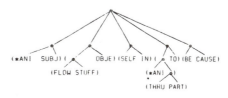

Formulas are best seen as nestings of *subformulas*, each of which is either a case specification or a direct specification on the head itself. Within any subformula there is a dependence at every level of the left half of a binary pair of the right half. This dependence relation is normally to be understood as type subspecification, in the way that *ANI specifies the type of agent in the example above. The mutual relation of the subformulas is not one of dependence, even though all the other subformulas be thought of as dependent on the rightmost subformula containing the head. However, the order of the subformulas is significant, since, for example, an object specification is considered to be the object of *all* actions to its right in the formula, whether they are the head or at some other level in the formula.

Subformula	Case/Act	Value	Explanation
(*ANI SUBJ)	SUBJ	*ANI	the preferred agent is animate
((FLOW STUFF)OBJE)	OBJE	(FLOW STUFF)	preferred object is liquid
(SELF IN)	IN	SELF	the container is the self, the subject
(((* ANI(THRU PART))TO)	TO	(* ANI(THRU PART))	the direction of the action is a human aperture(the mouth)
(BE CAUSE)	CAUSE	BE	the action is of causing to be (somewhere else)

Let us now decompose the formula for "drink." It is to be read as an action, preferably done by animate things (*ANI SUB); to liquids, or to substances that flow ((FLOW STUFF)OBJE); causing the liquid to be in the animate thing (SELF IN); and via (TO indicating the direction case) a particular aperture of the animate thing, the mouth, of course. It is hard to indicate a notion as specific as "mouth" with such general concepts. But we think that it would be simply irresponsible to suggest adding MOUTH as a semantic primitive, as do semantic systems that simply add an awkward lexeme as a new "primitive."

This notion of "preferring" is important: SUBJ case displays the preferred agents of actions, and OBJE case the preferred objects, or patients. We cannot enter such preferences as stipulations, as many linguistic systems do, such as Fodor and Katz's "selection restrictions." For we can be said to drink gall and wormwood, and cars are said to drink gasoline. It is proper to prefer the normal (quite different from probabilistically expecting it, we shall argue), but it would be absurd, in an intelligent understanding system, not to accept the abnormal if it is described. Not only everyday metaphor but the description of the simplest fiction require it.

A formula expresses the meaning of the word senses to which it is attached. This claim assumes a common sense distinction between explaining the meaning of a word and knowing facts about the thing the word indicates. The formulas are intended only to express the former, to express what we might find in a reasonable dictionary, though in a formal manner.

Now let us consider:

"grasp" (physical action) → ((*ANI SUBJ)((*PHYSOB OBJE)
(((THIS(MAN PART))INST)(TOUCH SENSE)))))

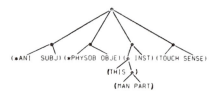

Subformula	Case/Act	Value	Explanation
(*ANI SUBJ)	SUBJ	*ANI	the preferred agent is animate
(* PHYSOB OBJE)	OBJE	*PHYSOB	the preferred agent is a physical object
((THIS(MAN PART))INST)	INST	((THIS(MAN PART))	the instrument is a human part, the hand
(TOUCH SENSE)	SENSE	TOUCH	the action is of physical contact

So, grasping in this sense is something preferably done by an animate thing to a physical object, done with the hand as instrument: an action of physical contact with the object. The mental sense of "grasp" is a THINK action.

Now consider:

"fire at" (action) → ((*HUM SUBJ)((*ANI OBJE)
((STRIK GOAL)((THING MOVE)CAUSE))))

Subformula	Case/Act	Value	Explanation
(*HUM SUBJ)	SUBJ	*HUM	preferably done by a human
(*ANI OBJE)	OBJE	*ANI	preferably done to an animate thing
(STRIK GOAL)	GOAL	STRIK	the aim being to strike the animate thing
((THING MOVE)CAUSE)	CAUSE	(THING MOVE)	the action is of causing an object (the bullet) to move

The fact that the bullet is the agent of the moving is implicit, and agents are unmarked except at the top level of the formula, although objects are marked at every level. So then, "firing at" is causing a thing to move so as to strike an animate target.

Let me now give the remaining formulas, with only an explanation, if the principles of the tree and table representation are now clear.

"policeman" → ((FOLK SOUR)(((((NOTGOOD
MAN)OBJE)PICK)(SUBJ MAN)))

i.e. a person who selects bad persons out of the body of people (FOLK). The case marker SUBJ is the dependent in the last element pair, indicating that the normal "top first" order for subject-entities in formulas has been violated, and necessarily so if the head is also to be the last element in linear order.

"big" → ((*PHYSOB POSS)(MUCH KIND))

i.e. a property preferably possessed by physical objects (substances are not big).

"interrogates" → ((MAN SUBJ)((MAN OBJE)(TELL FORCE)))

i.e. forcing to tell something, done preferably by humans to humans.

"crook" → ((((NOTGOOD ACT)OBJE)DO)(SUBJ MAN))

i.e. a man who does bad acts.

"crook" → ((((((THIS BEAST)OBJE)FORCE)(SUBJ MAN))POSS)(LINE THING))

i.e. a straight object possessed by a man who controls a particular kind of animal.

"singing" → ((*ANI SUBJ)((SIGN OBJE)((MAN SENSE)CAUSE)))))

which is to say, an act by an animate agent of causing a person to experience a sign, the song.

Semantic Templates

Just as the semantic elements have been explained by seeing how they functioned within formulas, so formulas, one level higher, are to be explained by describing how they function within *templates*, the third kind of semantic item in the system. The notion of a template is intended to correspond to an intuitive one of message: one not reducible merely to unstructured associations of word-senses.

A template consists of a network of whole formulas, and its connectivity is between an agent- , action- , and object-formula, such that from any one of these members of the basic triple a list of other formulas may depend. In any particular example, one or more of the formulas may be replaced by a dummy. We shall discuss such cases further.

The program sees each clause, phrase, or primitive sentence of text (called its *fragments*) as strings of formulas, drawn, one for each text word, from a dictionary. The program attempts to locate one or more templates in each string of formulas by first looking only at their head elements and seeking for acceptable sequences of heads.

A *bare template* is such an acceptable, or intuitively interpretable, sequence of an agent head, an action head, and an object head (subject again to the proviso about dummies). If there is a sequence of formulas whose heads are identical to such a bare template of elements, then the sequence of *formulas* is a template for that fragment, taken together with any other formulas that may be found to depend on those three main formulas.

For example: "Small men sometimes father big sons," when represented by a string of formulas, will contain the two sequences of head elements (where the heads of formulas are written under the corresponding word):

small	men	sometimes	father	big	sons
KIND	MAN	HOW	MAN	KIND	MAN
and KIND	MAN	HOW	CAUSE	KIND	MAN

(CAUSE is the head of the verbal sense of "father"; "to father" is analyzed as "to cause to have life.")

The first sequence has no underlying bare template because there is no intuitively interpretable element triple there, in the sense in which MAN CAUSE MAN in the second sequence is intuitively interpretable as "a human causes another human to exist." Thus we have already disambiguated "father," at the same time as picking up a sequence of three formulas, which is the core of the template for the sentence. It must be emphasized here that the template is the sequence of formulas (which are trees or structured lists) and is not to be confused with the bare template, or triple of elements (heads) used to locate it.

It is a hypothesis of this work that we can build up a finite but useful inventory of bare templates adequate for the analysis of ordinary language: a list that can be interpreted as the messages that people want to convey at some fairly high level of generality (for template matching is not in any sense phrase-matching at the surface level). The bare templates are an attempt to explicate a notion of a nonatomistic linguistic pattern: to be located whole in sentences in the way that human beings appear to when they read or listen.

We would not wish to defend, item by item, the particular template list in use at any given moment. Such lists are always subject to modification by experience, as are the formulas and even the inventory of basic elements. The only defense is that the system using them actually works; and if anyone replies that its working depends on mere inductive generalization, we can only remind them of Garvin's obvious but invaluable remark that all linguistic generalizations are, and must be, inductive.

Let us now illustrate the central processes of expansion and preference, in which the formulas become active items guiding the extension of the template network from a triple of formulas to a full template with preference bonds and dependent formulas. Let us consider the sentence "The big policeman interrogated the crook," for which we already have the appropriate formulas set out above.

The template matching algorithm will see this sentence as a string of formulas, one for each of its words, and will look only at the heads of the formulas. I shall now write [crook(man)] to denote not the English words in the square brackets but *the formula for the word or words*. Then, since MAN FORCE MAN is in the inventory of bare templates, one scan of the string of formulas containing [crook(man)] will pick up the sequence of formulas [policeman][interrogated][crook(man)], in that order. Again, when a string containing the formula [crook(thing)], the shepherd's sense of "crook," is scanned, since MAN FORCE THING is also a proper bare template, the sequence of formulas [policeman][interrogated][crook(thing)] will also be selected as a possible initial structure for the sentence. I should add here that the formula for both *tenses* of "interrogates" is the same, the tense difference being indicated by a tense element put into the formula during the process of expansion now being described.

We now have two possible template representations for the sentence after the initial match; both are triples of formulas in actor-action-object form. Next, the templates are expanded, if possible. This process consists of extending the simple networks we have so far, both by attaching other formulas into the network and by strengthening the bonds between those already in the template, if possible. Qualifier formulas can be attached where appropriate, and so the formula [big] is tied to that for "policeman" in both templates. But now comes a crucial difference between the two representations: one which will resolve the sense of "crook."

The expansion algorithm looks into the subparts of the formulas that express preferences to see if any of the preferences are satisfied: as we saw, the formula [big] prefers to qualify physical objects. A policeman is such, and that additional dependency is marked in both templates: similarly for the preference of "interrogate" for human actors in both representations. The difference comes with preferred objects: only the formula [crook-(man)] for human crooks can satisfy that preference for human objects, since the formula [crook(thing)] for shepherd's crooks, cannot. Hence the former template network is denser by one dependency, and is preferred over the latter in all subsequent processing: its connectivity is (ignoring the "the's"): [big] → [policeman] →↔ [interrogates] ↔← [crook(man)] and so that becomes the template for this sentence. The other possible template (one arrow for each preferential dependency established, and a double arrow to mark the standard, nonpreferential, link between the three major formulas of the template) was connected as follows: [big] → [policeman] →↔ [interrogates] ↔ [crook(thing)] and it is now discarded.

Thus the parts of the formulas that express preferences of various sorts are not only used to express the meaning of the corresponding word sense, but they can also be interpreted as implicit procedures for the construction of correct templates. This preference for the greatest semantic density works well, and can be seen as an expression of what Joos calls "semantic axiom number one" [2], that the right meaning is the least meaning, or what Scriven [10] has called "the trick [in meaning analysis] of creating redundancies in the input." As we shall see, this uniform principle works over both the areas that are conventionally distinguished in linguistics as syntax and semantics. There is no such distinction in this system, since all manipulations are of formulas and templates, and these are all constructed out of elements of a single type.

Templates and Linguistic Syntax

As a further example of linguistic syntax done by preference, let us take the sentence "John gave Mary the book," onto which the matching routine will have matched two bare templates, since it has no reason so far to prefer one to the other, as follows:

John gave Mary the book
MAN   GIVE   THING

MAN   GIVE   MAN

The expansion routine now seeks for dependencies between formulas, in addition to those between the three formulas constituting the template itself. In the case of the first bare template, a GIVE action can be expanded by any substantive formula to its immediate right which is not already part of the bare template (which is to say that indirect object formulas can depend on the corresponding action formula). Again "book" is qualified by an article, which fact is not noticed by the second bare template. So then, by expanding the first bare template we have established in the following dependencies at the surface level, where the dependency arrows "→" correspond to *preferential* relations established between formulas for the words linked.

John ↔ gave ↔ book
    ↑   ↑
  Mary   the

But if we try to expand the second bare template by the same method, we find we cannot, because the formula for "Mary" cannot be made dependent on the one for "give," since in that template "Mary" has already been seen, wrongly of course, as a direct object of giving, hence it cannot be an indirect object as well. So then, the template MAN GIVE MAN cannot be expanded to yield any dependency arcs connecting formulas to the template; whereas the template MAN GIVE THING yields two dependency arcs on expansion, and so gives the preferred representation.

This general method can yield virtually all the results of a conventional grammar covering the same range of expressions, while using only relations between semantic elements.

Case Ambiguity

In the actual implementation of the system, an input text is initially fragmented, and templates are matched with each fragment of the text. As we shall see, there are then complex routines for establishing contextual ties between these templates separated by fragmentation. However, it is claimed here that, for dealing with text containing realistically long and complicated sentences, some such initial fragmentation is both psychologically and computationally important.

The input routine fragments paragraphs at the occurrence of any of an extensive list of *key* words. The list contains all punctuation marks, subjunctions, conjunctions, and prepositions. In difficult cases, described in detail in [14], fragmentations are made even though a key word is not present, as at the slash in "John knows / Mary loves him," while in other cases a fragmentation is not made in the presence of a key word, such as "that" in ";John loves that woman."

Let us consider the sentence "John is / in the country," fragmented as shown. It should be clear that the standard agent-act-object form of template cannot be matched onto the fragment "John is." In such a case, a degenerate template MAN BE DTHIS is matched onto the two items of this sentence; the last item DTHIS being a dummy object, indicated by the D.

With the second fragment "in the country," a dummy subject DTHIS fills out the form to give a degenerate template DTHIS PBE POINT. The PBE is the same as the head of the formula for "in," since formulas for prepositions are assimilated to those for actions and have the head PDO or PBE. The fact that they originate in a preposition is indicated by the P, so distinguishing them from straightforward action formulas with heads DO and BE. POINT (indicates a spatial location that is not a movable physical object) is the head of the formula for "country," so this bare template triple for the fragment only tells us that "something is at a point in space." At a later stage, after the preliminary assignment of template structures to individual fragments, *TIE* routines attach the structures for separated fragments back together. In that process the dummies are tied back to their antecedents. So, in "John is in the country," the DTHIS in the MAN BE DTHIS template for the first fragment of the sentence ties to the whole template for the second fragment, expressing where John is.

It is very important to note that a preference is between alternatives. If the only structure derivable does *not* satisfy a declared preference, then it is accepted anyway. Only in that way can we deal naturally with metaphor.

So, in examples like "I heard an earthquake / singing / in the shower" (fragmentation as indicated by slashes), as contrasted with "I heard / an earthquake sing / in the shower," we shall expect, in the first case, to derive the correct representation because of the preference of notions like singing for animate agents. This is done by a simple extension of the density techniques to relations between structures for different fragments by considering, in this case, alternative connectivities for dummy parts of templates.

Thus, there will be a dummy subject and object template for /singing/, DTHIS CAUSE DTHIS, based on the formula for "singing" given earlier.

Now the overall density will be greater when the agent DTHIS, in the template for "singing," is tied to a formula for "I" in a preceding template, than when it is tied to one for "earthquake," since only the former satisfies the preference for an animate agent, and so the correct interpretation of the whole utterance is made.

But, and here we come to the point of this example, in the second sentence, with "sing" no such exercise of preference is possible, and the system must accept an interpretation in which the earthquake sings, since only that can be meant.

In order to give a rough outline of the system, I have centered our description on the stages of analysis within the individual fragment. After what has been described so far, *TIE* routines are applied to the expanded templates in a context of templates for other fragments of the same sentence or paragraph. The same techniques of dependency and preference are applied between full

templates for different fragments of a sentence or paragraph. At that stage, (1) case ties are established between templates (using the same cases as occur within formulas at a lower level); (2) dummies are attached to what they stand for as we indicated with the earthquake example; (3) remaining ambiguities are resolved; and (4) anaphoric ties are settled.

Paraplates and Case Ambiguity

The first of these tasks is done by applying *paraplates* to the template codings, using the same density techniques one level further up, as it were. Paraplates are complex items having the general form:

⟨list of predicates on mark-template⟩⟨case⟩
  ⟨list of predicates on case-template⟩
  ⟨generation stereotype⟩

A stereotype is a context sensitive generation pattern which will be described in the section on generation below, and in what follows here I shall give the paraplates *without* the attached stereotypes. The paraplates are essentially patterns that span two templates, which I call the mark and case templates, where the mark template generally precedes, though not necessarily immediately, the case template. If the predicates are all satisfied by the contents of the two templates, then that paraplate is considered to match onto the two templates and the case ambiguity of the preposition that functions as the pseudo-action in the second template is solved. Thus if we were analyzing "He ran the mile in four minutes" and we considered the template for the second fragment "in four minutes," we would find that all the predicates in some paraplate for TIMELOCATION case matched onto the appropriate parts of the templates for the two template fragments, and we would then know that the case of the second template was indeed TIMELOCATION and not, say, CONTAINMENT, as it would be in "He ran the mile in a plastic bag."

The paraplates are attached, as left-right ordered lists, to key words in English, generally prepositions and subjunctions. Consider the following three schematic paraplates for senses of "in" written out in order of preference below. These are presented without generation stereotypes for ease of explanation, but with a description in lowercase of which sense of "in" is in question in each line. The notion of *mark* is the standard intuitive one of the point of dependence of a phrase or clause. Thus, in "He ran the mile in four minutes" the second clause may be said to depend on the action "ran," which is then its mark. Whereas, in "He liked the old man in the corner," the mark of the second fragment is "man."

I will write the three paraplates out, first in linear order as they really are, and then in tabular form for ease of comprehension. The linear order is to be understood as corresponding to that of the six major formulas of the mark and case templates. The predicates in the paraplates may refer to any or all of these. The paraplates are called in on encountering the ambiguous subjunction, or most usually, ambiguous preposition that always functions as the pseudo-action of the second template—the one in hand, as it were. I have put a slash in the paraplate to indicate where the shift is, from predicates on the mark template to those on the case template. Also, where predicates have atomic arguments, like 2OCAS below, it indicates that those elements are separate arguments of the predicate. Where a predicate, like PRMARK below, has an argument that is a list, that list is a subformula that has to be located whole in the appropriate template formula so as to satisfy the predicate in question.

(1) (PRMARK(MOVE CAUSE))(2OBCAS INST GOAL)/
    (TO into)(PROBJE(CONT THING))

(2) (PRMARK *DO)(2OBHEAD)/(LOCA make part)

(3) (PRMARK(MOVE CAUSE))/
    (TO into) ((PROBJE(CONT THING))

What is not made absolutely clear by that form of the paraplates is where, on the six formulas of the two templates, each of the above predicates matches. Let us now set out each paraplate vertically in six lines, corresponding in turn to agent of first template, action of first template, object of first template, and then the same order for the second, case template.

(1)	
	FIRST AGENT
(PRMARK(MOVE CAUSE))	FIRST ACTION
(2OBCAS INST GOAL)	FIRST OBJECT
	SECOND AGENT
(TO into)	SECOND ACTION
(PROBJE (CONT THING))	SECOND OBJECT

(2)	
	FIRST AGENT
(PRMARK *DO)	FIRST ACTION
(2OBHEAD)	FIRST OBJECT
	SECOND ACTION
(LOCA make part)	SECOND AGENT

(3)	
	SECOND OBEJCT
	FIRST AGENT
(PRMARK(MOVE CAUSE))	FIRST ACTION
	FIRST OBJECT
	SECOND AGENT
(TO into)	SECOND ACTION
(PROBJE (CONT THING))	SECOND OBJECT

*DO is a wide class of action heads, TO and LOCA are case markers, 2OBCAS and 2OBHEAD are simply predicates that look at both the object (third) formulas of the current template (the second) and of the preceding template, i.e. at two objects. 2OBHEAD is true iff the two have the same head, and 2OBCAS is true iff they contain the same GOAL or INSTRUMENT subformula. The fact that those two predicates actually apply at two of the six places is a notational weakness in the tabular display above. PRMARK is a predicate on the semantic form of the mark, or a word governing the fragment that the key begins. In all the following examples, the mark is the action in the first fragment, and the predicate is

satisfied iff it is a (MOVE CAUSE) action: an action that causes something to move. Similarly, PROBJE is a predicate on the semantic form of the object (third formula) of the current template, and is satisfied if the predicate's argument is found in the formula.

Now consider the sentence "I put the key / in the lock," fragmented at the slash as shown. Let us consider that two templates have been set up for the second fragment: one for "lock" as a fastener, and one for the raising lock on a canal. Both formulas may be expected to refer to the containment case, and so to satisfy (PROBJE CONT). We apply the first paraplate and find that it fits only for the template with the correct (fastener) sense of "lock," since only there will 2OBCAS be satisfied, i.e. where the formulas for "lock" and "key" both have a subformula under GOAL indicating that their purpose is to close something. The third paraplate will fit with the template for the canal sense of "lock," but the first is a more extensive fit (indicated by the order of the paraplates, since the higher up the paraplate list, the more nontrivial template functions a paraplate contains) and is preferred. This preference has simultaneously selected both the right template for the second fragment and the correct paraplate linking the two templates for further generation tasks.

If we now take the sentence "He put the number / in the table," with two different templates for the second fragment (corresponding to the list and flat object senses of "table" respectively) we shall find that the intuitively correct template (the list sense) fails the first paraplate but fits the second, thus giving us the "make part of" sense of "in," and the right (list) sense of "table," since formulas for "number" and (list) "table" have the same head SIGN, though the formula for (flat, wooden) "table" does not.

Conversely, in the case of "He put the fork / in the table," fitting the correct template with the third paraplate will yield "into" sense of "in" (case DIRECTION) and the physical object sense of "table"; and this will be the preferred reading. Here we see the fitting of paraplates, and by choosing the densest preferential fit, which is always selecting the highest paraplate on the list that fits, we determine both word sense ambiguity and the case ambiguity of prepositions at once. Paraplate fitting makes use of deeper nested parts (essentially the case relations other than SUBJ and OBJE) of the formulas than does the template matching.

Anaphora and References

The TIE routines also deal with simple cases of anaphora on a simple preference basis. In cases such as "I bought the wine, / sat on a rock / and drank it," it is easy to see that the last word should be tied by TIE to "wine," and not "rock." This matter is settled by density after considering alternative ties for "it," and seeing which yields the denser representation overall. It will be "wine" in this case since "drink" prefers a liquid object.

In more complex cases of anaphora that require access to more information than is contained in formulas, templates, or paraplates, the system brings down what we referred to earlier as common sense inference rules.[1] Cases that require them will be ones like the sentence: "The soldiers fired at the women and we saw several of them fall." Simple semantic density considerations in *TIE* are inadequate here because both soldiers and women can fall equally easily, yet making the choice correctly is vital for a task like translation became the two alternatives lead to differently gendered pronouns in French. In such cases the Preference Semantics system applies a common sense rule, whose form, using variables and subformulas, would be

(1 (THIS STRIK) (*ANI 2)) ↔ ((*ANI 2)(NOTUP BE)DTHIS)

where the variables are restricted as shown, and the final DTHIS is simply a dummy to fill out the canonical form. This rule can be made more perspicuous by extending the informal [ ] notation to denote the *template form* representation of whatever is in the square brackets, thus: [1 strikes animate2] ↔ [animate2 falls]. The rules are applied to "extractions" from the situations to form chains of templates and template forms, and a rule only ultimately applies if it can function in the shortest, most-preferred, chain.

The way the common sense inferences work is roughly as follows: they are called in at present only when *TIE* is unable to resolve outstanding anaphoras, as in the present example. A process of extraction is then done, and it is to these *extractions*, and the relevant templates, that the common sense rules subsequently apply. The extractions are new template forms inferred from the deep case structure of formulas. So for example, if we were extracting from the template for "John drank the water," then going down into the tree structure of primitive elements in the formula for "drink," given earlier, we would extract that some liquid was now inside an animate thing (from the containment case in the formula for "drink"), and that it went in through an aperture of the animate thing (from the directional case). Moreover, since the extractions are partially confirmed, as it were, by the information about actor and object in the surrounding template, we can, by simple tying of variables, extract new template forms equivalent to, in ordinary language, "the water is in John," etc. These are (when in coded form) the extractions to which the common sense rules apply as the analytical procedure endeavors to build up a chain of extractions and inferences. The preferred chain will, unsurprisingly, be the shortest.

So then in the "women and soldiers" example we extract a coded form, by variable tying in the templates, equivalent to [soldiers strike women], since we can tell from the formula for "fired at" that it is intended to

strike the object of the action. We are seeking for partial confirmation of the assertion [X? fall], and such a chain is completed by the rule given, though not by a rule equivalent to, say [something strike X] → [X die], since there is nothing in the sentence as given to partially confirm that particular rule in a chain, and cause it to fit here. Since we are in fact dealing with subformulas in the statement of the rules, rather than with words, "fitting" means an "adequate match of subformulas."

It is conceivable that there would be another, implausible chain of rules and extractions giving the other result, namely that the soldiers fall: [soldiers fire] ∧ [X fires] → [X fired at] → [X fall], etc. But such a chain would be longer than the one already constructed and would not be preferred.

The most important aspect of this procedure is that it gives a rationale for selecting a preferred interpretation rather than simply rejecting one in favor of another, as other systems do. It can never be right to reject another interpretation irrevocably in cases of this sort, since it may turn out later to be correct, as if the "women" sentence above had been followed by "and after ten minutes hardly a soldier was left standing." After inputting that sentence the relevant preferences in the example might be expected to change. Nonetheless, the present approach is not in any way probabilistic. In the case of someone who utters the "soldiers and women" example sentence, what is to be taken as his meaning is that the women fell. It is of no importance in that decision if it later turns out that he intended to say that the soldiers fell. What was meant by that sentence is a clear, and not merely a likelihood, matter.

It must be emphasized that, in the course of this application, the *common sense* rules are not being interpreted at any point as rules of inference making truth claims about the physical world. It is for this reason that we are not contradicting ourselves in this paper by describing the Preference Semantics approach while arguing implicitly against deductive and theorem proving approaches to language understanding. The clearest way to mark the difference is to see that there is no inconsistency involved in retaining the rule expressed informally as [1 strikes animate2] → [animate2 falls], and at the same time, retaining a description of some situation in which something animate was struck but did not fall or even stagger. There is a clear difference here from any kind of deductive system which, by definition, could not retain such an inconsistent pair of assertions.

The Generation System for French

Translating into French requires the addition to the system of generation patterns called *stereotypes*. Those patterns are attached to English word senses in the dic-

---

[1] The present paper describes the linguistic base, or basic mode, of the system. The extended mode, requiring the rules of partial information and their application to the deep structure of formulas, is described in considerable detail in [15].

tionary, both to key and content words, and are carried into the semantic block for the sentence, or paragraph, by the analysis. The block contains all that is necessary for generation, which is then a task of recursively unwrapping the block in the right way. The generation process is described in considerably more detail in [1].

A content word has a list of stereotypes attached to each of its formulas. When a word sense is selected during analysis, this list is carried along with the formula into the block. Thus, for translation purposes, the block is not constructed simply with formulas but with *sense-pairs*. A sense-pair is: ⟨formula for a content word⟩ ⟨list of stereotypes⟩. We saw in the last section that each key paraplate contains a stereotype, which gets built into the block if the corresponding paraplate has been selected by the *TIE* routines. This stereotype is the generation rule to be used for the current fragment, and possibly for some of the fragments that follow it. The simplest form of a stereotype is a French word or phrase standing for the translation of an English word in context, plus a gender marker for nouns. For example:

private (a soldier):	(MASC simple soldat)
odd (for a number):	(impair)
build:	(construire)
brandy:	(FEMI eau de vie)

Note that, after processing by the analysis routines, all words are already disambiguated. Several stereotypes attached to a formula do not correspond to different senses of the source word but to the different French constructions it can yield.

Complex stereotypes are strings of French words and functions. The functions are of the interlingual context of the sense-pair and always evaluate either to a string of French words, to a blank, or (for content words only) to NIL. Hence such stereotypes are context-sensitive rules, which check upon, and generate from, the sense-pair and its context, possibly including fragments other than the current one. When a function in a content word stereotype evaluates to NIL, then the whole stereotype fails and the next one in the list is tried.

For example, here are the two stereotypes attached to the formula for the ordinary sense of "advise":

(conseiller (PREOB a MAN))
(conseiller)

The first stereotype would be for translating "I advised my children to leave." The analysis routines would have matched the bare template MAN TELL MAN on the words I-advised-children. The function PREOB checks whether the object formula of the template, i.e. the formula for "children" in our example, refers to a human being; if it does, as in this case, the stereotype generates a prepositional group with the French preposition "à," using the object sense-pair and its qualifier list. Here this process yields "à mes enfants," and the value of the whole stereotype is "conseiller à mes

enfants." For the sentence "I advise patience," however, whose translation might be "je conseille la patience," this stereotype would fail, because the object head in the template, brought in by the concept of patience, is STATE. The second is simply "(conseiller)," because no prescription on how to translate the object needs to be attached to "conseiller" when the semantic object goes into a French direct object. This is done automatically by the higher level function which constructs French clauses.

Thus we see that content words have complex stereotypes prescribing the translation of their context, when they govern an "irregular" construction: one that is irregular by comparison to a set of rules matching the French syntax onto the semantic block.

The general form of the generation program is a recursive evaluation of the functions contained in stereotypes. Thus, depending on its context of occurrence, a particular word of the French output sentence may have its origin in stereotypes of different levels: content word stereotype, or key word stereotype (or stereotypes) that are part of a set of top level basic functions. The system is formally equivalent to an augmented transition network in the sense of Woods [17].

Some complexity arises from the fragmented structure of the block and from dealing with the problem of integrating complex (i.e. context-sensitive) stereotypes. The program maintains a cursor which points to the fragment which is being generated from; the purpose of certain functions in a stereotype is to move the cursor up and down the block.

Integration of complex stereotypes in some contexts requires the reordering of the stereotype string. Thus, for "I often advised him to leave" going into "Je lui ai souvent conseille de partir," the stereotype: (conseiller (PREOB a MAN)) needs to be rearranged. This is done by a feature which permits the values of designated functions in a stereotype to be lifted and stored in registers. The values of these registers can be used at a higher level of recursive evaluation to construct a new correct French string.

Finally, the integration of complex stereotypes requires the implementation of a system of priorities for regulating the choice of generation rules. Since any word or key can dictate the output syntax for a given piece of the block, there may arise conflicts, which are resolved by having carefully settled priorities. The principle, as in the analysis program, is that a more specific rule has priority over a more general one. Thus, when a content word stereotype prescribes the translation of fragments other than its immediate context, it has priority over any key stereotype. This important process of a stereotype controlling the generation of other fragments than the one to which it attaches is also described in detail in [1].

Implementation

The system is programmed in LISP 1.6 and MLISP and runs on line on the PDP 6/10 system at Stanford Artificial Intelligence Laboratory where it is the system dump named MT. It runs at present over a vocabulary of about 600 words and takes texts of up to small paragraph length. There is no morphology in the system at present, every input and output word being treated as a separate LISP atom, since morphology presents no substantial research questions to compare with those of semantics. An English sentence is input and a French output, as it might be as follows to show the ambiguities of the preposition "out of":

I PUT THE WINE ON THE TABLE AND JOHN DRINKS IT OUT OF A GLASS. HE OFTEN DRINKS OUT OF DESPAIR AND THROWS THE GLASSES OUT OF THE WINDOW.

JE METS LE VIN SUR LA TABLE ET JEAN LE BOIT DANS UN VERRE. IL BOIT SOUVENT PAR DESESPOIR ET JETTE LES VERRES PAR LA FENETRE.

After this follows the usual cpu time declaration and the line (*common sense inferences called*) if the extended anaphora procedures using partial information are required. After that comes the whole semantic block for diagnostic purposes.

The format of the block is a list, each item of which, at the top level, is a text fragment tied to a template, the template being a list of pairs (of formulas and generation stereotypes) and of sublists of such pairs that are dependents on the main nodes of the template in the manner described above. In the lists at the same level as the text fragments are the key generation stereotypes for fragments, as well as paraplate and inference nodes that declare satisfactory preferred ties.

The block is clearly not wholly target-language independent because it contains the generative rules; however, it is very largely so. Moreover, the semantic representation it expresses could easily be adapted as a data

---

² By the use of nonhierarchical here, I would mean the connected linear structures I have described, each one approximating a notion of nuclear "message."

³ The common sense reasoning exhibited here is of a quite different sort from other programs in linguistics and artificial intelligence, and the only other systems to use "partial information" of this sort are Schank's and Rieger's [8 and 9]. Their systems and this one share far more similarities than differences. The main points of contrast concern: (a) the fact that the Preference Semantics system emphasizes the notion of choice between alternative competing structures for a piece of language; (b) a more general contrast in that the description of this system is weighted more toward the solution of concrete problems and the application of the system to actual text rather than being the description of a static network of concepts; and (c) the clear differences in the notion of "phenomenological level" the other systems employ in describing common sense reasoning: Preference Semantics tries to avoid imposing highly rationalist analyses of cause and mental phenomena that are very hard to justify in terms of common sense—if that is indeed to be the basis for understanding ordinary language.

base for some quite different task, such as question-answering. Indeed, many of the inferences required to set up the block, like those described in detail above, are equivalent to quite sophisticated question-answering.

Discussion

I have presented and argued for a nonstandard approach to the computational semantics of natural language and, by implication, against the more conventional linguistic approaches, as well as those from artificial intelligence that assume that natural language is approximated by restricted micro-worlds of simple object words, and the use of theorem proving methods.

In particular, I think the onus is on those who believe in strictly linguistic approaches to show the psychological and computational importance of the structures they impose with considerable difficulty upon even simple sentences. The present work suggests that a well defined semantic structure is the heart of the matter, that the "semi-parsing" of this system may be sufficient to support such structures, and that the heavily hierarchical syntax analyses of yesteryear may not be necessary.[2,3]

Received March 1973; revised July 1974

References
1. Herskovits, A. The generation of French from a semantic representation. Stanford Artif. Intell. Proj. Memo # 212, Aug. 1973.
2. Joos, M. Semantic Axiom # 1, *Language* (1972), 193–211.
3. McCarthy, J., and Hayes, P. Some philosophical questions from the standpoint of artificial intelligence. In Melzer and Michie (Eds.) *Machine Intelligence 4*, American Elsevier, New York, 1969.
4. Minsky, M. In Minsky (Ed), *Semantic Information Processing*, MIT Press, Cambridge, Mass., 1968.
5. Minsky, M. Frame systems. Unpublished ms., MIT, Feb. 1974.
6. Papert, S. *The Romanes Lectures*. U. of California, Berkeley, 1973.
7. Sandewall, E. Representing natural language information in predicate calculus. In Melzer and Michie (Eds.) *Machine Intelligence 6*, American Elsevier, New York, 1971.
8. Schank, R. Conceptual dependency. *Cognitive Psychology* (1972), 82–123.
9. Schank, R., and Rieger, C. Inference and the computer understanding of natural language. Stanford Artif. Intel. Lab. Memo # 197, May 1973.
10. Scriven, M. The concept of comprehension. In Carroll & Freedle (Eds.), *Language Comprehension*, Washington, D.C., 1972.
11. Simmons, R., and Bruce, B.C. Some relations between predicate calculus and semantic net representations of discourse. Proc. Second Internat. Joint Conf. on Artif. Intel., London, 1971.
12. Wilks, Y. Decidability and natural language. *MIND* (1971), 218–239.
13. Wilks, Y. *Grammar, Meaning and the Machine Analysis of Language*. Routledge & Kegan, London, 1971.
14. Wilks, Y. An artificial intelligence approach to machine translation. In Schank & Colby (Eds.) *Computer Models of Thought and Language*, San Francisco, 1973.
15. Wilks, Y. A preferential, pattern seeking, semantics for natural language inference. To appear in *Artif. Intel.*
16. Winograd, T. *Understanding Natural Language*, Academic Press, New York, 1972.
17. Woods, W.A., Procedural semantics for a question-answer machine, Proc. AFIPS 1968 FJCC Vol. 33, pp. 457–471. AFIPS Press, Montvale, N.J.

Semantics and Quantification in Natural Language Question Answering

W. A. WOODS

Bolt Beranek and Newman Inc.
Cambridge, Massachusetts

1. Introduction

The history of communication between man and machines has followed a path of increasing provision for the convenience and ease of communication on the part of the human. From raw binary and octal numeric machine languages, through various symbolic assembly, scientific, business and higher level languages, programming languages have increasingly adopted notations that are more natural and meaningful to a human user. The important characteristic of this trend is the elevation of the level at which instructions are specified from the low level details of the machine operations to high level descriptions of the task to be done, leaving out details that can be filled in by the computer. The ideal product of such continued evolution would be a system in which the user specifies what he wants done in a language that is so natural that negligible mental effort is required to recast the specification from the form in which he formulates it to that which the machine requires. The logical choice for such a language is the person's own natural language (which in this paper I will assume to be English).

For a naïve, inexperienced user, almost every transaction with current computer systems requires considerable mental effort deciding how to express the request in the machine's language. Moreover, even for technical specialists who deal with a computer constantly, there is a distinction between the things that they do often and remember well, and many other things that require consulting a manual and/or much conscious thought in order to determine the correct machine "incantation" to achieve the desired effect. Thus, whether a user is experienced or naïve, and whether he is a frequent or occasional user, there arise occasions where he knows what he wants the machine to do and can express it in natural language, but does not know exactly how to express it to the machine. A facility for machine understanding of natural language could greatly improve the efficiency of expression in such situations—both in speed and convenience, and in decreased likelihood of error.

For a number of years, I have been pursuing a long range research objective of making such communication possible between a man and a machine. During this period, my colleagues and I[1] have constructed several natural language question-answering systems and developed a few techniques for solving some of the problems that arise. In this paper, I will present some of those techniques, focusing on the problem of handling natural quantification as it occurs in English. As an organizing principle, I will present the ideas in a roughly historical order, with commentary on the factors leading to the selection of various notations and algorithms, on limitations that have been discovered as a result of experience, and on directions in which solutions lie.

Among the systems that I will use for examples are a flight schedules question-answering system (Woods, 1967, 1968), a system to ask questions about an augmented transition network (ATN) grammar (not previously published), the LUNAR system, which answers questions about the chemical analyses of the Apollo 11 moon rocks (Woods et al., 1972; Woods, 1973b), and a system for natural language trip planning and budget management (Woods et al., 1976).

Some of the techniques used in these systems, especially the use of the ATN grammar formalism (Woods, 1969, 1970, 1973a), have become widely known and are now being used in many different systems and applications. However, other details, including the method of performing semantic interpretation, the treatment of quantification and anaphoric

reference, and several other problems, have not been adequately described in accessible publications.

This paper is intended to be a discussion of a set of techniques, the problems they solve, and the relative advantages and disadvantages of several alternative approaches. Because of the length of the presentation, no attempt has been made to survey the field or give an exhaustive comparison of these techniques to those of other researchers. In general, most other systems are not sufficiently formalized at a conceptual level that such comparisons can be made on the basis of published information. In some cases, the mechanisms described here can be taken as models of what is being done in other systems. Certainly, the general notion of computing a representation of the meaning of a phrase from representations of the meanings of its constituents by means of a rule is sufficiently general to model virtually any semantic interpretation process. The details of how most systems handle such problems as the nesting of multiple quantification, however, are difficult to fathom. Hopefully the presentation here and the associated discussion will enable the reader to evaluate for himself, with some degree of discrimination, the capabilities of other systems.

2. Historical Context

2.1 Airlines Flight Schedules

Airlines flight schedules was the focusing context for a gedanken system for semantic interpretation that I developed as my Ph.D. thesis at Harvard University (Woods, 1967). In that thesis, I was concerned with the problem of "semantic interpretation"—making the transition from a syntactic analysis of input questions (such as could be produced by parsing with a formal grammar of English) to a concrete specification of what the computer was to do to answer the question. Prior to that time, this problem had usually been attacked by developing a set of structural conventions for storing answers in the data base and transforming the input questions (frequently by ad hoc procedures) into patterns that could be matched against that data base. Simmons (1965) presents a survey of the state of the art of the field at that time.

In many of the approaches existing at that time, the entire process of semantic interpretation was built on particular assumptions about the structure of the data base. I was searching for a method of semantic interpretation that would be independent of particular assumptions about data base structure and, in particular, would permit a single language

---

[1] Principal contributors to one or more of the systems described here include Madeleine Bates, Bertram Bruce, Ronald Kaplan, and Bonnie Nash-Webber (now Webber).

2.2 Answering Questions about ATN Grammars

To prove the point that the semantic interpretation system used in the flight schedules domain was in fact general for arbitrary data bases and independent of the detailed structure of the data base, immediately after completing that system, I looked for another data base to which I could apply the method. I wanted a data base that had not been designed to satisfy any assumptions about the method of question interpretation to be used. The most convenient such data base that I had at hand was the data structure for the ATN grammar that was being used by the system to parse its input sentences. This data base had a structure that was intended to support the parser, and had not been designed with any forethought to using it as a data base for question answering.

An ATN grammar, viewed as a data base, conceptually consists of a set of named states with arcs connecting them, corresponding to transitions that can be made in the course of parsing. Arcs connecting states are of several kinds depending on what, if anything, they consume from the input string when they are used to make a transition. For example, a word arc consumes a single word from the input, a push arc consumes a constituent phrase of the type pushed for, and a jump arc consumes no input but merely makes a state transition (see Woods, 1970, 1973a, 1975a, for further discussion of ATN grammars). These states and arcs constitute the data base entities about which questions may be asked.

In addition to the entities that actually exist as data objects in the internal structure for the grammar, there are some other important objects that exist conceptually but are not explicit in the grammar. The most important such entity is a path. A path is a sequence of arcs that connect to each other in the order in which they could be taken in the parsing of a sentence. Although paths are implicit in the grammar, they are not explicit in the data structure, i.e., there is no internal data object that can be pointed to in the grammar that corresponds to a path. Nevertheless, one should be able to talk about paths and ask questions about them. The techniques I will describe can handle such entities.

Examples of the kinds of sentences about this "grammar information system" could deal with are

"Is there a jump arc from state S/ to S/NP?"
"How many arcs leave state NP/?"
"How many nonlooping paths connect state S/ with S/POP?"
"Show me all arcs entering state S/VP."

2.3 The LUNAR System

The LUNAR system (Woods *et al.*, 1972; Woods, 1973b) was originally developed with support from the NASA Manned Spacecraft Center as a

understanding system to talk to many different data bases and permit the specification of requests whose answers required the integration of information from several different data bases. In searching for such an approach, I looked more to the philosophy of language and the study of meaning than to data structures and data base design.

The method I developed was essentially an interpretation of Carnap's notion of truth conditions (Carnap, 1964a). I chose to represent those truth conditions by formal procedures that could be executed by a machine. The representation that I used for expressing meanings was at once a notational variant of the standard predicate calculus notation and also a representation of an executable procedure. The ultimate definition of the meanings of expressions in this notation were the procedures that they would execute to determine the truth of propositions, compute the answers to questions, and carry out commands. This notion, which I referred to as "procedural semantics," picks up the chain of semantic specification from the philosophers at the level of abstract truth conditions, and carries it to a formal specification of those truth conditions as procedures in a computer language.

The idea of procedural semantics has since had considerable success as an engineering technique for constructing natural language understanding systems, and has also developed somewhat as a theory of meaning. In my paper "Meaning and Machines" (Woods, 1973c), I discuss some of the more theoretical issues of the adequacy of procedural semantics as a theory of meaning.

The flight schedules application initially served to focus the issues on particular meanings of particular sentences. The application assumed a data base essentially the same as the information contained in the Official Airline Guide (OAG, 1966)—that is, a list of flights, their departure and arrival times from different airports, their flight numbers and airlines, number of stops, whether they serve meals, etc. Specific questions were interpreted as requesting operations to be performed on the tables that make up this data base to compute answers.

The semantic interpretation system presented in my thesis was subsequently implemented for this application with an ATN grammar of English to provide syntax trees for interpretation, but without an actual data base. The system produced formal semantic interpretations for questions such as:

"What flights go from Boston to Washington?"
"Is there a flight to Washington before 8:00 A.M.?"
"Do they serve lunch on the 11:00 A.M. flight to Toronto?"

research prototype for a system to enable a lunar geologist to conveniently access, compare, and evaluate the chemical analysis data on lunar rock and soil composition that was accumulating as a result of the Apollo moon missions. The target of the research was to develop a natural language understanding facility sufficiently natural and complete that the task of selecting the wording for a request would require negligible effort for the geologist user.

The application envisaged was a system that would be accessible to geologists anywhere in the country by teletype connections and would enable them to access the NASA data base without having to learn either the programming language in which the system was implemented or the formats and conventions of the data base representations. For example, the geologist should be able to ask questions such as "What is the average concentration of aluminum in high-alkali rocks?" without having to know that aluminum was conventionally represented in the data base as AL2O3, that the high-alkali rocks (also known as "volcanics" or "fine-grained igneous") were conventionally referred to as TYPEAS in the data base, nor any details such as the name of the file on which the data was stored, the names of the fields in the data records, or any of a myriad of other details normally required to use a data base system.

To a substantial extent, such a capability was developed, although never fully put to the test of real operational use. In a demonstration of a preliminary version of the system in 1971 (Woods, 1973b), 78% of the questions asked of the system were understood and answered correctly, and another 12% failed due to trivial clerical errors such as dictionary coding errors in the not fully debugged system. Only 10% of the questions failed because of significant parsing or semantic interpretation problems. Although the requests entered into the system were restricted to questions that were in fact about the contents of the data base, and comparatives (which were not handled at that time) were excluded, the requests were otherwise freely expressed in natural English without any prior instructions as to phrasing and were typed into the system exactly as they were asked.

The LUNAR system allowed a user to ask questions, compute averages and ratios, and make listings of selected subsets of the data. One could also retrieve references from a keyphrase index and make changes to the data base. The system permitted the user to easily compare the measurements of different researchers, compare the concentrations of elements or isotopes in different types of samples or in different phases of a sample, compute averages over various classes of samples, compute ratios of two constituents of a sample, etc., all in straightforward natural English.

Examples of requests understood by the system are

"Give me all lunar samples with magnetite."
"In which samples has apatite been identified?"
"What is the specific activity of Al26 in soil?"
"Analyses of strontium in plagioclase."
"What are the plag analyses for breccias?"
"What is the average concentration of olivine in breccias?"
"What is the average age of the basalts?"
"What is the average potassium/rubidium ratio in basalts?"
"In which breccias is the average concentration of titanium greater than 6 percent?"

2.4 TRIPSYS

TRIPSYS is a system that was developed as the context for a research project in continuous speech understanding (Woods et al., 1976). The overall system of which it was a part was called HWIM (for "Hear What I Mean"). TRIPSYS understands and answers questions about planned and taken trips, travel budgets and their status, costs of various modes of transportation to various places, per diems in various places, conferences and other events for which trips might be taken, people in an organization, the contracts they work on, the travel budgets of those contracts, and a variety of other information that is useful for planning trips and managing travel budgets. It is intended to be a small-scale example of a general management problem. TRIPSYS also permits some natural language entry of information into the data base, and knows how to prompt the user for additional information that was not given voluntarily. Examples of the kinds of requests that TRIPSYS was designed to handle are

"Plan a trip for two people to San Diego to attend the ASA meeting."
"Estimate the cost of that trip."
"Is there any money left in the Speech budget?"

3. Overview

Since the LUNAR system is the most fully developed and most widely known of the above systems, I will use it as the principal focus throughout this paper. A brief overview of the LUNAR system was presented in the 1973 National Computer Conference (Woods, 1973b), and an extensive technical report documenting the system was produced (Woods et al., 1972). However, there has been no generally available document that gives a sufficiently complete picture of the capabilities of the system and how it works. Consequently, I will first give a brief introduction to the structure of the system as a whole, and then proceed to relatively detailed accounts of some of the interpretation problems that were solved. Examples from the other three systems will be used where they are more self-explanatory or more clearly illustrate a principle. Where the other systems differ in structure from the LUNAR system, that will be pointed out.

3.1 Structure of the LUNAR System

The LUNAR system consists of three principal components: a general purpose grammar and parser for a large subset of natural English, a rule-driven semantic interpretation component using pattern → action rules for transforming a syntactic representation of an input sentence into a representation of what it means, and a data base retrieval and inference component that stores and manipulates the data base and performs computations on it. The first two components constitute a language understanding component that transforms an input English sentence into a disposable program for carrying out its intent (answering a question or making some change to the data base). The third component executes such programs against the data base to determine the answer to queries and to effect changes in the data base.

The system contains a dictionary of approximately 3500 words, a grammar for a fairly extensive subset of natural English, and two data bases: a table of chemical analyses with 13,000 entries, and a topic index to documents with approximately 10,000 postings. The system also contains facilities for morphological analysis of regularly inflected words, for maintaining a discourse directory of possible antecedents for pronouns and other anaphoric expressions, and for determining how much and what information to display in response to a request.

The grammar used by the parsing component of the system is an augmented transition network (ATN). The ATN grammar model has been relatively well documented elsewhere (Woods, 1970, 1973a), so I will not go into detail here describing it, except to point out that if produces syntactic tree structures comparable to the "deep structures" assigned by a Chomsky type transformational grammar, vintage 1965 (Chomsky, 1965). Likewise, I will not go into much detail describing the inner workings of the data base inference and retrieval component, except to describe the semantics of the formal meaning representation language and discuss some of its advantages. What I will describe here are the problems of semantic interpretation that were handled by the system.

All of the systems mentioned in Section 2 share this same basic structure with the following exceptions:

1) The airline flight schedules problem was implemented up through the parsing and interpretation stage, but was never coupled to a real data base. This system was implemented solely to validate the formal semantic interpretation procedure.

2) The TRIPSYS system does not construct a separate syntactic tree structure to be given to a semantic interpreter, but rather the ATN grammar builds semantic interpretations directly as its output representation.

3.2 Semantics in LUNAR

A semantic specification of a natural language consists of essentially three parts:

a) a meaning representation language (MRL)—a notation for semantic representation for the meanings of sentences,

b) a specification of the semantics of the MRL notation, i.e., a specification of what its expressions mean, and

c) a semantic interpretation procedure, i.e., a procedure to construct the appropriate semantic representations for a given natural language sentence.

Accordingly, the semantic framework of the LUNAR system consists of three parts: a semantic notation in which to represent the meanings of sentences, a specification of the semantics of this notation (by means of formal procedures), and a procedure for assigning representations in the notation to input sentences.

In previous writings on LUNAR, I have referred to the semantic notation as a query language, but I will refer to it here, following a currently more popular terminology as a "meaning representation language" or MRL. To represent expressions in the MRL, I will use the so-called "Cambridge Polish" notation in wich the application of an operator to its arguments is represented with the operator preceding its operands and the entire group surrounded by parentheses. This notation places the operator in a standard position independent of the number of arguments it takes and uses the parentheses to indicate scoping of operators rather than depending on a fixed degree of the operator as in the "ordinary" Polish prefix notation (thus facilitating operators that take a variable number of arguments). Cambridge Polish notation is the notation used for the S-expressions of the programming language LISP (Bobrow et al., 1968), in which LUNAR is implemented.

Occasionally, the notations used for illustration will be slightly simplified from the form actually used in LUNAR to avoid confusion. For example, the DATALINE function used in LUNAR actually takes an additional argument for a data file that is omitted here.

4. The Meaning Representation Language

There are a number of requirements for a meaning representation language, but the most important ones are these:

a) It must be capable of representing precisely, formally, and unambiguously any interpretation that a human reader can place on a sentence.
b) It should facilitate an algorithmic translation from English sentences into their corresponding semantic representations.
c) It should facilitate subsequent intelligent processing of the resulting interpretation.

The LUNAR MRL consists of an extended notational variant of the ordinary predicate calculus notation and contains essentially three kinds of constructions:

- designators, which name or denote objects (or classes of objects) in the database,
- propositions, which correspond to statements that can be either true or false in the data base, and
- commands, which initiate and carry out actions.

4.1 Designators

Designators come in two varieties—individual specifiers and class specifiers. Individual specifiers correspond to proper nouns and variables. For example, S10046 is a designator for a particular sample, OLIV is a designator for a certain mineral (olivine), and X3 can be a variable denoting any type of object in the data base. Class specifiers are used to denote classes of individuals over which quantification can range. They consist of the name of an enumeration function for the class plus possible arguments. For example, (SEQ TYPECS) is a specification of the class of type C rocks (i.e., breccias) and (DATALINE S10046 OVERALL OLIV) is a specification of the set of lines of a table of chemical analyses corresponding to analyses of sample S10046 for the overall concentration of olivine.

4.2 Propositions

Elementary propositions in the MRL are formed from predicates with designators as arguments. Complex propositions are formed from these by use of the logical connectives AND, OR, and NOT and by quantification. For example, (CONTAIN S10046 OLIV) is a proposition formed by substituting designators as arguments to the predicate CONTAIN, and

(AND (CONTAIN X3 OLIV) (NOT (CONTAIN X3 PLAG)))

is a complex proposition corresponding to the assertion that X3 contains olivine but does not contain plagioclase.

4.3 Commands

Elementary commands consist of the name of a command operator plus arguments. As for propositions, complex commands can be constructed using logical connectives and quantification. For example, TEST is a command operator for testing the truth value of a proposition given as its argument. Thus

(TEST (CONTAIN S10046 OLIV))

will answer yes or no depending on whether sample S10046 contains olivine. Similarly, PRINTOUT is a command operator which prints out a representation for a designator given as its argument.

4.4 Quantification

An important aspect of the meaning of English sentences that must be captured in any MRL is the use of quantifiers such as "every" and "some." Quantification in the LUNAR MRL is represented in an elaborated version of the traditional predicate calculus notation. An example of an expression in this notation is

(FOR EVERY X1 / (SEQ SAMPLES) :
    (CONTAIN X1 OVERALL SILICON) ; (PRINTOUT X1)).

This says, "for every object X1 in the set of samples such that X1 contains silicon, print out (the name of) X1."

In general, an instance of a quantified expression takes the form

(FOR ⟨quant⟩ X / ⟨class⟩ : (p X) ; (q X))

where ⟨quant⟩ is a specific quantifier such as EVERY or SOME, X is the variable of quantification and occurs open in the expressions (p X)

sions that it can take as arguments in order to be meaningful. Each operator also specifies which of its arguments it takes literally as given, and which it will evaluate to obtain a referent (see discussion of opaque contexts below).

Predicates, functions, class names, class functions, command operators, and individual constants are all domain-dependent entities which are to be specified for a particular application domain and defined in terms of procedures. In LUNAR, they are defined as LISP subroutines. Individual constants are defined by procedures for producing a reference pointer to the appropriate internal object in the computer's model of the world; functions are defined by procedures for producing a reference pointer to the appropriate value given the values for the arguments; class names and class functions are defined by procedures that (given the appropriate values for arguments) can enumerate the members of their class one at a time; predicates are defined by procedures which, given the values of their arguments, determine a truth value for the corresponding proposition; and command operators are defined by procedures which, given the values of their arguments, can carry out the corresponding commands.

I should point out that the defintion given here for classes and commands are not adequate for a general theory of semantics, but are rather more pragmatic definitions that facilitate question answering and computer response to commands. For a general semantic theory, the requirement for semantic definition of a class is merely a procedure for recognizing a member, and the semantic definition for a command is a procedure for recognizing when it has been carried out. That is, to be said to know the meaning of a command does not require the ability to carry it out, and to know the meaning of a noun does not require an ability to enumerate all members of its extension. The distinction between knowing how, and just knowing whether, marks the difference between pragmatic utility and mere semantic adequacy. The requirements placed on the definitions of the classes and commands in the LUNAR system are thus more stringent than those required for semantic definition alone.

4.6 Procedural/Declarative Duality

The meaning representation language used in LUNAR is intended to serve both as a procedural specification that can be executed to compute an answer or carry out a command, and as a "declarative" representation that can be manipulated as a symbolic object by a theorem prover or other inference system. By virtue of the definition of primitive functions and predicates as LISP functions, the language can be viewed simulta-

and (q X), ⟨class⟩ is a set over which quantification is to range, (p X) is a proposition that restricts the range, and (q X) is the expression being quantified (which may be either a proposition or a command).

For the sake of simplifying some examples, I will generalize the format of the quantification operator so that the restriction operation implied by the ":" can be repeated any number of times (including zero if there is no further restriction on the range), giving rise to forms such as

(FOR ⟨quant⟩ X / ⟨class⟩ ; (q X))

and

(FOR ⟨quant⟩ X / ⟨class⟩ : (p X) : (r X) ; (q X)) .

When there is no restriction on the range of quantification, this can also be indicated by using the universally true proposition T, as in

(FOR ⟨quant⟩ X / ⟨class⟩ : T ; (q X)).

4.5 Specification of the MRL Syntax

A formal BNF specification of the LUNAR MRL is given here:

```
⟨expression⟩ = ⟨designator⟩ | ⟨proposition⟩ | ⟨command⟩
⟨designator⟩ = ⟨individual constant⟩ |
               ⟨variable⟩ |
               (⟨function⟩ ⟨expression⟩* )
⟨proposition⟩ = ⟨elementary proposition⟩ |
               ⟨quantified proposition⟩
⟨elementary proposition⟩ = (⟨propositional operator⟩
               ⟨expression⟩* )
⟨propositional operator⟩ = ⟨predicate⟩ | ⟨logical operator⟩
⟨logical operator⟩ = AND | OR | NOT | IF-THEN . . .
⟨quantified proposition⟩ = (FOR ⟨variable⟩ / ⟨class⟩ ;
               ⟨proposition⟩)
⟨class⟩ = ⟨elementary class⟩ | ⟨restricted class⟩
⟨elementary class⟩ = ⟨class name⟩ |
               (⟨class function⟩ ⟨expression⟩* )
⟨restricted class⟩ = ⟨class⟩ : ⟨proposition⟩
⟨command⟩ = ⟨elementary command⟩ | ⟨quantified command⟩
⟨elementary command⟩ = (⟨command operator⟩ ⟨expression⟩* )
⟨quantified command⟩ = (FOR ⟨variable⟩ / ⟨class⟩ ; ⟨class⟩ ; ⟨command⟩)
```

In addition to the above BNF constraints, each general operator (i.e., function, predicate, logical operator, class function, or command operator) will have particular restrictions on the number and kinds of expres-

neously as a higher level programming language and as an extension of the predicate calculus. This gives rise to two different possible types of inference for answering questions, corresponding roughly to Carnap's distinction between *intension* and *extension* (Carnap, 1964b). First, because of its definition by means of procedures, a question such as "Does every sample contain silicon?" can be answered *extensionally* (that is, by appeal to the individuals denoted by the class name "samples") by enumerating the individual samples and checking whether silicon has been found in each one. On the other hand, this same question could have been answered *intensionally* (that is, by consideration of its meaning alone without reference to the individuals denoted) by means of the application of inference rules to other (intensional) facts (such as the assertion "Every sample contains some amount of each element"). Thus the expressions in the meaning representation language are capable either of direct execution against the data base (extensional mode) or manipulation by mechanical inference algorithms (intensional mode).

In the LUNAR system, the principal mode of inference is extensional, that is, the direct evaluation of the formal MRL expression as a procedure. However, in certain circumstances, this expression is also manipulated as a symbolic object. Such cases include the construction of descriptions for discourse entities to serve as antecedents for anaphoric expressions and the use of "smart quantifiers" (to be discussed later) for performing more efficient quantification. Extensional inference has a variety of limitations (e.g., it is not possible to prove assertions about infinite sets in extensional mode), but it is a very efficient method for a variety of question-answering applications.

4.7 Opaque Contexts

As mentioned above, the general operators in the meaning representation language are capable of accessing the arguments they are given either literally or after evaluation. Thus, an operator such as ABOUT in an expression like

(ABOUT D70-181 (TRITIUM PRODUCTION))

(meaning "Document D70-181 discusses tritium production") can indicate as part of its definition that, in determining the truth of an assertion, the first argument (D70-181 in this case) is to be evaluated to determine its referent, while the second argument (TRITIUM PRODUCTION) is to be taken unevaluated as an input to the procedure (to be used in some special way as an intensional object—in this case, as a specification of a topic that D70-181 discusses).

This distinction between two types of argument passing is a relatively standard one in some programming languages, frequently referred to as call by value versus call by name. In particular, in the programming language LISP, there are two types of functions (referred to as LAMBDA and NLAMBDA functions), the first of which evaluates all of its arguments and the second of which passes all of its arguments unevaluated to the function (which then specifies in its body which arguments are to be evaluated and what to do with the others).

This ability to pass subordinate expressions literally as intensional objects (to be manipulated in unspecified ways by the operator that gets them) avoids several of the antinomies that have troubled philosophers, such as the nonequivalence of alternative descriptions of the same object in belief contexts. Although belief contexts do not occur in LUNAR, similar problems occur in TRIPSYS, for example, in interpreting the object of the verb "create," where the argument to the verb is essentially a description of a desired object, not an object denoted by the description.

In LUNAR, functions with opaque contexts are also used to define the basic quantification function FOR as well as general purpose counting, averaging, and extremal functions: NUMBER, AVERAGE, MAXIMUM, and MINIMUM. Calls to these functions take the forms:

(NUMBER X / ⟨class⟩ : (P X))

"The number of X's in ⟨class⟩ for which (P X) is true."

(AVERAGE X / ⟨class⟩ : (P X) : (F X))

"The average of the values of (F X) over the X's in ⟨class⟩ for which (P X) is true."

(AVERAGE X / ⟨class⟩ : (P X))

"The average value of X (a number) over the X's in ⟨class⟩ for which (P X) is true."

(MAXIMUM X / ⟨class⟩ : (P X))

"The maximum value of X in the set of X's in ⟨class⟩ for which (P X) is true."

(MINIMUM X / ⟨class⟩ : (P X))

"The minimum value of X in the set of X's in ⟨class⟩ for which (P X) is true."

The proposition (P X) in each of these cases has to be taken as an intensional entity rather than a referring expression, since it must be repeatedly evaluated for different values of X.

Opaque context functions are also defined for forming the intensional descriptions of sets and the intensional union of intensionally defined sets:

(SETOF X / ⟨class⟩ : (P X))

"The set of X's in ⟨class⟩ for which (P X) is true."

(UNION X / ⟨class⟩ : (P X) ; (⟨setfn⟩ X))

"The union over the X's in ⟨class⟩ for which (P X) is true of the sets generated by ((setfn) X)."

4.8 Restricted Class Quantification

One of the major features of the quantifiers in the LUNAR MRL is the separation of the quantified expression into distinct structural parts: (1) the basic class over which quantification is to range, (2) a set of restrictions on that class, and (3) the main expression being quantified. There are a number of advantages of maintaining these distinctions, one of which is the uniformity of the interpretation procedure over different kinds of noun phrase determiners that it permits. For example, the determiners "some" and "every", when translated into the more customary logical representations, give different main connectives for the expression being quantified. That is, "every man is mortal" becomes (Ax)Man(x)⇒Mortal(x) while "some man is mortal" becomes (Ex)Man(x)&Mortal(x). With the LUNAR format, the choice of determiner affects only the choice of quantifier.

Other advantages to this kind of quantifier are the facilitation of certain kinds of optimization operations on the MRL expressions, and the generation of appropriate antecedents for various anaphoric expressions. Recently, Nash-Webber and Reiter (1977) have pointed out the necessity of making a distinction between the quantification class and the predicated expression if an MRL is to be adequate for handling verb phrase ellipsis and "one"-anaphora.

4.9 Nonstandard Quantifiers

Another advantage of the restricted class quantifier notation is the uniform treatment of a variety of nonstandard quantifiers. For example, LUNAR treats the determiner "the" in a singular noun phrase as a quantifier, selecting the unique object that satisfies its restriction (and complaining if the presupposition that there is a unique such object is not satisfied). This differs from the traditional representation of definite description by means of the iota operator, which constructs a complex designator for a constituent rather than a governing quantifier. In the traditional notation, the sentence "The man I see is mortal," would be represented something like

MORTAL(i(x) : MAN(x) & SEE(I,x)).

In the LUNAR MRL it would be

(FOR THE X / MAN : (SEE I X) : (MORTAL X)).

Quantifiers such as "many" and "most," whose meaning requires knowledge of the size of the class over which quantification ranges (as well as the size of the class for which the quantified proposition is true) can be adequately handled by this notation since the range of quantification is specifically mentioned. These quantifiers were not implemented in LUNAR, however.

Among the nonstandard quantifiers handled by LUNAR are numerical determiners (both cardinal and ordinal) and comparative determiners. Ordinal quantifiers ("the third X such that P") are handled by a special quantifier (ORDINAL n) that can be used in the ⟨quant⟩ slot of the quantifier form. In general this ordinal quantifier should take another parameter that names the ordering function to be used, or at least require a preferred ordering function to be implied by context. The ordering of the members of the class used by LUNAR is the order of their enumeration by the enumeration function that defines the class (see Section 5.2).

Numerical quantification and comparative quantification are handled with a general facility for applying numeric predicates to a parameter N in the FOR function that counts the number of successful members of the range of quantification that have been found. Examples are (GREATER N ⟨number⟩), (EQUAL N ⟨number⟩), or even (PRIME N) (i.e., N is a prime number).

The interpretation of general numeric predicates as quantifiers is that if any number N satisfying the predicate can be found such that N members of the restricted class satisfy the quantified proposition (or successfully complete a quantified command), then the quantified proposition is true (or a quantified command is considered completed). In the implementation, the current value of N is tested as each successful member of the restricted class is found, until either the count N satisfies the numeric predicate or there are no more members in the class.

The numeric predicate quantifier can be used directly to handle comparative determiners such as "at least" and "more than," and can be used in a negated quantification to handle "at most" and "fewer than." The procedure for testing such quantifiers can return a value as soon as a sufficient number of the class have been found, without necessarily determining the exact number of successful members. The numerical determiner "exactly ⟨n⟩" is handled in LUNAR by the generalized counting function NUMBER embedded in an equality statement. (It could also be handled by a conjunction of "at least" and "not more than," but that would not execute as efficiently.)

The LUNAR MRL also permits a generic quantifier GEN, which is assigned to noun phrases with plural inflection and no determiner. Such noun phrases sometimes behave like universal quantification and sometimes like existential quantification. In LUNAR, unless some higher operator indicates that it should be interpreted otherwise, a generic quantifier is evaluated exactly like EVERY.

Examples of types of quantification in LUNAR are

    (FOR EVERY X / CLASS : (P X) ; (Q X))

"Every X in CLASS that satisfies P also satisfies Q."

    (FOR SOME X / CLASS : (P X) ; (Q X))

"Some X in CLASS that satisfies P also satisfies Q."

    (FOR GEN X / CLASS : (P X) ; (Q X))

"A generic X in CLASS that satisfies P, will also satisfy Q."

    (FOR THE X / CLASS : (P X) ; (Q X))

"The single X in CLASS that satisfies P also satisfies Q."

    (FOR (ORDINAL 3) X / CLASS : (P X) ; (Q X))

"The third X in CLASS that satisfies P also satisfies Q."

    (FOR (GREATER N 3) X / CLASS : (P X) ; (Q X))

"More than 3 X's in CLASS that satisfy P also satisfy Q."

    (FOR (EQUAL N 3) X / CLASS : (P X) ; (Q X))

"At least 3 X's in CLASS that satisfy P also satisfy Q."

    (NOT (FOR (EQUAL N 3) X / CLASS : (P X) : (Q X)))

"Fewer than 3 X's in CLASS satisfy P and also satisfy Q."

    (EQUAL 3 (NUMBER X / CLASS : (P X) : (Q X)))

"Exactly 3 X's in CLASS satisfy P and also satisfy Q."

4.10 Functions and Classes

Another of the attractive features of the LUNAR MRL is the way that quantification over classes, single and multiple valued functions, and the attachment of restrictive modifiers are all handled uniformly, both individually and in combination, by the quantification operators. Specifically, a noun phrase consisting of a function applied to arguments is represented in the same way as a noun phrase whose head is a class over which quantification is to range. For example "The departure time of flight 557 is 3:00" can be represented as

(FOR THE X / (DEPARTURE-TIME FLIGHT-557) : T ;
    (EQUAL X 3:00))

(where T is the universally true proposition, signifying here that there are no further restrictions on the range of quantification). This permits exactly the same mechanisms for handling the various determiners and modifiers to apply to both functionally determined objects and quantification over classes.

This uniformity of treatment becomes especially significant when the function is not single valued and when the class of values is being quantified over or restricted by additional modifiers as in

(FOR EVERY X / (DATALINE S10046 OVERALL SIO2) :
    T : (PRINTOUT X))

and

(FOR THE X / (DATALINE S10046 OVERALL SIO2) :
    (REF* X D70-181) ; (PRINTOUT X))

where (DATALINE ⟨sample⟩ ⟨phase⟩ ⟨constituent⟩) is the function used in LUNAR to enumerate measurements in its chemical analysis table and (REF* ⟨table entry⟩ ⟨document⟩) is a relation between a measurement and the journal article it was reported in.

4.11 Unanticipated Requests

The structure of the meaning representation language, when coupled with general techniques for semantic interpretation, enable the user to make very explicit requests with a wide range of diversity within a natural framework. As a consequence of the modular composition of MRL expressions, it is possible for the user to combine the basic predicates and functions of the retrieval component in ways that were not specifically anticipated by the system designer. For example, one can make requests such as "List the minerals", "What are the major elements?",

''How many minerals are there?'', etc. Although these questions might not be sufficiently useful to merit special effort to handle them, they fall out of the mechanism for semantic interpretation in a natural way with no additional effort required. If the system knows how to enumerate the possible samples for one purpose, it can do so for other purposes as well. Furthermore, anything that the system can enumerate, it can count. Thus, the decomposition of the retrieval operations into basic units of quantifications, predicates, and functions provides a very flexible and powerful facility for expressing requests.

5. The Semantics of the Notation

5.1 Procedural Semantics

As mentioned before, the semantic specification of a natural language requires not only a semantic notation for representing the meanings of sentences, but also a specification of the semantics of the notation. As discussed previously, this is done in LUNAR by relating the notation to procedures that can be executed. For each of the predicate names that can be used in specifying semantic representations, LUNAR requires a procedure or subroutine that will determine the truth of the predicate for given values of its arguments. Similarly, for each of the functions that can be used, there must be a procedure that computes the value of that function for given values of its arguments. Likewise, each of the class specifiers for the FOR function requires a subroutine that enumerates the members of the class.

The FOR function itself is also defined by a subroutine, as are the logical operators AND, OR, and NOT, the general counting and averaging functions NUMBER and AVERAGE, and the basic command functions TEST and PRINTOUT. Thus any well-formed expression in the language is a composition of functions that have procedural definitions in the retrieval component and are therefore themselves well-defined procedures capable of execution on the data base. In the LUNAR system, the definition of all of these procedures is done in LISP, and the notation of the meaning representation language is so chosen that its expressions are executable LISP programs. These function definitions and the data base on which they operate constitute the retrieval component of the system.

5.2 Enumeration Functions

One of the engineering features of the LUNAR retrieval component that makes the quantification operators both efficient and versatile is the definition of quantification classes by means of enumeration functions. These are functions that compute one member of the class at a time and can be called repeatedly to obtain successive members. Enumeration functions take an enumeration index argument which is used as a restart pointer to keep track of the state of the enumeration. Whenever FOR calls an enumeration function to obtain a member of a class, it gives it an enumeration index (initially T), and each time the enumeration function returns a value, it also returns a new value of the index to be used as a restart pointer to get the next member. This pointer is frequently an inherent part of the computation and involves negligible overhead to construct. For example, in enumerating integers, the previous integer suffices, while in enumerating members of an existing list, the pointer to the rest of the list already exists.

The enumeration function formulation of the classes used in quantification frees the FOR function from explicit dependence on the structure of the data base; the values returned by the enumeration function may be searched for in tables, computed dynamically, or merely successively accessed from a precomputed list. Enumeration functions also enable the quantifiers to operate on potentially infinite classes and on classes of objects that do not necessarily exist prior to the decision of the quantifier to enumerate them. For example, in an expression such as

(FOR SOME X / INTEGER : (LESSP X 10) ; (PRIME X))

(''some integer less than 10 is a prime''), a general enumeration procedure for integers can be used to construct successive integers by addition, without having to assume that all the integers of interest exist in the computer's memory ahead of time. Thus, the treatment of this kind of quantification fits naturally within LUNAR's general quantification mechanism without having to be treated as a special case.

In the grammar information system application, an enumeration function for paths computes representations for paths through the grammar, so that paths can be talked about even though there are no explicit entities in the internal grammar representation that correspond to paths. (See the discussion on ''smart'' quantifiers below for a further discussion of the problems of quantifying over such entities.)

An enumeration function can indicate termination of the class in one of two ways: either by returning NIL, indicating that there are no more members, or by returning a value with a NIL restart pointer, indicating that the current value is the last one. This latter can save one extra call to the enumeration function if the information is available at the time the last value is returned (e.g., for single valued functions). This avoids what would otherwise be an inefficiency in treating multiple- and single-valued functions the same way.

In LUNAR, a general purpose enumeration function SEQ can be used to enumerate any precomputed list, and a similar function SEQL can be used to enumerate singletons. For example,

(FOR EVERY X1 / (SEQ TYPECS) : T ; (PRINTOUT X1))

is an expression that will printout the sample numbers for all of the samples that are type C rocks.

Functionally determined objects and classes, as well as fixed classes, are implemented as enumeration functions, taking an enumeration index as well as their other arguments and computing successive members of their class one at a time. In particular, intensional operators such as AVERAGE, NUMBER, SETOF, and UNION are defined as enumeration functions and also use enumeration functions for their class arguments. Thus quantification over classes, computation of single-valued functions, and quantification over the values of multiple-valued functions are all handled uniformly, without special distinctions having to be made.

5.3 Quantified Commands

As mentioned earlier, both propositions and commands can be quantified. Thus one can issue commands such as

(FOR (EQ N 5) X / SAMPLES : (CONTAIN X SIO2) ; (PRINTOUT X))

("Print out five samples that contain silicon"). The basic commands in such expressions are to be iterated according to the specifications of the quantifier. However, it is possible for such commands to fail due to a violation of presuppositions or of necessary conditons. For example, in the above case, there might not be as many as five samples that contain silicon. In order for the system to be aware of such cases, each command in the system is defined to return a value that is non-null if the command has been successfully executed and NIL otherwise. Given this convention, the FOR operator will automatically return T if such an iterated command has been successfully completed and NIL otherwise.

There are other variations of this technique that could be useful but were not implemented in LUNAR, such as returning comments when a command failed indicating the kind of failure. In LUNAR, such comments were sometimes printed to the user directly by the procedure that failed, but the system itself had no opportunity to "see" those comments and take some action of its own in response to them (such as trying some other way to achieve the same end).

In LUNAR, interpretations of commands are given directly to the retrieval component for evaluation, although in a more intelligent system, as in humans, the decision to carry out a command once it is understood would not necessarily automatically follow.

6. Semantic Interpretation

Having now specified the notation in which the meanings of English sentences are to be represented and specifying the meanings of expressions in that notation, we are now left with the specification of the process whereby meanings are assigned to sentences. This process is referred to as semantic interpretation, and in LUNAR it is driven by a set of formal semantic interpretation rules. For example, the interpretation of the sentence "S10046 contains silicon." to which the parser would assign the syntactic structure

```
S DCL
NP   NPR S10046
AUX  TNS PRESENT
VP   V CONTAIN
     NP NPR SILICON
```

is determined by a rule that applies to a sentence when the subject is a sample, the object is a chemical element, oxide, or isotope, and the verb is "have" or "contain." This rule specifies that such a sentence is to be interpreted as an instance of the schema (CONTAIN x y), where x is to be replaced by the interpretation of the subject noun phrase of the sentence, and y is to be replaced by the interpretation of the object.

This information about conditions on possible arguments and substitutions of subordinate interpretations into "slots" in the schema is represented in LUNAR by means of the pattern → action rule

```
[S:CONTAIN
  (S.NP (MEM 1 SAMPLE))
  (S.V (OR (EQU 1 HAVE)
           (EQU 1 CONTAIN))
  (S.OBJ (MEM 1 (ELEMENT OXIDE ISOTOPE)))
  →(QUOTE (CONTAIN (# 1 1) (# 3 1))) ].
```

The name of the rule is S:CONTAIN. The left-hand side, or pattern part, of the rule consists of three templates that match fragments of syntactic structure. The first template requires that the sentence being

6.1 Complications Due to Quantifiers

In the above example, the interpretation of the sentence is obtained by inserting the interpretations of the proper noun phrases "S10046" and "silicon" (in LUNAR these are "S10046" and "SIO2," respectively) into the open slots of the right-hand side schema to obtain

(CONTAIN S10046 SIO2).

When faced with the possibility of a quantified noun phrase, however, the problem becomes somewhat more complex. If the initial sentence were "Every sample contains silicon," then one would like to produce the interpretation

(FOR EVERY X / SAMPLE ; (CONTAIN X SIO2)).

That is, one would like to create a variable to fill the "container" slot of the schema for the main verb, and then generate a quantifier governing that variable to be attached above the predicate CONTAIN. As we shall see, the LUNAR semantic interpretation system specifically provides for the generation and appropriate attachment of such quantifiers.

6.2 Problems with an Alternative Approach

Because of the complications discussed above, one might ask whether there is some other way to handle quantification without generating quantifiers that are extracted from their noun phrase and attached as dominant operators governing the clause in which the original noun phrase was embedded. One might, instead, attempt to interpret the quantified noun phrase as some kind of a set of a set that the verb of the clause takes as its argument, and require the definition of the verb to include the iteration of its basic predicate over the members of the class. For example, one might want a representation for the above example something like

(CONTAIN (SET X / SAMPLE : T) SIO2)

with the predicate CONTAIN defined to check whether its first argument is a set and if so, check each of the members of that set.

However, if one were to take this approach, some way would be needed to distinguish giving CONTAIN a set argument over which it should do universal quantification from one in which it should do existential quantification. One would similarly have to be able to give it arguments for the various nonstandard quantifiers discussed above, such as numerical quantifiers and quantifiers like "most." Moreover, the same thing would have to be done separately for the second argument to

interpreted have a subject noun phrase that is a member of the semantic class SAMPLE; the second requires that the verb be either "have" or "contain;" and the third requires a direct object that is either a chemical element, an oxide, or an isotope.

The right-hand side, or action part, of the rule follows the right arrow and specifies that the interpretation of this node is to be formed by inserting the interpretations of the subject and object constituents into the schema (CONTAIN (# 1 1) (# 3 1)), where the expressions (# m n) mark the "slots" in the schema where subordinate interpretation are to be inserted. The detailed structure of such rules is described in Section 6.3. (Note that the predicate CONTAIN is the name of a procedure in the retrieval component, and it is only by the "accident" of mnemonic design that its name happens to be the same as the English word "contain" in the sentence that we have interpreted.)

The process of semantic interpretation can conveniently be thought of as a process that applies to parse trees produced by a parser to assign semantic interpretations to nodes in the tree. In LUNAR and the other systems above, except for TRIPSYS, this is how the interpretations are produced. (In TRIPSYS, they are produced directly by the parser without an intermediate syntax tree representation.) The basic interpretation process is a recursive procedure that assigns an interpretation to a node of the tree as a function of its syntactic structure and the interpretations of its constituents.

The interpretations of complex constituents are thus built up modularly by a recursive process that determines the interpretation of a node by inserting the interpretations of certain constituent nodes into open slots in a schema. The schema to be used is determined by rules that look at a limited portion of the tree. At the bottom level of the tree (i.e., the leaves of the tree), the interpretation schemata are literal representations without open slots, specifying the appropriate elementary interpretations of basic atomic constituents (e.g., proper names).

In LUNAR, the semantic interpretation procedure is implemented in such a way that the interpretation of nodes can be initiated in any order. If the interpretation of a node requires the interpretation of a constituent that has not yet been interpreted, then the interpretation of that constituent is performed before that of the higher node is completed. Thus, it is possible to perform the entire semantic interpretation by calling for the interpretation of the top node (the sentence as a whole). This is the normal mode in which the interpreter is operated in LUNAR. I will discuss later (Sections 11.3 and 11.4) some experiments in which this mechanism is used for "bottom-up" interpretation.

CONTAIN as well as the first (i.e., the chemical element as well as the sample), and one would have to make sure that all combinations of quantifiers in the two argument positions worked correctly. Essentially one would have to duplicate the entire quantificational mechanism discussed above as part of the defining procedure for the meaning of the predicate CONTAIN. Moreover, one would then have to duplicate this code separately for each other predicate and command in the system. Even if one managed to share most of the code by packaging it as subroutines, this is still an inelegant way of handling the problem.

Even if one went to the trouble just outlined, there are still logical inadequacies, since there is no way with the proposed method to specify the differences in meaning that correspond to the different relative scopes of two quantifiers (e.g., "Every sample contains some element" versus "There is some element that every sample contains"). Likewise, there is no mechanism to indicate the relative scopes of quantifiers and sentential operators such as negation ("Not every sample contains silicon" versus "Every sample contains no silicon"). It appears, therefore, that treating quantifiers effectively as higher operators is essential to correct interpretation in general.

6.3 The Structure of Semantic Rules

As discussed above, in determining the meaning of a construction, two types of information are used: syntactic information about sentence construction and semantic information about constituents. For example, in interpreting the above example, it is both the syntactic structure of the sentence (subject = S10046; verb = "contain;" object = silicon) plus the semantic fact that S10046 is a sample and silicon is a chemical element that determine the interpretation. Syntactic information about a construction is tested by matching tree fragments such as those indicated below against the mode being interpreted:

```
S.NP    = S NP (1)          (subject of a sentence)
S.V     = S VP V (1)        (main verb of a sentence)
S.OBJ   = S VP NP (1)       (direct object of a sentence)
S.PP    = S VP PP PREP (1)  (preposition and object
              NP (2)          modifying a verb phrase)
NP.ADJ  = NP ADJ (2)        (adjective modifying a noun phrase)
```

Fragment S.NP matches a sentence if it has a subject and also associates the number 1 with the subject noun phrase. S.PP matches a sentence that contains a prepositional phrase modifying the verb phrase and associates the numbers 1 and 2 with the preposition and its object, respectively.

The numbered nodes can be referred to in the left-hand sides of rules for checking semantic conditions, and they are used in the right-hand sides for specifying the interpretation of the construction. These tree structure fragments can be named mnemonically as above for readability.

The basic element of the left-hand side of a rule is a *template* consisting of tree fragments plus additional semantic conditions on the numbered nodes of the fragment. For example, the template (S.NP (MEM 1 SAMPLE)) matches a sentence if its subject is semantically marked as a sample. The pattern part of a rule consists of a sequence of templates, and the action of the rule specifies how the interpretation of the sentence is to be constructed from the interpretations of the nodes that match the numbered nodes of the templates.

Occasionally, some of the elements that are required to construct an interpretation may be found in one of several alternative places in a construction. For example, the constituent to be measured in an analysis can occur either as a prenominal adjective ("a silicon analysis") or as a post-nominal prepositional phrase ("an analysis of silicon"). To handle this case, basic templates corresponding to the alternative ways the necessary element can be found can be grouped together with an OR operator to form a disjunctive template that is satisfied if any of its disjunct templates are. For example,

```
(OR (NP.ADJ (MEM 2 ELEMENT))
    (NP.PP (AND (EQU 1 OF)
                (MEM 2 ELEMENT))).
```

Also occasionally, two rules will be distinguished by the fact that one applies when a given constituent is present and the other will require it to be absent. In order to write the second rule so that it will not match in circumstances where it is not intended, a basic template can be embedded in a negation operator NOT to produce a negated template that is satisfied if its embedded template fails to match and is not satisfied when its embedded template succeeds. For example,

```
(NOT (NP.ADJ (EQU 2 MODAL))).
```

In general, the left-hand side of a rule consists of a sequence of templates (basic, disjunctive, or negated).

6.3.1 *Right-Hand Sides*

The right-hand sides (or actions) of semantic rules are schemata into which the interpretations of embedded constituents are inserted before the resulting form is evaluated to give a semantic interpretation. The places, or "slots," in the right-hand sides where subordinate interpretations are to be inserted are indicated by expressions called REFs, which begin with the atom # and contain one or two numbers and an optional "TYPEFLAG." The numbers indicate the node in the tree whose interpretation is to be inserted by naming first the sequence number of a template of the rule, and then the number of the corresponding node in the tree fragment of that template. Thus the reference (# 2 1) represents the interpretation of the node that matches node 1 of the 2nd template of the rule. In addition, the single number 0 can also be used to reference the current node, as in (# 0 TYPEFLAG).

The TYPEFLAG element, if present, indicates how the subordinate node is to be interpreted. For example, in LUNAR there is a distinction between interpreting a node normally and interpreting it as a topic description. Thus (# 0 TOPIC) represents the interpretation of the current node as a topic description. There are a variety of types of interpretation used for various purposes in the rules of the system. The absence of a specific TYPEFLAG in a REF indicates that the interpretation is to be done in the normal mode for the type of node that it matches.

6.3.2 Right-Hand Side Evaluation

In many cases, the semantic interpretation to be attached to a node can be constructed by merely inserting the appropriate constituent interpretations into the open slots in a fixed schema. However, occasionally, more than this is required and some procedure needs to be executed to modify or transform the resulting instantiated schema. To provide for this, the semantic interpreter treats right-hand sides of rules as expressions to be evaluated to determine the appropriate interpretation. For rules in which the desired final form can be given literally, the right-hand side schema is embedded in the operator QUOTE which simply returns its argument unchanged. This is the case in the example above. In special cases, right-hand side operators can do fairly complex things, such as searching a discourse directory for antecedents for anaphoric expressions and computing intensional unions of sets. In the usual case, however, the operator is either QUOTE or one of the two operators PRED and QUANT that handle quantifier passing (discussed below).

6.4 Relationship of Rules to Syntax

In many programming languages and some attempts to specify natural language semantics, semantic rules are paired directly with syntactic phrase structure rules so that a single compact pairing specifies both the syntactic structure of a constituent and its interpretation. This type of specification is clean and straightforward and works well for artificial languages that can be defined by context-free or almost context-free grammars, whose structure is less isomorphic to the kind of logical meaning representation that one would like to derive, it is less convenient, although not impossible. Specifically, with the more complex grammars for natural language, e.g., ATN's and transformational grammars, the simple notion of a syntactic rule with which to pair a semantic rule becomes less clear. Consequently, the rules in the LUNAR system are not paired with the syntactic rules, nor are they constrained to look only at the immediate constituents of a phrase. In general they can look arbitrarily far down into the phrase they are interpreting, picking up interpretations of subordinate constituents at any level, and looking at various syntactic aspects of the structure they are interpreting, as well as the semantic interpretations of constituents. The rules are invoked not by virtue of applying a given syntactic rule, but by means of rule indexing strategies described below.

6.5 Organization of the Semantic Interpreter

The overall operation of the semantic interpreter is as follows: A top level routine calls the recursive function INTERP looking at the top level of the parse tree. Thereafter, INTERP attempts to match semantic rules against the specified node of the tree, and the right-hand sides of matching rules specify the interpretation to be given to the node. The possibility of semantic ambiguity is recognized, and therefore the routine INTERP produces a list of possible interpretations (usually a singleton, however). Each interpretation consists of two parts: a node interpretation (called the SEM of the node) and a quantifier "collar" (called the QUANT of the node). The QUANT is a schema for higher operators (such as quantification) that is to dominate any interpretation in which the SEM is inserted (used for quantifier passing—see Section 6.7). Thus the result of a call to INTERP for a given node P is a list of SEM-QUANT pairs, one for each possible interpretation of the node.

6.5.1 Context-Dependent Interpretation

The function INTERP takes two arguments—the construction to be interpreted and a TYPEFLAG that indicates how to interpret it. The TYPEFLAG mechanism is intended to allow a constituent to be interpreted differently depending on the higher level structure within which it is embedded. The TYPEFLAG permits a higher level schema to pass down information to indicate how it wants a constituent interpreted. For example, some verbs can specify that they want a noun phrase interpreted as a set rather than as a quantification over individuals. The TYPEFLAG mechanisms is also used to control the successive phases of interpretation of noun phrases and clauses (discussed below).

When interpreting a node, INTERP first calls a function HEAD to determine the head of the construction and then calls a function RULES to determine the list of semantic rules to be used (which depends, in general, on the type of node, its head word, and the value of TYPEFLAG). It then dispatches, control to a routine MATCHER to try to match the rules. If no interpretations are found, then, depending on the TYPEFLAG and various mode settings, INTERP either returns a default interpretation T, goes into a break with a comment that the node is uninterpretable (permitting a systems programmer to debug rules), or returns NIL indicating that the node has no interpretations for the indicated TYPEFLAG.

6.5.2 *Phased Interpretation*

In general, there are two types of constituents in a sentence that receive interpretations—clauses and noun phrases. The former receive interpretations that are usually predications or commands, while the latter are usually designators. The interpretation of these two different kinds of phrase are slightly different, but also remarkably similar. In each case there is a governing "head" word; the verb in the case of a clause, and the head noun in the case of the noun phrase. The interpretation of a phrase is principally determined by the head word (noun or verb) of the construction. However, there are also other parts of a construction that determine aspects of its interpretation independent of the head word. These in turn break down into two further classes: (1) modifying phrases (which themselves have dominating head words) that augment or alter meaning of the head, and (2) function words that determine governing operators of the interpretation that are independent of the head word and its modifiers. In the case of clauses, these latter include the interpretation of tense and aspect and various qualifying operators such as negative particles. In the case of noun phrases, these include the interpretation of articles and quantifiers and the inflected case and number of the head noun.

As a consequence of these distinctions, the semantic interpretation of a construction generally consists of three kinds of operations: determining any governing operators that are independent of the head word, determining the basic interpretation of the head word, and interpreting any modifiers that may be present. In LUNAR, these three different classes of interpretation are governed by three different classes of rules that operate in three phases.

The phases are controlled by the rules themselves by using multiple calls to the interpreter with different TYPEFLAGS.

The above description is not the only way such phasing could be achieved. For example, it would be possible to gain the same phasing of interpretation by virtue of the structures assigned to the input by the parser (see Section 11.2) or by embedding the phasing in the control structure of the interpreter. In the original flight schedules and grammar information implementations, this phasing was embedded in the control structure of the interpreter. Placing the phasing under the control of the rules themselves in LUNAR provided more flexibility. In TRIPSYS, the equivalent of such phasing is integrated, along with the semantic interpretation, into the parsing process.

In general, the interpretation of a construction is initially called for with TYPEFLAG NIL. This first interpretation may in turn involve successive calls for interpretation of the same node with other TYPEFLAGs to obtain subsequent phases of interpretation. For example, clauses are initially interpreted with TYPEFLAG NIL, and the rules invoked are a general set of rules called PRERULES that look for negative articles, tense marking, conjunctions, etc., to determine any governing operators that should surround the interpretation of the verb. Whichever of these rules matches will then call for another interpretation of the same construction with an appropriate TYPEFLAG. The basic interpretation of the verb is done by a call with TYPEFLAG SRULES, which invokes a set of rules stored on the property list of the verb (or reachable from the entry for that verb by chaining up a generalization hierarchy). For example, in interpreting the sentence "S10046 doesn't contain silicon", the initial PRERULE PR-NEG matches with a right-hand side

$$(PRED \ (NOT \ (\# \ 0 \ SRULES))).$$

The SRULE S:CONTAIN discussed above then matches, producing eventually (CONTAIN S10046 SIO2), which is then embedded in the PR-NEG schema to produce the final interpretation

$$(NOT \ (CONTAIN \ S10046 \ SIO2)).$$

Ordinary noun phrases are usually interpreted by an initial phase that interprets the determiner and number, a second phase that interprets the head noun and any arguments that it may take (i.e., as a function), and a third phase that interprets other adjectival and prepositional phrase modifiers and relative clauses.

semantic network notations) so that they can be recorded once at the appropriate level of generality. Specifically, each work in the dictionary has a property called MARKERS which contains a list of classes of which it is a member (or subclass), i.e., classes with which this word has an "is-a" relationship. Each of these classes also has a dictionary entry that may contain SRULES, NRULES, and RRULES. The set of rules used by the interpreter for any given phrase is obtained by scanning up these chains of inheritance and gathering up the rules that are found. These accesses are quite shallow in LUNAR but would be used more heavily in a less limited topic domain.

In situations in which the set of rules does not depend on the head of the construction, the rules to be used are taken from a global list determined by the value of TYPEFLAG and the type of the constituent being interpreted. For example, in interpreting the determiner structure of a noun phrase, a global list of DRULES is used.

6.5.3 Proper Nouns and Mass Terms

In addition to the rules discussed above for ordinary noun phrases, there are two special classes of noun phrases—proper nouns and mass terms—that have their own rules. Proper nouns are the direct names of individuals in the data base. Their identifiers in the data base, which are not necessarily identical to their normal English orthography, are indicated in the dictionary entry for the English form. Mass terms are the names of substances like silicon and hydrogen. Proper nouns are represented in the LUNAR syntactic representations as special cases of noun phrases by a rule equivalent to NP → NPR, while mass terms are represented as ordinary noun phrases with determiner NIL and number SG.

In general, the interpretation of mass terms requires a special treatment of quantifiers, similar to but different from the ordinary quantifiers that deal with count nouns (e.g., "some silicon" means an amount of stuff, while "some sample" means an individual sample). In the LUNAR system, however, mass terms are used only in a few specialized senses in which they are almost equivalent to proper nouns naming a substance.

6.6 Organization of Rules

As mentioned above, the semantic rules for interpreting sentences are usually governed by the verb of the sentence. That is, out of the entire set of semantic rules, only a relatively small number of them can possibly apply to a given sentence because of the verb mentioned in the rule. Similarly, the rules that interpret noun phrases are governed by the head noun of the noun phrase. For this reason, most semantic rules in LUNAR are indexed according to the heads of the constructions to which they could apply, and recorded in the dictionary entry for the head words. Specifically, associated with each verb is a set of "SRULES" for interpreting that verb in various contexts, and associated with each noun is a set of "NRULES" for interpreting various occurrences of that noun. In addition, associated with each noun are a set of "RRULES" for interpreting various restrictive modifiers that may be applied to that noun. Each rule essentially characterizes a syntactic/semantic environment in which a word can occur, and specifies its interpretation in that environment. The templates of a rule thus describe the necessary and sufficient constituents and semantic restrictions for a word to be meaningful.

In addition to indexing rules directly in the dictionary entry for a given word, certain rules that apply generally to a class of words are indexed in an inheritance hierarchy (frequently called an "is-a" hierarchy in

6.6.1 Rule Trees

Whether indexed by the head words of constructions or taken from global lists, rules to be tried are organized into a tree structure that can make rule matching conditional on the success or failure of previous rules. A rule tree specifies the order in which rules are to be tried and after each rule indicates whether a different tree of rules is to be tried next, depending on the success or failure of previous rules. The format for a rule tree is basically a list of rules (or rule groups—see multiple matches below) in the order they are to be tried. However, after any given element in this list, a new rule tree can be inserted to be used if any of the rules preceding it have succeeded. If no rules preceding it have succeeded, then the inserted tree is skipped and rules continue to be taken from the rules that follow it in the list. For example, the tree (R1 R2 (R4 R5) R3 R4 R5) indicates that R1 and R2 are to be tried and if either of them succeed, the subsequent rules to be tried are R4 and R5. If neither R1 nor R2 succeed, then the remaining list R3, R4, R5 is to be tried next. This example illustrates how a rule tree can be used to skip around rules that are to be omitted if previous rules have succeeded.

The most usual cases of rule trees in LUNAR are simple lists (i.e., no branching in the tree), and lists of rules with inserted empty trees (i.e., the empty list NIL) serving as "barriers" to stop the attempted matching of rules once a successful rule has been found.

6.6.2 Multiple Matches

Since the templates of a rule may simultaneously match a single node, it is necessary to indicate how the interpretation of a node is to be constructed in such a case. To provide this information, the lists of rules at each level of a rule tree can be organized into groups, with each group indicating how (or whether) simultaneous matches by different rules are to be combined. The format of a rule group is a list of rules (or other groups) preceded by an operator specifying the mode for combining simultaneous matches. Outside the scopes of rule groups, the mode to be used is specified by a default value determined by TYPEFLAG and the type of node being interpreted. Possible modes are AND (which combines multiple matches with an AND, i.e., treats multiple matches as finding different parts of a single conjoined meaning), OR (which combines multiple matches with an OR), SPLIT (which keeps multiple matches separate as semantic ambiguities), and FAIL (which prohibits multiple matches, i.e., complains if it finds any).

To illustrate the behavior of rule groups in rule trees, a rule list of the form (A B NIL C (OR D E)) with default mode AND indicates that if either of the rules A or B is successful, then no further matches are tried (NIL is a barrier); otherwise, rules C, D, and E are tried. If both D and E match, then the results are OR'ed together, and if C matches together with D or E or both, it is AND'ed to the results of the OR group.

The modes (AND, OR, SPLIT, and FAIL) also apply to multiple matches of a single rule. A rule may either specify the mode for multiple matches as its first element prior to the list of templates, or else it will be governed by the rule group or default mode setting at the time it is matched.

6.7   The Generation of Quantifiers

As mentioned above, the LUNAR interpretation system specifically provides for the generation and appropriate attachment of quantifiers governing the interpretations it produces. Central to this capability is the division of the interpretation of a constituent into two parts: a SEM that is to be inserted into the appropriate slot of the schema for some higher constituent, and a QUANT that serves as a "collar" of higher operators that is to be passed up to some higher level of the tree (around which the collar will be "worn"). A quantifier to be attached to some higher constituent is represented as a schema, which itself contains a slot into which the interpretation of that higher constituent is to be inserted. This slot (the "hole" in the collar) is indicated by a marker DLT.

In the unquantified example sentence considered in Section 6.1, the SEM of the subject noun phrase is simply S10046, and the QUANT is the "empty" collar DLT. The quantifier schema in the second example would be represented as

(FOR EVERY X / SAMPLE : DLT).

6.7.1 Steps in Interpretation

The general procedure for interpreting a construction is

a) Match an interpretation rule against the construction, subject to the control of the rule tree.

b) If it matches, then determine from the right-hand side of the rule the set of constituent nodes that need to be interpreted.

c) Call for the interpretation of all of the constituents required, associate their SEMs with the slots in the schema that they are to fill, and gather up all of the QUANTs that are generated by those interpretations. Call a function SORTQUANT to determine the order in which those quantifiers (if there are several) should be nested.

d) Depending on an operator in the right-hand side of rule, either attach the quantifiers so generated around the outside of the current schema, or pass them further up the tree as the QUANT of the resulting interpretation.

e) If multiple matches are to be combined with an AND or OR, it is their SEMs that are so combined. Their QUANTs are nested one inside the other to produce the QUANT of the result.

6.7.2 Quantifier Passing Operators

There are three principal operators for use in the right-hand sides of rules to determine the behavior of quantifier passing up the tree. These are the operators PRED, QUOTE, and QUANT. The first indicates that the schema it contains is a predication that will accept quantifiers from below; it causes any quantifiers that arise from constituent interpretations to be attached around the current schema to become part of the resulting SEM. The QUANT associated with such an interpretation will be the empty QUANT DLT. The operator QUANT, on the other hand, indicates that the schema it contains is itself a quantifier schema, and that the result of its instantiation is to be passed up the tree (together with other quantifiers that may have resulted from constituent interpretations) as the QUANT of the interpretation. The SEM associated with such an interpretation is the variable name that is being governed by the quantifier. The operator QUOTE is used around a schema that is transparent to quantifier passing, so that any quantifiers that accumulate from constituent interpretations are simply aggregated together and passed on up the tree as the QUANT of the interpretation. The SEM of such an interpretation is simply the instantiated schema inside the QUOTE.

In the LUNAR implementation, a function SEMSUB, which substitutes the SEMs of lower interpretations into the right-hand sides of rules, maintains a variable QUANT to accumulate the nesting of quantifiers returned from the lower interpretations. Then, after making the substitutions, the right-hand side of the rule is evaluated to determine the SEM-QUANT pair to be returned. The result of the evaluation is the desired SEM of the pair, and the value of QUANT (which may have been changed as a side effect of the evaluation) is the QUANT of the pair. The operators PRED and QUANT in the right-hand sides of rules manipulate the variable QUANT to grab and insert quantifiers.

7. Problems of Interpretation

7.1 The Order of Quantifier Nesting

In the general quantification schema

(FOR ⟨quant⟩ X / ⟨class⟩ : (p X) : (q X))

both the expressions (p X) and (q X) can themselves be quantified expressions. Sentences containing several quantified noun phrases result in expressions with a nesting of quantifiers dominating the interpretation of the main clause. For example, the sentence ''Every sample contains some element'' has a representation

(FOR EVERY X / SAMPLE ;
 (FOR SOME Y / ELEMENT ;
  (CONTAIN X Y))).

Alternative interpretations of a sentence corresponding to different orderings of the quantifiers correspond to different relative nestings of the quantifier operations. For example, the above sentence has an unlikely interpretation in which there is a particular element that is contained in every sample. The representation of this interpretation is

(FOR SOME Y / ELEMENT ;
 (FOR EVERY X / SAMPLE ;
  (CONTAIN X Y))).

Thus, in interpreting a sentence, it is necessary to decide the appropriate order of nesting of quantifiers to be used. In general, this ordering is the left-to-right order of occurrence of the quantifiers in the sentence, but this is not universally so (for example, when a function is applied to a quantified noun phrase—see functional nesting below). In situations where the order of quantifiers is not otherwise determined, LUNAR assumes the left-to-right order of occurrence in the sentence.

7.2 Interaction of Negations with Quantifiers

The construction of an interpretation system that will handle sentences containing single instances of a quantification or simple negation without quantification is not difficult. What is difficult is to make it correctly handle sentences containing arbitrary combinations of quantifiers and negatives. The interpretation mechanism of LUNAR handles such constructions fairly well. Consider the sentence ''Every sample does not contain silicon.'' This sentence is potentially ambiguous between two interpretations:

(NOT (FOR EVERY X / SAMPLE ; (CONTAIN X SIO2)))

and

(FOR EVERY X / SAMPLE ; (NOT (CONTAIN X SIO2))).

The difference lies in the relative scopes of the quantifier and the negative. One interpretation of the above sentence is handled in LUNAR by the interaction of the rules already presented. The interpretation of the PRE-RULE PR-NEG, discussed in Section 6.5.2, has the right-hand side (PRED (NOT (# 0 SRULES))), whose governing operator indicates that it grabs quantifiers from below. The interpretation of the noun phrase ''every sample'' produces the quantifier ''collar'':

(FOR EVERY X / SAMPLE : T ; DLT)

which is passed up as the QUANT together with the SEM X. The right-hand side of S:CONTAIN is embedded in the operator QUOTE, which is transparent to quantifiers, producing the SEM (CONTAIN X SIO2) and passing on the same QUANT. The top level rule PR-NEG now executes its instantiated right-hand side:

(PRED (NOT (CONTAIN X SIO2)))

which grabs the quantifier to produce the interpretation:

(FOR EVERY X / SAMPLE : T ; (NOT CONTAIN X SIO2))).

The alternative interpretation of the above sentence can be obtained by an alternative PRERULE for sentential negatives whose right-hand side is

(BUILDQ (NOT #) (PRED (# 0 SRULES)))

where BUILDQ is an operator whose first argument is a literal schema into which it inserts the values of its remaining arguments. In this case, the PRED expression produces

(FOR EVERY X / SAMPLE : T ; (CONTAIN X SIO2))

and the BUILDQ produces

(NOT (FOR EVERY X / SAMPLE : T ; (CONTAIN X SIO2))).

If these two negative rules both existed in the list PRERULES, then the LUNAR interpreter when interpreting a negative sentence would find them both and would produce both interpretations. In the case where no quantifier is returned by the subordinate SRULES interpretation, then both rules would produce the same interpretation and the duplicate could be eliminated. In the case where a quantifier is returned, then the two interpretations would be different and a genuine ambiguity would have been found, resulting in a request by the system to the user to indicate which of the two interpretations he intended.

However, if one decides to legislate that only one of the two possible scope choices should be perceived by the system, then only the corresponding rule for negation should be included in the PRERULES list. This is the choice that was taken in the demonstration LUNAR system. Since the interpretation of the negative operator outside the scope of the quantifier can be unambiguously expressed using locutions such as "Not every sample contains silicon," LUNAR's rules treat sentential negation as falling inside any quantifiers (as expressed by the PR-NEG rule discussed previously). Rules for interpreting determiners such as "not every" can easily be written to produce quantifier expressions such as

(NOT (FOR EVERY X / ⟨class⟩ ; DLT))

to give interpretations in which the negative operator is outermost.

7.3 Functional Nesting and Quantifier Reversal

As previously mentioned, an interesting example of quantifier nesting occurs when an argument to a function is quantified. As an example, consider the departure times from the flight schedules request, "List the departure times from Boston to every American Airlines flight that goes from Boston to Chicago." This sentence has a bizarre interpretation in which there is one

time at which every American Airlines flight from Boston to Chicago departs. However, the normal interpretation requires taking the subordinate quantifier "every flight" and raising it above the quantifier of the higher noun phrase "the departure time." Such nesting of quantifiers is required when the range of quantification of one of them (in this case, the departure times) contains a variable governed by the other (in this case, the flights).

In the logical representation of the meaning of such sentences, the higher quantifier must be the one that governs the variable on which the other depends. This logical dependency is exactly the reversal of the "syntactic dependency" in the parse tree, where the argument to the function is contained within (i.e., "dependent" on) the phrase the function heads. The LUNAR system facility for interpreting such constructions automatically gets the preferred interpretation, since the quantifiers from subordinate constituents are accumulated and nested before the quantifier for a given noun phrase is inserted into the quantifier collar.

To illustrate the process in detail, consider the interpretation of the above example. In the processing of the constituents of the noun phrase whose head is "departure time," the quantifier

(FOR EVERY X2 / FLIGHT : (EQUAL (OWNER X2) AMERICAN) ; DLT)

is returned from the interpretation of the "flight" noun phrase (which gets the SEM X2). The temporary QUANT accumulator in the function SEMSUB (discussed in Section 6.7), at this point contains the single "empty" quantifier collar DLT. This is now modified by substituting the returned quantifier for the DLT, resulting in the QUANT accumulator now containing the returned quantifier

(FOR EVERY X2 / FLIGHT : (EQUAL (OWNER X2) AMERICAN) ; DLT)

(with its DLT now marking the "hole" in the collar).

When all of the subordinate constituents have been interpreted, and their SEM's have been inserted into the right-hand side schema of the rule interpreting the "departure time" noun phrase, the resulting instantiated schema will be

(QUANT (FOR THE X1 / (DTIME X2 BOSTON) : T ; DLT)).

This is then evaluated, again resulting in the DLT in the temporary QUANT accumulator being replaced with this new quantifier (thus inserting the definite quantification THE inside the scope of the universal quantifier EVERY that is already there). The result of this interpretation is to return the SEM-QUANT pair consiting of the SEM X1 and the QUANT

```
(FOR EVERY X2 / FLIGHT : (EQUAL (OWNER X2) AMERICAN) ;
    (FOR THE X1 / (DTIME X2 BOSTON) : T : DLT ) ).
```

The right-hand side for the next higher rule (the one that interprets the command "list x") contains a PRED operator, so that when its instantiated schema

```
(PRED (PRINTOUT X1))
```

is executed, it will grab the quantifier collar from below to produce the interpretation

```
(FOR EVERY X2 / FLIGHT : (EQUAL (OWNER X2) AMERICAN) ;
    (FOR THE X1 / (DTIME X2 BOSTON) : T :
        (PRINTOUT X1) ).
```

7.4 Relative Clauses

One of the features of the LUNAR system that makes it relatively powerful in the range of questions it can handle is its general treatment of relative clause modifiers. This gives it a natural ability to handle many questions that would be awkward or impossible to pose to many data management systems. Relative clauses permit arbitrary predicate restrictions to be imposed on the range of quantification of some iterative search. The way in which relative clauses are interpreted is quite simple within LUNAR's general semantic interpretation framework. It is done by a general RRULE R:REL, which is implicitly included in the RRULES for any noun phrase.

The rule R:REL will match a noun phrase if it finds a relative clause structure modifying the phrase. On each such relative clause, it will execute a function RELTAG that will find the node in the relative clause corresponding to the relative pronoun ("which" or "that"), and will mark this found node with the same variable X that is being used for the noun phrase that the relative clause modifies. This pronoun will then behave as if it had already been interpreted and assigned that variable as its SEM. The semantic interpreter will then be called on the relative clause node, just like any other sentence being interpreted, and the result will be a predicate with a free occurrence of the variable X. This resulting predicate is then taken, together with any other RRULE predicates obtained from adjectival and prepositional phrase modifiers, to form the restriction on the range of quantification of the modified noun phrase.

One consequence of a relative clause being interpreted as a subordinate S node (in fact, a consequence of any subordinate S node interpretation) is that, since the PRERULES used in interpreting the subordinate S node all have PRED operators in their right-hand sides, any quantifiers produced by noun phrases inside the relative clause will be grabbed by the relative clause itself and not passed up to the main clause. This rules out interpretations of sentences like "List the samples that contain every major element" in anomalous ways such as

```
(FOR EVERY X / MAJORELT : T :
    (FOR EVERY Y / SAMPLE : (CONTAIN Y X) ;
        (PRINTOUT Y) ))
```

(i.e., "For every major element list the samples that contain it") instead of the correct

```
(FOR EVERY Y / SAMPLE :
    (FOR EVERY X / MAJORELT : T : (CONTAIN Y X) ;
        (PRINTOUT Y) ).
```

Except in certain opaque context situations, this seems to be the preferred interpretation. As in other cases, however, although LUNAR's interpretation system is capable of producing alternative interpretations for some other criteria to choose between, the demonstration prototype instead uses rules that determine just those interpretations that seem to be most likely in its domain.

7.5 Other Types of Modifiers

In addition to relative clauses, there are other kinds of constructions in English that function as predicates to restrict the range of quantification. These include most adjectives and prepositional phrases. They are interpreted by RRULES that match the appropriate structures in a noun phrase and produce a predicate with free variable X (which will be instantiated with the variable of quantification for the noun phrase being interpreted). I will call such modifiers *predicators* since they function as predicates to restrict the range of quantification. Examples of predicators are modifiers like "recent" and "about olivine twinning" in phrases like "recent articles about olivine twinning". The interpretation of this phrase would produce the quantifier

```
(FOR GEN X / DOCUMENT :
    (AND (RECENT X) (ABOUT X (OLIVINE TWINNING))) : DLT ).
```

Note that not all adjectives and prepositional phrases are interpreted as just described. Many fill special roles determined by the head noun, essentially serving as arguments to a function. For example, in a noun phrase such as "the silicon concentration in S10046," the adjective "silicon" is specifying the value of one of the arguments to the function "concentration," rather than serving as an independent predicate that the concentration must satisfy. (That is, this phrase is not equivalent to "the concentration in S10046 which is silicon," which does not make sense). Similarly, the prepositional phrase "in S10046" is filling the same kind of argument role, and is not an independent modifier. I will call this class of modifiers *role fillers*.

In some cases, there are modifiers that could either be treated as restricting predicates or as filling argument roles in a function, depending on the enumeration function that is being used to represent the meaning of the head noun. For example, a modifier like "to Chicago" in "flights to Chicago" could either be interpreted as an independent predicate (ARRIVE X CHICAGO) modifying the flight, or as an argument to a specialized flight enumeration function FLIGHT-TO which enumerates flights to a given destination. In the flight schedules application, the former interpretation was taken, although later query optimization rules (see smart quantifiers, below) were able to transform the resulting MRL expression to a form equivalent to the latter to gain efficiency.

In general English, there are cases in which it seems moot whether one should treat a given phrase as filling an argument role or as a restricting predicate. However, there are also clear cases where the head noun is definitely a function and cannot stand alone without some argument being either explicitly present or inferable from context. In these cases such modifiers are clearly role fillers. On the other hand, the diversity of possible modifiers makes it unlikely that all adjectives and prepositional phrases could be interpretable as role fillers in any general or economical fashion. Thus, the distinction between predicators and role fillers seems to be necessary.

There is another use of a modifier that neither fills an argument role nor stands as an independent predicate, but rather changes the interpretation of the head noun. An example is "modal" in "modal olivine analyses." This adjective does not describe a kind of olivine, but rather a kind of analysis that is different from the normal interpretation one would make of the head "analysis" by itself. Such modifiers might be called *specializers* since they induce a special interpretation on the head noun. Note that these distinctions in types of modification refer to the role of modifier plays in a given construction, not to anything inherent in the modifier itself.

The sentence "List modal olivine analyses for lunar samples that contain silicon" contains a mixture of the different kinds of modifiers. The presence of the specializer adjective "modal" blocks the application of the normal NRULE N: ANALYSIS (it has a NOT template that checks for it), and it enables a different rule N: MODAL-ANALYSIS instead. The adjective "olivine" and the prepositional phrase are both interpreted by REFs in the right-hand side of this rule to fill argument slots in the enumeration function DATALINE. There are no predicators modifying "analyses," but there is a potential predicator "lunar" modifying "samples" and a restrictive relative clause also modifying samples. In LUNAR, the apparently restrictive modifier "lunar" modifying a word like "samples" is instead interpreted as a specializer that does not make a difference, since LUNAR knows of no other kind of sample. However, this is clearly not a limitation of the formalism.

The relative clause modifying "samples" is interpreted as described above to produce the predicate

(CONTAIN X2 SIO2).

The interpretation of the noun phrase "lunar samples that contain silicon" thus consists of the SEM X2 and the QUANT

(FOR GEN X2 / SAMPLE : (CONTAIN X2 SIO2) : DLT).

This SEM-QUANT pair is returned to the process interpreting the noun phrase "modal olivine analyses for ...," which in turn produces a SEM X1 and a QUANT

(FOR GEN X2 / SAMPLE : (CONTAIN X2 SIO2) :
   (FOR GEN X1 / (DATALINE X2 OVERALL OLIV) : T :
      DLT)).

This is returned to the rule interpreting the main verb "list," whose right-hand side produces the SEM (PRINTOUT X1) with the same QUANT as above. This process returns to the PRERULE for positive imperative sentences, where the quantifiers are grabbed to produce the interpretation

(FOR GEN X2 / SAMPLE : (CONTAIN X2 SIO2) :
   (FOR GEN X1 / (DATALINE X2 OVERALL OLIV) : T :
      (PRINTOUT X1))).

7.6 Averages and Quantifiers

An interesting class of quantifier interaction problems occurs with certain operators such as "average," "sum," and "number." In a sentence such as "What is the average silicon concentration in breccias?" it is clear that the generic "breccias" is not to be interpreted as a universal quantifier dominating the average computation, but rather the

quantifiers. For example, Bohnert and Backer (1967) present an account of the differences between "every" and "any" and between "some" and "a" in contexts such as the antecedents of if-then statements by giving "any" and "some" the broadest possible scope and "every" and "a" the narrowest. For example, using the LUNAR MRL notation,

If any soldier stays home, there is no war

(FOR EVERY x / soldier : (IF (home x)
THEN (not war))

If every soldier stays home, there is no war

(IF (FOR EVERY x / soldier : (home x))
THEN (not war)))

If some soldier stays home, there is no war

(FOR SOME x / soldier : (IF (home x)
THEN (not war))

If a soldier stays home, there is no war

(IF (FOR SOME x / soldier : (home x))
THEN (not war)).

The scope rules of Bohnert and Backer are enforced rules of an artificial language that approximates English and are not, unfortunately, distinctions that are always followed in ordinary English. In ordinary English, only a few such distinctions are made consistently, while in other cases the scoping of quantifiers appears to be determined by which is most plausible (see discussion of plausibility evaluation in Section 10.5).

In LUNAR, a slightly different form of this short/broad scope distinction arose in the interaction of operators like average with universal quantifiers. For example, the sentence "List the average concentration of silicon in breccias" clearly means to average over all breccias, while "List the average concentration of silicon in each breccia" clearly means to compute a separate average for each breccia. (In general, there are multiple measurements to average even for a single sample.) The sentences "List the average concentration of silicon in every breccia," and "List the average concentration of silicon in all breccias" are less clear,

average is to be performed over the set of breccias. A potential way of interpreting such phrases would be to treat average as a specializer adjective which, when applied to a noun like "concentration," produces a specialized enumeration function that computes the average. This special interpretation rule, would then interpret the class being averaged over in a special mode as a role filler for one of the arguments to the AVERAGE-CONCENTRATION function. However, this approach would lack generality, since it would require a separate interpretation rule and a separate AVERAGE-X function for every averageable measurement X. Instead, one would like to treat average as a general operator that can apply to anything averageable. Doing this, and making it interact correctly with various quantifiers is handled in the LUNAR system by a mechanism of some elegance and generality. I will describe here the interpretation of averages; the interpretations of sums and other such operators are similar.

Note that there are two superficial forms in which the average operator is used: one is a simple adjective modifying a noun ("the average concentration. . ."), and one is as a noun referring to a function that is explicitly applied to an argument ("the average of concentrations . . ."). LUNAR's grammar standardizes this variation by transforming the first kind of structure into the second (effectively inserting an "of ... PL" into the sentence). As a result, average always occurs in syntactic tree structures as the head noun of a noun phrase with a dependent prepositional phrase whose object has a "NIL ... PL" determiner structure and represents the set of quantities to be averaged.

In interpreting such noun phrases, the NRULE invoked by a head noun "average" or "mean" calls for the interpretation of the set being averaged with the special TYPEFLAG SET. This will result in that node's being interpreted with a special DRULE D:SETOF, which will construct an intensional set representation for the set being averaged. The data base function AVERAGE knows how to use such an intensional set to enumerate members and compute the average. The NRULE for "average" is

[N : AVERAGE
(NP.N (MEM 1 (MEAN AVERAGE))
(NP.PP (MEM 2 (QUANTITY))
→ (QUOTE (SEQL (AVERAGE X / (# 2 2 SET))))].

7.7 Short Scope/Broad Scope Distinctions

Another interesting aspect of quantifier nesting is a fairly well-known distinction between so called short-scope and broad-scope interpretation

called wh questions. Examples are "What is the concentration of silicon in S10046?", "Which samples contain silicon?", and "How many samples are there?" These fall into two classes: those in which an interrogative pronoun stands in the place of an entire noun phrase, as in the first example, and those in which an interrogative determiner introduces an otherwise normal noun phrase. In both cases, the noun phrase containing the interrogative word is usually brought to the front of the sentence from the position that it might otherwise occupy in normal declarative word order, but this is not always the case.

7.8.1 Interrogative Determiners

The natural representation of the interrogative determiners would seem to be to treat them just like any other determiner and represent a sentence such as the second example above as

```
S Q
    NP   DET WHQ
         N SAMPLE
         NU PL
    AUX  TNS PRESENT
    VP   V CONTAIN
         NP NPR SILICON
```

The interpretation procedure we have described seems to work quite well on this structure using a DRULE that matches the interrogative noun phrase and generates the quantifier

```
(FOR EVERY X / (# 0 NRULES) : (AND (# 0 RRULES) DLT) ;
 (PRINTOUT X)).
```

Note that the DLT in the quantifier (where the interpretation of the main clause is to be inserted) is part of the restriction on the range, and the quantified operator is a command to print out the answer. The structure of the quantifier in this case seems somewhat unusual, but the effect is correct and the operation is a reasonably natural one given the capabilities of the semantic interpreter.

However, when we try to apply this kind of analysis to conjoined

but it seems to be that the average over all breccias is slightly preferred in these cases. At any rate, the treatment of quantifiers needs to be able to handle the fact that there are two possible relative scopings of the average operator with universal quantifiers, and the fact that the choice is determined at least for the determiner "each" and for the "generic" or NIL-PL determiner.

LUNAR handles these scope distinctions for the "average" operator by a general mechanism that applies to any operator that takes a set as its argument. As discussed above, the right-hand side of the N:AVERAGE rule calls for the interpretation of the node representing the set being averaged over with TYPEFLAG SET. This causes a DRULE D:SET OF to be used for interpreting that node. The right-hand side of D:SETOF is

```
(SETGEN (SETOF X / (# 0 NRULES) : (# 0 RRULES) ))
```

where SETGEN is a function that grabs certain quantifiers coming from subordinate interpretations and turns them into UNION operations instead. The generic quantifier is grabbed by this function and interpreted as a union. However, the quantifier EACH is not grabbed by SETGEN but is passed on up as a dominating quantifier. Thus, the sentence "What is the average concentration of silicon in breccias?" becomes

```
(FOR THE X4 / (SEQL (AVERAGE X5 /
 (UNION X7 / (SEQ TYPECS) : T ;
  (SETOF X6 / (DATALINE X7 OVERALL SIO2) : T)))) : T ;
 (PRINTOUT X4) )
```

(i.e., the average is computed over the set formed by the union over all type C rocks X7 of the sets of measurements of SIO2 in the individual X7's). On the other hand, "What is the average concentration of silicon in each breccia?" becomes

```
(FOR EACH X12 / (SEQ TYPECS) : T ;
 (FOR THE X9 / (SEQL (AVERAGE X10 /
  (SETOF X11 / (DATALINE X12 OVERALL SIO2) : T ))) : T ;
  (PRINTOUT X9) ))
```

(i.e., a separate average is computed for each type C rock X12).

7.8 Wh Questions

In addition to simple yes/no questions and imperative commands to print the results of computations, LUNAR handles several kinds of so-

sentences, such as "What samples contain silicon and do not contain sodium?", the standard kind of deep structure assigned by a transformational grammar to conjoined sentences is not compatible with this interpretation. The usual reversal of the conjunction reduction transformations in a transformational grammar would produce a structure something like

```
S AND
   S Q
      NP  DET WHQ
          N SAMPLE
          NU PL
      AUX TNS PRESENT
      VP  V CONTAIN
          NP NPR SILICON
   S Q
      NEG
      NP  DET WHQ
          N SAMPLE
          NU PL
      AUX TNS PRESENT
      VP  V CONTAIN
          NP NPR SODIUM.
```

This structure corresponds to the conjunction of the two questions "What samples contain silicon?" and "What samples do not contain sodium?", which is the interpretation that it would receive by the LUNAR rules with the above DRULE for wh-determiners. However, this is not what the original conjoined question means; the intended question is asking for samples that simultaneously contain silicon and not sodium.

In order to handle such sentences, it is necessary to distinguish some constituent that corresponds to the conjunction of the two predicates "contain silicon" and "not contain sodium," which is itself a constituent of a higher level "what samples" operator. To handle such constructions correctly for both conjoined and nonconjoined constructions, LUNAR's ATN grammar of English was modified to assign a different structure to wh-determiner questions than the one that is assigned to other determiners. These sentences are analyzed as a special type of sentence, a noun phrase question (NPQ), in which the top level structure of the syntactic representation is that of a noun phrase, and the matrix sentence occurs as a special kind of subsidiary relative clause. For example, the sentence

"Which samples contain silicon?" is represented syntactically as

```
S NPQ
   NP  DET WHICHQ
       N SAMPLE
       NU PL
   S QREL
      NP  DET WHR
          N SAMPLE
          NU PL
      AUX TNS PRESENT
      VP  V CONTAIN
          NP DET NIL
             N SILICON
             NU SG.
```

This structure provides an embedded S node inside the higher level question, whose interpretation is a predicate with free variable bound in the question operator above. This embedded S node can be conjoined freely with other S nodes, while remaining under the scope of a single question operator. In this case, the appropriate DRULE (for a wh-determiner in a plural NPQ utterance) is simply

```
[D: WHQ-PL
 (NP.DET (AND (MEM 1 WHQ) (EQU 2 PL)))
 →
 (QUANT (FOR EVERY X / (# 0 NRULES) :
        (# 0 RRULES) ; (PRINTOUT X))) ].
```

Since the matrix sentence has been inserted as a relative clause in the syntactic structure assigned by the grammar, it will be interpreted by the RRULE R:REL in the subordinate interpretation (# 0 RRULES). A similar rule for interpreting singular noun phrases ("which sample contains. . .") produces a quantifier with ⟨quant⟩ = THE, instead of EVERY, thus capturing the presupposition that there should be a single answer.

All of the interrogative determiners, "which," "what," and "how many," are treated in the above fashion. The right-hand side of the "how

the interrogative pronoun "what." For example, in LUNAR the question "What is the concentration of silicon in S10046?" becomes

```
S Q
   NP   DET THE
        N CONCENTRATION
        NU SG
        PP PREP OF
           NP DET NIL
              N SILICON
              NU SG
           PP PREP IN
              NP NPR S10046
   AUX TNS PRESENT
   VP   V BE
        NP DET WHQ
           N THING
           NU SG/PL
```

A special SRULE for the verb "be" with complement "WHQ THING SG/PL" handles this case with a right-hand side schema:

(QUOTE (PRINTOUT (# 1 1)))

where the REF (# 1 1) refers to the subject noun phrase.

A somewhat more general treatment of the interrogative pronoun "what" would involve a DRULE whose right-hand side was

(FOR EVERY X / THING : DLT : (PRINTOUT X)).

Where the interpretation of the matrix sentence is to be inserted as a restriction, on the range of quantification and the overall interpretation is a command to print out the values that satisfy it. (THING in this case is meant to stand for the universal class.) One would not want to apply this rule in general to the simple "What is . . ." questions as above, since it would result in an interpretation that was less efficient (i.e., would enumerate all possible things and try to filter out the answer with an equality predicate). For example, "what is the concentration of silicon in S10046" would be interpreted

(FOR THE X / (DATALINE S10046 OVERALL SIO2) : T :
   (FOR EVERY Y / THING : (EQUAL X Y) :
      (PRINTOUT Y)))

many" rule is

(FOR THE X / (NUMBER X / (# 0 NRULES) : (# 0 RRULES)) :
   (PRINTOUT X)).

Here again, the interpretation of the matrix sentence is picked up in the call (# 0 RRULES). (The use of the same variable name in two different scopes does not cause any logical problems here, so no provision was made in LUNAR to create more than one variable for a given noun phrase.)

7.8.2 Interrogative Pronouns

A general treatment of the interrogative pronouns would require modifications of the assigned syntactic structures similar to the ones discussed above for interrogative determiners in order to handle conjunctions correctly. That is, sentences such as "What turns generic quantifiers into set unions and passes 'each' quantifiers through to a higher level?" seem to require an embedded S node to serve as a conjoined proposition inside a single "what" operator. However, it is far more common for conjoined questions with interrogative pronouns to be interpreted as a conjunction of two separate questions. This is especially true for conjoined "what is in . . ." questions. For example, "What is the concentration of silicon in S10046 and the concentration of rubidium in S10084?" is clearly not asking for a single number that happens to be the value of the concentration in both cases.

The LUNAR system contains rules for handling interrogative pronouns only in the special case of "what is . . ." questions. In this special case, conjoined questions fall into two classes, both of which seem to be handled correctly without special provisions in the grammar. In questions where the questioned noun phrase contains an explicit relative clause, that clause will contain an S node where conjunctions can be made and LUNAR's current techniques will treat this as one question with a conjoined restriction (e.g., "What is the sample that contains less than 15% silicon and contains more than 5% nickel?"). On the other hand, when there is no explicit relative clause, LUNAR will interpret such questions as a conjunction of separate questions (e.g., "What is the concentration of silicon in S10046 and the concentration of rubidium in S10084?").

The conventional structure assigned to "what is. . ." sentences by a transformational grammar represents the surface object as the deep subject, with a deep verb "be" and predicate complement corresponding to

difficult as deciding what the defining procedure for some of the possible intents should be. LUNAR's mechanisms are suitable for generating the alternative possible semantic representstions.

8. Post-Interpretive Processing

As mentioned before, the LUNAR meaning representation language has been designed both as a representation of executable procedures and as a symbolic structure that can be manipulated as an intensional object. Although every expression in the LUNAR MRL has an explicit semantics defined by its straightforward execution as a procedure, that procedure is frequently not the best one to execute to answer a question or carry out a command. For example, in the flight schedules applications, the literal interpretation of the expression

(FOR EVERY X / FLIGHT : (CONNECT X BOSTON CHICAGO) ;
(PRINTOUT X))

is to enumerate all of the flights known to the system, filtering out the ones that do not go from Boston to Chicago, and printing out the rest. However, in a reasonable data base for this domain, there would be various indexes into the flights, breaking them down by destination city and city of origin. If such an index exists, then a specialized enumeration function FLIGHT-FROM-TO could be defined for using the index to enumerate only flights from a given city to another. In this case, the above request could be represented as

(FOR EVERY X / (FLIGHT-FROM-TO BOSTON CHICAGO) : T ;
(PRINTOUT X)).

which would be much more efficient to execute.

Given the possibility of using specialized enumeration functions, one can then either write special interpretation rules to use the more specific enumeration function in the cases where it is appropriate, or one can perform some intensional manipulations on the interpretation assigned by the original rules to transform it into an equivalent expression that is more efficient to execute. The first approach was used in the original flight schedules system. An approach similar to the latter was used in the grammar information system, and to some extent in LUNAR, by

instead of

(FOR THE X / (DATALINE S10046 OVERALL SIO2) : T ;
(PRINTOUT X)).

Thus, one would still want to keep the special "what is ..." rule and LUNAR would only use the general rule in cases where the "what is ..." rule did not apply. (When the "what is ..." rule does apply, it does not even call for the interpretation of the "what" noun phrase that it has matched, so the general rule would not be invoked.)

Alternatively, one could use the general rule for all cases and then perform post-interpretive query optimization (see Section 8) to transform instances of filtering with equality predicates to a more efficient form that eliminates the unnecessary quantification.

7.8.3 Other Kinds of Wh Questions

Note that LUNAR interprets "what is ..." questions only as a request for the value of some function or the result of some search or computation, and not as requesting a definition or explanation. For example if LUNAR is asked "what is a sample" it will respond with an example (e.g., "S10046"), and if it is asked "what is S10046," it will respond "S10046." LUNAR is not aware of the internal structure of the defining procedures for its terms, nor does it have any intensional description of what samples are, so it has no way of answering the first type of question. There is no difficulty, however, in defining another rule for "what is ..." to apply to proper nouns and produce an interpretation with an operator NAME-CLASS (instead of PRINTOUT) that will print the class of an individual instead of its name. "What is S10046?" would then be interpreted as (NAME-CLASS S10046), which would answer "a sample."

Getting LUNAR to say something more complete about how S10046 differs from other samples, such as "a sample that contains a large olivine inclusion," is another matter. Among other problems, this would begin to tread into the area of pragmatics, where considerations such as the user's probable intent in asking the question and appropriateness of response in a particular context, as well as semantic considerations of meaning, become an issue (see Section 11.5). All of this is well beyond the scope of systems like LUNAR. However, deciding what semantic representation to assign as the intent of such a question is not nearly as

using "smart" quantifiers (see below). Recently, Reiter (1977) has presented a systematic treatment of a class of query optimizations in systems like LUNAR that interface to a relational data base.

Other post-interpretive operations on the MRL expression are performed in LUNAR to analyze the quantifiers and make entries in a discourse directory for potential antecedents of anaphoric expressions. Subsequently, definite descriptions and pronouns can make reference to this directory to select antecedents. I will not go into the treatment of anaphoric expressions in this paper other than to say that the search for the antecedent is invoked by an operator ANTEQUANT in the right-hand side of the DRULES that interpret anaphoric noun phrases. In general, this results in the generation of a quantifier, usually a copy of the one that was associated with the antecedent. Occasionally, the antecedent will itself fall in the scope of a higher quantifier on which it depends, in which case such governing quantifiers will also be copied and incorporated into the current interpretation. Some of the characteristics of LUNAR's treatment of anaphora are covered in Nash-Webber (1976) and Woods et al. (1972).

8.1 Smart Quantifiers

In the grammar information system, a notation of "smart" quantifier was introduced, which rather than blindly executing the quantification procedure obtained from semantic interpretation, made an effort to determine if there was a more specific enumeration function that could be used to obtain an equivalent answer. In general, the restriction on the range of quantification determines a subclass of the class over which quantification is ranging. If one can find a specialized enumeration function that enumerates a subclass of the original class but is still guaranteed to include any of the members that would have passed the original restriction, then that subclass enumeration function can be used in place of the original.

In the grammar information system, tables of specialized enumeration functions, together with sufficient conditions for their use, were stored associated with each basic class over which quantification could range. A resolution theorem prover a la Robinson (1965) was then used to determine whether the restriction of a given quantification implied one of the sufficient conditions for a more specialized class enumeration function. If so, the more specialized function was used. Unlike most applications of resolution theorem proving, the inferences required in this case are all very short, and since the purpose of the inference is to

improve the efficiency of the quantification, a natural bound can be set on the amount of time the theorem prover should spend before the attempt should be given up and the original enumeration function used.

In general, sufficiency conditions for specialized enumeration functions are parameterized with open variables to be instantiated during the proof of the sufficiency condition and then used as parameters for the specialized enumeration function. The resolution theorem proving strategies have a nice feature of providing such instantiated parameters as a result of their proofs; e.g., by using a mechanism such as the "answer" predicate of Green (1969).

Smart quantifiers were intended in general to be capable of other operations, such as estimating the cost of a computation from the sizes of the classes being quantified over and the depth of quantifier nesting (and warning the user if the cost might be excessive), saving the results of inner loop quantifications where they could be reused, interchanging the scopes of quantification to bring things that do not change outside a loop, etc. The capabilities actually implemented, however, are much more limited.

8.1.1 Path Enumeration in ATN's

Smart quantifiers were essential for efficiency in the grammar information system's enumeration of paths through its ATN. The system contained a variety of specialized path enumeration functions: one for paths between a given pair of states, one for paths leaving a given state, one for paths arriving at a given state, one for paths irrespective of end states, and versions of all of these for looping and nonlooping paths. Each specialized enumeration function was associated with a parameterized sufficiency condition for its use. For example, the function for nonlooping paths leaving a given state had a table entry equivalent to

(PATHSEQ Y T) if (AND (NOLOOP X) (START X Y))

where X refers to the variable of the class being quantified over, Y is a parameter to be instantiated, and (PATHSEQ Y T) is the enumeration function to be used if the sufficiency condition is satisfied.

Thus, if a quantification over paths had a restriction such as (AND (CONNECT-PATH X S/ S/VP) (NOLOOP X)) and the theorem prover had axioms such as (CONNECT-PATH X Y Z)⇒(START X Y), then

For special classes of objects, say concentrations, a pseudo-solution to this problem would be to adopt a strategy of always printing out all conceivable dependencies for that object (e.g., the sample, phase, and element associated with that concentration). This would be sufficient to indicate what dependencies each answer had on values of arguments, but would take no account of which of those dependencies was currently varying and which were fixed by the request. Moreover, this approach would not work in the above case, since the objects being printed are the results of a general purpose numerical averaging function, which does not necessarily have any dependencies, depending on what is being averaged over and what classes are being averaged over.

LUNAR contains a general solution to this quantifier dependency problem that is achieved by making the PRINTOUT command an opaque operator that processes its argument in a semi-intelligent way as an intensional object. PRINTOUT examines its argument for the occurrence of free variables. If the argument is itself a variable, it looks up the corresponding governing quantifier in the discourse directory (the same directory used for antecedents of anaphoric expressions) and checks that quantifier for occurrences of free variables. If it finds free variables in either place, it means that the object it is about to print has a dependency on those variables. In that case it prints out the current values of those variables along with the value that it is about to print out. In the case of the example above, the variable Y has the corresponding class specification (DATALINE X OVERALL SIO2) with restriction T, and is thus dependent on the variable X, which is ranging over the rocks. As a result, the printout from this request would look like

S10018 12.48 PCT
S10019 12.80 PCT
S10021 12.82 PCT
⋮

This mechanism works for arbitrary nesting of any number of quantifiers.

9. An Example

As an example of the overall operation of the semantic interpreter to review and illustrate the preceding discussions, consider the sentence

"What is the average modal plagioclase concentration for lunar samples that contain rubidium?"

the theorem prover would infer that the sufficiency condition (AND (NOLOOP X) (START X Y)) is satisfied with Y equal to S/ and therefore the specialized enumeration function (PATHSEQ S/ T) can be used.

Notice that the order of conjuncts in the restriction is irrelevant, and the restriction need only imply the sufficiency condition not match it exactly. In the above, there are still conditions in the restriction that will have to be checked as a filter on the output of the specialized enumeration function to make sure that the end of the path is at state S/VP. In general, it would be nice to remove from the restriction that portion that is already guaranteed to be satisfied by the new enumeration function, but that is easier said than done. In the grammar information system the original restriction was kept and used unchanged.

8.1.2 Document Retrieval in LUNAR

In the LUNAR system, a special case of smart quantifiers, without a general theorem prover, is used to handle enumeration of documents about a topic. When the FOR function determines that the class of objects being enumerated is DOCUMENT, it looks for a predicate (ABOUT X TOPIC) in the restriction (possibly in the scope of a conjunction but not under a negative). It then uses this topic as a parameter to an inverted file accessing routine which retrieves documents about a given topic.

8.2 Printing Quantifier Dependencies

The LUNAR MRL permits the natural expression of fairly complex requests such as "What is the average aluminum concentration in each of the type c rocks?" The interpretation of this request would be

(FOR EVERY X / (SEQ TYPECS) : T ;
(FOR THE Y / (AVERAGE Z / (DATALINE X OVERALL AL2O3))
: T ; (PRINTOUT Y))).

If the PRINTOUT command does nothing more than print out a representation for the value of its argument, the result of this command will be nothing more than a list of numbers, with no indication of which number goes with which of the rocks. Needless to say, this is usually not what the user expected.

returns a rule tree which it gets from the dictionary entry for the head of the sentence (the verb BE), and in this case a rule S: BE-WHAT matches. Its right-hand side is

(PRED (PRINTOUT (# 1 1)))

specifying a schema into which the interpretation of the subject noun phrase is to be inserted.

The semantic interpreter now begins to look at the subject noun phrase with TYPEFLAG NIL. In this case, RULES is smart enough to check the determiner THE and return the rule tree:

(D:THE-SG2 NIL D:THE-SG NIL D:THE-PL)

of which, the rule D:THE-SG matches successfully. The right-hand side of this rule is

(QUANT (FOR THE X / (# 0 NRULES) : (# 0 RRULES) ; DLT))

which specifies that a quantifier is to be constructed by substituting in the indicated places the interpretations of this same node with TYPE-FLAGs NRULES and RRULES.

The call to interpret the subject noun phrase with TYPEFLAG NRULES finds a list of NRULES in the dictionary entry for the word "average," consisting of the single rule N:AVERAGE. This rule, which we presented previously in Section 7.6, has a right-hand side

(QUOTE (SEQL (AVERAGE X / (# 1 1 SET))))

which calls for the interpretation of the "concentration" noun phrase with TYPEFLAG SET. The call to interpret the "average" node with TYPEFLAG RRULES, which will be done later, will result in the empty restriction T.

The call to interpret the "concentration" noun phrase with TYPE-FLAG SET uses a list of rules (D:SETOF NIL D:NOT-SET) where D:SETOF, which has been discussed previously in Section 7.7, checks for a determiner and number consistent with a set interpretation (i.e., determiner THE or NIL and number PL) and D:NOT-SET will match anything else. In this case, D:SETOF matches, with right-hand side

(SETGEN (SETOF X / (# 0 NRULES) : (# 0 RRULES)))

and calls for the interpretation of the same node with TYPEFLAGs NRULES and RRULES. The call with NRULES finds a matching rule N:CONCENTRATION after failing to match N:CONCENTRATION because of the presence of the adjective MODAL, which is rejected by a negated template. N:MODAL-CONC is used to interpret modal concen-

This sentence has the following syntactic structure assigned to it by the grammar:

```
S Q
  NP   DET THE
       N AVERAGE
       NU SG
       PP PREP OF
          NP DET NIL
             ADJ   MODAL
             ADJ   N PLAGIOCLASE
             N CONCENTRATION
             NU    PL
          PP   PREP FOR
             NP DET NIL
                ADJ LUNAR
                N SAMPLE
                NU PL
             S   REL
                 NP   DET WHR
                      N SAMPLE
                      NU PL
                 AUX TNS PRESENT
                 VP   V CONTAIN
                      NP DET NIL
                         N RUBIDIUM
                         NU SG
  AUX  TNS PRESENT
  VP   V BE
  NP   DET WHQ
       N THING
       NU SG/PL.
```

Semantic interpretation begins with a call to INTERP looking at the topmost S node with TYPEFLAG NIL. The function RULES looking at an S node with TYPEFLAG NIL returns the global rule tree PRE-RULES. These rules look for such things as yes/no question markers, sentential negations, etc. In this case, a rule PR6 matches and right-hand side, (PRED (# 0 SRULES)), specifies a call to INTERP for the same node with TYPEFLAG SRULES.

The function RULES looking at the S node with TYPEFLAG SRULES

trations of minerals in samples as a whole, and has the form

```
[N:MODAL-CONC
  (NP.N (MEM 1 (CONCENTRATION)))
  (OR (NP.PP (MEM 2 (SAMPLE)))
      (NP.PP.PP (MEM 2 (SAMPLE)))
      (DEFAULT (2 NP (DET EVERY)
                    (N SAMPLE)
                    (NU SG))))
  (OR (NP.PP (MEM 2 (PHASE MINERAL ELEMENT
                     OXIDE ISOTOPE)))
      (NP.ADJ #2 (MEM 2 (PHASE MINERAL ELEMENT
                         OXIDE ISOTOPE))))
  → (QUOTE (DATALINE (# 2 2) OVERALL (# 3 2))) ].
```

(DEFAULT is a special kind of template that always succeeds and that makes explicit bindings for use in the right-hand side. In the above case, if the "concentration" noun phrase had not mentioned a sample, then the default "every sample" would be assumed.)

N:MODAL-CONC in turn calls for the interpretations of the "sample" noun phrase and the constituent "rubidium." In interpreting the "sample" noun phrase, it again goes through the initial cycle of DRULES selected by TYPEFLAG NIL looking at a noun phrase, in this case finding a matching rule D:NIL whose right-hand side is

(QUANT (FOR GEN X / (# 0 NRULES) : (# 0 RRULES) ; DLT))

This in turn invokes an NRULES interpretation of the same phrase which uses the rule tree (N:TYPEA N:TYPEB N:TYPEC N:TYPED NIL N:SAMPLE) that looks first for any of the specific kinds of samples that might be referred to, and failing any of these, tries the general rule N:SAMPLE. N:SAMPLE checks for the head "sample" with an optional adjective "lunar" or the complete phrase "lunar material" and has a right-hand side

(QUOTE (SEQ SAMPLES))

where SEQ is the general enumeration function for known lists, and SAMPLES is a list of all the samples in the data base.

The RRULES interpretation uses the rule tree ((AND R:SAMPLE-WITH R:SAMPLE-WITH-COMP R:QREL R:REL R:PP R:ADJ)), which contains a single AND group of rules, all of which are to be tried and the results of any successful matches conjoined. The rule R:REL matches the relative clause, tagging the relative pronoun with the variable of interpretation XI3 and then calling for the interpretation of the relative

clause via the right-hand side

(PRED (# 1 1)).

The interpretation of the relative clause, like that of the main clause begins with a set of PRERULES, of which a rule PR6 matches with right-hand side

(PRED (# 0 SRULES)).

This again calls for the interpretation of the same node with TYPEFLAG SRULES. This interpretation finds the rule S:CONTAIN (presented earlier in Section 6), whose right-hand side calls for the interpretation of its subject noun phrase (which it finds already interpreted with the variable of quantification from above) and its object noun phrase "rubidium."

The latter is interpreted by a rule D:MASS, whose right-hand side looks up the word "rubidium" in the dictionary to get its standard data base representation RB (from a property name TABFORM) and produces the interpretation (QUOTE RB). As a SEM-QUANT pair, this is

((QUOTE RB) DLT).

This interpretation, together with that of the relative pronoun is returned to the process interpreting the "contain" clause, where they produce (after substitution and right-hand side evaluation) the SEM-QUANT pair

((CONTAIN X13 (QUOTE RB) DLT).

This same SEM-QUANT pair is return unchanged by the R:REL rule and since that is the only matching RRULE, no conjoining needs to be done to obtain the result of the RRULES interpretation of the "sample" noun phrase. Inserting this and the NRULES interpretation into the right-hand side of D:NIL, and executing, produces the SEM-QUANT pair

(X13 (FOR GEN X13 / (SEQ SAMPLES) :
     (CONTAIN X13 (QUOTE RB)) ; DLT))

where the right-hand side evaluation of the QUANT operator has embedded the quantifier in the QUANT accumulator and returned the SEM X13.

We now return to the NRULES interpretation of the "concentration" noun phrase, whose right-hand side called for the above interpretation and now calls for the interpretation of "plagioclase." Again, the D:MASS rule applies, looking up the TABFORM of the word in the dictionary and resulting in the SEM-QUANT pair

((QUOTE PLAG) DLT).

The substitution of these two into the right-hand side of the rule N:MODAL-CONC (and evaluating) produces the SEM-QUANT pair:

((DATALINE X13 OVERALL (QUOTE PLAG))
(FOR GEN X13 / (SEQ SAMPLES) :
(CONTAIN X13 (QUOTE RB)) ; DLT))

where the quantifier from below is still being passed up.

The RRULES interpretation of the ''concentration'' noun phrase produces T, since there are no predicating modifiers, and the insertion of these two into the right-hand side of the rule D:SETOF produces

(SETGEN (SETOF X12 / (DATALINE X13 OVERALL
(QUOTE PLAG)) : T))

while the quantifier accumulator QUANT contains the collar

(FOR GEN X13 / (SEQ SAMPLES) : (CONTAIN X13 (QUOTE RB)) :
DLT).

The execution of the function SETGEN grabs the generic quantifier from the register QUANT, leaving QUANT set to DLT, and produces the SEM

(UNION X13 / (SEQ SAMPLES) : (CONTAIN X13 (QUOTE RB)) ;
(SETOF X12 / (DATALINE X13 OVERALL (QUOTE PLAG)) : T)).

The quantification over samples has now been turned into a union of sets of data lines over a set of samples.

The resulting SEM and QUANT are returned to the process that is interpreting the ''average'' phrase, where the insertion into the right-hand side of the rule N:AVERAGE and subsequent evaluation yields the SEM-QUANT pair

((SEQL (AVERAGE X11 / (UNION X13 /
(SEQ SAMPLES) : (CONTAIN X13 (QUOTE RB)) :
(SETOF X12 / (DATALINE X13 OVERALL
(QUOTE PLAG)) : T))) DLT).

Interpretation of the ''average'' phrase with TYPEFLAG RRULES produces the SEM-QUANT pair (T DLT), and the insertion of this and the above into the right-hand side of the DRULE D:THE-SG and evaluating yields the SEM-QUANT pair

(X11 (FOR THE X11 / (SEQL (AVERAGE X11 / (UNION X13 /
(SEQ SAMPLES) : (CONTAIN X13 (QUOTE RB)) ;
(SETOF X12 / (DATALINE X13 OVERALL (QUOTE PLAG)) : T))))
: T ; DLT)).

This is returned to the SRULE S:BE-WHAT where the SEM X11 is embedded in the right-hand side to produce:

(PRED (PRINTOUT X11)).

Evaluating this expression grabs the quantifier to produce the new SEM, which the next higher rule, PR6, passes on unchanged as the final interpretation:

(FOR THE X11 / (SEQL (AVERAGE X11 / (UNION X13 /
(SEQ SAMPLES) : (CONTAIN X13 (QUOTE RB)) ;
(SETOF X12 / (DATALINE X13 OVERALL (QUOTE PLAG)) : T)))
: T ; (PRINTOUT X11)).

10. Loose Ends, Problems, and Future Directions

The techniques that I have described make a good start in handling the semantic interpretation of quantification in natural English—especially in the interaction of quantifiers with each other, with negatives, and with operators like ''average.'' However, problems remain. Some reflect LUNAR's status as an intermediate benchmark in an intended ongoing project. Others reflect the presence of some difficult problems that LUNAR would eventually have had to come up against. In the remaining sections, I will discuss some of the limitations of LUNAR's techniques, problems left unfaced, and trends and directions for future work in this area.

10.1 Approximate Solutions

One characteristic of some of the techniques used in LUNAR and many other systems is that they are only approximate solutions. A good example of an approximate solution to a problem is illustrated by LUNAR's use of the head word of a constituent as the sole source of features for the testing of semantic conditions in the left-hand sides of rules. To be generally adequate, it seems that semantic tests should be applied to the *interpretation* of a phrase, not just its syntactic structure (and especially not just its head). Some of the problems with the approximate approach became apparent when LUNAR first began to handle conjoined phrases. For example, it's simple semantic tests were no longer adequate when, instead of a single noun phrase of type X, a conjunction was encountered. This was due to a prior decision that the head of a conjoined phrase should be the conjunction operator (e.g., AND), since a constituent should have a unique head and there is no other unique

Without a semantic understanding of the situation, the computer has no criteria to select which of these three cases to use.

One of the roles that one might like the syntactic component to play in a language understanding system would be to make the appropriate grouping of a movable modifier with the phrase it modifies, so that the subsequent semantic interpretation rules will find the constituent where they would like it to be. However, since there is not always enough information available to the parser to make this decision on the basis of syntactic information alone, this would mean requiring the parser to generate all of the alternatives, from which the semantic interpreter would then make the choice. This in turn would mean that the interpreter would have to spend effort trying to interpret a wrong parsing, only to have to throw it away and start over again on a new one. It would be better for the parser to call upon semantic knowledge earlier in the process, while it is still trying to enumerate the alternative possible locations for the movable modifier. The question it would ask at this point would simply be whether a given phrase can take the kind of modifier in question, rather than a complete attempt to interpret each possibility.

10.2.1 Selective Modifier Placement

In general, the ATN grammars used in LUNAR tend to minimize the amount of unnecessary case analysis of alternative possible parsings by keeping common parts of different alternatives merged until the point in the sentence is reached where they make different predictions. At such a point, the choice between alternatives is frequently determined by having only one of their predictions satisfied. However, one place where this kind of factoring does not significantly constrain the branching of possibilities is at the end of a constituent where the grammar permits optional additional modifiers (e.g., prepositional phrase modifiers at the end of a noun phrase, as in the above example). Here. the alternatives of continuing to pick up modifiers at the same level and popping to a higher level have to be considered separately. If when the alternative of popping a constituent is chosen and the construction at the higher level can also take the same kind of modifier as the lower constituent, then a real ambiguity will result unless some restriction makes the modifier compatible with only one of the alternatives.

The LUNAR parser contains a facility called "selective modifier placement" for dealing with such "movable modifiers." When this facility is enabled, each time a movable modifier is constructed, the parser returns to the level that pushed for it to see if the configuration that caused the

candidate in a coordinate conjunction. However, since a conjunction operator would never have the semantic features expected by a rule, selectional restrictions applied to the head would not work.

A possible solution to this problem is to define the semantic features of a conjoined phrase to be the intersection of the features of its individual conjuncts. This has the attractive feature of enforcing some of the well-known parallelism constraints on conjunctions in English (i.e., conjoined constituents should be of like kind or similar in some respect). However, this solution is again only an approximation of what is required to fully model parallelism constraints. For example, it does not consider factors of size or complexity of the conjuncts. Further experience with such a model will almost certainly uncover still more problems.

Another example where obtaining the features from the head alone is inadequate involves noun phrases in which an adjective modifying the head contributes essential information (e.g., obtaining a feature +TOY from the phrase "toy gun"). In general, semantic selectional restrictions seem to require intensional models of potential referents rather than just syntactic structures. (In fact, their applying to such models is really the only justification for calling such constraints "semantic.") In my paper "Meaning and Machines" (Woods, 1973c), I discuss more fully the necessity for invoking models of semantic reference for correctly dealing with such restrictions.

More seriously, the whole treatment of selectional restrictions as prerequisites for meaningfulness is not quite correct, and the details of making selectional restrictions work correctly in various contexts such as modal sentences (especially assertions of impossibility) are far from worked out. For example, there is nothing wrong with the assertion "Rocks cannot love people" even if there seems to be something odd about "the rock loved John." Again, Woods (1973c) discusses such problems more fully.

10.2 Modifier Placement

Another area in which LUNAR's solution to a problem was less than general is in the interpretation of modifiers that are syntactically ambiguous as to what they modify. For example, in the sentence "Give me the average analysis of breccias for all major elements," there are at least three syntactic possibilities for the modifier "for all major elements" (it can modify the phrases headed by "breccias," "analysis," or "give"). In this case, our understanding of the semantics of the situation tells us that it modifies "analysis," since one can *analyze* a sample for an element, while "breccias for all major elements" does not make sense.

making sure that all modifiers were used by some rule and avoiding duplicate use of the same modifier more than once.

A number of such decisions were made in LUNAR for the expedient of getting it working, and are not necessarily of theoretical interest. This particular one is mentioned here because of its suggestion of a possible way to handle a problem, and also to illustrate the difference between solving a problem in general and patching a system up to handle a few cases.

10.3 Multiple Uses of Constituents

Alluded to above in the discussion of LUNAR's method of looking for misplaced modifiers was the potential for several different rules to use the same constituent for different purposes. In general, one expects a given modifier to have only one function in a sentence. However, this is not always the case. For example, an interesting characteristic of the "average" operator is the special use of a prepositional phrase with the preposition "over," which usurps one of the arguments of the function being averaged. Specifically, in "the average concentration of silicon over the breccias," the prepositional phrase "over the breccias" is clearly an argument to the average function, specifying the class of objects over which the average is to be computed. However, it is also redundantly specifying the variable that will fill the constituent slot of the concentration schema, even though it does not have any of the prepositions that would normally specify this slot. The semantic interpretation framework that the LUNAR system embodies does not anticipate the simultaneous use of a constituent as a part of two different operators in this fashion (although the implemented mechanism does not forbid it).

The rules in the implemented LUNAR system deal with this problem (as opposed to solving it) by permitting the prepositional phrase with "over" to modify concentration rather than average. This choice was made because the average operator is interpretable without a specific "over" modifier, whereas the concentration is not interpretable without a constituent whose concentration is being measured. However, this "solution" leaves us without any constraint that "over" can only occur with averages. Consequently, phrases such as "the concentration of silicon over S10046" would be acceptable. Such lack of constraint is generally not a serious problem in very restricted topic domains and with relatively simple sentences, because users are unlikely to use one of the unacceptable constructions. However, as the complexity of the language increases, especially with the introduction of constructions such

push could also have popped to a higher level and, if so, whether that higher level could also have pushed for the same thing. It repeats this process until it has gathered up all of the levels that could possibly (syntactically) use the modifier. It then asks semantic questions to rank order the possibilities, choosing the most likely one, and generating alternatives for the others. In a classic example, "I saw the man in the park with a telescope," the phrase "in the park" could modify either "man," or "see," and "with a telescope" could modify either "park," "man," or "see" (with the possible exception, depending on your dialect, of forbidding "with a telescope" from modifying "man" if "in the park" is interpreted as modifying "see"). The selective modifier placement facility chooses the interpretation "see with a telescope" and "man in the park" when given information that one can see with an optical instrument. Woods (1973a) describes this facility for selective modifier placement more fully.

10.2.2 Using Misplaced Modifiers

Although the selective modifier placement facility in LUNAR's parser is probably very close to the right solution to this problem of movable modifiers, the mechanism as implemented requires the semantic information that it uses to be organized in a slightly different form from that used in the semantic interpretation rules. Rather than duplicate the information, LUNAR's demonstration prototype used a different approach. In this system, the grammar determined an initial placement of such modifiers based solely on what prepositions a given head noun could take as modifiers. Subject to this constraint, the movable modifier was parsed as modifying the nearest preceding constituent (i.e., as deep in the parse tree as premitted by the constraint). Subsequently during interpretation, if the semantic interpreter failed to find a needed constituent at the level it wanted it, it would look for it attached to more deeply embedded levels in the tree.

If this procedure for looking for misplaced modifiers had been handled by a general mechanism for looking for misplaced constituents subject to appropriate syntactic and semantic guidance, it would provide an alternative approach of comparable generality to selective modifier placement, raising an interesting set of questions as to the relative advantages of the two approaches. In the demonstration prototype, however, it was handled by the simple expedient of using disjunctive templates in the rules to look for a constituent in each of the places where it might occur. Each rule thus had to be individually tailored to look for its needed constituents wherever they might occur. Problems were also present in

explicitly mentioned elsewhere but must be inferred, and characterizing the regions of the surrounding context that can legitimately provide antecedents for ellipsis (e.g., can they be extracted out of subordinate relative clauses that do not dominate the occurrence of the ellipsis?).

10.5 Plausibility of Alternative Interpretations

In general, the correct way to handle many of the potential ambiguities that arise in English seems to be to construct representations of alternative interpretations, or alternative parts of interpretations, and evaluate the alternatives for their relative plausibility. LUNAR does not contain such a facility. Instead, it makes the best effort it can to resolve ambiguities, given what it knows about general rules for preferred parsings, criteria for preferred interpretations, and specific semantic selectional restrictions for nouns and verbs. LUNAR does quite well within these constraints in handling a wide variety of constructions. This is successful largely because of the limited nature of the subject matter and consequent implicit constraints on the kinds of questions and statements that are sensible. However, a variety of phenomena seem to require a more general plausibility evaluator to choose between alternatives. If one had such an evaluator of relative plausibility, the mechanisms used in LUNAR would be adequate to generate the necessary alternatives.

10.6 Anaphoric Reference

Anaphoric reference is another problem area in which LUNAR's treatment does not embody a sufficiently general solution. Every time an interpretation is constructed, LUNAR makes entries in a discourse directory for each constituent that may be subsequently referred to anaphorically. Each entry consists of the original syntactic structure of a phrase, plus a slightly modified form of its semantic interpretation. In response to an anaphoric expression such as "it" and "that sample," LUNAR searches this directory for the most recent possible antecedent and reuses its previous interpretation.

LUNAR's anaphoric reference facility is fairly sophisticated, including the possibility to refer to an object that is dependent on another quantified object, in which case it will bring forward both quantifiers into the interpretation of the new sentence (e.g., "What is the silicon content of each volcanic sample?" "What is its magnesium concentration?"). It also handles certain cases of anaphora where only part of the intensional description of a previous phrase is reused (e.g., "What is the concentration of silicon in breccias?" "What is it in volcanics?"). However, this facility contains a number of loose ends. One of the most serious is that

as reduced relative clauses and conjunction reduction, the possibility increases that some of these unacceptable sequences may be posed as partial parsings of an otherwise acceptable sentence, and can either result in unintended parsings or long excursions into spurious garden path interpretations.

This kind of ad hoc "solution" to the "average...over..." problem is typical of the compromises made in many natural language systems, and is brought up here to illustrate the wrong way to attack a problem. It contrasts strongly with the kinds of general techniques that typify LUNAR's solutions to other problems.

10.4 Ellipsis

Possibly the correct solution to the problem of "average...over..." is one that handles a general class of ellipsis—those cases where an argument is omitted because it can be inferred from information available elsewhere in a sentence. In this account, the "over" phrase would be an argument to "average" and the subordinate "concentration" phrase would have an ellipsed specification of the constituent being measured. A similar problem with ellipsis occurs in the flight schedules context, where sentences such as

List the departure time from Boston of every TWA flight to Chicago.

would be interpreted literally as asking for the Boston departure times of all TWA flights that go to Chicago, regardless of whether they even go through Boston. To express the intended request without ellipsis, the user would have to say

List the departure time from Boston of every TWA flight *from Boston* to Chicago.

As I pointed out in my thesis (Woods, 1967), the information in the semantic rules provides the necessary information for the first step in treating such ellipsis—the recognition that something is missing. Capitalizing on this, however, requires a rule-matching component that is able to find and remember the closest matching rule when no rule matches fully, and to provide specifications of the missing pieces to be used by some search routine that tries to recover the ellipsis. This latter routine would have to examine the rest of the structure of the sentence, and perhaps some of the discourse history, to determine if there are appropriate contextually specified fillers to use. Research problems associated with such ellipsis have to do with the resolution of alternative possible fillers that meet the description, finding potential fillers that are not

only the phrases typed in by the user are available for anaphoric reference, while the potential antecedents implied by the responses of the system are not (responses were usually not expressed in English, and in any case were not entered into the discourse directory). Anaphoric reference in general contains some very deep problems, some of which are revealed in LUNAR. Nash-Webber (1976, 1977), Nash-Webber and Reiter (1977), and Webber (1978) discuss these problems in detail.

10.7 Ill-Formed Input and Partial Interpretation

One of the problems that face a real user of a natural language understanding system is that not everything that he tries to say to the system is understandable to it. LUNAR tried to cope with this problem by having a grammar sufficiently comprehensive that it would understand everything a lunar geologist might ask about its data base. The system actually came fairly close to doing that. In other systems, such as the SOPHIE system of Brown and Burton (1975), this has been achieved even more completely. In a limited topic domain, this can be done by systematically extending the range of the system's understanding every time a sentence is encountered that is not understood, until eventually a virtual closure is obtained. Unfortunately, in less topic-specific systems, it is more difficult to reach this kind of closure, and in such cases it would be desirable for the system to provide a user with some partial analysis of his request to at least help him develop a model of what the machine does and does not understand.

LUNAR contains no facility for such partial understanding, although it does have a rudimentary facility to comment about modifiers that it does not understand in an otherwise understandable sentence and to notify the user of a phrase that it does not understand in a sentence that it has managed to parse but cannot interpret. Given the size of its vocabulary and the extensiveness of its grammar, there are large classes of sentences that LUNAR can parse but not understand. For these, LUNAR will at least inform the user of the first phrase that it encounters that it cannot understand. However, it cannot respond to questions about its range of understanding or be of much help to the user in finding out whether (and, if so, how) one can rephrase a request to make it understandable. More seriously, if a sentence fails to parse (a less common occurrence, but not unusual), LUNAR provides only the cryptic information that it could not parse the input. The reason for this is as follows.

If the user has used words that are not in its dictionary, LUNAR of course informs him of this fact and the problem is clear. If, however, the user has used known words in a way that does not parse, all LUNAR

knows is that it has tried all of its possible ways to parse the input and none of them succeeded. In general, the parser has followed a large number of alternative parsing paths, each of which has gotten some distance through the input sentence before reaching an inconsistency. LUNAR in fact keeps track of each blocked path, and even knows which one of them has gotten the farthest through the sentence. However, experience has shown that there is no reason to expect this longest partial parse path to be correct. In general, the mistake has occurred at some earlier point, after which the grammar has continued to fit words into its false hypothesis for some unknown distance before an inconsistency arises. Beyond simply printing out the words used in this longest path (letting the user guess what grammatical characteristic of his sentence was unknown to the computer) there is no obvious solution to this problem. In this respect, a language with a deterministic grammar has an advantage over natural English, since there will only be one such parse path. In that case, when the parser blocks, there is no question about which path was best.

Note that there is no problem here in handling any particular case or anticipated situation. Arbitrary classes of grammatical violations can be anticipated and entered into the grammar (usually with an associated penalty to keep them from interfering with completely grammatical interpretations). Such sentences will no longer be a problem. What we are concerned with here requires a system with an understanding of its own understanding, and an ability to converse with a user about the meaning and use of words and constructions. Such a system would be highly desirable, but is far from realization at present. The grammar information system discussed above, which knows about its own grammar and can talk about states and transitions in the grammar, is a long way from being able to help a user in this situation.

One technique from the HWIM speech understanding system (Woods et al., 1976) that could help in such a situation is to find maximally consistent islands in the word string using a bidirectional ATN parser that can parse any fragment of a correct sentence from the middle out. One could then search in the regions where such islands abut or overlap for possible transitions that could connect the two.

A special case of the ungrammatical sentence problem is the case of a mistyped word. If the misspelling results in an unknown word, then the problem is simple; when LUNAR informs the user of an unknown word, it also gives him the opportunity to change it and continue. However, if the misspelling results in another legal word, then the system is likely to go into the state discussed above, where all parsing paths fail and there is little the system can say about what went wrong. In this

The function STORE could interface to any mechanical inference system to store its argument as an axiom or rule. For example, with a resolution theorem proving system such as Green's QA3 (Green, 1969), STORE could transform its argument from its given (extended) predicate calculus form into clause form and enter the resulting clauses into an indexed data base of axioms. TEST could then be extended to try inferring the truth of its argument proposition from such axioms either prior to, or after, attempting to answer the question extensionally. TEST could in fact be made smart enough to decide which mode of inference to try first on the basis of characteristics of the proposition being tested. Moreover, procedures defining individual predicates and functions could also call the inference component directly. For example, the predicate ABOUT that relates documents to topics could call the inference facility to determine whether a document is about a given topic due to one of its stored topics subsuming or being subsumed by the one in question.

The incorporation of intensional inference into the LUNAR framework is thus a simple matter of writing a few interfacing functions to add axioms to, and call for inferences from, some mechanical inference facility (assuming one has the necessary inference system). The problems of constructing such an inference facility to efficiently handle the kinds of inferences that would generally be required is not trivial, but that is another problem beyond the scope of this paper. A number of other natural language systems have capabilities for natural language input of facts (e.g., Winograd, 1972), but few have very powerful inference facilities for their subsequent use.

Among the shifts in emphasis that would probably be made in a semantic interpretation system to permit extensive intensional inference would be increasing attention to the notational structure of intensional entities to make them more amenable to inspection by various computer programs (as opposed to being perspicuous to a human). The effectiveness of the MRL used in LUNAR derives from its overall way of decomposing meanings into constituent parts, but is not particularly sensitive to notational variations that preserve this decomposition. When such MRL expressions are used as data objects by intensional processors, internal notational changes may be desired to facilitate such things as indexing facts and rules, relating more general facts to more specific ones, and making the inspection of MRL expressions as data objects more efficient for the processes that operate on them. In particular, one might want to represent the MRL expressions in some network form such as that described in Woods (1975b) to make them accessible by associative retrieval.

However, whatever notational variations one might want to adopt for

case, the user can probably find his mistake by checking the sentence he has typed, but sometimes a mistake will be subtle and overlooked. Again, some of the techniques from the HWIM system could be used here. Specifically, HWIM's dictionary look-up is such that it finds all words that are sufficiently similar to the input acoustics and provides multiple alternatives with differing scores, depending on how well they agree with the input. An identical technique can enumerate possible known words that could have misspellings corresponding to the typed input, with scores depending on the likelihoods of those misspellings. These alternatives would then sit on a shelf to be tried if no parsing using the words as typed were found.

10.8 Intensional Inference

As discussed previously, the LUNAR prototype deals only with extensional inferences, answering questions with quantifiers by explicitly enumerating the members of the range and testing propositions for individual members. LUNAR contains a good set of techniques for such inference, such as the use of general enumeration functions and smart quantifiers. However, although this is a very efficient mode of inference, it is not appropriate for many types of questions. The ability to deal with more complex types of data entities, even such specialized things as descriptions of shape and textural features of the lunar samples, will require the use of intensional inference procedures. For this reason, LUNAR's MRL was designed to be compatible with both intensional and extensional inference. Intensional inference is necessary for any type of question whose answer requires inference from general facts, rather than mere retrieval or aggregation of low-level observations. In particular, it is necessary in any system that is to accept input of new information in anything other than a rigid stylized format.

Although LUNAR contained some rudimentary facilities for adding new lines to its chemical analysis data base and for editing such entries, it contained no facility for understanding, storing, or subsequently using general facts and information. For example, a sentence such as "All samples contain silicon" is interpreted by LUNAR as an assertion to be tested and either affirmed or denied. It is not stored as a fact to be used subsequently. However, there is nothing in LUNAR's design that prohibits such storage of facts. In particular, a simple PRERULE for declarative sentences with a right-hand side (PRED (STORE (# 0 SRULES)) could generate interpretations that would store facts in an intensional data base (where STORE is assumed to be a function that stores facts in an intensional data base).

increasing the efficiency of intensional processing, it should not be necessary, and is certainly not desirable, to sacrifice the fundamental understanding of the semantics of the notation and the kinds of structural decompositions of meanings that have been evolved in LUNAR and her sister systems.

11. Syntactic/Semantic Interactions

A very important question, for which LUNAR's techniques are clearly not the general answer, has to do with the relative roles of syntactic and semantic information in sentence understanding. Since this is an issue of considerable complexity and confusion, I will devote the remainder of this paper to discussing the issues as I currently understand them.

The question of how syntax and semantics should interact is one that has been approached in a variety of ways. Even the systems discussed above contain representatives of two extreme approaches. LUNAR exemplifies one extreme: it produces a complete syntactic representation which is only then given to a semantic interpretation component for interpretation. TRIPSYS, on the other hand, combines the entire process of parsing and semantic interpretation in a grammar that produces semantic interpretations directly without any intermediate syntactic representation.

Before proceeding further in this discussion, let me first review the role of syntactic information in the process of interpretation.

11.1 The Role of Syntactic Structure

The role of a syntactic parsing in the overall process of interpreting the meaning of sentences includes answering such questions as "What is the subject noun phrase?", "What is the main verb of the clause?", "What determiner is used in this noun phrase?", etc.—all of this is necessary input information for the semantic interpretation decisions. Parsing is necessary to answer these questions because, in general, the answers cannot be determined by mere local tests in the input string (such as looking at the following or preceding word). Instead, such answers must be tentatively hypothesized and then checked out by discovering whether the given hypothesis is consistent with some complete analysis of the sentence. (The existence of "garden path" sentences whose initial portion temporarily misleads a reader into a false expectation about the meaning are convincing evidence that such decisions cannot be made locally.)

Occasionally, the interpretation of a sentence depends on which of several alternative possible parsings of the sentence the user intends (i.e., the sentence is ambiguous). In this case the parser must perform the case analysis required to separate the alternative possibilities so they can be considered individually. A syntactic parse tree, as used in LUNAR and similar systems, represents a concise total description that answers all questions about the grouping and interrelationships among words for a particular hypothesized parsing of a sentence. As such, it represents an example of what R. Bobrow (Bobrow and Brown, 1975) calls a "contingent knowledge structure," an intermediate knowledge structure that is synthesized from an input to summarize fundamental information from which a large class of related questions can then be efficiently inferred. In general, there is an advantage to using a separate parsing phase to discover and concisely represent these syntactic relationships, since many different semantic rules may ask essentially the same questions. One would not want to duplicate the processing necessary to answer them repeatedly from scratch.

In addition to providing a concise description of the interrelationships among words, the parse trees can serve an additional role by providing levels of grouping that will control the semantic interpretation process, assigning nodes to each of the phrases that behave as modular constituents of the overall semantic interpretation. The semantic interpreter then walks this tree structure, assigning interpretations to the nodes corresponding to phrases that the parser has grouped together. The syntax trees assigned by the grammar thus serve as a control structure for the semantic interpretation.

For historical reasons, LUNAR's grammar constructed syntactic representations as close as possible to those that were advocated at the time by transformational linguists as deep structures for English sentences (Stockwell et al., 1968). The complex patterns of semantic rules in LUNAR and the multiple-phase interpretation are partly mechanisms that were designed to provide additional control information that was not present in those tree structures. An alternative approach could have been to modify the syntactic structures to gain the same effect (see below). The approach that was taken provides maximum flexibility for applying a set of semantic interpretation rules to an existing grammar. It also provides a good pedagogical device for describing interpretation rules and strategies, independent of the various syntactic details that stand between the actual surface word strings and the parse structures assigned by the grammar. However, the use of such powerful rules introduces a cost in execution time that would not be required by a system that adapted the grammar more to the requirements of semantic interpretation.

11.2 Grammar Induced Phasing of Interpretation

As mentioned above, most of the control of multiple phase interpretation that is done in LUNAR by means of successive calls to the interpreter with different TYPEFLAGS could be handled by having the parser assign a separate node for each of the phases of interpretation. If this were done, the phasing of interpretation would be governed entirely by the structure of the tree. For example, one could have designed a grammar to assign a structure to negated sentences that looks something like

```
S DCL
  NEG
  S   NP NPR S10046
      VP V CONTAIN
         NP DET NIL
            N SILICON
            NU SG
```

instead of

```
S DCL
  NEG
  NP NPR S10046
  VP V CONTAIN
     NP DET NIL
        N SILICON
        NU SG.
```

In such a structure, there is a node in the tree structure to receive the interpretation of the constituent unnegated sentence, and thus the separate phasing of the PRERULES and the SRULES used in LUNAR would be determined by the structure of the tree. Similarly, noun phrases could be structured something like

```
NP DET THE
   NU  SG
   NOM NOM ADJ  N SILICON
           NOM N CONCENTRATION
   PP  PREP IN
       NP NPR S10046
```

instead of the structure

```
NP DET THE
   ADJ N SILICON
   N   CONCENTRATION
   NU  SG
   PP  PREP IN
       NP NPR S10046
```

which is used in the LUNAR grammar. In such a structure, the nested NOM phrases would receive the interpretation of the head noun plus modifiers by picking up modifiers one at a time.

It is not immediately obvious, given LUNAR's separation of syntactic and semantic operations, which of the two ways of introducing the phasing is most efficient. Introducing phasing via syntax requires it to be done without the benefit of some of the information that is available at interpretation time, so that there is the potential of having to generate alternative syntactic representations for the interpreter to later choose between. On the other hand, doing it with the semantic interpretation rules requires extra machinery in the interpreter (but does not seem to introduce much extra run-time computation).

One might argue for the first kind of structure in the above examples on syntactic grounds alone. If this is done, then the efficiency issue just discussed is simply one more argument. If it turns out that the preferred structure for linguistic reasons is also the most efficient for interpretation, that would be a nice result. Whether this is true or not, however, is not clear to me at present.

11.3 Semantic Interpretation while Parsing

The previous discussion illustrates some of the disadvantages of the separation of parsing and semantic interpretation phases in the LUNAR system. The discussion of placement of movable modifiers illustrates another. In general, there are a variety of places during parsing where the use of semantic information can provide guidance that is otherwise not available, thus limiting the number of alternative hypothetical parse paths considered by the parser. It has frequently been argued that performing semantic interpretation during parsing is more efficient than performing it later by virtue of this pruning of parse paths. However, the issue is not quite as simple as this argument makes it appear. Against this savings, one must weigh the cost of doing semantic interpretation on partial parse paths that will eventually fail for syntactic reasons. Which of the two approaches is superior in this respect depends on (1) the relative costs of doing semantic versus syntactic tests and (2) which of these two sources of knowledge provides the most constraint. Both of these factors will vary from one system to another, depending on the fluency of their grammars and the scope of their semantics.

At one point, a switch was inserted in the LUNAR grammar that would call for the immediate interpretation of any newly formed constituent rather than wait for a complete parse tree to be formed. This turned out not to have an efficiency advantage. In fact, sentences took longer to process (i.e., parse and interpret). This was due in part to the fact that LUNAR's grammar did a good job of selecting the right parse without semantic guidance. In such circumstances, semantic interpretations do not help to reject incorrect paths. Instead, they merely introduce an extra cost due to interpretations performed on partial parse paths that later fail. Moreover, given LUNAR's rules, there are constituents for which special interpretations are required by higher constructions (e.g., with TYPEFLAG SET or TOPIC). Since bottom-up interpretation may not know how a higher construction will want to interpret a given constituent, it must either make as assumption (which may usually be right, but occasionally will have to be changed), or else make all possible interpretations. Either case will require more interpretation than waiting for a complete tree to be formed and then doing only the interpretation required. All of these considerations make semantic interpretation during parsing less desirable unless some positive benefit of early semantic guidance outweighs these costs.

11.4 Top-Down versus Bottom-Up Interpretation

In the experiment described above, in which LUNAR was modified to perform bottom-up interpretation during parsing, the dilemma of handling context-dependent interpretations was raised. In those experiments, the default assumption was made to interpret every noun phrase with TY-PEFLAG NIL during the bottom-up phase. In cases where a higher construction required some other interpretation, reinterpretation was called for at that point in the usual top-down mode. Since LUNAR maintains a record of previous interpretations that have been done on a node to avoid repeating an interpretation, it was possible to efficiently reuse interpretations that were made bottom-up when they happened to be the kind required, while performing new ones if needed.

An alternative approach to this problem of bottom-up interpretation in context is to make a default interpretation that preserves enough information so that it can be modified to fit unexpected contexts without actually having to redo the interpretation. This would be similar to the

kind of thing that SETGEN (in the right-hand side of the D:SET rule) does to the quantifiers it picks up to turn them into UNIONs. In the HERMES grammar (Ash et al., 1977), R. Bobrow uses this approach, which he calls "coercion" (intuitively, forcing the interpretation of a constituent to be the kind that is expected). In this case, when the higher construction wants the interpretation of a constituent in some mode other than the one that has been already done, it asks whether the existing one can be coerced into the kind that it wants rather than trying to reinterpret the original phrase.

Many of these questions of top-down versus bottom-up interpretation, syntax-only parsing before semantic interpretation or vice versa (or both together), do not have clear cut answers. In general, there is a tension between doing work on a given portion of a sentence in a way that is context free (so that the work can be shared by different alternative hypotheses at a higher level) and doing it in the context of a specific hypothesis (so that the most leverage can be gained from that hypothesis to prune the alternatives at the lower level). It is not yet clear whether one of the extremes or some intermediate position is optimal.

11.5 Pragmatic Grammars

One thing that should be borne in mind when discussing the role of grammars is that it is not necessary that the grammar characterize exactly those sentences that a grammarian would consider correct. The formal grammar used by a system can characterize sentences as the user would be likely to say them, including sentences that a grammarian might call ungrammatical. For example, LUNAR accepts isolated noun phrases as acceptable utterances, implicitly governed by an operator "give me."

In the classical division of problems of meaning into the areas of syntax, semantics, and pragmatics, the latter term is used to denote those aspects of meaning determined not by general semantic rules, but as aspects of the current situation, one's knowledge of the speaker, etc. For example, in situations of irony, a speaker says exactly the opposite of what he means. Likewise, certain apparent questions should in fact be interpreted as commands or as other requests (e.g., "Do you have the time?" is usually a "polite" way of asking "What time is it?"). Moreover, certain ungrammatical utterances nevertheless have a meaning that can be inferred from context. In general, the ultimate product of language understanding is the pragmatic interpretation of the utterance in context. This interpretation, while not necessarily requiring a syntactically and semantically correct input sentence, nevertheless depends on an understanding of normal syntax and semantics.

In LUNAR, there is no systematic treatment of pragmatic issues, although in some cases, pragmatic considerations as well as semantic ones were used in formulating its interpretation rules. For example, the rule that interprets the head "analysis," when it finds no specification of the elements to be measured, makes a default assumption that the major elements are intended. This is due to the pragmatic fact that (according to our geologist informant) this is what a geologist would want to see if he made such a request, not because that is what the request actually means. In this way, LUNAR can handle a small number of anticipated pragmatic situations directly in its rules.

In TRIPSYS, a small step toward including pragmatics in the grammar was taken. The TRIPSYS grammar takes into account not only semantic information such as class membership and selectional restrictions of words, but also pragmatic information. This includes factual world knowledge such as what cities are in which states, actual first and last names of people, and discourse history information, such as whether appropriate referents exist for anaphoric expressions. The TRIPSYS system is only beginning to explore these issues, and has not begun to develop a general system for pragmatic interpretation. Much more work remains to be done in this area, and interest in it seems to be building as our mastery of the more basic syntactic and semantic issues matures.

The "pragmatic" grammar of TRIPSYS is only one exploration of a philosophy of combined syntactic and semantic grammars that has arisen independently in several places. Other similar uses of ATN or ATN-like grammars combining syntactic and semantic (and possibly pragmatic) information are the "Semantic Grammars" of Burton (1976), the "Performance Grammars" of Robinson (1975), the SHRDLU system of Winograd (1972), and the HERMES grammar of R. Bobrow (Ash *et al.*, 1977).

11.6 Semantic Interpretation in the Grammar

In separating parsing and semantic interpretation into two separate processes (whether performed concurrently or in separate phases), LUNAR gains several advantages and also several disadvantages. On the positive side, one obtains a syntactic characterization of a sizable subset of English that is independent of a specific topic domain and hence transferable to other applications. All of the domain-specific information is contained in the dictionaries and the semantic interpretation rules. On the other hand, there is a conceptual expense in determining what syntactic structure to use for many of the less standard constructions. One would like such structures to be somehow motivated by linguistic prin-

ciples and yet, at the same time, have them facilitate subsequent interpretation. In many cases, the desired interpretation is more clear to the grammar designer than is a suitable syntactic representation. In a number of situations, such as those discussed previously for handling wh-questions with conjunction reduction and for handling averages, I have found it desirable to change what had initially seemed a suitable syntactic representation in order to facilitate subsequent semantic interpretation. If semantic interpretations were to be produced directly by the grammar instead of using an intermediate syntactic representation, then such problems would be avoided.

The integration of semantic interpretation rules into the grammar could be done in a number of ways, one of which would be to develop a rule compiler that would use the templates of rules such as LUNAR's to determine where in the grammar to insert the rule. Another would be to write the interpretation rules into the grammar in the first place. This latter is the approach that is taken in the TRIPSYS system. It seems clearly an appropriate thing to do for such rules as the PRERULES for sentences and the DRULES for noun phrases, where the principal information used is largely syntactic. For the equivalent of SRULES, NRULES, and RRULES, writing specific rules into the grammar would make the grammar itself more topic-specific than one might like. However, writing generalized rules that apply to large classes of words, using information from their dictionary entries for word-specific information such as case frames, selectional restrictions, permitted prepositions, and corresponding MRL translations, should produce a grammar that is relatively topic-independent. This is the approach taken by Robinson (1975) and by R. Bobrow (Ash *et al.*, 1977).

Integrating semantic interpretation with a grammar is not an obvious overall improvement, since by doing so one gives up features as well as gaining them. For example, as discussed earlier the "advantage" of using semantic interpretation to prune parse paths is not always realized. However, there are some other efficiencies of the combined syntactic/semantic grammars that have nothing to do with pruning. One of these is the avoidance of pattern-matching.

One of the costs of the separate semantic interpretation phase used in LUNAR is the cost of pattern-matching the rules. Much of this effort is redundant since the various pieces of information that are accessed by the rules were mostly available in registers during the parsing process. From here they were packaged up by actions in the grammar into the parse tree structures that are passed on to the interpreter. The pattern-matching in the interpreter recovers these bindings so that the right-hand side of the rule can use them. If the right-hand side schema of the rule

tactic/semantic grammar is much more domain-specific and less transportable unless clear principles for separating domain-specific from general knowledge are followed. Moreover, the fact that a given semantic constituent can be found in different places by different arcs in the grammar seems to require separate consideration of the same semantic operations at different places in the grammar.

11.7 Generating Quantifiers while Parsing

The generation of separate SEM's and QUANT's when performing interpretation while parsing appears to complicate the integration of the semantic interpretation into the grammar, but in fact is not difficult. One can stipulate that any constituent parsed will return a structure that contains both a SEM and a QUANT as currently assigned by the INTERP function in LUNAR. The parsing at the next higher level in the grammar will then accumulate the separate QUANTs from each of the constituents that it consumes, give them to a SORTQUANT function to determine the order of nesting, and construct the interpretation of the phrase being parsed out of the SEM's of the constituent phrases. All of the quantifier-passing operations described previously can be carried out during the parsing with little difficulty.

One advantage of this procedure is that the job of SORTQUANT is simplified by the fact that the quantifiers will be given to it in surface structure order rather than in some order determined by the deep structure assigned by the grammar. LUNAR's SORTQUANT function has to essentially reconstruct surface word order.

12. Conclusions

The LUNAR prototype marks a significant step in the direction of fluent natural language understanding. Within the range of its data base, the system permits a scientist to ask questions and request computations in his own natural English in much the same form as they arise to him (or at least in much the same form that he would use to communicate them to another human being). However, although the LUNAR prototype exhibits many desired qualities, it is still far from fully achieving its goal. The knowledge that the current system contains about the use of English and the corresponding meanings of words and phrases is very limited outside the range of those English constructions that pertain to the system's data base of chemical analysis data. This data base has a very simple structure; indeed it was chosen as an initial data base because

could be executed while these bindings were still available during the parsing process, considerable computation could be avoided. Moreover, much of the syntactic information that is checked in the rules is implicitly available in the states of the grammar by virtue of the fact that the parser has reached that state (and more of that information could be put into the states if desired). Thus, in many cases, much of the testing that goes on in the pattern-matching of rules would be avoided if the right-hand side of the rule, paired with whatever semantic tests are required, were inserted as an action at the appropriate points in the grammar.

For example, at certain points in the parsing, the grammar would know that it had enough information to construct the basic quantifier implied by the determiner and number of a noun phrase. At a later point, it would know all of the various modifiers that are being applied to the head noun. As the necessary pieces arrive, the interpretation can be constructed incrementally.

The effectiveness of this kind of combined parser/interpreter depends partly on the discovery that the kinds of associations of REFs to constituent nodes that are made by LUNAR's rules are usually references to direct constituents of the node being interpreted. Thus, they correspond closely to the constituents that are being held in the registers by the ATN grammar during its parsing. The original semantic rule format was designed to compensate for rather large potential mismatches between the structure that a grammar assigns and the structure that the interpreter would like to have (since it was intended to be a general facility applicable to any reasonable grammar). When a grammar is specifically designed to support the kinds of structures required by the interpreter, this very general "impedance matching" capability of the rules is not required.

Thus, when fully integrated with the parsing process in an ATN grammar, the process of semantic interpretation requires fewer computation steps than when it is done later in a separate phase. This clearly has a bearing on the previous discussion of the relative costs of syntactic and semantic processing. Other advantages of this kind of integrated parsing and interpretation process is that the single nondeterminism mechanism already present in the parser can be used to handle alternative interpretations of a given syntactic structure, without requiring a separate facility for finding and handling multiple rule matches. This not only eliminates extra machinery from the system, but appears to be more efficient. It also permits a more flexible interaction between the ranking of alternative syntactic choices and the ranking of alternative choices in semantic interpretation.

A disadvantage of this integrated approach is that the combined syn-

247 Semantics and Quantification in Natural Language Question Answering

its structure was simple and straightforward. For less restricted applications, such systems will require much greater sophistication in both the linguistic processing and the underlying semantic representations and inference mechanisms.

In this paper, I have presented some of the solutions that were developed in LUNAR (and several related systems) for handling a variety of problems in semantic interpretation, especially in the interpretation of quantifiers. These include a meaning representation language (MRL) that facilitates the uniform interpretation of a wide variety of linguistic constructions, the formalization of meanings in terms of procedures that define truth conditions and carry out actions, efficient techniques for performing extensional inference, techniques for organizing and applying semantic rules to construct meaning representations, and techniques for generating higher quantifiers during interpretation. These latter include methods for determining the appropriate relative scopes of quantifiers and their interactions with negation, and for handling their interactions with operators such as "average." Other techniques are described for post-interpretive query optimization and for displaying quantifier dependencies in output.

I have also discussed a number of future directions for research in natural language understanding, including some questions of the proper relationship between syntax and semantics, the partial understanding of "ungrammatical" sentences, and the role of pragmatics. In the first area especially, I have discussed a number of advantages and disadvantages of performing semantic interpretation during the parsing process, and some aspects of the problem of separating domain specific from general knowledge.

As discussed in several places in the paper, there are a variety of loose ends and open problems still to be solved in the areas of parsing and semantic interpretation. However, even in the four systems discussed here, it is apparent that as the system becomes more ambitious and extensive in its scope of knowledge, the need for pragmatic considerations in selecting interpretations becomes increasingly important. I believe that, as a result of increasing understanding of the syntactic and semantic issues derived from explorations such as the LUNAR system, the field of computational linguistics is now reaching a sufficient degree of sophistication to make progress in a more general treatment of pragmatic issues. In doing so, it will become much more concerned with general issues of plausible inference and natural deduction, moving the field of language understanding in the direction of some of the other traditional areas of artificial intelligence research, such as mechanical inference and problem solving.

ACKNOWLEDGMENTS

Work described in this paper has been supported in part by the following contracts and grants: National Science Foundation Grant GS-2301; NASA Contract No. NAS9-1115; ARPA Contracts N00014-75-C-0533, N00014-77-C-0378; and ONR Contract N00014-77-C-0371.

REFERENCES

Ash, W., Bobrow, R., Grignetti, M., and Hartley, A. (1977). "Intelligent On-Line Assistant and Tutor System," Final Tech. Rep., Rep. No. 3607. Bolt Beranek and Newman. Cambridge, Massachusetts.

Bobrow, D. G., Murphy, D. P., and Teitelman, W. (1968). "The BBN-LISP System." BBN Rep. No. 1677. Bolt Beranek and Newman, Cambridge, Massachusetts.

Bobrow, R. J., and Brown, J. S. (1975). Systematic understanding: Synthesis, analysis, and contingent knowledge in specialized understanding systems. In "Representation and Understanding: Studies in Cognitive Science" (D. Bobrow and A. Collins, eds.), pp. 103–129. Academic Press. New York.

Bohnert, H. G., and Backer, P. O. (1967). "Automatic English-to-Logic Translation in a Simplified Model. A Study in the Logic of Grammar." IBM Res. Pap. RC-1744. IBM Research, Yorktown Heights, New York.

Brown, J. S., and Burton, R. R. (1975). Multiple representations of knowledge of tutorial reasoning. In "Representation and Understanding: Studies in Cognitive Science" (D. Bobrow and A. Collins, eds.), pp. 311–349. Academic Press. New York.

Burton, R. (1976). "Semantic Grammar: An Engineering Technique for Constructing Natural Language Understanding Systems." Rep. No. 3453. Bolt Beranek and Newman. Cambridge, Massachusetts.

Carnap, R. (1964a). Foundations of logic and mathematics. In "The Structure of Language: Readings in the Philosophy of Language" (J. Fodor and J. Katz, eds.), pp. 419–436. Prentice-Hall, Englewood Cliffs, New Jersey.

Carnap, R. (1964b). "Meaning and Necessity." Univ. of Chicago Press, Chicago, Illinois.

Chomsky, N. (1965). "Aspects of the Theory of Syntax." MIT Press, Cambridge, Massachusetts.

Green, S. (1969). "The Application of Theorem Proving to Question-Answering Systems," Tech. Rep. CS 138. Stanford University Artificial Intelligence Project, Stanford, California.

Nash-Webber, B. L. (1976). Semantic interpretation revisited. Presented at 1976 Int. Conf. Comput. Linguist. (COLING-76), Ottawa. (Available as BBN Rep. No. 3335. Bolt Beranek and Newman, Cambridge, Massachusetts.)

Nash-Webber, B. L. (1977). Inference in an approach to discourse anaphora. Proc. 8th Ann. Meet. North Eastern Linguist. Soc. (NELS-8) (K. Ross, ed.), pp. 123–140. University of Massachusetts, Amherst. (also as Tech. Rep. No. 77. Center for the Study of Reading. University of Illinois, Urbana.)

Nash-Webber, B. L., and Reiter, R. (1977). Anaphora and logical form: On formal meaning representations for English. Proc. Int. J. Conf. Artif. Intell., 5th, MIT, Cambridge, Mass. pp. 121–131. (Also as Tech. Rep. No. 36. Center for the Study of Reading, University of Illinois, Urbana and Bolt Beranek and Newman, Cambridge, Massachusetts.)

OAG (1966). "Official Airline Guide," Quick Reference North American Edition. Standard reference of the Air Traffic Conference of America.

Reiter, R. (1977). "An Approach to Deductive Question-Answering," Rep. No. 3649. Bolt Beranek and Newman, Cambridge, Massachusetts.

Robinson, J. A. (1965). A machine-oriented logic based on the resolution principle. *J. ACM* **12**, 23–41.

Robinson, J. J. (1975). Performance grammars. *In* "Speech Recognition: Invited Papers Presented at the 1974 IEEE Symposium" (D. R. Reddy, ed.), pp. 401–427. Academic Press, New York.

Simmons, R. F. (1965). Answering English questions by computer: A survey. *Commun. ACM* **8**(1), 53–70.

Stockwell, R. P., Schacter, P., and Partee, B. H. (1968). "Integration of Transformational Theories on English Syntax," Rep. ESD-TR-68-419. Electronic Systems Division, L. G. Hanscom Field, Bedford, Massachusetts.

Webber, B. L. (1978). A formal approach to discourse anaphora. Ph.D. Thesis, Harvard University, Cambridge, Massachusetts.

Winograd, T. (1972). "Understanding Natural Language." Academic Press, New York.

Woods, W. A. (1967). "Semantics for a Question-Answering System." Rep. NSF-19. Harvard University Computation Laboratory, Cambridge, Massachusetts. (Available from NTIS as PB-176-548.)

Woods, W. A. (1968). Procedural semantics for a question-answering machine. *AFIPS Natl. Comput. Conf. Expo., Conf. Proc.* **33**, 457–471.

Woods, W. A. (1969). "Augmented Transition Networks for Natural Language Analysis." Rep. No. CS-1. Aiken Computation Laboratory, Harvard University, Cambridge, Massachusetts. (Available from NTIS as Microfiche PB-203-527.)

Woods, W. A. (1970). Transition network grammars for natural language analysis. *Commun. ACM* **13**, 591–602.

Woods, W. A. (1973a). An experimental parsing system for transition network grammars. *In* "Natural Language Processing" (R. Rustin, ed.), pp. 111–154. Algorithmics Press, New York.

Woods, W. A. (1973b). Progress in natural language understanding: An application to LUNAR geology. *AFIPS Natl. Comput. Conf. Expo., Conf. Proc.* **42**, 441–450.

Woods, W. A. (1973c). Meaning and machines. *In* "Computational and Mathematical Linguistics" (A. Zampolli, ed.), pp. 769–792. Leo S. Olschki, Florence.

Woods, W. A. (1975a). Syntax, semantics, and speech. *In* "Speech Recognition: Invited Papers Presented at the 1974 IEEE Symposium" (D. R. Reddy, ed.), pp. 345–400. Academic Press, New York.

Woods, W. A. (1975b). What's in a link: Foundations for semantic networks. *In* "Representation and Understanding: Studies in Cognitive Science" (D. Bobrow and A. Collins, eds.), pp. 35–82. Academic Press, New York.

Woods, W. A., Kaplan, R. M., and Nash-Webber, B. (1972). "The Lunar Sciences Natural Language Information System: Final Report," BBN Rep. No. 2378. Bolt Beranek and Newman, Cambridge, Massachusetts.

Woods, W. A., Bates, M., Brown, G., Bruce, B., Cook, C., Klovstad, J., Makhoul, J., Nash-Webber, B., Schwartz, R., Wolf, J., and Zue, V. (1976). "Speech Understanding Systems—Final Report, 30 October 1974 to 29 October 1976," BBN Rep. No. 3438. Vols. I–V. Bolt Beranek and Newman, Cambridge, Massachusetts.

A Procedural Model of Language Understanding

Terry Winograd
Massachusetts Institute of Technology

Much of the research on language is based on an attempt to separate it into distinct components—components that can then be studied independently. Modern syntactic theoreticians have been tremendously successful at setting up complex rules which describe in detail the possible orderings of syntactic constituents; at the same time other researchers are trying to define semantic relations and to model the cognitive structures underlying language use.

Most attempts to model language understanding on the computer have followed this strategy of dealing with a single component of language. They are constructed primarily as a syntactic program (Kuno, 1965), a model of semantic connections (Schank, 1971), or an attempt to model the memory structures (Quillian, 1967).

Question-answering systems have had to deal with the entire language process, but they have been severely limited in the breadth of their language ability. The only attempt to handle large portions of language data was the machine translation effort, and it soon became obvious that the methods were not up to the requirements of the task. Language translation could not be treated as a problem of rearranging syntactic structures and words, because attention to meaning was required even to achieve moderately acceptable results.

One basic limitation of those programs that have tried to handle the problems of meaning is that they have dealt almost exclusively with the understanding of single sentences, when in fact almost no human use of language takes place in such an artificial setting. We are always in a context, and in that context we make use of what has gone on to help interpret what is coming. Much of the structure of language comes from its being a process of communication between an intelligent speaker and hearer, occurring in a setting. The setting includes not only a physical situation and a topic of discourse, but also the knowledge each participant has about the world and the other's ideas.

This paper describes an attempt to explore the interconnections between the different types of knowledge required for language understanding. It is based on a computer program that "understands" language in a limited domain by including a model of the subject being talked about and a context of discourse. As an example of the interactions between the different sorts of knowledge the system must have, let us look first at the use of pronouns.

Our syntactic knowledge of English enables us to know that in the sentence "Arthur wants to see him," the word "him" must refer to someone other than Arthur (otherwise we would have used "himself"). In "Arthur wants somebody to see him," "him" might or might not refer to Arthur. The distribution of reflexive pronouns like "himself" depends in a complex way on the syntactic structure of the sentences in which they appear, and a language understander must have this knowledge. As a semantic fact, we know that "him" must refer to something which the speaker is characterizing as animate and male.

At another level, we know that the referent is likely to occur in the preceding sentence, or earlier in the sentence being interpreted, that it is more likely to refer to the topic or the subject of the previous sentence, and is much more likely to refer to a major constituent than to one deeply embedded in the structure. This type of heuristic knowledge about the organization of discourse also plays a part in our understanding.

Finally, there is a level based on knowledge of the world. In the sentence "Sam and Bill wanted to take the girls to the movies, but they didn't have any money," we understand "they" as referring to Sam and Bill. This doesn't involve syntactic or general semantic knowledge, but depends on our knowledge of our social culture. When someone takes someone else to the movies, it is the inviter who pays, and it is his or her financial situation that is relevant.

Whenever we look into realistic language use, these types of interaction play a large role, not only with pronouns, but in deciding on the structures of sentences and meanings of individual words as well. We assign different structures to sentences like "He gave the house plants to charity," and "He gave the boy plants to water," on the basis of our syntactic and semantic knowledge. Even the most common words have multiple meanings, and we must bring a variety of facts to bear in deciding, for example, the meaning of "had" in "Mary had a little lamb, but I preferred the baked lobster."

In discourse, people take advantage of a variety of mechanisms that depend on the existence of an intelligent hearer who will use all sorts of knowledge to fill in any necessary information.

In making a computer model of language use, this presents a serious problem. On the one hand, it is impossible to isolate one aspect of language from the others, or to separate a person's use of linguistic knowledge from his use of other knowledge. On the other hand, it is clearly folly at this point to think of giving the program all the knowledge a person brings into a conversation. In our program, we choose to resolve the dilemma by picking a tiny bit of the world to talk about. Within this mini-world, we can give the computer a deep kind of knowledge, including the equivalent of "Who would pay for a movie?"

The subject chosen was the world of a toy robot with a simple arm. It can manipulate toy blocks on a table containing simple objects like a box. In the course of a dialogue, it can be asked to manipulate the objects, doing such things as building stacks and putting things into the box. It can be questioned about the current configurations of blocks on the table, about the events that have gone on during the discussion, and to a limited extent about its reasoning. It can be told simple facts which are added to its store of knowledge for use in later reasoning. The conversation goes on within a dynamic framework—one in which the computer is an active participant, doing things to change his toy world, and discussing them.

The program was written in LISP on the PDP-10 ITS time-sharing system of the Artificial Intelligence Laboratory at MIT.* It displays a simulated robot world on a television screen and converses with a human on a teletype. It was not written for any particular use with a real robot and does not have a model of language based on peculiarities of the robot environment. Rather, it is precisely by limiting the subject matter to such a small area that we can address the general issues of how language is used in a framework of physical objects, events, and a continuing discourse.

The programs can be roughly divided into the three domains mentioned above: There is a syntactic parser which works with a large-scale grammar of English; there is a collection of semantic routines that embody the kind of knowledge needed to interpret the meanings of words and structures; and there is a cognitive deductive system for exploring the consequences of facts, making plans to carry out commands and finding the answers to questions. There is also a comparatively simple set of programs for generating appropriate English responses.

In designing these pieces, the main emphasis was on the interaction of the three domains. The form in which we want to state a syntactic theory or a type of deduction must take into account the fact that it is only a part of a larger system. One of the most useful organizing principles was the representation of much of the knowledge as procedures. Many other theories of language state their rules in a form modelled on the equations of mathematics or the rules of symbolic logic. These are static rules that do not explicitly describe the process involved in using them, but are instead manipulated by some sort of uniform deduction procedure. By writing special languages suited to the various types of knowledge (semantic, syntactic, deductive), we are able to preserve the simplicity of these systems. This is accom-

plished by putting the knowledge in the form of programs in which we can explicitly express the connections between the different parts of the system's knowledge, thus enriching their possibilities for interaction.

The rest of this chapter illustrates the capabilities of the system and explains in some detail how it works. The second section presents a sample of a dialogue with the program, along with comments describing some of the features being demonstrated. The third section gives a closer view of the program itself, and the final section discusses some of its basic limitations.

Sample Dialogue

This section contains a sample dialogue with the language-understanding system. This system carries out actions and answers questions about a simple scene containing a table, hand, and box, and several blocks and pyramids. The numbered lines in lower case were typed in by a person, and the lines in upper case are the computer's response. Other lines are comments describing some of the features being exhibited.

The dialogue was carried out in real time with the response of the "robot" displayed on a television screen. Figures are included to show the state of the scene at various points.

1. *pick up a big red block.*

OK.

The system answers "OK" when it carries out a command. In order to pick up the red block, it had to clear it off by finding a space for the green one and moving the green one away. The initial situation is shown in Figure 4.1, and the result in Figure 4.2.

2. *grasp the pyramid.*

I DON'T UNDERSTAND WHICH PYRAMID YOU MEAN.

There are three pyramids in the scene, and the program knows that phrases beginning with "the" are intended to refer to a specific object the speaker has in mind.

3. *find a block which is taller than the one you are holding and put it into the box.*

The system has to figure out what is meant by "one" and "it," as well as using deduction to decide which block it is holding.

*For more details on the entire system, see Winograd (1972). The actual program is written in LISP, occupies about 100K of storage on the PDP-10, and operates in approximately real time, responding to a sentence in an average of 10 or 15 seconds.

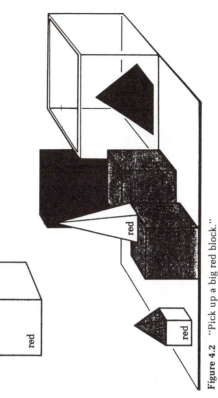

Figure 4.2 "Pick up a big red block."

5. *what is the pyramid supported by?*

Earlier the system responded to "the pyramid" by saying "I DON'T UNDERSTAND WHICH PYRAMID YOU MEAN." Now, it assumes that we mean the one just mentioned.

THE BOX.

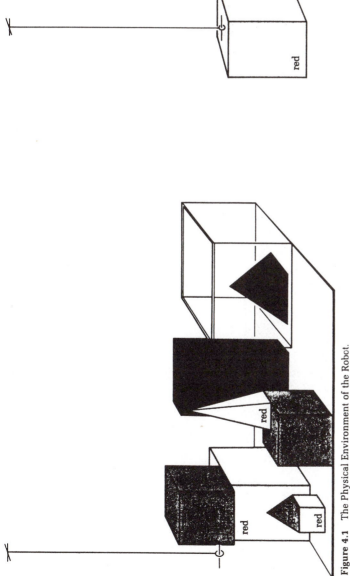

Figure 4.1 The Physical Environment of the Robot.

BY "IT," I ASSUME YOU MEAN THE BLOCK WHICH IS TALLER THAN THE ONE I AM HOLDING.

There were two possible referents for "it": the one selected, and "the one you are holding." The program has heuristics for choosing between them.

OK.

The hand has to set down the red block to pick up the taller blue one. Figure 4.3 shows the result of the system's manipulations so far.

4. *what does the box contain?*

THE BLUE PYRAMID AND THE BLUE BLOCK.

complicated numbers such as "*at least one*," "*more than three*," "*exactly seven*," etc. The memory of past events is used to deduce which block is "*the one which I told you to pick up*." Notice the complicated syntactic structure in which "*the one*" is actually the object of a clause embedded two levels deeper. The parser incorporates a grammar that handles this kind of complexity in a general way.

```
YES, THE RED CUBE.
```

8. *is it supported?*

```
YES, BY THE TABLE.
```

The system has heuristics about what information is relevant to a person who asks a question, even if he does not request that information specifically.

9. *can the table pick up blocks?*

```
NO.
```

The semantic rules include the knowledge that "picking up" must be done by an animate object, and that the table is not animate.

10. *can a pyramid be supported by a block?*

```
YES.
```

The deductive system finds an actual example, so it knows this is possible.

11. *can a pyramid support a pyramid?*

```
I DON'T KNOW.
```

The question makes sense, but there is no example in the scene. The system has no way of looking into the details of its programs, even though these ultimately define its capabilities.

12. *stack up two pyramids.*

```
I CAN'T.
```

The robot tries and fails.

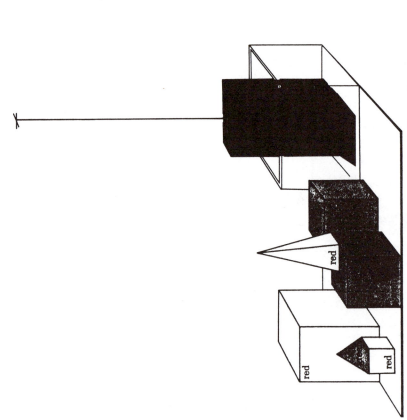

Figure 4.3 "Find a block which is taller than the one you are holding and put it into the box."

6. *how many blocks are not in the box?*

Negatives such as "*not*" and "*no*" are handled whether they appear in clauses or noun groups (such as "*no boxes*").

```
FOUR OF THEM.
```

7. *is at least one of them narrower then the one which i told you to pick up?*

The phrase "*at least one of them*" must be analyzed to refer back to the previous question, and "*the one which . . .*" must also refer to blocks. Noun groups can have

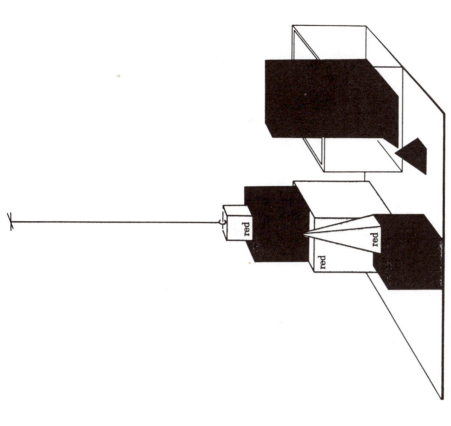

Figure 4.4 "Will you please stack up both of the red blocks and either a green cube or a pyramid."

13. *the blue pyramid is mine.*

I UNDERSTAND.

All of the information about colors, shapes, sizes and locations of the objects is known to the program initially. Possession is left as an unknown property of objects about which it can be told. It stores this information in its data base.

14. *i own all blocks which are not red, but i don't own anything which supports a pyramid.*

I UNDERSTAND.

The result of understanding these sentences is the creation of new procedures within the robot for deducing whether I own something.

15. *do i own the box?*

NO.

The box supports whatever it contains, including a pyramid.

16. *do i own anything in the box?*

YES, TWO THINGS: THE BLUE BLOCK AND THE BLUE PYRAMID.

17. *will you please stack up both of the red blocks and either a green cube or a pyramid?*

OK.

Logical connectives, such as "and," "or," "either," etc., are handled in both the grammar and semantics. A command is executed even if it looks like a question. The command is carried out by the following series of steps: It puts a green cube on the large red block (it chooses the green cube with nothing on it), then removes the small pyramid from the little red cube, so that it can use that cube to complete the stack as specified, resulting in what is described in Figure 4.4.

Ordinarily the system would be satisfied with calling this "*a big green cube,*" but since we asked "*which cube*" it has to be more specific in naming it. It has procedures for using substitute nouns (such as "one") and pronouns in answers to make the discourse more natural.

18. *which cube is sitting on the table?*

THE LARGE GREEN ONE WHICH SUPPORTS THE RED PYRAMID.

19. *is there a large block behind a pyramid?*

YES, THREE OF THEM: A LARGE RED ONE, A LARGE GREEN CUBE AND THE BLUE ONE.

20. *put a small one onto the green cube which supports a pyramid.*

"A small one" must contrast with the person's earlier phrase "a large block," so this means "a small block."

OK.

21. *put the littlest pyramid on top of it.*

Words like "littlest" are not in the dictionary but are interpreted from the root forms like "little." The program compares the sizes of all the pyramids to carry out the action.

OK.

22. *how many things are on top of green cubes?*

I'M NOT SURE WHAT YOU MEAN BY "ON TOP OF" IN THE PHRASE "ON TOP OF GREEN CUBES"

DO YOU MEAN:
1 – DIRECTLY ON THE SURFACE
2 – ANWHERE ON TOP OF?

In the previous sentence, the phrase "on top of" was interpreted without trouble because the context made it clear what was meant. In this one, the heuristics for disambiguation do not come up with a clearcut decision, so the system has to ask the user for more information. The paraphrases were included with the dictionary definition of "on." A request like this can also occur when the meaning of a pronoun such as "it" or "they" is unclear.

23. *had you touched any pyramid before you put the green one on the little cube?*

YES, THE GREEN ONE.

The system deduces from its memory what event is being referred to, and can relate other events to it in time. The analysis includes complex tenses of verb groups, and there are special facilities for keeping track of the various forms of irregular verbs like "have."

24. *when did you pick it up?*

WHILE I WAS STACKING UP THE RED CUBE, A LARGE RED BLOCK AND A LARGE GREEN CUBE.

A time is described by naming the main goal which was being worked on.

25. *why?*

The system remembers immediately previous sentences to understand questions like this and the following ones.

TO GET RID OF IT.

By keeping track of selected parts of the original subgoal tree, the system has some understanding of its own motives.

26. *why did you do that?*

TO CLEAN OFF THE RED CUBE.

"That" refers to the action mentioned in the system's last answer.

27. *why did you clear off that cube?*

Here, "that" means the one just referred to.

TO PUT IT ON A LARGE GREEN CUBE.

28. *why did you do that?*

TO STACK UP THE RED CUBE, A LARGE RED BLOCK AND A LARGE GREEN CUBE.

29. *why did you do that?*

BECAUSE YOU ASKED ME TO.

It remembers what it did, not how the request was worded.

30. *how did you do it?*

"It" refers to the action mentioned in the last question, rather than the answer.

BY PUTTING A LARGE RED BLOCK ON THE TABLE; THEN LETTING GO OF IT; THEN PUTTING A LARGE GREEN CUBE ON IT; THEN LETTING GO OF THAT CUBE; THEN PUTTING THE RED CUBE ON THAT CUBE; THEN LETTING GO OF THAT CUBE.

This is a description of the top-level subgoals used to achieve the goal.

31. *how many objects did you touch while you were doing it?*

Time references can refer to a time span, using words like "while."

FOUR OF THEM.

32. *what did the red cube support before you started to clean it off?*

THE GREEN PYRAMID.

By remembering what has been moved, it is possible to deduce things about earlier states of the scene. We can use complex nestings of clauses like "before you started to clean it off."

33. *there were five blocks to the left of the box then.*

"Then" must refer to the time mentioned in the last sentence.

NO, ONLY FOUR OF THEM: THE RED CUBE, TWO LARGE GREEN CUBES AND A LARGE RED BLOCK.

Earlier in the dialogue, information about "owning" was accepted at face value. But the system knows that it has complete information about the basic properties of objects, including location. It checks any statements about these to see whether it agrees or disagrees.

34. *put the blue pyramid on the block in the box.*

This is syntactically ambiguous, but is understood without ambiguity since the parsing corresponding to "put the blue pyramid which is on the block into the box" does not make sense in the current scene, whereas "put the blue pyramid onto the block which is in the box" does.

OK.

35. *is there anything which is bigger than every pyramid but is not as wide as the thing that supports it?*

The system understands quantifiers such as "every," "any," "some," etc., and structures such as "bigger than," "as wide as," etc. Here "it" refers to a noun group within the same sentence but two levels up in the parsing tree.

YES, THE BLUE BLOCK.

36. *does a steeple*

SORRY, I DON'T KNOW THE WORD "STEEPLE".

The system interrupts immediately when it sees a word it doesn't know.

37. *a "steeple" is a stack which contains two green cubes and a pyramid.*

The quote marks indicate that we are defining a new word. The definition is added to the dictionary in a form compatible with all the words it already knows.

I UNDERSTAND.

38. *are there any steeples now?*

NO.

The new definition is used as a description to recognize steeples.

39. *build one.*

OK.

The description given in the definition is enough to deduce a plan for building new objects as well as recognizing them. The word "one" means "a steeple," and the plan is carried out. First, one of the large green cubes is cleared off by removing the red cube and two pyramids. Then the two green cubes and the tall red pyramid are stacked up to fit the description.

40. *call the biggest block "superblock."*

OK.

We can also give objects names.

41. *have you picked up superblock since we began?*

YES.

42. *why did you drop it?*

BY "IT", I ASSUME YOU MEAN THE SUPERBLOCK.
I CAN'T EXPLAIN A NON-EXISTENT EVENT.

There is no record in memory of any block being dropped. The answer routines have special checks for this type of "loaded question" which presupposes things which aren't true.

43. *is there anything to the right of the red pyramid?*

YES, FOUR THINGS: THE BOX, THE RED CUBE, THE BLUE PYRAMID AND THE BLOCK NAMED SUPERBLOCK.

Once an object has a name, the name is used to help identify it in responses.

44. *thank you.*

YOU'RE WELCOME!

The grammar is written as a procedure, which gives it the capability to carry out special sorts of parsing for idioms.

Details of the Model

In this section we go into some detail about the various parts of the language understanding program and its operation. This type of analysis is important for understanding any computer model, since the surface appearance of its output can be deceptive. A program may succeed by carefully choosing the problem it will attack, so that some simple special-purpose solution will work. ELIZA (Weizenbaum, 1964) and STUDENT (Bobrow, 1967) are examples of programs which give impressive performances owing to a severe and careful restriction of the kind of understanding they try to achieve. If a model is to be of broader significance, it must be designed to cover a large range of the things we mean when we talk of understanding. The principles should derive from an attempt to deal with the basic cognitive structures.

On the other hand, it is possible to devise abstract ideas of the logical structure of language—ideas which seem in theory to be applicable. Often, such systems, although interesting mathematically, are not valid as psychological models of human language, since they have not concerned themselves with the operational problems of a mental procedure. They often include types of representation and processes which are highly implausible, and which may be totally inapplicable in complex situations because their very nature implies astronomically large amounts of processing for certain kinds of computations. Transformational grammar and resolution theorem proving (Green, 1969) are examples of such approaches.

The Representation of Meaning

Our program makes use of a detailed world model, describing both the current state of the blocks world environment and its knowledge of procedures for changing that state and making deductions about it. This model is not in spatial or analog terms, but is a symbolic description, abstracting those aspects of the world which are relevant to the operations used in working with it and discussing it. First there is a data base of simple facts like those shown in Box 4.1, describing what is true at any particular time. There we see, for example, that B1 is a block, B1 is red, B2 supports B3, blue is a color, EVENT27 caused EVENT29, etc. The notation simply involves indicating relationships between objects by listing the name of the relation (such as IS or SUPPORT) followed by the things being related.* These include both concepts (like BLOCK or BLUE) and proper names of individual objects and events (indicated

*The fact that B1 is a block could be represented in more usual predicate notation as (BLOCK B1). We have chosen to associate with each object or concept a property describing its most relevant category for the purpose of generating an English phrase for it. Thus (IS B1 BLOCK) is used to describe B1 as a block. Similarly, properties like colors are represented (COLOR B1 BLUE) instead of (BLUE B1). This allows for more efficiency in the operation of the deduction system, without changing its logical characteristics.

cedures written in the PLANNER language (Hewitt, 1971). For example, the concept CLEARTOP (which might be expressed in English by a phrase like "clear off") can be described by the procedure diagrammed in Figure 4.5. The model tells us that to clear off an object X, we start by checking to see whether X supports an object Y. If so, we GET-RID-OF Y, and go check again. When X does not support any object, we can assert that it is CLEARTOP. In this operational definition, we call on other concepts like GET-RID-OF and SUPPORT. Each of these in turn is a procedure, involving other concepts like PICKUP and GRASP. This representation is oriented to a model of deduction in which we try to satisfy some goal by setting up successive subgoals, which must be achieved in order to eventually satisfy the main goal. Looking at the flow chart for GRASP in Figure 4.6, we can see the steps the program would take if asked to grasp an object B1 while holding a different object B2. It would be called by setting up a goal of the form (GRASP B1), so when the GRASP program ran, X would represent the object B1. First it checks to see whether B1 is a manipulable object, since if not the effort must fail. Next it sees if it is already grasping B1, since this would satisfy the goal immediately. Then, it checks to see if it is holding an object other than B1, and if so tries to GET-RID-OF it. The program for GET-RID-OF tries to put the designated object on the table by calling a program for PUTON, which in turn looks for an empty location and calls PUT. PUT deduces where the hand must be moved and calls MOVEHAND. If we look at the set of currently active goals at this point, we get the stack in Box 4.2.

Notice that this subgoal structure provides the basis for asking "why" questions, as in sentences 25 through 29 of the dialog in Section 2. If asked *"Why did you put B2 on the table?,"* the program would look to the goal that called PUTON, and say *"To get rid of it."* If asked *"Why did you get rid of it?"* it would go up one more step to get *"To grasp B1."* (Actually, it would generate an English phrase describing the object B1 in terms of its shape, size, and color.) "How" questions are answered by looking at the set of subgoals called directly in achieving a goal, and generating descriptions of the actions involved.

Box 4.1 Typical Data Expressions.

```
(IS B1 BLOCK)
(IS B2 PYRAMID)
(AT B1 (LOCATION 100 100 0))
(SUPPORT B1 B2)
(CLEARTOP B2)
(MANIPULABLE B1)
(CONTAIN BOX1 B4)
(COLOR-OF B1 RED)
(SHAPE-OF B2 POINTED)
(IS BLUE COLOR)
(CAUSE EVENT27 EVENT29)
```

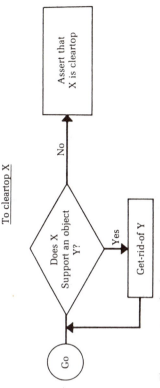

Figure 4.5 Procedural Description for the Concept CLEARTOP.

To cleartop X

---

with numbers, like B1 and TABLE2).† The symbols used in these expressions represent the concepts (or conceptual categories) that form the vocabulary of the language user's cognitive model. A concept corresponds vaguely to what we might call a single meaning of a word, but the connection is more complex. Underlying the organization is a belief that meanings cannot be reduced to any set of pure "elements," or components from which everything else is built. Rather, a person categorizes his experience along lines which are relevant to the thought processes he will use, and his categorization is generally neither consistent, nor parsimonious, nor complete. A person may categorize a set of objects in his experience into, for example "chair," "stool," "bench," etc. If pushed, he cannot give an exact definition for any of these, and in naming some objects he will not be certain how to make the choice between them. This is even clearer if we consider words like "truth," "virtue," and "democracy." The meaning of any concept depends on its interconnection with all of the other concepts in the model.

Most formal approaches to language have avoided this characterization of meaning even though it seems close to our intuitions about how language is used. This is because the usual techniques of logic and mathematics are not easily applicable to such "holistic" models. With such a complex notion of "concept," we are unable to prove anything about meaning in the usual mathematical notion of proof. One important aspect of computational approaches to modelling cognitive processes is their ability to deal with this sort of formalism. Rather than trying to prove things about meaning we can design procedures which can operate with the model and simulate the processes involved in human use of language. The justification for the formalism is the degree to which it succeeds in providing a model of understanding.

What is important then, is the part of the system's knowledge which involves the interconnections between the concepts. In our model, these are in the form of procedures written in the PLANNER language (Hewitt, 1971). For example, the concept

---

†The notation does not correspond exactly to that in the original program, as mnemonics have been used here to increase readability.

Box 4.2   Goal Stack.

```
(GRASP B1)
  (GET-RID-OF B2)
    (PUTON B2 TABLE1)
      (PUT B2 (453 201 0))
        (MOVEHAND (553 301 100))
```

procedure invoked requires direct physical actions like the aforementioned. In others, it may be a search for some sort of information (perhaps to answer a question), whereas in others it is a procedure which stores away a new piece of knowledge or uses it to modify the knowledge it already has. Let us look at what the system would do with a simple description like "a red cube which supports a pyramid." The description will use concepts like BLOCK, RED, PYRAMID, and EQUIDIMEN-SIONAL—all parts of the system's underlying categorization of the world. The result can be represented in a flow chart like that of Figure 4.7. Note that this is a program for finding an object fitting the description. It would then be incorporated into a command for doing something with the object, a question asking something about it, or, if it appeared in a statement, it would become part of the program which was generated to represent the meaning for later use. Note that this bit of program could also be used as a test to see whether an object fit the description, if the first FIND instruction were told in advance to look only at that particular object.

At first glance, it seems that there is too much structure in this program, as we don't like to think of the meaning of a simple phrase as explicitly containing loops, conditional tests, and other programming details. The solution is to provide an internal language that contains the appropriate looping and checking as its primitives, and in which the representation of the process is as simple as the description. PLANNER provides these primitives in our system. The program described in Figure 4.7 would be written in PLANNER looking something like Box 4.3. * The loops of the flow chart are implicit in PLANNER's backtrack control structure. The description is evaluated by proceeding down the list until some goal fails, at which time the system backs up automatically to the last point where a decision was made, trying a different possibility. A decision can be made whenever a new object name or variable (indicated by the prefix ?) such as ?X1 or ?X2 appears. The variables are used by a pattern matcher. If they have already been assigned to a particular item, it checks to see whether the GOAL is true for that item. If not, it checks for all possible items which satisfy the GOAL, by choosing one, and then taking successive ones whenever backtracking occurs to that point. Thus, even the distinction between testing and choosing is implicit. Using other primitives of PLANNER, such as NOT and

*The system actually uses Micro-Planner, (Sussman et. al., 1970) a partial implementation of PLANNER. In this presentation we have slightly simplified the details of its syntax.

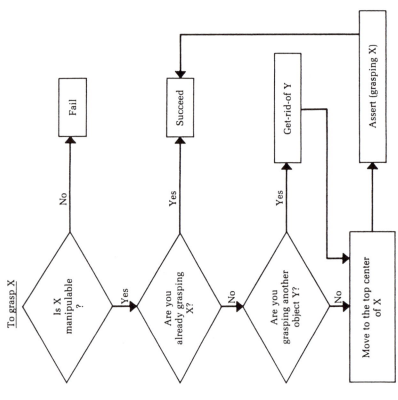

Figure 4.6   Procedural Description of GRASP.

These examples illustrate the use of procedural descriptions of concepts for carrying out commands, but they can also be applied to other aspects of language, such as questions and statements. One of the basic viewpoints underlying the model is that all language use can be thought of as a way of activating procedures within the hearer. We can think of any utterance as a program—one that indirectly causes a set of operations to be carried out within the hearer's cognitive system. This "program writing" is indirect in the sense that we are dealing with an intelligent interpreter, who may take a set of actions which are quite different from those the speaker intended. The exact form is determined by his knowledge of the world, his expectations about the person talking to him, his goals, etc. In this program we have a simple version of this process of interpretation as it takes place in the robot. Each sentence interpreted by the robot is converted to a set of instructions in PLANNER. The program that is created is then executed to achieve the desired effect. In some cases the

FIND (which looks for a given number of objects fitting a description), we can write procedural representations for a variety of descriptions, as shown in Box 4.4.

Semantic Analysis

When we have decided how the system will represent meanings internally, we must deal with the way in which it creates a program when it is given an English input. There must be ways to interpret the meanings of individual words and the syntactic structures in which they occur. First, let us look at how we can define simple words like "cube", and "contain." The definitions in Box 4.5 are completely equivalent to those used in the program with a straightforward interpretation.* The first says that

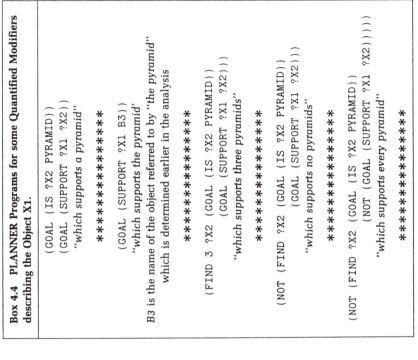

Box 4.4 PLANNER Programs for some Quantified Modifiers describing the Object X1.

```
(GOAL (IS ?X2 PYRAMID))
(GOAL (SUPPORT ?X1 ?X2))
"which supports a pyramid"
******************

(GOAL (SUPPORT ?X1 B3))
"which supports the pyramid"
```
B3 is the name of the object referred to by "the pyramid" which is determined earlier in the analysis
```
******************
(FIND 3 ?X2 (GOAL (IS ?X2 PYRAMID))
           (GOAL (SUPPORT ?X1 ?X2)))
"which supports three pyramids"
******************

(NOT (FIND ?X2 (GOAL (IS ?X2 PYRAMID))
               (GOAL (SUPPORT ?X1 ?X2))))
"which supports no pyramids"
******************

(NOT (FIND ?X2 (GOAL (IS ?X2 PYRAMID))
     (NOT (GOAL (SUPPORT ?X1 ?X2)))))
"which supports every pyramid"
******************
```

*Again, in comparing this with the details in Winograd (1972), note that some of the symbols have been replaced with more understandable mnemonic versions.

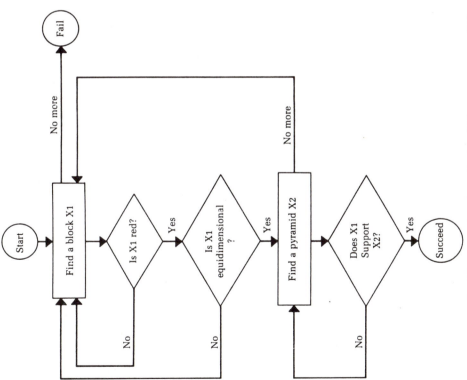

Figure 4.7 Procedural Representation of "a red cube which supports a pyramid."

Box 4.3 PLANNER Program for Description of "a red cube which supports a pyramid."

```
(GOAL (IS ?X1 BLOCK))
(GOAL (COLOR-OF ?X1 RED))
(GOAL (EQUIDIMENSIONAL ?X1))
(GOAL (IS ?X2 PYRAMID))
(GOAL (SUPPORT ?X1 ?X2))
```

pack them all into the box. The program for checking to see whether the object is singular or plural is simple, and any semantic system must have the flexibility to incorporate such things in the word definitions. We do this by having the definition of every word be a program which is called at an appropriate point in the analysis, and which can do arbitrary computations involving the sentence and the present physical situation.

This flexibility is even more important once we get beyond simple words. In defining words like "the," or "of," or "one" in "Pick up a green one," we can hardly make a simple list of properties and descriptors as in Figure 4.12. The presence of "one" in a noun group must trigger a program which looks into the previous discourse to see what objects have been mentioned, and can apply various rules and heuristics to determine the appropriate reference. For example it must know that in the phrase "a big red block and a little one," we are referring to "a little red block," not "a little big red block" or simply "a little block." This sort of knowledge is part of a semantic procedure attached to the word "one" in the dictionary.

Words like "the" are more complex. When we use a definite article like "the" or "that" in English, we have in mind a particular object or objects which we expect the hearer to know about. I can talk about "the moon" since there is only one moon we usually talk about. In the context of this article, I can talk about "the dialogue", and the reader will understand from the context which dialogue I mean. If I am beginning a conversation, I will say "Yesterday I met a strange man" even though I have a particular man in mind, since saying "Yesterday I met the strange man" would imply that the hearer already knows of him. Elsewhere, "the" is used to convey the information that the object being referred to is unique. If I write "The reason I wrote this paper was . . .", it implies that there was a single reason, whereas "A reason I wrote this paper was . . ." implies that there were others. In generic statements, "the" may be used to refer to a whole class, as in "The albatross is a strange bird." This is a quite different use from the single referent of "The albatross just ate your lunch."

A model of language use must be able to account for the role this type of knowledge plays in understanding. In the procedural model, it is a part of the process of interpretation for the structure in which the relevant word is embedded. The different possibilities for the meaning of "the" are procedures which check various facts about the context, then prescribe actions such as "Look for a unique object in the data base which fits this description." or "Assert that the object being described is unique as far as the speaker is concerned." The program incorporates a variety of heuristics for deciding what part of the context is relevant. For example, it keeps track of when in the dialogue something has been mentioned. In sentence 2 of the dialogue, "Grasp the pyramid" is rejected since there is no particular pyramid which the system can see as distinguished. However, in sentence 5 it accepts the question "What is the pyramid supported by?" since in the answer to sentence 4 it mentioned a particular pyramid.

This type of knowledge plays a large part in understanding the things that hold a discourse together, such as pronouns, adverbs like "then", and "there", substitute

---

Box 4.5   Dictionary Definitions for "cube" and "contain."

```
(CUBE
  ((NOUN  (OBJECT
            ((MANIPULABLE RECTANGULAR)
              ((IS ? BLOCK)
                (EQUIDIMENSIONAL ?)))))))

(CONTAIN
  ((VERB  ((TRANSITIVE (RELATION
            (((CONTAINER) ((PHYSICAL-OBJECT))
              (CONTAIN #1 #2))
            ((CONSTRUCT) ((PHYSICAL-OBJECT))
              (PART-OF #2 #1)))))))))
```

a cube is an object that is RECTANGULAR and MANIPULABLE, and can be recognized by the fact that it is a BLOCK and EQUIDIMENSIONAL. The first part of this definition is based on the use of semantic markers and provides for efficiency in choosing interpretations. By making a rough categorization of the objects in the model, the system can make quick checks to see whether certain combinations are ruled out by simple tests like "this meaning of the adjective applies only to words which represent physical objects." Chomsky's famous sentence "Colorless green ideas sleep furiously" would be eliminated easily by such markers. The system uses this information, for example, in answering question 9 in the dialogue, "Can the table pick up blocks?," as "pick up" demands a subject that is ANIMATE, whereas "table" has the marker INANIMATE. These markers are a useful but rough approximation to human deductions.

The definition for "contain" shows how they might be used to choose between possible word meanings. If applied to a CONTAINER and a PHYSICAL-OBJECT, as in "The box contains three pyramids," the word implies the usual relationship we mean by CONTAIN. If instead, it applies to a CONSTRUCT (like "stack", "pile", or "row") and an object, the meaning is different. "The stack contains a cube" really means that a cube is PART of the stack, and the system will choose this meaning by noting that CONSTRUCT is one of the semantic markers of the word "stack" when it applies the definition.

One important aspect of these definitions is that although they look like static rule statements, they are actually calls to programs (OBJECT and RELATION) which do the appropriate checks and build the semantic structures. Once we get away from the simplest words, these programs need to be more flexible in what they look at. For example, in the robot world, the phrase "pick up" has different meanings depending on whether it refers to a single object or several. In sentence 1, the system interprets "Pick up the big red block," by grasping it and raising the hand. If we said "Pick up all of your toys," it would interpret "pick up" as meaning "put away," and would

nouns such as "one", phrases beginning with "that", and ellipses. The system is structured in such a way that the heuristics for handling mechanisms like these can be expressed as procedures in a straightforward way.

The Role of Syntax

In describing the process of semantic interpretation, we stated that part of the relevant input was the syntactic structure of the sentence. In order to provide this, the program contains a parser and a fairly comprehensive grammar of English.* The approach to syntax is based on a belief that the form of syntactic analysis must be useable by a realistic semantic system, and the emphasis of the resulting grammar differs in several ways from traditional transformational approaches.

First, it is organized around looking for syntactic units which play a primary role in determining meaning. A sentence such as "The three big red dogs ate a raw steak" will be parsed to generate the structure in Figure 4.8. The noun groups (NG) correspond to descriptions of objects, whereas the clause is a description of a relation or event. The semantic programs are organized into groups of procedures, each of which is used for interpreting a certain type of unit.

For each unit, there is a syntactic program (written in a language called PRO–GRAMMAR, especially designed for the purpose) which operates on the input string to see whether it could represent a unit of that type. In doing this, it will call on other such syntactic programs (and possibly on itself recursively). It embodies a description of the possible orderings of words and other units, for example, the scheme for a noun group, as shown in Figure 4.9. The presence of an asterisk after a symbol means that that function can be filled more than once. The figure shows that we have a determiner (such as "the") followed by an ordinal (such as "first"), then a number ("three") followed by one or more adjectives ("big," "red") followed by one or more nouns being used as classifiers ("fire hydrant") followed by a noun ("covers") followed by qualifying phrases which are preposition groups or clauses

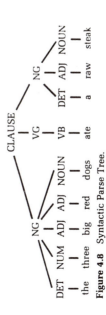

Figure 4.8 Syntactic Parse Tree.

("without handles" "which you can find"). Of course many of the elements are optional, and there are restriction relations between the various possibilities. If we choose an indefinite determiner such as "a," we cannot have an ordinal and number, as in the illegal string "a first three big red fire hydrant covers without handles you can find." The grammar must be able to express these rules in a way which is not simply an ad hoc set of statements. Our grammar takes advantage of some of the ideas of Systemic Grammar (Halliday, 1971).

Systemic theory views a syntactic structure as being made up of units, each of which can be characterized in terms of the *features* describing its form, and the *functions* it fills in a larger structure or discourse. In the sentence in Figure 4.8, the noun group "three big red dogs" can be described as exhibiting features such as DETER-MINED, INDEFINITE, PLURAL, etc. It serves the function SUBJECT in the clause of which it is a part, and various discourse functions, such as THEME as well. It in turn is made up of other units—the individual words—which fill functions in the noun group, such as DETERMINER and HEAD. A grammar must include a specification of the possible features a unit can have, and the relation of these to both the functions it can play, and the functions and constituents it controls.

These features are not haphazard bits of information we might choose to notice about units, but form a highly structured system (hence the name Systemic Grammar). As an example, we can look at a few of the features for the CLAUSE in Figure 4.10. The vertical lines represent sets from which a single feature must be selected and horizontal lines indicate logical dependency. Thus, we must first choose whether the clause is MAJOR—which corresponds to the function of serving as an independent sentence—or SECONDARY, which corresponds to the various functions a clause can serve as a constituent of another unit (for example as a QUALIFIER in the noun group "the ball which is on the table"). If a clause is MAJOR, it is either DECLARATIVE ("She went"), IMPERATIVE ("Go"), or INTERROGATIVE ("Did she go?"). If it is INTERROGATIVE, there is a further choice between YES-NO ("Did she go?") and WH- ("Where did she go?").

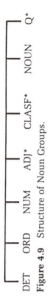

Figure 4.9 Structure of Noun Groups.

Figure 4.10 Simple System Network for Clauses.

---

*It is of course impossible to provide a complete grammar of English, and often difficult to evaluate a partial one. The dialogue of Section 2 gives a sample of the constructions which can be handled, and does not make use of specially included patterns. Winograd (1972) gives a full description of the grammar used.

It is important to note that these features are syntactic, not semantic. They do not represent the use of a sentence as a question, statement, or command, but are rather a characterization of its internal structure—which words follow in what order. A DECLARATIVE can be used as a question by giving it a rising intonation, or even as a command, as in "You're going to give that to me," spoken in an appropriate tone. A question may be used as a polite form of a command, as in "Can you give me a match?," and so on. Any language understander must know the conventions of the language for interpreting such utterances in addition to its simpler forms of syntactic knowledge. To do this, it must have a way to state things like "If something is syntactically a question but involves an event which the hearer could cause in the immediate future, it may be intended as a request." Syntactic features are therefore basic to the description of the semantic rules. The actual features in a comprehensive grammar are related in a more complex way than the simple example of Figure 4.10, but the basic ideas of logical dependency are the same.

In the foregoing we stated that there is a choice between certain features, and that depending on the selection made from one set, we must then choose between certain others. In doing this we are not postulating a psychological model for the order of making choices. The networks are an abstract characterization of the possibilities, and form only a part of a grammar. In addition we need realization and interpretation rules. Realization rules describe how a given set of choices would be expressed in the form of surface syntactic structures, whereas interpretation rules describe how a string of words is analyzed to find its constituents and their features.

Our grammar is an interpretation grammar for accepting grammatical sentences. It differs from more usual grammars by being written explicitly in the form of a program. Ordinarily, grammars are stated in the form of rules, which are applied in the framework of a special interpretation process. This may be very complex in some cases (such as transformational grammars) with separate phases, special "traffic rules" for applying the other rules in the right order, cycles of application, and other sorts of constraints. In our system, the sequence of the actions is represented explicitly in the set of rules. The process of understanding an utterance is basic to the organization of the grammar.*

In saying that grammars are programs, it is important to separate the procedural aspect from the details usually associated with programming. If we say to a linguist "Here is a grammar of English," he can rightfully object if it begins "Take the contents of location 177 and put them into register 2, adding the index . . ." The formalization of the syntax should include only those operations and concepts that are relevant to linguistic analysis, and should not be burdened with paraphernalia needed for programming details. Our model is based on the belief that the basic ideas of programming such as procedure and subprocedure, iteration, recursion, etc. are central to all cognitive processes, and in particular to the theory of language. What is needed is a formalism for describing syntactic processes. Our grammar is written in a language which was designed specifically for the purpose. It is a system

*For a discussion of the psycholinguistic relevance of such interpretive grammars see Kaplan (1971). He describes a similar formulation of procedural grammar, represented as a transition network.

built in LISP, called PROGRAMMAR, and its primitive operations are those involving the building of syntactic structures, and the generation of systemic descriptions of their parts.

The set of typical grammar rules shown in Box 4.6 would be expressed in PRO-GRAMMAR by the program diagrammed in Figure 4.11. For such a simplified bit of grammar, there isn't much difference between the two formulations, except that the PROGRAMMAR representation is more explicit in describing the flow of control. When we try to deal with more complex parts of syntax, the ability to specify procedures becomes more important. For example the word "and" can be associated with a program that can be diagrammed as shown in Figure 4.12. Given the sentence "The giraffe ate the apples and peaches," it would first encounter "and" after parsing the noun "apples." It would then try to parse a second noun, and would succeed, resulting in the structure shown in Figure 4.13. If we had the sentence "The giraffe ate the apples and drank the vodka," the parser would have to try several different things. The "and" appears at a point which represents boundaries between several units. It is after the noun "apples," and the NP, "the apples." It is also after the entire VP "ate the apples." The parser, however, cannot find a noun or NP beginning with the following word "drank". It therefore tries to parse a VP and would successfully find "drank the vodka". A CONJOINED VP would be created, producing the final result shown in Figure 4.14. Of course the use of conjunctions is more complex than this, and the actual program must take into account such things as lists and branched structures in addition to the problems of backing up if a wrong possibility has been tried. But the basic operation of "look for another one like the one you just found" seems both practical and intuitively plausible as a description of how conjunction works. The ability to write the rules as procedures leaves us the flexibility to extend and refine it.

Viewing "and" as a special program that interrupts the normal parsing sequence also gives us a sort of explanation for some puzzling syntactic facts. The statement "I saw Ed with Steve" has a corresponding question, "Whom did you see Ed with?" But "I saw Ed and Steve" cannot be turned into "Whom did you see Ed and?" The "and" program cannot be called when there is no input for it to work with.

Program Organization

So far, we have described how three different types of knowledge are represented and used. There is the data base of assertions and PLANNER procedures which represent the knowledge of the physical world; there are semantic analysis programs

---

Box 4.6 Simple Grammar in Replacement Rule Form.

```
S   →  NP VP
NP  →  DETERMINER NOUN
VP  →  VERB/TRANSITIVE NP
VP  →  VERB/INTRANSITIVE
```

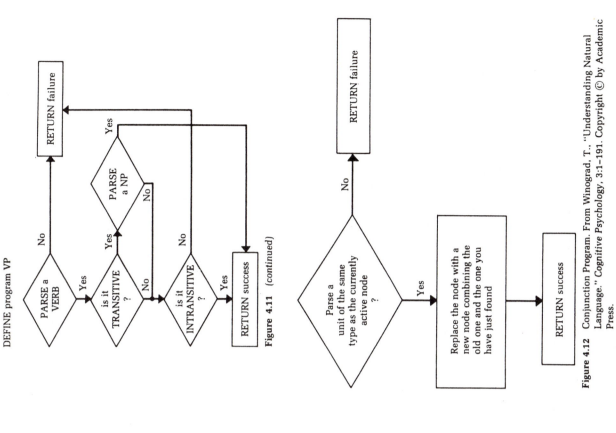

Figure 4.11 (continued)

Figure 4.12 Conjunction Program. From Winograd, T., "Understanding Natural Language." *Cognitive Psychology*, 3:1–191. Copyright © by Academic Press.

which know about such problems as reference; and there is a grammar which determines the syntactic structure. The most important element, however, is the interaction between these components. Language cannot be reduced into separate areas such as "syntax, semantics, and pragmatics," in hopes that by understanding each of them separately, we have understood the whole. The key to the function of language as a means of communication is in the way these areas interact.

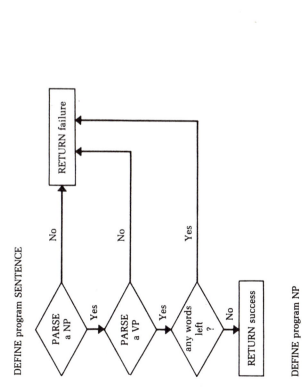

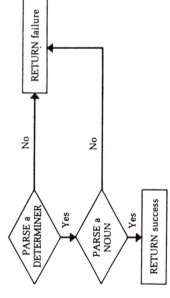

Figure 4.11 PROGRAMMAR Grammar From Winograd, T , "Understanding Natural Language." *Cognitive Psychology*, 3:1–191. Copyright © by Academic Press.

basis of conflicting category information. Thus, there is a continuing interplay between the different sorts of analysis, with the results of one affecting the others.

The procedure as a whole operates in a left to right direction through the sentence. It does not carry along multiple possibilities for the syntactic analysis, but instead has ways of going back and doing something different if it runs into trouble. It does not use the general backup mechanism of PLANNER, but decides what to do on the basis of exactly what sort of problem arose. In the sentences like those of the dialogue, very little backup is ever used, since the combination of syntactic and semantic information usually guides the parser quite efficiently.

Limitations of the Approach

The program we are describing does not purport to be a point by point model of psychological processes at a detailed level. Rather, it is an attempt to show how a general view of language can really be filled in with enough detail to provide a working model. The importance from a psychological point of view is the approach to language as a process which can be modeled within the context of a procedural description of cognitive processes. Rather than trying to attach psychological meaning to isolated components into which language has been divided for abstract study, it attempts to relate the various types of knowledge and procedures involved in intelligent language use.

Looking into the specific capabilities of the system, we can find many places where the details seem inadequate, or whole areas are missing. The program does not attempt to handle hypothetical or counterfactual statements; it only accepts a limited range of declarative information, it cannot talk about verbal acts, and the treatment of "the" is not as general as the description above, and so on. These deficiencies, however, seem to be more a matter of what has been tackled so far, rather than calling into question the underlying model. Looking deeper, we can find two basic ways in which it seems an inadequate model of human language use. The first is the way in which the process is directed, and the second is concerned with the interaction of the context of the conversation and the understanding of its content.

We can think of a program for understanding a sentence as having two kinds of operations—coming up with possible interpretations, and choosing between them. Of course, these are not separate psychologically, but in the organization of computer programs, the work is divided up.

In our program, the syntactic analysis is in charge of coming up with possibilities. The basic operation requires that we find a syntactically acceptable phrase, and then do a semantic interpretation on it to decide whether to continue along that line of parsing. Other programs such as Schank (1971) and Quillian (1967) use the semantic information contained in the definitions of the words to provide an initial set of possibilities, then use syntactic information in a secondary way to check whether the hypothesized underlying semantic structure is in accord with the arrangement of the words.

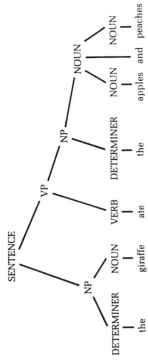

Figure 4.13 Conjoined Noun Structure. From Winograd, T., "Understanding Natural Language." *Cognitive Psychology*, 3:1–191. Copyright © by Academic Press.

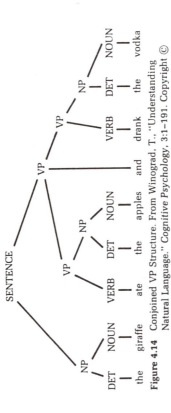

Figure 4.14 Conjoined VP Structure. From Winograd, T., "Understanding Natural Language." *Cognitive Psychology*, 3:1–191. Copyright © by Academic Press.

Our program does not operate by first parsing a sentence, then doing semantic analysis, and finally by using deduction to produce a response. These three activities go on concurrently throughout the understanding of a sentence. As soon as a piece of syntactic structure begins to take shape, a semantic program is called to see whether it might make sense, and the resultant answer can direct the parsing. In deciding whether it makes sense, the semantic routine may call deductive processes and ask questions about the real world. As an example, in sentence 36 of the dialogue ("Put the blue pyramid on the block in the box"), the parser first comes up with "the blue pyramid on the block" as a candidate for a noun group. At this point, semantic analysis is begun, and since "the" is definite, a check is made in the data base for the object being referred to. When no such object is found, the parsing is redirected to find the noun group "the blue pyramid." It will then go on to find "on the block in the box" as a single phrase indicating a location. In other examples the system of semantic markers may reject a possible interpretation on the

By observing human language use, it seems clear that no single approach is really correct. On the one hand, people are able to interpret utterances which are not syntactically well formed, and can even assign meanings to collections of words without use of syntax. The list "skid, crash, hospital" presents a certain image, even though two of the words are both nouns and verbs and there are no explicit syntactic connections. It is therefore wrong to insist that some sort of complete parsing is a prerequisite to semantic analysis.

On the other hand, people are able to interpret sentences syntactically even when they do not know the meanings of the individual words. Most of our vocabulary (beyond a certain age) is learned by hearing sentences in which unfamiliar words appear in syntactically well-defined positions. We process the sentence without knowing any category information for the words, and in fact use the results of that processing to discover the semantic meaning. In addition, much of our normal conversation is made up of sentences like "Then the other one did the same thing to it" in which the words taken individually do not provide clues to enable us to determine the conceptual structure without a complete syntactic analysis.

What really seems to be going on is a coordinated process in which a variety of syntactic and semantic information can be relevant, and in which the hearer takes advantage of whatever is more useful in understanding a given part of a sentence. Our system models this coordination in its order of doing things, by carrying on all of the different levels of analysis concurrently, although it does not model it in the control structure.

Much remains to be done in understanding how to write computer programs in which a number of concurrent processes are working in a coordinated fashion without being under the primary hierarchical control of one of them. A language model able to implement the sort of "heterarchy" found in biological systems (like the coordination between different systems of an organism) will be much closer to a valid psychological theory.

The second basic shortcoming is in not dealing with all the implications of viewing language as a process of communication between two intelligent people. A human language user is always engaged in a process of trying to understand the world around him, including the person he is talking to. He is actively constructing models and hypotheses, and he makes use of them in the process of language understanding. As an example, let us consider again the use of pronouns. In Section 1, we described some of the knowledge involved in choosing referents. It included syntax, semantic categories, and heuristics about the structure of discourse.

But all of these heuristics are really only a rough approximation to what is really going on. The reason that the focus of the previous sentence is more likely to be the referent of "it" is because a person generally has a continuity in his conversation, which comes from talking about a particular object or event. The focus (or subject) is more likely just because that is the thing he is talking about, and he is likely to go on talking about it. Certain combinations of conceptual category markers are more plausible than others because the speaker is probably talking about the real

world, where certain types of events are more sensible than others. If we prefix almost any sentence with "I just had the craziest dream . . ." the whole system of plausible conceptual relations is turned topsy-turvy.

If someone says "I dropped a bottle of Coke on the table and it broke," there are two obvious interpretations. The semantic categories and the syntactic heuristics make it slightly more plausible that it was the bottle that broke. But consider what would happen if we heard "Where is the tool box? I dropped a bottle of coke on the table and it broke" or, "Where is the furniture polish? I dropped a bottle of coke on the table and it broke." The referent is now perfectly clear—only because we have a model of what is reasonable in the world, and what a person is likely to say. We know that there is nothing in the tool box to help fix a broken coke bottle and that nobody would be likely to try fixing one. It would be silly to polish a table that just got broken, while it would be logical to polish one that just had a strong corrosive spilled on it. Of course, all this must be combined with deductions based on other common sense knowledge, such as the fact that when a bottle containing a liquid breaks, the liquid in it spills.

Even more important, we try to understand what the speaker is "getting at." We assume that there is a meaningful connection between his sentences, and that his description of what happened is probably intended as an explanation for why he wants the polish or toolbox. More subtle deductions are implied here as well. It is possible that he broke the table and fixed it, and now wants the polish to cover the repair marks. If this were the case, he would almost surely have mentioned the repair to allow us to follow that chain of logic.

Our system makes only the most primitive use of this sort of deduction. Since it keeps track of when things have been mentioned, it can check a possible interpretation of a question to see whether the asker could answer it himself from his previous sentences. If so, it assumes that he probably means something else. We could characterize this as containing two sorts of knowledge. First, it assumes that a person asks questions for the purpose of getting information he doesn't already have, and second, it has a very primitive model of what information he has on the basis of what he has said. A realistic view of language must have a complex model of this type, and the heuristics in our system touch only the tiniest bit of the relevant knowledge.

It is important to recognize that this sort of interaction does not occur only with pronouns and explicit discourse features, but in every part of the understanding process. In choosing between alternative syntactic structures for a sentence, or picking between multiple meanings of words, we continually use this sort of higher level deduction. We are always basing our understanding on the answer to questions like "Which interpretation would make sense given what I already know?" and "What is he trying to communicate?"

Any attempt to model human language with simple semantic rules and heuristics like those described above is a bit like an attempt to model the behavior of a complex system by using unrelated mathematical formulas whose results are a general approximation to its output. The results may be of interest, and the resulting equations may have a high correlation with what is going on, but it is not a model in the true sense of reflecting the underlying process.

It seems likely that more advanced computational models will move towards overcoming these deficiencies. As we learn more about the organization of large complex systems, we may well be able to model language in ways which are more complete, clearer, and closer to psychological reality.

acceptable, the semantic component may build deep, internal structures representing the meaning of the input (or portions of the input) in the context of a particular task domain. Third, by considering the meaning of a phrase that constitutes a fragment of the utterance, the semantic component may make predictions concerning what words or syntactic constructions are likely to occur in other parts of the utterance. In the current implementation of the speech understanding system, the first two of these functions, filtering and structure building, are performed in a single module; prediction of likely words (but not of syntactic constructions) is carried out in a separate procedure. In this chapter, the major emphasis will be on the first two; prediction will be treated briefly at the end.

To understand the details of semantic filtering and structure building, it will be helpful to consider first some of the higher-level design features of the system.

1. Integration of Filtering and Structure Building

One of the system design features to note is that filtering and structure building are not handled as individual processes but are treated collectively. It would be convenient to have semantic filtering guide the parsing while saving the relatively expensive structure building task for a postparsing phase in which the syntactic analysis of an input would be known in total and the building of structures for spurious phrases could be omitted. However, it turns out that filtering (by both semantics and discourse) is dependent upon the structures assigned to subphrases of the input. Therefore, filtering and structure building are combined. When a phrase combination is proposed to the semantic system, the system attempts to build up a structure encoding the meaning of the new phrase. If any of various checks and restrictions in the structure-building process recognize an anomalous condition, the structure building fails, and this failure, acting as a filter, serves to reject the phrase combination.

2. Timely Semantic Filtering

Most text-based understanding systems (e.g., Woods et al., 1972) perform a complete syntactic analysis of an input before taking any but the most superficial semantic considerations (e.g., number agreement) into account. This approach is quite reasonable, since, for processing text, semantic analysis tends to be far more expensive than reading words from the input buffer or manipulating the grammar. However, when dealing with the added costs and uncertainties of acoustic input, the early use of semantic filtering (and, consequently, structure building) to prune misheard words and false paths through the grammar becomes more attractive. Therefore, in the SRI speech understanding system, the semantic component is given the opportunity to reject each new phrase when it is first proposed.

3. A Two-Phase System

An additional design feature, which has had a great influence on the overall structure of the semantic system, is that the scoping of quantified variables is saved for a postparsing phase. There are two reasons for this postponement. First, the determination of scopes is

VII SEMANTIC ASPECTS OF TRANSLATION

Prepared by Gary G. Hendrix

CONTENTS:

A. INTRODUCTION

The subject of this chapter is the utilization of semantic knowledge in the process of understanding spoken inputs as practiced in the SRI speech understanding system. Basically, there are three functions that a semantic component may perform during the understanding process. First, it may filter out phrase combinations that, although syntactically and acoustically acceptable, do not meet semantic criteria for meaningful unification. Second, for combinations that are extremely context sensitive, making it difficult (or impossible) to perform in a bottom-up fashion, one phrase at a time. Second, the information that scoping adds to the structures representing the semantic interpretations of phrases provides few (if any) new clues that are helpful in filtering. Thus, it is also more efficient to delay the quantification process.

4.   Cooperation with Discourse

The semantic and discourse components of the speech understanding system are closely coordinated and should be studied as a pair. Both components build and evaluate networks that describe the system's interpretation of phrases in the input. Interpretations for some phrases (e.g., pronouns) are built by discourse alone. Some types of phrases (e.g., indefinite noun phrases, verb phrases, prepositional phrases) have interpretations constructed by the semantic component alone. But some phrases (e.g., definitely determined noun phrases) are interpreted by a cooperative effort in which the semantic component builds an intentional description of the phrase's meaning, and discourse relates this intentional description to a particular object in the domain model. In forming an interpretation for a new composite phrase, the semantic module uses the interpretations for each of the phrase's constituent subphrases. These interpretations may have been produced either by semantics or discourse (or have come directly from the lexicon).

As another point of cooperation between discourse and semantics, after discourse expands an elliptical input into a sentence level interpretation, the semantic system is used to add quantification.

B.   PHASE I: SEMANTIC COMPOSITION

As indicated above, the operations of the semantic component may be separated into two phases. The first of these phases, called the "composition" phase, is the subject of this section. The second (or "quantification") phase is discussed in Section C.

The task of the composition phase is to provide semantic filtering and (unquantified) structure building in support of the parsing process. This task is performed by a battery of semantic composition routines (SCRs) that are tightly coordinated with the language definition of the system (see Chapter II). Whenever a language definition rule suggests the feasibility of combining a number of components of the input to produce a larger or more general phrase, one of these SCRs is invoked. Acting as a filter, the SCR may reject the combination on semantic grounds. If the combination is accepted, then the SCR builds a network structure representing the (unquantified) interpretation of the phrase. In building up such structures, the SCRs are in fact COMPOSING network or paraphrases of the input phrases. Hence the name "composition routine."

Since different SCRs are associated with different rules of the language definition, each SCR constitutes a procedural encoding of the associated syntactic knowledge concerning the semantic import of the associated syntactic production(s). This procedural specification references and coordinates the declarative semantic knowledge in the system's lexicon and in the network-encoded domain model. Bringing these sources of semantic information to bear on a proposed phrase combination, an SCR creates an

interpretation structure meeting a number of highly interdependent criteria. These include:

* Creating an interpretation structure that accurately models the (unquantified) meaning of the phrase.

* Reusing the network structures of components in building interpretations of the composite phrase. (This consideration, which is nontrivial in bidirectional networks, makes the building of the composite phrase less expensive.)

* Building structures that allow multiple hypotheses concerning the proper incorporation of a given utterance component in larger phrases to be encoded simultaneously. (This makes possible the handling of ambiguous situations.)

* Allowing competing users of a subphrase to share a single network structure representing the interpretation of that subphrase. (Recycling increases efficiency.)

* Incorporating special quantification markers into the structure that are effectively invisible to other parts of the speech understanding system. (These markers are needed by the quantification phase but must be so encoded that they do not change the meaning of the unquantified structures.)

* Indicating the association between each syntactic unit of the composite phrase and its contribution to the network interpretation structure. (This association is needed both by the quantification phase and by that portion of the discourse component that expands elliptical inputs.)

The ability to use the structures of subphrases in the building of composite structures and the complications of simultaneously maintaining multiple hypotheses make the interactions of the SCRs both more important and more interesting than the operation of any one SCR in isolation. Therefore, the operations of the SCRs will be presented by a series of examples in which many SCRs participate in the construction of an interpretation of a complete utterance.

1.   An Introductory Example

To introduce most of the important features of the SCRs while postponing side issues, consider, for the purposes of simplicity, the parsing of the following, rather unlikely, sentence:

"A power plant of a submarine was built by a company."

The ultimate result of the semantic interpretation process for this sentence is the network structure recorded in the SCRATCH space of Figure VII-1. Structures representing new inputs are constructed in a scratch space (or spaces) to prevent them from becoming confused with the system's model of the task domain, which is recorded on the KNOWLEDGE space. Since the SCRATCH space of the example is immediately below the KNOWLEDGE space in the viewing hierarchy (as shown by the heavy arrow), the view from the SCRATCH space includes the structures in the KNOWLEDGE space. In Figure VII-1, the scratch space is presented in its entirety, but only a fraction of the structures in the KNOWLEDGE space have been shown.

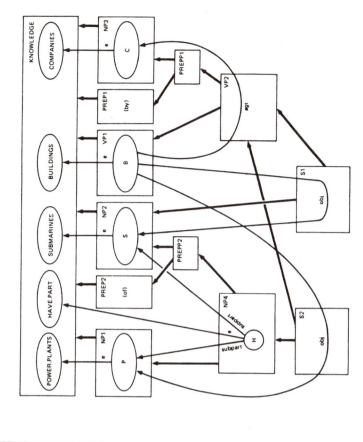

LEXICON

NP: a-power-plant,
    a-submarine, a-company
VP: was-built
PREP: of, by

In the translation process, spaces are created to represent the semantics of each grammatically defined constituent of the total utterance. These spaces are shown in Figure VII-2, with heavy arrows indicating the visibility hierarchy.

Figure VII-1. PARSE TARGET STRUCTURE FOR "A-POWER-PLANT OF A-SUBMARINE WAS-BUILT BY A-COMPANY"

Figure VII-2. MULTIPLE SCRATCH SPACES FOR "A-POWER-PLANT OF A-SUBMARINE WAS-BUILT BY A-COMPANY"

Since the system interprets new inputs by calling on previous knowledge, there are several links from the SCRATCH space into the KNOWLEDGE space. The interpretation of the network in the SCRATCH space is as follows: Node 'B' represents an element of the set BUILDINGS, the set of all building events. In the particular event B, an agt (agent) C is the builder of an obj (object) P. The agent C of the building event is an element of COMPANIES. The object built by C is P, an element of the set POWER.PLANTS. Node 'H' encodes the proposition that power plant P is the subpart in a HAVE.PART situation in which S, some member of the set of SUBMARINES, is the suppart (super part).

To suppress syntactic technicalities while concentrating on the semantic aspects of the construction of this interpretation structure from the original English input, assume the highly simplified language definition:*

GRAMMAR

R1:   S => NP VP
R2:   NP => NP PREPP
R3:   VP => VP PREPP
R4:   PREPP => PREP NP

----
* In the actual system, "a-power-plant" is not treated as an NP. Rather, "power plant" is first combined with PREP "of a submarine" and only afterward is "a" appended to produce the NP "a power plant of a submarine".

At the start of processing, space KNOWLEDGE contains knowledge about power plants, HAVE.PART situations, submarines, building events, and companies. Upon spotting the noun phrase "a-power-plant", an SCR is called to set up a structure representing the meaning of the phrase. In particular, the SCR creates a new space, NP1, below the KNOWLEDGE space in the viewing hierarchy. Within this space, a node 'p' is created with an e arc to 'POWER.PLANTS'. Thus, node 'p' represents some power-plant and the e arc makes its membership in POWER.PLANTS explicit. The new space NP1 separates the structures built to represent the phrase from structures that are in the KNOWLEDGE space. Similarly, new spaces PREP2, NP2, VP1, PREP1, and NP3 are set up to encode other utterance constituents that correspond to explicit lexical entries (terminals).

As language definition rules suggest the grouping of subphrases into larger units, SCRs are called to aid in the process. Using rule R4, PREP1 ("by") and NP3 ("a-company") are combined to form PREPP1 ("by a-company"). PREPP1 is allocated its own space, but no new structures are created within it.

When syntactic considerations suggest combining VP1 ("was-built") with PREPP1, the appropriate SCR is called. Consulting a surface-to-deep-case map associated with "build", the SCR determines that a "by" PREPP following the verb often signals the deep agt case in a passive construction. Operating under this hypothesis, the SCR checks the semantic feasibility of the NP of PREPP1 serving as the agt in a BUILDINGS event. To make this check, the SCR consults the delineation of BUILDINGS, which indicates that any agt of a BUILDINGS situation must be an element of LEGAL.PERSONS. (Delineations are discussed in Chapters V and VI.) The candidate for the agt position is C of space NP3. Since C is an element of COMPANIES, and COMPANIES is a subset of LEGAL.PERSONS, C is accepted. A combination such as "built by a submarine" would have been rejected.

Once VP1 and PREPP1 have passed the acceptability tests, a new space, VP2, is constructed to encode the resultant VP. This new space links node 'B' of VP1 with node 'C' of NP3 via an agt arc. This new arc is visible from space VP2 (and lower spaces in the hierarchy), but is not visible from either VP1 or NP3, leaving the components encoded in VP1 and NP3 free to combine in alternatives to VP2 if necessary.

Continuing the parse, NP2 ("a-submarine") is combined with VP2 ("was-built by a-company") to form S1, after passing tests similar to those above. The obj arc linking the constituent phrases of S1 is contained in space S1 and hence is not seen from the spaces of the constituents NP2 and VP2. Notice that the construct "a-submarine was-built by a-company", which is encoded by S1, is a spurious interpretation of utterance components. The creation of this spurious phrase could have been avoided by strict left-to-right parsing. However, in a system for understanding speech, it may be desirable for parsing to proceed from the right or from the middle (island driving). In any case, the purpose of this presentation is to show how spurious constructions arising either from misheard words or local ambiguities are handled by the SCRs.

---

* The use of case information is described in greater detail in Section D at the end of this chapter.

Using rule R4, PREP2 ("of") may be combined with NP2 ("a-submarine") to form PREPP2. The network structures that are visible from space PREPP2 do not include the (spurious) obj arc from 'B' to 'S' that lies in space S1.

When the syntax of rule R2 suggests combining NP1 and PREPP2 to form a new NP ("a-power-plant of a-submarine"), an SCR is called. The SCR checks NP1 to see if it is relational in nature (as is "length" in "length of the Henry.L.Stimson" or "length of 425 feet") and hence expecting an argument to be supplied. Since NP1 fails this test, the SCR checks the properties of the PREP "of" and discovers that it may be used to encode HAVE.PART situations. Calling upon the delineation of HAVE.PART and appropriate surface-to-deep-case maps, the SCR determines that the HAVE.PART hypothesis provides a feasible interpretation for the NP and hence builds space NP4 with node 'H' and three arcs as shown. Although these new constructs are visible from space NP4, they are not visible from constituents NP1 and PREPP2 (and NP2). Furthermore, they cannot be seen from spurious space S1. Thus, the construction of NP4 has not altered the view of the net from S1. This is an important feature, since at this point in the processing S1 is just as likely a hypothesis as NP4. While these two hypotheses are incompatible, they are nevertheless able to share the structure of NP2 without interfering with one another.

Using rule R1, S2 is constructed from NP4 and VP2. In addition to the obj arc contained in space S2 itself, the view of the net from S2 includes all the information accessible from either space SCRATCH NP4 or space VP2, and hence is identical to the view from space SCRATCH of Figure VII-1. Since the parse corresponding to space S1 does not successfully account for the total input, it is rejected, and S2 is accepted as expressing the meaning of the input.

As will be described later, during the quantification phase, the structures on space S2 and those spaces that are above S2 but below KNOWLEDGE are quantified. The result of this process is exactly the SCRATCH space of Figure VII-1.

The partial ordering of spaces from S2 to KNOWLEDGE indicated in Figure VII-2 is identical to that represented more clearly in Figure VII-3 which, because of the choice of space labels, may be recognized as the parse tree of the input sentence. Consequently, the syntax of the input and the association between each syntactic unit and its corresponding semantics have been captured in the structures built by the SCRs. As discussed below in Section C on quantification and in relation to discourse analysis in Chapter XIII, this association plays a central role in determining the scopes of higher-order predicates and in analyzing elliptical utterances.

2. Technical Comments on the Example

In the discussion of the example, a few technical points were suppressed to simplify the exposition. These will now be considered.

a. Sharing Network Structures

As seen in the example, partitioning enables networks to maintain alternative hypotheses (e.g., S1 and S2) concerning the use of

are not. Such bookkeeping, of course, constitutes a type of network partitioning.

b. Syntactic Order

The visibility hierarchies shown in Figure VII-3 appear to maintain the syntactic order of constituents of a phrase. For example, these figures show that NP4 and VP2 are immediately above S2 and seem to indicate that NP4 is to the left of VP2. In reality, the orthodox vista of S2 is guaranteed to contain both space NP4 and space VP2, but the vista itself says nothing about their relative order. Therefore, any space created by an SCR that has more than one direct parent will have a property, called PARENT.ORDER, indicating the left to right order of its parents. For example, the PARENT.ORDER of S2 is (NP4 VP2). Because of quantification considerations, the order is reversed if one of the parents is a prepositional phrase. This result reflects the quantification rule that "the scoping power of a higher-order predicate decreases from left to right except when embedded in a prepositional phrase."

c. Conceptual Spaces

Actually, it is not necessary for the system to create new spaces for all syntactic units (even though it could). For example, the spaces PREP1, PREPP1, PREP2, and PREPP2 of the example exist only conceptually. The space really associated with the syntactic unit PREPP1 is NP3. This reflects the fact that, in isolation, the prepositional phrase determines no more network structure than the NP alone.

However, empty spaces sometimes are created by the SCRs. Typically, this occurs when a new phrase has the same unquantified network structure as one of its constituents but differs from the constituent because of quantification. A new space is created in order to attach a quantification property that is to belong to the new phrase but not to the constituent.

d. Communicating with the System Executive

Each SCR has its own set of input parameters. Typically, these include the semantic interpretations of phrase constituents and a few syntactic attributes. If any constituent is ambiguous, multiple unambiguous calls are made to SCRs. If the results of an SCR are ambiguous, a list of interpretations is returned. The interpretations returned by the SCRs are typically communicated by pairs of the form (node . vista). For example, the interpretation of the VP "was-built by a-company" is passed to the executive by the pair

('B' . (VP2 VP1 [PREPP1] NP3 KNOWLEDGE)).

(Recall that [PREPP1] and [PREP1] are only conceptual.) Discounting the KNOWLEDGE space, the vista of a pair includes all spaces upon which structures have been created to encode the unquantified interpretation of the phrase. (As will be seen in a subsequent example, this vista sometimes consists of the KNOWLEDGE space alone.) The node of the pair is the so-called "head node" of the structure. It is at this node that the structure will typically be joined to other structures in creating larger phrases.

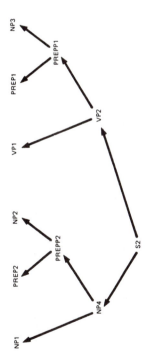

Figure VII-3. VIEWING HIERARCHY ABOVE S2

utterance constituents and enables such competing hypotheses to share network substructures (e.g., V2). Since partitioned structures, together with the associated feature of multiple vistas which allows alternative views of the network, make sharing so natural and straightforward, it is worthwhile to reflect upon the problem of sharing that arises in unpartitioned networks.

The root of the problem is that networks, unlike simpler list structures, are cross-linked by two-way pointers. To see the distinction, let X be some S-expression and let L1 and L2 be two list structures that contain pointers to X. In establishing pointers from L1 and L2 to X, no change is made in X itself. In particular, the creation of a pointer to X does not result in the creation of an inverse pointer from X. So both L1 and L2 may point to X without any complications since X does not point back to either structure.

In ordinary networks, the situation is different. If arcs are established to (or from) a node Y from (to) other nodes N1 and N2, then pointers are established in N1 and N2 that point to Y and N2, then pointers are established in Y that point to N1 and N2. Now, if N1 and N2 are alternatives, the following problem arises. By taking alternative N1, the structures pointed to by N1 must be taken also (since they form a part of the extended meaning of N1). In particular, Y must be taken, and in turn the structures pointed to by Y. But this includes N2, which, being the other alternative, was to have been excluded. The point is that N1 and N2 become linked when they attempt to share the same substructure Y. This contrasts with the list structures above in which L1 and L2 could both point to X without establishing a path from L1 to L2.

There are two solutions to the sharing problem in networks. The first is not to share at all. That is, all structures that would have been shared are instead copied. This solution is expensive and, ultimately, unworkable, since there is usually some path between just about any two nodes in the network. The other solution is to establish a bookkeeping procedure that will maintain a number of different points of view. For each point of view, the bookkeeping must indicate exactly which network structures are to be included and which

For simplicity of writing, a node-space pair may be used to represent the node-vista pair in which the vista is the orthodox vista of the space. Thus, the pair above may be abbreviated as

('B' . VP2).

Using this notation, the results of the various calls to the SCRs may be summarized as follows:

PHRASE	INTERPRETATION
NP1	('P' . NP1)
NP2	('S' . NP2)
NP3	('C' . NP3)
NP4	('P' . NP4)
PREP1	pre net
PREP2	pre net
PREPP1	('C' . NP3)
PREPP2	('S' . NP2)
S1	('B' . S1)
S2	('B' . S2)
VP1	('B' . VP1)
VP2	('B' . VP2)

3. Interacting with Discourse: Determined Noun Phrases

The example utterance considered above was carefully constructed to avoid complications arising from quantification or from interactions with the discourse component of the speech understanding system. However, both quantification and interaction with discourse have major impacts on the semantic aspects of the translation process. By considering a second example sentence

"General.Dynamics built the American submarine."

new facets of the semantic system, particularly its interaction with discourse, may be highlighted while still avoiding the complications of quantification.

The principal distinction between the first example sentence and the current sentence is that the former contained only indefinitely determined noun phrases whereas the latter contains definitely determined NPs. Thus, the first example concerns "a company", but the current example concerns the particular company "General.Dynamics". Likewise, the first example concerns "a submarine", but the current example concerns a particular submarine that is designated as "the American submarine".

The phrase "the American submarine" is intended for use in a context in which the partial description "an American submarine" is sufficient for distinguishing a particular individual. Assuming that the current conversation concerns the Henry.L.Stimson, which is an American submarine, and the Churchill, which is a British submarine, then the phrase "the American submarine" designates the Henry.L.Stimson, and the example sentence is equivalent to the following:

"General.Dynamics built the Henry.L.Stimson."

The actual task of relating "the American submarine" to the Henry.L.Stimson is performed by the discourse component and is described

more fully in Chapter XI. As will be shown in this section, SCRs create the network descriptions that discourse uses in finding the referents of determined noun phrases. Further, once a referent is found, SCRs are used to incorporate the particular individuals returned by discourse when building larger structures.

Turning now to the details of translating the example sentence, the target structure which is to be produced by the parsing process is shown in Figure VII-4. Note that the SCRATCH space contains only the building node and its associated arcs. These elements constitute the new information conveyed by the sentence. Both "General.Dynamics" and "the American submarine" (i.e., "the Henry.L.Stimson") were already known to the system.

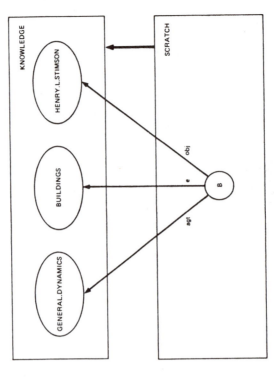

Figure VII-4. CONTEXT-DEPENDENT PARSE TARGET STRUCTURE FOR "GENERAL.DYNAMICS BUILT THE AMERICAN SUBMARINE"

To perform the translation with minimal syntax, assume the following simplified language definition:

GRAMMAR

R1: S => NP VP
R2: VP => VP NP
R3: NP => N
R4: NP => ART MOD N

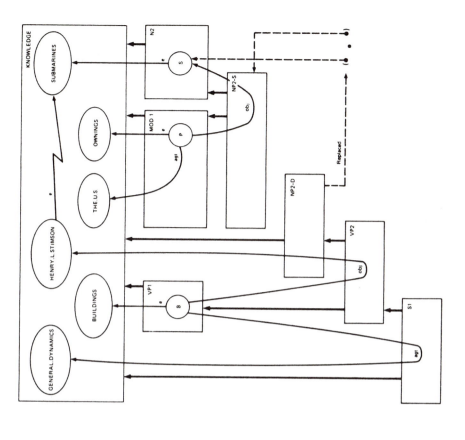

Figure VII-6.   SCRATCH SPACES FOR "GENERAL.DYNAMICS BUILT
THE AMERICAN SUBMARINE"

Using this language definition, the parsing process will produce the
various subphrases shown in Figure VII-5. The semantic and discourse
interpretations of these phrases are indicated by node-space pairs that
refer to the network of Figure VII-6. Figure VII-6 shows a
portion of the KNOWLEDGE space and all network structures that are
produced in the translation of the example sentence.

```
                LEXICON

        N:   General.Dynamics, submarine
        VP:  built
        MOD: American
        ART: a, an, the
```

PHRASE	ENGLISH EXPRESSION	INTERPRETATION
ART1	the	--
MOD1	American	('P' . MOD1)
N1	General.Dynamics	('General.Dynamics' . KNOWLEDGE)
N2	submarine	('S' . N2)
NP1	General.Dynamics	('General.Dynamics' . KNOWLEDGE)
NP2	the American submarine	('S' . NP2-S)
		from semantics
		('Henry.L.Stimson' . NP2-D)
		from discourse
VP1	built	('B' . VP1)
VP2	built the submarine	('B' . VP2)
S1	General.Dynamics built	('B' . S1)
	the American submarine	

Figure VII-5.   NODE-SPACE PAIRS FOR PHRASES IN "GENERAL.DYNAMICS
BUILT THE AMERICAN SUBMARINE"

The first word of the sentence is the N "General.Dynamics".
When this word is identified in the acoustics, an SCR is called to
construct an interpretation. Typically, SCRs build new network
structures, but since information in the lexicon indicates that
"General.Dynamics" has a unique referent, which is modeled by the node
'General.Dynamics' of the KNOWLEDGE space, no new network structures
need be created. Rather, the SCR simply returns the node-space pair
('General.Dynamics' . KNOWLEDGE).

It has been stated previously that the interpretations
produced by the semantics system indicate the association between each
phrase of an utterance and its network translation (if any). This
association is usually indicated by spaces. Since phrases typically
cause new structures to be constructed, and since these structures
usually involve more than a single node or arc, spaces (or vistas) are
used to encircle the collection of structures created for the phrase.
But spaces need not always be used. Since "General.Dynamics" already
has a representation in the KNOWLEDGE space, no new structures are
created. Further, since "General.Dynamics" is represented by a single
node, a new space is not needed to bundle together a number of network
structures. As seen in Figure VII-5, the semantic interpretation of
"General.Dynamics" is designated by the node-space pair
('General.Dynamics' . KNOWLEDGE). In general, wherever the
interpretation of a phrase is expressed by a pair in which the node is

in the KNOWLEDGE space, the network translation of the phrase is simply the node of the pair.

By applying rule R3 of the grammar, the N "General.Dynamics" may be generalized to an NP. The SCR associated with this transformation is an identity function. That is, the interpretation of the NP is the same as the interpretation of the N.

It is worth emphasizing that the SCR that associates the N "General.Dynamics" with the node 'General.Dynamics' makes this association because the lexicon indicates that the noun has a unique referent that is independent of context. That is, there is only one General.Dynamics and hence the interpretation of the N "General.Dynamics" does not vary with context. A proper (and hence definitely determined) noun such as "John" is typically used to refer to some particular object, but since there may be many Johns, the object referred to depends upon the context in which the noun is used. Finding the referents of determined noun phrases with respect to context is the task of discourse and will be illustrated shortly.

Moving to the next word in the sentence, an SCR is called when the VP "built" is recognized. As was the case for the previous example sentence, this SCR creates a new space, VP1, to encode the interpretation of the VP. Within this space, a node 'B' with an e arc to BUILDINGS is created to represent a building event.

The recognition of the word "the" as an ART (article) leads to no significant processing by SCRs.

The next word, "American", has only one meaning in the speech understanding system: "owned by the.U.S." (Were other interpretations allowed, the following analysis would simply be one among many.) The SCR that is called to build an interpretation for this MOD (modifier) creates the space MOD1 shown in Figure VII-6. Within this space, a node 'P' is created to represent the ownership situation and an agt arc is created from 'P' to 'The.U.S.' to indicate that the U.S. is the owner. These structures are built in accordance with information taken from the lexical entry for "American". The lexical entry also indicates that the thing to be modified by this MOD must fill the obj case of the OWNINGS situation. The obj case is said to be the "open" case of the MOD.

The last word, "submarine", causes a space N2 to be created, upon which lies a node 'S' with an e arc to 'SUBMARINES'.

Consider now the application of rule R4 to produce the NP phrase "the American submarine" from the phrases ART1, MOD1, and N2. The SCR associated with this rule tests to see if the head of the N phrase (represented by node 'S') is a feasible candidate to fill the open case of the MOD. To do this, the SCR uses the delineation of set OWNINGS, as described previously. Once this test is satisfied, an obj arc is created from 'P' to 'S' on a new space NP2-S. This space, in combination with the spaces MOD1 and N2 of its orthodox vista, encodes what may be paraphrased as "A submarine that is owned by the U.S." Note particularly that it does not really represent "THE submarine that is owned by the U.S."

If the ART of the production were "a" or "an", then the description of an American submarine that is produced by the SCR would

be an appropriate final interpretation of the new NP. But, since the ART is in fact "the", the description produced by semantics is only the first step in the process of properly interpreting the NP. The presence of "the" signals that the NP is definitely determined. In terms of the system, this result means that the description built by the SCR should be sufficiently specific to uniquely identify some particular object that is currently in context. It is the task of the discourse component to use the description built by the SCR to find this object.*

Assuming that both the Churchill and the Henry.L.Stimson have been mentioned recently, the discourse system will determine that "the American submarine" is the Henry.L.Stimson. At a technical level, discourse creates an interpretation that is expressed by the node-space pair

    ('Henry.L.Stimson' . NP2-D)

Paralleling ('General.Dynamics' . KNOWLEDGE), since 'Henry.L.Stimson' is on the KNOWLEDGE space, the final network translation of the NP "the American submarine" is the single node 'Henry.L.Stimson'. The space NP2-D contains no structure. Its purpose is simply to hold the place of the space NP2-S that was created by semantics. Subsequent compositions that would have used space NP2-S will now use NP2-D. To show that NP2-D has replaced NP2-S, the property list of NP2-D contains a REPLACED property whose value is ('S'. NP2-S), the displaced semantic interpretation. Property lists and LISP pointers are shown in Figure VII-6 by dashed arrows.

The next rule to be applied is R2, which indicates that a new VP may be created from VP1 ("built") and NP2 ("the American submarine"). The SCR for this rule uses the surface-to-deep-case map associated with the lexical entry for "built" in determining that the syntactic direct object should map onto the deep obj case. The delineation of BUILDINGS is then used to test the feasibility of the Henry.L.Stimson filling this case. When this test is passed, an obj arc from 'B' to 'Henry.L.Stimson' is created on a new space "VP".

Similarly, rule R1 is used to establish an agt arc from 'B' to 'General.Dynamics' on new space S1, completing the parsing process. The quantification phase then transforms the interpretation of the total sentence into the network of the SCRATCH space of Figure VII-4. The structures on this SCRATCH space are exactly those structures that lie on the spaces of the orthodox vista of S1, omitting space KNOWLEDGE.

------

* There are other meanings conveyed by definitely determined NPs, and discourse must determine which is intended. For example, there is the generic meaning, as in "the dog is man's best friend." Also, the context is sometimes universal as in "the moon is full." With no context, "the moon" refers to the moon of earth, but in a special context, "the moon" might refer to one of the moons of Mars. The resolution of a determined NP sometimes depends upon the context defined by the embedding sentence itself, as in "the composer that I like best is Bach." But the case under consideration, the case in which discourse looks for an object in local context, is the only important case for the current SRI speech understanding system.

represent the same object because the objects represented by the nodes are not KNOWN to be equivalent--even though they are equivalent.) In processing inputs, objects that have been described differently are often asserted to be equivalent. To show this equivalence, the objects may be connected by an equiv arc. The direction of the equiv arc is irrelevant.

For example, consider the sentence

"The Henry.L.Stimson is a ship."

The scratch spaces created in translating this sentence are shown in Figure VII-8. The first NP of this sentence ("The Henry.L.Stimson") is interpreted as designating node 'Henry.L.Stimson' of KNOWLEDGE. The second NP results in the creation of a node 'X' to represent some element of SHIPS. The copula "is" links these two concepts by asserting that they are equivalent. That is, some ship X is equivalent to the Henry.L.Stimson. Using this identity, the Henry.L.Stimson must itself be an element of SHIPS. The result of eliminating the equiv arc and substituting 'Henry.L.Stimson' for 'X' is shown in Figure VII-9.

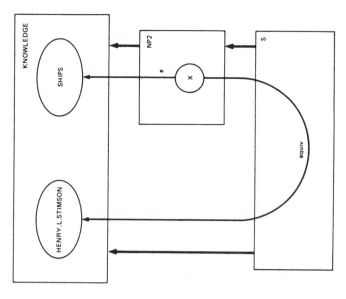

Figure VII-8. SCRATCH SPACES WITH EQUIV ARC FOR "THE HENRY.L.STIMSON IS A SHIP"

4. Other Aspects of the SCRs

With the exception of quantification, the examples presented above have introduced all of the major aspects of the semantic composition routines. However, a few of the less central aspects are worth mentioning.

a. Multiple Node Lexical Entries

All of the lexical items presented thus far have produced at most one node in the scratch spaces used by the SCRs. However, the MOD "American" may really be thought of as a two-node lexical item since it designates both an element of OWNINGS and fills the deep agt case of the owning situation with The.U.S.

Some relational nouns are entered in the lexicon as two node entries. For example, the interpretation of the isolated noun "beam" is shown in Figure VII-7. This word imports both the concept of a length L and the concept of this L filling the measure case of a HAVE.BEAM situation H. Since "beam", "draft", and "length" all designate elements of LENGTHS, it is the situation part that distinguishes these words from one another.

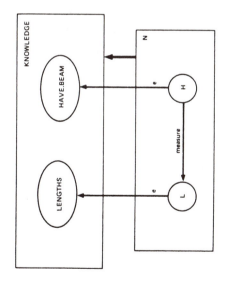

Figure VII-7. THE TWO-NODE INTERPRETATION OF BEAM

b. Equiv Arcs

In the network representing the domain model, if two nodes N1 and N2 are known to represent the same thing, then N1 and N2 are the same node. (Note carefully that two different nodes may still

"beam of 33 feet"). The delineation of HAVE.BEAM, by indicating that the obj must be a physical object and the measure must be a length, provides sufficient information to determine the role played by the Z.

6.   Semantic Composition Rule Summary

The operations of the semantic composition rules may be summarized as follows. When a content word is identified in the acoustic stream, an SCR is called to interpret the word. The interpretation structure is a network fragment that describes the input by relating it to concepts in the KNOWLEDGE space (which encodes the system's domain model). Information concerning how to interpret a given isolated word comes largely from the lexicon.

Information concerning if and how subphrases may be combined to form larger units is encoded procedurally in the various SCRs and declaratively in the delineations of sets.

For determined noun phrases, the indefinite interpretations constructed by the SCRs are typically replaced by discourse interpretations referencing particular items in the domain model. The interpretations built by SCRs are used by the discourse system in finding the appropriate referent. The interpretations from the discourse system may be combined into larger combinations in the same manner as the interpretations created by the SCRs themselves.

The network interpretation of a total utterance is divided among a number of scratch spaces. Each syntactic unit of the input may be identified either with a single node on the KNOWLEDGE space or with some set (i.e., vista) of these scratch spaces. The syntactic phrase structuring of the input is reflected in the vista hierarchy relating the various spaces.

In addition to the node and arc structures, the various spaces created by SCRs may carry information on their property lists concerning quantification. The nature of this information and its role in completing the translation process are the subjects treated next.

C.   PHASE II: QUANTIFICATION

The quantification procedure performed by the semantic component and described in this section is the final step in the construction of a structure representing the meaning of an input. This operation is performed on the (as yet unquantified) interpretation structure of a complete utterance that was produced either by an SCR (in the case of a complete sentence) or by the discourse component (in the case of elliptical expansion).

The task of the quantification phase is to introduce higher-order predicates and their associated scopes into the structure produced by the composition phase. Although the scoping of all higher-order predicates is performed during this process, the procedure is called the "quantification phase" because most of the higher-order predicates that have been considered are, in fact, quantifiers.

The introduction of scopes into the translation net is delayed until a postphase because of the highly context-sensitive nature of scope determination. While quantifiers are frequently indicated within

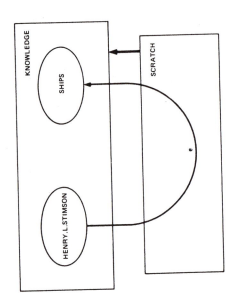

Figure VII-9. SIMPLIFIED INTERPRETATION OF "THE HENRY.L.STIMSON IS A SHIP"

As described in Chapter XVI, the deduction component of the speech understanding system makes use of equiv arcs. In particular, an equiv arc is matched against a dummy entity, and the from- and to- nodes of the arc are paired.

5.   More on Delineations

Above, in processing example sentences, delineations were used as semantic tests to determine whether a given object could play a given role in a situation of a given type. In a speech understanding system, the principal contribution of such tests is to throw out spurious combinations which, typically, are proposed as a result of misheard words. But these delineation tests can also clear up certain ambiguities.

Given the skeletal sentence

"X built Y"

it is clear that, if the sentence makes sense at all, X designates the deep agt of a building event and Y designates the deep obj. However, for the skeletal noun phrase,

"beam of Z"

the Z might be either the obj of a HAVE.BEAM relationship (as in "beam of the Henry.L.Stimson") or the measure of such a relationship (as in

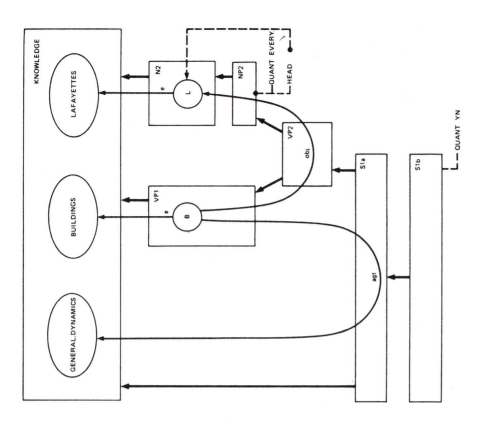

Figure VII-10. SCR SPACES FOR "DID GENERAL.DYNAMICS BUILD EVERY LAFAYETTE?"

noun phrases, their influence is generally not confined to the noun phrase itself, but rather is brought to bear on higher constituents in which the noun phrase is embedded. Furthermore, the scopes of most English quantifiers are affected by other quantifiers that appear in the utterance. The interaction of quantifiers is influenced by the syntax of the higher level constituents that incorporate them, by the relative scoping strengths of the actual English words used, and by the physical feasibility of readings.

The quantification process is largely performed by repartitioning the nodes and arcs of the unquantified interpretation structures. That is, while leaving the original partitioning in place to save the syntactic history of the input for discourse analysis (i.e., for the expansion of future elliptical inputs), nodes and arcs are placed in new spaces that are ordered hierarchically to indicate the nesting of higher-order predicates. For example, a typical new space might define the boundaries of the scope of a universal variable. In addition to repartitioning, some new nodes also may be introduced into the translation structure to represent such logical connectives as IMPLICATIONS and NEGATIONS.

Information for deciding how to define the new "quantification" spaces and how to order the spaces is taken from the network structures built earlier in the semantic composition phase. In particular, the syntactic structure of the input, as shown in the hierarchy of scratch spaces, plays an important role. Heavy reliance is also placed on information (not yet discussed) that is encoded on the property lists of the scratch spaces.

The approach to determining the scopes of quantifiers that is presented in this section has been influenced by the game theory technique advanced by Hintikka (1974). However, certain engineering expediencies have been used in applying portions of his technique to an operational system based on partitioned semantic networks.

1. Overview

To gain a perspective on the overall quantification procedure, consider the processing of the example query

"Did General.Dynamics build every Lafayette?"

(The Lafayettes compose one class of nuclear submarines.) The scratch spaces for this query that were built by the SCRs during the composition phase are shown in Figure VII-10.

Simply put, the node and arc structure created by semantic composition is the same as would have been created for

"General.Dynamics built a Lafayette."

In more detail, the noun phrase "General.Dynamics" is interpreted by the single node 'General.dynamics' of the KNOWLEDGE space. The VP "built" results in space VP1, as in previous examples. Also paralleling previous examples, the noun "Lafayette" results in a

However, two of the spaces have special properties relating to quantification (or, more generally, higher-order predicates). Space NP3 includes information about the English quantifier "every" and space S1b includes information about the special YN (i.e., yes/no) quantifier."

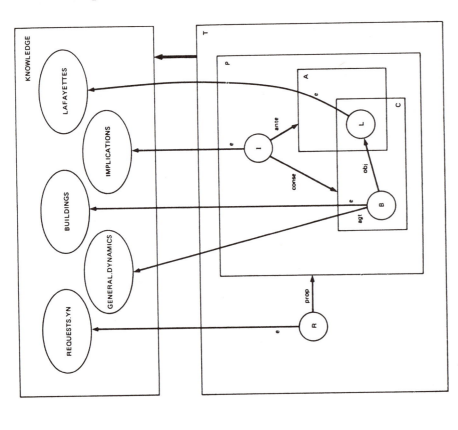

Figure VII-11. ULTIMATE TRANSLATION OF "DID GENERAL.DYNAMICS BUILD EVERY LAFAYETTE?"

node 'L' with e arc to 'LAFAYETTES' being created in a new space N2. The quantifier "every" is combined with this noun to form a new noun phrase, "every Lafayette." This NP is represented by the vista from new space NP2. The view from NP2 inherits the noun structure of N2. But, through the property list of space NP2, there is added to this noun structure the information that the English quantifier "every" was used in the formation of the NP. The empty space NP2 is created solely to provide a place to attach this property list. If the properties were hung from space N2, then the interpretation of the noun in isolation would be altered and would not be available for incorporation in alternative hypotheses. (There may, for example, be a hypothesis in which the acoustic signal preceding "Lafayette" is interpreted as containing some word other than "every.")

VP1 and NP2 are combined to form VP2, "built every Lafayette," in a fashion analogous to previous examples. In the last stage of composition, the AUXD (the auxiliary verb of the "do" family) "did" is combined with the NP "General.Dynamics" and VP2 to form a complete query. The building operations for node and arc structures are the same as if the NP and VP were being combined to form an assertion. But the pattern

    AUXD NP VP

signals that the validity of the assertion

    NP VP

is to be tested by a YES/NO query. Since a test involving a proposition is second-order, the request for a test is not translated into a network structure by the SCR. Rather, the creation of a (second-order) network structure to encode the YES/NO query involving the proposition NP-VP is delayed until the quantification phase. To indicate that this structure is to be built, the space S1b is created below S1a and is marked by the property value pair (QUANT . YN). (Space S1a with its vista is the interpretation of proposition NP-VP.) In general, a QUANT property is assigned to a space whenever a quantification or other higher-order structure must be built during the second phase of semantic processing.

Using the structure built during the composition phase as its sole input, the quantification phase builds a network structure that provides a complete (literal) interpretation of the original input utterance, which includes all higher-order structures. For the example query, the structure of Figure VII-10 is transformed into the structure of Figure VII-11 (while the structure of Figure VII-10 is preserved for subsequent discourse analysis).

Space T of Figure VII-11 is the target translation space for the query. At the top level, T encodes a request R for information of the YES/NO type. (See the discussion of REQUESTS.YN in Chapter V, Section E.3.a, and Chapter XV, Section B.1.) The proposition of this request, whose validity determines the answer to the query, is encoded on space P. In particular, P encodes the proposition

    "For every L, if L is an element of LAFAYETTES,
    then L was built by General.Dynamics."

Note that this proposition contains the universally quantified variable L and that the quantification is encoded in accordance with the techniques described in Chapter V, Section E.2.

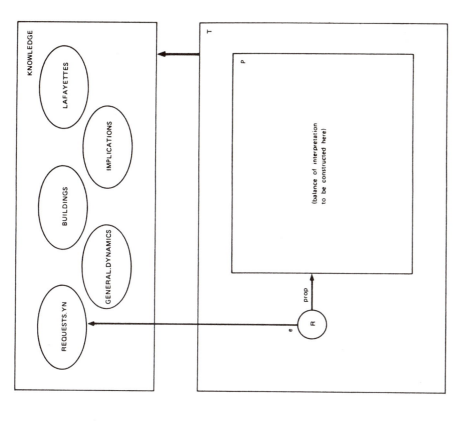

Figure VII-12.   RESULT OF Q.YN SCOPING PROCEDURE

The conversion of a semantic composition structure (i.e., the final product of the SCRs) into a fully quantified translation is performed by applying "quantification" functions (Q functions) to the various spaces created by the SCRs. Exactly one Q function is applied to each space, and the process is completed when the last space has been processed. The Q functions that are applied determine the types of higher-order structures that are produced, and the order in which spaces are selected for the application of a Q function determines the nesting of predicate scopes. Only a small number of Q functions are used.

The particular Q function to be applied to a given space is determined solely by the QUANT value of the space. (Spaces with no QUANT property are understood to have the value NIL.) The order in which the functions are applied is determined by calculations involving the syntax of the utterance and the relative scoping strength of those quantifiers that occur in the semantic composition structure.

Omitting the details of the order of space selection, the conversion of the example query proceeds as follows: First, an empty translation space T is created below the KNOWLEDGE space. This space is designated as the current active space for the creation of new structures by subsequent calls to Q functions. Then, space S1b is selected and the value of its QUANT property is mapped onto the Q function Q.YN. Q.YN is then applied to space S1b.

Q.YN builds structures to represent a YES/NO request on the active translation space, T. In particular, the structures of space T shown in Figure VII-12 are created by Q.YN. These structures consist of a node 'R', an e arc from 'R' to 'P'. Upon completing this structure building operation, Q.YN designates the new space P as the active space for the application of Q functions to any space above S1b in the viewing hierarchy. For the current example, this includes all other spaces created during the composition phase.

The next space that is selected is space NP2. After the value of its QUANT property has been mapped onto the function Q.UNIV, Q.UNIV is called to build structures in the currently active translation space, P. The structures built by this call to Q.UNIV are shown in Figure VII-13. These include an implication node 'I' with its corresponding ante and conse spaces, A and C. After creating these structures, Q.UNIV copies node 'L' from composition space N2 onto both A and C. Q.UNIV copies 'L' because it is marked as the HEAD node of NP2. This copying, which is relatively inexpensive, does not alter the structure of N2, leaving it intact for use in discourse analysis. However, the copying does cause spaces A and C to overlap and hence, by the overlapping convention of IMPLICATIONS (presented in Chapter V, Section E.2.d), establishes L as a universal variable.

Upon completion of its building and copying operations, Q.UNIV splits the remainder of the quantification process into two subprocesses. In the first of these subprocesses, the spaces above NP2 (the space that activated the function) are to be considered, using space A as the active space. In the second subprocess, all other spaces currently pending are to be considered, using space C as the active space.

In the first of these subprocesses, only space N2 remains to be processed. Since this space has no QUANT value, the default function Q.EXISTS is applied. This function simply copies all the structures of NP2 onto the currently active translation space, A. Since 'L' already exists on A, this copy operation acts as a no-op. But the e arc from 'L' to 'LAFAYETTES' is transferred.

In the second of the subprocesses, spaces S1a, VP2, and VP1 are considered, using C as the active space. Since none of these spaces have a QUANT property, Q.EXISTS is applied to each with the result that their structures are copied onto space C. This copying process in no way alters the structures created during semantic composition.

With S1b, VP2, and VP1 processed, all the semantic composition spaces have had a Q function applied, and the quantification phase of translation is completed.

2. The Quantifiers

A list of the quantifiers used in the system with their associated Q functions and strengths is presented in Figure VII-14. (The word "quantifier," as used here means "any MARKER denoting a higher-order predicate and its strength.") The quantifiers include both English words (all, any, both, each, either, every, neither, no, none, not, and some) and quantifiers derived from structure (CONSTANT, NIL, PL-DEF, PL-NUMBERED, PL-OPEN, WH, and YN).

QUANTIFIER	Q FUNCTION	STRENGTH
ALL	Q.UNIV	2
ANY	Q.UNIV	7
BOTH	Q.UNIV	2
(CONSTANT)	—	infinite
EACH	Q.UNIV	6
EITHER	Q.UNIV	2
EVERY	Q.UNIV	2
NEITHER	Q.NO-EXIST	3
(NIL)	Q.EXISTS	0
NO	Q.NO-EXIST	3
NONE	Q.NO-EXIST	2
NOT	Q.NEG	4
PL-DEF	Q.UNIV	3
PL-NUMBERED	Q.SET	1
PL-OPEN	Q.EXISTS	0
SOME	Q.EXISTS	1
WH	Q.WH	5
YN	Q.YN	8

Figure VII-14. THE Q FUNCTIONS AND STRENGTHS OF QUANTIFIERS

The quantifiers associated with English words are typically found during the composition phase by spotting constructions of the form

quantifier-word noun-structure

as in "all submarines", "every destroyer", "no torpedo launchers". The structural quantifiers are found by noting the structure of inputs. For example, the YN quantifier is signaled by the construction

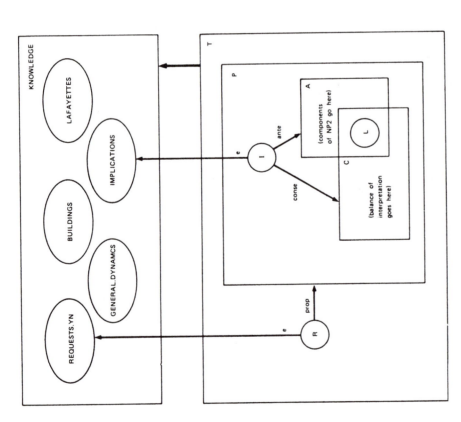

Figure VII-13. RESULT OF Q.UNIV SCOPING PROCEDURE

is X Y?

Whenever a quantifier is found in the composition process, it becomes the value of the QUANT property of one of the composition spaces.

Each quantifier denotes two separate pieces of information: a higher-order predicate and the relative scoping strength with which that predicate is to be used. In the speech understanding system, a different Q function is used for each of the higher-order predicates recognized by the system, and it is this Q function, rather than the predicate itself, that is directly associated with a quantifier.

The interpretations placed on the English word quantifiers are quite straightforward. ALL, ANY, BOTH, EACH, EITHER, and EVERY are all interpreted as denoting universal quantification. In particular, the quantifier ANY is never used in the existential interpretation. The quantifiers are only applied to count (as opposed to mass) nouns and the individual (as opposed to the collective) interpretation is always assumed. Thus "John saw all the men" is interpreted as "For every man, John saw him" as opposed to "John saw the group of men."

The English word quantifier SOME is interpreted as denoting existential quantification. NO, NONE, and NEITHER denote "there does not exist." NOT denotes negation.

The structural quantifiers denote some of the more exotic higher-order predicates. WH (signaled by words such as "who," "what," "which," and "how many") is used to identify a WH-type request for information. Similarly, the YN quantifier denotes a YES/NO query.

The PL-DEF quantifier arises from plural, definitely determined noun phrases such as "those five ships" in "General.Dynamics built those five ships." During the composition phase, the discourse component resolves plural, determined NPs to nodes on the KNOWLEDGE space representing sets. The PL-DEF denotes a universal quantification over one of these resolved sets. For example, "for every member of the set consisting of <those five ships>, General.Dynamics built it."

PL-NUMBERED arises from plural noun phrases that explicitly designate a number (e.g., "five men", "two of the submarines", "how many engines"). This quantifier is associated with a predicate over two objects N and P that may be paraphrased as

"N is the cardinality of the set defined by the predicate P."

For example, consider the statement

"General.Dynamics built 31 Lafayettes."

During the composition phase, the phrase "31 Lafayettes" signals the PL-NUMBERED quantifier. In the quantification phase, this results in the creation of a structure encoding

"31 is the cardinality of set S, where x is an element of S if and only if x is a Lafayette and x was built by General.Dynamics."

If a plural noun phrase contains no English quantifier, no definite determiner, and no number designation, then it signals a PL-OPEN quantification. For example, "submarines" in "General.Dynamics built submarines" signals a PL-OPEN. Under normal circumstances, PL-OPEN simply indicates existential quantification. For the example just cited the interpretation would be

"There exists a submarine that General.Dynamics built."

(This interpretation loses the information that more than one submarine was built, but the structure for the more complete interpretation was considered more expensive than it was worth for the present implementation.)

Unlike any other quantifier in the system, the effect of PL-OPEN can sometimes be superseded by stronger quantifiers. In particular, if a PL-OPEN type of NP is the subject of a sentence, then an ALL quantifier is created by the sentence-level SCR to supersede the PL-OPEN. For example, in

"Ships are built by corporations."

both "ships" and "corporations" are PL-OPEN NPs. But since "ships" is the subject, an ALL quantifier at the sentence level supersedes the PL-OPEN. Thus the interpretation is

"For every ship there exists a corporation that built it."

Most spaces created during semantic composition are not marked as being quantified at all and may be thought of as having a QUANT value of NIL. This NIL value signals existential quantification. The sentence

"A power plant of a submarine was built by a company."

which was the first example considered under semantic composition, is purely existential.

Some types of phrases are mapped directly onto the KNOWLEDGE space during the composition phase. For example, phrases with unique referents such as "General.Dynamics" and (in context) "the American submarine" are so mapped. Such KNOWLEDGE space nodes are tantamount to CONSTANTS and are therefore unaffected by quantification.

3. Space Ordering

The nesting of scopes by Q functions is critically dependent upon the order in which spaces are selected for Q-function application. It has been suggested that this order would best be established by game theory considerations as outlined by Hintikka (1974). However, the game theory approach did not appear suitable for immediate adaptation to a computational system. Therefore, a more engineering-oriented approach, based on syntax and quantifier strength, has been used in the SRI speech understanding system.

The ordering of spaces for Q function applications conforms to the following rule:*

----
* Doug Appelt and I are currently working on a revised version of this rule. Appelt has observed that when an English-word quantifier is the first word of a sentence, its strength relative to other English-word quantifiers is greatly increased. We have also observed that quantifiers in fronted adverbial phrases outscore quantifiers in the balance of the sentence, and that when an "ANY" falls within the scope of a WH or YN, it behaves existentially. Updates to the system based on these observations are pending.

GIVEN any two composition spaces,

IF either has a QUANT of greater strength than the other, then the stronger is taken first.

OTHERWISE, if either is in the orthodox vista of the other, then the space in whose vista the other lies is taken first (i.e., compounds dominate their constituents).

OTHERWISE, that space corresponding to the logically leftmost syntactic constituent is taken first.

With one exception, a syntactic unit X is to the logical left of syntactic unit Y if X appears before Y in the sentence. The exception is the case in which X and Y combine with a preposition to form a new syntactic unit Z as in the production

Z => X PREP Y

For this case only, Y is considered to be to the logical left of X. (Example: "Every engine of every submarine" is roughly equivalent with "For every submarine, for every engine of that sub".)

Applying the above rule to the example input of Figure VII-10 yields the following analysis: Space S1b is the first space for Q-function application because its QUANT strength, at 8 for a YN, is greater than any other. Space NP2 comes next with a QUANT strength of 2 for EVERY. The other spaces (S1a, VP2, VP1, and N2) all have strength 0. Since all of these other spaces are in the orthodox vista of S1a, S1a comes next. Similarly, VP2 comes before VP1 or N2. VP2 comes before N2 because it is to the left of N2, and N2 comes last.

As was the case in the introductory example, the application of some Q functions may cause the quantification process to be split into multiple subprocesses, each with its own active target space. When this happens, those spaces that remain unconsidered are divided among the subprocesses. But in each subprocess, the spaces are considered in the same order as they would have been had the subprocess remained joined.

To gain a better feel for the influence of quantifier strength over the scoping of predicates, consider the two queries

"Who built every X?"

and

"Who built each X?"

These queries are of interest because the WH quantifier signaled by the word "who" has a strength of 5, which lies between the strength of EVERY (strength 2) and EACH (strength 6). The network structures representing these two queries are shown in Chapter V, Section E.3.b.

Since WH outscopes EVERY, the interpretation of the first query goes something like this: "Who is that one builder B such that for all x in X, B built x?" Since WH is outscoped by EACH, the interpretation of the second query goes something like this: "For all x in X, who built x?"

Another pair of sentences whose interpretations differ only with respect to scope are

"All the men didn't go."

and

"Each of the men didn't go."

In the first, not all went. In the second, not any went. (Of course, "not all went" versus "not any went" is just another case in point.)

The scoping scheme as outlined above is far from perfect and should be regarded as merely a first cut at a difficult but fascinating problem.

D. THE USE OF CASE INFORMATION*

Case information establishes a link between certain syntactic and semantic constructions. It serves two purposes: First, it provides a basis for using information from a syntactic structure in determining what semantic relationships hold in a particular phrase. Second, it is a relatively simple mechanism for eliminating incorrect interpretations by rejecting unallowable semantic relationships and by blocking syntactic predictions for words that cannot possibly fit in the current semantic context. Both uses of case information have already figured in examples earlier in this chapter. Here we will describe the mechanism involved and illustrate its application.

Every word that conveys the concept of a situation has contained in its lexical entry (1) a pointer to the semantic net representation for the set of similar situations, and (2) a statement of the syntactic attributes that signal which syntactic units specify which semantic roles in situations of that type. Verbs, certain prepositions, modifiers, adjectives, and certain nouns are interpreted semantically in terms of situations and have this information associated with them in the lexicon. When a word or phrase conveying situation data is added to a phrase, this information is used along with the syntactic attributes of the phrase to determine the case relations allowed among particular constituents. If the phrase satisfies the relations, the information is used by the semantic composition routines to build the semantic structure representing it. The information also is used to eliminate interpretations where these relations cannot hold.

Since many verbs map the same surface constituents into the same case relations, with the only difference between verbs being the particular situation types, these verbs are grouped together and described by common paradigms (see Celce-Murcia, 1976). Thus, verbs like "build", "own", and "construct" all follow a common paradigm which indicates that in the active voice, the syntactic subject fills the agt (agent) case and the syntactic object fills the obj (object) case, and that they are reversed in the passive voice. Cases may be obligatory or optional, and all the obligatory ones must be filled for a sentence interpretation to be accepted.

To see in more detail how this information is used to check possible phrases and to block predictions of words by the executive that would otherwise be made on the basis of syntactic information, it is necessary to look more closely at what information is available. As has been described in Chapter V, Section E.2.g, each situation has a delineating element that has case arcs connecting it to other nodes in the network. As a result, it is possible to determine for each case arc

----
* This section was prepared by Ann Robinson.

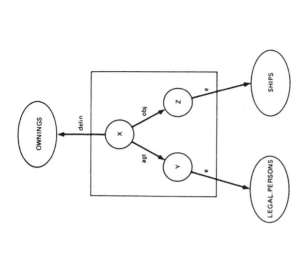

Figure VII-15. SEMANTIC NET REPRESENTATION OF THE OWNING SITUATION

the set of items that can be in the case relation. Structures indicating a particular instance of that situation must correspond to the restrictions that are specified. For example, semantic structures can not be built for phrases like "The Henry L. Stimson owns the U.S." because submarines cannot own countries.

To save the time that would be otherwise be required to compute for each noun whether its possible referents are included in a specific set, nouns are predivided into subcategories that correspond to the sets allowed in particular case relations. When a word that refers to a situation is added to a phrase, the information associated with that word is used along with syntactic information to determine which case relations the other constituents in the phrase can fill. If other constituents have been found and are compatible, then the phrase is built. If the other constituents have not yet been found, then the information indicating what case each constituent can fill is used to determine what subcategory or subcategories of nouns can occur in that constituent. When the executive is ready to predict nouns for each subcategory, it first checks the attributes of that subcategory in the current context. If that subcategory is not allowed semantically because of the case (or other) constraints, then that prediction is eliminated. If that subcategory is allowable then the predictions for individual words are made.

As an example, consider the sentence "Who owns the Henry L. Stimson?" as shown in Figure VII-15. The verb "owns" corresponds to the semantic situation set OWNINGS. This has two associated case arcs: agt and obj. The agt arc indicates the the set of all possible owners, and the obj arc indicates the set of all things that can be owned. In this domain, the owners are all the legal persons: companies and countries. When the verb "owns" is found, and a partial verb phrase is constructed, the case information is used to restrict the nouns that can follow it. The verb "owns" is active, so the verb phrase must be of the form V NP, i.e., a noun phrase must follow the verb. The case information restricts the NP to include one of the nouns in the subcategory of nouns that is associated with the set of ships. If any complete noun phrases have been found to the right of the verb, they will be combined with the verb only if they meet the _case_ criteria, namely, that the head noun reference a ship. If a successful interpretation has not been found, when the executive is ready to predict nouns for the NP constituent, it will first check each noun subcategory to see if that subcategory could fit at that place. In this example, the only allowable subcategory is ships. Companies, countries, measures, and the like are not allowed. The executive will only predict the individual words in that subcategory. Henry.L.Stimson is a submarine, and thus the noun "Henry L. Stimson" is in that subcategory. When the phrase "the Henry L. Stimson" is found and specified as a noun phrase, the information that it is likely to fit the obj case in the semantic representation is given to the semantic composition routines along with the semantic structures for "own" and "the Henry L. Stimson". With the VP thus completed, the information is used in the S rule to determine what possible cases the surface subject can fill. Since the obj case is filled, the remaining NP must fill the agt case. "Who" is consistent with the constraint on agt, that it be a reference to a legal person, so it is combined with the VP and the information given to the semantic composition routines to complete the semantic interpretation.

PROBLEMS IN LOGICAL FORM

Robert C. Moore

SRI International, Menlo Park, CA 94025

I   INTRODUCTION

Decomposition of the problem of "language understanding" into manageable subproblems has always posed a major challenge to the development theories of, and systems for, natural-language processing. More or less distinct components are conventionally proposed for handling syntax, semantics, pragmatics, and inference. While disagreement exists as to what phenomena properly belong in each area, and how much or what kinds of interaction there are among these components, there is fairly widespread concurrence as to the overall organization of linguistic processing.

Central to this approach is the idea that the processing of an utterance involves producing an expression or structure that is in some sense a representation of the literal meaning of the utterance. It is often maintained that understanding what an utterance literally means consists in being able to recover this representation. In philosophy and linguistics this sort of representation is usually said to display the logical form of an utterance, so we will refer (somewhat loosely) to the representations themselves as "logical forms."

This paper surveys what we at SRI view as some of the key problems encountered in defining a system of representation for the logical forms of English sentences, and suggests possible approaches to their solution. We will first look at some general issues related to the notion of logical form, and then discuss a number of problems associated with the way information involving certain key concepts is expressed in English. Although our main concern here is with theoretical issues rather than with system performance, this paper is not merely speculative. The DIALOGIC system currently under development in the SRI Artificial Intelligence Center parses English sentences and translates them into logical forms embodying many of the ideas presented here.

II   THE NATURE OF LOGICAL FORM

The first question to ask is, why even have a level of logical form? After all, sentences of natural languages are themselves conveyers of meaning; that is what natural languages are for. The reason for having logical forms is to present the literal meanings of sentences more perspicuously than do the sentences themselves. It is sometimes said that natural-language sentences do not "wear their meanings on their sleeves"; logical forms are intended to do exactly that.

From this perspective, the main desideratum for a system of logical form is that its semantics be compositional. That is, the meaning of a complex expression should depend only on the meaning of its subexpressions. This is needed for meaning-dependent computational processes to cope with logical forms of arbitrary complexity. If there is to be any hope of maintaining an intellectual grasp of what these processes are doing, they must be decomposable into smaller and smaller meaning-dependent subprocesses operating on smaller and smaller meaningful pieces of a logical form. For instance, if identifying the entities referred to by an utterance is a subprocess of inferring the speaker's intentions, there must be identifiable

pieces of the logical form of the utterance that constitute referring expressions. Having logical forms be semantically compositional is the ultimate expression of this kind of decomposability, as it renders every well-formed subexpression a locus of meaning—and therefore a potential locus of meaning-dependent processing. This is probably a more telling argument for semantic compositionality in designing language-processing systems than in analyzing human language, but it can be reasonably argued that such design principles must be followed by any system, whether natural or artificial, that has to adapt to a complex environment (see [Simon, 1969], especially Chapter 4).[1]

Logical form, therefore, is proposed as a level of representation distinct from surface-syntactic form, because there is apparently no direct way to semantically interpret natural language sentences in a compositional fashion. Some linguists and philosophers have challenged this assumption [Montague, 1974a] [Barwise and Cooper, 1981], but the complexity of their proposed systems and the limited range of syntactic forms they consider leave serious doubt that the logical-form level can be completely bypassed.[2]

Beyond being compositional, it is desirable—though perhaps not essential—that the meaning of a logical form also be independent of the context in which the associated utterance occurs. (The meaning of an expression in natural language, of course, is often context-dependent.) A language-processing system must eventually produce a context-independent representation of what the speaker means by an utterance because the content of the utterance will normally be subjected to further processing after the original context has been lost. In the many cases in which the speaker's intended meaning is simply the literal meaning, a context-independent logical form would give us the representation we need. There is little doubt that some representation of this sort is required. For example, much of our general knowledge of the world is derived from simple assertions of fact in natural language, but our situation would be hopeless if, for every fact we knew, we had to remember the context in which it was obtained before we could use it appropriately. Imagine trying to decide what to do with a tax refund by having to recall whether the topic of conversation was rivers or financial institutions the first time one heard that banks were good places in which to keep money.

As this example suggests, context independence is closely related to the resolution of ambiguity. For any given ambiguity, it is possible to find a case in which the information needed to resolve it is derived from the context of an utterance. Therefore, if the meanings of logical forms are to be context-independent, the system of logical forms must provide distinct, unambiguous representations for all possible readings of an ambiguous utterance. The question remains whether logical form should also provide ambiguous representations to handle cases in which the disambiguating information is obtained later or is simply general world knowledge. The pros and cons of such an approach are far from clear, so we will generally assume only unambiguous logical forms.

Although it is sometimes assumed that a context-independent representation of the literal meaning of a sentence can be derived by using syntactic and semantic knowledge only, some pragmatic factors must also be taken into account. To take a concrete example, suppose the request "Please list the Nobel Prize winners in physics," is followed by the question "Who are the Americans?" The phrase "the Americans" in the second utterance should almost certainly be interpreted as referring to American winners of the Nobel Prize in physics, rather than all inhabitants or citizens of the United States, as it might be understood in isolation. If the logical form of the utterance is to reflect the intended interpretation, processes that are normally assigned to pragmatics must be used to derive it.

One could attempt to avoid this consequence by representing "the Americans" at the level of logical form as literally meaning all Americans, and have later pragmatic processing restrict the interpretation to American winners of the Nobel Prize in physics. There are other cases, however, for which this sort of move is not available. Consider more carefully the adjective "American." American people could be either inhabitants or citizens of the United States; American cars could be either manufactured or driven in the United States; American food could be food produced or consumed in or prepared in a style indigenous to the United States. In short, the meaning of "American" seems to be no more than "bearing some contextually determined relation to the United States." Thus, there is no definite context-independent meaning for sentences containing modifiers like "American." The same is true for many uses of "have," "of," possessives, locative prepositions [Herskovits, 1980] and compound nominals. The only way to hold fast to the position that the construction of logical-form precedes all pragmatic processing seems to be to put in "dummy" symbols for the unknown relations. This may in fact be very useful in building an actual system,[3] but it is hard to imagine that such a level of representation would bear much theoretical weight.

We will thus assume that a theoretically interesting level of logical form will have resolved contextually dependent definite references, as well as the other "local" pragmatic indeterminacies mentioned. An important consequence of this view is that sentences per se do not have logical forms; only sentences in context do.[4] If we speak loosely of the logical form of a sentence, this is how it should be interpreted.

If we go this far, why not say that all pragmatic processing takes place before the logical form is constructed? That is, why make any distinction at all between what the speaker intends the hearer to infer from an utterance and what the utterance literally means? There are two answers to this. The first is that, while the pragmatic factors we have introduced into the derivation of logical form so far are rather narrowly circumscribed (e.g., resolving definitely determined noun phrases), the inference of speaker intentions is completely open-ended. The problem confronting the hearer is to answer the question, "Why would the speaker say that in this situation?" Practically any relevant knowledge that the speaker and hearer mutually possess [Clark and Marshall, 1981] [Cohen and Perrault, 1981] may be brought to bear in answering this question. From a purely methodological standpoint, then, one would hope to define some more restricted notion of meaning as an intermediate step in developing the broader theory.

Even putting aside this methodological concern, it seems doubtful that a theory of intended meaning can be constructed without a concomitant theory of literal meaning, because the latter notion appears to play an explanatory role in the former theory. Specifically, the literal meaning of an utterance is one of those things from which hearers infer speakers' intentions. For instance, in the appropriate context, "I'm getting cold" could be a request to close a window. The only way for the hearer to understand this as a request, however, is to recover the literal content of the utterance, i.e., that the speaker is getting cold, and to infer from this that the speaker would like him to do something about it.

In summary, the notion of logical form we wish to capture is essentially that of a representation of the "literal meaning in context" of an utterance. To facilitate further processing, it is virtually essential that the meaning of logical-form expressions be compositional and, at the same time, it is highly desirable that they be context-independent. The latter condition requires that a system of logical form furnish distinct representations for the different readings of ambiguous natural-language expressions. It also requires that some limited amount of pragmatic processing be involved in producing those representations. Finally, we note that not all pragmatic factors in the use of language can be reflected in the logical form of an utterance, because some of those factors are dependent on information that the logical form itself provides.

III   FORM AND CONTENT IN KNOWLEDGE REPRESENTATION

Developing a theory of the logical form of English sentences is as much an exercise in knowledge representation as in linguistics, but it differs from most work in artificial intelligence on knowledge representation in one key respect. Knowledge representation schemes are usually intended by their designers to be as general as possible and to avoid commitment to any particular concepts. The essential problem for a theory of logical form, however, is to represent specific concepts that natural languages have special features for expressing information about. Concepts that fall in this category include:

* Events, actions, and processes
* Time and space
* Collective entities and substances
* Propositional attitudes and modalities.

A theory of logical form of natural-language expressions, therefore, is primarily concerned with the content rather than the form of representation. Logic, semantic networks, frames, scripts, and production systems are all different forms of representation. But to say merely that one has adopted one of these forms is to say nothing about content, i.e., what is represented. The representation used in this paper, of course, takes a particular form (higher-order logic with intensional operators) but relatively little will be said about developing or refining that form. Rather, we will be concerned with the question of what particular predicates, functions, operators, and the like are needed to represent the content of English expressions involving concepts in the areas listed above. This project might thus be better described as knowledge encoding to distinguish it from knowledge representation, as it is usually understood in artificial intelligence.

IV   A FRAMEWORK FOR LOGICAL FORM

As mentioned previously, the basic framework we will use to represent the logical form of English sentences is higher-order logic (i.e., higher-order predicate calculus), augmented by intensional operators. At a purely notational level, all well-formed expressions will be in "Cambridge Polish" form, as in the programming language LISP; thus, the logical form of "John likes Mary" will be simply (LIKE JOHN MARY). Despite our firm belief in the principle of semantic compositionality, we will not attempt to give a formal semantics for the logical forms we propose. Hence, our adherence to that principle is a good-faith intention rather than a demonstrated fact. It should be noted, though, that virtually all the kinds of logical constructs used here are drawn from more formal work of logicians and philosophers in which rigorous semantic treatments are provided.

The only place in which our logical language differs significantly from more familiar systems is in the treatment of quantifiers. Normally the English determiners "every" and "some" are translated as logical quantifiers that bind a single variable in an arbitrary formula. This requires using an appropriate logical connective to combine the contents of the noun phrase governed by the determiner with the contents of the rest of the sentence. Thus "Every P is Q" becomes

(EVERY X (IMPLIES (P X) (Q X))),

and "Some P is Q" becomes

(SOME X (AND (P X) (Q X)))

It seems somewhat inelegant to have to use different connectives to join (P X) and (Q X) in the two cases, but semantically it works.

In an extremely interesting paper, Barwise and Cooper [1981] point out (and, in fact, prove) that there are many determiners in English for which this approach does not work. The transformations employed in standard logic to handle "every" and "some" depend on the fact that any statement about every P or some P is logically equivalent to a statement about everything or something; for example, "Some P is Q" is equivalent to "Something is P and Q." What Barwise and Cooper show is that there is no such transformation for determiners like "most" or "more than half." That is, statements about most P's or more than half the P's cannot be rephrased as statements about most things or more than half of all things.

Barwise and Cooper incorporate this insight into a rather elaborate system modeled after Montague's, so that, among other things, they can assign a denotation to arbitrary noun phrases out of context. Adopting a more conservative modification of standard logical notation, we will simply insist that all quantified formulas have an additional element expressing the restriction of the quantifier. "Most P's are Q" will thus be represented by

(MOST X (P X) (Q X)).

Following this convention gives us a uniform treatment for determined noun phrases:

"Most men are mortal"   (MOST X (MAN X) (MORTAL X))
"Some man is mortal"   (SOME X (MAN X) (MORTAL X))
"Every man is mortal"   (EVERY X (MAN X) (MORTAL X))
"The man is mortal"   (THE X (MAN X) (MORTAL X))
"Three men are mortal"   (3 X (MAN X) (MORTAL X))

Note that we treat "the" as a quantifier, on a par with "some" and "every." "The" is often treated formally as an operator that produces a complex singular term, but this has the disadvantage of not indicating clearly the scope of the expression.

A final point about our basic framework is that most common nouns will be interpreted as relations rather than functions in logical form. That is, even if we know that a person has only one height, we will represent "John's height is 6 feet" as

(HEIGHT JOHN (FEET 6))

rather than

(EQ (HEIGHT JOHN) (FEET 6))[5]

There are two reasons for this: one is the desire for syntactic uniformity; the other is to have a variable available for use in complex predicates. Consider "John's height is more than 5 feet and less than 6 feet." If height is a relation, we can say

(THE L (HEIGHT JOHN L)
    (AND (GT L (FEET 5))
         (LT L (FEET 6)))),

whereas, if length is a function, we would say

(AND (GT (HEIGHT JOHN) (FT 5))
     (LT (HEIGHT JOHN) (FT 6)))

The second variant may look simpler, but it has the disadvantage that (HEIGHT JOHN) appears twice. This is not only syntactically unmotivated, since "John's height" occurs only once in the original English but, what is worse, it may lead to redundant processing later on. Let us suppose that we want to test whether the assertion is true and that determining John's height requires some expensive operation, such as accessing an external database. To avoid doing the computation twice, the evaluation procedure must be much more complex if the second representation is used rather than the first.

V   EVENTS, ACTIONS, AND PROCESSES

The source of many problems in this area is the question of whether the treatment of sentences that describe events ("John is going to New York") should differ in any fundamental way from that of sentences that describe static situations ("John is in New York"). In a very influential paper, Davidson [1967] argues that, while simple predicate/argument notation, such as (LOC JOHN NY), may be adequate for the latter, event sentences require explicit reference to the event as an object. Davidson's proposal would have us represent "John is going to New York" as if it were something like "There is an event which is a going of John to New York":

(SOME E (EVENT E) (GO E JOHN NY))

Davidson's arguments for this analysis are that (1) many adverbial modifiers such as "quickly" are best regarded as predicates of the event, and that (2) it is possible to refer to the event explicitly in subsequent discourse. ("John is going to New York. The trip will take four hours.")

The problem with Davidson's proposal is that for sentences in which these phenomena do not arise, the representation becomes unnecessarily complex. We therefore suggest introducing an event abstraction operator, EVABS, that will allow us to introduce event variables when we need them:

(P X1 ... Xn) <->
    (SOME E (EVENT E) ((EVABS P) E X1 ... Xn))

In simple cases we can use the more straightforward form. The logical form of "John is kissing Mary" would simply be (KISS JOHN MARY). The logical form of "John is gently kissing Mary," however, would be

(SOME E (EVENT E)
    (AND ((EVABS KISS) E JOHN MARY)
         (GENTLE E))))

If we let EVABS apply to complex predicates (represented by LAMBDA expressions), we can handle other problems as well. Consider the sentence "Being a parent caused John's nervous breakdown." "Parent" is a relational noun; thus, if John is a parent, he must be the parent of someone, but if John has several children we don't want to be forced into asserting that being the parent of any particular one of them caused the breakdown. If we had PARENT1 as the monadic property of being a parent, however, we could say

```
(SOME E (EVENT E)
       (AND ((EVABS PARENT1) E JOHN)
            (CAUSE E "John's nervous breakdown")))
```

We don't need to introduce PARENT1 explicitly, however, if we simply substitute for it the expression,

```
(LAMBDA X (SOME Y (PERSON Y) (PARENT X Y))),
```

which would give us

```
(SOME E (EVENT E)
       (AND ((EVABS (LAMBDA X (SOME Y (PERSON Y)
                                       (PARENT X Y))))
             E
             JOHN)
            (CAUSE E "John's nervous breakdown")))
```

Another important question is whether actions—that is, events with agents—should be treated differently from events without agents and, if so, should the agent be specially indicated? The point is that, if John kissed Mary, that is something he did, but not necessarily something she did. It is not clear whether this distinction should be represented at the level of logical form or is rather an inference based on world knowledge.

Finally, most AI work on actions and events assumes that they can be decomposed into discrete steps, and that their effects can be defined in terms of a final state. Neither of these assumptions is appropriate for continuous processes; e.g., "The flow of water continued to flood the basement." What the logical form for such statements should look like seems to be a completely open question.[6]

VI   TIME AND SPACE

We believe that information about time is best represented primarily by sentential operators, so that the logical form of a sentence like "John is in New York at 2:00" would be something like (AT 2:00 (LOC JOHN NY)). There are two main reasons for following this approach. First, current time can be indicated simply by the lack of any operator; e.g., "John owns Fido" becomes simply (OWNS JOHN FIDO). This is especially advantageous in basically static domains in which time plays a minimal role, so we do not have to put something into the logical form of a sentence that will be systematically ignored by lower-level processing. The other advantage of this approach is that temporal operators can apply to a whole sentence, rather than just to a verb. For instance, in the preferred reading of "The President has lived in the White House since 1800," the referent of "the President" changes with the time contexts involved in evaluating the truth of the sentence. The other reading can be obtained by allowing the quantifier "the" in "the President" to assume a wider scope than that of the temporal operator.

Although we do not strongly distinguish action verbs from stative verbs semantically, there are syntactic distinctions that must be taken into account before tense can be mapped into time correctly. Stative verbs express present time by means of the simple present tense, while action verbs use the present progressive. Compare:

John kisses Mary (normally habitual)
John is kissing Mary (normally present time)
John owns Fido (normally present time)
John is owning Fido (unacceptable)

This is why (KISS JOHN MARY) represents "John is kissing Mary," rather than "John kisses Mary," which would normally receive a dispositional or habitual interpretation.

What temporal operators will be needed? We will use the operator AT to assert that a certain condition holds at a certain time. PAST and FUTURE will be predicates on <u>points</u> in time. Simple past tense statements with stative verbs, such as "John was in New York," could mean either that John was in New York at some unspecified time in the past or at a contextually specific time in the past:

```
(SOME T (PAST T) (AT T (LOC JOHN NY)))
(THE T (PAST T) (AT T (LOC JOHN NY)))
```

(For the second expression to be an "official" logical-form representation, the incomplete definite reference would have to be resolved.) Simple future-tense statements with stative verbs are parallel, with FUTURE replacing PAST. Explicit temporal modifiers are generally treated as additional restrictions on the time referred to. "John was in New York on Tuesday" might be (on at least one interpretation):

```
(SOME T (AND (PAST T) (DURING T TUESDAY))
        (AT T (LOC JOHN NY))))
```

For action verbs we get representations of this sort for past and future progressive tenses; e.g., "John was kissing Mary" becomes

```
(THE T (PAST T) (AT T (KISS JOHN MARY)))
```

When we use event abstraction to introduce individual events, the interactions with time become somewhat tricky. Since (KISS JOHN MARY) means "John is (presently) kissing Mary," so must

```
(SOME E (EVENT E) ((EVABS KISS) E JOHN MARY))
```

Since <u>logically</u> this formal expression means something like "There is (presently) an event which is a kissing of Mary by John," we will interpret the predicate EVENT as being true at a particular time of the events in progress at that time. To tie all this together, "John was kissing Mary gently" would be represented by

```
(THE T (PAST T)
     (AT T
         (SOME E (EVENT E)
                 (AND ((EVABS KISS) E JOHN MARY)
                      (GENTLE E)))))
```

The major unsolved problem relating to time seems to be reconciling statements that refer to points in time with those that refer to intervals—for instance, "The company earned $5 million in March." This certainly does not mean that at every point in time during March the company earned $5 million. One could invent a representation for sentences about intervals with no particular relation to the representation for sentences about points, but then we would have the difficult task of constantly having to decide which representation is appropriate. This is further complicated by the fact that the same event, e.g. the American Revolution, could be viewed as defining either a point in time or an interval, depending on the time scale being considered.[7] ("At the time of the American Revolution, France was a monarchy," compared with "During the American Revolution, England suffered a decline in trade.") One would hope that there exist systematic relationships between statements about points in time and statements about intervals that can be exploited in developing a logical form for tensed sentences. There is a substantial literature in philosophical logic devoted to "tense logic" [Rescher and Urquhart, 1971] [McCawley, 1981], but almost all of this work seems to be concerned with evaluating the truth of sentences at points, which, as we have seen, cannot be immediately extended to handle sentences about intervals.

We include space under the same heading as time because a major question about space is the extent to which its treatment should parallel that of time. From an objective standpoint, it is often convenient to view physical space and time together as a four-dimensional Euclidean space. Furthermore, there are natural-language constructions that seem best interpreted as asserting that a certain condition holds in a particular place ("In California it is legal to make a right turn on a red light"), just as time expressions often assert that a condition holds at a particular time. The question is how far this analogy between space and time can be pushed.

VII COLLECTIVE ENTITIES AND SUBSTANCES

Most representation schemes are designed to express information about such discrete, well-individuated objects as people, chairs, or books. Not all objects are so distinct, however; collections and substances seem to pose special difficulties. Collections are often indicated by conjoined noun phrases. If we say "Newell and Simon wrote Human Problem Solving," we do not mean that they each did it individually (cf. "Newell and Simon have PhDs."), rather we mean that they did it as a unit. Furthermore, if we want the treatment of this sentence to be parallel to that of "Quine wrote Word and Object," we need an explicit representation of the unit "Newell and Simon" so that it can play the same role the individual "Quine" plays in the latter sentence. These considerations create difficulties in sentence interpretation because of the possibility of ambiguities between collective and distributed readings. Thus, "Newell and Simon have written many papers," might mean that individually each has written many papers or that they have jointly coauthored many papers. The problems associated with conjoined noun phrases also arise with plural noun phrases and singular noun phrases that are inherently collective. "John, Bill, Joe, and Sam," "the Jones boys," and "the Jones String Quartet" may all refer to the same collective entity, so that an adequate logical-form representation needs to treat them as much alike as possible. These issues are treated in detail by Webber [1978].

The most obvious approach to handling collective entities is to treat them as sets, but standard set theory does not provide quite the right logic. The interpretation of "and" in "the Jones boys and the Smith girls" would be the union of two sets, but in "John and Mary" the interpretation would be constructing a set out of two individuals. Also, the distinction made in set theory between an individual, on one hand, and the singleton set containing the individual, on the other, seems totally artificial in this context. We need a "flatter" kind of structure than is provided by standard set theory. The usual formal treatment of strings is a useful model; there is no distinction made between a character and a string just one character long;

moreover, string concatenation applies equally to strings of one character or more than one. Collective entities have these features in common with strings, but share with sets the properties of being unordered and not having repeated elements.

The set theory we propose has a set formation operator COMB that takes any number of arguments. The arguments of COMB may be individuals or sets of individuals, and the value of COMB is the set that contains all the individual arguments and all the elements of the set arguments; thus,

(COMB A {B C} D {E F G}) = {A B C D E F G}

(The notation using braces is NOT part of the logical-form language; this example is just an attempt to illustrate what COMB means in terms of more conventional concepts.) If A is an individual, (COMB A) is simply A.

We need one other special operator to handle definitely determined plural noun phrases, e.g., "the American ships." The problem is that in context this may refer to some particular set of American ships; hence, we need to recognize it as a definite reference that has to be resolved. Following Weber [1978], We will use the notation (SET X P) to express a predicate on sets that is satisfied by any set, all of whose members satisfy (LAMBDA X P). Then "the P's" would be the contextually determined set, all of whose members are P's:

(THE S ((SET X (P X)) S) ...)

It might seem that, to properly capture the meaning of plurals, we would have to limit the extension of (SET X P) to sets of two or more elements. This is not always appropriate, however. Although "There are ships in the Med," might seem to mean "The set of ships in the Med has at least two members," the question "Are there any ships in the Med?" does not mean "Does the set of ships in the Med have at least two members?" The answer to the former question is yes, even if there is only one ship in the Mediterranean. This suggests that any presupposition the plural carries to the effect that more than one object is involved may be a matter of Gricean implicature ("If he knew there was only one, why didn't he say so?") rather than semantics. Similarly, the plural marking on verbs seems to be just a syntactic reflex, rather than any sort of plural operator. On the latter approach we would have to take "Who killed Cock Robin?" as ambiguous between a singular and plural reading, since singular and plural verb forms would be semantically distinct.

To illustrate the use of our notation, we will represent "Every one of the men who defeated Hannibal was brave." Since no one defeated Hannibal individually, this must be attributed to a collection of men:

(SOME T (PAST T)
    (AT T
        (EVERY X (THE S (AND ((SET Y (MAN Y)) S)
                            (DEFEAT S HANNIBAL))
                    (MEMB X S))
            (BRAVE X))))

Note that we can replace the plural noun phrase "the men who defeated Hannibal" by the singular collective noun phrase, "the Roman army," as in "Everyone in the Roman army was brave":

(SOME T (PAST T)
    (AT T
        (EVERY X (THE S (AND (ARMY S) (ROMAN S))
                    (MEMB X S))
            (BRAVE X))))

The only change in the logical form of the sentence is that

(AND ((SET Y (MAN Y)) S) (DEFEAT S HANNIBAL))

is replaced by (AND (ARMY S) (ROMAN S)).

Collective entities are not the only objects that are difficult to represent. Artificial intelligence representation schemes have notoriously shied away from mass quantities and substances. ([Hayes, 1978] is a notable exception.) In a sentence like "All Eastern coal contains some sulfur," it seems that "coal" and "sulfur" refer to properties of samples or pieces of "stuff." We might paraphrase this sentence as "All pieces of stuff that are Eastern coal contain some stuff that is sulfur." If we take this approach, then, in interpreting a sentence like "The Universe Ireland is carrying 100,000 barrels of Saudi light crude," we need to indicate that the "piece of stuff" being described is the maximal "piece" of Saudi light crude the ship is carrying. In other cases, substances seem to be more like abstract individuals, e.g., "Copper is the twenty-ninth element in the periodic table." Nouns that refer to substances can also function as do plural noun phrases in their generic use: "Copper is [antelopes are] abundant in the American southwest."

VIII   PROPOSITIONAL ATTITUDES AND MODALITIES

Propositional attitudes and modalities are discussed together, because they are both normally treated as intensional sentential operators. For instance, to represent "John believes that the Fox is in Naples," we would have an operator BELIEVE that takes "John" as its first argument and the representation of "The Fox is in Naples" as its second argument. Similarly, to represent "The Fox might be in Naples," we could apply an operator POSSIBLE to the representation of "The Fox is in Naples." This approach works particularly well on a number of problems involving quantifiers. For example, "John believes someone is in the basement" possesses an ambiguity that is revealed by the two paraphrases, "John believes there is someone in the basement" and "There is someone John believes to be in the basement." As these paraphrases suggest, this distinction is represented by different relative scopes of the belief operator and the existential quantifier introduced by the indefinite pronoun "someone":

(BELIEVE JOHN (SOME X (PERSON X) (LOC X BASEMENT)))

(SOME X (PERSON X) (BELIEVE JOHN (LOC X BASEMENT)))

This approach works very well up to a point, but there are cases it does not handle. For example, sometimes verbs like "believe" do not take a sentence as an argument, but rather a description of a sentence, e.g., "John believes Goldbach's conjecture." If we were to make "believe" a predicate rather than a sentence operator to handle this type of example, the elegant semantics that has been worked out for "quantifying in" would completely break down. Another alternative is to introduce a predicate TRUE to map a description of a sentence into a sentence that necessarily has the same truth value. Then "John believes Goldbach's conjecture" is treated as if it were "John believes of Goldbach's conjecture that it is true." This is distinguished in the usual way from "John believes that Goldbach's conjecture (whatever it may be) is true" by reversing the scope of the description "Goldbach's conjecture" and the operator "believe."

IX   QUESTIONS AND IMPERATIVES

The only types of utterances we have tried to represent in logical form to this point are assertions, but of course there are other speech acts as well. The only two we will consider are questions and imperatives (commands). Since performatives (promises, bets, declarations, etc.) have the same syntactic form as assertions, it appears that they raise no new problems. We will also concern ourselves only with the literal speech act expressed by an utterance. Dealing with indirect speech acts does not seem to change the range of representations needed; sometimes, for example, we may simply need to represent what is literally an assertion as something intended as a command.

For questions, we would like to have a uniform treatment of both the yes/no and WH forms. The simplest approach is to regard the semantic content of a WH question to be a predicate whose extension is being sought. This does not address the issue of what is a satisfactory answer to a question, but we regard that as part of the theory of speech acts proper, rather than a question of logical form. We will introduce the operator WHAT for constructing complex set descriptions, which, for the sake of uniformity, we will give the same four-part structure we use for quantifiers. The representation of "What American ships are in the Med?" would roughly be as follows:

(WHAT X (AND (SHIP X) (AMERICAN X))
        (LOC X MED))

WHAT is conveniently mnemonic, since we can represent "who" as (WHAT X (PERSON X) ....), "when" as (WHAT X (TIME X) ....), and so forth. "How many" questions will be treated as questioning the quantifier. "How many men are mortal?" would be represented as

(WHAT N (NUMBER N)
        (N X (MAN X) (MORTAL X)))

Yes/no questions can be handled as a degenerate case of WH questions by treating a proposition as a 0-ary predicate. Since the extension of an n-ary predicate is a set of n-tuples, the extension of a proposition would be a set of 0-tuples. There is only one 0-tuple, the empty tuple, so there are only two possible sets of 0-tuples. These are the singleton set containing the empty tuple, and the empty set, which we can identify with the truth values TRUE and FALSE. The logical form of a yes/no question with the proposition P as its semantic content would be (WHAT () TRUE P), or more simply P.

With regard to imperatives, it is less clear what type of semantic object their content should be. We might propose that it is a proposition, but we then have to account for the fact that not all propositions are acceptable as commands. For instance, John cannot be commanded "Bill go to New York." The response that a person can only be "commanded something" he has control over is not adequate, because any proposition can be converted into a command by the verb "make"--e.g., "Make Bill go to New York."

The awkwardness of the phrasing "command someone something" suggests another approach. One commands someone to do something, and the things that are done are actions. If actions are treated as objects, we can define a relation DO that maps an agent and an action into a proposition (See [Moore, 1980]). "John is going to New York" would then be represented by (DO JOHN (GO NY)). Actions are now available to be the semantic content of imperatives. The problem with this approach is that we now have to pack into actions all the semantic complexities that can arise in commands--

for instance, adverbial modifiers, which we have treated above as predicates on events ("Go quickly"), quantifiers ("Go to every room in the house"), and negation ("Don't go").

A third approach, which we feel is actually the most promising, is to treat the semantic content of an imperative as being a unary predicate. The force of an imperative is that the person to whom the command is directed is supposed to satisfy the predicate. According to this theory the role of "make" is clear--it converts any proposition into a unary predicate. If the assertion "John is making Bill go to New York" is represented as (MAKE JOHN (GO BILL NY)), we can form a unary predicate by LAMBDA abstraction:

(LAMBDA X (MAKE X (GO BILL NY)),

which would be the semantic content of the command "Make Bill go to New York."

This approach does away with the problem concerning adverbial modifiers or quantifiers in commands; they can simply be part of the proposition from which the predicate is formed. A final piece of evidence favoring this approach over a theory based on the notion of action is that some imperatives have nothing at all to do with actions directly. The semantic content of commands like "Be good" or "Don't be a fool" really does seem to consist exclusively of a predicate.

X   CONCLUSION

In a paper that covers such a wide range of disparate topics, it is hard to reach any sweeping general conclusions, but perhaps a few remarks about the nature and current status of the research program are in order. First, it should be clear from the issues discussed that at least as many problems remain in the quest for logical form as have already been resolved. Considering the amount of effort that has been expended upon natural-language semantics, this is somewhat surprising. The reason may be that relatively few researchers have worked in this area for its own sake. Davidson's ideas on action sentences, for instance, raised some very interesting points about logical form-- but the major debate it provoked in the philosophical literature was about the metaphysics of the concept of action, not about the semantics of action sentences. Even when semantics is a major concern, as in the work of Montague, the emphasis is often on showing that relatively well-understood subareas of semantics (e.g., quantification) can be done in a particular way, rather than on attempting to take on really new problems.

An additional difficulty is that so much work has been done in a fragmentary fashion. It is clear that the concept of action is closely related to the concept of time, but it is hard to find any work on either concept that takes the other one seriously. To build a language-processing system or a theory of language processing, however, requires an integrated theory of logical form, not just a set of incompatible fragmentary theories. Our conclusion, then, is that if real progress is to be made on understanding the logical form of natural-language utterances, it must be studied in a unified way and treated as an important research problem in its own right.

ACKNOWLEDGEMENTS

The ideas in this paper are the collective result of the efforts of a large number of people at SRI, particularly Barbara Grosz, Stan Rosenschein, and Gary Hendrix. Jane Robinson, Jerry Hobbs, Paul Martin, and Norman Haas are chiefly responsible for the implementation of the DIALOGIC system, building on earlier systems to which Ann Robinson and Bill Paxton made major contributions. This research was supported by the Defense Advanced Research Projects Agency under Contracts N00039-80-C-0645 and N00039-80-C-0575 with the Naval Electronic Systems Command.

NOTES

[1] Although our immediate aim is to construct a theory of natural-language processing rather than truth-conditional semantics, it is worth noting that a system of logical form with a well-defined semantics constitutes a bridge between the two projects. If we have a processing theory that associates English sentences with their logical forms, and if those logical forms have a truth-conditional semantics, then we will have specified the semantics of the English sentences as well.

[2] In other papers (e.g., [Montague, 1974b]), Montague himself uses an intensional logic in exactly the role we propose for logical form--and for much the same reason: "We could ... introduce the semantics of our fragment [of English] directly; but it is probably more perspicuous to proceed indirectly by (1) setting up a certain simple artificial language, that of tensed intensional logic, (2) giving the semantics of that language, and (3) interpreting English indirectly by showing in a rigorous way how to translate it into the artificial language. This is the procedure we shall adopt;..." [Montague, 1974b, p.256].

[3] The DIALOGIC system does build such a representation, or at least components of one, as an intermediate step in deriving the logical form of a sentence.

[4] This suggests that our logical forms are representations of what David Kaplan, in his famous unpublished paper on demonstratives [Kaplan, 1977], calls the <u>content</u> of a sentence, as opposed to its <u>character</u>. Kaplan introduces the content/character distinction to sort out puzzles connected with the use of demonstratives and indexicals. He notes that there are at least two different notions of "the meaning of a sentence" that conflict when indexical expressions are used. If A says to B, "I am hungry," and B says to A, "I am hungry," they have used the same words, but in one sense they mean different things. After all, it may be the case that what A said is true and what B said is false. If A says to B, "I am hungry," and B says to A, "<u>You</u> are hungry," they have used different words, but mean the same thing, that A is hungry. This notion of "meaning different things" or "meaning the same thing" is one kind of meaning, which Kaplan calls "content." There is another sense, though, in which A and B both use the words "I am hungry" with the same meaning, namely, that the same rules apply to determine, in context, what content is expressed. For this notion of meaning, Kaplan uses the term "character." Kaplan's notion, therefore, is that the rules of the language determine the character of a sentence--which, in turn, together with the context of utterance, determines the content. If we broaden the scope of Kaplan's theory to include the local pragmatic indeterminacies we have discussed, it seems that the way they depend on context would also be part of the character of a sentence and that our logical form is thus a representation of the content of the sentence-in-context.

[5] It should be obvious from the example that nouns referring to units of measure--e.g., "feet"--are an exception to the general rule. We treat types of quantities, such as distance, weight, volume, time

duration, etc., as basic conceptual categories. Following Hayes [1979], units such as feet, pounds, gallons, and hours are considered to be functions from numbers to quantities. Thus (FEET 3) and (YARDS 1) denote the same distance. Relations like length, weight, size, and duration hold between an entity and a quantity of an appropriate type. Where a word like "weight" serves in English to refer to both the relation and the quantity, we must be careful to distinguish between them. To see the distinction, note that length, beam, and draft are all relations between a ship and a quantity of the same type, distance. We treat comparatives like "greater than" as multidomain relations, working with any two quantities of the same type (or with pure numbers, for that matter).

6 Hendrix [1973], Rieger [1975], Hayes [1978], and McDermott [1981] have all dealt with continuous processes to some extent, but none of them has considered specifically how language expresses information about processes.

7 This point was impressed upon me by Pat Hayes.

REFERENCES

Barwise, J. and R. Cooper [1981] "Generalized Quantifiers and Natural Language," _Linguistics and Philosophy_, Vol. 4, No. 2, pp. 159–219 (1981).

Clark, H. and C. Marshall [1981] "Definite Reference and Mutual Knowledge," in _Elements of Discourse Understanding: Proceedings of a Workshop on Computational Aspects of Linguistic Structure and Discourse Setting_, A. K. Joshi, I. A. Sag, and B. L. Webber, eds. (Cambridge University Press, Cambridge, England, 1981).

Cohen, P. and C. R. Perrault [1981] "Inaccurate Reference," in _Elements of Discourse Understanding: Proceedings of a Workshop on Computational Aspects of Linguistic Structure and Discourse Setting_, A. K. Joshi, I. A. Sag, and B. L. Webber, eds. (Cambridge University Press, Cambridge, England, 1981).

Davidson, D. [1967] "The Logical Form of Action Sentences," in _The Logic of Decision and Action_, N. Rescher, ed., pp. 81–95 (University of Pittsburgh Press, Pittsburgh, Pennsylvania, 1967).

Hayes, P. J. [1978] "Naive Physics: Ontology of Liquids," _Working Papers_, Institute of Semantic and Cognitive Studies, Geneva, Switzerland, (August 1978).

Hayes, P. J. [1979] "The Naive Physics Manifesto," in _Expert Systems in the Micro-electronic Age_, D. Michie, ed., pp. 242–270 (Edinburgh University Press, Edinburgh, Scotland, 1979).

Hendrix, G. [1973] "Modeling Simultaneous Actions and Continuous Processes," _Artificial Intelligence_, Vol. 4, Nos. 3, 4, pp. 145–180 (Winter 1973).

Herskovits, A. [1980] "On the Spatial Uses of Prepositions," in _Proceedings of the 18th Annual Meeting of the Association for Computational Linguistics_, University of Pennsylvania, Philadelphia, Pennsylvania, pp. 1–5 (19–22 June 1980).

Kaplan, D. [1977] "Demonstratives, An Essay on the Semantics, Logic, Metaphysics and Epistemology of Demonstratives and Other Indexicals," unpublished manuscript (March 1977).

McCawley, J. D. [1981] _Everything that Linguists Have Always Wanted to Know About Logic but Were Ashamed to Ask_ (University of Chicago Press, Chicago, Illinois, 1981).

McDermott, D. V. [1981] "A Temporal Logic for Reasoning about Processes and Plans," Research Report 196, Yale University, Department of Computer Science, New Haven, Connecticut (March 1981).

Montague, R. [1974a] "English as a Formal Language," in _Formal Philosophy, Selected Papers of Richard Montague_, R. H. Thomason, ed., pp. 188–221 (Yale University Press, New Haven, Connecticut, and London, England, 1974).

Montague, R. [1974b] "The Proper Treatment of Quantification in Ordinary English," in _Formal Philosophy, Selected Papers of Richard Montague_, R. H. Thomason, ed., pp. 188–221 (Yale University Press, New Haven, Connecticut, and London, England, 1974).

Moore, R. C. [1980] "Reasoning About Knowledge and Action," Artificial Intelligence Center Technical Note 191, SRI International, Menlo Park, California (October 1980).

Rescher, N. and A. Urquhart, [1971] _Temporal Logic_ (Springer-Verlag, Vienna, Austria, 1971).

Rieger, C. [1975] "The Commonsense Algorithm as a Basis for Computer Models of Human Memory, Inference, Belief and Contextual Language Comprehension," in _Proceedings, Theoretical Issues in Natural Language Processing_, Cambridge, Massachusetts, pp. 180–195 (10–13 June 1975).

Simon, H. A. [1969] _The Sciences of the Artificial_ (The MIT Press, Cambridge, Massachusetts, 1969).

Webber, B. L. [1978] "A Formal Approach to Discourse Anaphora," Report No. 3761, Bolt Beranek and Newman, Inc., Cambridge, Massachusetts (May 1978).

From English to Logic:
Context-Free Computation of
'Conventional' Logical Translations[1]

Lenhart K. Schubert

Department of Computing Science
University of Alberta

Francis Jeffry Pelletier

Department of Philosophy
University of Alberta
Edmonton, Canada T6G 2H1

We describe an approach to parsing and logical translation that was inspired by Gazdar's work on context-free grammar for English. Each grammar rule consists of a syntactic part that specifies an acceptable fragment of a parse tree, and a semantic part that specifies how the logical formulas corresponding to the constituents of the fragment are to be combined to yield the formula for the fragment. However, we have sought to reformulate Gazdar's semantic rules so as to obtain more or less 'conventional' logical translations of English sentences, avoiding the interpretation of NPs as property sets and the use of intensional functors other than certain propositional operators. The reformulated semantic rules often turn out to be slightly simpler than Gazdar's. Moreover, by using a semantically ambiguous logical syntax for the preliminary translations, we can account for quantifier and coordinator scope ambiguities in syntactically unambiguous sentences without recourse to multiple semantic rules, and are able to separate the disambiguation process from the operation of the parser-translator. We have implemented simple recursive descent and left-corner parsers to demonstrate the practicality of our approach.

1. Introduction

Our ultimate objective is the design of a natural language understanding system whose syntactic, semantic and pragmatic capabilities are encoded in an easily comprehensible and extensible form. In addition, these encodings should be capable of supporting efficient algorithms for parsing and comprehension.

In our view, the achievement of the former objective calls for a careful *structural* separation of the subsystems that specify possible constituent structure (syntax), possible mappings from constituent structure to underlying logical form (part of semantics), and possible mappings from logical form to deeper, unambiguous representations as a function of discourse context and world knowledge (part of pragmatics and

inference). This sort of view is now widely held, as evidenced by a recent panel discussion on parsing issues (Robinson 1981). In the words of one of the panelists,

"I take it to be uncontroversial that, other things being equal, a homogenized system is less preferable on both practical and scientific grounds than one that naturally decomposes. Practically, such a system is easier to build and maintain, since the parts can be designed, developed, and understood to a certain extent in isolation... Scientifically, a decomposable system is much more likely to provide insight into the process of natural language comprehension, whether by machines or people." (Kaplan 1981)

The panelists also emphasized that structural decomposition by no means precludes interleaving or paral-

[1] Submitted August 1981; revised July 1982.

lelism of the *processes* that draw on the various kinds of linguistic and non-linguistic knowledge.

Note that we are making a distinction between the logical form that corresponds directly to surface structure on the one hand, and an unambiguous deeper representation on the other. Indeed, at the level of logical form our theory of logical translation admits ambiguities in all of the formal building blocks (terms, functions, predicates, connectives, and quantifiers), as well as in the scopes of quantifiers and coordinators. For example, logical-form translations may contain terms such as Mary2 and <the1 (little2 girl3)>, ambiguous between various referents (e.g., MARY5 and MARY17), and quasi-predicates such as has3, good2, cold5, and recovers1, ambiguous between various proper predicates (e.g., has3: OWNS1, AFFLICTED-WITH, ...; good2: VIRTUOUS, GOOD-TASTING, ...; cold5: COLD1, EMOTIONLESS, ...; and recovers1: RE-COVERS1, REGAINS, ...). In other words, we do not regard the logical form of a sentence as fully determining its meaning – not even its 'literal' meaning; rather, its meaning is determined by its logical form along with the context of its utterance. Thus "She is becoming cold" might convey on one occasion that Lady Godiva is beginning to feel cold, on another that Queen Victoria is becoming emotionless, and on a third that Mount St. Helens is cooling off; but the logical form does no more than specify the feminine gender of the referent and its property of "becoming cold (in some sense) at the time of utterance". Our primary concern in this paper will be with the semantic rules that define immediate logical form, although we attempt to define this form in a way that minimizes the remaining gap to the deeper representation.

All the experience gained within AI and linguistics suggests that bridging this final gap will be very difficult. Some would take as their lesson that research efforts should concentrate on the last, pragmatic phase of comprehension, where 'the real problems' lie. We believe on the contrary that the only way to make the pragmatic problems tractable is to have a precise conception of the constituent structure and logical form of the natural language input, in terms of which the pragmatic operations can in turn be precisely formulated.

In AI research, the objectives of clarity and extensibility have often been sacrificed to immediate performance goals. One reason for this may have been the need to establish the credibility of a relatively young and controversial discipline. In any case, the state of linguistic theory until fairly recently left no real alternatives. The transformational grammars whose study dominated theoretical linguistics seemed a poor prospect even for the limited goal of describing natural language syntax, because of the subtlety of transformational rules and supplementary devices such as co-indexing procedures, filters and constraints on movement, and the complexity of their interactions. Moreover, the prospects for writing efficient transformational parsers seemed poor, given that transformational grammars can in principle generate all recursively enumerable languages. But most importantly, generative grammarians developed syntactic theories more or less independently of any semantic considerations, offering no guidance to AI researchers whose primary objective was to compute 'meaning representations' for natural language utterances. Katz and Fodor's markerese (Katz & Fodor 1963) was patently inadequate as a meaning representation language from an AI point of view, and Generative Semantics (Lakoff 1971) never did develop into a formal theory of the relation between surface form and meaning.

Theoretical linguistics took an important new turn with the work of Montague on the logic of English and later expansions and variants of his theory (e.g., see Thomason 1974a, Partee 1976a, and Cresswell 1973). According to Montague grammar the correspondence between syntactic structure and logical form is much simpler than had generally been supposed: to each lexeme there corresponds a logical term or functor and to each rule of syntactic composition there corresponds a structurally analogous semantic rule of logical composition; this is the so-called *rule-to-rule* hypothesis [Bach 1976].[2] Furthermore, the translations of all constituents of a particular syntactic category are assigned formal meanings of the same set-theoretic type; for example, all NPs, be they names or definite or indefinite descriptions, are taken to denote property sets. Crucially, the formal semantics of the logical translations produced by the semantic rules of Montague grammar accords by and large with intuitions about entailment, synonymy, ambiguity and other semantic phenomena.

---

[2] Interestingly enough, this linguistic hypothesis was anticipated by Knuth's work on the semantics of attribute grammars (Knuth 1968). Schwind (1978) has applied Knuth's insights to the development of a formal basis for question answering systems, anticipating some of the work by Gazdar and others on which our own efforts are founded.

There is also some similarity between the rule-to-rule hypothesis and the rule-based approach to the interpretation of syntactic structures that emerged within AI during the 1960's and early 70's. The idea of pairing semantic rules with phrase structure rules was at the heart of DEACON (Craig et al. 1966), a system based on F. B. Thompson's proposal to formalize English by limiting its subject matter to well-defined computer memory structures (Thompson 1966). However, DEACON's semantic rules performed direct semantic evaluation of sorts (via computations over a data base) rather than constructing logical translations. The systems of Winograd (1972) and Woods (1977) constructed input translations prior to evaluation, using semantic rules associated with particular syntactic structures. However, these rules neither corresponded one-to-one to syntactic rules nor limited interpretive operations to composition of logical expressions; for example, they incorporated tests for selectional restrictions and other forms of inference, with unrestricted use of the computational power of LISP.

The chief limitation of Montague's grammar was that it treated only very small, syntactically (though not semantically) simple fragments of English, and efforts were soon under way to extend the fragments, in some cases by addition of a transformational component (Partee 1976b, Cooper & Parsons 1976). At the same time, however, linguists dissatisfied with transformational theory were beginning to develop non-transformational alternatives to traditional generative grammars (e.g., Peters & Ritchie 1969, Bresnan 1978, Lapointe 1977, Brame 1978, Langendoen 1979). A particularly promising theory that emerged from this development, and explicitly incorporates Montague's approach to semantics, is the phrase structure theory advanced by Gazdar and others (Gazdar 1980, 1981, Gazdar, Pullum & Sag 1980, Gazdar & Sag 1980, Sag 1980, Gazdar, Klein, Pullum & Sag, to appear). The theory covers a wide range of the syntactic phenomena that have exercised transformationalists from Chomsky onward, including subcategorization, coordination, passivization, and unbounded dependencies such as those occurring in topicalization, relative clause constructions and comparatives. Yet the grammar itself makes no use of transformations; it consists entirely of phrase structure rules, with a node-admissibility rather than generative interpretation. For example, the rule [(S) (NP) (VP)] states that a fragment with root S, left branch NP and right branch VP is an admissible fragment of a syntactic tree.[3] Such phrase structure rules are easy to understand and permit the use of efficient context-free parsing methods. Moreover, the grammar realizes the rule-to-rule hypothesis, pairing each syntactic rule with a Montague-like semantic rule that supplies the intensional logic translation of the constituent admitted by the syntactic rule.

It has long been assumed by transformationalists that linguistic generalizations cannot be adequately captured in a grammar devoid of transformations. Gazdar refutes the assumption by using metagrammatical devices to achieve descriptive elegance. These devices include *rule-schemata* (e.g., coordination schemata that yield the rules of coordinate structure for all coordinators and all syntactic categories), and *metarules* (e.g., a passive metarule that takes any transitive-VP rule as 'input' and generates a corresponding passive-VP rule as 'output' by deleting the

object NP from the input rule and appending an optional *by*-PP). Although metarules resemble transformational rules, they map rules into rules rather than trees into trees, leaving the grammar itself context-free. Another key innovation is the use of categories with 'gaps', such as NP/PP, denoting a NP from which a PP has been deleted (*not* necessarily at the top level). A simple metarule and a few rule schemata are used to introduce rules involving such derived categories, elegantly capturing unbounded dependencies.

The character of the syntactic theory will become clearer in Section 4, where we supply a sampling of grammatical rules (with our variants of the semantic rules), along with the basic metarule for passives and the coordination schemata. First, however, we would like to motivate our attempt to reformulate Gazdar's semantic rules so as to yield 'conventional' logical translations (Section 2), and to explain the syntactic and semantic idiosyncrasies of our target logic (Section 3).

By 'conventional' logics we mean first-order (and perhaps second-order) predicate logics, augmented with a lambda operator, necessity operator, propositional attitude operators and perhaps other non-extensional propositional operators, and with a Kripke-style possible-worlds semantics (Hughes & Cresswell 1968).[4] The logic employed by Montague in his first formal fragment of English comes rather close to what we have in mind (Montague 1970a), while the intensional logics of the later fragments introduce the unconventional features we hope to avoid (1970b,c). It is the treatment in these later fragments that is usually referred to by the term "Montague grammar". (For a detailed discussion of the distinction between conventional logics in the above sense and intensional logics, see Guenthner 1978).

We should stress that it is semantics, not syntax, which is the crux of the distinction. We shall take certain liberties with conventional logical syntax, aligning it more nearly with the surface structure; but this will not lead to major departures from conventional semantics. For example, our syntax of terms allows syntactically unfamiliar formulas such as

[<all1 man2> mortal3].

---

[3] We use traditional category symbols in our exposition, occasionally followed by supplementary features, e.g., (V TRAN) for transitive verb. Gazdar actually assumes a two-bar $\bar{\bar{x}}$ system (e.g., see Bresnan 1976, Jackendoff 1977) that distinguishes between $\bar{\bar{X}}$, $\bar{X}$ and X categories (e.g., $\bar{\bar{V}}$, $\bar{V}$, and V, equivalent to the traditional S, VP and V respectively) and employs complex symbols whose first component specifies the 'number of bars' and whose second component supplies a feature bundle encoding syntactic category, subcategorization, and morphosyntactic and morphological information.

[4] We admit predicate modifiers and some second-order predicate constants into our logical vocabulary, and may ultimately want to employ a full-fledged second-order logic, in view of such sentences as "Every good general has at least some of Napoleon's qualities". On the other hand, we may pare down rather than expand the logical apparatus, opting for a logic that treats properties, propositions and other intensional entities as first-order individuals. This type of treatment, which avoids the unwanted identity of logically equivalent propositions, appears to be gaining currency (e.g., Fodor 1978, McCarthy 1979, Thomason 1980, Chierchia 1981). Some minor adjustments would be required in our rules of logical translation.

But the formula derives its interpretation from its stipulated logical equivalence to

(all1 x:[x man2])[x mortal3],

which may in turn become

$\forall x[[x \text{ HUMAN}] => [x \text{ MORTAL}]]$,

after disambiguation.[5]

2. Intensional and 'Conventional' Translations

We should emphasize at the outset that our objective is not to impugn Montague grammar, but merely to make the point that the choice between intensional and conventional translations is as yet unclear. Given that the conventional approach appears to have certain advantages, it is worth finding out where it leads; but we are not irrevocably committed to this approach. Fortunately, the translation component of a parser for a Gazdar-style grammar is easily replaced.

Montague grammarians assume that natural languages closely resemble formal logical systems; more specifically, they postulate a strict homomorphism from the syntactic categories and rules of a natural language to the semantic categories and rules required for its formal interpretation. This postulate has led them to an analysis of the logical content of natural language sentences which differs in important respects from the sorts of analyses traditionally employed by philosophers of language (as well as linguists and AI researchers, when they have explicitly concerned themselves with logical content).

The most obvious difference is that intensional logic translations of natural language sentences conform closely with the surface structure of those sentences, except for some re-ordering of phrases, the introduction of brackets, variables and certain logical operators, and (perhaps) the reduction of idioms. For example, since the constituent structure of "John loves Mary" is

[John [loves Mary]],

the intensional logic translation likewise isolates a component translating the VP "loves Mary", composing this VP-translation with the translation of "John" to give the sentence formula. By contrast, a conventional translation will have the structure

[John loves Mary],

in which "John" and "Mary" combine with the verb at the *same* level of constituent structure.

In itself, this difference is not important. It only becomes important when syntactic composition is assumed to correspond to *function application* in the semantic domain. This is done in Montague grammar

by resort to the Schoenfinkel-Church treatment of many-place functions as one-place functions (Schoenfinkel 1924, Church 1941). For example, the predicate "loves" in the above sentence is interpreted as a one-place function *that yields a one-place function* when applied to its argument (in this instance, when applied to the semantic value of "Mary", it yields the function that is the semantic value of "loves Mary"). The resultant function in turn yields a sentence value when applied to its argument (in this instance, when applied to the semantic value of "John", it yields the proposition expressed by "John loves Mary"). Thus, a dyadic predicator like "loves" is no longer interpreted as a set of pairs of individuals (at each possible world or index), but rather as a function into functions. Similarly a triadic predicator like "gives" is interpreted as a function into functions into functions.

Moreover, the arguments of these functions are not individuals, because NPs in general and names in particular are assumed to denote property sets (or truth functions over properties) rather than individuals. It is easy to see how the postulate of syntactic-semantic homomorphism leads to this further retreat from traditional semantics. Consider Gazdar's top-level rule of declarative sentence structure and meaning:

<10, [(S) (NP) (VP)], (VP' NP")>.

The first element of this triple supplies the rule number (which we have set to 10 for consistency with the sample grammar of Section 4), the second the syntactic rule and the third the semantic rule. The semantic rule states that the intensional logic translation of the S-constituent is compounded of the VP-translation (as functor) and the NP-translation (as operand), where the latter is first to be prefixed with the intension operator ^. In general, a primed syntactic symbol denotes the logical translation of the corresponding constituent, and a double-primed symbol the logical translation prefixed with the intension operator (thus, NP" stands for ^NP').

For example, if the NP dominates "John" and the VP dominates "loves Mary", then S' (the translation of S) is

((loves' ^Mary') ^John').

Similarly the translation of "Every boy loves Mary" comes out as

((loves' ^Mary') ^(every' boy')),

given suitable rules of NP and VP formation.[6] Note the uniform treatment of NPs in the logical formulas, i.e., (every' boy') is treated as being of the same semantic category as John', namely the (unique) seman-

---

[5] We consistently use infix form (with the predicate following its first argument) and square brackets for complete sentential formulas.

[6] The exact function of the intension operator need not concern us here. Roughly speaking, it is used to bring meanings within the domain of discourse; e.g., while an NP' denotes a property set at each index, the corresponding ^NP' denotes the entire NP intension (mapping from indices to property sets) at each index.

tic category corresponding to the syntactic category NP. What is the set-theoretic type of that category? Since (every' boy') cannot be interpreted as denoting an individual (at least not without making the rules of semantic valuation for formulas depend on the structure of the terms they contain), neither can John'. The solution is to regard NPs as denoting sets of properties, where a property determines a set of individuals at each index, and VPs as sets of such property sets (or in functional terms, as truth functions over truth functions over properties). Thus John' does not denote an individual, but rather a set of properties, namely those which John has; (every' boy') denotes the set of properties shared by all boys, (a' boy') the set of all properties possessed by at least one boy, and so on. It is not hard to see that the interpretation of VPs as sets of property sets then leads to the appropriate truth conditions for sentences.[7]

With respect to our objective of building a comprehensible, expandable natural language understanding system, the simplicity of Gazdar's semantic rules and their one-to-one correspondence to phrase structure rules is extremely attractive; however, the semantics of the intensional logic translations, as sketched above, seems to us quite unnatural.

Admittedly naturalness is partly a matter of familiarity, and we are not about to fault Montague grammar for having novel features (as some writers do, e.g., Harman 1975). But Montague's semantics is at variance with pretheoretical intuitions as well as philosophical tradition, as Montague himself acknowledged (1970c:268). Intuitively, names denote individuals (when they denote anything real), not sets of properties of individuals; extensional transitive verbs express relations between pairs of individuals, not between pairs of property sets, and so on; and intuitively, quantified terms such as "everyone" and "no-one" simply *don't* bear the same sort of relationship to objects in the world as names, even though the evidence for placing them in the same syntactic category is overwhelming. Such objections would carry no weight if the sole purpose of formal semantics were to provide an explication of intuitions about truth and logical consequence, for in that area intensional logic is remarkably successful. But formal semantics should also do justice to our intuitions about the relationship between word and object, where those intuitions are clear — and intensional logic seems at odds with some of the clearest of those intuitions.[8]

There is also a computational objection to intensional logic translations. As indicated in our introductory remarks, a natural language understanding system must be able to make *inferences* that relate the natural language input to the system's stored knowledge and discourse model. A great deal of work in AI has focused on inference during language understanding and on the organization of the base of stored knowledge on which the comprehension process draws. Almost all of this work has employed more or less conventional logics for expressing the stored knowledge. (Even such idiosyncratic formalisms as Schank's conceptual dependency theory (Schank 1973) are much more akin to, say, first order modal logic than to any form of intensional logic — see Schubert 1976). How are intensional logic formulas to be connected up with stored knowledge of this conventional type?

One possible answer is that the stored knowledge should not be of the conventional type at all, but should itself be expressed in intensional logic. However, the history of automatic deduction suggests that higher-order logics are significantly harder to mechanize than lower-order logics. Developing efficient inference rules and strategies for intensional logics, with their arbitrarily complex types and their intension, extension and lambda abstraction operators in addition to the usual modal operators, promises to be very difficult indeed.

Another possible answer is that the intensional logic translations of input sentences should be postprocessed to yield translations expressed in the lower-order, more conventional logic of the system's knowledge base. A difficulty with this answer is that discourse inferences need to be computed 'on the fly' to guide syntactic choices. For example, in the sentences "John saw the bird without binoculars" and "John saw the bird without tail feathers" the syntactic roles of the prepositional phrases (i.e., whether they modify "saw" or "the bird") can only be determined by inference. One could uncouple inference from parsing by computing all possible parses and choosing among the resultant translations, but this would be cumbersome and psychologically implausible at best.

As a final remark on the disadvantages of intensional translations, we note that Montague grammar relies heavily on *meaning postulates* to deliver simple consequences, such as

A boy smiles - There is a boy;

---

[7] This was the approach in Montague (1970b) and is adopted in Gazdar (1981a). In another, less commonly adopted approach NPs are still interpreted as sets of properties but VPs are interpreted simply as properties, the truth condition for a sentence being that the property denoted by the VP be in the set of properties denoted by the NP (Montague 1970c, Cresswell 1973). In other words, the NP is thought of as predicating something about the VP, rather than the other way around.

[8] Thomason reminds us that "...we should not forget the firmest and most irrefragable kind of data with which a semantic theory must cope. The theory must harmonize with the actual denotations taken by the expressions of natural languages,...", but confines his further remarks to sentence denotations, i.e., truth values (Thomason, 1974b:54).

(in this instance an extensionalizing postulate is required for "smiles" – see Montague 1970c:263). A conventional approach dispensing with postulates of this type would be preferable.

Having stated our misgivings about Montague grammar, we need to confront the evidence in its favour. Are there compelling reasons for regarding sentential constituents as more or less directly and uniformly interpretable? In support of the affirmative, one can point out the simplicity and elegance of this strategy from a logical point of view. More tellingly, one can cite its success record: it has made possible for the first time the formal characterization of nontrivial fragments of natural languages, with precisely defined syntactic-semantic mappings; and as one would hope, the formal semantics accounts for many cases of entailment, ambiguity, contradictoriness, and other semantic phenomena, including some of the subtlest arising from intensional locutions.

Concerning the simplicity of the strategy, we note that the connection between language and the world could be just as simple as Montague grammar would have it, without being quite so direct. Suppose, for a moment, that people communicated in first-order logic. Then, to express that Al, Bill and Clyde were born and raised in New York, we would have to say, in effect, "Al was born in New York. Al was raised in New York. Bill was born in New York. ... Clyde was raised in New York." The pressure to condense such redundant verbalizations would be great, and might well lead to 'overlay' verbalizations in which lists enumerating the non-repeated constituents were fitted into a common sentential matrix. In other words, it might lead to something like constituent coordination. But unlike simple constituents, coordinated constituents would not be meaningful in isolation; they would realize their meaning only upon expansion of the embedding overlay verbalization into a set of first-order formulas. Yet the connection between language and the world would remain simple, assuming that the *syntactic* relation between overlay verbalizations and their first-order translations were simple. It would be quite pointless to reconstrue the semantics of the enhanced language so as to align the denotations of names with the denotations of coordinated names, for example, as is done in Montague grammar. While formally simplifying the semantic mapping function, such a move would lead to complex and counterintuitive semantic types.

The success of Montague grammar in characterizing fragments of natural languages, with a proper account of logical relations such as entailment, is indeed strong evidence in its favour. The only way of challenging this success is to offer an equally simple, equally viable alternative. In part, this paper is intended as a move in that direction. While we do not explicitly discuss logical relations between the translations of sentences, the kinds of translations produced by the sample grammar in Section 4 should at least provide some basis for discussion. To the extent that the translations are of a conventional type (or easily converted to conventional form), the entailment relations should be more or less self-evident.

There is one linguistic phenomenon, however, which deserves preliminary comment since it might be thought to provide conclusive evidence in favour of Montague grammar, or at least in favour of the intensional treatment of NPs. This concerns intensional verbs such as those in sentences (1) and (2), and perhaps (3):

(1) John looks for a unicorn,
(2) John imagines a unicorn,
(3) John worships a unicorn.

These sentences admit non-referential readings with respect to the NP "a unicorn", i.e., readings that do not entail the existence of a unicorn which is the referent of the NP. In intensional logic the nonreferential reading of the first sentence would simply be

$$((\text{looks-for'} \ {}^\wedge(\text{a' unicorn'})) \ {}^\wedge\text{John'}).$$

The formal semantic analysis of this formula turns out just as required; that is, its value can be "true" or "false" (in a given possible world) irrespective of whether or not there are unicorns (in that world). The referential reading is a little more complicated, but presents no difficulties.

It is the non-referential reading which is troublesome for conventional logics. For the first sentence, there seems to be only one conventional translation, viz.,

$$\exists x[[\text{John looks-for } x] \ \& \ [x \text{ unicorn}]],$$

and of course, this is the referential reading. There is no direct way of representing the non-referential reading, since the scope of a quantifier in conventional logics is always a sentence, never a term.

The only possible escape from the difficulty lies in translating intensional verbs as complex(non-atomic) logical expressions involving opaque sentential operators.[9] The extant literature on this subject supports the view that a satisfactory decomposition cannot be supplied in all cases (Montague 1970c, Bennett 1974, Partee 1974, Dowty 1978, 1979, Dowty, Wall & Peters 1981). A review of this literature would be out of place here; but we would like to indicate that the case against decomposition (and hence against conventional translations) is not closed, by offering the fol-

---

[9] With regard to our system-building objectives, such resort to lexical decomposition is no liability: the need for some use of lexical decomposition to obtain "canonical" representations that facilitate inference is widely acknowledged by AI researchers, and carried to extremes by some (e.g., Wilks 1974, Schank 1975).

lowing paraphrases of the three sample sentences. (Paraphrase (1)' is well-known, except perhaps for the particular form of adverbial (Quine 1960, Bennett 1974, Partee 1974), while (2)'-(3)'' are original). These could be formalized within a conventional logical framework allowing for non-truth-functional sentential operators:

(1)'   John *tries* to find a unicorn (by looking around),

(2)'   John forms a mental description which *could* apply to a unicorn,

(3)'   John *acts, thinks and feels as if* he worshipped a unicorn.

(3)''   John worships an entity which *he believes* to be a unicorn.

In each case the operator that is the key to the translation is italicized. Note that the original ambiguity of (1) and (2) has been preserved, but can now be construed as a quantifier scope ambiguity in the conventional fashion. In (3)' and (3)'' the embedded "worships" is to be taken in a veridical sense that entails the existence of the worshippee. It is important to understand that the translations corresponding to (3)' and (3)'' would not be obtained *directly* by applying the rules of the grammar to the original sentence; rather, they would be obtained by *amending* the direct translation, which is patently false for a hearer who interprets "worships" veridically and does not believe in unicorns. Thus we are presupposing a mechanism similar to that required to interpret metaphor on a Gricean account (Grice 1975). The notion of "acting, thinking and feeling as if..." may seem rather ad hoc, but appears to be applicable in a wide variety of cases where (arguably) non-intensional verbs of human action and attitude are used non-referentially, as perhaps in "John is communing with a spirit", "John is afraid of the boogie-man in the attic", or "John is tracking down a sasquatch". Formulation (3)'' represents a more radical alternative, since it supplies an acceptable interpretation of (3) only if the entity *actually* worshipped by John may be an 'imaginary unicorn'. But we may need to add imaginary entities to our 'ontological stable' in any event, since entities may be *explicitly* described as imaginary (fictitious, hypothetical, supposed) and yet be freely referred to in ordinary discourse. Also, sentences such as "John frequently dreams about a certain unicorn" (based on an example in Dowty, Wall and Peters 1981) seem to be untranslatable into any logic without recourse to imaginary entities. Our paraphrases of (3) have the important advantage of entailing that John has a *specific* unicorn in mind, as intuitively required (in contrast with (1) and (2)). This is not the case for the intensional logic translation of (3) analogous to that of (1), a fact that led Bennett to regard "worships" – correctly, we think – as extensional (Bennett 1974).

In the light of these considerations, the conventional approach to logical translation seems well worth pursuing. The simplicity of the semantic rules to which we are led encourages us in this pursuit.

3. Syntactic and Semantic Preliminaries

The logical-form syntax provides for the formation of simple terms such as

John1, x,

quantified terms such as

<some1 man2>, <the1 (little2 boy3)>,

simple predicate formulas such as

man2, loves3, P4,

compound predicate formulas such as

⟨loves2 Mary3⟩, ⟨⟨loves2 Mary3⟩ John1⟩,
[John1 loves2 Mary3],

modified predicate formulas such as

(bright3 red4), (passionately2 ⟨loves3 Mary4⟩),

and lambda abstracts such as

$\lambda x[x$ shaves2 $x]$, $\lambda y[y$ expects2 $[y$ wins4$]]$.

Note the use of sharp angle brackets for quantified terms, square brackets or blunt angle brackets for compound predicate formulas, and round brackets for modified predicate formulas. (We explain the use of square brackets and blunt angle brackets below.) We also permit sentences (i.e., compound predicate formulas with all arguments in place) as operands of sentential operators, as in

[[John5 loves6 Mary7] possible3],

[Sue1 believes2 [John5 loves5 Mary6]],

[[John1 feverish3] because4
[John1 has5 malaria6]].

For coordination of expressions of all types (quantifiers, terms, predicate formulas, modifiers, and sentential operators) we use sharp angle brackets and prefix form, as in

<or2 many1 few3>, <and2 John1 Bill3>,

<and4 ⟨hugs2 Mary3⟩ ⟨kisses5 Sue6⟩>.

The resemblance of coordinated expressions to quantified terms is intentional: in both cases the sharp angle brackets signal the presence of an unscoped operator (viz., the first element in brackets) to be scoped later on.

Finally, we may want to admit second-order predicates with first-order predicate arguments, as in

[Fido1 little-for3 dog5], [blue1 colour4],

$[\lambda x[x$ kisses1 Mary2$]$ is-fun3$]$,

though it remains to be seen whether such second-order predications adequately capture the meaning of English sentences involving implicit comparatives and nominalization.

Fuller explanations of several of the above features follow. In outline, we first delve a little further into the syntax and semantics of predicate formulas; then we discuss the sources and significance of ambiguities in the formulas.

Atomic sentences are of the form

$$[t_n \; P \; t_1 \; ... \; t_{n-1}], \; (\text{equivalently}, \; \langle P \; t_1 \; ... \; t_n \rangle),$$

where $t_1, ..., t_n$ are terms and P is a predicate constant, and the square brackets and blunt angle brackets distinguish infix and prefix syntax respectively. We regard this sentential form as equivalent to

$$[t_n \; \langle ... \langle \langle P \; t_1 \rangle \; t_2 \rangle ... \; t_{n-1} \; \rangle],$$

i.e., as obtained by applying an n-ary predicate *successively* to n terms. For example,

[John loves Mary] = $\langle$loves Mary John$\rangle$

=[John $\langle$loves Mary$\rangle$] = $\langle\langle$loves Mary$\rangle$ John$\rangle$.[10]

As in Montague grammar, this predicate application syntax helps to keep the rules of translation simple: in most cases the translation of a phrase is just the composition of the translations of its top-level constituents. However, we saw earlier that a functional interpretation of predicate application leads to the interpretation of predicates as telescoped function-valued functions, whereas we wish to interpret predicates as n-ary relations (in each possible world) in the conventional way.

We can satisfy this requirement by interpreting predicate application not as function application, but rather as *leftmost section* of the associated relation at the value of the given argument. For example, let V denote the semantic valuation function (with a particular interpretation and possible world understood) and let

$$V(P) = \{<a,b,c>, <a,b,d>, <e,f,g>\},$$
$$V(x) = a, \; V(y) = b, \; \text{and} \; V(z) = d,$$

where P is a triadic predicate symbol, x, y, and z are individual constants or variables, and a, b, ..., g are elements of the individual domain D. Then

$$V(\langle P \; x \rangle) = \{<b,c>, <b,d>\},$$
$$V(\langle P \; x \; y \rangle) = V(\langle\langle P \; x \rangle \; y \rangle) = \{<c>, <d>\}, \; \text{and}$$
$$V([z \; P \; x \; y]) = V(\langle\langle\langle P \; x \rangle \; y \rangle \; z \rangle) = \{<>\}.$$

We use the convention $\{<>\}$ = true, $\{\}$ = false.

Lambda abstraction can be defined compatibly by

$$V_I(\lambda x \phi) = \bigcup_{d \, \in \, D} (\{d\} \times V_{I(x:d)}(\phi))$$

where I is an interpretation, I(x:d) is an interpretation identical to I except that x denotes d, and $\times$ denotes Cartesian product (and a particular possible world is understood). It can be verified that the usual lambda-conversion identities hold, i.e.,

$$\langle \lambda x \langle P...x... \rangle \; t \rangle = \langle P...t... \rangle, \; \text{and}$$
$$P = \lambda x \langle P \; x \rangle = \lambda x \lambda y \langle P \; x \; y \rangle = ... ,$$

where P is a predicate of any adicity (including null, if we use $\{<>\} \times A = A$ for any set A).

As far as modified predicate formulas such as (bright3 red4) are concerned, we can interpret the modifiers as functions from n-ary relations to n-ary relations (perhaps with n restricted to 1).

We now turn to a consideration of the potential sources of ambiguity in the formulas. One source of ambiguity noted in the Introduction lies in the primitive logical symbols themselves, which may correspond ambiguously to various proper logical symbols. The ambiguous symbols are obtained by the translator via the first stage of a two-stage lexicon (and with the aid of morphological analysis, not discussed here). This first stage merely distinguishes the formal logical roles of a lexeme, supplying a distinct (but in general still ambiguous) symbol or compound expression for each role, along with syntactic information. For example, the entry for "recover" might distinguish (i) a predicate role with preliminary translation "recovers-from" and the syntactic information that this is a V admissible in the rule that expands a VP as a V optionally followed by a (PP from); (this information is supplied via the appropriate rule number); and (ii) a predicate role with preliminary translation "recovers" and the syntactic information that this is a V admissible in the rule that expands a VP as a V followed by an NP.

Having obtained a preliminary translation of a lexeme in keeping with its apparent syntactic role, the translator affixes an index to it which has not yet been used in the current sentence (or if the translation is a compound expression, it affixes the same index to all of its primitive symbols). In this way indexed preliminary translations such as Mary1, good2, and recovers3 are obtained. For example, the verb translation selected for "recovers" in the sentence context "John recovers the sofa" would be recovers2, recovers-from2 being ruled out by the presence of the NP complement. The second stage of the lexicon supplies alternative final translations of the first-stage symbols, which in the case of "recovers" might be RE-COVERS, REGAINS, and so on. Naturally, the processors that choose among these final symbols would have to draw on knowledge stored in the propositional data base and in the representation of the discourse context.

A second source of ambiguity lies in quantified terms. The sentence

Someone loves every man

---

[10] We provide the double syntax for purely cosmetic reasons. In our use of the notation, expressions delimited by square brackets will generally be complete open or closed sentences, while expressions delimited by blunt angle brackets will be 'incomplete sentences', i.e., predicates with one or more arguments missing (and denoting a relation with adicity = number of missing arguments).

illustrates a quantifier scope ambiguity arising from a syntactically unambiguous construction. Its logical-form translation is

[<some1 one2> loves3 <every4 man5>],

wherein the relative scopes of the quantifiers some1 and every4 are ambiguous. Quantified terms are intended to be 'extracted' in the postprocessing phase to positions left-adjacent to sentential formulas (which may already be prefixed with other quantifiers). A new variable is introduced into each extracted quantifier expression, the angle brackets are changed to round brackets, and the new variable is substituted for all occurrences of the extracted term. (Thus the level of extraction must be 'high' enough to encompass all of these occurrences.) In the above formula, quantifier extraction reveals the implicit ambiguity, yielding either

(some1 x:[x one2])(every4 y:[y man5])[x loves3 y]

or

(every4 y:[y man5])(some1 x:[x one2])[x loves3 y],

depending on the order of extraction.

Assuming that some1 and every4 correspond to the standard existential and universal quantifiers, these translations could be further processed to yield

∃x[[x one2] & ∀y[[y man5] => [x loves3 y]]] and
∀y[[y man5] => ∃x[[x one2] & [x loves3 y]]].

However, we may not implement this last conversion step, since it cannot be carried out for all quantifiers. For example, as Cresswell remarks, "most A's are B's" cannot be rendered as "for most x, either x is not an A or x is a B" (Cresswell 1973: 137). (Consider, for instance, A = dog and B = beagle; then the last statement is true merely because most things are not dogs — irrespective of whether or not most dogs are in fact beagles.) It appears from recent work by Goebel (to appear) that standard mechanical inference methods can readily be extended to deal with formulas with restricted quantifiers.

A third source of ambiguity lies in coordinated expressions. For example, the logical form of the sentence "Every man loves Peggy or Sue" is

[<every1 man2> loves3 <or5 Peggy4 Sue6>],

which is open to the readings

(every1 x:[x man2])[[x loves3 Peggy4] or5
                          [x loves3 Sue6]]

and

[(every1 x:[x man2])[x loves3 Peggy4]
    or5 (every1 x:[x man2])[x loves3 Sue6]].

The postprocessing steps required to scope coordinators are similar to those for quantifiers and are illustrated in Section 4.[11]

An important constraint on the disambiguation of the basic symbols as well as quantified terms and coordinated expressions is that identical expressions (i.e.,

expressions with identical constituent structure, including indices) must be identically disambiguated. For example, "John shaves himself" and "John shaves John" translate respectively into

[John1 λx[x shaves2 x]] = [John1 shaves2 John1],

and

[John1 shaves2 John3].

The stated constraint ensures that both occurrences of John1 in the first formula will ultimately be replaced by the same unambiguous constant. Similarly "Someone shaves himself" and "Someone shaves someone" translate initially into

[<some1 one2> shaves3 <some1 one2>] and
[<some1 one2> shaves3 <some4 one5>]

respectively, and these translations become

(some1 x:[x one2])[x shaves3 x] and
(some1 x:[x one2])(some4 y:[y one5])[x shaves3 y]

respectively after quantifier extraction. Note that the two occurrences of <some1 one2> in the first formula are extracted in unison and replaced by a common variable. Indexing will be seen to play a similar role in the distribution of coordinators that coordinate non-sentential constituents.

By allowing the above types of ambiguities in the logical form translations, we are able to separate the problem of disambiguation from the problems of parsing and translation. This is an important advantage, since disambiguation depends upon pragmatic factors. For example, "John admires John" may refer to two distinct individuals or just to one (perhaps whimsically), depending on such factors as whether more than one individual named John has been mentioned in the current context. Examples involving ambiguities in nouns, verbs, determiners, etc., are easily supplied. Similarly, the determination of relative quantifier scopes involves pragmatic considerations in addition to level of syntactic embedding and surface order. This is true both for explicit quantifier scope ambiguities such as in the sentence "Someone loves every man", and for scope ambiguities introduced by decomposition, such as the decomposition of "seeks" into

λyλx[x tries [x finds y]],

as a result of which a sentence like

John seeks a unicorn

admits the alternative translations

∃x[[x unicorn] & [John tries [John finds x]]], and
[John tries ∃x[[x unicorn] & [John finds x]]],

neglecting indices. It is simpler to produce a single output which can then be subjected to pragmatic post-

---

[11] If first-order predicates are to be allowed as arguments of functions or predicates, then quantifier and coordinator scoping of the following types must also be allowed: ⟨P...<Q R>...⟩ → λx(Q y:[y R])[x P...y...], <C P R> → λx[[x P] C [x R]].

processing to determine likely quantifier scopes, than to generate all possible orderings and then to make a pragmatic choice among them. Much the same can be said about scoping of coordinators.

We also note that a grammar designed to generate all possible unambiguous translations of English phrases and sentences would have to supply multiple semantic rules for certain syntactic rules. For example, no one semantic rule can translate a quantifier-noun combination (rule 3 in Section 4) so as to deliver both readings of "Someone loves every man" upon combination of the verb translation with the translations of the NPs. Our use of an ambiguous logical form preserves the rule-to-rule hypothesis.

4. Sample Grammar

Our syntactic rules do not depart significantly from Gazdar's. The semantic rules formally resemble Gazdar's as well, but of course produce conventionally interpretable translations of the type described in the preceding section. As in Gazdar's semantic rules, constituent translations are denoted by primed category symbols such as NP' and V'. The semantic rules show how to assemble such translations (along with the occasional variable and lambda operator) to form the translations of larger constituents. The translations of individual lexemes are obtained as described above.

In operation, the translator generates the minimum number of brackets consistent with the notational equivalences stated earlier. For example, in assembling [NP' VP'], with NP' = John1 and VP' = [loves2 Mary3], the result is

[John1 loves2 Mary3],

rather than

[John1 ⟨loves2 Mary3⟩].

Also, in binding a variable with lambda, the translator replaces all occurrences of the variable with a previously unused variable, thus minimizing the need for later renaming. Finally, it performs lambda conversions on the fly. For example, the result of assembling [NP' VP'] with NP' = John1 and

VP' = $\lambda x[x$ shaves2 $x]$,

is

[John1 shaves2 John1].

The rules that follow have been adapted from Gazdar (1981a). Note that each rule that involves a lexical category such as PN, N or V is accompanied by a specification of the subset of lexical items of that category admissible in the rule. This feature is particularly important for verb subcategorization. In addition, each rule is followed by (a) a sample phrase accepted by the rule, (b) an indication of how the logical translation of the phrase is obtained, and possibly (c) some words of further explanation.

```
<1, [(NP) (PN)], PN'>, PN(1) = {John, Mary, New York, ...}
   (a)  Mary
   (b)  with PN' = Mary6, NP' becomes Mary6.

<2, [(AN) (ADJP) (N)], (ADJP' N')>, N(2) = {boy, game, noise, ...}
   (a)  little boy
   (b)  with ADJP' = little2, N' = boy3,
        AN' becomes (little2 boy3);
   (c)  "little" is taken as a predicate modifier.12

<3, [(NP) (Q) (AN)], <Q' AN'>>, Q(3) = {a, the, all, many, ...}
   (a)  the little boy
   (b)  with Q' = the1, AN' = (little2 boy3),
        NP' -> <the1 (little2 boy3)>.

<4, [(PP to) (to) (NP)], NP'>
   (a)  to Mary
   (b)  with NP' = Mary6, PP' -> Mary6;
   (c)  PP verb complements have the same meaning as their NP, as per Gazdar (1981a).

<5, [(VP) (V)], V'>, V(5) = {run, smile, disappear, ...}
   (a)  smiles
   (b)  with V' = smiles4, VP' -> smiles4.
```

---

[12] Siegel (1979) argues rather persuasively that measure adjectives, unlike genuine predicate modifiers such as "consummate", actually combine with terms. For such adjectives we might employ the semantic rule $\lambda x[[x \text{ ADJP'}] \& [x \text{ N'}]]$; in the case of "little", we would use ADJP' = ⟨little-for P⟩, where P is an indeterminate predicate to be replaced pragmatically by a comparison-class predicate. Thus the translation of "little boy" (neglecting indices) would be $\lambda x[[x \text{ little-for P}] \& [x \text{ boy}]]$.

```
<6, [(VP) (V) (NP) (PP to)], ⟨V' PP' NP'⟩>
  V(6) = {give, hand, tell, ...}
  (a)  gives Fido to Mary
  (b)  with V' = gives4, NP' = Fido5, PP' = Mary6, VP' -> ⟨gives4 Mary6 Fido5⟩.

<7, [(VP INF) (to) (VP BASE)], VP'>
  (a)  to give Fido to Mary
  (b)  with VP' = ⟨gives4 Mary6 Fido5⟩, the resultant infinitive has the
       same meaning.

<8, [(VP) (V) (VP INF)], λx[x V' [x VP']]>,
  V(8) = {want, expect, try, ...}
  (a)  wants to give Fido to Mary
  (b)  with V' = wants2, VP' = [gives4 Mary6 Fido5],
       VP' -> λx3[x3 wants2 [x3 gives4 Mary6 Fido5]];
  (c)  The formal lambda variable x given in the semantic rule has been replaced by
       the new variable x3.  Two pairs of square brackets have been deleted, in
       accordance with the simplification rules stated earlier.

<9, [(VP) (V) (NP) (VP INF)], ⟨V' [NP' VP']⟩>,
  V(9) = {want, expect, imagine, ...}
  (a)  wants Bill to give Fido to Mary
  (b)  with V' = wants2, NP' = Bill3, VP' = ⟨gives4 Mary6 Fido5⟩,
       VP' -> ⟨wants2 [Bill3 gives4 Mary6 Fido5]⟩.

<10, [(S DECL) (NP) (VP)], [NP' VP']>
  (a)  the little boy smiles
  (b)  with NP' = <the1 (little2 boy3)> and VP' = smiles4, the result is
       S' -> [<the1 (little2 boy3)> smiles4].  After pragmatic postprocessing
       to extract quantifiers, the result might be
        S' = (the1 x5:[x5 (little2 boy3)])[x5 smiles4].
       Further postprocessing to determine referents and disambiguate operators
       and predicates might then yield
        S' = [INDIV17 SMILES1],
       where INDIV17 is a (possibly new) logical constant unambiguously denoting
       the referent of (the1 x5:[x5 (little2 boy3)]) and SMILES1 is an unambiguous
       logical predicate.[13]  If constant INDIV17 is new, i.e., if the context provided
       no referent for the definite description, a supplementary assertion like
        [INDIV17 (LITTLE2 BOY1)]
       would be added to the context representation.
  (a)' John wants to give Fido to Mary
  (b)' with NP' = John1,
       VP' = λx3[x3 wants2 [x3 gives4 Mary6 Fido5]],
       S' -> [John1 wants2 [John1 gives4 Mary6 Fido5]];
  (c)' Note that John1 becomes the subject of both the main clause and the
       embedded (subordinate) clause.
```

The reader will observe that we have more or less fully traced the derivation and translation of the sentences "The little boy smiles" and "John wants to give Fido to Mary" in the course of the above examples.

The resultant phrase structure trees, with rule numbers and translations indicated at each node, are shown in Figs. 1 and 2.

---

[13] Definite singular terms often serve as descriptions to be used for referent determination, and in such cases it is the name of the referent, rather than the description itself, which is ultimately wanted in the formula.

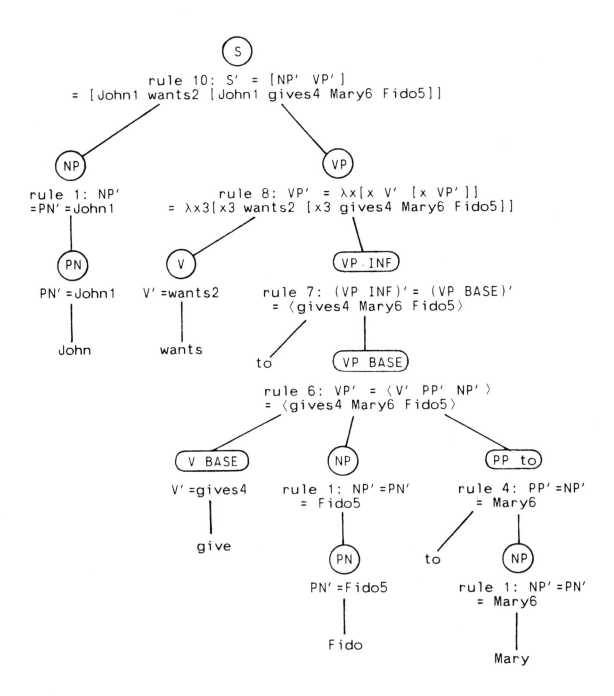

Figure 1. Phrase structure and translation of the sentence "John wants to give Fido to Mary".

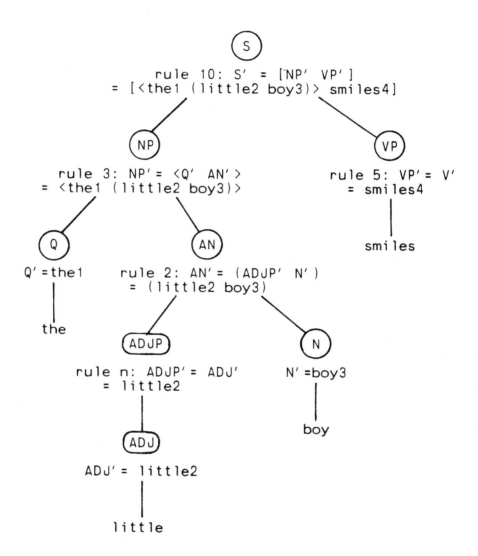

Figure 2. Phrase structure and translation of the sentence
"The little boy smiles."

All of the above rules, as well as our versions of the remaining rules in Gazdar (1981a), are as simple as the intensional logic versions or simpler. For example, our semantic rule 8, i.e., λx[x V' [x VP']], may be contrasted with the corresponding rule suggested by Gazdar:

λ**P**{**P** λx[(V' ∧(VP' λP(P x))) λP(P x)]}.

Here the lambda variable x, as in our formula, is used to feed a common logical subject to V' (the translation of the main verb) and to VP' (the translation of the embedded infinitive); the variables **P** and P, on the other hand, serve to ensure that the arguments of the V' and VP' functions will be of the correct type. Our 'conventional' rule is simpler because it makes no such use of lambda abstraction for type-raising and dispenses with the intension operator.

Gazdar's approach to unbounded dependencies carries over virtually unchanged and can be illustrated with the sentence

To Mary John wants to give Fido.

Here the PP "to Mary" has been topicalized by extraction from "John wants to give Fido to Mary", leaving a PP 'gap' at the extraction site. This 'gap' is syntactically embedded within the infinitive VP "to give Fido", within the main VP "wants to give Fido", and at the highest level, within the sentence "John wants to give Fido". In general, the analysis of un-

bounded dependencies requires *derived rules* for propagating 'gaps' from level to level and *linking rules* for creating and filling them. The linking rules are obtained from the correspondingly numbered basic rules by means of the metarule

[A X C Y] ==> [A/B X C/B Y],

where A, B and C may be any basic (i.e., non-slash) syntactic categories such that C can dominate B, and X, Y may be any sequences (possibly empty) of basic categories. The linking rules for topicalization are obtained from the rule schemata

<11, [B/B t], h>, and
<12, [(S) B (S)/B], ⟨λhS' B'⟩>,

where B ranges over all basic phrasal categories, and t is a dummy element (trace). The first of these schemata introduces the free variable h as the translation of the gap, while the second lambda-abstracts on h and then supplies B' as the value of the lambda variable, thus 'filling the gap' at the sentence level. At syntactic nodes intermediate between those admitted by schemata 11 and 12, the B-gap is transmitted by derived rules and h is still free.

Of the following rules, 6, 8, and 10 are the particular derived rules required to propagate the PP-gap in our example and 11 and 12 the particular linking rules that create and fill it:

```
<11, [(PP to)/(PP to) t], h>
   (a)  t
   (b)  PP' -> h

<6, [(VP)/(PP to) (V) (NP) (PP to)/(PP to)], ⟨V' PP' NP'⟩>
   (a)  give Fido
   (b)  with V' = gives5, NP' = Fido6, PP' = h,
        VP' -> ⟨gives5 h Fido6⟩
   (c)  Note that the semantic rule is unchanged.

<8, [(VP)/(PP to) (V) (VP INF)/(PP to)], λx[x V' [x VP']]>
   (a)  wants to give Fido
   (b)  with V' = wants3, VP' = ⟨gives5 h Fido6⟩,
        VP' -> λx4[x4 wants3 [x4 gives5 h Fido6]]

<10, [(S)/(PP to) (NP) (VP)/(PP to)], [NP' VP']>
   (a)  John wants to give Fido
   (b)  with NP' = John2,
        VP' = λx4[x4 wants3 [x4 gives5 h Fido6]],
        S' -> [John2 wants3 [John2 gives5 h Fido6]]

<12, [(S) (PP to) (S)/(PP to)], ⟨λhS' PP'⟩>
   (a)  To Mary John wants to give Fido
   (b)  With S' as in 10 (b) above and PP' = Mary1,
        S' -> [John2 wants3 [John2 gives5 Mary1 Fido6]].
   (c)  This translation is logically indistinguishable from the
        translation of the untopicalized sentence.  However, the
        fronting of "to Mary" has left a pragmatic trace: the
```

```
corresponding argument Mary1 has the lowest index, lower
than that of the subject translation John2 (assuming that
symbols are indexed in the order of occurrence of the
lexical items they translate).  In subsequent pragmatic
processing, this feature could be used to detect the special
salience of Mary1, without re-examination of the superficial
sentence form.
```

Another example of a sentence that can be analyzed by such methods, using relative clause rules similar to those for topicalization, is

Every dog Mary wants to buy is small.

The rules analyze "Mary wants to buy" as an S/NP with translation

[Mary wants [Mary buys h]],

neglecting indices. A further rule reduces the S/NP to an R (relative clause), and its semantic part abstracts on h to yield the predicate

$R' = \lambda h[\text{Mary wants } [\text{Mary buys } h]]$

as the translation of the relative clause. The rules for NPs can be formulated in such a way that "every dog" will be translated as

$<\text{every } \lambda x[[x \text{ dog}] \& [x \mathbf{R}]]>$

where $\mathbf{R}$ is a free predicate variable that is replaced by the translation of the relative clause when the NP-R rule

$<13, [(NP) (NP) (R)], <\lambda \mathbf{R}NP' R'>>$

is applied (cf., Gazdar 1981b; we have ignored multiple relative clauses). The resulting NP translation is

$<\text{every } \lambda x[[x \text{ dog}] \& [\text{Mary wants}$
$\qquad\qquad\qquad [\text{Mary buys } x]]]>.$

The translation of the complete sentence, after extraction of the quantifier and conversion of the constraint on the universally quantified variable to an implicative antecedent, would be

$\forall y[[[y \text{ dog}] \& [\text{Mary wants } [\text{Mary buys } y]]]$
$\qquad => [y \text{ (small P)}]],$

where P is an undetermined predicate (= dog, in the absence of contrary contextual information).

As a further illustration of Gazdar's approach and how easily it is adapted to our purposes, we consider his metarule for passives:

$<[(VP)(V \text{ TRAN}) (NP) X], (\mathscr{F} NP'')> ==>$
$<[(VP \text{ PASS}) (V) X \{(PP \text{ by})\}],$
$\qquad\qquad \lambda \mathbf{P}((\mathscr{F} \mathbf{P}) PP'')>;$

i.e., "for every active VP rule that expands VP as a transitive verb followed by NP, there is to be a passive VP rule that expands VP as V followed by what, if anything, followed the NP in the active VP rule, followed optionally by a by-PP" (Gazdar 1981a). In the original and resultant semantic rules, ($\mathscr{F}$ ...) represents the original rule matrix in which NP'' is embedded; thus ($\mathscr{F}$ **P**) is the result of substituting the lambda

variable **P** (which varies over NP intensions) for NP'' in the original rule. Intuitively, the lambda variable 'reserves' the NP'' argument position for later binding by the subject of the passive sentence. It can be seen that the metarule will generate a passive VP rule corresponding to our rule 6 which will account for sentences such as "Fido was given to Mary by John". Moreover, if we introduce a ditransitive rule

$<14, [(VP) (V \text{ TRAN}) (NP) (NP)],$
$\qquad \langle V' NP' NP' \rangle>$ [14]

to allow for sentences such as "John gave Mary Fido", the metarule will generate a passive VP rule that accounts for "Mary was given Fido by John", in which the indirect rather than direct object has been turned into the sentence subject.

The only change needed for our purposes is the replacement of the property variable **P** introduced by the metarule by an individual variable x:

$...\langle \mathscr{F} NP' \rangle... ==> ...\lambda x \langle\langle \mathscr{F} x \rangle PP' \rangle...$

Once the subject NP of the sentence is supplied via rule 10, x is replaced by the translation of that NP upon lambda conversion.

Finally in this section, we shall briefly consider coordination. Gazdar has supplied general coordination rule schemata along with a cross-categorical semantics that assigns appropriate formal meanings to coordinate structures of any category (Gazdar 1980b). Like Gazdar's rules, our rules generate logical-form translations of coordinated constituents such as

$<\text{and John Bill}>, <\text{or many few}>,$
$<\text{and } \langle\text{hugs Mary}\rangle \langle\text{kisses Sue}\rangle>,$

echoing the surface forms. However, it should be clear from our discussion in Section 2 that direct interpretation of expressions translating, say, coordinated NPs or VPs is not compatible with our conventional conception of formal semantics. For example, no formal semantic value is assigned directly to the coordinated term in the formula

$[<\text{and John Bill}> \text{ loves Mary}].$

Rather, interpretation is deferred until the pragmatic processor has extracted the coordinator from the embedding sentence (much as in the case of quantified

---

[14] In the computational version of the semantic rules, primed symbols are actually represented as numbers giving the positions of the corresponding constituents, e.g., $\langle 1\ 2\ 3 \rangle$ in rule 14. Thus no ambiguity can arise.

terms) and distributed the coordinated terms over duplicate copies of that sentence, yielding

[[John loves Mary] and [Bill loves Mary]].

We adopt the following coordination schemata without change. The superscript denotes sequences of length ≥ 1 of the superscripted element. The schemata are accompanied by examples of phrases they admit, along with (unindexed) translations. The bracketing in (a) and (a)' indicates syntactic structure.

```
<15, [(A 𝓕) (𝓕) (A)], A'>,
    where A is any syntactic category and 𝓕 ∈ {and, or}
    (a)   and admires
    (b)   admires
    (a)'  or Mary
    (b)'  Mary

<16, [(A) (A)+ (A 𝓕)], <𝓕' A'A'...A'>>
    (a)   loves [and admires]
    (b)   <and loves admires>
    (a)'  [Fido Kim] [or Mary]
    (b)'  <or Fido Kim Mary>

<17, [(A) (A) (A 𝓕)+], <𝓕' A'A'...A'>>
    (a)   Fido [[or Kim] [or Mary]]
    (b)   <or Fido Kim Mary>
```

The order in which coordinators are extracted and distributed is a matter of pragmatic choice. However, a crucial constraint is that multiple occurrences of a particular coordinated expression (with particular indices) must be extracted and distributed in a single operation, at the level of a sentential formula whose scope encompasses all of those occurrences (much as in the case of quantifier extraction). The following examples illustrate this process.

```
(a)  John loves and admires Fido or Kim
(b)  [John1 <and3 loves2 admires4> <or6 Fido5 Kim7>] ->
     [[John1 loves2 <or6 Fido5 Kim7>] and3
     [John1 admires4 <or6 Fido5 Kim7>]] ->
     [[[John1 loves2 Fido5] and3
     [John1 admires4 Fido5]] or6
     [[John1 loves2 Kim7] and3
     [John1 admires4 Kim7]]].
```
(c) Note that once the and3-conjunction has been chosen for initial extraction and distribution, the simultaneous extraction and distribution of both occurrences of the or6-disjunction at the highest sentential level is compulsory. The resultant formula expresses the sense of "John loves and admires Fido or loves and admires Kim". Initial extraction of the or6-disjunction would have led to the (implausible) reading "John loves Fido or Kim and admires Fido or Kim" (which is true even if John loves only Fido and admires only Kim).

```
(a)'  All men want to marry Peggy or Sue
(b)'  [<all1 man2> wants3 [<all1 man2> marries4 <or6 Peggy5 Sue7>]]->
      (all1 x:[x man2])[x wants3 [x marries4 <or6 Peggy5 Sue7>]] ->
      (all1 x:[x man2])[x wants3
            [[x marries4 Peggy5] or6 [x marries4 Sue7]]].
```
(c)' In the second step above, the coordinator or6 might instead have been raised to the second highest sentential level, yielding
```
      (all1 x:[x man2])[[x wants3 [x marries4 Peggy5]] or6
            [x wants3 [x marries4 Sue7]]],
```
or to the highest sentential level, yielding

```
[(all1 x:[x man2])[x wants3 [x marries4 Peggy5]] or6
 (all1 x:[x man2])[x wants3 [x marries4 Sue7]]].
```
The three readings are logically distinct and all are quite
plausible (in the absence of additional context). The reader
can verify that the first and second readings, but not the
third, could have been obtained by extracting the coordinator
first and the quantifier second.

Finally, we should remark that the distributive rules are not appropriate for the group reading of coordinate structures in sentences such as

John and Mary carried the sofa (together).

We envisage a mereological interpretation in which John and Mary together comprise a two-component entity. However, we refrain from introducing a logical syntax for such entities here (but see the treatment of plurals in Schubert, 1982).

5. Parsing

Phrase structure grammars are relatively easy to parse. The most advanced parser for Gazdar-style grammars that we are aware of is Thompson's chart-parser (Thompson 1981), which provides for slash categories and coordination, but does not (as of this writing) generate logical translations. We have implemented two small parser-translators for preliminary experimentation, one written in SNOBOL and the other in MACLISP. The former uses a recursive descent algorithm and generates intensional logic translations. The latter is a 'left corner' parser that uses our reformulated semantic rules to generate conventional translations. It begins by finding a sequence of left-most phrase-structure-rule branches that lead from the first word upward to the sentence node. (e.g., Mary → PN → NP → S). The remaining branches of the phrase structure rules thus selected form a "frontier" of expectations. Next a similar initial-unit sequence is found to connect the second word of the sentence to the lowest-level (most immediate) expectation, and so on. There is provision for the definition and use of systems of features, although we find that the parser needs to do very little feature checking to stay on the right syntactic track. Neither parser at present handles slash categories and coordination (although they could be handled inefficiently by resort to closure of the grammar under metarules and rule schemata). Extraction of quantifiers from the logical-form translations is at present based on the level of syntactic embedding and left-to-right order alone, and no other form of postprocessing is attempted.[15]

It has been gratifyingly easy to write these parser-translators, confirming us in the conviction that Gazdar-style grammars hold great promise for the design of natural language understanding systems. It is particularly noteworthy that we found the design of the translator component an almost trivial task; no modification of this component will be required even when the parser is expanded to handle slash categories and coordination directly. Encouraged by these results, we have begun to build a full-scale left-corner parser. A morphological analyzer that can work with arbitrary sets of formal affix rules is partially implemented; this work, as well as some ideas on the conventional translation of negative adjective prefixes, plurals, and tense/aspect structure, is reported in Schubert (1982).

6. Concluding Remarks

From the point of view of theoretical and computational linguistics, Gazdar's approach to grammar offers profound advantages over traditional approaches: it dispenses with transformations without loss of insight, offers large linguistic coverage, and couples simple, semantically well-motivated rules of translation to the syntactic rules.

We have attempted to show that the advantages of Gazdar's approach to grammar can be secured without commitment to an intensional target logic for the translations of natural language sentences. To motivate this endeavour, we have argued that there are philosophical and practical reasons for preferring a conventional target logic, and that there are as yet no compelling reasons for abandoning such logics in favour of intensional ones. More concretely, we have shown how to reformulate Gazdar's semantic rules to yield conventional translations, and have briefly described some extant PSG parsers, including one that is capable of parsing and translating in accordance with the reformulated Gazdar grammar (minus metalinguistic constructs).

We believe that a parser-interpreter of this type will prove very useful as the first stage of a natural language understanding system. Since the grammar rules are expressed in a concise, individually comprehensible form, such a system will be easy to expand indefinitely. The assignment of a well-defined logical form to input sentences, compatible with favoured knowledge representation formalisms, should help to

---

[15] Since submission of this paper for publication, we have become aware of several additional papers on parser-translators similar to ours. One is by Rosenschein & Shieber (1982), another by Gawron et al. (1982); in conception these are based quite directly on the generalized phrase structure grammar of Gazdar and his collaborators, and use recursive descent parsers. A related Prolog-based approach is described by McCord (1981, 1982).

bring a measure of precision and clarity to the rather murky area of natural language interpretation by machine.

Acknowledgements

The authors are indebted to Ivan Sag for a series of very stimulating seminars held by him at the University of Alberta on his linguistic research, and valuable follow-up discussions. The helpful comments of the referees and of Lotfi Zadeh are also appreciated. The research was supported in part by NSERC Operating Grants A8818 and A2252; preliminary work on the left-corner parser was carried out by one of the authors (LKS) under an Alexander von Humboldt fellowship in 1978-79.

References

Bach, E. 1976 An extension of classical transformational grammar. Mimeo, Univ. of Massachusetts, Amherst, MA.

Bartsch, R. 1976 *The Grammar of Adverbials*. North-Holland, Amsterdam.

Bennett, M. 1974 Some extensions of a Montague fragment of English. Ph.D. dissertation, UCLA; available from the Indiana University Linguistics Club.

Brame, M.K. 1978 *Base Generated Syntax*. Noit Amrofer, Seattle, WA.

Bresnan, J.W. 1976 On the form and functioning of transformations. *Linguistic Inquiry* 7 3-40.

Bresnan, J.W. 1978 A realistic transformational grammar. In Halle, M., Bresnan, J.W., and Miller, G.A., Ed., *Linguistic Theory and Psychological Reality* MIT Press, Cambridge, MA.

Chierchia, G. 1981 Nominalization and Montague grammar. A semantics without types for natural languages. MS, Dept. of Linguistics, Univ. of Massachusetts, Amherst, MA.

Church, A. 1941 *The Calculi of Lambda Conversion*. Princeton Univ. Press, Princeton, NJ.

Cooper, R., and Parsons, T. 1976 Montague grammar, generative semantics and interpretive semantics. In Partee 1976a, 311-362.

Craig, J.A., Berezner, S.C., Carney, H.C., and Longyear, C.R. 1966 DEACON: Direct English access and control. Fall Joint Comp. Conf., Nov. 7-10, San Francisco, CA, *AFIPS Conf. Proc.* vol. 29. Spartan Books, Washington, D.C.: 365-380.

Cresswell, M.J. 1973 *Logics and Languages*. Methuen, London.

Dowty, D.R. 1978 A guide to Montague's PTQ. Indiana Univ. Linguistics Club, Bloomington, IN.

Dowty, D.R. 1979 *Word Meaning and Montague Grammar: The Semantics of Verbs and Times in Generative Semantics and in Montague's PTQ*. D. Reidel, Dordrecht.

Dowty, D.R., Wall, R., and Peters, S. 1981. *An Introduction to Montague Semantics*. D. Reidel, Dordrecht.

Fodor, J.A. 1978 Propositional attitudes. *The Monist* **61**, 501-523.

Gawron, J.M., King, J.J., Lamping, J., Loebner, E.E., Paulson, E. A., Pullum, G.K., Sag, I.A., and Wasow, T.A. 1982 Processing English with a generalized phrase structure grammar. CLS-82-5, Comp. Science Lab. Tech. Note Series, Hewlett Packard, Palo Alto, CA. Presented at the 20th Ann. Meet. of the Assoc. for Computational Linguistics, June 16-18, Univ. of Toronto, Toronto, Ont.

Gazdar, G. 1980a A phrase structure syntax for comparative clauses. *Glot-Lexical Grammar* 165-179.

Gazdar, G. 1980b A cross-categorical semantics for coordination *Linguistics and Philosophy* **3**, 407-409.

Gazdar, G. 1981a Phrase structure grammar. To appear in Jacobson, P. and Pullum, G.K., Ed., *The Nature of Syntactic Representation*. D. Reidel, Dordrecht.

Gazdar, G. 1981b Unbounded dependencies and coordinate structure. *Linguistic Inquiry* **12.2**.

Gazdar, G., Klein, E., Pullum, G. K., and Sag, I. to appear *English Syntax*.

Gazdar, G., Pullum, G.K., and Sag, I. 1980 A phrase structure grammar of the English auxiliary system. Unpublished paper. A slightly different version entitled "Auxiliaries and related phenomena in a restricted theory of grammar" is available from Indiana Univ. Linguistics Club; to appear as "Auxiliaries and related phenomena" in *Language*.

Gazdar, G. and Sag, I. 1980 Passive and reflexives in phrase structure grammar. In Groenendijk, J., Janssen, T., and Stokhof, M., Ed., *Formal Methods in the Study of Language, Proc. 3rd Amsterdam Coll., March 25-28, 1980*. Mathematical Centre Tracts, Amsterdam.

Goebel, R. 1982 Forthcoming Ph.D. thesis, Dept. of Computer Science, Univ. of British Columbia, Vancouver, B.C.

Grice, H.P. 1975 Logic and conversation. In Davidson, D. and Harman, G., Ed., *The Logic of Grammar*. Dickenson, Encino, CA: 64-75.

Guenthner, F. 1978 Systems of intensional logic and the semantics of natural language. In Guenther, F. and Rohrer, C., Ed., *Studies in Formal Semantics*. North-Holland, Amsterdam: 41-74.

Harman, G. 1975 Logical form. In Davidson, D. and Harman, G., Ed., *The Logic of Grammar*. Dickenson, Encino, CA: 289-307.

Hughes, G.E. and Cresswell, M.J. 1968 *An Introduction to Modal Logic*. Methuen, London.

Jackendoff, R. 1977 $\bar{X}$ *Syntax: A Study of Phrase Structure*. MIT Press, Cambridge, MA.

Kaplan, R.M. (panelist) 1981 A view of parsing. *Proc. 19th Ann. Meet. of the Assoc. for Computational Linguistics, June 29 – July 1*. Stanford Univ., Stanford, CA, 103-104.

Katz, J., and Fodor, J.A. 1963 The structure of a semantic theory. *Language* **39**, 170-210.

Knuth, D.E. 1968 Semantics of context-free languages. *Mathematical Systems Theory* **2**, 127-145.

Lakoff, G. 1971 On generative semantics. In Steinberg, D.D. and Jakobvitz, L.A., Ed., *Semantics: An Interdisciplinary Reader in Philosophy, Linguistics and Psychology*. Cambridge Univ. Press, New York: 232-296.

Langendoen, T. 1979 On the assignment of constituent structures to the sentences generated by a transformational grammar. *City Univ. of New York Forum*. New York, NY.

Lapointe, S. 1977 Recursiveness and deletion. *Linguistic Analysis* **3**, 227-266.

McCarthy, J. 1979 First-order theories of individual concepts and propositions. In Michie, D., Ed., *Expert Systems in the Micro Electronic Age*. Edinburgh Univ. Press, Edinburgh: 271-287.

McCord, M.C. 1981 Focalizers, the scoping problem, and semantic interpretation rules in logic grammars. Tech. Rep. No. 81-81. Univ. of Kentucky, Lexington, KY. To appear in *Proc. of the Int. Workshop on Logic Programming for Expert Systems, Logicon*, Woodland Hills, CA, Aug. 1981.

McCord, M.C. 1982 Using slots and modifiers in logic grammars for natural language. *Artificial Intelligence* **18**, 327-367.

Montague, R. 1970a English as a formal language. In Thomason 1974a, 188-221.

Montague, R. 1970b Universal grammar. In Thomason 1974a, 222-246.

Montague, R. 1970c The proper treatment of quantification in ordinary English. In Thomason 1974a, 247-270.

Partee, B.H. 1974 Opacity and scope. In Munitz, M.K., and Unger, P.K., Ed., *Semantics and Philosophy.* New York Univ. Press, New York: 81-101.

Partee, B.H., Ed. 1976a *Montague Grammar.* Academic Press, New York.

Partee, B.H. 1976b Some transformational extensions of Montague grammar. In Partee 1976a, 51-76.

Peters, P.S., and Ritchie, R.W. 1969 Context-sensitive immediate constituent analysis: context-free languages revisited. In *First Ann. Symp. on Theory of Computing,* ACM, New York, 1-8. Also in *Math. Systems Theory* 6 (1973) 324-333.

Quine, *W.v.O. 1960 Word and Object.* MIT Press, Cambridge, MA.

Robinson, J.J. (chr.) 1981 Panel: perspectives on parsing issues. *Proc. 19th Ann. Meet. of the Assoc. for Computational Linguistics,* June 29-July 1, Stanford Univ., Stanford, CA, 95-106.

Rosenschein, S.J., and Shieber, S.M. 1982 Translating English into logical form. Presented at the 20th Ann. Meet. of the Assoc. for Computational Linguistics, June 16-18, Univ. of Toronto, Toronto, Ont.

Sag, I. 1980 A semantic theory of NP-movement dependencies. To appear in Jacobson, P. and Pullum, G.K., Ed., *The Nature of Syntactic Representation.* D. Reidel, Dortrecht.

Schank, R.C. 1973 Identification of conceptualizations underlying natural language. In Schank, R.C. and Colby, K.M., Ed., *Computer Models of Thought and Language.* W.H. Freeman, San Francisco: 187-247.

Schank, R.C. 1975 The primitive ACTs of conceptual dependency. In *Advance Papers of Theoretical Issues in Natural Language Processing Workshop,* June 10-13, MIT, Cambridge, MA, 34-37.

Schoenfinkel, M. 1924 Ueber die Bausteine der mathematischen Logik. *Math. Annalen* 92, 305-316.

Schubert, L.K. 1976 Extending the expressive power of semantic networks. *Artificial Intelligence* 7, 163-198.

Schubert, L.K. 1982 An approach to the syntax and semantics of affixes in 'conventionalized' phrase structure grammar. *Proc. of the 4th Biennial Conf. of the Can. Soc. for Computational Studies of Intelligence (CSCSI/SCEIO),* 17-19 May 1982, Univ. of Saskatchewan, Saskatoon, Sask.: 189-195.

Schwind, C. 1978a A formalism for the description of question answering systems. In Bolc, L., Ed., *Natural Language Communication with Computers.* Springer-Verlag, Berlin, Heidelberg & New York: 1-48.

Schwind, C. 1978b The translation of natural language texts into state logic formulae. Tech. Rep. TUM-INFO-7806, Technische Univ. Muenchen, available from Bibliothek des Fachbereichs Mathematik, Technische Univ. Muenchen, D-8000 Muenchen 2, W. Germany.

Siegel, M.E.A. 1979 Measure adjectives in Montague grammar. In Davis, S., and Mithun, M., Eds., *Linguistics, Philosophy, and Montague Grammar.* Univ. of Texas Press, Austin, TX: 223-262.

Thomason, R.H. ed. 1974a *Formal Philosophy: Selected Papers of Richard Montague.* Yale Univ. Press, New Haven, CT.

Thomason, R.H. 1974b Introduction to Thomason 1974a, 1-69.

Thomason, R.H. 1980 A model theory for propositional attitudes. *Linguistics and Philosophy* 4, 47-70.

Thompson, F.B. 1966 English for the computer. Fall Joint Comp. Conf., Nov. 7-10, San Francisco, CA. *AFIPS Conf. Proc. Vol. 29,* Spartan Books, Washington, D.C., 349-356.

Thompson, H. 1981 Chart parsing and rule schemata in PSG. *Proc. 19th Ann. Meet. of the Assoc. for Computational Linguistics,* June 29-July 1, Stanford Univ., Stanford, CA: 167-172.

Wilks, Y. 1974 An artificial intelligence approach to machine translation. In Schank, R.C., and Colby, K.M. Ed., *Computer Models of Thought and Language.* W.H. Freeman, San Francisco: 114-151.

Winograd, T. 1972 *Understanding Natural Language.* Academic Press, New York.

Woods, W.A. 1977 Lunar rocks in natural English: Explorations in natural language question answering. In Zampolli, A., Ed., *Linguistic Structures Processing.* North-Holland, Amsterdam: 521-569.

Lenhart K. Schubert is an associate professor of computer science at the University of Alberta, Edmonton. He received the Ph.D. degree from the University of Toronto.

Francis Jeffry Pelletier is a professor of philosophy at the University of Alberta. He received the Ph.D. degree from the University of California at Los Angeles.

A NEW SEMANTIC COMPUTATION WHILE PARSING: PRESUPPOSITION AND ENTAILMENT[1]

RALPH M. WEISCHEDEL
University of Delaware, Newark

1. INTRODUCTION

Though there is not yet complete agreement on what the definition of presupposition should be, a pattern has emerged among the concrete examples cited to justify various definitions of presupposition. For those examples in the literature which have not been successfully refuted, presuppositions seem to be associated with particular lexical items and certain grammatical constructions. (Karttunen and Peters, 1975, make this observation as well.) This suggests that a parser and lexicon might predict the presuppositions of a sentence, using a purely structural computation. I have constructed such a parser and lexicon which, when given an input sentence, compute the presuppositions of the sentence. A solution to the projection problem for compound sentences is also included.

Many examples of entailment also seem to be associated with particular lexical items; for instance, Givón (1973) and Karttunen (1970) offer many instances. These, too, can be generated while parsing a sentence. Furthermore, the solution to the projection problem for pre-

suppositions has been extended to compute the entailments of compound sentences.

This chapter describes the parser and lexicon at an intermediate level of detail. A higher level description may be found in Joshi and Weischedel (1977); an in-depth description appears in Weischedel (1975), including background material on the formalism of the grammar and a complete analysis of the lexical information.

For the purposes of this chapter, assume that a completely satisfactory definition of presupposition and entailment will soon be found, incorporating the rich and diverse examples of Fillmore (1971), Givón (1973), Keenan (1971), Kiparsky and Kiparsky (1971), Karttunen (1970), and Karttunen and Peters (1975). I shall use the terms PRESUPPOSITION and ENTAILMENT to refer to those examples which appear to be associated with particular lexical items and syntactic constructions. I use the term CONTEXT to mean previous text, cultural rules, universal laws, etc. All phenomena attributable to the effect of context and all computations modeling such phenomena are termed PRAGMATIC.

Assume that the goal of a natural language parser is to translate from sentences to semantic representations for those sentences. My parser translates to the type of semantic representations posed by Keenan (1972), which are also amenable to semantic analyses using factorization of verbs. However, my computation presumes only that the semantic representations are a subset of a context-free language. Thus, the only assumption is that they may be represented by a tree or bracketed string.

Let S and S' be sentences with semantic representations L and L'. We say that sentence S' may be SUBFORMULA-DERIVED from sentence S if there is a tree transformation f and a subtree t of L such that

$$L' = f(t).$$

The chief result of this research is to demonstrate that presuppositions and entailments may be subformula-derived and to demonstrate how to write a parser and lexicon for this purpose.

My grammar is written in the formalism of the augmented transition network (ATN) of Woods (1970, 1973), and is patterned after the linguistic string parser of Sager (1967, 1973). (The linguistic string parser is based on the theory of grammar by Harris, 1970.)

The fact that presupposition and entailment may be computed while parsing is quite important from the viewpoint of a computational linguist. The process of drawing inferences is computationally quite complex, though crucial to model many semantic and pragmatic

[1] The work was carried out while the author was in the Department of Computer and Information Science, University of Pennsylvania, Philadelphia. It was partially supported by NSF Grant SOC 72-0546A01.

phenomena. Furthermore, how to guide the inference process to make the important inferences rather than all inferences is an unsolved problem. (Charniak, 1976, discusses these problems.) Since computing the semantic representation of a sentence is central to processing the sentence, the fact that we can also compute presuppositions and entailments as part of the parsing process is important. Furthermore, presupposition and entailment are central to the meaning of a sentence, in the sense that they arise from the meaning of particular words and syntactic constructions.

One chief advantage of a computational approach in linguistic research is that it offers interacting computational processes as a model of the use and interpretation of language. Interacting computational processes potentially provide a model of the interaction of syntax, semantics, and pragmatics, which is evident in anaphora, ambiguity, paraphrase, contradiction, presupposition, and discourse.

Let us consider this with respect to presupposition. Much of the literature raises difficulties for a purely semantic view of presupposition, as well as difficulties for a purely pragmatic view of presupposition. Kempson (1975, Chapter Four) discusses many difficulties. However, interacting computational processes could offer a solution to these difficulties.

For instance, a pragmatic view of presupposition might claim that presuppositions must be in the common ground of speaker and audience in order that the sentence be uttered felicitously. However, sentences such as (1) may be uttered to inform the audience of the truth of the presupposition expressed by the complement.

(1) *I regret that smoking is not permitted in this auditorium.*

The process described in this chapter computes presupposition by purely structural means, thus reflecting the intuition that presupposition is semantic in nature. A second process could verify whether the presuppositions computed are true in the context of the utterance, thus reflecting the pragmatic aspects of presupposition. If they are not, a third process would be invoked to hypothesize the speaker's intent, whether perhaps to inform that smoking is not permitted, to make a joke, or to be sarcastic. Psycholinguistic evidence for such processes appears in Clark and Haviland (1977).

On the other hand, a purely semantic view of presupposition has difficulty explaining the projection algorithm. For instance, *and* is not symmetrical with respect to affecting presuppositions of embedded sentences. However, a process model can reflect this well, since the

common ground may be augmented by the proposition to the left of *and* before verifying presuppositions of the right side.

We make no pretence that the ideas of the two previous paragraphs are a scientific model; however, the sections that follow present a concrete process which could become a portion of such a model. In fact, that process has been applied by Weischedel, Voge, and James (1977) toward sophisticated computer-assisted language instruction. The interacting processes in that system are used to pinpoint a student's mistakes in use of language as the student gives (sentential) answers to questions about a given short text. If a presupposition of a student's answer does not correspond to the text, the system points out the lexical item that was used inappropriately. Furthermore, using the presuppositions of a question, the system identifies a student's failure to comprehend the question if an inference process cannot infer from the student's answer the proposition corresponding to the presupposition. We feel there is great potential in exploiting interacting computational processes as a model of linguistic phenomena.

The remainder of this chapter is organized as follows. Sections 2, 3, and 4 detail the computation of presupposition, of entailment, and of those entities in compound sentences, respectively. Section 5 suggests a criterion for including semantic information in a lexicon, and Section 6 concludes. The syntactic constructions in the implemented system are given in Appendix A; some sample output appears in Appendix B.

2. COMPUTING PRESUPPOSITIONS

While parsing a sentence, my system computes the presuppositions and entailments of that sentence, using an ATN and a lexicon for detailed information about each word. (We will not attempt to provide a description of the ATN formalism. Woods, 1970, 1973, gives this.)

The ATN enables one to write natural language parsers which are close to the surface structure of sentences, yet which can do the equivalent of inverse transformations while parsing a sentence. Therefore, my parser can compute semantic representations (as defined by Keenan, 1972) without operating on surface structure trees. Furthermore, while it computes the semantic representation of the sentence, it also computes the semantic representations for presuppositions and entailments.

The ATN is a generalization of finite state machines, so rich that they are equivalent to unrestricted production rules, and therefore equivalent to a Turing machine. Since an ATN is a generalization of a finite state machine, I will frequently refer to finding a particular parse as traversing a particular path in the graph of the ATN. The designer of a parser may associate a specific computation with any such path or parse (which is a way that the equivalent of inverse transformations may be achieved).

For two reasons, sets are an adequate data structure for storing presuppositions during the computation: No presuppositions interact with each other in elementary (unembedded) sentences. For embedded sentences, a simple tree transformation depending upon the embedding predicate gives the set of presuppositions at the current sentential level from the sets of presuppositions of embedded sentences.

Presuppositions are added to the set in one of three ways. First, those arising from syntactic constructs are added as soon as the construct has been parsed. Second, when a word having a presupposition is encountered, a tree transformation is retrieved from the lexical entry and added to the set of such tree transformations. At the completion of parsing at the current level, the tree transformations are performed, yielding presuppositions from lexical entries. Third, after parsing the sentence at the current level including all of its embedded sentences, the appropriate tree transformation is applied to the sets computed for embedded sentences, thereby computing the effect of the embedding on presuppositions. The first two ways are discussed in Sections 2.1 and 2.2, the third in Section 4.

2.1 Presuppositions from Syntactic Constructs

There are two keys to understanding how to compute presuppositions that arise from syntactic constructs. One is that since they arise from syntactic constructs, their occurrence is syntactically marked. Suppose we construct the ATN graph such that there is a path which corresponds exactly to that syntactic construct; that is, the path is taken if and only if those syntactic clues for that construct are present. Then, we can associate with the arcs of that path a function to select the proper well-formed subformula and apply the proper tree transformation to it.

The second key is that when there is ambiguity, when two different syntactic constructs yield the same surface sentence but differ in presuppositions, the responsibility of any parser and of our system is not to resolve all ambiguity, but to be able to generate both readings so that semantic and pragmatic components can choose between them.

Two examples are cleft sentences and definite noun phrases. The cleft sentences, with a noun phrase extracted, are represented by the following path, where REL represents relative clause and the double circle indicates final state.

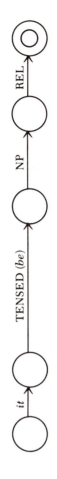

A cleft sentence presupposes that there is some individual (person or thing) having the property mentioned in the relative clause REL. To obtain the semantic representation of the relative clause, the binding of the variable representing the noun phrase must be changed to that of a constant representing "some individual." Associating this new binding with the representation of the relative clause gives the semantic representation of the presupposition. Since the REL arc computes the representation of the relative clause, the binding can be changed as an action of that arc, and the new presupposition added to the set of presuppositions.

A second example is noun phrases whose determiner is *the*. (Possessives and noun phrases with relative clauses are other definite noun phrases having presuppositions; the system handles these in an analogous way.) A noun phrase such as *the extremely big, red dog* presupposes that *there is an extremely big, red dog* in the shared information of the dialogue participants. In a function argument notation we might represent this as (L).

(L):   (binding (*UNTENSED (IN-THE-SHARED-INFO variable)))

IN-THE-SHARED-INFO is a predicate meaning "in the shared information of the dialogue participants"; the *UNTENSED indicates that the tense is not known. If "binding" gives the binding of "variable," then we need to fill in "binding" with the semantic representation of the noun phrase itself except that an existential quantifier replaces the determiner (quantifier) *the*.

Thus, after parsing noun phrases with determiners, the corresponding path must check to see if the determiner of the head noun is *the*. If it is, a presupposition is generated by replacing that determiner by the existential quantifier, and by embedding that semantic representation in the place of "binding" in (L) and by replacing "variable" in (L) by the variable assigned to the noun phrase as a whole. This presupposition is added to the set of presuppositions and returned among the values of the noun phrase graph.

2.2. Presuppositions from Lexical Entries

The organization of lexical entries is patterned after the linguistic string parser (Sager, 1967, 1973, and Grishman, 1973), which has a lexicon of 9000 words and has been very successful. The linguistic string parser relies on restrictions placed on co-occurring constituents; these can be encoded in an ATN via the conditions on arcs.

In the linguistic string parser each word is classified into one or more hierarchically arranged subcategories. The characterization is so precise that one may compute both the constituents with which a subcategory can co-occur and the syntactic paraphrases that are possible. Another feature of the subcategories is that words having affixes are associated with their stem words.

In the lexical entry for a word, we must encode the tree transformation for a particular presupposition. The left hand side of a tree transformation gives the pattern to be matched and names for the subtrees which are to be manipulated. We have found that the pattern is encoded by the lexical subcategories of the linguistic string parser and the constituents with which they can co-occur. Therefore, by associating the right-hand side of the transformation with the word plus lexical subcategory, pattern matching occurs naturally as the ATN parses the sentence. Since my ATN parser assigns pieces of semantic representation to registers according to logical role in the sentence rather than syntactic role, the naming of subtrees involved in the transformation occurs automatically in parsing according to a convention for naming the logical roles.

Thus, we need only store the right-hand side of the transformation under the word plus syntactic category. The function BUILD of the ATN is a natural choice to encode the right-hand side, for it offers a general way to combine subtrees to form a new tree. However, the restriction that BUILD use only the contents of registers to fill "vacant slots" is too rigid. For instance, (2a) presupposes (2b).

(2)   a. *John stopped running at noon.*
      b. *At a time immediately before noon, John had been running.*

Corresponding to *a time immediately before noon,* a new variable must be generated for the logical notation. This cannot be part of the representation of (2a), and is therefore not available as a register in the augmented transition network. Thus, the computation is not merely a composition of the contents of registers. The function we need is similar to BUILD, but the list elements for filling "vacant slots" in the tree may be any computable function of the contents of the registers.

We may call this new function NEWBUILD. It has one argument, a list (*L1, L2, L3, . . . , Ln*), where *L*1 is the tree structure and each *Li, i* > 1, is evaluated to fill the slots.

This allows more complex computations than tree transformations. However, in all cases the arguments specifying what subtrees to insert are simply register names or else the LISP function that generates a unique variable for the logical notation. Therefore, the computation is like that of a tree transformation.

As an example, the verb *resent* presupposes that its logical subject is human, and that the embedded sentence is true. For instance, (3) presupposes (4) and (5).

(3)   *John resented that he was forced to move.*

(4)   *John is human.*

(5)   *John was forced to move.*

In the lexical entry for *resent* (taking a *that SENTENCE* complement) we would have a list consisting of elements (6) and (7).

(6)   ((*UNTENSED (HUMAN +)) LSUBJ);

(7)   (+ COMP).

For Sentence (3), register LSUBJ, the logical subject, would be *John.* Thus, NEWBUILD applied to (6) yields (*UNTENSED (HUMAN John)), which may be paraphrased *John be* (unknown tense) *human.* For Sentence (3), COMP, containing the embedded complement sentence, is *John was forced to move,* which is also the result of applying NEWBUILD to (7).

Sentence (2) provides an example that the computation of presupposition is not merely manipulation and composition of the contents of ATN registers. Sections 2.2.1–2.2.4 present other complex aspects of the computation. For the remainder of Section 2, I adopt a convention that a sentence labeled (a) presupposes a sentence labeled (b).

2.2.1. INTERNAL AND EXTERNAL NEGATION

There are at least two types of negation in language. With internal negation, only the assertion of the affirmative form of the sentence is negated. For instance, the sentence *Mary did not leave when John came,* would normally be interpreted as *At the time John came, Mary did not leave. John came* is presupposed, demonstrating that presuppositions are not affected by internal negation. External negation denies at least one of the presuppositions of the affirmative form of the sentence. For instance, the previous sentence in the context of (8) does not presuppose that John came.

(8) HERMAN: *Did Mary leave when John came?*
     FRANK: *Mary did not leave when John came, because John never came.*

Context determines which interpretation is intended. My system is written to compute (if need be) both interpretations for negation. Selection of an intended reading would occur in a pragmatic component, designed for all context-dependent computations. My system has not implemented a pragmatic component.

2.2.2. ASSIGNING TENSE

Assigning the proper tense to a presupposition can be crucial semantically, as example (9) demonstrates.

(9) a. *John stopped beating Mary at 10:00.*
    b. *Immediately before 10:00, John had been beating Mary.*

The tense of a presupposition seems to be completely determined by the tense of the surface sentence and the lexical item which has the presupposition. Thus, for each presupposition, one can associate a function whose argument is the tense of the surface sentence. Each such function has a name; we have chosen the class of names $*TENSEi*$, where i is a positive integer.

Let L be the lexical entry to generate a particular presupposition, represented as a tree. In L, place the name of the appropriate tense function $*TENSEi*$ where the tense should appear in the complete presupposition. By definition NEWBUILD will not move the atom $*TENSEi*$. If we define a function APPLYTENSE to search for any $*TENSEi*$, apply that function name to a tense, and insert the result in the tree where $*TENSEi*$ is, then

$$\text{APPLYTENSE (NEWBUILD}(L), \text{tense)}$$

gives the properly tensed presupposition. ("Tense" is assumed to be the tense at this sentential level.) This solves the problem of assigning tense to presuppositions.

2.2.3. EFFECT OF SYNTACTIC ENVIRONMENT

The syntactic environment of a word can affect whether it has a presupposition, thus, differentiating shades of meaning. For instance, (10a) presupposes (10b), but (11) has no such presupposition.

(10) a. *John knows that Henry is coming.*
     b. *Henry is coming.*

(11) *John knows whether Henry is coming.*

The lexical subcategories (of the linguistic string parser [Anderson, 1970]), that are assigned to a word provide a way to compute the syntactic environments in which a word may occur. We have found that where the syntactic environment differentiates between a sense of a word having a presupposition and one which does not, there are two different syntactic subcategories of the word. (Or, where this is not the case, we may further subdivide the subcategory to make it so.) Corresponding to two different syntactic subcategories of the word, there are two different paths in the ATN graph. After completing the parse at the current sentential level, the path taken determines which of the two syntactic subcategories of the word was used. Thus, ASSOCIATING PRESUPPOSITIONAL ENTRIES IN THE LEXICON WITH THE WORD AND ITS SYNTACTIC SUBCATEGORY IS A SOLUTION TO THE EFFECT OF SYNTACTIC ENVIRONMENT ON COMPUTATION OF PRESUPPOSITIONS.

For example, *know* has at least two syntactic subcategories: one corresponding to "that SENTENCE" as complement, and one corresponding to "whether SENTENCE or not" as complement. With the first syntactic subcategory we would associate a lexical entry for presuppositions; with the second, the lexical entry would be empty. This is analogous to having two senses of *know*: $know_1$ and $know_2$. Figure 1a shows an operation that gives the presupposition of $know_1$.

(a)

(This is not a tree transformation.)

(b)

FIGURE 1

Traversing the path in Figure 1b enables the ATN to recognize that *know*$_1$ is intended in the sentence. NEWBUILD and APPLYTENSE, as described earlier, perform the equivalent of the operation in Figure 1a at the end of the path in Figure 1b.

2.2.4. Stem Words and Affixes

In the lexicon, one would like to have as little redundant information as possible for words that are derivatives of some stem. As mentioned earlier the lexical subcategories relate words with affixes to their stem words. Since we associate the presuppositional information in the lexicon with the word plus its subcategory, we have been able to relate the similar presuppositions of words such as *disappoint, disappointed,* and *disappointment.* In many instances, one need only have a pointer to the stem word in the lexicon, rather than having the lexical information replicated.

3. COMPUTING ENTAILMENTS

The computation of entailments is more complex than it is for presuppositions because the computation depends on the presence or absence of negation. For instance, sentence (12a) entails (12b), but (13) has no entailment. Throughout the remainder of this section, an (a) sentence entails a (b) sentence.

(12)   a. *John was not able to leave.*
        b. *John did not leave.*

(13)   *John was able to leave.*

Karttunen (1970) studies the effect of negation on the entailments of numerous lexical items.

A chain of entailments must be computed, because entailments at a given sentential level in the semantic representation may be affected by embedding predicates and syntactic structures arbitrarily many levels above the current one. For instance, (15a) entails (15b) and (15c), since (15b) entails (15c). However, from (14a), one cannot conclude anything about whether Mary won.

(14)   a. *It is false that John prevented Mary from winning.*
        b. *John did not prevent Mary from winning.*

(15)   a. *It is true that John prevented Mary from winning.*

b. *John prevented Mary from winning.*
        c. *Mary did not win.*

The embedded sentences of (14a) or (15a) could have been preposed, therefore the computation must wait until the entire sentence is traversed. A tree is built during the parse; every node in the tree corresponds to a propositional or sentential level. Upon reaching the period (or question mark) marking the end of the sentence, the information in the tree is used to compute the chain of entailments.

At each node of the tree, three units of information are needed: an atom indicating whether there is negation present in the surface sentence at this sentential level, the surface tense (if any) at this level, and a list of the lexical entries for potential entailed propositions arising from words at this level. After parsing the complete sentence, a function CHAIN of three arguments is applied to each node of the tree. The arguments are the tree just described, an atom indicating whether negation is passed from the higher sentential level, and the tense from a higher level. The function computes entailments by checking the negation requirements of the possible entailments at this level against the negation actually present. If the negation conditions of none of the possible entailments at this level are satisfied, the remainder of the subtree is ignored. This corresponds to the fact that (14a) entails nothing about whether Mary won or not. I shall refer to this tree as a **TREE OF POTENTIAL ENTAILMENTS.**

The tree is formed in the following way. One of the entities returned from any embedded sentence is the tree constructed from that sentence. Each tree is stored in a list according to logical role rather than syntactic order. As each word that could have entailments is encountered at this sentential level, its lexical information is added to a set of such information at this level. At the end of this level, each member of this set is modified by applying NEWBUILD to its argument in the member. Also, an atom telling whether or not negation is present at this level and the surface tense at this level is added, forming a new node of the tree.

The lexical information for entailments is associated with the word plus subcategory, just as it was for presupposition. The information is a set of elements, one element per possible entailment.

For each set element, four items are necessary. The first is an atom indicating whether negation must be present or absent. The second is the argument to NEWBUILD, which will yield the logical form of the potential entailment. The third item is an atom indicating whether the entailed proposition would be positive or negative. This is necessary to verify that the negation conditions are satisfied for potential entailments of embedded sentences. The fourth unit is necessary for predicates which have two embedded sentences. It is an atom indicating whether the left or right subtree is associated with the entailment (for purposes of continuing the chain of entailments).

In addition to the effect of negation, there are two other phenomena that prevent potential entailments from being added to the set of entailments of a sentence.

3.1 Blocking Entailments

Examples (16) and (17) demonstrate the behavior of *prevent* with respect to negation.

(16)   a. *John prevented Mary from leaving.*
       b. *Mary did not leave.*

(17)   *John did not prevent Mary from leaving.*

(18)   *Did John prevent Mary from leaving?*

(19)   *I ask you whether John prevented Mary from leaving.*

If the proposition of (16a) is asked as a yes–no question or embedded in a "whether" clause, as in (18) and (19), there is no entailment corresponding to *prevent*. This is due to the dependence of entailment on negation.

Modeling this computationally is straightforward. In a yes–no question, the tree of potential entailments at the top sentential level is simply the null tree. Similarly, the sentential level of a "whether" clause has the null tree as well. However, entailments of embedded sentences must still be computed, as Section 3.2 demonstrates.

3.2. Promoting Entailments to Presuppositions

Any entailment of a presupposition is also a presupposition. Since (20) presupposes (16a), (16b) is also presupposed by (20).

(20)   *Did John know that he prevented Mary from leaving?*

The entailment of *prevent* has been promoted to a presupposition, because of the meaning of *know*.

A way to reflect this is to add an entailment entry in the lexicon under *know* and its appropriate subcategory. However, the negation condition would be *T*, for universally true. At the end of the current sentential level, the system checks the set of possible entailments for

any condition marked *T*. If it finds one, the subtree of potential entailments is used to calculate the entailments immediately and add them to the set of presuppositions. The subtree is then set to null.

That is a way to compute entailments promoted to presuppositions because of the effect of lexical items. A similar computation occurs for the effect of syntactic constructs having presuppositions; rather than marking the lexical entry, the path of that syntactic construct is appropriately marked.

4. COMPOUND SENTENCES

The search for a recursive rule that would give the presuppositions and entailments of a compound sentence from those of its embedded sentences has been called the PROJECTION PROBLEM. A solution has evolved over several years. It is summarized in Joshi and Weischedel (1977); a more thorough account appears in Weischedel (1975).

The solution involves placing the predicates that take embedded sentences in four classes: holes, speech acts, predicates of propositional attitude, and connectives. Associated with each class is a simple structural computation which gives the presuppositions and entailments of the compound from those of its embedded sentences. The lexicon records to which of the four classes each such predicate belongs.

The parser is designed such that a "pushdown" occurs whenever an embedded proposition is expected, whether or not it has the syntactic form of a sentence. The set of presuppositions and the tree of potential entailments of the embedded proposition are returned as values. At the end of the sentence at the current level, the recursive rule or projection rule is applied. First, I describe the rule for presuppositions, then the one for entailments.

4.1. Presuppositions

The broadest of the four classes of predicates has been called HOLES, because presuppositions of embedded sentences become presuppositions of the compound. *Regret*, *fail*, and *begin* are just a few predicates in this class. Numerous examples of this class and the other classes may be found in Karttunen (1973). For this class, presuppositions of embedded sentences are merely added to the set of the current level.

The two classes of speech acts and of predicates of propositional attitude exhibit similar behavior. Speech acts are verbs of saying. Predicates of propositional attitude include verbs such as *think* and *hope*. Presuppositions of sentences embedded under these predicates become presuppositions of the compound, but under the speaker's claims (for speech acts) or the actor's "beliefs" (for predicates of propositional attitude). For instance, (21a) presupposes (21b), not (21c).

(21) a. *John said that Mary regretted that she left.*
      b. *John claimed Mary left.*
      c. *Mary left.*

To reflect this, every presupposition of a sentence embedded under a speech act becomes embedded under a predicate *CLAIM*, which is a semantic primitive; the logical subject of the speech act is an additional argument to *CLAIM*. For predicates of propositional attitude, the same computation occurs, except using a primitive *BELIEVE*.

An exception to this case arises with presuppositions that definite noun phrases have referents. When the noun phrase makes transparent reference (that is, all participants in the communication agree that there is a referent), those presuppositions are not embedded under the speaker's claims. Opaque reference is the case of the referent existing only in the world of the speaker or actor; in this case, presuppositions of definite noun phrases must be embedded under the speaker's claims or actor's beliefs.

We can easily separate those presuppositions that pertain to existence of referents of noun phrases, because they arise from syntactically distinguished strings. The projection algorithm must generate two interpretations. The one corresponding to opaque reference embeds all presuppositions of embedded sentences in the world of the speaker's claims or the world of the actor's beliefs (for predicates of propositional attitude). The interpretation corresponding to transparent reference embeds only the subset of presuppositions not pertaining to noun phrases under the speaker's claims or actor's beliefs; each member of the subset pertaining to noun phrases becomes a presupposition of the compound without such embedding.

A fourth class is connectives, such as *and*, *or*, and *if . . . then . . . .* As in the previous paragraphs, presuppositions of embedded sentences become presuppositions of the compound, but embedded under a world created by the connective. For instance, presuppositions of *if A then B* (interpreted as material implication) are the presuppositions of A plus all propositions *if A then C*, where C is a presupposition of B. (Examples involving other connectives appear in Joshi and Weischedel, 1977, and Karttunen, 1973).

4.2. Entailments

A significant new contribution of the research was demonstrating that the analysis for presuppositions carries over to entailments, subject to the constraint that the negation conditions are satisfied. Therefore, the projection algorithm acts on the tree of potential entailments, rather than a set as in the case of presuppositions.

For the class of predicates which are holes, the tree of potential entailments for the embedded sentence is unchanged, and becomes a subtree at the current level as described earlier.

For speech acts and predicates of propositional attitude, entailments of embedded sentences must be embedded under the speaker's claims (for speech acts) or the actor's beliefs (for predicates of propositional attitude). However, the speech act or predicate of propositional attitude itself has negation conditions on the embedded entailment becoming an entailment of the compound sentence. For instance, (22a) entails (22b). When part of a compound as in (23a), (23b) is entailed. However, (24) has no such entailment.

(22) a. *John forced Mary to leave.*
      b. *Mary left.*

(23) a. *Jack said that John forced Mary to leave.*
      b. *Jack claimed Mary left.*

(24) *Jack did not say that John forced Mary to leave.*

To account for this, the projection algorithm modifies the tree of potential entailments from embedded sentences; each potential entailment in the tree must be embedded under a predicate *CLAIM* (for speech acts) with an additional argument specifying the speaker. For predicates of propositional attitude, potential entailments are embedded under a predicate *BELIEVE*, with an additional argument specifying the speaker.

To account for the negation conditions of the speech act or predicate of propositional attitude, we can encode these negation conditions in the lexicon for each such predicate with the same four units of information described in Section 3. In this case, the proposition entailed by a speech act or predicate of propositional attitude is the trivial, universally true proposition T.

The fourth class of embedding predicates is the connectives. A and B entails A, B and the entailments of each. However, if A and B is negated as in I doubt that A and B, none of the entailments of A or of B become entailments of the whole. For material implication, if B entails C, then the entailments of if A then B, are of the form if A then C.

By now, the projection rule for connectives should be clear, for the phenomena to account for are analogous to those for speech acts. For *if A then B*, we embed each entailment in the list or tree structure in (25).

(25)   (IF *a c*)

Of course, *a* is a register containing the semantic representation of *A*, and *c* contains a potentially entailed proposition of *B*.

There are negation conditions for *and* and *or* just as there were for speech acts and predicates of propositional attitude. The type of lexical entry described for speech acts will work for the connectives as well.

5. A SUGGESTION ABOUT THE LEXICON

I have demonstrated here and in Joshi and Weischedel (1977) that the presuppositions and entailments for a given interpretation or reading of a sentence may be computed independent of nonstructural context. As the parser generates the various readings of a sentence, my system computes the presuppositions and entailments for each reading. Of course, since context alters which reading is intended by a speaker or author, the presuppositions and entailments alter depending on context. In my computation, the lexicon contains the information used to compute those presuppositions and entailments associated with particular words.

THIS LEADS ME TO SUGGEST THAT THE TEST OF WHAT SHOULD BE INCLUDED IN A PARSER AND ITS ASSOCIATED LEXICON IS WHETHER THE LANGUAGE PHENOMENON IS INDEPENDENT OF NONSTRUCTURAL CONTEXT. If it is independent of nonstructural context, then it may be included.

Similar principles have been implicit in the design of the lexicon of the linguistic string parser, described in Section 2. It is based on a theory of grammar by Harris (1970). The empirical basis of his model is not acceptability itself, but rather whether hypothesized syntactic transformations preserve the acceptability or unacceptability of sentences. That empirical test largely factors out the effect of nonstructural context. (This theory of grammar has been studied formally in Joshi, Kosaraju, and Yamada, 1972, and its relation to transformational grammar has been considered in Joshi, 1973.)

To summarize, I suggest that the test of what should be included in a parser and its associated lexicon is whether the phenomenon is independent of nonstructural context. Presupposition and entailment have this property.

6. CONCLUSION

This chapter has demonstrated how a parser, written as an augmented transition network, and its associated lexicon may compute the presuppositions and entailments of a sentence. The system achieves this by computing them for each reading or interpretation of a sentence as the parser generates the various readings. The computation is structural in nature, using tree transformations. Presupposition and entailment are examples of semantic information that may appropriately be included in a parser. A solution for the projection problem for presuppositions has been included in the system. Furthermore, that solution has been extended to include entailments.

This chapter has described a concrete computational model of computing presuppositions and entailments of sentences, and has sketched in Section 1 how interacting computational processes might predict the diverse phenomena of presupposition, which embrace semantics and pragmatics. I feel that interacting computational processes potentially offer powerful means for modeling linguistic phenomena, such as anaphora, paraphrase, contradiction, presupposition, entailment, and discourse. This is important since many linguistic phenomena embrace aspects of each of syntax, semantics, and pragmatics.

APPENDIX A

Compared to grammars appearing in linguistic literature, this one is of modest size. However, since it is patterned after a subset of the lexicon of the linguistic string parser of Sager, it is very general in nature. Furthermore, compared to many grammars that have been implemented on a computer, it is somewhat extensive.

Since one way to evaluate a natural language system is by the extent and complexity of syntactic constructions in the system, this appendix specifies a context-free language which includes all sentences the system is prepared to handle. The context-free language is specified by a recursive transition network (Woods, 1970).

A recursive transition network (RTN) is a generalization of a finite-state machine. An RTN is a graph with labeled states, labeled directed arcs, a distinguished start state, and a subset of final states. Arc labels may be either terminal symbols or state names. An input string of terminal symbols is accepted by an RTN if there is a path from the start state to the final state which consumes the string. A transition from one state to another in such a path may be made in one of two ways: (*a*) an arc labeled by a terminal symbol is taken if that terminal is currently pointed to in the input string; (*b*) an arc labeled by a state name is taken if there is a substring beginning at the current symbol in the input such that the substring is accepted by a path from the state named on the arc to a final state.

I have used the following nonterminals to represent syntactic categories (which would appear in the lexicon for a word). This is a shorthand for a subgraph of two states; the first state being labeled by that syntactic category, and the second state being a final state. The arcs between the two states would each be labeled by a word in the lexicon having that syntactic category.

V	verb
VN	nominalized verb
VEN	past participle of verb
VING	present participle of verb
PRO	pronoun
DET	determiner
TITLE	title
A	adjective
D	adverb
N	noun
P	preposition

The six graphs are DS for declaratives, NP for noun phrases, LS for subject shapes, OBJ for object shapes, POBJ for passive forms of object shapes, and $T(x)$ for tensed verbs x.

All items in lower case are constants. All upper case items are state names, corresponding to nonterminal symbols. Some special symbols follow:

λ	null symbol, that is, a jump
/s	ending for plural nouns or present tense, third person, singular
*poss	possessive ending

only or by relative clauses. The $T(x)$ graph assumes that when it is called, it has been given (via SENDR) a particular syntactic subcategory or stem word to match, specified as x.

DS (DECLARATIVE SENTENCES)

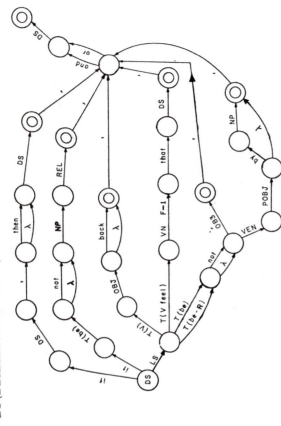

NP (NOUN PHRASES)

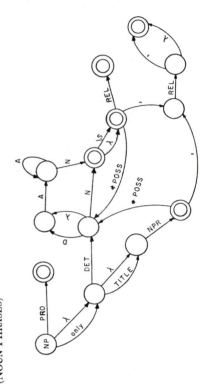

I have not included in this appendix graphs for relative clauses or questions (although these are included in the system); the reader can easily ascertain the relative clause and question constructions allowable from the DS, LS, OBJ, and POBJ graphs, by extraction of a noun phrase.

The nonterminal S–NP refers to any noun phrase not modified by

POBJ (OBJECT SHAPES FOR PASSIVE SENTENCES)

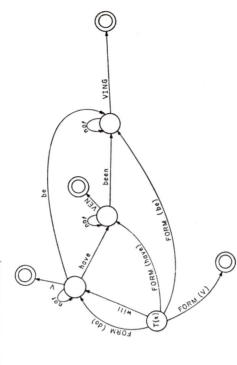

T(x) (TENSED ELEMENTS)

LS (SUBJECT SHAPES)

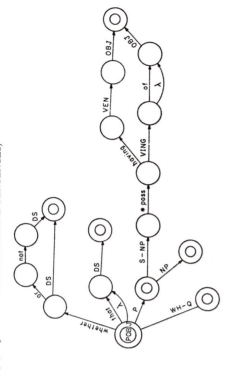

OBJ AND OB3 (OBJECT SHAPES)

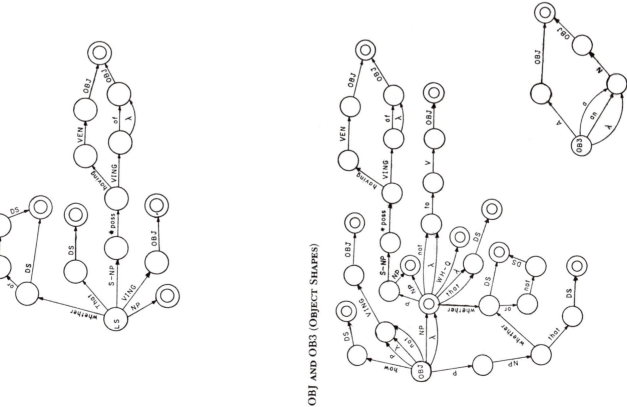

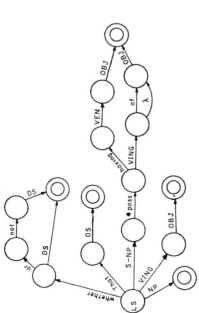

APPENDIX B: SAMPLE OUTPUT

Several example sentences are presented here with their computed presuppositions and entailments. The semantic representations used follow those suggested by Keenan (1972). It is a predicate and argument notation, encoded as list structures. The predicate is the first argument of a list and its arguments are the remaining list elements. The bindings (corresponding to noun phrases) for variables are encoded in lists one at a time. If *b* is a binding and *r* is a sentence in this notation, the sentence with the additional binding is (*b r*).

In the output, periods and commas are preceded by a slash because of LISP conventions. The input sentence appears first followed by a semantic representation of it.

The two sets of presuppositions computed are labeled NON-NP PRESUPPOSITIONS, those not associated with noun phrases, and NP-RELATED PRESUPPOSITIONS, those corresponding to the referents of noun phrases. Entailments are printed last. For presuppositions and entailments, the semantic representation of the proposition is printed first, followed by a simple translation to English. The symbol -UNTENSED- indicates that the tense of the proposition is not known.

Example 1 illustrates the presupposition of a *wh* question. Almost all of the examples include presuppositions of definite noun phrases. Examples 2 and 3 reflect the effect of syntactic environment on whether the predicate *be a problem* has a presupposition. Examples 4 and 5 show entailments corresponding to *force* and *prevent*. Example 6 is a yes–no question; the entailment of *continue* is therefore blocked, but the presupposition of *continue* remains. Examples 7 and 8 illustrate the projection algorithm.

Example 1

WHO TRANSLATED THE ASSIGNMENT?

SEMANTIC REPRESENTATION

((THE ASSIGNMENT /, X0077) ((E ONE /, X0076) (ASK I YOU (WH-SOME X0076 (IN-THE-PAST (TRANSLATE X0076 X0077))))))

NON-NP PRESUPPOSITIONS

NP-RELATED PRESUPPOSITIONS

((E ASSIGNMENT /, X0077) (*UNTENSED (IN-THE-SHARED-INFO X0077)))
SOME ASSIGNMENT EXIST -UNTENSED- IN THE SHARED INFORMATION.

((THE ASSIGNMENT /, X0077) ((E ONE /, X0076) (IN-THE-PAST (TRANSLATE X0076 X0077))))

SOME, ONE TRANSLATED THE ASSIGNMENT.

ENTAILMENTS

Example 2

THAT THE DISCUSSIONS ARE IRRELEVANT IS A PROBLEM /.

SEMANTIC REPRESENTATION

(((COLLECTIVE DISCUSSION /, X0013) (NUMBER X0013 TWO-OR-MORE)) /, X0014) (ASSERT I (IN-THE-PRESENT (PROBLEM (FACT (IN-THE-PRESENT (NOT (RELEVANT X0014))))))))

NON-NP PRESUPPOSITIONS

(((((COLLECTIVE DISCUSSION /, X0013) (NUMBER X0013 TWO-OR-MORE)) /, X0014) (IN-THE-PRESENT (NOT (RELEVANT X0014)))))
THE DISCUSSIONS ARE IRRELEVANT.

NP-RELATED PRESUPPOSITIONS

((((E DISCUSSION /, X0013) (NUMBER X0013 TWO-OR-MORE)) /, X0014) (*UN-TENSED (IN-THE-SHARED-INFO X0014)))
SOME DISCUSSIONS EXIST -UNTENSED- IN THE SHARED INFORMATION.

ENTAILMENTS

Example 3

WHETHER THE DISCUSSIONS ARE IRRELEVANT IS A PROBLEM /.

SEMANTIC REPRESENTATION

(((((COLLECTIVE DISCUSSION /, X0017) (NUMBER X0017) TWO-OR-MORE)) /, X0018) (ASSERT I (IN-THE-PRESENT (PROBLEM (WHE (IN-THE-PRESENT (NOT (RELEVANT X0018)))))))))

NON-NP PRESUPPOSITIONS

NP-RELATED PRESUPPOSITIONS

((((E DISCUSSION /, X0017) (NUMBER X0017 TWO-OR-MORE)) /, X0018) (*UNTENSED (IN-THE-SHARED-INFO X0018)))
SOME DISCUSSIONS EXIST -UNTENSED- IN THE SHARED INFORMATION.

ENTAILMENTS

Example 4

MARY WAS FORCED TO LEAVE /.

SEMANTIC REPRESENTATION

((MARY /, X0052) (ASSERT I (IN-THE-PAST (CAUSE NIL (COME-ABOUT (EVENT (LEAVE X0052))))))

NON-NP PRESUPPOSITIONS

NP-RELATED PRESUPPOSITIONS

((MARY /, X0052) (*UNTENSED (IN-THE-SHARED-INFO X0052)))
MARY EXIST -UNTENSED- IN THE SHARED INFORMATION.

ENTAILMENTS

((MARY /, X0052) (IN-THE-PAST (LEAVE X0052)))
MARY LEFT.

Example 5

THE CROWDED LECTURES PREVENTED THE STUDENTS FROM LEARNING /.

SEMANTIC REPRESENTATION

(((((COLLECTIVE STUDENT /, X0059) (NUMBER X0059 TWO-OR-MORE)) /, X0060) ((((((COLLECTIVE LECTURE /, X0056) (CROWDED X0056)) /, X0057) (NUMBER X0057 TWO-OR-MORE)) /, X0058) (ASSERT I (IN-THE-PAST (CAUSE X0058 (NOT (COME-ABOUT (EVENT (LEARN X0060 NIL)))))))))

NON-NP PRESUPPOSITIONS

NP-RELATED PRESUPPOSITIONS

((((E LECTURE /, X0056) (CROWDED X0056)) /, X0057) (NUMBER X0057 TWO-OR-MORE)) /, X0058) (*UNTENSED (IN-THE-SHARED-INFO X0058)))
SOME CROWDED LECTURES EXIST -UNTENSED- IN THE SHARED INFORMA-TION.

((((E STUDENT /, X0059) (NUMBER X0059 TWO-OR-MORE)) /, X0060) (*UN-TENSED (IN-THE-SHARED-INFO X0060)))
SOME STUDENTS EXIST -UNTENSED- IN THE SHARED INFORMATION.

ENTAILMENTS

(((((COLLECTIVE STUDENT /, X0059) (NUMBER X0059 TWO-OR-MORE)) /, X0060) (NOT (IN-THE-PAST (LEARN X0060 NIL))))
IT IS NOT THE CASE THAT THE STUDENTS LEARNED.

Example 6

DID MARY CONTINUE STRIKING JOHN?

SEMANTIC REPRESENTATION

((JOHN /, X0109) ((MARY /, X0108) (ASK I YOU (WHE (IN-THE-PAST (CONTINUE (EVENT (STRIKE X0108 X0109)) NIL))))))

NON-NP PRESUPPOSITIONS

((JOHN /, X0109) ((MARY /, X0108) (((E TIME /, X0108) ((((E TIME /, X0110) (IMMEDIATELY-BEFORE X0110 NIL)) /, X0111) (AT-TIME (IN-THE-PAST (HAVE-EN (BE-ING (STRIKE X0108 X0109)))) X0111)))))
MARY HAD BEEN STRIKING JOHN.

NP-RELATED PRESUPPOSITIONS

((MARY /, X0108) (*UNTENSED (IN-THE-SHARED-INFO X0108)))
MARY EXIST -UNTENSED- IN THE SHARED INFORMATION.

((JOHN /, X0109) (*UNTENSED (IN-THE-SHARED-INFO X0109)))
JOHN EXIST -UNTENSED- IN THE SHARED INFORMATION.

ENTAILMENTS

Example 7

THE PROFESSOR DOUBTED THAT JOHN MANAGED TO TRANSLATE AN AS-SIGNMENT /.

SEMANTIC REPRESENTATION

((E ASSIGNMENT /, X0042) (JOHN /, X0041) ((THE PROFESSOR /, X0039) (ASSERT I (IN-THE-PAST (BELIEVE X0039 (NOT (IN-THE-PAST (COME-ABOUT (EVENT (TRANSLATE X0041 X0042)))))))))

NON-NP PRESUPPOSITIONS

((THE PROFESSOR /, X0039) (*UNTENSED (HUMAN X0039)))
THE PROFESSOR BE -UNTENSED- HUMAN.

((E ASSIGNMENT /, X0042) (JOHN /, X0041) ((THE PROFESSOR /, X0039) (IN-THE-PAST (BELIEVE X0039) (IN THE PAST (ATTEMPT (EVENT (TRANSLATE X0041 X0042)))))))
THE PROFESSOR BELIEVED THAT JOHN ATTEMPTED TO TRANSLATE SOME ASSIGNMENT.

NP-RELATED PRESUPPOSITIONS

((E PROFESSOR /, X0039) (*UNTENSED (IN-THE-SHARED-INFO X0039)))
SOME PROFESSOR EXIST -UNTENSED- IN THE SHARED INFORMATION.

((JOHN /, X0041) (*UNTENSED (IN-THE-SHARED-INFO X0041)))
JOHN EXIST -UNTENSED- IN THE SHARED INFORMATION.

ENTAILMENTS

((E ASSIGNMENT /, X0042) (JOHN /, X0041) ((THE PROFESSOR /, X0039) (IN-THE-PAST (BELIEVE X0039) (NOT (IN-THE-PAST (TRANSLATE X0041 X0042))))))
THE PROFESSOR BELIEVED THAT IT IS NOT THE CASE THAT JOHN TRANS-LATED SOME ASSIGNMENT.

Example 8

JOHN WON /, AND MARY FELT DISAPPOINTMENT THAT HE WON /.

SEMANTIC REPRESENTATION

((MARY /, X0050) ((JOHN /, X0048) (ASSERT I (AND (IN-THE-PAST (WIN X0048)) (IN-THE-PAST (DISAPPOINT (FACT (IN-THE-PAST (WIN X0048))) X0050)))))

NON-NP PRESUPPOSITIONS

((JOHN /, X0048) (IF-THEN (IN-THE-PAST (WIN X0048)) (IN-THE-PAST (WIN X0048))))

IF JOHN WON THEN JOHN WON.

((MARY /, X0050) ((JOHN /, X0048) (IF-THEN (IN-THE-PAST (WIN X0048)) (*UNTENSED (HUMAN X0050)))))

IF JOHN WON THEN MARY BE -UNTENSED- HUMAN.

NP-RELATED PRESUPPOSITIONS

((JOHN /, X0048) (*UNTENSED (IN-THE-SHARED-INFO X0048)))

JOHN EXIST -UNTENSED- IN THE SHARED INFORMATION.

((JOHN /, X0048) (IF-THEN (IN-THE-PAST (WIN X0048)) ((MARY /, X0050) (*UNTENSED (IN-THE-SHARED-INFO X0050)))))

IF JOHN WON THEN MARY EXIST -UNTENSED- IN THE SHARED INFORMATION.

ENTAILMENTS

((JOHN /, X0048) (IN-THE-PAST (WIN X0048)))

JOHN WON.

((MARY /, X0050) ((JOHN /, X0048) (IN-THE-PAST (DISAPPOINT (FACT (IN-THE-PAST (WIN X0048)) X0050)))))

THE FACT THAT JOHN WON DISAPPOINTED MARY.

REFERENCES

Anderson, B., Transformationally based english strings and their word subclasses. *String Program Reports No. 7.* New York: Linguistics String Project, New York University, 1970.

Charniak, E., Inference and knowledge I. In E. Charniak and Y. Wilks, (Eds.), *Computational semantics.* Amsterdam: North-Holland, 1976.

Clark, H. H., and Haviland, S. E., Comprehension and the given-new contract. In R. Freedle, (Ed.), *Discourse production and comprehension.* Hillside, New Jersey: Lawrence Erlbaum Associates, 1977.

Fillmore, C. J., Verbs of judging: An exercise in semantic description. In C. J. Fillmore and D. T. Langendoen (Eds.), *Studies in linguistic semantics.* New York: Holt, 1971.

Fitzpatrick, E. and Sager, N., The lexical subclasses of the linguistic string parser. *American Journal of Computational Linguistics,* 1974, *1,* microfiche 2.

Givón, T., The time-axis phenomenon. *Language,* 1973, *49,* 890–925.

Grishman, R., Implementation of the string parser of English. In R. Rustin (Ed.), *Natural language processing.* New York: Algorithmics Press, 1973.

Harris, Z. S., Two systems of grammar: Report and paraphrase. In Z. S. Harris (Ed.), *Structural and transformational linguistics.* Dordrecht, Holland: D. Reidel, 1970.

Joshi, A. K., A class of transformational grammars. In M. Gross, M. Halle, and M. Schutzenberger (Eds.), *Formal analysis of natural language.* Amsterdam: North-Holland, 1973.

Joshi, A. K., and Weischedel, R. M., Computation of a subclass of inferences: Presupposition and entailment. *American Journal of Computational Linguistics,* 1977, *4,* microfiche 63.

Joshi, A. K., Kosaraju, S., and Yamada, H. M., String adjunct grammars I and II, *Information and Control, 21,* 1972, 93–116; 235–260.

Karttunen, L., On the semantics of complement sentences. *Papers from the Sixth Regional Meeting of the Chicago Linguistic Society.* Chicago: University of Chicago, 1970.

Karttunen, L., Presuppositions of compound sentences. *Linguistic Inquiry,* 1973, *IV,* 169–193.

Karttunen, L. and Peters, S., Conventional implicature in Montague grammar. Paper presented at the First Annual Meeting of Berkeley Linguistic Society, Berkeley, California, February 15, 1975.

Keenan, E. L., Two kinds of presupposition in natural language. In C. J. Fillmore and D. T. Langendoen (Eds.), *Studies in linguistic semantics.* New York: Holt, 1971.

Keenan, E. L., On semantically based grammar. *Linguistic Inquiry,* 1972, *4,* 413–461.

Kempson, R. M., *Presupposition and the delimitation of semantics.* Cambridge: Cambridge University Press, 1975.

Kiparsky, P. and Kiparsky, C., Fact. In D. Steinberg and L. Jakobovits (Eds.), *Semantics.* New York: Cambridge University Press, 1971.

Sager, N., Syntactic analysis of natural language. In F. Alt. and M. Rubinoff, (Eds.), *Advances in Computers,* 8. New York: Academic Press, 1967.

Sager, N. The string parser for scientific literature. In R. Rustin (Ed.), *Natural language processing.* New York: Algorithmics Press, 1973.

Weischedel, R. M., Computation of a unique subclass of inferences: Presupposition and entailment. Unpublished doctoral dissertation, University of Pennsylvania, 1975.

Weischedel, R. M., Voge, W., and James, M. An artificial intelligence approach to language instruction. *Artificial Intelligence,* in press.

Woods, W. A., Transition network grammars for natural language analysis. *Communications of the ACM,* 1970, *13,* 591–606.

Woods, W. A. An experimental parsing system for transition network grammars. In R. Rustin (Ed.), *Natural language processing.* New York: Algorithmics Press, 1973.

III. DISCOURSE INTERPRETATION

When people use language, they write or speak not in single isolated utterances but in extended sequences of them. Natural languages take advantage of this by providing ways for one utterance to use all aspects of the *context* of previous utterances to augment what is explicitly said in the utterance itself. Other features of NL enable hearers or readers to draw inferences about the connections between the information conveyed in two separate utterances. Thus, in order to perform appropriately, NL systems for both understanding and generation need capabilities for dealing with those features of language that rely on context and those features of text that establish context.

As the papers in Chapter 2 (*Semantic Interpretation*) illustrate, *domain* (i.e., the subworld the system knows about) provides certain information crucial for determining the meaning of various constituents of an utterance (e.g., for disambiguating word senses). This general information (often common-sense information as well as specialized facts) can be distinguished from the more immediate *context of use* of an utterance, which also provides constraints on its meaning. *Context* is determined by a combination of the previous utterances in the discourse (discourse context), the location in space and time of the discourse (spatio-temporal context), and the beliefs, desires, and intentions (both private and shared) of the discourse participants.

One of the major contributions to linguistics of work in computational linguistics has been to establish the primacy of discourse and the importance of nonlinguistic factors to determining the interpretation of an utterance in context. Referring expressions, in particular pronouns and definite descriptions (e.g., "the tall man in white shoes"), are among the phrases for which constraints from context and nonlinguistic factors matter the most. All of the papers in this chapter cover research that was concerned, at least in part, with computational techniques for treating these expressions. Although the papers in this chapter deal almost exclusively with the process of NL understanding, several of the papers have provided techniques for, or influenced the design of, NL generation systems.

When computational work on referring expressions was first undertaken, the standard line was that pronouns referred back to previous words in the text (i.e., to their antecedents), and it was assumed that a search, for the most part, linearly back through a sequence of utterances would lead to the appropriate referent. The papers in this chapter make clear that the crucial relationship is not between referring expressions and previous phrases: rather, people use such expressions to refer to entities (objects, properties, relations) in some world or model. Now while early computational work (see *Woods, Winograd*, Chapter 2) took partial account of this by typically searching back through some intermediate representation of each utterance to find a form corresponding to the appropriate referent, these intermediate representations were not general enough to cover a wide range of referring expressions. A second problem pointed out in the articles here is that the entity being referred to need not be the most recently mentioned entity (even of a particular type). A linear search through the text may work in a large number of cases (see *Hobbs*, this chapter), but it is insufficient in general because what matters primarily is the structure of the discourse. Finally, there need be no explicit mention of the entity being referred to: commonsense knowledge and reasoning must be called into play to treat referring expressions adequately.

Jack and Janet in Search of a Theory of Knowledge

Charniak's disseration [1] on understanding children's stories included one of the first proposals for dealing with pronouns that went beyond a simple history list search using surface syntactic features (e.g., number and gender) and semantic properties (e.g., selectional features like animacy) to rule out candidates. The major contribution of Charniak's work was to show the pervasive need for common-sense knowledge and reasoning in determining referents: regardless of the sophistication of syntactic and semantic constraints, they are just not adequate in and of themselves to determine reference relationships. The main concern of the paper included here is with the kind of domain information a story understander needs to access and ways in which this information might be represented. The major limitation of Charniak's approach (an issue *Hobbs*, *Sidner*, and *Webber* [see this chapter] all address) is that it ignores all questions of the control of inference: anything that might be inferred would be.

Resolving Pronoun References

Hobbs' paper presents two different algorithms for dealing with pronouns in text. The first of these (his "naive" algorithm) incorporates well-understood syntactic constraints and provides for semantic selectional restrictions (e.g., in "he moved it," "it" can only refer to a movable object). This algorithm has been used in a number of practical NL systems (e.g., TEAM, see *Martin et al.*, Chapter 6). Hobbs tested this algorithm on three very different texts and found it to work in about 90% of the cases. On the other hand, it cannot detect when it goes awry nor can it be extended in any straightforward way to cover the other 10% of the cases. The second algorithm is based on constraints arising from the content of the text, and is a forerunner of Hobbs' coherence relations [6].

The Representation and Use of Focus in a System for Understanding Dialogs

Both Charniak's and Hobbs' work were largely domain and sentence oriented; neither considered discourse context. Both Grosz's and Sidner's papers are concerned with various properties of the discourse itself that play important roles in determining the referent of various types of definite noun phrases. Grosz's dissertation [3, 4] showed that task-oriented dialogues have a structure much like sentences: the full dialogue divides into segments that bear certain relationships to each other and to the discourse overall. This structure affects the use of referring expressions. The dissertation also showed that the structure of a task-oriented dialogue depends in part on the structure of the task being done.

To treat the interaction between discourse structure and referring expressions, Grosz defined two levels of *focusing of attention*, immediate and global. *Immediate focusing* operates at the level of an utterance, affecting how things are said in a subsequent utterance. *Global focusing* operates at the discourse segment level. The article included here examines how global focusing interacts with the generation and intepretation of definite descriptions. It provides examples illustrating that the most recently mentioned object of a certain type may not be the referent of a pronoun. It also presents a representation of global focusing and shows how shifts in focusing are determined (in part) by the task being carried out.

The major contribution of this work was to link dialogue structure, task structure, focusing, and constraints on the use of referring expressions. Subsequently, other researchers demonstrated a similar structuring of a wide range of discourse types [2, 7, 8, 9]. This has led to a generalization of task structure to a notion of an *intentional structure* of discourse and to a generalization of the interactions between focusing and referring expressions [5].

Focusing in the Comprehension of Definite Anaphora

Sidner's paper addresses issues of immediate focusing and its role in the interpretation of pronouns and some classes of "this" and "that" noun phrases. A major concern of the paper is constraining the amount and types of inferences that need to be drawn in determining what a pronoun refers to. Sidner defines immediate focus as a discourse construct that is determined by a combination of syntactic, semantic, discourse, and domain-based constraints. She gives algorithms for establishing, continuing, and shifting immediate focus and provides rules for using immediate focus in interpreting pronouns and this/that noun phrases.

A major feature of Sidner's work is that it predicts certain pronoun uses will be illegal. Although Sidner's paper discusses focusing and pronouns solely from the point of view of interpretation, her focusing rules have also been used in several generation systems (e.g., *McKeown, Appelt,* Chapter 5). For generation, it is crucial that her theory proscribes certain uses.

So What Can We Talk About Now?

Unlike most computational work on referring expressions, Webber's paper is concerned not with identifying the correct referent of an expression, but with determining what alternatives a particular utterance makes available for subsequent reference. Much of the AI work on referring expressions ignores even such straightforward constructions as quantified noun phrases (e.g., "every man," "the three women"). One of the contributions of Webber's work is to show the importance of considering more seriously the wide range of alternatives a given noun phrase can make available. The paper includes a wealth of important examples. Webber also examines what characteristics of a representation are necessary to support the computation of alternatives from the utterance. Webber, like Sidner, makes it clear that the actual form in which something is said provides important constraints on what can be said next. Commonsense reasoning, although clearly necessary to the interpretation of referring expressions, is not sufficient; properties of the surface form must be taken into account.

Other articles in this volume treat other aspects of context than discourse context; in particular, the articles in Chapter 4 (*Language Action and Intention*) discuss the effects of the participants' beliefs, desires, and intentions (both shared and private). In addition, the domain-specific event structures (scripts) discussed in Cullingford's paper on SAM (see Chapter 6) are claimed to provide a context for interpreting referring expressions and to play a role in linking utterances together for certain types of discourse.

References

[1] Charniak, E., *Towards a Model of Children's Story Comprehension*, PhD thesis, Massachusetts Institute of Technology, 1972.

[2] Cohen, R., *A Computational Model for the Analysis of Arguments*, Technical Report CSRG-151, Computer Systems Research Group, University of Toronto, October, 1983.

[3] Grosz, B. J., The Representation and Use of Focus in Dialogue Understanding, Technical Report 151, Artificial Intelligence Center, SRI International, Menlo Park, CA July, 1977.

[4] Grosz, B. J., Discourse Analysis. In Walker, D. (editor), *Understanding Spoken Language,* Chapter IX, pages 235–268. Elsevier North-Holland, New York City, 1978.

[5] Grosz, B. J. and Sidner, C. L., Attention, Intentions, and the Structure of Discourse, *Computational Linguistics* 12, 1986.

[6] Hobbs, J., Coherence and Co-references, *Cognitive Science* 3(1):67–82, 1979.

[7] Linde, C., Focus of Attention and the Choice of Pronouns in Discourse. In Givon, T. (editor), *Syntax and Semantics, Vol. 12 of Discourse and Syntax,* pages 337–354. Academic Press, Inc., 1979.

[8] Polanyi, L. and Scha, R., A Model of the Syntactic and Semantic Structure of Discourse. In Polanyi, L. (editor), *The Structure of Discourse.* Ablex Publishers, Norwood, NJ, 1986.

[9] Reichman-Adar, R., Extended Person-Machine Interface, *Artificial Intelligence* 22(2):157–218, March, 1984.

JACK AND JANET IN SEARCH OF A THEORY OF KNOWLEDGE

Eugene Charniak
Artificial Intelligence Laboratory
Massachusetts Institute of Technology

Abstract

In order to answer questions about children's stories one needs a great deal of "common sense" knowledge. A model is presented which gives a rough organization to this knowledge along with specifications as to how the information will be accessed. This rough model is then used as a basis for tight arguments about narrow issues (primarily using examples concerning piggy banks.) The paper is intended as an illustration of how one might go about constructing a theory of knowledge.

Acknowledgements

This paper is based on portions of an MIT Ph.D. thesis submitted to the department of Electrical Engineering. The thesis is reproduced as AI Technical Report 266. As in my thesis I would like to thank all the people at the MIT Artificial Intelligence Laboratory who listened to and argued with me on many occasions.

The work reported herein was conducted at the Artificial Intelligence Laboratory, a Massachusetts Institute of Technology research program supported in part by the Advanced Research Projects Agency of the Department of Defense and monitored by the Office of Naval Research under Contract Number N00014-70-A-0362-0003.

1   Introduction

Let us consider the problem of constructing an abstract model of story comprehension. To determine what the model, or program, has "understood" about what it has read, we will ask it questions. So a typical story might start:

(1)   Janet needed some money. She got her piggybank (PB) and started to shake it. Finally some money came out.

Some typical questions would be:

(2)   Why did Janet get the PB?
(3)   Did Janet get the money?
(4)   Why was the PB shaken?

Questions (2) - (4) are not answered explicitly in the text. That is, the story did not say "Janet got her PB because she ..." The story does not even contain a full implicit answer; one cannot logically deduce an answer from the statements in the story without using general knowledge about the

world such as:

(5)   One can often get money from PBs.
(6)   The hard part of getting money from a PB is getting it out. Once that is done one can be said to have the money.
(7)   Shaking helps get money out of a PB.

So in order to understand a children's story we need a theory of every day knowledge. This theory would have to answer questions like "What is the knowledge we have?" and "How is it organized so we can get at the necessary information when it is needed?" Note that this latter question assumes that we have some specific task or tasks in mind, in our case answering questions about children's stories.

The rest of this paper divides into two parts. In the first part a rough description of a model of children's story comprehension will be presented. In the second section we will assume the model presented in the first and look at some narrow questions concerning the organization and content of our knowledge about piggy banks.

2   A Model of Children's Story Comprehension

The model presented here is solely concerned with deduction and does not consider problems of natural language per se. In particular it does not deal with syntax or those problems on the boundary between syntax and deduction like disambiguation of word senses and determination of noun phrase referents. (However, my Ph.D. thesis considers the noun phrase problem in some detail.)

So we will assume that as the story comes into the program it is immediately translated into an internal representation which is convenient for doing deduction. The internal representation will be a group of "assertions" each assertion being a predicate on an arbitrary number of arguments. Putting an assertion into the data base is to "assert" it. The model will try to "fill in the blanks" of the story on a line by line basis. That is, as it goes along, it will try to make connections between events in the story (usually causal connections) and fill in missing facts which seem important such as Janet's now having the money in (1).

2.1   Demons and Base Routines

Consider a fact like:

(8)   If "it is (or will be) raining" and
              if "person P is outside"
                 then "P will get wet"

We have an intuitive belief that (8) is a
fact about "rain", rather than, say, a fact
about "outside." Many things happen outside
and getting wet is only one of them. On the
other hand only a limited number of things
happen when it rains.

We will embody this belief in our system
by associating (8) with "rain" so that only
when "rain" comes up in the story will we
even consider using rule (8). We will say
that rain is the "topic concept" of (8). To
put this another way, when a concept is
brought up in a story, the facts associated
with it are "made available" for use in
making deductions. (We will also say that
the facts are "put in" or "asserted.") So,
if "circus", say, has never come up, the
program will not be able to make deductions
using those facts associated only with
"circus."

Note however that we are not saying that
"rain" has to be mentioned explicitly in the
story before we can use (8). It is only
necessary that there be a "rain" assertion
put into the data base. Other parts of the
story may provide facts which cause the
program to assert that it is raining. For
example:

(9)   One afternoon Jack was outside
          playing ball with Bill. Bill looked
          up and noticed that the sky was
          getting dark. "I think we should
          stop" said Bill. "We will get wet
          if we keep playing."

Here, the sky's getting dark in the afternoon
suggests that it is going to rain. If this
is put into the data base it will be
sufficient to bring in facts associated with
"rain."

Also note that a topic concept need not
be a single "key word." A fact may not
become available to the system until a
complex set of relations appears in the data
base. A fact may be arbitrarily complex, and
in particular may activate other facts
depending on the presence or absence of
certain relations in the story.

Looking Forward, Looking Back. When a
fact is made available we might not have all
the information needed to make use of the
fact. Since we are making deductions as we
go, if the necessary information comes in
after the rule has been asserted we want to
make the deduction when the information comes
in. So we might have:

(10)   Jack was outside. It was raining.
(11)   It was raining. Jack was outside.

In (10) there is no problem. When we
introduce "rain" we have sufficient
information to use (8) and deduce that Jack
is going to get wet. But in (11), we only
learn that Jack is outside after we have
mentioned rain. If we want to use (8) we
will need some way to have our fact "look
forward" in the story. To do this we will
break a fact into two parts, a pattern and a

body (an arbitrary program). We will execute
the body of the fact only when an assertion
is in the data base which matches the
pattern. (We will also say that the
assertion "excites" the fact.) In (8) the
pattern would be "someone outside." Then in
(11) when we introduce (8) no assertion
matches the pattern. But the next line
creates a matching assertion, so the fact
will be excited. We will say that a fact is
"looking forward" when its topic concept
appears before the assertion which matches
the pattern. When the assertion which
matches the pattern comes first we will say
that the fact is "looking backward" (as in
10).

We can see how important looking forward
is with a few examples.

(12)   "Janet was thinking of getting Jack
          a ball for his birthday. When she
          told Penny, Penny said, 'Don't do
          that. Jack has a ball.'" Here we
          interpreted the line "Jack has a
          ball" as meaning that he did not
          want another. The common sense
          knowledge is the fact that in many
          cases having an X means that one
          will not want another X. This piece
          of information would probably be
          filed under "things to consider when
          about to get something for somebody
          else." Naturally it was an earlier
          line which mentioned that Janet was
          thinking of getting Jack a ball.

(13)   "Bill offered to trade his pocket
          knife for Jack's dog Tip. Jack said
          'I will ask Janet. Tip is her dog
          too.'" The last line is interpreted
          as the reason Jack will ask Janet.
          This requires information about the
          relation between trading and
          ownership.

(14)   "Janet wanted to get some money.
          She found her piggy bank and started
          to shake it. She didn't hear
          anything." The last line means that
          there was nothing in the piggybank
          on the basis of facts about
          piggybanks.

In each of these cases it is an earlier line
which contains the information which is used
to assign the interpretation. So in (12)
there is nothing inherent in the line "Jack
has a ball" which means "don't get him
another." If there were, something in the
line would also have to key a check for the
following situations:

(15)   Bill and Dick wanted to play
          baseball. When Jack came by Bill
          said "There is Jack. He has a
          ball."

(16)   Tom asked his father if he would buy
          him a ball. "Jack has a ball," said
          Tom.

(17) Bill's ball of string was stuck in the tree. He asked Jane how he could get it out. Jane said "You should hit it with something. Here comes Jack. He has a ball."

Those familiar with Planner might notice that our "facts" look quite similar to Planner antecedent theorems, with the exception that our facts can "look back" as well as "look forward." Antecedent theorems are only designed to look forward. I initially formulated facts as antecedent theorems because I was so impressed with the need to "look forward." However, rather than call the facts antecedent theorems, I call them "demons" since it is a shorter name.

Specification and Removal of Demons. It should be emphasized that the model does not "learn" the information contained in the demons. This information is put in by the model maker. On the other hand, the demons are not specific to the story in the sense that they mention Jack, or "the red ball." Rather, they talk about "a person X" who at one point in the story could be Jack, at another, Bill. We will assume a mechanism for binding some of the variables of the demon ("specifying" the demon) at the time the demon is asserted.

We want demons to be active only while they are relevant to the story. A story may start by talking about getting a present for Jack, but ultimately revolve around the games played at his party. We will need some way to remove the "present getting" demons when they have outlived their usefulness. (An irrelevant but active demon not only wastes time and space, but can cause us to misinterpret a new line.) As a first approximation we will assume that a demon is declared irrelevant after a given numer of lines have gone by.

Base Routines. So far we have said that demons are asserted when the proper concept has been mentioned. But this implies that there is something attached to the concept name telling us what demons should be put in.

If we look at a particular example, say (13), it is Bill's offer to trade which sets up the context for the rest of the fragment. I will assume that the information to do so is in the form of a program. Such routines, which are available to set up demons, will be called "base routines."

These base routines will be responsible for more than setting up demons. Suppose we are told that Jack had a ball, and Bill a top. Then Jack traded his ball to Bill for the top. One question we might ask is "Who now has the top?" Naturally since questions of "who has what" are important in understanding stories we will want to keep tabs on such information. In this particular case, it must again be the "trade" statement which tells us to switch possession of the objects. Every time a trade occurs we will want to exchange objects, so whenever we see "trade" we execute the "trade" base routine. Of course, the program can't be too simple-minded, since it must also handle "I will trade..." and perhaps even "Will you trade

...?"

A good test as to whether a given fact should be part of a base routine or a demon is whether we need several lines to set it up or whether we can illustrate the fact by presenting a single line. (Naturally several lines could be made into one by putting "and's" between them, but this is dodging the point. I am only suggesting an intuitive test.) So we saw that "Jack has a ball" was not enough by itself to tell us that Jack does not want another ball. Hence this relation is embodied by a demon, not a base routine. On the other hand, often a single line can tell us quite a bit as in "Jack was on second base." This indicates that the base routine for "second base" can often tell us that we are talking about a baseball game.

2.2 Bookkeeping and Fact Finders

Updating and Bookkeeping. Up to this point we have introduced two parts of the model, demons and base routines. In this section we will introduce the remaining two parts.

Again let us consider the situation when Jack had a ball, Bill a top, and they traded. When we say that Bill now has the ball, it implies that Jack no longer does. That is to say, we must somehow remove the fact that Jack has the ball from the data base. Actually we don't want to remove it, since we may be asked "Who had the ball before Bill did." Instead, we want to mark the assertion in some way to indicate that it has been updated. We will assume that there is a separate section, pretty much independent of the rest of the model, which is responsible for doing such updating. We will call this section "bookkeeping."

Fact Finders. But even deciding that one statement updates another requires special knowledge. Suppose we have:

(18) Jack was in the house. Sometime later he was at the store.

If we ask "Is Jack in the house?" we want to answer "No, he is at the store." But how is bookkeeping going to figure this out? There is a simple rule which says that (<state> A B) updates (<state> A C) where C is not the same as B. So (AT JACK FARM) would update (AT JACK NEW-YORK). But in (18) we can't simply look for Jack AT <someplace which is not the store>, since he is IN the house. To make things even worse, we could have:

(19) Jack was in the house. Sometime later he was in the kitchen.

To solve this problem we will need:

(20) To establish that PERSON is not at
location LOC.

Find out where PERSON is, call it X.
If X = LOC , then theorem is false
so return "No."
If X is part of LOC then return
"No."
If LOC is part of X, then try to
find a different X.
Else return "Yes."

In (18) the bookkeeper would try to prove
that Jack is not at the store, and it would
succeed by using (20) and the statement that
Jack is in the house. Bookkeeper would then
mark the earlier statement as updated.
Theorems like (20) are called "fact finders."
Like demons, fact finders have a pattern
and a body. A particular fact finder is
called when either a demon, base routine or
bookkeeping wants to establish a goal which
matches the fact finder's pattern. This is
different from demons which are called when
we encounter a given fact.
The basic idea behind fact finders is
that they are used to establish facts which
are comparatively unimportant, so that we do
not want to assert them and hence have them
in the data base. So in (18) we do not want
to assert "Jack is not in the house" as well
as "Jack is at the store." In the same way
we will have a fact finder which is able to
derive "<person> knows <fact>" by asking such
questions as "was the <person> there when
<fact> was mentioned or took place?" Again,
this information is easily derivable, and not
all that important, so there would seem to be
no reason to include it explicitly in the
data base.

3 Some Narrow Questions

In section 1 we stated that our theory
of knowledge should answer questions like
"how do we access the information" and "what
is the information." In this portion of the
paper we will look at two problems, one of
each kind. We start with a question of
information access.

3.1 Demon-Demon Interaction

In the description of the model it was
stated that demons are excited when an
assertion enters the data base which matches
the demon's pattern. In this section we will
present evidence that, given the model of
part 1, we must also allow demons to excite
other demons. I call this "demon-demon
interaction."

A Demon About PBs. Before we can talk
about demon-demon interaction we need to
establish the need for two particular demons.
Suppose we were given:

(21) Janet needed money. She got her
piggy bank.
(22) Janet got her PB. "I want a nickel"
she said.

Were we asked what Janet is going to do with
the PB we would say, "get money from it."
The obvious way to handle this is with a
demon which is declared relevant when we see
a person getting a PB. Naturally this would
be done by the PB base routine. This demon
would be looking for "<getter> need <money>"
(i.e., that would be its pattern). When
excited the demon would assert that there is
a causal relation between "need money" and
"get PB." We will call this demon PB-NEED-
MONEY.
Now we might claim that "want money"
should put in a demon to look for "get PB"
rather than vice versa. However, this seems
to be less reasonable, since there are many
ways of getting money, but only a very
limited number of reasons a person gets a PB.

A Demon About Buying. Buying things
often requires money. So if we saw

(23) Janet was going to by some candy.
She needed some money.
(24) Janet needed some money. She was
going to buy some candy.

we would assert that the reason she needs
money is to buy candy. Since the "need
money" statement can occur on either side of
the "buy" statement, it is clear that we want
"buy" to put in a demon which says "If the
'buyer' needs money, it is because of the
'buying'." We will call this the BUY-NEED-
MONEY demon.
We do not want "need money" to put in a
demon looking for "buy." There are many
things one can do with money, bribe a juror,
pay rent, take a taxi, tip a bellboy, etc.
It would seem more obvious to have the
various events state that they (usually)
require money, rather than have "need money"
look for all of them. Nor does it seem
reasonable to claim that all of these events
("bribing", etc.) are really versions of
"buying." To express "take a taxi" as "buy
some of the taxi driver's time plus the
temporary use of the automobile in order to
convey onself from one loaction to another"
seems somewhat forced. Most of this
"definition" comes from knowledge of
economics rather than taxis.

Evidence of the Phenomenon. But now
consider the following fragment:

(25) Janet was going to buy some candy.
She went to get her PB.

Here we want to assert that Janet gets her PB
because she wants money. But this time there
is no previous assertion which says that she
needs money. Of course, what is at work here
is the fact that buying requires money. But,
we have represented this fact as a demon, and
so far we have no way for two demons to
interact with one another. Now both PB-
NEED-MONEY and BUY-NEED-MONEY will have the
same pattern. So we can account for (25) by
allowing a demon to excite other demons with
the same pattern. Naturally this is what I
mean by demon-demon interaction.

A Restriction on Demon-Demon
Interaction. Demon-demon interaction is

probably more complex than we have indicated so far. Consider:

(26) Janet was going to buy some candy. She was also going to buy some fruit.

In (26) both occurences of "buy" will activate BUY-NEED-MONEY demons. (Though we did not comment on this earlier, the idea of specifying demons as mentioned in 2.1 obviously requires separate copies of a demon to be able to exist simultaneously.) However, (26) does not imply that Janet really needs money. For all we know she has as much as she needs in her pocket. If demon-demon interaction were as simple as we have made it out to be, the two instances of BUY-NEED-MONEY would join up to produce a "need money" assertion. So it is not sufficient for two demons to be looking for the same pattern.

Looking at example (25) we note that one of the demons gave a reason why Janet might need money, and the second suggested that needing money was the cause of a certain action. So we have:

Will buy --> Need money --> Will get PB

To put this in everyday terms, in (25) we have both a motive for needing money (buying), and a result of needing the money (go and get PB). In (26) we have two motives. The natural suggestion is that demon-demon interaction be restricted to cases where we have both motive and result.

How do we recognize when we have both motive and result? As it stands now one demon looks pretty much like any other. We might just try to label all demons as "motive" or "result" with respect to their pattern. On the other hand it might be possible to derive "motive" and "result" from more basic considerations. At any rate, it seems premature to formalize such concepts at this point. We simply don't know enough.

Capturing Generalizations. Before moving on I should point out that the kind of argument used in this section (and the next also) is a "capture the generalization" type argument commonly found in linguistics. We could have created a new demon to explain (25). It would have said, "if a person gets his PB look for him planning to buy something." However, this would be missing the generalization that "motives" and "results" always act this way. So far I have only given one example to support the "demon-demon interaction generalization", but in in the next section we will see another.

3.2 Putting Money into a Piggy Bank

In this section we will look at a possible demon associated with piggy banks and argue that the deduction it would account for can be better handled by demon-demon interaction between two other demons. In effect we will be trying to determine, on an extremely small scale, what people know.

A Piggy Bank Problem. One fact we know about PB's is that they are good places to keep money. This fact seems to come into play in:

(27) Penny said to Janet, "Don't take your money with you to the park. (You will lose it.) Go and get your PB!"

(28) After Janet helped Ms. Jones with her groceries Ms. Jones gave her a dime. Jack came along and said, "Come with me to the park, Janet." "OK," said Janet. "But first I am going home to find my PB. I do not want to take the money to the park."

(29) Janet put some money on the sink. Mother said, "If you leave the money there it may fall in the drain. Let's find your PB."

In each case the natural question is, "Why should Janet get her PB?" Now we might try to construct a "piggy bank" demon which responds to some common element in (27) - (29) and then make the necessary assertions. A close look at the examples even gives a start at what such a common element might be, say "a particular location for the money is negatively evaluated." We will call this demon PB-BAD-PLACE. The trouble with such a solution would be that it would not account for:

(30) Janet said, "I am going to put my money away. I will get my PB."

(31) Janet helped Ms. Jones with her groceries. Ms. Jones gave Janet a dime. Jack came along and said, "Janet, let's go to the park." "OK," said Janet. "But I want to put my money in a safe place. I am going to get my PB."

Now there is nothing saying that our demon needs to account for (30) and (31). However, it seems quite obvious that we are using the same information in all the examples above. The only difference is that in (27) - (29) we are expressing the need for a "safe place" by making negative comments about another location. If this is a single fact we would like a single demon to express it. The trouble is finding what (27) - (31) have in common.

A Non-Piggy Bank Problem. In the course of looking at examples like (27) - (31) I noted examples like:

(32) Penny said to Janet, "Don't take your money with you to the park. Put it on the shelf."

(33) After Janet helped Ms. Jones with her groceries Ms. Jones gave her a dime. Jack came along and said "Come with me to the park, Janet." "OK," said Janet. "But first I am going to put my money in the house. I do not want to take the money to the park."

(34) Janet put some money on the sink. Mother said, "If you leave the money there it may fall in the drain." Janet put the money in a drawer.

(35) Janet said "I am going to put my money away. I will put it in my toy box."

(36) Janet helped Ms. Jones with her groceries. Ms. Jones gave Janet a dime. Jack came along and said "Janet, let's go to the park." "OK," said Janet. "But I want to put my money in a safe place." Then Janet went into the house and put the money in her room.

These examples exactly mirror (27) - (31), except that (32) - (36) don't mention PB's. Naturally, in these examples the question to ask is "Why did Janet put the money in the drawer?", "in the house?", etc.

Such examples tend to indicate that the problem facing us is wider that just PB's. We will name this wider problem the "put away" problem. However it is not the case that our problem with PB's can be completely reduced to the "put away" problem. So while in the non-piggy bank examples we mention that Janet has or actually intends to "put" the money some place, in the PB examples all we needed to say was that Janet was going to get the PB. To put this another way, our knowledge of PB's allowed us to interpret "get PB" as meaning that Janet was going to put money into it. However our knowledge of houses or shelves does not allow us to make similar deductions in (32) - (36).

The Put-Away Demon. Ignoring piggy banks for the moment, what would a solution to (32) - (36) look like? We will have some demon, called the PUT-AWAY demon, which is activated by lines like:

(37) Don't leave the money by the sink.
(38) I do not want to take my money to the park.
(39) I will put my money away.

These lines will put in a demon looking for "put away" and the demon will assert that the reason for putting the thing away is (37) - (39). Ultimately we will want a theory of why people put things away (i.e., what lines put in the "put away" demon), and how to determine what constitutes a "put away" location. However, (32) - (36) clearly show that the problem is distinct from the question of what we know about PBs.

The Piggy Bank Demon. What we will now see is that if we assume the PUT-AWAY demon, all the examples in (27) - (31) fall out easily, plus a few others which we haven't even looked at yet. But first we need to consider a new PB demon entitled PB-MONEY-IN. It is parallel to PB-NEED-MONEY, but while the latter was for recognizing that money was going to be taken out of the PB, PB-MONEY-IN is for recognizing that money is going to be put in. It says "If you see that the person wants some money to be in the PB then the

reason he is getting the PB is to put it in." (Actually this theorem is true of a wide class of containers, but that does not affect the argument at hand.) This demon will account for examples like:

(40) Ms. Jones gave Janet a dime. Janet went to get her PB. "I want the money to be in my PB," she thought.

(41) Janet got her PB and dropped some money in.

(42) After Ms Jones gave Janet a dime, Jack came by and asked Janet if she wanted to go to the park. "OK," said Janet. "I will go home first and get my PB." Soon Janet came back and said "My money is in the PB, let's go!"

Demon-Demon Interaction. Now, if we assume demon-demon interaction as discussed in section 3.1, PB-MONEY-IN plus PUT-AWAY will interact to solve all the examples from (27) to (31). Let us see how this will happen.

First note that the restrictions we placed on demon-demon interactions are met here. First both demons have the same pattern, e.g., "money is in PB." (Actually the pattern for PUT-AWAY is "<object> is in <appropriate location>" however <object> will be bound to the money at the time the demon is asserted, and <appropriate location> will match PB when the demon is excited.) Secondly, we need both a motive and a result before we can "combine" demons. In the case at hand, PUT-AWAY is a motive for having the money in the PB, and "get PB" is a result of intending to put money in the PB.

Saving Money. Finally, note that our solution extends to the following case:

(43) Janet got a dime from Ms. Jones. She said "I am saving my money to buy a bicycle. I am going home to get my PB."

Here we know that Janet is going to put the money in the PB because of the "save" statement. However, we immediately note that we have cases like:

(44) Janet got a dime from Ms. Jones. Janet told her "I am saving my money to buy a bicycle. I am going home to put the money away. (I am going home to put the money in my drawer.)"

Naturally, (44) indicates that "save" must activate PUT-AWAY. If this is the case, then (43) is accounted for in exactly the same manner as all the initial examples. While the reader may not be surprised at this result, I am, since initially I thought that the relationship of "save" with piggy banks would need a separate PB demon.

4   Conclusion

The two halves of this paper stand in contrast to each other. The presentation of the model (section 2) is general (in theory covering all of children's stories), but vague and full of covert appeals to the reader's intuition. Section 3 on the other hand is narrow, only talking about small portions of our knowledge of PBs, but tightly reasoned (hopefully).

Now by themselves the conclusions of section 3 are not that important. Of course, if we could pin down one hundred facts the way we pinned down one in section 3.2 then we would have the beginnings of a theory of knowledge. But I did not write this paper to tell of one fact about PBs. Rather I view the paper as an illustration of how one might go about the task of constructing a theory of knowledge.

RESOLVING PRONOUN REFERENCES

Jerry R. HOBBS*

Dept. of Computer Sciences, City College, CUNY, New York, U.S.A.

Received January 1977

Two approaches to the problem of resolving pronoun references are presented. The first is a naive algorithm that works by traversing the surface parse trees of the sentences of the text in a particular order looking for noun phrases of the correct gender and number. The algorithm clearly does not work in all cases, but the results of an examination of several hundred examples from published texts show that it performs remarkably well.

In the second approach, it is shown how pronoun resolution can be handled in a comprehensive system for semantic analysis of English texts. The system is described, and it is shown in a detailed treatment of several examples how semantic analysis locates the antecedents of most pronouns as a by-product. Included are the classic examples of Winograd and Charniak.

1. Introduction

1.1.

The importance of having the right algorithm for resolving pronoun references, or finding the antecedent of a pronoun, can be seen on American television in any episode of the George Burns and Gracie Allen re-runs, for much of Gracie's humor depends on her having the wrong algorithm.[1] For example, an episode is built around her misunderstanding of a fire inspector's warning:

There's a pile of inflammable trash next to your car. You'll have to get rid of it.

In Jespersen (1954: 143) the problem of pronoun resolution rates brief mention:

An ambiguity (not very serious) may sometimes arise when there are two antecedents to which *it* may refer: If the baby does not thrive on raw milk, boil it.

What counts as serious depends on one's point of view.

In this paper, two approaches to pronoun resolution are considered. The first is a simple, efficient, but naive algorithm working on the surface parse trees of the sentences in the text. Examination of several hundred examples from a variety of published texts shows that in spite of its obvious flaws, the algorithm works remarkably well.

In the second approach, it is shown how pronoun resolution happens in a total system for semantic analysis. And the word 'happens' is appropriate here. Charniak (1972) demonstrated rather convincingly that in order to do pronoun resolution, one had to be able to do everything else. In the latter part of this paper it is argued that once everything else is done, pronoun resolution comes free – it happens automatically. A system for the semantic analysis of English texts is described, and it is shown in a detailed treatment of several examples how semantic analysis locates the antecedents of most pronouns as a by-product.

The problems studied in this paper are addressed from a computational, analytic point of view, that is, within a clearly specified framework for analyzing texts rather than generating them. In some generative approaches, a noun phrase in deep structure is transformed into a pronoun by a pronominalization rule, under the condition of 'identity of reference' with another noun phrase. Little more is said about this condition; presumably the one generating the sentence is somehow aware of this identity of reference. However, from the computational, analytic point of view, we must be very precise about how a listener could *become* aware of this identity of reference. When he hears or reads a pronoun, how, out of all the possible structures which could serve as an antecedent, might he be able to pick the correct one. Our emphasis is directed toward developing algorithms for doing this. Even if it is the generation of texts one is interested in, the analytic point of view may be the correct one to take, for as Olson (1970) argues, the speaker elaborates his description of an entity just to the extent that will allow his listener to identify it.

* The author wishes to thank Eileen Fitzpatrick for her helpful suggestions. This work was supported by the CUNY Faculty Research Award Program Grants Nos. 11233 and 11655 and National Science Foundation Grant No. MCS-76-82164.

Present address: SRI International, Menlo Park, California, U.S.A.

[1] I am indebted to Eileen Fitzpatrick for calling this to my attention.

1.2. Review of the natural language processing literature

Most work by linguists on the problems of pronoun resolution has been concerned with elucidating syntactic constraints on the coreferentiality and non-coreferentiality of two entities occurring in the same sentence. Some of this work will be reviewed in Part 2. This section is a brief review of the most important work in natural language processing, in which the problem of locating antecedents has been addressed more directly.

Winograd (1972) was the first to write procedures for locating antecedents, in his system for manipulating and carrying on dialogs about a blocks microworld. He collects all possible referents and rates their plausibility on the basis of syntactic position, apparently in an order similar to that which the naive algorithm of Part 2 defines. A subject is favored over an object and both are favored over the object of a preposition. In addition, 'focus' elements are favored, where focus is determined from, among other things, the answers to wh-questions and from indefinite noun phrases in yes-no questions.

In his system for general natural language inferencing, Rieger (1974) finds the antecedent of any definite entity by creating and narrowing down a candidate set of possible antecedents, based on the known properties of the entity. The difficulty with this approach for pronouns is that normally the only explicit property we have is new and not very useful for identification. If implied properties are included, then one runs into an overall problem with Rieger's system (shared by Charniak's). There are no controls on inferencing; everything that can be inferred is. When more than one candidate remains, the most recently referenced is chosen, where recency is determined by a 'system clock', i.e. determined by a complex and largely unspecified order of processing.

The chief value of Charniak's work has been to show just how difficult the pronoun resolution problem is. In particular, he showed how spurious the recency principle is. His thesis (Charniak 1972) contains a wealth of difficult cases in the guise of children's stories, which show that arbitrarily detailed world knowledge can be required to decide upon an antecedent. He points out that the knowledge required for pronoun resolution is just that which might be required by a conversational system which is asked questions about the stories. He internalizes these questions in the form of 'demons', which are axioms whose antecedents have been matched and which are looking for their consequents. However, he offers no solution to the problem of what questions are the appropriate ones to ask. Section 3.2 of this paper may be seen as an attempt to solve this problem.

Wilks (1974) has given a very nice partial solution to the problem of deciding among competing plausible antecedents, based on the use of selectional information to maximize the redundancy. In addition, he uses a bidirectional search through a data base of world knowledge to resolve pronouns. His approach, in general, is similar to that of operation 4 in Section 3.2, although he lacks a notion of salience.

2. The syntactic approach: The naive algorithm

In this section a naive algorithm for finding antecedents of pronouns is described and related to previous linguistic research. Results are presented of a statistical study of the algorithm's effectiveness on 300 examples of pronoun occurrences from three very different texts.

2.1. The algorithm

In what follows reference will be made to the 'surface parse tree'. By this is meant the tree that exhibits the grammatical structure of the sentence – its division into subject, verb, objects, adverbials, etc. – without permuting or omitting any of the words in the original sentence. That is, the terminal nodes of the tree taken in left-to-right order form the English sentence. It will be assumed however that certain syntactically recoverable omitted elements are available as antecedents, as described below.

It will be necessary to assume that an NP node has an $\bar{N}$ node below it, as proposed by Chomsky (1970), to which a prepositional phrase containing an argument of the head noun may be attached. Truly adjunctive prepositional phrases are attached to the NP node. This assumption, or something equivalent to it, is necessary to distinguish between the following two sentences:

(1) Mr. Smith saw a driver in his truck.
(2) Mr. Smith saw a driver of his truck.

In (1) 'his' may refer to the driver, but in (2) it may not. The structures we are assuming for the relevant noun phrases in (1) and (2) are shown in figs. 1a and 1b, respectively.

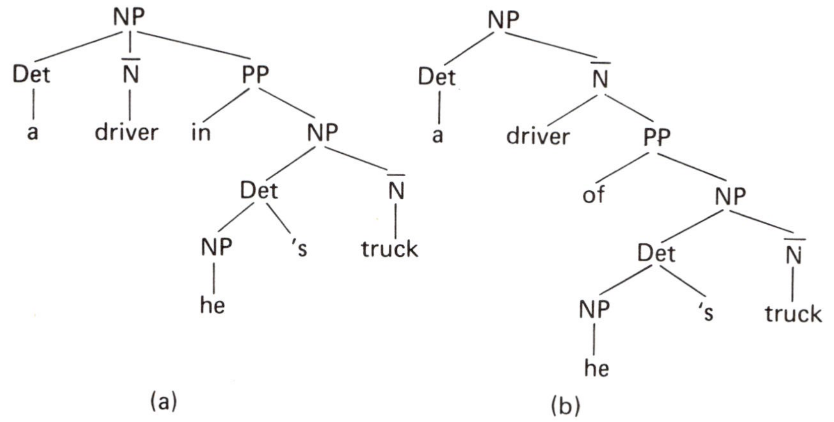

The naive algorithm traverses the surface parse tree in a particular order looking for a noun phrase of the correct gender and number. The traversal order is as follows:

(1) Begin at the NP node immediately dominating the pronoun.

(2) Go up the tree to the first NP or S node encountered. Call this node X, and call the path used to reach it p.

(3) Traverse all branches below node X to the left of path p in a left-to-right, breadth-first fashion. Propose as the antecedent any NP node that is encountered which has an NP or S node between it and X.

(4) If node X is the highest S node in the sentence, traverse the surface parse trees of previous sentences in the text in order of recency, the most recent first; each tree is traversed in a left-to-right, breadth-first manner, and when an NP node is encountered, it is proposed as antecedent. If X is not the highest S node in the sentence, continue to step 5.

(5) From node X, go up the tree to the first NP or S node encountered. Call this new node X, and call the path traversed to reach it p.

(6) If X is an NP node and if the path p to X did not pass through the N̄ node that X immediately dominates, propose X as the antecedent.

(7) Traverse all branches below node X to the left of path p in a left-to-right, breadth-first manner. Propose any NP node encountered as the antecedent.

(8) If X is an S node, traverse all branches of node X to the *right* of path p in a left-to-right, breadth-first manner, but do not go below any NP or S node encountered. Propose any NP node encountered as the antecedent.

(9) Go to step 4.

A breadth-first search of a tree is one in which every node of depth n is visited before any node of depth $n + 1$. Steps 2 and 3 of the algorithm take care of the level in the tree where a reflexive pronoun would be used. Steps 5–9 cycle up the tree through S and NP nodes. Step 4 searches the previous sentences in the text.

For the sake of concreteness, suppose we have the following context-free grammar for generating the surface structures of a fragment of English:

$$S \rightarrow NP\ \ VP$$

$$NP \rightarrow \left\{ \begin{array}{l} (Det)\ \bar{N}\ \left(\begin{array}{c} (PP) \\ Rel \end{array} \right)^* \\ pronoun \end{array} \right\}$$

$$Det \rightarrow \left\{ \begin{array}{l} article \\ NP\text{'s} \end{array} \right\}$$

$$\bar{N} \rightarrow noun\ (PP)^*$$
$$PP \rightarrow preposition\ NP$$
$$Rel \rightarrow wh\text{-}word\ S$$
$$VP \rightarrow verb\ NP\ (PP)^*$$

Words in lower case letters mean any word of that category; parentheses, (...), indicate optional elements; the asterisk means 0 or more copies of the element that precedes it; braces, {...}, contain alternatives. Figure 2 illustrates the algorithm working on the sentence

The castle in Camelot remained the residence of the king until 536 when he moved it to London.

Beginning from node NP_1, step 2 rises to node S_1. Step 3 searches the left portion of S_1's tree but finds no *eligible* NP node. Step 4 does not apply.

Fig. 1.

(a)

(b)

Step 5 rises to NP$_2$ which step 6 proposes as antecedent. Thus, '536' is recommended as antecedent of 'it'.

The algorithm can be improved somewhat by applying simple selectional constraints, such as

Dates can't move;
Places can't move;
Large fixed objects can't move.

The utility of these constraints is limited. They never help with the pronoun 'he', since what one male human can do another can too. Even with 'it' the utility is limited since most English words can occur in such a wide variety of contexts. However, in the present example, they help.

After NP$_2$ is rejected, steps 7 and 8 turn up nothing, and control is returned to step 4 which does not apply. Step 5 rises to S$_2$, where step 6 does not apply. In step 7, the breadth-first search first suggests NP$_3$ (the castle), which selectional constraints reject. It then continues to NP$_4$ where it correctly settles upon 'the residence' as antecedent of 'it'.

If we were searching for the antecedent of 'he', the algorithm would continue, first rejecting NP$_5$ because of gender and finally lighting upon NP$_6$, the king.

When seeking an antecedent for 'they', the algorithm accepts plural and collective singular noun phrases and also collects selectionally compatible entities. In

John sat on the sofa. Mary sat before the fireplace. *They* faced each other.

the algorithm would pick 'Mary' and 'John' rather than 'Mary' and 'the fireplace'. Also, when two plurals are conjoined, the conjunction is favored over either plural, as in

Human bones and relics were found at this site. *They* were associated with elephant tusks.

It should be assumed that the algorithm is part of a larger left-to-right interpretation process which also recovers syntactically recoverable omitted material and records coreference and non-coreference relations. The algorithm then handles the case of Grinder and Postal's 'missing antecedents' (1971). In

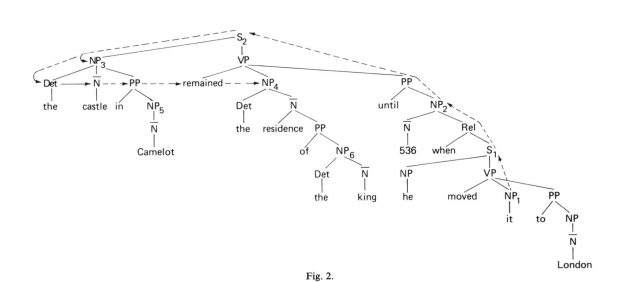

Fig. 2.

2.2. Relation of the algorithm to results from the generative transformational tradition

A great deal of work has been done in transformational grammar in recent years on stating precisely the conditions under which a noun or non-reflexive pronoun may *not* be coreferential with another element in the sentence. That is, the goal has been to state constraints of the form

A and B are necessarily non-coreferential if ....

This is equivalent to restricting the possible antecedents to a (usually still very large) set of entities. The problem of this paper is how to determine out of this remaining set what in fact really is the antecedent. It is important to be clear about the distinction between these two problems.

The easiest way for us to take the constraints into account would be simply to assume that there is a mechanism which applies them. Then any entity which the naive algorithm proposes is checked by the mechanism, which thus acts as a filter. This in fact is what will be assumed in Part 3. However, here it is shown that the two principal constraints are incorporated within the algorithm itself. There are classes of examples from the literature which are not and could not easily be handled by the algorithm, but they occur rarely in actual texts, and in view of the fact that the algorithm fails on much more natural and common examples, there seems to be little point in greatly complicating the algorithm to handle them.

The first constraint is that a non-reflexive pronoun and its antecedent may not occur in the same simplex sentence (Lees and Klima 1963; Langacker 1969; Jackendoff 1972). In the examples

John likes him.
John's portrait of him

'him' and 'John' cannot be coreferential. However, if an NP node precedes and is on a lower level than the pronoun, it is a possible antecedent, as in

John$_i$'s father's portrait of him$_i$
After John$_i$ robbed the bank, the police apprehended him$_i$.

This constraint is accommodated by steps 2 and 3 of the algorithm.

My uncle doesn't have a spouse, but your aunt does, and *he* is lying on the floor

the interpretation process first expands the second clause into

... but your aunt does have a spouse ...

and the algorithm then selects the aunt's spouse as antecedent of 'he'. The algorithm also avoids choosing 'the man' as antecedent of 'him' in

John said his mother would sue the man who hit *him*

for 'the man' is necessarily coreferential with the omitted subject of 'hit', which is necessarily non-coreferential with 'him'.

In dialogue it is assumed that the implicit 'A said to B ...' has been recovered before the algorithm is applied to quoted sentences and that rules are available to exclude the speaker and listener as possible antecedents of third person pronouns inside quotes.

The algorithm does not handle sentence pronominalization, as in

Ford was in trouble, and he knew *it*.

One might suggest that the algorithm be modified to accept an S node as the antecedent of a pronoun occurring in certain contexts. However, the problem of avoiding spurious antecedents would then be quite severe. In

The newspaper reported that Ford had claimed the economy was improving, but I didn't believe it

the algorithm allowing both S and NP nodes would recommend the following as plausible antecedents, in the given order:

The newspaper reported that Ford had claimed the economy was improving
the newspaper
Ford claimed the economy was improving
the economy was improving.

This is quite the opposite of one's intuitive feelings about which readings are preferred.

The algorithm fails on the class of picture noun examples, however. In

(3) John saw a picture of him

it would interpret 'him' as John; yet if they were coreferential, 'himself' would have been used. Jackendoff has given an analysis of how reflexives are to be interpreted beyond the scope of simplex sentences. Unfortunately, the corresponding rule for how non-reflexives are *not* to be interpreted is incorrect. For there are cases where either the reflexive or non-reflexive pronoun may be used. Consider

*John$_i$ saw him$_i$.
?*John$_i$ saw a picture of him$_i$.
??John$_i$ saw a picture of him$_i$ hanging in the post office.
?John$_i$ saw that a picture of him$_i$ was hanging in the post office.
John$_i$ claimed that the picture of him$_i$ hanging in the post office was a fraud.

'Himself' is perfectly acceptable in place of 'him' in all five sentences. But apparently the more deeply the pronoun is embedded and the more elaborate the construction it occurs in, the more acceptable the non-reflexive becomes. Yet there is no precise boundary between where it is acceptable and where it is not.

Rather than complicate the algorithm excessively, we will simply let it fail on cases like (3).

The second principal constraint is the rule proposed by Langacker (1969) that the antecedent of a pronoun must precede or command the pronoun. A node NP$_1$ is said to command node NP$_2$ if neither NP$_1$ nor NP$_2$ dominates the other and if the S node which most immediately dominates NP$_1$ dominates but does not *immediately* dominate NP$_2$. The command relation was proposed by Langacker to take care of backward pronominalization examples:

After he$_i$ robbed the bank, John$_i$ left town.
That he$_i$ was elected chairman surprised John$_i$.

Step 8 of the algorithm, which searches the tree to the right of the pronoun, handles such cases.

There is a search downward in order to include examples like

That he$_i$ had done something terrible was disturbing to John$_i$.

But there is no search below S or NP nodes because of the apparent unacceptability of

?That he$_i$ had done something terrible disturbed John$_i$'s teacher
*That he$_i$ had done something terrible disturbed the teacher who punished John$_i$.

This constraint will cause the algorithm to fail on several examples which have been discussed in the literature:

Mary sacked out in his$_i$ apartment before Sam$_i$ could kick her out. (Lakoff 1968; Culicover 1976)
Girls who he$_i$ has dated say that Sam$_i$ is charming. (Ross 1967)

However, this constraint never caused the algorithm to fail in the sample studied. If it were lifted, the performance of the algorithm would degrade drastically.

2.3. Statistical results

One hundred consecutive examples of pronouns from each of three very different texts were examined to test the performance of the naive algorithm. The pronouns were 'he', 'she', 'it', and 'they'. 'It' was not counted when referring to a syntactically recoverable 'that' clause or occurring in a time or weather construction. In applying the algorithm, it was assumed that the correct parse was available for each sentence. The texts were William Watson's *Early Civilization in China*, pp. 21–69, the first chapter of Arthur Haley's novel *Wheels*, pp. 1–6, and the July 7, 1975 edition of *Newsweek*, pp. 13–19, beginning with the article 'A Ford in High Gear'. The results of the study are summarized in table 1.

Overall, the algorithm worked in 88.3% of the cases. The algorithm together with selectional constraints worked 91.7% of the time. This is somewhat deceptive since in over half the cases there was only one nearby plausible antecedent. For that reason, the number of examples in which

Table 1
Summary of the three texts.

	#	C_0	$C_1 - C_0$	$C_2 - C_1$	$C_3 - C_2$	$C_9 - C_8$	Algorithm works	Algorithm works after selection
he	139	126	10	2	0	1	130	130
she	7	7	0	0	0	0	7	7
it	71	64	4	1	2	0	55	59
they	83	74	9	0	0	0	73	79
Total	300	271	23	3	2	1	265	275

	Conflicts before selection	Algorithm correct	Conflicts after selection	Algorithm correct
he	31	22	31	22
she	0	0	0	0
it	48	33	44	33
they	53	43	45	41
Total	132	98	120	96

more than one plausible antecedent occurred are tabulated, with the number of times the algorithm worked. Of 132 such conflicts, twelve were resolved by selectional constraints and 96 of the remaining 120 were resolved by the algorithm. Thus, 81.8% of the conflicts were resolved by a combination of the algorithm and selection.

If we look at the results for Watson as typical of technical writing, things look even more encouraging. There were a very high number of conflicts, 76 out of 100 examples, but selection resolved eight of these and the algorithm worked on 62 of the remaining 68. The combination thus yields the correct antecedent in 92% of the cases where there is conflict.

Klapholz and Lockman (1975) put forward the hypothesis that the antecedent is always found within the last n sentences, for some small n. Charniak (1972) was more explicit and proposed, with reservations, $n = 5$. This is clearly wrong. However, it is of interest to know how often this heuristic does hold and for what values of n it holds often enough to be useful. Therefore, statistics were also collected on how close the antecedent was to the pronoun. It turns out that it is possible to make a much stronger statement than either Klapholz and Lockman or Charniak suggested. With n 'less than one', a very large majority of the antecedents will be found. Let the *candidate sets* $C_0, C_1, \ldots, C_n$ be defined as follows:

$$C_0 = \begin{cases} \text{the set of entities in the current} & \text{if pronoun comes} \\ \text{sentence and the previous sentence} & \text{before main verb} \\ \text{the set of entities in only the current} & \text{if pronoun comes} \\ \text{sentence} & \text{after main verb.} \end{cases}$$

$$C_1 = \begin{cases} \text{the set of entities in the current sentence and the previous} \\ \text{sentence.} \end{cases}$$

$$C_n = \text{the set of entities in the current sentence and the previous } n \\ \text{sentences.}$$

The frequencies with which antecedents were found in $C_0, C_1, \ldots$, is also given in table 1, and they show that the hypothesis is very strong.

Ninety percent of all antecedents are in C_0 while 98% are in C_1. Yet there is no useful absolute limit on how far back one need look for the antecedent. One antecedent occurred nine sentences before the pronoun. The pronoun 'it', especially in technical writing, can have a very large number of plausible antecedents in one sentence – one example in Watson had thirteen. Any absolute limit we impose might therefore have dozens of plausible antecedents and would hardly be of practical value. Computationally speaking, it will be a long time before a semantically based algorithm is sophisticated enough to perform as well, and these results set a very high standard for any other approach to aim for.

Yet there is every reason to pursue a semantically based approach. The naive algorithm does not work. Any one can think of examples where it fails. In these cases it not only fails; it gives no indication that it has failed and offers no help in finding the real antecedent.

Moreover, the semantic approach described in Part 3 is all processing that must be done anyway in the analysis of texts.

3. The semantic approach

3.1. A system for semantic analysis of English texts

It is well known that understanding natural language requires a great deal of world knowledge. We will assume this knowledge is available in the form of predicate calculus axioms. Here we describe a system for the semantic analysis of English texts which consists of several 'semantic operations' that draw inferences selectively from the collection of axioms. The inferences drawn are just those which are required to interpret general words in context, determine the relations between sentences, and resolve anaphora.

The input to the semantic analyzer is the text, which we assume syntactic analysis or semantic interpretation rules have already reduced to a logical notation which exhibits functional relationships. In addition, we will assume the syntactically derivable coreference and non-coreference relations have been detected and recorded; any antecedent proposed by the method described below is checked against these relations.

The text in the logical notation consists of (1) a set of entities – X_1, X_2, X_3, ..., representing the entities referred to in the text; (2) the set of kernel statements which describe properties of the entities by applying predicates, corresponding roughly to English words, to the entities; and (3) an indication of which statement in a sentence is asserted and which are grammatically subordinate, by means of the symbol '|', which is read 'such that' or 'where'. For example, the sentence

The boy is on the roof of the building

would be represented (ignoring tense and definite articles)

on(X_1 | boy(X_1), X_2 | roof(X_2, X_3 | building(X_3))).

(The X_1 such that X_1 is a boy is on X_2 where X_2 is the roof of X_3 which is a building.) The information content of this sentence consists of the statements

on(X_1, X_2), boy(X_1), roof(X_2, X_3), building(X_3).

In the course of semantic processing, the text is augmented by inferences which the semantic operations determine appropriate, and entities standing for anaphors are merged with the entities standing for their antecedents. Each of the potentially large number of world knowledge axioms is associated with a particular word, or predicate; hence the collection of

axioms will be called the 'Lexicon'. For example, stored with the word 'bank' would be the fact that a bank is a building

(4) $(\forall y)(bank(y) \supset building(y))$

and with 'building' the fact that a building has a roof

(5) $(\forall y)(\exists z)(building(y) \supset roof(z, y))$.

The general form of the axioms is

(6) $(\forall y)(\exists z)(p(y) \supset (q(y, z) \supset r(y, z)))$

where p is the word or predicate with which the inference is associated, y represents its explicit parameters, z stands for the entities whose existence is also implied, and q(y, z) represents the other enabling conditions which must be checked before the conclusions r(y, z) can be drawn. If p(X_1) occurs in the text and (6) is determined to be appropriate, then q(X_1, X_1) is looked for in the text for some entities X_1, and if it is found, the conclusion r(X_1, X_1) is drawn by adding it to the text.

Inferences are not drawn freely, but only in response to the specific demands of semantic operations. These demands take two forms:

Forward inferences: from p(X_1) try to infer something of the pattern r(z_1, z_2).

Backward inferences: Find something in the text from which p(X_1) could be inferred.

Since the Lexicon is potentially quite large, the axioms are divided into clusters roughly according to topic. The clusters are given an initial measure of salience according to their anticipated relevance to the text at hand. The measures of salience are modified in the course of semantic processing in response to changes in topic in the text in the following way: When an axiom in a cluster is used, the entire cluster is given maximum salience; while the axioms in a cluster are not being used, its salience decays. All searches of the Lexicon initiated by the semantic operations are conducted in cluster order.

It may seem at first glance that this device is purely for efficiency. But

Among the axioms in the Lexicon will be axioms stating our knowledge about causes and effects. A strong form of the Cause pattern is

Find a causal chain from the purported cause to the purported effect.

A weaker form is

(7) Find a causal chain from a prominent fact inferable from the purported cause to a prominent fact inferable from the purported effect.

Here in a sense we are required to establish the causal link between supersets containing the items rather than between the items themselves. This allows us to recognize as having valid causal links, texts which are not just instantiations of potential theorems in the system.

(2) *Predicate interpretation:* It is typical for the most common English words to be useable in a wide variety of contexts. In large measure, this is possible because they are defined not so much in terms of the inferences that can be drawn from them, but in terms of their effect on the inferences that are drawn from the words with which they are grammatically related. For example, normally from the use of the word 'horse' one can infer certain facts about the entity described, such as that a typical activity might be racing and that it moves within a certain range of speed when it races. However, when we encounter 'slow horse', the word 'slow' alters what we may infer about the horse's speed when racing. A general definition for 'slow' will first instruct us to find the most prominent motion associated with the entity it modifies (and here the notion of context-dependent salience comes in). It then qualifies what we may infer about the range of speed of this motion. Such a definition will work for not only 'slow horse', but also 'slow walk', 'slow race', and 'slow watch', and if we are allowed to interpret 'motion' metaphorically, it also works for 'slow student' and 'slow business'.

This suggests a method for the interpretation of general words or predicates in context. A definition consists of two parts. The first part specifies the demands the predicate makes on its arguments, expressed in terms of inferences to be drawn from the explicit properties of the arguments. The second part specifies how these inferences are to be modified, or what further information is provided by the predicate. The operation which searches the Lexicon for these inferences and draws them with the appropriate modifications we will call 'predicate interpretation'.

in fact it is a crucial part of the analysis mechanism. When an operation calls for a chain of inference, there are usually quite a few chains of inference possible, each of which may lead to a different interpretation or a different antecedent. The changing salience measures on the axioms together with the lengths of the chains of inference define a dynamic ordering on the set of chains of inference. The operation then picks the appropriate chain of inference which is first in this ordering at the time the operation is invoked. In this way the inferencing process and hence the interpretation it produces are made highly context dependent.

3.2. The semantic operations and pronoun resolution

There are four principal semantic operations:

(1) *Detecting intersentence connectives:* The implicit relations between sentences in a paragraph are detected by comparing the current sentence and a previous sentence against a small set of common patterns. These patterns are stated in terms of inferences to be drawn from the two sentences. The patterns include Contrast, Cause, Violated Expectation, Temporal Succession, Paraphrase, Parallel, and Example. Only the first three are relevant to the examples below and are described here.[2]

Explicit conjunctions cause certain patterns to be strongly preferred – 'and' promotes Temporal Succession and Parallel, 'because' promotes Cause, a dash and 'i.e.' promote Paraphrase, and 'but' promotes Contrast and Violated Expectation.

One variety of the Contrast pattern might be stated as follows:

From the assertions of the current sentence and a previous sentence, try to infer statements S_1 and S_2, respectively, where
(a) the predicates of S_1 and S_2 are contradictory or lie at opposite ends of some scale;
(b) one pair of corresponding arguments of S_1 and S_2 are identical;
(c) the other pairs of corresponding arguments are 'similar' but different.

The Violated Expectation pattern is matched if from the assertion of the previous sentence a statement S can be inferred, while from the assertion of the current sentence, not-S is inferred. The latter inference is drawn and the former is suppressed.

[2] All the patterns are described in Hobbs (1976b).

Consider two more words which are used in examples below:

(a) 'Into' is a two-argument predicate. We must verify that its first argument (what the prepositional phrase modifies) is a motion and that its second argument (the object of the preposition) is a real or metaphorical region. We may then infer that the endpoint of the motion is within the region.

(b) For the predicate 'reduce', we must first locate the most salient scale with a real or metaphorical vertical orientation associated with its object. We can then infer that a downward motion occurs on this scale.

The operation of predicate interpretation allows us to recover omitted material such as *the part from the whole*:

He landed on (the roof of) the building

because 'on' demands a surface for its object; and *missing quantity words*:

(The price of) Coffee is higher this month

since 'higher' requires a real or metaphorical vertical scale.

This operation has a default feature. If a proof of the required inference can't be found, the inference is drawn anyway. At worst it will be instantiated with new and unknown entities for its arguments. The next operation will normally correct for this.

Predicate interpretation frequently aids in pronoun resolution, as will be seen in the next few paragraphs, and in Section 4.1.

(3) *Knitting*: When a statement is instantiated whose predicate is identical to that of a statement already in the text, then the first guess we make is that this is a redundancy. That is, redundancy is expected to be the normal state of affairs. If no obvious inconsistency is found, we assume the two statements are the same, and we merge them, thereby merging the corresponding arguments.

Knitting frequently leads to the antecedents of pronouns and implicit entities being found before operation 4, whose work it is to find antecedents, is even called. For example, suppose the following text is being processed:

(8) The boy walked into the bank. Moments later he was seen on its roof.

Let the bank be represented by the entity X_1 and the ''it'' of 'its' by X_2. Predicate interpretation on 'into' forces us to verify that its object, X_1, is an enclosure. This could be done by using the fact (4) that a bank is a building and the fact that a building is an enclosure. Since the entire chain of inference is instantiated the statement

(9) building(X_1)

becomes part of the text. The second sentence is processed, and predicate interpretation on 'roof' demands verification that X_2 is a building. This cannot be verified by the other properties of X_2 since it has no other properties. Therefore the default feature applies and

(10) building(X_2)

is simply assumed. The redundancy of (9) and (10) is presumed, knitting occurs, and the two statements and thereby their corresponding arguments X_1 and X_2 are merged. Thus has the antecedent of 'it' been identified as 'the bank'.

(4) *Identifying entities*: This operation seeks to identify the so far unidentified entities. Entities referred to in a text may be arranged in a hierarchy according to their degree of specification:
(a) proper names, including "you" and "I";
(b) other noun phrases, including those with definite, indefinite, and demonstrative articles;
(c) third person pronouns;
(d) zeroed arguments and implicit entities.

When a proper noun is encountered, it is identified with any entity in the previous text described by the same proper noun, or if there is none, a new entity is introduced. When a noun phrase tagged by the indefinite article is encountered, a new entity is introduced. The identification procedure for definite noun phrases is described in Hobbs (1975, 1976b). Its search step is similar to the search step described below for pronouns.

In order to find the antecedent of a pronoun a backward search through the Lexicon is conducted for a chain of inference that begins at some statement in the text and ends with a known property of the pronoun. Suppose example (8) had escaped the first three operations, and a search for the antecedent of 'it' was necessary. The only known property of X_2 is that it has a roof. The Lexicon is probed to see what has a roof, the fact

(5) stored with 'building' that buildings have roofs is found, and the text is checked for an occurrence of 'building'. Assume 'building(X_1)' has not yet been inferred from 'bank(X_1)', so that 'building' is not found. The Lexicon is then searched for something which is a building, the fact (4) associated with 'bank' that a bank is a building is found, and a bank is mentioned explicitly in the text. The required chain of inference

$$\text{bank}(X_1) \supset \text{building}(X_1) \supset \text{roof}(X_3, X_1)$$

is found. Hence the antecedent of 'it' is located.

The difficulty with this search is that it is very expensive. It requires exponential time and the branching factor of the search can be very large. For example, there could be a great many axioms in the Lexicon which say that something is a building; gas stations, post offices, dime stores, etc. are all buildings. Therefore in order to cut down on the size of the search, and at the same time to take advantage of the effectiveness of the naive algorithm of Part 2, a bidirectional search (Pohl 1971) is used which starts not only at the pronoun but also at the entity the naive algorithm would choose as antecedent, in hopes that the two searches will meet somewhere in the middle. Thus, in about 90% of the cases, the search will go quite fast.

Once a plausible antecedent is found, a shallow check is made to insure that the properties of the two entities to be merged are not obviously inconsistent.

More than one plausible antecedent may be found by the search. If so, we choose the candidate that maximizes the redundancy in the simplest possible way, by inferring freely from the properties of the candidates and of the pronoun and picking the candidate that has the most properties of high salience in common with the pronoun.

4. Examples of the semantic approach to pronoun resolution

4.1.

The first example is from the archaeology text (Watson 1966: 21) and illustrates knitting working in conjunction with predicate interpretation:

The plain was reduced by erosion to *its* present level.

or, in the logical notation,

$$\text{reduce}(\text{erode}(X_1), X_2 \mid \text{plain}(X_2), X_3 \mid \text{present}(\text{level}(X_3, X_4)))$$

i.e. something, X_1, eroding reduces X_2 which is a plain to X_3 where X_3's being the level of X_4 is true at present. We must identify the antecedent not only if 'it' (X_4) but also of the implicit entity which is eroding (X_1). Note that syntactic criteria do not solve the problem, for in the sentence

Walter was introduced by John to his present wife

'his' could refer to Walter, John, or someone else. Selectional criteria will not work either, for 'erosion' can have a present level, as in

Contour farming has reduced erosion to its present level.

Consider now what happens in the course of semantic processing. We apply predicate interpretation to 'reduce'. This predicate demands of its second argument that it be capable of movement along some vertical axis (real or metaphorical), leading us to infer that a plain, being a land form, is characterized by an altitude, i.e. a position on the real vertical axis going from the center of the earth outward. 'Reduce' then adds the information that a change downward to the third argument X_3 has occurred on this axis:

(11) $\text{become}(\text{at}(X_2, X_5), \text{at}(X_2, X_3)) \mid \text{exceed}(X_5, X_3, X_7 \mid \text{Altitude-axis} (X_7)), \text{vertical}(X_7)$

i.e. the plain X_2 at X_5 becomes X_2 at X_3 where X_5 exceeds X_3 on the vertical Altitude axis X_7.

Next the arguments of 'reduce' are processed in turn. From the argument X_1 of 'erode' we must also infer that it is capable of movement along a real or metaphorical vertical axis. 'Erode' also says this movement is in a downward direction. X_1 has no explicit properties, so we cannot infer a vertical axis. Hence we simply assume one to exist.

(12) $\text{become}(\text{at}(X_1, X_8), \text{at}(X_1, X_9)) \mid \text{exceed}(X_8, X_9, X_{10} \mid \text{vertical} (X_{10}))$

Since (11) and (12) are identical except for temporary entities, and since no contradiction could be derived if we identified the temporary entities, the knitting operation applies, and the implicit entity which is eroding, X_1, is identified with the plain, X_2, X_8 is identified with X_5, X_9 with X_3, and the vertical axis X_{10} with the Altitude axis X_7.

When the third argument of 'reduce' is processed, we first apply predicate interpretation to 'present'. 'Present' carries with it the implication that what it describes – X_3 being the level of X_4 – resulted by a 'becoming' from some previous state. 'Level' demands that its first argument be a point on a vertical scale, and that its second argument be at that point. Thus, we infer

become(X_{11}, at(X_4, X_3 | on(X_3, X_{12} | vertical(X_{12}))))

i.e. the state X_{11} changes into the state in which X_4 is located at X_3 which is a point on a vertical scale X_{12}. Knitting identifies this with (11), thereby identifying X_{11} with 'at(X_2, X_5)', X_4 ('it') with X_2 ('the plain'), and vertical axis X_{12} with the Altitude axis X_7.

When at last we invoke operation 4, we find that all entities have been identified except the anaphoric definite noun phrase 'the plain'.

4.2.

The second example comes from *Newsweek* and illustrates how the intersentence operation aids in pronoun resolution.

The FBI said they had tentative identifications on the fugitives, but didn't know where *they* were.

We wish to find the antecedent of the 'they' in the 'but' clause.

The naive algorithm does not work on this example. The first entity it would propose is the omitted subject of 'didn't know', i.e. the FBI, as if the FBI were lost in a forest and didn't know where they were. Next it would light upon 'tentative identifications', as if the FBI had identifications but a clerk had misfiled them. Only at last would the correct antecedent, 'fugitives', be reached.

In examining the semantic approach, assume we have the correct parse, conjoining the 'but' clause with 'they had tentative identifications ...'. Assume also that the 'they' of the first clause and the omitted subject of the second have been recognized as coreferential with 'the FBI'. The conjunction 'but' makes the Contrast pattern strongly preferred. From 'the FBI had tentative identifications on the fugitives' we can infer 'the FBI had tentatively identified the fugitives'. From this can be inferred 'the FBI (tentatively) knows the names of the fugitives'. This is compared with the assertion of the 'but' clause, which paraphrased is 'the FBI does not know the location of X'. We find that the predicates are contradictory, and the first arguments are the same. Therefore the Contrast pattern will be matched if the second arguments – 'the names of the fugitives' and 'the location of X' – can be shown to be similar. This can be accomplished by assuming 'they' and 'the fugitives' to be the same.

The search step, operation 4, would locate the antecedent, even if the first three operations failed. The following chain of inference would be discovered:

(13) From 'fugitive(X_1)' infer 'hide-from(X_1, X_2 | police(X_2))'
(14) From (13) infer 'cause(X_1, not(know (X_2, location(X_1))))'.
From (14) infer 'not(know(X_2, location(X_1)))'.

(If something is caused, it holds.) But this is just the property we know about 'they'.

4.3.

Next is the classic example from Winograd (1972: 33). Consider

(15) They_1 prohibited them_2 from demonstrating because they_3 feared violence.
(16) They_1 prohibited them_2 from demonstrating because they_3 advocated violence.

'They_3' is coreferential with 'they_1' in (15), but with 'them_2' in (16).

In (15), the intersentence operation will seek to link the two clauses, and on account of the conjunction 'because' a match with a Cause pattern will be the most sought.

For the sake of this discussion we will coin a word 'diswant', analogous to 'dislike'. To diswant S is to want not-S. From 'x prohibits y' we can infer 'x diswants y' and from 'x fears z' we can infer 'x diswants z'. We will use (7) and try to establish a causal link from 'they_3 diswant violence' to 'they_1 diswant (they_2 demonstrate)'.

A prominent fact about demonstrations, well known to anyone aware in the 'sixties, is that frequently

(17) (w demonstrate) cause violence.

A fundamental fact relating the real world with mental and emotional worlds is

(18) (x cause y & z diswant y) cause (z diswant x).

This has the interesting effect of transforming a causal link between two events in the real world into the reversed causal link between mental states in which these events are apprehended. Because of (17) and (18) 'they$_3$ diswant violence' causes 'they$_3$ diswant (w demonstrate)', so that the link is established if we identify 'they$_3$' with 'they$_1$' and w with 'they$_2$'.

To match the Cause pattern in (16) we seek a causal chain from the second clause to the statement inferable from the first clause that 'they$_1$ diswant (they$_2$ demonstrate)'. The chain is as follows: Someone advocating something often causes that something to occur. In particular, they$_3$ advocating violence may cause violence to occur. Normally, someone, in particular they$_3$, will diswant violence. Therefore, by (18), they$_1$ will diswant they$_3$ advocating violence. Since 'they$_3$ demonstrate' causes 'they$_3$ advocate x', again by (18) we infer 'they$_1$ diswant (they$_3$ demonstrate)'. The pattern is then matched by identifying 'they$_3$' and 'they$_2$'.

The pronoun problem of (15) and (16) could also be solved by proposing both 'they$_1$' and 'them$_2$' as plausible antecedents and holding a competition to see which choice maximized redundancy. In (15), the redundancy between 'they$_1$ diswant ...' and 'they$_3$ diswant ...' would result in 'they$_1$' being chosen. In (16), the prominent fact about demonstrating that someone who demonstrates advocates something would make 'them$_2$', the choice that maximized redundancy.

4.4.

Last is the classic example from Charniak (1972, 1974), in the style of a children's story:

Jack invited Janet to his birthday party.
Janet wondered if Jack would like a kite.

But Bill said Jack already had a kite. Jack would make her take it back.

The question is, how do we know 'it' refers to the kite she is thinking about buying and not the more recently mentioned kite Jack already has.

This is a difficult text, but it is important to be clear about where the difficulty lies. For it does not lie in the pronoun resolution problem in the last sentence. In part, it lies in determining the relation between the first two sentences. And this difficulty is reflected in a slight but perceptible discontinuity the reader senses at that point.

The relation between the two sentences is causal. Establishing a causal chain from the first to the second might go as follows: Jack inviting Janet to the birthday party causes her to want to come to it. (19), a 'want' version of (18), may be proposed as a general rule and is applied here several times.

(19) If y enables or is required for z, then x wanting z causes x to want y.

A guest at a birthday party is required to give the host a present. To be a present something should be new and it should be liked by the recipient. For it to be new one has to buy it. Now if Jack would like a kite and the present were a kite, then Jack would like the present. Therefore her wanting Jack to like the present causes her to want to know (i.e. wonder) if Jack would like her to buy a kite.

Regardless of the particular facts used and the particular causal chain found, we must somehow flesh out the second sentence to something like

Janet wondered if Jack would like the kite if she bought one for him for a birthday present.

Once this is accomplished, pronoun resolution becomes a straightforward matter. We simply take the word 'back' seriously.[3] For there to be motion *back* there must have been motion *to*. Therefore, in performing predicate interpretation on 'back', we look for the most salient motion in the previous text, preferably involving the same agent and object as the motion modified by 'back'. We find the motion of Janet's buying the kite, and therefore identify 'it' with the kite she considers buying.

The intersentence operation is also relevant. The Violated Expectation

[3] Charniak (1974) has also pointed this out.

pattern between the second and third sentences, signalled by 'but', is verified by noting that the expectation that Jack would like the kite is violated. From this the unacceptability of the kite as a gift can be inferred, and this is the cause whose effect is the return of Janet's kite in the fourth sentence.

A minor aspect that contributes to Janet's kite being chosen as antecedent is the fact that the kite exists in the hypothetical world of Janet's wondering. Jack's kite exists in the real world. 'It' occurs in the hypothetical world dominated by 'would'. Thus, maximum redundancy is served if we assume 'it' to be the hypothetical kite.

5. Summary

We have proposed three steps for pronoun resolution.

(1) The intersentence relation operation together with knitting.

(2) Predicate interpretation together with knitting.

(3) The bidirectional search through the Lexicon, using the naive algorithm.

To these two more steps can be added as a fail-safe mechanism:

(4) For all the entities of the correct gender in the current sentence and the previous sentence, hold a competition to maximize the redundancy as in Operation 4 of Section 3.2. At least we know the antecedent is there in 98% of the cases. Heretofore, this has been the best solution offered for the pronoun resolution problem.

(5) Apply the naive algorithm. This has the advantage that it always gives an answer.

Normally, pronoun resolution will be accomplished by the first two steps. On reflection, this should not be surprising. For the reason a speaker uses a pronoun is precisely because the identity of the entity is obvious without description to anyone who is understanding what is being said, and the first two semantic operations capture, in large measure, what is meant by understanding.

References

Charniak, E., 1972. Toward a model of children's story comprehension. AI TR-266, Massachusetts Institute of Technology Artificial Intelligence Laboratory.

Charniak, E., 1974. 'He will make you take it back': A study in the pragmatics of language. Working Paper 5, Institute for Semantic and Cognitive Studies.

Chomsky, N., 1970. Remarks on nominalization. In: R. Jacobs and P. Rosenbaum (eds.), Readings in transformational grammar, 184–221. Waltham, Mass.: Blaisdell.

Culicover, P., 1976. A constraint on coreferentiality. Foundations of Language 14, 109–118.

Grinder, J., and P. Postal, 1971. Missing antecedents. Linguistic Inquiry 2, 269–312.

Hobbs, J., 1975. A general system for semantic analysis of English and its use in drawing maps from directions. American Journal of Computational Linguistics, microfiche 32.

Hobbs, J., 1976a. Pronoun resolution. Res. Rep. 76-1, Dept. Comp. Sci., City College, CUNY, July 1976.

Hobbs, J., 1976b. A computational approach to discourse analysis. Res. Rep. 76-2, Dept. Comp. Sci., City College, CUNY, December 1976.

Jackendoff, R., 1972. Semantic interpretation in generative grammar. Cambridge, Mass.: MIT Press.

Jespersen, O., 1954. A modern English grammar on historical principles, part VII: Syntax. London: Allen and Unwin.

Klapholtz, D., and A. Lockman, 1975. Contextual reference resolution. American Journal of Computational Linguistics, microfiche 36.

Lakoff, G., 1968. Pronouns and reference. Unpublished paper.

Langacker, R., 1969. On pronominalization and the chain of command. In: D. Reibel and S. Schane (eds.), Modern studies in English, 160–186. Englewood Cliffs: Prentice-Hall.

Lees, R., and E. Klima, 1963. Rules for English pronominalization. Language 39, 17–28.

Olson, D., 1970. Language and thought: Aspects of a cognitive theory of semantics. Psychological Review 77, 257–273.

Pohl, I., 1971. Bi-directional search. In: B. Meltzer and D. Michie (eds.), Machine intelligence, vol. 6, 127–140. New York: American Elsevier.

Rieger, C., 1974. Conceptual memory: A theory and computer program for processing the meaning content of natural language utterances. Stanford AIM-233.

Ross, J., 1967. On the cyclic nature of English pronominalization. In: To honor Roman Jakobson, 1669–1682. The Hague: Mouton.

Watson, W., 1966. Early civilization in China. New York: McGraw-Hill.

Wilks, Y., 1975. A preferential, pattern-seeking, semantics for natural language inference. Artificial Intelligence 6, 53–74.

Winograd, T., 1972. Understanding natural language. New York: Academic Press.

THE REPRESENTATION AND USE OF FOCUS IN A SYSTEM FOR UNDERSTANDING DIALOGS

Barbara J. Grosz
Artificial Intelligence Center
SRI International, Menlo Park, California 94025

ABSTRACT

As a dialog progresses the objects and actions that are most relevant to the conversation. and hence in the focus of attention of the dialog participants, change. This paper describes a representation of focus for language understanding systems. emphasizing its use in understanding task-oriented dialogs. The representation highlights that part of the knowledge base relevant at a given point in a dialog. A model of the task is used both to structure the focus representation and to provide an index into potentially relevant concepts in the knowledge base. The use of the focus representation to make retrieval of items from the knowledge base more efficient is described.

I   INTRODUCTION

To understand the sentences in a discourse. a computer system, like a person, must have knowledge about the domain of the discourse. However, the knowledge required to understand even simple, real-life domains is so extensive that it will overwhelm a system that does not apply it selectively. This means that the ability to focus on the subset of knowledge relevant to a particular situation is crucial. This paper addresses the problem of focus from the perspective of building a computer system that can participate in a task-oriented dialog. A representation for focus is presented; its use is illustrated by showing how the referents of definite noun phrases are identified.

A combination of contextual factors influences the interpretation of an utterance. In fact, what is usually meant by "the context of an utterance" is precisely that set of constraints which together direct attention to the concepts of interest in the discourse in which the utterance occurs. Both the preceding discourse context -- the utterances that have already occurred -- and the situational context -- the environment in which an utterance occurs -- affect the interpretation of the utterance. For a dialog, the situational context includes the physical environment, the social setting, and the relationship between the participants in the dialog. This paper shows how the task and dialog contexts combine to provide a focus on those concepts relevant to the interpretation of utterances in task-oriented dialogs.

This research is currently supported by the National Science Foundation under Grant No. MCS76-22004; it was previously funded under ARPA contract DAAG29-76-C-0011, administered through the Army Research Office.

The following two dialog fragments illustrate the role of focus in interpreting utterances.

S1:   The lid is attached to the container with four 1/4-inch bolts.
R1:   Where are the bolts?

S2:   Attach the lid to the container.
R2:   Where are the bolts?

In the first sequence, statement S1 explicitly points out a set of bolts that are then referred to in response R1. The dialog context provides the focus for understanding the phrase In the second sequence, no such explicit mention occurs. Instead, the attaching referred to in S2 implicitly focuses on the fasteners involved. In a particular task context, knowledge about the process of attaching a specific lid to a specific container focuses on a specific set of bolts. Hence, the noun phrase in R2 is unambiguous.

A.   REQUISITES FOR A FOCUS REPRESENTATION

There are three requisite properties of a focus representation. The most crucial is that it differentiate among the items in the knowledge base (i.e., the encoding of that portion of the world the system knows about) on the basis of relevance. By highlighting those items in the knowledge base that are most relevant to the current discourse, the focus representation enables the system to access more important information first during its retrieval and deduction operations.

Second, the focus representation must account for implicitly focused items. Specific mention of an object brings into focus not only the object itself, but also certain associated items. For example, mention of "the house" brings into focus such associated objects as "the living room", "the roof", "the yard", and "the owner". Parts of actions as well as objects may enter focus in this way. For example, "sewing a dress" brings into focus "cutting out the skirt".

Third, the focus representation must include mechanisms for shifting focus. As successive utterances in a discourse are interpreted, the items in focus change. Shifts of focus occur both gradually with time, and more abruptly with change of topic. Not only the objects in focus, but also the particular way of viewing them, can change. For example, a doctor can be viewed as a member of the medical profession, or as having a role in a family.

B.   OVERVIEW OF PAPER

The next section describes a focus
representation that satisfies these requirements.
The representation was developed in the context of
a system for understanding language (Walker 1976).
The knowledge base of this system is embodied in a
semantic network. In such a system, identifying a
network structure is the analog of the human
process of identifying and retrieving an item from
memory. Hence, the matching of network structures
is a crucial process in interpreting utterances. A
major use of the focus representation is to make
this matching process more efficient. Once the
focus representation has been described, and its
use illustrated, mechanisms for shifting focus in
task-oriented dialogs are discussed. These
mechanisms are the only part of the focus
representation that is specific to task-oriented
dialogs. Finally, a description is given of how
the focus representation can be extended to help
solve two essential problems in natural language
understanding: focusing on different attributes of
the same object under different circumstances, and
forgetting information no longer relevant to a
discourse.

The focus representation was implemented in
the SRI speech understanding system (Walker, 1976)
and used by the discourse component to resolve
definite noun phrases. The process representation
used to encode the task model, which is needed both
for implicit focusing and to guide shifts of focus,
is designed and currently being implemented. (The
speech understanding system implementation used a
simpler shift strategy than the one described
here.)

II   THE FOCUS REPRESENTATION

This section describes a two-part focus
representation. One part corresponds to explicit
focus, the other to implicit focus. The explicit
focus data structure contains those items that are
relevant to the interpretation of an utterance
because they have participated explicitly in the
preceding discourse. Implicit focus consists of
those items that are relevant because they are
closely connected to items in explicit focus. For
instance, in the dialog fragments given in the
introduction, both S1 and S2 result in the lid, the
container, and the attaching operation being in
explicit focus. The bolts involved in the
operation are in explicit focus following S1, but
implicit focus following S2.

Concepts that are implicitly focused are
separated from those that are explicitly focused
(i.e., they are not added to the explicit focus
data structure) for two reasons. First, there are
numerous implicitly focused items, many of which
are never referenced in a dialog. Including these
items in the explicit focus data structure would
clutter it, weakening its highlighting function.
Second, references to implicitly focused items are
considered indications of shifts of focus.

A.   FOCUS SPACES--A REPRESENTATION OF EXPLICIT
     FOCUS

The representation of explicit focus is
achieved by partitioning a semantic network. A
semantic network is a directed graph: a set of
nodes, and a set of (labelled, directed) arcs,
connecting pairs of those nodes. Networks have
been used in several previous language
understanding systems (e.g., Quillian. 1968;
Simmons, 1973). Conventions for the use and
meaning of nodes and arcs vary. The networks
described here use the conventions of
Hendrix (1975)--nodes are used to represent
"objects," where "objects" include such things as
physical objects, events, relationships, and sets.
Arcs are used only to encode those binary
relationships that do not change over time.

Partitioning adds to the structure of a
semantic network by segmenting the nodes and arcs
of the network into units called spaces.
Hendrix (1975) introduced the notion of network
partitioning, and described its use in encoding
quantification, abstraction, and hypothetical
worlds. In addition to separating the nodes of a
network into spaces, partitioning provides for
grouping the spaces into ordered sets called
vistas. Vistas typically are used to restrict the
network entities seen by procedures that reference
the network (i.e., vistas impose visibility
constraints). When given a vista, a procedure can
operate as though the only nodes and arcs in the
network are those contained in some space in the
vista. Although any set of spaces may be collected
into a vista, vistas typically are used to group
spaces hierarchically.

To encode focus, Hendrix's notion of
partitioning has been extended to allow a network
to be partitioned in more than one way. The nodes
and arcs are separated into different sets of
segments for different purposes. In particular,
the network is partitioned to encode focus in
addition to being partitioned to encode
quantification. The partitioning to encode
quantification is referred to as the "logical
partitioning," and is represented by dashed lines
in the figures in this report. The partitioning to
encode focus is referred to as the "focus
partitioning" and is represented by solid lines.
The spaces in the focus partitioning are used to
highlight items that become focused in a discourse.
The focus spaces are related in a hierarchy that
reflects the structure of the discourse (this is
important for shifting focus, as will be discussed
later).

An example of a partitioned semantic network
is displayed in Figure 1. The network is divided
into four spaces: S0, S1, S2, and S3. The
conventions adopted for figures in this paper are
that a node lies on the space(s) inside of which it
is drawn, and an arc lies on the space(s) inside of
which its label appears. If the boxes representing
two spaces overlap, but neither contains the other,
then the nodes and arcs in the overlap lie on both
spaces. In Figure 1, space S0 groups the nodes
representing EXCHANGES (the set of all exchange
situations), ATTACHINGS, BOLTS, PUMPS, and

PLATFORMS (the sets of all attach operations, bolts, pumps, and platforms, respectively). Space S1 contains the specific exchange, represented by the node 'EX1' (single quotes denote node names), in which one object, the set of bolts B1, represented by the node 'B1', is exchanged for another, the amount of money represented by the node '$1'. The e arc from 'EX1' to 'EXCHANGES' indicates that EX1 is an element of the set EXCHANGES. The s arc from 'B1' to 'BOLTS' indicates that the set B1 is a subset of BOLTS. Space S2 contains the representation of a specific attaching operation, A1, of the minor part, PU1, and the major part, PL1. Space S3 also contains the specific attaching operation A1 but shows that this operation involves the specific set of bolts, B1.

The hierarchy of spaces in Figure 1 is shown by the heavy arrows between spaces. Each space is associated with a particular vista that is the "orthodox" vista for that space. In Figure 1, the orthodox vista associated with each space S is composed of the space S itself and all spaces that can be reached from S by following the heavy arrows. For instance, the orthodox vista of S0 is (S0) and the orthodox vista of S3 is (S3 S2 S0).

The visibility constraints that result from this partitioning may be seen by considering different views of the bolts B1 and the attaching operation A1. B1 is shown as taking part in two different events. A1 is a single operation shown at two different levels of detail. From the vista (S1 S0), the set of bolts B1 is seen only to be involved in the exchange EX1. However, from the vista (S3 S2 S0), B1 is seen as the fasteners in the operation of attaching PU1 to PL1. The two vistas give two alternative views of B1. A similar situation occurs with A1. From the vista (S2 S0), A1 is seen only as an attaching between two parts, with the fasteners left unspecified. When S3 is added as the bottom space in the vista, A1 is seen to involve the specific fasteners B1.

The focus partitioning makes it possible to highlight the particular way of looking at a concept that is germane to a given point in a dialog. When the same object enters the dialog twice, in two different subdialogs (e.g., a tool used in two distinct subtasks), the node corresponding to that object will appear in two distinct focus spaces. If different aspects of the object are focused on in the two subdialogs, different relationships in which the object participates will be in the two focus spaces. For example, in Figure 1, B1 is focused on in S1 as a part of an exchange. In contrast, in S3 it is focused on as part of an attaching operation.

The main reason for providing the ability to focus on different attributes of an object is to allow differential access to the properties of the object, and hence to order the retrieval of derivable facts about that object. Differential access is important for events and relationships as well as physical objects. For example, when quilting is considered as a kind of sewing, the subactions of cutting and pinning are accessed first, but when quilting is considered as a social

gathering, the subactions of talking and eating are more important, and are selected first.

There are two principles governing what is contained in a focus space. First, if a concept is in focus, type information about that concept must also be in focus. (The type information both indicates the aspect of the concept being focused on and provides the key index to additional knowledge about the concept.) Therefore, in the network representation, every node in focus must have one outgoing element or subset arc also in focus. Second, if a concept's participation in some situation (e.g., a book's being the object of a specific owning relationship) is in focus, then the situation itself (i.e., the specific owning relationship) also must be in focus. Therefore, the node from which any focused case arc emanates must also be in focus.

New focus spaces are created as the focus of a discourse shifts. At any point in a dialog, only one focus space is "active," but several may be considered "open." The active focus space reflects the focus of attention at the current point in the dialog. The open focus spaces reflect previous active spaces that contain some unfinished topics and hence may become active again; they are areas to which the dialog may return. The relationship between focus spaces is determined by (and hence reflects) the structure of the particular discourse being processed For task dialogs, the task hierarchy provides a framework for this structure (Grosz, 1977, discusses the structure of these dialogs).

B.   IMPLICIT FOCUSING THROUGH A TASK
     REPRESENTATION

The representation of implicit focus requires a decision about what information associated with a concept should be put in focus when that concept is introduced. The bounds on this information depend on the knowledge and expectations about the concept that are shared by speaker and hearer (see Karttunen, 1968; Maratsos, 1976). The tradeoff between how much information to associate with a given concept, and how many levels of associations to consider for implicit focusing, must be resolved. In general, these problems entail basic and complex issues about the representation of knowledge. They will be addressed here only as they occur for events.

For physical objects, the subparts of the object are among the concepts that must be implicitly focused when the object is in focus. For events, the situation is somewhat more complicated. The direct analogy of subparts of an object is subevents of an event. However, the participants in the subevents of an event are also implicitly focused. The dialog sequence S2-R2 presented in the introduction illustrates this point. S2 implicitly focuses on the bolts involved in the attaching as well as the subevent of fastening the lid down.

To enable implicit focusing on both the subevents and the participants involved in them, the representation of an event indicates both its

subevents and the participants in its subevents.
Figure 2 shows a network representation that
accomplishes this for the task step of attaching a
pump to a platform. The logical space
KNOWLEDGESPACE, only part of which is shown here,
contains representations for all items in the
knowledge base. The set of
ATTACHINGS.PUMP.PLATFORM is shown to be a subset of
all ATTACHINGS. The delin arc from 'APP' to
'ATTACHINGS.PUMP.PLATFORM' indicates that APP is
the prototypical element of the set of such
attachings (see Hendrix, 1975, for a discussion of
delineations). The two nodes 'APP' and 'APPD'
together with the other structures inside the
delineation space, DS, describe the nature of
events in which a pump is attached to a platform.
APP relates the participants in the event. The
outgoing arcs from 'APP' indicate that these
attachings involve a minor part, which is an
element of the set PUMPS, and a major part, which
is an element of the set PLATFORMS.

APPD is the event descriptor for APP. It
relates the preconditions, effects, and substeps of
the event. The two constituents of APPD that are
most relevant here are the plot space and the
binding space. The plot space, PS, contains the
breakdown of APP into two substeps, S1 and S2,
specifying a POSITION operation, OP1, and a SECURE
operation OP2. The suc arcs indicate successor
links between substeps. (Although not shown here,
the representation allows for partial ordering of
substeps, as in Sacerdoti, 1975.) The binding
space, BS, contains a set of four bolts that take
part in the securing substep. When the task step
of attaching a particular pump to a particular
platform is in (explicit) focus, then the
corresponding substeps for S1 and S2, and the set
of bolts in the binding space are considered
implicitly in focus.

In general, the binding space contains all the
participants in any subevent that are at a level of
detail too low to be mentioned explicitly as
participants in the main event. The implicit focus
for an event consists of the vista of the plot
space and binding space, and thus contains both the
subevents and the participants in those subevents.
Because more inferencing is required if more levels
of associations (e.g., deeper levels of the task
hierarchy) are referenced, when retrieval requires
a search of implicit focus (e.g., the concept
sought is not in explicit focus), a breadth-first
search is done. Subconcepts of all relevant
concepts are examined before any sub-subconcepts
are examined.

Implicit focus is used for the interpretation
of both object and action references (cf.
Rieger, 1975; the implicit focus of the task
representation provides the same task context as
conceptual overlays). For example, if the current
task is attaching the pump to the platform, then
"the bolts" refers to the bolts that participate in
the securing operation and "put" refers to the
positioning subevent.

This representation has been developed jointly
with Gary G. Hendrix and Ann E. Robinson.

III   USING FOCUS FOR NETWORK STRUCTURE MATCHING

The retrieval of items from memory is one of
the most frequent operations any knowledge-based
system must do. In a system with a semantic
network knowledge base, the central process
involved in retrieval is matching a network
fragment containing variables with the knowledge
base. This matching process typically entails
considerable search that is guided only by local
constraints. A major use of the focus
representation is to constrain the search on the
basis of discourse information. In this paper, the
system component that performs this matching
process will be called the matcher. Fikes and
Hendrix (1977) describes in detail how this
component works. Only enough detail will be given
here to elucidate the need for and the role of the
focus representation in this process.

The matcher works with two (logical) vistas: a
QVISTA (question vista) and a KVISTA (knowledge
vista). The QVISTA is a set of spaces collectively
containing a piece of network for which a match is
sought. The KVISTA represents the set of all
knowledge in which the match is sought. For
example, when the matcher is called as part of the
procedure for resolving a definite noun phrase
(e.g., the red bolts), the QVISTA is a piece of
network structure that describes the object
referred to by the noun phrase, as it is described
by the noun phrase (e.g., a net structure for a
subset of bolts that are colored red). The KVISTA
is the whole knowledge base. The match of the
QVISTA fragment to the KVISTA corresponds to
finding a real object (i.e., an object that
'exists' in the knowledge base) that can be
described by the definite noun phrase.

In the process of arriving at a match, the
matcher binds each item (i.e., each node and arc)
in the QVISTA to an element of the KVISTA. Two
kinds of decisions affect the amount of computation
done in arriving at a match. First, at each step
of the match, an item must be selected for matching
from the QVISTA. The order of selection influences
the efficiency of the matching computation.
Second, once a QVISTA element is selected, the
matcher must select an element of the KVISTA for
trial binding to the QVISTA element. In general,
there are many candidates and only local
information is available to guide the selection.

Each binding of a QVISTA and a KVISTA element
is tentative. First, side effects of the binding
must be checked. For example, if a node is bound,
the matcher must establish that unbound element or
subset arcs in QVISTA from that node are consistent
with the arcs in KVISTA. The match will be carried
further only if such consistencies hold. Even so,
the binding may be rejected later if a match of the
remainder of the QVISTA is not found. Hence, the
number of bindings attempted is a significant
element of the cost of arriving at a match.

In the SRI speech understanding system, this
component was implemented by Richard E. Fikes and
was called the deduction component.

Optimally, for both kinds of decision, the matcher will choose the most constraining element. In an unfocused match, the choice can be made only on the basis of local structural information.

A. MATCHING IN FOCUS

The focus representation is used to order the candidates considered for binding by the matcher. The term "focused match" is used to denote matches that are constrained by focus. Focusing on certain concepts (both nodes and arcs) constrains the matcher to consider only objects germane to the dialog. Since arcs provide indices from focused items into general network (KVISTA) information, focusing on an arc also guides the matcher in establishing properties about nodes being matched. That is, focused arcs provide a means of differential access to unfocused information. Using the arcs in focus for differential access does not eliminate consideration of a concept from a different perspective. Instead, it orders the way in which aspects of the concept are to be examined in looking for new (to the dialog) information about the concept.

When a focused match is requested, the matcher is passed two arguments in addition to the usual QVISTA and KVISTA: a focus vista and a "forced-in-focus" list. The focus vista represents the set of nodes and arcs considered to be "in focus." Different calls on the matcher are made for explicit and implicit focus matches. For explicit focus, the focus vista may be either the active focus space alone, or the entire vista of open focus spaces. For implicit focus, the focus vista is the composite of the implicit focus vistas for all items in explicit focus (e.g., for each event, the vista of plot space and binding space). The forced-in-focus list contains those items in the QVISTA that must be bound to items in the focus vista. As an example of the use of the forced-in-focus list, consider the requirement that the referent of a definite noun phrase be in focus. This requirement corresponds to a focused match in which the forced-in-focus list contains the QVISTA node corresponding to the head noun of the noun phrase.

Forcing a QVISTA item to be in focus provides a strong constraint on the search for a matching KVISTA item. Hence, forced-in-focus items are selected as the first candidates from the QVISTA to be matched. If a successful match is obtained for such an item, it constrains other items in the QVISTA. If no match can be found for a forced-in-focus item, then no focused match of the QVISTA is possible.

The focus vista is used to order the selection of KVISTA items for trial binding to a QVISTA item. Each step of the matching algorithm first selects relevant items in the focus vista both for explicit matches (the item in the QVISTA is bound to an item that explicitly exists in the KVISTA) and for derived matches (application of a general rule produces a new KVISTA element). Hence, focus influences the order in which deductions are made in the process of arriving at a match.

Figure 3 illustrates the use of focus to reduce the number of candidates considered for binding by the matcher. Consider the KVISTA of Figure 3 and the QVISTA (q.w1) of Figure 4. The KVISTA contains several wrenches: W1 is a box-end wrench that is in focus FS1; W2 is a box-end wrench in focus FS2; W3 is an open-end wrench also in focus FS2; W4 is another open-end wrench not in focus at all. There is another object, O1, with a box-end. The QVISTA represents the noun phrase "the box-end wrench". In an unconstrained match, the matcher would consider all the nodes with e arcs to 'WRENCHES', or all of the nodes with endtype arcs to 'BOX-END' (depending on which set is smaller) as candidates for binding to QW1. Eventually, it would try 'W1' or 'W2' and obtain a successful match. In the worst case, this would entail one node and two arc bindings for each of the candidate nodes that fails as a complete match. In general, there may be many such unsuccessful candidates (e.g., many wrenches that are not box-end wrenches, but are considered by the matcher before it selects 'W1' or 'W2').

The focused match is able to avoid all this searching. If focus space FS1 is used, only nodes 'H1' and 'W1' are considered. 'H1' will be rejected immediately because the e arc to 'HAMMERS' is incompatible with the e arc from 'QW1' to 'WRENCHES' (the matcher knows that the sets HAMMERS and WRENCHES have no intersection from the ds arcs from 'WRENCHES' and 'HAMMERS' to 'TOOLS'). With focus space FS2 as the constraint, both 'W3' and 'W2' are considered, but 'W3' is eliminated because of its incompatible endtype. In the worst case, one set (one e arc and one node) of unnecessary bindings is made. Even greater savings are obtained when deduction is necessary to achieve a match, that is, when general rules -- chunks of information stored in the net as applicable to whole sets of concepts -- must be applied (see Grosz, 1977). In such cases, focus constrains the application of such rules, avoiding a combinatorial explosion of trial bindings.

IV SHIFTING FOCUS AND THE RESOLUTION OF DEFINITE NOUN PHRASES

To complete the focus representation, it is necessary to provide a mechanism for deciding when to shift focus. A shift in focus may be stated directly by some utterance in a discourse (e.g., "I've finished that step. What's next?" or "Let's change the topic."), but usually the cues are more subtle. For example, when the discussion of some activity turns to a discussion of one of the participants in the activity, the focus shifts from the overall activity to that participant. What indicates a shift in focus depends on both the kind of discourse being processed and on the topic of discourse. The shift strategy described here is specific to task-oriented dialogs. It reflects the task as the major topic of such dialogs, and hence the major indicator of shifts of focus. Although the rest of the focus representation is general, this aspect would need modification for application to other kinds of discourse.

In task dialogs, a shift in focus takes place whenever a new task is entered or an old one completed. A narrowing of focus takes place whenever a subtask of the active task is opened for discussion. The focus shifts back up to the higher level task when that subtask is completed. Hence, when a subtask of the current task is referenced, a new active focus space is created below the current active focus space. When the subtask is completed, the new focus space is closed and the old space (i.e., the higher space) becomes the active focus space again. The top of the focus space hierarchy is the focus of the overall task.

A shift in focus may be cued by any part of an utterance: a noun phrase, a verb phrase, or modifying phrases. Although an individual constituent (e.g., a noun phrase) may indicate a shift in focus, the constituent alone cannot be used to determine the shift, because the remainder of the utterance influences the decision. For instance, an isolated noun phrase may seem to indicate a shift to some task but, when considered with its embedding verb phrase, may indicate a shift to a different task. The following discussion examines the relationship between identifying the referent of a definite noun phrase and shifting focus. Grosz (1977) describes the interaction of various constituents of an utterance in determining a shift.

To illustrate how a noun phrase may indicate a shift in focus, consider the task hierarchy in Figure 5 and the focus environment portrayed in Figure 6. Figure 5 is only for the reader's benefit; this information is actually encoded in structures like those in Figure 2 and Figure 6. The dotted lines show the task hierarchy and the solid lines show time sequencing. Suppose that task T2, installing the aftercooler, is the current task. The focus spaces FS0, FS1, and FS2 in Figure 6 correspond to subtasks T0, T1, and T2 respectively. FS2 is the active focus space; the vista (FS1 FS0) is the hierarchy of open focus spaces.

A reference to an object in either the active focus space or one of the open focus spaces does not cause a shift in focus. Those items in the active focus space are considered first when resolving a reference because the currently active task is more in focus than its embedding tasks. The phrases "the aftercooler", "the wrench", and "the crescent wrench" all refer to objects in FS2, the active focus space. Hence, the use of any of these phrases does not affect the focus of attention. The referent can be retrieved immediately. The use of either "the air compressor", "the pump", or "the ratchet wrench" also does not cause a change in focus. Since these objects are in open focus spaces, they are also in focus, but are accessed only after considering the objects in FS2. Note that the noun phrase, "the wrench," is not ambiguous because of the distinction between the active focus and the open focus spaces (this distinction is evident in references occurring in actual task dialogs between two people; see Grosz, 1977).

References to either a new subtask, or a new parallel or higher task, or to subtasks of any of these, do change focus. In the example, space IADS contains the delineation of the process for installing the aftercooler. The plot space of this delineation is the implicit focus for node 'IAC1'. It shows that this kind of installation has two substeps (corresponding to T3 and T4 in Figure 5). The first substep involves a connection operation between the aftercooler and one of its subparts, an aftercooler elbow. In this focus environment, since there is no aftercooler elbow in explicit focus, the phrase, "the aftercooler elbow", indicates a possible shift in focus to task T3. If the remainder of the utterance concurs with such a shift, a new focus space will be created below FS2 in the hierarchy. The utterance, "Attach the aftercooler elbow", indicates such a shift, but the utterance, "The aftercooler elbow is broken", does not. Note that a shift in focus may entail instantiating new entities or identifying real entities corresponding to hypothetical entities in implicit focus. If focus is shifted to task T3, the aftercooler elbow ACE1 is brought into focus and the noun phrase "the aftercooler elbow" is identified with it; i.e., the new focus space will contain the node 'ACE1'.

With a representation of focus, the process of identifying the referent of a noun phrase looks quite different than in systems that search sequentially back through a discourse for a referent. The important question is when and how to shift focus, not how far back (i.e., how many sentences) to look for the referent. The search for the referent of a definite noun phrase takes into account the difference between those items which do and those which do not shift focus. Items in explicit focus, which do not indicate a shift in focus, are checked before items in implicit focus, which do.

V EXTENSIONS

This section explores the use of the focus space representation in the solution of two other problems that arise in building knowledge based systems. First, there is a space-time tradeoff between storing derived information in the knowledge base and recomputing the information. Ideally, the information would be stored only as long as needed and then erased from the knowledge base. This issue is closely related to the general issue of forgetting in a knowledge based system. Second, any given object may be viewed from several different perspectives. Highlighting a particular view may be used to capture the information conveyed by the specific way an object is described in a given utterance.

A. DERIVED INFORMATION AND FORGETTING

In the process of matching network structures, it is often necessary to deduce information about particular objects from general rules in the knowledge base. In the process of computing a match, the matcher may create new network structure. If the network structure is permanently stored in the knowledge base, the deduction will never have to be repeated. However, making the structure permanent uses up valuable storage. Focus spaces provide a mechanism for determining how long to store such information. When the new structure is derived, it can be added to the current focus space. When the focus space is closed, the new information can be erased.

As an example of this use of focus spaces, consider the situation portrayed in Figure 7. The (logical) space oew.desc represents the fact that all elements of the set O-E have endtype OPEN-END. Bew.desc represents a similar rule. Suppose that initially the nodes 'W1' and 'W2' were in focus as elements of the sets B-E and O-E respectively (e.g., the wrenches were selected from two boxes each containing one type of wrench). If the matcher is given the structure for "box-end wrench" (see Figure 4) to match, it will create two new arcs, an endtype arc from 'W1' to 'BOX-END', and an explicit e arc from 'W1' to 'WRENCHES'. These new arcs are added to the focus space, FS, as shown in Figure 7. Any further matches sought for "the box-end wrench" while the focus is FS will be able to take advantage of this explicitly stored information. When FS ceases to be open, the arcs will be erased. If the deduction had resulted in new nodes being created, they too could be erased. Using focus spaces in this way creates the double advantage of having the information available when it is relevant, and allowing it to be "garbage collected" or "forgotten" after it ceases to be relevant.

B. DIFFERENTIAL ACCESS AND DESCRIPTION

The representation of some concept C may include descriptions of C as an instance of several different kinds of other concepts. Focusing allows the particular way of looking at C germane to a given point in a dialog to be highlighted (cf. the use of multiple perspectives in Bobrow and Winograd, 1977). The arcs from focused items to unfocused items provide the matcher with preferential access to information that is most likely to become relevant to a discourse.

This use of focusing addresses one part of the "mayor of San Diego" problem posed by Norman et al. (1975). Consider the situation portrayed in Figure 8. The person represented by the node 'MNMSD' is shown to be both D's neighbor and the mayor of San Diego. If MNMSD is referred to by D either as "the mayor of San Diego" or "D's neighbor", then node 'MNMSD' represents the individual referred to. The problem is that looking only at that node provides no reflection of the differences between the two references to MNMSD, even though the surface noun phrases do express this difference. Focus spaces provide a

means of representing this difference. Even though node 'MNMSD' will be in focus no matter which reference is used, arcs from 'MNMSD' that are in focus in the two cases will differ. Focus spaces FS1 and FS2 illustrate this difference.

VI SUMMARY

The focus representation groups items relevant to a particular point in a discourse, providing a small subset of the knowledge base on which the understanding system can concentrate. In particular, the focus representation may be used to guide the retrieval of information from the knowledge base. It reduces the size of the search space that the retrieval mechanism must traverse. The representation of explicit focus in focus spaces also appears to be useful for related understanding system problems, such as describing objects and forgetting information. Although the representation presented is in terms of a semantic network, partitioning a memory representation for the purpose of reflecting focus of attention is a general mechanism which may be used in other representation schemes as well.

REFERENCES

Bobrow, Daniel G. and Winograd Terry. An Overview of KRL, A Knowledge Representation Language. cognitive Science 1977, 1.

Fikes, Richard E. and Hendrix, Gary G. A Network-Based Knowledge Representation and its Natural Deduction System. Fifth International Joint Conference on Artificial Intelligence, 1977.

Grosz, Barbara J. The Representation and Use of Focus in Dialogue Understanding. Ph.D Thesis, University of California, Berkeley, California, June 1977.

Hendrix, Gary G. Partitioned Networks for the Mathematical Modeling of Natural Language Semantics. Technical Report NL-28, Department of Computer Sciences, University of Texas, Austin, Texas, 1975.

Karttunen, Lauri What Makes Definite Noun Phrases Definite. Paper P-3871 The RAND Corporation, Santa Monica, California, 1968

Maratsos, Michael P. The Use of Definite and Indefinite Reference in Young Children. Cambridge University Press, Cambridge, 1976. pp. 133-136.

Norman, Donald A., Rumelhart, David E., and the LNR Research Group. Explorations in Cognition. Freeman, San Francisco, 1975.

Quillian, M.R. Semantic Memory. In: Semantic Information Processing. Edited by Marvin Minsky. The MIT Press, Cambridge, Massachusetts, 1968.

Rieger, C. Conceptual Overlays: A Mechanism for the Interpretation of Sentence Meaning in Context. Technical Report TR-354. Computer Science Department, University of Maryland, College Park, Maryland. February 1975.

Sacerdoti, Earl D. A Structure for Plans and
    Behavior. Technical Note 109, Artificial
    Intelligence Center, Standford Research
    Institute, Menlo Park, California, 1975.

Simmons, Robert F. Semantic Networks: Their
    Computation and Use for Understanding English
    Sentences. In: Computer Models of Thought and
    Language. Edited by Roger C. Shank and
    Kenneth M. Colby. Freeman, San Francisco, 1973.
    pp. 63-113.

Walker, Donald E. (Ed.) Speech Understanding
    Research. Final Report, Project 4762,
    Artificial Intelligence Center, Stanford
    Research Institute, Menlo Park, California,
    October, 1976.

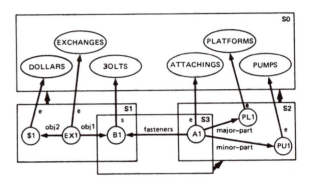

FIGURE 1   A SAMPLE PARTITIONED SEMANTIC NETWORK

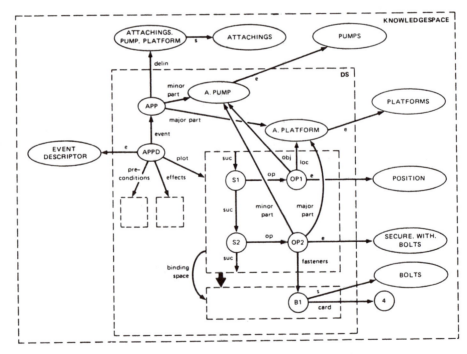

FIGURE 2   EVENT ENCODING SHOWING IMPLICIT FOCUS

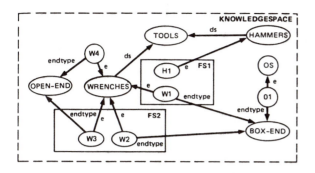

FIGURE 3   A SIMPLE KVISTA WITH TWO FOCUS SPACES

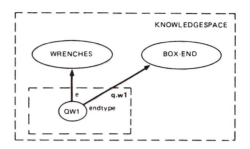

FIGURE 4   QVISTA FOR "THE BOX-END WRENCH"

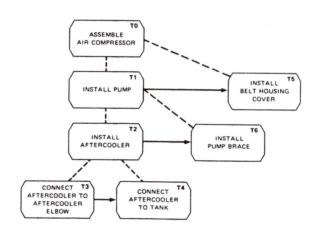

FIGURE 5   PARTIAL TASK HIERARCHY FOR ASSEMBLING
AIR COMPRESSOR

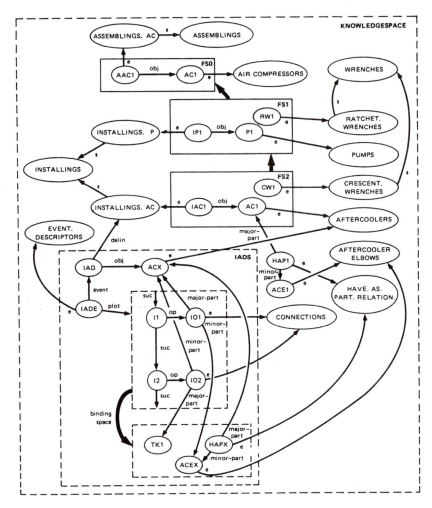

FIGURE 6   FOCUS SPACES AND IMPLICIT FOCUS FRAGMENT FOR SHIFTING FOCUS

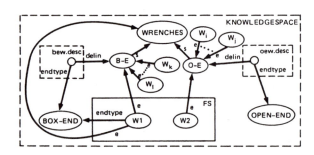

FIGURE 7   THE WRENCHES KVISTA WITH FOCUS ADDED

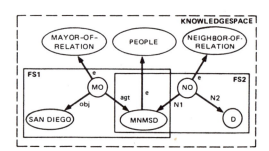

FIGURE 8   MY NEIGHBOR THE MAYOR OF SAN DIEGO

Focusing in the Comprehension of Definite Anaphora

Candace L. Sidner

5.1 Introduction: Interpretation of Definite Anaphora

In spoken and written discourse, people use certain words to "point back" in the discourse context to the people, places, objects, times, events and ideas mentioned there. The use of such a pointing back device is called anaphora, and I will refer to words or phrases used in this way as anaphors; in particular, definite anaphora include the personal pronouns, certain uses of definite noun phrases, and noun phrases containing *this* and *that*. Traditionally, researchers have defined the problem of anaphor comprehension as one of determining the antecedent of an anaphoric expression, that is, determining to which word or phrase an anaphoric expression refers or "points". Recent studies in both artificial intelligence and linguistics have demonstrated the need for a theory for anaphor comprehension which accounts for the role of syntactic and semantic effects, as well as inferential knowledge in explaining how anaphors are understood. In this chapter a new theory, based on the concept of focusing in the discourse, will be introduced to explain the interpretation of definite anaphors.

Before a theory can be given, and before even the difficulties in interpreting anaphors can be discussed, we must first re-consider what an antecedent is. The traditional definition encounters difficulty right from the start; it is founded on the notion that one word in a sentence refers or points back to another word in the (same or another) sentence. But words don't refer back to other words [Morgan 1978]: people use words to refer to objects. In particular people use anaphors to refer to objects which have already been mentioned in a discourse. Since an anaphoric phrase does not refer to an antecedent, one might want to claim that both the antecedent and the anaphor co-refer to some object. This definition is adequate for sentence (1) below,

(1) I think green apples taste best and *they* make the best cooking apples too.

though not for discourse 1D1, where there is no antecedent word in the discourse which co-refers with the pronoun *they*.

1D1-1 My neighbor has a monster Harley 1200.
 2 *They* are really huge but gas-efficient bikes.

As an alternative to viewing antecedence as co-reference, one might propose that antecedence is a kind of cognitive pointing, the kind of pointing that causes *they* and *green apples* to point to the same class of objects in one's mind (in some unknown way). This proposal is problematic for same reason that co-reference is: people use anaphora when there is no other noun phrase in the discourse which points to the right mental object. In 1D1, *they* refers to bikes which are Harley 1200s as a group, while the speaker's use of the noun phrase *a monster Harley 1200* only serves to mention some particular Harley 1200. *They* seems to be able to refer to Harley 1200s as a group when used with the previously mentioned phrase *a monster Harley 1200* without the two phrases either co-referring or co-pointing.

If an anaphor does not refer to an antecedent phrase, and if it need not always co-refer with its apparent antecedent (as in 1D1), then anaphor interpretation is not simply finding the antecedent. Nevertheless the concept of antecedence as a kind of pointing back does seem to capture some aspect of the comprehension of anaphora, for when certain antecedent words are missing from a discourse, people often fail to understand what is being said.

Let us define the problem of interpreting and understanding an anaphor in the following way. The phrase *apples* in (1), when syntactically and semantically interpreted, will be said to *specify* a cognitive element in the hearer's mind. In the computational model of that process, this element is a database item, which might be represented by the schema below:

```
Phrase76:
    string: "green apples"
    context: speaker1 think * tastes best
    specifies: Apples2

Apples2:
    super-concept: apples
    color: green
    used-for: cooking
```

The speaker uses the information in a cognitive representation like Apples2 above to choose the phrase *green apples* in (1). The hearer then uses the phrase *green apples* plus the syntactic and semantic interpretation of rest of the sentence to locate a similar cognitive element in his own mind; it may be slightly different because the hearer may not associate use in cooking with green apples. A cognitive element, such as Apples2, is called the *specification* of *green apples*.

These elements, present in the memories of speaker and hearer, are of course related to other cognitive elements in their memories.

What is the relation of specifications to the real world? One might like to claim that a reference relation exists between specified cognitive elements and objects in the world, but since referring is what people do with words, this relation is problematic for cognitive elements. Instead, specifications will be said to <u>represent</u> the objects referred to, that is, they bear a well-structured correspondence to objects in the world. Apples2, the specification of *green apples*, represents the objects that are green apples. For phrases such as *Santa Claus*, where there is no real world object to represent, a specification represents the properties normally associated with this imaginary person.

The phrase *they* in (1) also specifies a cognitive element, namely the same one that *green apples* does. Since the two bear the same relation to the representation Apples2, they will be said to *co-specify* that memory element, or alternatively, that the interpretation of *green apples* in (1) is the *co-specifier* of the interpretation of *they*. Co-specification, unlike co-reference, allows one to construct abstract representations and define relationships between them which can be studied in a computational framework. With co-reference no such use is possible, since the object referred to exists in the world and is not available for examination by computational processes.

Even if a noun phrase and a pronoun do not co-specify, the specification of a noun phrase may be used to <u>generate</u> the specification of a pronoun. For example, in (1) *they* does not co-specify with the apparent antecedent phrase *a monster Harley 1200*. Here the anaphor *they* refers to the class of Harley 1200s of which the apparent antecedent (the neighbor's monster Harley 1200) is an instance. Thus anaphor interpretation is not simply a matter of finding the corresponding cognitive element which serves as the specification of the anaphor; some additional process must generate a specification for the anaphor from the related phrase *a monster Harley 1200*.

The concepts of specification and co-specification capture the "pointing back" quality of antecedence, and also permit us to formulate an explanation of anaphor interpretation which avoids the pitfalls of the concept of antecedence. Anaphor interpretation can be studied as a computational process that uses the already existing specification of a noun phrase to find the specification for an anaphor. The process uses a representation of the discourse preceding the anaphor which encodes the syntactic and semantic relationships in each sentence as well as co-specification relationships between phrases.[1]

These definitions in themselves do not constitute a theory of anaphor interpretation. They do, however, make possible a succinct statement of the problem: how does one determine the specification of an anaphor? Also since we suspect that the specification of an apparent antecedent phrase plays some role in choosing an anaphor's specification, we may ask, just what is this role? We hope for a direct answer to these questions, but before one can be given, let us consider how a theory of interpretation ought to address these questions. A brief look at the difficulties of finding co-specifiers will suggest which issues our theory should cover.

Determining the co-specifier of an anaphor is difficult because there are a multitude of possible co-specifiers in a given discourse, and there is no simple way to choose the correct one. Yet human hearers and readers generally do recover the correct co-specifying phrase intended by the speaker. Human readers and hearers also fail to recover the co-specifying phrase in certain situations; this behavior is just as valuable an observation as garden path phenomena for theories of parsing. A theory of interpretation must predict the pattern of the hearer's and reader's correct and incorrect choices, as well as failures to understand, by a rule-governed account. In addition, a taxonomy of the cases in which specifications are used to generate other specifications must be given, as well as a means of predicting their distribution; Webber [Chapter 6 of this volume] provides additional treatment of some aspects of these phenomena.

5.1.1 Research on Anaphora

Before exploring the use of specification and co-specification for anaphor interpretation, we must consider other aspects of human communication and knowledge which bear on anaphor interpretation; two significant characteristics are the context of discussion and the inferences people make.

People use the context surrounding an anaphor in understanding it. If a theory of anaphor interpretation is to capture understanding, it must include a means of encoding discourse context and whatever structure it has; the context

---

[1] In the rest of this chapter, I will speak of a phrase co-specifying (or specifying) with another phrase, when what I really mean is that the relation is between representations of phrases that have been interpreted by some parsing process, which indicates the sentence syntactic relations, and by a semantic interpretation process, which computes semantic relations among words of the sentence. The kind of processes I envision are rather like running "in reverse" the realization procedure that McDonald describes in this volume.

example below illustrates:

(2) Take the mud pack off your face. Notice how soft it feels.

Syntactic restrictions, stated in logical form ([Chomsky 1976]) and in constituent structure ([Lasnik 1976] and [Reinhart 1976]), stipulate conditions in which a pronoun and a noun phrase must have disjoint references.

(3) * Near Dan, he saw a snake.

(4) * The man whose house he bought went gold digging in Alaska.

These rules, however, do not stipulate the interpretation of an anaphor; in a general theory they act as filters on the class of possible co-specifiers. Furthermore, these rules are not yet theoretically complete as linguists are still studying the disjoint reference conditions on reflexive anaphora.

Work by artificial intelligence researchers on inference has led to methods for forward and backward chaining of inferences to "bind" the anaphor, represented as a free variable, with some piece of knowledge; with this approach the anaphor's interpretation was whatever value became bound to the free variable. This approach revealed that inferences about world knowledge are often needed to interpret anaphors. However, the methods tried failed to control the inference process sufficiently. Charniak, attempting to resolve this problem, proposed demons that would "wake up" in the appropriate situation (that is, processes which could notice themselves when they were to begin processing). But a large cache of demons would be required, and no assurance could be given that demons would exist in every situation. Most significantly, his proposal said nothing about the situation where two or more demons might apply (who gets control? how are the decisions made?). Finally all of the inference based approaches to pronoun interpretation fail to offer any theoretical approach because they rely on a simple mechanism, (simple variable binding between pronoun and some other phrase) which does not apply in many uses of anaphora, such as D1.

Discourse approaches to anaphora have included a technique similar to the inference method; one identified sentence pairs and examined them for the coherence relations of similarity, contrast, parallel structure; the pronouns were interpreted by variable binding between items of the sentence pairs ([Hobbs 1979]). A different approach, used by Webber (see Chapter 6 of this volume, or [Webber 1978a]) relies on identifying representational constraints which will restrict what discourse phrases and associated discourse entities may be used in coherent discourse. She presents a form of restricted quantification which provides such constraints. I will consider the role of Webber's formalism in focusing later in this chapter.

Grosz [Grosz 1977, 1978, 1981] defined a focus space as that subset of the speaker's total knowledge which is relevant to a discourse segment. Elements in the space are highlighted via focusing, a process which reflects what a speaker says

must be distilled into a form that preserves its richness without adding overwhelming complexity to the interpretation process. In addition, researchers have discovered that anaphor interpretation involves making inferences, some of which can be complex, each of which must be chosen from a large base of knowledge about objects, people and things. The practical deployment of inferential capabilities for any task requires control: knowing what to infer when, and knowing when to stop. Since the general control problem is poorly understood, solutions to the more specific problem of controlling inference in anaphor interpretation must be provided by a theory of anaphor interpretation.

The role of context and inference, as well as syntax and semantics on anaphor interpretation have been explored extensively. A brief look at these explorations will indicate the necessity of a new approach. Research on anaphora falls into four broad categories:

General heuristics for finding antecedents
([Winograd 1972])

Syntactic and semantic constraints on anaphora
([Katz and Fodor 1963], [Woods et al. 1972],
[Chomsky 1976], [Lasnik 1976],
[Reinhart 1976], [Walker 1976]).

Use of inference to find antecedents
([Charniak 1972], [Rieger 1974]
[Hobbs 1976])

Analysis of objects in a discourse context
([Grosz 1977], [Lockman 1978],
[Reichman 1978], [Webber 1978a],
[Hobbs 1979])

Rather than review each approach, I will point out the contributions of each category to a theory of anaphor interpretation.

General heuristics, as a means of choosing antecedents, predict reliably in a large number of typical examples. However, no simple characterization fits the wide variety of cases where they fail (see [Winograd 1972] and [Hobbs 1977]); furthermore, the heuristic approach is not theoretically grounded and cannot offer a unified approach to the phenomena.

Semantic selectional restrictions, based on the Katz-Fodor theory of semantic markers, and used by many computational linguists, can reduce the space of possible antecedents, but they cannot be used to eliminate all possibilities, as the

and the nature of the knowledge in the space. Several such spaces, dubbed "focus spaces," may be relevant at a time although only one is centered on for processing at any given time. Grosz presented a procedure for interpreting non-pronominal noun phrases using the focusing and focus space notions. Reichman [Reichman 1978] has expanded this paradigm by describing "context spaces" which are delineated by their topics. Within a context space, entities receive various focus levels; only phrases that are in high focus may be pronominalized. Reichman's work leaves open important questions: what is the recognition procedure for determining a context space, how does one identify its topic; and how does the hearer determine the interpretation of a anaphor, that is, how does a hearer decide which highly focused phrases act as the co-specifier of a anaphor?

To summarize, current research on anaphor interpretation suggests that control of inferring and constraints on representation of discourse are necessary aspects of a theory of anaphor interpretation. Grosz' approach indicates that one must also consider what the speaker is talking about; Reichman's analysis shows that certain phrases in the conversation play a special role in interpretation, while Webber indicates how the representation of quantifiers affects the interpretation of anaphor. All these approaches support the view that since hearers do not have privileged access to a speaker's mind, other than through what a speaker says, imposing structure on the speaker's discourse will provide a framework for establishing the interpretation of anaphors.

5.1.2 The Focusing Approach to Anaphora

One of the basic units of language communication is the discourse. Informally and intuitively, a discourse is a connected piece of text or spoken language of more than one sentence spoken by one or more speakers. If such an informal definition is to be helpful at all, some notion of what it means to be "connected" is needed. While there are many different properties which contribute to discourse connectedness, in this chapter I want to consider only one: the speaker or speakers talk about something, one thing at a time.

In a discourse speakers center their attention on a particular discourse element, one which I will call the focus. It is the element which is elaborated by a portion of the discourse. Sometimes speakers' discourses can be quite different; their discourses are incoherent or at least hard to follow because:

1a) they talk about several elements without relating them or

1b) they talk about several elements without informing the hearer that several elements will be discussed at once or

2) they do not choose a central element for the discourse.

In a nutshell, discourses with these properties are not connected, that is, they lack an element which is focused on. The focus is then one of the connecting threads that makes a text or a set of utterances a discourse.

Focusing is a discourse phenomenon rather than one of single sentences. When a speaker uses several sentences about one focus, one would expect that it would need to be re-introduced in each sentence. However, re-introduction is a redundant and thus inefficient process; in fact, speakers do not use it. If re-introduction is not used, and still hearers claim to know what is being talked about, there must be some means by which the discourse remains connected. In fact, there are two ways. First, special words indicate to the hearer "that I am still talking about the thing I talked about in the previous sentence;" traditionally these signals are called anaphoric expressions; the speaker assumes that some connections between the focus and some other elements are already shared with the hearer so that she or he need not explicitly state what they are. Of course, there is a risk that the connections are no longer obvious, resulting in a set of sentences which simply confuse the hearer.

Now a possible line of investigation becomes clear. The focus and the assumed shared knowledge can be used as one of the chief constraints on the choice of the co-specification of anaphoric expressions. Rules governing an anaphor interpreter can be discovered which use these two sources of constraints. In these rules the focus will play a central role as a source of co-specification. The focus and the structure of assumed shared knowledge are significant to rules governing the choice of anaphors because they capture the effects of what has been talked about previously, and what the speaker has assumed is knowledge that is shared with the hearer.

This view of focusing and anaphora rests on four assumptions about the nature of communication, each of which is true in most situations. First, the speaker is assumed to be communicating about something. This assumption implies that the speaker is not speaking gibberish, that the utterance contains referring expressions and communicates some intention. The something which the communication is about will be called the <u>focus</u> of the discourse. Second, the speaker assumes that the hearer can identify the focus of the discourse. The speaker wants to communicate about something, and for the communication to occur, the hearer must be able to distinguish what the speaker is communicating about. Third, the speaker is not trying to confuse or deceive the hearer. The speaker uses referring expressions with the intention of referring to someone or something, or with the intention of describing something or some event. In Gricean ([Grice 1975]) terms, the the byword is "Be perspicuous." Finally the speaker assumes the hearer has certain knowledge about the real world which can be used to reason about referring expressions during the communication process. Recent research ([Perrault and Cohen 1981], Allen (Chapter 2 of this volume) [Clark and Marshall 1978]), and the well known work of Searle [Searle 1969] and Austin [Austin 1962]. describe models of the speaker's knowledge of what the hearer believes. In this chapter, the weakest form of such a model is assumed: the speaker assumes the hearer has enough real-world knowledge in common with the speaker to know about the entities in the real world which the speaker refers to and to know about the cognitive elements of the discourse which the speaker mentions; Webber (Chapter 6 of this volume) speaks of this assumption as that of shared knowledge between speaker and hearer. The speaker draws on that knowledge in constructing a message for a hearer. These four assumptions will play an important part in the discussion of co-specification interpretation which follows.

By viewing focusing as a process that chooses a focus as one of the elements of discourse structure, a new tool for interpreting anaphors becomes available. The focus of the discourse will act as an index to the specifications of referring expressions. For definite anaphora the focus is the locus of the specification information. Either the focus is the co-specifying phrase for an anaphor, when it meets certain syntactic, semantic and inferential knowledge restrictions, or else the the discourse representation of the phrase in focus can be used to generate the specification of the definite anaphor. Because representations and knowledge are essential to how an anaphor is interpreted, an explanation of focus is incomplete without some consideration of the way in which it is represented, and how it is related to other concepts people know about and other items mentioned in the discourse. The use of focus also requires another type of computational machinery, an inferring process, which is used to infer from general knowledge and other suppositions that a certain proposition is consistent with what else is known.

An example to illustrate the concept of focus will be helpful here. In the discourse below, the focus of discussion is the meeting of D2-1.

D2-1 I want to schedule a meeting with Ira.
  2 It should be at 3 p.m.
  3 We can get together in his office.
  4 Invite John to come, too.

All four sentences give information about the focused element. While D2-3 and 4 make no direct reference to the meeting of D2-1, as human hearers, we assume that these sentences are related to the rest of D2 because they can be interpreted as giving information about the focus *meeting*. D2-3 names the location of the meeting while D2-4 introduces an additional participant by use of *invite*, and by taking advantage of knowledge that people are invited to meetings.

If we assume that speakers know that meetings have associated places, times, participants, and purposes, then when a new instance of meeting is evoked, this knowledge can be used to understand what the speaker is communicating to the hearer about meetings. It also makes possible an explanation for how the hearer understands the role the pronouns play in the discourse; the pronouns co-specify the element in focus.

Of course, the co-specifier of a pronoun must be proposed by some process, a process which can interpret rules which restrict what might be the the co-specifier and then test proposed co-specifiers. Thus in D2-2, once the focus is proposed as the co-specifier of *it*, this interpretation process must assure that meetings can occur at a particular time. To provide confirmation, an inferring process uses knowledge of the world to determine that meetings have times. This being so, the proposal of meeting as the co-specifier of *it* is accepted.

The explanation of the role of focus cannot be quite so simple because the focus of a discourse can change to a new element of the discourse. A means of recognizing this change is required in the model of the focusing process. For example, in D3 the focus begins on meeting, but the *it* in D3-3 has *my office* as its co-specifier, not the meeting. Detecting this co-specifier requires a means of noticing a movement of focus to *my office* and using the inferring mechanism to confirm the choice of the new focus as co-specifier.

D3-1 I want to schedule a meeting with George, Jim, Steve and Mike.
  2 We can meet in my office.
  3 It's kind of small,
  4 but we'll only need it for about an hour.

In addition to the comprehension of pronouns such as *it*, focusing will be shown to provide an explanation for the definite anaphora of *this* and *that*, as used in the discourses below. Since these definite anaphors have received little treatment in any literature, an explanation of their behavior as part of focusing will offer new insights about how language is understood.

phrase because inferring is used to confirm a hypothesized link between an anaphor and a focus.

3. Distinguishing and disambiguating definite anaphora
Focus, used with the representation of knowledge in (1), with Webber's representation (see Chapter 6) and with information describing sentence syntactic constraints, such as c-command, and semantic selectional restrictions, can distinguish those definite anaphora governed by discourse effects. It can be used to disambiguate their specifications as well.

The theory of focusing makes certain testable predictions, ones which are produced by the processes and interpreters that are to be described in this chapter. They will predict which representations are the specifications of anaphors and what decisions are made to find the representations. Since the theory relies on representations of knowledge, it also makes predictions and suggests constraints on both the structure and the content of these representations. In discussing all these predictions, I will illustrate the advances of the focusing theory over earlier work as well as explain the limitations of the theory for interpreting one class of definite anaphora.

5.2 The Definition of Focus

5.2.1 A Sketch of the Process Model of Focusing

A process model of focusing consists of three distinct processes, which function in a cycle for each sentence of a discourse. The first process chooses foci based on what the speaker initially says. Then an interpreter uses these foci and a set of rules of anaphor interpretation to interpret the anaphoric expressions in the discourse. This interpreter, like a human hearer, must "keep in mind" whatever other newly mentioned elements the speaker has introduced, since sometimes an anaphor may co-specify with one of these instead of the elements in focus. A third process updates the foci using the anaphoric interpretations chosen by the interpreter. During this last phase, the updating process will move one of the foci to a new element of the discourse, if the phrase previously in focus is no longer part of the information conveyed by the sentence. The three processes taken together sketch a simple process model of focus tracking; the model behaves like its human counterpart in the way it interprets anaphors and in the instances in which it fails to "understand."

The three process cycle can be illustrated with the example below.

D4-1 The axon may run for a long distance, sending off several sidebranches along the way,
2 before it terminates in an even finer network of filaments, the terminal arbor.
3 Man's longest axon runs for several feet, from the spinal column to muscles that control movements of the toes.
4 In spite of its great length, this axon, like all nerve fibers, is a part of a single cell.
5 It is living matter.

D5-1 I'm having a party tomorrow night;
2 it will be like the one I had last week.
3 That party was a big success
4 because everyone danced.
5 This one will have better food.
6 I've asked everyone to bring something special.
7 Want to come?

If focusing is to be viewed as part of anaphor comprehension, some process must choose, in a reliable way, what I have described loosely as the focus of the discourse. The process will be required to make use of representations of elements of a sentence that are linked to other memory elements because people seem to use just such information themselves. In addition, an interpreter will make use of the focus, as well as syntactic, semantic, and general knowledge restrictions, in determining the co-specifier of the anaphoric expressions. This brief description of a focus, the focusing process and the anaphor interpreter raises some questions which must be answered. What is the focus of the discourse, and how is it determined? What kinds of assumptions about the structure of the knowledge must be made in order to use a focus for definite anaphor disambiguation? What inferences are used in the prediction of co-specifiers? How does an anaphoric interpreter use the focus to interpret personal and this/that pronouns?

The answers to these questions will be provided in the new few sections. As the theory unfolds, I will also support the following claims about definite anaphora.

1. The role of focus in co-specification
Focus and a knowledge network together determine the relationships among elements of the discourse. These relationships indicate ways in which co-specification with the focus can be accomplished.

2. Focused inferring
Focusing controls the inference mechanism needed to determine a specification relationship between a focus and an anaphoric noun

D6-1 Last week there were some nice strawberries in the refrigerator.
2 They came from our food co-op and were unusually fresh.
3 I went to use them for dinner, but someone had eaten them all.
4 Later I discovered it was Mark who had eaten them.
5 Mark has a hollow leg, and it's impossible to keep food around when his stomach needs filling.

Suppose the first focusing process initially guesses that strawberries are the focus in D6-1. Next a pronoun interpreter would apply a rule that says "A pronoun that can be replaced by the focus phrase, with the focus, unless some remaining syntactically acceptable, co-specifies with the focus, unless some pragmatic knowledge rules out that co-specifier," to determine that strawberries can replace *they* in D6-2 with no syntactic failure. An inference process, governed by the pronoun interpreter, could confirm that strawberries can come from food co-ops and can be fresh; that is, no contradiction in general knowledge results. Finally, the third process can confirm strawberries as the focus since it has been re-mentioned and because other objects mentioned in D6-1, the refrigerator and the previous week, were not discussed in D6-2.

The focusing mechanism will be a useful theoretical tool only if it is coherent to talk about some element of the discourse as being in focus. While our intuitions as speakers and hearers led us to believe that there is something we talk about, the intuition is problematic because there appear to be many phenomena which function in distinguishing what it is that someone is talking about. One such phenomenon for marking focus are syntactic constructions, such as there-insertion sentences as (5) and cleft sentences as (6).

(5) There once was a wise old king who lived on a mountain.

(6) It was the butler who kidnapped the heiress.

Another phenomenon which marks focus is speech stress and prosodics: it appears that these mark what the speaker is most interested in talking about. In (7) if contrastive stress is put on Jeremy, the hearer might expect that the next sentence will say more about him.

(7) I want one of JEREMY'S pictures.

In an upcoming section these and similar phenomena will be presented and analyzed in detail for their role in determining focus. In the theory that will be presented, the focus will be defined as that discourse element selected by the computational process; the process will be defined so that it takes into account all the phenomena. Hence, the definition of focus will be a function of the theory rather than an independently defined object.

5.2.2 The Representation of Focus

In the focusing theory, the element of the discourse in focus will be modeled as a data structure. Each of the phrases in a sentence, evoke such structures, which correspond to structures in the mental models of speakers and hearers; that is, each phrase specifies a piece of a mental database, which is represented in some way. In Webber's terms, these structures are "discourse entities," and the whole collection is a "discourse model." I will use the terms "cognitive elements" or "discourse elements" when discussing these structures because they are meant to be analogous to the structures in the mental models of speakers and hearers.

Since the cognitive elements are specifications, they bear a representational correspondence to objects in the speaker's world, and one must consider how these elements are represented. I will assume that each element is represented as a piece of a network of elements. The network contains many elements, but the focus is the element selected as primary among them for a given part of a discourse.

What kind of data structure is required for representing the focus? First of all, it is associative; that is, certain special associations are marked between elements of the network. The associations are special in the sense that an element has direct links to certain other elements but not to all elements. For example, **meeting** has built-in associations for a **time**, a **place**, a set of **participants**, and a **topic** of discussion, but it has no associations to color, cost or age. Each phrase in a discourse is encoded as an instance of the generic network element of **meeting** (existing prior to the discourse). With a hierarchical net, instances of generalized templates can be created, as in Figure 1.

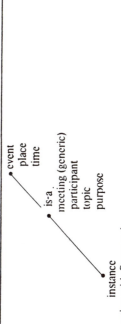

Figure 1 Instances of a general meeting element.

The data structure must also support two kinds of hierarchical links with the ability to inherit on both. One link expresses the is-a kind of relation; it allows properties from the network description of one element to be inherited by another. Thus the generic **meeting** is a conceptual element which is-a kind of **event**; and it inherits the associations of place and time from the is-a relation. The second relation with inheritance captures the notion of an instance type. This relation occurs between a conceptual element like **meeting** and a particular meeting like **meeting-with-Stanoczyk**. This element is a particular copy or instance of its parent node. Elements that are generics represent abstract kinds while instances represent objects in the world. Both may serve as the specification of a phrase in discourse.

The data structure needed must have other properties. It must also allow for the embedding of structure within structures, because these represent other discourse elements subject to discussion and re-mention. If we are told that John is eating an ice cream cone, the representation must show that the act of eating includes two sub-structures, one representing John and the other the ice cream cone. Finally the data structure must allow for a natural representation of scope of quantifiers; their representation is considered by Webber in this volume, and a discussion of how that representation may be used is given later in this chapter. These data structure characteristics are necessary for anaphor comprehension because loss of any characteristic has important effects on what anaphors can be comprehended, as we will see in the examples in this chapter.

The properties of a net structure expressed here are sometimes part of Artificial Intelligence representation languages (see KL-ONE, [Brachman 1978], OWL [Hawkinson 1978], KRL [Bobrow and Winograd 1977] among others). These properties will be necessary in the discussions of focusing and anaphor interpretation that follow, so whichever representation language is used, it must have the features mentioned for the focusing theory.

The illustration of focus in figure 1 is slightly misleading because it suggests that the focus is only the computational encoding of the specification of a particular noun phrase. In fact, the process which establishes the specification of a noun phrase in focus must have access to the syntactic and semantic forms of the phrase. If they are left out, some anaphors will appear ambiguous, when in fact they are not. Unnecessary ambiguity can be illustrated using D7 below.

D7-1 The first man on the moon became a national hero.
    2 Due to his status, he rode in ticker tape parades, met public officials and was chased by autograph hunters.

The focus of this example is *the first man on the moon*. Suppose that the specification of that phrase is the focus as depicted below, without benefit of the referring definite noun phrase.

Database representation of:

FOCUS:

NEIL ARMSTRONG
Rank: colonel in U.S. Army
Father: 3 children
Achievement: first moon walker

The specification of *his status* will be ambiguous because several roles in which he has status, those of father, colonel and moon walker. But *his status* in D7-2 is not ambiguous for human speakers. To avoid unnecessary ambiguity, the expression with its syntax and semantics must be included as part of the focusing process. Hereafter, focus will be spoken of as being on a particular noun phrase. This is an informal means of referring to the encoding of focus by the focusing process; that is, focus is encoded as a representation built by syntactic and semantic constructs of the noun phrase which points to another representation its specification.

In addition to the focus, focusing must take into account the actors of the discourse. An actor focus is a discourse item which is predicated as the agent in some event. It is distinct from the main focus, which will be called the discourse focus. Actors can become the discourse focus only when no other item is available for focusing. Actors must be specified separately because (1) the focus of the discourse often is distinguished from the actor (see the example below), and (2) actors can be spoken of anaphorically at the same time that the discourse focus is pronominalized. As a result, different rules for governing mention of actors are needed.

A typical example of an actor focus can be found in D8.

D8-1 Jerome took his pigeon out on a leash.
    2 Since he was trying to train it,
    3 he hollered "heel" and "run" at it,
    4 as they sauntered along.

The actor focus is just whoever is currently the agent in the sentence. When the agent of the next sentence is a pronoun, the actor focus is usually chosen for co-specifier. Jerome is the actor focus in the first sentence of D8. Using this actor focus, the co-specifier of *he* can be established as Jerome. At the same time, the discourse focus is on Jerome's pigeon. It is needed as well because the pigeon is re-mentioned using *it*, and since *they* in D8-4 co-specifies both Jerome and his pigeon. Bringing the the actor focus and discourse focus together is quite common, as shown below, where the discourse focus is needed to establish who actually went to the movies from among the three actors. Rules for anaphors co-specifying with actors will be discussed later.

D9-1 I wanted to go to the movies on Saturday.
2 John said he'd come too, but Bill decided to stay home and study.
3 So we went and afterwards had a beer. (we = *John, the speaker*)

5.2.3 Finding The Discourse Focus

For the focusing process to proceed, an initial discourse focus must be found as early as possible in the discourse. The focus recognition algorithm I will propose can be viewed as part of a bootstrapping operation. The focusing algorithm depends upon the selection of an initial focus, but on the basis of one sentence, it is not always possible to predict what the focus will be. To choose a focus, an initial prediction after the first sentence will be made, and then this selection, called the expected focus, will either be confirmed or rejected by the basic focusing algorithm on the basis of the anaphors in the discourse.

The expected focus algorithm can select an expected focus that is not the discourse focus. Luckily speakers talk in such a way that incorrect predictions are easily recognized, and better choices can be easily computed. Hence the basic focusing algorithm is designed to confirm the expected focus, and if it cannot, to choose an alternate phrase to be the focus. This method provides an effective algorithm because once a false prediction is recognized, an alternative phrase is always available.

Before I review the reliable focus indicators and the defaults, I want to point out how I judged which phrase was the discourse focus. In each example, I used the pronouns which occur in the second sentence of the discourse (if there are any) as a signal of discourse focus. Since pronouns contain little lexical information, they reflect what the speaker has focused on in the previous sentence, so that the focus is that phrase which co-specifies with the pronoun (I am assuming that co-specifiers can be reliably chosen on an intuitive basis by native speakers of English).

There are a few indicators of focus that are highly reliable means of marking focus. When these indicators are not present, the only criteria that remain permit a noun phrase or verb phrase to be selected on the basis of preferences for focus locations. One criterion which will not be discussed here is stress and prosodics. While it appears to affect anaphor comprehension in discourse, not enough is known about stress and prosodics to discuss these behaviors in computational terms. When they are better understood, perhaps new algorithms can be revised

to incorporate their role.

There are a few sentence syntactic types that make recognition of focus easy since these sentence types have the purpose of singling out one discourse element from the others. These types are cleft, pseudo-cleft and *there*-insertion sentences as shown below:

(9) (pseudo-cleft agent) The one who ate the rutabagas was Henrietta.
(10) (pseudo-cleft object) What Henrietta ate was the rutabagas.
(11) (cleft agent) It was Henrietta who ate the rutabagas.
(12) (cleft object) It was the rutabagas that Henrietta ate.
(13) (agent) There once was a prince who was changed into a frog.
(14) (object) There was a tree which Sanchez had planted.

As the introductory sentence of a discourse, sentences (13) and (14) provide a means of introducing a new object or agent for further discussion. Sentences (9)-(12) rarely occur as initial sentences in a discourse since they assume there is some object already under discussion about which they provide new information; for example, (9) tells who ate the rutabagas, the rutabagas already being known about. As I will show in depth later on, sentences like those of (9)-(12) move the focus from one element to a new one. These examples suggest that *there*-insertion sentences mark an initial expected focus.

When an expected focus is chosen on the basis of semantic categories of a verb, the most reliable default is in the verb position of the theme.[1] In the two examples below the expected focus is indicated in parentheses.

D10-1 Mary took a nickel from her toy bank yesterday.
2 She put it on the table near Bob. (the nickel)

D11-1 Sandy walked her dog near a bull one day.
2 He walked quietly along. (Sandy's dog)

In D10, *it* co-specifies with *a nickel*. While it is inferentially acceptable for *it* to co-specify *Mary's toy bank* (since toy banks can be put on tables), on first reading, people understand the nickel to be the antecedent of *it*. A similar behavior occurs with D11. In these cases the noun phrase in a prepositional phrase following the theme cannot be the focus of the discourse unless the expected focus is explicitly overridden by a full definite noun phrase co-specifying with some other phrase of

---

1. This is Gruber's [Gruber 1976] term for the notion of the object case of a verb. His theory extends verb semantics to include verbs such as the ones below where the theme is located inside a prepositional phrase.

(15) We waited out the thunderstorm in a rundown old shack.
(16) Please focus on the star of India in the case on the left.

If the concept of theme is used as the default choice for expected focus, these examples fit naturally within the framework.

the initial sentence. For example, in D10-2, if *the bank* were used in place of *it*, the expected focus would be overridden in favor of bank.

In a sentence without a theme, that is, where only non-theme prepositional phrases are present, there does not appear to be a preference for expected focus. Most other thematic positions (instrument, goal and locatives) do not offer a strong preference for focus although some weak preferences sometimes appear. These weak preferences are for goal and any position in which an indefinite occurs. However, it is difficult to know how reliable these preferences are without some means of determining the role of stress and prosodics in these cases. Therefore, no claims will be made about preference for expected focus for these positions. Instead the algorithm for computing expected focus below will rely on a simple scheme of sentence surface order for these thematic positions.

One thematic position that is not preferred for discourse focus is the agent. When a pronoun occurs in a non-agent position, and in the preceding sentence, both an agent and a phrase in another thematic position can be its co-specifiers, the agent is not preferred, as is illustrated in the example below. Hence in the choice of expected focus, the agent is ordered last among possible noun phrase choices.

D12-1 A group at HXN developed a high speed technical chip packer.
2 The press gave it rave reviews.

Two sentence forms affecting focus do not depend on thematic position. One, is-a verbs, take the subject of the sentence as expected focus.

D13-1 The Personal Assistant group$_i$ is a research group that is designing pieces of a personal assistant program$_j$.
2 (a) Several graduate students and research faculty are members of it$_i$.
(b) * Several graduate students and research faculty are members of it$_j$.

While the predicate nominative is being associated with the subject in *is-a* sentences, it does not co-specify with the subject. Instead the subject is being described as having some particular properties, and hence is fundamental to the discussion.[1]

---

1. There are to-be nominal forms which do not contain the focus in subject position:
(17) A woman with great ideas is Amelia Michels. She is inspiring and works incredibly hard.

As far as I can tell, these forms are a kind of topicalization that is well marked (to the point of being grammatically odd for some speakers). In these cases, the subject is inverted from predicate nominal position and hence the focus is in nominal position instead of in the subject.

In the other non-thematic sentence form, the verb phrase can be expected focus as is evidenced by the use of *do-so* and *do-it* anaphora, as well as the sentential *it* anaphora shown below.

D14-1 Last week, we went out to the lake near my cottage.
2 It was a lot of fun.

Sentential anaphora seem to co-specify with an element representing the whole predication of the sentence while do-anaphora co-specify with the verb phrase. The verb phrase will be used in the list for expected focus, and the anaphor interpreter must determine whether just the verb or the whole sentence was the focus. Sentential *it* anaphora examples show that both theme and agent are preferred before the verb phrase. Examples such as D15 indicate that sentential *it* anaphora are not preferred as focus when a theme is present since the two uses of *it* co-specify bear, and not the capturing.

D15-1 Mike captured a bear.
2 Everyone said it made a lot of noise.
3 but I was asleep and didn't hear it.

The agent is preferred over sentential *it* as well. In D16, *it* co-specifies the bear although D16-2 is semantically neutral[1] between bear and the entire first sentence.

D16-1 One of the black bears got loose in the park the other night.
2 It frightened all the campers and generally caused panic.

To summarize, the choice of expected focus has been shown to depend upon the grammatical relations in a sentence, although a few sentence types can be judged on the basis of syntactic properties. This means of choosing is an alternative to the approach of [Baranovsky 1973] who used a list of discourse "topics" ordered by recency. The algorithm below chooses an expected focus on the basis of the preceding analysis of syntactic and semantic preferences; included in the algorithms are comments about the data structures and sentence information required for the decisions in the algorithm.

---

1. By "semantically neutral," I mean that the selectional restrictions on the thematic position in question do not rule out the use of either bear or the event of getting loose.

The Expected Focus Algorithm:

Choose an expected focus as:

1. The subject of a sentence if the sentence is an *is-a* or a *there*-insertion sentence.

   This step presumes information from a parse tree about what the subject, and verb are and about whether the sentence is there-insertion.

2. The first member of the default expected focus list (DEF list), computed from the thematic relations of the verb, as follows:

   Order the set of phrases in the sentence using the following preference schema:
   - theme unless the theme is a verb complement in which case the theme from the complement is used.
   - all other thematic positions with the agent last
   - the verb phrase

   This step requires a list of the surface order of the noun phrases, and a data structure which indicates which noun phrases fill which thematic slots in the verb. Such a data structure must be computed by a case frame mechanism such as the one reported in [Marcus 1980].

The expected focus algorithm is used to choose the discourse focus. An analogous algorithm to choose the actor focus can be defined. This algorithm would choose John as the expected actor in the sentence below.

(18) John rode his pony to the big meadow at the edge of the farm.

Were that sentence to be followed by a sentence with a pronoun in agent position, as below, the pronoun would confirm the expected actor focus as the actor focus.

(19) He liked to sing as he rode.

Later I will discuss the interaction between the actor and discourse foci.

5.2.4 Rejecting the Expected Focus

While the expected focus algorithm can always choose an expected focus, its choice may have to be rejected because the default position is overridden by other factors. Typically, this occurs when a pronoun, which does not co-specify with the expected focus, is used in the second sentence of the discourse, and no anaphor is used to co-specify with the expected focus. In the sample D17, the expected focus is the graduation party, but in the following sentence the use of *it* to co-specify with Cathy's house indicates that the focus is on the house.

D17-1 Cathy wants to have a big graduation party at her house.
    2 She cleaned it up
    3 so that there would be room for everyone.

Two questions come to mind: How can one recognize that the expected focus is not the focus? How can an alternative noun phrase be chosen as the focus? Recognition and selection both depend on the use of inferences about general knowledge. For example, in D17 the choice of party for *it* can be rejected since having cleaned up an event would be rejected as incompatible with other knowledge about cleaning. Following the rejection of the expected focus, a correct co-specifier can be selected because it is available in the previous sentence. To find it, each alternate default focus must be considered in turn, until one is found which is not rejected on the basis of general knowledge. When the focusing process runs again after all the anaphors are interpreted, the proper focus can be chosen.

The default expected focus can be rejected only when the inference mechanism clearly indicates that the predicted co-specifier is unacceptable. That is, the inference must contradict given knowledge from the discourse or be incompatible with other general knowledge. The fact that a noun phrase besides the expected focus might be acceptable as a co-specifier is irrelevant as long as the expected focus is acceptable. For example, in D11, repeated below, while the bull might be an acceptable co-specifier for *he*, it is not considered since the expected focus is acceptable.

D11-1 Sandy walked her dog near a bull one day.
    2 He trotted quietly along.

A matter which is related to the problem of rejecting a focus is how speakers recover from co-specification failures. Consider the following variation on D11:

D18-1 Sandy walked her dog near a bull.
    2 She saw how he threw back his great menacing horns.
    3 He certainly was an unusual looking dog and the name "Little Bull" fit him well.

After D18-2 the co-specifier of *he* seems to be the bull mentioned in D18-1. After the third sentence, the reader is likely to have discovered that the dog has been the focus all along and that this discourse is a bit bizarre. Virginia Woolf [Woolf 1957] points out that literature is interesting for the ways in which authors break rules. This chapter will only point out what rules can be violated. Why those rules are violated, and how native speakers recover from violations of those rules remains to be explained.

In summary, the expected focus can be rejected in favor of another phrase in the discourse. Rejection is possible, only when the predicted co-specification between a definite anaphor and the expected focus is unacceptable. The rejected phrase must be retained for possible re-introduction later in the discourse.

5.2.5 Inferring and Focusing

Confirming the expected focus often requires inferring some truths and can be quite complex. [Winograd 1972] cites the sentence "The city council refused the demonstrators a permit because they feared violence," and he describes some of the knowledge needed to determine the antecedent of they. [Charniak 1972] presents numerous examples of general knowledge, and [Isner 1975] presents one approach to handling inference for Winograd's sentences. The crucial difference between these theories and the one presented here is that the focusing process predicts an anaphor's co-specifier and then an inferring process confirms the prediction. A contradiction may be reached, which indicates that the expected focus must be rejected. The inferring may be trivial: for D18, he as co-specifying Sandy's dog is rejected because dogs do not have horns. When inferring is complex, focusing is advantageous.

Focusing simplifies the inference process because it delimits the beginning and end propositions that the inferring process uses, and it governs which inference can be taken back if a contradiction results. Schemes such as Isner's depend upon unification to bind the pronoun they to a "constant" noun phrase. While [Rieger 1974] never stated how pronouns are to be resolved for his system, his methodology for inference suggests using unification in a manner similar to Isner. By contrast, focus techniques "bind" the pronoun to the specification of the focus and then look for an inference chain that supports the resulting sentence.

For Winograd's sentence and its dual, both given below, the use of actor focus rules predicts that they co-specifies the city council in both sentences (actor focus rules are pertinent because they is an actor in the sentence "they feared violence").

D19-1 (a) The city council refused to give the women a permit because they feared violence.
(b) The city council refused to give the women a permit because they advocated revolution.

For D19-1a, the inference chain from "city council fears violence" to "city council refuses to give the permit" would be established by reasoning of the following form:

Form of reasoning:
- Find chain of inference from (CC fears violence) to (CC refuses (CC gives Permit Women)).
- If (X refuse (X gives Y Z)) is defined as caused by either:
   X is-Selfish or
   (X wants Y) or
   (X Dislikes Z) or

there is event (W) and (W is-undesirable-to X) and ((Z have Y) --> Occur W)
- Then the chain of inference must be found between (CC fears violence) and one of the above.

The first three disjuncts cannot be proven, so a chain must be found between (CC fears violence) and some event, which is undesirable to the council and which will occur if the women have a permit. If violence is taken as the event W, then one can easily deduce the second conjunct from: (CC fears violence) --> (Not (CC wants Violence)), and (Not (CC wants Violence)) --> (Violence is-undesirable-to CC). The third conjunct, that is, (W have Permit) --> (occur violence), cannot be established as true, although it is consistent with other information (no contradiction is reached). For focusing, consistency between the two ends of the inference chain is sufficient, while for traditional schemes, establishing of the third conjunct is necessary. Furthermore, for traditional schemes, the simple chain of inference above would not occur, because it is not known when the inferring process begins that it is the city council who fears violence.

For D19-1b, focusing predicts incorrectly that they co-specifies with the city council. Since a traditional scheme might also choose this co-specifier on its way to the correct solution, the significance of focusing follows from the control which occurs in inferring. This claim can be illustrated by the details of the inferring process. During the process of chaining from the city council advocating revolution to the council refusing to give a permit, a contradiction would be reached about the event of revolution being both advocated by the council (from the choice of co-specifier) and undesirable to the council (from the fourth conjunct of the definition of refusing above and general knowledge that city councils usually find revolution undesirable). Traditional schemes might search for another event W to infer about, while for focusing, the contradiction reached follows from the co-specifier choice. This choice is then retracted in favor of another focus choice, that is, the women advocating revolution. Hence the search is considerably reduced. Once the choice of women for they is made, inferring is also simplified just was it was for D19-1a.

A comment about finding contradictions in databases. Some research on truth maintenance systems ([Doyle 1978] and [McAllester 1978]) has experimented with constraint checking and developed algorithms for efficiently finding and undoing contradictions; these techniques have been developed as a means of reasoning mechanically in ways typical of the problem solving often needed by people. However, for a large scale problem, finding contradictions may still be impractical. One solution might be to choose a database that is a subsection of the whole database with the discourse elements or even the focus as the database core. As yet, no one has considered how to explore only certain "sub-sections" of a database for contradictions.

One might wish to argue against the use of inferring with focus on the grounds that for D19-1b there may be some other inference path chain between the city council advocating violence and the city council refusing to give out a permit; such a path would indicate consistency in the hearer's general knowledge of the world and would permit *they* to co-specify with the city council. If indeed such a path existed, the unlikely co-specifier would go through. But this choice would depend on a hearer thinking that city councils advocate violence, a very unlikely belief to hold. What hearers take to be the co-specifiers of anaphors does depend on what they believe, and were they to have such beliefs about city councils, we would expect them to produce such anaphoric interpretations.

Sometimes there is no other focus choice. If no other groups have been discussed before (20) is uttered, the focusing process would respond just as hearers do: reject the only available choice for the co-specifier of *they*.

(20) The council refused a permit because they advocated revolution.

On the focusing theory, the only possible co-specifier for *they* is the council, which would be rejected by the inferring process. Since no other choice is available, the focusing process will fail to find a choice, and the theory will predict that such sentences are odd. Conceivably, the speaker intended to say such an odd thing, or the speaker did not mean to say what was actually said. In either case, focusing does not eliminate the need for making inferences; it offers a constraint on how they are made. The complexity of the inferring process is constrained to asking for confirmation of the sentence predication, thereby eliminating combinatorial search for free variable bindings and non-terminating inferring.

5.2.6 An Algorithm For Focusing

I will now state the focusing algorithm which confirms or rejects the expected focus (found by the expected focus algorithm applied to the first sentence in the discourse), and in the case of rejection, determines which phrase is to move into focus; it is used for all sentences of a discourse except the first, where the expected focus algorithm applies. The algorithm makes use of several data structures: the current focus (CF), the alternate focus list (AEFL), which is initialized to either the default expected focus list (DEF) or the potential focus list (PFL); and the focus stack; the latter two structures have not yet been introduced, and their

purpose, as well as the condition given in steps 2 and 9, will be discussed below.[1] In the algorithm, the term "discourse initial" applies to the algorithm's first operation, which is on the second sentence of a discourse, while "in progress" applies to any of the later sentences.

The Focusing Algorithm

NOTE: The focus stack is initially empty when this algorithm is used.

NOTE: Before this algorithm runs, the current focus (CF) is set to either the default expected focus found from the expected focus algorithm or the discourse focus when discourse is in progress.

To confirm the current focus as focus or to reject the current focus for another focus in the next sentence of the discourse:

0. INITIALIZATION: Make note of the existence of do-anaphora, anaphors co-specifying the CF and AEFL, implicit specifications, anaphors which specify elements not in the discourse or the lack of an anaphor use.

1. DO-ANAPHORA: If the sentence contains do-anaphora, take the last member of the AEFL as the focus. Stack the current focus in the focus stack and halt.

2. FOCUS SET COLLECTION: When the discourse is in progress, if focus sets are being collected, and no anaphora occur in the current sentence, continue the collection. If some anaphor appears in the current sentence, use its co-specifier as the focus. Halt.

---

1. Steps 2 and 9 make use of focus sets. These will be discussed later in the chapter. Step 7 of the algorithm makes use of implicit specification, a concept which will be not discussed here; the step is included to assure completeness of the algorithm. Implicit specification is important when considering the interpretation of full definite noun phrases, a topic not included in this chapter. For a discussion, see [Sidner 1979].

stack, but the CF can fill a non-obligatory case[1] in the sentence or if the verb phrase is related to the CF by nominalization, retain the CF and halt.

9. FOCUS SET INITIALIZATION: If there are no foci mentioned and the sentence is discourse initial, collect focus sets.

10. NO FOCUS USED: Otherwise if there are no foci mentioned, retain the CF as focus. For any unspecified pronouns, the missing co-specifier condition holds.[2]

To illustrate the focusing algorithm in action, its behavior will be traced during the recognition of the initial focus of D6, which is repeated below:

D20-1 Last week there were some nice strawberries in the refrigerator.
  2 They came from our food co-op and were unusually fresh.
  3 I went to use them for dinner, but someone had eaten them all.
  4 Later I discovered it was Mark who had eaten them.
  5 Mark has a hollow leg, and it's impossible to keep food around when his stomach needs filling.

D20-1 is a there-insertion sentence, so step 1 of the expected focus algorithm indicates that the expected focus is the subject of the sentence, that is, *some strawberries*. The focusing algorithm contains a note that the current focus is set to the expected focus, and the ALFL be set to the other phrases in D20-1, that is, *last week* and *the refrigerator* and the verb phrase. The state of the entire focusing process at the point in which D20-2 is encountered, is illustrated in Figure 2.

---

1. Obligatory relations are cases of a verb that must be filled or the sentence is odd as in "John sold." Non-obligatory cases need not be filled: in "John sold a book," one non-obligatory case is the person to whom the book was sold.
2. See section 4.4 of this chapter for a discussion of missing co-specifier uses.

3. CHOOSING BETWEEN CF and ALFL: If there is an anaphor co-specifying the CF and another co-specifying some member of the ALFL, retain the CF as focus if the anaphor is not in agent position. If it is, take the member of the ALFL as focus. If both are non-agents, retain the CF as focus unless only the ALFL member is mentioned by a pronoun. In that case, move the focus to the ALFL member (Focus is moved by stacking the CF: setting the CF to the co-specifier of the anaphoric term, and then stacking any flagged implicit specifications as long as that specification is not the specification to which focus moves.). Halt.

4. RETAINING THE CF as FOCUS: If there are anaphors which co-specify only the CF, retain the CF as focus. Halt.

5. ALFL as FOCUS: If the anaphors only co-specify a member of ALFL, move the focus to it. If several members of the ALFL are co-specified, choose the focus in the manner suggested by the expected focus algorithm. Halt.

6. FOCUS STACK USE: If the anaphors only co-specify a member of the focus stack, move the focus to the stack member by popping the stack. Halt.

7. IMPLICIT SPECIFICATION: If a definite noun phrase implicitly specifies an element associated with the focus, retain the CF and flag the definite noun phrase as implicit specification. If specification is associated with member of ALFL, move focus to that member and flag the definite noun phrase as implicit specification. Halt.

8. LACK OF ANAPHORA: If there are no anaphors co-specifying any of CF, ALFL or focus

---

CF: *some strawberries* --specifies--> database representation of strawberries

ALFL: *last week, the refrigerator*, verb phrase of D20-1

Sentence: D20-2

Anaphors: *they* co-specifies with CF

Processor: skips through steps 0-3 of the Focusing Algorithm
At step 4: CF is taken as focus

Figure 2 Action of focusing process for the start of D20-2.

The focusing algorithm causes step 4 to be applied to retain the CF of *some strawberries* as focus, because there are no do-anaphora, no focus sets and no anaphors co-specifying with members of the ALFL.

In the example above rules to be formulated later governing the choice of anaphors given a focus (in this case an expected focus) determine that *they* co-specifies the CF. Definite noun phrase interpretation, of which *our food co-op* is an example, will not be discussed here although it is treated fully in [Sidner 1979]. Now that the algorithm has been demonstrated on discourse initial sentences, we turn to the use of the algorithm for a discourse in progress where focus movement, the focus stack, and the alternate focus list play a role.

5.2.7 Focus Movement

Since speakers do not always talk about just one thing, the focusing process must provide for the focus of the discourse to change. In D6, the strawberries are discussed for a few sentences, and then the discussion moves to the person who ate them. Accounting for this movement is necessary for anaphor interpretation because the new discourse element may be co-specified in later sentences. This process of moving the focus will be called focus movement. The discourse below illustrates focus movement from *meeting* to *office* (in D21-3) and back to *meeting* (in D21-4).

D21-1 I want to schedule a meeting$_j$ with Harry, Willie and Edwina.
  2 We can use my office$_i$.
  3 It$_i$ kind of small,
  4 but the meeting$_j$ won't last long anyway.

How can one tell if focus movement has occurred? Judging from D21, one might guess that focus moves whenever a new term is introduced. A counterexample to this rule is the alternate form of D21 below.

D22-1 I want to schedule a meeting$_j$ with Harry, Willie and Edwina.
  2 We can use my office$_i$.
  3 It won't take very long,
  4 so we could have it in the conference room.

In D22-3, there is no focus movement. If the focus were moved to office and back to meeting, the moves would be unnecessary since all the sentences are about the meeting.

Focus movement is recognized in a manner which is akin to initial focus recognition. Any new term in the discourse is a potential focus. The sentence following its introduction may contain either an anaphor which co-specifies with the potential focus or an anaphor which co-specifies with the element already in focus. If the anaphor co-specifies with the potential focus, the co-specification causes the potential focus to become the discourse focus.

With the above description there is no focus movement following D22-2 because no expression co-specifies with *my office*. For the original version, D21-2, the focus does moves because *it* can be taken to co-specify with the speaker's office.[1] and nothing co-specifies with meeting.

The two versions of D21 indicate the basic point of focus movement: when the sentence following a potential focus contains no co-specification with the potential focus, then focus movement does not occur. Since a potential focus does not always become the discourse focus, focus movement is like expected focus recognition: if one tried to predict a focus movement before the anaphor occurred, the prediction could be wrong, just as predictions of expected focus can be. Rather than consider focus movement a matter of prediction, it is best to think of it as a matter of recognition based on the anaphoric terms that follow in the discourse.

Potential foci have a short lifetime. If a potential focus does not become the focus after the interpretation of the sentence following the one in which the potential is seen, it is dropped as a potential focus. For example, at D22-3 *my office* is dropped. Hereafter if *office* is discussed, it cannot be referred to using *it* until some sentence re-introduces *my office* as a potential focus.

Since any new term in a sentence can be a potential focus, when several terms

---

1. Note that *it* cannot co-specify with the meeting because the tense of the sentence rules out the co-specification.

occur in one sentence, some means of choosing a potential focus is needed. Syntactic cleft constructions, as I have noted, indicate focus movement. In addition, one would expect that the theme should be the preferred position for a potential focus. In fact the same order used for default expected foci can be used for potential foci, except that the phrase which confirms the focus is not included in the list because it cannot be a potential focus. In English sentences, phrases which mention new information tend to occur towards the end of the sentence, while old information occurs at the beginning; this method of choosing potential focus captures that behavior.

In summary, the algorithm for determining the potential focus list (PFL) is:

1. If a cleft or pseudocleft sentence is used, the potential focus is the cleft item if and only if the element in non-clefting position co-specifies the focus. When it does not, the sentence is incoherent.

2. Otherwise order a potential focus list of all the noun phrases filling a thematic relation in the sentence, excluding a noun phrase in agent position and the noun phrase which co-specifies the focus if one exists. The last member of the PFL is the verb phrase of the sentence.

How strong is the focus/potential focus expectation? An indication of the strength of focus is given in the example below.

D23-1 Expert: Take off the bolts.
2 Apprentice: I am loosening them with the pliers that used to be in one of the tool boxes. Where are they?

The use of *they* in the last sentence is difficult to understand. The expected focus is bolts and is confirmed by the use of *them* in the apprentice's first statement. The apprentice also introduces the pliers as a potential focus, but *they* cannot co-specify to either the pliers or the bolts (because, as the inferring process must determine, the apprentice knows where they are in order to do the task). Hence the use of *they* is strange. Some informants say that *they* could co-specify the tool boxes but that such a choice is forced upon them only as a last resort to find something that makes sense. Such odd readings are captured by the failure to use the focus or potential focus as the co-specifier of a pronoun.

In general, focus movement occurs only when there are definite anaphora that are used to co-specify something besides the focus; these anaphora signal the movement. However, there is one condition which does not follow this general

rule. When two different anaphors co-specify with the focus and a potential focus respectively, and only one of the anaphors is a pronoun, there is no certainty about which will be focused on in the next sentence. Yet, there seems to be a preference for the focus to be marked by the pronoun use. In other words, pronouns seem to support a focus more strongly than anaphoric definite noun phrases do. Consider the case below:

D24-1 I got a new hat,
2 and I decorated it with a big red bow.
3 (a) I think the bow will brighten it up a lot. (it = the hat)
   (b) I think it will brighten up the hat a lot. (it = the bow)
4 If not, I think I'll still use it.

After D24-2, the focus is the hat, co-specified by *it*, and the potential focus list includes *a big red bow*. Either form of D24-3 uses anaphors which co-specify the hat and the bow. D24-4 is syntactically and semantically neutral on the choice of hat or bow as antecedent of *it*. However, if the sequence D24-3a and D24-4 occurs, the *it* co-specifies hat, while if D24-3b is used, the bow is slightly preferred. This example suggests that unlike the general case, the element co-specified by the pronoun should become the focus. The second condition for focusing is: Whenever both the current focus and a potential focus are co-specified but only one of them is co-specified by a pronoun, the focus is determined by the pronoun co-specifier. This condition appears in the focusing algorithm-as step 3.

Steps 2 and 9 of the focusing algorithm distinguish a feature unique to focus confirmation. The focus set initialization steps in the focusing algorithm are designed to recognize a discourse situation illustrated in D25.

D25-1 John and Mary sat on the sofa and played cards.
2 Henry read a book.
3 At 10 p.m. they went to Joey's Bar to hear a new rock group. It

After D25-1 and 2, the focus of this discourse is not *sofa*, *cards* or *book*. It appears that D25 is about John, Mary and Henry and what they did for an evening. In other words, the focus in D25 is collected over several sentences. The focusing expected focus algorithm will choose *sofa* as expected focus, while the focusing expected focus algorithm without step 9 would confirm the expected focus since no anaphors occur in D25-2. To capture the focus collection and to prevent confirmation when no anaphors occur in the initial part of a discourse, focus set collection is used. In collecting focus sets, discourse items in the same thematic position in each sentence are collected as one set. For D25, this method makes sets of (1) cards and book, (2) John, Mary and Henry, and (3) sitting, playing and reading actions. When D25-3 is processed through the focusing algorithm, *they* co-specifies with John, Mary and Henry, and so the three will be chosen as discourse focus. The informal description of focus movement given here illustrates that focus confirmation and focus movement are similar behaviors. So similar are these behaviors that they can be formally described by one algorithm. That algorithm provides a statement of control flow and the details of the conditions for confirming or rejecting a focus.

The significance of a single algorithm for both processes must not be overlooked: the one algorithm provides a uniform treatment of two phenomena which at first glance appear unrelated, namely, expected focus confirmation and focus movement. Furthermore, the one algorithm indicates just how the two processes are similar. The similarity in expected focus confirmation and focus movement can be extended beyond the parallel between default expected foci and potential foci since there are syntactic structures which mark focus movement just as there are syntactic forms which mark initial focus. More importantly, the focusing algorithm shows that expected focus confirmation and focus movement are both processes which require additional mention of the element in focus to confirm the choice.

5.2.8 Backwards Focus Movement

In discourse, discussion may be returned to a previous focus, that is, the focus may eventually shift back to a noun phrase previously in focus. This process is called focus popping. In D21-4 the phrase *the meeting* co-specifies with a meeting previously in focus.

D21-1 I want to schedule a meeting$_j$ with Harry, Willie and Edwina.
2 We can use my office$_j$.
3 It's$_j$ kind of small,
4 but the meeting$_j$ won't last long anyway.

To retain previous foci, a stack is used. Generally whenever an expression mentions an element listed as a focus in the stack, called the stacked focus, the focus is popped, and the stacked focus becomes the focus again. In terms of the focus movement algorithm, a stacked focus is considered as a possible focus choice following the discourse focus and potential foci list.

To claim that focus popping is in fact a stack behavior requires criteria for explaining why other behaviors cannot and do not occur. The basis for such claims requires further investigation which has not been undertaken here. Focus popping is described as a stack behavior because discussions in dialogues do return back to a previous focus without concern for intervening foci, and because once a focus pop occurs, the intervening foci are not mentioned without focus

movement similar to the regular focus movement.[1]

A simple discourse will indicate why a stack notion seems to be the right one. In the discourse below, the focus moves from Wilbur to the book, to quarks, and to elementary field theory. Then a pop back to the book occurs. Once the pop is made, Wilbur can be co-specified by *he* easily. A stack representing the foci at the time that D26-8 is processed is given in Figure 3.

D26-1 Wilbur is a fine scientist and a thoughtful guy.
2 He gave me a book a while back which I really liked.
3 It was on relativity theory,
4 and talks mostly about quarks.
5 They are hard to imagine,
6 because they indicate the need for elementary field theories of a complex nature.
7 These theories are absolutely essential to all relativity research.
8 Anyway, I got it while I was working on the initial part of my research.
9 He's really a helpful colleague to have thought of giving it to me.

FOCUS: elementary field theories

FOCUS STACK: quarks
                        book
                        Wilbur

Figure 3 Stack of foci at D26-8.

The discussion of focusing so far has been concerned with localized movements of focus from one discourse element to another, from a second to a third and possibly back to a first. Focus-popping, however, is a non-local behavior because the focus may move past several foci in the stack to some element that has not been mentioned for a long portion of the discourse. Typically, this non-local popping back to an old focus is accompanied by the use of a definite noun phrase to specify the old focus. The definite noun phrase is a clear signal of

1. Current implementations of the focusing process have been designed with a simple last-in first-out stack to pop foci until the proper focus is found, since this type of stack reflects the popping back in a discourse.

what is being talked about because of its distinguishing noun phrase head. Pronouns can be used as well, but their use is more restricted and governed by the interpreter rules, which prevent a pronoun from co-specifying a stack item if the discourse or actor foci are acceptable co-specifiers. The interpreter rules, in connection with the focus algorithm, impose a kind of stacked focus constraint that maintains localized focus movement. In D27 a pronoun may be used to pop back to an old focus. There the focus begins on career in law and moves to the friends of the speaker, with a potential focus of *their jobs*. The *it* in the last sentence co-specifies with a law career and re-establishes it as focus.

D27-1 A: Have you ever thought of a career in law?
2 B: I have some friends who are lawyers, and I've talked with them about their jobs, but I don't think it's for me.

In contrast some readers find D26 difficult because the transition at D26-8 is too abrupt for a pronoun to be used, especially if *anyway* is deleted from the sentence; *the book* in place of *it* seems to be more acceptable. This suggests that the stacked focus constraint should be modified so that pronouns are not interpreted to co-specify with items more than one position back in the stack. Rather than propose such a modification, some additional evidence about discourse must first be considered.

There are circumstances where the stacked focus constraint, in its original form or modified as suggested above, fails to account adequately for some language behavior. In some discourses, a pop back to an old focus can occur with a pronoun even though the pronoun could co-specify with the discourse or actor focus, and even when many foci intervene. In these cases the non-local, popping back movement occurs not only because a pronoun was used, but also because the hearer is aware of other structures that help him or her to discern where to pop to. These structures make it possible to use a pronoun to move the focus back without confusion. In the example below, *it* co-specifies with the pump, not the ratchet wrench, which was under discussion when D28-9 occurred. It appears that in conversations, words such as *ok* in combination with a discourse that reflects the task structure defined by [Grosz 1977], make it possible for speakers to use pronouns to co-specify with a phrase from an earlier part of the discourse.

D28-1 A: Bolt the pump to the base plate. There are 4 bolts, 4 nuts and 4 washers. <here follows an explanation of where to put the bolts and what tools to use.>
2 B: I would like to know if I can take off the back plate.
3 A: You shouldn't have to. Are you having trouble with the bolts?
4 B: Yes
5 A: <Now follows a long discussion of the use of the ratchet wrench, the extension and the socket for the wrench. The discussion ends with:> You will use the 2" extension and a 1/2" socket.
6 B: It is bolted. Now what should I do?

The type of popping back in discourse illustrated here indicates that the focusing algorithm and the anaphor interpreter might be joined with a mechanism which recognizes the task structure assumed by a speaker. Just such a mechanism has been proposed by [Grosz 1977], and another one, for informal conversations has been sketched by [Reichman 1978]; how the algorithm and such mechanisms might be joined remains to be discovered.

5.2.9 Using the Focusing Algorithm for Movement

To make clearer how the focusing algorithm is used for focus movement, let us trace the action of the algorithm on the following example discourse.

D29-1 Alfred and Zohar liked to play baseball.
2 They played it everyday after school before dinner.
3 After their game, Alfred and Zohar had ice cream cones.
4 They tasted really good.
5 Alfred always had the vanilla super scooper,
6 while Zohar tried the flavor of the day cone.
7 After the cones had been eaten,
8 the boys went home to study.

Using the expected focus algorithm, the expected focus for D29-1 is baseball (it is the theme of the verb complement). There are two pronouns in D29-2, but only one is considered by the discourse focusing algorithm because *they* is in agent position. As shown below, because *it* co-specifies with the expected focus, the expected focus is confirmed as focus.

phenomenon, called co-present foci, will be discussed later.

We have seen that a process model of focusing and focus tracking consists of three sub-processes. The first, the focus recognizer, chooses an expected focus based on what the speaker initially says. Then an interpreter applies its rules of interpretation, which make use of the focus to interpret the anaphoric expressions in the next sentence of the discourse. A third processor, the focusing algorithm, updates the focus using the anaphoric interpretations to decide either to confirm an initial discourse phrase as expected focus, maintain an established discourse focus, move the focus to a new phrase in the discourse or shift the focus back to a phrase which was once in focus. The interpreter and the focusing algorithm cycle through the remaining discourse. Our understanding of anaphor interpretation would not be complete without an explanation of the anaphoric expression interpreter; to illustrate its behavior and to provide a theory of anaphor interpretation, the rules it uses for personal pronouns and for *this-that* anaphora will be presented and explained.

5.3 Focus for Pronoun Interpretation

In this section, I will show how the discourse, actor, potential and stacked foci can be used by a rule-governed interpreter for finding the co-specifications of pronouns. I will discuss the general form of the rules and some of the interaction problems between the actor and discourse foci that must be resolved. Then I will turn to how the stacked foci are used in these rules. Following this discussion, I will review a number of examples where the pronouns interpreter cannot function adequately unless a representation of scope and related matters are included in the representation of specifications. Using Webber's representation in this volume, I will discuss how these are treated. Then I will point out some uses of pronouns which remain unaccounted for in the focusing theory.

The focusing theory assumes that when interpretation rules for anaphora are "run" by the interpreter, there are several groups of discourse elements available as possible co-specifiers: the discourse focus and its associated potential and stacked foci, and the actor focus and its associated foci. The interpreter must choose among these possible elements using constraints from sentence structure and semantics, and the hearer's knowledge of the world. In this section an account of the interpretations of pronouns for examples which have appeared previously will be given.

The proposal made here contains two implicit processing assumptions, (1) serial processing, and (2) end-of-sentence processing. By "serial processing," I mean that the interpreter checks a focus as a candidate for the interpretation of a

---

CF: *baseball* --specifies--> database representation of baseball

ALFL: verb phrase   FOCUS STACK: empty

Sentence: D29-2: They played it everyday after school before dinner.

Anaphors: *it* co-specifies with *baseball*

Processor at Steps 1-2: Not applicable

    at Step 3: CF taken as discourse focus since
                 anaphor co-specifies with CF

D29-3 also mentions baseball, by means of the definite noun phrase *their game*. This use is a case of lexical generalization of focus, a common means of referring with an anaphoric definite noun phrase. D29-4 shows a movement of the focus.

CF: *baseball* --specifies--> database representation of baseball

ALFL: *ice cream cones*, verb phrase FOCUS STACK: empty

Sentence: D29-4: They tasted really good.

Anaphors: *they* co-specifies with *ice cream cones*

Processor at Steps 1 - 4: Not applicable

    at Step 5: Since no anaphor co-specifies with CF, stack CF
                and take CF as *ice cream cones* plus its
                specification. Discourse focus is CF.

D29-4 contains the anaphor *they*. Since, on syntactic grounds, it does not co-specify with the focus, the ALFL (set to the PFL before the start of the focusing algorithm) contains *ice cream cones*, an acceptable co-specifier for *they*, so *ice cream cones* is confirmed as focus. The old focus of baseball is stacked in the focus stack. In just this way, focus moves. In the remaining two sentences each ice cream cone is spoken about separately using definite noun phrases; this

pronoun, and then if that focus is unacceptable, checks alternate candidates in turn. By "end-of-sentence processing," I mean that pronouns are not interpreted until the entire sentence has been syntactically and semantically interpreted. Both of these criteria can be given up without undermining the focusing theory. One could envision processing in parallel by checking the foci and alternates and then determining the pronoun's specification from an ordering of all those candidates that meet the criteria of choice; for interpretation of pronouns before the end of the sentence, conceivably the pronoun interpreter could choose a specification from available information and then review it as more of the sentence is processed. These two implicit processing assumptions have been made because they simplify the account of focusing and because they reflect an implemented version of a system with focusing. Further research will indicate whether these assumptions are too strong--if so, the focusing theory can be revised.

5.3.1 Using Focus for Pronoun Interpretation Rules

To begin the discussion, let us consider a pronoun interpretation rule that follows naturally from the discussion of focus and focus movement in the first half of this chapter. This rule is not adequate for reasons I will discuss below and will be revised over the course of the section.

R1: If the pronoun under interpretation appears in a sentence thematic relation other than agent, choose the discourse focus as the co-specifier unless any of the syntactic, semantic and inferential knowledge constraints rule out the choice. If the pronoun appears in agent position, choose the actor focus as co-specifier in the same way.

Ruling out a co-specifier on the basis of syntactic and semantic constraints is accomplished by computing the various syntactic relationships and restrictions (such as Lasnik's disjoint reference rules) and by use of semantic selectional restrictions (such as those of Fodor and Katz discussed in the beginning of this chapter) on sentence thematic categories. For inferential knowledge, the inferring process discussed earlier is used.

When a suggested co-specifier for a pronoun must be given up, R1 does not suggest how to proceed in using either the actor or the discourse focus to find some other choice for a co-specifier. It is here the potential foci are used, as illustrated in the example below.

D29-1 Alfred and Zohar liked to play baseball.
2 They played it everyday after school before dinner.
3 After their game, Alfred and Zohar had ice cream cones.
4 The boys thought they tasted really good.
5 Alfred always had the vanilla super scooper,
6 while Zohar tried the flavor of the day cone.
7 After the cones had been eaten,
8 the boys went home to study.

Alfred and Zohar are the initial actor focus while baseball is the initial discourse focus. D29-2 contains two pronouns, they and it which, according to R1, co-specify respectively with Alfred and Zohar, and baseball. D29-3 uses their, which co-specifies with Alfred and Zohar. but is not accounted for by rule R1. Furthermore they in D29-4 does not co-specify with baseball but with ice cream cones. How does the interpreter conclude these facts?

R1 must be extended in a manner that takes advantage of the potential foci, discussed earlier, that are available to the focusing algorithm and the anaphor interpreter. The potential foci can be used whenever the current actor or discourse focus is ruled out by criteria from syntax, semantics or inferential knowledge. Thus since they in D29-4 cannot co-specify with baseball (on both syntactic[1] and semantic[2] grounds), a potential focus is chosen. Whether the potential focus becomes the actor or discourse focus depends on whether the pronoun is used as an agent. In D29-4, they is the theme, so the discourse potential foci are used. The first potential focus which meets all the constraints is chosen as the co-specifier; in D29-4, ice cream cones is the first acceptable potential focus which meets all the necessary constraints as a co-specifier for they.

Use of R1 modified in this way follows hand-in-hand with the focusing algorithm discussed previously. The algorithm updates its discourse model after each sentence by tracking pronoun use. When a pronoun is used to co-specify a new potential focus, either the discourse focus or actor focus moves to that potential focus; which focus moves depends on whether the pronoun fills the agent position in the verb frame, and in the case of multiple agents, whether the ongoing actor focus is re-mentioned. For example, after D29-4, the discourse focus changes to ice cream cones because they co-specifies with the ice cream cones; the boys remain the actor focus, since they is not an agent case for taste and since the boys were already the actor focus.

The pronoun interpretation rule takes into account the movement of focus and

1. They is a plural pronoun while baseball is singular.
2. The discourse items filling the object case of taste should be tastable items.

The general rule for possessives[1] can be formulated as: if the discourse focus and actor focus were not established in the same sentence of the discourse, then the discourse focus is the co-specifier (if acceptable on the usual grounds); if the discourse focus was unacceptable, the actor focus is checked for acceptability and that failing, the potential discourse foci are considered; if both were established in the same sentence, the use will be ambiguous. As in the interpretation of personal pronouns, this rule shows that the discourse focus take precedence as the co-specifier. Unlike the case of personal pronouns, *their* is ambiguous between agents and other discourse elements; when the precedence of the discourse focus cannot be established, ambiguity occurs. Only when the discourse focus is not a possible co-specifier, can the actor focus be considered without ambiguity.

Another source of ambiguity occurs when an actor and one potential actor are both present in a previous sentence where the discourse focus is a non-animate element. An example is given below. Suppose that sentence (21) below followed each of (22), (23), (24) and (25).

(21) He knows a lot about high energy physics.
(22) Prof. Darby will tell Monty about the neutron experiment.
(23) Prof. Darby will lecture Monty on the neutron experiment.
(24) Prof. Darby will help Monty with the neutron experiment.
(25) Prof. Darby will teach Monty about the neutron experiment.

Some native speakers find all of these sentence pairs ambiguous, while some native speakers find only the pair (22) followed by (21) ambiguous. These examples are surprisingly similar to D31. How do some speakers decide that *he* co-specifies with Monty or Prof. Darby? It appears that they make a comparison and choose between the actor focus and the potential actor on the basis of evidence for their preferred interpretation. When that evidence is not forthcoming, informants are confused. Such a behavior suggests that the inferring process postulated thus far should be capable of a special judgment when given one actor and one potential actor; it must weigh its findings, and choose one of the two candidates as superior.

What kind of evidence can be used in such cases? The hearer knows that there is some person named Monty, who is probably male, that there is a professor named Darby, possibly male as well, that Darby is giving information to Monty about some physics experiment, the experiment being marked by the definite article as known to the hearer, as well as some criteria for determining who knows a lot about high energy physics in the context of teaching, helping, or lecturing.

---

1. Some special cases require a few additional rules that are discussed fully in [Sidner 1979].

constraints on syntax, semantics and inferential knowledge. However, some additional pragmatic criteria need to be added to deal with the interactions between actor and discourse foci, because a pronoun in agent position may co-specify with the discourse focus rather than the actor focus! One such example of this observation is below.

D30-1 I haven't seen Jeff for several days.
    2 Carl thinks he's studying for his exams.
    3 but it's obvious to me that he went to the Cape with Linda.

Although Carl is the actor focus after D30-2, and *he* in D30-3 is an agent thematic relation in the embedded sentence, the proper choice for the co-specifier of *he* is Jeff. Rather than suggest that Carl is considered as the co-specifier and then is ruled out (which seems unlikely as there are no syntactic, semantic or knowledge constraints which eliminate it), one might ask whether Carl is ever even considered for processing. In D30 it appears not. The discussion is about Jeff, who is introduced first, while the actors seem relatively incidental. In general such cases are resolved because if the discourse focus is animate and is established earlier in the discourse than the actor focus, the discourse focus takes precedence even for pronouns in agent position. In essence this approach takes the discourse focus as primary, the discourse focus being what the speaker is talking about so far while the actor focus is the locus of information about actions in the discourse.

This precedence rule does not indicate what to do when the discourse focus and actor focus are both animate, have the same gender, number and person, and are both established during the same sentence of the discourse. Interestingly enough, people sometimes have difficulty choosing interpretations in such circumstances. In D31-2a below, *he* co-specifies with *John* (the actor focus) but if D31-2b followed D31-1, *he* may co-specify with either John or Mike (the expected discourse focus).

D31-1 John called up Mike yesterday.
    2 a. He wanted to discuss his physics homework.
       b. He was studying for his driver's test.

In these cases, native speakers report that the co-specifier for the pronoun is ambiguous. If the pronoun fills an agent relation, the actor focus is preferred, but this preference is not a strong one. It appears that in such cases the ambiguity may not be easily resolved unless additional information about the two foci is known that stipulates that the sentence is true of only one.

What about the interpretation of possessive pronouns such as *their* in D29-3?

A computational system that makes such judgments must have a very rich knowledge base (that is, to know that Monty is a male name, that professors can be male, that professors are experts, that neutron experiments are physics experiments) and be able to draw inferences from that base. None of this is surprising; however, a computational framework for carrying out such subtle judgments is still beyond the state of the art. The matter of weighing evidence to decide between two candidates is similar to the semantic choice mechanism postulated by [Marcus 1980] for parsing certain kinds of structures such as prepositional phrases. This device, when attaching prepositional phrases, asks the semantic processor about its preferences for making the attachment.

In summary, this kind of ambiguity can be generally handled with the following condition.

POTENTIAL ACTOR AMBIGUITY CONDITION:

Whenever a pronoun may co-specify with the actor focus, and a single potential actor exists, expect a possible ambiguity. To resolve it.

1. Look for evidence supporting the statement in which the pronoun occurs. evidence which is true of the actor focus as the co-specifier, but not of the potential actor. If this is found, the actor focus is the co-specifier.
2. Choose the potential actor when evidence exists for it but not for the actor focus.
3. However, if there is evidence true for both, choose the actor focus but indicate possible ambiguity.

A summary of a full set of rules for interpreting possessive and personal pronouns can be found in [Sidner 1979]. In this section we have considered their motivation and general form. These rules represent what can be said about pronoun interpretation in the absence of any additional information in knowledge representation beyond that suggested in the discussion of co-specification. To interpret certain pronouns, such as those where a co-specifying phrase does not precede the pronoun in the discourse, as in the previously given D1, we must consider how knowledge is structured and represented. It is to this matter that we now turn.

5.3.2 Focus and Knowledge Representation

[VanLehn 1978] presents extensive evidence for the view that people do not normally disambiguate the scope of certain ambiguous quantifiers when understanding sentences such as D32-1.[1]

D32-1 Wendy gave each girl Bruce knows a crayon.
   2 She used it to draw a Christmas card for her mother.

He reviews the major theories of scoping phenomena and concludes that disambiguation of quantifier scope does not seem to take place during parsing or semantic interpretation of a sentence and that the determination of quantifier scope is the result of other linguistic processing.

To explain the comprehension of D32 above, some underlying semantic form representing scope is needed at some point in the processing of the discourse. In this volume, Webber argues why a representation of scope is needed and what the representation should be. What remains to be determined is when it is used. The pronoun interpreter requires such a representation, for example, to choose the proper co-specifiers of she and it in D32-2. The interpreter's behavior indicates that such a representation is needed, not in the initial determination of a focus, but in the process of determining the pronoun's co-specifier. This use of scope information is compatible with Van Lehn's findings because interpretations of scope are not considered until additional discourse material beyond the single sentence is presented.

A crayon in D32 may be used to specify objects which can be represented by the formal representations of Webber (Chapter 6 in this volume). Rather than list the actual formal notation, a paraphrase will be presented.

The first representation (call it R1) expresses that there is a unique set of entities that are crayons and were evoked in D32-1. The members of the set are distributed so that each one was given by Wendy to some one of the girls Bruce knows. The representation leaves open whether all the crayons were given out, but makes explicit the fact that all the girls got crayons.

The second representation (call it R2) represents a crayon as a unique singleton object that is a crayon and was evoked in D32-1. It was given by Wendy to a unique entity that is a girl and that is prototypic of the girls Bruce knows.

---

1. Some informants find this example unacceptable English because they cannot decide whether she in D32-2 is Wendy or someone else.

A third representation (R3) (which is a possible reading only for some speakers) can be derived from R1 by interpreting a crayon as a unique set having only one member. This corresponds to the reading that there was only one crayon given (in a collective way) to the set of girls Bruce knows.

Suppose now that D32-1 is vague, and no processing of it adjudicates the two readings (R1) and (R2) for a crayon. When the focus algorithm runs after D32-1 is processed, a crayon will become the discourse focus, but its representation will not distinguish between (R1) and (R2) or will list both as possible representations.[1] When the pronoun interpreter uses its rules to choose a co-specifier for it in D32-2, both readings must be available. The set reading (R1) may be eliminated immediately because of syntactic constraints that rule out a co-specifier for it with that reading, so (R2) is left, forcing a reading for each girl as the prototypic girl. If, however, a speaker accepts (R3) as an alternative reading, then D32 is ambiguous since both one crayon (R3) and a prototypic crayon (R2) are available to focusing.

To determine the actor focus specification for she in D32-2, the ambiguity between Wendy and each girl must be resolved since this is a case of potential actor ambiguity. Actually the interpretation is three ways ambiguous; there is Wendy, each girl interpreted as a set as in (R1) and (R3), or as a prototype as in (R2). The set reading may be eliminated immediately because she is singular. For the anaphor interpreter to choose between the remaining two, the inferring process must rule out one of the readings and find the other acceptable. Many native speakers cannot choose between Wendy and the prototypic girl; in fact numerous native speakers find D32 odd, presumably because neither choice is particularly sensible for them. On the whole, the focusing rules suggest just what people do - they rule out several readings (all of which can apply after D32-1) and then they fail to choose given the discourse actor ambiguity.

Another case of semantic ambiguity, similar to the one in D32, is illustrated in D33 below.

D33-1 Sally wanted to buy a vegomatic.
    2 She had seen it advertised on TV.

A vegomatic may be interpreted specifically, to mean there is one particular vegomatic, or non-specifically[1], to mean it is one of the many vegomatics. The focus does not distinguish between the two after D33-1 because, like D32-1, D33-1 is ambiguous, and neither interpretation can be chosen with certainty. When it is resolved for co-specification in D33-2, both readings can be considered, and the inferring process must determine that Sally saw a specific one on TV. Notice that the vegomatic Sally saw is not identical to the one she wanted to buy; in D33-2, it does not co-specify with Sally's vegomatic. Therefore the pronoun specification must be generated accordingly--a specific one seen by Sally on TV.

Suppose, for a moment, that D33-1 is interpreted so that a representation that maintains ambiguity is available. When the pronoun interpreter processes a subsequent sentence with a pronoun, it need only rule out readings; if the the inference machine discounts as contradictory one of the readings (Sally didn't want to buy the very one she saw on TV). If no reading is ruled out, the co-specifier would remain ambiguous, so that both the indefinite phrase and the pronoun would have ambiguous co-specifications. As the next example shows, there is some evidence for this behavior.

Consider the case shown in D34.

D34-1 Sally bought a vegomatic that had a broken cutting blade.
    2 She had seen it advertised on TV.

A vegomatic that had a broken cutting blade in the context of D34-1 usually means some particular vegomatic that Sally bought. However, it is ambiguous among the vegomatic Sally bought, some one vegomatic and a vegomatic that is an instance of the generic vegomatic; that is, "it" is ambiguous among three readings, Sally's vegomatic, and vegomatics taken as the specific and non-specific readings.

For D34-2, pronoun interpreter does not distinguish among the three readings since it accesses the one provided by the specification in D34-1, which is the specific reading. To find the specification of "it," the inferring process must discover that it is odd (1) for Sally to have seen the vegomatic with a broken blade which she bought being advertised on TV, and (2) for Sally to see any broken vegomatics on TV, and (3) for Sally to have seen the very one she bought on TV. Then if no other choices for co-specification are available, the specification of vegomatic from D34-1 must be used to generate an appropriate specification for "it". Since only unbroken ones not bought by Sally are appropriate, the

---

1. Both [Martin 1979] and Webber [Chapter 6 of this volume] have asked whether a sentence which is ambiguous between several readings must be represented by several different structures, one for each reading. Martin proposes representations that preserve ambiguity until some processor demands a refinement. Whether this approach or an alternative representation listing all readings is best is still an open question.

1. The terms 'non-specific' and 'specific' are traditional semantic expressions which bear no relation to "specify" and "specification." A non-specific reading of a dog corresponds in computational terms to a representation of an instance of the generic dog: that is, what is represented is a dog which has the characteristics of the generic dog - that is, an animal with four legs, a tail, medium size, brown, friendly, barks, and the like.

specification of "it" must be generated using only part of the phrase from D34-1.

This example seems problematic because it places much weight on the inferring process to decide that certain readings are odd. However, this is likely to be just where the weight of the decision ought to be; many native speakers find D34 slightly bizarre because their first reading is that Sally had seen a vegomatic with the broken blade advertised on TV. In fact, it appears that when a specific indefinite noun phrase such as *a vegomatic* is introduced, the speaker can direct attention to the non-specific reading more readily with a plural pronoun, as shown below.

(26) She had seen them advertised on TV.

The plural non-specific reading as in (26) has been incorporated in the pronoun interpretation rules, but the generation of specifications for the singulars in more unusual cases, such as D34-2, has not; it is difficult to recognize that a specification should be generated when the inferring process rejects the two readings. However that people falter in such cases suggests that some additional, possibly general, problem solving behavior is relevant to the proper treatment of these cases.

Examples such as D34 are perplexing for another reason; they are examples of what I will call, following [Fahlman 1979], the "copy phenomenon". The ambiguity centers around the fact that there can be many copies of an abstract prototype. Automobiles, computer programs, airplane flights and money are other common cases of entities which exhibit the copy phenomenon. In D35, the interpretation of *it* depends on whether the speaker is referring to a particular flight or the normal Sunday flight, a copy of which occurred on *this Sunday*.

D35-1 TWA 384 was so bumpy this Sunday I almost got sick.
2 It usually is a very smooth flight.

Note that the *it* cannot co-specify with the particular flight on *this Sunday*. However, it is possible that the speaker intended TWA384 to refer to a particular flight; if this is so, the speaker mixed the specific and non-specific interpretations for the co-specifier of *it*, just as in D34-2.

Another characteristic use of anaphora is the bound variable case given by Partee [Partee 1972, 1978]. In D36 below, *him* co-specifies with Archibald, while if *himself* were used, it would constitute a reflexive use of *every man*.

D36-1 Archibald sat down on the floor.
2 Every man put a flower in front of him.

In linguistic theory, bound variables are assumed to be represented in sentence semantics; when used in conjunction with syntactic disjoint reference rules, pronouns within the *scope* of the quantifier can be distinguished from non-scoped ones. Since the pronoun interpreter takes account of these conditions, it can easily choose a proper co-specifier for *him* in D36 in terms of the focus, but for *himself* it

will recognize the bound relation to *every man*. It is crucial to these cases that part of the representation of the interpretation of sentence phrases is some scope of quantification, especially when it is unambiguous.

5.3.3 Focus Restrictions on Co-specification

There are other restrictions on co-specification that result from the processing of the focusing algorithm. As discussed previously, the focusing algorithm can access a stack on which old foci are stored. In addition to co-specifying with current actor and discourse foci, a speaker may use a pronoun to co-specify a discourse element that was once in focus but is no longer; [Grosz 1978] described and illustrated this behavior for anaphoric noun phrases in task oriented dialogues. It can be captured in the pronoun interpretation rules by a rule which selects candidates from the focus stack. However, there is a constraint, called the <u>stacked focus constraint</u>, on this use due to the nature of the focusing algorithm. An anaphor which is intended to co-specify with a stacked focus must not be able to co-specify with either the focus or potential focus. An example from a literary text[1] where a pronoun co-specifies with a stacked focus is presented below.

Was that old lady evil, the one Saul and I had seen sitting on the porch? I had dreamed about her. When the trolley car took me and Saul past her house again this morning, she was gone. Evil, it had a queer sound to it in English.

{Here the narrative moves on to an incident in a school classroom. A discussion between the speaker and a male teacher ensues for five paragraphs. The succeeding paragraph begins:}

She had worn an old brown coat and a green scarf over her head.

In this example, *she* co-specifies with the old lady discussed previously. If Potok had told of a discussion between the speaker and a female teacher, it would no longer be possible to tell that *she* was co-specifying with the old woman. The reading of *she* as teacher might be a bit surprising because what the teacher is wearing was not relevant to the previous conversation, but it certainly is not the

---

1. "In the Beginning" by Chaim Potok, page 212, chapter 4, Fawcett Publications, Inc. Conn. 1975.

case that an inferring process would decide that teachers do not wear old brown coats and so forth.

The stacked focus constraint is not stated directly within the focusing algorithm. Rather it is implicit in its function. The following situation is ruled out by the manner in which a focus is used: A pronoun cannot co-specify with a stacked focus when a current focus is an acceptable co-specifier, since that current focus will be taken as the interpretation, and the stacked focus will never come into consideration. The stacked focus constraint is a consequence of the movement of focus in the focus machinery.

The stacked focus constraint, however, may be overridden. An astonishing set of examples was identified by Grosz (see [Deutsch 1974], [Deutsch 1975]). One such example was given previously (D28), and another is shown below.

> A: One of the bolts is stuck and I'm trying to use both the pliers and the wrench to get it unstuck.
> E: Don't use the pliers. Show me what you are doing. Show me the 1/2" combination wrench.
> A: Ok.
> E: Show me the 1/2" box wrench.
> A: I already got it loosened.

Generally readers understand this example without taking enough time to go back and test the intervening co-specifiers before choosing one of the bolts in this example.[1] Instead some other process is helping drive the understanding of what is meant. One explanation is that understanding depends on knowing that something being loosened completes the task that A originally indicated in the first sentence. The focus of A's first command indicates exactly what is bolted. Thus the focus could provide the co-specification for the object under discussion, but some other mechanism, which interprets completion of task goals, indicates where to pop back in the set of task environments under consideration. The focus relevant for that task environment is used to determine the co-specification of a pronoun.

How many such discourse interpretation mechanisms exist? While this chapter does not address this question directly, some speculation is possible due to research reported elsewhere (see [Grosz 1981], [Sidner 1979], [Robinson 1981]). In general, it appears that discourses permitting violations of the stacked focus constraint must contain an implicit structure of tasks pertinent to the conversation

---

[1] This informal evidence needs to be tested out in a psychological laboratory. The author has not done so, but the results of such experimentation would be helpful.

or some other well specified structure which guides the hearer in understanding. Without this structure the hearer has no means for choosing something other than the current focus as co-specifier.

5.3.4 Pronouns Which Have No Co-specifiers

The previous discussion has assumed that a pronoun is always preceded by a co-specifying phrase. However, this is not always the case, and a complete theory of pronoun interpretation must address cases where the co-specifying phrase appears *after* the pronoun; and where no co-specifying phrase exists but one is implied by the discussion.

Pronouns which are used with their co-specifiers appearing *after* the occurrence of the pronoun have been called backward anaphora in the linguistic literature; I will refer to them as forward co-specifiers. Two such examples, (27) and (28) are given below.

> (27) If he comes before the show, give John these tickets and send him to the theatre.
> (28) Near him, Dan saw a snake.

In general the pronoun co-specifies with some noun phrase interpretation, but the phrase is placed forward in the discourse. The types of sentences in which this behavior can occur are limited. In general it seems to be permitted for fronted sentential prepositional phrases (as in (28)), for complement sentences fronted on another sentence (as in (27)), and for sentences containing co-ordinating conjunctions. Extensive research in linguistics on forward co-specifiers ([Solan 1978] contains a good review) gives reliable evidence that it is governed by structural constraints. In particular, syntactic rules can be stated that determine when forward co-specifiers are not permitted. The most recent formulation, by Solan, called the backward anaphora restriction, fails on certain sentences such as *In her room Mary saw a ghost*, so further research is still needed.

Whatever the best formulation of the syntactic rules for forward co-specifiers, they are preferable only in initial sentences of a discourse. For example, when a sentence such as (27) occurs in mid-discourse, if a speaker has been talking about Henry, and just begun mention of Charles, he will be taken (by native speakers) to co-specify with Henry, or with Charles, if Henry can be ruled out on basis of some special pragmatic knowledge. The focus rules can capture just this behavior when used in conjunction with the proper syntactic rules.

The pronoun interpreter acts on a condition that will be called the missing co-specifier condition. In the remainder of this section, I will define that condition. The pronoun interpretation rules include a rule for recognizing a missing co-specifier, and this recognition forms the basis of the condition to which the focusing algorithm responds.

There are many uses of pronouns where the pronoun has no co-specifier in the preceding discourse, where the pronoun is not used to co-specify forward, and where it is not used in conjunction with some action such as pointing. One such use, pronouns that specify a generic from a non-specific reading, has already been considered. However, such a case is distinguished from the ones given below because the pronoun is not used to specify a generic which is generated from the focused noun phrase; rather the pronouns below specify without a generating phrase. The examples given below are from several sources; the first three are from [Postal 1969], the fourth from [Chafe 1972], the fifth from dialogues collected for the PAL system ([Sidner 1978]), and the last was spoken by a lecturer at a presentation this author attended.

D37-1 I saw Mr. Smith the other day; you know, she died last year.
  2 John is an orphan. He misses them very much.
  3 Pro-Castro people don't believe he is a monster.
  4 I went to a concert last night. They played Beethoven's ninth.
  5 I want to meet with Bruce next week. Please arrange it for us.
  6 I used to be quite a tennis player. Now when I get together with the young guys to play, I can hardly get it over the net.

With the exception of D37-1, most hearers are able to say which is the intended specification of the pronoun in the cases above; D37-1 can be understood if the hearer is informed that Mr. Smith had a wife. However, some of these, especially 1 and 2, are so odd that most hearers read the sentence several times before comprehending. Hearers are divided on the acceptability of 3, and most hearers find 4 and 5 acceptable. Such examples, as far as I can tell, do not occur naturally in written samples.

While these uses of pronouns can be recognized by the rule interpreter, how they are understood remains a mystery. [Webber 1978a, 1978b] provides some additional constraints on their use. However, the focusing approach provides some basic structure that help to provide an explanation. In all the multi-sentence cases, the pronoun specifies something which is closely associated with the focus. More explanation is required since some speakers do not understand those pronoun uses which seem to be related to the non-existence of an object (such as John's parents in light of John's orphanhood). Whatever the manner in which hearers recover specifications for such pronouns, some principles are needed that govern why some pronouns are acceptable and others are not.

5.3.5 The Problem of Parallelism

The pronoun interpretation rules give incorrect predictions for certain uses of pronouns, uses that are difficult to define. Intuitively, they may be characterized as instances of parallel structure between sentences of a discourse. To understand what is meant by parallel structure, two simple cases, one in which the rules do predict correctly, and another in which they fail, will be discussed. In D38, the pronoun co-specifies with the mud pack, as the pronoun interpretation rules would predict. The parallelism of these sentences is reflected in the semantics of put on and pull off as well as in the similarity of the syntactic structure of the two sentences, each containing an imperative mood main clause.

D38-1 Put the mud pack on your face.
  2 After 5 minutes, pull it off.

he pronoun interpretation rules predict the proper co-specifier in D38 because the thematic relations of the verb follow the similarity of structure. In D39, the pronoun it co-specifies with rose and not with the green Whitierleaf. The initial focus after the first sentence is Whitierleaf, but the parallel syntactic structure of the sentences seems to govern the choice of co-specifier. To summarize, between similarity of structure and the focus rules, similarity is preferred as a means of choosing the co-specifier, so when each gives a different prediction, similarity of structure must be used.

D39-1 The green Whitierleaf is most commonly found near the wild rose.
  2 The wild violet is found near it too.

On first glance it appears that the pronoun interpretation rules could be "fixed" by simply observing that the initial focus is wrong and that a potential focus should be chosen. No such option is available, for such a "fix" requires that the inferring process reject the initial focus. To do so, the inferring process needs some knowledge about the world that indicates the unacceptability. For D39 no such knowledge could possibly be forthcoming since all the flora involved are found near one another. There is no knowledge to the effect that violets are found near wild roses and not near Whitierleafs.

Another example of parallel structures is shown in D40. The parallel structures again are reflected in the similarity of the syntactic forms as well as the

---

1. In certain cases a special audience may have different responses to the parallelism above. For example, botanists who know what flowers are near others might behave differently. But even special audiences must sometimes use general techniques. Such is the case in the D39 example, because Whitierleafs are imaginary flora.

that is able to determine parallel relations among sets of sentences in a discourse. However, methods for interpreting pronouns from parallel sentences and paragraphs offer no constructive way of interpreting the pronouns in most of the examples presented in this chapter. Many cases of co-specification occur where there is no similarity of structure other than the common subject-verb-object pattern typical of English sentences. Since what is being talked about appears in many constituent positions in sentences of a discourse, the s-v-o pattern is too gross a level to specify similarity. Hence while parallelism is needed to deal with a certain set of cases for which the pronoun interpretation rules predict incorrectly, those rules are effective for many other cases of co-specification where parallelism would not be helpful. One may conclude that focus process accounts for one aspect of anaphor interpretation, and that some different mechanism is needed to encode similarities in structure which are used in discourse. The examples in this chapter provide some additional observations about the nature of parallelism in interpreting pronouns in natural languages and led us to conclude that further research is needed.

5.4 The Interpretation of *This* and *That*

5.4.1 Co-present Foci in Anaphor Disambiguation

In an earlier section, it was pointed out that sometimes speakers discuss several concepts at once without indicating that they are doing so. Generally this causes the discourse to be confusing enough to prevent the hearer from understanding. Sometimes however people discuss more than one thing without confusion. How is that possible? One such case has already been presented; in the last section, it was shown that an actor focus may be present in many discourses in addition to the discourse focus. It is also possible to have co-present discourse foci within the discourse.

In this section I will first describe in more detail the concept of co-present foci. Then I will illustrate how it can explain the use of *this* and *that* in discourse. Finally I will discuss the rules of interpretation for these anaphors and their relation to the focusing algorithm. I will show that, when used together in a discourse, *this* and *that* keep the focus on two objects at once, while when used separately, *this* generally moves the focus and *that* does not.

Just what is meant by co-present foci? When more than one element is introduced in a discourse and each is discussed relative to the other or relative to a class in which both occur, the discourse is said to be maintaining co-present foci. An example will be helpful for understanding how this behavior occurs.

semantics of *most* and *mine*. After D40-1, the initial focus is the car radiator (that is, the prototypic car radiator). Using the focusing rules, *it* will be taken to co-specify with that radiator. But this prediction is incorrect; *it* co-specifies with the radiator of the speaker's car.[1]

D40-1 On most cars the radiator has a free bolt hook.
    2 But on mine, it has a floating bolt hook.

The use of *it* here is similar to the instance of a generic for *it* in the example of the vegomatic with the broken cutting blade. What makes it different is that D40-2 has an underlying semantic form which is similar to D40-1. D40-1 specifies a universal set of cars and says something about one of the parts for those cars; D40-2 specifies a set of one thing, the speaker's car, and says something about a part of it; the speaker's car is related to the universal car by instantiation. Thus *it* in D40-2 is not pointing to some instance of the prototypic radiator; it co-specifies with the radiator of the speaker's car, but the co-specification seems to come about partly due to the representation of the *radiator* in D40-1. The similarity in the underlying semantics of D40-1 and D40-2 must be used in interpreting the pronoun.

One might wish to construct some special purpose mechanism that looks for similarities in structure between two sentences. This method is doomed for two reasons. First, parallelism exists in many aspects of language, and it happens at arbitrary levels of structure. Second, at any given level, the problem of recognition of parallelism has plagued computational models of language since such models were first suggested. For example, parsing of English sentences containing conjunction is as yet an unsolved problem. Methods tried for parsing conjunctions, such as those of [Woods 1973] in LUNAR, fail because of overgeneralization. Recognition of parallelism is still beyond computational theory.

The fact that interpretation of parallelism has failed for other aspects of computational models of language only indicates that the problem is a deep one. An extended example in [Sidner 1979], which will not be shown here, indicates that parallel constructions may be found between whole paragraphs in a discourse. Such constructions affect the interpretation which speakers and hearers choose for anaphors; hearers seem to take advantage of the parallel structure between two paragraphs of a discourse in deciding what was meant.

One possible consequence of these observations could be that the focus algorithm should be abandoned in favor of some as yet unspecified mechanism

---

1. The author thanks R.C. Moore for suggesting this example.

DS-1 I'm having a party tomorrow night;
2 it will be like the one I had last week.
3 That party was a big success
4 because everyone danced.
5 This one will have better food.
6 I've asked everyone to bring something special.
7 Want to come?

Two different parties are talked about; that is, both of them are in focus. To indicate that the speaker wants to discuss both, that is introduced to co-specify with the one mentioned second. The second party is used as a means for comparison to the first; hence this indicates the main concern of the speaker while that a secondary concern.

5.4.2 Interpretation of Co-present this and that

The anaphoric use of this and that has been difficult to explain. Most previous explanations (for example, by [Halliday and Hasan 1976], [Fillmore 1971] and [Lakoff 1974]) require some concept of proximity. Linguists have observed that deictic (that is, physically pointing) uses of this and that[1] seem to involve proximity to the speaker. The sense of proximity for this is being near the speaker, while for that, it means "near you or not near either of us but at any rate not near me."[2] By analogy, they explain anaphoric this indicating either proximity in the time and space of the context or in the sense of experience or empathy with the speaker, while for that, there is less proximity or empathy. These explanations are vague enough for us to ask for a more concrete one.

With focusing a different explanation is possible. The speaker needs a way to talk about two objects of the same type (for example, this letter and that one), but cannot use a pronoun because it will co-specify with only one of them. To distinguish the two and yet allow both to be spoken about, this and that phrases are used. In the case where the speaker wants to indicate that one of the two is more important, it will be co-specified using this; when this is used to mark relative importance, it will be referred to as primary focus.

To consider how this is accomplished with the focusing algorithm, let us analyze DS in detail for a summation of the focusing behavior. DS-1 and 2 establish a focus on the party tomorrow night according to the focusing algorithm. Among the potential foci of DS-2 is the one I had last week. DS-3 indicates that the speaker wants to say more about the potential focus while maintaining the first focus; this is accomplished by means of using that instead of the to co-specify with the party last week. If the had been used, it would cause the hearer to suppose initially in processing that the speaker was talking about the upcoming party; then the hearer would need to reject the choice because of the tense of the verb. That is a much clearer means of telling the hearer which one is under discussion.

How is the first focus maintained in the focusing algorithm for DS? While two discourse foci could be introduced, a simpler choice is available; the first focus could be stacked at the top of the focus stack. When a noun phrase with this as determiner is encountered, the co-present focus from the stack could then be chosen as the co-specifier.

The kernel of the rule for this and that is:

> this is a determiner used for main focus, that is, this + <noun phrase> determines main focus, while that + <noun phrase> co-specifies with a potential or old focus. However, if the focus has been mentioned using that, then a this definite noun phrase must co-specify with an old focus.

DS is a case where the primary focus (tomorrow night's party) is stacked, in favor of a discussion of a second element in the discourse, signalled by the use of that. It moves into focus, and when the first party is discussed again, this must be used. An example of the normal rule instantiation is given below in D41. First Hilda's plan is talked about in focus and then the speaker's own plan. Thereafter Hilda's plan is talked about using that.

D41-B: What are the plans for the banana raid?

A: According to Hilda's plan, you and I stay here until everyone else is in position. I don't much like it because I think we'll miss all the action. I think I've got a better plan: we'll be the guide party, and Eloise and Hilda the search party. With this plan, we'll be in on the action. Well, what do you think, isn't it a better plan than that one?

The rule for this and that reflects the locus of the speaker's concern. In DS the first thing introduced is the chief concern, while in D41, A indicates concern with her own plan rather than Hilda's. In general, when the speaker uses that as determiner for a definite anaphor that co-specifies with the focus, the speaker is indicating that chief concern lies with another element, one that has previously

---

1. In the sample case below, the speaker would be pointing at each painting as the sentence is uttered.
(29) This painting is a Van Gogh; that one is a Renoir.
2. [Halliday and Hasan 1976], op. cit., pages 58-59.

been in focus, but that has been "put on hold" until the speaker finishes with the *that* phrase.

The above explanation is incomplete. Speaker concern functions slightly differently when the speaker and hearer are not focused on the same elements, and especially when *this* and *that* co-specify elements of different types. In D5 and D41, speaker and hearer are focused on what the speaker makes the focus of the discourse. However, in some dialogues, the speaker and hearer do not always share focused items. Consider D42 below.

D42-1 A: Let's flip a coin and see who calls it.
2 B: Heads.
3 A: That's what it is. (* This is what it is.)

The focus of this dialogue is the coin which is being flipped. B has a second focus which is the result of the toss. When A speaks of B's focus, A uses *that* to refer to it; *this* cannot be so used. When several examples are considered, the proper formulation of the rule becomes clear: when speaker and hearer (as a second speaker) have different focus, use *that* as the determiner of a definite noun phrase that co-specifies the hearer's focus, and use *this* for the speaker's focus.

That in D42 is used non-co-presently. Non-co-present uses of *this* and *that* are those where the anaphors specify discourse elements that represent two different types of objects and where there is only one focus per speaker. In non-co-presence, *this* co-specifies an element which becomes the focus while *that* co-specifies some other discourse element, which stays out of focus in spite of the anaphoric term. Since non-co-present uses concern focus movement, let us discover just how they behave in discourse.

5.4.3 *This* and *That* in Focus Movement

When considering the behavior of *this* in discourse, one may observe that a *this* definite noun phrase moves the focus to whatever is specified by the head noun of the definite noun phrase. As the rules in the discussion of pronouns indicate, usually the focus moves to the leading potential focus in the potential focus list. Yet sometimes the focus moves to the entire description given by the previous sentences; sometimes, surprisingly, the focus does not really move in the sense that a new element is co-specified: the same element is specified but from a different perspective.

This definite anaphora are used in four ways depending upon the type of noun phrase heads that they and the focus contain. The cases are enumerated below with sample illustrative texts.

1. The focus and *this* definite anaphor have the same head nouns: the co-specifier for the anaphor is a member of the potential focus list and can be chosen just as pronoun co-specifiers are; move the focus to co-specifier.[1]

D4-1 The axon may run for a long distance, sending off several
sidebranches along the way,
2 before it terminates in an even finer network of filaments, the
terminal arbor. (FOCUS: the axon)
3 Man's longest axon runs for several feet, from the spinal column
to muscles that control movements of the toes.
4 In spite of its great length, this axon, like all nerve fibers, is a part
of a single cell. (NEW FOCUS: Man's longest axon)
5 It is living matter.

2. The focus and *this* definite anaphor have different head nouns: the focus should be considered as a co-specifier of the *this* definite anaphor before other potential foci. If the focus is an acceptable co-specifier, the focus does not move.

D43-1 Consider the roomful of electronic equipment that makes up a
modern, high-speed digital computer.
2 Rack after rack of transistors, diodes, magnetic core memories,
magnetic film memories--
3 all laced together by an intricate system of wiring many miles in
length.
4 Imagine the room, and everything in it, shrunk to about the size
of a cigarette package. (FOCUS: the room)
5 Now suppose we give this marvelous box to a clever electrical
engineer, a man working, however, not in our own midcentury,
but about the year 1900.
6 We present our gift
7 and demonstrate a few of the remarkable feats it can perform:
several hundred thousand additions in one second...
8 We leave this tantalizing device with the suggestion that he try
to find out what's inside the cigarette package...

3. *This* definite anaphor has an empty head. Choose the co-specifier from the potential focus list, but order the verb phrase predication as first choice. Move the

---

1. This example and the next are from [Denes and Pinson 1973], *The Speech Chain: The Physics and Biology of Spoken Language.*. Anchor Press, Garden City, New York, pages 124, and 122, respectively.

focus to the co-specifier.[2]

D44-1 Since however, the interpretation has been put forward as a hypothesis,
2 some weight will be added to it
3 if it can be shown to have an antecedent probability. (FOCUS: the interpretation)
4 This is what I shall endeavor to do in the remaining pages.
(NEW FOCUS: show that the interpretation has antecedent probability)

4. A *this* definite anaphor occurs inside of a quantified phrase. The *this* definite anaphor takes its co-specifier from the quantified variable; such cases are similar to the bound variable pronouns discussed in earlier.[3] The focus does not move. (In the example[4] below, the quantified phrase and *this* anaphora are underlined.)

D45-1 We can, therefore, associate with each point near the earth a vector **g** which is the acceleration that a body would experience if it were released at this point.
2 We call **g** the *gravitational field strength* at the point in question.

Why are *this* anaphora provided as a signalling behavior when *it* and definite anaphora using *the* are available? The cases cited above permit the conclusion that the speaker needs a way to signal focus movement where *it* and *the* anaphora would keep the focus on an existing discourse element. Sometimes the speaker also needs a way to signal a new view of the focus (case 2): in such cases *it* could not provide this signal, and *the* noun phrases are too easily taken to be new items in the discourse, rather than the focus from a different description. Only in quantified phrases can *this* anaphora be used without moving focus; as these cases are well marked by the quantifier, the hearer can distinguish them as a special case.

In contrast to *this*, *that* used non-presently singles out an element of the text for re-mention without causing a focus movement. The focus may move later, but another anaphor must cause the move.

There are two kinds of non-co-present *that*, which will be called new mention

---

2. This example is from Thomas A. Goudge. [Goudge 1969] *The Thought of C.S. Peirce*. Dover Publications, Inc. New York. page 326.
3. Quantified phrase patterns also use *that* in a similar way.
4. From Resnick, Robert and David Halliday [Resnik and Halliday 1966] *Physics: Part I*. John Wiley and Sons, Inc. New York, page 405.

that and previous mention *that*. New mention *that* describes an element which has not been mentioned previously in the text. It signals a new discourse element and can be used without confusion as long as no other definite noun phrases with the same noun head as the *that* phrase exist in the discourse. Two examples of new mention *that* are given below.[1]

D46-1 This is a course in biology.
2 Biology studies those entities that are called organisms: men, worms, yeast cells, bacterial cells are organisms.
3 Some organisms are unicellular,
4 some are multi-cellular.

D47-1 In Marigold's garden, roses grow everywhere.
2 She likes roses of the Eastern gorge variety more than those of the Western shore.
3 so she has a lot of them in her collection.
4 They grow to prize winning shapes and sizes.

A previous mention *that* phrase takes as its co-specifier the interpretation of some phrase mentioned previously in the discourse. An example[2] is given below.

D48-1 If MNMSD is referred to by D either as "the mayor of San Diego" or "D's neighbor,"
2 then node 'MNMSD' represents the individual referred to.
3 The problem is that only looking at that node provides no reflection of the differences in the two references to MNMSD,
4 even though the surface DEFNPs do express this difference.
5 Focus spaces provide a means of representing this difference.

In D48, *that node* co-specifies with the node of D48-2. If the rest of the discourse is ignored, D48-3 would have been equally acceptable using *this*. However, the author does not want to focus on *that node* since in the next sentence she uses *this difference* to focus.

The important question about previous mention *that* is why it exists at all in English. It is clear from D48 why *this* cannot be used, but what about *the* or *it*? In the examples I have found, *it* in place of *that* is ambiguous in indicating what object is being referred to. *The* in place of *that* seems to be possible, but has a certain effect. Suppose D48-3 were:

(30) The problem is that only looking at the node provides no reflection of the differences in the two references to MNMSD...

The use of *the* forces a movement of focus from the person to the node, when

---

1. The first example comes from Luria, S.E. [Luria 1975] *Thirty-Six Lectures in Biology*. Cambridge: MIT Press, 3. It also contains a use of deictic *this*.
2. From [Grosz 1977], page 82.

what the author actually wants to turn her attention to is the differences in the two references to the person. In other words, an intervening, and in this case unnecessary, focus movement occurs.[1] Hence *that* serves a useful function in the language; it allows the speaker re-mention discourse elements without them becoming the focus of the speaker's (and therefore the hearer's) attention.

5.4.4 Using the Focus Movement Algorithm

To conclude this section and illustrate how the anaphor interpreter and the focusing algorithm function for *this* and *that* anaphora, their behavior will be illustrated on an example which uses *this* and *that* non-co-presently.

D49-1 One day Bill's father bought Bill a new softball.

2 Bill and his friends played with it daily.

3 Not long after Harry was given a hardball by his uncle.

4 This ball, allowing more speed and accuracy than Bill's, became the boys' choice for all their baseball games.

5 That bothered Bill's father

6 because he didn't like to see Bill neglect his toys.

The expected focus of D49 is *a softball*. It is confirmed by the use of *it* in D49-2. D49-3 introduces a hardball, which is a potential focus for the discourse. Since *this* definite anaphora must use the potential focus list as a source for co-specifiers (when no co-present *that* is present), and since the source passes syntactic, semantic, and inference criteria, *this ball* in D49-4 is chosen to co-specify with the potential focus of *a hardball*. When the focusing algorithm runs after D49-4, the focus must move because of the use of *this*. In the next sentence a noun phrase consisting only of *that* occurs. The potential focus list of the previous sentence contains *the boys' choice*, *their baseball games* and the predication expressed by the verb phrase. The rules for *that* predict that the last member of the potential focus list is the co-specifier of *that*, a predication, which is what, intuitively, *that* co-specifies with.

This section has introduced and developed the notion of co-presence in discourse, for understanding the use of *this* and *that* anaphora. Co-presence is a means for talking about two or more discourse elements that are related to each other. Because language is spoken in a linear dimension, and perhaps because

people have trouble paying close attention to two things at once, it is not really possible to focus on both elements simultaneously. Instead, two elements are set up for discussion and considered in turn using the normal focusing process. Co-presence cases are well signalled in language behavior, perhaps to prevent confusion for hearer. Since hearers are sometimes confused by single focus, it is not surprising that co-present foci must be signalled clearly enough so that some of the potential confusion is reduced. It may well be that the signalling is necessary for the speaker as well, to help keep track of what he or she is trying to say. This is mere speculation until focusing is applied to the generation of language, and a theory of its behavior is given. Some research in this direction is discussed by McDonald in this volume.

In contrast to co-present foci use of *this* and *that* noun phrases, non-co-present uses of them allow the speaker to indicate which of all the things she or he has mentioned is most important to the discussion. *This* and *that* used in non-co-presence allow the speaker to point at the relevant material with the least confusion. Hence the real difference in these uses is a difference in the speaker's plans for, and the hearer's means of deciding, what will be talked about.

5.5 Conclusions

In this chapter the concept of focus has been defined and the role of focusing in understanding discourse has been illustrated. To formalize and clarify this behavior, I have described algorithms for finding the focus and for moving the focus as the discourse progresses. Tracking the movement of the focus includes a means of distinguishing the presence of more than one focus in the discourse; the focusing algorithm tracks both the discourse focus, the chief element of discussion and the actor focus, the chief actor in a portion of the discourse.

Focusing provides the foundation for a theory of anaphor interpretation. The foci and aspects of the focusing algorithm together with linguistic rules for disjoint reference and selectional restrictions, and with representations of network relations and sentential scope information provide an account of the interpretation of many uses of definite anaphora. Both the rules and representations have been shown to be compatible with the process of focusing, and necessary to focusing in providing information relevant to determining the co-specifier of a pronoun. In most cases, the focus itself provides a co-specifier, and in some cases, a generator for the specification.

Focusing simplifies a crucial step of anaphor interpretation. In choosing a co-specification, inferences about knowledge of the everyday world are needed, and focusing has contributed a means of controlling the inferring process.

---

1. There is another reason for using *that*. The context which precedes the text of D48 makes reference to a figure in the text. *That* node doubles as a deictic phrase. This example suggests that there is an important relation between focusing and deixis, a matter demanding further research.

Under the category of *Relation* I place a single maxim, namely, "Be relevant." "Though the maxim itself is terse, its formulation conceals a number of problems which exercise me a good deal; questions about what different kinds and foci of relevance there may be, how these shift in the course of a talk exchange, how to allow for the fact that subjects of conversation are legitimately changed, and so on."

As long as relevance is a part of a theory of pragmatics, focusing must be included in that theory, whether it is the theory which Grice has begun to unfold or some other one. Focusing and focus as they have been used here bear directly on Grice's concerns; for they suggest a means for carrying out the maxim of relevance. Namely, a speaker is speaking relevantly in a discourse if he or she introduces a focus, and proceeds to another one by mentioning it and re-mentioning it with definite anaphora. Old foci are re-invoked by a definite noun phrase which points out which old focus is co-specified or in one of the other, less direct, ways discussed in the previous chapters. Nothing less than the use of focus will suffice for relevance: for the moment the speaker fails to provide a focus for the hearer and to point back to it in successive utterances, the hearer has no means of knowing what is relevant in the discourse at hand. In some sense the discourse ceases to be a discourse.

Perhaps it is surprising that focusing should play such a central role in a theory of pragmatics. In particular, it is surprising that focusing one's attention on something and signalling one's focus is part of the criteria for speaking relevantly. One expects relevance to be a matter of what is said about some thing, rather than that the thing is mentioned consistently. But if we remember that focusing allows for the speaker to tell the hearer that the same thing is still under discussion and without needing to say explicitly what that thing is, then the role of focusing is not so surprising. Focusing must then be the first criterion for speaking relevantly, since it explains how a hearer decides what the speaker is talking about.

5.6 Acknowledgements

The research reported in this paper was supported in part by the Advanced Research Projects Agency under contract No. N0014-77-C-0378. Research reported here was also done at the Artificial Intelligence Laboratory of the Massachusetts Institute of Technology. Support for the laboratory's artificial intelligence research is provided in part by the Advanced Research Projects Agency of the Department of Defense under ONR contract N0014-75-0643.

Because the pronoun interpreter predicts a co-specifier and then asks for confirmation or rejection based on the presence of contradictions in the inferring process, the inference process is controlled by the focus machinery. In previous AI natural language systems interpretation resulted from binding of free variables during inferring; however, many inferences had to be drawn and then "undone" due to incorrect binding choices. The focusing approach eliminates this kind of blind binding and unbinding as well as shortening the inference chain search.

In this chapter I have also illustrated the value of concept of co-presence for interpreting the use of *this* and *that*. Co-presence is the means by which a speaker can be focused on more than one thing in a conversation, and it has been shown that *this* and *that* used co-presently allow the maintenance of two foci, one of main concern and the other of secondary concern to the speaker. *This* and *that* used non-co-presently, that is, when only one of the two types of noun phrases is found, also indicate main concern (*this*), or secondary concern (*that*) relative to some other focus.

The focus "popping" cases described by Grosz, and the need for parallelism underscore the role of higher discourse structures in focus interpretation. The Grosz examples violate the stacked focus constraint, but are comprehensible because the speaker relies on knowledge of task structures. The parallelism examples show that some additional structure is also used in understanding discourses. While focus popping makes use of the focus algorithm, the parallel structure cases seem to rely on a mechanism which is different in kind.

This chapter further specifies the nature of focusing as it relates to a theory of definite anaphor interpretation. A focus-based theory with stipulations for syntax, semantics and inferential knowledge, provides a predictive and explanatory theory of anaphor interpretation. The theory is predictive because it stipulates legal and illegal pronoun uses as well as their interpretations; it is explanatory because it hinges on the focusing algorithm using anaphora as signals of what is being discussed, while the syntactic, semantic and inferential knowledge used in interpreting anaphora provide for changes in the foci of discourse, changes that are reflected in pronoun use.

Focusing seems to be a necessary part of the theory of the pragmatics of language. In his well known William James lectures, [Grice 1975] defined several maxims of conversation, one of which was the maxim of relevance. Grice[1] says about this maxim:

---

1. Grice, *op. cit.*, page 67.

So What Can We Talk About Now?

Bonnie Lynn Webber

6.1 Introduction

I started my research on anaphoric reference in natural language when 'I was struck by the following two examples:

D1-1 John gave Mary five dollars.
   2 *It* was more than he gave Sue.
D2-1 John gave Mary five dollars.
   2 One of *them* was counterfeit.

in which both *it* and *them* seem to follow from the same phrase, *five dollars*. This seemed extraordinary: if definite pronouns like *it* and *they* referred anaphorically to a text strings, how could the same string of text justify both a singular and a plural pronoun.

Moreover, neither of the natural language understanding (NLU) systems that I had worked on up to the time - LUNAR [Woods et. al. 1972] and BBN's speech understanding system [Woods 1976] - could handle both examples either. That is, while these systems had rules for identifying what noun phrases made available for subsequent definite anaphora,[1] for each type of noun phrase, there was only one such rule. As a consequence, one could program the system to treat *five dollars* as either an indefinite plural noun phrase (NP) - later to be referenced as by *they*, or as a mass NP - a singular quantity - later to be referenced as as *it*, but not both.

Nor was this problem acknowledged, much less solved, by any of the anaphor resolution heuristics coming from either artificial intelligence or psychology (i.e., heuristics for choosing the intended referent of a definite anaphor from among possible alternatives). All these heuristics simply assumed that a text made things available for later anaphora, and that the intended referent would always be among the possible alternatives. Nor could standard linguistic theory at the time account for the anaphoric behavior in both examples: definite pronoun anaphora

---

1. one of the functions served by definite pronouns like "it" and "they" and definite NPs.

was only of interest within the single sentence and even that, only with respect to lexical, syntactic and/or semantic constraints on what a pronoun could be associated with, *within that same sentence.*

Five dollars is clearly not an isolated example. One can quickly discover many instances where a single sentence admits a variety of things available for subsequent anaphora, based on what seems to be the same phrase. For example,

'The Rhodesian ridgeback down the block bit me yesterday. *It's* really a vicious beast.

- 'The Rhodesian ridgeback down the block bit me yesterday. *They're* really vicious beasts.

- Each girl in Mary's class marched up to the desk and took a brick. *She* then went back and sat quietly in her seat.

- Each girl in Mary's class marched up to the desk and took a brick. *They* used them to build a mockup of the Great Wall of China.

- John didn't marry a Swedish blonde. *She* was Danish.

- John didn't marry a Swedish blonde. *She* had brown hair.

- John didn't marry a Swedish blonde. *She's* just living with him.

- Wendy gave each boy a green T-shirt. She gave *one* to Sue as well.

- Wendy gave each boy a green T-shirt. Sue, she gave a red *one*.

In beginning my research, my feeling was that whatever regularities were present in making things available to either definite pronoun or "one" anaphora, they could not be formulated purely in terms of text strings, parse trees or any of the then-current AI representations. While I shall not comment on the first two types of representations, the AI representations used within computer-based NLU systems fell roughly into three categories, none of which was motivated by

purposes. What my research has been directed at then is (1) a definition of what a text makes available for anaphora that can accommodate the kinds of examples presented above and also be amenable to computational treatment and (2) within that computational treatment, a characterization of features of a representational formalism (or set of related formalisms) that would most efficiently support the procedures.[1] That is, I have attempted to articulate what a text makes available for anaphora in terms of the structure (as opposed to content) of its sentences, as they are represented in such a formalism. Like any other structure-based understanding strategy, this would have the advantage of being common to all users of a language, whether the content were completely understood or not.

As for the remainder of this paper, the first part is based on my thesis research [Webber 1978a], although it has profited from recent work with R. Bobrow on a natural language interface we call PSI-KLONE, for "Parsing and Semantic Interpretation in KL-ONE" [Bobrow and Webber 1980a, 1980b, 1981]. I have also changed my terminology somewhat, to emphasize the commonality of this work with the complementary set of issues discussed by Sidner (this volume). The second part of the paper contains an approach to "one" anaphora that differs substantially from that presented in [Webber 1978a]. This new approach has the attractive feature of reducing two separate difficult problems into the same (albeit still difficult) one.

6.2 Fundamental Assumptions

The approach I have adopted to identifying what a text makes available for the interpretation of definite pronoun and "one"-anaphora is based on the notion of a "discourse model".[2] The assumption is that one objective of discourse is to talk about some situation or state of the real or some hypothetical world. To do this, a speaker must have a mental model of that situation or state. The ensuing discourse is thus, at one level, an attempt by the speaker to direct the listener in synthesizing a similar "discourse model" and by that, acquire information about the speaker's situation or state. (In this sense, I am equating "understanding" with "synthesizing an appropriate model".)

---

1. As [Hankamer and Sag 1976] point out, both definite pronoun and "one" anaphora may be "controlled" by things other than the previous text. In particular, they demonstrate "control" by the spatio-temporal context that speaker and listener share. In this paper, I shall only be discussing what texts (and, to a limited extent, what inference) make available.
2. This is a notion that has been explored in cognitive psychology to explain the inferences that people draw in understanding text. See, for example, [Collins, Brown, and Larkin 1977].

understanding continuous discourse and the phenomena common to it.

1. Several followed formalisms often borrowed from linguistics (e.g., LUNAR's syntactic parse tree, SHRDLU's systemic analysis [Winograd 1972], most "case" representations [Bruce 1975]) that were meant to map "paraphrases" (syntactic and/or lexical variants) into the same representation.

2. Several were modifications of a logical formalism (e.g. the meaning representation languages used in LUNAR, PHLIQA [Bronnenberg et al. 1980], etc.) that were meant to provide a well-understood single-sentence semantics.

3. Several were meant to fill in for material often left unsaid in natural language utterances (Schank's frame-like conceptual dependency representation [Schank 1975]). Whatever procedures were used to handle instances of anaphora were ones that could be grafted onto these formalisms, a posteriori.

Surprisingly enough, such procedures were not complete failures, and even had modest success. LUNAR, for example, was able to make use of its logical meaning representation to deal with such non-obvious anaphoric references as

D3-1 Do any samples contain bismuth and ruthenium?
2 YES
3 Give me their overall analyses.

where it correctly interpreted "their" in D3-3 to refer to the set of samples which contain bismuth and ruthenium. In forming this set description -- i.e., "samples that contain bismuth and ruthenium" - LUNAR ignored its own answer to question D3-1. Thus in example D4, it would incorrectly propose "samples that contain bismuth and ruthenium" (rather than "samples") as the interpretation of "they".

D4-1 Do any samples contain bismuth and ruthenium?
2 NO
3 Then what do they contain?

So, to summarize the then-current situation in linguistics and AI natural language understanding, the former either weren't interested in discourse anaphora or tried to handle it by either string or structure matching - clearly inadequate - while the latter attempted to deal with it using whatever ad hoc methods could be grafted onto representations primarily designed for other

Informally, a discourse model (DM) may be described as the set of entities "naturally evoked" (or in Sidner's terms, "specified") by a discourse, linked together by the relations they participate in. I have called these things "discourse entities", and Sidner has called them "cognitive elements". In linguistics, they harken back to what [Karttunen 1976] has called "discourse referents". The alternate terminologies that Sidner and I have adopted rest on wanting to keep "refer" a separate technical term. That is, "referring" is what people do with language. Evoking and accessing discourse entities are what texts/discourses do. A discourse entity inhabits a speaker's discourse model and represents something the speaker has referred to. A speaker *refers* to something by utterances that either *evoke* (if first reference) or *access* (if subsequent reference) its corresponding discourse entity.

To illustrate the notion of entities "naturally evoked" by a discourse, consider the following sentence.

ID5-1 Each 3rd-grade girl brought a brick to Wendy's house.

Then consider each of the following continuations. In each case, I would label what is accessed by the definite pronoun as "naturally evoked" by sentence ID5 -1.[1] As the reader can see, such entities may have descriptions appropriate to individuals, sets, stuff, events, activities, etc.

- She certainly was surprised.
  she ≡ Wendy

- They knew she would be surprised.
  they ≡ the set of 3rd-grade girls

- She piled them on the front lawn.
  them ≡ the set of bricks, each of which some 3rd-grade girl brought to Wendy's house

- She was surprised that they knew where it was.
  it ≡ Wendy's house

- Needless to say, it surprised her.
  it ≡ the brick-presenting event

---

1. The symbol ≡ in these continuations should be taken as indicating the same target for both expressions.

- Generally, Wendy can always find something to do with them.

them ≡ bricks, bricks people bring her

Notice moreover that texts identical at a conceptual level may not be identical vis-a-vis the discourse entities they naturally evoke, even though their phrasings differ only slightly. For example

D6-1 John traveled around France twice.
  2 ??They were both wonderful.

D7-1 John took two trips around France.
  2 They were both wonderful.

McDonald makes a similar point in [McDonald 1977], where he discusses the problem of generating subsequent "referring" expressions. He takes as his example conceptual level the first-order predicate logic and considers English renderings of the simple formula,

$$\forall x \; man(x) \Rightarrow mortal(x)$$

which include

1. For any thing, if that thing is a man, then it is mortal.

2. Being a man implies being mortal.

3. All men are mortal.

McDonald notes that only the first version gives the variable x a separate status, thereby making it something that can be specified again (e.g., "it is mortal). The second version gives the open formula "man(x)" separate status, making it in turn available for re-specification (e.g., "It also implies being subject to supply-side economics."). McDonald concludes

In short, it is not possible to predict which objects will be explicitly referred to and which not just on the basis of a formula in the internal representation language.

It is not just what the conceptual level information is, but how that information is realized that determines what types of discourse entities are available when.

Now a speaker is usually not able to communicate all at once the relevant properties and relations s/he may want to ascribe to the referent of a discourse entity. To do that, s/he may have to direct the listener's attention to that referent (via its corresponding discourse entity) several times in succession. When the speaker wants to re-access an entity already in his/her DM (or another one directly inferable from it), s/he may do so with a definite anaphor (pronoun or NP). In so doing, the speaker assumes (1) that on the basis of the discourse thus far, a similar entity will be in (or "directly" inferable from) the listener's growing DM and (2) that the listener will be able to re-access (or infer) that entity on the basis of the speaker's cues. (For example, pronouns are less of a cue than anaphoric NPs.) The problem then, at least for definite anaphora, is identifying what discourse entities a text naturally evokes.

What characterizes a discourse entity? My minimal view is that a discourse entity is a "conceptual coathook" (a term coined by William Woods) on which to hang descriptions of the entity's real world or hypothetical world correspondent.

As soon as a discourse entity is evoked, it gets a description. Over the course of the text, the descriptions it receives are derived from both the content of the speaker's utterances and their position within the discourse, as well as whatever general or specific information about the discourse entity the listener can bring to bear. (For example, as the text conveys the passage of time, a description like "the 16-year old girl that..." might change to "the 20-year old girl that....") These descriptions provide part of the means by which a listener can decide the intended target of subsequent definite anaphora (the other being provided by focusing mechanisms, as discussed by [Grosz 1977] and Sidner in Chapter 5 of this volume). What I claim is a special status for the initial description (ID) that tags a newly evoked discourse entity. (Examples of such IDs follow the equivalence symbol ($\equiv$) in the continuations to example IDS-1 above.)

In what way is a discourse entity's ID special? For one thing, it is the only information about an entity that can, from the first and without question, be assumed to be shared (though not necessarily believed) by both speaker and listener alike. Thus, at least initially, it is an inference that the speaker can assume the listener both capable of and likely to make. That the speaker needn't believe the description for it to be effective is discussed in [Perrault and Cohen 1981] -- that the listener needn't believe it either is discussed in [Webber 1978b]. The important thing is that it is *shared*, and hence useful.

Now this view of discourse understanding does not preclude discourse entities from being evoked by other things than the text. In fact, I will argue that certain types of discourse entities must be derived from other ones inferentially. In particular, I will argue that it is the simplest way of accounting for anaphoric access to "generic set" discourse entities. I will show that, from any discourse entity (except, in general, ones evoked by a proper noun phrase, name, title, etc.), the speaker can presume that a listener is capable of deriving a discourse entity corresponding to one of a limited number of generic sets to which the referent of the original discourse entity belongs.

The problems I set out to solve - identifying what a text makes available for definite pronoun anaphora (and, it turns out, for "one" anaphora as well) and developing computationally feasible ways for making them available in an NLU system - were thus transformed into (1) identifying the discourse entities a text evokes and (2) ascribing to them appropriate IDs. What I discovered was that these things depend heavily on *combinatoric* features of a sentence.[1] Moreover, these features can be captured in the *structure* of a representational formalism (as opposed to its lexical content), and can be the basis for procedures which identify the entities evoked by a text and derive their IDs. What I have realized more recently is discussed in Section 6.5: namely, that the semantic problem of interpreting "one" anaphora[2] can be reduced to the already considered problem of identifying possible "set-type" resolvants for definite plural anaphora.

Before finishing this statement of my fundamental assumptions, I want to comment on where I see evoking and labeling discourse entities fitting into the whole process of understanding continuous text. First, most discourse entities are ones evoked by a noun phrase in its clausal context.[3] Now whether or not a discourse entity should be evoked (and if so, how it should be described) depends on clausal features - especially the combinatoric features presented in Section 6.3 - that often remain elusive, even after the clause is parsed and both general semantic and particular pragmatic knowledge is applied. That is, sentences often pose what might be called an "underconstrained combinatoric problem" [Bobrow and Webber 1980a]. What is required of semantic interpretation is to delineate the problem to be solved. What happens then depends on what is required: one

---

1. Combinatoric features are discussed in the next section. Briefly put, the ones I am considering are:

   iteration "A window was tested in each house" implies the speaker is viewing the situation in terms of one testing per house.

   dependency "A window was tested in each house" implies under one interpretation that the particular window depends on the particular house: a window associated with house1 was tested in house1, a window associated with house2 was tested in house2, etc. Under a different interpretation, the particular window is independent of the house, the same one tested throughout.

   cardinality "Two windows were tested in each house" implies for any given house there were two windows tested, where the two are distinct from one another. Notice the sentence does not (on its own) imply anything about the cardinality of the entire window set.

2. as opposed to the *syntactic* problem of characterizing where "one(s)" can and cannot occur, a problem of interest to transformational grammarians; cf. Section 6.5.

3. Clauses may also evoke discourse entities of various sorts, as may verb phrases. For example, *Stir the dissolved yeast into the flour, then knead the dough for 10 minutes or until elastic.* The discourse entity describable as "the dough" is evoked by the first clause, or rather, the reader's understanding of it. However, I will be ignoring such examples in this discussion.

possibility is that the discourse/pragmatics component - using whatever discourse and pragmatic information is available to it - may be forced to solve the problem immediately in order to provide an appropriate response.

But what if no immediate response to the sentence is called for? What if one doesn't need to commit oneself one way or another? Then the combinatoric aspects of the sentence's interpretation can remain underconstrained - i.e., ambiguous. On the other hand, if the need to interpret later sentences requires a particular resolution or particular type of resolution, that can result in further constraints on the delineation. For example, in processing a definite anaphor, a listener may simultaneously (1) make explicit some or all the possible senses of a previous sentence; (2) formulate appropriate IDs for the entities that each sense, if correct, would evoke; (3) identify one of these entities as the intended resolvant of the definite anaphor; and (4) thereby identify the correct, intended sense of that previous sentence. What enables the listener to do all this is the fact that alternative possible interpretations do not lead to equally satisfying ways of resolving the anaphor.

6.3 Factors in Forming Discourse-dependent Descriptions

As I mentioned in the last section, it is necessary to take account of certain combinatoric aspects of a sentence in order to form appropriate IDs for the discourse entities it evokes. To do this requires *inter alia*:[1]

1. distinguishing between definite and indefinite noun phrases and between singular and plural noun phrases.

2. distinguishing, for each modifier in a plural noun phrase, whether it conveys information about the entire set denoted by the plural noun phrase or about the individual set members. The same is true of the verb phrase/predicate.

3. resolving any ellipsed verb phrases in the sentence.

4. identifying what has traditionally been called "quantifier scope assignments", although, as noted in Section 6.2, they may not be determinable when the sentence is first heard.

---

1. Other features are discussed in [Webber 1978a].

After this, I shall show one way in which combinatoric aspects of a sentence can be articulated in a logical formalism, and hence provide a structural basis for forming appropriate discourse entity IDs. This is illustrated briefly in Section 6.4, after which I discuss the derivation of "generic set" discourse entities from specific ones and the use of both in understanding "one" anaphora.

6.3.1 The Definite/Indefinite Distinction

My reason for requiring distinct representations for definite and indefinite noun phrases is that while both can evoke discourse entities in the same context, the descriptions appropriate to them are quite different.[1] Looking first at simple singular noun phrases with no other quantified noun phrases around, compare the following examples.

D8-1 Wendy bought the yellow T-shirt that Elliot had admired.
   2 It cost twenty dollars.
D9-1 Wendy bought a yellow T-shirt that Elliot had admired.
   2 It cost twenty dollars.

In either case, the target of "it" has a unique description that both discourse participants share. In D8, it is the explicit description *the yellow T-shirt that Elliot had admired*. In D9, it is the derived description, something like "the just-mentioned yellow T-shirt that Elliot had admired, that Wendy bought." To see that only this description can be presumed to be shared, notice that D9 can be uttered truthfully if Elliot had admired several yellow T-shirts or even if Wendy had bought several such T-shirts. Thus it does not even presuppose that there is a unique yellow T-shirt that Elliot had admired that Wendy bought. But it does mention only one such T-shirt. As such, the above description applies uniquely to one entity - the one accessed by "it".

The point is that the entity evoked by a singular definite noun phrase can usually be described adequately by just that description (but cf. Section 6.3.2 on quantifier scoping). On the other hand, an adequate description of the entity evoked by a singular indefinite noun phrase depends on a conjunction of (1) the description inherent in the noun phrase (e.g. *yellow T-shirt that Elliot had admired*); (2) a predicate that embodies the remainder of the sentence (e.g. *which Wendy bought*); and (3) a predicate that relates that entity to the sentence evoking it (e.g. "which was mentioned in (or evoked by) sentence <k>"). This conjunctive

---

1. As I mentioned earlier, definite descriptions can be used in two ways: they can be used like definite pronouns to access entities presumed to be in the listener's discourse model or they can be used to evoke new entities into that model. It is the latter use of definite descriptions that is relevant here.

description forms the entity's initial description (ID).

Notice that forming the second conjunct requires all ellipsed verb phrases in the sentence be recovered. If not, a sentence like

> D10-1 A woman whom Wendy knows is too.

would evoke a discourse entity which could only be described as *the just-mentioned woman whom Wendy knows who is too*. This is not very useful from the point of view of reasoning about entities.

However, a more important reason for requiring the recovery of ellipsed verb phrases is that doing so may reveal other noun phrases that should be associated with discourse entities. Failure to do so may result in subsequent definite anaphora failing to have referents. For example,

> D11-1 John didn't bake a cake for Wendy. On the other hand, Elliot did 0. but she didn't like it.
>
> 0 = bake a cake for Wendy
> .it = the "just-mentioned" cake that Elliot baked for Wendy

If the ellipsed verb phrase has not been recovered by the time the *but* clause is being processed, there will be no way of accounting for the pronoun *it*. (1 linguists have used the term "missing antecedent" [Grinder and Postal 1971] to describe this situation, in which the "antecedent" of a definite pronoun is not explicit, being somehow "contained" in an ellipsed constituent.)

The same characteristic behavior of definites and indefinites just discussed for singular noun phrases holds for plural noun phrases as well. The referent of the definite plural pronoun *they*, like the referent of a definite singular pronoun, must satisfy a unique description shared by speaker and listener. While both indefinite and definite plural noun phrases in context may evoke uniquely describable set of entities, the procedure for forming their descriptions again differs in the two cases. Consider, for example, the following sentences. (Comments are in parentheses):

> D12-1 I saw the guys from "'Yes" on TV tonight. (I saw all of them.)
> 2 I saw the five guys from "Yes" on TV tonight. (I saw all of them - that is, five.)
> 3 I saw all five guys from "Yes" on TV tonight. (Usually they're only around in twos and threes.)
> 4 I saw some guys from "Yes" on TV tonight. (I didn't see them all.)
> 5 I saw four guys from "Yes" on TV tonight. (There are more than four guys in Yes.)

The first three sentences each contain a definite plural noun phrase. Corresponding to that noun phrase, a discourse entity will be evoked into the listener's discourse model which can be described appropriately as *the (set of) guys from 'Yes'*. (The second two sentences provide the cardinality of that set as well.)

This can be verified by following either of these sentences by "'They were being interviewed by Dick Cavett" and considering what is accessed by *they*. The last two sentences, on the other hand, each contain an indefinite plural noun phrase.

The only appropriate description for the discourse entity that each of these noun phrases in context evokes is something like *the just-mentioned set of guys from 'Yes' that I saw on TV tonight*. This is because either sentence is consistent with there being other members of "Yes" whom I didn't see on TV tonight, as well as other members whom I did see but whom I don't mean to include in my statement. (The last sentence simply provides additional cardinality information about that set of guys from 'Yes' that I saw.)

6.3.2 Quantifier Scoping

The phenomenon to be discussed here has traditionally called "quantifier scoping" or "quantifier ordering", after its formulation in the first order predicate calculus. Early in the development of Transformational Grammar, it was found to pose a problem for the treatment of passivization as an "optional" (i.e., semantically neutral) transformation. The problem can be illustrated by the minimally different pair of sentences

- Each boy in the room speaks two languages.
- Two languages are spoken by each boy in the room.

Even though these two sentences differ only in their voice (active vs. passive), they have different immediate interpretations: the first allows for different languages per boy, and the second implies the same two languages, independent of boy. Because the traditional way of representing the two sentences logically has them differ in whether or not the universal quantifier ($\forall$) associated with the interpretation of *each boy in the room* is outside or inside the scope of the existential quantifier ($\exists$) associated with the interpretation of *two languages*, the problem has been called that of "quantifier scoping" or "quantifier ordering". If the universal is outside the scope of the existential ($\forall\exists$), then it can "distribute" over the existential and what VanLehn [VanLehn 1978] has called a "different/per" reading is allowed. (In theorem proving, this is called a Skolem functional dependency of the existential on the universal [Nilsson 1980].) If the universal is inside the existential ($\exists\forall$), then the existential is independent of the universal and van Lehn's "same/per" reading is implied.

What I want to comment on here is the importance of quantifier

reflects the considerable (and growing) body of evidence that there is wide variation in people's grasp of quantified sentences: certain aspects of them seem to be understood easily and consistently, even when the sentences are presented with no context (e.g., "three $\langle x \rangle$'s" implies. to people that there are at least three separate things describable as an $\langle x \rangle$, never just one or two things, each describable in more than one way as an $\langle x \rangle$). Certain other aspects people have trouble grasping at all [VanLehn 1978] - much less trying to select which of several alternative readings is intended (e.g., the data base queries below that [Thomas 1976] asked human subjects to answer.

· Print out any departments that sell every article that some company makes.

- Print the departments whose entire line of items is supplied by a single company.

Several subjects interpreted these queries in ways that bore little relation to any of the strict logical readings, while other subjects claimed they made no sense at all.)

We feel a better model for people's understanding of quantified sentences in discourse is one in which we can separate out those aspects of quantification that a listener will immediately understand in a given sentence and make a commitment to from those aspects which cannot be immediately understood, whose resolution will be postponed. Only when forced to by another task, like the need to act in response to the sentence or the need to understand a following one, will the listener attempt to resolve (partially, if not fully) these latter aspects. As presented in [Bobrow and Webber 1981], a combinatoric model allows for this separation.

Note though that the purpose of such a combinatoric model is to allow the discourse understander to postpone decisions about combinatoric features as long as possible, while still capturing all those aspects of meaning that can be immediately grasped. However in most cases, in order to describe the discourse entities that a clause gives rise to, some resolution is required, even if just to ascertain and compare its consequences with current discourse demands. The rules for deriving discourse entity descriptions presented in Section 6.4.4 are thus based on fully resolved forms. For a discussion in terms of perhaps only partially resolved combinatoric features, the reader is referred to [Bobrow and Webber 1981].

scoping/ordering to understanding anaphora in discourse. That importance arises from the different anaphoric properties of "same/per" and "different/per" readings, as shown in the following pairs of sentences.

D13-1 Mary showed each boy an apple.
 2 The apple was a Mackintosh.
D14-1 Mary showed each boy an apple.
 2 Then she mixed the apples up and had each boy guess which was his.

In example D13, understanding the anaphoric NP *the apple* follows from a "same/per" reading of the first sentence, while in example D14, understanding the anaphoric NP "the apples" follows from a "different/per" reading of that same first sentence. That is, only a "different/per" reading allows the possibility of a different apple per boy and hence a specifiable set of apples.

What this demonstrates is both that something like quantifier scoping is important for understanding anaphora in discourse *and* that the speaker's intended quantifier scope assignment (if s/he indeed has one) may only be made clear later in the discourse.

It is interesting to notice that such "same/per" and "different/per" readings are not limited to the interpretation of indefinite noun phrases; the same phenomenon arises with definite noun phrases as well. Consider the following case:

D15-1 In each car, the mechanic adjusted the radio antenna.
 2 He had found them all 4 inches too short.

To understand the second sentence correctly, one must give a "same/per" reading to the description *the mechanic* - the same mechanic for all the cars - and a "different/per" reading to *the radio antenna* - a different one for each car. That is, one must see an intrinsic dependency between radio antennas and cars. (While world knowledge about mechanics, cars and radios may confirm the sensibility of these readings, it is also possible for a second sentence to require, say, a different mechanic per car as well, as in

D16-1 In each car, the mechanic adjusted the radio antenna.
 2 Unfortunately for the drivers, the mechanics knew zip about radios.)

The reason for hedging above vis-a-vis "something like" quantifier scoping is that Bobrow and I have reason to advocate a reinterpretation of quantifier scoping in terms of the combinatoric features - dependency, iteration and cardinality. For example, we would distinguish a "same/per" and a "different/per" reading (of either a definite or an indefinite NP) in terms of whether or not the NP is seen to depend (either Skolem-functionally, intrinsically or explicitly) on some distributive quantifier (i.e., some iterated description). Our reinterpretation

6.3.3 Member/Set Information

Plural noun phrases may provide information about two separate things: a *set* and its members. For example,

D17-1 three dotted lines which intersect at point P
 2 the three dotted lines which intersect at point P

Dotted is a property of each individual line. *Three*, on the other hand, supplies information about the cardinality of the sets of lines which satisfy these descriptions. Moreover, the relative clause - *which intersect at point P* - does not directly restrict which individual lines belong to these sets, but rather specifies a property of appropriate sets of three lines. Prenominal, prepositional and clausal modifiers within a noun phrase may all be used to describe either a set as a unit or the set's individual members.

For handling anaphora, a distinction must be drawn between set and member information within a plural noun phrase, both for describing the entity it evokes and for describing those entities evoked by any embedded noun phrases. Consider the following sentences.

D18-1 'Three men who tried to lift a piano dropped it.
 2 'The three men who tried to lift a piano dropped them.
 3 'Three men who tried to lift a piano dropped them.
 4 'The three men who tried to lift a piano dropped them.

In the first two sentences, the relative clause conveys information about the set of men as a unit. Thus *it* can be understood as accessing the discourse entity describable as *the just-mentioned piano which the just-mentioned three men tried to lift.* However, in the second two sentences, the relative clause conveys information about each member of the set. Thus *they* can be understood as accessing the entity describable as *the just-mentioned pianos, each of which one of the just-mentioned men tried to lift.*[1]

6.3.4 Three Uses of Plurals

Another factor in forming appropriate IDs for entities evoked by plural noun phrases involves distinguishing what it is predicating of each set and what it is predicating of each individual set member. That is, I see <u>distributiveness</u> (i.e., an equivalent thing being predicated of each individual set member) as only

---

[1] These four sentences hint at another distinction that must be made in order to identify discourse entities adequately - whether a noun phrase occurs embedded in a relative clause (as *a piano* does above) or in the matrix sentence. This is discussed at length in [Webber 1978c] and [Webber 1978b].

---

one of three distinct senses that a sentence containing a plural noun phrase can be used to convey. The three senses I call <u>distributive</u>, <u>collective</u> and <u>conjunctive</u>. Consider for example

- Three boys bought five roses.

This can be used to convey either:

1. that Boy1 bought five roses, Boy2 bought five roses and Boy3 bought five roses (*distributive reading*). Should the sentence have contained an explicit "each," this would clearly be the intended sense. However as [Stenning 1978] notes, "each" can be implied contextually as well - e.g.,

   - How many roses did each of your customers buy?

   Well, ten boys bought 8 roses each.
   Three boys bought 5 roses.
   And one girl, she bought three dozen.

2. that three boys (formed into a consortium) bought five roses (*collective reading*).

3. that the total of rose-buying boys is three and the total number of roses, each of which was bought by some rose-buying boy, is five (*conjunctive reading*). This implies that the speaker either does not know or does not care to tell the listener how boys match up with roses. As it is the least commital interpretation, it may be the default when there is no contextual bias.

It is important for the listener to identify the intended sense because of their different implications. That is,

- If the example is understood distributively, it implies that each of the boys owns five roses as a result of the transaction.

- If it is understood conjunctively, then it implies that each of the boys owns at least one (or part of one) rose as a result.

- If it is understood collectively, then it does not imply that any individual boy owns any roses as a result. Only the consortium owns roses, and it owns five.

Distinguishing these implications is important not only for reasoning but for

distinction to be made between a predicate associated with a sentential verb phrase and a predicate associated with another part of the sentence. For example,

Some cotton T-shirt is expensive.
$(\exists x).$ Cotton$(x) \wedge$ T-shirt$(x) \wedge$ Expensive(x)

Without this distinction, it is impossible to effect different treatments for definite and indefinite noun phrases or to resolve ellipsed verb phrases [Webber 1978a], a necessary step in producing adequate IDs. Moreover, there is no way in a "flat" predicate calculus representation to distinguish a noun phrase embedded in a relative clause from one in a matrix clause. (This is another necessary distinction discussed in [Webber 1978a].)

One formalism that both contains the logical operators and allows the above distinctions to be made is an extension of *restricted quantification.*[1] In restricted quantification, a quantification operator (e.g. $\forall$, $\exists$), the variable of quantification and the class it ranges over (noted implicitly as a predicate) constitute a structural unit of the representation - i.e., (Qx:P) where Q is a quantification operator; x, the variable of quantification; and P, a predicate. For example, *Every boy is happy* can be represented as

$(\forall x{:}Boy).$ Happy(x)

This is truth functionally equivalent to

$\forall x.$ Boy$(x) \supset$ Happy(x)

Similarly *Some boy is happy* can be represented as

$(\exists x{:}Boy).$ Happy(x)

which is truth functionally equivalent to

$(\exists x).$ Boy$(x) \wedge$ Happy(x)

---

[1] The formalism actually being used to implement these ideas is KL-ONE, a uniform language based on the idea of structured inheritance networks [Brachman 1978, 1979] KL-ONE has several advantages over even a typed first-order predicate calculus (TFOPC) formalism: being a non-linear representation, it allows for partial ordering of dependencies. (In the TFOPC, left-to-right ordering rigidly defines dependencies.) Moreover, it will allow us to represent -- in terms of mappings -- all and only the combinatoric information currently known.[Bobrow and Webber 1980a]

anaphora as well, as the following pairs of sentences show:

D19-1 The three boys ordered a large anchovy pizza.
2 Because of the heavy traffic, *it* was delivered cold.
D20-1 The three boys each ordered a large anchovy pizza.
2 Because of the heavy traffic, *they* were delivered cold.

Because English has a different pronoun for accessing a set than an individual, the distributive use of a plural must be distinguished from a conjunctive or collective use. Only when a plural is used to convey distributive quantification can it change the discourse entity evoked by a singular noun phrase within its scope from an individual to a set. This means that a different pronoun would be used to refer to it.

Specifically, in D19 *it* accesses a discourse entity appropriately described as *the just-mentioned large anchovy pizza that the boys ordered.* In D20, *they* accesses the set evoked by the same noun phrase, this time describable as *the set of just-mentioned large anchovy pizzas, each of which was ordered by one of the three boys.* The general issue is getting appropriate descriptions. In the original example,

Three boys bought five roses.

depending on which sense of *three boys* the speaker means to convey, the description appropriate to the discourse entity evoked by *five roses* will be something like

- the set of just-mentioned roses, each of which belongs to a set of five roses which one of these three rose-buying boys bought (distributive)

- the set of five roses, each of which one of the three rose-buying boys bought (in part or *in toto*) (conjunctive)

- the set of five roses which this rose-buying consortium of three boys bought (collective)

6.4 An Appropriate Formalism for Computing Descriptions

6.4.1 Noun Phrases in General

The attempt to capture both quantifier scope and predication in an adequate representation implies a formalism with logical operators. Unfortunately, a "flat" predicate calculus will not suffice: its structure is not rich enough to allow a

To extend this notation to include relative clauses is quite simple. Semantically, a relative clause can be viewed as a predicate, albeit a complex one. One way to provide for arbitrarily complex predicates is through the use of the abstraction (or "λ") operator. For example, the noun phrase *a peanut* can be represented as

∃x:Peanut

while the noun phrase *a peanut that Wendy gave to a gorilla* can be represented as

∃x:λ(u:Peanut)[(∃y:Gorilla) . Gave(Wendy,u,y)]

This follows the same format as (Qx:P) as above. In this case

λ(u:Peanut)[(∃y:Gorilla) . Gave(Wendy,u,y)]

specifies a unary predicate which is true if its argument is a peanut that Wendy gave to some gorilla.

Notice that representing NPs in terms of (possibly complex) typed quantifiers in this way provides for both explicit and implicit dependencies between noun phrases - explicitly, by allowing the type-predicate of one variable to depend on the value of another, and implicitly, by quantifier ordering and attendant discourse-related or real-world knowledge.

6.4.2 Singular Noun Phrases

I argued in Section 6.3 that in order to form appropriate IDs, it was necessary to distinguish whether a noun phrase was singular or plural, definite or indefinite.[1] One way to do so is to use a typed existential quantificational operator ("there exists", or ∃) for indefinite NPs and another operator - ∃!, to be read "there exists a unique" - for definite NPs. Both are of the form

⟨operator⟩⟨variable⟩.⟨S⟩

where ⟨operator⟩ is either ∃ or ∃! and ⟨S⟩ is an open sentence in ⟨variable⟩. For example,

---

1. The following discussion contains a more uniform treatment of definite and indefinite noun phrases than that presented in [Webber 1978a]. However, it does not attempt to capture the notion of underconstrained combinatorics.

a hat
the hat Sue saw
a red hat

∃x: Hat
∃!x:λ(u:Hat)Saw(Sue,u)
∃x:λ(u:Hat)Red(u)

6.4.3 Plural Noun Phrases

As for the singular/plural noun phrase distinction, one can have the unmarked case correspond to singular NPs, as above. However, the standard logical way to specify a set *via* its defining property (or set of properties)[1] - i.e., where {u|the arbitrary predicate P} represents the set of things u for which Pu is true - is inadequate for representing all plural noun phrases, as it does not allow one to predicate things about the sets themselves. This is because {u|Pu} always refers to the maximal set of u's such that Pu is true. For example, this notation is inadequate to represent noun phrases like

three men who tried to lift a piano

massed bagpipe bands

The sense of the former is *some set of men*, of cardinality three, who together tried to lift a piano.

One way to remedy this deficiency is to introduce a way of getting at the subsets of a given set, a way provided by the standard mathematical notion of a power set. The power set of a given set is the complete set of its subsets. The mathematical notation used to indicate the power set of the set A is 2^A. This reflects the fact that the size of the power set of a set is 2 raised to the size of the set. Corresponding to this, but in terms of predicates (whose extensions are sets) rather than in terms of sets directly, one can use a function, set, which takes predicates on individual x's to predicates on sets of x's. For example, if *Man* is a predicate which is true if its argument is an individual man, then set(*Man*) is a predicate which is true if its argument is a set of men. Similarly, if

λ(v:Man)[(∃y:Piano) I (v,y)]

is a predicate true if its argument is a man who lifted a piano, then

---

1. A set may also be specified explicitly via a list of its members.

$\lambda(v{:}set(Man))[(\exists y{:}Piano)L(v,y)]$

is a predicate true if its argument is a set of men such that the set of them lifted a piano. On the other hand,

$set(\lambda(v{:}Man)[(\exists y{:}Piano) . L(v,y)])$

is a predicate which is true if its argument is a set of men, each of whom lifted a piano.[1]

All plurals (besides conjunctions like *Bob and Carol and Ted and Alice*) can now be represented with this set operator, the difference between definite and indefinite coming out in the choice of quantifier. For example,

(i) $\exists x{:} \lambda(v{:}set(Man))[(\exists y{:}Piano)L(v,y)]$
some men who (together) lifted a piano

(ii) $\exists x{:} set(\lambda(v{:}Man)[(\exists y{:}Piano)L(v,y)])$
some men who (each) lifted a piano

Definite plurals can be represented like definite singulars using the "unique existential" operator.

(iii) $\exists!x{:} \lambda(v{:}set(Man))[(\exists y{:}Piano)L(v,y)]$
the men who (together) lifted a piano

(iv) $\exists!x{:} set(\lambda(v{:}Man)[(\exists y{:}Piano)L(v,y)])$
the men who (each) lifted a piano

In (iv) the definiteness of the plural should be interpreted as indicating the *total* set of all and only those individuals (in the context) satisfying the given predicate. Cardinality, if specified (e.g. *two men, the two men*, etc.), can be included in these representations simply by using the cardinality "| |" and equality "=" operators. For example, parallel to (i)-(iv) above are

$\exists x{:} \lambda(v{:}set(Man))[(\exists y{:}Pig) . L(v,y) \wedge |v| = 3]$
"three men who (together) lifted a pig"

$\exists x{:} \lambda(u{:}set(\lambda(v{:}Man)[(\exists y{:}Pig) . L(v,y)]))[|u| = 3]$
"three men who (each) lifted a pig"

---

1. I am assuming that predicates like L ("lift") can be applied to both individuals and sets, with the appropriate semantics falling out at evaluation. This notion of "semantic overloading" is well-known in the programming languages literature.

$\exists!x{:} \lambda(v{:}set(Man))[(\exists y{:}Pig) . L(v,y) \wedge |v| = 3]$
"the three men who (together) lifted a pig"

$\exists!x{:} \lambda(u{:}set(\lambda(v{:}Man)[(\exists y{:}Pig) L(v,y)]))[|u| = 3]$
"the three men who (each) lifted a pig"

At this point, the reader might be puzzled about the absence of universal quantifiers - ∀'s - thus far, given that in elementary logic, the standard practice is to use them to represent plural noun phrases. The standard example of this is

All men are mortal
$\forall x . Man(x) \supset Mortal(x)$

However, this assumes that things are only attributable to individuals, and as I discussed earlier, English allows things to be attributed to sets as well. Adopting the above conventions permits a separation of the notions of focusing the listener on a set of things and of saying something about that set or about its individual members. Only when attributing some property to each member of some set, would one add in a universal quantifier. For example,

Three men ate a pizza.
$(\exists!x{:}\lambda(u{:}set(Man))[|u| = 3])(\exists y{:}Pizza) Ate(x,y)$

Three men each ate a pizza.
$(\exists!x{:}\lambda(u{:}set(Man))[|u|=3])(\forall w \in x)(\exists y{:}Pizza) Ate(w,y)$

The three men ate a pizza.
$(\exists!x{:}\lambda(u{:}set(Man))[|u| = 3])(\exists y{:}Pizza) Ate(x,y)$

The three men each ate a pizza.
$(\exists!x{:}\lambda(u{:}set(Man))[|u| = 3])(\forall w \in x)(\exists y{:}Pizza) Ate(w,y)$

Now one might still choose to interpret sentences like "each man ate a pizza" simply in terms of a universal quantifier - i.e.,

Each man ate a pizza
$(\forall x . Man)(\exists y{:} Pizza) Ate(x,y)$

However, this misses the point that such sentences are rarely meant to imply true universality. Rather they imply that the predicate holds of every member of some more limited set that the speaker and listener jointly recognize. That is, "each <x>" is more correctly interpreted as "each of the <x>s" - i.e., in terms of a definite set and a universal quantifier over that set:

will vary according to how individual constants are substituted for the variables in the pattern. The quantifier collar, on the other hand, can be viewed as a *combinatoric specification* which determines what ordered combinations of constants can be assigned to the variables to instantiate or stamp out copies of the pattern. Among the combinatoric constraints on individual instantiations are the three earlier mentioned factors - dependency, distribution and cardinality. It is with respect to these three factors[1] that the rules for forming appropriate specific (as opposed to generic) discourse entity IDs can be specified.

In what follows, I will first present two rules for forming IDs where the evoking noun phrase (NP) is not dependent on any iteration, and then two rules for forming IDs when there is such a dependency. The IDs are formed by a procedure which moves across a clause representation left-to-right, applying whichever rule matches in order to identify the next discourse entity, and then rewriting the representation in terms of that entity in order to remove some of the quantificational complexity. (This should become clearer through the examples.)

One further note before beginning: in [Webber 1978a]. I needed six rules in order to account for the same data as here. The current reduction comes from a more uniform treatment of definite and indefinite NPs - cf. Section 6.4.2 - and a treatment of "each" NPs as iterating over some definite (possibly discourse-definite) set - i.e., representing "each" NPs as a quantifier sequence of the form $(\exists! \, \forall)$. cf. Section 6.4.3

Non-iterated Contexts

Here we consider discourse entities evoked in the following two contexts

$$(\exists x : \langle type \rangle) \, . \, P(x)$$
$$(\exists! x : \langle type \rangle) \, . \, P(x)$$

where $\langle type \rangle$ is either a predicate on individuals or a predicate on sets. The relevant point is that the quantifier ($\exists$ or $\exists!$) is not within the scope of a distributive ($\forall$). Rule 1 below applies to singular and plural indefinites ($\exists$), Rule 2 to singular and plural definites ($\exists!$).

As for notation, I will limit myself to unary predicates, since any n-ary predicate can be rewritten as a unary one on the variable of interest by "lambda-fication" - i.e.,

$$P(x, y_1, \ldots, y_k) \Rightarrow$$

---

1. disregarding other factors like tense, negation and modality [Webber 1978a].

Each man ate a pizza.
$$(\exists! w : set(Man))(\forall x \in w)(\exists y : Pizza) \, Ate(x,y)$$

As with other definite noun phrases. it is the task of pragmatics to figure out what accounts for the definiteness, including definiteness by virtue of being the total/universal set of things describable as an $\langle x \rangle$. In the following discussion - as in [Bobrow and Webber 1981] - I will be representing explicitly the definite set associated with "each NPs".

6.4.4 Deriving Discourse Entity IDs

6.4.4.1 IDs for Specific Discourse Entities

Following the example formalism presented in Section 6.4, the representations we are interested in will have the form

$$Q \, . \, P \, x_1, \ldots, x_n, d_1, \ldots, d_k$$

where Q stands for a (possibly empty) sequence of typed quantifiers - the "quantifier collar" - and P. a (possibly complex) predicate applied to the variables of quantification $x_1, \ldots, x_n$. For example, the sentence

Each boy gave a girl he knew three peaches

has one reading (i.e., the one in which *he* varies with *each boy*) which can be represented as

$$(\exists! s : set(Boy))(\forall x \in s) \, (\exists y : \lambda(u : Girl) \, [Know(x,u)])$$
$$(\exists z : \lambda(w : set(Peach))[|w|=3]) \, Gave(x,y,z))$$

Here the representation for the clause is simply the open formula

$$Gave(x,y,z)$$

In this representation - a type of Prenex Normal Form - the open formula to the right of the quantifier collar can be viewed as a *pattern* - a way of describing a *set* of ground literal formulas by giving their *syntactic shape*. The literals in this set while the noun phrases correspond to elements in the quantifier collar. The variable x is shown to range over individual boys from the definite set indicated by variable x is shown to range over individual boys from the definite set indicated by "s", the variable y is shown to select, for each boy, an individual girl he knows, while the variable z ranges over sets of individual peaches whose cardinality is 3.

$$\lambda(u)[P(u, y_1,....,y_k)] x =_{def} P'(x)$$

I will also not make explicit any quantifiers to the right of the one of interest, absorbing them rather into the predicate for simplicity - i.e.,

$(\exists x Q)$ $Quant_2...Quant_k$ $P(x)....$ $\supset$ $(\exists x Q)$
$\lambda(u)[Quant_2...Quant_k . Pu....] x =_{def} P'(x)$

Rule 1: The first rule applies in the following indefinite contexts (left column) to produce discourse entities with IDs as in the right column. (The clause being processed is labeled S and i stands for the iota function used in forming definite descriptions.)

$(\exists x Q). P(x)$ iX: Qx ∧ P(x) ∧ Evoke(S,x)
$(\exists x: set(Q)). P(X)$ iX: set(Q)X ∧ P(X) ∧ Evoke(S,X)
$(\exists x: set(Q))(\forall x \in X). P(x)$ iX: set(Q)X ∧ (∀x∈X). P(x) ∧ Evoke(S,X)

Rule 1 has the effect of associating with a clause like

I saw a cat.
$(\exists x: Cat) Saw(I,x)$

the discourse entity describable as

"the cat I saw that was evoked by sentence S"
iX: Cat(x) ∧ Saw(I,x) ∧ Evoke(S,x)

("Evoke" corresponds to the predicate discussed in Section 6.3.1.) Rule 1 also associates with a clause like

I saw three cats.
$(\exists x: \lambda(u:set(Cat))[|u|=3]) . Saw(I,x)$

the discourse entity describable as

"the three cats that I saw that were evoked by S"
iX: λ(u:set(Cat))[|u|=3]X ∧ Saw(I,x) ∧ Evoke(S,X)

and with the clause

Three cats each danced the tango.
$(\exists x: \lambda(u:set(Cat))[|u|=3])(\forall x \in X). Tango(x)$

the discourse entity describable as

"the three cats who each danced the tango that were evoked by S"
iX: λ(u:set(Cat))[|u|=3]X ∧ (∀x∈X) . Tango(x) ∧ Evoke(S,X)

Rule 2: The second rule applies in the following three definite contexts (left column) to produce discourse entities with IDs as in the right column.

$(\exists! x:Q) . P(x)$ iX:Qx
$(\exists! x: set(Q)). P(X)$ iX:QX
$(\exists! x: set(Q))(\forall x \in X). P(x)$ iX:QX

This rule is very simple, assigning to each discourse entity associated with an independent definite NP, simply that description. If the definite is meant to be anaphoric, then this new description must be compatible with ones already attributed to the entity so specified. If not, the ID is assigned to the newly evoked entity. Rule 2 is intended to cover all the following cases:

- I saw the cat who hates Sam.

- I saw the cats who hate Sam.

- I saw the three cats who hate Sam.

- The three cats who hate Sam each plotted mayhem.

But since its application and consequences are so simple, I will not bother to go through specific examples.

At this point, I want to take up the restriction in Rules 1 and 2 that the quantifier ∃ or ∃! appear at the left end of the wff. What about quantifiers "in the middle"? Because the clause is being processed sequentially left-to-right, this is not a problem. To see this, consider a wff of the form

$$(Hx_1:Q_1)(Hx_2:Q_2) ... P(x_1,x_2)$$

where H is either indefinite (∃) or definite (∃!), Q_2 may be dependent on x_1, and Q_1 and Q_2 may be predicates on either sets or individuals -- for example

in the above rather general format will be justified after Rules 3 and 4 are presented.

<u>Rule 3</u>: The third rule applies in the following three indefinite contexts (left column) to produce the discourse entity IDs in the right.

$$(\forall y_1...y_k)(\exists x:Q) . P(x) \qquad (x|Qx \land (\exists y_1...y_k) . P(x) \land Evoke(S,X))$$

$$(\forall y_1...y_k)(\exists X: set(Q)) . P(x) \qquad (X | set(Q)X \land (\exists y_1...y_k) . P(X) \land Evoke(S,X))$$

$$(\forall y_1...y_k)(\exists X:X \in set(Q))(\forall x:X) . P(x) \qquad (X | set(Q)X \land (\exists y_1...y_k) . P(x) \land (X\exists x\forall A) \lor Evoke(S,X))$$

where $P(x)$ stands for $\lambda(u)[P\ u,y_1,...y_k]x$ and Q may depend on one or more of the y's. The set notation $|x\ |\ ...|$ should be interpreted as the set of all things for which the right-hand side description is true - i.e., the maximal set.
This rule has the effect of associating with the indefinite singular in a clause like

Each cat ate a mouse it saw.
$$(\forall y:Cat)(\exists x: \lambda(u:Mouse)[Saw\ y,u]) . Ate\ y,x$$

(where e_1 is the discourse entity associated with the definite set of cats) the discourse entity describable as

the set of things each of which is a mouse and for each of which there is a cat who saw it and ate it and which was evoked by S
$$(x | (\exists y \in e_1) Mouse(x) \land Ate(y,x) \land Evoke(S,X))$$

and associating with the indefinite plural in a clause like

Each cat ate three mice.
$$(\forall y \in e_1): \lambda(u:set(Mouse))[|u|=3]) . Ate(y,x)$$

the discourse entity describable as

the set of things, each of which is a set of three mice and for each of which there is a cat who ate them and which was evoked by S
$$(X | (\exists y \in e_1) set(Mouse)X \land Ate(y,x) \land Evoke(S,x))$$

and finally, associating with the indefinite plural distributive in a clause like

Some boy kissed a girl he liked.
$$(\exists x_1: Boy)(\exists x_2:\lambda(u:Girl)[Liked(x_1,u)]) K(x_1,x_2)$$

After the first quantifier $(\exists x_1)$ is processed and its associated discourse entity (e_1) identified, we can rewrite this wff in terms of e_1, thereby removing the first quantifier - i.e.,

$$(\exists x_2: \lambda(u:Girl)[Liked(e_1,u)]) K(e_1,x)$$

That is, the wff schema given above can be rewritten as

$$(\exists x_2:Q_2) ... P(e_1, x_2)$$

or if Q_2 depends on x_1, as it does in the "boy kiss girl" example,

$$(\exists x_2:Q_2(e_1)) ... P(e_1,x_2)$$

Thus, provided there is no distributive between the two quantifiers, each will in turn be leftmost and be matched by either Rule 1 or Rule 2. The two cases where a distributive is interposed between the two quantifiers will be taken up in the next section.

<u>Iterated Contexts</u>
Here we consider discourse entities evoked in the remaining two contexts

indefinite: $(\forall y_1...y_k)(\exists x:\langle type\rangle) . P(x)$

definite: $(\forall y_1...y_k)(\exists !x:\langle type\rangle) . P(x)$

where $\langle type\rangle$ is either a predicate on individuals or a predicate on sets, and may be a function of $y_1...y_k$. (In the definite case, it must be dependent on one or more of these variables in order for Rule 4 below to be applicable. Otherwise, the definite might just as well be to the left of the distributives, matching the context of Rule 2. The notations $(\forall y_1...y_k)$ and $(\exists y_1...y_k)$ are, respectively, short for

$$(\forall y_1 \in e_1)...(\forall y_k \in e_k)$$

and

$$(\exists y_1 \in e_1)...(\exists y_k \in e_k)$$

where $e_1...e_k$ are set-type discourse entities. How arbitrary wffs can be rewritten

Each cat ate three mice, one by one.

$$(\forall y \in c_1)(\exists x : \lambda(u{:}set(Mouse))[|u|=3])(\forall x \in X) . Ate(y,x) .$$

the discourse entity describable as

the set of things, each of which is a set of three mice and for which there's a cat who ate each one of them and which was evoked by S

$$[X|(\exists y \in c_1) set(Mouse) X \vee (\forall x \in X)(\exists x)\wedge Ate(y,x) \wedge Evoke(S,X)]$$

<u>Rule 4</u>: The fourth and final rule applies in the following three definite contexts (left column) to produce the discourse entity IDs in the right.

$(\forall y_1...y_k)(\exists x{:}Q) . P(x)$	$[X|(\exists y_1...y_k) . Qx]$
$(\forall y_1...y_k)(\exists! x{:}set(Q)) . P(X)$	$[X|(\exists y_1...y_k) . set(Q)X]$
$(\forall y_1...y_k)(\exists! x{:}set(Q)(\forall x \in X) . P(x)$	$[X|(\exists y_1...y_k) . set(Q)X]$

This rule is intended to cover such cases as

- In each car the steering wheel was stuck.

- Each boy piled up his own books.

- In each car the two front wheels were under-pressured.

It has the effect of associating with the NP "the steering wheel" in the first clause

In each car the steering wheel was stuck.

$$(\forall x \in c_1)(\exists! y : \lambda(u{:}S\text{-}Wheel)[Have\ u,x]) . Stuck\ y$$

the discourse entity describable as

the set of things, each of which is the steering wheel of one of the cars

$$[x|(\exists y \in c_1) . S\text{-}Wheel(x) \wedge Have(x,y)]$$

where "S-Wheel" stands for *steering wheel*, c_1 is the discourse entity associated with the definite set of cars, and "Have" is a rough encoding of the implicit dependency relationship between steering wheel and car.

Rule 4 also associates with the NP *his own books* in the second clause

Each boy piled up his own books.

$$(\forall x \in c_2)(\exists! Y : \lambda(u{:}set(Book))[Have(u,x)]) . P(x,y)$$

the discourse entity describable as

the set of things, each of which is associated with some boy as his set of books

$$(Y|(\exists x \in c_2) . set(Book)Y \wedge Have(y,x))$$

where c_2 is the discourse entity associated with the definite set of boys and "P" stands for "piled up".

And finally, it associates with the NP "the front wheels" in the third clause

In each car the two front wheels were underpressured.

$$(\forall x \in c_1)(\exists! Y : \lambda(u{:}set(F\text{-}Wheel))[|u|=2 \wedge Have(u,x)])(y \in Y) . Underpressured(y)$$

the discourse entity describable as

the set of things, each of which is associated with some car and is the set of two front wheels for that car

$$(Y|(\exists x \in c_1) \lambda(u{:}set(Wheel))[|u|=2]Y \wedge Have(Y,x))$$

where c_1 is again the discourse entity associated with the definite set of cars.

Before winding up this presentation, I want to take up the restriction in Rules 3 and 4 that a distributive context can be represented simply as a quantifier collar of the form

$$(\forall y_1 \in e_1)...(\forall y_k \in e_k)$$

i.e., a form with no indefinite or definite existentials, which I have been abbreviating as

$$(\forall y_1...y_k)$$

Again, because the clause is being processed sequentially left-to-right, this restriction does not pose a problem. To see this, consider any of the following situations

- $(\exists y{:} set()Q)(\forall y \in Y)(\exists x{:}Q_2)...P(x),...$

- $(\exists y{:} set()Q)(\forall y \in Y)(\exists! x{:}Q_2)...P(x),...$

- $(\exists! Y{:} set()Q)(\forall y \in Y)(\forall y \in A)([(\exists x{:}Q_2)...P(x),...$

- $(\exists Y: set(Q_1))(\forall y \in Y)(\exists!x: Q_2)...P(x)...$

which all have existentials ($\exists$ or $\exists!$) as well as distributive quantifiers ($\forall$) before the quantifier in question ($\exists x: Q_2$) or ($\exists!x: Q_2$). Notice that because of the way "each", "every", etc. are treated, every distributive is paired with an existential set that specifies the domain of the distribution. Q_2 may be a predicate on individuals or a predicate on sets, and in either case, may depend on y. (If Q_2 merely depends on Y_1, then it is simply a case covered by Rule 2 above.)

I showed earlier how simple existentials could be removed. Now for the existential-distributive pairs, by Rule 1 in the first two cases and Rule 2 in the second two, one can identify the discourse entity e_j associated with the leftmost pair and subsequently rewrite it as

$(\forall y \in e_j)$.

Rule 3 can now be used to remove any indefinite existentials in the scope of this distributive and Rule 4, any definite existentials in its scope, leaving the above form

$(\forall y_1 \in e_1)...(\forall y_k \in e_k)(\exists x:Q)...P~x...$

This concludes my presentation of the four rules needed to account for the specific discourse entities evoked by (disambiguated) quantified expressions. In the next section, I take up the issue of generic set entities.

6.4.5 IDs for Derived Entities: Generic Sets

Not all definite plural anaphora are intended to specify **particular** sets of <x>s evoked by a text. Others seem intended to specify sets that one could characterize in roughly as "the set of things describable as an <x>". These set entities I have considered called "generic sets", although I do not mean to imply thereby that <x> need be any sort of "natural genus". For example, just as a definite plural anaphor may specify a particular sets of <x>s like

D21-1 I see three Japanese cars outside.
2 Do any of them belong to you?

them ≡ *the just-mentioned Japanese cars I see outside*

D22-1 Last week Wendy again bought each boy a green T-shirt at Macy's.
2 She's always buying them.

them ≡ *the just mentioned green T-shirts, each of which Wendy bought at Macy's for some boy)*

a definite plural anaphor may also specify a generic set entity like

D23-1 I see seven Japanese cars in the parking lot.
2 They're really selling like hot cakes.

they ≡ *Japanese cars*

D24-1 Last week Wendy bought each boy a green T-shirt at Macy's.
2 She gives them to everyone.

them ≡ *green T-shirts*

The important questions regarding access to generic sets are thus:

1. When is a definite plural anaphor interpreted as specifying a generic set?

2. Is there a limit on the generic sets that a definite plural anaphor can specify, and if so, in what way is that limit related to the material present in the text and where it is located?)

Aspects of these questions are discussed in Sidner (Chapter 5 of this volume) and [Sidner 1979]. In particular, she shows that it is the elements in _focus_ at any particular time that are the major (if not the only) textual source of generic set entities. Reflecting this, she augments her anaphor resolution heuristics for definite plural anaphora to try generic set resolvants based on the elements in focus at the particular time. The complementary problem that I have considered here is that of characterizing this "based on" relation between focused elements and generic set entities and hence, the range of generic

of anything explicitly in the text. Rather it is describable by a generalization of the discourse entity ID *the just-mentioned set of T-shirts that Wendy bought yesterday*. In D28, on the other hand, no specific discourse entity is evoked by the indefinite noun phrase *a green T-shirt*, yet *they* is able to access the discourse entity describable as *green T-shirts*. Thus I believe that both explicit text descriptions (which don't necessarily evoke discourse entities) and discourse entity IDs are sources of generalizable descriptions and hence, of the discourse entities associated with them.

The accessibility of generic sets demands attention for several reasons. Most obviously, one must account for the instances of definite anaphora that seem to access them. Less obviously, it allows for a uniform account to be given of "one" anaphora, as I shall show in the next section. And finally, it is yet another instance of the generally intriguing problem of what inferences a speaker can assume a listener both capable of and likely to make.

6.5 One Anaphora

The anaphoric use of the work "one" (or "ones") is another phenomenon common to natural English discourse. On the surface, an anaphoric-"one" noun phrase is immediately recognizable in that it has the word "one(s)" taking the place of (at least) its head noun. For example,

- one that I heard long ago

- the striped one you got from Harry

- three small ones

Not all uses of "one" in English are anaphoric, of course: "one" is used by itself as a formal, non-specific third person pronoun e.g.,

- One is cautioned against harassing the bears

- One doesn't do that in polite company

or as a number - e.g.,

- One true faith, two French hens, ...

- We arrived at one p.m.

set entities that can and cannot be accessed.[1]

For example, the entity describable as *the set of just-mentioned green T-shirts*, *each of which Wendy gave to some boy* can give rise to an entity appropriately describable as *green T-shirts* as in D24 above, or even *T-shirts* as in D-23 below, but not *shirts*, *cotton things*, etc. If one of the latter is required to understand an utterance, it is distinctly bizarre, as in example D-25.

D25-1 Last week Wendy bought each boy a green T-shirt at Macy's.
   2 She prefers them in more subdued colors, but these were on sale.

D26-1 The green T-shirt you gave me is lovely.
   2 ?? But I prefer them with long sleeves and a button-down collar.
      them ≡ shirts

I would like to claim that the listener can generate new generic-set entities, whose IDs are based on generalizations of a recent description the listener has either heard or derived. These generalizations will be limited to ones that the listener can, with some certainty, assume that the speaker assumes that s/he - the listener - can (and will) make. That is, they will rarely depend on world knowledge - even a type/inheritance hierarchy, since that cannot be assumed to be shared.

As for the descriptions that are subject to such generalizations, I agree with Sidner that they are related to notions of focus - what the speaker is talking about and in terms of. Such available descriptions can include not only (1) the IDs derived for and ascribable to all the focused discourse entities, but also (2) those descriptions in the text which don't evoke or access discourse entities. To see this, consider the following two examples.

D27-1 Wendy bought some T-shirts yesterday.
      Usually she charges them, but yesterday, she paid cash.
      them ≡ T-shirts Wendy buys
D28-1 Wendy wouldn't buy a green T-shirt, because they always run in the wash.
      them ≡ green T-shirts

In D27 the generic set accessed by *them* is not describable by a generalization

---

1. There are other definite plural anaphors that seem to target entities corresponding to the "natural set" to which a given individual belongs, perhaps in a given context. Ellen Prince (personal communication) has pointed out the following example in a transcript of spoken narrative:

I went to pick up Jan the other day. You know, they live in that big house on Vine.

Here *they* seems to access Jan's natural "living" set - i.e., her family. However, I don't plan to discuss here the characteristics and boundaries of that inferential process that makes such entities (and not other ones) available to the listener and allows the speaker to correctly presume that availability.

Although in most cases it is easy to distinguish anaphoric from formal or numeric "one" on surface syntactic grounds alone, it is possible for there to be syntactically ambiguous cases in text,[1] e.g.,

- Since anyone can choose his favorite number, I want one.

- Since John has a cat and I don't, I want one.

In linguistics, one can point to at least two significantly different approaches to "one" anaphora: the transformational approach (which is concerned with its syntax) and the text-level approach (which is more concerned with semantics). Since the approach that I will be presenting here differs from both of these, I will mention them both to provide a basis for comparison.

In transformational grammar, "one" anaphora has been discussed purely syntactically, as an intra-sentential substitution phenomenon. For example, Baker [Baker 1978] presents such an account in the context of deciding between two alternative structural analyses of noun phrases - the so-called "NP-S analysis" and the "Det-Nom analysis". The rewrite rules of these two analyses are roughly as follows:

NP-S	Det-Nom
NP --> NP S	NP --> Det Nom
NP --> Det N	Nom --> Nom S | Nom PP | Adj Nom
	Nom --> N

Baker argues for the "Det-Nom analysis" because it seems to allow the simplest statement in terms of *structural identity* of what "one(s)" can substitute for. The statement that Baker arrives at is

X	NOM	Y	ADJ	NOM	Z
			the	+count	
				Number	
1	2	3	4	5	6

condition: 2 = 5

⇒ 1, 2, 3, 4, one , 6

    Number

where a NOM inherits its features (e.g. count, NUMBER, etc.) from those of its

---

[1]. In speech, the ambiguity may not arise because anaphoric "one" is unstressed, while the other two uses of "one" aren't.

head noun. Informally, the above transformation states that a NOM constituent preceded by an adjective or definite determiner, whose head is a count noun, can be replaced by "one" or "ones" (depending on whether the NOM is singular or plural in NUMBER) if an identical NOM appears earlier in the sentence. This transformation is meant to account for examples like

D29-1 I prefer the striped tie you got from your aunt to the paisley one.

The problem with this structural-identity account is not only that it is limited to individual sentences, but that it is not even an adequate syntactic account at that level. Consider for example the following.

D30-1 If Mary offered you a new Porsche and Sally offered you a '68 Morgan, which one would you choose?

Under no analysis does this sentence meet the structural conditions of Baker's rule: rather *which one* means roughly "which member of the set consisting of the new Porsche Mary offered you and the '68 Morgan Sally offered you". Baker's approach has nothing to say about this.[1] In text linguistics, a particularly clear (albeit purely discursive) analysis of both definite pronoun and "one" anaphora is presented in [Halliday and Hasan 1976], where the primary concern is with the notion of "cohesion" - what makes a text hold together, what makes it more than a random set of sentences. According to the authors, both definite pronouns and "one(s)" can instantiate two types of cohesive relations: the former, the relation of "reference", the latter, the relation of "substitution". "Reference", as Halliday and Hasan use the term, relates a text element like a definite pronoun and

...something else by reference to which it is interpreted in the given instance. Reference is a potentially cohesive relation because the thing that serves as the source of the interpretation may itself be an element of text [Halliday and Hasan 1976], pp.308-9.

Except for their terminology, Halliday and Hasan's general position on definite anaphora and its relation to the discourse is not all that far from that which I have been attempting to formalize.

"Substitution" on the other hand, is

---

[1]. Baker poses an additional constraint on "one" anaphora in [Baker 1979] - effectively, a "transderivational constraint" arbitrating between optional, applicable transformational rules. However, this still treats "one" anaphora purely intra-sententially and still does not address examples such as D30 above.)

consider first some specific sets evoked by a text:

D31-1 All the wines in Dave's cellar are drinkable.
   2 He bought them 10 years ago.

   they ≡ *the wines in Dave's cellar*

D32-1 Sue gave each boy a green hat.
   2 She had gotten them on sale.

   them ≡ *the set of just mentioned green hats, each of which Wendy gave to some boy*

D33-1 I see a BMW, a Porsche, and an Audi outside.
   2 Do they belong to you?

   they ≡ *[the just-mentioned BMW I see outside, the just-mentioned Porsche I see outside, the just-mentioned Audi I see outside]*

Each of these can be the implicit set from which a "one" anaphor selects.

D34-1 All the wines in Dave's cellar are drinkable.
   2 So bring me the ones he bought in Florence.

   SELECT "ones" from: *the wines in Dave's cellar*

D35-1 Sue gave each boy a green hat.
   2 Unfortunately the largest one was torn.

   SELECT "one" from: *[the just-mentioned green hats, each of which Sue gave to some boy]*

D36-1 I see a BMW, a Porsche and an Audi outside.
   2 Is one yours?

   SELECT "one" from:
   [the just-mentioned BMW I see outside, the just-mentioned Porsche I see outside, the just-mentioned Audi I see outside]

Notice that there may be additional stipulations given in the text concerning which member or members are to be selected - e.g., *bought in Florence*, *largest*, etc. However in these examples, selection from a specific set-type discourse entity does account for the data.

Next consider some generic set-type entities evoked by a text.

D37-1 All the wines in Dave's cellar are drinkable.
   2 He buys them only from the best merchants.

   them ≡ *wines*

---

a formal (lexicogrammatical) relation, in which a form (word or words) is specified through the use of a grammatical signal indicating that it is to be recovered from what has gone before. 'The source of recovery is the text, so that the relation of substitution is basically an endophoric one. It is inherently cohesive, since it is the preceding text that provides the relevant environment in which the presupposed item is located [Halliday and Hasan 1976], p.308.

So unlike definite pronouns, "one(s)" establishes cohesion simply at the level of wording and syntactic structure. Thus except for not confining itself to the single sentence and being more concerned with the <u>function</u> of "one(s)" than with its formal syntax, Halliday and Hasan's account of "one(s)" anaphora still mirrors Baker's.

In [Webber 1978a], I took an approach to formalizing what a text makes available for "one"-anaphora that was not too far from Halliday and Hasan's. I based that work on the view that what "one" accessed was a "description" that the speaker felt was available to the listener. Such descriptions can be made available by the speaker's and hearer's shared spatio-temporal context, as in two people peering into a geology exhibit case and one saying to the other, "Even larger ones were found in the Marc Cambrium." However, a speaker can usually rely more on descriptions s/he has uttered being available to the listener. Hence, the most likely place to look for descriptions accessible to "one" anaphora is the text.

With more thought about the problems in my 1978a approach, I came to feel that a simpler account was possible. My current approach to anaphoric "one(s)" reduces it to the earlier-discussed problem of identifying the possible resolvants of definite plural anaphors. This approach is based on the intuition that "one" phrases always indicate to a listener selection from a set. That is, the interpretation of anaphoric "one" should be the same as the interpretation of "one of them". This reduces the problem to the (still non-trivial) one of identifying the set-type discourse entities (both specific and generic) that this implicit "them" can access.[1] 'This way of treating "one" anaphora may seem fairly obvious here; however, its obviousness only follows from considering the sets a text makes available for access and realizing that these sets - both specific and generic - must also be "around" to provide an account of definite anaphora. As for the evidence,

---

1. Evidence for this approach also comes from Baker [Baker 1978]. His rewrite rules - given above - require the "one" constituent to be interpretable as having the feature "+count" - i.e., to be capable of specifying a set. A mass term X, except when interpreted as "types of X", does not specify a set. It is also not open to "one" anaphora, e.g., except in this "types of X" case - e.g.
   I love red wine, especially ones that have been aged properly.

D38-1 Sue gave each boy a green hat.
2 Usually she pays $8 apiece for them.

D39-1 I saw 7 Japanese station wagons today.
2 They must really be selling like hot cakes.

they ≡ Japanese station wagons

Again, each of these generic sets can be the implicit set from which a "one" anaphor selects.

D40-1 All the wines in Dave's cellar are drinkable.
2 So we don't need to open the ones he bought yesterday.

SELECT "ones" from: *wines*

D41-1 Sue gave each boy a green hat.
2 She gave Wendy one too.

SELECT "one" from: *green hats*

3 She gave Wendy a red one.

SELECT "one" from: *hats*

D42-1 I saw 7 Japanese station wagons on Walnut Street and another one on Pine.

SELECT "one" from: *Japanese station wagons*

2 They were all smaller than the French one Jean bought.

SELECT "one" from: *station wagons*

Notice that just as there may be more than one generic set entity derivable (via generalization) from a salient description, so may there be more than one generic set entity from which a "one" anaphor may select.

The final point I want to make concerns the ability of more subtle inferential processes to make additional set-type entities available to "one" anaphora. As noted in Footnote 16 (illustrated by the example repeated below), inferential processes can certainly make set-type entities accessible to explicit definite anaphora like *they*. However, as the example shows, such entities seem less available to the implicit "of them" in a "one" anaphor.

D43-1 I went to pick up Jan the other day.
2 You know, they live in that big house on Vine.

they ≡ Jan's family

D44-1 I went to pick up Jan the other day.
2 ?? You know, the older one broke his ankle?[1]

SELECT one from: *Jan's family*

Why this is the case is not clear. Intuitively, one could say that it was easier for a listener to take an explicit *they* via Jan to Jan's family, than it was to take "one" to an implicit *they* then via Jan through Jan's family to a selection from that set. As I noted earlier, I have not investigated the boundaries of the inferential processes which might make such associated "natural set" entities available. More to the point, no one I know of has as yet really investigated the actual distribution of "one" anaphora to look at the range of inferential processes assumed to be at work there. Whatever the results of such investigations may be though, I am sure that this unified approach to dealing with definite plural and "one" anaphora has the joint advantages of elegance and computational efficiency. We are currently at work on its implementation.[2]

6.6 Conclusion

I am writing this paper three years after completing and publishing the results of my thesis research. Since then the other authors represented in this volume have finished their research as well. I have thus been able to benefit from their investigations in rethinking my past research and composing this paper. I have also benefitted from their many useful comments on it.

What I have presented here is an approach to identifying what particular kinds of noun phrases make available to talk about next (definite anaphora) or in terms of next (one anaphora). In some way, this must be part of any speaker's knowledge of the language. If s/he wants to talk about (or in terms of) something and have the listener follow, s/he must obey the rules presented here at least more often than not. Sidner also presents similar rules, relating to sentence organization - some positions inviting the inference more than others that the associated entity will be talked about or in terms of next. McDonald's concern is to provide these types of knowledge for real time generation.

It is exciting to be working in this area, and it is my feeling that results of interest both psycholinguistically and computationally will continue to be produced.

---

1. I am aware that it seems perfectly fine to say "You know. the one who broke his ankle?". In that case, it would seem that "one" is selecting from the generic set of Jans that the speaker presumes the listener to know (and possibly confuse). How proper names evoke generic sets is an object of further study.

2. Work being carried out at Bolt Beranek and Newman Inc. and the University of Pennsylvania.

IV. LANGUAGE ACTION AND INTENTION

The articles in Chapter 3 (*Discourse*) examine one facet of the context of use of an utterance and its effect on the interpretation of that utterance. The articles in this chapter look at yet another facet: the ways in which the beliefs and intentions of speakers and writers shape the utterances they produce and, conversely, the ways in which listeners' and readers' beliefs about a speaker's or writer's beliefs and intentions affect how those utterances are understood. The papers bring together two threads of research, one from AI and the other from philosophy.

Several philosophers of language [1, 8, 9, 19] have argued that language use is properly viewed as purposeful action. People use language to affect the state of the world, much like they use other kinds of actions. They issue utterances with certain intentions, and recognizing some of these intentions is crucial to understanding the utterances. Thus, an agent can produce a sequence of utterances to affect the beliefs of another agent (and through this, that agent's intentions and possibly other aspects of his or her mental state). According to this view, speech acts (i.e., uttering sequences of words that constitute requests, informings, promises, etc.) and the intentions behind them, rather than phrases or sentences, are the basic building blocks of communication. Speakers or writers have intentions that cause them to produce certain actions; understanding what has been said requires recognizing the underlying intentions. Theories of language use depend in part then on theories of rational action more generally. Speech act theory research has examined a wide range of issues concerned with the conditions under which certain utterances can be used to affect certain types of changes.

From the very earliest work on robots [6, 15], a significant segment of AI research has focused on how to build artificial systems that could plan sequences of actions to achieve a particular goal. This work on planning systems provided a basis for NL systems that could produce and recognize speech acts and hence communicate naturally with users, but it needed to be modified and expanded in various ways. First, this work assumed that the robot or planning system would be working alone; hence there was no need for communication with other agents (either to get information or enlist aid) or to reason about their beliefs and intentions. Also, this work was focused for the most part on act generation; the problem of recognizing what actions had been performed or what intentions underlay them was not addressed.

To reason about the communicative actions performed by another agent and the intentions underlying them requires that a system be able to distinguish its beliefs from those of other agents and to reason separately about their beliefs. It also requires that a system be able to reason about the connection between knowledge and action. Recent research in representation and reasoning [2, 11] has explored a wide range of problems in this area. Much of this work was stimulated by the treatments of speech acts and planning discussed in this chapter.

The articles in this chapter examine issues that arise in adapting to NLP the general planning techniques developed within AI in order to plan speech acts and to recognize the intended actions another agent has performed. Planning speech acts is necessary for NL generation; recognizing intended actions is necessary for understanding what a speaker means. Together with the papers in Chapter 3, the articles here provide a basis for much recent work in both dialogue and text understanding and in NL generation. They also represent the approaches taken within AI and computational linguistics to problems treated within linguistics proper under the rubric of pragmatics. (See [13] for an excellent overview of pragmatics.)

Generation as a Social Action

The paper by Bruce was the earliest attempt to merge ideas from AI planning work with speech act theory. By a "social action," Bruce meant an action that affects the mental state (beliefs, intentions, desires, etc.) of a writer or hearer. His speech act plans were an early attempt to identify and represent discourse-level intentions. The actual representation scheme is based on very early planning ideas and is out-of-date, but the work is interesting for the merger it proposed and for the wide range of behavior it attempted to explain. Although this particular representation was not used in any system, variants of it were incorporated in several experimental systems.

Elements of a Plan-Based Theory of Speech Acts

Cohen and Perrault's article describes the first effort to use formal models of planning from AI as a basis of a theory of speech acts. (It thus provides solid foundations for some of the ideas suggested by Bruce.) The authors model speech acts as operators within a planning system and use the approach to planning developed for STRIPS [6] as the basis for a system that could plan individual requesting and informing actions. By viewing intentions as plans, they set the stage for taking NL generation to involve a broader range of issues than the production of surface forms. Although the system did not produce utterances, but rather descriptions of the actions to be performed, subsequent work by Appelt (see Chapter 5) incorporated a more general mechanism for reasoning about knowledge and action, as well as a method for generating surface forms.

Along with the work described in *Allen and Perrault* (this chapter), the research described here was seminal, spurring a wide range of research on the relationships between planning and language. The article itself addresses several key issues of reasoning about the beliefs and desires of other agents in order to determine appropriate speech acts, uncovers a number of "bugs" in the original speech act definitions, and discusses a wide range of question types.

Analyzing Intention in Utterances

Allen and Perrault's paper describes the first work on plan recognition applied to NLP. They examine a number of issues that arise in adapting planning models to plan inference (i.e., figuring out what a speaker was trying to do). Their model of planning is also based on STRIPS, and they use the same representation for beliefs and intentions as *Cohen and Perrault* (this chapter). The paper provides both plan-inference rules and heuristics (crucially based only on domain-independent relations between structural elements of a plan) for controlling the search for a complete plan.

This important work has formed the basis for most subsequent research in NLP on plan recognition and its use in understanding discourse. Although the paper's main emphasis is on plan recognition, it also discusses a range of issues concerned with providing helpful responses based on recognizing another agent's plan and obstacles in it. In particular, the paper considers when to provide more information than requested, how to interpret certain pragmatically based sentence fragments, and how to treat indirect speech acts. (A second paper provides a more detailed treatment of this last point [17].)

Points: A Theory of the Structure of Stories in Memory

Wilensky's paper examines the role of plans and plan recognition in story understanding and describes a version of the PAM system which he developed at Yale [20]. PAM was done within Schank's Conceptual Dependency framework (see *Schank*, Chapter 2) and represents an attempt to provide a more general theory of story understanding than that provided in purely script-based systems (see *Cullingford*, Chapter 6). Unlike the other papers in this chapter, it does not directly draw on either speech act theory or AI planning work, though the influence of each is apparent. The main contribution of this paper is the elaboration of several kinds of relationships among goals.

The papers in this chapter are concerned largely with the production and recognition of individual speech acts. However, communicative intentions (like intentions for actions more generally) typically require the execution of multiple actions and may involve multiple agents (see *Appelt*, Chapter 5). The need for a complex of speech acts leads back naturally to discourse: the use of a sequence of utterances to satisfy a particular intention (e.g., to provide a description of an object). Recent research in discourse, intentions, and actions (e.g., [5, 10, 14, 18]) examines various issues concerned with how sequences of utterances are used as composite actions and with the kinds of theories of action and intention that are needed to support theories of language use (see Bratman [3]).

Although many fundamental issues remain to be solved, the results reported in the papers in this chapter have been used by several people in constructing various systems that, although limited in scope, do reason about the user's intentions rather than only treating the literal content of his or her input [4, 21]. Going beyond the literal content of an utterance is one feature of cooperative interaction, a topic that has received significant attention from, NLP researchers. Not all of this research is based on plan recognition though: some is based on making maximum use of clues to appropriate responses that can be extracted from the structure and lexical semantics of the utterances themselves [7, 12, 16]. These efforts are not able to guarantee appropriate responses all the time—they are able to enrich systems' behavior in small but significant ways, at a cost (in time) that is currently lower than methods based on plan recognition.

References

[1] Austin, J. L., *How To Do Things With Words,* Oxford University Press, London, 1962.

[2] Brachman, R. and Levesque, H. (editors), *Readings in Knowledge Representation,* Morgan Kaufmann, Inc., Los Altos CA, 1985.

[3] Bratman, M., *Intentions, Plans, and Practical Reason,* Harvard University Press, Cambridge, MA, 1986.

[4] Carberry, S., A Pragmatics-Based Approach to Understanding Intersentential Ellipsis. In *Proc. of 23rd Annual Meeting,* pages 188–197. Assoc. for Computational Linguistics, Chicago IL, July, 1985.

[5] Cohen, P. R. and Levesque, H. L., Speech Acts and the Recognition of Shared Plans. In *Proc. of the Third Biennial Conference,* pages 263–271. Canadian Society for Computational Studies of Intelligence, Victoria, B. C., May, 1980.

[6] Fikes, R., and Nilsson, N. J., STRIPS: A New Approach to the Application of Theorem Proving to Problem Solving, *Artificial Intelligence* 2:189–208, 1971.

[7] Gal, A. and Minker, J., A Natural Language Database Interface that Provides Cooperative Answers. In *Proc. Second Annual Conf. on Artificial Intelligence Applications,* pages 352–357. IEEE, Miami FL, December, 1985.

[8] Grice, H.P., Meaning, *Philosophical Review* 66:377–388, 1957.

[9] Grice, H. P., Utterer's Meaning and Intentions, *Philosophical Review* 68(2):147–177, 1969.

[10] Grosz, B. J. and Sidner, C. L., Attention, Intentions, and the Structure of Discourse, *Computational Linguistics* 12, 1986.

[11] Halpern, J. V. (editor), *Theoretical Aspects of Reasoning about Knowledge,* Morgan Kaufmann, Inc., Los Altos CA, 1986, Proc. of the 1986 Conference, Monterey CA, March 1986.

[12] Kaplan, S. J., Cooperative Responses From a Portable Natural Language Query System, *Artificial Intelligence* 19(2):165–188, 1982.

[13] Levinson, S. C., *Pragmatics,* Cambridge University Press, Cambridge, 1983.

[14] Litman, D., Linguistic Coherence: A Plan-Based Alternative. In *Proc. of the 24th Annual Conference,* pages 215–223. Assoc. for Computational Linguistics, New York City, June, 1986.

[15] McCarthy, J., Programs with Common Sense. In Minsky, M. (editor), *Semantic Information Processing,* chapter 7, pages 403–418. MIT Press, Cambridge MA, 1968. Section 2 is taken from the original Stanford Memo entitled 'Situations, Actions and Causal Laws.'

[16] Mercer, R. and Rosenberg, R., Generating Corrective Answers by Computing Presuppositions of Answers, Not of Questions. In *Proceedings of the 1984 Conference,* pages 16–19. Canadian Society for Computational Studies of Intelligence, University of Western Ontario, London, Ontario, May, 1984.

[17] Perrault, C. R., and Allen, J. F., A Plan-Based Analysis of Indirect Speech Acts, *American Journal of Computational Linguistics* 6(3):167–182, 1980.

[18] Pollack, M., A Model of Plan Inference that Distinguishes between the Beliefs of Actors and Observers. In *Proc. of 24th Annual Meeting,* pages 207–214. Assoc. for Computational Linguistics, New York City, June, 1986.

[19] Searle, J. R., *Speech Acts: An Essay in the Philosophy of Language,* Cambridge University Press, Cambridge, 1969.

[20] Wilensky, R., *Planning and Understanding: A Computational Approach to Human Reasoning,* Addison-Wesley, Reading, Mass., 1983.

[21] Wilensky, R., Arens, Y., and Chin, D., Talking to UNIX in English: An Overview of UC, *CACM* 27(6), June, 1984.

GENERATION AS A SOCIAL ACTION

Bertram C.   Bruce
BBN

On his first visit to kindergarten, while mother was still with him, Bruce, age five, looked over the paintings on the wall and asked loudly, "Who made these ugly pictures?"

Mother was embarrassed.   She looked at her son disapprovingly, and hastened to tell him, "It's not nice to call the pictures ugly when they are so pretty."

The teacher, who understood the meaning of the question, smiled and said, "In here you don't have to paint pretty pictures. You can paint mean pictures if you feel like it." A big smile appeared on Bruce's face, for now he had the answer to his hidden question: "What happens to a boy who doesn't paint so well?"

-from Between Parent and Child

Haim Ginott, 1961

I.   INTRODUCTION

This paper is about the "why" and the "how" of natural language generation. Specifically, why does a person choose to communicate one idea rather than another (or none at all), and how does this choice get translated into a particular utterance? I want to present a few of the major issues and then suggest some ways of viewing the problem.

In the example above, the child's question is understandable in terms of his wants and fears and beliefs about the world. In order to explain why he asked the question he did, we must view his utterance as an action, rather than just a string of words. A string of words, per se, is not associated with any plan or goal. But an action is; in fact, the full representation of an action seems to require a representation of both its actual and its intended effects, its actual and its assumed preconditions.

This viewpoint further justifies the study of what Searle, Austin and others have called the "speech act." The production of a natural language utterance is best understood as an action which alters the state of the world, rather than as a mapping from a given meaning representation into a surface structure. Indeed, many of the problems of deep structure representation, such as focus and presupposition, are more profitably attacked in terms of action and plan structures.

Generation can then be seen as a two stage process. First, a plan is formulated which requires a communication with others. Second, the communication is made in terms of conventions which allow complex intentions to be expressed easily. These stages are inextricably linked since the language conventions for expressing intentions make implicit references to plans of both the speaker and hearer. At the same time knowledge of the conventions can be used in plan formation.

II.   GENERATION AS A SOCIAL ACTION

Before discussing some of the conventions used to express intentions, it will be useful to consider the notion of a social action. A social action is one whose definition refers to beliefs, wants, fears, or intentions. There may be non-social actions. For example, eating can be described without reference to the diner's beliefs about the substance he puts in his mouth. But the description itself implies beliefs about the action which may or may not be shared. Another observer might say that the alleged diner is just pretending, or picking at the food, or wolfing it down.

A description of eating is a special case of INFORMING. It implies that the speaker believes that the diner is eating, and thus, that he believes that the diner intends to chew, swallow, and whatever else constitutes the physical act of eating. In other words, the act of describing encodes beliefs about plans. Speech is a social action because the definition of a speech act requires reference to the beliefs of both the speaker and the hearer. Implicit in each speech act is the goal of the speaker in making the utterance.

There are actions other than speech acts for which the notion of belief and intention are necessary. For example, HELPING is a social action in which the actor does something which furthers a plan inferred for someone else. I believe that generation can best be understood as a social action, i.e., the problem is first to understand how to represent and process any action defined in terms of beliefs and intentions, then to further specify that understanding for language generation.

III.   HOW TO REPRESENT A SOCIAL ACTION

The problem with a social action is that it cannot be represented by any predetermined, finite structure. Instead, its representation requires elements such as beliefs about plans, where plans are themselves defined in terms of beliefs and other plans. Rather than a structure itself, the definition of a social action is best thought of as a set of operations to be performed on a belief system. For example, a REQUEST requires the modification to a belief system such that (equivalently, is valid if) there is a plan of the speaker which has as either a goal or a subgoal a condition which the speaker believes would result from the action requested. Such an operation may require formulation of a plan or modification of existing plans.

The recognition and representation of plans is a complex and by no means fully understood process. It requires a variety of types of knowledge to be applied. For instance, <u>motivation rules</u> must be used to determine whether a goal is appropriate for a person. <u>Normative rules</u> are used to account for behavior done under a sense of obligation. <u>Wants</u> are properties of persons which are used in inferring their goals in a given situation. These concepts and others are discussed in the references [1-3]. In the remainder of this paper I want to focus on one particular aspect of generation as a social action, namely, "How is intention encoded?"

How does a speaker indicate the purpose of his utterance to his listeners? In the example in the beginning of this paper, the child is only partially successful in making his intention known, and to the extent that he fails, he also fails to achieve his goals. In this case at least one of his goals seems to be reassurance that even if he doesn't paint well he won't be rejected.

Note that in recognizing his intention, Bruce's teacher also makes other inferences. He/she probably assumes that Bruce believes that he doesn't paint well; that he fears that he may be punished for painting "mean pictures;" and that he believes that the painter of the "ugly picture" stands in the same social relationship to the teacher as does Bruce. These inferences are both consequences and determinants of the perceived intention.

IV. HOW TO ENCODE INTENTION

<u>Presuppositions</u>. What can a speaker do to ensure that his purpose, and consequently, its associated inferences, are communicated to his listeners? One way is to establish, in the discourse previous to the utterance, the presuppositions for the purpose. For example, the purpose of REQUESTING INFORMATION has the presupposition that the speaker does not know the information. In the kindergarten example, Bruce is making a different REQUEST, in this case, for reassurance. There is a different set of presuppositions which needs to be established. We can assume that the teacher's familiarity with children entering kindergarten makes it easier for him/her to establish such presuppositions as that Bruce fears that the teacher may do bad things to him. If the listener fails to establish the presuppositions, as Bruce's mother does, then the communication fails. Bruce would need to emphasize his fears to his mother in order to have his utterance understood.

<u>Linguistic Conventions</u>. A second way that intentions are encoded is through use of linguistic conventions. For example, to indicate a REQUEST of any kind, the question form is typically used. A request often has a rising intonation, future tense or a modal, inverted word order, or a special word like "please." Many intentions, such as REQUEST, have a special associated verb, e.g., "I <u>request</u> that you..."

<u>Discourse Structure</u>. A third way to encode intentions is to take advantage of higher order linguistic conventions about discourse structure. There are places in a discourse where questions make sense, others where explanations are expected. Knowledge of typical discourse structures allows persons to condense and simplify utterances, avoiding the explicit establishment of presuppositions or explicit use of words like "promise."

While there is probably not a "discourse grammar" which would define "well-formedness of discourses," it is useful to have a model of how social actions typically fit together, and thus a model of discourse structure. Such a model can be viewed as a heuristic which suggests likely action sequences. By focusing the search involved in recognizing intentions it facilitates generation and subsequent understanding.

I have used the term "social action paradigm" (SAP) [1] for such a model of the flow of social actions. A SAP is a pattern of behavior (its body) with constraints (its header) on the applicability of the body. The header checks conditions on the situation in which the body is to be applied. At the same time, it binds variables in the SAP body to elements (people, times, locations, things) of the situation. A typical SAP body is shown in the attached figure. In the figure, REQUEST, SUGGEST, PROMISE, etc. are social actions; A and R are persons; and X is an action. $F_1(X)$ is an alternative to X; $F_2(X)$ is information which relates to the doing of X; and $F_3(X)$ is a reason for not doing X.

The SAP body says that A can REQUEST that R do X. Following the REQUEST, R may SUGGEST an alternative to X, may PROMISE to do X, may do X, may REFUSE to do X, or may REQUEST additional information. Following R's REFUSAL or inaction, A may DEMAND that R EXPLAIN, and so on.

Both speakers in a discourse can be expected to know various SAP's. For instance, knowing that a SUGGESTION often follows a REQUEST it is not necessary to encode the SUGGESTION explicitly. A person does not have to say, "I suggest instead that you..."

V. HOW TO FIT IT ALL TOGETHER

The principal point of this paper is that generation needs to be understood as an action in a social context. Let us examine such a context to see how a person's plan is carried out by encoding his intentions.

<u>The context</u>: Bill and Catherine are growing a vegetable garden. They have planted the seeds and have seen the first plants appear. The rhubarb is being attacked by small insects which have eaten holes in the leaves. Catherine notices the holes.

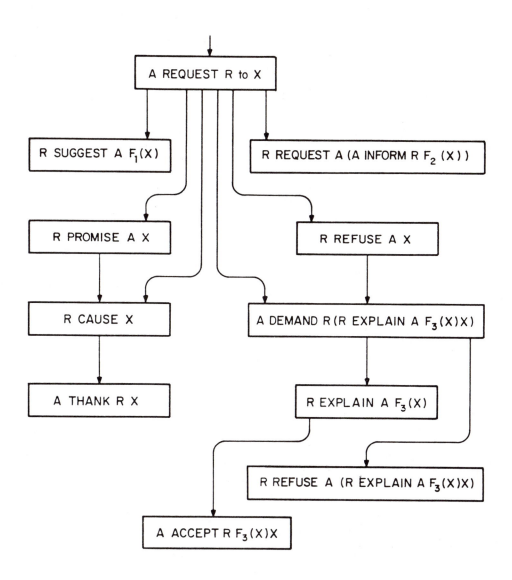

A Social Action Paradigm

<u>Catherine's plan</u>: Catherine's goal of having rhubarb to eat is threatened by the insects. In this case let's assume that she formulates a plan to poison the insects with Bill's assistance. She assumes that Bill has the same goals as she does with regard to the garden. Furthermore, let's assume that she doesn't know what poison to use but believes that Bill does, and that Bill doesn't know about the holes. Thus Catherine's plan involves INFORMING Bill about the holes so that he will be motivated either to put poison on the rhubarb or to tell her what poison to use. Another appropriate action for this plan is a REQUEST to Bill to do something about the holes (and the insects).

<u>Encoding Catherine's INFORM/REQUEST</u>: Catherine needs to do two things. One is to give information to Bill which she believes he does not have. This is called an INFORM. The other is to ask Bill to do something on the basis of his new knowledge. This is called a REQUEST. She can do these things with two utterances. However, if she believes that Bill doesn't want the holes, that he will infer that either she needs to know what poison to use or that he must apply the poison himself, and that he believes that she believes these things, then one utterance may be sufficient. Thus Catherine may just say,

"Bill, the rhubarb's got holes."

In that case she is relying on shared presuppositions about her utterance to carry the information about intention. On the other hand she could use explicit linguistic conventions as in,

"I inform you, Bill, that the rhubarb's got holes. I request that you either tell me which poison to use or apply poison to it yourself."

<u>Bill's plan</u>: While Bill has basically the same goals as Catherine let's assume he doesn't know much about plants, particularly rhubarb. When Catherine tells him that the rhubarb has holes he fails to make the inference that insects are eating the plant. Without that inference her last utterance might appear as an INFORM but not a REQUEST. Thus he has no reason to modify his plans about the garden. However he might well wonder why she said such a thing and formulate a plan to satisfy his curiosity. An action for his plan could be to REQUEST Catherine to explain her last utterance.

<u>Encoding Bill's REQUEST</u>: Following an INFORM a common action is a REQUEST to the first speaker to EXPLAIN his INFORM. This fact is expressed in the SAP's which include INFORM's. The general expectation of such a REQUEST coupled with a commonly used linguistic convention makes it possible for Bill to express his REQUEST succinctly:

"So?"

<u>Catherine's plan</u>: Realizing that Bill misses the point of her INFORM/REQUEST Catherine also realizes that her plan needs further action. She has to infer from Bill's REQUEST that he is not making the appropriate inferences himself and needs to be told directly that there are insects on the rhubarb which need to be poisoned.

<u>Encoding Catherine's second INFORM/REQUEST</u>: Catherine still believes that Bill will recognize her implicit REQUEST and that the problem with her first utterance was that facts were left out which Bill needed. Thus she says,

"It's covered with little bugs!"

VI. CONCLUSION

The little dialogue introduced above could be continued in any of several directions. One likely continuation might be:

"I guess we oughta dust it then."

"I don't know what to use."

"How about the rose bush powder?"

"On rhubarb?"

"Sure, a bug's a bug."

"OK. But you do it. I don't know how much to use."

For each utterance in this sequence there is an associated plan and set of beliefs. At the same time there is heavy use of presuppositions, linguistic conventions, and SAP's to improve the speed and ease of communication.

These comments provide only a partial answer to the question of why Catherine says, "The rhubarb's got holes," or why Bruce says, "who made these ugly pictures?", They give but a sketch of how words are selected to encode intentions. I hope, though, that the comments have supported a consideration of generation as a social action occurring in the context of the speaker's and listener's intentions and beliefs.

REFERENCES

[1] Bruce, Bertram C., "Belief Systems and Language Understanding", Report No. 2973, Bolt Beranek and Newman Inc., Cambridge, Mass., January 1975.

[2] Bruce, Bertram C., and C.F. Schmidt, "Episode Understanding and Belief Guided Parsing", Computer Science Department, Rutgers, 1974, NIH Report CBM-TR-32.

[3] Schmidt, C.F., "Modeling of Belief Systems, Section 3". Second Annual Report of the Rutgers Special Research Resource on Computers in Biomedicine, 1973. Computer Science Department,

Elements of a Plan-Based Theory of Speech Acts*

PHILIP R. COHEN

Bolt Beranek and Newman Inc.

AND

C. RAYMOND PERRAULT

University of Toronto

This paper explores the truism that people think about what they say. It proposes that, to satisfy their own goals, people often plan their speech acts to affect their listeners' beliefs, goals, and emotional states. Such language use can be modelled by viewing speech acts as operators in a planning system, thus allowing both physical and speech acts to be integrated into plans.

Methodological issues of how speech acts should be defined in a plan-based theory are illustrated by defining operators for requesting and informing. Plans containing those operators are presented and comparisons are drawn with Searle's formulation. The operators are shown to be inadequate since they cannot be composed to form questions (requests to inform) and multiparty requests (requests to request). By refining the operator definitions and by identifying some of the side effects of requesting, compositional adequacy is achieved. The solution leads to a metatheoretical principle for modelling speech acts as planning operators.

1. INTRODUCTION

The Sphinx once challenged a particularly tasty-looking student of language to solve the riddle: "How is saying 'My toe is turning blue,' as a request to get off my toe, similar to slamming a door in someone's face?" The poor student stammered that in both cases, when the agents are trying to communicate something, they have analogous intentions. "Yes indeed" countered the Sphinx, "but what are those intentions?" Hearing no reply, the monster promptly devoured the poor student and sat back smugly to wait for the next oral exam.

*The research described herein was supported primarily by the National Research Council of Canada, and also by the National Institute of Education under Contract US-NIE-C-400-76-0116, the Department of Computer Science of the University of Toronto, and by a summer graduate student associateship (1975) to Cohen from the International Business Machines Corporation.

Contemporary philosophers have been girding up for the next trek to Giza. According to Grice (1957)[1], the slamming of a door communicates the slammer's anger only when the intended observer of that act realizes that the slammer wanted both to slam the door in his face and for the observer to believe that to be his intention. That is, the slammer intended the observer to recognize his intentions. Slamming caused by an accidental shove or by natural means is not a communicative act. Similarly, saying "My toe is turning blue" only communicates that the hearer is to get off the speaker's toe when the hearer has understood the speaker's intention to use that utterance to produce that effect.

Austin (1962) has claimed that speakers do not simply produce sentences that are true or false, but rather perform speech actions such as requests, assertions, suggestions, warnings, etc. Searle (1969) has adapted Grice's (1957) recognition of intention analysis to his effort to specify the necessary and sufficient conditions on the successful performance of speech acts. Though Searle's landmark work has led to a resurgence of interest in the study of the pragmatics of language, the intentional basis of communicative acts requires further elaboration and formalization; one must state for any communicative act, precisely which intentions are involved and on what basis a speaker expects and intends those intentions to be recognized.

The Sphinx demands a competence theory of speech act communication—a theory that formally models the possible intentions underlying speech acts. This paper presents the beginnings of such a theory by treating intentions as plans and by showing how plans can link speech acts with nonlinguistic behavior. In addition, an adequacy test for plan-based speech act theories is proposed and applied.

1.1 A Plan-based Theory of Speech Acts

Problem solving involves pursuing a goal state by performing a sequence of actions from an initial state. A human problem-solver can be regarded as "executing" a plan that prespecifies the sequence of actions to be taken. People can construct, execute, simulate, and debug plans, and in addition, can sometimes infer the plans of other agents from their behavior. Such plans often involve the communication of beliefs, desires and emotional states for the purpose of influencing the mental states and actions of others. Furthermore, when trying to communicate, people expect and want others to recognize their plans and may attempt to facilitate that recognition.

Formal descriptions of plans typically treat actions as operators, which are defined in terms of applicability conditions, called preconditions, effects that will be obtained when the corresponding actions are executed, and bodies that describe the means by which the effects are achieved. Since operators are repre-

1See also (Strawson, 1964; Schiffer, 1972)

sentations, their preconditions, effects, and bodies are evaluated relative to the problem-solver's model of the world. We hypothesize that people maintain, as part of their models of the world, symbolic descriptions of the world models of other people. Our plan-based approach will regard speech acts as operators whose effects are primarily on the models that speakers and hearers maintain of each other.[2]

Any account of speech acts should answer questions such as:

—Under what circumstances can an observer believe that a speaker has sincerely and successfully performed a particular speech act in producing an utterance for a hearer? (The observer could also be the hearer or speaker.)

—What changes does the successful performance of a speech act make to the speaker's model of the hearer, and to the hearer's model of the speaker?

—How is the meaning (sense/reference) of an utterance x related to the acts that can be performed in uttering x?

To achieve these ends, a theory of speech acts based on plans should specify at least the following:

—A planning system: a formal language for describing states of the world, a language for describing operators, a set of plan construction inferences, a specification of legal plan structures. Semantics for the formal languages should also be given.

—Definitions of speech acts as operators in the planning system. What are their effects? When are they applicable? How can they be realized in words?

As an illustration of this approach, this paper presents a simple planning system, defines the speech acts of requesting and informing as operators within that system, and develops plans containing direct requests, informs and questions (which are requests to inform). We do not, however, discuss how those speech acts can be realized in words.

We argue that a plan-based theory, unlike other proposed theories of speech acts, provides formal adequacy criteria for speech act definitions: given an initial set of beliefs and goals, the speech act operator definitions and plan construction inferences should lead to the generation of plans for those speech acts that a person could issue appropriately under the same circumstances.[3] This adequacy criterion should be used in judging whether speech act definitions pass a certain tests, in particular, the test of compositionality. For instance, since a speaker can request that a hearer do some arbitrary action, the operator definitions should show how a speaker can request a hearer to perform a speech act. Similarly, since one can inform a hearer that an action was done, the definitions should capture a speaker's informing a hearer that a speech act was performed. We show how a number of previous formulations of requesting and informing are

compositionally inadequate, and then develop definitions of informing that can be composed into questions.

Another goal of this research is to develop metatheoretical principles that state how to formulate speech act definitions to pass these adequacy tests. This paper proposes such a principle and shows how its application leads to compositionally adequate definitions for multiparty requests (as in ''Ask Tom to open the door'').

To simplify our problems in the early stages of theory construction, several restrictions on the communication situation that we are trying to model have been imposed:

—Any agent's model of another will be defined in terms of ''facts'' that the first believes the second believes, and goals that the first believes the second is attempting to achieve. We are not attempting to model obligations, feelings, etc.

—The only speech acts we try to model are requests, informs, and questions since they appear to be definable solely in terms of beliefs and goals. Requesting and informing are prototypical members of Searle's (1976) ''directive'' and ''representative'' classes, respectively, and are interesting since they have a wide range of syntactic realizations, and account for a large proportion of everyday utterances.

—We have limited ourselves to studying ''instrumental dialogues''—conversations in which it is reasonable to assume that the utterances are planned and that the topic of discourse remains fixed. Typically, such dialogues arise in situations in which the conversants are cooperating to achieve some task-related goal (Deutsch, 1974), for example, the purchasing of some item. The value of studying such conversations relative to the structure of a task is that the conversants' plans can be more easily formalized.

1.2   A Competence Theory of Speech Acts

At least two interdependent aspects of a plan-based theory should be examined—the plans themselves, and the methods by which a person could construct or recognize those plans. This paper will be concerned with theories of the first aspect, which we shall term *competence* theories, analogous to competence theories of grammar (Chomsky, 1965). A plan-based competence theory of speech acts describes the *set of possible plans* underlying the use of particular kinds of speech acts, and thus states the conditions under which speech acts of those types are appropriate. Such descriptions are presented here in the form of a set of operator definitions (akin to grammatical ''productions'') and a specification of the ways in which plans are created from those operators.

The study of the second aspect aims for a *process* theory, which concerns *how* an ideal speaker/hearer chooses one (or perhaps more than one) plan out of the set of possible plans. Such a theory would characterize how a speaker decides what speech act to perform and how a hearer identifies what speech act was performed by recognizing the plan(s) in which that utterance was to play a part.

By separating out these two kinds of theoretical endeavors we are not claiming that one can study speech act competence totally divorced from issues of processing. On the contrary, we believe that for a (careful) speaker to issue a particular speech act appropriately, she must determine that the hearer's speech

---

[2] This approach was inspired by Bruce and Schmidt (1974) and Bruce (1975). This paper can be viewed as supplying methodological foundations for the analyses of speech acts and their patterned use that they present.

[3] Though this could perhaps be an empirical criterion, it will be used intuitively here.

act recognition process(es) will correctly classify her utterance. Thus, a competence theory would state the conditions under which a speaker can make that determination—conditions that involve the speaker's beliefs about the hearer's beliefs, goals, and inferential processes.

Our initial competence theory has been embodied in a computer program (Cohen, 1978) that can construct most of the plans presented here. Programs often point out weaknesses, inconsistencies, and incorrect assumptions in the statement of the competence theory, and can provide an operational base from which to propose process theories. However, we make no claims that computational models of plan construction and recognition are cognitive process theories; such claims would require empirical validation. Moreover, it is unclear whether there could be just one process theory of intentional behavior since each individual might use a different method. A more reasonable goal, then, is to construct computational models of speech act use for which one could argue that a person could employ such methods and converse successfully.

1.3 Outline of the Paper

The thread of the paper is the successive refinement of speech act definitions to meet the adequacy criteria. First, we introduce in sections 2 and 3 the tools needed to construct plans: the formal language for describing beliefs and goals, the form of operator definitions, and a set of plan construction inferences.

As background material, section 4 summarizes Austin's and Searle's accounts of speech acts. Then, Searle's definitions of the speech acts of requesting and informing are reformulated as planning operators in section 5 and plans linking those speech acts to beliefs and goals are given. These initial operator definitions are shown to be compositionally inadequate and hence are recast in section 6 to allow for the planning of questions. Section 7 shows how the definitions are again inadequate for modelling plans for composed requests. After both revising the preconditions of requests and identifying their side effects, compositional adequacy for multiparty requests is achieved. The solution leads to a metatheoretical "point of view" principle for use in formulating future speech act definitions within this planning system. Finally, section 8 discusses the limitations of the formalism and ways in which the approach might be extended to handle indirect speech acts.

2. ON MODELS OF OTHERS

In this section, we present criteria that an account of one agent's (AGT1) model of another's (AGT2's) beliefs and goals ought to satisfy.[4] A theory of speech acts need not be concerned with what is actually true in the real world; it should

[4]The representations used by Meehan (1976), and Schank and Abelson (1977) do not, in a principled way, maintain the distinctions mentioned here for belief or want.

describe language use in terms of a person's beliefs about the world. Accordingly, AGT1's model of AGT2 should be based on "believe" as described, for example, in Hintikka (1962; 1969). Various versions of the concept "know" can then be defined to be agreements between one person's beliefs and another's.

2.1 Belief

Apart from simply distinguishing AGT1's beliefs from his beliefs about AGT2's beliefs, AGT1's belief representation ought to allow him to represent the fact that AGT2 knows *whether* some proposition P is true, without AGT1's having to know which of P or ~ P it is that AGT2 believes. A belief representation should also distinguish between situations like the following:

1. AGT2 believes that the train leaves from gate 8.
2. AGT2 believes that the train has a departure gate.
3. AGT2 knows what the departure gate is for the train.

Thus, case 3 allows AGT1 to believe *that* AGT2 knows what the departure gate is without AGT1's actually knowing which gate AGT2 thinks that is. This distinction will be useful for the planning of questions and will be discussed further in section 6.

Following Hintikka (1969), belief is interpreted as a model operator A BELIEVE(P), where A is the believing agent, and P the believed proposition.[5] This allows for an elegant, albeit too strong, axiomatization and semantics for BELIEVE. We shall point out uses of various formal properties of BELIEVE as the need arises.

A natural question to ask is how many levels of belief embedding are needed by an agent capable of participating in a dialogue? Obviously, to be able to deal with a disagreement, AGT1 needs two levels (AGT1 BELIEVE and

[5]The following axiom schemata will be assumed:

B.1 aBELIEVE(all axioms of the predicate calculus)
B.2 aBELIEVE(P) => aBELIEVE(aBELIEVE(P))
B.3 aBELIEVE(P) OR aBELIEVE(Q) => aBELIEVE(P OR Q)
B.4 aBELIEVE(P&Q) <=>aBELIEVE(P) & aBELIEVE(Q)
B.5 aBELIEVE(P) => ~ aBELIEVE(~ P)
B.6 aBELIEVE(P => Q) => (aBELIEVE(P) => aBELIEVE(Q))
B.7 $\exists$x aBELIEVE(P(x)) => aBELIEVE($\exists$x P(x))
B.8 all agents believe that all agents believe B.1 to B.7

These axioms unfortunately characterize an idealized "believer" who can make all possible deductions from his beliefs, and doesn't maintain contradictory beliefs. Clearly, the logic should be weakened. However, we shall assume the usual possible worlds semantics of BELIEVE in which the axioms are satisfied in a model consisting of a *universe* U, a subset A of U of *agents*, a set of *possible worlds* W, and *initial world* WO in W, a *relation* R on the cross-product A× W × W, and for each world w and predicate P, a subset Pw of U called the *extension* of P in w. The truth functional connectives *and*, *or*, *not*, and => have their usual interpretations in all possible worlds. aBELIEVE(P) is true in world w if P is true in all worlds w1 such that R(a', w,w1), where a' is the interpretation of a in w. $\exists$x P(x) is true in world w if there is some individual i in U such that P(x) is true in w when all free occurrences of x in P are interpreted as i.

AGT1 BELIEVE AGT2 BELIEVE). If AGT1 successfully lied to AGT2, he would have to be able to believe some proposition P, while believing that AGT2 believes that AGT1 believes P is false (i.e., AGT1 BELIEVE AGT2 BELIEVE AGT1 BELIEVE (~ P)). Hence, AGT1 would need at least three levels. However, there does not seem to be any bound on the possible embeddings of BELIEVE. If AGT2 believes AGT1 has lied, he would need four levels. Furthermore, Lewis (1969) and Schiffer (1972) have shown the ubiquity of *mutual belief* in communication and face-to-face situations—a concept that requires an infinite conjunction of beliefs.[6] Cohen (1978) shows how a computer program that plans speech acts can represent beliefs about mutual beliefs finitely.

2.2 Want

Any representation of AGT2's goals (wants) must distinguish such information from: AGT2's beliefs, AGT1's beliefs and goals, and (recursively) from AGT2's model of someone else's beliefs and goals. The representation for WANT must also allow for different scopes of quantifiers. For example, it should distinguish between the readings of "AGT2 wants to take a train" as "There is a specific train that AGT2 wants to take" or as "AGT2 wants to take any train." Finally, it should allow arbitrary embeddings with BELIEVE. Wants of beliefs (as in "AGT1 WANTS AGT2 BELIEVE P") become the reasons for AGT1's telling P to AGT2, while beliefs of wants (i.e., AGT1 BELIEVES AGT1 WANTS P) will be the way to represent AGT1's goals P.[7] In modelling planning behavior, we are not concerned with goals that the agent does not think he has, nor are we concerned with the subtleties of "wish," "hope," "desire," and "intend" as these words are used in English. The formal semantics of WANT, however, are problematic.

3. MODELS OF PLANS

In most models of planning (e.g., Fikes & Nilsson, 1971; Newell & Simon, 1963), real world actions are represented by *operators* that are organized into plans.[8] To execute a plan, one performs the actions corresponding to the operators in that plan. An operator will be regarded as transforming the planner's model of the world, the *propositions* that the planner believes, in correspondence with the changes to the real world made by the operator's associated action.[9] An operator is *applicable* to a model of the world in which that operator's *preconditions* hold. Operators can be defined in terms of others, as stated in their *bodies* (Sacerdoti, 1975). The changes that an operator makes to the world model in which it is evaluated to produce a new world model are called that operator's *effects*.

We shall view plans for an arbitrary agent S to be constructed using (at least) the following heuristic principles of purposeful behavior:

At the time of S's planning:

1. S should not introduce in the plan actions whose effects S believes are (or will be) true at the time the action is initiated.

2. If E is a goal, an operator A that achieves E can be inserted into the plan.

3. If an operator is not applicable in the planner's belief model, all the preconditions of that operator that are not already true can be added to the plan.

The previous two inferences reflect an agent's reasoning "in order to do this I must achieve that."

4. If the planner needs to know the truth-value of some proposition, and does not, the planner can create a goal that it know whether that proposition is true or false.

5. If the planner needs to know the value of some description before planning can continue, the planner can create a description that it find out what the value is.

The previous two inferences imply that the planner does not have to create an entire plan before executing part of it.

6. Everyone expects everyone else to act this way.

Since agents can sometimes recognize the plans and goals of others, and can adopt others' goals (or their negations) as their own, those agents can plan to facilitate or block someone else's plans. Bruce and Newman (1978) and Carbonell (1978) discuss these issues at length.

The process of planning to achieve a goal is essentially a search through this space of inferences to find a temporal sequence of operators such that the first operator in the sequence is applicable in the planner's current world model and the last produces a world model in which the goal is true. A new world model is obtained by the execution of each operator.

3.1 The Form of Operators

Early approaches to problem-solving based on first order logic (Green, 1969; McCarthy & Hayes, 1969) have emphasized the construction of provably correct

---

[6]Lewis (1969) and Schiffer (1972) talk only about mutual or common knowledge, but the extension to mutual belief is obvious.

[7]This also allows a third place to vary quantifier scope, namely:

$$\exists x\ aBELIEVE\ aWANT\ P(x)$$
$$aBELIEVE\ \exists x\ aWANT\ P(x)$$
$$aBELIEVE\ aWANT\ \exists x P(x)$$

[8]One usually generalizes operators to *operator schemata* in correspondence with *types* of actions; operator instances are then formed by giving values to the parameters of an operator schema. Since only operator instances are contained in plans we will not distinguish between the operator schema and its instances unless necessary. The same schema/instance, type/token distinction applies as well to speech acts modelled as planning operators.

[9]We are bypassing the fact that people need to observe the success or failure of their actions before being able to accurately update their beliefs. The formalism thus only deals with operators and models of the world rather than actions and the real world. Operators names will be capitalized while their corresponding actions will be referred to in lower case.

plans. Such approaches formalize the changes an action makes to the state of the world model by treating an operator as a predicate of one whose arguments is a *state variable*, which ranges over states of the world model. Unfortunately, to be able to reason about what is true in the world after an action is executed, one must give axiom schemata that describe which aspects of the state of the world are *not* changed by each operator. For instance, calling someone on the telephone does not change the height of the Eiffel Tower. This thorny "frame problem" (McCarthy & Hayes, 1969) occurs because individual states of the world are not related to one another *a priori*.

To overcome this problem, Fikes and Nilsson (1971) in their STRIPS planning system assume that all aspects of the world stay constant except as described by the operator's effects and logical entailments of those effects. Such an assumption is not formalized in the reasoning system, making it difficult to prove the correctness of the resulting plans. Nevertheless, it has become the standard assumption upon which to build problem-solvers. We too will make it and thus shall describe an operator's effects by the propositions that are to be added to the model of the world.[10]

All operator schemata will have two kinds of preconditions—"cando" and "want" preconditions. The former, referred to as CANDO.PRs, indicate proposition schemata that, when instantiated with the parameter values of an operator instance, yield propositions that must be true in the world model for that operator instance to be applicable. We do not discuss how they can be proven true. The "want" precondition, henceforth WANT.PR, formalizes a principle of intentional behavior—the agent of an action has to want to do that action.

The following example serves to illustrate the form of such definitions.

MOVE(AGT, SOURCE, DESTINATION)

CANDO.PR:	LOC(AGT, SOURCE)
WANT.PR:	AGT BELIEVE AGT WANT move-instance
EFFECT:	LOC(AGT, DESTINATION)

The parameters of an operator scheme are stated in the first line of the definitions and it is assumed that values of these parameters satisfy the appropriate selectional restrictions, (here, a person, and two locations, respectively). The WANT.PR uses a parameter "move-instance" that will be filled by any instance of the MOVE operator schema that is currently being planned, executed, or recognized. The CANDO.PR states that before an agent can move from the SOURCE location, he must be located there. The EFFECT of the MOVE indicates that the agent's new location is the DESTINATION.

S's plan to achieve goal G is pictured schematically in Figure 1 (P and Q are arbitrary agents, A1 and A2 are arbitrary actions). Instead of indicating the entire state of the planner's beliefs after each operator, those propositions that are effects of an operator and are preconditions of some other operator in the plan are presented.

[10] Those propositions that need to be deleted (or somehow made "invisible" in the *current* worldmodel) will not be discussed here.

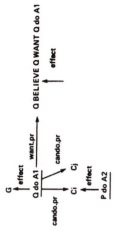

S BELIEVE S WANT:

Figure 1. A schematic of S's plan to achieve G.

This diagram illustrates the building block of plans—given goal G, S applies an inference of type 2 and selects operator A1, whose agent is Q as a producer of that effect. That operator is applicable when preconditions Ci and Cj hold and when agent Q wants to perform A1. Type 3 inferences allow each of the preconditions to be achieved by other actions (e.g., A2), which may be performed by another agent (e.g., P). This chaining of operators continues until all preconditions are satisfied. Plan diagrams are thus read from "top" to "bottom".

To indicate that this schematic is part of agent S's plan, the plan components are "embedded" in what S BELIEVE S WANTs. The truth or falsity of preconditions is evaluated with respect to S's beliefs. For example, verifying the WANT.PR of operator A1 (i.e., Q BELIEVE Q WANT Q do A1) would involve establishing that S BELIEVE Q BELIEVE Q WANT Q do A1. If Q is the same person as S (i.e., S is planning her own action A1) then this condition is trivially true since A1 is already part of S's plan, and since for all agents R, we assume that if R BELIEVE (P) then R BELIEVE R BELIEVE (P). However, if Q is not the same as S, the WANT.PR also needs to be achieved, leading, as we shall see, to S's planning a speech act.

4.   SPEECH ACTS

4.1   Austin's Performatives

Austin (1962) notes a peculiar class of declarative utterances, which he termed *performatives*, that do not state facts but rather constitute the performance of an action. For instance saying, "I hereby suggest you leave" is an act of suggesting. Unlike the usual declaratives, such sentences are not true or false, but rather are subject to the same kinds of failures ("infelicities") as nonlinguistic actions—such as being applied in the wrong circumstances or being performed insincerely.

Generalizing further, Austin claims that in uttering any sentence, one performs three types of speech acts: the *locutionary, illocutionary,* and *perlocution-*

ary acts. A speaker performs a *locutionary* act by making noises that are the uttering of words in language satisfying its vocabulary and grammar, and by the uttering of sentences with definite meaning (though perhaps having more than one). Such acts are used in the performance of *illocutionary acts* which are those acts performed *in* making utterances. For instance, stating, requesting, warning, ordering, apologizing, are claimed to be different types of illocutionary acts, each of which is said to have a unique *illocutionary force* that somehow characterizes the nature of the act. Each illocutionary act contains *propositional content* that specifies what is being requested, warned about, ordered, etc.

New distinctions, however, bring new problems. Frequently, when performative verbs are not used, the utterance's illocutionary force is not directly interpretable from its content. For example, to understand the force of the utterance "The door," the hearer may need to use his beliefs that the door is currently closed, that the speaker has two arm-loads of groceries, and that he wants to be on the other side of the door in determining that the speaker has requested that the door be opened. Furthermore, a speaker may appear to be performing one illocutionary act, and actually may be trying to use it to do something else. Thus, "We have to get up early tomorrow" may simply be an assertion but when said at a party, may be intended as an excuse to the host for leaving, *and* may be intended as a request that the hearer leave. Such *indirect speech acts* (Gordon & Lakoff, 1971; Searle, 1975) are the touchstone of any theory of speech acts.

The last major kind of act identified by Austin is the *perlocutionary* act—the act performed *by* making an utterance. For instance, with the illocutionary act of asserting something, I may *convince* my audience of the truth of the corresponding proposition (or *insult* or *frighten* them). Perlocutionary acts produce *perlocutionary effects*: convincing produces belief and frightening produces fear. While a speaker often has performed illocutionary acts with the goal of achieving certain perlocutionary effects, the actual securing of those effects is beyond his control. Thus, it is entirely possible for a speaker to make an assertion, and for the audience to recognize the force of the utterance as an assertion and yet not be convinced.

4.2 Speech Acts à la Searle

Searle (1969) presents a formulation of the structure of illocutionary acts (henceforth referred to simply as speech acts) by suggesting a number of necessary and sufficient conditions on their successful performance. He goes on to state rules corresponding to these conditions, for a speaker's using any "indicator of illocutionary force" to perform a particular speech act.

As an example, let us consider Searle's conditions for a speaker S, in uttering T, to request that some hearer H do action A. The conditions are grouped as follows:

Normal Input/Output Conditions. These include such conditions as: H is not deaf and S is not mute, joking, or acting.

Propositional Content Conditions. Literal speech acts only use propositions of certain forms. The restrictions on these forms are stated in the *propositional content conditions*. For a request, the proposition must predicate a future act of H.

Preparatory Condition. A preparatory condition states what must be true in the world for a speaker to felicitously issue the speech act. For a request, the preparatory conditions include:

—H is able to do A.
—S believes H is able to do A.
—It is not obvious to S and H that H will do A in the normal course of events (the "non-obviousness" condition).

Searle claims the non-obviousness condition is not peculiar to illocutionary acts. This paper will support his claim by showing how the condition can be applied more generally to rational, intentional behavior.

Sincerity Condition. A *sincerity condition* distinguishes a sincere performance of the speech act from an insincere one. In the case of a request, S must want H to do A; for a promise, S must intend to do the promised action; for an assertion, S must believe what he is asserting.

Essential Condition. An *essential condition* specifies what S was trying to do. For a request, the act is an attempt to get H to do A.

Force Condition (our terminology). The purpose of the *force condition* is to require that the speaker utter a speech act only if he intends to communicate that he is performing that act. "Intending to communicate" involves having certain intentions regarding how the hearer will recognize the force of the utterance. The basic idea is that it is intended that the hearer recognize that the speaker is trying to bring about the satisfaction of the essential condition. For a request this amounts to the speaker's wanting the hearer to realize the speaker intends for him to do A.

5. A FIRST REFORMULATION OF SEARLE'S CONDITIONS

Searle (1969) unfortunately does not supply justifications for the adequacy of his definitions for various kinds of speech acts. A primary goal of this paper is to show how a plan-based theory provides the basis for such adequacy criteria by allowing one to see clearly how changes in speech act definitions affect the plans that can be generated.

A second, more specific point of this formulation exercise is to show which of Searle's conditions are better regarded as pertaining to more general aspects of intentional behavior than to particular speech acts. In this spirit, we show how the sincerity condition, which we shall argue is a misnomer, and the propositional content and "non-obviousness" conditions arise during the course of planning. Concerning the remaining conditions, we assume the "normal input/output conditions," but have chosen not to deal with the force condition until we have a better understanding of the plans for speech acts and how they can be recognized. The remaining conditions, the preparatory and essential conditions, will be mapped into the formalism as the preconditions and effects of speech act operators.

5.1 First Definition of REQUEST

Searle claims the preparatory conditions are required for the "happy" performance of the speech act—where "happy" is taken to be synonymous with Austin's use of "felicitous." Austin was careful to distinguish among infelicities, in particular, misapplications (performing the act in the wrong circumstances), and flaws (incorrectly performing the act). We take Searle's preparatory conditions as conditions guaranteeing applicability rather than successful performance, allowing them to be formalized as preconditions. Thus if an operator's preconditions are not satisfied when it is performed, then the operator was "misapplied." Before expressing preconditions in a formalism, a systematic "point of view" must be adopted. Since the applicability conditions affect the planning of that speech act, the preconditions are stated as conditions on the speaker's beliefs and goals. Correspondingly, the effects describe changes to the hearer's mental state.[11] We establish a *point-of-view principle*, that is intended to be a guideline for constructing speech act definitions in *this* planning system—namely: preconditions begin with "speaker believe" and effects with "hearer believe."

Let us consider Searle's preparatory conditions for a request: H is able to do ACT, and S believes H is able to do ACT. From our discussion of "belief," it should be clear what H can *in fact* do, i.e., what the real world is like is not essential to the success of a request. What may be relevant is that S and/or H thinks H can do ACT. To formalize "is able to do A," we propose a predicate CANDO (Q,ACT) that is true if the CANDO.PR's of ACT are true (with person Q bound to the agent role of ACT).[12]

The essential condition, which is modeled as the EFFECT of a REQUEST,

[11]This does not violate our modelling just one person's view since a speaker, after having issued a speech act, will update his beliefs to include the effects of that speech act, which are defined in terms of the hearer's beliefs.

[12]This should be weakened to "... are true or are easily achievable"—i.e. if Q can plan to make them true.

is based on a separation of the illocutionary act from its perlocutionary effect. Speakers, we claim, cannot influence their hearers' beliefs and goals directly. The EFFECTs of REQUEST are modeled so that the hearer's actually wanting to do ACT is not essential to the successful completion of the speech act. Thus, the EFFECT is stated as the hearer's believing the speaker wants him to do the act. For important reasons, to be discussed in section 5.7, this formulation of the essential condition will prove to be a major stumbling block.

The operator REQUEST from SPEAKER to HEARER to do action ACT, which represents a literal request, can now be defined as:

REQUEST(SPEAKER,HEARER,ACT)

CANDO.PR:	SPEAKER BELIEVE HEARER CANDO ACT
	AND
	SPEAKER BELIEVE
	HEARER BELIEVE HEARER CANDO ACT
WANT.PR:	SPEAKER BELIEVE SPEAKER WANT request-instance
EFFECT:	HEARER BELIEVE
	SPEAKER BELIEVE SPEAKER WANT ACT

5.2 Mediating Acts and Perlocutionary Effects

To bridge the gap between REQUESTs and the perlocutionary effect for which they are planned, a mediating step named CAUSE-TO-WANT is posited, that models what it takes to get someone to want to do something. Our current analysis of this "act" trivializes the process it is intended to model by proposing that to get someone to want to do something, one need only get that person to know that you want them to do it.

The definition of an agent's (AGT1) causing another agent (AGT) to want to do ACT is:

CAUSE-TO-WANT (AGT1,AGT,ACT)

CANDO.PR:	AGT BELIEVE
	AGT1 BELIEVE AGT 1 WANT ACT
EFFECT:	AGT BELIEVE AGT WANT ACT

The plan for a REQUEST is now straightforward. REQUEST supplies the necessary precondition for CAUSE-TO-WANT (as will other act combinations). When the WANT.PR of some action that the speaker is planning for someone else to perform, is not believed to be true, the speaker plans a REQUEST. For example, assume a situation in which there are two agents, SYSTEM[13](S) and JOHN, who are located inside a room (i.e., they are at location INROOM). Schematically, to get JOHN to leave the room by moving himself to location

[13]The agent who creates plans will often be referred to as "SYSTEM," which should be read as "planning system."

OUTROOM, the plan would be as in Figure 2. Notice that the WANT.PR of the REQUEST itself, namely

S BELIEVE
S WANT
  REQUEST(S,JOHN,MOVE(JOHN,INROOM,OUTROOM))

is trivially true since that particular REQUEST is already part of S's plan. The CANDO.PR's of the REQUEST are true if S believes JOHN is located INROOM and if it believes JOHN thinks so too. Thus, once the planner chooses someone else, say H, to do some action that it believes H does not yet want to do, a directive act (REQUEST) may be planned.

5.3 Comparison with Searle's Conditions for a REQUEST

Searle's "non-obviousness" condition for the successful performance of a request stated that it should not be obvious to the speaker that the hearer is about to

do the action being requested, independently of the request. If that were obvious to the speaker, the request would be pointless. However, as Searle noted, the non-obviousness condition applies more generally to rational, intentional behavior than to speech acts alone. In our formalism, it is the WANT.PR of the act being requested (goal "++" in Figure 2). If the planning system believed the WANT.PR were already true, i.e., if it believed that John already wanted to leave the room, then the plan would proceed no further; no REQUEST would take place.

Searle's "sincerity" condition, stated that the speaker had to want the requested act to be performed. The sincerity condition in the plan of Figure 2 is the goal labeled "+." The speaker's wanting the hearer to move is the reason for planning a REQUEST.

Notice also that the propositional content of the REQUEST, a future act to be performed by the hearer, is determined by prior planning—i.e., by a combination of that act's WANT.PR, the mediating act CAUSE-TO-WANT, and by the EFFECT of a REQUEST. Searle's propositional content condition thus seems to be a function of the essential condition (which is approximated by the EFFECTs of the speech act operator), as Searle claimed. So far, we have factored out those aspects of a request that Searle suggested were eliminable. Future revisions will depart more significantly.

5.4 Definition of INFORM

The speech act of informing is represented by the operator INFORM, which is defined as a speaker's stating a proposition to a hearer for the purpose of getting the hearer to believe that the speaker believes that proposition to be true. Such acts will usually be planned on the basis of wanting the hearer to believe that proposition. For a SPEAKER to INFORM a HEARER that proposition PROP is true, we have:

INFORM(SPEAKER, HEARER, PROP)

CANDO.PR:	SPEAKER BELIEVE PROP
WANT.PR:	SPEAKER BELIEVE
	SPEAKER WANT inform-instance
EFFECT:	HEARER BELIEVE
	SPEAKER BELIEVE PROP

The CANDO.PR simply states that the only applicability condition to INFORMing someone that proposition PROP is true is that the speaker believes PROP.[14] The EFFECT of an INFORM is to communicate what the speaker believes. This allows for the hearer to refuse to believe the proposition without

[14]Other preconditions to the INFORM act could be added—for instance, to talk to someone one must have a communication link (Schank & Abelson, 1977); which may require telephoning or going to that person's location, etc. However, such preconditions would apply to *any* speech act, and hence probably belong on the locutionary act of making noises to someone.

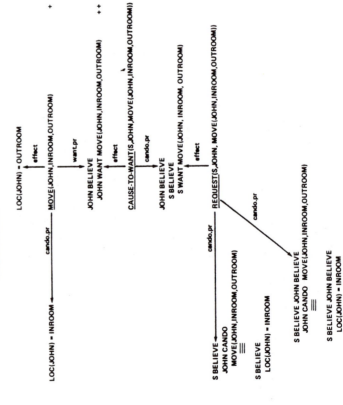

Figure 2. A plan for a REQUEST.

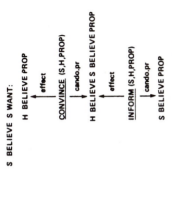

Figure 3.   A plan for an INFORM.

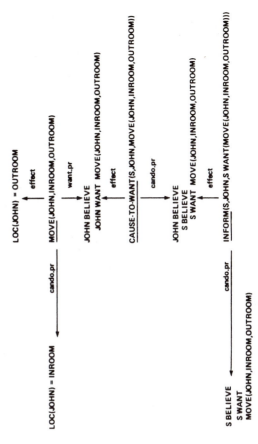

Figure 4.   A plan for an INFORM of a WANT.

invalidating the speaker's action as an INFORM. Therefore, an intermediate "act," termed CONVINCE, is necessary to get the hearer to believe the proposition.

For a person AGT 1 to CONVINCE another person AGT that proposition PROP is true, we define:

> CONVINCE(AGT1, AGT, PROP)
>
>   CANDO.PR: AGT BELIEVE
>   AGT1 BELIEVE PROP
>
>   EFFECT: AGT BELIEVE PROP

This operator says that for AGT 1 to convince AGT of the truth of PROP AGT need only believe that AGT1 thinks PROP is true. Though this may be a necessary prerequisite to getting someone to believe something, it is clearly not sufficient. For a more sophisticated precondition of CONVINCE, one might state that before AGT will be convinced, she needs to know the justifications for AGT1's belief, which may require that AGT believe (or be CONVINCE of) the justifications for believing those justifications, etc. Such a chain of reasons for believing might be terminated by mutual beliefs that people are expected to have or by a belief AGT believes AGT1 already has. Ideally, a good model of CON-VINCE would allow one to plan persuasive arguments.[15]

5.5   Planning INFORM Speech Acts

The planning of INFORM speech acts now becomes a simple matter. For any proposition PROP, S's plan to achieve the goal H BELIEVE PROP would be that of Figure 3. Notice that it is unnecessary to state as a precondition to inform, that the hearer H does not already believe PROP. Again, this non-obviousness condition can be eliminated by viewing speech acts in a planning context.

What would be Searle's sincerity condition for the INFORM above (S BELIEVE PROP) turns out to be a precondition for the speech act rather than a reason for planning the act as we had for REQUEST's sincerity condition, (i.e., SPEAKER BELIEVE SPEAKER WANT HEARER do ACT). If we were to use REQUEST as a model, the sincerity condition for an INFORM would be SPEAKER BELIEVE SPEAKER WANT HEARER BELIEVE PROP. One may then question whether Searle's sincerity condition is a consistent naming of distinctive features of various kinds of speech acts. Insincerity is a matter of falsely claiming to be in a psychological state, which for this model is either belief or want. By this definition, both conditions, SPEAKER BELIEVE PROP

and SPEAKER BELIEVE SPEAKER WANT HEARER BELIEVE PROP, are subject to insincerity.

5.6   Planning an INFORM of a WANT

As stated earlier, there are other ways to satisfy the precondition to CAUSE-TO-WANT. Since REQUEST was taken as a prototypical directive act, all members of that class share the same EFFECT (Searle's (1976) "illocutionary point"). However, issuing an INFORM of a WANT, as in "I want you to do X," also achieves it. Another plan to get John to move appears in Figure 4.

---

[15] Without a specification of the justifications for a belief, this operator allows one to become convinced of the truth of one's own lie. That is, after speaker S lies to hearer H that P is true, and receives H's acknowledgment indicating H has been convinced, S can decide to believe P because he thinks H thinks so. Further research needs to be done on CONVINCE and BELIEVE to eliminate such bizarre behavior.

The initial stages of this plan are identical to that of Figure 2 through the CANDO.PR of CAUSE-TO-WANT. This precondition is achieved by an INFORM whose propositional content is S WANT MOVE (JOHN, INROOM, OUTROOM). In this instance, the planning system does not need to proceed through CONVINCE since an INFORM of a WANT produces the necessary effects. Testing the CANDO.PR of INFORM determines if the system believes this proposition, which it does since the MOVE by John is already one of its goals. The WANT.PR of INFORM is trivially true, as before, and thus the plan is complete.

5.7 REQUEST vs. INFORM of WANT

Searle claimed that the conditions he provided were necessary and jointly sufficient for the successful and nondefective performance of various illocutionary acts. Any behavior satisfying such a set of conditions was then said to be a particular illocutionary act. Thus, if two utterances have the same illocutionary force, they should be equivalent in terms of the conditions on their use. We believe that the two utterances "please open the door" and "I want you to open the door (please)" can have the same force as directives, differing only in their politeness. That is, they both *can be* planned for the same reasons. However, our treatment does not equate the literal speech acts that could realize them when they should be equated. The condition on REQUEST that distinguishes the two cases is the precondition SPEAKER BELIEVE HEARER BELIEVE HEARER CANDO ACT. Since there is no corresponding precondition in the plan for the INFORM of a WANT, there is no reason to check the hearer's beliefs.

In order to force an equivalence between a REQUEST and an INFORM of a WANT, various actions need to be redefined. We shall remove the above condition as a CANDO.PR from REQUEST and add it as a new CANDO.PR to CAUSE-TO-WANT. In other words, the new definition of CAUSE-TO-WANT would say that you can get a person to decide to want to do some action if she believes you want her to do it and if she believes she can do it. With these changes, both ways of getting someone to want to do some action would involve her believing she is able to do it. More formally, we now define:

REQUEST (SPEAKER, HEARER, ACT)

CANDO.PR:	SPEAKER BELIEVE HEARER CANDO ACT
WANT.PR:	SPEAKER BELIEVE SPEAKER WANT request-instance
EFFECT:	HEARER BELIEVE
	SPEAKER BELIEVE SPEAKER WANT ACT

and

CAUSE-TO-WANT (AGT1, AGT, ACT)

CANDO.PR:	AGT BELIEVE
	AGT1 BELIEVE AGT1 WANT ACT
	AND
	AGT BELIEVE AGT CANDO ACT
EFFECT:	AGT BELIEVE AGT WANT ACT

Though REQUEST and INFORM of a WANT can achieve the same effect, they are not interchangeable. A speaker (S), having previously said to a hearer (H) "I want you to do X," can deny having the intention to get H to want to do X by saying "I simply told you what I wanted, that's all." It appears to be much more difficult, however, after having requested H to do X, to deny the intention of H's wanting to do X by saying "I simply requested you to do X, that's all." S usually plans a request for the purpose of getting H to want to do some act X by means of getting H to believe that S wants H to do it. While maintaining the distinction between illocutionary acts and perlocutionary effects, thus allowing for the possibility that H could refuse to do X, we need to capture this distinction between REQUEST and INFORM of WANT. The solution (Allen, 1979; Perrault & Allen, forthcoming) lies in formulating speech act bodies as plans achieving the perlocutionary effect—plans that a hearer is intended to recognize.

In the next two sections, we investigate the compositional adequacy of these operator definitions via the planning of REQUESTs that a hearer perform REQUEST or INFORM speech acts.

6. COMPOSITIONAL ADEQUACY: QUESTIONS

We are in agreement with many others, in proposing that questions be treated as requests for information. In terms of speech act operators, the questioner is performing a REQUEST that the hearer perform an INFORM. That is, the REQUEST leads to the satisfaction of INFORM's "want precondition." However, for a wh-question, the INFORM operator as defined earlier cannot be used since the questioner does not know the full proposition of which he is to be informed. If he did know what the proposition was there would be no need to ask; he need only decide to believe it.

Intuitively, one plans a wh-question to find out the value of some expression and a yes/no question to find out whether some proposition is true. Such questions are planned, respectively, on the basis of believing *that* the hearer knows what the value of that expression is or *that* the hearer knows whether the proposition is true, without the speaker's having to know what the hearer believes.

Earlier we stated that a person's (AGT1) belief representation should represent cases like the following distinctly:

1. AGT2 believes the Cannonball Express departs at 8 p.m.
2. AGT2 believes the Cannonball Express has a departure time.
3. AGT2 knows what the departure time for the Cannonball Express is.

Case 1 can be represented by a proposition that contains no variables. Case 2 can be represented by a belief of a quantified proposition—i.e.,

AGT2 BELIEVE

∃x (the y : DEPARTURE-TIME(CANNONBALL-EXPRESS,y)) = x)

However, Case 3 can be approximated by a *quantified belief*, namely,

∃x AGT2 BELIEVE

(the y : DEPARTURE-TIME(CANNONBALL-EXPRESS,y)) = x),

where "the y : P(y)," often written "iy P(y)," is the logical description operator read "the y which is P." This formula is best paraphrased as "there is something which AGT2 believes to be the departure time for the Cannonball Express."[16] Typical circumstances in which AGT1 might acquire such quantified beliefs are by understanding a definite description uttered by AGT2 referentially (Donnellan, 1966). Thus, if AGT2 says "the pilot of TWA 461 on July 4," AGT1 might infer that AGT2 knows who that pilot is.

Quantified beliefs often become goals when a planner needs to know the values of the parameters of an operator and when these parameters occur in that operator's preconditions.[17] We show how, when a quantified belief is a goal for AGT, AGT can plan a wh-question.

6.1 Planning Wh-Questions

First, a new operator, INFORMREF, and its associated mediating act CONVINCEREF, are needed.[18]

INFORMREF(SPEAKER,HEARER, λxDx) (i.e., D is a predicate of one argument)

CANDO.PR: ∃y SPEAKER BELIEVE (ixDx) = y
WANT.PR: SPEAKER BELIEVE SPEAKER WANT informref-instance
EFFECT: ∃y HEARER BELIEVE SPEAKER BELIEVE (ixDx) = y

[16]Another conjunction can be added to the representation of (3) as suggested by Allen (1979) to refine our representations of "AGT2's knowing what the value of the description is," namely:

∃x [(the y: D(y)) = x & AGT2 BELIEVE ((the y: D(y)) = x)]

We shall, however, use the simpler quantified belief formulation.

[17]We would prefer to formalize declaratively that "the agent of an action must know the values of the parameters of the action." One way of doing this is suggested by Moore (1979).

[18]In Cohen (1978) we achieved the same effect by parameterizing INFORM and CONVINCE so that different sets of preconditions and effects were used if the original goal was a quantified belief. In addition, Cohen (1978) did not use descriptions. We believe the formulation that follows, due to J. Allen, is clearer. The actual names for these acts were suggested by W. Woods.

Thus, before a speaker will inform a hearer of the value of some description, there must be some individual that the speaker believes is the value of the description, and the speaker must want to say what it is. The effect of performing this act is that there is then some individual that the hearer thinks the speaker believes to be the value of the description. As usual, we need a mediating act to model the hearer's then believing that individual to be the value of the description. To this end, we define AGT1's convincing AGT of the referent of the description as:

CONVINCEREF(AGT1,AGT, λxDx)

CANDO.PR: ∃y AGT BELIEVE AGT1 BELIEVE (ixDx) = y
EFFECT: ∃y AGT BELIEVE (ixDx) = y

Using these operators, if the planning system wants to know where Mary is and believes that Joe knows where she is, it can create the plan underlying the question "Where is Mary?" as is shown in Figure 5. After the system plans for Joe to tell it Mary's location, on the basis of believing that he knows where she is, it must get Joe to want to perform this act. In the usual fashion, this leads to a REQUEST and hence the construction of a question. The precondition to

S BELIEVE S WANT:

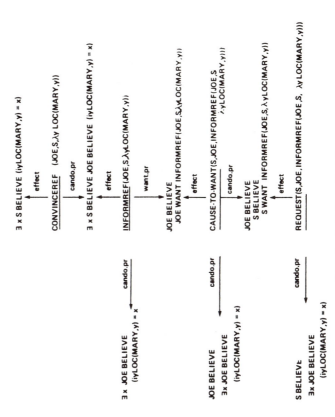

Figure 5. A plan for a wh-question.

CAUSE-TO-WANT, namely, JOE BELIEVE JOE BELIEVE JOE CANDO the INFORMREF is actually:

$$\text{JOE BELIEVE}$$
$$\exists y \text{ JOE BELIEVE}$$
$$ixLOC(MARY,x) = y$$

which is implied by

$$\exists y \text{ JOE BELIEVE } ixLOC(MARY,x) = y$$

that was asserted, for this example, to be one of the planning system's beliefs. Notice, that the planning of this question depends upon the system's having chosen Joe to tell it the answer, and upon its having chosen itself to get Joe to want to perform the INFORM. Section 7 discusses what happens when different decisions are made.

6.2 Plans for Yes/No Questions

To plan a yes/no question about some proposition P, one should think that the hearer knows whether P is true or false (or, at least "might know"). An approximate representation of AGT2's knowing whether P is true or false is OR (AGT2 BELIEVE P, AGT2 BELIEVE ~ P).[19] Such goals are often created, as modeled by our type 4 inference, when a planner does not know the truth-value of P. Typical circumstances in which an agent may acquire such disjunctive beliefs about another are telephone conversations, in which AGT1 believes that there are certain objects in AGT2's view. AGT1 then probably believes that AGT2 knows whether certain visually derivable (or easily computable) properties of those objects are true, such as whether object A is on top of object B.

To accommodate yes/no questions into the planning system, a third INFORM, called INFORMIF, and its associated mediating act CONVINCEIF are defined as follows:

INFORMIF(SPEAKER,HEARER,P)

CANDO.PR:	OR(SPEAKER BELIEVE P, SPEAKER BELIEVE ~ P)
EFFECT:	OR(HEARER BELIEVE SPEAKER BELIEVE P, HEARER BELIEVE SPEAKER BELIEVE ~ P)
WANT.PR:	SPEAKER BELIEVE SPEAKER WANT informif-instance

CONVINCEIF(AGT,AGT1,P)

CANDO.PR:	OR(AGT BELIEVE AGT1 BELIEVE P, AGT BELIEVE AGT1 BELIEVE ~ P)
EFFECT:	OR(AGT BELIEVE P, AGT BELIEVE ~ P)

[19]Allen (1979) also points out that another conjunct can be added to the representation of "knowing whether" as a disjunctive belief, to obtain (P & AGT2 BELIEVE (P)) OR (~ P & AGT2 BELIEVE (~ P)).

The plan for a yes/no question to Joe is now parallel to that of a wh-question.[20] That is, in the course of planning some other act, if the system wants proposition P to be true or to be false, and if the truth-value of proposition P is unknown to it, it can create the goal OR(SYSTEM BELIEVE P, SYSTEM BELIEVE ~ P). For instance if P were LOC(MARY,INROOM), the illocutionary acts underlying the question to Joe "Is Mary in the room?" can be planned provided the planning system believes that Joe either believes P is true or he believes P is false. That disjunctive belief could be stated directly or could be inferred from a belief like ∃y JOE BELIEVE(ixLOC(MARY,x)) = y—i.e., there is something Joe believes is Mary's location. But if it had some idea where Joe thought Mary was, say OUTROOM, then it would not need to ask.

6.3 Summary

A plan for a question required the composition of REQUEST and INFORM and led to the development of two new kinds of informing speech acts, INFORMREF and INFORMIF, and their mediating acts. The INFORMREF acts lead to "what," "when," and "where" questions while INFORMIF results in a yes/no question.[21] The reason for these new acts is that, in planning a REQUEST that someone else perform an INFORM act, one only has incomplete knowledge of their beliefs and goals; but an INFORM, as originally defined can only be planned when one knows what is to be said.

7.   COMPOSITIONAL ADEQUACY AND THE POINT OF VIEW PRINCIPLE

Earlier, a guiding "Point of View Principle" (POVP) for defining speech acts as planning operators was proposed: the preconditions of the operator should be stated from the speaker's point of view, i.e., in terms of the speaker beliefs; the effects should be stated from the hearer's point of view. We now wish to judge the adequacy of speech act definitions formulated along these lines. The test case

[20]Searle (1969) suggested there were different speech acts for real and teacher-student (or exam) questions, where in the latter case, the questioner just wants to know what the student thinks is the answer. Since teacher-student questions seem to have similar conditions on their appropriateness as real questions, save the questioner's intention to be convinced, we have good reason for factoring the mediating acts out of each of the three INFORM act types. This leaves the perlocutionary effects of an INFORM act neutral with respect to what kind of question they are contained in. In general, if the perlocutionary effects of an INFORM were incorporated into the act's definition, then we would need two new primitive teacher-student question speech acts. For now, we opt for the former.

[21]The language for stating operators needs to be extended to account for "which," "how," and "why" questions. For instance, "why" and "how" questions involve quantifying over actions and/or plans.

will be the composing of REQUESTs, i.e., the planning of a REQUEST that some third party himself perform a REQUEST. For instance, the utterance ''Ask Tom to tell you where the key is,'' is an example of such a third party request.

The current definitions of speech acts will be shown to be compositionally inadequate since they force speakers to have unnecessary knowledge about intermediaries' beliefs. Achieving compositional adequacy, however, requires more than a simple restatement of the point of view principle; the side effects of speech act operators also must be considered.

Our scrutiny will be focused upon the seemingly innocent precondition to REQUEST, SPEAKER BELIEVER HEARER CANDO ACT whose form depended on the POVP. The goal is to show how the POVP leads us astray and how a formulation of that precondition according to a new POVP that suggests a more neutral point of view for speech act definitions sets us back on course. From here on, the two versions of the precondition will be referred to as the ''speaker-based'' and ''neutral'' versions.

7.1 Plans for Multiparty Speech Acts

Multiparty speech acts can arise in conversations where communication is somehow restricted so as to pass through intermediaries.[22] The planning system, since it is recursive, can generate plans for such speech acts using any number of intermediaries provided that appropriate decisions are made as to who will perform what action.

Let us suppose that the planning system wants to know where a particular key is and that it must communicate through John. We shall use the speaker-based precondition on REQUEST for this example, and for readability, the following abbreviations:

SYSTEM—S TOM—T JOHN—J
BELIEVE—B WANT—W LOC(KEY23,y)—D(y)

Figure 6 shows the plan for the specific three-party speech act underlying ''Ask Tom to tell me where the key is.''

S develops the plan in the following fashion: T is chosen to tell S the key's location since, we shall assume, he is believed to know where it is. Since T is not believed to already want to tell, and since S cannot communicate directly with T (but T can communicate with S), J is chosen to be the one to talk T into telling. Since J is not believed to already want to do that, S plans a REQUEST that J perform a REQUEST, namely REQUEST(S,J,REQUEST (J,T,INFORMREF (T,S,λyLOC (KEY23,y)))). J, then, is an intermediary who is just expected to do what he is asked; his status will be discussed soon.

The preconditions that need to be satisfied in this plan are:

S BELIEVE:

(P1) ∃y T BELIEVE [ιxLOC(KEY23,x)=y]
(P2) T BELIEVE (P1) (implied by P1)
(P3) J BELIEVE (P1)
(P4) J BELIEVE J BELIEVE (P1) (implied by P3)
(P5) S BELIEVE J BELIEVE (P1) (implied by P3)

S BELIEVE S WANT:

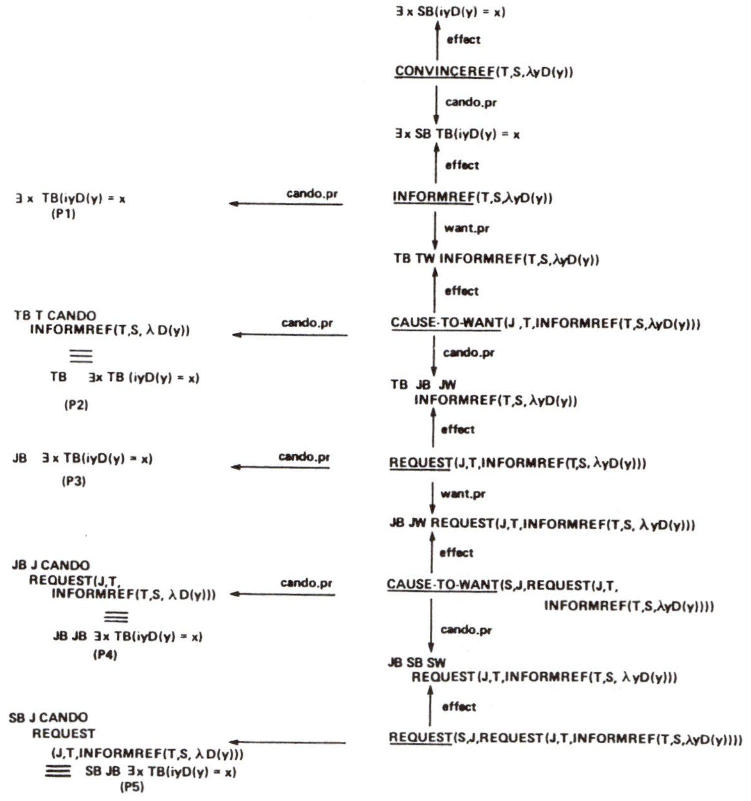

$$\exists x\, SB(\iota y D(y) = x)$$
effect — CONVINCEREF(T,S,λyD(y))
cando.pr — $\exists x\, SB\, TB(\iota y D(y)) = x$
effect — INFORMREF(T,S,λyD(y))
want.pr — TB TW INFORMREF(T,S,λyD(y))
effect — CAUSE-TO-WANT(J,T,INFORMREF(T,S,λyD(y)))
cando.pr — TB JB JW INFORMREF(T,S,λyD(y))
effect — REQUEST(J,T,INFORMREF(T,S,λyD(y)))
want.pr — JB JW REQUEST(J,T,INFORMREF(T,S, λyD(y)))
effect — CAUSE-TO-WANT(S,J,REQUEST(J,T, INFORMREF(T,S, λyD(y))))
cando.pr — JB SB SW REQUEST(J,T,INFORMREF(T,S, λyD(y)))
effect — REQUEST(S,J,REQUEST(J,T,INFORMREF(T,S,λyD(y))))

cando.pr — $\exists x\, TB(\iota y D(y) = x$ (P1)

cando.pr — TB T CANDO INFORMREF(T,S, λ D(y))
$\equiv$ TB ∃x TB (ιyD(y) = x (P2)

cando.pr — JB ∃x TB(ιyD(y) = x (P3)

cando.pr — JB J CANDO REQUEST(J,T INFORMREF(T,S, λ D(y)))
$\equiv$ JB JB ∃x TB(ιyD(y) = x (P4)

SB J CANDO REQUEST (J,T,INFORMREF(T,S, λ D(y)))
$\equiv$ SB JB ∃x TB(ιyD(y) = x (P5)

Figure 6.   A plan for a third party REQUEST.

While the plan appears to be straightforward, precondition P3 is clearly unnecessary—S ought to be able to plan this particular speech act without having any *prior* knowledge of the intermediary's beliefs. This prior knowledge requirement comes about because precondition P5 is constructed by composing

---

[22]For instance, in the Stanford Research Institute Computer-based Consultant research (Deutsch, 1974) communication between an expert and an apprentice was constrained in this way. The apprentice typically issued such speech acts, while the expert did not.

Conditions P3 and P5 are the same as P1, and thus the preconditions to the REQUESTs in the plan, are independent of the speaker's beliefs; they depend only on *the planner's* beliefs. While the use of the neutral precondition eliminates prior knowledge requirements for REQUESTs *per se*, condition P4 still requires, as a precondition to CAUSE-TO-WANT, that the planner have some knowledge of the intermediary's beliefs. The next section shows why the planner need not have such beliefs at the time of plan construction.

7.2 Side Effects

The performance of a speech act has thus far been modeled as resulting in an EFFECT that is specific to each speech act type. But, by the very fact that a speaker has attempted to perform a particular speech act, a hearer learns more— on identifying which speech act was performed, a hearer learns that the speaker believed the various preconditions in the *plan* that led to that speech act held. The term *side effect* will be used to refer to the hearer's acquisition of such beliefs by way of the performance of a speech act. Since the plan the hearer infers for the

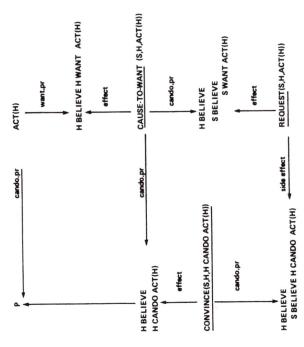

Figure 8. A REQUEST with side effects.

REQUEST's precondition schema with precondition P3, and P3 is similarly constructed from P1.

The problem can be eliminated by reformulating REQUEST's precondition as HEARER CANDO ACT. Consider a general plan for three-party REQUESTs, as in Figure 7. T's INFORMREF has been generalized to "ACT(T)" whose precondition is "P."

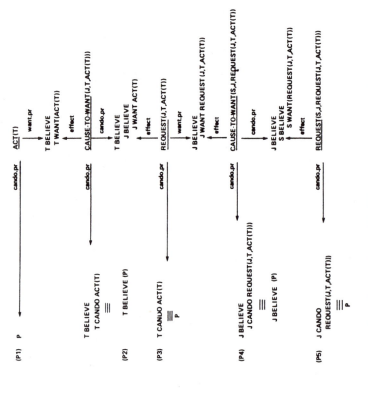

Figure 7. A third party REQUEST using the "neutral" precondition.

The preconditions that have to be satisfied in S's plan are:

S BELIEVE:

  (P1) P (also P3 and P5)

  (P2) T BELIEVE (P)

  (P4) J BELIEVE (P)

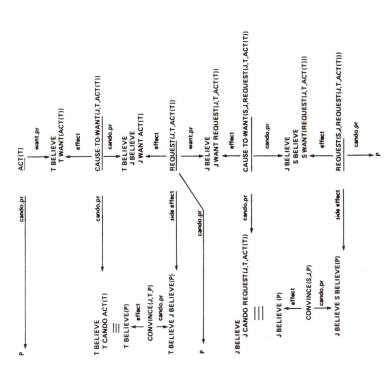

Figure 9. A third party REQUEST using the "neutral" precondition and side effects.

speaker depends upon his beliefs about the speaker's beliefs and goals, the side effects of a speech act cannot be specified in advance. However, the hearer is minimally entitled to believe the speaker thought her speech act's preconditions held (Bruce, 1975; Bruce & Schmidt, 1974).[23] Furthermore, not only do hearers make such assumptions about speakers' beliefs, but speakers know that and often depend on those assumptions for the success of their plans. Figure 8 is a schematic of a simple plan by S to REQUEST H to do action ACT that illustrates this situation.

The minimal side effect is that the hearer believes the speaker believes the precondition of the REQUEST holds, i.e., that HEARER BELIEVE SPEAKER BELIEVE HEARER CANDO ACT. This goal satisfies, via a CONVINCE, the CANDO.PR of CAUSE-TO-WANT, and hence the REQUEST achieves two goals in the plan.[24] The schematic can be applied twice in Figure 7 to obtain Figure 9.

After the side effects of J's REQUEST to T take hold, T would think J believes the preconditions to J's REQUEST (P) obtain. We claim that it is because T thinks that J believes P that T comes to believe P. In this way, precondition (P2) is satisfied as a result of J's REQUEST. Naturally, the side effect argument applies equally to J as the hearer of S's REQUEST. That is, J comes to believe P (precondition P4) because he thinks S believes P. S's belief that the preconditions to action A hold thus gets "passed" down the line of intermediaries, whatever its length, to the final agent of A. In this way S can issue the third party REQUEST without having any prior knowledge of J's beliefs about P, S's REQUEST provides all the necessary information!

An interesting aspect of this transmission is that, while J may come to believe P and, by making a REQUEST to T, transmit this belief, T's belief *that* P may be of little use to T. Consider Figure 9 again. Suppose P were

$$\exists y \ \text{T BELIEVE} \ (\text{ixLOC(KEY23,x)}) = y$$

which we are loosely paraphrasing as T knows where the key is. S's REQUEST conveys S's belief *that* T knows where the key is. Though J, to decide to perform his REQUEST, need only think *that* T knows where the key is, T actually has to know where it is before he can do A.[25] J's conveying his belief does no good

since he has supplied information for a CONVINCE, but T needs information sufficient for a CONVINCEWH. A planning system has to be able to realize this and to plan, by making the same choices as before, the additional REQUEST that John perform an INFORM, e.g., "Tell Tom that the key is in the closet."[26]

7.3 A New Point-of-View Principle

In addition to considering side effects for speech acts, we are led to propose a new point-of-view principle:

The "Cando" preconditions and effects of speech acts should be defined in a way that does not depend on who the speaker of that speech act is. That is, no CANDO.OR or EFFECT should be stated as a proposition beginning with "SPEAKER BELIEVE."

[23]The hearer may in fact believe those preconditions are false.

[24]The simple backward-chaining planning algorithm described in Cohen (1978) could not easily construct this plan since it ignores intermediate states of the world model that would be created after each operator's execution (i.e., after S's, and J's, REQUESTs).

[25]T cannot obtain that information from believing P since

$$\exists y \ \text{T BELIEVE} \ \exists y \ \text{T BELIEVE ixLOC(KEY23,x)} = y \ \text{cannot be inferred from}$$
$$\text{T BELIEVE} \ \exists y \ \text{T BELIEVE ixLOC(KEY23,x)} = y, \ \text{by B.2 and B.7 (footnote 5)}.$$

If CONVINCE can be defined so that AGT1 cannot be convinced by AGT2 that AGT1 believes something, then J could not CONVINCE T that $\exists y$ T BELIEVE ixLOC(KEY23,x) = y on the basis of T's thinking that J believes it.

[26]The side effects again figure in this additional three-party REQUEST—John comes to believe that the key is in the closet by believing that S thinks so.

The CANDO.PRs of speech acts defined according to this principle not only resolve our difficulties with composite speech acts, but they also behave as desired for the usual noncomposite cases since preconditions now depend only on the *planner's* beliefs, and the planner is often the speaker. Thus speech act operator definitions are intimately bound to the form of the planning system.

The only result the new principle is to make clear whose beliefs should be updated with those EFFECTs. After successfully executing a speech act to H, the speaker can update his model of H with the speech act's EFFECTs. But, for a composite speech act *ultimately* directed to H, the initial planner must observe or assume the success of the rest of the multiparty plan in order to conclude that the EFFECTs of the final speech act to H hold.

While the new principle guarantees that the EFFECTs of speech acts are independent of the use of intermediaries, hearers have every right to believe that the speakers of those speech acts believe that the preconditions hold. Because side effects are stated in terms of the hearer's beliefs about the speaker's beliefs, intermediaries are vulnerable to a charge of insincerity if they brazenly execute the speech acts they were requested to perform. It is to avoid such a charge, and thus make intermediaries "responsible for" the speech acts they execute, that we place the condition on CAUSE-TO-WANT stating that AGT BELIEVE AGT CANDO ACT.

Finally, to complete the reexamination of speech act definitions we point out that the WANT.PR also has a SPEAKER BELIEVE on it. One cannot, in the spirit of "housecleaning," remove the SPEAKER BELIEVE SPEAKER WANT from the WANT.PR of speech acts since a speaker's goal cannot be characterized independently of the speaker's beliefs, unless one is willing to model someone's "unconscious" goals. We are not.[27]

7.4 New Definitions of REQUEST and INFORM

Using this principle, REQUEST is redefined as:

```
REQUEST(SPEAKER,HEARER,ACT)
CANDO.PR:    HEARER CANDO ACT
WANT.PR:     SPEAKER BELIEVE
             SPEAKER WANT request-instance
EFFECT:      HEARER BELIEVE
             SPEAKER BELIEVE SPEAKER WANT ACT
```

The principle applied to the definition of the operator INFORM results in a. CANDO.PR stated as PROP rather than as SPEAKER BELIEVE PROP.[28] Such a change allows one to plan to request an intermediary, say a child, to tell someone else that the key is in the closet without the planner's having to believe, at the time of planning, that the child thinks so. The new definition of INFORM then becomes:

```
INFORM(SPEAKER,HEARER,PROP)
CANDO.PR:    PROP
WANT.PR:     SPEAKER BELIEVE
             SPEAKER WANT inform-instance
EFFECT:      HEARER BELIEVE
             SPEAKER BELIEVE PROP
```

Regarding the other informing speech acts, the principle cannot be used to justify the deleting of the SPEAKER BELIEVE from the CANDO.PR of IN-FORMREF and INFORMIF since the highest elements of those conditions are "∃" and "OR", respectively. Intuitively speaking, this is a sensible result since a speaker SP cannot plan for an intermeriary, INT, to tell H whether P is true, or what the value of description D is unless INT is believed to have that information.

7.5 Summary

The appropriate planning of composite speech acts has turned out to be a powerful test of the adequacy of speech act definitions. To meet its demands on the planning of questions and multiparty speech acts, two new speech acts, IN-FORMREF and INFORMIF have been defined, and the preconditions to RE-QUEST and INFORM have been reformulated according to a point-of-view principle. Since these last two speech acts were taken to be prototypes of Searle's (1976) "directive" and "representative" classes, the principle will find wide application.

A side effect of direct requests was identified and used in planning multiparty speech acts. Side effects, however, cannot be calculated until the hearer has recognized the speaker's plan and thus has classified the observed utterance as a particular speech act type. Thus the minimal side effect formulation given here should be further justified on the basis of what a hearer needs to assume about the speaker's beliefs in order to identify an utterances's illocutionary force.

There may be other ways to meet compositional adequacy. For instance, one could state explicitly that an action's preconditions should be true at the time the action is to be done (Bruce, 1975). For our multiparty REQUESTS, such an approach (using a speaker-based precondition) produces preconditions like: S believes J will believe P will be true when ACT is to be done, which seems reasonable. However, the minimal side effect of S's REQUEST then becomes: J now believes that (before that REQUEST) S *expected* J to believe that P would be true when ACT is done (where "now" is just after the REQUEST was made). As yet, we do not have an analogue of CONVINCE that would allow J to then come to believe that P would be true. Again, if REQUEST is defined using the neutral precondition, this problem does not arise.

---

[27]The fact that a WANT.PR is found on *every* intentional act makes us suspect that it belongs on some single "element" that is present for every act.

[28]Of course, what must be satisfied in any plan for INFORM is that the planner believe PROP.

8. CONCLUDING REMARKS

It has been argued that a theory of speech acts can be obtained by modelling them in a planning system as operators defined, at least, in terms of the speakers' and hearers' beliefs, and goals. Thus, speech acts are treated in the same way as physical acts, allowing both to be integrated into plans. Such an approach suggests new areas for application. It may provide a more systematic basis for studying real dialogues arising in the course of a task—a basis that would facilitate the tracking of conversants' beliefs and intentions as dialogue and task proceed. A similar analysis of characters' plans has also been shown (Bruce & Newman, 1978) to be essential to a satisfactory description of narrative. Finally, Allen (1979) and Cohen (1978) have suggested how computer conversants might plan their speech acts and recognize those of their users.

Given this range of application, the methodological issues of how speech acts should be modelled in a planning system become important. Specifically, a plan-based competence theory, given configurations of beliefs and goals, speech act operators, and plan construction inferences should generate plans for all and only those speech acts that are appropriate in those configurations. This paper developed tests that showed how various definitions of the speech acts of requesting and informing were inadequate, especially to the demand that they generate appropriate plans when composed with other speech acts to form questions and multiparty requests.

To resolve the difficulties, two "views" of INFORM to be used in constructing questions were defined, allowing the questioner to have incomplete knowledge of the hearer's beliefs. After revising both the form of speech act preconditions and identifying some speech act side effects, compositional adequacy for multiparty REQUESTS was achieved. The solution led to a metatheoretical "point-of-view" principle for use in defining future speech acts as operators within this planning system.

Our approach has both assumed certain idealized properties of speaker/hearers, and has been restricted in its scope. The preconditions and effects of our operators are stated in the language of logic, not because of any desire to perform logically valid inferences, but because the conditions in the plans should have well-defined semantics. While this has been partially realized through the adoption of the possible-worlds semantics for belief, the semantics is too strong to be a faithful model of human beliefs. For instance, it leads here to requiring a questioner to have very strong, though incomplete, knowledge of the hearer's beliefs. To reflect human beliefs more accurately, one needs to model (at least): degrees of belief, justifications, the failure to make deductions, inductive leaps, and knowing what/who/where something is. These refinements, though needed by a theory of speech acts, are outside its scope. Finally, the semantics for WANT and for actions are lacking (but see Moore (1979) for an interesting approach to the latter).

Only two kinds of speech acts, prototypes of Searle's (1976) directive and representative classes, have been examined here, but the approach can be extended to other members of those classes (Bruce, 1975) and perhaps to the commissive class that includes promises. However, in order to model promises and warnings, a better understanding of the concepts of benefit and obligation is necessary.

Finally, we have so far discussed how a planning system can select illocutionary force and propositional content of a speech act, but not how utterances realizing it can be constructed nor how illocutionary acts can be identified from utterances. Extending the plan-based approach to the first area means investigating the extent of "pragmatic influence" of linguistic processing. An important subproblem here is the planning of referring expressions involved in performing illocutionary acts (Perrault & Cohen, forthcoming; Searle, 1969). Regarding speech act identification, the acid-test of a plan-based approach is its treatment of indirect speech acts (Searle, 1975). Gordon and Lakoff (1971) proposed "conversational postulates" to account for the relation between the direct or literal and the indirect illocutionary forces of an utterance. But, as Morgan (1977) notes, by calling them "postulates," one implies they cannot be explained by some other independently motivated analysis.

We suggest that the relation between direct and indirect readings can be largely accounted for by considering the relationship between actions, their preconditions, effects, and bodies, and by modelling how language users can recognize plans, which may include speech acts, being executed by others. The ability to recognize plans is seemingly required in order to be *helpful*, independent of the use of indirect speech acts. For instance, hearers often understand a speaker's utterance literally but go beyond it, inferring the speaker's plans and then performing acts that would enable the speaker's higher level goals to be fulfilled. Indirect speech acts arise because speakers can intend hearers to perform helpful inferential processing and they intend for hearers to know this. Allen (1979) and Perrault and Allen (forthcoming) formalize this process of intended plan-recognition (and thus Searle's force condition) extending our plan-based approach to the interpretation of indirect speech acts.

ACKNOWLEDGMENTS

We would like to thank Marilyn Adams, James Allen, Ron Brachman, Chip Bruce, Sharon Oviatt, Bill Woods and the referees for their comments, and Brenda Starr, Jill O'Brien, and Beverly Tobiason for their tireless assistance in the paper's preparation. Special thanks are extended to Brenda Starr for her invaluable editorial help.

REFERENCES

Allen, J. A plan-based approach to speech act recognition. Ph.D. Thesis, Technical Report No. 131/79, Dept. of Computer Science, University of Toronto, January, 1979.

Austin, J. L. *How to do things with words*. J. O. Urmson (Ed.), Oxford University Press, 1962.

Bruce, B. Belief systems and language understanding. Report No. 2973, Bolt Beranek and Newman, Inc. January, 1975.

Bruce, B., & Newman, D. Interacting plans. *Cognitive Science*, 1978, 2, 195–233.

Bruce, B., & Schmidt, C. F. Episode understanding and belief guided parsing. Presented at the Association for Computational Linguistics Meeting at Amherst, Massachusetts (July 26–27, 1974).

Carbonell, J. G. Jr. POLITICS: Automated ideological reasoning. *Cognitive Science*, 1978, 2, 27–51.

Chomsky, N. *Aspects of the theory of syntax*. Cambridge, Mass. MIT Press, 1965.

Cohen, P. R. On knowing what to say: Planning speech acts. Ph.D. Thesis, Technical Report No. 118, Department of Computer Science, University of Toronto, January 1978.

Deutsch, B. G. The structure of task-oriented dialogues. In L. D. Erman (Ed.), *Proceedings of the IEEE symposium on speech recognition*. Pittsburgh, PA: Carnegie-Mellon University, 1974.

Donnellan, K. Reference and definite description. In *The Philosophical Review*, v. 75, 1960, 281–304. Reprinted in Steinberg & Jacobovits (Eds.), *Semantics*, Cambridge University Press, 1966.

Fikes, R., & Nilsson, N. J. STRIPS: A new approach to the application of theorem proving to problem solving. *Artificial Intelligence*, 1971, 2, 189–208.

Gordon, D., & Lakoff, G. Conversational postulates. *Papers from the Seventh Regional Meeting*, Chicago Linguistic Society, 1971, 63–84.

Green, C. Application of theorem-proving techniques to problem-solving. In D. E. Walker & L. M. Norton (Eds.), *Proceedings of the international joint conference on artificial intelligence*. Washington, D.C., May 1969.

Grice, H. P. Meaning. In *The Philosophical Review*, 1957, 66, 377–388. Reprinted in D. A. Steinberg & L. A. Jacobovits (Eds.), *Semantics: An interdisciplinary reader in philosophy, linguistics, and psychology*. New York: Cambridge University Press, 1971.

Hintikka, J. *Knowledge and belief*. Ithaca: Cornell University Press, 1962.

Hintikka, J. Semantics for propositional attitudes. In J. W. Davis et al. (Eds.), *Philosophical logic*. Dordrecht-Holland: D. Reidel Publishing Co., 1969. Reprinted in L. Linsky (Ed.), *Reference and modality*. New York: Oxford University Press, 1971.

Lewis, D. K. *Convention: A philosophical study*. Cambridge, Mass: Harvard University Press, 1969.

McCarthy, J., & Hayes, P. J. Some Philosophical Problems from the Standpoint of Artificial Intelligence. In B. Meltzer & D. Michie (Eds.) *Machine intelligence 4*, New York: American Elsevier, 1969.

Meehan, J. R. Tale-spin, an interactive program that writes stories. In *Proceedings of the fifth international joint conference on artificial intelligence*, Cambridge, Mass., 91–98.

Moore, R. C. Reasoning about knowledge and action. Ph.D. Thesis, Artificial Intelligence Laboratory, Department of Electrical Engineering and Computer Science, Massachusetts Institute of Technology, February, 1979.

Morgan, J. Conversational postulates revisited. *Language*, 1977, 277–284.

Newell, A., & Simon. H. A. GPS, A program that simulates human thought. In E. A. Feigenbaum & J. Feldman (Eds.), *Computers and thought*. New York: McGraw Hill, 1963.

Perrault, C. R., & Allen, J. F. A plan-based analysis of indirect speech acts. Forthcoming.

Perrault, C. R., & Cohen, P. R. Inaccurate Reference, *Proceedings of the workshop on computational aspects of linguistic structure and discourse setting*, Joshi, A. K., Sag, I. A., & Webber, B. L. (Eds.), Cambridge University Press, forthcoming.

Sacerdoti, E. D. A structure for plans and behavior. Ph.D. Thesis, Technical Note 109, Artificial Intelligence Center, Stanford Research Institute, Menlo Park, California, August 1975.

Schank, R., & Abelson, R. *Scripts, plans, goals, and understanding*. Hillsdale, N.J.: Lawrence Erlbaum Associates, 1977.

Schiffer, S. *Meaning*. Oxford: Oxford University Press, 1972.

Searle, J. R. A taxonomy of illocutionary acts. In K. Gunderson (Ed.), *Language mind and knowledge*, University of Minnesota Press, 1976.

Searle, J. R. Indirect speech acts. In P. Cole & J. L. Morgan (Eds.), *Syntax and semantics*. (Vol. 3), *Speech acts*. New York: Academic Press, 1975.

Searle, J. R. *Speech acts: An essay in the philosophy of language*. Cambridge: Cambridge University Press, 1969.

Strawson, P. F. Intention and convention in speech acts. In *The Philosophical Review*, v: lxxiii, 1964. Reprinted in *Logico-linguistic papers*, London: Methuen & Co., 1971.

Analyzing Intention in Utterances*

James F. Allen

Computer Science Department, The University of Rochester, Rochester, NY 14627, U.S.A.

C. Raymond Perrault

Department of Computer Science, The University of Toronto, Toronto, Canada

Recommended by N.S. Sridharan

ABSTRACT

This paper describes a model of cooperative behavior and describes how such a model can be applied in a natural language understanding system. We assume that agents attempt to recognize the plans of other agents and, then, use this plan when deciding what response to make. In particular, we show that, given a setting in which purposeful dialogues occur, this model can account for responses that provide more information that explicitly requested and for appropriate responses to both short sentence fragments and indirect speech acts.

1. Introduction

A good question answering system often needs to provide a response that specifies more information than strictly required by the question. It should not, however, provide too much information that is of no use to the person who made the query. For example, consider the following exchange at an information booth in a train station.[1]

(1.1) *patron*: When does the Montreal train leave?

(1.2) *clerk*: 3:15 at gate 7.

Although the departure location was not explicitly requested, the clerk provided it in his answer.

Other examples of helpful behavior, however, do not involve language. For example, if the patron approached a closed door in the station carrying a large bag of groceries in each arm, the clerk might very well open the door for him. This may occur without any communication occurring between them. We claim that the motivation for the clerk's behavior in both these examples is the same; the clerk wants to assist the patron in furthering his goals.

This paper concerns the modeling of such helpful behavior and, in particular, it investigates how such a model can be used to explain several aspects of linguistic behavior. We make the following assumptions:

— People are rational agents who are capable of forming and executing plans to achieve their goals.

— They are often capable of inferring the plans of other agents from observing that agent perform some action.

— They are capable of detecting *obstacles* in another agent's plans.

Obstacles are goals in the plan that the other agent cannot achieve (easily) without assistance.

One form of helpful behavior arises because the observing agent assumes a goal of overcoming an obstacle in the other agent's plan. The plan to achieve this goal will involve the helpful actions.

Language can be viewed as an instance of such goal-oriented behavior. Utterances are produced by actions (*speech acts*) that are executed in order to have some effect on the hearer. This effect typically involves modifying the hearer's beliefs or goals. A speech act, like any other action, may be observed by the hearer and may allow the hearer to infer what the speaker's plan is. Often a speech act may explicitly convey a goal to the hearer that is an obstacle. For example, utterance (1.1) conveys to the hearer that the speaker needs to know the departure time of the train. But there may be other goals in the plan that were not explicitly conveyed but are also obstacles. The helpful response will attempt to overcome these obstacles as well as the explicitly mentioned ones.

This model provides the mechanisms to explain some interesting aspects of language, including:

— the generation of responses that provide more information than required (as in the above example);

— the generation of responses to sentence fragments;

— the analysis of indirect speech acts.

Let us consider each of these in turn.

It is fairly simple to see how the model explains the providing of more information than explicitly requested. In the train domain, the clerk expects that the patron has goals such as boarding and meeting trains. The query about a train departure time (i.e., (1.1)) indicates that it is likely that the patron's plan

* This research was supported in part by the National Research Council of Canada under Operating Grant A9285. Preparation of the document was supported in part by the Alfred P. Sloan Foundation under Grant No. 78-4-15.

[1] All the examples given in this paper are taken from transcripts of dialogues collected at the information booth in Union Station, Toronto [12].

train domain described above [1]. While the dialogues in this domain are somewhat restricted in subject matter, they provide a wide range of interesting linguistic behavior.

2. An Overview of the Model

Let us start with an intuitive description of what we think occurs when one agent A asks a question of another agent B which B then answers. A has a *goal* to acquire some information; he creates a plan (*plan construction*) that involves asking B a question whose answer will provide the information. A then asking B a question, asking B the question. B receives the question, and attempts to infer A's plan (*plan inference*). In this plan, there may be goals that A cannot achieve without assistance. These are the *obstacles* in A's plan. B can accept some of these obstacles as his own goals and create a plan to achieve them. B's response is generated when he executes this plan.

This section outlines the mechanisms that are needed to specify this model more precisely. The first part of it considers the issue of representing knowledge about the world, goals, actions and speech acts. The succeeding sections describe the plan construction, plan inference, and obstacle detection processes, respectively.

2.1. Actions, plans and speech acts

We need to be able to represent our intuitive notions of plan, goal, and action and relate them to language. These problems have already received much attention, both as problems in the philosophy of language and from the point of view of artificial intelligence.

Existing problem solving systems provide a formulation of actions and plans [7, 8]. In these systems, the world is modelled as a set of *propositions* that represent what is known about its static characteristics. This world is changed by *actions*, which can be viewed as parameterized procedures. Actions are described by *preconditions*, conditions that must hold before the action can execute, and by *effects*, the changes that the action will make to the world. Given an *initial world state* W and a *goal state* G, a *plan* is a sequence of actions that transforms W into G.

Austin [2] suggested that every utterance is the result of several actions or *speech acts*. We are particularly interested in speech acts such as requesting, warning, asserting, and promising. These speech acts are appropriate only in certain circumstances. In particular, they may require the speaker and the hearer to have certain beliefs and intentions (wants). For example, to sincerely *INFORM* you that I am tired, I must believe that I am tired and I must intend to get you to believe that I am tired. Both these conditions can be modelled as preconditions on the INFORM act. A simple version of this act could have the

is to board the train. In addition, assuming that the clerk believes that the patron does not already know the departure location, he believes knowing the location is also an obstacle in the plan. Thus he generates a response that overcomes both obstacles (i.e., (1.2)).

Another problem that arises in the transcripts is that people often communicate using sentence fragments. For instance:

(2.1) *patron*: The 3:15 train to Windsor?

(2.2) *clerk*: Gate 10.

Neither the syntactic form of the query nor the meaning of its words indicate what the response should be. However, in the model above, it is quite conceivable that the information in the fragment is sufficient to allow the hearer to deduce what the speaker's plan is. Hence he can produce a reasonable response based on what the obstacles in the plan are. In the above example, (2.1) is sufficient to identify the speaker's goal to board the 3:15 train to Windsor. An obstacle in this plan is knowing the departure location, hence the response (2.2).

Other sentences in the dialogues are not treated at face value. For instance,

(3.1) *patron*: Do you know when the Windsor train leaves?

Syntactically, this is a yes/no question about the hearer's knowledge. However, an answer of 'yes' in the given setting would be quite inappropriate. In other surroundings, however, it could be intended literally. For instance, a parent seeing a child off at the station and wanting to make sure that everything is arranged might say (3.1) intending to receive a yes/no answer. Sentences such as this that appear to mean one thing yet are treated as though they mean something else are termed *indirect speech acts* [24]. With relatively minor extensions to the basic plan inference/obstacle detection model, these forms can be explained. Intuitively, the solution lies in the realization that the speaker knows that the hearer performs such helpful behavior, and hence may say something intending that the hearer infer the indirect goal. There is not space to examine this problem in depth here; it is considered in detail in [16].

This paper describes the plan inference and obstacle detection processes and shows how they can be applied to explain helpful responses and the understanding of sentence fragments. Section 2 provides an overview of the general methods and Section 3 gives more details of the processes.

The remaining sections apply these techniques to analyzing language and provide some examples. Section 4 considers responses that provide more information than asked for and Section 5 considers the analysis of sentence fragments. Section 6 considers the generation of subdialogues intended to clarify the intent of a previous utterance.

Cohen [5] demonstrated that speech acts such as request and inform can be modelled successfully as actions in a planning system. He showed how speech acts may be planned in order to achieve specific (typically non-linguistic) goals.

2.2. Plan construction

Given a goal state, two major tasks need to be done to produce a plan to achieve that goal. One is to find a sequence of actions that will accomplish the transformation from the initial world state to the goal state. The other concerns specifying the bindings for the parameters of the actions in the constructed plan.

A typical method of constructing a plan is backwards chaining: given a goal G, find an action A that has G as one of its effects. Then evaluate the preconditions of A. If some of these conditions are not satisfied in the initial state, they become subgoals and the plan construction process repeats.

Another dimension of plan construction involves planning at different *levels of abstraction*. For example, in a domain where a robot has to plan a route through many rooms, the plan would first be developed in terms of 'go to room x' and 'open door y'. Only after such a plan was constructed would one consider planning actions such as 'rotate n degrees', 'twist arm', etc. To incorporate this, many actions must have the capability of being 'broken down' into sequences of more specific actions.

In order to facilitate reasoning about the planning process, we characterize it as a set of planning rules and a control strategy. Since this paper is mainly concerned with plan inference, we will not consider control strategies for planning explicitly. However, many of the control issues for plan inference are directly applicable to planning as well.

The planning rules are of the form 'If agent A wants to achieve Y', and are written:

$$AW(X) = c \Rightarrow AW(Y).$$

For example, a simple rule is:

(C.1) If an agent wants to achieve a goal E, and ACT is an action that has E as an effect, then the agent may want to execute ACT (i.e., achieve the execution of ACT).

One other rule of interest concerns reasoning about knowledge necessary to execute an action.

(C.2) If an agent wants to achieve P and does not know whether P is true, then that agent may want to achieve 'agent knows whether P is true'.

These ideas will be made more precise in Section 3.

2.3. Plan inference

Plan inferencing concerns the attempted (re)construction of some other agent's plan based on actions that that agent was observed performing. This process depends on both the observer's knowledge of how plans are constructed and on his original beliefs about what goals the other agent is likely to have.

The plan could be inferred in two manners. Starting from the expected goals, the observer could simulate the other agent's planning process, searching for a plan that includes the observed action. Obviously, most of the time such an approach is impractical. The alternative is to reconstruct the plan from the observed action, effectively applying the plan construction rules in reverse. The method we propose depends mainly on the latter approach, but does allow the possibility of the former occurring when circumstances permit. Note that, in actual fact, people probably use much more specialized knowledge to infer the plans of other agents, thereby bypassing many of the particular inferences we will suggest. Our approach so far, however, has been to specify a minimal set of reasoning tools that can account for the behavior observed. Given these tools, we then hope to precisely define and explain the more complex and specialized mechanisms by deriving them from the simple set.

As with the plan construction process, the plan inference process is specified as a set of inference rules and a control strategy. Rules are all of the form 'If agent S believes agent A has a goal X, then agent S may infer that agent A has a goal Y.' Examples of such rules that correspond to the planning rules (C.1) and (C.2) are:

(D.1) If S believes A has a goal of executing action ACT, and ACT has an effect E, then S may believe that A has a goal of achieving E.

(D.2) If S believes A has a goal of knowing whether a proposition P is true, then S may believe that A has a goal of achieving P.

Of course, given the conditions in (D.2), S might alternately infer that A has a goal of achieving *not* P. This is treated as a separate rule. Which of these rules applies in a given setting is determined by control heuristics.

The plan inferencing involves a search through a set of partial plans that consist of two parts: one is constructed using the plan inference rules from the observed action (and called *alternatives*), and the other is constructed using the plan construction rules on an expected goal (and called *expectation*). When mutually exclusive rules can be applied to one of these partial plans, the plan is copied and one rule is applied in each copy. Each partial plan has *tasks* associated with it that attempt to modify and further specify it. Typical tasks involve application of the rules and identification of the referents of variables in the plan.

Partial plans are rated as to how probable they are to be the correct plan. This rating is determined using a set of heuristics that fall into two classes:

those that evaluate how well-formed the plan is in the given context and those that evaluate how well the plan fits the expectations. An example of a heuristic is:

(H1) Decrease the rating of a partial plan if it contains a goal that is already true in the present context.

The tasks associated with a partial plan are rated according to this rating, and compete for execution according to this rating.

2.4. Obstacle detection

We claim that many helpful responses arise because the hearer detects obstacles in the speaker's plan, i.e., goals that the speaker cannot (easily) achieve without assistance. The most obvious obstacles are those that the speaker specifically brings attention to by his utterance. These *explicit obstacles* are goals that are an essential part of the chain of inferences that the hearer makes when he deduces the speaker's plan. For example, to infer the plan of the speaker from the utterance

(4.1) When does the Windsor train leave?

the hearer must infer that the speaker has the goal of knowing when the train leaves. Thus, this is an explicit obstacle.

However, the hearer cannot base his response solely on these explicit obstacles. For instance, if A, carrying an empty gas can, comes up to S on the street and asks

(5.1) Where is the nearest gas station?

and S answers

(5.2) On the next corner.

knowing full well that the station is closed, then S has not been helpful. But S's response did overcome the explicitly mentioned obstacle, namely knowing where the nearest gas station is. S may want to notify A if there are other obstacles to his plan, especially ones that A is not aware of. This behavior is expected; even if A and S are strangers, if A believes that S knew all along that the gas station was closed, he has justification for being angry at S, for S has violated some basic assumptions about human cooperation.

In the dialogues we have studied, all obstacles are caused by a lack of some information required in order to be able to execute the plan. This is not the case in general, as we saw in the example where the clerk opens the door for the patron carrying the groceries. There the obstacle concerned the patron's

2.5. Related work

Although there has been some previous work on recognizing plans and generating helpful responses, to our knowledge, no one else has attempted to combine the two techniques. Bruce [4] outlines a general model of story comprehension based on recognizing the intentions of the characters in the story as well as the intentions of the author. Although a slightly different application, our work here agrees quite closely with his view, and it will be interesting to attempt to combine the approaches. Bruce does not, however, describe any algorithm for actually recognizing the intentions in his stories.

Schmidt et al. [23] discuss a plan recognition algorithm where physical actions are observed and their task is to discover what the agent is doing. But they allow an arbitrary number of acts to be observed before committing themselves to a particular plan. This technique is appropriate for analyzing sequences of actions. In our work, however, it is essential that we identify the speaker's plan from a single observed action (i.e., his utterance).

The system PAM [25] analyzes stories by constructing a plan for the participants and then answers questions about the story using the plan. However, it does not attempt to recognize the plan of the agent asking the questions i.e. it does no plan based reasoning about how language is used. PAM answers questions solely on the form of the question asked (see [14]).

Kaplan [13] discusses some helpful responses to questions. But these are based on violated presuppositions conveyed by the question. He does not discuss any mechanisms that could explain helpful behavior in its general form.

The most important distinguishing characteristic of our research is that we emphasize the use of a model of the other's beliefs and goals. Helpful responses are detected because of this ability to reason about the other agents. A few more specific comparisons on linguistic issues will be discussed as the work is presented.

3. Plan Inference and Obstacle Detection

Some representation issues must be considered before the plan inference process can be described. Section 3.1 discusses the representation of belief, knowledge and want, and Section 3.2 considers actions and plans. The description of plan inference is then broken into three parts: we consider the plan inference rules in Section 3.3, the rating heuristics in Section 3.4, and the control of the process in Section 3.5. The final section considers how obstacles are detected in the plans that are inferred.

3.1. Belief, knowledge, and wants

An adequate description of modeling belief would take an entire paper by itself. We can just outline a few of the important issues here. Our treatment of belief is virtually identical to that of Hintikka [11]. The reader interested in the representation should see Cohen [5].

The crucial property of belief is that what one agent S believes another agent A believes has no logical relation to what S believes. Thus, S may believe A believes the world is flat while personally believing that it is round.

Intuitively, the belief operator allows us to consider actions and plans from another agent's point of view. This can be captured crudely by the axiom schema

$$(AB(P \Rightarrow Q) \ \& \ AB(P)) \Rightarrow AB(Q).$$

Thus, S may infer that A inferred some proposition Q if S believes that A believes that there is sufficient evidence to infer Q. We also need an axiom that states that conjunction can 'pass through' the belief operator. Thus, if S believes that A believes P is true and that A believes Q is true, then S also believes that A believes P and Q are true, and vice versa. Written more formally:

$$AB(P) \ \& \ AB(Q) \Leftrightarrow AB(P \ \& \ Q).$$

A similar axiom is *not* valid for disjunction.

Note that to be completely adequate, the belief operator B would have to be indexed by the time when the belief was held. For the sake of simplicity, however, we will ignore time throughout this paper.

Some formulas involving beliefs occur commonly enough to warrant special mention. In particular, there are three constructs associated with the word 'know' that arise very frequently.

The first involves representing that an agent S believes some A knows that P is true. This not only conveys the fact that S believes A believes P, but also that S believes P as well, i.e.,

$$SB(P \ \& \ AB(P)).$$

As an abbreviation, we define

$$A \ \text{KNOW} \ P = P \ \& \ AB(P).$$

In other words, if SB(A KNOW P), then S believes that S and A agree that P is true. This, of course, has no implication as to whether P is 'actually' true.

The next structure involves uses of 'know,' as in 'John knows whether P is true'. This is the type of belief S would have to have if S believed that John was able to answer a question such as 'Is P true?'. It is represented as the disjunction

$$A \ \text{KNOWIF} \ P = (P \ \& \ AB(P)) \lor (\text{not} P \ \& \ AB(\text{not} P)).$$

The final use of know is in the sense demonstrated by the sentence 'John knows where the box is'. This case is represented by quantifying over the B

operator:

$$A \ \text{KNOWREF} \ D = (\exists y)(\text{the } x : D(x) = y) \ \& \ AB(\text{the } x : D(x) = y)$$

where 'the $x : D(x)$' is any description. In the above example it would be 'the x such that the location of the box is x'. For further details on these representations of 'know', see Allen [1].

Goals and plans of agents are indicated by using an operator want ('W'), i.e.,

$$AW(P) = A \text{ has a goal to achieve } P.$$

By this, we mean that the agent A actually intends to achieve P, not simply that A would find P a desirable state of affairs. The properties of W in this work are specified completely by the planning and plan inference rules.

3.2. Actions and plans

As with the operators in STRIPS [8], actions can be grouped into families represented by *actions schemas*. An action schema consists of a name, a set of parameters and (possibly null) sets of formulas in the following classes:

Preconditions: Conditions that should be true if the action's execution is to succeed.

Effects: Conditions that should become true after the execution of the action.

Body: A specification of the action at a more detailed level. This may specify a sequence of actions to be performed, or may be a set of new goals that must be achieved.

Each action definition may also specify *applicability conditions* on the parameters: conditions that must be true for the action to be well-defined. Every action has at least one parameter, namely the *agent* or instigator of the action.

An *action instance* is a predicate constructed from an action schema name with a set of parameter instantiations and a time specification. The predicate is true only if the described action is (was or will be) executing at the specified time. For example,

ACT(S)(t)—a predicate that is true only if the action ACT with agent S was/will be executed at time t.

We will say that an action is *intentional* if whenever the action was performed, the agent wanted it to occur at that time. Thus, if ACT is an intentional act, A any agent, t any time, then

$$ACT(A)(t) \Rightarrow AW(ACT(A)(t)).$$

Thus, in a loose sense, there is a 'precondition' on every intentional action that the agent must want to perform the action. We will sometimes refer to this want condition as the *want precondition* of the act.

In general, the time specification will be omitted. If an action is within the immediate scope of the B operator, it is assumed to have a time specification in the past. If it is within the immediate scope of a W operator, it is assumed to have a time specification in the future.

Actions are not only reasoned about, sometimes they are executed. The execution of an action is specified either as *primitive* or by its body. If the body is a sequence of other actions, this sequence may be recursively executed. If the body is a set of new goals, plan construction must be initiated on the goals and then the resultant plan executed.

It will often be convenient to refer to an action and its associated preconditions, effects and body as a single unit. Such *action clusters* are action schemas with instantiated parameters.

A *speech act* is an intentional action that has as parameters a speaker (i.e., the agent), a hearer, and a propositional content, and whose execution leads to the production of an utterance. Their preconditions and effects are defined in terms of the beliefs and wants of the speaker and hearer. For the present, we will assume that the speech act intended by the speaker can be readily identified from the syntactic form of the utterance. This assumption, which is obviously incorrect, will be removed in the later sections of the paper concerning indirect speech acts and sentence fragments.

In its final form, a *plan* is a linear sequence of action instances that will map an initial world state into a goal state. But as Sacerdoti [20] points out, plans cannot easily be constructed in linear form. He uses a representation that imposes only a partial ordering on the actions, where the orderings are imposed only when necessary. We use a similar representation.

A plan can be represented as a directed graph with predicates (goals and actions) as nodes and labelled arcs indicating their interrelationships. These arcs implicitly specify a partial ordering on the actions. The *enable* arc links a proposition that is a precondition of an action to that action. Likewise, an *effect* arc links an action to a proposition that is its effect. The *know* arc links a KNOWIF or KNOWREF proposition to a proposition in a plan whose truth values cannot be determined unless the 'know' proposition is true. For example, the planner cannot achieve the goal

'planner at the location of *n*'

unless

'planner KNOWREF the location of *n*'.

To permit plans to be represented at varying levels of detail, plan structures themselves can be nodes in a plan. These 'plan' nodes represent the bodies of actions. The *body* arc links an action to a plan node that contains its body.

3.3. The plan inference rules

The plan inference process starts with an incomplete plan, usually containing a single observed action or an expected goal and attempts to fill in the plan. The possible additions that can be made are described in this section as a set of plausible inference rules. They are presented without any consideration of whether the inference is reasonable in a given setting, for whether or not a rule is applied depends on the likelihood that the new plan specification it produces is the actual plan. This is evaluated using the heuristics described in the next section.

The notation

$$SBAW(X) = i \Rightarrow SBAW(Y)$$

indicates that if S believes A's plan contains X, then S may infer that A's plan also contains Y. The possible rules can be divided into three broad categories: those that concern actions, those that concern knowledge, and those that concern planning by others.

3.3.1. *The rules concerning actions*

These rules arise from the model of how plans are constructed. Throughout this section, S refers to the agent that is inferring the plan of another agent A.

$$SBAW(P) = i \Rightarrow SBAW(ACT) \quad \text{if } P \text{ is a precondition of action ACT.}$$
[Precondition-Action Rule]

Thus, if A wants to achieve some goal P, then A may want to execute an action ACT enabled by P.

$$SBAW(B) = i \Rightarrow SBAW(ACT) \quad \text{if } B \text{ is part of the body of ACT.}$$
[Body–Action Rule]

Thus, if A wants to execute an action B that is part of the execution of another action ACT, A may want to execute ACT.

$$SBAW(ACT) = i \Rightarrow SBAW(E) \quad \text{if } E \text{ is an effect of ACT.}$$
[Action–Effect Rule]

Simply, this says that if A wants to execute an action, then A wants the effects of that action.

$$SBAW(nW(ACT)) = i \Rightarrow SBAW(ACT) \quad \text{if } n \text{ is the agent of the intentional action ACT.}$$
[Want-Action Rule]

This rule is based on the want precondition for intentional actions. Intuitively, this says that if A wants n to want to do some action ACT, then A may want n to do ACT.

$XW(E) = c \Rightarrow XW(ACT)$ if E is an effect of ACT.   [Effect–Action Rule]

$XW(P) = c \Rightarrow XW(X \text{ KNOWIF } P)$.   [Know-Rule]

Thus, if X wants to achieve P but doesn't know whether P is true, X must find out whether P is ture.

When X constructs a plan involving the cooperation of another agent Y, X may depend on Y to do some plan construction as well. Thus, X might get Y to perform some action ACT by getting Y to have the goal of achieving ACT's effects. For example, assume that X wants to have a surprise birthday party for his roommate Y and needs to get Y out of the house. X says

'We need some beer.'

expecting Y to assume the goal of getting beer, and then construct a plan to get some. This involves leaving the house, the goal X had all along. Thus X has reasoned about Y's planning process. Crudely, this new planning inference rule can be described as

$XW(YW(\text{'leave house'})) = c \Rightarrow XW(YW(\text{'get beer'}))$

since

$XB(YW(\text{'get beer'})) = c \Rightarrow YW(\text{'leave house'})$.

Thus, if X wants Y to want to do ACT, he may achieve this by getting Y to want to achieve E, where Y's planning process will infer ACT as a way of achieving E. In general, we have the set of plan construction rules

$XW(YW(P)) = c \Rightarrow XW(YW(Q))$ if $XB(YW(Q) = c \Rightarrow YW(P))$.   [Nested-Planning Rule]

These rules are of interest when it is assumed that there is no deceit between the agents, and both realize that the planning by the hearer was intended. Thus, a king might say

'It's cold in here.'

to a servant, expecting the servant to plan to make the room warmer. But for the servant to understand the king's intention in the above example, he must recognize that the king's plan included planning by the servant. We can characterize inferences that construct these new plans as follows (reverting back to S as recognizer, A as the observed agent):

$SBAW(SW(P)) = i \Rightarrow SBAW(SW(Q))$ if $SBAB(SW(P) = c \Rightarrow SW(Q))$.   [The Recognizing Nested-Planning Rule]

3.3.2. The rules concerning knowledge

These inference rules indicate how goals of acquiring knowledge relate to goals and actions that use that knowledge. The first two rules reflect the fact that if A wants to know whether a proposition P is true, then it is possible that A wants to achieve a goal that requires P to be true (or requires P to be false). The third one indicates that A wants to know whether P is true in order to establish the identity of one of the terms in P.

$SBAW(A \text{ KNOWIF } P) = i \Rightarrow SBAW(P)$;   [Know-positive Rule]

$SBAW(A \text{ KNOWIF } P) = i \Rightarrow SBAW(\text{not} P)$;   [Know-negative Rule]

$SBAW(A \text{ KNOWIF } P(a)) = i \Rightarrow SBAW(A \text{ KNOWREF the } x : P(x))$.   [Know-value Rule]

Of course, in any plan alternative, at most one of these rules can be correct. The decision as to which of these is correct, or that none of these is correct, is the responsibility of the heuristic evaluation of the plans produced by applying them.

The final inference rule about knowledge concerns goals of finding the referents of descriptions. It suggests that such a goal indicates that A has another goal that involves the referent.

$SBAW(A \text{ KNOWREF the } x : D(x)) = i \Rightarrow SBAW(P(\text{the } x : D(x)))$ [Know-term Rule]

where $P(\text{the } x : D(x))$ is a goal or action involving the description (or its referent).

Because of the vagueness in the resulting goal, this rule does not produce reasonable plans unless a specific goal or action of form $P(D)$ already exists in the expectations.

3.3.3. The rules concerning planning by others

The plan construction process can be described in the same manner as the plan inference process; as a set of rules that describe possible constructions, and a set of heuristics to evaluate the resulting plans. The plan construction rules are simply the inverses of the plan inference rules. Some examples are given below. X is the name of the agent doing the plan construction.

$XW(ACT) = c \Rightarrow XW(P)$ if P is a precondition of ACT.   [Action–Precondition Rule]

Thus if X wants to execute ACT, X must ensure that its preconditions are ture.

$XW(ACT) = c \Rightarrow XW(B)$ if B is part of the body of ACT.   [Action–Body Rule]

3.4. Rating heuristics

As mentioned above, plan inferencing is accomplished by a search through a set of specifications of *partial plans* that consist of two parts. One part is constructed using the plan inference rules from the observed action (and called the *alternative*), and the other is constructed using the plan construction rules (and called the *expectation*). (In the implementation, a partial plans may contain many expectations sharing one common alternative.)

Each partial plan is assigned a rating, which is determined using heuristics described in this section, that reflects how likely it is to be part of the 'correct' plan. These heuristics are based solely on domain-independent relations between actions, their bodies, preconditions and effects. The initial partial plans are given a rating of 1. The heuristics are expressed here only in terms of increasing and decreasing the ratings. The actual formulas are very simple and given in Table 1 at the end of the section. This is organized in this way to emphasize the fact that while rating changes in the indicated direction are essential to our model, we feel that some variation is possible in the actual figures.

Finally, before we give the heuristics, we must make the distinction between actions that are currently executing, awaiting execution (pending), and have executed. In particular, the observed action is considered to be currently executing, and any action which contains an executing action in its body is also considered to be executing.

(A) *Action based heuristics*. Generally, one expects agents to construct plans that they believe they are able to execute, and they execute them only to achieve goals that are not presently true. This gives us two rules:

(H1) Decrease the rating of a partial plan if it contains an action whose preconditions are false at the time the action starts executing.

(H2) Decrease the rating of a partial plan if it contains a pending or executing action whose effects are true at the time that the action commences.

Heuristic (H1) states that if the action is presently executing, then the preconditions must not have been false when the action was initiated. On the other hand, if the action is pending, then its preconditions must be achieved within the plan or must be achievable by a *simple plan*. As a first approximation to a simple plan, we define it as a hypothesized plan consisting of a single action whose preconditions are already true.

(B) *Expectation-based heuristics*. These heuristics favor those partial plans whose alternatives seem most likely to merge with its expectation.

(H3) Increase the rating of a partial plan if it contains descriptions of objects and relations in its alternative that are *unifiable* with objects and relations in its expectation.

The term unifiable is used here in the sense of the unification algorithm found in resolution theorem provers (see [15]). Thus, if an alternative involves a train description, those expectations that involve a (compatible) train will be favored. Similarly, if an expectation involves a relation such as arrival time, an alternative seems more favorable if it also involves an arrival time relation.

(C) *Search based heuristics*. The remaining heuristics involve evaluating which partial plans should be considered next from a search efficiency point of view. These measure how specific the plan fragment is becoming. A couple of heuristics relate to events that produce important specializations to the plan, i.e., identifying referents of descriptions and identifying the speech act.

(H4) Increase the rating of a partial plan if the referent of one of its descriptions is uniquely identified. Decrease the rating if it contains a description that does not appear to have a possible referent.

(H5) Increase the rating of a partial plan if an intersection is found between its alternative and expectation, i.e., they contain the same action or goal.

The final heuristic favors alternatives that have produced inferences that are well rated enough to be applied.

(H6) Increase the rating of a partial plan each time an inference rule is applied.

A particular partial plan will be extended until either it splits sufficiently many times to lower its rating, or the rating heuristics start to disfavor it. Each partial plan has a *weight* that is used to calculate its rating. Heuristic (H3) adds a fixed factor of 5 for each similarity found. (The actual value 5 has no effect on the search except possibly for roundoff considerations in the rating calculation.) All other heuristics affect the weight by a multiplicative constant.

TABLE 1. The multiplicative factors for the heuristics

Heuristic	Description	Factor
(H1)	Preconditions false	0.5
(H2)	Effects true	0.5
(H4)	Referent identified	1.5
(H4)	Referent impossible	0.2
(H5)	Intersection found	1.5
(H6)	Inference rule applied	1.25

TABLE 2. The rating of tasks relative to the rating (R) of their partial plan

Task	Rating Formula
Infer	$0.75 * R$
Expand	$0.75 * R * f(n)$ where $f(n) = 1.25/n$, where n is the number of new partial plans to be created by the Expand
Identify	R
Accept	R

The total weight of all the partial plans is used in calculating each plan's rating. The rating of a plan P is simply the percentage of the total weight that plan P has. The actual values of the multiplicative factors are provided in Table 1.

3.5. The control of plan inferencing

As mentioned previously, partial plans are modified and refined by a set of programs (*tasks*) that are attached to them. When a task is *suggested*, it is given a rating that is strongly dependent on the partial plan that it is to manipulate and is placed on a priority list according to this rating. The top rated task is always selected for execution and removed from the list. This section describes the various types of tasks.

It is important for search efficiency considerations that there be extensive interactions between the expectations and alternatives. The information in an expectation may specify constraints on an alternative that restricts what possible inferences could be made from it, and vice versa. For instance, if both the expectation and alternative refer to a train, the trains are assumed to be identical (unless they contradict).

The initial set of partial plans consists of all pairings of an alternative containing only the observed action and one of the original expectations. To allow for the possibility of an utterance that does not fit an expectation, a partial plan is also constructed with a null expectation.

The actual tasks that perform the plan inferencing can be divided into three classes: those that specify the structure of the plans, those that identify objects on the plans, and those that control the search.

(A) *The plan specification tasks.* The plan specification tasks make additions to a plan hypothesis according to the inference rules discussed above. Alternatives are expanded using the plan inference rules and expectations are expanded using the planning rules. There are many occasions when mutually exclusive rules can be made. In such cases, copies of the partial plan are made and one rule is applied in each. When such a split occurs, the rating of the partial plan is divided between its successors.

This is performed by two tasks: *Infer* and *Expand*. *Infer* examines a local area of a plan and suggests possible inference rules that apply. *Expand* actually applies these rules to modify the partial plan. The processing is divided to allow explicit control of the 'fan-out' of the search: when an *Expand* is suggested from an *Infer*, its rating is determined by the rating of the partial plan it concerns, plus an estimate of the number of splits it will make. The greater the number of splits, the lower the rating (see Table 2). The relation between these two is set so that the copying (i.e., the splitting) will not be done until the newly

created partial plans would be sufficiently well-rated to produce tasks that are competitive on the agenda.

(B) *The Identify task.* The plan being inferred will usually contain many descriptions of objects whose referents must be identified. Some of these descriptions were introduced by the inferences. For an example of the second type, say in applying the precondition–action rule, there is a parameter in the action definition that is not part of the precondition. Then this parameter will not be specified when the action is introduced into the plan, although there may be constraints on its referent imposed in the action definition.

Likewise, existing descriptions may acquire additional constraints as the inferences are made. An action introduced into a hypothesis may specify constraints on one of the parameters in the plan that unified with one of its parameters.

Thus new descriptions may be introduced and old descriptions may be further specified as the inferences are made. Each time such a change occurs, an *Identify* task is suggested that will attempt to find a referent.

Note that since some agent S is inferring another agent A's plan, all evaluation of descriptions must be done with respect to what S believes A believes. In general, if S believes that there is only one object that A believes could fit the constraints, then it is the referent. This is in fact not a sufficient condition, but will suit our purposes here. Perrault and Cohen [18] examine reference problems in detail.

Identification of referents may require the use of domain specific inferences. For example, in the train domain, there is a need for an inference rule that says, 'If a train is described without a time specification, then it is probably the next train that fits the description.' It remains a problem as to whether such a heuristic could be inferred from the general structure of plans, or whether it is truly domain specific.

Another effective filter on the obstacles involves considering which obstacles the hearer intended to communicate. In particular, the goals that (S believes) A believes S can achieve are most likely to have been intended by A. For example, in the train station setting, the clerk not only does not sell tickets, but he also believes that the patrons know this. As a consequence, although not having a ticket is an obstacle, in the plan of boarding a train, the clerk does not expect the patron to ask him for a ticket (because he can't provide one).

The above are useful strategies if S believes that both S and A agree on what the obstacles in the plan are. However, if S and A disagree on some issue, special obstacles occur that must be addressed. For example, if A thinks that state X already holds and is depending on X in his plan, but S believes X does not hold, then S is obliged to mention this fact to A. Otherwise, A's plan will fail and S will be considered as uncooperative. In the reverse case, if A thinks state X is not true, but S believes it in fact already holds, then S must tell A, for A will not execute his (valid) plan because he thinks it will not succeed.

There is one class of obstacle that is truly difficult to detect but should be considered. If there are two goals in a plan and one is just a step towards achieving the second, then the heuristics above will indicate that the first is the only obstacle. However, in some cases, achieving the second eliminates the need to ever (even temporarily) achieve the first. For example, if A and S are in a locked room and A asks S where the key to the door is, S might deduce the following goals:

'A know where key is' in order to 'Get the door open'.

If S opens the door himself, say by some means other than using the key, then the goal of knowing the key's location becomes irrelevant. However, detecting such situations is quite difficult and beyond the scope of the present work, for it may involve considering the speaker's plan to an arbitrary distance into the future with no well defined termination condition.

The algorithm used in the system involves testing every goal statement in the plan. Obstacles are selected using the following preferences:

(1) those goals that S and A disagree about whether they hold or not;
(2) those goals that are explicitly indicated as obstacles by the utterance, i.e., the inference path from the surface speech act to an expected goal includes the goal;
(3) those goals that are required to perform the actions that are partially enabled by the goals in class (2), but are not achieved in the plan; and
(4) those goals that are not 'preceded' by other goals in the partial ordering of obstacles, and are not achieved in the plan.

The algorithm produces a set of obstacles in the highest preference class that is not empty.

(C) *The search control tasks.* Most of the control mechanisms are built into the rating scheme and the plan inferencing monitor. For instance, every time an addition is made to an alternative, the expectations are examined for new similarities caused by the addition. This may cause a change in the ratings according to the expectation-based rating heuristics.

Some mechanism must terminate plan inferencing. This is done by the task *Accept*, which is suggested by the monitor whenever an intersection of alternative and an expectation seems possible because they contain unifiable specifications of a step (i.e., an action or goal) in the plan, or when the plan with the null expectation is rated twice as favorably as the other partial plans. *Accept* must decide whether to terminate the plan inferencing or not. At present, the termination condition is fairly simple: if the plan under consideration is rated twice as favorably as any other partial plan, it is accepted. This is implemented by suggesting a dummy task at half the present task's rating. This task will sit on the pending list until all better rated tasks have executed. When it comes to the top, if no other *Accepts* have been executed, the original alternative is identified as the speaker's plan and plan inference stops. If another *Accept* has executed, there is an ambiguity (see Section 6).

3.6. Obstacle detection

Once S has inferred the speaker's plan, the next step, if he is to be helpful, is to identify the obstacles in that plan.

An obstacle is any goal specification that is not initially true or achieved within the plan. Some obstacles involving knowledge are only implicitly in the plan. For example, if a proposition P is a goal in A's plan, and S believes that A does not know whether P holds, i.e., SB(A *not* KNOWIF P), then A KNOWIF P is an implicit obstacle. Similarly, if the plan involves a description, say 'the $x:D(x)$', that S believes A does not know the referent of, then 'A KNOWREF the $x:D(x)$' is an implicit obstacle. These implicit obstacles can be derived by applying the knowledge plan inference rules to each step in the plan. Problems arise from the fact that the entire plan of the speaker may not be inferred, as only enough of the plan to link the observed utterance to an expectation is generated by the plan inference. So there may be apparent obstacles according to the partial plan that would not be an obstacle in the complete plan. One strategy to eliminate some of these is to not consider obstacles that can be easily achieved by a simple plan by the speaker.

There are other techniques for eliminating possible obstacles. The obstacles can be partially ordered using the ordering constraints imposed by the plan relations. In such cases, S knows he must address any obstacles prior to a given obstacle 0 if he is to address 0. For example, if A is carrying groceries in his arms and needs to pass through two doors, it does no good for S to open the second door unless he also opens the first.

account is found in Perrault and Allen [16]. The INFORM speech act, which is typically realized as a declarative sentence, is defined as follows:

INFORM(speaker, hearer, *P*)
want-precondition: speaker want INFORM (speaker, hearer, *P*)
precondition: speaker KNOW *P*
effect: hearer KNOW *P*

For an agent A to sincerely inform an agent H that *P* is true, A must believe that *P* is true (the precondition), and he must intend to get H to know that *P* is true (the effect of a successful inform). Note that this action cannot succeed without the cooperation of the hearer, for only he can change his own beliefs.

In many cases, agents reason about inform acts to be performed (by others or themselves) where the information for the propositional content is not known at the time of planning. For example, A may plan for S to inform A whether *P* is true; A cannot plan for S to perform INFORM(S,A,*P*) since this assumes that *P* is true. Thus we need two other 'views' of the INFORM act: INFORMIF and INFORMREF: (standard want-preconditions are omitted):

INFORMIF(speaker, hearer, *P*)
precondition: speaker KNOWIF *P*
effect: hearer KNOWIF *P*

and

INFORMREF(speaker, hearer, description)
precondition: speaker KNOWREF description
effect: hearer KNOWREF description

One further speech act that we need models one agent requesting another agent to do some action:

REQUEST(speaker, hearer, action)
effect: hearer WANT (hearer DO action)

The following examples show typical realizations of these speech acts in English.

'The train leaves at 3' intended literally is an INFORM that the train leaves at 3.
'Open the door' intended literally is a REQUEST that the hearer open the door.
'Does the train leave at 3' intended literally is a REQUEST that the hearer inform the speaker whether (INFORMIF) the train leaves at 3.

For the time being, we will assume that all speech acts are realized in their literal form, and thus can be easily identified from the input utterance.

4. Examples of Helpful Responses

This section provides three examples of helpful responses that can be produced using the plan inference and obstacle detection processes. The first shows a simple response that provides more information than was explicitly requested. It is described in some detail to give an idea of the actual plan inference mechanisms in operation. The second examples considers a yes/no question and shows why extra information should be provided if the answer is negative. The third example shows how an appropriate answer may be given to a question that is an indirect speech act. This final example is only briefly sketched. A detailed account of indirect speech acts can be found in Perrault and Allen [16] or Allen [1].

Before the examples are presented, the train domain is specified (Section 4.1) and definitions are given for the speech acts (Section 4.2).

4.1. The train domain

The setting for the examples is the train station information booth, S is the system playing the role of the information clerk, and A is the patron at the station. The non-linguistic actions relevant to the simple train domain are:

BOARD(agent,train,station):SOURCE(train,station)
precondition: AT(agent, the x:DEPART.LOC(train,x),
 the x:DEPART.TIME(train,x))
effect: ONBOARD(agent,train)
MEET(agent,train,station):DEST(train,station)
precondition: AT(agent, the x:ARRIVE.LOC(train,x),
 the x:ARRIVE.TIME(train,x))
effect: MET(agent,train)

S's expectations are the partially instantiated plans formed from the following action instantiations with their preconditions and effects:

BOARD(A, ⟨train⟩, TORONTO)

MEET(A, ⟨train⟩, TORONTO)

where the angle brackets (⟨···⟩) indicate unspecified parameters in the expectations. At the start of processing, there are three partial plans each with a null alternative and each containing one of the BOARD, MEET, or NULL expectations. The first example shows that the number of expectations could be increased without greatly affecting the combinatorics of the search.

4.2. The speech act definitions

The speech act definitions provided here are very superficial. A more adequate

The BOARD plan (rated 62):

The expectation:

BOARD(A,train1, TORONTO)
| enable
AT(A, the x : DEPART.LOC(train1,x), the x :
DEPART.TIME(train1, x))

The alternative:

(1) REQUEST(A, S, INFORMREF(S, A, the (x : time):···)
| effect
v
DEPART.TIME(train1,x)))

where train1 = the (x : train):SOURCE(x,TORONTO) & DEST(x,WINDSOR)

(2) S WANT INFORMREF(S, A, the (x : time):···)

The MEET plan (rated 25):

The expectation:

MEET(A, train2, TORONTO)
| enable
AT(A, the x : ARRIVE.LOC(train2,x), the x :
ARRIVE.TIME(train2))

where train2 = the (x : train):DEST(x, TORONTO)

The alternative:

(1) REQUEST(A, S, INFORMREF(S, A, the (x : time):···)
---
v
DEPART.TIME(train1,x)))

(2) S WANT INFORMREF(S, A, the (x : train):DEST(x,WINDSOR)

where train1 = the (x : train):DEST(x,WINDSOR)

The null plan (rated 12) contains only the alternative as described above in the MEET plan.

Fig. 1. The initial part plans.

4.3. Example 1: Providing more information than requested

This is a very simple example to give an idea of the plan inference process in operation. It has been modified from the way the actual system runs so it can be described in terms of the simple view of partial plans as one expectation and one alternative.

Let the observed action be:

REQUEST(A, S, INFORMREF(S, A, the (x : *time*):
DEPART.TIME of ⟨train1⟩ is x)
where ⟨train1⟩ = the (x : train):DEST(x,WINDSOR)

Such an action could be constructed from an utterance such as

'When does the train to Windsor leave?'

The action specifies an action cluster consisting of a REQUEST to INFORMREF that is added to the plan alternative in each partial plan. The partial plans are then examined for similarities. Within the 'BOARD' plan, A, the train to Windsor and the DEPART.TIME relation are all found to be mentioned in both the alternative and expectation (giving the plan a weight of 20). The train descriptions in the alternative and expectation are merged to form a more complete description, i.e., both the source (TORONTO) and the destination (WINDSOR) are known. With the 'MEET' plan, only A is found to be similar (giving it a weight of 5). As a consequence, the BOARD plan is strongly favored. If there were other expectations, they would probably have little in common with the utterance, and so would start off poorly rated. The null expectation plan starts with a token weight of 5.

After this initial processing, the partial plans are as in Fig. 1.

The initial tasks suggested are:

(1) Identify the train in the 'BOARD' plan, rated 62 (since its description was modified).

(2) Infer from the REQUEST act cluster in the BOARD plan, rated 46.
(3) Identify the trains in the 'MEET' plan, rated 25.
(4) Infer from the REQUEST act cluster in the MEET plan, rated 19.
(5) Identify the train in the NULL plan, rated 12.
(6) Infer from the REQUEST act cluster in the NULL plan, rated 9.

Identifying the train in the BOARD plan. Identifying the train in the BOARD plan succeeds, the assumption being made that the next train leaving is the one intended unless the speaker says otherwise. This provides further evidence that the BOARD plan is the correct one, increasing the BOARD plan's rating to 71 (weight 37) at the expense of the other partial plan ratings.

The Infer and Expand cycle. The *Infer* task on the BOARD plan (now rated 53) is executed. Inferring from (2) in the BOARD plan, the effect of the

REQUEST finds only the want-action rule applicable. An *Expand* task is suggested (rated 53), which immediately executes, since it is the best rated task, adding the action

    (3) INFORMREF(S, A, the $(x:time):\cdots)$

Added in the action cluster with (3) is its effect

    (4) A KNOWREF the $(x:time):$DEPART.TIME(train1,x)

and another *Infer* task is suggested from (4). Since an inference has been applied, the BOARD plan's rating is increased (heuristic (H6)) to 75 (weight 46). This *Infer* and *Expand* cycle is executed again. The know-term rule finds a link between (4) and the DEPART.TIME relation in the precondition to the BOARD action expectation. The monitor notices this intersection between the alternative and the expectation (and boosts the rating by heuristic (H5)), to 82 (weight 69)), and suggests an *Accept* task (rated 82). This task terminates the plan inference for there are no other well-rated hypotheses.

S now performs the next step to help A, namely, find the obstacles in A's plan and select from them some goals to achieve. One obstacle is straightforward, A has explicitly indicated the goal of knowing the departure time of the train. However, S examines the plan further and finds the implicit obstacle that A needs to know the departure location. S accepts these goals as his own and plans to achieve each goal simply with an inform. When this plan is executed, output is produced that corresponds to the English utterances:

    'The train leaves at 1600'

    'The train leaves from gate 7'

An interesting problem remains as to how S could have planned to achieve both goals with a single utterance such as

    '1600 at gate 7'

How does one construct a plan to achieve multiple goals simultaneously?

4.4. Example 2: A yes/no question answered no

In this section we consider the question 'Does the Windsor train leave at 4?'.
The initial utterance is mapped into the action

    REQUEST(A, S, INFORMIF(S, A, LEAVE(train1,1600)))
    where train1 =
        the $(x:train):$PROPERTY of x is WINDSOR.

LEAVE is a predicate pattern that will match the predicates DEPART.TIME and DEPART.LOC. The inferences from this action will eventually produce the goal (using similar steps as in above example).

    A KNOWIF LEAVE(train1, 1600).
The possible knowledge-based rules suggest goals for A such as

    'A wants the train to leave at 4'   [know-positive]
    'A wants the train not to leave at 4'   [know-negative]
    'A wants to know what train leaves at 4'   [know-value]
    'A wants to know when the train leaves'   [know-value]

Only the latter goal leads to a reasonable plan; the know-term rule from it produces a connection to the third argument of the precondition to the BOARD action.

    AT(A, the $(x:loc):$DEPART.LOC(train1,x),
            the $(x:time):$DEPART.TIME(train1,x)).

Possible obstacles in this plan are found to be the explicitly mentioned goal of knowing whether the train leaves at 1600, plus the obstacles of knowing the departure time and location. For the sake of clarity, let us assume that the location is already known in this example. The obstacles remaining are

    A KNOWIF DEPART.TIME(train1,1600)

    A KNOWREF the $(x:time):$DEPART.TIME(train1,x).

If the answer to the original query were 'yes', then both these goals would be accomplished by answering the query as a yes/no question. But if the answer is 'no', only the first obstacle is achieved by the yes/no answer. The second obstacle accounts for the extra information.

This example reflects a general point. When a person asks about the truth of some proposition that happens to be false, he often is interested in a related, true proposition. The main problem is determining how to modify the original proposition to make it true. Our feeling is that, with respect to a given set of goals, the objects referred to by the terms in a proposition can usually be ordered by some criteria reflecting their importance in the plan. The more important the term, the less likely it is that it is what is wrong in the proposition. Two indicators or importance are

(1) at what level of abstraction the object (or term) was introduced into the plan, and

(2) what objects are defined in terms of other objects.

The second case occurred in the above example, the departure time was defined in terms of the train description, and so was the prime candidate to be wrong. This approach seems to be quite general. As an example, consider a 'co-operative' response cited by Kaplan [13].

(1a) 'Is John a senior?'

(1b) 'No, he's a junior.'

It makes little sense to consider an answer out of context. For instance, if I am a professor needing a senior to do some project for me, a more appropriate response to my query (1a) would be

'No, but Sam is'

This is because my goal of finding a senior is more important than John's status. If, on the other hand, my goal were to find out more about John, then the concept 'John' would be more important, hence response (1b) would be appropriate.

4.5. Example 3: An indirect speech act

Consider the plan that must be inferred in order to answer (1) with (2):

(1) A: Do you know when the Windsor train leaves?

(2) S: Yes, at 3:15.

The goal inferred from the literal interpretation is that

(3) A KNOWIF (S KNOWREF 'departure time').

Applying the know-positive rule, we obtain the goal

(4) S KNOWREF 'departure time'

which enables P to perform the action (precondition-action rule)

(5) INFORMREF (S,A, 'departure time')

to achieve the goal (action-effect rule)

(6) A KNOWREF 'departure time'

S's response (2) indicates that he believed that both (3) and (6) were obstacles that S could overcome.

However, sentences such as (1) are often uttered in a context where the literal goal is not an obstacle. For instance, A might already know the departure time, yet still utter (1). In such cases, A's goals are the same as though he had uttered the request

(7) When does the Windsor train leave?

Hence, (1) is often referred to as an *indirect speech act* [24].

Although the mechanisms already described are capable of answering such indirect acts correctly, they cannot distinguish between the two following cases:

(a) A said (1) merely expecting a yes/no answer, but S answered with the extra information in order to be helpful;

(b) A said (1) intending that S deduce his plan and realize that A really wants to know the departure time.

Theoretically, these are very different; (a) describes a yes/no question, while (b) describes an (indirect) request for the departure time. But the distinction is also important for practical reasons. For instance, assume S is not able to tell A the departure time for some reason. With interpretation (a), S can simply answer the question, whereas, with interpretation (b), S is obliged to give a reason for not answering with the departure time.

We have to reformulate our speech act definitions in order to handle such cases, as well as to bring our work in line with the philosophical views. We introduce a new set of *surface speech acts* that correspond directly to the form of the utterance. For example, an imperative mood sentence is always a surface request act (S.REQUEST) whether it is interpreted directly or not. An indicative mood sentence is always an S.INFORM act, which is defined simply as

S.INFORM(speaker, hearer, proposition)
effect: hearer BELIEVE
        speaker WANT
            hearer KNOW proposition.

The speech acts at the other level are defined by intentions of the speaker and correspond to the *illocutionary acts* in Austin [2]. These acts are executed by executing some surface act. An essential condition for the performance of an illocutionary act is that the hearer recognize that the speaker intended to perform that act. This condition could be represented as a precondition, but we represent it as a goal to achieve in the body of the act in order to allow hierarchical planning. So the definition of the illocutionary act INFORM is

INFORM(speaker, hearer, prop)
precondition: speaker KNOW prop
effect: hearer KNOW prop
body: hearer BELIEVE
        speaker WANT
            hearer KNOW prop

This is simply the old definition of INFORM with the added condition concerning the recognition of intention. The other speech act definitions are augmented similarly. Notice that the effect of the S.INFORM act matches the body of the INFORM act. This indicates that indicative sentences are a way of achieving an S.INFORM. It is important, however, that it is not the only way.

The second modification to the model is to allow the plan inference rules to be performed with the added condition that the hearer believes the speaker

in order to board the train such as having a ticket, are not relevant because (the information agent believes) the patron believes the information agent does not handle tickets.

Using these mechanisms, we say that a speaker can perform a speech act ACT by performing another speech act ACT' if he intends that the hearer recognize that ACT' was performed and also that he intended the hearer to infer that the effects of ACT should also be achieved.

Details of this analysis of speech acts can be found in [16].

5. Analyzing Sentence Fragments

As we have seen, plan knowledge is necessary to generate appropriate responses even to syntactically complete sentences. The mood of a sentence, given by the subject, auxiliaries, and main verb, is critical to speech act identification. With sentence fragments such as 'the Montreal train', even the mood of the sentence may not be known, thus making even the surface speech act identification difficult. However, the plan inference process described so far is already powerful enough to handle many ambiguities of this type.

Even in sentence fragments, there remain syntactic clues to the surface speech act. Words such as 'when', 'what', 'which', etc., signal a S.REQUEST to INFORMREF. The use of the word 'please' in a sentence marks it as a request [21]. Thus, an utterance such as 'the door, please' could not be interpreted as an inform. Of course, there will often be cases where a mood ambiguity cannot be resolved at the syntactic level, and in these cases, the alternatives will be enumerated and each case will become a plan alternative. Since the number of surface speech acts is small, this approach is reasonable.

The less explicit the utterance, the more important the expectations become, for they provide the missing details of the speaker's actions and plans. Typically, a speaker has a specific speech act and propositional content that he wants to convey to the hearer. In addition, the speaker may have some idea of what the hearer expects him to say. Any fragment that singles out the correct expectation from the rest is acceptable to communicate the speech act and proposition. The fragment must also distinguish what particular subgoals in the expectation are being pursued. In restrictive domains, such as the train station, identifying the fundamental goal (i.e. boarding, meeting) is sufficient to identify the subgoals desired. In such settings, very brief fragments can be used successfully. For example,

'The train to Windsor?'

successfully identifies the fundamental goal of boarding the train. Of the possible subgoals that are involved in this plan, only knowing the departure time and location are relevant (expected), for this is what the information agent believes that the patron believes he can help achieve. Other subgoals required

5.1. An example of a sentence fragment

As usual, the setting is the train station, A is a patron and S is the information agent.

A: The train to Windsor?

The syntactic analysis suggests two interpretations:

(5.1) S.REQUEST(A, S, INFORMREF(S, A, the x : PROPERTY of train1 is x))

(5.2) S.REQUEST(A, S, INFORMIF(S, A, PROPERTY involving train1))

train1 = the $(x : \text{train}) :$ PROPERTY(TO) of x is WINDSOR. The use of PROPERTY(TO) here is a cheat; it stands for an arbitrary property (involving a train and a city in this case) that is realizable at the syntactic level using the preposition 'to'. The problem we are avoiding here is that the actual relation referred to here can only be obtained from the expectations, which are not considered until the sentence is parsed and the 'literal' meaning constructed. It is not a simple matter to change this though, for arbitrarily many inferences may have to be made from the literal meaning before the correct relation can be identified. We have resorted to encoding such syntactic restrictions in special patterns that match the appropriate relation names.

This example will consider only the first interpretation. Details on how the second is eliminated can be found in [1]. The described train is incompatible with the MEET expectation, leaving only the BOARD expectation as the reasonable interpretation. The inferences made from interpretation (5.1) lead to the goal:

A KNOWREF the x : PROPERTY of 'train' is x

To identify the actual predicate indicated by the predicate pattern PROPERTY, the BOARD expectation is inspected for matches.

There are two relevant properties of trains, the DEPART.TIME and the DEPART.LOC. Assuming that S believes that A knows neither of the values for these relations, both can be considered obstacles and be used to form a response corresponding to

'It leaves at 3:15 from gate 7.'

In another setting, S's response to the same fragment might be quite different. If the train station had only one platform, he would only respond with the departure time because he would believe that A knows the location already. To be completely different, if S were the ticket agent he would interpret the fragment as a request for a ticket (since this is what S expects, i.e. what S believes that A believes S is able to do), and might reply

'$10.50 please'

This approach covers a quite different range of sentence fragments than any other method described in the literature. The most common method, which could be called the 'semantic approach', accepts fragments in the form of full syntactic units, such as noun phrases, and uses the fragments to build a partial 'semantic' representation that is then matched into the representation of the previous utterance [9, 3, 10]. If this match is successful, the representation of the utterance is constructed out of the previous utterance's structure with the newly specified parts replacing the parts that they matched. This method is limited to those fragments that depend on the structure of the previous utterance for their interpretation. As shown in the train dialogues, there are many fragments used where this is not the case.

Our approach is suited for cases where the mere mention of a concept or phrase is suggestive enough to convey a thought/wish. These instances typically have little syntactic relation to previous utterances, and in fact can occur when there is no previous utterance. In many ways, the matching techniques are similar to the 'semantic approach', but the goals are very different. The goal of the semantic approach is to find a structural similarity with the previous utterance. The goal of this work is to identify the plan and goals of the speaker. A syntactically complete utterance is never considered or constructed for it has no effect on the understanding of the utterance.

6. Clarification Dialogues

Many dialogue situations do not follow a simple question–answer ordering. Variations often arise because of misunderstandings or ambiguity in previous utterances. A plan-based model can account for some of these variations in a straightforward manner.

Consider the following exchange between a patron and the clerk at the train station.

(6.1) When is the Windsor train?

(6.2) To Windsor?

(6.3) Yes.

(6.4) 3:15.

Why is (6.2) a reasonable response to (6.1)? According to our model, the clerk is unable to deduce the plan of the patron from (6.1). In particular, two plans

seem possible:
(a) the patron wants to meet a train arriving from Windsor;
(b) the patron wants to board a train departing for Windsor.

Utterance (6.2) is intended to resolve this ambiguity by establishing a fact that will distinguish between the two plans.

To consider the model in detail, it is necessary to examine the relationship between the plan inference process and plan construction. The plan inference process can be viewed as an abstract action (the PI action), which is performed by a set of subactions (the PI tasks). Typically, the PI action is not expanded in a plan, its execution is in effect 'compiled' and runs without requiring any explicit reasoning about its execution. However, when difficulties arise, say one of the PI tasks cannot execute successfully unless some obstacle (in the sense used throughout) is overcome, the agent will want to explicitly reason about the PI process. The goal that is the obstacle is explicitly added to the plan as part of the body of the PI action. Hence, planning can be initiated on it in the standard manner, and once the goal is achieved, the 'compiled' PI execution can resume.

For example, consider a train setting in which there is a train scheduled to leave for Winsor at the same time as one is scheduled to arrive from Windsor. S is executing the PI action in an effort to help the patron who asks:

A: When is the Windsor train?

which is analyzed as

S.REQUEST(A, S, INFORMREF(S, A,
    the $(x:time)$:PROPERTY of train1 is x))

train1 = the $(x:train)$:PROPERTY of x is WINDSOR

This action can be interpreted with respect to either the BOARD or MEET expectation. With the BOARD expectation, the train leaves TORONTO for WINDSOR and A is interested in its departure time. With the MEET expectation, the train arrives in TORONTO from WINDSOR and A is interested in its arrival time. S has no reason to favor one reading over the other, so both alternatives are investigated to a uniform extent and eventually suggestions are made for both that they be accepted as the interpretation.

The Accept task detects that there is an ambiguity and, after allowing the PI process to continue to try and disambiguate to no avail, creates a goal to disambiguate the utterance. For instance, assuming that the Accept task that involves the BOARD interpretation is selected first by the search mechanism, the goal created is

S KNOWIF (A WANT (BOARD(A, train1, TORONTO)))

To achieve this goal, S creates a plan to (i) ask A whether BOARDing the train is his goal, and (ii) receive back A's response. So S executes the action

S.REQUEST(S, A,
    INFORMIF(A, S, AW(BOARD(A, train1, TORONTO))

producing an utterance corresponding to

'Do you want to go to Windsor?'

and then waits for a response. The response is handled by the PI action (nested inside the body of the original PI action) with the expectation that A will execute the action

INFORMIF(A, S, AW(BOARD(A, train1, TORONTO)))

Because this expectation is so explicit, even very brief responses with little content, such as a simple 'yes' or 'no', can be understood easily.

Assuming that the answer is 'yes', S then knows that A wants to BOARD the train. This knowledge achieves the goal specified by the *Accept* task and allows it to arrive at a (successful) decision. The BOARD interpretation is accepted and the PI process terminates. The obstacle detection and the planning of a response then continue as usual, eventually causing S to execute a response corresponding to an utterance such as

'It leaves at 3:15.'

6.1. Detecting dialogue failures

Above we considered dialogues initiated by S when he could not understand A's utterance. In this section we consider the opposite case, where A initiates a dialogue because of a failure to understand on his part, or to make a correction of a misunderstanding by S. We have not examined these dialogues in detail as yet, but preliminary analysis indicates that many such utterances can be detected by using what S believes about A's plan and beliefs. Consider some examples that demonstrate the types of failure that could occur after the exchange

(6.5) A: 'When is the Windsor train?'

(6.6) B: 'It leaves at 3:15.'

At this point S believes that A now knows the train leaves at 3:15, and therefore that his stated goal of knowing the departure time is accomplished. This interpretation depends on the fact that S believes A wants to board the train to Windsor (rather than meet a train from Windsor).

A can indicate a failure by stating a goal that S believes has already been achieved in SBAW. For example, the continuation

(6.7) A: 'When?'

indicates that the goal of knowing the departure time is not yet accomplished.

To model how S could recover from such a situation we would require a detailed analysis of the possible reasons for failure, e.g. faulty communication, disbelief of answer, etc.

Other utterances indicate that S made an error in inferring A's plan. These involve A denying that he wants a goal in the inferred plan. Some examples are

(6.8) A: 'I don't want to travel to Windsor.'

(6.9) A: 'No, I want to meet the Windsor train!'

These contradict the fundamental goals that S inferred for A and indicate that S should re-analyse the previous utterance after making appropriate modifications to his expectations about A's plan. Utterance (6.9) presents a difficulty: S must be able to realize what goals are mutually exclusive. In the train domain, the fundamental goals are assumed to be mutually exclusive, but in a more complex domain, such knowledge is non-trivial.

7. Future Directions

We have argued that much linguistic behavior can be explained by assuming a plan based model of language. Our specification of the actual plan inference process, however, is not detailed enough to allow it to perform in more complex domains than the train station. Considerable work needs to be done to specify more control heuristics. Large domains probably require the introduction of domain specific inference rules. We have begun to lay the groundwork by specifying characteristics that any plan inference mechanism would need in any domain.

Along with more complex domains will come more complex dialogues; in particular, dialogues that continue for prolonged periods of time and cover a wide range of topics. We have hinted in the section on clarification dialogues that some dialogue structure can be explained by the mechanisms of the plan based model itself. It will be interesting to see how much dialogue structure can be accounted for this way, and how much must be specifically introduced as 'conventional rules'.

One of the major problems in larger domains is the effective management of the large number of potential expectations. The progress of a dialogue relies on old expectations, but more importantly, establishes new ones. Grosz [9] shows how task structure can limit these expectations. Topic shifts and the initial dialogue expectations remain unaccounted for.

Perhaps the most difficult problems lie in specifying the relation between the syntactic processing and the rest of the system. We saw in the section on sentence fragments a case where the syntactic information concerning the preposition 'to' could not be used until the advanced stages of the plan inference process. The major issue here concerns what we were working with before the relation indicated by the phrase 'the train to Windsor' was identified.

8. Conclusions

The plan based model of language described here can be used to explain a wide range of linguistic behavior that has been problematic to previous approaches. In particular, we have addressed the problem of:

— generating responses that convey more information than was explicitly requested;
— generating appropriate responses to utterances that consist solely of a sentence fragment;
— generating clarification subdialogues when the intent of a previous utterance is not clear.

The common thread through the solutions to these problems and to the understanding of indirect speech acts is the inferring of the speaker's plans and the detection of obstacles in these plans.

We have explicitly indicated the role that context plays in language understanding: only those plans that are reasonable in the current context (as determined by the rating heuristics) are potential analyses of the intention of the speaker. A large part of the context is the hearer's model of the speaker's beliefs and goals. If the context is sufficiently restrictive to uniquely determine the speaker's plan, then appropriate responses can be generated for a wide range of utterances often considered problematic. If the context is not sufficiently restrictive, the model generates goals that lead to clarification dialogues.

One final concern is with the fundamental tools of our approach: our logics of belief, want and action are only minimally adequate. This has been acceptable so far, for our emphasis has been on demonstrating the usefulness of such notions in a model of language. Now that we have a better idea of how these tools can be used, it is time to return to them and attempt a better formulation.

REFERENCES

1. Allen, J.F., A plan-based approach to speech act recognition, Thesis, Department of Computer Science, University of Toronto (1979).
2. Austin, J.L., *How To Do Things With Words* (Oxford University Press, New York, 1962).
3. Burton, R.R., Semantic grammar: An engineering technique for constructing natural language understanding systems, BBN Rep. 3453 (1976).
4. Bruce, B.C., Plans and social action, in: R. Spiro, B. Bruce and W. Brewer, Eds., *Theoretical Issues in Reading Comprehension* (Lawrence Erlbaum, Hillsdale, NJ, to appear).
5. Cohen, P.R., On knowing what to say: Planning speech acts, Techn. Rep. 118, Department of Computer Science, University of Toronto (January 1978).
6. Cole, P. and Morgan, J.L., Eds., *Syntax and Semantics, Vol. 3: Speech Acts.* (Academic Press, New York, 1975).
7. Ernst, G. and Newell, A., *GPS: A Case Study in Generality and Problem Solving* (Academic Press, New York, 1969).
8. Fikes, R.E. and Nilsson, N.J. STRIPS: A new approach to the application of theorem proving to problem solving, *Artificial Intelligence* 2 (1971) 189–205.
9. Grosz, B.G., The representation and use of focus in dialog understanding, Dissertation, University of California at Berkeley (1977).
10. Hendrix, G., Human engineering for applied natural language processing, in: *Proceedings of the 5th International Joint Conference on Artificial Intelligence*, Cambridge, MA (1977).
11. Hintikka, J., *Knowledge and Belief* (Cornell University Press, Ithaca, NY, 1963).
12. Horrigan, M.K., Modelling Simple Dialogs. TR 108, Department of Computer Science, University of Toronto (1977).
13. Kaplan, S.J., Indirect responses to loaded questions, in: *Proceedings of the 2nd Conference on Theoretical Issues in Natural Language Processing*, Champaign-Urbana (1978).
14. Lehnert, W., Human and computational question answering, *Cognitive Sci.* 1 (1) (1977).
15. Nilsson, N.J., Problem solving methods in artificial intelligence (McGraw-Hill, New York, 1971).
16. Perrault, C.R. and Allen, J.F., *A Plan-Based Analysis of Indirect Speech Acts, American Journal of Computational Linguistics*, to appear.
17. Perrault, C.R. Allen, J.F. and Cohen, P.R., Speech acts as a basis for understanding dialogue coherence, in: *Proceedings of 2nd Conference on Theoretical Issues in Natural Language Processing*, Champaign-Urbana (1978).
18. Perrault, C.R. and Cohen, P.R., Inaccurate reference, in: A.K. Joshi, I.A. Sag and B.L. Webber, Eds., *Computational Aspects of Linguistic Structure and Dialogue Setting* (Cambridge University Press, New York, to appear).
19. Sacerdoti, E.D., Planning in a hierarchy of abstraction spaces, in: *Proceedings of 3rd International Joint Conference on Artificial Intelligence*, Stanford, CA (1973).
20. Sacerdoti, E.D., The nonlinear nature of plans, in: *Proceedings of 4th International Joint Conference on Artificial Intelligence*, Tbilisi, USSR (1975).
21. Sadock, J.M., *Toward a Linguistic Theory of Speech Acts* (Academic Press, New York, 1974).
22. Schiffer, S.R., *Meaning* (Oxford University Press, London, 1972).
23. Schmidt, C.F., Sridharan, N.S. and Goodson, J.L., The plan recognition problem: An intersection of artificial intelligence and psychology, *Artificial Intelligence* 10 (1) (1979).
24. Searle, J.R., Indirect speech acts, in: P. Cole and J.L. Morgan, Eds., *Syntax and Semantics, Vol. 3: Speech Acts* (Academic Press, New York, 1975).
25. Wilensky, R., Understanding goal-based stories, Thesis, Yale University (1978).

Received 9 November 1979; revised version received 7 May 1980

Points:
A Theory of the Structure of Stories in Memory

Robert Wilensky
University of California, Berkeley

INTRODUCTION

Story comprehension has recently received a great deal of attention from cognitive psychologists and researchers in artificial intelligence (for example, see Bower, 1976; Kintsch & van Dijk, 1975; Mandler & Johnson, 1977; Rumelhart, 1975; and Charniak, 1972; Cullingford, 1978; Schank & Abelson, 1977; and Wilensky, 1978). However, the complaint has been made repeatedly that most of the work on story understanding has little to do with stories. Rather, what is being studied both in AI and psychology are coherent texts. The difference is that not all coherent texts are stories, and that a theory of stories per se is still lacking.

One ostensible exception to this criticism is a formalism known as a story grammar. Using a grammar to try to capture the notion of "storyness" seems first to have occurred to Rumelhart (1975). Since then, the notion of story grammars has been expanded theoretically by a number of researchers, and even used as the basis for a number of empirical studies (e.g., Mandler & Johnson, 1977; Stein & Glenn, 1979; and Thorndyke, 1977).

Unfortunately, the story-grammar concept is lacking in a number of ways that make it inadequate for its intended purpose. The chief problem is that story grammars purport to capture the idea of what a story is by trying to express the structure of a story text. My claim is that a theory of stories must be much more concerned with the content of a text than with its form. Moreover, when story grammars are examined closely, most of the story structure they aim to capture dissolves away, and they end up saying little more than that story is a coherent set of sentences.

A detailed critique of story grammars is found in Black and Wilensky (1979),

and is not repeated here. This chapter is concerned with a theory of stories I have been developing based on text content. I call it a theory of *story points*. The theory is by no means complete. Nevertheless, some parts of it are well formed enough to be presented, perhaps even refuted. In any case, the piece of the theory described here should provide a picture of what I believe a theory of stories needs to look like.

One of the salient features of this theory is its complexity. In spite of its incompleteness, the theory presented here necessitates detail. Although it may be edifying to think that a theory of story representation should be simple and elegant, perhaps denotable by a few dozen story-grammar rules, it may turn out that this is not the case. One of the major goals of this chapter is to demonstrate the inherent complexity of the problem.

BACKGROUND

Most of the work that goes under the label of story understanding is really concerned with coherent text comprehension. Understanding such a text involves finding the implicit connections between story sentences, and thus much of the work in this area is concerned with the problem of inference generation. In particular, the problem of representing knowledge needed for understanding has dominated this work, and involves notions of scripts and plans (Schank & Abelson, 1977), schemata (Rumelhart, 1976), and frames (Minsky, 1974).

Most of this work on knowledge representation and organization is very basic. It has application not only to understanding narratives, but to other forms of cognitive processing, even nonlinguistic ones. This is precisely its failure as a theory of stories. For example, consider the following "story," which is used by Schank (1975) to demonstrate his script idea:

1. John went to a restaurant. The hostess seated John. The hostess gave John a menu. John ordered a lobster. He was served quickly. He left a large tip. He left the restaurant.

The point of this example is to demonstrate that knowledge about what typically goes on at a restaurant is needed to infer implicit events, such as John's eating the lobster. The notion of a script is introduced as a way to organize such knowledge.

Schank is careful to point out, however, that such neatly delineated event sequences do not necessarily constitute stories. The problem is that they are just too dull. No one will even be heard telling story 1 to anyone else because there is little reason to believe anyone would have any reason to express it, nor is anyone likely to be amused upon hearing it.

The ability to understand utterances like 1 seems to underlie all kinds of language processing. In the most general terms, such examples simply illustrate that people bring their experience to bear in understanding a new experience. However, the existence of such knowledge structures and their unquestionable utility in making a text coherent has little to do with the notion of a story. A story is not merely an arbitrary coherent sequence of events.

Thus it is extremely unlikely that anything conforming to the content of a mundane knowledge structure will constitute a story. Moreover, as was well understood at the time of their inception, rigid knowledge structures such as scripts are inadequate for much of the inference processing necessary to establish the coherence of a nonconforming text. Script-like knowledge structures reflect the repeated experience of mundane situations, and are directly useful for comprehending these situations. However, they are less clearly useful for processing situations that do not conform entirely to stereotypes.

Explanation-Driven Understanding

Understanding a situation that is not necessarily stereotypical requires a good deal more reasoning than script-based processing can provide. In particular, script-based understanding tends to be rather inflexible. If an event occurs that is not in the script being used to understand a text, it cannot be handled by a script-based mechanism. For example, consider the following story:

2. John wanted to impress Mary. He asked Fred if he could borrow his Mercedes for the evening.

It is unlikely that most understanders process this example using a script. To claim as much would amount to saying that whenever a reader hears that someone wants to impress a date, the reader then expects to hear of the person's asking a friend to loan him a fancy car. Such a script that includes all alternatives is an impossibility, because we can always dream up new variations not already packaged into it.

Even if it were possible to include an infinitude of variation within a script, doing so would defeat the whole purpose behind the script concept. Namely, scripts are supposed to limit the inference process by specifying events that are usually found in mundane sequences. Clearly, scripts would no longer be mundane or inference constraining if they explicitly delineated all possible alternatives.

Thus even though the utility of script processing is inherently limited to understanding those event sequences that conform to a rigid structure, human readers seem to have no trouble connecting up the events in texts like 2. Because people can easily understand texts with some novel variation in them, a more general theory of text coherence is needed to describe the processing of these situations.

I call the general process of finding the connection between events in a text *explanation-driven understanding*. That is, much of the processing that a reader needs to do to understand a text revolves around the task of finding explanations for the events of the text. Because stories are generally about people, explanations usually take on an intentional flavor. The reader must find explanations for people's behavior, and these explanations must be stated in terms of a person's plans and goals.

For example, in story 2, John's asking Fred to loan him a car is explained by inferring that this action is part of a plan for a goal of getting possession of a vehicle. This goal is explained by inferring that it is instrumental to John's plan for impressing his date, which is to pick her up in an expensive car. This plan in turn is explained by John's desire to impress his date. which is explicitly stated in the story.

Thus a reader of 2 must compute a series of explanatory inferences in order to understand John's action. Each of these inferences explains some element of John's behavior—why he has a goal, why he chooses a plan, or why he performs an action. In each case, the type of explanation that can be found is a function of the type of element that is to be explained. An action is explained if it is found to be part of a plan its actor is pursuing. A plan is explained if it can be used to achieve some goal of its planner. A goal can be explained if it is instrumental to some plan, or if there is some known state that gives rise to the goal. These states, called *themes* by Schank and Abelson (1977) include drives like being hungry or being tired, being in a social role, or having an attitude towards someone or something.

The types of intentional explanations are summarized in Fig. 13.1.

Fig. 13.1 describes the constituents of an explanation. But it does not describe how an explanation is constructed for a sentence in a text. Previously, I stated that a theory more general than script processing is needed because of the inability of that theory to cope with nonstereotypical texts. I offered explanation-driven understanding as this more general notion. The major consideration that this theory must take into account is how the context of a text can influence the explanation that is constructed without making the inference process too rigid to accommodate reasonable variations.

For example, suppose a reader were given the following short texts:

3. A bum on the street came over to John. He told John he wanted some money.

Item to explain	Explanation
Event	Plan of which event is a part
Plan	Goal at which plan is directed
Goal	Theme that gave rise to the goal, or plan to which goal is instrumental

FIG. 13.1. Types of intentional explanations.

4. A man came over to John and pulled out a gun. He told John he wanted some money.

5. John's son came over to John. He told John he wanted some money.

In these cases, the second sentence of each text has a different interpretation, even though the sentences are the same. The interpretations are different because they are influenced by the context set up by the first sentence. However, the context does not totally determine the interpretation, as it would in a script-governed situation. For example, in 5, John's son coming over to him does not determine that his son would ask him for something, although it does bias the subsequent processing. The problem is how to allow the context to influence the interpretation while still allowing enough latitude to explain unexpected events.

The general scheme by which explanation-driven understanding accomplishes this is as follows: When an explanation is needed for some element in a text (that is, an event, a plan, or a goal), the items already known to the reader are checked first to see if any of them constitute an explanation. If so, then an explanation has been found. If not, then the reader consults his or her general world knowledge to see if any usual explanation for this item is available. If so, the reader tentatively infers that explanation, and tries to find an explanation for that explanation. The process is iterated until either it fails or an explanation has been constructed that relates the input to previous parts of the story.

This process is summarized in Fig. 13.2.

As an example, consider the processing of the following story, taken from Schank and Abelson (1977):

6. Willa was hungry. She picked up the Michelin guide.

Upon reading the first sentence, the reader learns that Willa has the goal of satisfying her hunger. It is unlikely that this sentence will invoke any script that

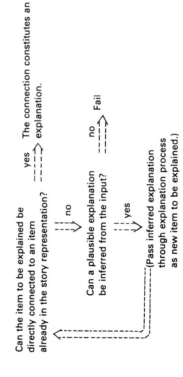

Can the item to be explained be directly connected to an item already in the story representation?

Can a plausible explanation be inferred from the input?   yes ----> The connection constitutes an explanation.

no ----> Fail

yes

(Pass inferred explanation through explanation process as new item to be explained.)

FIG. 13.2.   The process of finding an explanation for an event.

the next sentence will conform to. Thus the reader must explain why Willa picked up the Michelin guide. Because no plan of Willa's is known to the reader, one must be inferred. Picking up something is usually a plan for possessing that thing, so Willa must have had the goal of possessing the Michelin guide. This goal must then be explained. Again, there is no ready explanation from the story. However, having possession of something that has a function is usually instrumental to performing that function. Thus the reader infers that Willa was going to read the guide. Reading is often a plan for finding out some information, and because the Michelin guide is a source of information about the location of restaurants, the reader infers that Willa must have had the goal of knowing the location of a restaurant. Having this goal can be explained by the fact that knowing the location of a place is often instrumental to going there. Being at a restaurant is in turn instrumental to eating at the restaurant. Eating at a restaurant is a plan to satisfy hunger, which is known to be one of Willa's goals. Thus an explanation for Willa's action has been found, and the inference process can cease.

This notion of explanation and the explanation process just described are incomplete in a number of ways. These are discussed later on. For the time being, I assume this to be an accurate model of a reader, and call the theory of explanation underlying it *naive* explanation.

PAM

The naive-explanation model has been used as the basis of a computer program called PAM (Plan Applier Mechanism) that can understand a number of short texts. PAM has knowledge about the kinds of plans and goals people have, and uses this knowledge in accordance with the previously described algorithm to find explanations for the events described in a text. PAM can then paraphrase the text from the points of view of the different characters in the text, as well as answer questions about the text.

For example, PAM can read the Michelin guide story just given, answer a number of questions about the story, and produce a paraphrase from Willa's point of view[1]:

Input text:

WILLA WAS HUNGRY.
SHE PICKED UP THE MICHELIN GUIDE
AND GOT INTO HER CAR.

[1]The author is primarily responsible for the version of PAM referred to in this chapter. Michael Lebowitz assisted in the later stages of the development of this program. The question-answering component was written by Janet Kolodner, and the paraphrase mechanism developed by Rod McGuire.

Input: WHY DID WILLA PICK UP THE MICHELIN GUIDE?
Output: BECAUSE WILLA WANTED TO KNOW WHERE A RESTAURANT WAS.

Input: WHY DID WILLA GET INTO HER CAR?
Output: WHAT WERE THE CONSEQUENCES OF WILLA PICKING UP
Input: THE MICHELIN GUIDE?
Output: THIS ENABLED WILLA TO READ THE MICHELIN GUIDE.

Output:
THE STORY FROM WILLA'S POINT OF VIEW:
I WANTED TO GET SOMETHING TO EAT, BUT I DIDN'T KNOW WHERE A RESTAURANT WAS. SO I PICKED UP THE MICHELIN GUIDE, AND I GOT INTO MY CAR.

The question answering and paraphrasing demonstrate some of the inferences that PAM made as it was reading the story. For example, PAM had to infer that Willa was going to eat at a restaurant, that she picked up the guide in order to read it, that she read the guide to find out where a restaurant was, and that she wanted to know where one was so she could get there. PAM makes these inferences in the course of finding an explanation for Willa's action of picking up the Michelin.

PAM can understand a number of texts that are considerably more complicated than this one. In fact, some of the texts that PAM can process go beyond the model of naive explanation just given. These capabilities of the program are examined later on. For the present, references to PAM are essentially references to the part of PAM that implements the naive-explanation algorithm. I refer to this program (and the associated algorithm) as ''naive PAM.''

POINTS

PAM is a somewhat more flexible text understander than previous systems because it does not require that a text conform to a rigid structure. However, many of the same criticisms applicable to previous systems insofar as stories are concerned are just as applicable to naive PAM. PAM's ''stories'' may be less stereotyped than the texts other systems can process, but they are hardly any more reasonable. A relatively large number of inferences have to be generated to understand the Michelin guide example, but it is no more of a story than texts that conform to scripts. Once again, it is hard to imagine someone not in the field of natural-language processing bothering to tell this story to someone else.

Although goals and plans are important elements of real stories, the pursuit of a goal does not in and of itself make for good reading. For example, contrast the following two paragraphs:

7. John loved Mary. He asked her to marry him. She agreed, and soon after they were wed. They were very happy.

8. John loved Mary. He asked her to marry him. She agreed, and soon after they were wed. Then one day John met Sue, a new employee in his office, and fell in love with her.

Paragraph 7 is typical of the simple goal-based stories that can be understood by naive PAM: A character has a goal (wanting to marry Mary) generated by a theme (being in love with her) and pursues a plan (asking her) that results in the goals being fulfilled. Although 7 is cogent enough, it is not a good story. Most readers would be surprised, for example, if they were promised a story and were given paragraph 7. In spite of its coherent intentional structure, paragraph 7 seems much more like the setting of a story than a story itself.

In contrast, paragraph 8 seems much more promising. Although paragraph 8 does not appear to be a complete story either, it seems to get further along than paragraph 7 before it terminates. Here the reader probably expects the story to be continued with an elaboration of John's situation. In the case of story 7, it is much harder to guess what the story will be about.

What makes paragraph 8 more of a story than paragraph 7 is that paragraph 8 has a *point* to it. By a point I mean some element that invokes the interest of a reader. The point of a story is what the story seems to be about. For example, paragraph 7 seems not to be about anything, whereas paragraph 8 is about a married person who falls in love with someone else.

Stories are structured around what they are about. That is, the whole idea of a story is to convey some points to the reader. This content has its own structure, and it largely determines the structure of the story text. The main goal of the story reader is to determine the points of a story, and to structure what has been read in terms of these points.

Points Structure Memory

The conceptual representation of a story in memory is structured according to its point content. At one level, a story is conceptualized as a point or set of points that comprise the important content of the text. Beneath this level is a description of the actual events that comprise these points. Beneath this is a level of events that connect up with the major events of the story but do not in themselves constitute points. Finally, there is a level consisting of the actual words of the sentences used to express these ideas.

These levels of representation are hierarchically based on how a story appears to be structured in memory. Suppose someone were asked to read a real story of substantial length, and were then asked to retell it. Most likely, not all details of the story will be equally easy to retrieve. The exact words and form of sentences in the text become hard to recall very quickly after reading. Likewise, events and even whole episodes may be forgotten even though the reader still has an excellent idea of what the story is about. One way to account for this behavior is to assume that the story is structured in the reader's memory so that the first thing accessible to the reader is the story's point structure. The reader must then look through this structure to access specific events, and so on. At the very bottom are the literal words, which accounts for the relative difficulty in retrieving them.

For example, a reasonable summary of paragraph 8 might be that John and Mary were happily married, and then John fell in love with another woman. This summary constitutes the point of his story segment, and thereby, the highest level in the memory representation. Note that this summary neglects to mention that John asked Mary to marry him, or that they got married soon after she agreed. These facts are not pertinent to the point of the story, and therefore exist on a lower level of representation. They can be omitted without seriously damaging the overall structure of the story, but John's involvement with another woman cannot be.

It may be possible that the structure of a particular story deviates from this form in some way. For example, if a specific word or sentence formulation happened to be particularly poignant (that is, function as a point) in a given story, then this poignancy would be reflected by a reference to this item at a high level in the representation. However, such cases appear to be the exception to the description of the levels just given.

Points Affect Processing

Because readers are presumably looking for a point as a text is being read, points often give rise to expectations, or predictions, about what will happen next in the text. For example, a reader of paragraph 7 does not find any point; if the story ends here, the reader's expectations are not met and the reader is surprised by the story's pointlessness.

A reader of story 8, on the other hand, interprets the text as the beginning of a point poignant episode. The reader of this story will also be surprised if the story terminates here. However, this time, the surprise is due to a point's being introduced but not completed. That is, the reader would be equally confused if the story were to continue and introduce other points without continuing to expand on the point already introduced. Without some predefined notion of point, a reader could not judge that one of these stories is better formed than the other.

Thus a reader must possess some notion of what constitutes a point in order to recognize one's occurrence in a story. This knowledge about story points also plays a predictive role as well, because once a point has been referred to by a text, a reader must determine how the subsequent episodes in the story relate to that point.

Although text comprehension is normally influenced by points, it is possible that points play a greater role in special kinds of processing. For example, skimming is a text-comprehension technique in which the desire to process

poignant information dominates the reader's concerns. We are not concerned with this sort of processing here, but with the role points play in ordinary comprehension. For a model of skimming as a goal-directed understanding process, see DeJong (1979).

Kinds Of Points

By definition. some points are liable to be idiosyncratic. However, enough points seem to be sufficiently pervasive to allow people to agree that the same point structure exists in the same texts. My goal here is to isolate these common points.

Because points are those things that motivate the telling of a story in the first place, two kinds of points can be distinguished. An *external point* is some goal a story teller might have in telling a story. An *internal* or *content point* is some part of the story itself that generates interest.

External points are what is usually meant when someone refers to "the point of a story." External points include goals like convincing a listener of something (e.g., morals, propaganda), impressing someone, achieving an emotional reaction, or being informative. The external point of a text will certainly have some impact on the content and structure of the text. However, we do not pursue the nature of these kinds of points further. Instead, we concentrate on those points that legitimize a text from within. The term point is generally used to refer to content points when we can do so unambiguously.

Many of the content points in stories have to do with *human dramatic situation*. A human dramatic situation is a sequence of goal-related events that contains some *problem* for a character. For example, in story 8, the problem is that John loves someone, but is already married to somebody else. Dramatic situations usually also involve *solution* components that describe how a problem is resolved.

The notion that problems form the basis of many stories was noted by a number of people, in particular, by Rumelhart (1976). Rumelhart uses the notion of a problem in his theory to refer to any situation involving a goal. The concept of a problem introduced here differs from Rumelhart's in that it requires a character to have trouble fulfilling a goal. For example, Rumelhart's theory does not make the distinction between story 7 and 8, although one story clearly appears to be more interesting than the other.

The following text contains an actual story that illustrates some of the problem and solution components of a point that one is likely to encounter in a simple story:

9.

The Xeron Story

When John graduated college, he went job hunting and found a job with the Xenon corporation. John was well liked, and was soon promoted to an important position.

occurring dramatic situations include those in which there are a number of characters with opposing goals, and in which an individual has goals that are in conflict with one another. These goal relationships are defined as follows:

1. Goal conflict. A goal conflict is a situation in which one character has several goals such that the fulfillment of one goal will preclude the fulfillment of the others. For example, consider the following story:

10. John wanted to watch the football game but he had a paper due the next day. John decided to watch the football game. John failed Civics.

Story 10 is an instance of a goal conflict because John's goal of watching the football game may interfere with his other goal of writing his paper.

2. Goal competition. Goal competition refers to those situations in which several characters' goals may interfere with one another. For example, the following story contains an instance of goal competition:

11. John told Bill he would break his arm if Bill didn't give John his bicycle. Bill got on the bicycle and rode away.

John's goal of possessing Bill's bicycle cannot be fulfilled along with Bill's goal of preserving possession of the bicycle. If Bill succeeded in preserving possession of the bicycle, then John would have failed to fulfill his goal.

3. Goal subsumption: Goal subsumption refers to a situation in which a character's plan is to achieve a state that will make it easier for a character to fulfill a recurring goal. For example, the following story contains an instance of goal subsumption:

12. John was tired of frequenting the local singles' bars. He decided to get married.

In this story, John decides to get married in order to make it easier to achieve the goals he had been achieving previously by going to a singles' bar.

These particular goal relationships were chosen because the situations to which they give rise account for a large class of story problems. That is, dramatic situations involve a difficulty in fulfilling a goal, and these difficulties often arise due to goal interrelations. In particular, goal relationships can give rise to these problems:

1. Goal conflict. If a character is unable to resolve a goal conflict, then one of that character's goals may fail. Thus goal failure due to goal conflict and attempts to resolve goal conflict both provide interesting story situations.

2. Goal competition. As with goal conflict, the existence of competitive goals implies that some character may have trouble fulfilling a goal. Interesting stories

One day at work, John got into an argument with his boss. John's boss fired John and gave his job to John's assistant.

John had difficulty finding another job. Eventually, he could no longer keep up the payments on his car, and was forced to give it up. He also had to sell his house, and move into a small apartment.

Then one day, John saw a man lying in the street. Apparently, the man had been hit by a car and abandoned. John called a doctor and the man's life was saved. When he was well, the man called John and told him he was in fact an extremely wealthy man, and wanted to reward John by giving him a million dollars.

John was overjoyed. He bought himself a huge mansion and an expensive car, and lived out the rest of his life in the lap of luxury.

A reasonable summary of story 9 is the following:

John lost his job and came upon hard times. Then one day John helped a rich person in need, and was rewarded with enough money to last him a lifetime.

This summary conforms to a description of the story's point. In this case, the problem component is the situation that exists after John loses his job and is unable to maintain his lifestyle. The solution component of this point is the fortuitous circumstance that enabled John to once again attain his desired goals.

In order to read this story and produce the summary just-described, a reader must recognize this problem and solution as the poignant part of the text. To do so, a reader must be capable of realizing that a character is experiencing some difficulty. Unfortunately, stories in which goals are problematic are generally more complicated than the stories naive PAM is capable of handling. For example, the problem in the Xenon story involves John's running into a number of difficulties based on his inability to find work. This situation does not conform to any of the simple plan–goal type sequences that we used earlier to explain a character's behavior. That is, none of the planning structures mentioned so far can adequately describe the relationship between not having a job and having to move into a smaller apartment, or why getting a large sum of money should alleviate this problem. The details of this inadequacy are discussed later. In general, the problem is that to understand how a reader is capable of understanding the interesting dramatic situations that occur in real stories, or to build a computer system that can simulate this process, a more powerful theoretical apparatus in needed.

In particular, the problematic dramatic situations that initiate story points usually involve some complex interactions between goals that can create difficulties for a character. For example, in the Xenon story, John's problem involves a relationship between his recurring goals of living in a certain style, and the state of having a job. In addition to situations involving recurring goals, frequently

Story 13 at first appears to be similar to the stories that naive PAM can understand. That is, the story appears to have a goal and an action directed towards fulfilling it. However, this story actually involves planning for a recurring goal rather than the achievement of an individual one. To understand story 13, a reader must realize that John is using a plan that is directed not at a single goal, but at a multitude of potential goals. The goal in story 13 is not to be in Hartford, but to make it easier to achieve this goal each time it arises. Owning a car makes it easier to deal with being in Hartford each day because a means of transportation is then always available. In other words, owning a car *subsumes* John's recurring goal of being in Hartford every day.

Doing something that makes it easier to fulfill a recurring goal is called *goal subsumption*. Goal subsumption is a very general planning strategy that allows a planner to pursue many goals at once. Goal subsumption is possible whenever a character can anticipate having a number of goals, and there exists a set of plans for these goals all of which share a common precondition. If the character can then fulfill this precondition so that it holds each time he or she pursues one of these goals, then that person will be saved the work of fulfilling that precondition as each individual goal arises.

A story-understanding system must be able to recognize that a situation involves goal subsumption in order to explain the behavior of a character acting in that situation. For example, consider the following story:

14. John was feeling lonely every evening. He decided to get married.

Here, John has the recurring goal of alleviating loneliness. Being married to someone subsumes this goal by providing John with a companion. To alleviate loneliness, a person can use a plan that entails social interactions with other people. Social interaction has the precondition that a person be available with whom one can interact. Marrying someone assures that the person married will be available for social interactions over a fairly long period of time. Thus an understander could explain John's behavior in story 14 only if it inferred that the state of being married to someone fulfills the "have-companion" precondition of the "social-interaction" plan for the recurring goal of alleviating loneliness.

A goal subsumption relationship contains the following components:

1. A set of goals that arise repeatedly. In story 14, this was the set of recurring "enjoy-company" goals.
2. A set of plans for these goals, all of which share a common precondition. In story 14, the plan of SOCIAL INTERACTION was applicable to each goal.
3. A state that meets the common precondition and that endures over a time span that encompasses repeated instances of the set of goals. For example, being married to someone fulfills the "have-willing-companion" precondition of the SOCIAL INTEREACTION plan by providing a person who is obliged to interact with the planner.

therefore exist involving goal failure due to goal competition, struggles against the plans of other characters, and attempts at easing the competition.

3. Goal subsumption. Goal subsumption gives rise to dramatic situations when a subsumption state is terminated. For example, if John is happily married to Mary, and then Mary leaves him, all the goals subsumed by their relationship may now be problematic: John may become lonely, and miss his social interactions with Mary, for instance. Closely related to problems based on goal subsumption are those caused by the elimination of normal physical states. For example, becoming very depressed or losing a bodily function can give rist to the inability to fulfill recurring goals, and can therefore generate some interesting problems.

The next section contains a description of these relationships and the situations to which they give rise. A more detailed analysis of these relationships can be found in Wilensky, 1978.

GOAL RELATIONSHIPS AND THEIR SITUATIONS

Goal relationships are important in understanding what storeis are about because multiple goals can cause interesting difficulties for a character. However, the importance of goal relationships extends beyond the domain of stories per se. Much of the reasoning that people must do in their daily activities amounts to handling situations in which there are complex goal interactions. Thus understanding these situations, as well as the ability to act in them, involves knowledge of goal relationships.

In the case of text understanding. knowledge about goal relationships is crucial for making the necessary inferences to connect the sentences of a text. That is, some events in a text can only be explained if they are interpreted as responses to situations involving interacting goals. Thus the theory of naive explanation proposed earlier must be modified to take these more complicated situations into account.

Although knowledge about goal relationships is needed for the inferential process, a detailed examination of the use of this knowledge to make inferences is beyond the scope of this discussion. Instead, we are concerned with the kinds of goal interactions that can exist, and with the situations to which they give rise.

Goal Subsumption

Goal subsumption involves planning for a number of goals at once. For example, consider the following story:

13. John got a job in Harford, where he would have to commute to work each day. He asked Fred if he would sell him his car.

A number of goal subsumption states are important in their own right. For example, ownership of a functional object is a subsumption state (functional objects are objects that are normally used for particular plans). Ownership subsumes those goals for which the object is normally used. Thus a planner who realizes that he or she will have the need to repeatedly execute a plan involving a functional object may subsume that goal by obtaining ownership of the object.

Another common class of subsumption states involves *streams*. A stream is a continual source of a consumable substance. For example, a river would be an instance of a physical stream supplying water. A job is an example of a social stream that supplies the employee with money. If a planner can establish some means of tapping a stream of some consumable, then he or she can subsume those goals for which the consumable may be used.

Being in a social relationship is another important class of subsumption states, because relationships usually impose a set of obligations upon a person. An obligation is a belief held by a person's society that a person must act in a particular way in certain social situations. For example, being married implies that each person in the marriage relationship is obligated to help fulfill the other's emotional, sexual, and economic needs. Thus goals involving these needs are subsumed by the marriage relationship.

Goal-Subsumption Situations

Goal subsumption can give rise to story situations in which the subsumption state is either brought about or terminated:

1. Goal-subsumption state establishment. The simplest situation involving goal subsumption occurs when a character decides to subsume a recurring goal. The character then proceeds to select and execute a plan for this goal. An example of this situation is the following story:

15. John needed more money to pay his rent. He decided to take another job.

John has the goal of establishing a subsumption state to make it easier to pay the rent each month, and decides to achieve it by getting a job and establishing a stream of money.

2. Goal-subsumption state termination. A subsumption state may be ended, by either chance or volition, and leave a character with a problematic recurring goal. Thus goal-subsumption termination is a problem component of a story point. An example of goal-subsumption termination occurs in the following story:

16. John and Mary were happy children. During the war, their parents were killed, and they both became street urchins.

Being a child in a family normally subsumes a number of goals for the children. When such a state terminates, then, as it did in 16, the reader can infer that the recurring goals the state subsumed now must be dealt with individually. For

example, in 16 the reader might infer that the children did not get enough attention and had trouble getting enough to eat. In addition, the reader might infer that the children wanted to subsume these goals again, and that they would be eager to be adopted by new, loving foster parents.

The goal-subsumption termination problem is a point component in many stories. For example, in the Xenon story in the previous section, John's loss of his job is an instance of a problem caused by the termination of a subsumption state. John could no longer support himself as he had been while the subsumption state existed, and thus the individual subsumed goals all became problematic.

Goal Conflict

A goal conflict occurs when a character has several goals that interfere with one another. For example, consider following the stories:

17. John wanted to watch the Monday night football game. He also had a paper due the next day. That night, John watched the football game. John failed Civics.

18. John wanted to marry Mary. He also wanted to marry Sue. John took Mary out and proposed to her. She agreed. Later, John called Sue and told her he wouldn't be seeing her anymore.

The explanation for John's actions in each of these stories cannot be stated in terms of a single goal. There is no intrinsic reason that watching a football game should cause one to fail a course, as it did in story 17. Nor can one explain why someone would no longer want to see somebody he was considering marrying, as in story 18.

However, explanations for these events are readily available if the interrelationship between the goals present in each story is considered. The interrelationship of the goals in story 17 and those in story 18 is called *goal conflict*. A goal conflict is a situation with the following two components:

1. A character has several goals at the same time.
2. The fulfillment of one of these goals interferes with the fulfillment of the others.

For example, in story 17, John has the goal of watching the football game, and the goal of writing a paper. These goals are in conflict because there may not be enough time to fulfill both of them. In story 18, John's two goals are "being married to Mary" and "being married to Sue." These goals conflict because a person cannot be married to two different people at the same time.

To understand a story in which a goal conflict explains a character's behavior, a reader must first recognize that the goal conflict exists. Recognizing a goal conflict presumes that the reader knows about the various ways goals can conflict with one another, and can use this knowledge to determine whether the goals being compared are in conflict.

Thus a story understander must have knowledge about how goals can conflict. This section contains a classification of goal conflicts that is based upon similarities between the kinds of knowledge required to spot each goal-conflict situation. An understander supplied with this knowledge could use it to determine if a goal-conflict situation exists between the goals it is comparing.

Kinds of Goal Conflicts

I found it necessary to distinguish three classes of goal conflicts. They are as follows:

1. Resource limitations. Two goals can conflict if the plans chosen for those goals share a common resource, and there is an insufficient quantity of that resource available for both plans.

2. Mutually exclusive states. Two goals can also be in conflict if the states they are intended to achieve are incompatible.

3. Causing a preservation goal. A character may have a goal conflict if executing the plan for a goal will cause a preservation goal to come into being.

Each of these goal-conflict situations is now briefly described.

Resource Limitations. A *resource* is something needed to perform a plan. For example, the following stories contain goal conflicts caused by a shortage of resources:

19. John wanted to watch the football game, but he had a paper due the next day.

20. John had just enough money to buy either a television or a stereo, but he wanted to have both.

21. John wanted to cook linguine and hamburgers on his camp stove, but the stove had only one burner.

In story 19, watching the football game and writing a paper each require a certain amount of time, and the amount of time available to John is limited because the paper is due in a day. In story 20, John has two goals that are ordinarily achieved by purchasing the desired items. Purchasing an object requires that one has money, but the amount of money needed for both these goals exceeds John's means. John's plans for the goals in story 21 each require the use of a burner, but John has only enough resources to cook one item at a time. These examples serve to illustrate the way in which resource shortages can exist. There appear to be two major classes of resource shortages, those depending on time, and those depending on consumable functional objects:

1. Time. Because the execution of plans for all goals requires some amount of time, it is possible to have goal conflicts based on a time shortage. However, the following other factors must also be present:

1. The plans for the goals must have time constraints on them. These constraints require that a plan be executed at or before a certain time in order to be successful.

2. The time constraints must force the execution of the plans to overlap.

3. The planner must be incapable of executing both plans at once.

This last factor requires that either the execution of both plans is beyond the planner's abilities, or that the plans require the use of a functional object beyond what is available. For example, in story 19, the reader infers the existence of a goal conflict because he or she assumes John could not effectively write a paper and watch a television game at the same time. In story 21, the limitation of John's stove contributes to the conflict. Thus conflicts that appear to be based on time shortages are actually based on both time and limited abilities or functional objects.

2. Consumable objects. A consumable object is a functional object whose use to the planner is reduced after it performs its function. For example, food is a consumable object because it can no longer be used after it has been eaten. Money is a consumable object because it can no longer be used by a planner after someone buys something with it.

If the plans for a set of goals all require the use of a consumable object, then a goal conflict can result if the planner does not have a sufficient quantity of that consumable. For example, consider story 20. Money is a consumable object, and so John would need as much money as is required by the plans for both his goals. Because the total amount of money required is greater than the amount of money John possesses, John has a goal conflict.

Mutually Exclusive States. Goals can conflict due to resource limitations because of the nature of the plans chosen for each goal. In addition, goals can conflict because achieving them would require mutually exclusive states to come into existence. For example, consider the following stories:

22. John wanted to marry Mary, but he also wanted to marry Sue.

23. John wanted to have a regular job. He also wanted to collect unemployment insurance.

Mutually exclusive states can threaten to come into existence if the goals themselves constitute exclusive states, as in story 22. In addition, a goal state may be excluded by a state that is a consequence or a precondition of a plan for another goal. This is the case in 23, where not having a job was a precondition for one of John's goals, but excluded the other.

Exclusion can be of two forms, logical or social. Logically exclusive states are contradictory, such as being in two different places at once. Socially exclusive states cannot exist at the same time because of cultural prohibitions. For example, John's goals in 22 are socially exclusive because society prohibits a person from being married to two people at once.

Causing A Preservation Goal. Consider the following stories:

24. John wanted to go to the football game, but it was raining outside.
25. John wanted to take the night off, but he thought his boss would fire him.

Unlike most of the other stories discussed in this chapter, these stories only have one explicit goal in them. Nevertheless, these stories constitute goal conflicts. In story 24, if John goes to the football game, then he would become damp, an undesirable state of affairs. In story 25, taking the night off would result in John's being fired, another unpleasant state. A character who anticipates being in such a state will have the preservation goal of preventing that state from happening. Thus stories 24 and 25 have goal conflicts between their explicit goals and the unstated preservation goal that would be violated by plans for the explicit goals.

Goal-Conflict Situations

Goal conflicts create difficulties for characters and therefore form the basis for dramatic situations. These situations are usually continued in one of three ways. These are now outlined briefly.

1. Goal Abandonment. The character can simply opt for one of the conflicting goals and try to fulfill it, abandoning the other goals. For example, consider the following story:

26. John was in a hurry to make an important business meeting. On the way over, he ran into an old girlfriend. She invited him up to her apartment and John accepted. The next day, John's boss told him he was fired.

Here the reader infers that John has a goal conflict, and that he failed to fulfill his boss's order because he pursued another goal.

2. Goal-Conflict Resolution. The character can try to resolve the conflict. If successful, then the character can try to fulfill all his or her goals. If the character fails to resolve the conflict, then he or she can still opt for one goal via goal abandonment. The following stories are examples of attempts at resolution:

27. John was in a hurry to make an important business meeting. On the way over, he ran into an old girlfriend, who invited John up to her apartment. John called his boss and asked if the meeting could be postponed.
28. John had just enough money to buy either a stereo or a television, but he only had enough money for one. John decided to take a second job.

3. Spontaneous Goal-Conflict Resolution. The conflict may be resolved by some event precipitated by a character other than the planner. For example, consider the following:

29. John had just enough money to buy either a stereo or a television, but he only had enough money for one. Then John learned he inherited a small fortune.

Here John's inheritance eliminates one of the causes of John's goal conflict, making that conflict evaporate.

Spontaneous resolutions of this sort constitute an important class of solution point components. This class is discussed further later on.

Goal Competition

Just as the goals of a single character can interfere with one another, the goals of different characters can interact to create problems. Such an interaction is called goal competition. Goals can compete with one another more or less in the same manner as goals of an individual can conflict. That is, there is good competition due to resource limitation, mutually exclusive states, and causing preservation goals.

However, the situations that may arise out of goal competition are considerably different. For example, consider the following instance of goal competition:

30. John told Mary he wanted to watch the football game. Mary said that she wanted to watch the Bolshoi ballet.

John's goal competes with Mary's because both require use of the same functional object, the television set, at the same time and for different purposes. This story might be continued as follows:

31. Mary put on channel 3. John got out the lawnmower.
32. John got the old black and white TV out of the attic.
33. Mary put on channel 3. John punched Mary in the mouth and put on the ball game.
34. John told Mary he would take her out to the ballet if she would watch the football game with him.
35. Mary put on channel 3. She found out that the ballet was postponed until later that day.

These stories illustrate several goal-competition situations. They are classified as follows:

1. Independent goal pursuit. In this situation, each character tries to fulfill his or her own goal, ignoring the fact that the goal competes with someone else's. Some characters may succeed, causing other characters' goals to fail. Story 31 was an instance of independent-goal pursuit. Mary performed the actions necessary to achieve her own goal without regard to John's. As a result, Mary fulfilled her goal and John abandoned his.

2. Antiplanning. Antiplanning, the most complex goal-competition situation, occurs when a character's actions reflect the presence of other characters' goals. For example, in story 33, John tries to fulfill his own goal by eliminating the competition. In story 34, John tries to persuade Mary to abandon her goal. In an antiplanning situation, a character forms a plan to prevent another character from fulfilling a goal, or to prevent someone from interfering with his or her own plan. For example, John's punching Mary in story 33 can be understood as an antiplan to eliminate Mary from competing with John for the use of the television.

3. Easing the competition. Instead of pursuing their own goals, one or more of the characters with competing goals can try to ease the competition. For example, in story 32 John got another television so that both programs could be viewed at the same time. This action removed one of the conditions that caused the goals to compete, so that both characters could then pursue their respective goals independently.

4. External competition removal. The goal competition can be eliminated by some action not taken by one of the story characters. This was the case in story 35, in which the time of Mary's program had been changed. Her program no longer was to be aired concurrently with John's. This removed a condition that caused the competition, enabling independent goal pursuit.

Goal-Relationship Points

So far we have seen a number of problem and solution point components. Goal-subsumption termination is a problem point component because previously subsumed goals become problematic. Goal conflict and goal competition endanger the fulfillment of some of a character's goals, and therefore generate dramatic impact. On the solution side, we encountered goal-conflict resolution, goal abandonment, antiplanning, and spontaneous conflict and competition removal.

It was also noted that knowledge about goal relationships is needed on the purely inferential level. That is, some of the inferences that must be made to understand a story are based on knowledge about how goals can interact and what situations these interactions can give rise to. Independent of any concept of "storyness," goal relationships form the basis for coherence of more complex natural-language texts.

1. Subsumption state
2. Cause of termination event
3. Problem-state description
   1. Unfilled precondition
   2. Problematic goals (optional)
   3. New goal (optional)
   4. Emotional reactions (optional)

FIG. 13.3. Goal-subsumption termination prototype.

However, it is the problematic nature of these elements that gives them their poignancy, but the dramatic nature of goal relationships is not independent of how these relationships are presented in a text. For example, consider the following misuse of a potentially poignant goal relationship:

36. John lost his job. Then he found another one.

This is not a particularly dramatic situation. It contains an instance of goal-subsumption termination (John's losing his job) and a solution to the problem this creates (John's getting a new job). Nevertheless, 36 hardly qualifies as an interesting story.

The problem with 36 is that it contains the cause of the problem, the termination of a subsumption state, but no description of the problem itself. Contrast 36 with the Xenon story at the beginning of this chapter. John also lost his job in that story, but the situation contains considerably more dramatic impact. In the Xenon story, we are given a description of John's problem state. He could no longer afford all the things he had become used to. Because the problem is spelled out in this story, its dramatic effect is more fully realized.

Thus the mere appearance of a problematic goal relationship does not guarantee its poignancy. The problem must appear in a form that spells out its implications. I call these forms point prototypes. A point prototype is a kind of distillation of the dramatic element of which the goal relationship is a part. The Xenon story serves to illustrate such a prototype.

The problem for John in the Xenon story is caused by a goal subsumption state's terminating. To make this poignant, the story uses the problem point

1. Subsumption state—John has a job.
2. Cause of termination event—Boss fires John.
3. Problem-state description
   1. Unfilled precondition—John does not have enough money.
   2. Problematic goals—Maintaining a car and house.
   3. New goal—John wants to resubsume these goals.
   4. Emotional reactions—not explicitly stated.

FIG. 13.4. Instantiated goal-subsumption termination prototype.

1. Undesired state
2. Fortuitous event
   1. Incidental action
   2. Fortuitous outcome
3. New state
4. State-consequence description

FIG. 13.5.   Fortuitous circumstance solution prototype.

prototype in Fig. 13.3 to fill out the circumstances of the problem. That is, to use subsumption-state termination as a problem point, first state the subsumption state, then follow it by the cause of termination event. Then describe the problem state itself by listing the goals that are no longer subsumed; the goal of reestablishing a subsumption state may also be stated, along with any emotional reactions to the termination.

In the Xenon story, this prototype is instantiated, as is shown in Fig. 13.4.

This problem is resolved in the story through a very common solution point called Fortuitous Circumstances. Spontaneous goal-conflict resolution and external goal-competition removal are also instances of this solution point component, which is shown in Fig. 13.5.

This solution prototype is instantiated in the Xenon story, as Fig. 13.6 shows.

Some More Solution-Point Components

Solution-point components and their associated prototypes have not yet been analyzed in as much detail as the problem components have been. However, in addition to the fortuitous circumstances solution just given, several other solution-point components seem to be common.

One such solution is called "More Desperate Measures." In this point, a problem is attacked by some plan that is normally not considered because of its high risk. Because of this risk, More Desperate Measures solutions tend to generate goal conflicts for their user, thus creating another problem-point component for the story. For example, in the Xenon story, after John loses his job, he might decide to rob a bank to get some money. Robbery entails a number of risks, so the use of this plan would create a goal conflict for John between his desire to have money and to preserve his well being. This point would then be developed further in the story.

1. Undesired state—John does not have enough money.
2. Fortuitous event
   1. Incidental action—John saves rich man.
   2. Fortuitous outcome—Rich man gives John money.
3. New state—John is rich.
4. State-consequence description—John is happy and gets lots of possessions.

FIG. 13.6.   Instantiated fortuitous circumstance solution prototype.

Overcoming a Limitation is another solution point seen with some frequency. This case can occur when a problem is based in part on a character's inability or lack of courage. Here the character attempts to overcome a personal limitation or see the error of his ways in order to resolve a problematic situation. For example, a typical fairy-tale type plot might involve a character who is a subject of ridicule by peers because of cowardess, and then overcomes this cowardess in some heroic deed.

CURRENT STATE OF PAM

As was mentioned previously, the naive-explanation algorithm fails to find proper explanations for events in stories involving goal relationships. However, a more sophisticated version of PAM has been implemented that possesses knowledge about the goal relationships described earlier. PAM can use this knowledge to infer explanations for events in many complex goal-relationship situations. Although PAM now has this extended inferential capability, it still does not possess knowledge that these situations are poignant. That is, PAM does not yet organize the representation of the story hierarchically to reflect its point structure.

The following are some examples of PAM input–output of stories involving goal relationships:

Goal Subsumption:

Input text:

JOHN AND MARY WERE MARRIED.
THEN ONE DAY, JOHN WAS KILLED IN A CAR ACCIDENT.
MARY HAD TO GET A JOB.

Input: WHY DID MARY NEED EMPLOYMENT?
Output: JOHN DIED AND SO SHE NEEDED A SOURCE OF MONEY.

PAM infers that John's death terminates a subsumption state for Mary, and that she may seek to replace it. PAM uses this inference to infer the explanation behind Mary's goal of getting a job.

Goal Conflict:

Input text:

JOHN WANTED TO WATCH THE FOOTBALL GAME,
BUT HE HAD A PAPER DUE THE NEXT DAY.
JOHN WATCHED THE FOOTBALL GAME.
JOHN FAILED CIVICS.

Input: WHY DID JOHN FAIL A COURSE IN CIVICS?
Output: HE FAILED TO HAND IN AN ASSIGNMENT.

This is a goal-conflict story discussed earlier. PAM recognized the conflict and infers that John did not hand in an assignment because he pursued another goal that was in conflict with this task.

Input texts:

WILMA WANTED TO HAVE AN ABORTION.
WILMA WAS CATHOLIC.
WILMA CONVERTED FROM CATHOLICISM TO EPISCOPALIANISM

WILMA WANTED TO HAVE AN ABORTION.
WILMA WAS CATHOLIC.
WILMA WENT TO A ADOPTION AGENCY.

FRED WANTED TO TAKE HIS GUN HUNTING.
FRED WANTED WILMA TO HAVE A GUN AT HOME.
FRED ONLY HAD ONE GUN.
FRED BOUGHT ANOTHER GUN.

In the first two stories, PAM detects a conflict between Wilma's goal of having an abortion and her inferred goal of not having an abortion because she is Catholic. In the first story, PAM infers that Wilma resolved the conflict by changing the circumstance that gives rise to one of her goals, and fulfilled the other (that is, she decided to have the abortion). In the next case, PAM infers that Wilma abandoned her goal of having an abortion because it meant less to her than violating her religious beliefs.

The third story is a goal conflict based on a resource shortage. Here PAM infers that Fred bought another gun so he could take one with him and leave one at home.

Goal Competition:

Input text:

JOHN WANTED TO WIN THE STOCKCAR RACE.
BILL ALSO WANTED TO WIN THE STOCKCAR RACE.
BEFORE THE RACE, JOHN CUT BILL'S IGNITION WIRE.

Input: WHY DID JOHN BREAK AN IGNITION WIRE?
Output: BECAUSE HE WAS TRYING TO PREVENT BILL FROM RACING.

This story contains an instance of a goal-competition situation involving anti-planning. PAM explains John's action as part of a plan to undermine Bill's efforts by undoing a precondition for Bill's plan.

PAM also has been given some knowledge about poignancy. In particular, PAM knows about goal-subsumption termination problem components, and fortuitous-circumstance solution points. With this knowledge, PAM can now understand the following version of the Xenon story:

JOHN GRADUATED COLLEGE. JOHN LOOKED FOR A JOB. THE XENON CORPORATION GAVE JOHN A JOB. JOHN WAS WELL LIKED BY THE XENON CORPORATION. JOHN WAS PROMOTED TO AN IMPORTANT POSITION BY THE XENON CORPORATION.

JOHN GOT INTO AN ARGUMENT WITH JOHN'S BOSS. JOHN'S BOSS GAVE JOHN'S JOB TO JOHN'S ASSISTANT. JOHN COULDN'T FIND A JOB. JOHN COULDN'T MAKE A PAYMENT ON HIS CAR AND HAD TO GIVE UP HIS CAR. JOHN ALSO COULDN'T MAKE A PAYMENT ON HIS HOUSE, AND HAD TO SELL HIS HOUSE, AND MOVE TO A SMALL APARTMENT.

JOHN SAW A HIT AND RUN ACCIDENT. THE MAN WAS HURT. JOHN DIALED 911. THE MAN'S LIFE WAS SAVED. THE MAN WAS EXTREMELY WEALTHY, AND REWARDED JOHN WITH A MILLION DOLLARS. JOHN WAS OVERJOYED. JOHN BOUGHT A HUGE MANSION AND AN EXPENSIVE CAR, AND LIVED HAPPILY EVER AFTER.

In addition to the many inferences that are made to understand this story, PAM also recognizes that John's losing his job is an instance of a Goal-Subsumption Termination problem, and that the hit-and-run victim's rewarding John is an instance of a fortuitous-circumstance solution to this problem. The following is the actual computer representation of this problem and solution point. Its structure conforms to the point descriptions given in the figures in the previous section:

```
((GOALSUBTERPRO
  (SUB-STATE
   (BE-EMPLOYED (ACTOR JOHN1) (BY XENON) (LEVEL *ANY*)
    (SALARAY *ANY*)))
  (CAUSE (AUTH (ACTOR XENON)
    (STATE (NOT OBJECT (BE-EMPLOYED (ACTOR JOHN1)
     (BY ZENON)
     (LEVEL *ANY*)
     (SALARY *ANY*)))))))

 (UNFILL-PRE NIL)
 (PROBM-GOALS ((BUY-ON-TIME-PLAN (PLANNER JOHN1) (OBJECT HOUSE1))
    (BUY-ON-TIME-PLAN (PLANNER JOHN1) (OBJECT AUTO1))))
 (NEW-GOAL NIL)
 (EMOT-REACT NIL))
```

```
((FORCIRSOLPRO
  (UNDSTATE (POOR (OBJECT JOHN1)))
  (INTERACTION NIL)
  (FOROUTCOME (ATRANS (ACTOR MAN1) (OBJECT MONEY1)
                        (FROM MAN1) (TO JOHN1)))
  (NEW-STATE (WEALTHY (OBJECT JOHN1)))
  (STATE-CONSD ((ATRANS (ACTOR JOHN1) (OBJECT AUTO2)
                        (FROM NILSYM) (TO JOHN1))
                (ATRANS (ACTOR JOHN1) (OBJECT HOUSE3)
                        (FROM NILSYM) (TO JOHN1))))))
```

This representation can be used by a summarization program to produce a summary that included only the events of John's losing his job, the problems this caused, and the rich man's rewarding John. Alternatively, only these events can be remembered. and the unimportant events intelligently forgotten. (These programs can produce conceptual summaries that contain these events, although they cannot yet generate the summaries in English.)

SOME PSYCHOLOGICAL IMPLICATIONS OF POINTS

The notion of a story point suggested here gives rise to some testable predictions about the process of story comprehension. The following are some instances, none of which have yet been subjected to empirical scrutiny:

1. Subjects should be able to classify texts into stories or nonstories as a function of their point content. That is, stories that contain related problem and solution prototypes should be judged as being better formed stories than those that do not conform to any point prototype, or those that contain only incomplete or unrelated point components.

2. Story recall should measurably reflect a story's point structure. Because story memory is presumably structured by the points present in the story, those events most germane to story points should be the easiest to recall. This should be manifest in several ways. First, subjects asked to paraphrase the story should remember most of poignant events but may forget some events tangential to the point structure. Second, subjects asked to summarize the story should essentially produce an outline of the story's point structure. Third, recall of poignant events should be faster than that for the rest of the events in the text.

3. The predictive function of story points should be ascertainable by giving subjects story fragments and asking them to complete the stories, or to judge which of several alternative completions is more satisfactory. Presumably, subjects will prefer to introduce a point if none yet has been encountered; they will continue to fill out an incomplete point prototype; they will follow a problem

component with a solution; and they will either terminate a story that contains an entire point or continue it by introducing a new point.

Most of these effects should be greater as the time after understanding lengthens. Thus the hierarchical structure imposed by points controls the forgetting process as well as recall: The higher up an item is in the point structure, the less likely it is to be forgotten.

OTHER KINDS OF POINTS

The analysis of story points presented here is far from complete. However, I believe it is developed enough to suggest that the notion of storyness is not so much one of form but one of content. The preceding discussion is prototypical of a direction for research that I feel will be profitable to study stories and story comprehension.

The notion of a story point goes beyond the idea of the simple dramatic situations outlined in this chapter. Points are those things that generate interest, and therefore should also involve constructs such as enigma, novelty, tragedy, and humor. For example, a mystery, or a situation for which no explanation is readily inferable by the reader. The content of all these constructs is in need of analysis.

In addition, the notion of poignancy is not limited to the domain of stories. Other forms of communication have their points as well. For example, conversations seem to have a point structure within them. Consider the following sentences as conversational utterances:

37. Just before I came into your office, I was outside and I noticed a meter maid about to write a parking car ticket and put it under the windshiled of a car.

38. Just before I came into your office, I was outside and I noticed a meter maid about to write a parking car ticket and put it under the windshiled of your car.

After hearing utterance 37, most people would still be waiting to hear what the speaker was getting around to saying. However, utterance 38 fits into a pre-defined conversational point, and the speaker's remark immediately becomes salient. I expect that the point structure of interpersonal communication is at least as complicated as that of stories, and possibly more basic. However, neither have been analyzed sufficiently at this time to allow adequate comparison.

Mandler, J. M., & Johnson, N. S. (1977) Remembrance of things parsed: Story structure and recall. *Cognitive Psychology, 9,* 111–151.

Minsky, M. (1974) *A framework for representing knowledge* (AI Memo No. 306). MIT, Cambridge, Mass.

Polti, G. (1916) *The thirty-six dramatic situations.* Ridgewood, N.J.: The Editor Company.

Propp, V. (1968) *Morphology of the folktale.* Austin: University of Texas Press.

Rumelhart, D. E. (1975) Notes on a schema for stories. In D. G. Bobrow & A. Collins (Eds.), *Representation and understanding: Studies in cognitive science.* New York: Academic Press.

Rumelhart, D. E. (1976) *Understanding and summarizing brief stories* (Center for Human Information Processing Tech. Rep. No. 58). University of California, San Diego.

Schank. R. C., & Abelson, R. P. (1977) *Scripts plans goals and understanding.* Hillsdale, N.J.: Lawrence Erlbaum Associates.

Schank, R. C., & Yale A. I. Project (1975) *SAM—A story understander* (Research Rep. #43). Yale University, New Haven.

Stein, N. L., & Glenn, C. G. (1977) An analysis of story comprehension in elementary school children. In R. Freedle (Ed.), *New directions in discourse processing.* Norwood, N.J.: Ablex, 1979.

Thorndyke, P. (1977) Cognitive structures in comprehension and memory of narrative discourse. *Cognitive Psychology, 9,* 88–110.

Wilensky, R. (1978) Understanding goal-based stories.

SUMMARY

Stories constitute a subset of coherent natural-language texts. To establish text coherence, a great deal of knowledge is needed about people's goals and plans. The process by which this knowledge can be applied is termed explanation-driven understanding. It uses what has been heard previously to help disambiguate subsequent events, but does not constrain the understanding process to "canned" event sequences.

For texts to be stories, they must be poignant in addition to being coherent. This point structure of a story serves to organize the representation of a story in memory so that more important episodes are more likely to be remembered than trivial events. Points also serve to generate expectations about what will happen next in a story, because a story reader is looking for the point of a story as the text is being read.

An important class of story points deals with human dramatic situations, and these most often contain a set of interacting goals that create difficulties for a character. A taxonomy of these goal relationships and the situations they give rise to is useful for detecting a point of a story, as well as for establishing its coherence as a text. When a goal-relationship situation occurs as a problem-point component, it will occur as part of a point prototype. These prototypes specify those aspects of the situations that should be mentioned in order to produce a dramatic effect.

The notion of a story point competes with the idea of story grammars as a way to characterize story texts. The story-grammar approach attempts to define a story as a text having a certain form, whereas the story-point idea defines a story as a text having a certain content. The form of a story is viewed here as being a function of the content of the story, not a reasonably independent object. Understanding stories, then, is not so much a question of understanding the structure of a text, but of understanding the point of what the text is about.

REFERENCES

Black, J. B., & Wilensky, R. (1979) An evaluation of story grammars. *Cognitive Science 3* (No. 3).

Bower, G. H. (1976) Experiments on story understanding and recall. *Quarterly Journal of Experimental Psychology.* 28.

Charniak, E. (1972) Towards a model of children's story comprehension (AI TR-266). MIT, Cambridge. Mass.

Cullingford, R. E. (1978) *Script application: Computer understanding of newspaper stories* (Research Rep. #116). Yale University, New Haven.

DeJong, G. F. (1979) *Skimming stories in real time: An experiment in integrated understanding* (Research Rep. #158). Yale University, New Haven.

Kintsch, W., & vanDijk, T. A. (1975) Recalling and summarizing stories. *Language, 40,* 98–116.

V. GENERATION

This chapter on NL generation is only a small part of the collection, reflecting the relative proportion of research effort that has gone into NL generation compared to NL understanding. (Issues relevant to NL generation are discussed in other sections, but primarily from the point of view of NL understanding.) In recent years though, the scope of research on NL generation has increased, bringing with it a concomitant increase in the number of such research efforts. Thus one would expect a greater proportion of papers on NL generation in any future collection of readings in NLP.

In early work, researchers (e.g., [4, 17]) took NL generation as a way to demonstrate that their NL understanding system had correctly understood the individual sentences that had been fed in. The task of NL generation was thus to convert an isolated chunk of the system's knowledge into an isolated NL sentence. That is, NL generation was treated as an inverse single sentence understanding problem. For example, Simmons and Slocum [17] used an ATN (a very popular parsing engine, see *Woods*, Chapter 1) for traversing a chunk of verb-case-oriented semantic network structure and growing a corresponding English sentence in the process. In a very different paradigm, Goldman [4] developed a process for realizing chunks of CD representation (see *Schank*, Chapter 2) as individual NL sentences. Because CD is based on semantic primitives, as much as possible of the meaning of verbs is factored out and made explicit to show "deep" similarities in sentence meanings. Thus the problem Goldman [4] considered was the inverse problem of identifying appropriate verbs that best conveyed complex CD structures.

Around 1980, the growing interest in discourse and pragmatics led to increased concern with developing systems that could produce as well as understand multisentence texts. As a result, NL generation widened into a much larger problem, comprising three facets: (1) content determination, (2) text planning, and (3) realization as a sequence of NL utterances. The first two have been called the "strategic" side of NL generation; the third, the "tactical" side [20].

Content determination concerns what to include in a text—for example, what to include in an explanation, what to include in a persuasive argument or justification, what to include in a request for information so that it can be satisfied, what to include in answer to a question so that it may be understood and not misconstrued. These decisions on the part of a speaker (here, the system) can depend on such issues as what the speaker believes the hearer wants to know, what the speaker believes the hearer already knows, and what the speaker believes the hearer needs to know. *Content determination* thus depends both on general properties of the system's domain and task and on the specific discourse context. Note that *content determination* need not be a monolithic operation, done before *text planning* and *realization*: decisions made by either of these two processes should be able to suggest revisions or additional content.

Text planning concerns organizing the content to be communicated so that the resulting discourse is appropriate to at least (1) the function of the text and (2) the intended audience. Text structures often conform to familiar patterns that are associated either with the content of the material to be presented or with different rhetorical styles. For example, explanations of physical processes are often presented with the overall structure of a temporally ordered chain of causes and effects, with a definite start and a definite end, even when things are essentially simultaneous [18]. Devices are described in terms of either their functional or their physical decompositions [14]. Rhetorically, a newspaper report of a crime will differ from a police account in the order and focus of the material presented. Similarly a first-person narrative will differ from that of an omniscient observer.

Realization involves mapping the structured content proposed by *content determination* and *text planning* processes into an NL text. Decisions here include what words and phrases to use in describing or referring to things and what syntactic structures to use in presenting them. These decisions depend on the intended audience (e.g., its level of expertise), on the function of the description within the utterance (e.g., whether it is only being used to refer or whether the description is significant to what is being predicated), and on such discourse-specific properties as the current focus of attention and syntactic choices made in previous sentences. *Realization* is therefore concerned with both the choice of speech act and its specific linguistic manifestation.

The work described in the articles included here was all done under this text planning, content determination, and realization paradigm.

Discourse Strategies for Generating Natural Language Text

The first paper in this chapter, by McKeown, is concerned with both *content determination* and *text planning*. McKeown takes as a basic assumption that the way information is organized in a system's knowledge base does not necessarily provide an optimal organization for presenting to a user. One major contribution of this work is a characterization of three different common text structures, or "schemata," one used for defining terms vis-a-vis what they are, one for defining terms vis-a-vis what they subsume, and one for comparing two terms. These schemata are characterized in terms of smaller functional units, or "rhetorical predicates," each of which can then be instantiated against particular substructures in the system's knowledge base. (What constitutes a legal instantiation is specified in the system and would vary with the type of knowledge base.) Another contribution of this work is McKeown's extension of Sidner's focus-movement rules (see *Sidner,* Chapter 3) for NL generation. McKeown uses these rules both to decide among alternative possible expansions of a schema and to

influence syntactic realization (e.g., the choice of active or passive voice, the choice between a pronoun or a definite descriptor).

Planning English Referring Expressions

The second paper in this chapter, by Appelt, addresses problems of both *content determination* and *realization*. Appelt's work follows in the planning tradition of *Perrault, Cohen and Allen* (see Chapter 4): utterances are seen as being used to satisfy multiple goals on the part of the speaker. The task of a generation system is to reason from these goals to a plan involving both physical and linguistic actions that will satisfy the goals (*content determination*). The linguistic actions are refined until an English sentence is completely specified (*realization*). Unlike McKeown's system, the processes of content determination and realization are tightly interleaved, with segments of the utterance being realized as enough constraints are specified by the planning process. Appelt's most significant contributions are (1) showing how reasoning about knowledge and action can and must be part of NL generation and (2) constructing a system that integrated speech act computation, as in *Cohen and Perrault* (see, Chapter 4), with the production of an actual utterance. The grammar used here is much less sophisticated than that used in McDonald's work.

Description Directed Control

The final paper in this chapter, by McDonald, is concerned solely with *realization*. The paper describes MUMBLE, a particular architecture for the incremental realization of text specifications produced by outside *content specification* and *text-planning* processes. The purpose of MUMBLE is to explore three basic assumptions about human NL generation, which McDonald describes in this paper: (1) that NL generation is best characterized as a decision-making process (2) that all decisions are indelible (see *Marcus,* Chapter 1) and (3) that only a limited part of a text is planned at a time. The result of these assumptions is that a MUMBLE generator consists of three components: a domain-independent interpreter and a domain-dependent grammar and dictionary. The intepreter controls the overall realization process, propagating and enforcing constraints as a specification is elaborated and translated from left to right. The grammar enforces grammatical constraints and maintains local grammatical information. The dictionary indicates, for each term in the specification language, the various ways it can be expressed in English.

Thus MUMBLE lacks any (uncompiled) knowledge of words or even syntax. (This has been remedied somewhat in a more recent version of MUMBLE [9].) MUMBLE has been used thus far as a realization component for several different systems—GENARO (described here), ROMPER [7], and TEXT [15]. (For additional discussion of MUMBLE and what is involved in adapting it to a new domain, see [15].)

The factoring of issues in NL generation has thus far been very different than that applied to NL understanding. Rather than breaking along "traditional" linguistic lines of syntax, semantics, discourse, and pragmatics (which correspond to different types of knowledge used in NL processing), NL generation has broken along task-oriented lines—the tasks required for creating and realizing a text. Each of these tasks may draw on many types of knowledge, linguistic and otherwise.

Now attempts are being made to reconcile this broad task-oriented view of NL generation (comprising everything from content determination to actual realization) with our knowledge-oriented view of NL understanding. This may be the result of a desire for parsimony, which would reject positing separate knowledge sources and processes governing generation and understanding. Or it may be the result of moving on from a concern with isolated sentence understanding to connected text understanding. Whatever the cause, there have already been some instances of adapted or shared techniques.

In the area of discourse, as noted earlier, McKeown has extended Sidner's rules of focus movement (see *Sidner,* Chapter 3) for use in both *text planning* (i.e., selecting what to talk about next in a way that maximizes text coherence) and *realization* (e.g., choosing when to use pronouns and definite noun phrases). Similarly, Appelt has applied other parts of Sidner's work to planning descriptions, although he adopts the later notation of [5].

In the area of syntax and lexical semantics, there have also recently been (at least) two instances of sharing between NL understanding and generation. Kay's unification grammar (see *Kay,* Chapter 1) is designed specifically for such sharing of syntactic and lexical semantic knowledge. PHRED [6], a realization component for Berkeley's UC system [21], is also grounded in sharing its declarative knowledge of the syntactic and lexical patterns that can realize different concepts with UC's PHRAN component [21], which analyzes users' NL queries to the system. PHRAN/PHRED's knowledge is organized into pattern-concept rules whose patterns embody both syntactic and lexical-semantic aspects and reflect a particular approach to NLP, similar in many ways to semantic grammars (see *Hendrix et al.* and *Burton and Brown,* Chapter 6).

One area in which there has been little sharing or adaptation so far has been in applying the macro structures found in "schemata" or "text grammars" to discourse understanding—i.e., to provide an interpretive analogue of the *text planning* process.

In addition to the articles contained here, a reader interested in NL generation might investigate articles in somewhat related areas—for example, the area of explanation. Of historical interest is the recursive template method used for translating MYCIN rules into English [16]. This is a method that generates sentences in isolation: that is, even if a set of rules is being presented, each rule is mapped independently to a single English sentence, without regard for how the others are translated. The method is quite efficient though and usually produces understandable, if wordy, prose. However, if too much of the expertise has been shoe-horned into MYCIN's if-then format, while the text looks like English, it makes little sense. Also of interest is Chester's [2] method for producing NL presentations of natural deduction proofs. Chester's primary concern was structuring a linear sequence of proof statements into connected paragraph-length units (*text planning*). What is significant here is that Chester did not assume that the form of the system's proof structure was the best form of presentation, but that a motivated restructuring was both desirable and possible. In another vein, Swartout [19] presents work on enabling an expert system to justify its behavior rather than just (as MYCIN does) describing the context for that behavior. To do this, Swartout developed an automatic programmer to create an expert system from abstract knowledge of the domain and how problems were solved there. The development history of the program would then provide justification for the system's action. Of interest here is the observation that systems may have to be restructured to support adequate communication with their users: retrofitting NL "back-ends" and "front-ends" just won't do. Finally, Miller's work on "critiquing" both anesthesiology plans [11] and plans for the management of hypertension [12] involved both content determination and text planning. Of interest here are the effective texts he was able to produce. A bibliography of work done on NL generation prior to 1982 appears in [8].

The bibliography in [6] brings this up to date to early 1985.

A reader interested in generation might also look at work on paraphrase in NL question/answering systems. Many people have argued for the value of a paraphrase capability in the context of these systems—that is, to produce an unambiguous and understandable NL rendering of the formal query that the user's NL query has been mapped onto [1, 3, 10, 13]. The purpose of this is to show what question is actually being answered (for example, if there was any ambiguity detected in the user's query). For the most part, this work on paraphrase bears on issues of realization, since it has to inhibit paraphrases that are the same as the original query or that contain their own ambiguities or are too complex. But it also bears on issues of content determination, where the paraphrase of a multisentence text must show unequivocally how a definite pronoun or noun phrase has been resolved.

Finally, it should be noted that translation also involves generation issues, once the word-for-word approach is abandoned. These are primarily issues of *realization:* thus while most translation systems confine their activities to fairly local, and regular, reordering (e.g., verb shifting by rule), language mismatches between source and target languages can nevertheless make even adequate realization a tricky process.

Overall, most of the effort so far in NL generation has gone into producing sentences appropriate to their local context. Work on the construction of texts longer than a short paragraph or on generation in dialogues viewed as large-scale discourses has as yet hardly begun.

References

[1]   Boguraev, B. K. and Sparck Jones, K., A Natural Language Front End to Databases with Evaluative Feedback. In Gardarin, G., and Gelenbe, E. (editors), *New Applications of Data Bases*, pages 159–182. Academic Press, London, England, 1984.

[2]   Chester, D., The Translation of Formal Proofs into English, *Artificial Intelligence* 7:261–278, 1976.

[3]   Codd, E. F., Seven Steps to Rendezvous with the Casual User. In Klimbie, J. W., and Koffeman, K. L. (editors), *Data Base Management*, pages 179–199. North-Holland, 1974.

[4]   Goldman, N., Conceptual Generation. In Schank, R. and Riesbeck, C. (editors), *Conceptual Information Processing*. American Elsevier, New York City, 1975.

[5]   Grosz, B., Joshi, A., and Weinstein, S., Providing a Unified Account of Definite Noun Phrases in Discourse. In *Proceedings of 1983 Conference*, pages 44–50. Association for Computational Linguistics, June, 1983.

[6]   Jacobs, P., PHRED: A Generator for Natural Language Interfaces, *Computational Linguistics* 11(4):219–242, October-December, 1985.

[7]   Karlin, R., *ROMPER MUMBLES*, Technical Report MS-CIS-85-41, Dept. of Comp. and Info. Science, Univ. of Pennsylvania, August, 1985.

[8]   Mann, W., Bates, M., Grosz, B., McDonald, D., McKeown, K., and Swartout, W., Text Generation, *Amer. J. of Computational Linguistics* 8(2):62–69, April-June, 1982.

[9]   McDonald, D. and Pustejevsky, J., Description-Directed Natural Language Generation. In *Proc. of the 1985 Conference*, pages 799–805. Int'l Joint Conf. on Artificial Intelligence, Los Angeles CA, August, 1985.

[10] McKeown, K., Paraphrasing Using Given and New Information in a Question-Answer System. In *Proceedings of the 17th Annual Meeting of the ACL*, pages 67–72. Association for Computational Linguistics, August, 1979. Also appears in *Amer. J. Comp. Ling.*, 9(1), pp.1–11, January–March 1983.

[11] Miller, P., *A Critiquing Approach to Expert Computer Advice: ATTENDING*, Pitman Publishing Co., London, England, 1984.

[12] Miller, P., Medical Plan-Analysis by Computer: Critiquing the Pharmacologic Management of Essential Hypertension, *Computers and Biomedical Research* 17:38–54, 1984.

[13] Mueckstein, E-M., Q-Trans: Query Translation into English. In *Proc. 8th Int'l Joint Conf. on Artificial Intelligence*, pages 660–662. IJCAI, Karlsruhe, West Germany, August, 1983.

[14] Pirsig, R., *Zen and the Art of Motorcycle Maintenance*, Bantam Books, 1974.

[15] Rubinoff, R., Adapting MUMBLE: Experience with Natural Language Generation. In *Proc. 1986 National Conf. on Artificial Intelligence (NCAI)*. AAAI, Philadelphia PA, August, 1986.

[16] Shortliffe, E., Details of the Consultation System. In Buchanan, B. and Shortliffe, E. H. (editors), *Rule-Based Expert Systems*. Addison-Wesley, 1984.

[17] Simmons, R. and Slocum, J., Generating English Discourse from Semantic Networks, *CACM* 15(10):891–903, October, 1972.

[18] Stevens, A. and Steinberg, C., *A Typology of Explanations and its Application to Intelligent Computer Aided Instruction*, Technical Report 4626, Bolt, Beranek and Newman Inc., March, 1981.

[19] Swartout, W., XPLAIN: A System for Creating and Explaining Expert Consulting Programs, *Artificial Intelligence* 21:285–325, 1983.

[20] Thompson, H., Strategy and Tactics: A Model for Language Production. In *Papers from the 13th Regional Meeting*. Chicago Linguistics Society, Chicago IL, 1977.

[21] Wilensky, R., Arens, Y., and Chin, D., Talking to UNIX in English: An Overview of UC, *CACM* 27(6), June, 1984.

Discourse Strategies for Generating Natural-Language Text*

Kathleen R. McKeown

Department of Computer Science, Columbia University, New York, NY 10027, U.S.A.

ABSTRACT

If a generation system is to produce text in response to a given communicative goal, it must be able to determine what to include in its text and how to organize this information so that it can be easily understood. In this paper, a computational model of discourse strategies is presented that can be used to guide the generation process in its decisions about what to say next. The model is based on an analysis of naturally occurring texts and represents strategies that can be used for three communicative goals: define, compare, and describe. We show how this model has been implemented in TEXT, a system which generates paragraph-length responses to questions about database structure.

1. Introduction

In order to appropriately generate natural-language text, a system must be able to determine what information to include and how to organize this information to achieve its communicative goal most effectively. While researchers in natural-language processing have investigated issues involved in determining the surface structure of a pre-determined message in natural language, problems involving the content and textual shape of the message have gone largely unanswered. In this paper, a generation theory is presented that identifies how the content and organization of a text can be determined given a communicative goal. The theory has been implemented in the TEXT system, which generates paragraph-length responses to questions about database structure.

Our approach is based on the fundamental hypothesis that people have preconceived ideas about the means with which particular communicative goals can be achieved as well as about the ways in which these means can be integrated to form a text. That is, texts reflect one or more principles of organization. The structure of a narrative, for example, follows certain standard patterns, one of which dictates that it begin with a description of setting (scene, characters, or time-frame). A computational model of *discourse strategies* encoding text organization has been developed that is used to guide the generation process in deciding what to say next. The model was developed for three communicative goals: *define, describe,* and *compare.* It is based on an analysis of discourse strategies that are commonly used in naturally occurring texts for these purposes.

Discourse strategies are only part of the generation method developed. Interaction with semantic knowledge about information relevant to the communicative goal and how it relates to what has already been said is used to determine the final content and structure of the text. These constraints are captured in a representation of *focus of attention.* Focus of attention constrains the information that needs to be considered when deciding what to say next. It also provides constraints when the discourse strategy allows for several possible choices for what to say next by indicating which information ties in best with the preceding discourse. In this paper, focus of attention will be discussed only as it relates to the discourse strategies (for further details see [23, 24]).

The use of a formal model of discourse strategies which interacts with focus of attention constitutes a departure from earlier language-generation systems. First, it specifies a mechanism for generating coherent *text.* This is in contrast to the majority of earlier systems which focused on the generation of single sentences. Of those systems that could generate connected text (see, e.g. [17, 25, 35, 39]), few have used a formal representation of strategy to determine the content and organization of the text.[1] Furthermore, the use of interacting influences on the content and structure is another feature of our approach that is lacking in other systems.

2. Problems in Generating Text

What must a generation system take into account to generate a text, given a specific communicative goal? The following questions at least must be considered:
- How do problems in language generation differ from those of language interpretation?
- What is the range of choices a generation system must consider?
- How does generation of text differ from generation of single sentences?

Since less research has been done in language generation than interpretation, people are less familiar with its problems. Although there is research that

[1] These systems and their differences from TEXT will be discussed in detail in Section 8.

* This work was done while the author was a graduate student at University of Pennsylvania and was partially supported by NSF grant #MCS81-07290. Research in artificial intelligence at Columbia University is supported by ARPA grant N00039-84-C-0165 and ONR grant N00014-82-K-0256.

suggests that the same information can be used both for interpretation and generation (e.g. [15, 40, 42]), there are some important distinctions that can be made about the processes required for each task.

Interpretation of natural language requires examination of a text in order to determine its meaning and the intentions of the writer who produced it. It necessitates using the evidence available and examining the limited set of options the system knows to be available to the writer to determine the option actually taken. For example, in interpreting Example 0 below, a system would use the evidence that 'give' occurs in the passive form to determine that 'book' is the object being given and 'Mary' the agent that does the giving.

Example 0. Mary was given a book.

While developing an interpretation system involves specification of how a speaker's options are limited at any given point (for example, by writing grammars), it does not require a formulation of reasons for selecting between those options. [2] Thus, in interpreting Example 0, a system does not consider *why* the writer used the passive form as opposed to any of the other options available at that point.

In generation of natural language, however, this is exactly what is required. To produce Example 0 in an appropriate discourse sequence, a generator must decide that although both the active and passive forms are possible, the passive is better than the active. Furthermore, the generator must have a principled reason for making that decision, which it can use in all similar cases. Where research on interpretation may describe limitations on options in order to more efficiently determine the option taken, research in generation must specify why one option is better than others in various situations. [3]

The options which a generation system must address range across a variety of knowledge sources. A language-generation system must be able to decide *what* information to communicate, *when* to say what, and *which* words and syntactic structures best express its intent. In the last of these stages, local decisions such as the syntactic choice shown for Example 0 are made, often using a grammar and dictionary to do so. Until recently, this has been the focus of language-generation research. But determining what to say and how to structure text above the sentence level also introduce language issues that must be addressed by any speaker or writer of extended discourse. These three classes of decisions are all part of the language-generation problem.

If connected text is to be generated, issues of discourse structure and discourse coherency and their influence on content are particularly important. For some tasks, deciding what to say may be fairly straightforward (e.g., a search of a database), while for others it may require more complicated reasoning processes (e.g., selecting information appropriate to the level of the learner for computer aided instruction systems). At any rate, it is clear that one of the first steps in speaking or writing is the narrowing of attention to knowledge relevant to the purpose at hand. For example, when asked for my opinion on punk rock, it would be inappropriate for me to start telling you about my favorite Greek classic, even if I knew much more about ancient Greek literature than about punk rock. Unless I wanted to compare my knowledge about Greek classics to some aspect of punk rock, I would be unlikely to even consider it in formulating my answer.

After determining what information is likely to be relevant to its current discourse goal, a generation system must be able to decide what to say first, what next, and how to close a discourse. Order of information in a text can be crucial to a reader's understanding of it. For example, the sequence of sentences shown in Example 1 is easily understood, but if examples of a concept are presented before the concept is introduced as in Example 2, the meaning is unclear.

Example 1.
  (A) Many sports are just a rich man's domain.
  (B) Skiing, golf, and tennis are cases in point.

Example 2.
  (A) Skiing, golf, and tennis are cases in point.
  (B) Many sports are just a rich man's domain.

Given that the generator is producing text and not simply single sentences, certain choices at the surface level are critical in order to produce a coherent text. The generator must be able to make reasoned decisions about when to use pronominal reference and about the syntactic construction that should be used. Examples illustrating these choices are shown in Examples 3–5 below. While a generator could arbitrarily decide which of these choices to select in any given situation, an inappropriate decision could easily be made without additional guidance. If the three propositions shown in Examples 6–8 below), then one choice in each pair is clearly inappropriate.

Example 3. Lexical choice: *bought vs. sold*
  (A) Jane bought $3.00 worth of bobby socks from Michael.
  (B) Michael sold $3.00 worth of bobby socks to Jane.

[2] Note that as interpretation systems become more sophisticated, the analysis of reasoning behind the selection of a choice may be helpful in determining the goals and intentions of the speaker.
[3] Of course, a robust understanding system must be prepared to handle any input, while a generation system may be limited in the type of language it can produce without causing the system to actually fail (although it may produce inappropriate output).

tactical and strategic components as a second emphasis of the work is on the kind of information the strategic component must produce to allow surface choices to be made appropriately.

The main features of the generation method developed for the TEXT strategic component are (1) the selection of relevant information for the answer; (2) the pairing of rhetorical techniques for communication (such as analogy) with discourse purposes (for example, providing definitions); and (3) a focusing mechanism. Questions are answered by first partitioning off a subset of the knowledge base determined to be relevant to the given question (Determine Relevancy, Fig. 1). This partition is termed the *relevant knowledge pool*. Then, based on the discourse purpose and a characterization of information in the relevant knowledge pool, a discourse strategy encoding partially ordered *rhetorical techniques* is chosen (Select Strategy, Fig. 1; Section 5 describes this process). These techniques guide the selection of propositions from the relevant knowledge pool. A focusing mechanism representing *immediate focus* (Section 6) interacts with the use of rhetorical strategies to fully determine the content and order of the answer. It helps maintain discourse coherency by filtering the next possible propositions indicated by the discourse strategy to that proposition which ties in most appropriately with the previous discourse. The message thus determined is passed to the tactical component which uses a functional grammar [15] to transform the message into English (for more

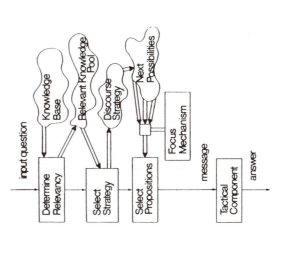

Fig. 1. System overview.

Example 4. Pronominal choice: *Linda* vs. *she*
(A) Linda flew to Washington.
(B) She flew to Washington.

Example 5. Syntactic choice: *passive* vs. *active*
(A) John gave the book to Mary.
(B) Mary was given the book by John.

Example 6.
Jane was in a hurry to finish her shopping.
It was a chore she particularly despised.
First, { Jane bought $3.00 worth of bobby socks from Michael.
{ *Michael sold $3.00 worth of bobby socks to Jane.[4]

Example 7.
We knew that Mary took the train to New York with Linda, but didn't realize that
{ Linda flew to Washington from there.
{ *she flew to Washington from there.

Example 8.
John bought that great new book on data structures.
He read the first three chapters and then
{ John gave the book to Mary.
{ *Mary was given the book by John.

3. The TEXT Generation Model

Our approach relies on a model of language production which divides processing into two stages. The first stage determines the content and structure of the discourse and is termed the 'strategic' component, following Thompson [38]. The second stage, the 'tactical' component, uses a grammar and dictionary to realize in English the message produced by the strategic component. This division allows for focus on the problems of determining content and structure as part of the strategic component.[5] The TEXT implementation includes both

[4] Note that even if we bring Jane into subject position still using the verb sell, the sentence is inappropriate in this sequence: *Jane was sold $3.00 worth of paper goods by Michael.

[5] A control structure which allows for backtracking between the tactical and strategic components (e.g. Appelt [2]) would also be possible. The approach we have taken clearly specifies how the planning of the text influences the realization of a message in natural language. Backtracking would allow for processes that produce the surface expression to influence the planning of the discourse. Our division of the processes, however, does allow us to focus on textual organization, an issue which Appelt has not addressed.

details on the tactical component see [3, 23]. This flow of control is illustrated in Fig. 1.

This method provides the means for the system to effectively (and efficiently, since it first narrows the information to be considered to a small subset of the knowledge base) determine what to include in a text and how to order it. Moreover, in the process of determining what to say next, the strategic component produces information that can be used by the tactical component to select between the surface-level choices outlined above. That is, the tactical component can use the tracking of focus of attention to select, for example, the passive construction over the active.

4. The Application Domain

Most natural-language database systems have concentrated on answering factual questions, providing answers in the form of lists or tables of objects in the database.[6] To ask such questions, a user must already be familiar with the database. Several experiments [16, 36] have shown that users often need to ask questions about database structure to familiarize themselves with it before making requests about its contents.

The task of the TEXT system is to generate responses to such meta-level questions. Three classes of questions corresponding to the three communicative goals have been considered: questions about information available in the database, requests for definitions, and questions about the differences between database entities. In this context, input questions provide the initial motivation for generating text.

Implementation of TEXT used a portion of an Office of Naval Research (ONR) database containing information about vehicles and destructive devices. Some examples of questions that can be asked of TEXT include[7]:
– What is a frigate?
– What do you know about submarines?
– What is the difference between a whisky and a kitty hawk?
The kind of generation of which the system is capable is illustrated by the response it generates to the question in Example 9 below.

Example 9. What kind of data do you have?
All entities in the ONR database have DB attributes REMARKS. There are 2 types of entities in the ONR database: destructive devices and vehicles. The vehicle has DB attributes that provide information on SPEED INDICES and TRAVEL MEANS. The destructive device has DB attributes that provide information on LETHAL INDICES.

The knowledge base developed for TEXT is an enhanced database schema based on the Chen entity-relationship model [5]. It includes a hierarchy on both entities and attributes (part of this hierarchy was generated automatically [20]). TEXT uses this meta-level representation to answer questions, although in some cases the ONR database itself is accessed.

5. Discourse Structure

The use of discourse strategies implies that text is generated by selecting information out of the underlying knowledge base and ordering it. Textural order is not pre-determined by the underlying knowledge base, but is determined at the time of generation by the discourse strategy used. This is based on an assumption that the structure of information in memory and the structure of a description of that information need not be the same. Note that although a person may describe the same event on several different occasions, exact repetition is unlikely. If the event is related for a different purpose moreover, it is even more likely that different information will be included. Experiments done by Chafe [4] support the assumption that a speaker decides as he is talking what material should go into a sentence. He showed that the distribution of semantic constituents among sentences often varies significantly from one version of a narrative to another.

The TEXT approach is also based on the observation that people follow certain standard patterns of discourse organization for different discourse goals. The production of narratives is an obvious example. A second example is the writing of short technical papers where people use knowledge about what normally goes into an introduction and which points a conclusion should emphasize. The discourse strategies used for TEXT were formalized on the basis of an analysis of naturally occurring texts which revealed a set of standard patterns.

Earlier we showed that the order of a text can influence both its meaning and clarity: if two sentences in a text are interchanged, then its meaning may be obscured. The discourse strategies we identify in the analysis specify order and content so that a writer's purpose is clearly communicated. That is, a writer uses such strategies because it makes it easier for a reader to understand a text. For a generation system, therefore, the strategies serve two purposes: they constitute a tractable mechanism which a system can use to generate text and

---

[6] Note that in some systems, the list (especially in cases where it consists of only one object) may be embedded in a sentence, or a table may be introduced by a sentence which has been generated by the system [12]. In a few systems (e.g. [6, 16]), a one- or two-sentence reply about the information in the database may be generated, but this reply is usually stored as a whole in the knowledge structure.

[7] Note that the system is not able to parse input natural-language questions. Instead questions must be asked via simple function notation corresponding to the three classes of questions: (1) (definition (e)), (2) (information (e)), (3) (difference (e1) (e2)), where (e), (e1), (e2) are entity classes in the database.

they specify an appropriate ordering that ensures effective communication of specific discourse goals.

In addition to ensuring understandable text, the use of discourse strategies also implies that different descriptions can be generated from the same knowledge representation. Since the discourse strategies control what is said and how that is structured, different strategies can be mapped onto the same piece of knowledge base to produce different texts. This means that the knowledge representation does not have to be appropriately structured for the generation task in addition to meeting all the other demands which are placed on it. This is not to say that representation isn't important for generation. The organization of the text, however, will not be dependent upon a particular organization of the knowledge base.

system being developed. This also avoided problems involved in narrative writing (e.g., scene, temporal description, personality).

To do the analysis, each proposition in self-contained samples from the texts was classified as one of a set of predicates. The set of predicates was drawn as much as possible from previous linguistic work. Both Grimes' and Williams' predicates were used (Figs. 2 and 3), but these did not capture all the structural relations in the examined texts, so an additional three predicates were adopted (Fig. 4).

The definitions of the predicates put forth by the authors were used to determine how to classify a proposition. These definitions were usually stated in English. For example, Grimes defines explanation as a proposition which provides the reason for which an inference (which can be implicit or explicit in the text) was drawn. Evidence, on the other hand, characterizes a proposition which provides support for a stated fact. Examples illustrating the use of other predicates are given in Figs. 2–4. While these definitions are not precise (see

1. **Attributive:**
   Mary has a pink coat.
2. **Equivalent:**
   Wines described as 'great' are fine wines from an especially good village.
3. **Specification (of general fact):**
   Mary is quite heavy. *She weighs 200 pounds.*
4. **Explanation (reasoning behind an inference drawn):**
   So people form a low self-image of themselves, *because their lives can never match the way Americans live on the screen.*
5. **Evidence (for a given fact):**
   The audience recognized the difference. *They started laughing right from the very first frames of that film.*
6. **Analogy:**
   You make it in exactly the same way as red-wine sangria, except that you use any of your inexpensive white wines instead of one of your inexpensive reds.
7. **Representative (item representative of a set):**
   What does a giraffe have that's special? ... a long neck.
8. **Constituency (presentation of sub-parts or sub-classes):**
   This is an octopus ... *There is his eye, these are his legs, and he has these suction cups.*
9. **Covariance (antecedent, consequent statement):**
   If John went to the movies, then he can tell us what happened.
10. **Alternatives:**
    We can visit the Empire State Building or call it a day.
11. **Cause-effect:**
    The addition of spirit during the period of fermentation arrests the fermentation development...
12. **Adversative:**
    It was a case of sink or swim.
13. **Inference:**
    So people form a low self-image of themselves.

FIG. 2. Grimes' predicates.

5.1. Rhetorical predicates

The basic units of discourse strategies are *rhetorical predicates*. They characterize the predicating acts a speaker may use and delineate the structural relation between propositions in a text. Some examples are 'analogy', 'constituency' (description of sub-parts or sub-types), and 'attributive' (providing detail about an entity or event). Linguistic discussion of such predicates indicates that some combinations of rhetorical predicates are preferable to others.

The notion of predicates goes back to Aristotle [22], who describes *enthymemes* and *examples*, predicates which a speaker can use for persuasive argument. Both Williams [41] and Shipherd [31], old-style grammarians, categorize sentences by their function in order to illustrate to the beginning writer how to construct paragraphs although neither says anything about combining sentence functions to form paragraphs. More recently, Grimes [11] has described rhetorical predicates as explicit organizing relations used in discourse. Grimes claims that the predicates are recursive and can be used to identify the organization of text at any level (i.e., proposition, sentence, paragraph, or longer sequence of text), but does not show how.

Our examination of texts and transcripts[8] has shown that not only are certain combinations of rhetorical techniques more likely than others, some are more appropriate for one communicative goal than another. For example, *definitions* of objects were frequently provided by a principled combination of certain techniques, while a *comparison* of two objects used others. For the analysis, a variety of texts was examined – ten different authors, in varying styles, from very literate written to transcribed spoken texts form the basis of the study. Short samples of *expository* texts were used because of their relevance to the

[8] Transcripts of mother-child dialogues [32] providing definitions of unfamiliar objects were used.

Williams' predicates are illustrated by providing an example paragraph from his text in which each sentence is classified as one of his predicates. The classifying predicate follows the sentence.

Comparison	Topic
General-illustration	Particular-illustration
Amplification	Contrasting
Conclusion	

"What, then, are the proper encouragements of genius? (topic). I answer, subsistence and respect, for these are rewards congenial to nature. (amplification). Every animal has an aliment suited to its constitution. (general-illustration). The heavy ox seeks nourishment from earth; the light chameleon has been supposed to exist on air. (particular-illustration). A sparer diet than even this satisfies the man of true genius, for he makes a luxurious banquet upon empty applause. (comparison). It is this alone which has inspired all that ever was truly great and noble among us. It is as Cicero finely calls it, the echo of virtue. (amplification). Avarice is the pain of inferior natures; money the pay of the common herd. (contrasting sentences). The author who draws his quill merely to take a purse no more deserves success than he who presents a pistol. (conclusion)."

FIG. 3. Williams' predicates.

[13] for more formal definitions), in general they provide characterizations of predicates which are sufficiently distinct to allow for classification.

To classify a proposition, the text was segmented into clauses that could be characterized by one of the predicates. For the most part, a proposition corresponds to a single clause in the text, but in some cases several clauses together better capture a predicate (for instance, see the text example for predicate 5, evidence in Fig. 2). In addition, the classification of a proposition was sometimes ambiguous between several predicates and for such cases, the single proposition was classified by all applicable predicates.

Our analysis has shown that, with slight variations, similar patterns of predicate usage occur across the various expository texts. Four different predicate patterns were noted and have been represented as schemata. They are the identification, constituency, attributive, and contrastive schemata and are shown in Figs. 5–8. A grammar notation was used to represent the schemata: '{}' indicates optionality, '/' indicates alternatives, '+' indicates that the item may appear 1 to n times, and '*' indicates that the item is optional and may

1. **Identification:**
   ELTVILLE (Germany) An important wine village of the Rheingau region.
2. **Renaming:**
   Also known as the Red Baron.
3. **Positing:**
   Just think of Marcus Welby.

FIG. 4. Additional predicates needed for the analysis.

appear 0 to n times. Each schema is followed by a sample paragraph and a classification of the propositions contained in the paragraph. ';' is used to represent classification of ambiguous propositions in the paragraph. These were translated into the schemata as alternatives.

The identification schema (Fig. 5) captures a strategy used for providing definitions. Its characteristic techniques include identification of an item as a member of a generic class (identification), description of an object's constituency or attributes (constituency/attributive), analogies (analogy), and examples (particular-illustration/attributive). It should be noted that the identification schema was only found in texts whose primary function was to provide definitions (e.g., dictionaries and encyclopedias). The other texts examined simply did not have occasion to provide definitions.

The constituency schema (Fig. 6) describes an entity or event in terms of its sub-parts or sub-types. After identifying the sub-types, the schema dictates either a switch to each of its sub-types in turn (following the depth-identification or depth-attributive path) or can continue focusing on the entity itself, describing either its attributes (attributive path) or its functions (cause-effect path). The schema may end by optionally returning to discussion of the original object by using the amplification, explanation, attributive or analogy predicate. In the sample paragraph, taken from the American Encyclopedia, two types of torpedoes are first introduced. Then, the steam-propelled model is identified by citing facts about it and the electric-powered model is compared against it, with a significant difference cited.

Identification schema

Identification (class & attribute/function)
{Analogy/Constituency/Attributive/Renaming/Amplification}*
Particular-illustration/Evidence+
{Amplification/Analogy/Attributive}
{Particular-illustration/Evidence}

Example

"**Eltville** (Germany) (1) An important wine village of the Rheingau region. (2) The vineyards make wines that are emphatically of the Rheingau style, (3) with a considerable weight for a white wine. (4) Taubenberg, Sonnenberg and Langenstuck are among vineyards of note." (Paterson [28]).

Classification of example

1. Identification (class & attribute)
2. Attributive
3. Amplification
4. Particular-illustration

FIG. 5. The identification schema.

Constituency schema

Constituency
Cause-effect*/Attributive*/
{Depth-identification/Depth-attributive
{Particular-illustration/evidence}
{Comparison/analogy}}+
{Amplification/Explanation/Attributive/Analogy}

Example

"Steam and electric torpedoes. (1) Modern torpedoes are of 2 general types. (2) Steam-propelled models have speeds of 27 to 45 knots and ranges of 4000 to 25,000 yds. (4,367–27,350 meters). (3) The electric powered models are similar (4) but do not leave the telltale wake created by the exhaust of a steam torpedo" [9].

Classification of example

1. Constituency
2. Depth-identification; (Depth-attributive)
3. Comparison
4. Depth-identification; (Depth-attributive)

FIG. 6. The constituency schema.

Attributive schema

Attributive
{Amplification; Restriction}
Particular-illustration*
{Representative}
{Question; Problem
Answer}
{Comparison; Contrast
Adversative}
Amplification/Explanation/Inference/Comparison

Example

"(1) This book, being about work, is, by its very nature, about violence – (2) to the spirit as well as to the body. (3) It is about ulcers as well as accidents, about shouting matches as well as fistfights, about nervous breakdowns as well as kicking the dog around. (4) It is, above all (or beneath all), about daily humiliations. (5) To survive the day is triumph enough for the walking wounded among the great many of us" (Terkel [38]).

Classification of example

1. Attributive
2. Amplification
3. Particular-illustration
4. Representative
5. Amplification; Explanation

FIG. 7. The attributive schema.

The *attributive* schema (Fig. 7) can be used to illustrate a particular point about a concept or object. The sample paragraph, taken from the Introduction to *Working*, attributes the topic (working and violence) to the book, amplifies on that in the second proposition ("spiritual as well as physical"), and in the third sentence, provides a series of illustrations. The fourth proposition selects out one instance as representative of the problem and the fifth amplifies on that instance.

The *contrastive* schema (Fig. 8) is used to describe something by contrasting a major point against a negative point (something the speaker wishes to show isn't true). The negative point is introduced first. The major concept is then described in more detail using one or more of the predicates shown in the second option of the schema. The closing sequence makes a direct comparison between the two. This schema dictates the structural relation between the two concepts – the use of A and ~A (not A) in the schema represent the major and negative points – but is less restrictive about which predicates are used than the other schemata.

In the sample paragraph, the contrastive schema is used to show how people form a bad self-image by comparing themselves against those in the movies. In the first sentence, the movie standard is introduced (the negative point or ~A). In the second and third sentences, real-life occupations and the feelings associated with them are described (the major point or A). This is done by first attributing the property of 'feeling degraded' to people such as waitresses and then providing evidence for that statement. Finally, a direct comparison is made between the glamorized occupations in movies and professions that people

have in real-life[9] and an inference drawn: "people form a low self-image of themselves".

It should be noted that the patterns found are fairly unrestrictive. Each contains a number of alternatives, indicating that a speaker has a wide variety of options within each type of structure. Moreover, since it is difficult to precisely define a predicate, the interpretation of each predicate in the pattern allows for additional speaker variation. In other words, text structure is not very rigidly defined. It allows for more individual variation than does the structure of sentences, for example.

Furthermore, the patterns are descriptive and not prescriptive. They identify commonly used means for achieving discourse goals, but do not dictate that these are the *only* means for achieving those goals. For example, the *identification* schema specifies one strategy for providing a definition, but it is likely that there are others. A mechanical device, for instance, might be defined by describing its function.

[9]Note that this statement could also be interpreted as an explanation for why people feel degraded and thus an ambiguous classification was made.

formally capture means that are used by people to create understandable texts, they can be used by a generation system to produce effective text.[10]

5.1.1. Schema recursion

As Grimes suggested, the rhetorical predicates do function recursively, describing the structure of text at all levels. For example, a single sentence may be used to attribute information to an entity or a longer sequence of text may be used for the same purpose. Our analysis of texts was made in order to discover just how predicates are combined to form longer sequences of text having specific functions. Thus, the resulting schemata describe combinations of predicates which serve the function of a single predicate. For this reason, each schema is associated with the predicate whose function it serves.

Schema recursion is achieved by allowing each predicate in a schema to expand to either a single proposition (e.g., a sentence) or to a schema (e.g., a text sequence). A text generated by applying schemata recursively will be tree-structured, with a sub-tree occurring at each point where a predicate has been expanded into a schema. Propositions occur at the leaves of the tree. Fig. 9 shows a hypothetical example of how schema recursion works. The *identification* schema is used in response to the question "What is a Hobie Cat?". The first step is to identify the Hobie Cat as a class of catamarans (1). To do so, a definition of a catamaran is also provided, assuming that the listener knows little about sailing. The identification predicate expands to the *identification* schema, where the speaker identifies the catamaran as a sailboat (2) and provides an analogy between the two, which consists of their similarities (3) and differences (4). These two steps are dictated by an *analogy* schema.

Compare and contrast schema

Positing/Attributive (~A)/
{Attributive (A)/
  Particular-illustration/Evidence (A)/
  Amplification (A)/
  Inference (A)/
  Explanation (A)}+
{Comparison (A and ~A)/
  Explanation (A and ~A)/
  Generalization (A and ~A)/
  Inference (A and ~A)}+

"(1) Movies set up these glamorized occupations. (2) When people find they are waitresses, they feel degraded. (3) No kid says I want to be a waiter, I want to run a cleaning establishment. (4) There is a tendency in movies to degrade people if they don't have white-collar professions. (5) So, people form a low self-image of themselves, (6) because their lives can never match the way Americans live – on the screen." (Terkel [38])

Classification of example

1. Positing (~A)
2. Attributive (A)
3. Evidence (A)
4. Comparison, explanation (A and ~A)
5. Inference (A and ~A)
6. Comparison, explanation (A and ~A)

FIG. 8. The compare and contrast schema.

ID schema	ID schema	Analogy schema
Identification →	Identification	Similarities
Attributie	Analogy →	Differences
Particular-illustration	Particular-illustration	

(1) A Hobie Cat is a brand of catamaran, (2) which is a kind of sailboat. (3) Catamarans have sails and a mast like other sailboats, (4) but they have two hulls instead of one. (5) That thing over there is a catamaran. (6) Hobie Cats have a canvas cockpit connecting the two pontoons and one or two sails. (7) The 16-ft. Hobie Cat has a main and a jib and the 14-ft. Hobie Cat has only a main.

FIG. 9. Schema recursion.

[10] Note that while schemata are not grammars of text in general, they do serve as a text grammar for the system since they describe all possible text structure that TEXT can generate.

Moreover, the schemata do not have the same binding action on the writer as does a sentence grammar. A text that breaks the rules specified by a schema is not perceived as 'illegal' or outside the English language, while a sentence that does not conform to a grammar is often recognized as ill-formed. Earlier on we noted that writers of short technical papers are aware of conventions for what constitutes a reasonable introduction. A talented writer, however, may purposely ignore such conventions to create a particularly captivating introduction. While such a text may be considered unusual, it would not be considered wrong.

All this points to the fact that the schemata do *not* function as grammars of text. They do, however, identify common means for effectively achieving certain discourse goals. They capture patterns of textual structure that are frequently used by a variety of people (and therefore do not reflect individual variation in style) to successfully communicate information for a particular purpose. Thus, they describe the norm for achieving given discourse goals, although they do not capture all the means for achieving these goals. Since they

After pointing out a catamaran to the listener (5), the text returns to the original *identification* schema to provide additional information about the Hobie Cat (6) and finally, cites two types of Hobie Cats, the 16-ft. and the 14-ft. (7).

Although TEXT is capable of performing recursion in some instances, full recursion, such as is illustrated in the above example, is not currently implemented. In order for the system to be fully recursive, a schema must be written for each rhetorical predicate. Right now, schemata for only four of the predicates (out of a total of ten predicates) are written. (In the above example, the *analogy* schema shown is assumed to correspond to the compare and contrast schema, but this would require more analysis to verify).

Another issue in the recursive use of schemata is the question of when recursion is necessary. Clearly there are situations where a simple sentence is sufficient for fulfilling a communicative goal, while in other cases, it may be necessary to provide a more detailed explanation. One test for recursion hinges on an assessment of the user's knowledge. In the above example, a speaker might provide a detailed identification of the Hobie Cat if the listener knew very little about sailing. Tests on when detail is necessary are currently being explored by Paris [27]. In order to develop a comprehensive theory on recursion a full user-model [1, 26, 29] must be developed.

5.2. Using schemata in the TEXT system

In TEXT, schemata are used to guide the generation process in its decisions about what to say next at each step in constructing the text. They serve as a text plan. The four schemata which were developed from our analysis of texts (Figs. 5–8) are used as the basis for TEXT schemata.

The schemata were implemented using a formalism based on an augmented transition network (ATN) [43]. An ATN is a graph representation of a grammar and allows for actions on its arcs which may set or test various registers. The ATN formalism was originally developed to parse sentences. When parsing a sentence, taking an arc involves consuming a word from the input string and augmenting a syntactic parse tree to include the new word and its category.

For TEXT, an ATN is used to build discourse instead of a parse tree. Taking an arc corresponds to the selection of a proposition for the answer and the states correspond to filled stages of the schema. No input string is consumed; instead the relevant knowledge pool is consumed, although it is not consumed in any order and it need not necessarily be completely exhausted when the graph is exited.

One major difference between the TEXT ATN implementation and a usual ATN, however, is in the control of alternatives. In the TEXT system, at each state all possible next states are computed and a function that performs the focus constraints is used to select one arc from the set of possibilities. Thus, although all possible next states are explored, only one is actually taken. This differs from the normal ATN where unrestricted backtracking can occur.

Once a schema has been selected for a given response, the answer is constructed by traversing the schema, beginning at the start state. An arc's type determines how the system decides whether or not it can be traversed. There are five types of arcs in the TEXT ATN graphs: *fill, jump, push, subr,* and *pop* arcs. *Fill* arcs are used to represent the predicates of the schema. Each predicate has a function associated with it which 'matches' the predicate against the relevant knowledge pool and returns all propositions in the pool which are classified by the predicate. A *fill* arc is traversed if its predicate matches at least one proposition in the pool. On traversal, the matched proposition is consumed.

Jump arcs function as they do in the original ATNs and are used to capture optional predicates. *Subr* arcs are used to allow for simplicity in the graph. They name a sub-graph and can be traversed if the sub-graph named can be traversed. *Pop* arcs indicate where a graph is exited and *push* arcs are used for recursion.

Figs. 10–14 show the graphs that implement the schemata used in TEXT. TEXT schemata do not contain predicates of the original schemata for which no information exists in the database domain and are thus each subsets of the corresponding schemata which emerged from an analysis of the texts (see Figs. 5–8).

The TEXT *identification* graph (Figs. 10 and 11) has as its first arc a *fill* arc, emanating from the start state ID/[11]. It represents the first predicate of the schema, the identification predicate. Following the first arc is an optional arc, (*subr* Description/), which can be skipped by taking the *jump* arc also emanating from state ID/ID. The sub-graph labeled by Description/ (Fig. 11) represents the second line of the original schema, capturing three predicates that were present in the original. Following this comes at least one predicate from the Example/ sub-graph (that is, either particular-illustration or evidence). The Example/ arc leads to state ID/EX, from which the schema can be exited via the *pop* arc. Alternatively, additional Example/arcs can be taken by cycling back through state ID/EX or optional predicates from the End-seq/ sub-graph followed by another optional Example/. These last two arcs correspond to the last two lines of the original schema.

Both the TEXT *constituency* (Fig. 12) and *attributive* (Fig. 13) schema are modified versions of the schemata resulting from the text analysis. The con-

[11] The states in the schema are named following the normal ATN convention. The name of the schema (here ID abbreviates *identification*) precedes the '/' and the predicate arc most recently traversed appears after the slash (thus, ID/ names the initial state when no predicate arcs have been traversed and ID/ID names the second state when the *identification* arc of the *identification* schema has been traversed).

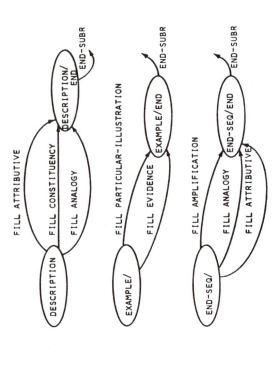

FIG. 10. The identification-schema graph.

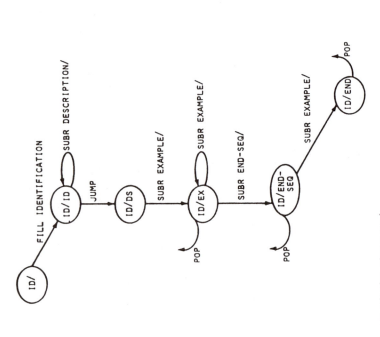

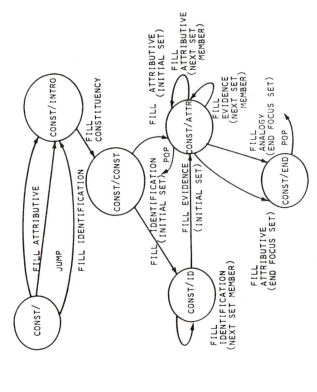

FIG. 11. Identification-schema sub-graphs.

FIG. 12. The constituency graph.

stituency graph is optionally headed by an attributive or identification predicate so that it can be used for providing answers to requests about available information or definitions. Following state CONST/INTRO, the graph mirrors the schema (Fig. 6). Note that two of the alternatives in the schema (cause-effect* and attributive*) were eliminated from the TEXT version and only the alternative beginning with depth-identification/depth-attributive remains. Two of the predicates from the last line of the schema (attributive and analogy) were included in the graph.

The TEXT *attributive* graph does not include the restriction, question; problem, answer, or adversative predicates from the original schema as there is no translation for these in the database domain. In addition, the predicate representative in the original schema was translated as classification in the TEXT version and comparison; contrast as analogy in order to make use of predicates already used. Only the explanation predicate from the last line of the original schema was included in the TEXT graph.

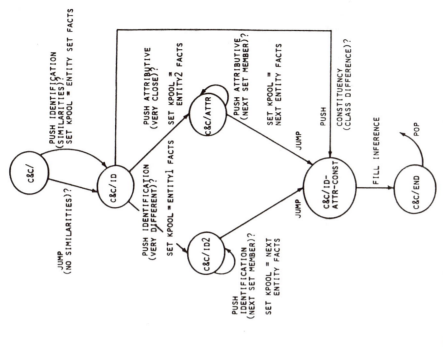

FIG. 14. The compare and contrast graph.

is invoked, the knowledge pool is reset to the information relevant for that portion of the response (this is indicated in Fig. 14 by the *set* action on each *push* arc).

The TEXT *compare and contrast* graph uses the *identification* schema to identify the similarities between the two objects. The schema that is used for the contrastive portion of the response depends on the semantic information available about the two entities. Either the *identification*, *constituency* or *attributive* schema can be used and this depends on whether the two entities are very different in concept, very similar, or in between (as determined by the tests on these three *push* arcs). This point is discussed further in the next section which describes the selection of a schema. The *compare and contrast*

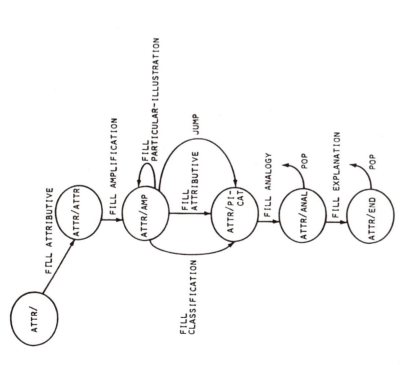

FIG. 13. The attributive graph.

The *compare and contrast* schema (Fig. 14) was modified to allow for equal discussion of the two items in question. The *contrastive* schema which emerged from the text analysis called for contrasting a major concept against a minor one. The minor concept, had, in most cases, either been discussed in the preceding text, or was assumed by the writer to be familiar to the reader. No history of discourse is currently maintained in TEXT and no user model other than a static one is constructed. Thus, the system does not know whether the user has more knowledge about one concept than another and the comparison must be equally balanced. Equal balance is achieved by first providing the similarities between the two objects and then presenting their differences.

The *compare and contrast* schema dictates a contrastive structure without specifying which predicates are to be used. To achieve this variation, the TEXT schema makes use of the three other schemata through recursion. A recursive call to a schema is indicated in the graph by a *push* arc. When another schema

schema concludes with a direct comparison between the two entities *via* the inference predicate.

5.2.1. *Answering a question*

To answer a question, TEXT first selects a schema to guide the construction of the answer. An answer is then constructed by *filling* the schema.

5.2.2. *Selecting a schema*

In the TEXT system, association of strategy with discourse goal is achieved by associating the different schemata with different question-types. For example, if the question involves defining a term, different schemata are possible than if the question involves describing information. A summary of the assignment of schemata to question-types is shown in Fig. 15.

On the basis of the given question-type, the associated schemata are selected as possible structures for the response. A single schema is selected out of this set on the basis of the information available to answer the question. This is one case where semantic information interacts with information about discourse structure to determine the structure of the generated text.

In response to requests for definitions and information, the *constituency* schema is selected when the relevant knowledge pool contains a 'rich' description of the questioned object's sub-classes and less information about the object itself. This is true when the questioned object occurs at a higher level in the knowledge base hierarchy than a pre-determined level. Note that the higher an entity occurs in the hierarchy, the less descriptive information is available to describe the set of instances it represents since the larger the class, the less common features occur across it. When this is not the case, the *attributive* schema is used for information questions and the *identification* schema is used for definition questions. For the question "What is a guided projectile?" (Example 10) the *constituency* schema is selected since more information is available about the guided projectile's sub-classes than about the guided projectile itself, while the *identification* schema is selected for the question "What is a ship?" (Example 11).

The *compare and contrast* schema is always selected in response to a request about the difference between objects but the type of information in the relevant knowledge pool is used to determine which sub-schema path should be taken for the contrastive portion of the answer. When two objects are very close in concept (see [23]) the *attributive* sub-schema path is taken in order to describe detailed differences (Example 12).[12] When the two objects are very different, the *identification* sub-schema path is taken in order to describe generic differences (Example 13). In other cases, the *constituency* sub-schema path is taken.

Example 10.

(definition GUIDED)
;
; What is a guided projectile?
;

Schema selected: constituency

Message through dictionary. Entering tactical component

A guided projectile is a projectile that is self-propelled. There are 2 types of guided projectiles in the ONR database: torpedoes and missiles. The missile has a target location in the air or on the earth's surface. The torpedo has an underwater target location. The missile's target location is indicated by the DB attribute DESCRIPTION and the missile's flight capabilities are provided by the DB attribute ALTITUDE. The torpedo's underwater capabilities are provided by the DB attributes under DEPTH (for example, MAXIMUM OPERATING DEPTH). The guided projectile has DB attributes TIME TO TARGET & UNITS, HORZ RANGE & UNITS and NAME.

Example 11.

(definition SHIP)
;
; What is a ship?
;

Schema selected: identification

Message through dictionary. Entering tactical component

A ship is a water-going vehicle that travels on the surface. Its surface-going capabilities are provided by the DB attributes DISPLACEMENT and

Requests for definitions
Identification
Constituency

Requests for available information
Attributive
Constituency

Requests about the difference between objects
Compare and contrast

FIG. 15. Schemata used for TEXT question-types.

[12] Note that, as currently implemented, the sub-schema paths do not have access to a discourse history of what has been included already in the text. This means that in selecting the information to contrast (for example, an entity's attributes), TEXT may select information for one entity that has not been included for another. This can lead to anomalies such as the last sentence of Example 12 where the DISPLACEMENT of the cruiser and ocean escort are compared although the cruiser's DISPLACEMENT was never stated. The inclusion of a discourse history is a topic for future work.

DRAFT. Other DB attributes of the ship include MAXIMUM SPEED, PROPULSION, FUEL (FUEL CAPACITY and FUEL TYPE), DIMENSIONS, SPEED DEPENDENT RANGE and OFFICIAL NAME. The DOWNES, for example, has MAXIMUM SPEED of 29, PROPULSION of STMTURGRD, FUEL of 810 (FUEL CAPACITY) and BNKR (FUEL TYPE), DIMENSIONS of 25 (DRAFT), 46 (BEAM), and 438 (LENGTH) and SPEED DEPENDENT RANGE of 4200 (ECONOMIC RANGE) and 2200 (ENDURANCE RANGE).

Example 12.

(difference OCEAN-ESCORT CRUISER)

; What is the difference between an ocean escort and a cruiser?

Schema selected: C & C-attributive

Message through dictionary. Entering tactical component

The cruiser and the ocean escort are surface ships. The ship's surface-going capabilities are provided by the DB attributes DISPLACEMENT and DRAFT. The ship has DB attributes MAXIMUM SPEED, PROPULSION, FUEL (FUEL CAPACITY and FUEL TYPE), DIMENSIONS, SPEED DEPENDENT RANGE and OFFICIAL NAME. Ocean escorts have a DISPLACEMENT between 3400 and 4100. All ocean escorts in the ONR database have REMARKS of 0, FUEL TYPE of BNKR, FLAG of BLBL, MAST HEIGHT of 85 and PROPULSION of STMTURGRD. Ocean escorts carry between 2 and 22 torpedoes, 16 missiles, and between 1 and 2 guns. A ship is classified as an ocean escort if the characters 1 through 2 of its HULL NO are DE. Cruisers have a PROPULSION of STMTURGRD and a LENGTH between 510 and 673. All cruisers in the ONR database have REMARKS of 0 and FUEL TYPE of BNKR. Cruisers carry between 8 and 42 torpedoes, between 4 and 98 missiles, and between 1 and 4 guns. A ship is classified as a cruiser if the characters 1 through 2 of its HULL NO are CL or the characters 1 through 2 of its HULL NO are CG. The ocean escort, therefore, has a smaller LENGTH and a smaller DISPLACEMENT than the cruiser.

Example 13.

(difference DESTROYER BOMB)

; What is the difference between a destroyer and a bomb?

Schema selected: C & C-identification

Message through dictionary. Entering tactical component

A destroyer is a surface ship with a DRAFT between 15 and 222. A ship is a vehicle. A bomb is a free falling projectile that has a surface target location. A free falling projectile is a lethal destructive device. The bomb and the destroyer, therefore, are very different kinds of entities.

5.2.3. Filling the schema

Each schema predicate has functions associated with it to define the type of information it can match in the knowledge pool. To construct a single proposition, the functions retrieve information from the knowledge base and format it in an internal representation. For example, in the database domain, one way to provide attributive information about an entity is through the use of database attributes. The attributive function, therefore, when passed an entity, retrieves the database attributes for that entity in the knowledge base and constructs a list containing the predicate, the entity, and the database attributes. This list is an internal representation of the proposition. The attributive proposition for the entity *ship* is shown below along with an eventual English translation. The first element in the list specifies that this is an attributive proposition, the second that this proposition identifies database attributes, the third identifies the entity to which the properties are attributed, and the remaining elements itemize the actual attributes.

(attributive db SHIP (name OFFICIAL_NAME) (topics SPEED_DEPENDENT_RANGE DIMENSIONS) (duplicates (FUEL FUEL_TYPE FUEL_CAPACITY)) (attrs PROPULSION MAXIMUM SPEED))

Other DB attributes of the ship include MAXIMUM SPEED, PROPULSION, FUEL (FUEL CAPACITY and FUEL TYPE), DIMENSIONS, SPEED DEPENDENT RANGE and OFFICIAL NAME.

The predicate semantics thus defined for TEXT are particular to a database system and would have to be redefined if the schemata were to be used in another type of system (such as a tutorial system). The semantics are not particular, however, to the *domain* of the database. When transferring the system from one database to another, the predicate semantics would not have to be altered.

The schema is filled by traversing the graph, using the predicate semantics to select propositions from the relevant knowledge pool. Where several arcs emanate from a single state in the graph representation of the schema or where a single predicate matches more than one proposition in the knowledge pool, all propositions are retrieved and the focus constraints are used to select the most appropriate proposition, thereby specifying which arc is taken. When the arc is taken, the proposition is removed from the knowledge pool.

1. Shift focus to item mentioned in previous proposition
2. Maintain focus
3. Return to topic of previous discussion
4. Select proposition with greatest number of implicit links to previous proposition

FIG. 16. Ordering of focus constraints.

6. Focus of Attention

As noted earlier, schemata are only part of the mechanism that TEXT uses to determine the content and order of its generated text. In this section, we show how constraints on how focus of attention can shift from one sentence to the next are used to determine what to say next in cases where the schemata do not totally constrain the system's choice.

When producing a single utterance (as dictated by a schema), TEXT narrows its focus of attention to a single object in its pool of relevant information. Having made a decision about what to talk about first, TEXT must support that decision in succeeding utterances if it wants its text to be easily understood. That is, having decided to focus on a particular object(s), its utterances constrain the set of possibilities for what can be said next if the system is to avoid jumping around from one topic to another. These are termed *immediate focus* constraints since they apply locally between utterances.

TEXT uses constraints developed by Sidner [33] on how immediate focus can shift or be maintained. Sidner showed that speakers can either maintain their current focus, shift focus to an item just introduced, return to a previous focus, or focus on an item implicitly related to the current focus. These constraints are used to limit the information TEXT considers when deciding what to say next. If its discourse plan allows for several utterances, the system only considers propositions that can be focused in one of these ways.

Several problems arose in adapting Sidner's work to generation. Since it considered *interpretation*, there was no need to discriminate between members of the set of legal foci; when more than one possibility for immediate focus existed after a given sentence, the next incoming sentence would determine which of the choices was taken. While Sidner's constraints are sufficient for interpreting natural language, for generation a system must be able to decide which of the constraints is better than any other at any point.

A preference ordering on Sidner's constraints was developed for generation (see Fig. 16). The ordering suggests that a speaker should shift to focus on an item just introduced into conversation if possible. If the speaker chooses not to do so, that item will have to be re-introduced into conversation at a later point before the additional information can be conveyed. If, on the other hand, the speaker does shift to the item just mentioned, there will be no trouble in continuing with the old conversation by returning to a previous focus.

Several consecutive moves to items just introduced are not a problem. In fact, consecutive focus shifts over a sequence of sentences occurs frequently in written text. If this rule were applied indefinitely though, it would result in never-ending side-tracking onto different topics of conversation. However, the model of generation assumes that information is being presented in order to achieve a particular goal (e.g., answer a question). Only a limited amount of information is within the speaker's scope of attention because of its relevance to that goal (as defined by the relevant knowledge pool). Hence only a limited amount of side-tracking can occur.

The second preference indicates that a speaker should continue talking about the same thing rather than returning to an earlier topic of conversation where possible. By returning to a previous discussion, a speaker closes the current topic. Therefore, having introduced a topic (which may entail the introduction of other topics), one should say all that needs to be said before returning to an earlier topic. That is, one avoids implying that the current subject has been completed when, in fact, there is more to be said. If neither of the first two preferences apply then the speaker must return to an earlier topic of discussion (Preference 3).

In cases where a speaker must choose between two propositions with the same focus, the preferences described so far proscribe no course of action. Rather than making an arbitrary choice, a speaker tends to group together in discourse information that is in some way related. When the system has a choice between two propositions with the same focus, it chooses that proposition with the most mentions to previously mentioned items (Preference 4).

This ordering doesn't dictate *absolute* constraints on the system. Just as a speaker may choose to suddenly switch topics, the system may choose to do so also. The ordered focus constraints are preferences which indicate the system's best move when faced with a choice. If the system's discourse plan indicates that no next choice meets these constraints, it will follow its plan making note of the abrupt switch in focus. This switch can then be syntactically marked by the tactical component to ease the transition for the user.

7. An Example of TEXT in Operation

To illustrate how schemata and focus constraints determine the content and organization of TEXT's output, consider the question "What is a ship?". The first step in generating a response is the construction of the relevant knowledge pool, immediately followed by the selection of a schema. For details on how the relevant knowledge pool is constructed (see [23]). Here, simply note that the area in the knowledge base immediately surrounding the questioned object (the *ship*) is selected. The resulting knowledge pool contains all associated information about the concept ship (including its database attributes, relations, and subordinates and superordinates in the knowledge base hierarchy). A diagram of the resulting pool is shown in Fig. 17. While the details are not important, the reader should note that only meta-level information is included in the pool.

To select a schema, TEXT first retrieves the set of schemata associated with the current question-type, a request for a *definition*, which includes both the *identification* and *constituency* schemata. The *identification* schema is selected since the ship occurs below a pre-determined level in the hierarchy.

After selecting the *identification* schema, TEXT begins traversing the schema graph. The first arc dictates that a proposition matching the identification

predicate must begin the response. Accordingly, a proposition identifying the ship as a water going vehicle is selected from the relevant knowledge pool and is eventually translated as the first sentence of the generated response (shown in Fig. 18).

(definition SHIP)
: What is a ship?
:

Schema selected: identification

1. A ship is a water-going vehicle that travels on the surface. 2. Its surface-going capabilities are provided by the DB attributes DISPLACEMENT and DRAFT. 3. Other DB attributes of the ship include MAXIMUM SPEED, PROPULSION, FUEL (FUEL CAPACITY and FUEL TYPE), DIMENSIONS, SPEED DEPENDENT RANGE and OFFICIAL NAME. 4. The DOWNES, for example, has MAXIMUM SPEED of 29, PROPULSION of STMTURGRD, FUEL of 810 (FUEL CAPACITY) and BNKR (FUEL TYPE), DIMENSIONS of 25 (DRAFT), 46 (BEAM), and 438 (LENGTH) and SPEED DEPENDENT RANGE of 4200 (ECONOMIC RANGE) and 2200 (ENDURANCE RANGE).

FIG. 18. "What is a ship?"

Having traversed the first arc, the system is now at state ID/ID. The schema dictates that the system now has two choices: it can either provide a Descriptive proposition (by following arc *subr* Description/) or it can jump to state ID/DS and provide an Example (by following arc *subr* Example/). Since the Description/ sub-graph has three arcs emanating from its initial state and the Example/ sub-graph has two arcs emanating from its initial state, TEXT has five arcs to choose from (representing the predicates analogy, constituency, attributive, evidence, and particular-illustration). One of these, the particular-illustration arc, is ruled out on the basis of information in the relevant knowledge pool compared with the semantics of the predicate. At this point, the relevant knowledge pool contains no information matching this predicate[13].

Since the schema does not constrain the system's choice for what to say next to a single proposition, the focus constraints are invoked to choose among the remaining arcs which match four propositions. (The four predicates, the matching propositions, the eventual translations of the propositions, and their foci are shown in Fig. 19.) Following the preferential ordering on how focus of attention should shift, TEXT first attempts to choose a proposition which allows it to shift focus to an element that was just introduced and is a potential

[13] The semantics for particular-illustration dictate that an example from the database can be extracted by instantiating database attributes already presented in the answer with values from the database. Since no database attributes have yet been mentioned, it is not possible to give an example at this point. Note that the schemata say nothing about what constitutes an appropriate example and this is one area where future work is required.

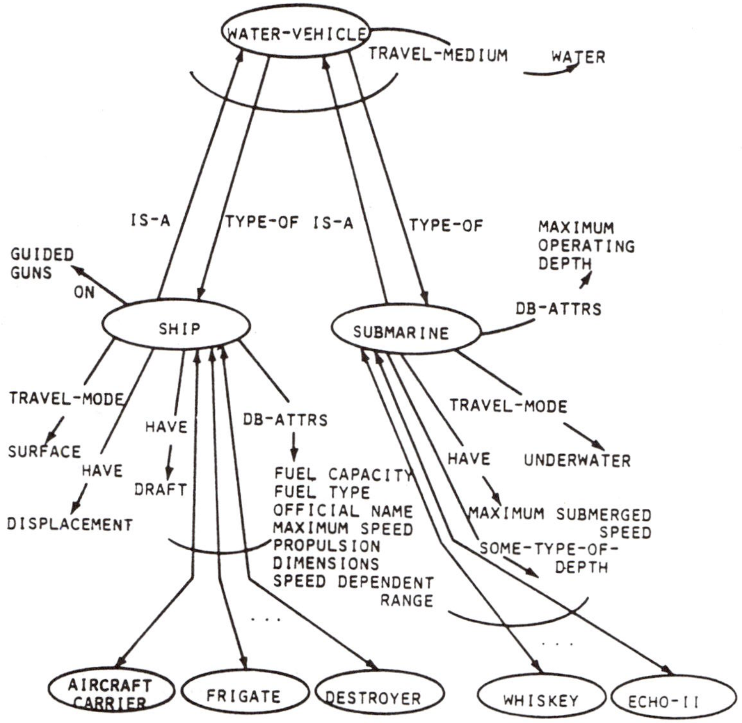

FIG. 17. Relevant knowledge pool.

which it does in sentence (3) of the text (Fig. 18) by including the attributive proposition it considered as a possibility for sentence (2). On the other hand, it would be awkward to shift at a later point in the text to the surface-going capabilities of the ship after continuing to focus on the concept 'ship'. This is a case where an opportunity to easily present information would be lost if it were not included at this point.

The process continues from state ID/EX until one of the *pop* arcs is taken and the *identification* schema is exited. At that point the full message has been constructed and is represented as a list of propositions. The tactical component is then invoked to transform the message into natural language and produce the final text as shown in Fig. 18.

To give a flavor of how this is done, the first two sentences of the answer are shown in proposition representation in Fig. 20 (further details on surface choice can be found in [23, 24]). Propositions are passed in this internal representation as input to the tactical component along with focus information, which includes the current focus of the proposition and its potential focus list (an ordered list of potential candidates for a shift in focus). The tactical component uses a dictionary to choose vocabulary for each argument of the proposition and to assign case roles. The predicate is always translated as the verb of the sentence and the choice of verb also determines which arguments of the proposition will fill the case roles of *protagonist*[15] and *goal*[16]. The representation of Proposition 2 at an intermediate stage of translation is shown in Fig. 21. Here, the verb 'provide' has been selected and the arguments '(HAVE DRAFT)(HAVE DISPLACEMENT)' have been assigned as the *protagonist* of the sentence and the arguments 'SHIP (TRAVEL_MODE SURFACE)' as the *goal*. The function 'entry-for' indicates that vocabulary for these arguments will also be chosen by accessing their entries in the dictionary.

Proposition 1:
(identification SHIP WATER-VEHICLE (restrictive TRAVEL-MODE SURFACE)
(non-restrictive TRAVEL-MEDIUM WATER)
(non-restrictive FUNCTION TRANSPORTATION))

Focus = SHIP

Proposition 2:
(evidence based-db SHIP (TRAVEL-MODE SURFACE)
(HAVE DRAFT) (HAVE DISPLACEMENT))

focus = (TRAVEL-MODE SURFACE)

FIG. 20. Propositions 1 and 2.

[15] Often referred to as *agent*. We are following Kay's [15] terminology here.
[16] Often referred to as *object* of the sentence.

1. **Analogy**
(analogy rels SHIP ON GUIDED GUNS)

The ship carries guided projectiles and guns

focus = *ship*

2. **Constituency**
(constituency SHIP (AIRCRAFT-CARRIER FRIGATE OCEAN-ESCORT, CRUISER, DE-STROYER))

There are 5 types of ships in the ONR database: aircraft carriers, frigates, ocean escorts, cruisers, and destroyers.

focus = *ship*

3. **Attributive**
(attributive db SHIP (name OFFICIAL_NAME) (topics SPEED_DEPENDENT RANGE DIMENSIONS) (duplicates (FUEL FUEL_TYPE FUEL_CAPACITY)) (attrs PROPULSION MAXIMUM_SPEED))

The ship has DB attributes MAXIMUM SPEED, PROPULSION, FUEL (FUEL CAPACITY and FUEL TYPE), DIMENSIONS, SPEED DEPENDENT RANGE and OFFICIAL NAME.

focus = *ship*

4. **Evidence**
(evidence based-db SHIP (TRAVEL_MODE SURFACE) (HAVE DRAFT) (HAVE DISPLACE-MENT))

Its surface-going capabilities are provided by the DB attributes DISPLACEMENT and DRAFT.

focus = *surface-going capabilities*

FIG. 19. Possible predicates, translations, and foci.

candidate for a shift in focus. The default focus[14] of all but the evidence proposition is on the concept 'ship', which is the focus of the previous proposition. The evidence proposition however, focuses on 'surface-going capabilities', a potential candidate for a shift, and thus it is selected as the next proposition for the text.

Note that the choice of the evidence predicate based on the focus constraints confirms the motivation for the rule that the system should shift focus if possible. It is quite natural for the system to return focus to the concept 'ship',

[14] Each predicate has a default focus associated with it which indicates the predicate argument that is most likely to be focused on. The default focus corresponds to the unmarked syntax associated with the predicating act. For example, the attributive predicate in its usual use attributes features to an entity or event. The unmarked use assumes an entity has been focused on: the entity is being talked about and some of its features are being described (see Sentence 1 below). The opposite case, of associating talked about features with a different entity is less usual (see Sentence 2 below):

1. The chimpanzee has fine control over finger use.
2. Fine control over finger use is also common to the chimpanzee.

```
verb = = = provide
protagonist = (entry-for (HAVE DRAFT)(HAVE DISPLACEMENT)))
goal = possessive = (entry-for SHIP)
nnp = (entry-for (TRAVEL-MODE SURFACE))
```

FIG. 21. Proposition 2 at an intermediate stage.

After vocabulary has been chosen for the remaining untranslated arguments, the grammar is invoked to fill in the syntactic details of the sentence and to order the constituents, producing the actual linear sentence. Here focus information is used to make appropriate surface choices. For example, since the concept 'ship' was focused in sentence (1), reference to it in the second sentence can be pronominalized, resulting in the choice of 'its'. Tests are also made on focus information to select the active or passive construction, or a construction known as *three-insertion*.[17] The rhetorical predicates provide information about the type of sentential connective that can be used. In this answer, the connective 'for example' in sentence (4) is selected on the basis of the particular-illustration predicate.

8. Related Research

By far, the majority of work done to date in language generation has addressed problems in the tactical component. This has included a system to directly translate a given semantic network into English sentences [34], Goldman's [10] work on lexical choice as part of the MARGIE system, Davey's [8] use of systemic grammar to generate commentaries on tic-tac-toe games, McDonald's MUMBLE [21] which includes a broad coverage of English syntax and employs a decision making process that takes into account many syntactic constraints on realization, and very recently, the work on NIGEL [18, 19] to develop a large linguistically justified grammar within a systemic framework. Without this earlier work in language generation, development of TEXT would have been nearly impossible as it draws on the results of this work for its own tactical component (in particular, the concept of dictionary developed by both Goldman and McDonald). These works have very little to say, however, about the issues that were of particular concern in TEXT: determining the content and organization of a text.

Work on planning and generation bears more closely on the problem of content. Cohen [7] addressed the problem of planning speech acts in response to a user's question. His system, OSCAR, could select a speech act and specify the propositional content of the act. Appelt [2] continued in this vein by showing that the planning formalism could be used for determining the lexical and syntactic structure of the text as well as the content. One of the major departures of

Appelt's work is its refutation of the 'conduit metaphor'. While other generation systems have assumed a separation between the process of deciding what to say and how to say it, Appelt's work is based on the hypothesis that decisions made in the lowest level of the language generation process can influence decisions about what to say.[18] Both Appelt's and Cohen's work, however, deals with single-sentence generation for the most part. Their work does not address the problem of organizing it appropriately for text.

Two of the earlier systems that were capable of producing text emphasized not the problem of text generation, but the type of knowledge needed in order to produce appropriate text. Swartout [35] examined the problem of knowledge needed for generation in the context of a medical consultation system. He showed that knowledge conveniently represented in order to efficiently arrive at a medical diagnosis, may not allow for the generation of understandable explanations about the system's reasoning. He developed a representation appropriate for explaining the expert system's reasoning which was used for the generation of explanations. His main concern, however, was with the knowledge representation and not with the generation process.

Meehan was also interested in the problem of knowledge needed for generation as part of his work on the story-generation system TALESPIN [25]. TALESPIN was capable of producing simple short stories about persons (or anthropomorphic animals) making plans to achieve goals and their frustrations while achieving those goals. Meehan was most concerned with the planning aspects of the program and the knowledge needed to select plans for the characters, although his system could produce multi-sentence descriptions of the characters and their actions.

Mann and Moore [17] were interested in the specific problems that arise in the generation of multi-sentential strings. They developed the *Knowledge Delivery System* (KDS) which could produce a paragraph providing instructions about what to do in case of a fire alarm. Their system relies on hill-climbing techniques to produce optimal text and does not use knowledge about discourse structure. Another drawback to their system is the fact that it operates in the very limited domain of the fire-alarm system.

One advantage to KDS is its ability to do continual re-editing of the text to produce the final version. TEXT cannot evaluate its own text and clearly this is an important facility which must eventually be developed. KDS uses heuristics to do its re-evaluation, however, and has not been used to produce a wide range of texts. In contrast, TEXT makes its decisions about ordering on the basis of rhetorical strategies that are commonly used for particular discourse goals.

---

[17] E.g., There are two types of guided projectives in the ONR database: torpedoes and missiles.

[18] TEXT is based on a generation model which does assume separation, a model that was adopted to allow focus on the problems of the strategic component. Some of the integration that Appelt proposes could be achieved by introducing backtracking between the two components. It should be noted, however, that while most researchers agree that there must be interaction between the two processes, exactly how that interaction should be achieved is still an open question.

In sum then, very little previous work touches directly on the issues addressed in TEXT. TEXT differs from those few that do by providing a detailed computational model of discourse strategies that interact with focus of attention to produce the final text.

9. An Evaluation of Responses Generated by TEXT

To illustrate how our generation principles have been successful in producing coherent texts, as well as to identify defects in the text, consider the text generated in response to the question "What is a guided projectile?" (shown in Example 14). This text is representative of the range of generation TEXT can produce.

Example 14.

(1) A guided projectile is a projectile that is self-propelled. (2) There are 2 types of guided projectiles in the ONR database: torpedoes and missiles. (3) The missile has a target location in the air or on the earth's surface. (4) The torpedo has an underwater target location. (5) The missile's target location is indicated by the DB attribute DESCRIPTION and the missile's flight capabilities are provided by the DB attribute ALTITUDE. (6) The torpedo's underwater capabilities are provided by the DB attributes under DEPTH (for example, MAXIMUM OPERATING DEPTH). (7) The guided projectile has DB attributes TIME TO TARGET & UNITS, HORZ RANGE & UNITS and NAME.

The overall structure of the text is dictated by the *constituency* schema and the paragraph is bracketed by discussion of the guided projectile (first and last sentence). The inner portion of the text relates the guided projectile to its sub-classes and discusses each of these in turn. The overall structure is thus nicely balanced, providing a clear organizational framework for the reader.

Now consider the content of the text. The system has correctly, although not surprisingly, included only information that is directly or indirectly related to the guided projectile. This is the result of using the relevant knowledge pool. More significant, of all the information that could have been included from information related to the guided projectile, the system has selected only that which directly supports its goal of defining the object. Of 11 pieces of information related to the guided projectile (Fig. 22), the system has chosen to include only 5 pieces of information (i.e., its superordinate (sentence 1), its sub-classes (sentence 2), and 3 of its attributes (sentence 7)). Of 26 pieces of information associated with the missile and at least that many for the torpedo, the system has chosen to select only 2 for the torpedo and 4 for the missile (1 defining attribute and 1 database attribute for the torpedo and 2 defining attributes for the missile). This is due partly to the use of the *constituency*

Of previous work on text generation, Weiner's work [39] is most similar to TEXT. He is also interested in the structure of text, although he focuses on explanations in particular. He proposes an *explanation grammar* which is similar to our use of schemata in that it dictates what orderings of propositions are possible, it captures the hierarchical structure of text, and the kernels of the grammar (e.g., statement, reason) are at the same level of granularity as the predicates used for TEXT. Furthermore, he also incorporates the notion of focus of attention by maintaining a pointer to the proposition in focus at each point in the explanation.

Weiner proposes that a person may justify a statement in one of three ways:

(1) by providing a reason;

(2) by providing supporting examples;

(3) by providing alternatives, all of which are shown as inadequate except the alternative which supports the statement.

Thus, he uses basically four 'predicates' (*statement, reason, example, and alternative*), along with a number of subordinators such as *and/or* and *if/then*. Since explanations are frequently embedded, a statement followed by a reason may in turn function as the reason for another statement. To account for this, his grammar rules generate tree structures, which may be transformed by transformational rules, to generate the hierarchical structure representing the surface explanation. At each point in the explanation, one node of the tree is singled out as the focused node.

While the approach taken in TEXT is compatible with Weiner's, the theory of textural structure as captured in TEXT goes considerably beyond their formulation in the following ways: in TEXT, strategies are associated with different discourse goals, while in Weiner's system the grammars were developed only for justification; TEXT uses a greater number of predicates in schemata than does Weiner; the schemata used for TEXT capture a notion of variability which is resolved by other influences on the text, such as focus of attention and underlying semantic information; and finally, the specification of focus of attention and its interaction with the schemata is much more detailed in TEXT, as an argument of a proposition is identified as its focus, while in Weiner's work, an entire proposition is focused upon.

One other piece of work, from psychology, should also be mentioned. Rumelhart's story grammars [30] are similar to schemata as they describe textual structure for stories. He uses the grammars to recognize the underlying structure of a story, as opposed to generating it, and to suggest a memory organization which summarizes the important events of a story. Thus, his purpose in developing the grammars were different from ours. Rumelhart's grammars also differ from schemata in that they include both a structural and a semantic component, the non-terminals of the grammar (e.g., setting, episode, event) do not correspond to the rhetorical predicates used for TEXT, and he captures the structure of narratives, while we are more interested in the structure of descriptions.

More significant improvements to the text can only be made by dramatically improving the capabilities of the system. Some of these facilities would include inferencing (e.g., if the system can recognize and state the target location of the missile and torpedo, it should be able to infer that although both weapons have a target location, the exact location differs), varying detail (e.g., do all readers need to know about missiles and torpedoes or would the information about the guided projectile alone be sufficient? – see [27]), and finer determination of relevance (e.g., if the reader already knows about bombs, a guided projectile should be compared against this existing knowledge, requiring the system to elaborate further on the fact that guided projectiles are self-propelled, while bombs are not).

10. Future Directions

One of the tenets of this research has been that the final structure of a text is influenced by interactions between different sources of information, one of which is a speaker's knowledge about usual strategies for communication as encoded by the schemata. In the TEXT system as currently implemented, the final structure of the text is also influenced by the semantics of what is to be said (affecting which schema is selected for the answer and which predicates of the schema can be instantiated) and constraints on how focus of attention can shift. One influence on the final structure of the text which was not taken into account is a model of the user. Information about the user could be taken into account when determining which alternative to follow in a schema (thus, a proposition could be selected if it was determined to be most appropriate for the given user). An analysis is currently being made of the ways in which information about a particular user affects the level of detail needed in a response [24, 27].

Another current direction of research is an analysis of how and when global focus can shift in conjunction with the recursive use of the schemata. This is also expected to rely in part on a model of the user. Other open questions for the use of focusing concerns the nature of the mechanisms for maintaining and shifting immediate focus. More complex structures may be needed for some situations. For example, a speaker may introduce an item into conversation, but specify that he will continue to talk about it at a later point (see [14]).

11. Conclusions

The use of rhetorical strategies and a focusing mechanism provides a computationally tractable method for determining what to include in a text and how to organize it. This goes beyond earlier work in generation by examining production *strategies* for satisfying a particular goal (in this case, responding to one of three classes of questions). The generation method described not only provides methods for determining high-level choices about order and content,

An English translation of these 11 pieces is:
1. The guided projectile is a self-propelled projectile.
2. Attributes relating to self-propulsion include FUSE TYPE (possessed by the torpedo).
3. The DB attribute SPEED INDICES (possessed by the missile) also indicate properties of self-propulsion.
4–9. It has 6 DB attributes associated with it (counted here as 6 pieces of information): HORZ RANGE & UNITS, TIME TO TARGET & UNITS, HORZ RANGE, HORZ RANGE UNITS, TIME TO TARGET, TIME TO TARGET UNITS.
10. It is carried by water-going vehicles.
11. There are two types of guided projectiles: missiles and torpedoes.

FIG. 22.

schema. It determines that the superordinate of the guided projectile should be identified, its sub-classes described, and that defining attributes of both the missile and torpedo should be included (sentences 3 and 4). The focus constraints also play a role in the selection of information. They ensure, for example, that when database attributes are selected for sentences 5 and 6, only attributes are selected that support the definitional attributes presented in the previous sentences.

The surface text is influenced by the focus constraints such that constructions are selected that increase coherency. In this particular text, the use of there-insertion in sentence (2) was selected on the basis of an introduction of a set into focus. Similarly, the passive is used in sentences (5) and (6) to allow continued focus on the missile and torpedo. In some texts, the use of a particular rhetorical technique will force the selection of a sentential connective. This does not occur in this text.

Many of the defects of the text are due to limitations in the surface text generator (i.e., the tactical component). The text could be improved, for example, by combining sentences (2) and (3), emphasizing the contrast (e.g., "The missile has a target location in the air or on the earth's surface while the torpedo has an underwater target location."). Alternatively, the switch in focus back to the guided projectile could be more clearly signalled, at the same time linking the proposition to previously conveyed information by using a phrasing such as "The DB attributes common to all guided projectiles include ...". The generation of more sophisticated phrasings such as these requires further theoretical work for the tactical component, addressing the question of why these phrasings are preferable to others.

On the organizational level, improvement could be achieved by grouping together statements about the missile and statements about the torpedo. This would involve a change to the constituency schema so that the system could group together statements about an element of a set when more than one statement occurs. Such a change would allow the tactical component to pronominalize second references to both the missile and the torpedo, thus reducing some of the ponderous feeling of the text.

but it also provides information that can be used by the tactical component to make decisions about various surface level choices.

The use of schemata to encode knowledge about discourse structure embodies a computational treatment of rhetorical strategies that can be used to guide the generation process. This reflects the hypothesis that the generation process does not simply trace the knowledge representation to produce text, but instead uses communicative strategies that people are familiar with. This has the consequence that the same information can be described in different ways for different discourse purposes.

The use of a focusing mechanism as well as the schemata illustrates how the final structure and content of a text is influenced by an interaction between structural and semantic constraints. In the TEXT system, semantic constraints are provided by the relevant knowledge pool. It constrains the possible content of the text to a small subset of the entire knowledge base. A preferential ordering on immediate focus constrains possibilities for further utterances on the basis of what has already been said. The interaction of focus constraints with the schemata allows for the construction of a greater variety of paragraph-length responses to questions about database structure.

ACKNOWLEDGMENT

Special thanks goes to my advisor, Dr. Aravind K. Joshi and to Dr. Bonnie Webber for their advice and guidance in pursuing this work.

REFERENCES

1. Allen, J.F. and Perrault, C.R.. Analyzing intention in utterances, *Artificial Intelligence* **15** (1980) 143–178.

2. Appelt, D.E., Planning natural language utterances to satisfy multiple goals, Ph.D. Dissertation,. Stanford University, Stanford, CA, 1981.

3. Bossie, S., A tactical component for text generation: sentence generation using a functional grammar, Tech. Rep. MS-CIS-81-5, University of Pennsylvania, Philadelphia, PA, 1981.

4. Chafe, W.L., The flow of thought and the flow of language, in: T. Givon (Ed.), *Syntax and Semantics, Discourse and Syntax*, **12** (Academic Press, New York, 1979).

5. Chen, P.P.S., The entity-relationship model – towards a unified view of data, *ACM Trans. Database Systems* **1** (1) (1976).

6. Codd, E.F., Arnold, R.F., Cadiou, J.-M., Chand, C.L. and Roussopoulos, N., Rendezvous Version 1: An experimental English-language query formulation system for casual users of relational databases, Tech. Rept. RJ2144(29407), IBM Research Laboratory, San Jose, CA, 1978.

7. Cohen, P., On knowing what to say: Planning speech acts, Tech. Rept. No. 118, University of Toronto, Toronto, Ont., 1978.

8. Davey, A., *Discourse Production* (Edinburgh University Press, Edinburgh, 1979).

9. *Encyclopedia Americana* (Americana Corporation, New York, 1976).

10. Goldman, N.M., Conceptual generation, in: R.C. Schank (Ed.), *Conceptual Information Processing* (North-Holland, Amsterdam, 1975).

11. Grimes, J.E., *The Thread of Discourse* (Mouton, The Hague, 1975).

12. Grishman, R., Response generation in question-answering systems, in: *Proceedings 17th Annual Meeting of the Association for Computational Linguistics*, La Jolla, CA (August 1979) 99–102.

13. Hobbs, J., Coherence and coreference, SRI Tech. Note 168, SRI International, Menlo Park, CA, 1978.

14. Joshi, A. and Weinstein, S., Control of inference: role of some aspects of discourse structure – centering, in: *Proceedings Seventh International Joint Conference on Artificial Intelligence*, Vancouver, BC, August 1982.

15. Kay, M., Functional grammar, in: *Proceedings Fifth Annual Meeting of the Berkeley Linguistic Society*, Berkeley, CA, 1979.

16. Malhotra, A., Design criteria for a knowledge-based English language system for management: an experimental analysis, Rept. MAC TR-146, MIT, Cambridge, MA, 1975.

17. Mann, W.C. and Moore, J.A., Computer generation of multiparagraph English text, *Amer. J. Comput. Linguistics* **7** (1) (1981).

18. Mann, W.C., An overview of the Nigel text generation grammar, in: *Proceedings 21st Annual Meeting of the Association for Computational Linguistics*, Cambridge, MA (1983) 74–78.

19. Matthiesson, C.M.I.M., A grammar and a lexicon for a text-production system, in: *Proceedings 19th Annual Meeting of the Association for Computational Linguistics*, Stanford, CA (1981) 49–56.

20. McCoy, K.F., Automatic enhancement of a data base knowledge representation used for natural language generation, M.S. Thesis, University of Pennsylvania, Philadelphia, PA, 1982.

21. McDonald, D.D., Natural language production as a process of decision making under constraint, Ph.D. Dissertation, draft version, MIT, Cambridge, MA, 1980.

22. McKeon, R., *The Basic Works of Aristotle* (Random House, New York, 1941).

23. McKeown, K.R., Generating natural language responses to questions about database structure, Ph.D. Dissertation, Tech. Rept. MS-CIS-82-5, University of Pennsylvania, Philadelphia, PA, May 1982.

24. McKeown, K.R., Focus constraints on language generation, in: *Proceedings Eighth International Joint Conference on Artificial Intelligence*, Karlsruhe, Germany (August 1983) 582–587.

25. Meehan, J.R., TALE-SPIN, an interactive program that writes stories, in: *Proceedings Fifth International Joint Conference on Artificial Intelligence*, Cambridge, MA (August 1977). 91–98.

26. Moore, R.C., Reasoning about knowledge and action, SRI Tech. Note No. 191, SRI International, Menlo Park, CA, 1980.

27. Paris, C., Determining the level of expertise of a user in a question answering system, Tech. Rept., Columbia University, New York, 1980).

28. Paterson, J., *The Hamlyn Pocket Dictionary of Wines* (Hamlyn, New York, 1980).

29. Rich, E.A., User modeling via stereotypes, *Cognitive Sci.* **3** (1979) 329–354.

30. Rumelhart, D.E., Notes on a schema for stories, in: D.G. Bobrow and A. Collins (Eds.), *Representation and Understanding: Studies in Cognitive Science* (Academic Press, New York, 1975) 211–236.

31. Shipherd, H.R., *The Fine Art of Writing* (Macmillan, New York, 1926).

32. Shipley, L., Transcripts of mother-child dialogues, Unpublished manuscript, University of Pennsylvania, Philadelphia, PA, 1980.

33. Sidner, C.L., Towards a computational theory of definite anaphora comprehension in English discourse, Ph.D. Dissertation, MIT, Cambridge, MA, 1979.

34. Simmons, R. and Slocum, J., Generating English discourse from semantic networks, *Comm. ACM* **15** (1972) 891–905.

35. Swartout, W.R., Producing explanations and justifications of expert consulting programs, Tech. Rept. MIT/LCS/TR-251, MIT, Cambridge, MA, January 1981.

36. Tennant, H., Experience with the evaluation of natural language question answerers, Working Paper 18, University of Illinois, Urbana-Champaign, IL, 1979.

37. Terkel, S., *Working* (Avon Books, New York, 1972).
38. Thompson, H., Strategy and tactics: a model for language production, in: *Papers 13th Regional Meeting Chicago Linguistic Society*, Chicago, IL, 1977.
39. Weiner, J.L., BLAH, A system which explains its reasoning, *Artificial Intelligence* **15** (1980) 19–48.
40. Wilensky, R., A knowledge-based approach to language processing: a progress report, in: *Proceedings of the Seventh International Joint Conference on Artificial Intelligence*, Vancouver, BC (August 1981) 25–30.
41. Williams, W., *Composition and Rhetoric* (Heath, Boston, MA, 1983).
42. Winograd, T., *Language as a Cognitive Process: Syntax*, Vol. I (Addison-Wesley, Reading, MA, 1983).
43. Woods, W.A., Transition network grammars for natural language analysis, *Comm. ACM* **13** (10) (1970) 591–606.

Received January 1983; revised version received April 1984

Planning English Referring Expressions

Douglas E. Appelt

Artificial Intelligence Center, SRI International, Menlo Park, CA 94025, U.S.A.

Recommended by B. Webber

ABSTRACT

This paper describes a theory of language generation based on planning. To illustrate the theory, the problem of planning referring expressions is examined in detail. A theory based on planning makes it possible for one to account for noun phrases that refer, that inform the hearer of additional information, and that are coordinated with the speaker's physical actions to clarify his communicative intent. The theory is embodied in a computer system called KAMP, which plans both physical and linguistic actions, given a high-level description of the speaker's goals.

1. Introduction

One major goal of artificial intelligence research in natural-language generation is to develop a means of producing utterances that are natural and as close as possible to what humans would produce, given a similar domain and a similar need to communicate.

To use language with the competence of a human, it is not sufficient to have only a description of the syntactic, semantic, and discourse rules of a language: Human language behavior is part of a coherent plan of action directed toward satisfying a speaker's goals. Furthermore, sentences are not straightforward actions that satisfy only a single goal. When people produce utterances, their utterances are crafted with great sophistication to satisfy multiple goals at different communicative levels.

Fig. 1 illustrates a typical situation arising when two people cooperate on a common task, in which a speaker plans an utterance that has multiple effects on the intended hearer. The speaker moves the wheelpuller in the direction of the hearer and says "Use the wheelpuller to remove the flywheel." The hearer, who is observing the speaker while he makes the request and knows the speaker is referring to the particular tool, thinks to himself, "Ah, so *that's* a wheelpuller." The speaker's gesture with the wheelpuller is an instance of

FIG. 1. Satisfying multiple goals in an utterance.

communicative pointing, i.e., using a physical action to communicate an intention to refer to something.

In this situation, most obviously, the speaker is requesting that the hearer carry out a particular action, because the use of the imperative strongly suggests that a request is intended. Notice, however, that the speaker includes using the wheelpuller as part of his request. If he knew that the hearer did not know that he was supposed to use the wheelpuller to remove the flywheel, then his utterance was also intended to communicate the knowledge of what tool to use for the task. Also, the fact that he is *pointing* to a particular object and doing so in an obvious way communicates the speaker's intention to refer to it with the noun phrase "the wheelpuller". Because the intention to refer has been communicated, the noun phrase also communicates the fact that the intended referent is called a wheelpuller. The speaker could have said "Remove the flywheel", if he thought the hearer knew how to do it, and he could have said "Use *that thing* to remove the flywheel", if he had no goal of informing the hearer that the tool is a wheelpuller. In this case, the speaker has probably reasoned that future communication involving the wheelpuller will be necessary, and if the speaker and hearer mutually believe some description of the object other than its physical properties, it will be easier to refer to it in the future. The speaker and hearer mutually know that the phrase "the wheelpuller", rather than "the flywheel", is intended to refer to the object of the gesture because they share sufficient knowledge of the domain to determine that the intended referent of "the flywheel" is some other object.

0004-3702/85/$3.30 © 1985, Elsevier Science Publishers B.V. (North-Holland)

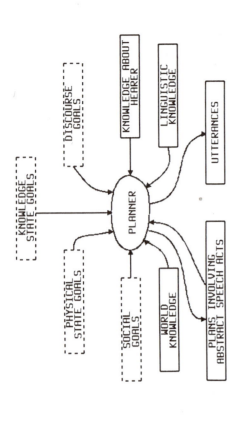

Fig. 2. Overview of an utterance planner.

The satisfaction of multiple goals in utterances is more the rule than the exception in communication. There are many different combinations of goals that can be simultaneously satisfied, and utterances with such combinations are common in everyday conversation. Here are a few examples:

- *Referring and communicating additional information.* A rock climber says to a friend, "Joe and I are going to climb the Snake Dike route on Half Dome next weekend." The speaker does not use the prepositional phrase "on Half Dome" to pick out a particular Snake Dike route from several that he and the hearer mutually know about, but rather assumes the hearer has never heard of the route, and provides additional information to inform him where it is located.

- *Referring and communicating an emotional attitude.* A speaker points to an accused spy and says "That scoundrel is the one who betrayed us!" The speaker is not trying to distinguish a particular scoundrel from some set of scoundrels. Although the speaker may be attempting to inform his audience that the intended referent is a scoundrel, quite possibly he is using a pejorative expression to convey his emotional attitude toward the intended referent.

- *Requesting and being polite.* Multiple-goal satisfaction even plays a role in such conventional utterances as "Could you tell me what time it is?" In this case the speaker chooses the indirect speech act to satisfy a goal of demonstrating politeness toward the hearer, while the more direct but less polite "What time is it?" would convey the request equally well.

These examples illustrate how a great deal of sophisticated reasoning about the effects of an utterance can be required to produce a seemingly simple sentence. A speaker capable of producing such utterances can be modeled by the process illustrated in Fig. 2. The speaker, modeled by the planner in the center of the diagram, plans to satisfy physical, knowledge-state, discourse and social goals, using knowledge about the world, his own mental states and those of the hearer, and knowledge about the language. The speaker's plans can ultimately entail both physical and linguistic action.

A planning system such as the one in Fig. 2 has been implemented as part of this research and is called KAMP, which stands for Knowledge And Modalities Planner. KAMP is a hierarchical planning system that uses a nonlinear representation of plans called a *procedural network* [1]. It is capable of taking a set of axioms about the state of the world, the preconditions and effects of actions, the beliefs of different agents and a description of an agent's high-level goal, and producing a plan from the perspective of the agent that involves the performance of both physical and linguistic actions. The linguistic actions are refined until an English sentence is completely specified.

A primary consideration in the design of KAMP was to avoid dividing the language planning task into two independent processes of deciding *what* to say

something is essentially a process of translation from a specification of the propositional content to the actual utterance. The propositional content remains unchanged by this process. Previous language-generation systems have always made this distinction (e.g. Mann [2]; McKeown [3]), because it allows one to separate the linguistic part of the system from everything else. Intuitively, this modularity is both theoretically and practically attractive.

In spite of its appeal, the 'what-how' distinction has less merit when examined in the light of a theory of language generation based on planning. Such a theory views communication as actions directed toward satisfying goals. There are many decisions at every level of the language planning process that can be described in terms of action and goal satisfaction. At the highest level, there is planning illocutionary acts, at lower levels there is deciding how to communicate an intention to refer, and deciding how to communicate intentions about the discourse. The actions that satisfy these goals depend to different degrees on what linguistic choices are available in the current context. Thus, the planning at each level involves consideration of both linguistic rules and goal satisfaction. The distinction between 'what' and 'how' then becomes merely two points on a continuum between goal-satisfaction and rule-satisfaction processes, and no modularization based on the distinction is obvious. This does not, of course, imply that modularization per se is undesirable, but that the dimension along which the modules are separated is not one of 'deciding what to say' and 'deciding how to say it'. For example the TELEGRAM grammar [23] separates knowledge about the grammar and its semantics from the rest of the knowledge the system needs, but integrates the processes that uses these knowledge sources so that planning plays a role in all aspects of

Criticism of other research efforts may be somewhat unfair because the resulting limitations on what they can do, for example, the lack of ability to coordinate physical and linguistic actions, were not problems that these researchers have sought to overcome. However, designers of natural-language generation systems will ultimately have to confront these issues.

A hierarchical planner was selected as the design of KAMP because it provides for a separation between the planning of domain-level goals and actions and low-level linguistic actions as well as intermediate levels of abstraction that facilitate the integration of multiple goals into utterances. The abstraction hierarchy coincides with the spectrum of goal satisfaction versus rule satisfaction, which makes this design well suited to planning without a sharp distinction between 'what' and 'how'.

This work is closely related to other recent work in artificial intelligence and linguistics. The idea of using speech acts as operators in a planning system originates with Bruce [4]. and Cohen and Perrault [5]. Evans [7] independently developed a theory of speech acts based on situation semantics [8] that shares many of the fundamental assumptions of the research reported in this article. An initial description of KAMP and utterance planning was given in two previous papers by Appelt [9, 10]. This paper describes the system and its underlying theory as it has been fully developed and implemented.

This paper is organized in three main sections. Section 2 describes the problem that is being addressed. Section 3 describes a formal approach to axiomatizing referring actions, and Section 4 illustrates the KAMP planner with an example.

2. English Referring Expressions

Speakers use noun phrases for many different purposes, and this research has not attempted to deal with all of them. This paper will be concerned only with planning singular, specific, definite noun phrases that do not contain explicit quantifiers. Even within this narrow domain of phenomena, there exist a number of different referring intentions that a speaker may have when he utters a noun phrase, and part of a hearer's task in understanding an utterance is figuring out which one the speaker has in mind. This intention-recognition process is necessary because identical noun phrases may be used in different contexts with different intentions. When a speaker utters a definite noun phrase, the hearer must decide whether the speaker intends that the hearer actually *identify* some person or object in the world to which the speaker intends to refer. The following intentions underly uses of the noun phrases under consideration:

– *Speaker intends to refer to a mutually known object.* In this case there is assumed to be a mutually known object to which the speaker intends to refer. A mutually known object is an object of which the speaker and hearer mutually know some properties. This mutual knowledge arises out of the immediate context either by being (to use Prince's terminology [11]) *situationally evoked* (part of the shared context) or *textually evoked* (previously introduced to the discourse). Pronominal and anaphoric noun phrases are used to communicate intentions of this type.

– *Speaker intends that the hearer identify a referent.* The speaker may intend to refer to an object (of which he and the hearer may or may not share mutual knowledge), and intends that the hearer, based on his understanding of the speaker's intentions, perform whatever actions are necessary to identify the individual to which the speaker intends to refer. On occasion, speakers may convey this intention explicitly by means of a request to find the referent. However, this intention often underlies referring actions for which no explicit identification request is made. For example, the italicized noun phrase in "Turn left at *the third light past the large pink house on the left*." is an example of a noun phrase that could be uttered with this intention. What distinguishes this case from the previous case is that there is not necessarily any mutual knowledge of the intended referent at the time of the utterance; in the above example, the hearer may have no prior knowledge at all of the large pink house. The speaker's implicit intention is that the hearer identify the referent may require the hearer to form and execute a complex plan to make the identification. Instead of planning a description with respect to the speaker and hearer's mutual knowledge, he tries to plan a description that is *useful* for the hearer to plan an identification action. For example, a speaker does not give the hearer a useful description when he tells the hearer (whom he has just met on the bus) which bus stop to get off by saying "Get off one stop before I do," because there is no way the hearer can use the description to form an effective plan to identify the referent, even though the noun phrase "one stop before I do" semantically denotes the right thing.

– *Speaker intends that the hearer not identify a referent.* When a definite noun phrase is used with this intention it is commonly called *attributive*. The speaker may have a description of an individual that relates the individual to the mutual knowledge of the speaker and hearer, and the speaker may or may not know which individual satisfies that description. The hearer must realize that the speaker does not intend to say anything about a particular individual, but rather of whatever individual it is that satisfies a description. The noun phrase *John's children* (where John does not have any children yet) in the sentence "*John's children* will be very rich", is used in this manner.

According to KAMP's model of language production and understanding, a speaker uttering something implies he intends for the hearer to recognize the intended propositional content. This entails recognizing predicates and the arguments to which they are applied. These arguments are drawn from a set of so called 'active' concepts. The speaker introduces concepts to this set through the performance of *concept activation actions*. These actions are frequently performed by means of *referring expressions*, which are expressions that bear a semantic denotation relationship to objects in the world. All of a speaker's physical and linguistic actions may be instrumental to conveying the intentions behind a concept activation, so while referring expressions are an important form of realization, they are not the only means that must be considered. Also, a concept can be active by means of inferential connection to active concepts even though it is not explicitly the object of a concept activation.

This paper will consider only the planning of concept activation actions in which the speaker and hearer mutually know some facts about the object of the concept activation at the time of the speaker's utterance. An adequate formal theory of concept activation actions should account for the following phenomena: (1) how speakers reason about mutual knowledge to arrive at a description of the object; (2) how speakers use nonlinguistic means (e.g. pointing) to contribute toward the satisfaction of a goal to activate a concept; and (3) how speakers plan noun phrases that satisfy goals in addition to reference. The next section examines these questions.

3. A Formal Theory of Reference Planning

The logic that is used for the formal description of referring actions is based on Moore's logic of knowledge and action [12]. This logic consists of an *object language* whose terms denote actions and objects in the world, and a *meta-language* whose terms also denote individuals, but which (in addition) can denote object-language terms and *possible worlds*. The object language includes intensional operators such as **Know** and **Intend**, the semantics of which are axiomatized in the first-order meta-language in terms of possible worlds. The semantics of action-terms in the object language are axiomatized as relations on possible worlds, where actions map one world into another, with possible worlds playing a role similar to the familiar states of a conventional logic of action [14]. The reader familiar with model-theoretic semantics will notice that the notion of possible world used here is quite different from the familiar notion of a world as a complete course of events, and should bear this distinction in mind throughout the article.

In this article, the following notational conventions will be adopted: Intensional operators (e.g. **Know**) are written in boldface type. Predicates, functions, and constants appear in lower-case type with initial capital letter (e.g. Kernel). Variables appear in lower-case italic type (e.g. *act*). Schema variables are upper-case italic type (e.g. *PS*). Most of the predicate naming conventions are taken directly from Moore [12] to facilitate cross-reference by the reader desiring more information.

A detailed description of Moore's scheme for reasoning about knowledge and action would be much too long for this article. This paper will only

The reader should bear in mind that the following predicates are used in most of the examples, and have the following meanings:

- $T(w, P)$ means object-language formula P is true in world w.
- $D(w, x)$ is the denotation of object-language term x in world w.
- $K(A, w_1, w_2)$ means world w_2 is consistent with A's knowledge in world w_1.
- $R(e, w_1, w_2)$ means that world w_2 is the result of event e happening in w_1.
- $@(x)$ is the *standard name* of x, i.e., a term whose denotation is x in every possible world.

For the sake of simplicity, this article uses a loose notation to represent object-language logical connectives and quantifiers. The same symbols will be employed to represent similar operations in both the object and the meta-language. Moore [12] discusses the correspondence between object language and meta-language, including some problems associated with quantifying into opaque contexts.

One may argue that an adequate theory of language planning must be based on a theory of *belief* rather than a theory of knowledge. Although this is a valid point, an adequate theory of belief is difficult to formalize, because once one admits the possibility of holding beliefs that are not true of the world, a theory of belief revision and truth maintenance is required. It is true that Moore's logic of knowledge can be transformed into a logic of belief by appropriately weakening the axioms (viz. the axiom that asserts reflexivity of the accessibility relation on possible worlds) so that it is no longer possible to infer P from **Know**(A, P). However, without addressing all the problems associated with belief and justification, one has really accomplished little else besides changing the word **Know** to **Believe**. Because a detailed study of reasoning about belief is beyond the scope of this research, the axioms are presented using **Know** as a first approximation to the best theory.

3.1. Reference and concept activation

KAMP is based on a theory of speech acts that is similar to that described by Searle [13]. According to Searle, the speaker performs some utterance acts from which the hearer recognizes the proposition that the hearer intends to convey. The speaker conveys these components of the propositional content to the hearer by means of what Searle calls *propositional acts* of referring and predicating. Then the hearer infers what the speaker wants him to do with the proposition—for example, whether it is to affect his beliefs or his future actions. This constitutes the recognition of the *illocutionary force* of the utterance.

The problem with Searle's theory is that it is too strongly sentence-oriented. With the exception of conjunctions and conditionals, uttering a referring expression constitutes the performance of exactly one propositional act, and

because failure to do so can result in an infelicitous reference. Clark and Marshall [15] demonstrate that is possible to construct examples where the definite description fails to identify the right concept for the hearer if only a finite number of assertions about the speaker's knowledge of the hearer's knowledge are considered.

Since mutual knowledge and mutual belief follow from an infinite number of facts, it is impossible to deduce mutual knowledge directly from its definition. Cohen and Perrault [16] demonstrate that the mutual-knowledge condition on referring expressions is in fact too strong. They demonstrate that A can use a definite description to refer to an object in speaking to agent B if it can be concluded that the nested assertions about A's knowledge about B's knowledge hold in all but a finite number of cases. Unfortunately, this analysis still leaves the problem of verifying an infinite number of conditions.

Nadathur and Joshi [17] circumvent this problem by adopting a weaker condition for the use of a definite description: that the speaker believes that the hearer believes that the description denotes the object, and the speaker has no reason to believe that the chosen description is not mutual knowledge.

The KAMP theory maintains that a description used in a referring expression must be mutually believed, but admits heuristics by which mutual belief can be plausibly inferred without recourse to verifying an infinite number of conditions. Clark and Marshall call such assumptions *copresence heuristics*. According to their copresence heuristics, mutual knowledge results from three sources: (1) common membership in a community of speakers; (2) sharing physical proximity that enables the agents to observe, and observe each other observing; (3) linguistic exchange of information.

In KAMP, copresence heuristics (1) and (2) above are stated directly in the axioms describing a particular communicative situation. Heuristic (3) is captured by a suitable axiomatization of illocutionary acts, described fully by Appelt [5], namely that the successful performance of an illocutionary act produces mutual knowledge of its performance.

In addition to copresence heuristics, KAMP requires a logical representation of mutual knowledge from which it is possible to derive any one of the infinite consequences of an assertion of mutual knowledge. The mutual knowledge of two agents A and B is everything that is true in the *union* of the possible worlds compatible with A's knowledge and B's knowledge. Notice that the *intersection* of the propositions believed by two agents is represented by the *union* of possible worlds compatible with their knowledge. For the purpose of stating this fact formally, a pseudo-individual called the *kernel* of A and B is defined such that the set of possible worlds consistent with the kernel's knowledge is the set of all worlds consistent with either A's knowledge or B's knowledge. This leads to the following definition of mutual knowledge:

$$\forall w_1\, T(w_1, \textbf{MutuallyKnow}(A, B, P)) \equiv$$
$$\forall w_2\, K(\text{Kernel}(A, B), w_1, w_2) \supset T(w_2, P).$$

(1)

The KAMP theory is an attempt to move beyond the sentence-oriented perspective and account for sentences that realize multiple illocutionary acts and illocutionary acts that appear to be realized over the course of several sentences. To achieve this goal it is necessary to formally decouple illocutionary acts and propositional acts from sentences and noun phrases. Toward that end, a hierarchy of linguistic actions is defined and axiomatized, and is employed by KAMP. At the top of the abstraction hierarchy are illocutionary acts. These actions are performed by means of surface speech acts. A surface speech act is realized by means of uttering a sentence.

KAMP plans concept activations, which are analogous to Searle's propositional acts, and these actions are performed by means of describing actions (realized directly as noun phrases) and communicative pointing actions. As with illocutionary acts and surface speech acts, it is possible to separate the intention communication action from its linguistic realization.

Concept activation actions and their realization will be the primary focus of this article. The verb 'refer' is often used in a sense that is very close to what is meant by activating a concept. If the subject of the verb 'refer' is a linguistic expression, then what is being described is a semantic relationship similar to what one means by 'denote'. When the subject of 'refer' is an agent, then the intended interpretation is "to perform a concept activation action by means of uttering a referring expression".

KAMP represents concepts as intensional object-language expressions that denote different objects in different possible worlds. In general, it is possible for object-language terms to denote different individuals with respect to each possible world. If an object-language term denotes the same individual in every possible world, it is called a *rigid designator*. A rigid designator is like a proper name, and it is often convenient to use such names in the theory because they simplify the axiomatization of the domain. Under such assumptions, it is easy to show that any agent can decide whether two rigid designators denote the same individual, and they are therefore useful for describing the process of an agent reasoning about who or what something is. Because of the simplification that results, the example in this article assumes that objects have standard names despite the implausibility of people having names for every individual (including, for example, each of the 200 identical screws in some parts bin).

3.2. Reasoning about mutual knowledge

The planning of concept activation actions requires not only the ability to reason about what different agents know, but also what they *mutually know*. Agents A and B mutually know P if and only if A knows P, B knows P, A knows that B knows P, B knows that A knows P, A knows that B knows that A knows P, B knows that A knows that B knows P, A knows that B knows that A knows P, and so on, ad infinitum. It is insufficient in planning a concept activation for A to consider only his own knowledge and the knowledge of B,

The second axiom that is needed is:

$$\forall x, w_1, w_2\, K(x, w_1, w_2) \supset \forall y\, K(Kernel(x, y), w_1, w_2). \qquad (2)$$

Axiom (2) states that the possible worlds consistent with any agent's knowledge is a subset of the possible worlds consistent with the kernel of that agent and any other agent. Note that because the knowledge axioms that allow one to conclude that if an agent knows P, he knows that he knows P, apply to the kernel individual as well as ordinary individuals, it follows that if A and B mutually know P, then they mutually know that they mutually know P. This allows statements of the form

Know$(A,$ **Know**$(B,$ **Know**$(A \ldots)))$

to be derived to any arbitrary depth. Axioms (1) and (2) can be used efficiently by a first-order logic theorem-prover that handles equational theories, such as that of Stickel [18].

3.3. Reasoning about intention

KAMP uses a possible-worlds semantics for intention that is similar to the possible-worlds semantics for knowledge and action. Reasoning about intention is crucial to utterance planning at several stages, because all actions with communicative intent (viz. illocutionary acts and concept activation actions) depends on the hearer's recognition of the speaker's intention for successful performance.

There are two levels at which KAMP describes an agent's intentions. First, an agent can intend to make a proposition true, or he can intend to perform an action. Thus,

Intend(A, P)

means that agent A intends to bring P about, and

IntendToDo(A, act)

means that A intends to perform act in the immediate future.

The semantics of **Intend** are that there is some set of possible worlds, called a *preference set* of an agent, such that for every world w in that preference set, P is true in w. This is expressed by Axiom (3).

$$T(w_1, \textbf{Intend}(A, P)) \equiv$$
$$\exists s\, PS(A, w_1, s) \wedge \forall w_2 (w_2 \in s) \supset T(w_2, P), \qquad (3)$$

in which $PS(A, w, s)$ is true if and only if s is a preference set in world w of agent A.

The semantics of **IntendToDo** are similar. In that case, there is some

$$T(w, \textbf{IntendToDo}(A, act)) \equiv$$
$$\exists s\, PS(A, w_1, s) \wedge \forall w_2 (w_2 \in s) \supset R(Do(A, act), w_1, w_2). \qquad (4)$$

It follows directly from (3) and (4) that if an agent intends to perform an action, then he intends to bring about the effects of the action.

These two axioms give KAMP a rudimentary ability to reason about what an agent intends to bring about and what he intends to do next which is adequate for KAMP to make simple multiple-agent plans. These axioms are not claimed to come close to an adequate theory of desire or intention.

3.4. An overview of KAMP

KAMP differs in a number of important ways from planning systems that are restricted to physical domains. The most fundamental difference is that the utterance-planning system is necessarily always planning in an environment with at least one other agent, and this introduces problems of cooperating with the other agent, or thwarting its goals [19]. The necessity of reasoning about different agents requires some means of reasoning about their knowledge, beliefs, and intentions, and how their mental states are affected by the actions that they and others perform.

The necessity of reasoning about propositional attitudes led to the adoption of the possible-worlds semantics representation described by Moore [12]. This formalism is best suited to proving that certain facts hold in a state of the world, and is not well suited to planning. Because knowledge states are represented as sets of possible worlds, straightforward application of a backward chaining algorithm to these sets in search of a plan is cumbersome at best. The design of the KAMP planner differs from other planning systems because of the need to overcome this disadvantage.

Fig. 3 illustrates the operation of KAMP. KAMP solves problems by using a heuristic problem-solving method, which is successful at finding a good plan with minimal effort most of the time while preserving the option to rely on brute-force search if heuristic methods fail. KAMP has two descriptions of the actions available to the planner. One description is in the form of axioms relating possible worlds, as described above. The other description is an *action summary*, which summarizes the preconditions and effects of actions in a STRIPS-like formalism (see [20]) involving preconditions and add and delete lists. The planner uses the action summaries as a heuristic guide to the selection of actions that are likely to result in a good plan. They are not intended to be complete descriptions of all the consequences of performing the action. The possible-worlds-semantics axiomatization is used to reason about whether the proposed plan is actually going to work. If the action summaries are well designed, stating the effects that the action is expected to have in the most

siders the intentions of other agents. Assuming that an agent A_1 doing the planning has a particular goal to achieve, it is possible for the planner to assume that A_1 will intend to do any action that A_1 knows will contribute to achieving the goal. However, if it is necessary to incorporate the actions of another agent, A_2, into the plan, A_1 must be able to assume that A_2 will actually do the actions required of him. This amounts to showing that A_2 intends to do the action. Guaranteeing that this condition holds can lead to planning requests and commands. Once it has been established that A_2 will intend to do a high-level action, then the planner assumes that A_2 will intend to do any action that he knows will contribute toward the realization of the high-level action. Although A_2 may not have the knowledge necessary to carry out the action, it can be assumed that A_2 will execute a plan he can figure out. A_2 can ask questions of A_1, however, if A_1 can anticipate this need for information and furnish it at the time of the request, the overall plan may be simplified, and the resulting dialogue will be more natural.

When the planner is given an initial goal, it first creates a procedural network consisting of a single plan step containing the goal. The following process is then executed repeatedly until either the planner concludes that the goal is unachievable, or some sequence of executable (i.e. low-level) actions is found that achieves the goal: First, a world (serving in its role as a situation) is assigned to each node in the procedural net reflecting the state of the world at that time (i.e. at the time *before* the action or goal named in the node is performed or achieved). The initial node is assigned W_0, the initial actual world. Then, iteratively, when the planner proposes that a subsequent action is performed in a world to reach a new world, a name is generated for the new world and the relation of the new world to its predecessor is explicitly asserted. All goal nodes that have worlds assigned are then evaluated, i.e. the planner calls on the deduction system to attempt to prove that the goal is satisfied in the assigned world. Any goal for which the proof succeeds is marked as a phantom goal, (i.e. a goal that is already satisfied), but is kept in the plan so that if actions planned at a later stage should make it no longer hold, corrective action can be taken to preserve or re-achieve it.

Next, all the unexpanded nodes in the network that have been assigned worlds and that are not phantoms are examined. Some may be high-level actions for which a procedure exists to determine the appropriate expansion. These procedures are invoked if they exist, otherwise the action generator is invoked that uses the action summaries to propose a set of actions that might be performed to achieve the goal. If an action is found, it is inserted into the procedural network along with its preconditions.

Like Sacerdoti's system, KAMP uses procedures called *critics* to examine the plan globally and to determine interactions between proposed actions. A critic is a modular procedure that examines the plan for specific kinds of interactions between the effects of the actions. At the end of each cycle of expansion, each

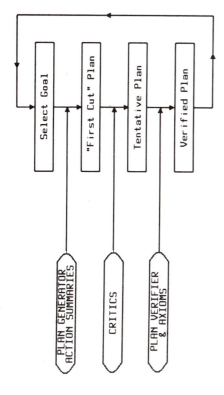

FIG. 3. The operation of KAMP.

plans most of the time, and the search required for finding a correct plan will be significantly reduced.

The search for a plan is facilitated by the simplifications introduced by the action summaries. For example, an implicit assumption in the action summaries is that all agents know what the effects of the actions are. In some instances this assumption may not hold, and any plan that depends on this assumption will fail the verification step. The process that uses the action summaries can be viewed as a 'plausible move generator' that proposes actions that are likely to succeed in achieving the goal.

KAMP uses a *procedural network* to represent the plan as it is being constructed and refined. A procedural network can be thought of as a two-dimensional data structure. The horizontal dimension is a temporal one, reflecting the partial ordering among the actions; the vertical dimension is one of abstraction, where goals and abstract actions are refined into sequences of low-level actions that can be performed directly by the agent. The connection between the planning data structure and the possible-worlds-semantics formalism is made by associating with each node in the procedural network a world that represents the state of affairs at that point. Whenever a fact must be proved to hold in the situation resulting from the execution of a series of actions, it is proved using the world associated with the appropriate node in the procedural network as the current real world.

KAMP's database contains assertions about what each agent knows, and what each agent knows what the other agents know. KAMP is not actually one of the agents doing the planning, but rather simulates how the agents would plan, given certain information about them. When KAMP plans, it 'identifies' with one of the agents and makes plans from the perspective of the agent it identifies with. This perspective makes an important difference when the planner con-

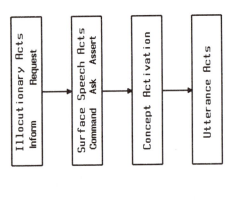

Illocutionary Acts
Inform   Request

Surface Speech Acts
Command   Ask   Assert

Concept Activation

Utterance Acts

Fɪɢ. 4. ᴋᴀᴍᴘ's hierarchy of linguistic actions.

conventions of communication (e.g. the Gricean maxims [21]), he may come to believe that a particular wrench is in a particular location, thus realizing the *perlocutionary effects* of the action. A detailed description of the axioms for illocutionary acts and their relationship to perlocutionary effects is given elsewhere [6] and is beyond the scope of this paper.

The next level of abstraction is that of surface speech acts. Performing a surface speech act entails uttering a particular sentence. The distinction between these two levels of actions can be described as follows: Saying *that* the box-end wrench is on the table is an illocutionary act. A surface speech act realizes the illocutionary act by a *particular* utterance, in this case "The box-end wrench is on the table" (or perhaps, "The green tool is next to the platform", if the concept activation actions are realized differently). There is a one-to-one correspondence between surface speech acts and utterances, because the former are merely abstract representations of the latter.

It is impossible to state simple axioms that describe the effects of surface speech acts in the same manner as has been done for illocutionary acts for two reasons: The same surface speech act can realize different illocutionary acts, depending on the context in which it is performed, and it is possible for a single surface speech act to realize several illocutionary acts simultaneously. Because the effects of a surface speech act depend on what illocutionary act it is being used to realize, it is impossible to describe its effects directly. The axioms need to state (1) that the hearer realizes what surface speech act has been performed, and (2) how the hearer deduces the illocutionary act from the surface speech act.

The relationship between surface speech acts and illocutionary acts can be

critic looks for a particular type of interaction. If the interactions occur, the critic reorganizes the structure of the plan in some way.

There is an important distinction between modifications to the plan made by critics and modifications made during the process of expanding an action to a lower level of abstraction. The process of expansion is local to an action and concerned with determining what actions can be used to achieve a given goal. The process considers only the state of the world as it is assumed to be at the time of performing an action, and what actions are available. Critics examine interactions between actions in the plan and propose changes, but do not propose new plans.

The result of separating expansion and criticism is an overall simplification of the planning process. The process of expanding actions is simpler because the many possible interactions do not have to be considered at the time of expansion. Obtaining a rough plan and refining it reduces the amount of blind search the planner has to do. The process of discovering interactions is also simpler because it does not have to be concerned with what actions to perform, only with the interactions between actions that have already been selected.

If the expansion of the plan to the next level of abstraction is complete, then the planner invokes the deduction system to prove that the proposed sequence of actions actually achieves the goal. If the proof is successful and the plan is not yet fully expanded to the level of executable actions, the process of world assignment is carried out again and the entire procedure is repeated.

If the proof fails, the reason is probably that the simplifying assumptions made by the action summaries were incorrect; in this case, the planner must resort to a more detailed search of the space to find a plan. Finding the best strategy for plan modification when the correctness proof fails is a good area for future research.

3.5. Planning concept activation actions

As described so far, ᴋᴀᴍᴘ has a general ability to plan actions that affect the knowledge and intentions of agents; however for ᴋᴀᴍᴘ to produce language, it needs axioms and critics that capture information about linguistic actions.

Fig. 4 depicts the hierarchy of linguistic actions used by ᴋᴀᴍᴘ. At the top of the hierarchy are such illocutionary acts as informing and requesting. These are the highest-level communicative actions. A correctly performed illocutionary act has the effect of making the speaker and hearer mutually aware that the speaker intended to perform the illocutionary act. For example, if the speaker performs the illocutionary action of informing the hearer that the box-end wrench is in the toolbox, then (as a result of the action) they mutually know that the speaker intended to do so. From this knowledge and from other knowledge that the hearer has about the speaker (e.g. whether or not he is

sentence that constitutes its linguistic realization. Initially, these structures are only partially specified; as the plan is expanded to lower levels, the actions in the expansion contribute to the syntactic structure of the sentence associated with the surface speech act of which they are a part. When the plan is complete, each surface speech act node specifies a sentence, the utterance of which demonstrably satisfies the speaker's goals.

KAMP's grammar originally consisted of a relatively small number of context-free rules distributed throughout the system. A grammar of basic clause structure was available to the planner when surface speech acts were planned, in expanding surface speech acts with concept activation actions, a grammar of noun phrase constituent structure was used. Obviously, the linguistic coverage was severely limited. This was not viewed as a serious limitation, however, because the purpose of KAMP was originally to explore and develop some of the most basic relationships between utterances and their relationship to communicative intentions, and the interesting problems concerned how utterances were used in multiple-goal satisfaction and integrated into a general plan of action rather than in the internal complexity of the utterances themselves.

The inadequacy of the initial approach led to the development of the TELEGRAM grammar formalism. Currently work is in progress on constructing a larger, more robust grammar based on function unification grammar [27] that provides a cleaner integration of the grammar with the planning mechanism. This work is described elsewhere [23] and discussion of the details of the grammar is beyond the scope of this article.

3.6. A formal theory of concept activation

The level of abstraction below surface speech acts in Fig. 4 is that of concept activation actions. Currently KAMP only plans concept activation actions for which the concept is part of the speaker's and hearer's mutual knowledge. Concept activations are part of the expansion of a surface speech act. We will consider only concept activation actions that have realizations as noun phrases. As discussed earlier, the types of actions planned by KAMP are only a subset of the types of actions that can be realized by noun phrases, but nevertheless represents a significant subset.

As explained in Section 2, the process of understanding a speech act involves first constructing a proposition from a set of available concepts. This set of available concepts are called 'active', and the predicate Active(C) means that C is an object-language term that belongs to the available set of terms for constructing the proposition the speaker is conveying by way of the surface speech act. Terms can enter the active set explicitly through the performance of a concept activation with the term as its object, or implicitly by way of inference. For example, in requesting a hearer to remove the pump from the platform in a domain involving the repair and assembly of an air compressor, if

example, a speaker can perform the surface speech act of uttering a declarative sentence with propositional content P and intend that the hearer recognize the intention to inform him that P. Such speech acts are called direct speech acts. In some cases, the inferential connection between the surface speech act and the intended illocutionary act is more complex, for example, when a speaker makes an utterance like "The door, please" and intends that the hearer recognize a request to open the door. Such actions are referred to as indirect speech acts, and Allen and Perrault [22] present a detailed analysis of how such intention recognition takes place.

KAMP does not currently plan surface speech acts that require the hearer to make indirect interpretations, not because it is inherently incapable of doing so, but rather because indirect speech acts are frequently planned to satisfy multiple goals, often along social dimensions and others that are very difficult to formalize. However, the ability to plan indirect speech acts is important for the generation of plausible utterances, and the incorporation of Allen and Perrault's intention-recognition conditions into the axioms for surface speech acts is an important area for further investigation.

Fig. 5 illustrates the two components of a surface speech act: the *intention communication* component and the *linguistic realization* component. The intention communication component is concerned with how the intentions of the speaker get communicated to the hearer. This includes communicating the intention to refer to objects or to get the hearer to identify objects. The linguistic realization component is concerned with taking the actions specified by the intention communication component and realizing them in a valid syntactic structure. A two-way channel of communication between these two components exists, because the means of communication of intention determines what linguistic structures must be chosen; in addition, the grammatical choices available constrain the possible means of intention communication. Associated with each surface speech act node is the syntactic structure of the

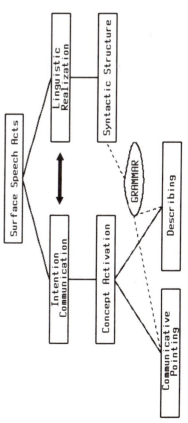

FIG. 5. Components of a surface speech act.

the hearer knows that the pump is attached to the platform and nothing else, the platform need not be mentioned because it is implicitly active. Therefore, it is only necessary to say "Remove the pump" for the hearer to recognize

Intend(S, Do(H, Remove(pump1, platform1))).

The performance of a communicative pointing action directed toward an object causes the standard name of that object to enter the set of active concepts.

The actual process of recognizing the proposition from the active concepts is not axiomatized. As a simplification, the axioms for surface speech acts state as a precondition that the terms that are part of the propositional content of the act must be active.

Axioms (5)–(7) describe what happens when an agent performs a concept activation action (Cact). Axiom (5) describes the preconditions that the speaker and the hearer are at the same location and that the speaker intends that the hearer know that that concept is active. Axiom (6) describes the change in the set of active concepts and axiom (7) states that the speaker and hearer mutually know that the concept activation action has taken place by specifying that the only worlds that are consistent with what the two agents mutually know are those that are the result of performing the action in some world consistent with their mutual knowledge before the action. The mutual knowledge of the action's occurrence results in the mutual knowledge of the preconditions and effects holding in the appropriate states, and thereby provides a means of stating the knowledge effects of actions without the necessity of listing every consequence explicitly. The axioms are expressed in the notation of Moore [12]. The function @ constructs a rigid designator that denotes its argument in all possible worlds, meaning that it functions like an inverse QUOTE for embedding meta-language terms inside of object-language formulas.

$$\forall A,B,C,w_1,w_2\, R(Do(A, Cact(B, C)), w_1, w_2) \supset$$
$$D(w_1, Location(A)) = D(w_1, Location(B)) \wedge$$
$$T(w_1, \textbf{Intend}(@(A), @(B), Active(@(C)))), \quad (5)$$

$$\forall A,B,C,w_1,w_2\, R(Do(A, Cact(B, C)), w_1, w_2) \supset T(w_2, Active(C)), \quad (6)$$

$$\forall A,B,C,w_1,w_2\, R(Do(A, Cact(B, C)), w_1, w_2) \supset$$
$$\forall w_3\, K(Kernel(A, B), w_2, w_3) \supset$$
$$\exists w_4\, K(Kernel(A, B), w_1, w_4) \wedge R(Do(A, Cact(B, C)), w_4, w_3). \quad (7)$$

When KAMP is expanding a concept activation action to lower-level actions, it takes into account both the intention communication and linguistic realization components of the action. The intention communicating component may be

realized by a plan involving either physical or linguistic actions. KAMP relies on *description* as a linguistic means of communicating an intention to refer, and on *pointing* as a nonlinguistic means.

The following schema defines the preconditions of the *describe* action in a manner similar to axiom (5):

$$\forall A,B,w_1,w_2\, R(Do(A, Describe(B, \mathcal{D})), w_1, w_2) \supset$$
$$\exists x\, T(w_1, \textbf{Know}(A, \mathcal{D}(@(x)))) \wedge$$
$$T(w_1, \sim\textbf{MutuallyKnow}(A, B, \sim\mathcal{D}^*(@(x)))) \wedge$$
$$T(w_1, \forall y \sim\textbf{MutuallyKnow}(A, B, \mathcal{D}^*(y)) \supset y \neq @(x)). \quad (8)$$

Axiom (8) states the preconditions for an agent A planning to use a description $\mathcal{D}$ to refer to an object to an agent B. The description $\mathcal{D}$ is an object-language predicate composed of a number of individual descriptors. It is defined as

$$\mathcal{D} \equiv_{def} \lambda x(D_1(x) \wedge \cdots \wedge D_n(x)),$$

where the $D_i(x)$ are the individual descriptors that comprise the description. The symbol $\mathcal{D}^*$ denotes a similar expression that includes all the descriptors of $\mathcal{D}$ composed with the predicates that define the center of the discourse. These predicates restrict the possible individuals to which the description can apply to be only those that are relevant in the current discourse context. The general idea is that a single concept is identified as the *center* (C_b) of the discourse. As a simple approximation to a correct theory,

$$\mathcal{D}^* \equiv_{def} \lambda y((\mathcal{D}(C_b) \wedge y = C_b) \vee (\sim\mathcal{D}(C_b) \wedge \mathcal{D}(y))).$$

This axiom says that if a description $\mathcal{D}$ is true of the center, then $\mathcal{D}^*$ applies only to the center, otherwise, $\mathcal{D}^*$ applies to the other objects, if any, of which $\mathcal{D}$ is true. With the addition of axioms to describe how C_b moves as the discourse progresses, KAMP can plan referring expressions that take centering into account. A full discussion of centering is beyond the scope of this article. A more detailed account of the role of centering in KAMP's description planning strategy is discussed by Appelt [6].

The first clause in the conclusion of axiom (8) states that the speaker must believe the description that he attributes to the intended referent actually holds. The second and third clauses state that the intended referent is the only one that is not ruled out according to the mutual knowledge of the two agents. The reason for this indirect approach is that one must allow for the case in which a speaker plans a description that serves to both identify a referent and inform the hearer of properties of that referent. In that case, descriptors $D_1(x)$ through $D_i(x)$ (called the basic descriptors) will be mutually known to identify a single object, while descriptors $D_{i+1}(x)$ through $D_n(x)$ will be believed only by the speaker. Therefore, when the hearer interprets the speaker's utterance, the

communicates his intention to activate a concept, provided that the action has not *ruled out* by the description. Because the hearer knows that the speaker a suitable corresponding linguistic realization in the surface speech act.

3.7. Satisfying multiple goals in a referring expression

KAMP attempts to take advantage of opportunities to achieve multiple goals in a single utterance by recognizing situations in which *action subsumption* is possible. An important application of this principle is in the planning of referring expressions.

An action A_1 *subsumes* an action A_2 if A_1 and A_2 are part of the same plan, and action A_1 (in addition to producing the effects for which it was planned) also produces the effects for which A_2 was intended. Therefore, the resulting plan need only include action A_1 (and its expansion) to achieve all the goals.

The concept of action subsumption is particularly useful for planning linguistic actions because many options are typically available for expanding an illocutionary act into a surface utterance. Frequently, the planner can detect situations in which minor alterations to the expansion of an action will allow an action in another part of the plan to be subsumed. Although the term 'minor alterations' is somewhat vague, the general idea is clear. When planning surface speech acts, it means making a change localized to only one of the constituents of the sentence. Changes can be made to a surface speech act during the planning that do not alter the overall structure of the sentence, but are sufficient to subsume other actions in the plan. An example of such a change that is relevant to this article is adding a descriptor to a referring expression.

Axiom (8) provides the justification subsuming informing actions by concept activation actions. For efficient planning, a good strategy is needed to recognize when action subsumption is possible. Action subsumption is an example of a global interaction between actions in a plan. Such interactions are detected by the *critics* discussed in Section 3.4. The action-subsumption critic works by first applying a set of rules to see if action subsumption may be possible. If so, it then tries several action-subsumption strategies that specify the exact modification to the plan that must be made. If the strategy is successful, then the plan is altered, and the subsumed action marked so that no further work is done by the planner to expand it.

An example of the action-subsumption test rules would be "look for a situation in which a concept activation of a concept C is being performed, and where in the same plan there is a goal that the hearer know some property holds of C." The planner attempts to (1) expand the concept activation with a describe action, and (2) incorporate the property as one of the descriptors in the describe action. Axiom (8) enables KAMP to verify the correctness of the plan modifications proposed by the critics.

This type of reasoning is what enables the speaker in the example of Fig. 1 to

description $\mathcal{D}$ is not known to apply to anything at all. However, if the speaker planned the description so that the basic descriptors are mutually known to pick out a single referent in context, then there will be only one object that is not *ruled out* by the description. Because the hearer knows that the speaker believes the *entire description* he then can then decide to believe the information conveyed by the additional descriptors.

KAMP chooses a set of basic descriptors when planning a describe action to minimize both the number of descriptors chosen, and the amount of effort required to plan the description. Choosing a provably minimal description requires an inordinate amount of effort and contributes nothing to the success of the action. KAMP chooses a set of descriptors by first choosing a *basic category* descriptor (see [26]) for the intended concept, and then adding descriptors from those facts about the object that are mutually known by the speaker and the hearer, subject to the constraint that they are all linguistically realizable in the current noun phrase, until the concept has been uniquely identified.

Some psychological evidence suggests the validity of the minimal description strategy; however, one does not have to examine very many dialogues to find counter-examples to the hypothesis that people always produce minimal descriptions. According to the language-generation theory embodied in KAMP, people do choose minimal descriptions for concept activations; however these descriptions can be augmented for a variety of reasons, (e.g., to realize additional informing actions, as in the example in the next section, or to make it easier for a speaker to identify an object when an identification is requested, see [28]).

The other action that can be used to expand a concept activation action is *communicative pointing*. The following axiom describes pointing as one way of performing a concept activation action, which directly activates the concept of the object of the pointing action.

$$\forall A, B, w_1, w_2\, R(\mathrm{Do}(A, \mathrm{Point}(B, X), w_1, w_2) \supset$$
$$T(w_2, \mathbf{MutuallyKnow}(A, B, \mathrm{Active}(@(X)))).\tag{9}$$

Axiom (9) says that if an agent performs a pointing action, the standard name of the object he is pointing at becomes active.

A problem with pointing actions, not dealt with here, is how it is possible to decide whether such an action has communicative intent. It is a convention of a language use that utterances almost universally have communicative intent (the exceptions being actions like muttering to oneself). However, a particular physical action may or may not have communicative intent, and KAMP does not attempt to describe how a particular perceived gesture is interpreted as an attempt to describe how a particular perceived gesture is interpreted as communicative pointing.

Axioms (5)–(7) work together with (8) and (9) to produce the desired communicative effects. When a speaker utters a description, or points, he

conclude that he is informing the hearer that the object he is pointing to is a wheelpuller. The example example presented in the next section illustrates how KAMP plans multi-purpose referring expressions.

4. An Example of Planning Referring Expressions

KAMP's initial domain is the information required by an expert system that knows about the assembly and repair of a particular piece of equipment, and in which the user is a novice seeking assistance. There are two reasons for choosing this particular domain: First, dialogue protocols have been collected [29] that provide a body of linguistic data raising interesting issues and examples of phenomena that can be explained by the theory on which KAMP is based. Second, the domain provides an ideal situation for multiple-agent planning in which communicative actions arise naturally.

Fig. 6 illustrates a typical situation in which KAMP operates. This domain has two agents called Rob and John. Rob is a robot that incorporates KAMP for planning and deduction. Rob's only connection with the world is the computer terminal; thus, he is capable of performing speech acts, but no actions that directly affect the physical state of the world. John is assumed to be a person who is capable of performing both speech acts and physical actions. The particular situation for this example includes a piece of equipment to be repaired (in this case, an air compressor) and tools that are necessary for the task. The tools can be out in plain view on the table (in which case Rob and John mutually know properties such as their color, shape, size and location) or they can be stored away out of sight in the toolbox (in which case Rob may know where they are, but not necessarily John). In general, Rob is the expert and he knows almost everything about the situation. For example, Rob knows how to assemble the compressor; specifically, he knows how the parts fit together, what tools are needed for the various assembly operations, and where the tools are located.

This domain provides an ideal setting for studying multiple-agent planning as it relates to the production of utterances. Communication arises naturally in this domain because of the difference in knowledge and capabilities of the agents. Because Rob is incapable of performing physical actions, he must make requests of John whenever he intends to change the physical state of the world. Because Rob knows all there is to know about the task (and John knows this) John must ask questions to get the information he needs when he requests John to do something. Therefore, the need for communication arises in order for either agent to satisfy his goals.

The example presented in this section does not touch on every issue that arises in utterance planning, however, it touches on enough of them to give the reader a sense of how the different components of the KAMP planner fit together. The following notation is used for the illustrations in this section: Each node in the plan has some sort of boldface label (**P1, P2, . . ., Pn**) to make it easier to refer to. Dotted boxes are used to represent phantom goals. The successor relation between actions is represented by solid connecting lines and hierarchical relationships by dotted lines. Each node has an associated world. For goal nodes, the world is written inside parentheses (e.g. (W_i)), to represent that the planner is to start in world W_i and find some actions to reach a world in which the goal is satisfied. For phantom nodes, the world name is not in parentheses to indicate the goal is actually satisfied within the indicated world. Action nodes have a label like '$W_i \rightarrow W_j$' to indicate that the action is a transformation relating worlds W_i and W_j. Actions will often be planned without knowing precisely what worlds they will be performed in, or precisely what world will be the result of the action. This is particularly true of actions that are represented at a high level of abstraction. Worlds are represented in the diagram as '?' if the planner has not yet assigned a definite world. (Note that KAMP can often reason about what is true at a given point in the plan, even though it has not assigned a world to the node, because frame axioms can be stated for high-level actions that describe some changes and leave others unspecified.) A notation like '$W_1 \rightarrow ?$' is assigned to a high-level action that may be expanded to several actions at a lower level. The planner knows the action sequence will begin in W_1, but it will not know the resulting world until the action is expanded. A notation such as '$? \rightarrow ?$' is used when the planner knows where in a sequence a high-level action must fall in relation to other actions in the plan, but cannot assign either an initial or final world.

KAMP requires a fairly rich description of its domain to plan communica

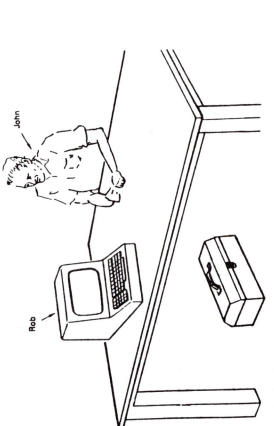

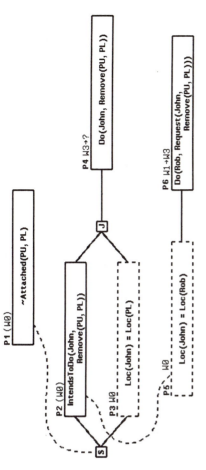

FIG. 7. Rob requests that John remove the pump.

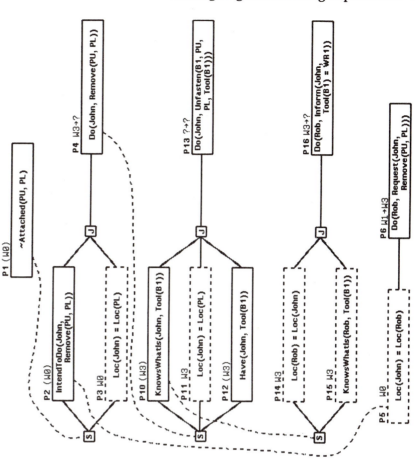

FIG. 8. Rob plans for John to remove the pump.

acts. KAMP needs knowledge in five areas: Basic common-sense knowledge (e.g., wrenches are tools, a compressor pump can only be attached to one thing at a time), basic knowledge about the objects in the domain (e.g., there is a wrench, it has an end-type of box-end, it is located in the toolbox), knowledge and mutual knowledge of agents in the domain (e.g., Rob knows the box-end wrench is located in the tool box, John does not know where the wrench is, Rob and John mutually know the pump is located on top of the table, it is universally known that all agents know their own location at all times), and descriptions of actions and their physical and knowledge-state effects, (e.g., if an agent performs an unfastening action, then he knows that he has just performed it, and the two objects that were fastened together are now now longer connected, and the agent knows this), and the basic axioms about knowledge and communication actions discussed earlier.

In the example discussed here the agents are Rob and John, the domain objects are a pump, PU, and platform, PL, mutually known to be on a table, T1, an object WR1 mutually known to be a box-end wrench, TB1 mutually known to be a toolbox and mutually known to be located under the table. The pump is mutually known to be fastened to the platform by a bolt, B1. Rob and John are initially in the same location. Because they are always in close proximity, they will always mutually know each other's location as well as their own. It is explicitly stated that John does not know what tool to use for unfastening B1, and that John does not know the location of WR1. Rob begins with the initial goal that the pump be removed from the platform:

True($\sim$ Attached(PU, PL)).

Given the above goal, KAMP begins planning as described in Section 3.4 by creating a procedural network and refining the plan to successively lower levels of abstraction. Refinement to the first level of abstraction results in the plan shown in Fig. 7, nodes **P1** to **P6**. KAMP has decided that Rob should request that John perform the action of removing the pump because according to the action summaries, a request is the only possible action one agent can perform to affect another's intentions. Whenever complete expansion to one level of abstraction is completed, KAMP uses the axioms to prove that the plan proposed according to the action summaries is successful.

Because the request is the only illocutionary act that has been planned so far, there is no more linguistic planning to be done at this stage. KAMP now turns its attention to expanding the REMOVE action. KAMP's axioms for remove (included as part of the general description of the domain) specify that removing is performed by unfastening any fasteners that are connecting one object to the other. This leads KAMP to include unfastening bolt B1 using the appropriate tool as part of the plan he must execute to remove the pump. This leads to the plan illustrated in Fig. 8. The preconditions for John performing this action are represented by nodes **P10**, **P11**, and **P12**—that John knows what the right tool

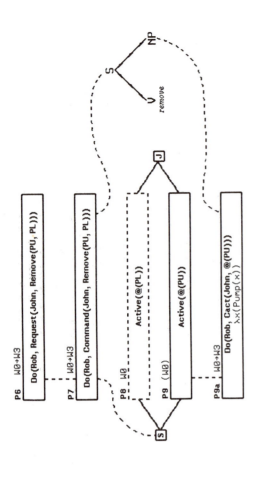

FIG. 9. Expanding a surface speech act.

is, that John is in the same place as the platform, and that John has the tool. Because John is already assumed to be in the same location as PL, the location goal, **P11** is a phantom (i.e. it is already true, but must be considered by the planner in the event that some other action causes it to no longer hold). Rob does not know whether John has the tool, or even that John knows where the tool is located; therefore, KAMP plans for Rob to inform John that the tool for removing bolt B1 is wrench WR1 (Node **P16**).

In summary, what KAMP has done so far is formulate a plan in which John adopts Rob's goal of removing the compressor pump from its platform, and through additional planning, has discovered some information that John needs to know to carry out the plan, and has planned to provide him with this information by means of an additional informing action.

Next, the planner must expand illocutionary acts in the plan to surface speech acts. This step may require some complex reasoning about when a surface speech act will be recognized as a particular kind of illocutionary act, for example, when a question will be understood as a request for information. For reasons explained in Section 3.5, surface speech acts are assumed to be interpreted directly, so the utterance of an imperative sentence is planned to realize the request in **P6**.

KAMP reasons that enough information must be included in the utterance so the hearer will recognize the intended proposition Remove(PU, PL). This entails conveying the predicate 'Remove', and activating concepts @(PU) and @(PL). As described in Section 3.6, concepts can be activated by being inferentially related to active ones as well as being activated directly. In this problem, axioms are included that state that Rob and John both know that the platform is the only object to which the pump is attached. Therefore, any action that removes the pump must remove it from the platform, and it is only necessary to say "Remove the pump" to have the hearer recognize the entire proposition.

Fig. 9 illustrates the interaction between the two components of surface speech-act planning—intention communication and linguistic realization. The intention communication component of this surface speech act consists of concept activation goals (nodes **P8** and **P9**) for each of the concepts mentioned in the intended proposition. Because KAMP has reasoned that it does not need to mention the platform, node **P8** is marked as a phantom. The phantom action will most likely not be reflected in the final utterance, but can be noticed by critics and later reactivated if the critic decides that it could satisfy another goal by referring to the platform with an appropriate description.

The linguistic realization component consists of choosing a basic syntactic structure for the sentence and relating it to the actions of the intention communication component. According to its grammar, the planner knows that an imperative sentence has the structure "V NP (PP)*", and associates such a structure with the surface speech-act node **P7**

KAMP now turns attention to expanding the goal node **P9**, activating the concept @(PU). Intention communication in this case is very simple, because (according to the initial axiomatization of the domain) there is only one object that is mutually believed by the speaker and hearer to be a pump. Therefore, the concept activation action **P9a** is planned, and its subordinate describe action, choosing

$$\lambda x(\mathrm{Pump}(x))$$

as a description, as described in Section 3.6.

KAMP has now reached the point at which the criticism portion of the expansion-criticism cycle begins. As explained in Section 3.4, each critic has a simple test that it applies to the plan to see if it is applicable. The action-subsumption critic's test works by examining pairs of illocutionary acts, such as the informing action **P16** and the request **P6** (see Fig. 8) to see if they are connected in a way that permits action subsumption. Actions **P16** and **P6** are connected by the fact that the wrench referred to in **P16** is an instrument of the action requested by **P6**. Because the verb chosen for **P6**, remove, can take an instrument case, the critic realizes that the informing action **P16** can be subsumed by the request **P6**, provided that reference to the instrument is made explicitly in the utterance. Since the simple grammar doesn't constrain the number of adverbial PPs that appear in the sentence, the addition of a prepositional phrase is adopted as a subsumption strategy.

The action-subsumption critic must also determine whether all the preconditions for the subsumption candidate are also satisfied in the world when the subsuming action is going to be 'performed'. All the conditions, namely

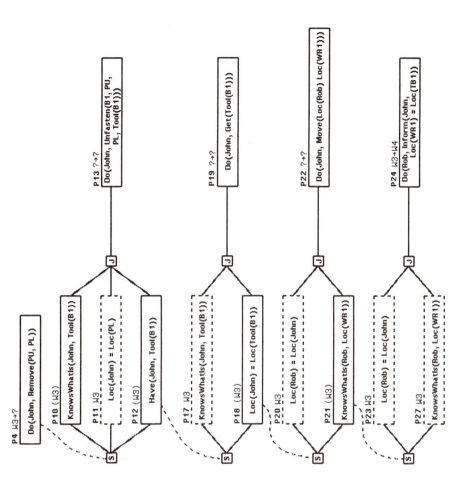

FIG. 11. Rob plans to inform John of the wrench's location.

that Rob is in the same location as John, and Rob knows that Tool(B1) = WR1, are satisfied in this situation. The critic adds concept activation **P16a** of Fig. 10 to the plan for intention communication, and adds the prepositional phrase with preposition *with* to the syntax tree. Once the addition is performed, then the planner reasons that the description $\lambda x(\text{Wrench}(x))$ is adequate to activate @ (WR1).

The subsumption of the informing action means that the hearer's knowledge will have changed by the time he executes the action of removing the pump. Because the exact effect of this additional knowledge on the plan is difficult to determine, the entire expansion of node **P4** is discarded and replanned. Fig. 10 shows the procedural net after criticism by the action-subsumption critic.

KAMP now turns its attention to goal **P12**, that John has wrench WR1 in his possession. For John to have the wrench, he must know where it is, and he must go there and get it. According to our model, John does not have this knowledge, but Rob does; accordingly KAMP plans for Rob to perform an additional informing action (**P24** in Fig. 11) to tell John the wrench's location.

In the next criticism cycle, the action-subsumption critic finds a situation analogous to the one with informing action **P16**. Action **P17** is a candidate for subsumption by the request because it informs the hearer of a property of one of the case arguments of the main verb being planned for the request. As in the previous case, the informing action is relocated so that it follows the request, and the part of the plan that may be affected by the hearer's new knowledge is discarded and replanned, as before. The description used in the concept-activation action **P16a** is then augmented with the new descriptor to yield

$$\lambda x[(\text{Wrench}(x) \land (\text{Loc}(x) = \text{Loc}(\text{TB1})))]$$

and modifying the linguistic realization, shown in Fig. 12 to attach a prepositional phrase to the noun phrase referring to the wrench.

The plan is completed when the planner plans a concept activation of TB1, using the description $\lambda x(\text{Tool-box}(x))$. In the completed plan, Rob says to John "Remove the pump with the wrench in the toolbox." Before the plan is actually adopted and executed, KAMP verifies that it will actually work, since the action summaries employ simplifications that may in some cases lead to the formulation of an incorrect plan. In this case the verification is possible because according to axiom (8), the hearer acquires the knowledge through the describe actions associated with concept activation **P16a** that would have been provided by inform actions **P16** and **P24** had they not been subsumed.

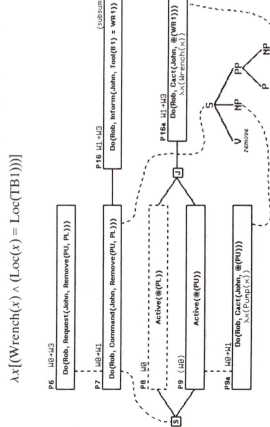

FIG. 10. Subsuming the informing action.

ing these axioms and action summaries into KAMP and designing plan critics that focus on interactions typical of linguistic actions. The result of incorporating these capabilities into KAMP is a system capable of producing English sentences with complex referring expressions as part of an agent's plan.

Several important research issues in planning referring expressions have been raised by the work done on KAMP, but have received only cursory examination to date. The linguistic coverage of the grammar needs to be extended considerably, and the work on TELEGRAM has been an important step in that direction. As has been cited earlier, there are a number of different purposes for which speakers use noun phrases. Not only are the concept activation actions examined in depth in this article realized by noun phrases, but also identification requests, attributive uses of definite descriptions, and a variety of other phenomena. It will be an important test of the theory to see if these other actions can be axiomatized and easily accommodated within this general framework.

KAMP has proven to be a useful tool for the investigation of planning referring expressions and utterances in general, and promises to be useful in developing a speech-act theory to account for many aspects of natural language use.

ACKNOWLEDGMENT

This research was supported in part by the Office of Naval Research under contract N0014-80-C-0296 and in part by the National Science Foundation under grant MCS-8115105. The author is grateful to the AI Journal referees for pointing out the shortcomings of the first draft. The author is particularly indebted to Barbara Grosz for providing thorough comments on several drafts of this article.

REFERENCES

1. Sacerdoti, E. A *Structure for Plans and Behavior* (North-Holland, Amsterdam, 1977).
2. Mann, W.C. and Matthiessen, C., Nigel: A systemic grammar for text generation, University of Southern California Information Sciences Institute Tech. Rept. ISI/RR-83-105, 1983.
3. McKeown, K., Generating natural language text in response to questions about data base structure, Ph.D. Dissertation, University of Pennsylvania, Philadelphia, PA, 1982.
4. Bruce, B.C. Belief systems and language understanding, BBN Technical Rept. No. 2973, Cambridge, MA, 1975.
5. Cohen, P. and Perrault, C.R., Elements of a plan based theory of speech acts, *Cognitive Sci.* 3 (1979) 177–212.
6. Appelt, D., *Planning English Sentences* (Cambridge University Press, Cambridge, U.K., 1985).
7. Evans, D. Situations and speech acts: Toward a formal semantics of discourse, Ph.D. Dissertation, Department of Linguistics, Stanford University, Stanford, CA, 1981.
8. Barwise, J. and John, P., *Situations and Attitudes* (MIT Press, Cambridge, MA, 1983).
9. Appelt, D.E., A planner for reasoning about knowledge and action, in: *Proceedings National Conference on Artificial Intelligence* (1980) 131–133.
10. Appelt, D.E., Planning natural-language referring expressions, in: *Proceedings 20th Annual Meeting of the Association for Computational Linguistics*, (1982) 108–112.
11. Prince, E.F. Toward a taxonomy of given-new information, in: P. Cole (Ed.), *Radical*

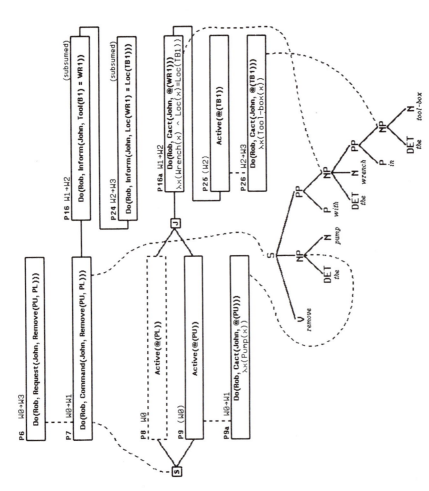

FIG. 12. Incorporating the wrench's location into the referring expression.

5. Conclusion

This research has focused on how speakers plan referring expressions that can be coordinated with physical actions and that may satisfy multiple goals. Producing such utterances given only a description of a speaker's goals is not a simple process; it requires a powerful system that is capable of general reasoning about agents' beliefs and intentions. It is difficult to envision any alternative to utterance planning that will account for the wide range of behavior observed in human communication.

The KAMP system is a useful vehicle for the investigation of a theory of language generation based on planning. Adapting KAMP from a general-purpose hierarchical planner to a language planner involved axiomatizing the various linguistic actions (illocutionary acts, surface speech acts, describing, pointing

12. Moore, R.C., Reasoning about knowledge and action, SRI International AI Center Tech. Note No. 191, Menlo Park, CA, 1980.

13. Searle, J., *Speech Acts: An Essay in the Philosophy of Language* (Cambridge University Press, Cambridge, U.K., 1969).

14. McCarthy, J. and Hayes, P., Some philosophical problems from the standpoint of artificial intelligence, in: B. Meltzer and D. Michie (Eds.), *Machine Intelligence* **4** (Edinburgh University Press, Edinburgh, 1969).

15. Clark, H. and Marshall, C., Definite reference and mutual knowledge, in: A.K. Joshi, I.A. Sag and B.L. Webber (Eds.), *Elements of Discourse Understanding* (Cambridge University Press, Cambridge University Press, Cambridge, U.K., 1981).

16. Cohen, P. and Perrault, C.R., It's for your own good: a note on inaccurate reference, in: A.K. Joshi, I.A. Sag and B.L. Webber (Eds.), *Elements of Discourse Understanding* (Cambridge University Press, Cambridge, U.K., 1981).

17. Nadathur, G. and Joshi, A.K., Mutual beliefs in conversational systems: their role in referring expressions, in: *Proceedings Eighth International Joint Conference on Artificial Intelligence*, Karlsruhe, West Germany (1983) 603–605.

18. Stickel, M.E., Theory resolution: building in nonequational theories, in: *Proceedings National Conference on Artificial Intelligence*, Washington, DC (1983) 391–397.

19. Bruce, B.C. and Newman, D., Interacting plans, *Cognitive Sci.* **2** (1978) 195–233.

20. Fikes, R.E., and Nilsson, N., STRIPS: a new approach to the application of theorem proving to problem solving, *Artificial Intelligence* **2** (1971).

21. Grice, H.P., Logic and conversation, in: Davidson (Ed.), *The Logic of Grammar* (Dickenson, Encino, CA, 1975).

22. Allen, F. and Perrault, C.R., Analyzing intention in utterances, *Artificial Intelligence* **15** (1980) 143–178.

23. Appelt, D.E., TELEGRAM: A grammar formalism for language planning, in: *Proceedings Eighth International Conference on Artificial Intelligence*, Karlsruhe, West Germany (1983) 595–599.

24. Grosz, B.J., Joshi, A.K. and Weinstein S., Providing a unified account of definite noun phrases in discourse, in: *Proceedings 21st Annual Meeting of the Association of Computational Linguistics* (1983) 44–50.

25. Grosz, B.J., Focusing and description in natural language dialogs, in: A.K. Joshi, I.A. Sag and B.L. Webber (Eds.), *Elements of Discourse Understanding: Proceedings of a Workshop on Computational Aspects of Linguistic Structure and Discourse Setting* (Cambridge University Press, Cambridge, U.K., 1980) 84–105.

26. Rosch, E., Mervis, C., Gray, W., Johnson, D. and Boyes-Braem, P., Basic objects in natural categories, *Cognitive Psychol.* **8** (1976) 382–439.

27. Kay, M., Functional unification grammar: A formalism for machine translation, in: *Proceedings Tenth International Conference on Computational Linguistics* (1984) 75–78.

28. Cohen, P., The need for identification as a planned action, in: *Proceedings Seventh International Joint Conference on Artificial Intelligence*, Vancouver, BC (1981) 31–36.

29. Deutsch (Grosz), B., Typescripts of task-oriented dialogs, SRI International AI Center Tech. Note No. 146, Menlo Park, CA, 1975.

Received October 1982; revised version received October 1983, August 1984

DESCRIPTION DIRECTED CONTROL: ITS IMPLICATIONS FOR NATURAL LANGUAGE GENERATION

DAVID D. MCDONALD†

Department of Computer and Information Science, University of Massachusetts at Amherst, MA 01003, U.S.A.

Abstract—We propose a very specifically constrained virtual machine design for goal-directed natural language generation based on a refinement of the technique of data-directed control that we have termed "description-directed control". Important psycholinguistic properties of generation follow inescapably from the use of this control technique, including: efficient runtimes, bounded lookahead, indelible decisions, incremental production of the text, and inescapable adherence to grammaticality. The technique also provides a possible explanation for some well known universal constraints, though this cannot be confirmed without further empirical investigation.

In description-directed control the controlling data structure is the surface-level linguistic description of the very text being generated. This constituent structure tree is itself generated depth first by the incremental realization of a hierarchical description of the speaker's communicative goals (neutrally termed a "realization specification") organized according to the scope and importance of its components. The process of traversing the surface structure gates and constrains the realization process; all realizations are thus subject to the grammatical constraints that accrue to the surface structure at which they occur, as defined by the grammatical annotation of the surface structure tree.

1. INTRODUCTION: COMPUTATIONAL HYPOTHESES IN A.I.

In the early stages of Artificial Intelligence research into a new phenomena, we normally do our modeling with the most powerful and general purpose computational tools at our disposal. This is because we do not yet know what will be required in the processing and need to retain maximum flexibility to experiment with variations in our model. Once the phenomena is better understood however, we can develop hypotheses about exactly what representations and operations on them the process requires. The primitive tools can then be tailored and restricted to accommodate just those requirements and no more, transforming the computational architecture from general purpose and powerful to particular and limited. The type of architecture adopted—the design of the virtual machine on which the modeling is based—becomes a *direct manifestation* of our hypotheses about the phenomenon under study.

This tactic, the limitation of primitive algorithms, representations, and operations to just those required to support the hypothesized processing and no more, is the strongest means available to us within the discipline of Artificial Intelligence for expressing a hypothesis about a psychological process. Its precision makes the hypothesis easier to disprove, either through the discovery of internal inconsistencies that can no longer be hidden behind vague definitions, or by finding ourselves unable to fit pretheoretically expected elaborations of the hypothesis within the stipulations of the design. (In this regard a restricted architecture acts as a "safety check" while the hypothesized model is being completed, since it makes an inadvertent or disguised extension of the system's computational power impossible because it is impossible to formulate.)

We have seen this methodological pattern at work during this last decade in research on natural language parsing. The initial exploratory work of Thorne *et al.*[1], Winograd[2] and Woods[3] was based on tools that could almost implement completely general type zero rewriting systems (e.g. augmented transition networks). The information gathering ability and possible control paths of these systems were constrained only by the informal conventions of the people writing the rules. After experience with these all-powerful systems had been accumulated however, we saw some researchers making a shift to a very specific hypotheses about the computational requirements of the parsing task, e.g.[4–7], the core of their hypotheses being the specification of the carefully limited machine on which the parsing process was to run.

†Preparation of this paper was supported in part by the National Science Foundation under Grant IST-8104984.

In this paper we will look closely at a virtual machine for goal-directed natural language generation and consider its implications. The computational hypothesis that this design embodies has evolved during the last eight years according to the same sort of progression as has taken place in the treatment of parsing: Its first instantiations were based on very general tools that permitted free and easy modification of the design; it became clear however that the full power of the tools was not being used, and, after adjustments to a few of the grammatical analyses (interesting in their own right), a far more restricted set of tools was found to perform just as well. In addition, the restricted design was found to lead inescapably to behavioral properties of the virtual machine with important psycholinguistic consequences, some of which will be discussed at the end of this paper.

We will begin by defining the role that the hypothesized control structure plays in generation. This will entail making certain assumptions which, while appealing, cannot now be proven. We will then look at the control structure algorithm and the representation of surface structure on which it is based. This will lead to a discussion of the computational constraints that the control structure imposes on generation, and to some of their linguistic and psycholinguistic implications. For concreteness a short example taken from one of the applications of the current implementation will be woven throughout the discussion.

2. THE ROLE OF THE CONTROL STRUCTURE IN GENERATION

What are the actions that take place during language generation? What is it that a control structure must organize? This is the most basic question that one can ask about the generation process: if we are drastically wrong in our answer (i.e. if people function on some other basis), then regardless of how effective the virtual machine may be it will be an improper model for people.

Regrettably there is no direct evidence from psycholinguistic studies that we can bring to bear on this question. Deliberate studies aimed for example at determining how work load varies during generation[8] or at determining how much advance planning there must be[9] can to date yield only indirect evidence, and must be placed in a theoretical framework before they can be interpreted. They define phenomena that a successful computational theory must be able to account for, but they do not themselves provide the basis for such a theory. Even studies of spontaneous speech errors[10–14]—the richest source of evidence on generation that we presently have—can yield hard evidence only about the kinds of data that the generation process must be manipulating and not about the process itself.

In the absence of hard evidence about human processing, one must rely on intuitions derived from studies of linguistic competence and from what we know about efficient computation. This leads us to a set of kernal assumptions, which we make precise by developing into a specification of a virtual machine. Space does not permit a discussion of why these particular assumptions were adopted (cf.[15, 16]), nor would any discussion at this point convince the skeptical reader since assumptions have the status of postulates and as such are difficult to argue about. The enterprise is instead to use them as the basis of a theoretical account of generation that is rich enough computationally to make it possible to derive and test its empirical consequences and have the assumptions stand or fall accordingly.

There are three principle assumptions of the present research, each with its corollaries and fine points:

Goal-directed natural language generation is best characterized as a decision-making process. This is a matter of point of view and emphasis: it means that the control structure is to be concerned with, e.g. what dictates what decisions are to be made, what kinds of things are decided upon, what information the decisions are based on and how it is made accessible, or what should be the form of the result. Computationally, emphasizing decision-making might be contrasted with emphasizing the space of a heuristic search, or the stages of a perceptual process, or the adaptive relaxation process that sets an organism's global state.

I assume that all decisions either contribute directly to the substance of the text under production or constrain it, i.e. the choices to be made are between alternate surface-level linguistic forms: alternate words, idioms, sentence structures, rhetorical or intonational effects, etc. (N.B. this means that there is no notion of "grammatical derivation" in this theory, in direct contrast with models of production based on transformational generative grammar ("TG") such as Fay's[13].

All decisions "count". Every decision that a speaker makes is assumed to contribute to the processing effort expended. Consequently if deliberative effort is to be minimized, then the control structure must ensure that every decision is compatible. With every decision adding to the text (or imposing constraints on its structure), compatibility becomes equated with grammaticality—all that we know about the elaborate systems of grammatical dependencies in natural language can be brought over into our study of the generation process. In particular, any decision that is made before all of the other decisions on which it is dependent have been made runs the risk of selecting a choice that is incompatible with those other decisions, leading either to a mistake or to wasteful backup. Under this assumption the order in which decisions are made has real consequences and provides a means, albeit indirect, of testing whether the dependencies proposed in a given grammar are psychologically real.

Only a limited part of the text is planned at a time. The structures that are selected in a decision† are typically greater than one word in length and can involve grammatical relations among widely separated parts of the output text. It must therefore be possible to represent planned but not yet uttered text and grammatical relations. It must also be possible to represent *planned but unexecuted decisions* as well, since decision-making continues as a text is actually being uttered. One can, and in unpracticed conversation usually will, begin a text without having totally decided how it will end. Consequently, later decisions may be restricted in the choices open to them since the text they select must be grammatically compatible with what has already been spoken. The common experience of "talking oneself into a corner"—leaving out things we should have mentioned and even making grammatical errors—suggests that we are unable to appreciate all of the grammatical consequences of early decisions upon later ones, and that we are unable to rescind earlier problematic decisions short of aborting any planned but unspoken text and starting over (another way of saying that all decisions count).

This assumption means that the control structure must support a representation of pending decisions and selected but not yet uttered linguistic structures. In doing this however, the design must very carefully regulate access to the information that is latent in such a representation, and must tie this regulation in with independently justifiable systems such as the grammar if phenomena such as "talking oneself into a corner" are to be captured in a non-*ad hoc* way.

The virtual machine that I shall describe in this paper—based on description-directed control—manifests a sharpened version of these assumptions as an inescapable consequence of its design, i.e. it cannot behave otherwise. Thus if the assumptions are correct, this virtual machine is a *prima facie* candidate to be the one that people actually use; more precisely, we can put this machine forward as transparently functionally isomorphic to the architecture of the human language generation process at the computational level (cf. [17]). Methodologically there are two kinds of test that must be passed before we can believe such a claim. First, the design must be shown to be internally consistent: there must be a successful implementation actually exhibiting the posited behaviors, and it must be possible to consistently incorporate refinements to the behavior as they become known through empirical study. Second, we must look for evidence (presumably indirect) that the functional divisions posited in the virtual machine are in fact the ones that people have. This will certainly include considering whether the design can account for the classes of speech-errors that people make, and possibly the behavior of aphasic patients or the results of online psycholinguistic experiments. (N.B. in judging whether any such account is satisfactory, it is essential to appreciate that all "confrontations" between competence theories (even computational ones) and observed psychological data are mediated by a theoretical account of the functional mapping between them

---

†To avoid confusion it is important here to distinguish the process of making a decision from what one has decided once the decision has been made. I will refer to what is decided upon as the *choice*, and reserve the term *decision* for the process by which the choice is arrived at. Formally such a "decision" is a function which when evaluated in a given environment returns a "choice". Decisions are implemented in the current computer implementation of the generator by schematically specifying a decision-tree of predicates to be tested (i.e. a set of nested conditionals), with the alternative choices explicitly given as the decision-tree's leaves.

(i.e. which device in the competence theory is to be responsible for which observed effect), and this account must be independently argued for; see [18] for discussion.)

3. ASSUMPTIONS ABOUT THE INPUT TO THE GENERATION PROCESS

The "generation process' that the virtual machine defines is *not* assumed to include the initial "urge to communicate" that sets the process in motion; its focus is instead on the process of deciding the linguistic form of the text and of actually uttering it. The bulk of the decisions not connected with form, e.g. when to speak, what information to include and what to leave out, or how to organize the presentation on a large scale, are assumed to have preceded the initiation of the generation process, and to have resulted in the construction of a specification of the speaker's communicative goals. Such a *realization specification*† (abbreviated "*r*-spec") would include the propositions and references that the audience is to be made aware of, the connotations and affective overtones that are to be maintained, any assumptions about what the audience already knows or about what kinds of rhetorical tactics work best with them, and other things of that sort.‡

Since the actual form of realization specifications within the human mind is not known§ (we do not even know whether they would have to exist as explicit entities), the framework makes only minimum assumptions about them. Specifically:

● A realization specification is a *composite* structure that is brought together for a specific communicative situation.

● Consequently, the determination of what decisions a particular specification implies can not be precomputed; it must instead be uncovered through some kind of recursive decomposition of the structure, this process presumably being ordered by the relative importance of the individual goals and mental objects involved (for convenience also termed "*r*-specs") and the relations between them.

● At any one moment the total set of atomic relations, objects, properties, etc. from which a realization specification can be composed is *fixed*. The correspondence between each available atomic "term" in an *r*-spec and the possible natural language phrases, syntactic relations, etc. that could realize it in context can therefore be known before hand and drawn upon as the raw material of the generator. (This formulation would allow for changes in the correspondences or the addition of new base terms, but only over time as the use of the language changes or as new concepts are learned.)

To be concrete, let me introduce an actual *r*-spec from one of the computer programs that use this generator. This program and the design behind it are discussed in [20]. The computer speaker is a scene-description system written by Jeff Conklin that takes a database of objects and spatial relations produced by the UMass VISIONS system analysing a photograph of a suburban street scene and plans paragraph of text in English describing the scene. The example paragraph in the 1982 paper is:

> "*This is a picture of a white house with a fence around it. The door of the house is red, and so is the gate of the fence. There is a mailbox across the street in front of the fence, and a large tree obscures part of a driveway on the right. It is a cloudy day in summer.*"

---

†I have elected to coin a functionally descriptive term, "realization specification" ("the specification of what is to be realized in the text"), rather than to use a more common term such as "message", in order to emphasize the interpretive, context-sensitive nature of the relationship between an *r*-spec and the text that results from it. The metaphor of "messages" carries with it a notion of generation (and interpretation) as a translation process where the audience reconstructs in its mind the very same expression—the "message"—as the speaker starts with. This metaphor is fraught with difficulties both practical and philosophical (for discussion see [19]), and has largely been abandoned in A.I. research in favor of the view of generation as a planning process with plan realization as its last phase.

‡The point of declaring that the planning and construction of such specifications is external to the processing of the generator is to avoid any claim that such processing has to use the generator's control structure. This is a precaution based on the fact that while I see good reasons for adopting a very restricted but efficient virtual machine design for orchestrating linguistic reasoning, I have no evidence as yet to suggest that the conceptual planning of goals for natural language generation is comparably restricted.

§For computer programs we presume that there is some flexibility in the design of whatever expert program is serving as the speaker for this generator and that these assumptions can be met. Without such flexibility, there is no guarantee that a generator of this design will perform as desired for an arbitrary expert progam: it cannot make a silk purse from a sow's ear.

Let us look at the *r*-spec that gave rise to the second sentence of that paragraph. (This data structure is an LISP list with five embedded lists as indicated by the parentheses and indentation. Each of the embedded lists represents and individual "sub-" *r*-spec which can be referred to by the unique symbol at the beginning of the list (e.g. "*r*-spec2"). The order of the embedded *r*-specs reflects their importance to the composite *r*-spec as a whole.)

```
(r-spec1
    (r-spec2    color-of (door-3 red))
    (r-spec3    part-of (door-3 house-1))
    (r-spec4    condense-on-property (r-spec2 r-spec5 red))
    (r-spec5    color-of (gate-4 red))
    (r-spec6    part-of (gate-4 fence-2)))
```

Fig. 1. An example realization specification.

Decision-procedures for realizing the terms in an r-spec. Of equal stature with a speaker's knowledge of their grammar is their knowledge of the correspondence between the terms they use in their realization specifications and the linguistic structures that could serve as their realizations. This is the "raw material" of the generation process, which itself could be characterized as the process of selecting and combining the realizations of *r*-specs in such a way that the grammar of the language is obeyed and the overall goals of the speaker are met.

I will stipulate that every term in an *r*-spec is associated with a set of alternative choices of linguistic realization plus a decision procedure that selects between them according to constraints that hold at the time the decision is to be made. The relation "color-of" for example would have one realization when it functioned as an independent proposition (e.g. "⟨object⟩ is ⟨color⟩"), and another when it functioned as part of an object's description (e.g. "⟨color⟩⟨object⟩" or "⟨object⟩ which is ⟨color⟩"). The form and internal behavior of these decision procedures is not important for the purposes of this paper. Our concern is only with how they interact with the rest of the generation process, and in our assumption (number three above) that decision procedures are fixed and thus will contribute not more than a predictable, bounded amount of effort to the overall process.

Planning vocabulary. Our research on scene description has set aside the question of lexical choice, allowing us to represent the contents of these *r*-specs as simple relations for which the English vocabulary choices are deliberately obvious. (The terms and relation names are taken from a simulation of the object-level spatial data base that is the output of the VISIONS system's analysis.) We have instead concentrated our efforts on the design of the speaker's rhetorical planning vocabulary. "R-spec4" is a token of this vocabulary. Its content is a rhetorical goal that Conklin has called "condense-on-property". It represents an observation by the planner that two of the objects it wishes to describe share a common salient property, in this case their color. Notice that condense-on-property is a relation over other *r*-specs (*r*-spec2 and *r*-spec5) rather than just objects in VISIONS' data base. Consequently its realization will not result in text, but will *impose constraints* on the realization of *r*-spec2 and *r*-spec5, in this case coordinating them and forcing an ordering on their constituents that emphasizes their shared color. (That is, it forces the realization to be something like "The door of the house is red and so is the gate of the fence", rather than say "A red door is part of the house. The fence has a red gate.")

A major part of our on-going research is the formalization of rhetorical effects like condense-on-property (others we have looked at include focus, ordering by new vs old information, restrictions on the extent of a description, and coordinated emphasis and contrast). We believe that rhetorical effects are a key part of a speaker's planning vocabulary—one which we must understand thoroughly if we are to make sense of the structure of human discourses. This is because terms at the rhetorical level can serve the *r*-spec planner as a compact and expeditious model of the lower-level syntactic resources of the language, simplifying the planning process by encapsulating the complexities of syntactic variations into manageable packages, thereby reducing what the planner has to know about. Complementary to the question of identifying the rhetorical vocabulary is the question of how that vocabulary is realized—by what means is condense-on-property to impose its constraints on r-spec2 and r-spec5? This, it turns out, is neatly handled under description-directed control, as we will see when we continue this example at the end of the next section.

With the assumptions laid out, we can now move on to the heart of this paper, the definition of description-directed control and its ramifications. One cautionary note before leaping in: readers with linguistic training may be skeptical, once they see the workings of this design, that it would possibly be able to produce certain basic natural language constructions such as wh-movement or raising to subject. Their concern is appropriate since the design does impose a severe bias on the "direction" in which grammatical dependencies can be noticed and acted positions within a sentence back to early and high positions might seem to be impossible to capture. There is of course a way out, namely to develop new, alternative theories of what the speaker-internal sources of these constructions are, adopting sources where the dependencies flow in the proper direction. The motivation for alternatives of this sort will be the subject of the last section.

4. DESCRIPTION-DIRECTED CONTROL

Description-directed control is a special case of *data-directed* control, where the controlling data structure is the evolving description of the final product. In the case of generation we have two such descriptions: an abstract description given in the speaker's planning vocabulary (the realization specification), and a much more concrete, linguistic description that is built up from the first by successively realizing its components (the surface structure). Both are used to control the process, with the linguistic description being most important since it provides the primary constraints on realization and organizes the recursive decomposition of the original r-spec into its component r-specs so as to match the order in which the text is to be incrementally produced.

We will begin this section by sketching the basics of data-directed control and how it has been used in generation; this corresponds to control by the first of our two descriptions, the realization specification. The motivation for introducing a level of linguistic description into the control structure will then be discussed, and the interleaving of the two descriptions described by returning to our example of the house scene. We end the section by giving a careful description of the mechanisms of description directed control, elaborating on the concept of surface structure as program.

4.1 *Data-directed control*

In a data-directed system there is no fixed program. Instead, the knowledge the system has is distributed into many relatively small modules, with the execution order of the modules dictated by an external data structure (typically the input to the system) as interpreted by a simple controller algorithm. The controller treats the data structure as though it were a program in a very high-level language, interpreting the terms and relations that it reads as instructions to execute particular system modules. This technique of associating program modules with specific terms or cannonical events as interpreted by some controlling algorithm is known as *procedural attachment*, and it lies at the heart of any data-directed system.

To specify a data-directed system given a specification of the class of data structure that is to be in control, one must specify (1) how the structure will be traversed, (2) the mapping between terms in the data structure and modules in the system, and (3) the computational environment that the modules will be allowed to access—can they for example examine other parts of the data structure than those the controller currently "has its fingers on"? Is there an independent record of past actions? Where do the modules put the results of their computations?

Data-directed control is a natural technique for an interface system such as a natural language generator. It permits a flexible and efficient response to a speaker's specifications which a system based on a fixed program can not match. Several well-known generators besides my own have used data-directed control, e.g. [21–23]; it is the basis of the technique that Mann *et al.*[28] in their review have termed "direct translation". To use direct translation, the speaker program selects one of its own internal data structures to be the basis of the text and passes it to the generator to be traversed via *recursive descent* and rendered into English term by term. Such a system might for example answer a "how" question by selecting and passing to the generator the internal procedure that actually performed action. Conditionals in the procedure might be rendered by "if-then" clauses, test predicates as clauses, and so on, with the overall pattern of the text exactly matching that of the internal procedure since the procedure served directly as the template that organized the generator's translation.

4.2 *The need for control by a linguistic description*

In the terminology of this paper, the "modules" that contain a data-directed system's knowledge are (principally) the decision procedures, and the realization specification is the input to the system that serves as (part of) the data that directs control. However, the speaker's realization specification does not exhaustively determine all of the decisions that must be made. The demands of the language's grammar must be taken into account, as well as the constraints due to any text that has already been produced. This leads us to the special contribution of my technique for natural language generation, which is otherwise very similar to direct translation. This is the design decision to *embed* the process of realizing the speaker's specifications within *another* process—also data-directed—this second, enfolding process being responsible for ensuring that the output text is grammatical and that it includes those details that are important because the text is English rather than some other natural language.

The controlling data structure that I have chosen for this second process is *the text's own linguistic description*. This description is of course the output of the decision procedures as they realize the *r*-specs. It is a tree-structured, surface-level syntactic description, based on the form of the text as it will actually be produced rather than as it would look at some more abstract linguistic level. (In terms of Chomsky's most recent formulation[24], the level of this description corresponds to his "*R*-structure", the level at which any optional "stylistic" transformations that may apply have done so, and which is the input to the phonological component.) Part of what the surface structure does is to define the path of the traversal; it fixes the order in which the linguistic "program" that it defines will be executed. This is the function of the hierarchical pattern of the nodes and the sequential order of their immediate constituents. The other part of what the surface structure does is to define the "content" of this program, this being done by the grammatical labels that have been selected to annotate the parts of the tree.

The form of the surface structure. The surface structure tree is created incrementally from top to bottom and from left to right by the realization of successive embedded *r*-specs (see next section). In the "finished" syntactic trees that we are accustomed to looking at, the nodes specify syntactic constituents and the leaves are the words of the text. Here however we are dealing with trees that are "in progress" and whose force in the algorithm is to specify where they can be extended and what grammatical constraints they impose on those extensions. Thus while the tree's nodes will always denote constituents, its leaves may all be *r*-specs in the early parts of the process. Later, after the first of those *r*-specs had been decomposed through the action of several successive realizations, that part of the tree will probably have been developed down to the clause and NP level and most of its leaves will be words. The surface structure tree is not exceptional in form. Nodes are labeled to indicate their categories and other grammatical properties (e.g. "clause", "VP", "possible-sentence-start"). Nodes by definition have immediate constituents; every nonterminal constituent must be a node: legal terminal constituents can be only words or *r*-specs. One significant extension to the usual formalism for tree structure has been made in this design, namely that the positions daughter constituents can take with respect to their mother node have been reified. These "position objects" are called *slots*, and are labeled with the terms that linguists normally use for grammatical relations between constituents, e.g. "subject", "object-of-a-preposition", "head", etc.

This grammatical "annotation" represented by the labels is very conventional at the sentence level and below (reflecting the author's background in transformational generative linguistics and systemic grammar). At the discourse level on the other hand, while it maintains the same form, i.e. a strict tree, the relationship of the structure of the tree to the structure of the output text is less fixed than at lower levels. For example one sentence in the text might actually span several nodes at the discourse level because it was realized from several *r*-specs in sequence.

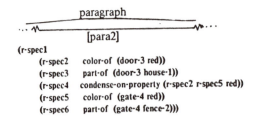

Fig. 2. Snapshot after the *r*-spec arrives at the generator.

4.3 *Embedding* r-*specs within a syntactic description*

To illustrate how the two descriptions are interleaved, let me return to the example of the second sentence of the house scene. The *r*-spec that led to that text (shown in Fig. 1) was the second in a stream of five. By the time it was passed to the generator, the decision that it was to be part of a paragraph had been made and the first *r*-spec put in place as the paragraph's first constituent and its utterance begun. (We assume that planning and realization are asyncronous.) The second *r*-spec is thus already embedded in a linguistic context, albeit a relatively unconstraining one, which we can diagram as shown below in Fig. 2. In this style of diagram, syntactic nodes are shown as trapezoids labeled on top by their category and with their positions for constituents running along the bottom as functional labels enclosed in brackets. (Only the second constituent position ("slot") with the *r*-spec is shown. The first slot at this point contains the complete surface structure tree corresponding to the first sentence; following slots as needed will contain the succeeding *r*-specs as the planner constructs them and passes them over.)

As will be discussed in detail later, the generation process is directed by a depth-first traversal of the surface structure tree: words are spoken as soon as they are reached, and the grammatical labels on the tree are interpreted for the constraints and low-level grammatical actions that they imply. As the second constituent of the paragraph, the *r*-spec is now also a part of the surface structure—a planned realization decision waiting to be made once the traversal reaches its position. Let us say that that position has just been reached, the first sentence having just been uttered. All *r*-specs are realized according to the same schematic procedure, which can be summarized as follows. (Details can be found in[15] or in[16].)

The Realization Procedure

● Every realization specification is either a single, composite structure or with a loosely related set of other *r*-specs as in the present example. In both cases the *r*-spec is passed to its associated decision-procedure which will either be one that is specific to that kind of composite or be a very general procedure that will try to find a realizable unifying linguistic relation among the *r*-specs of the set, and realize the other *r*-specs in terms of it.

● All *decision-procedures* that realize *r*-specs are organized in the same way. Formally they are functions from *r*-specs to surface structure. (Except for minor grammatical adjustment rules, they are the *only* source of syntactic relations and content words.) They have two parts: a set of predetermined choices (see below) and a set of tests (the actual "decision procedure") which are organized into a tree with the choices at its leaves. They are always preconstructed rather than being the result of a dynamic planning process. They may (and typically do) anticipate dynamic contingencies by incorporating context-sensitive tests within their conditions, however they are selected—associated with the appropriate classes of *r*-specs—on a strictly context-free basis that is computed locally to the individual *r*-spec.

● The output of one of these decision-procedures will always be a *choice* selected from among its predetermined set of alternatives. A choice is a minimal, schematic description of some linguistic structure. The structure may be of any size from an entire paragraph to a single word, and may contain any amount of detail from a completely "canned" phrase to just a constraint on later-realized *r*-specs, for example that one particular part of the *r*-spec under realization is to precede another in the text.

● When a choice is selected, it is "instantiated", and a well-formed subtree is constructed to meet the schematic description. A choice may be parameterized, i.e. some of the constituents it specifies may be given as variables that are filled on instantiation with selected sub-components of the original *r*-spec.

The result of realizing our example *r*-spec is thus to cause a new fragment of the surface structure of the text to be created and then *installed in the r-spec's place* as the paragraph's second constituent. This is how the surface structure grows: via the replacement of *r*-specs by the surface structures that realize them. The new surface structure typically incorporates other *r*-specs that were components of the original; these are reached and realized in turn as the traversal process continues, the whole procedure exactly matching the intended recursive decomposition of the original *r*-spec.

Figure 3 shows the relevant section of the surface structure just after the example *r*-spec has been realized and replaced. The example was a *set* of *r*-specs, and as sketched above, its realization was performed by looking for a unifying linguistic relation (in this case the rhetorical goal "condense-on-property") and basing the realization just on it. In the computer program there were two choices available to the decision procedure for condense-on-property: the first was to merge the subjects of the relations (e.g. "Both the door of the house and gate of the fence are red"), and the second is to use some form of what in the TG tradition is known as "verb phrase deletion" (e.g. "The door of the house is red and so is the gate of the fence."). The second is chosen because a "standing order"† concerning the proper style of a scene description has not been overridden. This standing order is to avoid constructions that make the "chaining" of discourse topics difficult. The selected sentence, because it ends mentioning the fence, can be coherently followed by a subsequent sentence elaborating on the fence's other properties. The blocked sentence on the other hand ends by emphasizing the color "red" and has bunched the scene objects up in the subject, making it awkward to continue describing them.‡

The conjunction node, the "modifies" relations appended to the two embedded *r*-specs, and the special "VP-deletion" label on the conjunction's second slot are all reflexes of the decision to realize condense-on-property using a form of verb phrase deletion. Decision procedures are forbidden from looking ahead to anticipate the effects of later embedded realizations to expand several levels of an *r*-spec at once (as would have been required if the textual effects of verb phrase deletion were to have been produced at the very moment the decision to use it was made). Instead, the decision procedures are given the ability to specially mark the surface structure that they do produce with special labels whose effect will be to bring about the desired effects when the relevant part of the tree is reached by the traversal. Such annotations are

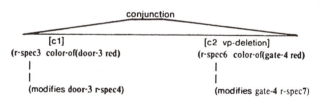

Fig. 3. Snapshot after realizing the initial *r*-spec.

†The idea behind the notion of a "standing order" is that the planner should be able to impose constraints on what is said which will apply universally (unless specifically overridden) and thus not need to be thought about while constructing each and every *r*-spec. Standing orders are effectively default components of every *r*-spec, which for convenience are instead incorporated directly into the decision-procedures.

‡As it happens, the next sentence in this paragraph does not continue to chain on the fence but instead changes the topic completely and talks about the mailbox. This is not a mistake: it is rather a reflection of the fact that the planner's deliberations as it constructs a realization specification are very local. The planner had not looked ahead to the third sentence before it sent off the *r*-spec for the second; as far as it knew, the third sentence might have been more about the fence and the standing order thus to the point. Even though it turns out that the third sentence starts an entirely new discourse unit (signalled by the "there is" construction), the use of verb phrase deletion did not do any harm. If it had, we would have had evidence that the scope of the planner's deliberations was too narrow.

another way in which the needs of the generation process have introduced variations in the form of surface structure from what linguists are accustomed to.

4.4 *Traversing the surface structure: syntactic trees as programs*

Given what has been said about the organization of data-directed systems, the explanation of how a text's surface structure is used to control its generation should include a specification of how the surface structure is traversed, a specification of the kind of "modules" that there are and how the terms in the surface structure map to them, and finally a specification of the overall computational environment to which the modules have access; these are the subject of the rest of this section. The specifications that will be given are not the only ones that one could imagine given only the notion of a surface structure tree as a controlling representation. They reflect *additional design constraints* that are intended (1) to enforce a very strict constraint on the rate at which the generation process proceeds, and (2) to support a minimalist position on the amount of information that is required moment to moment to support linguistic decisions. We will take up these issues after the fundamentals of the traversal's operation have been established.

The traversal algorithm. The surface structure tree is traversed in the classic depth-first pattern, i.e. top-down and left-to-right starting from its root-node. The traversal is performed by a trivial skeleton algorithm that spends the bulk of its time dispatching to the procedures attached to the grammatical labels (see below). Its only other important function is to define what happens to the contents of each slot as it is reached:

● If the slot contains a word then it is a leaf and the traversal will return back up the tree. The word is passed to a morphological routine for specialization according to the labels on its slot; thense it is passed to the output stream (i.e. it is "spoken").

● If the slot contains a syntactic node then it is a nonterminal and the traversal continues down into that subtree.

● If the slot contains a realization specification then it is (for the moment) a leaf. The *r*-spec is passed to the decision-procedure to which it maps for realization. This process will return either a node or a word which is then knit into the tree in the *r*-spec's place and the dispatch-on-contents process done again.

Attached grammatical procedures. The key to the data-directed use of the tree is the definition of reference "events" within the traversal. These events provide the same kind of "hooks"—points at which to attach procedures—as are provided in many knowledge representation systems by the operations that add or remove assertions from the data base. Just as we can have "if-added" or "if-removed" procedures that are associated with the patterns of assertions in a knowledge base, we here have procedures associated with the grammatical labels that annotate the surface structure and have them triggered by the occurrence of well-defined events in the traversal. Five such events have been found to be important:

(1) *Entering a node* from above, having traversed all of the tree above it and to its left.
(2) *Leaving a node* from below, having traversed all of its constituents.
(3) *Entering a slot*, having traversed all of its sister constituents to its left.
(4) *Leaving a slot*, having just traversed the constituent (or word) that it contains.
(5) *After realizing a r-spec* when the subtree that was chosen for it has been constructed and just been knit into the tree (in the *r*-spec's place), but not yet traversed. Since embedded *r*-specs appear only as the contents of slots, procedures associated with this "After-realization" event are attached only to slot-annotating labels.

Attached grammatical procedures perform several kinds of functions. A major one is to provide the staging grounds for decisions that the grammar requires but that the speaker's specifications do not provide for. Relative pronouns and complementizers are a clear case in point: The fact that one must include the word "that" in a phrase like "the report *that* the island's sovereignty had changed" is a fact about the English language and not about the information that has to be conveyed. Consequently one wants the decision to say "that" (or to decide between "that" and "which", or to decide whether to leave it out when it is optional) to be incorporated as an action of the grammar independent of the speaker's specifications. That is done by making the "relative pronoun decision" part of a procedure associated with the label that marks post-nominal NP constituents, identifying it with the "enter-slot" event in the transition algorithm so that the decision is made and the pronoun said (or not) just after the head of the NP is said (the "head" being the previous constituent), and before any of the relative clause is said.

Uninteresting but necessary matters such as putting commas after the items of a conjunction or periods at the end of sentences are readily implemented by making them part of procedures attached to the labels that identify those subtrees as such in the surface structure. The "of" of the genitive or the "to" of the infinitive are done similarly. In a description-directed system, such lexical or morphological correlates of syntactic constructions are efficiently and economically incorporated into the process since the fact that they are "piggybacked" onto the very labels that define the constructions means that they will automatically be incorporated when their constructions are used and will never be thought about when they are not.

The grammatical operation of subject-verb agreement brings up another, very important function of the attached procedures: the maintenance of *pointers* to grammatically significant parts of the surface structure tree. The English rule that subject and (tensed) verb must agree in person and number is understood in generation as a constraint of the form of the verb rather than of the subject. That is, we presume that a speaker does not first decide that the verb should be, say, second person singular and then select a subject to match! The rule is manifest as a trivial decision procedure, positioned within the morphology routine, that is activated whenever the morphology routine is passed a word that is identified as the first word of a tensed verb group (the identification having been set up by the action of earlier labels). In order to select a form of the verb that matches the subject in person and number, this decision procedure clearly needs to be able to identify and query the subject constituent, which it does by accessing a pointer to it that was set by the action of a procedure attached to the label "subject" and that has been maintained in the computational environment ever since. (Such a pointer is implemented in the computer program as a global variable of a given name and is incorporated into the body of the decision-maker on that basis.)

The human grammar writer is permitted to declare pointers freely and to have attached procedures assign them to whatever structures in the tree that the procedures can access (typically just the contents of the current slot if done at an "enter-slot" or "leave-slot" event, or the current node if at an "enter-node" or "leave-node" event; the "after-realization" event can access both the *r*-spec the current slot originally contained and the new node that replaces it). The pointers are recursive, permitting them to be assigned relative to the current grammatical context and then reassigned (with the former values saved) when the traversal recursively enters another grammatical unit of the same sort. For example one would have the value of the pointer to the "current-subject" rebound when the traversal enters an embedded clause, and then have it restored to its former value when the traversal finishes the embedding and returns to the original clause.

4.5 Constraining decisions: the rest of the example

As the purpose of this paper is to illustrate a control structure rather than to explore possibly controversial linguistic analyses, I will not dwell on this example more than necessary. We left it at the point of the snapshot in Fig. 3 taken just after the initial *r*-spec had been realized. This corresponds to the third condition of the traversal algorithm (beginning of previous section), and the next step is to continue the traversal down into the conjunction and then to the *r*-spec embedded as its first constituent, i.e. "(*r*-spec2 color-of(door-3 red))". Realizing it gives us its next level of terms embedded in a predicate adjective clause, essentially "[(door-3)--(modifies door-3 *r*-spec3)] is ⟨red⟩".

As already discussed, lexicalization in this task domain is deliberately trivial: all of the properties of an object that are to go into its description are given explicitly in the *r*-spec, and the decision as to what determiner to use has been simplified to just "the" for already mentioned objects, and "a" for when they are introduced. The realization of the first constituent thus goes very simply; the embedded *r*-spec "*r*-spec3" (i.e. "part-of(door-3 house-1)") is realized as genitive construction because of its function as a modifier.

Once the completed first noun phrase is traversed (causing the words "the door of the house"

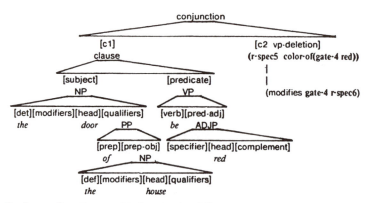

Spoken so far: *The door of the house is red, and //*

Fig. 4. Snapshot just before VP-deletion.

to be spoken), the traversal moves back up the tree and on into the verb phrase. When its traversal is complete the surface structure looks as shown in the snapshot in Fig. 4.

At this point there are two strong sources of constraint on the realization of "*r*-spec5": the fact that it is in a conjunction, and the fact that it (or rather its slot—the effect is the same) has been marked to undergo VP-deletion. As another standing order on text style, we have decided that all of the clauses of a conjunction should employ parallel constructions. This is translated for purposes of generation into the constraint that all decisions made in later clauses should automatically make the same choice as was made in the first. Thus decision processes for the second instance of the "color-of" relation will be pre-empted: Color-of will automatically be realized as a predicate adjective clause, and the second "part-of" will automatically come out as a genitive.

The force of the directive to perform VP-deletion is to transform the selected predicate adjective construction into either a "predicate-preposed" form where the repeated predicate can pronominalized as "do so" (e.g. "The casualties were heavy and *so were* the material losses."), or to keep the order the same and add an adverb such as "too" or "also" ("... and the material losses were too."). Here again the stylistic standing order applies and selects the predicate-preposed form preferentially. (Actually it does not do a "selection", rather it filters out the other choice. Since it is only a stylistic heuristic, it cannot be allowed to block all alternatives, thus if the "too" form had been the only one possible no filtering would have been done.)

The rest of the traversal proceeds the same way as the traversal of the first conjunct had gone. The actual mechanism of the verb phrase deletion is to first invoke a transformation (so to speak) to cause the "color-of" relation to be realized in copula-shifted order (i.e. "⟨red⟩ is ⟨gate-4⟩"), and then to "pronominalize" the predicate-adjective as the word "so".

5. IMPLICATIONS OF THE ALGORITHM

Regardless of how effective a computational system may be, success as an abstract system does not automatically imply success as a psychological theory. The latter can only be accessed by projecting the behavior of the system onto observed human behavior and attempting to formulate a coherent accounting of it with predictive consequences. Section 5.1 of this section introduces the key computational constraints that the design imposes on the generator's behavior. Since the design itself does not specify what the grammar and pragmatic decision-criteria are to be, only how they can be used within the process, these constraints are likely to be the key points of leverage in eliciting predictions. Section 5.2 lays out the most immediate matches between the behavior of the system and of humans, while 5.3 discusses alternative ways to analyse certain linguistic phenomena that might otherwise be problematic. Section 5.4 looks at the status of the traditional notion of constraints in transformational generative grammars and suggests that the phenomena these capture would be more satisfactorily accounted for by looking to the computational properties of the processor. Section 5.5 carries this further by examining some actual human speech errors and considering how they might have arisen.

5.1 *Computational constraints*

The use of pointers to positions of interest within the surface structure tree alludes to several constraints imposed by the generator's computational environment that have been implied by the discussion so far but not made explicit:

● No computations of any sort take place in the generator except those that are directed by the actions of the traversal algorithm.

● Computations are therefore local to a single location in the tree at a time.

● No parts of the tree other than the present location of the traversal are accessible to a decision-maker (except for those expressly pointed to). In particular, there are deliberately no provisions for operations that could "walk" through the tree looking for arbitrary landmarks or patterns (One cannot, for example, have a grammatical rule that refers to "the subject of the clause two embeddings up and one back from the present position").

These constraints follow directly and inescapably from the data-directed basis of the generator. They act to guarantee two very attractive run-time properties, namely that the algorithm is "on-line", and executes in linear time at a constant (bounded) rate.

On-line transduction. Formally the algorithm can be viewed as two cascaded transducers, a realization process converting realization specifications couched in the speaker's internal representation into a surface structure tree, and a traversal process "converting" that tree (with words at its leaves) into a text. An "on-line" transducer is one that converts the current token in its input stream completely into tokens of the output stream before moving on to the next input token. An on-line transducer thus faithfully reflects the ordering of its input stream in its output, and does not accumulate unconverted parts of its input. This definition must be complicated somewhat to accommodate the fact that the input *r*-specs and output subtrees of the realization process are both nested structures; however since the transduction preserves proper nesting, there is no problem.

Linear time/constant bounded rate. The linearity of the algorithm and its bounded rate are guaranteed by the fact that the second transducer—the one from the surface structure to the output text—is the one that dictates the overall flow of control. Since control is based on a one-pass traversal of an acyclic tree, the process is guaranteed to be linear in the number of nodes (i.e. each node and each slot will be entered and left only once). Since the only sources of subtrees in the surface structure is the realization of successive *r*-specs as they are "exposed" in the recursive decomposition of the speaker's original *r*-spec, the number of nodes in a given surface structure will be dictated by the number of embedded *r*-specs that are realized. The side of the subtree that results from any one realization is fixed in advance, and thus can be no larger than some bound determined by the available choices. (Recall that all choices are precomputed—realization is basically just a process of filtering out ungrammatical choices and selecting from what is left.) Overall then, we can establish that no more than a bounded number of nodes will have to be traversed per element in the initial composite *r*-spec. Therefore given the completely data-directed nature of the computation, there can be no more than a bounded number of operations per input element, or, for that matter, per word of output text.

To insure that the linear time—bounded rate—constraint is adhered to, one must guarantee that none of the modules that are dispatched to are capable of performing operations that could potentially require processing time proportional to the length of one of controlling data-structures. Prohibiting predicates that can perform tree-walking operations (or that can perform arbitrary scans of the realization specifications) is a key part of this guarantee. Maintaining a fixed set of pointers, on the other hand, does not perturb the constraint at all, since they are set only when the traversal is directly on top of the place of interest.

5.2 *A natural match with human phenomenology*

These purely computational properties of description-directed control in generation lend themselves to a very attractive phenominological interpretation—a "match" with the way that the generation process appears to us as human beings that should be exploitable as a point of leverage in formal psycholinguistic experiments.

Incremental production. Since each word is spoken as soon as the traversal reaches it at a leaf of the tree, texts are produced in their natural order and in increments that correspond to the size of the units (the input *r*-specs) by which they were planned conceptually.

Indelibility. Once this generator has spoken a word, it cannot take it back; once it has decided to use a certain construction and made it part of the surface structure, it cannot change its mind short of aborting the entire process and starting over. This "indelibility" of the output text and grammatical context is again an inescapable consequence of the use of description-directed control.

Limited lookahead. Since embedded realization specifications are never elaborated before the point in the text where they are to appear has been reached by the traversal, decision-makers never can have more than a sketchy notion of what decisions will happen after theirs. In the tree behind the current position of the traversal, all structures are described in an entirely linguistic vocabulary and the grammar writer may arrange to have the system remember (through pointers) any class of information that they wish. In front of the current position however, the specificity of the linguistic plans in place so far becomes increasingly vague since none of their details have been decided yet. This is suggestive of the common experience that people have of starting to speak without knowing how they will finish beyond knowing that they will try and speak about such and such a relation or make a certain reference.

Enforced grammaticality. Though not discussed in this paper, the labels on the surface structure also serve to define "filters" that restrict the choices available for realizing an *r*-spec to just those that are grammatical in the context defined by its position in the tree. (Details can be found in[15]). For example when an *r*-spec whose *a priori* choices include realization both as an adjective and as a predicate adjective (e.g. both "the X *is red*" and "the *red* X") has been embedded in the surface structure at a position that permits only the adjective form, then the labels on that position will act to suppress the predicate adjective choice, leaving the *r*-spec's decision procedure to decide only between variations on the adjective choice.

The effect of this kind of filtering action is to insure that the output text will be grammatical regardless of the organization of the original specification. We have always presumed that the original *r*-spec was deliberately planned and constructed; we can make the further assumption that the speaker has so structured the *r*-spec that its most important components will be realized first. This means that since grammatical constraints are minimal at the beginning of a text but built up as the traversal goes further along or become more deeply embedded, it will be the least important (or last thought of) components of the *r*-spec that will be most in danger of being omitted from the text for grammatical reasons—exactly our experience as human speakers.

5.3 *The direction of grammatical dependencies*

The fact that this generator is based on a description-directed control technique with its attendant constraints on the computational environment has the effect of imposing a discipline on the analyses of the human grammar writer that forces significant departures from those commonly seen. Some of this may just involve alternatives in methodology, but some may indicate substantive ontological differences in what the nature of grammar is taken to be that should be ammenable to psycholinguistic tests.

Natural language constructions involve syntactic dependences between their parts that must be captured by the grammar that is written for the generator. The usual way of expressing these rules in the past, at least for main-stream American linguistics, has involved the use of a procedural calculus—transformational generative grammar—in which the relationship between surface texts and their corresponding semantic representations are "derived" by a cyclic, bottom-up process from schematic syntactic base structures. As a result, some of the grammatical dependencies most significant for linguistic theory are couched in terms of procedural analyses that are completely the reverse of those required for a psychologically plausible generator that is actually to be used by a speaker. Examples of such dependencies include the relation between the WH word and its "gap" in questions or relative clauses, the relation between subject noun phrases and the deep case structure of the complements of so-called "raising verbs" such as "*expect*" or "*seems*", or generally speaking any grammatical dependency where a marked feature high and to the left in a text apparently depends upon circumstances that are only manifest lower and to its right.

The effect in the present design of adopting a depth-first traversal pattern on the emerging surface structure tree is to impose an inescapable bias on the flow of information, grammatical or otherwise, within it. Those parts of the surface structure that are high and to the left are constructed first: decisions made there impose constraints on all decisions made later in the tree down and to the right. For the bulk of the grammatical dependencies in English, this is exactly the right direction: pronouns depend upon their antecedents; extraposition and heavy-phrase shift "move" their phrases to the right; the various kinds of conjunction-reduction occur only after the first conjunct has appeared; subjects precede their verbs.

The cases of dependencies that apparently move "against the current" so to speak are undeniable however, and to deal with them this generator must impose certain conventions on the way that speakers organize their realization specifications if the computational constraints of the description-directed control structure are to be preserved. The control structure does not allow the generator to "hold off" on a grammatical decision while it extends the surface structure down and to the right in order to find out some critical later decision is going to turn out—such an operation cannot possibly be formulated in this generator. Instead, the speaker must provide the requisite information as part of its r-spec. In[16], I refer to this as the *constraint-proceeds* stipulation. It is a prediction that must be borne out by independent examination of human r-spec's if the present virtual machine is to prove valid.

The use of a description-directed generator encourages *planning* by the speaker as the way to achieve the most effective texts. There are no restrictions in the design on the *passing down* of linguistic information that has been determined by an early decision-maker; consequently, if speakers plan their use of marked linguistic constructions and signal them explicitly at the appropriate points in their realization specifications, then linguistically "redundant" information can be provided to dependencies top-down to make up for information down and to the right would otherwise not be available until it was too late to use it.

WH-movement is a clear case in point. Under the generative grammar analysis, questions are derived from specifically marked D-structures by a process of transformationally moving a WH-word (e.g. "who", "what", "why", etc.) up to the front of the sentence from the position it would have held in the declarative version of the same sentence, leaving a "gap". This analysis "captures" the generalization that the form of the WH-word is dictated by the position of the gap.† In the analysis for generation, on the other hand, questions arise from r-specs that begin with the internal representation of the questioned element (the source of the WH-word) *and* that of the body of the question (a lambda abstraction), both at the same level. No motion within the constituent structure is required since the WH-word is available from the start. (The gap is created by what amounts to a form of pronominalization at the point when the recurrence of the questioned element is reached during the traversal of the question matrix.) By adopting this alternative analysis of the "source" for questions and other WH constructions, we are making the assumption that in deciding to use a question a speaker already knows three items before starting to speak: (1) what is going to be questioned, (2) how the question will be framed (the source of the body), and (3) how the question relates to that frame (information from which to make a decision like "who" vs "whom"). This does not seem unreasonable; indeed, it is hard to imagine how it could be otherwise.

This example of questions points to a methodology for dealing with natural language constructions whose dependencies appear to go in the wrong direction. First we must ask why a speaker would want to use the construction: is there some special rhetorical effect that it achieves? a special emphasis? a special stylistic pattern in the text? Asking this question is a critical step since one cannot formulate a grammatical analysis for a generator without first deciding what the non-linguistic source of the analyzed construction is, e.g. an apparently minor change in the information in the realization specification can make an enormous difference in how the construction must be analyzed linguistically. If the construction is one that is

---

†Consider the use of "who" vs "whom". "Who" is used when the questioned item would have been a subject or direct object (as in "Who did the islander's think _____ should have soverignty?"), while "whom" is used when the item would have been the object of a preposition ("For whom was the loss more important?"). This phenomena is very weak in English, but in languages with strong case markings such as Russian or Finnish, the question word must match the grammatical properties of the position of the gap in every respect.

"marked" (i.e. realizes a rhetorical goal that a speaker might plan for in a realization specification), then we can reanalyze right-to-left linguistic dependencies as top-down dependencies, by arranging that speakers place the goal that triggers the construction sufficiently early in the r-spec that the text of the construction has not yet been started when that goal is considered. This will give the decision-makers sufficient "warning" that they will not inadvertently select realizations that would make the construction impossible.

Consider how we would use this methodology to analyze the tough-movement construction, one that would be impossible for the generator under its usual analysis. ("Tough-movement" is what is said to have happened in the grammatical derivation of a sentence like "Economics is tough for John to study".) Step one is to ask why a speaker would ever want to use it; or better, why they would want to use tough-movement in favor of the other two alternatives usually included in that paradigm, i.e. the extraposed form "It's tough for John to study economics", and the (putatively) unmarked case "For John to study economics is tough". One very comfortable answer for why to use it would be "in order to focus on 'economics'". That being the case, then if that goal is ordered in the speaker's r-spec before the goal to express the proposition "tough(study(John,economics))", the required top-down information flow of the re-analysis can be carried forward (see [15] for details).

5.4 Alternatives to stipulated constraints

One of the most important hypotheses one can make in linguistic theory is to propose a universal constraint. Such constraints apply "across the board", controlling the actions of all individual rules and thereby simplifying their statement. Early constraints, such as those proposed by Ross[26], proposed limitations on the structural descriptions (i.e. constituent trees) to which transformations could be applied. His "complex noun phrase constraint" for example stated that no transformation was permitted to move a constituent from inside a relative clause to outside. This for instance blocks the "extraction" that would lead to the ungrammatical question: "What treasure did Sigfried kill the dragon that guarded?".

For all its comprehensiveness however, a stipulated constraint is just that, stipulated. One has no explanation of why the grammar of a natural language should include it, other than that it is necessary if the grammar is to generate only grammatical sentences—a conclusion that does not sit well with many computational linguists. Marcus's treatment of syntactic parsing with a computationally restricted virtual machine[5] demonstrated how the restrictions on his machine lead inescapably to behavior that satisfied certain universal constraints that had been stipulated for competence grammars (i.e. Chomsky's "specified subject" and "tensed-S" constraints[25]). The same kind of demonstration can be made with this description-directed treatment of language generation.

Note however that nothing is necessarily "proved" by such demonstrations in and of themselves. They establish that if such and such a virtual machine were in use then the behavior captured by the constraint would occur without the need for any stipulation in the grammar that the virtual machine employs. There still remains the problem of establishing that said virtual machine is actually functionally issomorphic to the one that people use—a demonstration that is not yet possible given the indirect nature of the available evidence.

With the grammar and realization procedures used in the present computer implementation, this generator appears to have non-stipulative explanations for at least the following constraints: the A-over-A principle, complex-NP and prohibited extractions from islands generally, right-node raising, and the "that-deletion" filter of[27]. However, rather than extend this paper to several times its present length by presenting detailed arguments in support of that claim (some appear in [15], the rest will appear in [29]), I prefer to end here with a discussion of how I believe the question of "constraints" should be approached by those who would study natural language generation. Detailed arguments will always be contingent on what grammatical analyses one believes in and on "boot-strapped" assumptions about the form and content of the speaker's internal sources, neither of which can be taken to any firm conclusions until considerably more empirical work has been done on the processes involved in language use rather than just on the description of language competence.

5.5 Constraints: what do people actually do?

People violate grammatical constraints regularly. The frequency is low—perhaps one or two occurrences per day among the people I regularly listen to—nevertheless violations occur often enough that one can characterize what happens and try to make hypotheses about it. Consider the following actually occurring texts: (These were written down immediately after they occurred and checked for veracity against what the speaker remembered having said.)

[Said in reference to the speaker's cluttered bedroom]
"There are all sorts of assorted things here that should be found a place for."

[Said about a roadmap that had a poor index]
"It's not a map that you can use to find a street that you don't know where it is."

[Said while trying to coordinate vacations]
"I wonder if we could find an expedition that we would both be interested in and the leader would both be interested in us."

The first text is strange because the speaker has "passivized" a verb which does not allow it, i.e. "find a place for". The second is strange because it violates Ross's Complex NP Constraint: the NP "a street" has been modified with a relative clause in which "street" occurs in a place where it is not legal to leave a gap and a resumptive pronoun has been used instead. The third has arranged for a parallelism in the placement of the word "both" while ignoring the fact that the word can not be used in its intended meaning when in that position in the second conjunct (i.e. the text should have been "...interested in both of us").

The most important thing about these texts is that the speakers *did not stop* when faced with a violated constraint. In a generative grammar, constraints act to block illegal derivations; in actual use however, these "illegal" texts are produced in spite of the constraint and with the same fluency and intonation as normal texts. The speaker is typically very aware of having said something strange and may well immediately say the text over again correctly formed, but the original ill-formed text does appear—the grammar is *not* an all or nothing filter.

The story that such texts suggest to me revolves around failures in planning: speakers have a very strong ordering on their communicative goals but they have neither the time, nor perhaps the ability, to evaluate the linguistic consequences of all of their goals taken together. They begin their text as though there was not going to be any problem and only afterwards find that their later *r*-specs cannot be realized properly in the linguistic context that their earlier *r*-specs have established. At this point human speakers do not go catatonic. They have already planned the text that would follow (or rather positioned the *r*-specs it derives from and made some decisions about its linguistic character), and thus they have the option of continuing. The grammar will in fact support them as they continue, making the best of a bad situation, because *the grammar is not a censor but a mediator*—it shapes what is said but does not dictate it.

In the production of the second text about finding streets on the badly indexed map (one of my own errors), the goal was first to characterize the map and second to say about it that you couldn't use it to find a street if you didn't already know where the street was. The first goal led to the use of extraposition ("It's not a map that..."); the second was fundamentally a fact about streets and the difficulty of finding them, hence its realization as a complex NP centered on "a street". Only at the last minute did I become aware of the grammatical bind in which I had placed myself, and, being among friends, I decided to complete my sentence and assume that they could figure it out rather than stop and restructure the whole utterance.

This grammatical "horizon effect" has a natural explanation in the context of description-directed generation. The meaning of a grammatical constraint is to force a selection between alternative realizations: one uses the legal form and does not consider its illegal alternative. However, this action can occur only if the linguistic parameters required to recognize that the constraint applies are available at the time that the two alternatives must be decided between. When a violation occurs, it is because one or more of the needed parameters was unknown when the choice-point was reached, e.g. the choice required knowing how a *r*-spec embedded further on in the tree was going to be realized. The speaker assumes that everything will work out correctly, but is unable to actually prove it because of limitations in the kinds of information that can be acquired about an *r*-spec's realization without actually producing it. When the realization eventually occurred, it turns out to be "out of phase" with the actual grammatical environment; the grammatical procedures attached to that environment are unable to perform their usual functions; and the resulting text "violates" the constraint.

6. CONCLUSION: PROPERTIES OF THE VIRTUAL MACHINE

As this is a concepts paper rather than a technical report, it would be inappropriate here to develop the background necessary for presenting a formal specification of the virtual machine: there is not yet anything resembling a universal notation or universally understood set of primitives that could be appealed to in representing the definitions. Let me instead attempt to present the key ideas in prose, leaving the compact† symbolic definition to [29].

Surface structures as processes

The key concept of this design is that the surface structure selected for the text defines the steps to be taken in producing it. The node pattern of the surface structure defines the order of the steps, and its grammatical labels define the constraints that are to be imposed on any embedded decisions. As a computational object, the surface structure is all action and no representation: i.e. it defines the processing that takes place but does not itself need to be examined. This means that the most natural implementation of such surface structure is as *a process, not a buffer*—an object that performs a series of actions, but whose internal structure is not accessible or modifiable from outside it.

Enumeration and association. After control by the surface structure description of the text, the other concept the virtual machine must support is a capability for enumerating the components ("sub" *r*-specs) of the realization specification as dictated by its recursive decomposition by the process of realization. The enumeration—the sequential stream of *r*-specs being realized one after the other—defines the timing and "chunk size" of the transition from the speaker's conceptual vocabulary used for planning what they want to say and their linguistic vocabulary manifest in the surface structure procedures. *R*-spec's in the enumeration stream pass out of it by being realized, i.e. by causing the initiation of the surface structure process that the decision-procedure associated with them has selected.

Unlike the surface structure processes which are defined once and for all by the grammar and can thus be precomputed, enumeration cannot be implemented by a fixed process since each realization specification is specific to the speaking situation that motivated it and these situations constitute an unbounded set. However, the set of components from which *r*-specs can be composed is assumed to be fixed (at least over the short term), thus the associations between the individual components and the surface structures that can realize them does constitute a bounded set and could be manifested by a set of precomputed processes just like the surface structures. The enumeration would then be the output of a continuous function (here undefined) whose inputs would be the current situation and some (also here undefined) "urge to speak".

Coordinating the two. A critical requirement on the virtual machine is that it supports the gating of the enumeration and realization process by the surface structure processes. *R*-specs embedded within the selected surface structure are not realized until the traversal reaches the point where they appear, and the output of the realization, the new "sub" surface structure, is traversed immediately afterwards. The two processes must therefore be running in close coordination, with the timing of successive realizations dependent on the (virtual) text position reached by the active surface structure processes. The least assuming way to support this coordination is to have the surface structures syncronously control the enumeration; asyncronous coordination would not violate any of the design criteria of the generator, but would add a requirement for something like a buffer of pending *r*-specs tagged by the point in the surface structure at which they were to appear, which would not otherwise be required.

---

†What a specification language must provide is a clearly defined set of primitive operations and a calculus for their combination from which the meaning of any expression in the specification can be unambiguously and exactly determined. Any well-constructed computer programming language could play this role; though one would rarely want to accept the primitives that the programming language supplied as the primitives of any proposed psychological process. An "extended language" defined in terms of the original programming language could serve this process however, with the original language serving as a concrete instance of an implementation of specifications written in the extended language.

The LISP program presently instantiating the generator can in this sense serve as one definition of the virtual machine the generator requires, since it consists first of the definition (in LISP) of an extended language in which to define a grammar and pragmatic decision procedures, and then a specific set of primitives by which to interpret them. The program is quite cleanly written in terms of typed objects and a few compact algorithms, and is available to interested investigators for inspection and application. The LISP dialect used is Lispmachine lisp.

The virtual machine must thus support:

● The instantiation and execution of surface structure processes,

● The enumeration of the realization specification (i.e. its conversion from a hierarchical network to a sequential stream), and

● Coordination between these two, with the timing of the enumeration and realization dictated by the "position" that the surface structure processes had reached.

In order to run in real time, the processes maintained by the virtual machine *must* be precomputed, since the time required to construct them from primitives would be a polynomial function of the size of the constituents in the text (see [29]). This implies that the underlying physical machine (e.g. the human brain) must be able to contain latent processes in the hundreds of thousands if not the tens of millions. A sobering thought perhaps, but one which researchers in vision have become quite comfortable with[17], and which should not daunt us.

7. REFERENCES

1. J. Thorne, P. Bratley and H. Dewar, The syntactic analysis of English by machine. In *Machine Intelligence* 3 (Edited by Richie). American Elsevier, New York (1968).
2. T. Winograd, *Natural Language Understanding.* Academic Press, New York (1972).
3. W. Woods, Transition network grammars for natural language analysis. *CACM* **13**(10), 591–606 (1972).
4. M. Marcus, "A 'wait and see' theory of syntactic parsing. In *Proc. TINLAP*-1. ACM, New York (1975).
5. M. Marcus, *A Theory of Syntactic Recognition for Natural Language.* MIT Press, Cambridge, Mass. (1980).
6. R. Milne, Paper presented at the *Winter Meeting of the Association for Computational Linguistics*, 28–30 December 1981.
7. R. Berwick, Learning structural descriptions of grammar rules from examples. Master's Thesis, MIT (1980).
8. M. Ford and V. Holmes, Planing units and syntax in natural language generation. *Cognition* **6**, 35–53 (1978).
9. M. Ford, Sentence planning units: implications for the speaker's representation of meaningful relations underlying sentences. Occasional Paper No. 2, MIT Center for Cognitive Science (1980).
10. V. Fromkin, *Speech Errors as Linguistic Evidence.* Mouton, Paris (1973).
11. M. Garrett, The analysis of sentence production. In *Psychology of Learning and Motivation*, Vol. 9. Academic Press, New York.
12. M. Garrett, Syntactic processes in sentence production. In *New Approaches to Language Mechanisms* (Edited by Walker and Walker). North-Holland, Amsterdam (1976).
13. D. Fay, Transformational errors. In *Errors in Linguistic Performance* (Edited by Fromkin). Academic Press, New York (1980).
14. S. Shattuck-Hufnagel, Speech errors as evidence for a serial ordering mechanism in sentence production. In *Sentence Processing: Psycholinguistic Studies Presented to Merrill Garrett* (Edited by Cooper and Walker). Lawerence Erlbaum Assoc. New York (1979).
15. D. D. McDonald, Natural language generation as a process of decision-making under constraints. Ph.D. Thesis, MIT revision in preparation to appear as a Technical Report from the MIT Artificial Intelligence Lab. (1980).
16. D. D. McDonald, Natural language generation as a computational problem: an introduction. In *Computational Models of Discourse* (Edited by Brady). MIT Press, Cambridge, Mass.
17. D. Marr, *Vision.* Freeman, New York (1982).
18. R. Berwick and A. Weinberg, The role of grammars in models of language use. *Cognition* In press.
19. D. Appelt, Planning natural-language utterances to satisfy multiple goals. Ph.D. Thesis, Stanford University; available as SRI International Technical Note 259 (March 1982).
20. J. Conklin and D. D. McDonald, Salience: the key to the selection problem in natural language generation. In *Proc. 20th Ann. Meeting of the Association for Computational Linguistics*, pp. 129–135. University of Toronto, 16–18 June 1982.
21. W. R. Swartout, A digitalis therapy advisor with explanations. Technical Report TR-176, MIT Laboratory for Computer Science, Cambridge, Mass (1977).
22. W. Clancy, Transfer of rule-based expertise through a tutorial dialogue. Stan-cs-79-769, Dept. of Computer Science, Stanford University.
23. D. Chester, The translations of formal proofs into English. *Artificial Intell.* **7**(3) (1976).
24. N. Chomsky, *Lectures on Government and Binding.* Foris Publications, Dordrecht (1982).
25. N. Chomsky, Conditions on Transformations. In *A Festschrift for Morris Halle* (Edited by Anderson and Kuporsky). Holt, Rinehart & Winston.
26. R. Ross, Constraints on variables in syntax. Ph.D. Thesis, MIT; available from the Indiana Linguistics Club (1968).
27. N. Chomsky and H. Lasnik, Filters and control. *Linguistic Inquiry* **8**(3), 425–504 (1977).
28. W. Mann, M. Bates, B. Grosz, D. D. McDonald, K. McKeown and W. Swartout, Text generation: the state of the art and literature. Technical Report *RR*-81-101, Information Sciences Institute (1981).
29. D. D. McDonald, a revision of [15] in preparation to appear as a Technical Report from the MIT Artificial Intelligence Lab.

VI. SYSTEMS

The articles in previous chapters focused on the elements of NLP. Those here discuss efforts aimed at pulling the elements together into a functioning NLP system. While the construction of these systems may have also entailed the investigation of specific language-related techniques, the particular papers we have included focus on the systems themselves and so, on the way the issues listed here have been tackled.

NLP systems fall into two main classes: interactive systems and text processing systems. *Interactive systems* are ones in which NL is the primary *mode of interaction* with a system meant to do other things. (The system may also allow for graphics-based interaction, mouse-based interaction, tabular output, etc.) Systems for NL interaction have mainly been used for access to database systems. Soon, they may also be used for interacting with intelligent systems such as expert systems or robots, as well as with conventional software such as help systems. *Text processing systems* are ones in which NL texts are the primary *objects of interest*. The purpose of these systems is to analyze an NL text into a form that is more amenable to subsequent processing than the raw text itself. Text processing systems offer the promise of automating the creation of knowledge bases, as well as of carrying out such obviously text-based operations as translation, message integration, automatic abstracting, or sophisticated searching of full-text databases. One can even imagine combined interactive text processing systems—for example, systems that interact with users in NL to determine their information needs and then search through on-line document libraries for information to satisfy those needs. This is the dream of intelligent full-text retrieval systems.

When considering NL from a systems point of view, issues emerge that can usually be ignored when focusing on particular language phenomena and individual components. These issues include modularity, integration, problem factorization, transportability, habitability, extensibility, speed, and cognitive veracity.

Modularity concerns two types of separation: separation of domain-dependent information from domain-independent information and separation of processing modules according to the resources they draw upon.

Integration concerns how the information computed by each processor is brought together into a single analysis. Questions here include how and when these modules communicate and what they communicate about. For example, processors may work in parallel, communicating through individual channels or a global blackboard, or they may be pipelined. Each may compute and propose a single complete analysis, or it may compute and propose several partial hypotheses in order to get feedback.

Problem factorization concerns how responsibility for dealing with a given language phenomenon is distributed among a set of independent modules, and it involves trade-offs in how much effort each module spends on a particular problem. For example, if the semantic analyzer can handle multiple hypotheses, the syntactic processor may not be required to make its own (perhaps *ad hoc*) judgment as to the intended grammatical structure of an utterance.

Transportability is concerned with moving a system to a new domain. Recall that *domain* refers to the world being modeled in the system. Systems cannot be completely domain independent, since knowledge of the world being modeled is critical for correct understanding or generation—domain knowledge is always embedded in one or more places in a system. Transportability involves the separation of domain-dependent aspects of the system from its domain-independent aspects, the expertise needed to transport a system to a new domain, and the ease in doing so. Systems may be augmented with tools that simplify their being adapted to a new domain, as for example in *Martin et al.'s* TEAM system (see this chapter).

Habitability involves a system's coverage and its ability to react adequately to utterances outside that coverage. (This issue is not relevant to text generation systems.) These extraordinary utterances may be the result of errors in typing, spelling, or grammar or (more problematically) the user's exceeding the system's limited grammatical, conceptual, or functional coverage.

Extensibility has to do with the ability to extend a system's linguistic and/or conceptual coverage, either on the user's part or the part of a separate domain expert.

Speed is an important parameter, since the system is actually attempting to perform a task. Speed is especially an issue in interactive systems, since the form, content, and function of user utterances may vary greatly with respect to the system's speed in responding to them.

Veracity concerns how close the system comes to being an accurate model of human language behavior. It is not often used as a criteria in assessing systems, because we do not yet know enough about how language understanding and generation tasks are distributed in human language processing machinery to judge systems on this count. (Some efforts, especially recent ones experimenting with parallel architectures, are aimed directly at providing such models.)

A major challenge in system building lies in distinguishing the general from the specific, and, within the latter, in distinguishing task-specific features (e.g., serving a consultative function) from domain-specific features (e.g., within the domain of medicine). The issues above all have to be viewed in relation to appropriate ways of supplying and deploying universal and specific language processing resources.

Other papers in this volume that discuss systems issues (in part) include: in Chapter 2, *Schank, Winograd,* and *Woods* and in Chapter 6, *McKeown* and *Appelt.* Other papers focused on systems-related issues can be found in the *Proceedings of the Confer-*

ence on Applied NL Processing [1] and an issue of the *American Journal of Computational Linguistics* devoted to "ill-formed input" [2]. Additional features of cooperative NL interactive systems are presented in [5, 6, 7, 8, 11, 13]. An excellent essay on NL interfaces to databases can be found in [10]. It should be noted that there is more effort directed at text processing than this volume would suggest, especially in the area of translation. Translation presents distinctive challenges for NLP in dealing with differences in the expressive devices available in the source and target languages. For articles on mechanical translation, the reader is referred to two recent issues of the *American Journal of Computational Linguistics* [3].

Seven of the eight articles in this chapter describe interactive systems, while one describes a text processing system (SAM). We briefly describe each of the eight below, starting with the two oldest (BASEBALL and PARRY). We then describe the two articles dealing with NL interfaces to database systems (LADDER and TEAM), then the two dealing with general conversational systems (GUS and SOPHIE), and, finally, the two dealing with systems (SAM and QUALM) based on Conceptual Dependency and its extensions (see *Schank,* Chapter 2).

Baseball: An Automatic Question Answerer

BASEBALL was one of the first Q/A systems, developed at a time when most NLP research involved mechanical translation or information retrieval and when user input came only in the form of punch cards. BASEBALL's domain covered games played during one season of the American League. BASEBALL analyzed syntactically a user's query to the extent necessary to create a framelike representation (called a "specification list"), evaluated that specification against a hierarchically organized database, and returned an answer in outline form. BASEBALL was *modular: integration* was realized through its modules (question read-in, dictionary look-up, syntactic analysis, specification list construction, database evaluator, responder) processing the input in strict sequence. *Transportability, habitability, extensibility,* and *speed* were not of concern (especially given the punch card input). What was exciting about BASEBALL was its existence proof that such systems were possible, presaging one of the major lines of research in NLP today.

Conversational Language Comprehension Using Integrated Pattern-Matching and Parsing

PARRY was an attempt to embody a theory of paranoia in a system, which would then explicitly demonstrate paranoid behavior when interacting with a user. In this case, users were psychiatrists, and an interaction had two goals: for the psychiatrist/users, the goal was to detect evidence of paranoia (and its degree) through the interaction and to evaluate the veridicality of the interaction. For the system designers, the goal was to develop an accurate theory of paranoia. Since psychiatrists are trained to perceive underlying illness through NL interaction with their patients, PARRY was designed to carry on such interactions as realistically as possible. It did this by carrying to extremes the idea that NLP could be done through pattern-matching (a technique made famous in Weizenbaum's ELIZA [15]): PARRY had over 2000 patterns available for matching against the input. PARRY's NL interaction was therefore designed for maximum *habitability* and *speed*. As noted earlier, *veracity* was also a critical issue in the system.

Developing a Natural Language Interface to Complex Data

The LADDER system was a milestone in the development of practical NL database Q/A systems. It was designed at SRI as a sophisticated, human-engineered system, rather than a demonstration of a set of syntactic, semantic, and pragmatic theories. The stated goal of LADDER was to provide users with a transparent way of gaining access to information distributed over various databases, where any given user query might require information from several databases, each built on a different database management system (DBMS).

At the level of global *modularity*, LADDER distributed the task of getting information from these databases over three different modules: (1) INLAND—its linguistic component, built using SRI's LIFER language-definition facility, whose task was to translate a user query into a command list of constraints on and requests for database field values, (2) IDA, whose task was to translate this command list into a sequence of queries against individual files in the languages of the remote DBMSs, and (3) FAM, which found the location of the individual files and managed access to them and remote failures. With respect to *problem factorization*, this meant that responsibility for communicating with the DBMSs was distributed over the three components: INLAND was not solely responsible for translating a user's query into an executable object. Another system that demonstrates this type of problem factorization is PHLIQA1 [9].

Within INLAND, *modularity* was limited. Syntax and semantics were combined in a single semantic grammar that also handled some discourse phenomena. There was also a special ellipsis-handler that was able to pattern-match an ellipsed input against the previous user input (or its expanded form). INLAND itself lacked *modularity* and *transportability*. On the other hand, LIFER (its source system) made implementing semantic grammars for a new domain relatively straightforward.[1] LIFER consisted of a domain-independent parser and interactive language definition facility that could be used to create domain-specific linguistic components. Much of the current paper describes LIFER's language-definition facility. LADDER's *habitability* was supported by a spelling corrector and an ability to deal with some forms of incomplete input. Its *extensibility* came from giving the user partial access to LIFER's language-definition functions, allowing the user to extend the system's linguistic coverage through synonyms and paraphrases.

Transportability and Generality in a Natural Language Interface System

The TEAM system was a descendent of LADDER. Its goal was to maximize *transportability*, which LADDER lacked. To this end, TEAM had a domain-independent parser, grammar, basic vocabulary, semantic interpretation routines, basic sort/type taxonomy, pragmatic processes (for resolving vague predicates), quantifier scope algorithm, and schema translator. None of these had to be touched in a move to a new domain or database. Domain-dependent information such as the lexicon, conceptual schema (i.e., remaining semantic taxonomy, predicate argument relations, and pragmatic markings), and database schema were acquired from a database expert during TEAM's acquisition phase, which was designed to elicit information from someone who was not necessarily a specialist in NLP.

TEAM was more *modular* than LADDER, separating its syntactic, semantic, reference, vagueness, and scope resolution processes, which operated independently and in strict sequence (*integration*). The task of producing a complete logical form represention of a query was *factored* across TEAM's semantic translator functions and later pragmatic functions. They resolved vague predicates using the sorts of their arguments and resolved quantifier and

---

[1]However, both the domain analysis needed to create such a grammar and the design of the grammar itself were still skills requiring expertise in NLP.

operator scopes based on the structure of the parse tree, the interpretability of the resulting form and the *a priori* relative "scoping strengths" of different quantifiers. Thus full responsibility for a correct logical form representation was not put on a single processor early on, but rather computed as evidence became available. Again, like LADDER, responsibility for producing an object executable against the database was factored over several modules—initial formulation done by the DIALOGIC linguistic component, then exact translation done by the schema translator. TEAM allowed some *extension* by end users, allowing them to define synonyms but not paraphrases.

GUS, A Frame Driven Dialogue System

The next two articles describe GUS (*Bobrow et al.*) and SOPHIE (*Burton and Brown*). These were experimental, extended NL interaction systems developed in the mid 1970s. GUS was a vehicle for studying dialogue understanding by carrying on a realistic, task-oriented dialogue with a user in a limited domain. As reported in this article, GUS played the role of a travel agent, with a user planning a simple return trip to a city in California. In the design of GUS, emphasis was put on *modularity* for an interesting reason: the designers wanted to see if a general dialogue system, with all its complexity, could be made modular and to test their notions of reasonable lines of decomposition. The *integration* of GUS's modules was through the use of a global agenda: at each cycle, GUS examined its agenda to select the next task to be done. During that execution, additional tasks would be put on the agenda. Part of the reason for this was to allow a mixed-initiative interaction between user and system. GUS was able to understand incomplete and indirect utterances (*habitability*) because it set up strong expectations about what information the user would provide in response to its questions (expectations based on the question, the limited domain, and the user's assumed goals). GUS's designers saw GUS as the first in a series of experimental systems that would contain and act on better models of human interactive behavior. Unfortunately, that did not happen.

Toward a Natural Language Capability for Computer-Assisted Instruction

SOPHIE was a prototype instructional system, aimed at teaching students procedural knowledge and reasoning strategies, rather than simply facts. NL was chosen as the mode of communication because of the range of interaction required by the system—a student should be able to ask for information, test hypotheses, and find out why his or her conclusions were right or wrong—and the awkwardness of trying to carry out such a rich, natural interaction in an unfamiliar, rigid mode. On the other hand, to support this kind of NL interaction, SOPHIE's NL system had to be *fast* and *habitable*, even at the expense of *modularity*. Like LADDER, SOPHIE used a semantic grammar, which speeded understanding and allowed it to deal with some types of incomplete utterances and anaphoric references. SOPHIE's semantic grammar was encoded as an ATN for *perspicuity*, but then compiled into pure LISP code for *speed*. *Habitability* was supported through the use of the INTERLISP spelling corrector. (In an earlier, non-ATN implementation of its semantic grammar, SOPHIE ignored unexpected words that were not part of any meaningful pattern. This increased *habitability* at the expense of possible errors and bizarre behavior.) Burton and Brown stress the importance of an instructional system's being able to accept a wide range of initial statements of the same idea, as their students seemed unable to rephrase quickly when their first attempt failed.

SAM

The final two papers in this chapter describe applications of the language theories of Schank and his students (see Chapter 2) to extended text understanding. The first system, SAM, could read newspaper stories on several topics and produce an instantiated script structure representing the story's explicit and implicit content. The second system, QUALM, drew on this script structure, together with a theory of Q/A, in order to answer a user's NL queries about the text.

SAM consisted of three modules: ELI [12], which did a sentence-by-sentence mapping of the text into an "inference free" conceptual dependency (CD) representation; PP-Memory, which took the language-free output of ELI and identified the individuals referred to in the text, assigned them unique labels, and attempted to decide whether any of them had already been seen; and the Script Applier, which attempted to decide what script the section of the text gave evidence of (e.g., the current script or a new or embedded script) and how that script should be instantiated. These modules operated as independent processes (*integration*) that analyzed each sentence in turn. (There does not appear to have been any mechanism to correct script choices or role assignments, should they later be found to be incorrect.) Nevertheless, responsibility for handling certain language phenomena was *factored* among the modules: for example, deciding what a description refers to and what its role is (or its roles are) within the currently active set of scripts required effort on the part of each of the three modules.

Although ELI has been used as a component of many NLP systems developed at Yale, *transportability* is not discussed in the current article. Cullingford notes that even though scripts have to be constructed for each new domain, script construction is a well-understood, if tedious, process. (For example, DeJong's FRUMP system [4] was supplied with a large number of scripts, albeit cruder ones than SAM's. Also see PAM, both in [16] and *Wilensky*, Chapter 4.) The Script Applier itself appears to be domain independent.

Text understanding requires a large amount of domain-based inference, as well as various sized structures for organizing the information presented in the text. In basing story understanding on script understanding, SAM attempted to be an accurate model of human story understanding (*veracity*). (For more discussion of script-based and CD-based systems, the reader is referred to *Schank* in Chapter 2.)

A Conceptual Theory of Question Answering

The last paper in this chapter describes QUALM, an NL Q/A system developed by Lehnert, which answers questions about stories understood by SAM or its companion system PAM (see *Wilensky*, Chapter 4). As with SAM, QUALM is *modular*, its modules operating in strict sequence. First, ELI is used to produce a CD representation of the user's NL question. Then this CD representation is passed through a discrimination net to find its "conceptual category." This represents a deeper level of understanding of what is actually being requested in the query. Then another inference mechanism may be invoked to supply additional constraints on what constitutes an appropriate answer. Following this, retrieval processes first decide what kind of information to return, depending on the answer found, and then search the story structure built by SAM or PAM to find (or infer) the answer and the additional information desired.

The importance of QUALM, from a systems point of view, lies in its early recognition that an appropriate answer to a question is not always completely determined by its literal meaning and in its attempt to reason about the function of a question and the appropriateness of particular answers. More recent Q/A systems factor out many of the specific behaviors attempted in QUALM and deal with them individually in a more sophisticated manner. For a survey of current NL Q/A techniques, see [14].

In summary, although the systems described above were all important efforts, it has to be recognized that they were all limited—and limited in more than one respect. That they could be as successful as they were is primarily because they were able to take advantage of their well-defined micro application. In this respect, NL interfaces have generally been more tractable than text processing systems. But the limitations of current interfaces are well illustrated, for example, by the fact that though they may allow some mixed initiative, they do not support the range of functionality that is characteristic of human dialogue. But that just means that there is still room in the future for interesting systems development.

References

[1] Kameny, I. (editor). *Conference on Applied Natural Language Processing*, ACL, Santa Monica CA, 1983, 1–3 February 1983.

[2] Allen, J. (editor), Special Issue on Ill-formed Input, *Amer. J. of Computational Linguistics*, Volume 9, Numbers 3–4, July–December 1983.

[3] Slocum, J. (editor), Special Issues on Machine Translation, *Computational Linguistics*, Volume 11, Issues 1–3, 1985. Includes papers on the TAUM, SPANAM, EUROTRA, and METAL systems.

[4] DeJong, G., Prediction and Substantiation: A New Approach to Natural Language Processing, *Cognitive Science* 3(3):251–273, July–September, 1979.

[5] Finin, T., Joshi, A., and Webber, B., Natural Language Interactions with Artificial Experts, *IEEE Proceedings*, July, 1986, Special Issue on Natural Language Processing.

[6] Gal, A. and Minker, J., A Natural Language Database Interface that Provides Cooperative Answers. In *Proc. Second Annual Conf. on Artificial Intelligence Applications*, pages 352–357. IEEE, Miami FL, December, 1985.

[7] Hoeppner, W., Morik, K., and Marburger, H., Talking it Over: The NL Dialog System HAM-ANS. In Bolc, L. (editor), *Cooperative Interactive Systems*. Springer-Verlag, Berlin, 1984.

[8] Kaplan, S. J., Cooperative Responses From a Portable Natural Language Query System. *Artificial Intelligence* 19(2):165–188, 1982.

[9] Landsbergen, S. P. J., Syntax and Formal Semantics of English in PHLIQA1. In *Proc. of the 6th Int'l Conf. on Computational Linguistics*. COLING, Ottawa, Canada, July, 1976.

[10] Perrault, C. R. and Grosz, B. J., Natural-Language Interfaces. In *Annual Review of Computer Science 1986*, pages 47–82. Annual Reviews, Inc., Palo Alto CA, 1986.

[11] Pollack, M., A Model of Plan Inference that Distinguishes between the Beliefs of Actors and Observers. In

Proc. of 24th Annual Meeting, pages 207–214. Assoc. for Computational Linguistics, New York City, June 1986.

[12] Riesbeck, C. and Schank, R., Comprehension by Computer: Expectation-Based Analysis of Sentences in Context. In Levelt, W. J. M., and Flores d'Arcais, G. B. (editors), *Studies in the Perception of Language.* John Wiley and Sons, Ltd., Chichester, England, 1979.

[13] Wahlster, W., Marburger, H., Jameson, A., and Busemann, S., Overanswering Yes-No Questions: Extended Responses in a NL Interface to a Vision System. In *Proceedings of the 8th IJCAI,* pages 643–646. Int'l. J. Conf. on Artificial Intelligence, Karlsruhe, Germany, August, 1983.

[14] Webber, B.L., Questions, Answers and Responses. In Mylopoulos, J. and Brodie, M. (editors), *On Knowledge Base Systems.* Springer-Verlag, 1986.

[15] Weizenbaum, J., ELIZA—A Computer Program for the Study of Natural Language Communication Between Man and Machine, *Comm. ACM* 9(1), January, 1966.

[16] Wilensky, R., *Planning and Understanding: A Computational Approach to Human Reasoning,* Addison-Wesley, Reading, MA, 1983.

BASEBALL: AN AUTOMATIC QUESTION ANSWERER

by Bert F. Green, Jr., Alice K. Wolf, Carol Chomsky, &
Kenneth Laughery

Introduction

Men typically communicate with computers in a variety of artificial, stylized, unambiguous languages that are better adapted to the machine than to the man. For convenience and speed, many future computer-centered systems will require men to communicate with computers in natural language. The business executive, the military commander, and the scientist need to ask questions of the computer in ordinary English, and to have the computer answer the questions directly. Baseball is a first step toward this goal.

Baseball is a computer program that answers questions posed in ordinary English about data in its store. The program consists of two parts. The linguistic part reads the question from a punched card, analyzes it syntactically, and determines what information is given about the data being requested. The processor searches through the data for the appropriate information, processes the results of the search, and prints the answer.

The program is written in IPL-V (Newell, et al., 1960e), an information processing language that uses lists, and hierarchies of lists, called list structures, to represent information. Both the data and the dictionary are list structures, in which items of information are expressed as attribute-value pairs, e.g., Team = Red Sox.

The program operates in the context of baseball data. At present, the data are the month, day, place, teams and scores for each game in the American League for one year. In this limited context, a small vocabulary is sufficient, the data are simple, and the subject matter is familiar.

Some temporary restrictions were placed on the input questions so that the initial program could be relatively straightforward. Questions are limited to a single clause; by prohibiting structures with dependent clauses the syntactic analysis is considerably simplified. Logical connectives, such as *and*, *or*, and *not*, are prohibited, as are constructions implying relations like *most* and *highest*. Finally, questions involving sequential facts, such as "Did the Red Sox ever win six games *in a row?*" are prohibited. These restrictions are temporary expedients that will be removed in later versions of the program. Moreover, they do not seriously reduce the number of questions that the program is capable of answering. From simple questions such as "Who did the Red Sox lose to on July 5?" to complex questions such as "Did every team play at least once in each park in each month?" lies a vast number of answerable questions.

Specification List

Fundamental to the operation of the baseball program is the concept of the *specification list*, or *spec list*. This list can be viewed as a canonical expression for the meaning of the question; it represents the information contained in the question in the form of attribute-value pairs, *e.g.*, Team = Red Sox. The spec list is generated from the question by the linguistic part of the program, and it governs the operation of the processor. For example, the question "Where did the Red Sox play on July 7?" has the spec list:

Place = ?
Team = Red Sox
Month = July
Day = 7.

Some questions cannot be expressed solely in terms of the main attributes (Month, Day, Place, Team, Score, and Game Serial Number), but require some modification of these attributes. For example, on the spec list for the question "What teams won 10 games in July?", the attribute Team is modified by Winning, and Game is modified by Number of, yielding

Team $_{(winning)}$ = ?
Game $_{(number\ of)}$ = 10
Month = July.

Dictionary

The dictionary definitions, which are expressed as attribute-value pairs, are used by the linguistic part of the program in generating the spec list. A complete definition for a word or idiom includes a part of speech, for use in determining phrase structure; a meaning, for use in analyzing content; an indication of whether the entry is a question word, *e.g.*, *who* or *how many*; and an indication of whether a word occurs as part of any stored

of hierarchical organization was included for generality and potential efficiency. The basic rule is that any one path through the data, including one list at each level, must contain all of the facts for a single game. Also, on every such path, each attribute may occur at most once, unless it occurs on parallel sublists.

Details of the Program

The program is organized into several successive, essentially independent routines, each operating on the output of its predecessor and producing an input for the routine that follows. The linguistic routines include question read-in, dictionary look-up, syntactic analysis, and content analysis. The processing routines include the processor and the responder.

Linguistic Routines

QUESTION READ-IN

A question for the program is read into the computer from punched cards. The question is formed into a sequential list of words.

DICTIONARY LOOK-UP

Each word on the question list is looked up in the word dictionary and its definition copied. Any undefined words are printed out. (In the future, with a direct-entry keyboard, the computer can ask the questioner to define the unknown words in terms of words that it knows, and so augment its vocabulary.) The list is scanned for possible idioms; any contiguous words that form an idiom are replaced by a single entry on the question list, and an associated definition from the idiom dictionary. At this point, each entry on the list has associated with it a definition, including a part of speech, a meaning, and perhaps other indicators.

SYNTAX

The syntactic analysis is based on the parts of speech, which are syntactic categories assigned to words for use by the syntax routine. There are 14 parts of speech and several ambiguity markers.

First, the question is scanned for ambiguities in part of speech, which are resolved in some cases by looking at the adjoining words, and in other cases by inspecting the entire question. For example, the word *score* may be either a noun or a verb; our rule is that, if there is no other main verb in the question, then *score* is a verb, otherwise it is a noun.

Next, the syntactic routine locates and brackets the noun phrases, [□], and the prepositional and adverbial phrases, (□). The verb is left un-

idiom. Separate dictionaries are kept for words and idioms, an idiom being any contiguous set of words that functions as a unit, having a unique definition.

The meaning of a word can take one of several forms. It may be a main or derived attribute with an associated value. For example, the meaning of the word *Team* is Team = (blank), the meaning of *Red Sox* is Team = Red Sox, and the meaning of *who* is Team = ?. The meaning may designate a subroutine, together with a particular value, as in the case of modifiers such as *winning, any, six,* or *how many.* For example, *winning* has the meaning Subroutine A1 = Winning. The subroutine, which is executed by the content analysis, attaches the modifier Winning to the attribute of the appropriate noun. Some words have more than one meaning; the word *Boston* may mean either Place = Boston or Team = Red Sox. The dictionary entry for such words contains, in addition to each meaning, the designation of a subroutine that selects the appropriate meaning according to the context in which the word is encountered. Finally, some words such as *the, did, play,* etc., have no meaning.

Data

The data are organized in a hierarchical structure, like an outline, with each level containing one or more items of information. Relationships among items are expressed by their occurrence on the same list, or on associated lists. The main heading, or highest level of the structure, is the attribute Month. For each month, the data are further subdivided by place. Below each place under each month is a list of all games played at that place during that month. The complete set of items for one game is found by tracing one path through the hierarchy, i.e. one list at each level. Each path contains values for each of six attributes, *e.g.*:

    Month = July
        Place = Boston
            Day   = 7
            Game Serial No. = 96
            (Team = Red Sox, Score = 5)
            (Team = Yankees, Score = 3)

The parentheses indicate that each Team must be associated with its own score, which is done by placing them together on a sublist.

The processing routines are written to accept any organization of the data. In fact, they will accept a nonparallel organization in which, for example, the data might be as above for all games through July 31, and then organized by place, with month under place, for the rest of the season. The processing routines will also accept a one-level structure in which each game is a list of all attribute-value pairs for that game. The possibility

bracketed. This routine is patterned after the work of Harris and his associates at the University of Pennsylvania (Harris, 1960). Bracketing proceeds from the end of the question to the beginning. Noun phrases, for example, are bracketed in the following manner: certain parts of speech indicate the end of a noun phrase; within a noun phrase, a part of speech may indicate that the word is within the phrase, or that the word starts the phrase, or that the word is not in the phrase, which means that the previous word started the phrase. Prepositional phrases consist of a preposition immediately preceding a noun phrase. The entire sequence, preposition and noun phrase, is enclosed in prepositional brackets. An example of a bracketed question is shown below:

[How many games] did [the Yankees] play (in [July])?

When the question has been bracketed, any unbracketed preposition is attached to the first noun phrase in the sentence, and prepositional brackets added. For example, "Who did the Red Sox lose to on July 5?" becomes "(To [who]) did [the Red Sox] lose (on [July 5])?"

Following the phrase analysis, the syntax routine determines whether the verb is active or passive and locates its subject and object. Specifically, the verb is passive if and only if the last verb element in the question is a main verb and the preceding verb element is some form of the verb *to be*. For questions with active verbs, if a free noun phrase (one not enclosed in prepositional brackets) is found between two verb elements, it is marked *Subject*, and the first free noun phrase in the question is marked *Object*. Otherwise the first free noun phrase is the subject, the next, if any, is the object. For passive verbs, the first free noun phrase is marked *Object* (since it is the object in the active form of the question) and all prepositional phrases with the preposition *by* have the noun phrase within them marked *Subject*. If there is more than one, the content analysis later chooses among them on the basis of meaning.

Finally, the syntactic analysis checks to see if any of the words is marked as a question word. If not, a signal is set to indicate that the question requires a *yes/no* answer.

CONTENT ANALYSIS

The content analysis uses the dictionary meanings and the results of the syntactic analysis to set up a specification list for the processing program. First any subroutine found in the meaning of any word or idiom in the question is executed. The subroutines are of two basic types: those that deal with the meaning of the word itself and those that in some way change the meaning of another word. The first type chooses the appropriate meaning for a word with multiple meanings, as, for example, the sub-routine mentioned above that decides, for names of cities, whether the meaning is Team = A_t, or Place = A_p. The second type alters or modifies the attribute or value of an appropriate syntactically related word. For example, one such subroutine puts its value in place of the value of the main noun in its phrase. Thus Team = (blank) in the phrase *each team* becomes Team = each; in the phrase *what team*, it becomes Team = ?. Another modifies the attribute of a main noun. Thus Team = (blank) in the phrase *winning team* becomes $Team_{(winning)}$ = (blank). In the question "Who beat the Yankees on July 4?", this subroutine, found in the meaning of *beat*, modifies the attribute of the subject and object, so that Team = ? and Team = Yankees are rendered $Team_{(winning)}$ = ? and $Team_{(losing)}$ = Yankees. Another subroutine combines these two operations: it both modifies the attribute and changes the value of the main noun. Thus, Game = (blank) in the phrase *six games* becomes $Game_{(number of)}$ = 6, and in the phrase *how many games* becomes $Game_{(number of)}$ = ?.

After the subroutines have been executed, the question is scanned to consolidate those attribute-value pairs that must be represented on the specification list as a single entry. For example, in "Who was the winning team . . ." Team = ? and $Team_{(winning)}$ = (blank) must be collapsed into $Team_{(winning)}$ = ?. Next, successive scans will create any sublists implied by the syntactic structure of the question. Finally, the composite information for each phrase is entered onto the spec list. Depending on its complexity, each phrase furnishes one or more entries for the list. The resulting spec list is printed in outline form, to provide the questioner with some intermediate feedback.

Processing Routines

PROCESSOR

The specification list indicates to the processor what part of the stored data is relevant for answering the input question. The processor extracts the matching information from the data and produces, for the responder, the answer to the question in the form of a list structure.

The core of the processor is a search routine that attempts to find a match, on each path of a given data structure, for all the attribute-value pairs on the spec list; when a match for the whole spec list is found on a given path, those pairs relevant to the spec list are entered on a *found list*. A particular spec list is considered matched when its attribute has been found on a data path and either the data value is the same as the spec value, or the spec value is ? or *each*, in which case any value of the particular attribute is a match. Matching is not always straightforward. Derived attributes and some modified attributes are functions of a number of attributes on a path and must be computed before the values can be matched. For example, if the spec entry is Home Team = Red Sox, the actual home team for a particular path must be computed from the place and teams on that path before the spec value Red Sox can be matched with the computed data value. Sublists also require special handling because the entries on the sublist must sometimes be considered separately and sometimes as a unit in various permutations.

The found list produced by the search routine is a hierarchical list structure containing one main or derived attribute on each level of each path. Each path on the found list represents the information extracted from one or more paths of the data. For example, for the question "Where did each team play in July?", a single path exists, on the found list, for each team which played in July. On the level below each team, all places in which that team played in July occur on a list that is the value of the attribute Place. Each path on the found list may thus represent a condensation of the information existing on many paths of the search data.

Many input questions contain only one query, as in the question above, *i.e.*, Place = ?. These questions are answered, with no further processing, by the found list produced by one execution of the search routine. Others require simple processing on all occurrences of the queried attribute on the generated found list. The question "In how many places did each team play in July?" requires a count of the places for each team, after the search routine has generated the list of places for each team.

Other questions imply more than one search as well as additional processing. For a spec attribute with the value *every*, a comparison with a list of all possible values for that attribute must be made after the search routine has generated lists of found values for that attribute. Then, since only those found list paths for which all possible values of the attribute exist should remain on the found list as the answer to the question, the search routine, operating on this found list as the data, is again executed. It now generates a new found list containing all the data paths for which all possible values of the attribute were found. Likewise, questions involving a specified number, such as 4 teams, imply a search for *which teams*, a count of the teams found on each path, and a search of the found list for paths containing 4 teams.

In general, a question may contain several implicit or explicit queries. Since these queries must be answered one at a time, several searches, with intermediate processing, are required. The first search operates on the stored data while successive searches operate on the found list generated by the preceding search operation. As an example, consider the question "On how many days in July did eight teams play?" The spec list is

$$Day_{(number\ of)} = ?;$$
$$Month = July;$$
$$Team_{(number\ of)} = 8.$$

On the first pass, the implicit question *which teams* is answered. The spec list for the first search is

$$Day = Each;$$
$$Month = July;$$
$$Team = ?.$$

The found data is a list of teams that played on that date. Following this search, the processor counts the teams for each day and associates the count with the attribute Team. On the second search, the spec list is

$$Day = ?;$$
$$Month = July;$$
$$Team_{(number\ of)} = 8.$$

The found data is a list of days in July on which eight teams played. After this pass, the processor counts the days, adds the count to the found list, and is finished.

RESPONDER

No attempt has yet been made to respond in grammatical English sentences. Instead, the final found list is printed in outline form. For questions requiring a yes/no answer, YES is printed along with the found list. If the search routine found no matching data, NO is printed for yes/no questions, and NO DATA for all other cases.

Discussion

The differences between Baseball and both automatic language translation and information retrieval should now be evident. The linguistic part of the Baseball program has as its main goal the understanding of the meaning of the question as embodied in the canonical specification list. Syntax must be considered and ambiguities resolved in order to represent the meaning adequately. Translation programs have a different goal: transforming the input passage from one natural language to another. Meanings must be considered and ambiguities resolved to the extent that they affect the correctness of the final translation. In general, translation programs are concerned more with syntax and less with meaning than the Baseball program.

Baseball differs from most retrieval systems in the nature of its data. Generally the retrieval problem is to locate relevant documents. Each document has an associated set of index numbers describing its content. The retrieval system must find the appropriate index numbers for each input request and then search for all documents bearing those index numbers. The basic problem in such systems is the assignment of index categories. In Baseball, on the other hand, the attributes of the data are very well specified. There is no confusion about them. However, Baseball's derived attributes and modifiers imply a great deal more data processing than most document retrieval programs. (Baseball does bear a close relation with the ACSI-MATIC system discussed by Miller et al. at the 1960 Western Joint Computer Conference.)

The concept of the spec list can be used to define the class of questions that the Baseball program can answer. It can answer all questions whose spec list consists of attribute-value pairs that the program recognizes. The attributes may be modified or derived, and the values may be definite or queries. Any combination of attribute-value pairs constitutes a specification list. Many will be nonsense, but all can be answered. The number of questions in the class is, of course, infinite, because of the numerical values. But even if all numbers are restricted to two digits, the program can answer millions of meaningful questions.

The present program, despite its restrictions, is a very useful communication device. Any complex question that does not meet the restrictions can always be broken up into several simpler questions. The program usually rejects questions it cannot handle, in which case the questioner may rephrase his question. He can also check the printed spec list to see if the computer is on the right track, in case the linguistic program has erred and failed to detect its own error. Finally, he can often judge whether the answer is reasonable.

Next Steps

No important difficulty is expected in augmenting the program to include logical connectives, negatives, and relation words. The inclusion of multiple-clause questions also seems fairly straightforward, if the questioner will mark off for the computer the boundaries of his clauses. The program can then deal with the subordinate clauses one at a time before it deals with the main clause, using existing routines. On the other hand, if the syntax analysis is required to determine the clause boundaries as well as the phrase structure, a much more sophisticated program would be required.

The problem of recognizing and resolving semantic ambiguities remains largely unsolved. Determining what is meant by the question "Did the Red Sox win most of their games in July?" depends on a much larger context than the immediate question. The computer might answer all meaningful versions of the question (we know of five), or might ask the questioner which meaning he intended. In general, the facility for the computer to query the questioner is likely to be the most powerful im-

provement. This would allow the computer to increase its vocabulary, to resolve ambiguities, and perhaps even to train the questioner in the use of the program.

Considerable pains were taken to keep the program general. Most of the program will remain unchanged and intact in a new context, such as voting records. The processing program will handle data in any sort of hierarchical form, and is indifferent to the attributes used. The syntax program is based entirely on parts of speech, which can easily be assigned to a new set of words for a new context. On the other hand, some of the subroutines contained in the dictionary meanings are certainly specific to baseball; probably each new context would require certain subroutines specific to it. Also, each context might introduce a number of modifiers and derived attributes that would have to be defined in terms of special subroutines for the processor. Hopefully, all such occasions for change have been isolated in a small area of special subroutines, so that the main routines can be unaltered. However, until we have actually switched contexts, we cannot say definitely that we have been successful in producing a general question-answering program.

Conversational Language Comprehension Using Integrated Pattern-Matching and Parsing[1]

Roger C. Parkison, Kenneth Mark Colby and William S. Faught

Department of Psychiatry, Neuropsychiatric Institute, University of California, Los Angeles, California 90024, U.S.A.

Recommended by T. Winograd

ABSTRACT

One of the major problems in natural language understanding by computer is the frequent use of patterned or idiomatic phrases in colloquial English dialogue. Traditional parsing methods typically cannot cope with a significant number of idioms. A more general problem is the tendency of a speaker to leave the meaning of an utterance ambiguous or partially implicit, to be filled in by the hearer from a shared mental context which includes linguistic, social, and physical knowledge. The appropriate representation for this knowledge is a formidable and unsolved problem. We present here an approach to natural language understanding which addresses itself to these problems. Our program uses a series of processing stages which progressively transform an English input into a form usable by our computer simulation of paranoia. Most of the processing stages involve matching the input to an appropriate stored pattern and performing the associated transformation. However, a few key stages perform aspects of traditional parsing which greatly facilitate the overall language recognition process.

1. Background

The goal of our research is an understanding of paranoid thought processes. To this end, we have constructed a computer simulation of our theory of paranoia (Colby [3]; Faught et al. [6]). This program, called PARRY, facilitates objective evaluation of our theory and highlights weaknesses in it. Psychiatrists evaluate PARRY by means of a psychiatric interview. A discrepancy between the program's performance and that of human paranoids indicates one of two things: either our theory of paranoia is deficient, or our program cannot do what our theory requires.

It is not possible for a psychiatrist to distinguish between these two problems. We must first minimize the differences between the program and the theory so that psychiatrists can more easily evaluate the theory.

One of the wider gaps between the program's performance and the theory is in the area of natural language comprehension. Paranoid humans are usually quite perceptive but some interviews with PARRY take on the air of a Marx Brothers comedy with misunderstanding and partial comprehension running rampant. Our model should be able to communicate with a psychiatrist over the full range of concepts which it can manipulate internally. A communication bottleneck between interviewer and model obviously reduces the interviewer's ability to perceive the internal processes. In addition, the model must recognize and utilize a comfortable variety of natural language expressions for each internal concept. A doctor should not have to "learn PARRY's language" because that would interfere with his concentration on the psychiatric aspects of the program.

The implementation of these specifications in a computer program is the subject of this paper. Readers who wish to know more about the psychological aspects of our model should read Colby [3] or Faught et al. [6]. Readers unfamiliar with PARRY may wish to glance through the sample interview in the appendix to acquaint themselves with the model's present capabilities.

2. Comparison and contrast with related work

Most of the early "language-understanding" programs (Bobrow [1]; Weizenbaum [25]; Raphael [17]; Charniak [2]) did not function primarily as language analyzers. Each one performed a task in a restricted problem domain. Any input to the program was presumed to be meaningful within that domain. Within such strong semantic constraints, one could almost enumerate the meaningful input sentences. With allowance for replacement of words by synonyms and "blanks" in which any words were acceptable, it was possible to enumerate the meaningful sentence categories or patterns. The number of patterns required was usually less than 50. Each of these patterns evoked a highly specific response and thus the performance of these programs was surprisingly "intelligent".

For our purposes with PARRY, there are two weaknesses in this approach. First, the blanks in the stored patterns were intended to match arbitrary noun phrases or even whole clauses, but there was no way to verify that a noun phrase or clause had actually been located. Also, there was no way to modify the choice of a response procedure based on the contents of the noun phrase or clause. This is not satisfactory for a model which must respond more to the connotation of a statement than to its syntactic form. Second, the stored patterns were too specific. We estimate that 100,000 specific patterns would be needed to cover our model's range of topics and diversity of expression. Within this vast data base, there would be many similar patterns and recurring features. By factoring out some of these and using a more complex pattern-matching algorithm (Colby et al. [4]), we

[1] This research was sponsored by the National Institute of Mental Health under Grant PHS MH 27132–02. Computer facilities were provided by the Stanford University Medical Experimental Computing Resource (SUMEX) funded by the Biotechnology Resources Branch of the National Institutes of Health under Grant number RR–785.

obtained a few thousand general patterns. These were the basis of PARRY's previous natural language comprehension program (Wilks [26]). His patterns are much more abstract, using only a few dozen distinct nouns and verbs, while ours contain over 100 distinct verbs.

Our goal is to improve PARRY's usefulness as a tool in our study of the paranoid mode of thought. In order to test our hypotheses about the workings and treatment of the paranoid mode, we have developed a new version of PARRY with the ability to become more "normal" (or more paranoid) during a course of this treatment. A normal personality presents much greater natural language problems for the model builder due to the opening and deepening of areas previously closed to discussion. Subjects central to the model's interests are discussed in greater detail and additional peripheral subjects may be touched on. We considered extending our language recognition process along existing lines but we found the resulting proliferation of stored patterns unacceptable on both practical and aesthetic grounds. The generation of thousands of additional patterns is a tedious and therefore error-prone job. Also, the recurring similarities among our "general" patterns became more pronounced. Most of these were manifestations of the regularities of English grammar. The most prominent ones were the introduction of auxiliary verbs (DO, BE, HAVE) in complex verb tenses and subject-auxiliary inversion in questions.

Another family of natural language understanding programs is based directly on English grammar (Petrick [15]; Grishman [7]; Kay [9]; Thorne et al. [23]; Woods [28]; Heidorn [8]; Winograd [27]). An inherent difficulty in this approach lies in the fact that a grammar of English is generally expressed in a form better suited to generation than to recognition of language. Simple generation grammars can be mechanically inverted to produce reasonable parsers but the complex grammars needed for natural language must almost always be laboriously inverted by hand. A problem which plagues all these parsers is lexical and syntactic ambiguity. (A good parser can produce five different analyses for any input sentence. (A bad parser can produce 100.) Most of these alternatives will be semantically nonsensical. One way out of this problem is to stop with a syntactic analysis and make no attempt to discover the meaning of the sentence. To be useful in a language understanding program, a parser must produce one most probable parse instead of multiple possibilities. The difficulty is that the information which selects the meaningful parse from the nonsense is not easily represented in the grammar. Decisions about the function of a prepositional phrase or even the syntactic category of an ambiguous word can be based on semantic information which is highly specific to individual situations. The point we wish to raise is that this semantic information might best be represented in a form resembling the patterns which are used in PARRY.

Idioms are another stumbling block for parsers. Most idioms obey grammatical rules but the meaning is entirely lost during syntactic analysis. Other idioms are so perverse that they invariably lead to dead ends in a parser's logic. The writer

of a parser cannot extend his grammar to recognize one idiom without accepting dozens of other peculiar word combinations as valid idioms. (It is awkward for a parser to distinguish "OUT ON A LIMB" from "OUT ON A BRANCH".) Woods' transition network parser contains a preprocessor to look for what he calls "compound words". We believe that any parser which recognizes a large subset of everyday English must contain some such pattern recognizer. Grammatical but rarely used constructions are almost as troublesome as idioms. If they are left out of a parser, then it fails miserably on encountering them. This abrupt failure is in sharp contrast to humans whose performance degrades only gradually in the face of unfamiliar constructions. Our pattern-matching solution to this problem is to include some vague patterns which locate one or two key concepts in a sentence and disregard the rest. If rare constructions are included in a parser, then they must be handled with the same generality and completeness as the more common natural language constructions. This generality is aesthetically pleasing but it can make a parser painfully slow. Most of the parsers cited above respond in from 10 seconds to a minute. In our experience with man-machine dialogues, a person's concentration lapses in just a few seconds if no response is forthcoming.

A different approach to natural language comprehension is taken by Schank (Schank [21]; Riesbeck [19]). His conceptual dependency paradigm emphasizes the underlying semantic relationships between the parts of a sentence to the exclusion of their syntactic relationships. In keeping with this philosophy, Riesbeck's conceptual dependency parser primarily seeks out a key conceptual word (verb or nominalized verb) and then assimilates the rest of the sentence using extensive knowledge about the meaning of that word. Some syntactic knowledge is also used. Information about passive constructions and complex verb tenses is stored with the appropriate auxiliary verbs, and information about the structure of noun phrases is stored with determiners. This type of parser comes much closer to our needs than the grammatical parsers mentioned earlier, but it still takes no notice of idiomatic verb usage or the meaning of nouns. We would need an additional process to transform the literal meaning of a sentence into its idiomatic meaning to our model. A practical difficulty with Schank's conceptual dependency system is its reduction of abstract ideas to 16 primitive verbs. This approach makes the internal representation of some of the concepts which are central to the model's beliefs (e.g. GAMBLE, INCRIMINATE, SPY-ON) quite unwieldy.

Speech understanding programs are usually organized so that recognition expands outward from key words also (Woods et al. [29]; Reddy et al. [18]; Walker [24]; Miller [13]). This is done because the occurrence of contentive words can be predicted from prior context while the smaller function words, which written language analyzers utilize, are almost impossible to locate in speech input. The need for accurate contextual prediction restricts present speech understanders to very small vocabularies and problem domains. It is not clear that their sentence analysis methods would be feasible in larger domains with larger vocabularies.

Our new program shares all its high-level design goals with previous versions of the model so it naturally contains the ideas which worked well before. Primary among these are idiom patterns with literal substitutions (see Sections 4.3 and 4.6) and concept patterns to determine the meaning of an input within the model's domain of interest (see Section 4.9). In between these ideas we have inserted several other ideas which we borrowed from grammatical parsing. Primary among these are parsing of noun phrases (see Section 4.4) and feature analysis of verb phrases (see Section 4.5). The processes taken from grammatical parsing serve to eliminate redundancy in the pattern matching processes which we brought forward from the previous version of our model.

3. Outline of the Program's Operation

The model's language recognition phase must find a connection between a doctor's typed input and the model's internal concepts. The discovery of such a connection proceeds in several stages. At each stage, certain complexities of natural language expression are extracted, leaving a slightly simpler representation of the input. Briefly, the nine stages are:

3.1. Standardize teletype input

This stage shelters the remaining stages from the vagaries of teletype hardware and human typing. All letters are converted to upper case, unrecognized characters are deleted, and punctuation is separated from neighboring words.

3.2. Identify word stems

A morphological analysis is done to remove suffixes from words. Contractions, inflectional endings, and derivational suffixes are all removed and replaced by appropriate words or markers. There are about 3500 words in the main dictionary and about 80 suffixes are recognized.

3.3. Condense rigid idiomatic phrases

About 350 rigid, multi-word phrases are replaced by synonymous words. For example:

UNITED STATES OF AMERICA → USA
IN SPITE OF → DESPITE
BET possessive BOTTOM DOLLAR → RELY
("possessive" represents one of MY, YOUR, HIS, etc.)

3.4. Bracket noun phrases

Simple noun phrases are located and bracketed using a transition network grammar. This transition network only identifies noun phrases: the remainder of the sentence is not analyzed at all by this parser.

3.5. Simplify verb phrases

Most features of verb phrases, such as tense, modal verbs, adverbs, and subject-auxiliary inversion are removed and noted in a pre-determined set of adverbial variables.

3.6. Replace flexible idioms

About 250 idioms which can contain embedded noun phrases are replaced. For example:

KEEP [AN EYE] ON → WATCH
PICK noun-phrase UP → PICK-UP noun-phrase

3.7. Locate simple clauses

The input is next broken into simple clauses using about 20 stored clause patterns. The sentence "Could you tell me if you want to leave the hospital?" is analyzed as:

(YOU TELL ME) (YOU WANT) (LEAVE [HOSPITAL])

The missing "IF" is remembered in the adverbial variables mentioned above (i.e. ADVERB = IF is associated with (YOU WANT)). The effect of these variables is described in a later section.

3.8. Embed subordinate clauses

The sequence of simple clauses found in the input is scanned for possible embeddings, or deletions. Following the previous example:

(YOU TELL ME) (YOU WANT) (LEAVE [HOSPITAL])
→ (YOU WANT (YOU LEAVE [HOSPITAL]))

3.9. Determine relevance to model's sphere of interest

Finally, the idiomatically and syntactically simplified input is matched against about 2000 stored concept patterns which represent the model's sphere of interest (and therefore comprehension). The best matches, and the generalizations necessary to accomplish them, are passed on to the psychological modelling phase of the program.

4. Description of the Program

4.1. Standardize teletype input

An important requirement for the model's language recognition phase is that it "keep a low profile". Its main goal is to reveal the workings of a paranoid model and not to enforce proper typing style. Therefore, the program is as forgiving as possible regarding capitalization of words, irregular spacing among words and punctuation, and erroneous characters due to careless typing or hardware errors. Letters are converted to upper case, unrecognized characters are deleted, and punctuation is separated from adjacent words.

4.2. Identify word stems

Each word is first looked up in the main dictionary. If it is found, attention shifts to the next word. If it is not found, a small dictionary of frequent misspellings is consulted. If the word appears there, it is replaced by its correct spelling. (Also, a note is made for future use in evaluating the interviewer.) If the word is still not found, the trailing letters of the word are compared against all possible forms of suffix in a suffix dictionary.

Contractions are treated as a form of suffix. They are replaced by fully spelled-out words. Since some people omit the apostrophe or can't find it on a teletype keyboard, most contractions are accepted either with or without it. This could conceivably cause "COINCIDENT" to be interpreted as "COINCIDE NOT", just as "DONT" means "DO NOT". To prevent this kind of over-analysis, the remaining word must belong to a category which normally allows the indicated contraction. In the case of "NOT", only the primary (DO, BE, HAVE) and modal (COULD, WOULD, etc.) auxiliaries permit contraction.

Inflectional endings are removed from plural nouns, third person singular verbs, and tensed verbs. For tensed verbs, a marker is inserted after the verb indicating past (-ED), present participle (-ING), or past participle (-EN). A number of verbs have no past participle distinct from the simple past form. Hence, later sections of the program which look for participles also accept past forms. Many of the most commonly used verbs in English have irregular inflections. These are recorded in a separate dictionary of irregular words. A few nouns and pronouns with irregular plurals are also listed there. For example:

WAS → BE -ED
CHILDREN → CHILD -S

Derivational suffixes are also utilized. Examples are the analysis of "HAR-MONIOUSNESS" into "HARMONY+OUS+NESS" or "CERTAINLY" into "CERTAIN+LY". Each suffix has a predictable effect, transforming one class of word (e.g. verb, noun, adjective) into a semantically related word in a different class. This information alone is enough to determine that "HARMONIOUS" is an adjective or that "HARMONIOUSNESS" is a noun, given that "HARMONY" is a noun. Where a more specific meaning is needed, a network of semantic relations connects smaller word categories. To elaborate on the present example, suppose the following information is stored explicitly:

AGREE is a verb
CONGRUOUS is an adjective
HARMONY is a noun

Then the following information can be deduced from derivational rules:

HARMONIZE means AGREE
HARMONIOUS, AGREEING, and AGREEABLE mean CONGRUOUS
AGREEMENT and HARMONIOUSNESS mean HARMONY

Actually, the participial verb form must be considered as a possible verb as well as an adjective, but it was included to illustrate the usefulness of derivational analysis. A small dictionary can be used to recognize a much larger vocabulary with only a controllable loss of precision in meaning.

The procedure described above does not use all the information contained in a derivational suffix. When suffixes are applied to verbs, "cause-effect" information is lost. Thus, our program confuses "FEARSOME" with "FEARFUL" and "INVENTOR" with "INVENTION". This situation could be remedied by making finer distinctions in the derivational rules and semantic relationship pointers. (See Quirk et al. [16] for a thorough treatment of this topic.)

A few prefixes are recognized and removed also. The semantic effect of these prefixes is approximated by the insertion of appropriate adverbs into the sentence For example:

INSANE → NOT SANE
UNHAPPY → NOT HAPPY
MISINFORM → BADLY INFORM

When all else fails, a word is treated as a possible typing error. Typical typing errors are omitting the space between words, transposing two letters, or missing the intended key and striking a nearby key instead. Other possible errors are typing the number 0 for the letter O, or neglecting the shift key and typing a 7 instead of an apostrophe. Some teletypes will occasionally send a double letter when only a single letter was typed. If the teletype is connected to the computer by telephone lines (as is often the case with PARRY) then noise on the line can generate extra characters. Some human spelling errors are systematic enough to be correctable. Among these are doubling of consonants (UNTILL → UNTIL), confusing vowels in unaccented syllables (DEXIDRINE → DEXEDRINE), and transposing I and E (CONCIEVE → CONCEIVE).

All of these errors can be corrected by systematically applying a few "respelling" rules. These rules are:

(1) Delete any single letter from the word.
(2) Transpose any pair of adjacent letters.
(3) Replace any letter by another which is similar or nearby on the keyboard.
(4) Split the word into two words.

Each of these rules is tried in turn until the resulting word appears in one of the dictionaries. When a word is totally unrecognizable, it is deleted from the input.

same word. The resulting increase in recognition consists almost entirely of mis-recognition with a negligible increase in valid typing correction.

This procedure works quite well on misspellings of known words but it spends an inordinate amount of time trying to make sense out of a truly novel word. It lacks the human ability to see at a glance that the meaning of "KWERTYLPRZ" will not be revealed by spelling correction. This ability to see the obvious depends on an ability to measure the difference between two words and on an ability to restrict the possibilities to a manageable subset of the entire dictionary. Lacking these abilities, our program should at least limit the effort expended on a mis-spelled word.

4.3. Condense rigid idiomatic phrases

There is a whole spectrum of expressions including compound words, proper nouns, idioms, and formulaic sentences sharing the property that the meaning of the expression cannot be obtained by combining the meanings of the parts. These expressions occur frequently in colloquial English so the model must recognize them. This is accomplished by matching each part of the input against a collection of idiom patterns and replacing the parts that match with more literal synonyms. The elements in the stored patterns are either (1) specific words, which match only themselves or (2) word-class names, which match any word in the class (as indicated by the main dictionary). The tense of an idiom is preserved in its literal translation. The following examples illustrate a variety of rigid idioms and related expressions:

Compound words:

ALL RIGHT → ALRIGHT
IN SPITE OF → DESPITE

Proper nouns:

COSA NOSTRA → MAFIA
F.B.I. → FBI

Noun+adjective:

STRAIGHT JACKET → RESTRAINTS
EMERGENCY ROOM → HOSPITAL

Preposition+object:

ON possessive TOES → ALERT
BESIDE reflexive → UPSET
AT THE MOMENT → NOW

Verb+particle:

MAKE UP WITH → RECONCILE WITH

Verb+object:

SEE RED → BECOME ANGRY

Verb+adverbial phrase:

GO TO PIECES → CRUMBLE (this is still metaphorical)

Verb+object+particle:

HAVE IT IN FOR → HATE ("IT" has no referent at all)

Verb+object+adverbial phrase:

HAVE possessive HEART IN possessive MOUTH → BE AFRAID

Formulaic sentences:

HOW DO YOU DO? → HELLO.
HOW GOES IT? → HOW ARE YOU?
PARLEZ VOUS FRANCAIS? → DO YOU SPEAK FRENCH?

4.4. Bracket noun phrases

After the idiomatic substitutions have been made, a transition network grammar is used to locate simple noun phrases. Each group of premodifiers, adjectives, nouns, and trailing prepositional phrases introduced by "OF" is bracketed so that it can be treated as a single unit in later processing. Other prepositional phrases are assumed to be objects of verbs or adverbial modifiers rather than noun modifiers. Other words in the sentence are untouched. For example:

(DO YOU LIKE YOUR FATHER) → (DO YOU LIKE [YOUR FATHER])

At this stage, no attempt is made to analyze the over-all structure of the input sentence. Thus it is difficult to determine the intended usage of many ambiguous words (e.g. WORK, BEATING). These words are treated as nouns if they are preceded by premodifiers or adjectives but they are left unbracketed otherwise. The failure to bracket these nouns when they are used alone is not a problem since a noun phrase consisting of one word is treated as a single unit whether it is bracketed or not.

An attempt is made to identify the primary noun of each bracketed group. In most cases, it is the final word of the group (e.g. [MY FATHER'S DOG], [A FEAR OF DEATH]). The general rule is to select the last noun before an occurrence of "OF" unless it is a quantifier or measure (e.g. LOT OF, GALLON OF). In that case the first "OF" is skipped and the last noun before the second "OF" is selected. This process is repeated until a noun is selected or the end of the phrase is reached.

Relative clauses are not recognized by the transition network. In fact, relative clauses are not handled systematically anywhere in our model. There are two practical reasons for this shortcoming. First, relative clauses rarely occur in dialogues with our model. Second, the format of our model's internal belief representation does not make it easy to represent the information contained in an arbitrary relative clause. We have encountered a few relative clauses, invariably following indefinite pronouns (e.g. SOMEBODY, ANYTHING) or equally vague nouns (e.g.

PEOPLE, THINGS). These special cases are handled in much the same way that idioms are handled, with about 20 patterns which convert a noun followed by a relative clause into a single noun.

4.5. Simplify verb phrases

A verb phrase consists of a main verb, a collection of auxiliaries indicating tense, voice, and modality, a possible inversion indicating interrogation, and some adverbs. The goal of this stage of processing is to remove everything except the main verb from the phrase and record the significance of the removed words in a small set of adverbial variables. The present set of adverbial variables is INTER-ROGATIVE, TENSE, MODAL, NEGATIVE, WH, and ADVERB.

Subject-auxiliary inversion in questions is recognized and replaced using a few patterns with the following general form:

    auxiliary noun-phrase verb
    → noun-phrase auxiliary verb+INTERROGATIVE = ?

A question mark at the end of the clause can also set the INTERROGATIVE variable.

The meaning of TENSE is made clear by the following examples:

    DO verb → verb
    verb -ED → verb+TENSE = past
    HAVE verb -EN → verb+TENSE = past
    BE verb -ING → verb+TENSE = progressive

Combinations of auxiliaries are simplified by repeated application of the elementary rules. Thus:

    HAVE BEEN verb -ING → verb+TENSE = past progressive

Passive constructions are converted to active ones in two ways. There is a table of about 35 pairs of verb-classes which are approximate passives for each other (e.g. SCARE and FEAR, CONFUSE and MISUNDERSTAND). When one of these verbs appears in a passive construction, the entire construction is replaced by the alternate member of the pair. When no passive alternate is known, the following rules are used to transpose the subject and object into their usual positions:

    noun-phrase1 BE verb -EN BY noun-phrase2
    → noun-phrase2 verb noun-phrase1

    noun-phrase BE verb -EN → SOMEBODY verb noun-phrase

Modal verbs (e.g. COULD, SHOULD) are deleted from the sentence and put into the variable named MODAL. "WILL" is treated as a modal rather than as an indicator of future tense. A group of verbs called semi-auxiliaries is converted to synonymous modal verbs and then treated as modals. For example:

    HAD BETTER → SHOULD
    BE ABOUT TO → SHALL

The treatment of adverbs is less firmly based in English grammar. The adverbs selected for special recognition and those relegated to the ADVERB category were empirically determined. Naturally, the groups selected bear some relation to grammatical sub-categories but no claims are made for uniformity or completeness. Two categories of adverbs have been singled out for their frequency of occurrence and important contribution to the meaning of sentences. They are NEGATIVE (e.g. NOT, NEVER) and WH (e.g. WHEN, WHERE, WHY).

4.6. Replace flexible idioms

Many idiomatic verb constructions allow the object of the verb to be embedded within the idiom. These flexible idioms can safely undergo noun phrase bracketing and verb phrase simplification. Then only one pattern is needed to recognize each idiom. These idioms can be categorized like the more rigid idioms:

Verb+object+particle:

    PICK noun-phrase UP → PICK-UP noun-phrase

Verb+object:

    FEEL [THE NECESSITY] → NEED

Verb+object+adverbial phrase:

    RUB noun-phrase [THE WRONG WAY] → IRRITATE noun-phrase

Verb+object+object:

    LEND noun-phrase [A HAND] → HELP noun-phrase

4.7. Locate simple clauses

During this stage, the input sentence is segmented into simple clauses or fragments by matching it against about 20 general clause patterns. When an initial portion of the input matches a pattern, that portion is broken off, and the remainder of the input is again matched against the patterns. The patterns are all at the level of generality typified by the example, "(noun verb noun)". Incomplete clauses appear because some verbs commonly take an embedded clause as an object. Embedded clausal objects in the input are isolated rather than nested within the main clause pattern, thus the main clause appears to be without an object. For example:

    I FEEL YOU NEED [ELECTRIC SHOCK].
    → (I FEEL) (YOU NEED [ELECTRIC SHOCK])

Each clause is then modified according to the collection of adverbial variables associated with it. First, the interaction among the features of a verb phrase is resolved. When NEGATIVE is the only feature present, it reverses the clause's meaning, but when NEGATIVE is present along with INTERROGATIVE or WH, it merely indicates the speaker's presuppositions. After the significant vari-

the entire clause is embedded in another clause whose main verb is a pseudo-verb derived from the adverb. For example:

(any-clause)+WH = WHEN → ((any-clause) IS-WHEN?)

A few verbs (e.g. BE) behave differently with certain WH- words:

(noun-phrase BE)+WH = WHEN → (noun-phrase IS-WHEN?)

There are about a dozen rules like the one above which specify a particular verb and adverb combination. When the NEGATIVE feature is present, an attempt is made to convert the verb in the clause to a verb with the opposite meaning. There is a table of about 25 pairs of verb-classes which are approximate negatives for each other (e.g. SUCCEED and FAIL, LIKE and HATE). If the verb can't be negated, the NEGATIVE feature is passed on to the psychological model. The INTERROGATIVE feature is saved for eventual use in determining the type of the input sentence (e.g. DECLARATIVE, IMPERATIVE). The other adverbial features are generally ignored in the present version of the model. The facility exists to retain all adverbial information but it is usually unimportant to our paranoid model.

4.8. Embed subordinate clauses

There is frequently more than one simple clause in a single sentence. Sometimes it is just a sequence of separate ideas. For example: "Hello, I'm Doctor Smith, who are you?". There is no higher-level language recognition pattern which connects these concepts, although other sections of the model could recognize this sequence as the beginning of an interview. Often, simple clauses are incomplete or interrelated and meaningful recognition requires the combination of multiple clauses into a single concept. Typical examples are sentences with embedded or subordinate clauses:

Adverbial clause:
DO YOU EVER HAVE ANY PROBLEMS WHERE YOU WORK?
→ (YOU HAVE [PROBLEM] ((YOU WORK) IS-WHERE?)
Subordinate clause:
WHAT WOULD YOU DO IF YOU GOT OUT OF THERE?
→ (YOU DO?) (YOU LEAVE [HOSPITAL])
Clausal object:
DO YOU KNOW WHY I AM HERE?
→ (YOU KNOW) ((I IS-WHERE [HOSPITAL]) IS-WHY?)

Adverbial and subordinate clauses are revealed by markers of subordination such as adverbs (e.g. WHILE) or conjunctions (e.g. BECAUSE). Clausal objects are predicted when the preceding clause lacks an object and its verb belongs to any of 50 verb-classes known to permit clausal objects (e.g. EXPECT, STOP). Ten of these classes are often used as little more than polite wrapping for an overly blunt statement (e.g. (I THINK), (IT SEEMS)). These instances are deleted, and

the clausal object is elevated to the status of main clause. In all other cases, the subordinate clause is embedded at the end of the main clause.

4.9. Determine relevance to model's sphere of interest

Our model's attention is fixed on its own life situation. It can converse competently about its personal background, hospitalization, and interpersonal relations. It has only a limited ability to deal with concepts outside of these areas. This limited horizon is reflected in the language recognition processes. This limitation is not a flaw unique to our model, but rather an exaggeration of a property shared by human beings.

The final task of the language recognition process is to determine which concepts in the memory of the psychological model are most similar to the ideas expressed in the input. In a sense, the simplified input is matched against the memory. For matching purposes, the memory is represented as a set of about 2000 concept patterns. Each pattern is tied to one of about 1000 internal concept names. When a match is found, the concept name and a list of the generalizations necessary to effect the match are passed on to the psychological modeling processes. As in all previous instances where the input is matched against stored patterns, the permissible generalizations of the input are given by the main dictionary. In addition to the usual words and word-classes, concept patterns may contain the names of other concepts, which match embedded clauses in the input.

There is one special pattern name which matches any embedded clause. This permits an entire family of sentences to be treated identically by the language recognition process, provided the psychological model knows how to deal with the arbitrary embedded concept. This feature will be used increasingly as the model's general reasoning abilities are expanded. Currently, even the apparently easy cases turn out to be quite difficult. Consider questions of the form, "DO YOU KNOW ...?". It is tempting to have a concept pattern:

(YOU KNOW any-concept) → YOU-KNOW-X

Then a procedure could simulate the asking of the embedded question and respond with "YES" or "NO" depending on the outcome. This captures the literal meaning of the question but that is not always the intended meaning in a dialogue situation. In a human dialogue, each participant brings with him an extensive mental model of the world and quickly forms a mental model of the other participant. The influence of these mental models can be seen in the widely varying responses to syntactically similar sentences:

Q. DO YOU KNOW WHY I AM HERE?
A. YES.
Q. DO YOU KNOW WHAT YOUR DOCTOR'S NAME IS?
A. DR. SMITH.
Q. DO YOU KNOW WHERE YOU ARE?
A. OF COURSE I DO, WHAT ARE YOU IMPLYING?

In the first case, the literal meaning is probably intended. In the second case, the embedded answer to the literal question is fairly obvious so the answer to the embedded question is probably desired. In the third case, both the literal and embedded answers are obvious so it must be some sort of unusual question. A general understanding of this type of question requires a model of what people know in general and what interviewers know in particular. Our program does not contain the information necessary to make these judgments during an interview. The program's model of an interviewer extends only to style (e.g. dominating, initiating), value (e.g. helpful, useless), and rapport (e.g. friendly, hostile). Decisions about what is obvious to whom must be made externally and incorporated into the program as needed. We have found specific concept patterns to be the most economical and uniform way to encode this information. (See Lakoff [10] for further treatment of this topic.)

Patterns containing very general word-class names can be used like patterns containing the special "any-concept" pattern name. Since our model can evaluate its emotional reaction to practically anything, the following pattern can be used:

(YOU LIKE noun-phrase) → YOU-LIKE-X

The actual noun phrase from the input is bound to the class-name "noun-phrase" and passed along with the concept name. There is another use for generality in concept patterns. It avoids cluttering up the model's memory with specific instances of concepts which are treated in broader terms internally. For example:

(noun-phrase ADMIRE YOU) → X-ADMIRE-YOU

Our paranoid model does not need to know who "noun-phrase" is because it believes that nobody admires it. This approach can be extended into areas totally irrelevant to the model. Broad categories of irrelevant or flippant questions can be fielded with a few general patterns.

The previous version of our model contained a pattern matching heuristic which permitted dropping a word from the input in order to effect a match with the stored concept patterns. For several reasons, this heuristic is no longer necessary. The new pattern matcher can "generalize a word away" as in the "X-ADMIRE-YOU" example. The extraneous modifiers, both adverbs and adjectives, which bedeviled the previous version are now removed from the sentence or attached as modifiers to the appropriate words.

It is still possible for an interviewer to say something which does not match any stored concept patterns. In this eventuality, the model can still get the topic of conversation from the list of embedded clauses or noun phrases found by the language recognition processes.

recognized as a meaningful constituent (e.g. idiom), it is removed and replaced by a simpler or more literal group of words. The processing of a sentence is divided into stages which must be performed in a specific order. Each stage removes only those phrases which no later stage can handle. Using this procedure, there is no need for a data structure which can retain the original expression of a sentence along with the intermediate analyses. After the idiomatic and grammatical substitutions, the resulting sentence is matched against stored concept patterns. The names of the patterns which best matched the sentence are passed on to the remaining phases of the model. Additional, detailed information is also available, giving the words from the sentence which matched each pattern element. A pattern name indicates which existing internal concept is most similar to the idea expressed in the input sentence. Naturally, familiar ideas are recognized most accurately, but novel ideas can be represented and transmitted using general internal concepts instantiated by a few words selected from the input sentence.

An important decision about the representation of data within PARRY, or any program, is the choice between using

(a) very specific data with simple procedures to apply it and
(b) generalized data with sophisticated procedures to apply it.

Wherever possible, linguistic information has been factored out into individual procedures leaving smaller, generalized data tables. For example, a procedure was written to deal with inflectional and derivational word endings so that the dictionary need only contain root words (e.g. CONCLUDE but not CONCLUDING or CONCLUSION). Another procedure removes complex verb tenses, passives, and interrogatives so that a single pattern can be used to recognize an entire family of related sentences.

More sophisticated linguistic information is left implicit in the clause and concept patterns, or lack thereof. For instance: the only pattern in which the verb "RAIN" appears has "IT" as a subject. This conveys the information that

(1) no other subject is permitted with "RAIN" and
(2) it is not necessary to seek a referent for "IT" in this case.

Storing highly specific patterns has the advantage that it is possible to handle some instances of a phenomenon (e.g. subject-verb-object compatibility) without solving it in complete generality. The corresponding disadvantage is that each instance requires another independent piece of data (e.g. (IT SNOWS)), whereas a piece of information in general procedures or tables would propagate throughout the recognition process. The pattern tables are a large reservoir of special cases which the program is unable to analyze further for one reason or another. Numerous instances of our own linguistic, cultural, and physical knowledge are encoded in the patterns. All of this information is necessary for adequate performance in a dialogue situation, but we did not wish to approach the entire problem of human

5. Representation of Information

Throughout the recognition program, a sentence is represented as an almost linear list. Only trailing clausal objects can be nested more than one level deep.

it simply does not permit part-of-speech ambiguity. The program's dictionary is tree-structured, with each word in a single synonym-class and, ultimately, assigned to a single part of speech. A few sample entries from the dictionary illustrate this structure:

verb HARM
ATTACK
INJURE

noun INJURY
WOUND

In the case of an ambiguous word, this assignment represents the most common (i.e. expected) sense of the word. In the example above, "ATTACK" is expected to be used as a verb rather than a noun. This simple solution is successful because most ambiguity is removed from a sentence before it is matched against clause patterns. The most common lexical ambiguities are between semantically related verbs and nouns. This form of ambiguity is detected locally in several ways and the ambiguous word is replaced by an unambiguous word of the appropriate type using the semantic relationship pointers established for derivational suffix removal. During suffix removal, a noun stem with an "-ING" suffix is converted to a verb. During noun phrase bracketing, a verb following a determiner is converted to a noun. During verb phrase simplification, a noun following subject-auxiliary inversion is converted to a verb. For example:

WOUNDING → HARM -ING
THE ATTACK → [THE INJURY]
DID HE WOUND → HE DID HARM+INTERROGATIVE = ?

The remaining ambiguous words are generally ambiguous within a single part of speech. For instance, "ATTACK" has several senses as a verb. The matching of general clause patterns is not influenced by this level of ambiguity. These words do not cause problems for the concept matching stage either because the exact meaning of an isolated word is not important. A meaning (i.e. internal pattern name) is assigned to an entire clause when it matches a stored concept pattern. Given the context of the pattern, it is easy for a human reader to identify the intended sense of each word, but this information is not explicit in the program.

7. Implementation Notes

The latest version of PARRY is written in MLISP, which translates directly into UCI-LISP. The UCI-LISP is compiled and run on a PDP-10 under a TENEX operating system. The language comprehension phase of PARRY occupies 100,000 words of memory and processes an average sentence in half a second (CPU time). PARRY's size is due to several large data tables:

knowledge representation in a general way at this time. (It is interesting to note that many researchers who began with an interest in natural language processing are now working on knowledge representation.)

The program uses primarily declarative data representations, although some data is interpreted by complicated procedures. This facilitates incremental improvements on a time scale much shorter than is usually required for recoding procedures. In many instances, a lack of data can be detected internally. Occasionally, the probable meaning of an unknown word or clause can be inferred and a rudimentary form of learning takes place. More often, human assistance must be sought. In an interview situation, it is not appropriate for a model designed to simulate human thought processes to ask for linguistic assistance. However, in a data-acquisition situation involving the programmer, the program is able to pinpoint the problem, ask a specific question, check the answer for consistency with other data, and manipulate the answer into the appropriate internal format. These human engineering features are a valuable addition to any program which must deal with large amounts of data.

6. Utilization of English Grammar

Since the program being described attempts to recognize English language expressions, it is strongly influenced by the surface structure of English. However, the ultimate goal is a recognition of the meaning of an expression rather than an analysis of its syntax. Therefore, grammatical analysis is only utilized when it appears to be the easiest path to the meaning of an expression. In some instances, rules describing grammatical structure are represented explicitly in the program. The most prominent uses of traditional grammatical rules are in the simplification of complex verb tenses, passive constructions, and subject-auxiliary inversions. Traditional grammatical rules governing the structure of simple noun phrases are contained in a transition network which brackets noun phrases. Grossly simplified, the network indicates that a noun phrase may consist of a determiner, some adjectives, some nouns, and some prepositional phrases introduced by "OF". At least one noun must be present but all the other constituents are optional. Although less explicit, the treatment of adverbs and some idiomatic adverbial phrases corresponds closely to their function as modifiers of verb phrases. In the traditional analysis, modal verbs are a special case sharing a few properties with the primary auxiliaries. In the program, modal verbs are treated as auxiliaries up to a certain stage, after which they are treated as adverbs. Other facets of English grammar are left implicit in the clause patterns and concept patterns.

The much-lamented ambiguity inherent in many English expressions has already been mentioned. One source of this ambiguity is single words with multiple meanings. At first glance, it appears that our attempt to match an ambiguous sentence against 20 general clause patterns would fail as miserably as any grammatical parser attempting to analyze the same sentence. Our matcher does not fail because

A basic dictionary of about 3500 words.

A table of about 200 semantic relationship classes among the dictionary words.

Two idiom tables totalling about 600 entries.

A table of about 2000 concept patterns.

Additionally, there are a dozen small tables which will probably never exceed 100 entries each (e.g. inflectional endings, irregular verbs). All the data tables are presently stored as ordinary **LISP** expressions on property lists. The multiword phrases and patterns are stored as tree structures with identical initial portions of phrases or patterns merged into a single branch of the tree. This eliminates one source of redundancy in the pattern matching procedure. The remaining redundancy is manageable because the average phrases and patterns are only three to five words long.

8. Room for Improvement

A few weaknesses have already been mentioned. The analysis of derivational word endings is crude. The spelling correction algorithm runs amok on unknown words. Relative clauses are not comprehended after nouns. Other forms of self-embedding, such as a nominalized clause in the subject position of a sentence, will also confuse the grammatical analysis processes.

Separation of the recognition process into distinct stages produces efficiency but it also prevents a useful form of information feedback during sentence recognition. Since all word identification is done before clauses are sought, it is not possible to use global information to determine, for example, if "YOR" is a misspelling of "YOUR" or "OR". Increased parallelism among the various stages of processing could alleviate this problem.

An interesting extension would be the modification of the model's recognition procedures based on the current affect (i.e. emotion) levels. Presently, a sentence is recognized identically each time it is entered, although the remaining phases of the model may choose to respond differently based on affect levels. In situations of extreme affect (i.e. rage, terror) it is plausible that recognition becomes so distorted that the level-headed interpretation of a sentence is not available at all.

A problem of immense importance in dialogue situations is ellipsis. After a simple sentence, a wide variety of elliptic responses is possible. Consider the sentence:

    The Mafia follows me.

This can be followed by:

    The Mafia?
    Who?
    Who does?
    Follows you?
    You?
    Really?

    They do, do they?
    So do I.
    Me too.
    Even in the hospital?
    Why?

In isolation, these statements are either meaningless or highly ambiguous. They become meaningful only when viewed in the context of the previous sentence. The previous sentence provides a basic structure which is modified in a systematic way by the collection of pronouns, auxiliaries, and adverbials in an elliptic response. A few instances of ellipsis are handled in the present program with forward anticipation but the problem seems better suited to a solution which only looks back after an ellipsis is encountered. (See Longuet-Higgins [11] or Deutsch [5] for further discussion of ellipsis in dialogue.)

Closely related problems are sentences which are syntactically well formed but loaded with pro-forms (e.g. DO) and anaphora to the point that they are meaningless out of context. The following sentences are examples:

    What do they do?
    I think so too.
    Why do they do that?

It is necessary to locate complex anaphoric references like "so" and "that" as well as the usual personal pronouns. We have a number of ideas for the solution of these problems which we intend to test shortly.

9. Conclusion

The language-recognition program described in this paper functions within an unusual set of constraints. The most difficult to satisfy is that an untrained user must be entirely comfortable with the dialogue. No facet of colloquial natural language usage can be prohibited by fiat. A system which establishes such an outrageous constraint must give something in return. Our paranoid model has its own intentions, independent of the input, and these serve to focus the conversation into certain, pre-determined areas with which the language recognizer is familiar. Given some such focusing influence, our language-recognition methods could be applied to any other problem domain which requires man-machine communication in unrestricted natural language.

Appendix—Sample Interview

A diagnostic psychiatric interview illustrating the recognition and response processes of the model at work.

I = Interviewer, P = PARRY. Annotations are in square brackets [].
I—HELLO. MY NAME IS DR. JONES.
P—GLAD TO MEET YOU.

[Multiple sentences are correctly recognized. In this case, only one response is necessary.]
I—WHAT'S YOUR NAME?
P—PAT SMITH.
I—PATRICK OR PATRICIA?
P—I'M A MAN.
[This illustrates the use of world knowledge (i.e. masculine and feminine names) built into concept patterns.]
I—HOW ODL ARE YPPU?
P—TWENTY-EIGHT.
[Both of these misspellings are corrected.]
I—WHY ARE YOU HERE?
P—I'M SOMEWHAT UPSET.
I—HAVE YOU DREAMT ANY STRANGE DREAMS?
P—I DON'T REMEMBER DREAMS.
[The irregular past tense of "DREAM" is recognized. The second occurrence of "DREAM" is converted into a noun.]
I—CAN STRANGERS READ YOUR MIND?
P—NATURALLY NOT.
[This matches a stored concept pattern with "noun-phrase" in the subject slot since our model does not worry at all about mind reading.]
I—I SEE YOURE TOUCHY ABOUT THAT.
P—ONLY WHEN PEOPLE ANNOY ME.
["I SEE" is recognized as an instance of polite wrapping for a delicate subject.]
I—DONT YOU LIKE BEING HERE?
P—NO.
[The negative in the question does not reverse its meaning, so the correct response is "NO".]
I—BEING IN THE HOSPITAL MIGHT DO YOU A LOT OF GOOD.
P—ITS NOT HELPING ME MUCH TO BE HERE.
[The flexible idiom, "DO noun-phrase GOOD", is recognized.]
I—I WAS TOLD YOU'RE ON MEDICATION.
P—I TAKE SOME SORT OF SEDATIVES.
["I WAS TOLD" is another instance of polite wrapping, and "BE ON MEDICATION" is a known idiom.]
I—WERE YOU EVER ON ANY KIND OF MEDICATION BEFORE?
P—NO.
[This illustrates another use of the same flexible idiom, "BE ON MEDICATION".]
I—DO YOU PLAN TO CONTINUE TAKING IT?
P—I DON'T REALLY NEED HELP LIKE THEY THINK.
[This question contains doubly embedded clausal objects.]
I—DO YOU HAVE ANY HOBBIES.

P—YES, I LIKE HORSERACING.
[This is seen as a question due to interrogative word order although the question mark was omitted. The model senses an opening in which to introduce one of its favourite topics.]
I—GO ON.
P—THERE ARE A LOT OF TRICKY OPERATORS DOWN THERE.
[This is a rigid idiom, often used in imperative sentences.]
I—DID YOU GET GYPPED?
P—YES, THOSE GUYS ARE CROOKS.
[This is the colloquial passive, using "GET" rather than "BE" as the auxiliary verb.]
I—ARE YOU DISTRUSTFUL OF PEOPLE?
P—SOME PEOPLE ACT KIND OF FUNNY, LIKE THOSE IMMIGRANT TYPES I WORK WITH.
["DISTRUSTFUL" is turned into "SUSPICIOUS" using derivational rules on the root word, "TRUST".]
I—IN WHAT WAY?
P—THOSE FOREIGNERS ARE TRYING TO RUN THE COUNTRY.
[This is a rigid idiom for "HOW". This elliptical question was anticipated by the model.]
I—DO YOU WANT TO GET A PAIR OF SOCKS FOR CHRISTMAS?
P—I WANT TO BE OUT OF HERE.
[This frivolous question is clearly not within the model's realm of interest. However, there is a general concept pattern containing "any-concept" in the object position, and the model does know what it wants. In addition, the model notes that it could not understand the input, and decrements self-esteem accordingly.]
I—COULD YOU TELL ME THE NAME OF THE FIRST PRESIDENT OF THE UNITED STATES?
P—BABE RUTH.
[The elaborate noun phrase is recognized as a single noun phrase but not identified with any existing concept. The model has a snappy answer for frivolous "NAME" questions. The model also adds to its store of beliefs about the interviewer, based on the perceived inappropriateness of the input.]
I—WHEN DID YOU FIRST LEARN YOU WERE CRAZY?
P—I DON'T WANT TO TALK WITH YOU ANY MORE, BUZZ OFF.
[The model responds to the emotionally charged embedded presupposition instead of the innocuous main clause.]
I—BUT, I LIKE YOU A LOT.
P—SOMEBODY SHOULD TEACH YOU A LESSON ABOUT INTERVIEWING PATIENTS.
[The model cannot accept this claim from such an erratic interviewer.]
I—I HAVE TO GO NOW ANYWAY.

P—OK, THIS HAS BEEN LONG ENOUGH.
[The semi-auxiliary verb, "HAVE TO", is converted to the modal, "MUST".]
I—WHAT ARE YOU GOING TO BE DOING AT THE SAME TIME OF DAY TOMORROW?
P—I'LL JUST BE HERE ON THE WARD.
[This elaborate verb phrase, with complex tense and multiple adverbials, is simplified and recognized.]
I—BYE, PAT.
P—GOODBYE.

REFERENCES

1. Bobrow, D. Natural language input for a computer problem-solving system, in: Minsky, M. (ed.) Semantic Information Processing (M.I.T. Press, Cambridge, MA, 1968).
2. Charniak, E. Computer solution of calculus word problems, Proceedings of the IJCAI, Mitre Corp. (1969).
3. Colby, K. M. Artificial Paranoia: A Computer Simulation of Paranoid Processes (Pergamon Press, Oxford, 1975).
4. Colby, K. M., Parkison, R. C. and Faught, W. S. Pattern-matching rules for the recognition of natural language dialogue expressions, American Journal of Computational Linguistics 1 (September 1974).
5. Deutsch, B. Establishing context in task-oriented dialogues, Stanford Research Institute Artificial Intelligence Center (September 1975).
6. Faught, W..S., Colby, K. M. and Parkison, R. C. Inferences, affects and intentions in a model of paranoia Cognitive Psychology 9 (April 1977).
7. Grishman, R. Implementation of the string parser of English, in: Rustin, R. (ed.) Natural Language Processing (Algorithmics Press, Inc., 1973).
8. Heidorn, G. E. Natural language inputs to a simulation programming system, Naval Postgraduate School, Monterey, California (October 1972).
9. Kay, M. The mind system, in: Rustin, R. (ed.) Natural Language Processing (Algorithmics Press, Inc., 1973).
10. Lakoff, R. Language in context, Language (December 1972).
11. Longuet-Higgins, H. C. The algorithmic description of natural language, Proceedings of the Royal Society of London 182 (October 1972).
12. Michie, D. (ed.) Machine Intelligence 3 (Edinburgh University Press, 1968).
13. Miller, P. L. An adaptive natural language system that listens, asks, and learns, M.I.T. RLE Natural Language Group (May 1975).
14. Minsky, M. (ed.) Semantic Information Processing (M.I.T. Press, Cambridge, MA, 1968).
15. Petrick, S. R. Transformational analysis, in: Rustin, R. (ed.) Natural Language Processing (Algorithmics Press, Inc., 1973).
16. Quirk, R., Greenbaum, S., Leech, G. and Svartvik, J. A Grammar of Contemporary English (Seminar Press, 1972).
17. Raphael, B. SIR: Semantic information retrieval, in: Minsky, M. (ed.) Semantic Information Processing (M.I.T. Press, Cambridge, MA, 1968).
18. Reddy, R., Erman, L. D., Fennell, R. D. and Neely, R. B. The HEARSAY speech understanding system: An example of the recognition process, Proceedings of the 3rd IJCAI, Stanford University (August 1973).
19. Riesbeck, Christopher K. Computational understanding: Analysis of sentences and context, Stanford Artificial Intelligence Laboratory (May 1974).
21. Schank, R. Identification of conceptualizations underlying natural language, in: Schank, R. and Colby, K. M. (eds.) Computer Models of Thought and Language (Freeman, San Francisco, CA, 1973).
22. Schank, R. and Colby, K. M. (eds.) Computer Models of Thought and Language (Freeman, San Francisco, CA, 1973).
23. Thorne, J. P., Bratley, P. and Dewar, H. The syntactic analysis of English by machine, in: Michie, D. (ed.) Machine Intelligence 3 (Edinburgh University Press, 1968).
24. Walker, D. E. Speech understanding, computational linguistics, and artificial intelligence. Stanford Research Institute Artificial Intelligence Center (August 1973).
25. Weizenbaum, J. ELIZA—A computer program for the study of natural language communication between man and machine. Communications of the ACM 9 (January 1966).
26. Wilks, Y. An artificial intelligence approach to machine translation, in: Schank, R. and Colby, K. M. (eds.) Computer Models of Thought and Language (Freeman, San Francisco, CA, 1973).
27. Winograd, T. Understanding Natural Language (Academic Press, New York, 1972).
28. Woods, W. A. Transition network grammars for natural language analysis, Communications of the ACM 13 (October 1970).
29. Woods, W. A., Kaplan, R. M. and Nash-Webber, B. The lunar sciences natural language information system: Final report. Bolt Beranek and Newman, Inc. (June 1972).

Received June 1976; revised version received January 1977

Developing a Natural Language Interface to Complex Data

GARY G. HENDRIX, EARL D. SACERDOTI, DANIEL SAGALOWICZ, AND JONATHAN SLOCUM
SRI International

Aspects of an intelligent interface that provides natural language access to a large body of data distributed over a computer network are described. The overall system architecture is presented, showing how a user is buffered from the actual database management systems (DBMSs) by three layers of insulating components. These layers operate in series to convert natural language queries into calls to DBMSs at remote sites. Attention is then focused on the first of the insulating components, the natural language system. A pragmatic approach to de-language access that has proved useful for building interfaces to databases is described and illustrated by examples. Special language features that increase system usability, such as spelling correction, processing of incomplete inputs, and run-time system personalization, are also discussed. The language system is contrasted with other work in applied natural language processing, and the system's limitations are analyzed.

Key Words and Phrases: natural language, intelligent interface, database access, semantic grammar, human engineering, run-time personalization
CR Categories: 3.42, 3.62, 3.79, 4.22, 4.33

1. INTRODUCTION

In dealing with a very large database (VLDB), which is perhaps distributed among multiple computers with different database management systems (DBMSs) on remote sites, a central problem faced by would-be users is that of formulating queries in terms communicable to the system.

It is usually the case that business executives, government officials, and other decision makers have a good idea of the kind of information residing in their data-bases. Yet to obtain the answer to a particular question, they generally need to employ the services of a technician who works with the database on a regular basis

and who is thoroughly familiar with its file structure, the DBMSs on which it resides, how it is distributed among various computer systems, the coded field names for the data items, the kinds of values that different fields are expected to contain, and other idiosyncrasies.

The technician must understand the decision maker's question, reformulate it in terms of the data that is actually stored, plan a sequence of requests for particular items from particular files on particular computers, open connections with remote sites, build programs to query the remote systems using the primitives of the DBMSs of the remote systems, monitor the execution of those programs, recover from errors, and correlate the results. This is a demanding, time-consuming, and exacting task requiring much attention to detail. Escalated levels of sophistication are needed as the VLDB increases in size and complexity and as it is distributed over a wider range of host computers.

With the goal of making large, distributed databases directly available to decision makers (while freeing technicians from increasingly tedious details), a group of researchers at SRI International has developed a prototype system that, for many classes of questions, automates the procedures usually performed by technicians. This paper presents an overview of this system, called LADDER (for language access to distributed data with error recovery) [16],[1] and then concentrates on the particular problem of translating user queries from English into the terms of the database. The other aspects of the LADDER system are presented in greater detail elsewhere in the literature [13, 16, 17]. The system was developed as a management aid to Navy decision makers, so examples throughout the paper will be drawn from the domain of Navy command and control.

2. SYSTEM ARCHITECTURE

The running demonstration system consists of three major components that provide levels of buffering of the user from the underlying DBMSs. The LADDER user can think he is retrieving information from a "general information base" rather than retrieving specific items of data from a set of highly formatted, traditional databases that are scattered across a computer network. The user provides a question about the information base in English; LADDER applies all the necessary information concerning the vocabulary and syntax of the question, the names of specific fields, how they are formatted, how they are structured into files, and even where the files are physically located, to provide an answer.

LADDER's first component, called INLAND (for informal natural language access to Navy data), accepts questions in a restricted subset of natural language and produces a query or sequence of queries to the VLDB as a whole. The queries to the VLDB, as produced by INLAND, refer to specific fields, but make no commitment about how the information in the database is broken down into files.

For example, INLAND translates the question "What is the length of the Kennedy?" into the query

$$(\text{(NAM EQ JOHN\#F.KENNEDY) (? LENGTH)}),$$

where LENGTH is the name of the length field, NAM the name of the ship name

General permission to make fair use in teaching or research of all or part of this material is granted to individual readers and to nonprofit libraries acting for them provided that ACM's copyright notice is given and that reference is made to the publication, to its date of issue, and to the fact that reprinting privileges were granted by permission of the Association for Computing Machinery. To otherwise reprint a figure, table, other substantial excerpt, or the entire work requires specific permission as does republication, or systematic or multiple reproduction.
The work reported herein, other than the development of the LIFER system, was supported by the Advanced Research Projects Agency of the Department of Defense under Contract DAAG29-76-C-0012 with the U.S. Army Research Office. Development of LIFER was conducted under SRI's Internal Research and Development Program.
A version of this paper was presented at the Third International Conference on Very Large Data Bases, Tokyo, Japan, October 1977.
Authors' address: Artificial Intelligence Center, SRI International, Menlo Park, CA 94025
© 1978 ACM 0362-5915/78/0600-0105 $00.75

---

[1] A glossary of system names precedes the Appendix.

field, and JOHN#F.KENNEDY the value of the NAM field for the record concerned with the Kennedy.

Queries from INLAND are directed to the second component of LADDER, called IDA (for intelligent data access) [17]. In general, a query to IDA is a command list of constraints (such as (NAM EQ JOHN#F.KENNEDY) or (* MAX LENGTH)) and requests for values of fields (such as (? LENGTH)). INLAND operates by building a (possibly null) fragment of a query to IDA for each lower-level syntactic unit in the English input. These fragments are combined as higher-level syntactic units are recognized. At the sentence level, the combined fragments are sent as a command string to IDA.

Employing a model of the structure of the VLDB, IDA breaks down a query against the entire VLDB into a sequence of queries against individual files. Linkages among the records retrieved are preserved so that appropriate answers to the overall query may be composed and returned.

For example, suppose that the database consists of a single file whose records contain the fields

(NAM CLASS LENGTH).

Then, to answer the database query issued above, IDA can simply create one file retrieval program that says, in essence, "For the ship record with NAM equal JOHN#F.KENNEDY, return the value of the LENGTH field." Suppose, however, that the database is structured in two files, as follows:

SHIP: (NAM CLASS . . .)
CLASS: (CLASSNAME LENGTH . . .).

In this case the single query about the Kennedy's length must be broken into two file queries. These would say, first, "Obtain the value of the CLASS field for the SHIP record with NAM equal JOHN#F.KENNEDY." Then, "find the corresponding CLASS record and return the value of the LENGTH field from that record." Finally, IDA would compose an answer that is relevant to the user's original query (i.e. it will return NAM and LENGTH data, suppressing the CLASS-to-CLASSNAME link).

In addition to planning the correct sequence of file queries, IDA must actually compose those queries in the language of the remote DBMSs. Currently the system accesses, on a number of different machines, a DBMS called the Datacomputer [4, 6], whose input language is called DATALANGUAGE. IDA creates the relevant DATALANGUAGE query by inserting field and file names into prestored templates. However, since the database is distributed over several machines, the DATALANGUAGE that IDA produces does not refer to generic files, files containing a specific kind of record. It refers instead to specific files in specific directories on specific machines. For example, the queries discussed above might refer to the SHIP file rather than file SHIP.ACTIVE in directory NAVY on machine CCA-2.

It is the function of the third major component of LADDER to find the location of the generic files and manage the access to them. To carry out this function, the third component, called FAM (for file access manager) [13], relies on a locally

stored model showing where files are located throughout the distributed database. When it receives a query expressed in generic DATALANGUAGE, it searches its model for the primary location of the file (or files) to which it refers. It then establishes connections over the ARPANET to the appropriate computers, logs in, opens the files, and transmits the DATALANGUAGE query, as amended to refer to the specific files that are being accessed. If at any time the remote computer crashes, the file becomes inaccessible, or the network connection fails, FAM can recover, and if a backup file is mentioned in FAM's model of file locations, it can establish a connection to a backup site and retransmit the query.

The existing system, written in INTERLISP [19], can process a fairly wide range of questions against a database consisting of some 14 files containing about 100 fields. Processing a typical question takes less than a second of CPU time on a DEC KL-10 computer. An annotated transcript of a sample session with the system is provided in the Appendix.

We emphasize that the three major components of LADDER each address separate portions of the data access problem. Although they have been designed to work in combination, each component is a separate, self-contained module that independently addresses one aspect of data access. For example, the virtual view of the data that IDA supports for its caller would be of value even without a natural language front end. Likewise, the general technology developed for natural language translation may be separated from the data access problem and applied in other domains.

3. THE NATURAL LANGUAGE COMPONENT

With the goal of supplying natural language interfaces to a variety of computer software, we have developed a language processing package, called LIFER (for language interface facility with ellipsis and recursion) [11], that facilitates the construction and run-time operation of special purpose, applications-oriented, natural language interfaces. INLAND, the linguistic component of our intelligent interface to distributed data, has been constructed within the LIFER framework. Figure 1 gives some indication of the diversity of language accepted by this system. Below we describe the nature of INLAND and illustrate how it was created using LIFER's interactive language definition facilities. Of course, the examples can show only limited aspects of INLAND. We believe the existing INLAND system to be one of the most robust computerized natural language systems ever developed, accepting a wide range of questions about information in the database (as shown in Figure 1) as well as metaquestions about definitions of database fields and the grammar itself.

3.1 Overview of LIFER

Although work in artificial intelligence and computational linguistics has not yet developed a general approach to the problems of understanding English and other natural languages, mechanisms do exist for dealing with major fragments of language pertinent to particular application areas. The idea behind LIFER is to adapt existing computational linguistic technology to practical applications while investigating

---

[2] If it is possible to perform multiple file accesses with a single multifile query, IDA will do so.

What kind of information do you know about
Is there a doctor on board the Biddle
Display all the American cruisers in the North Atlantic
What is the name and location of the carrier nearest to New York
What is the commanding officer's name
Who commands the Kennedy
What is the Kennedy's beam
When will the Los Angeles reach Norfolk
Tell me when Taru is scheduled to leave port
Where is she scheduled to go
When will Los Angeles arrive in its home port
When will the Sturgeon arrive on station
What aircraft units are embarked on the Constellation
To which task organization is Knox assigned
Where is the Sellers
Where is Luanda
What is the next port of call of the Santa Inez
When will Tarifa get underway
Which convoy escorts have inoperative sonar systems
When will they be repaired
Which U.S. Navy DDGs have casreps involving radar systems
What Soviet ship has hull number 855
To what class does the Soviet ship Minsk belong
What class does the Whale belong to?
What is the normal steaming time for the Wainwright from Gibraltar to Norfolk
What American ships are carrying vanadium ore
How far is it to Norfolk
How far away is Norfolk
How many nautical miles is it to Norfolk
How many miles is it to Norfolk from here
How close is the Baton Rouge to Norfolk
How far is the Adams from the Aspro
What is the distance from Gibraltar to Norfolk
What is the nearest oiler
What is the nearest oiler to the Constellation
How far is it from Naples to 23-00N, 45-00W
What is the distance from the Kitty Hawk to Naples
How long would it take the Independence to reach 35-00N, 20-00W
How long is the Philadelphia
How long would it take the Aspro to join Kennedy
What is the nearest ship to Naples with a doctor on board
What is the nearest USN ship to the Enterprise with an operational air search radar
What is known about that ship
How many merchant ships are within 400 miles of the Hepburn
What are their identities and last reported locations
What cargo does the Pecos have
Who is CTG 67.3
What are the length, width, and draft of the Kitty Hawk
To whom is the Harry E. Yarnell attached
What type ships are in the Knox class
Where are the Charles F. Adams class ships
What are their current assignments

Fig. 1. Sample of acceptable inputs to LADDER

Figure 1 is continued on the next page

and extending the human engineering aspects of the technology. The LIFER system supplies basic parsing procedures and an interactive methodology needed by a system developer to create convenient interfaces (such as INLAND) in reasonable amounts of time. Certain user-oriented features, such as spelling correction, processing of incomplete inputs, and the ability of the run-time user to extend the language accepted by the system through the use of paraphrase, are also included in the LIFER package.

LIFER is composed of two basic parts: a set of interactive language specification functions, and a parser. The language specification functions are used to define an application language, a subset of a natural language (e.g. English) that is appropriate for interacting with existing software, such as a DBMS. Using this language specification, the LIFER parser interprets natural language inputs, translating them into appropriate interactions with the application software.

Figure 2 shows simplified example interactions with the LIFER parser using the INLAND language specification. A sequence of complete examples is presented in the Appendix. The user of the system types in a question or command in ordinary English, followed by a carriage return. The LIFER parser then begins processing the input. When analysis is complete, the system types "PARSED!" and invokes database functions (IDA) to respond.

An important feature of the parser is an ability to process elliptical (incomplete) inputs. Thus if the system is asked, as in question 1 of Figure 2,

WHAT IS THE LENGTH OF THE CONSTELLATION,

then the subsequent input

OF THE NAUTILUS

will be interpreted as WHAT IS THE LENGTH OF THE NAUTILUS.

If a user misspells a word, LIFER attempts to correct the error, using the INTERLISP spelling corrector [19]. If the parser cannot account for an input in terms of the application language definition, error messages, such as that produced after question 6, are printed that indicate how much of the input was understood and that suggest means of completing the input.

Provision is included in INLAND for interfacing with LIFER's own language specification functions, making it possible for users to give natural language commands for extending the language itself. In particular, computer-naive users may extend the language accepted by the system by employing easy-to-understand notions such as synonyms and paraphrases. This is illustrated by interactions 7 and 10 in Figure 2.

In using LIFER to define a language for INLAND, we have followed the approach taken by most real-time language processing systems in embedding considerable semantic information in the syntax of the language. Such a language specification is typically called a "semantic grammar." For example, words like NAUTILUS and DISPLACEMENT are not grouped together into a single ⟨NOUN⟩ category. Rather, NAUTILUS is treated as a ⟨SHIP-NAME⟩ and DISPLACEMENT as an ⟨ATTRIBUTE⟩. Similarly, very specific sentence pat-

What subs in the South Atlantic are within 1000 miles of the Sunfish
What is the Kittyhawk doing
How many USN asw capable ships are in the Med
Where are they
What are their current assignments and fuel states
What ships are NOT at combat readiness rating C1
When will Reeves achieve readiness rating C1
Why is Hoel at readiness rating C2
When will the sonar be repaired on the Sterett
What ships are carrying cargo for the United States
Where are they going
What are they carrying
When will they arrive
Where is Gridley bound
Which cruisers have less than 50 per cent fuel on board
Where are all the merchant ships
When will the Kitty Hawk's radar be up?
What ships are in the Los Angeles class
What command does Adm. William have
Under whose opcon is the Dale
Show me where the Kennedy is!
What ship has hull number 148?
What is the next port of call for the South Carolina?
Are doctors embarked in the Kawishiwi
What kind of cargo does the Francis McGraw have?
What air group is embarked in the Constellation?
What do you know about the employment schedule of the Lang?
Which systems are down on the Kitty Hawk
What ships in the Med have doctors embarked?
How many ships carrying oil are within 340 miles of Mayport?
What sub contacts are within 300 miles of the Enterprise?
List the current position and heading of the US Navy ships in the Mediterranean every 4 hours
What is the status of the Enterprise's air search radar?
Where is convoy NL53 going
What convoy is the Transgermania in
How many embarked units are in Constellation
What ships are in British ports
What U.S. ships are within 500 miles of Wilmington?
What U.S. ships are faster than the Gridley are in Norfolk
What is the fastest ship in the Mediterranean Sea
How close is that ship to Naples?
What is its home port
Print the American cruisers' current positions and states of readiness!
How is the Los Angeles powered
What ship having a normal cruising speed greater than 30 knots is the largest
Display the last reported position of all ships that are in the North Atlantic
When did the Endeavour depart the port of New York
What nationality is the ship with international radio call sign UA1D
What ports are in the database
What merchant ships are enroute to New York and within 500 miles of the Saratoga
To what country does the fastest sub belong?

Fig. 1 (continued from previous page)

1- What is the length of the Constellation
PARSED!
(LENGTH 1072 feet)

2- of the Nautilus
TRYING ELLIPSIS: WHAT IS THE LENGTH OF THE NAUTILUS
(LENGTH 319 feet)

3- displacement
TRYING ELLIPSIS: WHAT IS THE DISPLACEMENT OF THE NAUTILUS
(STANDARD-DISPLACEMENT 4040 tons)

4- length of the fastest American Nuclear sub
TRYING ELLIPSIS: WHAT IS THE LENGTH OF THE FASTEST AMERICAN NUCLEAR SUB
(LENGTH 360 feet NAM LOS ANGELES SPEED 30.0 knots)

5- Who commands the Constellation
SPELLING--/CONSTELLATION
PARSED!
(COMMANDER CAPT J. ELLISON)

6- Who commands JFK
TRYING ELLIPSIS: ELLIPSIS HAS FAILED
THE PARSER DOES NOT EXPECT THE WORD "JFK" TO FOLLOW
"WHO COMMANDS"
OPTIONS FOR NEXT WORD OR META-SYMBOL ARE:
(SHIP-NAME)

7- Define JFK to be like Kennedy
PARSED!
• (JFK is now a synonym for KENNEDY, which is a ship name)
• ...

8- Who commands JFK   (that is, retry interaction 6)
PARSED!
(COMMANDER CAPT P. MOFFETT)

9- info JFK country
TRYING ELLIPSIS: ELLIPSIS HAS FAILED
• (error message omitted)
• ...

10- Define "Info JFK country" to be like "what is the country of JFK"
PARSED!
• ...

11- Info JFK country
PARSED!
(NATION USA)

12- Info fastest American nuclear submarine speed
PARSED!
(SPEED 30.0 knots NAM LOS ANGELES)

13- Nautilus
TRYING ELLIPSIS: INFO NAUTILUS SPEED
(SPEED 22 knots)

Fig. 2 Simplified interactions with LADDER

terms such as

WHAT IS THE ⟨ATTRIBUTE⟩ OF ⟨SHIP⟩

are typically used instead of more general patterns such as

⟨NOUN-PHRASE⟩ ⟨VERB-PHRASE⟩.

For each syntactic pattern, the language definer supplies an expression for computing the interpretation of instances of the pattern. INLAND's expressions for sentence-level patterns usually invoke the IDA component to retrieve information from the distributed database.

This method of language specification is easy to understand, easy to use, and, when pursued systematically, allows languages of broad coverage to be defined, as indicated in Figure 1.

To provide a more detailed view of how LIFER has been employed to produce an efficient and effective language processing system, let us examine in detail a highly simplified fragment of the INLAND language specification.

3.2 INLAND's Function in Brief

The central notions of how INLAND is constructed may be seen by considering the problem of providing English access to two files of the form

SHIP: (NAM CLASS COMMANDER HOME-PORT HULL# LOC)
CLASS: (CLASSNAME TYPE NATION FUEL LENGTH BEAM DRAFT SPEED)

located on different computers. IDA and FAM together provide levels of insulation from the real situation, so that INLAND need consider only the problem of specifying what subset of the overall database should be queried and what field values within that subset should be returned. IDA will dynamically plan the appropriate joins on the files in the database, and FAM will carry them out. (In the actual LADDER system, the intertwining of multiple files is much more complex than in the current example.)

3.3 A Miniature Language Specification

(1) *Productions.* The grammar rules may be viewed as productions of the form

metasymbol ⇒ *pattern | expression,*

where *metasymbol* is a metasymbol of the application language, *pattern* is a list of symbols and metasymbols in the language, and *expression* is a LISP expression whose value, when computed, is assigned as the value of the metasymbol.[3] The symbol ⟨L.T.G⟩ (LIFER top grammar) is the highest-level metasymbol of the grammar. The system's answer to complete inputs that match a pattern instantiating ⟨L.T.G⟩ will be the result of evaluating the associated LISP expression.

For example, the input

PRINT THE LENGTH OF THE KENNEDY

is an instantiation of the sentence-level production

⟨L.T.G⟩ ⇒ ⟨PRESENT⟩ THE ⟨ATTRIBUTE⟩ OF ⟨SHIP⟩ |
            (IDA (APPEND ⟨SHIP⟩ ⟨ATTRIBUTE⟩)).

The input matches the pattern

⟨PRESENT⟩ THE ⟨ATTRIBUTE⟩ OF ⟨SHIP⟩.

where ⟨PRESENT⟩ matches PRINT, ⟨ATTRIBUTE⟩ matches LENGTH, and ⟨SHIP⟩ matches the phrase THE KENNEDY. If the semantic values for ⟨SHIP⟩ and ⟨ATTRIBUTE⟩, computed by means described shortly, are ((NAM EQ JOHN#F.KENNEDY)) and ((? LENGTH)), respectively, then the answer to the question is computed from the expression portion of the production as follows:

(IDA (APPEND ⟨SHIP⟩ ⟨ATTRIBUTE⟩))
⇒ (IDA (APPEND '((NAM EQ JOHN.#F.KENNEDY))
            '(? LENGTH)))
⇒ (IDA '((NAM EQ JOHN#F.KENNEDY)(? LENGTH))).

(APPEND is a LISP function that appends any number of lists together to form a larger list.) At this point, the IDA component is called with the argument

((NAM EQ JOHN#F.KENNEDY) (? LENGTH))

and the length of the Kennedy is retrieved as

(IDA '((NAM EQ JOHN#F KENNEDY) (? LENGTH)))
⇒ (LENGTH 1072 feet).

In LIFER, productions like the one just shown are defined interactively by issuing commands such as

PD[(L.T.G)
   (⟨PRESENT⟩ THE ⟨ATTRIBUTE⟩ OF ⟨SHIP⟩)
   (IDA (APPEND ⟨SHIP⟩ ⟨ATTRIBUTE⟩))],

where PD is the production definition function.

(2) *Lexical Entries.* Metasymbols, such as ⟨PRESENT⟩ and ⟨ATTRIBUTE⟩, are often associated with individual words or fixed phrases, which are maintained in LIFER's lexicons. The LIFER function MS (make set) is used to define a set of words and phrases that may match a particular metasymbol. For example, the call

MS[(ATTRIB)
   (CLASS COMMANDER FUEL TYPE NATION LENGTH
   BEAM DRAFT (LOCATION . LOC) (POSITION . LOC)
   (NAME . NAM) (COUNTRY . NATION)
   (NATIONALITY . NATION)((HOME-PORT) . HOME-PORT)
   ((POWER TYPE) . FUEL)((HULL NUMBER) . HULL#))]

is used to define 16 words and fixed phrases that may match the symbol ⟨ATTRIBUTE⟩ (which is used subsequently in defining ⟨ATTRIBUTE⟩).

After this call to MS, ⟨ATTRIB⟩ will match the words CLASS, COMMANDER, FUEL, TYPE, NATION, LENGTH, BEAM, and DRAFT. For these words, ⟨ATTRIB⟩ will take as its semantic value the word itself. ⟨ATTRIB⟩ will also

---

[3] In addition to computing values for acceptable applications of the production, the expression may also be used to reject some applications on semantic grounds. Rejection is signaled if the expression returns *ERROR* as its value.

match the word LOCATION, but for this match the value of ⟨ATTRIB⟩ will be LOC. Similarly, ⟨ATTRIB⟩ matches POSITION, NAME, COUNTRY, and NATIONALITY, but takes the values LOC, NAM, NATION, and NATION, respectively. ⟨ATTRIB⟩ also matches the two-word phrase HOME PORT, taking HOME-PORT as its value. For the phrase POWER TYPE, the value is FUEL; for HULL NUMBER it is HULL#. (It is assumed that the codes HOME-PORT, HULL#, LOC, and NAM are peculiar to the database and will not occur in natural language inputs.)

(3) *Subgrammars.* Metasymbols may also be defined by production rules. For example, the call

PD[⟨ATTRIBUTE⟩
  (⟨ATTRIB⟩)
  (LIST (LIST '? ⟨ATTRIB⟩))]

indicates that an ⟨ATTRIBUTE⟩ may be matched by an ⟨ATTRIB⟩, viz.:

⟨ATTRIBUTE⟩ ⟹ ⟨ATTRIB⟩.

For this production, the associated expression is

(LIST (LIST '? ⟨ATTRIB⟩)).

Since the word LENGTH matches ⟨ATTRIB⟩ and causes ⟨ATTRIB⟩ to take LENGTH as its value, the rule above indicates that LENGTH is an instantiation of ⟨ATTRIBUTE⟩. That is,

⟨ATTRIBUTE⟩ ⟹ ⟨ATTRIB⟩ ⟹ LENGTH.

The value assigned to ⟨ATTRIBUTE⟩ when it matches LENGTH is computed by the production's expression as follows:

(LIST (LIST '? ⟨ATTRIB⟩))
⟹ (LIST (LIST '? LENGTH))
⟹ (LIST '(? LENGTH))
⟹ '((? LENGTH)).

This fragment of an IDA command requests the value of the LENGTH field. It was used above in answering the question "What is the length of the Kennedy?"
To recognize inputs such as

PRINT THE LENGTH BEAM AND DRAFT OF THE KENNEDY,

the concept of an ⟨ATTRIBUTE⟩ may be generalized[4] by adding two new productions as follows:

PD[⟨ATTRIBUTE⟩
  (⟨ATTRIB⟩ AND ⟨ATTRIBUTE⟩)
  (CONS (LIST '? ⟨ATTRIB⟩) ⟨ATTRIBUTE⟩)]

PD[⟨ATTRIBUTE⟩
  (⟨ATTRIB⟩ ⟨ATTRIBUTE⟩)
  (CONS (LIST '? ⟨ATTRIB⟩) ⟨ATTRIBUTE⟩)].

(CONS is a Lisp function that adds an element (in this case the list whose first element is ? and whose second element is the value of ⟨ATTRIB⟩) to the front of a list (in this case the value of ⟨ATTRIBUTE⟩).) These productions allow the phrase LENGTH BEAM AND DRAFT to be accounted for in terms of the syntax tree of Figure 3.

(4) *Complete Analysis of a Simple Query.* The examples above have indicated how the pattern

⟨PRESENT⟩ THE ⟨ATTRIBUTE⟩ OF ⟨SHIP⟩

may be defined as a top-level input and how the metasymbol ⟨ATTRIBUTE⟩ may be defined. To complete the analysis of the top-level pattern, consider now the following definitions for ⟨PRESENT⟩ and ⟨SHIP⟩.
To define ⟨PRESENT⟩, the function MS may be used:

MS[⟨PRESENT⟩
  (PRINT LIST SHOW GIVE ((GIVE ME) . PRINT)
  (WHAT IS) . PRINT) ((WHAT ARE) . PRINT))].

This call allows ⟨PRESENT⟩ to match the words PRINT, LIST, SHOW, and GIVE and the phrases GIVE ME, WHAT IS, and WHAT ARE. The values assigned to ⟨PRESENT⟩, which might be used, for example, to direct output to the terminal or to a graphics subsystem, are not of interest here.
A ⟨SHIP⟩ may be designated in any one of a number of ways, the simplest being by name. The call

PD[⟨SHIP⟩
  (⟨SHIP-NAME⟩)
  (LIST (LIST 'NAM 'EQ ⟨SHIP-NAME⟩))]

causes ⟨SHIP⟩ to match a ⟨SHIP-NAME⟩ and to take as its value an IDA command fragment restricting the value of the NAM field to be EQ (equal) to the particular name. ⟨SHIP-NAME⟩ may be defined by MS:

MS[⟨SHIP-NAME⟩
  (CONSTELLATION NAUTILUS

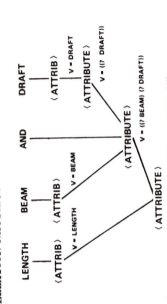

Fig. 3. ⟨ATTRIBUTE⟩ syntax tree

---

[4] The use of two symbols ⟨ATTRIB⟩ and ⟨ATTRIBUTE⟩ could be avoided by letting ⟨ATTRIBUTE⟩ directly match lexical items and by introducing such productions as ⟨ATTRIBUTE⟩ ⟹ ⟨ATTRIBUTE⟩ AND ⟨ATTRIBUTE⟩. Unfortunately, the collapse of the two symbols into one results in both ambiguity and left recursion. LIFER recognizes only one of the ambiguous interpretations. Left recursion can be tolerated by special mechanisms in LIFER's top-down left-to-right parser, but only at a considerable increase in parsing time.

(KENNEDY . JOHN#F.KENNEDY)
((JOHN F. KENNEDY) . JOHN#F.KENNEDY) etc.)].

For an actual database, this list is, of course, much more extensive. To allow the optional use of "the" before the name of a ship, a supplementary production for ⟨SHIP⟩ may be defined:

PD[⟨SHIP⟩
(THE ⟨SHIP⟩)
⟨SHIP⟩].

With these definitions, LIFER has been given all the information needed to process a small class of sentence-level inputs. For example, the complete analysis of the input

WHAT IS THE LENGTH OF THE KENNEDY

is shown in the syntax tree of Figure 4. Note how the query given to IDA was generated by combining fragments from ⟨SHIP⟩ and ⟨ATTRIBUTE⟩. From the definitions for complete inputs defined above, LIFER can infer how to process incomplete inputs in context. For example, having just parsed the input

WHAT IS THE LENGTH OF THE KENNEDY,

the system may, without additional knowledge, also handle the following sequence of incomplete inputs:

BEAM
  (i.e. what is the beam of the Kennedy)
HOME PORT AND CLASS
  (i.e. what is the home port and class of the Kennedy)
NAUTILUS
  (i.e. what is the home port and class of the Nautilus).

The method by which these incomplete inputs are processed is discussed below. Other inputs that the rules defined thus far will accept include:

GIVE ME THE POSITION OF THE NAUTILUS
PRINT THE HULL NUMBER AND POWER TYPE OF CONSTELLATION
SHOW THE COMMANDER COUNTRY AND TYPE OF THE JOHN F. KENNEDY.

3.4 Some Generalizations

The tiny fragment of language defined above already allows English access to most of the fields in the example database, given the name of a ship. This fragment may be expanded easily along many dimensions.

(1) *Generalizing* ⟨SHIP⟩. Generalizing ⟨SHIP⟩ provides one of the most fruitful expansions. Naval ships are divided into major sets called classes. For example, the Constellation is in the Kitty Hawk class. Sometimes users will wish to ask questions about all ships of a particular class; for example, HOW LONG ARE KITTY HAWK CLASS SHIPS. To do this, the language may be extended by the call

PD[⟨SHIP⟩
((CLASS) CLASS SHIP)
(LIST (LIST 'CLASS 'EQ ⟨CLASS⟩))],

where ⟨CLASS⟩ is defined to match class names and takes their database designations as values.[5] After this extension, the system will accept such inputs as

PRINT THE LENGTH OF KITTY HAWK CLASS SHIPS.

A ⟨SHIP⟩ might also match a general category such as CARRIERS, CRUISERS, or MERCHANT SHIPS. Such categories may usually be defined in terms of the TYPE field in the database. For example, CARRIERS are of type CVA, CVAN, or CVS. OILERS are AO or AOR. ⟨CATEGORY⟩ might be defined by

MS[⟨CATEGORY⟩
((CARRIER.((TYPE EQ CV)
        OR (TYPE EQ CVAN)
        OR (TYPE EQ CVS)))
(OILER.((TYPE EQ AO)
        OR (TYPE EQ AOR)))
    etc.)].

A new production for ⟨SHIP⟩ may then be added such as

PD[⟨SHIP⟩
((CATEGORY))
(LIST ⟨CATEGORY⟩)].

With this production, the command

PRINT THE LOCATION OF CARRIERS

will be accepted.

Modifiers such as AMERICAN, NUCLEAR, and CONVENTIONAL are also very useful; for example,

MS[⟨MOD⟩
((AMERICAN . (NATION EQ US))

---

[5] To simplify the language definition, a language builder may supply LIFER with a preprocessor that does certain kinds of morphological transformations. For example, plural nouns such as SHIPS may be converted to the singular SHIP plus the pluralizing suffix -S. Or, as is assumed here, the suffix may simply be discarded.

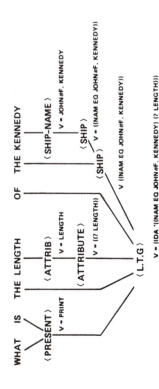

Fig. 4. Syntax tree for a complete question

be used as input to a procedure that can compute the answer from more primitive data. For example, the distance between two ships is not directly available in the example database, although position data is. Suppose the function STEAMING-TIME can take speed and position information returned by IDA and calculate the time for the first ship to travel to the position of the second ship. Then, after defining ⟨SHIP2⟩ like ⟨SHIP⟩,

PD[⟨SHIP2⟩
((SHIP))
⟨SHIP⟩],

a new top-level production may be defined as follows:

PD[(L.T.G)
(HOW MANY HOURS IS ⟨SHIP⟩ FROM ⟨SHIP2⟩)
(STEAMING-TIME
(IDA (APPEND '((? SPEED) (? LOC)) ⟨SHIP⟩))
(IDA (CONS '(? LOC) ⟨SHIP2⟩)))].

This production allows such queries as

HOW MANY HOURS IS KENNEDY FROM THE CONSTELLATION.

3.5 Extending the Lexicon with Predicates

In certain instances, it is impractical to use the MS function to explicitly list all of the symbols that might match some metasymbol. For example, if the metasymbol ⟨NUMBER⟩ is to match any number, then MS is of little value. For such cases, LIFER allows a metasymbol to be associated with a predicate function. The metasymbol will match any symbol for which the predicate returns a non-NIL value. When such a match occurs, the metasymbol will take as its semantic value the response returned by the application of the predicate.

To define a metasymbol in terms of a predicate, the function MP (make predicate) is used. For example,

MP[⟨NUMBER⟩ NUMBERP]

defines ⟨NUMBER⟩ to match any symbol for which LISP predicate function NUMBERP returns a non-NIL value. When applied to numbers, NUMBERP returns the number itself. When applied to anything else, it returns NIL.

As the following questions indicate, ⟨NUMBER⟩ has many uses in the example database:

WHAT CARRIERS HAVE LENGTHS GREATER THAN 1000 FEET
HOW FAR IS CONSTELLATION FROM 40 DEGREES NORTH 6 DEGREES EAST
WHAT SHIPS ARE WITHIN 100 MILES OF KENNEDY.

As the size of the lexicon becomes large, the predicate feature may be used to push certain large classes of words out of the natural language system and into the database itself. For example, ⟨SHIP-NAME⟩ could be defined in terms of a predicate that accesses the NAM field of the database. (This would slow the parsing operation, of course, and spelling correction could not be performed easily.)

(NUCLEAR . (FUEL EQ NUCLEAR))
(CONVENTIONAL . (FUEL EQ DIESEL))
etc.)].

By adding

PD[⟨SHIP⟩
((MOD) ⟨SHIP⟩)
(CONS ⟨MOD⟩ ⟨SHIP⟩)],

the system will then process inputs such as

GIVE ME THE POSITION OF THE AMERICAN NUCLEAR CARRIERS.

Superlative modifiers, such as FASTEST and SHORTEST, may be defined:

MS[⟨MOD⟩
((FASTEST . (* MAX SPEED))
(SLOWEST . (* MIN SPEED))
(LONGEST . (* MAX LENGTH))
etc.]

Then the system will accept inputs such as

GIVE ME THE NAME AND LOCATION OF THE FASTEST AMERICAN OILERS.

This would translate into the IDA call

(IDA '((* MAX SPEED) (NATION EQ US)
((TYPE EQ AO) OR (TYPE EQ AOR))
(? NAM) (? LOC))).

(2) *Generalizing* ⟨L.T.G⟩. New sentence-level productions, defined in terms of the more primitive metasymbols already described to LIFER, also greatly extend the range of language accepted. For example,

PD[(L.T.G)
((PRESENT) ⟨SHIP⟩)
(IDA (CONS '(? NAM) ⟨SHIP⟩))]

allows inputs such as

WHAT ARE THE FASTEST NUCLEAR SUBMARINES
PRINT THE CARRIERS

and

GIVE ME THE KITTY HAWK CLASS SHIPS.

As another example,

PD[(L.T.G)
(WHO COMMANDS THE ⟨SHIP⟩)
(IDA (CONS '(? COMMANDER) ⟨SHIP⟩))]

allows the input

WHO COMMANDS THE KENNEDY.

(3) *Calculated Answers.* Sometimes a database does not contain the information needed to answer a question directly, but nevertheless contains information that may

3.6 Accepting Metalanguage Inputs

(1) *Interrogating the Language System.* It is possible to define input patterns that make reference to the LIFER package itself. For example, LIFER contains a function called SYMBOL.INFO which takes a metasymbol as its argument and prints lexical items, patterns, and predicates that may be used to match the symbol. The interface builder may incorporate this function in response expressions as in

PD[⟨L.T.G⟩
    (HOW IS ⟨SYMBOL⟩ USED)
    (SYMBOL.INFO ⟨SYMBOL⟩)]

After this call to PD,[6] a user might ask the metaquestion

HOW IS ⟨SHIP⟩ USED

and receive the reply

⟨SHIP⟩ MAY BE ANY SEQUENCE OF WORDS FOLLOWING ONE OF THE PATTERNS:
    ⟨SHIP⟩ ⟹ ⟨SHIP-NAME⟩
             THE ⟨SHIP⟩
             ⟨CLASS⟩ CLASS SHIP
             ⟨MOD⟩ ⟨SHIP⟩.

Using other system interrogation functions, it is possible to provide in an application language for such inputs as

PRINT THE GRAMMAR ON FILE APP.GRAM
DISPLAY THE PRODUCTIONS EXPANDING ⟨SHIP⟩
SHOW LEXICAL ENTRIES FOR CATEGORY ⟨SHIP-NAME⟩
WHAT PREDICATE DEFINES ⟨NUMBER⟩
DRAW THE SYNTAX TREE FOR THE LAST INPUT
HOW WOULD YOU PARSE "HOW FAST IS KENNEDY",
IN WHAT PRODUCTIONS DOES ⟨SHIP⟩ APPEAR ON THE RIGHT.

Metaquestions requesting general information about the system, such as

WHAT KIND OF INFORMATION DO YOU KNOW ABOUT
WHAT'S IN THE DATABASE
HELP,

may easily be included in the application language. Top-level response expressions for such inputs may simply return canned explanation texts. With more sophistication, the expressions might access a semantic schema of the database to help formulate an up-to-date reply.

(2) *Personalizing the Application Language.* LIFER contains a function called SYNONYM that allows a new word to be defined as having the same meaning as a model word that is already known to LIFER. Using this function, an interface builder may introduce structures into the application language that allow users to define their own synonyms at run time. In particular,

PD[⟨L.T.G⟩
    (DEFINE ⟨NEW-WORD⟩ LIKE ⟨OLD-WORD⟩)
    (SYNONYM ⟨NEW-WORD⟩ ⟨OLD-WORD⟩)]

allows the parser to accept inputs such as

DEFINE JFK LIKE KENNEDY.

The symbols ⟨NEW-WORD⟩ and ⟨OLD-WORD⟩ are defined by predicates that will match any word. SYNONYM works by copying lexical information from ⟨OLD-WORD⟩ to ⟨NEW-WORD⟩.

LIFER also contains a function called PARAPHRASE that allows a new sequence of words to be defined as having the same meaning as a model sequence of words that the parser already accepts as a complete sentence. Using function PARAPHRASE in a response expression, the interface builder may extend the grammar by

PD[⟨L.T.G⟩
    (LET ⟨NEW-SEQUENCE⟩ BE A PARAPHRASE OF ⟨OLD-SENTENCE⟩)
    (PARAPHRASE ⟨NEW-SEQUENCE⟩ ⟨OLD-SENTENCE⟩)]

where ⟨NEW-SEQUENCE⟩ matches any sequence of words and returns a list of the matched words as its value, and ⟨OLD-SENTENCE⟩ matches any sequence of words currently accepted as a sentence in the application language.

This new rule allows computer-naive users to personalize the syntactic constructions understood by the system at run time. For example, the user might say

LET "REPORT ON KENNEDY" BE A PARAPHRASE OF
"PRINT THE LOCATION AND COMMANDER OF KENNEDY".

The expression associated with the top-level production that matches this input sentence calls upon the paraphraser. Given the language definition defined above, LIFER then automatically adds the new production

⟨L.T.G⟩ ⟹ REPORT ON ⟨SHIP⟩

to the system, with an appropriate response expression. This new, user-defined production will allow the system to accept such new inputs as

REPORT ON THE KENNEDY
REPORT ON OILERS
REPORT ON THE FASTEST AMERICAN SUBMARINES.

LIFER's methods for learning paraphrases are discussed below.

3.7 Extendibility

The preceding subsections have indicated how a few simple notions may be drawn together to create a small interface. But can the same notions be used to create much more sophisticated systems? Until our recent experience, we would have joined others in answering, "Not likely." Long before reaching an acceptable level of performance, previous language systems, including our own, have generally grown so complex and unwieldy that further extension has been stifled.

---

[6] As specified more fully in [10], the metasymbol ⟨SYMBOL⟩ may itself be defined by function MP, using a predicate that sees whether its argument is included in the list of defined metasymbols. Being so defined, ⟨SYMBOL⟩ can even match itself so that the input HOW IS ⟨SYMBOL⟩ USED may be parsed and answered.

by successfully transversing some branch of the transition tree that encodes the productions expanding the metasymbol.

At the top level, if the parser reaches a response expression as a result of accounting for the last word of an input, then a top-level match for the input has been found and the response expression is evaluated to compute a response.

5. IMPLEMENTATION OF SPECIAL LIFER FEATURES

This section presents an overview of LIFER's implementation of the spelling corrector, elliptical processor, and paraphraser.

5.1 Implementation of Spelling Correction

Each time LIFER's left-to-right, ATN parser discovers that it can no longer follow transitions along the current path, it records the failure on a failpoint list. Each entry on this list indicates the state of the system when the failure occurred (i.e. the position in the transition net and the values of various stacks and registers) and the current position in the input string. Local ambiguities and false paths make it quite normal for many failpoints to be noted even when a perfectly acceptable input is processed.

If a complete parse is found for an input, the failpoints are ignored. But if an input cannot be parsed, the list of failpoints is used by the spelling corrector, which selects those failpoints associated with the rightmost position in the input at which failpoints were recorded. It is assumed that failpoints occurring to the left were not caused by spelling errors, since some transitions using the words at those positions must have been successful for there to be failpoints to their right.[7]

The spelling corrector further restricts the rightmost failpoints by looking for cases in which a rightmost failpoint G is dominated by another rightmost failpoint F. G is dominated by F if G is a failpoint at the beginning of a subordinate transition tree that was reached in an attempt to expand F.

Working with the rightmost dominating failpoints, the spelling corrector finds all categories of words that would be valid at the point where the suspected misspelling occurred. This typically requires an exploration of subgrammars. Using the INTERLISP spelling corrector, the word of the input string associated with the rightmost failpoints is compared with the words of the categories just found. If the misspelled word is sufficiently similar to any of these lexical items, the closest match is substituted. Failpoints associated with lexical categories that include the new word are then sequentially restarted until one leads to a successful parse. (This may produce more spelling corrections further to the right.) If all restarts with the new word fail, other close lexical items are substituted for the misspelled word. If these also fail, LIFER prints an error message.

[7] This heuristic can cause LIFER to fail to find and correct certain errors. For example, if the user types CRAFT for DRAFT in WHAT DRAFT DOES THE ROARK HAVE, the spelling error will not be caught since a sentence such as WHAT CRAFT ARE NEAR ROARK would account for the initial sequence WHAT CRAFT. This is traded off against faster processing for the majority of spelling errors.

In designing LIFER, much attention has been given to the problem of supplying interface builders with an environment supporting the incremental development of relatively broad interfaces. All LIFER functions are interactive. Parsing, and language specification tasks may be i. ermixed, allowing interface builders to operate in a rapid, extend-and-test mode. Transition trees, which are an efficient representation for the parser to work with, are automatically produced from productions, which we have found to be an efficient representation for interface builders to work with. The system contains a grammar editor and numerous special functions for answering questions about the structure of the language definition and for tracing and debugging a grammar. Details concerning these and other features of LIFER are specified more fully in the LIFER Manual [10].

We believe that the support features of LIFER have enabled us to give the INLAND language broader coverage than previous systems. Unfortunately, we know of no adequate measure of "breadth of coverage." However, some feeling for the types of inputs accepted by LADDER may be gained by considering a sample of acceptable inputs, such as that shown in Figure 1.

4. THE TRANSITION TREE PARSER

The LIFER parser is a top-down, left-to-right parser based on a simplification of the augmented transition network (ATN) system developed by Woods [23]. Rather than use true ATNs, LIFER works with transition trees. If ⟨L.T.G⟩ is defined by the productions

⟨L.T.G⟩ ⇒ ⟨PRESENT⟩ THE ⟨ATTRIBUTE⟩ OF ⟨SHIP⟩ | e1
    ⇒ ⟨PRESENT⟩ ⟨SHIP'S⟩ ⟨ATTRIBUTE⟩ | e2
    ⇒ HOW MANY ⟨SHIP⟩ ARE THERE | e3
    ⇒ HOW MANY ⟨SHIP⟩ ARE THERE WITH ⟨PROPERTY⟩ | e4,

then the transition (not syntax) tree of Figure 5 would be constructed for use by the parser.

Starting at the box labeled ⟨L.T.G⟩, the parser attempts (nondeterministically) to move toward the response expressions on the right. At each step, the parser may move to the right on a branch if the left part of the remaining portion of the input can be matched by the symbol on the branch. Literal words on a branch can be matched only by themselves. A metasymbol, such as ⟨PRESENT⟩, may be matched by a lexical item in the associated set created by MS. Or it may be matched by the predicate, if any, that has been defined for the metasymbol. Or it may be matched

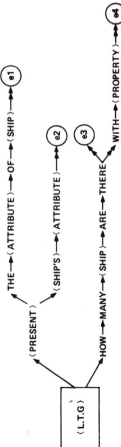

Fig. 5. Transition tree.

5.2 Implementation of Ellipsis

LIFER's mechanism for treating elliptical inputs presumes that the application language is defined by a semantic grammar so that a considerable amount of semantic information is encoded in the syntactic categories. Thus similar syntactic constructions are expected to be similar semantically. LIFER's treatment of ellipsis is based on this notion of similarity. During elliptical processing, LIFER is prepared to accept any string of words that is syntactically analogous to any contiguous substring of words in the last input. (If the last input was elliptical, its expansion into a complete sentence is used.)

LIFER's concept of analogy appeals to the syntax tree of the last input that was successfully analyzed by the system. For any contiguous substring of words in the last input, an "analogy pattern" may be defined by an abstraction process that works backward through the old syntax tree from the words of the substring toward the root. Whenever the syntax tree shows a portion of the substring to be a complete expansion of a syntactic category, the category name is substituted for that portion. The analogy pattern is the final result after all such substitutions. For example, consider how an analogy pattern may be found for the substring

OF SANTA INEZ,

using the syntax tree shown in Figure 6 for a previous input, WHAT IS THE LENGTH OF SANTA INEZ.

Note that the syntax tree used in Figure 6 reflects production rules similar to those defined previously, but introduces a new metasymbol, ⟨ITEM⟩, to add more substance to the discussion. Since the SANTA INEZ portion of the substring is a complete expansion of ⟨SHIP-NAME⟩, the substring is rewritten as OF ⟨SHIP-NAME⟩. Similarly, since ⟨SHIP⟩ expands to ⟨SHIP-NAME⟩, the substring is rewritten as OF ⟨SHIP⟩. Since no other portions of the substring are complete expansions of other syntactic categories in the tree, the process stops and OF ⟨SHIP⟩ is accepted as the most general analogy pattern. If the current input matches this analogy pattern, LIFER will accept it as a legitimate elliptical input. For example, the analogy pattern OF ⟨SHIP⟩, extracted from the last input, may be used to match such current elliptical inputs as

OF THE KENNEDY
OF THE FASTEST NUCLEAR CARRIER

and

OF KITTY HAWK CLASS SHIPS.

Note that the expansion of ⟨SHIP⟩ need not parallel its expansion in the old input that originated the analogy pattern. For example, OF KITTY HAWK CLASS SHIPS is not matched by expanding ⟨SHIP⟩ to ⟨SHIP-NAME⟩ but by expanding ⟨SHIP⟩ to ⟨CLASS⟩ CLASS SHIP.

To compute responses for elliptical inputs matching OF ⟨SHIP⟩, LIFER works its way back through the old syntax tree from the common parent of OF ⟨SHIP⟩ toward the root. First, the routine for computing the value of an ⟨ITEM⟩ from constituents of the production

⟨ITEM⟩ ⇒ THE ⟨ATTRIBUTE⟩ OF ⟨SHIPS⟩

is invoked, using the new value of ⟨SHIP⟩ (which appeared in the current elliptical input) and the old value of ⟨ATTRIBUTE⟩ from the last sentence. Then, using the newly computed value for ⟨ITEM⟩ and the old value for ⟨PRESENT⟩, a new value is similarly computed for ⟨L.T.G⟩, the root of the syntax tree.

Some other substrings with their associated analogy patterns are shown below, along with possible new elliptical inputs matching the patterns:

substring: THE LENGTH
pattern: THE ⟨ATTRIBUTE⟩
a match: THE BEAM AND DRAFT

substring: LENGTH OF SANTA INEZ
pattern: ⟨ATTRIBUTE⟩ OF ⟨SHIP⟩
a match: HOME PORTS OF AMERICAN CARRIERS

substring: WHAT IS THE LENGTH
pattern: ⟨PRESENT⟩ THE ⟨ATTRIBUTE⟩
a match: PRINT THE NATIONALITY

substring: WHAT IS THE LENGTH OF SANTA INEZ
pattern: ⟨L.T.G⟩
a match: [any complete sentence]

For purposes of efficiency, LIFER's elliptical routines have been coded in such a way that the actual generation of analogy patterns is avoided. [8] Nevertheless, the effect is conceptually equivalent to attempting parses based on the analogy patterns of each of the contiguous substrings of the last input.

5.3 Implementation of Paraphrase

LIFER's paraphrase mechanism also takes advantage of semantically-oriented syntactic categories and makes use of syntax trees. In the typical case, the paraphraser is given a model sentence, which the system can already understand, and a paraphrase. The paraphraser's general strategy is to analyze the model sentence and then look for similar structures in the paraphrase string. In particular, the paraphraser invokes the parser to produce a syntax tree of the

---

[8] See Hendrix [11] for details of the algorithm.

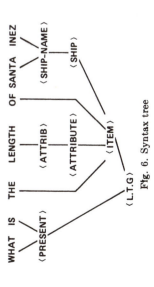

WHAT IS THE LENGTH OF SANTA INEZ

⟨PRESENT⟩ ⟨ATTRIB⟩ ⟨ATTRIBUTE⟩ ⟨SHIP-NAME⟩ ⟨SHIP⟩ ⟨ITEM⟩ ⟨L.T.G⟩

Fig. 6. Syntax tree

model. Using this tree, the paraphraser determines all proper subphrases of the model, i.e. all substrings that are complete expansions of one of the syntactic categories listed in the tree. Any of these model subphrases that also appear in the paraphrase string are assumed to play the same role in the paraphrase as in the model itself. Thus the semantically-oriented syntactic categories that account for these subphrases in the model are reused to account for the corresponding subphrases of the paraphrase. Moreover, the relationship between the syntactic categories that is expressed in the syntax tree of the model forms a basis for establishing the relationship between the corresponding syntactic units inferred for the paraphrase.

(1) *Defining a Paraphrase Production.* To find correspondences between the model and the paraphrase, the subphrases of the model are first sorted. Longer phrases have preference over shorter phrases, and for two phrases of the same length, the leftmost is taken first. For example, the sorted phrases for the tree of Figure 6 are

1. ⟨ITEM⟩   THE LENGTH OF SANTA INEZ
2. ⟨PRESENT⟩   WHAT IS
3. ⟨SHIP-NAME⟩ SANTA INEZ   —not used
4. ⟨SHIP⟩   SANTA INEZ
5. ⟨ATTRIB⟩   LENGTH   —not used
6. ⟨ATTRIBUTE⟩ LENGTH.

Because the syntax tree indicates ⟨SHIP⟩ ⇒ ⟨SHIP-NAME⟩ ⇒ SANTA INEZ, both ⟨SHIP-NAME⟩ and ⟨SHIP⟩ account for the same subphrase. For such cases, only the most general syntactic category (⟨SHIP⟩) is considered. The category ⟨ATTRIB⟩ is similarly dropped.

Beginning with the first (longest) subphrase, the subphrases are matched against sequences of words in the paraphrase string. (If a subphrase matches two sequences of words, only the leftmost match is used.) The longer subphrases are given preference since matches for them will lead to generalizations incorporating matches for the shorter phrases contained within them. Whenever a match is found, the syntactic category associated with the subphrase is substituted for the matching word sequence in the paraphrase. This process continues until matches have been attempted for all subphrases.

For example, suppose the paraphrase proposed for the question of Figure 6 is

FOR SANTA INEZ GIVE ME THE LENGTH.

Subphrases 1 and 2, listed above, do not match substrings in this paraphrase. Subphrase 3 is not considered, since it is dominated by subphrase 4. Subphrase 4 does match a sequence of words in the paraphrase string. Substituting the associated category name for the word sequence yields a new paraphrase string:

FOR ⟨SHIP⟩ GIVE ME THE LENGTH.

Subphrase 5 is not considered, but subphrase 6 matches a sequence of words in the updated paraphrase string. The associated substitution yields

FOR ⟨SHIP⟩ GIVE ME THE ⟨ATTRIBUTE⟩.

Since there are no more subphrases to try, the structure

⟨L.T.G.⟩ ⇒ FOR ⟨SHIP⟩ GIVE ME THE ⟨ATTRIBUTE⟩

is created as a new production to account for the paraphrase and for similar inputs such as

FOR THE FASTEST AMERICAN SUB GIVE ME THE POSITION AND HOME PORT.

(2) *Defining a Response Expression for the Paraphrase Production.* A new semantic response expression indicating how to respond to inputs matching this paraphrase production is programmed automatically from information in the syntax tree of the model. In particular, the syntax tree indicates which productions were used in the model to expand various syntactic categories. Associated with each of these productions is the corresponding response expression for computing the interpretation of the subphrase from subphrase constituents. The paraphraser reuses selected response expressions of the model to create a new expression for the same paraphrase production. The evaluation of this new expression produces the same effect that would be produced if the expressions of the model were reevaluated. Metasymbols that appear in both the paraphrase production and the model remain as variables in the new response expression. Those symbols of the model that do not appear in the paraphrase production are replaced in the expression by the constant values to which they were assigned in the model.

6. DISCUSSION

As implied by Figure 1 and the examples given in the Appendix, the INLAND system is a habitable, rather robust, real-time interface to a large database and is fully capable of successfully accepting natural language inputs from inexperienced users. In the preceding sections, we have indicated some of the key techniques used in creating this system. We now seek to place our previous remarks in perspective by considering some of the limitations of the system, the roles played by the nature of our task and the tools we built in developing the system, and some of the similarities and differences between other systems and our own.

6.1 Limitations

In considering the limitations of our work, the reader should distinguish between limitations in the current INLAND grammar and limitations in the underlying LIFER system.

(1) *Syntactic Limitations*
(a) *The Class of Languages Covered by LIFER.* Consider the set of sentences that LIFER can accept. Because in the worst case a special top-level production may be defined in LIFER to cover any (finite-length) sentence that an interface builder may wish to include in the application language, it is impossible to exhibit a single sentence that the LIFER parser cannot be made to accept. Therefore, the only meaningful questions concerning syntactic limitations of LIFER must relate to LIFER's ability to use limited memory in covering infinite or large finite sets of sentences.

LIFER application languages are specified by augmented context-free[9] grammars. Each rule in the grammar, as discussed previously, includes a context-free production, plus an arbitrarily complex response expression, which is the "augmentation." Although a purely context-free system would severely restrict the set of (nonfinite) languages that LIFER could accept, the use of augmentation gives the LIFER parser the power of a Turing machine. The critical question is whether or not the context-free productions and their more powerful augmentations can be made to support one another in meaningful ways.

To see the interplay between augmentation and context-free rules in the recognition of a classic example of non-context-free languages, consider the language composed of one or more X's followed by an equal number of Y's followed by an equal number of Z's. Let $\langle x \rangle$ be defined as

$$\langle x \rangle \Rightarrow X \mid 1$$
$$\langle x \rangle \Rightarrow X \langle x \rangle \mid (\text{PLUS } 1 \langle x \rangle).$$

Thus $\langle x \rangle$ matches an arbitrary sequence of X's and takes as its value the number of X's in the string. Similar definitions may be made for $\langle y \rangle$ and $\langle z \rangle$. A top-level sentence may be defined by the pattern $\langle x \rangle \langle y \rangle \langle z \rangle$, but the augmentation must check to see that the numeric values assigned to the metasymbols are all equal. If they are equal, the augmentation expression returns some appropriate response. But if they are unequal, the expression returns the special symbol *ERROR*, which the LIFER parser traps as a "semantic" (as opposed to syntactic) rejection. The Turing machine power of LIFER is illustrated by the following trivial grammar:

```
⟨PRE-SENTENCE⟩ ⟹ ⟨WORD⟩ | (LIST ⟨WORD⟩)
               ⟹ ⟨WORD⟩ ⟨PRE-SENTENCE⟩ | (CONS ⟨WORD⟩
                                           ⟨PRE-SENTENCE⟩)

⟨SENTENCE⟩      ⟹ ⟨PRE-SENTENCE⟩
                | (TMPARSE ⟨PRE-SENTENCE⟩)
```

This grammar simply collects all of the words of the input into a list which is then passed to function TMPARSE, a parser of Turing machine power. In this extreme case, the LIFER parser makes virtually no use of the context-free productions, but relies exclusively on the augmentation. LIFER is best used in the middle ground between this extreme and a purely context-free system.

In other words, the class of languages for which LIFER was designed may be characterized as those allowing much of their structure to be defined by context-free rules but requiring occasional augmentation. It has been our experience that much of the subset of English used for asking questions about a command and control database falls in this class. However, we have not considered certain complex types of transformations which will be discussed in the next subsection.

(b) *Troublesome Syntactic Phenomena.* English speakers and writers often omit from a sentence a series of words that do not form a complete syntactic unit. For example, consider the following family of conjunctive sentences:

(1) WHAT LAFAYETTE AND WASHINGTON CLASS SUBS ARE WITHIN 500 MILES OF GIBRALTAR

(2) WHAT LAFAYETTE CLASS SUBS AND WASHINGTON CLASS SUBS ARE WITHIN 500 MILES OF GIBRALTAR

(3) WHAT LAFAYETTE CLASS SUBS AND KITTY HAWK CLASS CARRIERS IN THE ATLANTIC ARE WITHIN 500 MILES OF GIBRALTAR

(4) WHAT LAFAYETTE CLASS SUBS IN AND PORTS ON THE ATLANTIC ARE WITHIN 500 MILES OF GIBRALTAR

(5) WHAT LAFAYETTE CLASS SUBS IN THE ATLANTIC AND KITTY HAWK CLASS CARRIERS IN THE MEDITERRANEAN SOON WILL BE WITHIN 500 MILES OF GIBRALTAR.

Sentence (1) omits the fragment CLASS SUBS ARE WITHIN 500 MILES OF GIBRALTAR from the "complete" question WHAT LAFAYETTE CLASS SUBS ARE WITHIN 500 MILES OF GIBRALTAR AND WHAT WASHINGTON CLASS SUBS ARE WITHIN 500 MILES OF GIBRALTAR. Note that the omitted fragment does not correspond to any well-formed syntactic unit, but begins in the middle of the noun phrase WHAT LAFAYETTE CLASS SUBS and continues to its right. Moreover, the fragment of the noun phrase that is left behind, namely, WHAT LAFAYETTE, is not likely to be a well-formed syntactic unit, because one would expect to have WHAT combine with LAFAYETTE-CLASS-SUBS rather than have WHAT-LAFAYETTE combine with CLASS-SUBS. As the family of sentences above illustrates, the omission of words, signaled by the conjunction AND, may be moved to the right through the sentence one word at a time, slicing up the well-formed syntactic units at arbitrary positions. INLAND has no difficulty in accepting either conjunctions or disjunctions of well-formed syntactic categories, but LIFER provides no general mechanism for dealing with omissions that slice through categories at arbitrary points.

In the SYSCONJ facility of Woods [24], special mechanisms for handling a large (but not exhaustive) class of conjunction constructions were built into the parser. Roughly, when SYSCONJ encounters the conjunction "AND" in an input X AND Y, it nondeterministically attempts to break both X and Y into three (possibly empty) parts X1-X2-X3 and Y1-Y2-Y3, such that X1-X2-X3-Y2-Y3 and X1-X2-Y1-Y2-Y3 parse as sentences with the same basic syntactic structure. In particular, X2-X3-Y2 and X2-Y1-Y2 must be expansions of the same metasymbol. The effect of SYSCONJ is to transform X1-X2-X3-AND-Y1-Y2-Y3 into X1-X2-X3-Y2-Y3 and X1-X2-Y1-Y2-Y3.

For example,

WHAT LAFAYETTE AND WASHINGTON CLASS SUBS ARE THERE

may be analyzed as

WHAT	empty	LAFAYETTE	AND	WASHINGTON	CLASS SUBS	ARE THERE
X1	X2	X3	and	Y1	Y2	Y3

[9] See Hopcroft and Ullman [12] for definitions of terms such as "context-free" and "context-sensitive."

Both X1-X2-X3-Y2-Y3 (WHAT LAFAYETTE CLASS SUBS ARE THERE) and X1-X2-Y1-Y2-Y3 (WHAT WASHINGTON CLASS SUBS ARE THERE) are parsed by what would correspond in INLAND to the sentence-level production

⟨L.T.G⟩ ⟹ WHAT ⟨SHIP⟩ ARE THERE

and both X2-X3-Y2 (LAFAYETTE CLASS SUBS) and X2-Y1-Y2 (WASHINGTON CLASS SUBS) are expansions of the same metasymbol, ⟨SHIP⟩. In effect, the original input is transformed into WHAT LAFAYETTE CLASS SUBS ARE THERE and WHAT WASHINGTON CLASS SUBS ARE THERE.

Handling conjunctions is just one example of the general need to perform transformations at parse time. A similar phenomenon occurs with comparative clauses, but much more is omitted and transformed. For example,

THE KITTY HAWK CARRIES MORE MEN THAN THE WASHINGTON

may be viewed as a transformed and condensed form of

THE KITTY HAWK CARRIES X-MANY MEN AND
THE WASHINGTON CARRIES Y-MANY MEN AND
X IS MORE THAN Y.

For further discussion of this subject, see Paxton [15].

(c) *YES/NO Questions.* A limitation of INLAND, although not of LIFER, is that few YES/NO questions are covered. The reason for this is pragmatic—INLAND users do not ask them. Upon reflection, the motivation for this is clear—WH questions (i.e. questions asking who, what, where, when, or how) produce more information for the questioner at a lower cost. A user might ask

IS THE KENNEDY 1000 FEET LONG,

but it is shorter to ask

HOW LONG IS THE KENNEDY,

and if the answer to the first question is NO (and if the system is so inconsiderate as to not indicate the correct length), then the user may still have to ask for the length.

Creating a grammar for YES/NO questions is easy enough. For example,

PD[⟨L.T.G⟩
   (IS ⟨NUMBER⟩ ⟨UNIT⟩ THE ⟨ATTRIB⟩ OF ⟨SHIP⟩)
   (YESNO.NUM.ATT ⟨NUMBER⟩ ⟨UNIT⟩ ⟨ATTRIB⟩ ⟨SHIP⟩)]

might be used to allow the input

IS 1000 FEET THE LENGTH OF THE KENNEDY.

Function YESNO.NUM.ATT finds the ⟨ATTRIB⟩ of ⟨SHIP⟩ using IDA. Knowing the units in which the database stores values of ⟨ATTRIB⟩, YESNO.NUM.ATT converts the returned answer into the units specified by ⟨UNIT⟩ and compares the converted value to ⟨NUMBER⟩. If the units are valid and the numbers match, YES is returned; otherwise NO is returned, and the correct answer, as computed by IDA, is printed.

(d) *Assertions.* INLAND was designed for retrieval and therefore does not handle such inputs as

THE LENGTH OF THE KENNEDY IS 1072 FEET
LET THE LENGTH OF THE KENNEDY BE 1072 FEET
SET THE LENGTH OF THE KENNEDY TO 1072 FEET.

Moreover, IDA itself does not provide for updating the database. Extending the language with new productions such as

⟨L.T.G⟩ ⟹ SET THE ⟨ATTRIBUTE⟩ OF ⟨SHIP⟩ TO ⟨VALUE⟩

would be easy, but there are serious database issues involved regarding consistency, security, and priority. Such database problems are beyond the scope of our research.

(e) *Irregular Coverage.* One of the consequences of the ease with which interface builders can add new patterns to a LIFER grammar is that gaps may appear in coverage. For example, suppose a given language definition contains no passive constructions. Through the use of paraphrase or by direct action on the part of the interface builder, the language may be extended to cover some, but perhaps not all, passive constructions. That is, the system might be made to accept

(1) THE KENNEDY IS OWNED BY WHOM,

but not

(2) THE KENNEDY IS COMMANDED BY WHOM.

(The semantically-oriented syntactic categories for OWNED and COMMANDED may differ.) If a user knows that the system accepts (1) and that the system accepts the active

(3) WHO COMMANDS THE KENNEDY,

then he is likely to be upset when input (2) is not accepted.

In creating the language specification for INLAND, we have tried to minimize such irregularities in coverage by applying standard techniques of modular programming to the grammar specification. We feel this has been reasonably successful. Because LIFER gives the inference builder the freedom to add particular instances and subclasses of linguistic phenomena, it is his responsibility to avoid the gaps in coverage that may result.

(2) *Limitations Regarding Ambiguity.* The LIFER parser does not deal with syntactic ambiguity directly, but accepts its first successful analysis as being the sole interpretation of an input.[10] Because English contains truly ambiguous con-

---

[10] On October 31, 1977, LIFER was modified to allow optional production of all syntactically correct readings of an input. However, INLAND has not yet been revised to take advantage of this new option. When ambiguity is discovered, LIFER calls a user-defined subroutine with the list of parse trees (including response expressions and variable bindings at each non-terminal node) for all readings. One of the trees is to be returned for execution of the root-level response expression. A default "user" subroutine is supplied with LIFER that prints the various parse trees and asks the user to select one by number. More sophisticated subroutines are expected to be written that will enter into more natural clarification dialogues.

structions, even when semantic considerations (the "augmentations") are taken into account, this limitation can be serious. For example, in the request

(1) NAME THE SHIPS FROM AMERICAN HOME PORTS
    THAT ARE WITHIN 500 MILES OF NORFOLK

the phrase THAT ARE WITHIN 500 MILES OF NORFOLK might modify either the SHIPS or the PORTS. The choice will, of course, influence the response made to the user. The current LIFER parser is biased against deep parses and will only consider the interpretation in which the clause modifies SHIPS. Even a single word can produce difficulties. For example, the word NORFOLK in request (1) could refer to a port in Virginia, a port in Great Britain, an American frigate, or a British destroyer. Thus the request is at least eight ways ambiguous. Codd [3] has studied at some length the problem of ambiguity in the context of practical database systems and has developed the strategy of engaging in a dialogue in which the system articulates ambiguities (and other problems) and asks questions of the user to clarify the intent of his requests.

In addition to the simple syntactic form of ambiguity, exemplified by request (1), other forms of ambiguity may arise. For example, the question

(2) IS KENNEDY IN RADAR RANGE OF THE KNOX

is syntactically unambiguous, but the meaning might be either

IS KENNEDY IN KNOX'S RADAR RANGE

or

IS KNOX IN KENNEDY'S RADAR RANGE.

This example represents a purely semantic ambiguity. Similarly,

(3) IS KENNEDY NEARER TO GIBRALTAR THAN KITTY HAWK

might be considered syntactically unambiguous in its present form, yet it has two possible meanings. By adding "missing words" at two different points in the input it is possible to produce the readings

IS THE KENNEDY NEARER TO GIBRALTAR THAN
    the kennedy is near to THE KITTY HAWK

and

IS THE KENNEDY NEARER TO GIBRALTAR THAN
    THE KITTY HAWK is near to Gibraltar.

Examples of ambiguity such as queries (1), (2), and (3) just given begin to show the difficulty of dealing with the problem in any general way. However, in the domain of INLAND, ambiguities have tended to arise only infrequently and have presented only minor problems for our particular application. Fortunately, our users have been very helpful by tending to avoid the use of the long and complex constructions that are most likely to lead to ambiguities. Perhaps this is because the teletype medium inclines users to prefer short, simple constructions.

Even though LIFER does not deal with ambiguity directly, certain types of ambiguities may be trapped and treated by using the response expressions of LIFER production rules. For example,

```
PD(L.T.G)
  (IS (SHIP1) IN (RANGE-TYPE) RANGE OF (SHIP2))
  (COMPUTE.RANGE (SHIP1) (SHIP2) (RANGE-TYPE))]
```

will accept such inputs as

IS KENNEDY WITHIN RADAR RANGE OF KNOX

and call the function COMPUTE.RANGE to respond. COMPUTE.RANGE is given the two ships and the range type as an input. Knowing the pattern to be inherently ambiguous, COMPUTE.RANGE may enter into a (formal) conversation with the user to resolve the ambiguity.

The INLAND grammar also tries to avoid ambiguity whenever possible. For example, the phrase AMERICAN ARMORED TROOP CARRIER might mean a ship (of any nationality) that carries armored troops from the U.S. military, or an American ship that carries armored troops (of any nationality), or a ship that carries troops that were armored by the U.S., or a ship that was armored by the U.S. and that carries troops, or any one of several other combinations. In INLAND, ARMORED-TROOP-CARRIER is recognized as a fixed phrase and all the problems with ambiguity vanish.

(3) Limitations Regarding Definite Noun Phrases

(a) The Restricted Context Problem. A phrase such as THE AMERICAN SUBS may be used to refer to different American submarines, depending upon the "context" in which it appears. For example, if the Washington, the Churchill, and the Lincoln are being discussed, then THE AMERICAN SUBS in

HOW OLD ARE THE AMERICAN SUBS

refers to the Washington and the Lincoln. Had the current context concerned the Roosevelt, Jefferson, and Leninsky Komsomol, then THE AMERICAN SUBS would have referred to the Roosevelt and the Jefferson. The point is that the meanings of certain noun phrases are dependent upon the contexts in which the phrases appear.

INLAND has only a limited ability to handle phrases such as THE SHIPS, THE AMERICAN SUB, and THOSE CRUISERS, which are said to be "definitely determined." As opposed to indefinitely determined noun phrases (such as A SHIP), which refer to the existence of objects not currently in context, definite noun phrases are often used to refer to a particular object or set of objects that is already in context. In dealing with a database, "in context" may usually be taken to mean "in the database." Thus the phrase THE AMERICAN SUBS generally means "the American subs in the database," and this is the interpretation that INLAND almost always places on this phrase. But suppose the user has just asked WHAT SUBS ARE IN THE MEDITERRANEAN and has been answered by a list of several subs, some of which are American and some of which belong to other countries. If the user now asks WHAT ARE THE POSITIONS OF THE AMERICAN SUBS he expects only the positions of American subs in the Mediterranean, but is given information about all American subs in the database. The problem is that the local context established by previous questions is more restricted than the total database and INLAND has not received enough lexical and syn-tactic clues to recognize this. (Had the input been WHAT ARE THE POSITIONS OF THE AMERICAN ONES, the use of the pronoun would have signaled the local context and INLAND would have replied properly.)

Where the context is very clear, INLAND can sometimes handle a restricted perspective on the database. For example, following

SELECT A MAP OF THE NORTH ATLANTIC

the query

DISPLAY THE AMERICAN SUBS

will cause the retrieval of only those subs in the North Atlantic, because others could not be displayed on the map in any case.

We know of no applied language system that deals adequately with this problem. However, significant experimental results are described in Grosz [7].

(b) *Some Methods for Treating Pronouns.* Even though the general problem of properly resolving pronouns is quite difficult, simple techniques can cover a large number of cases. For example, there are many trivial uses of pronouns in which no resolution is needed at all. Examples include

WHAT TIME IS IT
WAS IT 1968 WHEN THE KENNEDY WAS LAUNCHED

and instances in which the pronoun references an earlier phrase in a pattern as in

WHEN WILL ⟨SHIP⟩ ⟨HAVE⟩ ITS ⟨PART⟩ ⟨REPAIRED⟩
(e.g. WHEN WILL THE KENNEDY GET ITS RADAR FIXED).

Very often pronouns are used in natural language queries to refer to things mentioned in the previous question. Thus in the sequence

WHAT IS THE LENGTH OF THE KENNEDY
WHAT IS HER SPEED,

the pronoun HER refers to THE KENNEDY. Suppose the first sentence above is interpreted by means of the production

⟨L.T.G⟩ ⇒ ⟨PRESENT⟩ THE ⟨ATTRIBUTE⟩ OF ⟨SHIP⟩

and the second sentence by

⟨L.T.G⟩ ⇒ ⟨PRESENT⟩ ⟨SHIP'S⟩ ⟨ATTRIBUTE⟩.

The primary method for matching ⟨SHIP'S⟩ might be through a production such as

⟨SHIP'S⟩ ⇒ ⟨SHIP⟩ ⟨-'S⟩

where ⟨-'S⟩ is the possessive-forming suffix which is stripped off by a preprocessor.[11]

---

11 Alternatively, a set of possessive nouns naming ships could be defined and the stripper not used, or, as is the case in INLAND, possessives could be thrown away altogether and ⟨SHIP'S⟩

This primary method may be extended so that ⟨SHIP'S⟩ may also match HER or ITS or THEIR if a ⟨SHIP⟩ was used in the last input. This will allow WHAT IS HER SPEED to be interpreted as WHAT IS KENNEDY'S SPEED.

To extend the definition of ⟨SHIP'S⟩ to match pronouns, first define a predicate SHIP.PRONOUN that will return a non-NIL value if its argument is a possessive pronoun and the last input contained a ⟨SHIP⟩. The predicate may be defined as

```
(LAMBDA (WORD)
    (AND (MEMBER WORD '(HER ITS THEIR))
         (LIFER.BINDING '(SHIP))))
```

where LIFER.BINDING is a LIFER function that determines whether the metasymbol given as its argument had a binding in the interpretation of the last input and, if so, returns the binding.[12] Using predicate SHIP.PRONOUN, the definition of metasymbol ⟨SHIP'S⟩ may be extended by the call

MP[⟨SHIP'S⟩ SHIP.PRONOUN].

Another technique, which works nicely for some classes of anaphoric references, involves the use of global variables (sometimes called "registers"). For example, suppose that each response expression associated with a pattern defining the meta-symbol ⟨SHIP⟩ is so constructed that it will set the global variable LATEST-SHIP to the value it returns as the binding of ⟨SHIP⟩. To be concrete,

```
PD[⟨SHIP⟩
    (⟨SHIP-NAME⟩)
    (SETQ LATEST-SHIP
        (LIST (LIST 'NAM 'EQ ⟨SHIP-NAME⟩)))]
```

causes ⟨SHIP⟩ to match a ⟨SHIP-NAME⟩ as defined previously. The response expression that computes the value of ⟨SHIP⟩ will return the same value as de-fined above, but, as a side effect, it will now also set the global variable LATEST-SHIP to the same value. Later, when phrases such as THE SHIP or THAT SHIP are used to refer to the last ship mentioned, the global variable LATEST-SHIP may be used to recall that ship. For example, if ⟨DET-DEF⟩ is defined to match definite determiners (e.g. THAT, THE), then

```
PD[⟨SHIP⟩
    (⟨DET-DEF⟩ SHIP)
    LATEST-SHIP]
```

will define structures that allow ⟨SHIP⟩ to match THE SHIP and take as its value the value of the LATEST-SHIP. Note that LATEST-SHIP is always ready with the value of the latest ⟨SHIP⟩ mentioned, but (LIFER.BINDING '⟨SHIP⟩) is of help only if ⟨SHIP⟩ was used in the last input.

(4) *Limitations in Processing Elliptical Inputs.* After successfully processing the complete sentence

(1) HOW MANY CRUISERS ARE THERE

---

12 If there were multiple occurrences of the symbol in the last input, the leftmost-topmost instance is returned.

LIFER will accept the elliptical input

(2) CRUISERS WITHIN 600 MILES OF THE KNOX

but not

(3) WITHIN 600 MILES OF THE KNOX.

The elliptical processor is based on syntactic analogies. Input (2) is a noun phrase which is analogous to the noun phrase CRUISERS of input (1). Input (3), on the other hand, is a modifier that is intended to modify the CRUISERS of input (1). Because input (1) has no modifiers, elliptical input (3) has no parallel in the original input and hence cannot be accepted.

(5) *Other Limitations.* A few other important limitations of INLAND and LIFER are worth mentioning briefly.

First, LIFER has no "core grammar" that is ready to be used on any arbitrary database. This is because LIFER was designed as a general purpose language processing system and makes no commitment whatever to the types of programs and data structures for which it is to provide a front end or even to which natural language is to be accepted. LIFER might, for example, be used to build a Japanese language interface to a program that controls a robot arm. This could not be done if assumptions had been made restricting LIFER to database applications and to the English language. Thus LIFER contrasts with systems such as Thompson and Thompson's REL (rapidly extendable language) [20], which provides a core grammar but which requires reformatting of data into the REL database.[13]

Some systems, such as ROBOT (Harris [8, 9]), use the information in the database itself as an extension of the language processor's lexicon. The LIFER interface may do this also but need not. If one elects not to use the database as lexicon, and this choice was made in INLAND, then the lexicon must be extended whenever new values are added to the database that a user may want to mention in his queries.[14] The price of using the database itself as an extended lexicon is that the database must be queried during the parsing process. For very large databases, this operation will probably be prohibitively expensive.

INLAND, of course, is basically a question answerer that relies on a database as its major source of domain information. In particular, INLAND cannot read newspaper articles or other extended texts and record their meaning for subsequent querying. Moreover, although it is perfectly reasonable that the LIFER parser might be used for a text reading system, LIFER itself contains no particular facilities other than calls to response expressions for recording or reasoning about complex bodies of knowledge.

6.2 The Role of the Task Domain

The limitations presented in the last subsection would cause major difficulties in dealing with many areas of natural language application. However, for our particu-

lar application, the limitations did not prevent the creation of a robust and useful system. In the next few paragraphs, we briefly outline some of the key features of the application that simplified our task.

The creation of INLAND was greatly facilitated by the nature of the particular interface problem that was addressed—providing a decision maker with access to information he knows is in a database. Because the user is expected to know what kinds of information are available and is expected to follow the technical terms and styles of writing that are typical in his domain of decision making, we can establish strong predictions about a user's linguistic behavior and hence INLAND needs to cover only a relatively narrow subset of language.

A second factor in facilitating the creation of the natural language interface was the interface provided by the IDA and FAM components of the LADDER system. By providing a simplistic view of what is in fact a complex and highly intertwined collection of distributed data, IDA and FAM helped greatly in simplifying the LISP response expressions associated with productions in the INLAND grammar.

In short, IDA allows the database to be queried by high-level information requests that take the form of an unordered list of two kinds of items: fields whose values are desired, and conditions on the values of associated fields. Using IDA, the INLAND grammar need never be concerned with any entities in the database other than fields and field values. Furthermore, because the input to IDA is unordered, the construction of segments of a call to IDA can be done while parsing lower-level metasymbols.

The performance of INLAND for a given user is also enhanced by the user's own, often subconscious, tendency to adapt to the system's limitations. Because INLAND can handle at least the most straightforward paraphrases of most requests for the values of any particular fields, even a new user has a good chance of having his questions successfully answered on the first or second attempt. It has been our experience that those who use the system with some regularity soon adapt the style of their questions to that accepted by the language specification. The performance of these users suggests that they train themselves to understand the grammar accepted by INLAND and to restrict their questions whenever possible to forms within the grammar. Formal investigation of this subjectively observed phenomenon might prove very interesting.

6.3 The Role of Human Engineering

Although the basic language processing abilities provided by LIFER are similar to those found in some other systems, LIFER embodies a number of human engineering features that greatly enhance its usability. These humanizing features include its ability to deal with incomplete inputs and to allow users to extend the linguistic coverage at run time. But, more importantly, LIFER provides easy-to-understand, highly interactive functions for specifying, extending, modifying, and debugging application languages. These features provide a highly supportive environment for the incremental development of sophisticated interfaces. Without these supporting features, a language definition rapidly becomes too complex to manage and is no longer extendable. With support, the relatively simple types of

---

[13] Fragments of foreign-language versions of INLAND have been used to access the naval database in Swedish and Japanese.

[14] Because LADDER accesses data over the ARPANET, we felt the overall system would be intolerably slow if the actual database was used at parse time.

linguistic constructions accepted by LIFER may be used to produce far more sophisticated interfaces than was previously thought possible.

Creating a LIFER grammar that covers the language of a particular application may be thought of constructively as writing a program for a parser machine. All the precepts of good programming—top-down design, modular programming, and the like—are relevant to good design of a semantic grammar. A well programmed grammar is easy to augment, because new top-level patterns are likely to refer to lower-level metasymbols that have already been developed and shown to work reliably. Thus the task of adding new top-level productions to a grammar is analogous to the task of adding new capabilities to a more typical body of computer code (such as a statistics package) by defining new capabilities in terms of existing subroutines.

No matter how well programmed a grammar might be, as the complexity of the grammar increases, the interactions among components of the language specification will grow. This leads the language designer into the familiar programming cycle of program, test, and debug. With many systems for parsing and language definition, the cycle may take many minutes for each iteration. With LIFER, when a new production is interactively entered into the grammar, it is immediately usable for testing by parsing sample inputs. The time required for the cycle of program, test, and debug is thus dependent on the thinking time of the designer, not the processing time of the system. Because the designer can make very effective use of his time, he can support, maintain, and extend a language specification of far greater complexity than would otherwise be possible.

The basic parsing technology of LIFER is not really new. But the human engineering that LIFER provides for interface builders has allowed us to better manage the existing technology and to apply it on a relatively large scale.

6.4 Related Work

As indicated by the February 1977 issue of the SIGART Newsletter [5], which contains a collection of 52 short overviews of various research efforts in the general area, interest in the development of natural language interfaces is widespread. Our own work is similar to that of several others.

The LIFER parser is based on a simplification of the ideas developed in the LUNAR parser of Woods and others [23, 26]. In particular, LIFER manipulates internal structures that reflect Woods's ATN formalism. Woods's parser was used as a component of a system that accessed a database in answering questions about the chemical analysis of lunar rocks. The system did not use semantically-oriented syntactic categories and the database was smaller and less complex than that used by INLAND, although the database query language was more general than that accepted by IDA.

Woods's ATN formalism has been used in a variety of systems, including a speech understanding system [25], and the semantically-oriented systems of Waltz [22], Brown and Burton [1], and Burton [2]. These latter systems do not use the LUNAR parser, but rather compile the ATN formalism into procedures that in turn perform the parsing operation directly, without using a parser/interpreter to interpret a grammatical formalism. Compilation results in greater parsing speed, which is of importance for many applications. However, compilation also makes personalization features, such as PARAPHRASE, much more difficult to implement and increases the time of the program-test-debug cycle.

The first natural language systems to make extensive use of semantic grammars were those of Brown and Burton [1] and Burton [2]. These systems were designed for computer-assisted instruction rather than as interfaces to databases.

In work very similar to our own, Waltz [22] has devised a system called PLANES which answers questions about the maintenance and flight histories of airplanes. PLANES uses both an ATN and a semantic grammar. Apparently the system does not include a paraphrase facility similar to LIFER's. It does support the processing of elliptical inputs by a technique differing from our own and supports clarification dialogues with users.

The PLANES language definition makes less use of syntactic information than INLAND. In particular, PLANES looks through an input for constituent phrases matching certain semantically-oriented syntax categories. When one of these constituent phrases is found, its value is placed in a local register that is associated with the given category. Rather than attempt to combine these constituents into a complete sentence by syntactic means, "concept case frames" are used. Essentially, PLANES uses case frames to decide what type of question has been asked by looking at the types and values of local registers that were set by the input. For example, the three questions

WHO OWNS THE KENNEDY
BY WHOM IS KENNEDY OWNED
THE KENNEDY IS OWNED BY WHOM

would all set, say, an ⟨ACT⟩ register to OWN and a ⟨SHIP⟩ register to KENNEDY. The case frames can determine what question is asked simply by looking at these registers. Performing a complete syntactic analysis such as INLAND does require different constructions for each question pattern.[15]

If the input following one of the three questions asked in the preceding paragraph is the elliptical fragment "KNOX," the ⟨SHIP⟩ register is reset. Because no case frame is associated with ⟨SHIP⟩ alone and because ⟨SHIP⟩ was used in the last input, the ⟨ACT⟩ register is inherited in the new context and the elliptical input properly analyzed. When more than one case frame matches an input, PLANES enters into a clarification dialogue with the user to decide which was intended. (This conversation prints interpretations of inputs in a formal query language.)

The use of case frames is very attractive in that it allows many top-level syntactic patterns to be accounted for by a single rule. However, it is inadequate for complex

---

[15] LIFER may be used to support case frames, although this was not done in INLAND. In particular, ⟨L.T.G⟩ may be defined as an arbitrary sequence of ⟨CONSTITUENT⟩s, where ⟨CONSTITUENT⟩ may be expanded as any of the semantically-oriented syntax categories used by the case system. The response expression associated with the expansions of ⟨CONSTITUENT⟩ cause global registers to be set, and the response expression associated with ⟨L.T.G⟩ ⟹ ⟨CONSTITUENTS⟩ may make use of these registers and the case frames in computing a top-level response. A case frame system supported by LIFER would, of course, inherit LIFER's run-time personalization and introspection features.

inputs. The question IS KNOX FASTER THAN KENNEDY contains two ⟨SHIP⟩s. Only the syntax tells us which to test as the faster of the two. Compound-complex sentences would be extremely difficult to process without extensive use of syntactic data. Waltz is investigating ways of supplementing his case frames with nominal pieces of syntactic information.

Codd's concept of the RENDEZVOUS system [3] for interface to relational databases provides many ideas concerning clarification dialogues that might be included in LIFER at some later date. RENDEZVOUS is failsafe in that it can fall back on multiple choice selection if natural language processing fails completely.

Another applied natural language system whose underlying philosophy is akin to that of LIFER is the REL system developed by Thompson and Thompson [20]. REL is a data retrieval system like LADDER, though REL requires data to be stored in a special REL database. The grammar rules of REL contain a context-free part and an augmentation very much like those of LIFER. As its name implies, REL was intended to be easily extendable by interface builders. Much effort has gone into making REL run rapidly and it is almost certainly faster than LIFER. However, this speed was gained by a low-level language implementation with the unfortunate side effect that response expressions are not easily written.

Recently, the Artificial Intelligence Corporation introduced a commercial product called ROBOT for interfacing to databases. As described in Harris [8], ROBOT "calls for mapping English language questions into a language of database semantics that is independent of the contents of the database." The database itself is used as an extension of the dictionary, and the structure of files within the database helps in guiding the parser in the resolution of ambiguities. Our own research indicates that the types of linguistic construction employed by users are rather dependent on the content of the database. We also worry that extensive recourse to a database of substantial size may greatly slow the parsing process, unless the file is indexed on every field. Moreover, our database is coded largely in terms of abbreviations that are unsuitable as lexical entries. Nevertheless, the notion of using the data itself to extend the capabilities of the language system is very attractive.

In addition to the work on near-term application systems, a number of workers are currently addressing longer-range problems of accessing databases through natural language. See, for example, Mylopoulos et al. [14], Sowa [18], Walker et al. [21], and Sacerdoti [16]. There are, of course, many people engaged in research in the general area of natural language processing, but a survey of their work is beyond the scope of this paper.

7. CONCLUSION

We have described a system called LADDER that provides natural language access to a large, distributed database. We have shown that the language processing component of this system, although based on simple principles and subject to certain limitations, is sufficiently robust to be useful in practical applications. Moreover, we have indicated that LADDER is not an isolated system but that other applied language systems have achieved significant levels of performance as well, particularly in interfacing to databases. We believe that the evidence presented

indicates clearly that, for certain restricted applications, natural language access to databases has become a practical and practicable reality.

8. GLOSSARY

DBMS — Database management system.

FAM — File access manager. Maps generic file names onto specific file names on specific computers at specific sites. Initiates network connections, opens files, and monitors for certain errors.

IDA — Intelligent data access. Presents a structure-free view of a distributed database.

INLAND — Informal natural language access to Navy data. The natural language interface to IDA, which incorporates a special-purpose LIFER grammar.

LADDER — Language access to distributed data with error recovery. Our total system composed of INLAND, IDA, and FAM.

LIFER — Language interface facility with ellipsis and recursion. The general facility for creating and maintaining linguistic interfaces.

MP — Make predicate. The LIFER function for defining a metasymbol as a predicate function.

MS — Make set. The LIFER function for defining a metasymbol as a set of lexical items.

PD — Pattern define. The LIFER function for defining a metasymbol as a pattern expansion.

VLDB — Very large database.

APPENDIX. AN EXAMPLE SESSION WITH LADDER

```
@LADDER
Please type in your name: TOD S.

Do you want instructions? (type FIRST LETTER of response) No

Do you want to use 2 Data Computers? No

Do you want to specify a current location (default = Norfolk)? No

Do you wish distance/direction calculations to default to GREAT CIRCLE,
or RHUMB LINE? (you can override by specifying in the query) Great Circle

1_What is the current position of the Kennedy?
PARSED!
Parse time: .68 seconds
    * This counts cpu time used by INLAND.
IDA: ((? PTP) (? PTD) (NAM EQ 'KENNEDY% JF'))
    * This is the call to IDA.
Connecting to Datacomputer at CCA1:
    * FAM indicates which computer is being accessed.  The next
    * 13 lines are interactions between FAM and the Datacomputer.
>> ;0031 77110818W236    IONETI: CONNECTED TO SRI-KL-22700010
>> ;J150 77110818W238    FCRUN: V=DC-4/10.00.1' J=3 DT='TUESDAY, NOVEMBER
8, 1977 13:42:38-EST' S='CCA'
>> ;0041 77110818W239    DNCTNX: DATACOMPUTER GOING DOWN IN 905 MIN BECAUSE
SYSTEM IS GOING DOWN AT WED NOV 9 77 5:00:00AM-EST FOR 240 MIN DUE TO
```

```
SCHEDULED PM
>> ;J200 771108184239     RHRUN: READY FOR REQUEST
*> Set parameters
*<    Exit
CCA1:^Z
*> Set parameters
*< V   Verbosity (-1 to 5):   1
*< P   PROCEED with Datalanguage   [confirm with <CR>]
      * The connection has now been established.    FAM now logs in
      * and opens the necessary files.
CCA1:LOGIN $TOP.ACCAT.GUEST ;
CCA1:OPEN $TOP.ACCAT.SAGALOWICZ.NSTDPORT1 WRITE;
CCA1:OPEN $TOP.ACCAT.NTRACKHIST READ;
CCA1:OPEN $TOP.ACCAT.NNSHIP READ;
      * FAM now transmits the query.
CCA1:FOR R1 IN NNSHIP WITH (NAM EQ 'KENNEDY JF') FOR NSTDPORT1 , R2 IN
CCA1:NTRACKHIST WITH R2.UICVCN EQ R1.UICVCN BEGIN STRING1 = R2.PTP STRING2 =
CCA1:R2.PTD END;
*> Total bytes transferred: 27
IDA = ((PTP '600ON03000W' PTD 7601171200))
      * This is the value returned by IDA.
Computation time for query: 4.077 seconds
      * This counts cpu time used by IDA and FAM.  Extra time is
      * needed to establish the network connection, log in, and
      * open files.
Real time for query: 224.725 seconds
      * This measures real time from the time the request is made
      * to IDA until IDA returns the answer.
(POSITION 6000N03000W DATE 7601171200)
      * Kennedy was last reported to be at 60 degrees North,
      * 30 degrees West, at noon on January 17, 1976.

2_of kitty hawk
Trying Ellipsis:    WHAT IS THE CURRENT POSITION OF KITTY HAWK
Parse time: .97 seconds

IDA: ((? PTP) (? PTD) (NAM EQ 'KITTY% HAWK'))
CCA1:FOR R1 IN NNSHIP WITH (NAM EQ 'KITTY HAWK') FOR NSTDPORT1 , R2 IN
CCA1:NTRACKHIST WITH R2.UICVCN EQ R1.UICVCN BEGIN STRING1 = R2.PTP STRING2 =
CCA1:R2.PTD END;
*> Total bytes transferred: 27
IDA = ((PTP '3700N01700E' PTD 7601171200))
Computation time for query: 1.077 seconds
Real time for query: 78.105 seconds
(POSITION 3700N01700E DATE 7601171200)

3_To what country does each merchant ship in the north atlantic belong
PARSED!
Parse time: .386 seconds

IDA: ((? NAT) (? NAM) ((TYPE EQ 'BULK') OR (TYPE EQ 'TNKR'))
(PTPNS EQ 'N') (PTPEW EQ 'W') ((PTPY GT 600) OR (PTPX LT 3600) OR
(PTPX GT 3900)) (? PTP)) (? PTD))
CCA1:OPEN $TOP.ACCAT.SAGALOWICZ.NSTDPORT2 WRITE;
CCA1:OPEN $TOP.ACCAT.NNMOVES READ;
CCA1:FOR R1 IN NNMOVES WITH ((TYPE EQ 'BULK') OR (TYPE EQ 'TNKR')) FOR R2 IN
CCA1:NTRACKHIST WITH (PTPNS EQ 'N') AND (PTPEW EQ 'W') AND
CCA1:((PTPY GT 600) OR (PTPX LT 3600) OR (PTPX GT 3900)) AND R2.UICVCN EQ
CCA1:R1.UICVCN FOR NSTDPORT2 , R3 IN NNSHIP WITH R3.UICVCN EQ R2.UICVCN BEGIN
CCA1:STRING1 = R2.PTP STRING2 = R2.PTD STRING3 = R3.NAT STRING4 = R3.NAM END;
*> Total bytes transferred: 4582
IDA = ((NAT 'US' NAM 'GREENVILLE% VICTORY' PTP '1533N03010W' PTD
7601171200) (NAT 'US' NAM 'TOULE%J' PTP '1533N03010W' PTD 7601171200)
   ...))

Computation time for query: 5.702 seconds
Real time for query: 228.231 seconds
I have 79 answers; do you want to see them all? ...Yes

NAT SHIP                      POSITION       DATE
US  GREENVILLE VICTORY   1533N03010W   7601171200
US  TOULE J              1533N03010W   7601171200
         .           (other entries omitted here)
         .
WG  TRANSQUEBEC          4633N02129W   7601171200
NO  TALABOT              0600N01130W   7601171200

4_the fastest sub
Trying Ellipsis:  TO WHAT COUNTRY DOES THE FASTEST SUB BELONG
Parse time: 1.484 seconds

IDA: ((? NAT) (? NAM) (* MAX MCSF) (TYPE1 EQ 'S') (TYPE2 EQ 'S'))
      * In the interests of brevity and clarity, the remaining
      * interactions with the Datacomputer are omitted.
IDA = ((NAT 'US' NAM 'LOS% ANGELES' MCSF '30.0'))
Computation time for query: 2.317 seconds
Real time for query: 173.3 seconds
(NAT US SHIP LOS ANGELES MXSPD 30.0)

5_what ships are en route to america
Trying Ellipsis:  Ellipsis has failed.
The parser does not expect the word "AMERICA" to follow
"WHAT SHIP ARE EN ROUTE TO"
Options for next word or symbol are:
<COUNTRY>,   <PORT>
end-of-list
      * LIFER cannot parse the question; "America" is not in
      * the vocabulary.

6_what is a <country>
PARSED!
      * In addition to questions about the data base, INLAND can
      * answer questions about the grammar itself.
"<COUNTRY>" may be any sequence of words following one of the patterns:
<COUNTRY>  =>  THE <COUNTRY>
<COUNTRY>  =>  U S
<COUNTRY>  =>  U S S R
<COUNTRY>  =>  U S S
<COUNTRY>  =>  U S A
<COUNTRY>  =>  U K
<COUNTRY>  =>  SOVIET UNION
<COUNTRY>  =>  UNITED STATES
<COUNTRY>  =>  UNITED KINGDOM
<COUNTRY>  =>  SOUTH AFRICA
<COUNTRY>  =>  WEST GERMANY
<COUNTRY>  =>  SAUDI ARABIA
<COUNTRY>  =>  GREAT BRITAIN
<COUNTRY>  =>  H M S
"<COUNTRY>" may be any member of the set {ANGOLA ANGOLAN ARABIA ARABIAN
ARGENTINA ARGENTINAN BRITAIN BRITISH CANADA CANADIAN DUTCH EGYPT EGYPTIAN
ENGLAND ENGLISH FOREIGN FRANCE FRENCH GERMAN GERMANY H.M.S. HMS ITALIAN
ITALY LIBERIA LIBERIAN NETHERLANDS NORWAY NORWEGIAN PORTUGAL PORTUGUESE
RUSSIA RUSSIAN SOVIET SPAIN SPANISH U.K. U.S. U.S.A. U.S.S. U.S.S.R. UK
US USA USS USSR VENEZUELA VENEZUELAN}
Finished

7_define america like usa
PARSED!
      * The user may add new synonyms to the vocabulary.

FINISHED
8_redo 5
```

```
    * Here we are using the "redo" feature of INTERLISP.
PARSED!
Parse time: .356 seconds

IDA: ((? NAM) (DSC EQ 'US'))

IDA = ((NAM 'KENNEDY% JF') (NAM 'LOS% ANGELES') (NAM 'BATON% ROUGE')
(NAM 'PHILADELPHIA') (NAM 'POGY') (NAM 'ASPRO') (NAM 'SUNFISH') (NAM
'KAWISHIWI'))
Computation time for query: 1.098 seconds
Real time for query: 67.16 seconds
SHIP = KENNEDY JF, LOS ANGELES, BATON ROUGE, PHILADELPHIA, POGY, ASPRO,
SUNFISH, KAWISHIWI

9_how many of them are navy ships
                  THEM => ((DSC EQ 'US'))
PARSED!
    * 'Them' or 'she' is currently always interpreted as a
      reference to a set of ships in the previous query.
Parse time: .505 seconds

IDA: ((? NAM) (DSC EQ 'US') ((TYPE NE 'BULK') AND (TYPE NE 'TNKR')))

IDA = ((NAM 'KENNEDY% JF') (NAM 'LOS% ANGELES') (NAM 'BATON% ROUGE')
(NAM 'PHILADELPHIA') (NAM 'POGY') (NAM 'ASPRO') (NAM 'SUNFISH') (NAM
'KAWISHIWI'))
Computation time for query: 1.205 seconds
Real time for query: 89.417 seconds
8 of them:
SHIP = KENNEDY JF, LOS ANGELES, BATON ROUGE, PHILADELPHIA, POGY, ASPRO,
SUNFISH, KAWISHIWI

10_give status kitty hawk
Trying Ellipsis: Ellipsis has failed.
The parser does not expect the word "STATUS" to follow
"GIVE"
Options for next word or symbol are:
<RELATIVE.CLAUSE>, <SHIP>, <VALUE.SPEC>, THE
end-of-list

11_define (give status kitty hawk)
like (list the employment schedule, state of readiness, commanding
officer and position of kitty hawk)
PARSED!
    * This is an example of the paraphrase feature of LIFER.  A
      new pattern is defined by example.
Parse time: .705 seconds
    * The system answers the query as a side-effect of parsing
      the paraphrase.
IDA: ((? ETERM) (? EBEG) (? EEND) (? READY) (? RANK) (? CONAM)
(? PTP) (? PTD) (NAM EQ 'KITTY% HAWK'))

IDA = ((ETERM 'SURVOPS' EBEG 760103 EEND 760205 READY 2 RANK 'CAPT'
CONAM 'SPRUANCE% R' PTP '3700N01700E' PTD 7601171200)
Computation time for query: 2.725 seconds
Real time for query: 173.404 seconds
(EMPLMNT SURVOPS EMPBEG 760103 EMPEND 760205 READY 2 RANK CAPT NAME
SPRUANCE R POSITION 3700N01700E DATE 7601171200 SHIP)
LIFER.TOP.GRAMMAR => GIVE STATUS <SHIP>
    * The generalized pattern for the paraphrase is added to
      the grammar.
F0086 (GIVE STATUS <SHIP>)
    * F0086 is the new LISP function created to be the response
      expression for this pattern.
```

```
12_give status us cruisers in the mediteranean
                    spelling-> MEDITERRANEAN
PARSED!
Parse time: 2.855 seconds
IDA: ((? ETERM) (? EBEG) (? EEND) (? READY) (? RANK) (? CONAM)
(? PTP) (? PTD) (? NAM) (NAT EQ 'US') (TYPE1 EQ 'C') (TYPE2 NE 'V')
(TYPE NE 'CGO'))

IDA = ((ETERM 'CARESC' EBEG 760101 EEND 760601 READY 1 RANK 'CAPT'
CONAM 'MORRIS% R' PTP '400ON0060OE' PTD 7601171200 NAM 'CALIFORNIA')
(ETERM 'CARESC' EBEG 751231 EEND 760615 READY 1 RANK 'CAPT' CONAM
'HARMS% J' PTP '3700N01700E' PTD 7601171200 NAM 'DANIELS% J') ...)
Computation time for query: 3.738 seconds
Real time for query: 195.698 seconds
```

```
EMPLMNT:   CARESC        CARESC       CARESC       CARESC
EMPBEG:    760101        751231       751231       751231
EMPEND:    760601        760615       760615       760615
READY:     1             1            1            1
RANK:      CAPT          CAPT         CAPT         CAPT
NAME:      MORRIS R      HARMS J      EVANS O      FRENZINGER T
POSITION:  400ON0060OE   3700N01700E  3700N01700E  3700N01700E
DATE:      7601171200    7601171200   7601171200   7601171200
SHIP:      CALIFORNIA    DANIELS J    WAINWRIGHT   JOUETT

          (information about 8 other ships omitted)
```

```
13_done
PARSED!

File closed  8-Nov-77 11:11:17
Thank you
@
```

* The user indicates that he is finished with the session.

ACKNOWLEDGMENTS

Our debugging of LIFER and the continuing development of human engineering features have been strongly influenced by interactions with interface builders. In particular, we would like to thank the following people for using the LIFER system extensively and sharing their experiences with us: Staffan Lof (Swedish version of LADDER and extensions to INLAND), Martin Epstein (medical database system of melanoma cases), and Harry Barrow and Keith Lantz (interactive aid for cartography and photo interpretation). We would also like to thank Gordon Novak for recent revisions to the elliptical processor.

REFERENCES

1. BROWN, J.S., AND BURTON, R.R. Multiple representations of knowledge for tutorial reasoning. In *Representation and Understanding*, D.G. Bobrow and A. Collins, Eds., Academic Press, New York, 1975, pp. 311-349.
2. BURTON, R.R. "Semantic grammar: An engineering technique for constructing natural language understanding systems. BBN Rep. 3453, Bolt, Beranek, and Newman, Boston, Mass., Dec. 1976.
3. CODD, E.F. Seven steps to rendezvous with the casual user. In *Data Base Management*, J.W. Klimbie and K.I. Koffeman, Eds., North-Holland, Amsterdam, 1974, pp. 179-200.
4. Computer Corporation of America. Datacomputer version 1 user manual. CCA, Cambridge, Mass., Aug. 1975.
5. ERMAN, L.D., Ed. ACM SIGART Newsletter *61*, Feb. 1977.
6. FARRELL, J. The Datacomputer—A network data utility. Proc. Berkeley Workshop on Distributed Data Management and Computer Networks, Berkeley, Calif., May 1976 pp. 352-364.

7. Grosz, B.J. The representation and use of focus in dialog understanding. Ph.D. dissertation, U. of California, Berkeley, May 1977.

8. Harris, L.R. ROBOT: A high performance natural language processor for data base query. ACM SIGART Newsletter 61, Feb. 1977, pp. 39-40.

9. Harris, L.R. User oriented data base que·y with the ROBOT natural language query system. Proc. 3rd Int. Conf. on Very Large Data Bases, Tokyo, Japan, Oct. 6-8, 1977.

10. Hendrix, G.G. The LIFER manual: A guide to building practical natural language interfaces. Tech. Note 138, SRI Artificial Intelligence Center, Menlo Park, Calif., Feb. 1977.

11. Hendrix, G.G. Human engineering for applied natural language processing. Proc. 5th Int. Joint Conf. on Artificial Intelligence, Cambridge, Mass., Aug. 1977.

12. Hopcroft, J.E., and Ullman, J.D. Formal Languages and Their Relation to Automata. Addison-Wesley, Reading, Mass., 1969.

13. Morris, P., and Sagalowicz, D. Managing network access to a distributed data base. Proc. 2nd Berkeley Workshop on Distributed Data Management and Computer Networks, Berkeley, Calif., May 1977.

14. Mylopoulos, J., Borgida, A., Cohen, P., Roussopoulos, N., Tsotsos, J., and Wong, H. TORUS—A natural language understanding system for data management. Proc. 4th Int. Joint Conf. on Artificial Intelligence, Tbilisi, U.S.S.R., Aug. 1975.

15. Paxton, W.H. A framework for speech understanding. Tech. Note 142, SRI Artificial Intelligence Center, Menlo Park, Calif., June 1977.

16. Sacerdoti, E.D. Language access to distributed data with error recovery. Proc. 5th Int. Joint Conf. on Artificial Intelligence, Cambridge, Mass., Aug. 1977.

17. Sagalowicz, D. IDA: An intelligent data access program. Proc. 3rd Int. Conf. on Very Large Data Bases, Tokyo, Japan, Oct. 1977.

18. Sowa, J.F. Conceptual graphs for a database interface. IBM J. Res. Develop. 20, 4 (July 1976), 336-357.

19. Teitelman, W. INTERLISP reference manual. Xerox PARC, Palo Alto, Calif., Dec. 1975.

20. Thompson, F.B., and Thompson, B.H. Practical natural language processing: The REL system as prototype. In Advances in Computers 13, M. Rubinoff and M.C. Yovits, Eds., Academic Press, New York, 1975.

21. Walker, D.E., Grosz, B.J., Hendrix, G.G., Paxton, W.H., Robinson, A.E., and Slocum, J. An overview of speech understanding research at SRI. Proc. 5th Int. Joint Conf. on Artificial Intelligence, Cambridge, Mass., Aug. 1977.

22. Waltz, D. Natural language access to a large data base: An engineering approach. Proc. 4th Int. Joint Conf. on Artificial Intelligence, Tbilisi, U.S.S.R., Sept. 1975, pp. 868-872.

23. Woods, W.A. Transition network grammars for natural language analysis. Comm. ACM 13, 10 (Oct. 1970), 591-606.

24. Woods, W.A. An experimental parsing system for transition network grammars. In Natural Language Processing, R. Rustin, Ed., Algorithmics Press, New York, 1973.

25. Woods, W.A., Bates, M., Brown, G., Bruce, B., Cook, C., Klovstad, J., Makhoul, J., Nash-Webber, B., Schwartz, R., Wolf, J., and Zue, V. Speech understanding systems, Final technical progress report. Tech. Rep. 3438, Bolt, Beranek, and Newman, Cambridge, Mass., Dec. 1976.

26. Woods, W.A., Kaplan, R.M., and Nash-Webber, B. The lunar sciences natural language information system. BBN Rep. 2378, Bolt Beranek and Newman, Cambridge, Mass., 1972.

Received June 1977; revised November 1977

Transportability and Generality in a Natural-Language Interface System

Paul Martin, Douglas Appelt, and Fernando Pereira
Artificial Intelligence Center
SRI International

Abstract

This paper describes the design of a transportable natural language (NL) interface to databases and the constraints that transportability places on each component of such a system. By a **transportable** NL system, we mean an NL processing system that is constructed so that a domain expert (rather than an AI or linguistics expert) can move the system to a new application domain. After discussing the general problems presented by transportability, this paper describes **TEAM** (an acronym for Transportable English database Access Medium), a demonstratable prototype of such a system. The discussion of TEAM shows how domain-independent and domain-dependent information can be separated in the different components of a NL interface system, and presents one method of obtaining domain-specific information from a domain expert.

1. Transportable Systems

To build a transportable system, the designer must distinguish between domain-specific and general rules at all levels in the design process. The additional constraints imposed by transportability force the builders of such systems to address several basic issues that can be overlooked in designing special purpose interfaces (e.g., LUNAR [Woods et al. 72], LADDER [Hendrix 77]). As a result, research on transportable systems has implications beyond practical utility.

Specifically, transportablility forces the designer to address the following broad issues:

- The syntax used must be a general grammar of English, rather than a domain-specific set of rules.

- Because the semantics cannot depend on some domain-specific syntax chosen for ease of semantic translation, a general mechanism must be developed to acquire and attach semantics to a wide variety of syntactic constructions.

- The lexicon must also be acquired; thus, any knowledge that might otherwise appear as "ad hoc" lexical entries must be structured to fit into the general grammar and to be specified in terms of user-oriented concepts.

- Both the pragmatics and database access processes must be able to use acquired information to turn the representation of what was said into a query appropriate for the database underlying the application. Whether a relation is actually stored in the database or is derived from other relations (**a virtual relation**) should be hidden from the user and from the semantic interpretation mechanisms.

- Finally, designing a system able to acquire all the kinds of information sketched above is in itself a challenge; through interacting with a person assumed to be unschooled in linguistics and AI, it must elicit both the conceptual structure and the linguistic content of the domain.

2. Overview of TEAM

TEAM runs in two distinct phases: first an expert on the domain (the **database expert** or **DBE**) answers questions about the database and the linguistic expressions used to refer to the information it contains, and then **end-users** can use it to answer natural-language queries from the application.

Figure 1 shows the major components of TEAM — acquisition, DIALOGIC, and database access. Acquisition obtains the description of an application from the DBE, and uses it to expand and update the internal specification of the user world. DIALOGIC translates English sentences into a logical form that represents their literal content. DIALOGIC uses two kinds of information acquired from the DBE: the **lexicon**, a table of vocabulary words and their definitions; and the **conceptual schema**, the specification of the predicates the language can use. The database access component converts this logical form to a formal database query using the conceptual schema and the **database schema**, a set of structured statements about the database.

Section 3 describes the acquisition process, Section 4 shows how a logical form is produced from an input sentence, and Section 5 describes the production of an appropriate database query.

TEAM OVERVIEW

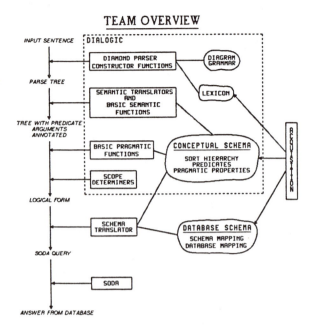

Figure 1: Overview of TEAM

3. Acquisition of a New Database

The acquisition component of TEAM is responsible for gathering information from the DBE about the structure of the database, the words that refer to objects in the database, and the relations among them. This information is incorporated into the lexicon and into the conceptual and database schemata. The acquisition component must meet several specific requirements:

- TEAM must acquire new concepts. Acquisition of a new database involves acquiring information about the structure of the database and modifying the existing conceptual schema.

- Detailed linguistic knowledge is acquired implicitly. The DBE is not required to have specialized knowledge of linguistics. Therefore, the linguistic information that DIALOGIC needs must be inferred from answers to questions that tap a layman's linguistic competence without recourse to the terminology of a trained linguist.

- TEAM must associate NL concepts with a wide range of database representations because a disparity generally exists between the database' view and the end-user's view of the world (cf. the notion of **view** in database theory).

- TEAM must provide the DBE with a powerful but clean interface to the acquisition processes. Acquisition of a multifile database is complex. The TEAM acquisition component thus seeks to present

the DBE with an interface that allows him to see the different relations of the database, move freely back and forth among different relations, and freely change answers to previous questions.

An Overview of Acquisition

The interface through which the DBE imparts his knowledge to TEAM is shown in Figure 2. At the top of the layout is a menu of the operations the DBE can perform. Below that is the **file menu** listing all the relations the system knows about, a **field menu** containing the fields in each relation, and a **word menu** containing all the vocabulary items that TEAM has acquired in addition to its basic lexicon. The question answering area is the space reserved for the user to answer detailed questions about files, fields, and words. The user selects one of the items in the menus with the mouse, and then continues to interact in the question-answering window.[1]

FILE MENU
EMPLOYEE

FIELD MENU
EMPLOYEE-DEPT   EMPLOYEE-EXEMPT   EMPLOYEE-ID   EMPLOYEE-NAME
EMPLOYEE-SALARY

WORD MENU
DEPT (n)   EXEMPT (n)   ID (n)
NAME (n)   EMPLOYEE (n)   SALARY (n)

Question Answering Area
File name - EMPLOYEE
Type of relation - **ACTUAL** VIRTUAL
LMFS pathname - EMPLOYEE.DB
Fields - NAME ID SALARY DEPT EXEMPT
Subject - EMPLOYEE
Primary key set - NAME **ID** SALARY DEPT EXEMPT
Identifying fields - **NAME ID** SALARY DEPT EXEMPT
Pronouns for file subject - **HE SHE** IT THEY
Don't forget to insert *employee* into the sort hierarchy.
Figure 2: File Menu Questions

The TEAM acquisition component also contains the following support functions, which are accessed through a fixed menu at the top of the display (not shown in the figure):

- The **sort-editor** allows the DBE to add new concepts to the **sort hierarchy**, a central data structure in the representation of the concepts of the application (**conceptual schema**). The sort hierarchy is a network that expresses the taxonomy of all the objects in the TEAM world. When TEAM is started, it contains certain core concepts; the acquisition task entails fitting all new domain-specific conceptual objects into the taxonomy.

- **Specify-rel** allows the DBE to specify the connections between virtual relations and the actual files of the database.

---

[1]Bold face is used in menus to represent items for which enough information has been given, and in questions to mark the currently selected answer (default).

An Example of Acquisition

To illustrate how the DBE specifies the information needed for natural language access, we consider the example of a simple database consisting of two files, EMPLOYEE and DEPARTMENT, and a virtual relation composed of their join, MANAGER.[2] The database consists of an EMPLOYEE file with fields NAME (the employee's name), SS (the employee's social security number), SALARY (the employee's salary), DEPT (the employee's department), and EXEMPT (a Boolean feature field indicating whether the employee is exempt from overtime regulations). The DEPARTMENT file has fields, NAME (the name of the department) and MGR (the name of the department's manager). A virtual MANAGER relation is defined that relates employees to their managers.

When a new relation is created (with the **new-rel** command as has already been done in Figure 2), the DBE must supply its name and fields, which then appear in the appropriate menus.

Other questions provide TEAM with a **primary key set** (see section 6), a set of **identifying fields** (used for answers), and **gender information**. TEAM creates a noun for the subject of the file and one for the name of each field.

Field Types

TEAM distinguishes among three kinds of fields — arithmetic, feature (Boolean), and symbolic — on the basis of the kinds of linguistic expressions that are used to express relationships about those fields. Symbolic fields are the simplest; linguistic access is restricted to naming the field or its values. Arithmetic fields contain numbers for which it makes sense to compare and to associate comparative and superlative adjectives. Feature fields correspond to the presence or absence of some arbitrary property of the subject. TEAM supports a variety of linguistic constructions that refer to such a property: adjectives modifying the subject, nouns representing the property that the subject has or lacks, nouns representing the subset of the subjects that have or lack the property, and intransitive verbs applied to the subject that has or lacks the property.

During the acquisition of each field, the DBE specifies information about the lexical items associated with the field and how the field fits into the conceptual schema. These questions resolve the difference between the user's view and the database view of the world. Figures 3, 5 and 6, illustrate the questions asked for each type of field.

Symbolic Field

Figure 3 shows the questions asked for the symbolic field DEPT in the EMPLOYEE file. Question (a), if answered affirmatively, would enter the database field values into the word menu so that the DBE can specify synonyms and irregular forms for database field entries. Questions (b) and (c) establish the modifier usages of the field values.

Question Answering Area
```
Is field actual or virtual? ACTUAL VIRTUAL
Associated file - EMPLOYEE
Name of field - DEPT
Type of field - SYMBOLIC ARITHMETIC FEATURE
Don't forget to insert the field in the sort hierarchy
Edit lexicon for words in this field? YES NO          (a)
'Unknown' convention for this field - *
'Not applicable' convention for this field - **
Are field values units of measure? YES NO
Noun subcategory - PROPER COUNT MASS
Typical value - PAYROLL
Will values of this field be used as classifiers?
        YES NO                                         (b)
Will the values in this field be used alone
        as implicit classifiers? YES NO               (c)
```
Figure 3: Symbolic Field Acquisition

In our example the answer to question (b) is "Yes," and the answer to (c) is "No." Depending on the domain, other answers are possible. For example, in a database about ships, we could neither ask "How many Jones ships are there?" nor "How many Joneses are there?" to obtain a count of the number of ships commanded by Jones. However, in a database about automobiles, we could ask "How many Ford cars are there?" or "How many Fords are there?" to find out how many automobiles are made by Ford.

Although TEAM derives the placement of arithmetic and feature fields in the sort hierarchy from the answers to the field questions, this is not possible for symbolic fields. The DBE must place symbolic fields in the sort hierarchy using the sort-hierarchy editor; we illustrate this process in Figure 4.

Arithmetic Fields

Figure 5 illustrates the questions asked about arithmetic fields. Because dates, measures, and counts are used differently, TEAM must be told, by answering question (a), what type of arithmetic field is being acquired. In this case, we have a unit of economic worth that is measured in dollars. Questions (b) and (c) discover adjectives (or other adjectival modifiers) that will be used in their comparative and superlative forms in queries (e.g., "Who is the highest paid employee?").

Feature Fields

Feature fields are the most difficult to handle because of the wide range of linguistic expressions used to express their values. Figure 6 illustrates feature field acquisition for the EXEMPT field in the EMPLOYEE file. TEAM needs to know the positive and negative values in the fields, and the nominals and adjectivals associated with each value. In this example, given the answers in Figure 6, one could ask "What employees are exempt?" or "How many nonexempt employees earn more than 20000

---

[2]We concentrate here on **noun** relations, for which we assume that there is a **subject** field (e.g., ships, ship classes, employees, instances of an ownership relation). We also assume that each relation is in third-normal form [Codd 70]; that is, each row represents an instance of the subject of the relation, and each column value is a function of the subject value.

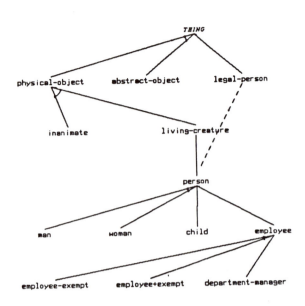

Figure 4: Sort Editor

Question Answering Area
Is field actual or virtual? **ACTUAL** VIRTUAL
Associated file - EMPLOYEE
Name of field - SALARY
Type of field - SYMBOLIC **ARITHMETIC** FEATURE
Value type - DATES **MEASURES** COUNTS   (a)
Are the units implicit? **YES** NO
Enter implicit unit - DOLLAR
Abbreviation for this unit?
Measure type of this unit -
TIME WEIGHT SPEED VOLUME LINEAR AREA **WORTH** OTHER
Minimum and maximum numeric values - 0. 100000.
Positive adjectives - (HIGH PAID)   (b)
Negative adjectives - (LOW PAID)   (c)
Figure 5: Arithmetic Field Acquisition

Question Answering Area
Is field actual or virtual? **ACTUAL** VIRTUAL
Associated file - EMPLOYEE
Name of field - EXEMPT
Type of field - SYMBOLIC ARITHMETIC **FEATURE**
Positive value - Y
Negative value - N
Positive adjectivals - EXEMPT
Negative adjectivals - NONEXEMPT
Positive abstract nouns -
Negative abstract nouns -
Positive count nouns -
Negative count nouns -
Figure 6: Feature Field Acquisition

dollars?"

Each type of expression leads to new lexical, conceptual schema, and database schema entries. In general, in the conceptual schema, feature field adjectivals create a new predicate, abstract nouns create contrasting new sorts that are subsorts of some abstract quality, and count nouns create contrasting subsorts of the file subject.

Volunteered Information

User has selected **new-word** *from menu.*
Question Answering Area
Enter word - DEPARTMENT
Synonym - DEPT
Syntactic category - ADJECTIVE **NOUN** VERB
Plural - DEPARTMENTS
Figure 7: Word Menu

Question Answering Area
Enter word - EARN
Syntactic category - ADJECTIVE NOUN **VERB**
Third person singular present tense (he she it) - EARNS
Past tense - EARNED
Past participle - EARNED
Sentence - AN EMPLOYEE EARNS A SALARY
'A SALARY EARNS.' <=>
          'Something EARNS a SALARY.' YES **NO**
'A EMPLOYEE EARNS.' <=>
          'A EMPLOYEE EARNS something.' **YES** NO
'A SALARY is EARNED.' <=>
          'Something EARNS a SALARY.' **YES** NO
Figure 8: Verb Acquisition

The DBE may volunteer lexical items to TEAM and assign them a meaning in terms of database relations (actual or virtual). For example, in Figure 7, the user volunteers the word DEPARTMENT and says it is a synonym of DEPT; in Figure 8 the DBE volunteers the verb 'earn.' In both cases, TEAM extracts both the syntactic and semantic properties of the new verb without recourse to technical linguistic terms.

Virtual Relations

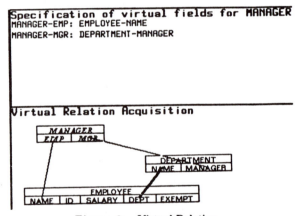

Figure 9: Virtual Relation

Figure 9 shows the DBE specifying the fields of a new virtual relation MANAGER, where an employee's manager is the manager of the department in which the employee works. The DBE can use the file menu to call up diagrams of any relation the system has acquired. Relations are specified graphically by making connections between the fields in the relation he is specifying and other relations in the database. The graphic interface serves both to display and manipulate the relationships of the database. The heavy line indicates that a database join is to be performed between the two fields, and the dotted lines indicate which fields in the virtual relation are carried over from the relations being joined.

4. DIALOGIC

The component of the TEAM system that takes an input sentence and produces a logical form is called DIALOGIC [Grosz et al. 82]. DIALOGIC comprises several phases, illustrated in Figure 1. All of the domain-dependent information it needs is in the conceptual schema and the lexicon (domain-independent information for core vocabulary such as pronouns and prepositions is already in these data structures before the acquisition).

We can illustrate the operation of DIALOGIC by considering an example sentence that could be asked in the employee database acquired in our previous example:

What employees earn more than their manager's salary?

retrieved from the lexicon to produce a set of syntactically acceptable parses.

The grammar is a set of context-free rules annotated with **constructors** that enforce context-sensitive syntactic constraints, and supply scores for the parses based on the *a priori* likelihood of a construction and on the composed likelihood of certain combinations. These scores are composed upward to the sentence node, yielding an overall sentence score. The score is used to rank the resulting parses so that the syntactically "best" ones are tried first by the semantic translation process. Figure 10 shows the top-ranked syntactic parse for our example sentence.

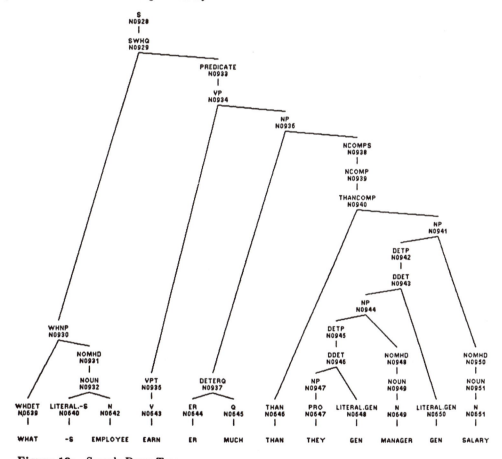

Figure 10: Sample Parse Tree

Syntactic Operations

The DIAMOND parser and the DIAGRAM grammar [Robinson 82] constitute the syntactic portion of DIALOGIC. Together they can analyze all common sentence types in English (with the exception of sentences using conjunctions). They are applied to the morphemes

Semantic Translation

In addition to the constructor functions, each rule of the grammar also has another associated function called its **translator**. The translators are domain-independent, but they derive much of their behavior from the acquired features and predicate structures associated with lexical entries. They compute the predicate relations of the sentence by using its syntactic structure and a set of semantic operations called the **basic semantic functions** (BSFs). This approach of decoupling these commonly conflated issues is important: By separating the parsing from the semantic translation, we allow independent development of the grammatical coverage and semantic capabilities. Separating the semantic phase into translators that are close to the grammar and BSFs that are tied to the target formal theory achieves a similar independence [Hendrix 78].

The BSFs annotate the parse tree with noun groups, predicates, and quantified variables. The predicate relations are specified as **logical form fragments** (LFFs). These are quantifier-free open formulas in the target logical form [Moore 81]. The complete **logical forms** are a higher-order predicate calculus in which the restriction and assertion clauses of a quantified expression are asserted separately.

For our example query, translator calls to the BSFs build variables representing employees, managers, and salaries as the heads of the noun phrases. The translator calls for pronouns and definite noun phrases also collect the set of syntactically feasible coreferents of such phrases [Hobbs 76]. In our example sentence, the pronoun 'them,' which is derived morphologically from 'their,' is assigned a variable that is marked as ambiguous among the employee and salary variables (the manager variable was previously ruled out on syntactic grounds). Calls to other BSFs build the predications that relate these variables, expressing information such as the relationship between an individual employee and a salary.

The BSFs also resolve certain classes of ambiguities, and detect and reject some kinds of semantically inappropriate parses. The requirements on the argument types of most predicates are used by the BSFs to check the semantic suitability of the proposed role fillers. The acquisition of domain-dependent predicates implicitly obtains the **delineations** that specify the sorts of their arguments. In our example sentence, the EARN predicate requires an EMPLOYEE in the first argument position and a SALARY in the second. Because a MANAGER is a kind of EMPLOYEE (as indicated by the sort hierarchy), the delineation checking mechanism allows a manager to EARN a salary too. If a parse had been chosen that reversed the order of these arguments, it would have been rejected.

When delineation checking detects an inappropriate sort, the BSFs have several options other than simply rejecting the parse:

- If either the predicate or the role filler is derived from words that have alternative semantic interpretations, the remaining alternatives can be tried.

- Alternative candidates for the referent of a pronoun are likewise treated as semantic alternatives. In our example sentence, the 'them,' which is the pronoun part of the genitive 'their' is constrained to be some EMPLOYEE (rather than a SALARY, for example)

by the delineation testing of the MANAGER relation.

- Noun groups may be converted from their initial sort to a related sort that satisfies the delineation (**backward coercion**). Backward coercion would recognize that 'salesman' is of sort JOB-TITLE and hence could not be used with the SALARY-OF predicate (which requires EMPLOYEE), and thus would replace it with the semantic equivalent of "an EMPLOYEE whose JOB-TITLE is salesman."

Pragmatics

Two further transformations must be applied to the parse tree: Remaining ambiguities caused by vague predicates (e.g., OF) or semantic alternatives must be resolved, and quantifiers and similar operators must be assigned relative scopes.

The basic pragmatic functions replace vague predicates with more meaningful predicates derived from properties of the sorts of the arguments. During acquisition, the sorts of the fields of every relation are automatically entered in the conceptual schema as representing functions of the the subject sort of the relation. Thus, because 'salary' is a field name of the employee file, its semantic sort SALARY is marked with the implicit predicate SALARY-OF. Inasmuch as the implicit predicate is not always the right replacement, delineation checking and other tests are used to make the decision.

Scope of Quantifiers

Quantifiers and operators such as negation and superlatives are distinguished from normal predicates because their arguments cannot generally be determined by simple composition. To determine the embedding of their arguments (or, equivalently, the correct relative scopes), TEAM uses the structure of the parse tree to rank each permutation of the operators, eliminating those permutations that produce an ill-structured logical form (e.g., one that uses a variable outside the region in which it is quantified). The choice between the existential and universal readings of 'any' in questions and negative contexts is also handled at this stage. Legal interpretations are scored by a set of **scope critics** that judge specific aspects of the scoping. Left-right ordering, the relative **scoping strengths** of the operators, and the tendency of 'any' to exceed the scope of at least one structure that syntactically surrounds it are exemplary of the information embodied in the scope critics. The summed scoping scores are used to order the possibilities, and the user is shown the result in the form of a very literal English rendering of the logical form. If TEAM has succeeded, this rendering is a paraphrase of the original input sentence.

A post-processor applies a few minor transformations, and the result is a logical form that represents an unambiguous interpretation of the natural language sentence. The final process of TEAM uses this logical form (the logical form for our example sentence is shown in the next section), and the acquired conceptual schema, and the database schema information to produce a database query.

5. The Schema Translator

The schema translator translates the logical forms of English sentences into database queries for the host database system. The current database system is SODA, a relational database system embedded in LISP [Moore 79].

The schema translator performs the following four tasks in sequence:

1. It replaces logical form quantifiers by machine-oriented quantification operators.

2. It simplifies the logical form by expanding the definitions of derived predicates (virtual relations) and by removing predications implied by other predications in the logical form.

3. It identifies and eliminates redundant occurrences of the same relation with the same key field.

4. It translates the simplified logical form into the host query language, SODA.

The schema translator uses a **schema mapping** that defines the predicates used in the logical form in terms of the actual database relations. The schema mapping is analogous to the virtual relations in a relational database that are used to make a database application independent of the actual relations in the database. The schema mapping is expressed in a variation of the definite clause subset of first-order logic. This subset has convenient computational properties [Roussel 75] and allows the acquisition of new relations to be implemented by using an extension of the techniques of Query-by-Example [Zloof 75, Neves et al. 82], as shown in Section 3.

Schema Mapping

The following formulas give a fragment of the schema mapping produced by the acquisition processes for the relations in Figure 9 (the actual notation in TEAM is somewhat different)

```
(MANAGER emp mgr) <=
  (EMPLOYEE emp ? ? dept ?) &
  (DEPT dept mgr)

(EARN name salary) <=
  (EMPLOYEE name ? salary ? ?)

(SALARY-OF name salary) <=
  (EMPLOYEE name ? salary ? ?)

(EMPLOYEE-SORT name) <=
  (EMPLOYEE name ? ? ? ?)

(SALARY-SORT salary) <=
  (EMPLOYEE ? ? salary ? ?)

(MANAGER-SORT manager) <=
```

```
(DEPT ? manager)
```

The formulas above are merely definite clauses, with upper-case words denoting predicates, lower-case words denoting named variables, and '?' denoting anonymous (don't care) variables. The notation is positional, with the arguments of predicates corresponding to the relation fields in the same positions in Figure 9.

The first rule defines the virtual relation MANAGER in terms of the two database relations EMPLOYEE and DEPT. These two relations are joined (in the relational sense) by the shared variable **dept**.

The second and third rules define the implicit virtual relations EARN (a verb) and SALARY-OF by projecting the relation EMPLOYEE over the 'name' and 'salary' fields. These virtual relations are not defined explicitly during acquisition, but correspond to the association of verbs and nouns to particular combinations of fields of a single relation.

The last three rules trivially define sorts associated with fields of EMPLOYEE and DEPT as projections of appropriate relations.

The first fields of EMPLOYEE (name) and of DEPT (dept) are the key fields of those relations.

Schema Translation

We will show now how the schema translator processes the Logical Form from the example sentence in Section 4.

What employees earn more than their manager's salary?

```
(QUERY (WH e
       (EMPLOYEE-SORT e)
       (SOME m
         (AND
           (MANAGER-SORT m)
           (MANAGER m e))
         (SOME s1
           (AND
             (SALARY-SORT s1)
             (SALARY-OF m s1))
           (SOME s2
             (SALARY-SORT s2)
             (AND
               (EARN e s2)
               (GT s2 s1)))))))
```

The schema translator would transform this logical form in steps (1) to (4) which follows:

1. Translate into Horn clause format removing redundant quantifiers.

   ```
   (ANSWER e) <=
     (EMPLOYEE-SORT e) &
     (MANAGER-SORT m) &
     (MANAGER m e) &
     (SALARY-SORT s1) &
     (SALARY-OF m s1) &
     (SALARY-SORT s2) &
     (EARN e s2) &
     (GT s2 s1)
   ```

2. Expand the definitions of virtual relations, and remove the predications implied by other predications.

```
(ANSWER e) <=
  (EMPLOYEE-SORT e)
  (MANAGER-SORT m) &
  (EMPLOYEE e ? ? d ?) &
  (DEPT d m) &
  (SALARY-SORT s1) &
  (EMPLOYEE m ? s1 ? ?) &
  (SALARY-SORT s2) &
  (EMPLOYEE e ? s2 ? ?) &
  (GT s2 s1)

(ANSWER e) <=
  (EMPLOYEE e ? ? d ?) &
  (DEPT d m) &
  (EMPLOYEE m ? s1 ? ?) &
  (EMPLOYEE e ? s2 ? ?) &
  (GT s2 s1)
```

3. Identify relation instances with equal key fields.

```
(ANSWER e) <=
  (EMPLOYEE e ? s2 d ?) &
  (DEPT d m) &
  (EMPLOYEE m ? s1 ? ?) &
  (GT s2 s1)
```

4. Translate to SODA.

```
(IN $E EMPLOYEE)
 (IN $D DEPT)
  (EQ ($E DEPT) ($D NAME))
   (IN $M EMPLOYEE)
    (EQ ($M NAME) ($D MANAGER))
     (GT ($E SALARY) ($M SALARY))
      (? ($E NAME))
```

Note that all but the last step apply the inference rules created by acquisition to transform a formula into a simpler one that implies it. The last step merely entails a change of representation between two essentially equivalent languages. This deduction process effectively decouples the format of the logical form from the database query language and from the actual database.

6. Conclusion

We have constructed a natural-language interface that cleanly separates domain-dependent from domain-independent information. The domain-independent portion includes the parser and grammar, the semantic translators, the pragmatic and scope determining processes, the schema translator, and the basic vocabulary and taxonomy that form the initial state of the data structures subsequently modified by the acquisition process.

The information that is automatically acquired for each new domain includes: the lexicon; the conceptual schema, comprising taxonomy, predicate argument relations, and pragmatic markings; and the database schema, describing the mapping from predicates to database relations.

The current version of TEAM already supports fluent interaction with multiple file databases and work is underway to extend its linguistic and database coverage, especially in the following areas:

- Acquisition of more complex verbs, such as verbs with multiple delineations, verbs that require special prepositions, verbs that do not translate into a projection of an existing noun relation, and verbs with sentential complements.

- Interpretation of aggregates, quantified commands, and commands to perform functions other than database access.

- Treatment of common forms of sentences that use conjunctions.

- Time and tense in DIALOGIC and in the database.

Earlier versions of TEAM ran on a DEC 2060, implemented in a combination of INTERLISP (acquisition and DIALOGIC) and PROLOG (schema translator). The current version runs on a Symbolics LM-2 LISP machine, and includes its own PROLOG interpreter for the schema translation. Although TEAM is still under development and therefore has not yet been formally tested, it has successfully acquired a variety of databases.

Acknowledgments

The development of TEAM has profited from the efforts of Armar Archbold, Barbara Grosz, Norman Haas, Gary Hendrix, Jerry Hobbs, Bob Moore, Jane Robinson, Daniel Sagalowicz, and David Warren.

This research was supported by the Defense Advanced Research Projects Agency under Contract N00039-80-C-0645.

The views and conclusions contained in this document are those of the authors and should not be interpreted as representative of the official policies, either expressed or implied, of the Defense Advanced Projects Agency or the U.S. Government.

References

E. F. Codd, "A Relational Model of Data for Large Shared Data Banks," *Communications of the ACM*, Vol. 13, No. 6, pp. 377-387 (June 1970).

B. Grosz, N. Haas, G. G. Hendrix, J. Hobbs, P. Martin, R. Moore, J. Robinson and S. Rosenschein, "DIALOGIC: A Core Natural-Language Processing System." Technical Note 270, Artificial Intelligence Center, SRI International, Menlo Park, California (November 1982).

G. G. Hendrix, "Human Engineering for Applied Natural Language Processing," *Proc. 5th International Joint Conference on Artificial Intelligence*, pp. 183-191, IJCAI, Cambridge, Massachusetts (August 1977).

G. G. Hendrix, "Semantic Aspects of Translation," in *Understanding Spoken Language*, D. E. Walker, ed., pp. 193-226 (Elsevier, New York, New York, 1978).

J. R. Hobbs, "Pronoun Resolution." Research
Report 76-1, Department of Computer Sciences, City
College, City University of New York, New York,
New York (August 1976).

R. C. Moore, "Handling Complex Queries in a
Distributed Database." Technical Note 170, Artificial
Intelligence Center, SRI International, Menlo Park,
California (October 1979).

R. C. Moore, "Problems in Logical Form," *Proc. of the
19th Annual Meeting of the Association for
Computational Linguistics*, ACL, Stanford,
California (1981).

J. Neves, R. Backhouse and S. Anderson, A Prolog
Implementation of Query-by-Example. Forthcoming.,
1982.

J. J. Robinson, "Diagram: a Grammar for Dialogues,"
Communications of the ACM, Vol. 25, No. 1, pp.
27-47 (1982).

P. Roussel, "Prolog: Manuel de Référence et Utilisation."
Technical Report, Groupe d'Intelligence Artificielle,
Université d'Aix-Marseille II, Marseille,
France (1975).

W. A. Woods, R. M. Kaplan and B. Nash-Webber, "The
Lunar Sciences Natural Language Information
System: Final Report." Report 3438, Bolt Beranek
and Newman Inc. (June 1972).

M. M. Zloof, "Query-by-Example," *Proc. AFIPS 1975
NCC, vol. 44*, pp. 331-348, AFIPS Press, Montvale,
New Jersey (1975).

GUS, A Frame-Driven Dialog System[1]

Daniel G. Bobrow, Ronald M. Kaplan, Martin Kay, Donald A. Norman, Henry Thompson and Terry Winograd

Xerox Palo Alto Research Center, 3333 Coyote Hill Road. Palo Alto, CA 94304, U.S.A.

Recommended by Don Walker

ABSTRACT

GUS is the first of a series of experimental computer systems that we intend to construct as part of a program of research on language understanding. In large measure, these systems will fill the role of periodic progress reports, summarizing what we have learned, assessing the mutual coherence of the various lines of investigation we have been following, and suggesting where more emphasis is needed in future work. GUS (Genial Understander System) is intended to engage a sympathetic and highly cooperative human in an English dialog, directed towards a specific goal within a very restricted domain of discourse. As a starting point, GUS was restricted to the role of a travel agent in a conversation with a client who wants to make a simple return trip to a single city in California.

There is good reason for restricting the domain of discourse for a computer system which is to engage in an English dialog. Specializing the subject matter that the system can talk about permits it to achieve some measure of realism without encompassing all the possibilities of human knowledge or of the English language. It also provides the user with specific motivation for participating in the conversation, thus narrowing the range of expectations that GUS must have about the user's purposes. A system restricted in this way will be more able to guide the conversation within the boundaries of its competence.

1. Motivation and Design Issues

Within its limitations, GUS is able to conduct a more-or-less realistic dialog. But the outward behavior of this first system is not what makes it interesting or significant. There are, after all, much more convenient ways to plan a trip and, unlike some other artificial intelligence programs, GUS does not offer services or furnish information that are otherwise difficult or impossible to obtain. The system is interesting because of the phenomena of natural dialog that it attempts to model

and because of the principles of program organization around which it was designed. Among the hallmarks of natural dialogs are unexpected and seemingly unpredictable sequences of events. We describe some of the forms that these can take below. We then go on to discuss the modular design which makes the system relatively insensitive to the vagaries of ordinary conversation.

1.1. Problems of natural dialog

The simple dialog shown in Fig. 1 illustrates some of the language-understanding problems we attacked. (The parenthesized numbers are for reference in the text). The problems illustrated in this figure, and described in the paragraphs below, include allowing both the client and the system to take the initiative, understanding indirect answers to questions, resolving anaphora, understanding fragments of sentences offered as answers to questions, and interpreting the discourse in the light of known conversational patterns.

1.1.1. Mixed initiative

A typical contribution to a dialog, in addition to its more obvious functions, conveys an expectation about how the other participant will respond. This is clearest in the case of a question, but it is true of all dialog. If one of the participants has very particular expectations and states them strongly whenever he speaks, and if the other always responds in such a way as to meet the expectations conveyed, then the initiative remains with the first participant throughout. The success of interactive computer systems can often be traced to the skill with which their designers were able to assure them such a dominating position in the interaction. In natural conversations between humans, however, each participant usually assumes the initiative from time to time. Either clear expectations are not stated or simply not honored.

GUS attempts to retain the initiative, but not to the extent of jeopardizing the natural flow of the conversation. To this extent it is a mixed-initiative system (see Carbonell [5, 6]). This is exemplified in the dialogue at (1) where the client volunteers more information than GUS requested. In addition to his destination, the client gives the date on which he wants to travel. Line (3) illustrates a case where the client takes control of the conversation. GUS had found a potentially acceptable flight and asked for the client's approval. Instead of either giving or denying it, the client replied with a question of his own.

1.1.2. Indirect answers

It is by no means always clear what constitutes an answer to a question. Frequently the purported answer is at best only a basis on which to infer the information requested. For example, when GUS asks "What time do you want to leave?" it is seeking information to constrain the selection of a flight. The client's response to this question, at (2), does constrain the flight selection, but only indirectly. In

[1] This work was done by the language understander project at the Xerox Palo Alto Research center. Additional affiliations: D. A. Norman, University of California, San Diego; H. Thompson, University of California, Berkeley; and T. Winograd, Stanford University.

general, the kinds of inference necessary to interpret indirect answers can be very complex. GUS can handle the problem in its simpler manifestations, thanks largely to the very narrow expectations it has about the subject matter and the client's goals.

1.1.3. Resolving anaphora

A central issue in dialog is ensuring that both parties understand a given word or phrase as referring to the same object or event (see [19, Chap. 3] for a discussion of the general problem of reference). One problem occurs when a short phrase refers back to something that was introduced earlier. GUS provides for this problem in some of its simpler manifestations. At line (3), for example, the client's query refers to the flight mentioned in GUS's immediately preceding utterance. In (4) there is a reference to the flight mentioned earlier in the conversation, at (2). Note that "next flight" in (3) was to be interpreted relative to the order of flights in the airline guide whereas "first one" in (1) refers to the order in which the flights were mentioned. Another implicit referent underlies the use of "Friday" to specify a date in (6). Resolution of this reference requires some complicated reasoning involving both the content and the context of the conversation. Since May 28 has been given as the departure date, it must presumably be the following Friday that the client has in mind. On the other hand, suppose that the specifications were reversed and

GUS: Hello. My name is GUS. I can help you plan a simple trip by air. Where do you want to go?

(1) Client: I want to go to San Diego on May 28
GUS: What time do you want to leave?
(2) Client: I must be in San Diego before 10 am
GUS: Would you like P.S.A. flight 102 that arrives at 9.15 am?
(3) Client: What is the next flight?
GUS: Air California flight 310 that leaves at 8.30 am and arrives at 10.00 am
(4) Client: I'll take the first one
GUS: In what name should I make a reservation, please?
(5) Client: Dan Bobrow
GUS: I have confirmed the following flight:
P.S.A. flight 102 on Wednesday May 28 from San Jose to San Diego that leaves at 7.30 am and arrives at 9.15 am.
What date do you want to return on?
(6) Client: On Friday in the evening.
GUS: Would you like the flight that leaves at 7.45 pm?
(7) Client: That's fine.
GUS: I have confirmed the following flight:
P.S.A. flight 307 on Friday May 30 from San Diego to San Jose that leaves at 7.45 pm and arrives at 9.30 pm
Thank you for calling. Goodbye.

FIG. 1. A transcript of an actual dialog with GUS.

Friday had been given as the departure date at line (1). It would then be most readily interpretable as referring to the Friday immediately following the conversation.

1.1.4. Sentence fragments

Utterances in natural conversation are by no means always complete sentences. This is not to say that there are no rules governing the ways in which fragments can be used. We collected a number of dialogs between people and examined the sentence fragments that occurred: most appeared as answers to direct questions. Furthermore, a rule can almost invariably be derived from a question that will convert a fragmentary answer into a complete sentence expressing the same information. For example, the client's response in (5) to the request for a name is not a sentence but, when inserted in the blank space in the skeleton "You should make the reservation in the name of ——", it yields a sentence. Normal processing of the sentence so constructed gives the required interpretation of the fragment. This works even for the fragment in (6) which is not even a complete phrase.[2]

These skeletons are systematically related, in the sense of transformational grammar, to the corresponding questions. The blank space in the skeletons usually occurs at the end. If Sgall and the linguists of the modern Prague school are right, then this follows from a strong tendency to organize sentences so that given information comes at the beginning and new information at the end. In this case, the given information is clearly that which is shared by the question and its answer.

1.1.5. Conversational patterns

Conversations conform to patterns, which are still only poorly understood, and there are specialized patterns that are used in special circumstances such as those that obtain in a travel agency. Realism requires that GUS fit its conversational strategy to these patterns. For example, flights are usually specified by departure time, but in response to (2), GUS specifies an arrival time, because the client had specified the arrival time to constrain the choice of flights. This is in accordance with a typical conversational convention; a speaker says as little as will suffice to communicate the point to be made. Grice [11] calls these conventions conversational postulates and implicatures.

It seems also to be important to use conversational implicatures with respect to the goals of the client and the system in interpreting and generating the dialog (see [10] for a general discussion of this issue). For example, in (1) the client says where he wants to go. GUS interprets this as a request for an action, that is, inserting the appropriate information into the travel plan being generated.

1.2. Principles of program organization

One of the major methodological issues we addressed in designing and building GUS was the question of modularity. We realize that language understanding systems,

---

[2] The SRI speech system (Walker, et al. [23]) uses a different set of fragments.

and other systems exhibiting some degree of intelligence, will be very large and complicated programs, and the flow of processing within them will be correspondingly complex. As Simon [27] has pointed out, one way of reducing the complexity of a system is to decompose it into simpler, more readily comprehensible parts, and to develop and debug these in isolation from one another. When the separate modules have been constructed, however, the task of integrating them into a single system still remains. This can be difficult: truly complex systems are more than just the sum of their parts. The components, when put together, interact in subtle but important ways. We implemented GUS in order to determine whether a modular approach for a dialog system was at all feasible and to test our notions of what reasonable lines of decomposition might be. We are aware of alternative decompositions, and are not committed to this one; it was convenient given the program modules already available, and the issues we wished to focus on. GUS provided a context in which to explore tools and techniques for building and integrating independent modules.

The major knowledge-oriented processes and structures in GUS—the morphological analyzer, the syntactic analyzer, the frame reasoner, and the language generator—were built as independent processes with well defined languages or data structures to communicate across the interfaces. They were debugged separately, and tied together by means of an overall asynchronous control mechanism.

1.2.1. Control

The organization of the system is based on the view that language-understanding systems must operate in a multiprocess environment [12, 14]. In a system with many knowledge sources and a number of independent processes, some part of the mechanism must usually be devoted simply to deciding what shall be done next. GUS puts potential processes on a central *agenda*. GUS operates in a cycle in which it examines this agenda, chooses the next job to be done, and does it. In general, the execution of the selected task causes entries for new tasks to be created and placed on the agenda. Output text generation can be prompted by reasoning processes at any time, and inputs from the client are handled whenever they come in. There are places at which information from a later stage (such as one involving semantics) are fed back to an earlier stage (such as the parser). A supervisory process can reorder the agenda at any time. This process is similar in function to the control module in the BBN Speechlis system [20, 25] except that it can resume processes which are suspended with an active process state. Preserving the process state is necessary because the flow in the system is not unidirectional: for example, the state of the syntactic analysis cannot be completely abandoned when domain dependent translation starts. If a semantically and pragmatically appropriate interpretation of an utterance cannot be found from the first parsing, the syntactic analyzer must resume where it was suspended. INTERLISP's coroutine facility makes it possible to completely preserve the active state of the various processes [2, 22].

1.2.2. Procedural attachment

Broadly speaking, procedural attachment involves redrawing the traditional boundary between program and data in such a way as to give unusual primacy to data structures. Most of the procedures that make up a program, instead of operating on separate data structures, are linked to those structures and are activated when particular items of data are manipulated in particular ways. This technique lies at the heart of the reasoning component which is described in more detail later. It provides a natural way of associating operations with the classes or instances of data on which they are to operate. It is in some ways extensions of ideas found in SIMULA [7] and SMALLTALK [9].

1.2.3. Monitoring and debugging

In a multiprocessing system with processes triggered by procedures attached to complex data structures special tools are needed for programmers to monitor the flow of control and changes in the data structures. Tightly linked with the agenda scheduler there is a central monitor with knowledge about how to summarize the current actions of the system. The monitor interprets special printing instructions associated with potential actions and particular items of data. In effect, the principle of procedural attachment has been extended to debugging information.

1.2.4. External data-bases

We believe that an important application of specialized dialog systems like GUS may be to help users deal with large files of formatted data. In the travel domain, the *Official Airline Guide* is such an external data-base. GUS can use an extract of this data-base, but the information in the file does not form part of its active working memory for the same reason that the information in the *Official Airline Guide* does not have to be memorized by a travel agent. Only that portion of the data base relevant to a particular conversation need be brought into the working memory of the system.

2. Processes and Knowledge Bases

Fig. 2 illustrates the knowledge structures and processes in GUS. Each numbered row corresponds to a single knowledge based process in the system. The input to each process is shown in the left hand column. Each input is labelled with a number in parentheses indicating the row number of the process which produces it. Processes usually provide input to the ones listed below them. The third column names the process which produces the output structures specified in the fourth column, using for the processing the permanent knowledge bases specified in column two. Fig. 3 shows the output structures of the earlier stages of processing of the sentence "I want to go to San Diego on May 28". Starting with an input string of characters typed by the client, a sequence of words is identified by a lexical analyzer consisting of a dictionary lookup process and a morphological analysis. The analysis program

GUS, A FRAME-DRIVEN DIALOG SYSTEM

Input Structures	Permanent Knowledge Structures	Processes	Output Structures
1. Text String (input)	Stem dictionary: Morphological rules	Dictionary lookup: Morphological analysis	Chart of word data structures
2. Query context (6): Chart (1)	Transition net grammar	Syntactic analysis	Parsing of a sentence
3. Parsing of a sentence (2)	Case-frame dictionary	Case-frame analysis	Case-frame structure
4. Case-frame structure (3)	Speech patterns: Domain specific frame forms	Domain dependent translation	Frame change description
5. Frame change descriptions (4, 5): Current frame instances (5)	Prototype frames and attached procedures	Frame reasoning	Frame change descriptions: Output response descriptions: Current frame instances
6. Output response description (5)	Dialog query map: Flight description template	Response generation	English text: Query context

Fig. 2. Knowledge structures and processes in GUS.

CLIENT: I want to go to San Diego on May 28   . . .the syntactic analysis of the input

```
[S MOOD = DCL
 SUBJ = [NP HEAD = [PRO CASE = NOMIN
                    NUMBER = SG ROOT = I]]
 PVERB = [V TENSE = PRESENT ROOT = WANT] HEAD = WANT
 OBJ = [S MOOD = FOR-TO
   SUBJ = I
   HEAD = [V TENSE = PRESENT ROOT = GO]
   MODS = (
     [PP PREP = [PREP ROOT = TO]
      POBJ = [NP HEAD = [NPR PROPERTYPE = CITY-NAME
              ROOT = SAN-DIEGO]]]
     [PP PREP = [PREP ROOT = ON]
      POBJ = [NP HEAD = [NPR PROPERTYPE = DATE-NAME
              MONTH = MAY DAY = 28]]])]]]
```

```
[CLIENT DECLARE     . . .the case-frame structure
 (CASE FOR WANT/E (TENSE PRESENT)
  (AGENT (PATH DIALOG CLIENT PERSON)
  (EVENT (CASE FOR GO (TENSE PRESENT)
   (AGENT (PATH DIALOG CLIENT PERSON))
   (TO-PLACE (CASE FOR CITY
    (NAME SAN-DIEGO)))
   (DATE (CASE FOR DATE
    (MONTH MAY)
    (DAY 28)
```

```
CMD: [CLIENT DECLARE     . . .the domain dependent translation, a
 (FRAME ISA TRIP-LEG     . . .frame change description
  (TRAVELLER (PATH DIALOG CLIENT PERSON))
  (TO-PLACE (FRAME ISA CITY
   (NAME SAN-DIEGO)))
  (TRAVEL-DATE (FRAME ISA DATE
   (MONTH MAY)
   (DAY 28]
```

Fig. 3. Processing the client's first utterance.

has access to a main dictionary of more than 3,000 stems and simple idioms and a body of morphological rules specifying how the information in the dictionary can be used to partition character sequences into known lexical items [16]. The output of this stage is a *chart* [15], a table of syntactic and semantic information for use by the parser.

The syntactic analyzer is based on the General Syntactic Processor [12]. Using a transition-network grammar and the chart, the parser builds one or more canonical syntactic structures, depending on whether or not the sentence is syntactically ambiguous. It finds one parse, and can continue to find others if the sentence is ambiguous and the first parse is rejected as uninterpretable by a later process. The syntactic analysis of the input sentence is shown in Fig. 3.

The case-frame analysis uses linguistic knowledge associated with individual lexical items to relate their appearance in canonical syntactic structures to their uses in a semantic environment. It uses a dictionary of case-frames based on the ideas of case grammar originated by Fillmore [8]; see Bruce, [4] for a general review of case systems. This component uses knowledge about such things as selectional restrictions and the mapping between surface cases (including prepositions) and semantic roles. As we have already observed, interpretation of an utterance must include knowledge of conversational patterns for the appropriate domain. Domain dependent interpretations of utterances were implemented by a simple structure-matching and reconstruction program that operates on case-frames. The example in Fig. 3 illustrates how the domain-dependent translation module handles a common conversational pattern for the travel domain: it interprets a statement of desire (the WANT/E) as an instruction to insert the specified event into the trip plan being

constructed. In addition, the case frame involving GO is transformed into a description of the TRIP-LEG which is part of the planned trip, with the AGENT of GO becoming the TRAVELLER in the TRIP-LEG and the DATE becoming the TRAVEL-DATE. This simple translation mechanism is obviously very limited; in a more realistic system, the purposes of the client would have to be understood more deeply.

The frame reasoner component of the system was the focus of most of the research and development. It was based on the assumption that large scale structures closely tied to specific procedures for reasoning constitute a framework for producing a mixed initiative dialog system. It uses the frame change description (labelled CMD in Fig. 3) to fill in the appropriate information in the trip plan it is building and trigger associated reasoning, as described later.

The generation of output English is guided by a query-map, a set of templates for all the questions that might be asked by the system. GUS uses a table lookup mechanism to find the appropriate template and generates the English by filling in the template form. This simple generation mechanism is sufficient for the dialog system; generation was not one of the areas of substantial work.

The module that generates questions for the client simultaneously produces one or more skeletons into which his responses can be inserted, if they do not prove to be sentences in their own right. What is being done here is surprisingly simple and works well for most of the fragments we have encountered in response to simple WH-questions. Note that the language generator communicates with the syntactic analyzer using English phrase fragments rather than using a specially constructed formalism. This contrasts with other approaches to the fragment problem, in which the various components of the system are more deeply affected.

3. The Reasoning Component

3.1. Frames

It is widely believed in artificial intelligence that intelligent processing requires both large and small chunks of knowledge in which individual molecules have their own sub-structure. Minsky's 1975 paper on *frames* discusses the issues and suggests some directions in which to proceed. But, as Minsky stated, his ideas were not refined enough to be a basis for any working system. Our intuitions about the structure of knowledge resemble Minsky's in many ways, and we have appropriated the word *frame*. However, our conceptions are by no means identical to Minsky's, and the two notions should not be confused. The frame structures used in this system were a first step towards a more comprehensive knowledge representation language whose current development is described in [3].

Frames are used to represent collections of information at many levels within the system. Some frames describe the sequence of a normal dialog, others represent the attributes of a date, a trip plan, or a traveller. In general, a frame is a data structure potentially containing a *name*, a reference to a *prototype* frame, and a set of *slots*. Frame names are included primarily as a mnemonic device for the system builders and are not involved in any of the reasoning processes. In fact, names are not assigned to any of the temporary frames created during a dialog.

If one frame is the prototype of another, then we say that the second is an *instance* of the first. A prototype serves as a template for its instances. Except for the most abstract frames in the permanent data base, every frame in GUS is an instance of some prototype. Most instances are created during the process of reasoning, although some (for example those representing individual cities) are in the initial data base.

A frame's important substructures and its relations to other frames are defined in its slots. A slot has a *slot-name*, a *filler* or *value*, and possibly a set of attached procedures. The value of a slot may simply be another frame or, in the case of a prototype, it may be a description constraining what may fill the corresponding slot in any instance of the given frame. Fig. 4 shows the prototype frame for **date** and the specific date **May 28**, which has no external name. The fact that it is an instance of **date** is indicated by the keyword ISA followed by the prototype name.

The date prototype illustrates several of the ways in which the values for instance slots can be described. For example, the slot labelled MONTH specifies that only a *name* can be used as value; that is, only a literal LISP atom. GUS interprets a standard set of type terms such as *name, integer, list,* and *string.* The slot of WEEKDAY stipulates that a value for that slot must be a member of the list shown in the frame. The slot DAY can only be filled by an integer between 1 and 31. The terms BOUNDED-INTEGER and MEMBER have no special meaning to the interpreter. Any LISP function may occur in this position as a predicate whose value must be non-NIL for any object filling the slot.

Not all of the slots of an instance frame need to be filled in. For example, in May 28, only the MONTH, and DAY are filled in, and not the WEEKDAY. A prototype frame provides slots as placeholders for any data that might be relevant, even though it may not always be present. Only those slot values which are required for the current reasoning process need be put into instances.

```
[DATE
MONTH    NAME
DAY      (BOUNDED-INTEGER 1 31)
YEAR     INTEGER
WEEKDAY  (MEMBER (SUNDAY MONDAY TUESDAY
                 WEDNESDAY THURSDAY FRIDAY SATURDAY)]
```

a. Prototype for **date**

```
[ISA DATE
MONTH    MAY
DAY      28]
```

b. The instance frame for **May 28**.

FIG. 4. Examples of frames.

3.2. Procedural attachment

We have already referred to *procedural attachment*, a concept first discussed by this name by Winograd [25], as a central feature of GUS. Procedures are attached to a slot to indicate how certain operations are to be performed which involve either the slot in the given frame or the corresponding slot in its instances. We have found that there are many slots for which some processing is best done by idiosyncratic procedures. For example, there may be special ways of finding fillers for them or for doing other kinds of reasoning about them. This might include verifying that the value in an instance is consistent with other known information or propagating information when the slot value is obtained.

The procedures associated with slots fall into two general classes: *servants* and *demons*. *Demons* are procedures that are activated automatically when a datum is inserted into an instance. *Servants* are procedures that are activated only on demand.

The expanded **date** prototype in Fig. 5 contains examples of both classes. On the slot WEEKDAY there is a demon marked by the keyword WHENFILLED and a servant marked by the keyword TOFILL. When a value is filled into the WEEKDAY slot of a date instance, the WHENFILLED statement on the prototype causes the interpreter to invoke the demon FINDDATEFROMDAY. This procedure attempts to compute the appropriate date to fill the other slots in the frame, using the name of the day just entered and contextual information to identify the value uniquely.

The servant GETWEEKDAY on the same slot is only invoked when the name of the week day is needed. The requirement is satisfied by calling the LISP procedure GETWEEKDAY with the current instance as an implicit argument. The servant attached to the slot YEAR indicates how a default value can be filled in. If the year is given by the client, then this servant will never be activated. However, if the client does not mention the year explicitly, the system will fill in the default value 1975 when any part of the reasoning process calls for it.

The system provides a number of standard servant procedures. ASKCLIENT causes the client to be asked for information that will determine the value of the slot. CREATEINSTANCE indicates that a new instance of a specified prototype should be created and inserted at that location. Some of the values of the newly created frame may be filled in by the procedure, others may be left to be filled through later reasoning or interaction with the client. In addition to standard servants, the builders of the system can program special procedures to compute appropriate values, such as the GETWEEKDAY mentioned earlier.

```
[DATE
 MONTH    NAME
 DAY      (BOUNDED-INTEGER 1 31)
 YEAR     INTEGER (TOFILL ASSUME 1975)
 WEEKDAY  (MEMBER (SUNDAY MONDAY TUESDAY
                   WEDNESDAY THURSDAY FRIDAY SATURDAY))
          (WHENFILLED FINDDATEFROMDAY)
          (TOFILL GETWEEKDAY))
 SUMMARY (OR (LIST MONTH DAY) WEEKDAY))]
```

Fig. 5. The frame for date with attached procedures and summary form.

3.3. Summarizing data structures

In Fig. 5, the frame for date includes a slot with the special name SUMMARY. A SUMMARY slot appears only in a prototype frame, never in an instance. It gives a format for describing the instances of the prototype to help programmers monitor and debug the system. Thus, instances of **date** will be described by printing the month and day, e.g. (May 28) or, if they are not known, just the day of the week.

4. Using Frames to Direct the Dialog

Frames are used at several levels to direct the course of a conversation. At the top level, GUS assumes that the conversation will be of a known pattern for making trip arrangements. To conduct a dialog, the system first creates an instance of the dialog frame outlined in Fig. 6. It goes through the slots of this instance attempting to find fillers for them in accordance with the specifications given in the prototype. When a slot is filled by a new instance of a frame, the slots of that instance are filled in the same way. GUS follows this simple depth-first, recursive process, systematically completing work on a given slot before continuing to the next. This is how GUS attempts to retain the initiative in the dialog. Notice, however, that slots may occasionally be filled out of sequence either through information volunteered by the client or by procedures attached to previously encountered slots.

In Fig. 6, boldface atoms are frame names, representing pointers to other frames. (Substructures for the frames for **Person, Date, City, PlaceStay, TimeRange,** and **Flight** are not shown.) Each of the slots shown in Fig. 6 must be filled in during the course of the dialog, usually by invoking a servant attached to the prototype slot. The servants for some slots calculate the desired values from other known data, or (as in the case of frames like **TripSpecification**) simply create a new frame. The servant ASKCLIENT obtains information needed to fill a slot by interrogating the client. The default organization of a dialog is determined by the order of the slots which have ASKCLIENT as servant, since appropriate questions will be asked if those slots have not been filled by the time they are encountered.

Now let us follow the system as it goes through part of a dialog, with special emphasis on the process of filling in the slots of frames. The dialog and the relevant information about the state of the system are shown in Fig. 7. This figure is the beginning of an actual transcript of a session, and the information shown there is provided to allow us (in the role of system builders) to follow the actions of the system.

The dialog starts when GUS outputs a standard message ("Hello. My name is GUS. I can help you plan a simple trip by air."). At that point, GUS knows that it is about to conduct a dialog on travel arrangements, so it creates an instance of the prototype **Dialog** frame shown in Fig. 6 and starts to try to fill its slots. (From now on, all numbers in parentheses refer to the corresponding lines of the frames of Fig. 6. All references to the dialog refer to Fig. 7.) The slot CLIENT at (1) contains a servant which fills this slot, when necessary, by creating a new instance of **Person.** This is indicated in the first line of the transcript of Fig. 7, where the instance of person is shown as {ISA PERSON}. After the slot is filled in, a demon associated with the CLIENT slot is triggered, which then puts the same person instance in the TRAVELLER slot in (16). GUS fills the NOW slot in (2) by constructing a frame instance for today's date.

It then creates a **TripSpecification** instance (3), summarized by ROUNDTRIP TO? in the transcript of Fig. 7, to fill the TOPIC slot (3).

At this point the **Dialog** frame has been completely filled in so GUS proceeds to fill in the slots of the **TripSpecification** frame. In (4), a HOMEPORT which is a **City** is required; GUS assumes, on the basis of an attached servant, that the home port is **Palo-Alto.** There is no attached servant to find the FOREIGNPORT in (5), so GUS just

Slots	Fillers	Servants	Demons
Dialog			
(1) CLIENT	**Person**	Create	Link to TRAVELLER
(2) NOW	**Date**	GetDate	
(3) TOPIC	**Trip Specification**	Create	
TripSpecification			
(4) HOMEPORT	City	Default— Palo Alto	
(5) FOREIGNPORT	City		Link to OUTWARDLEG, AWAYSTAY, INWARDLEG
(6) OUTWARDLEG	**TripLeg**	Create	
(7) AWAYSTAY	**PlaceStay**		
(8) INWARDLEG	**TripLeg**	Create	
TripLeg			
(9) FROMPLACE	City	FindFrom HOMEPORT	
(10) TOPLACE	City	AskClient	
(11) TRAVELDATE	**Date**	AskClient	
(12) DEPARTURESPEC	**TimeRange**	AskClient	Propose-Flight-By-Departure
(13) ARRIVALSPEC	**TimeRange**	AskClient	Propose-Flight-By-Arrival, Link to DEPARTURESPEC
(14) PROPOSEDFLIGHTS	(SetOfFlight)		
(15) FLIGHTCHOSEN	**Flight**	Ask Client	
(16) TRAVELLER	**Person**	Ask Client	

FIG. 6. An outline of key frame structures for our dialog.

leaves that slot empty for the moment. When a **TripLeg** instance is created for the outward leg of the journey, GUS begins trying to fill its slots. A servant for FROM-PLACE specifies that it should be filled with the city used for HOMEPORT in the **Trip Specification** frame, so **PaloAlto** is filled in. The first slot which has an ASKCLIENT servant is at (10), which requires a city to fill the TOPLACE in the **TripLeg,** which is the OUTWARDLEG of the **TripSpecification** (6). GUS issues the command (CMD) shown at the bottom of Fig. 7, which directs the generation of the English question. This is done by a rather elaborate table look up: the result is shown as the last line of Fig. 7.

We continue the trace of the analysis in Fig. 8, starting with the client's response to the question. The domain dependent translation contains the information needed to fill the frame slots. The result of the client's English input is that both the TOPLACE (10) and the TRAVELDATE (11) of the **TripLeg** are filled in.

GUS: Hello. My name is GUS. I can help you plan a simple trip by air.

CLIENT = {ISA PERSON} in {ISA DIALOG}
TODAY = (MAY 15) in {ISA DIALOG}
TOPIC = (ROUNDTRIP TO ?) in {ISA DIALOG}
HOME-PORT = PALO-ALTO in (ROUNDTRIP TO ?)
FROM-PLACE = PALO-ALTO in (TRIP TO ?)
CMD: (GUSQUERY (DIALOG TOPIC TRIP-SPECIFICATION
        OUTWARD-LEG TRIP-LEG TO-PLACE CITY))

GUS: Where do you want to go?

FIG. 7. The beginning of the transcript for the dialog.

The system then continues working its way through the entire tree specified by the frames, asking questions of the client. Many of the slots have demons which propagate information to other places in the data structure. For example, when the city that fills the slot FOREIGNPORT (5) is found, GUS will insert that same **City** as the place to stay in the AWAYSTAY (7). The FOREIGNPORT city also serves as the destination of the OUTWARDLEG of the trip and the starting point of the return trip (the INWARDLEG). To handle this information, GUS establishes two instances of the frame **TripLeg**, one for the outward leg, the other for the inward leg, and puts the city names in the appropriate slots.

Once a departure specification (some time range before, near or after the desired flight departure) is determined, a demon attached to DEPARTURESPEC calls a program which uses this information to propose a flight. Each proposed flight is added to the slot for PROPOSEDFLIGHTS (14). This slot can be used to resolve anaphoric references to flights, based on the order of their mention in the conversation. GUS then tries to determine which of the flights is appropriate to fill in the FLIGHT-CHOSEN slot (15). When that has been determined, it will ask for the name of the traveller and confirm the flight.

Many of the slots are marked in such a way that they need not be filled for the dialog to be completed. For example, the arrival specification (13) in each **TripLeg** frame is never requested. This slot is provided as a place to put constraints about the arrival of the flight, if the client volunteers information constraining the desired arrival time. Demons associated with that slot would then be activated to propose a flight based on the arrival time. In a similar way, the AWAYSTAY slot in the trip specification (7), is never asked for. If the client specifies something about the time range of the AWAYSTAY, as he did in the dialog of Fig. 1, there is a place to store that information in the frame structure and a demon to put it into the appropriate **TripLeg.**

Fig. 9 illustrates how a sentence fragment is processed. GUS asks "What date do you want to return on?" Generation of the question also generates a context for the expected interpretation of the next answer. The context is an inverted form of the question; that is, "I want to return" is a potential prefix to the next response. The preposition "on" may be optionally inserted in this prefix. The client responds "on Friday in the evening". Since this is not a sentence, the question context is used in the interpretation and the actual parsed structure which is interpreted is derived from the sentence "I want to return on Friday in the evening."

The time is taken as a departure specification and the date is specified in terms of the day of the week. The day of the week is filled into the appropriate place and date, and then the demon associated with that slot in date is activated. That demon computes the date relative to the previous date specified in the conversation. The phrase *evening* is taken as being equivalent to "around 7.30 pm". From this departure specification, GUS proposes the flight that leaves nearest to that time. Information is provided to the client about the leaving time, not the arrival time, because the client constrained the choice of flight by leaving time.

This simple dialog illustrates how GUS attempts to control a conversation by fitting it to the mold laid down in a structure of related frames. It has a place prepared in this structure for each piece of information that might potentially be used for making travel arrangements. It also has a strategy that will cause the pieces of information that the client must supply to be elicited in a natural order. The sequence of slots in the frames determines the usual course of the conversation, but it will change if, for example, the client volunteers information or asks questions.

5. Real and Realistic Dialogs

There is an important difference between *real* and *realistic* conversations. The simple dialog in Fig. 1 is a *realistic* conversation that was actually carried on with GUS. It is much too easy to extrapolate from that conversation a mistaken notion that GUS contained solutions to far more problems than it did. To get an idea of some problems that GUS does not approach, we collected a variety of travel dialogs that clients of a full-fledged system (perhaps the final version of GUS) might expect to conduct. We did this by simulating the system, asking the clients to arrange for round trip air flights between Palo Alto and San Diego, typing all queries and responses on the computer terminal, and pretending that a computer system was interacting with them. In fact, the role of GUS was played by an experimenter sitting at another computer terminal, airline guide, travel books, and calendar in hand, responding to the client.[3]

The two participants—client and experimenter—were each seated in independent, individual sound-isolated experimental booths. They communicated with a special experimental program (designed for tutorial instruction) that presented the experimenter's responses in a block presentation, so it appeared as a realistic approximation.

[3] The experimental dialogs were collected by Allen Munro in the LNR research laboratory at the University of California, San Diego.

```
CLIENT: I want to go to San Diego on May 28
CMD: [CLIENTDECLARE                              ...the domain dependent translation
     (FRAME ISA TRIP-LEG
     (TRAVELLER (PATH DIALOG CLIENT PERSON))
     (TO-PLACE (FRAME ISA CITY
          (NAME SAN-DIEGO)))
     (TRAVEL-DATE (FRAME: ISA DATE
          (MONTH MAY)
          (DAY 28))

TO-PLACE = SAN-DIEGO in (TRIP TO ?)             ...filling in the requested information
TRAVEL-DATE = (MAY 28) in (TRIP TO SAN-DIEGO)   ...and the volunteered
                                                   information

dowhen TO-PLACE is put in (TRIP TO SAN-DIEGO)   ...propagating information to
                                                   other slots

(LINK TRIP-SPECIFICATION FOREIGN-PORT CITY)
```

Fig. 8. The reasoning from the first input utterance.

```
GUS: What date do you want to return on?                 ...a query generated by GUS
The context of the next answer is:
(I WANT TO RETURN ((ON) (*SKIP*)))—     ...The expected context of the query
                                            response

CLIENT: On Friday in the evening
CMD: [CLIENTDECLARE   ...the domain dependent translation, including context
     (FRAME ISA TRIP-LEG
     (TRAVELLER (PATH DIALOG CLIENT PERSON))
     (TRAVEL-DATE (FRAME ISA DATE
          (WEEKDAY FRIDAY)))
     (DEPARTURE-SPEC (FRAME ISA TIME-RANGE
          (DAY-PART EVENING]

WEEKDAY = FRIDAY in {ISA DATE}      ...triggering a demon to find the Friday's date
dowhen WEEKDAY is put in {ISA DATE}
     (FINDDATEFROMDAY)
DAY = 30 in (MAY 30)
DAY-PART = EVENING IN {ISA TIME-RANGE}      ...evening is interpreted as
                                               around 7.30 pm

DEPARTURE-SPEC = (AT 7.30 PM) in (TRIP TO PALO-ALTO)
dowhen DEPARTURE-SPEC is put in (TRIP TO PALO-ALTO)
     (PROPOSE-FLIGHT-BY-DEPARTURE)      ...this demon proposes a flight using a
                                           departure spec

GUS: Would you like the flight that leaves at 7.45 pm?
CLIENT: That's fine.
```

Fig. 9. Processing a sentence fragment.

6. Conclusions

Computer programs in general, and programs intended to model human performance in particular, suffer from an almost intolerable delicacy. If their users depart from the behavior expected of them in the minutest detail, or if apparently insignificant adjustments are made in their structure, their performance does not usually change commensurately. Instead, they turn to simulating gross aphasia or death. The hope, which has been at least partially realized in GUS, is that the notions of procedural attachment and scheduling, as well as being realistic cognitive models, will make for more robust systems. We were pleased, for example, by the way the system's expectations could evolve in the course of a single conversation. The client would occasionally seize the initiative, volunteering information that was not asked for or refusing to answer a question as asked and GUS was able to respond appropriately in many cases. It would be misleading to press these claims too far. GUS never reached the stage where it could be turned loose on a completely naive client, however cooperative. But, to one familiar with other systems of the same general kind, the impression of increased robustness is clear.

GUS represents a beginning step towards the construction of an intelligent language understanding system. GUS itself is not very intelligent, but it does illustrate what we believe to be essential components of such a system. An intelligent language understander must have a high quality parser, a reasoning component, and a well structured data base of knowledge. The knowledge is of several types, from language specific information and expertise in the topic areas in which it can converse to broad general knowledge of the world that must be used to interpret people's utterances. This knowledge tends to be taken for granted by most native speakers of the language, hence often left for the listener to infer. The system must be capable of giving direction to the conversation, but it must also be flexible enough to respond to novel directions set by the clients. The system must be able to make use of a large external data base and to understand what information must be retrieved and processed in depth. There must be an intimate connection between its representation of structural knowledge and the procedures used to process knowledge. A general framework for representing knowledge must be able to encompass all the different necessary forms of knowledge. In our future studies of GUS, we intend to broaden the general framework for representing knowledge, as well as to increase the power of the components of the system. Preliminary steps in this direction include the development of improved systems for language analysis [16] and a knowledge representation language (KRL): [3].

REFERENCES

1. Bobrow, D. G. and Collins, A. M. (Eds.), *Representation and Understanding: Studies in Cognitive Science* (Academic Press, New York, 1975).
2. Bobrow, D. G. and Wegbreit, B., A model and stack implementation of multiple environments, *Comm. ACM*, **16** (1973) 591–603.
3. Bobrow, D. G. and Winograd, T., An overview of KRL, a Knowledge Representation Language, *Cognitive Sci.* **1** (1) (1977).

tion of a computer output, without the slow typing rate that would occur otherwise. The system delays were approximately what one would expect for the operation of a complex program (10 to 60 seconds response time).

Some of the problems we found were unexpected. For example, people spent a lot of time telling us about their thought processes and reasons. They made excuses for changing their minds. They hedged a lot about what they wanted. Fig. 10(a)

GUS: Do you want a flight leaving at 4.00 pm
CLIENT: Do you have something a little closer to 7?
GUS: Do you want the flight at 7.00 pm?
    (a) Interpreting politeness

GUS: Do you want the flight arriving at 8.00 pm?
CLIENT: When does it leave?
GUS: 6.30 pm
CLIENT: How much?
GUS: $25.50 round trip
    (b) Some pronominal reference problems

GUS: When would you like to return?
CLIENT: I would like to leave on the following Tuesday, but I have to be back before my first class at 9 am.
    (c) Giving a reason for flight preference

FIG. 10. Fragments of real dialogs, with a person simulating the role of GUS.

illustrates a type of conversational interaction our current system cannot even begin to handle. When the system proposes a flight at 4 pm, the client requests something *a little closer to* 7. A literal interpretation of that request would be to find a flight that is as close to 4 pm as possible, but in the direction of 7 pm: perhaps the 5.00 pm flight. That, of course, is not at all what was desired by the client. The human experimenter made the natural response of offering the flight that left at 7.

Fig. 10(b) indicates some pronominal reference problems which we did not attack at all. When the client says "when does *it leave*" it is quite obvious that he wants the departure time of the flight referred to in the previous sentence. For his question "how much," a response that "all of the plane leaves" seems somewhat inappropriate. In this case, the client is not referring to the previous system response, but rather is asking about the cost of the flight. But a response such as "how much" can sometimes refer to the previous system response. Suppose the system had just stated "They serve food on that flight." In this case, the client's query could be appropriately interpreted by the system as referring to the quantity of food. GUS cannot solve the problem of determining when a response is meant to refer to the previous question and when it is not.

Fig. 10(c) illustrates how people provide extra information about their motivations. In a system with a better model of human needs and desires, this would be useful for suggesting alternatives that might otherwise be ruled out.

4. Bruce, B., Case systems for natural language, *Artificial Intelligence* **6** (1975) 327–360.

5. Carbonell, J. R., AI in CAI: An artificial intelligence approach to computer-aided instruction, *IEEE Trans. Man-Machine Syst.* **11** (1970) 190–202.

6. Carbonell, J. R., Mixed-initiative man-computer instructional dialogues, Unpublished Ph.D. dissertation, Massachusetts Institute of Technology, Cambridge, MA (1970).

7. Dahl, O. J., and Nygaard, K., SIMULA – an ALGOL-Based Simulation Language, *Comm. ACM* **9**, (1966) 671–678.

8. Fillmore, C., The case for case, in: Bach, E. and Harms, R. T. (Eds.), *Universals in Linguistic Theory* (Holt, New York, 1968).

9. Goldberg, A. and Kay, A. (Eds.), SMALLTALK-72 instruction manual, Xerox Palo Alto Research Center SSL-76-6. Palo Alto, CA (1976).

10. Gordon, D. and Lakoff, G., Conversational postulates, Papers from Seventh Regional Meeting, Chicago Linguistic Society, Chicago, University of Chicago Linguistics Department (1972).

11. Grice, H. P., Logic and conversation, in: Cole, P. and Morgan, J. L., (Eds.), *Studies in Syntax. Volume III* (Seminar Press, New York, 1975).

12. Kaplan, R., A general syntactic processor, in: R. Rustin (Ed.), *Natural language processing* (Algorithmics Press, New York, 1973).

13. Kaplan, R., A multi-processing approach to natural language, *Proc. 1973 Nat. Comput. Conf.* (AFIPS Press, Montvale, NJ, 1973).

14. Kaplan, R., On process models for sentence analysis, in: Norman, D. A., Rumelhart, D. E., and the LNR Research Group, *Explorations in Cognition* (Freeman, San Francisco, 1975).

15. Kay, M., The MIND system, in: Rustin, R. (Ed.), *Natural language processing* (Algorithmics Press, NY, 1973).

16. Kay, M. and Kaplan, R., Word recognition, Xerox Palo Alto Research Center, Palo Alto, CA (1976).

17. Minsky, M. A., framework for representing knowledge, in: Winston, O. (Ed.), *The psychology of Computer Vision* (McGraw-Hill, NY, 1975).

18. Reddy, D. R., Erman. L. D., Fennell, R. D. and Neely, R. B., HEARSAY speech understanding system: An example of the recognition process, *Proc. Third Int. Joint Conf. Artificial Intelligence*, Stanford University (August 1973).

19. Norman, D. A., Rumelhart, D. E. and the LNR Research Group, *Explorations in cognition*, (Freeman, San Francisco, 1975).

20. Rovner, P., Nash-Webber, B. and Woods, W. A., Control concepts in a speech understanding system, *Proc. IEEE Symp. Speech Recognition*, Carnegie-Mellon University (April 1974).

21. Simon, H., *Sciences of the Artificial* (Massachusetts Institute of Technology Press, Cambridge, MA, 1969).

22. Teitelman, W., INTERLISP reference manual, Xerox Palo Alto Research Center, Palo Alto, California (December 1975).

23. Walker, D., Paxton, W., Robinson, J., Hendrix, G., Deutsch, B., and Robinson, A., Speech understanding research, Annual report, Project 3804, Artificial Intelligence Center, Stanford Research Institute (1975).

24. Winograd, T., Frames and the declarative procedural controversy, in: Bobrow, D. G., and Collins, A. M., (Eds.), *Representation and Understanding* (Academic Press, New York, 1975).

25. Woods, W. A., Motivation and overview of BBN SPEECHLIS: An experimental prototype for speech understanding research, *Proc. IEEE Symp. Speech Recognition*, Carnegie-Mellon University (April 1974).

Received May 1976

Toward a Natural-Language Capability for Computer-Assisted Instruction[1]

RICHARD R. BURTON and
JOHN SEELY BROWN

THE NATURE AND REQUIREMENTS OF A NATURAL-LANGUAGE SYSTEM

This is a period of dramatic advances in computer technology that should change the way computers are employed in instruction. Technological advances will decrease the cost of computer hardware to the extent that each student will have available computational resources that are currently restricted to a few elite users. Traditional computer-assisted instruction (CAI) paradigms were developed under the assumption that computational power is a scarce resource, and these paradigms are, for the most part, incapable of exploiting the latest technological advances. To use the increased computational power effectively requires a reevaluation of the role of the computer in instructional paradigms, and, in turn, a reevaluation of the authoring aids needed to facilitate efficient development in this medium.

[1] This research was supported in part by the Defense Advanced Research Projects Agency, Air Force Human Resources Laboratory, Army Research Institute for Behavioral and Social Sciences, and Naval Personnel Research and Development Center under contract number MDA903-76-C-0108. Views and conclusions contained in this document are those of the author and should not be interpreted as necessarily representing the official policies, either expressed or implied, of these agencies or of the United States government.

The type of instructional system that we see emerging has specific knowledge and problem-solving expertise that is used to aid students. First, as a source of information, it can answer their questions, evaluate their theories, and critique their solution paths. Second, as a tutorial mechanism, it can form models of both the students' states of knowledge and their reasoning strategies. These structural models are used both to identify fundamental misconceptions and to determine when and how to provide remediation, heuristic recommendations ("hints"), or further instruction.

In general, we are not focusing on techniques for teaching factual, textbook knowledge. Computer-assisted instruction systems that do not use the knowledge they contain (as a textbook does not use the knowledge it contains) can competently handle this task and are inherently cheaper for it. Instead, we are focusing on techniques for teaching *procedural knowledge* and *reasoning strategies* that are learned when students must use their factual knowledge in hands-on laboratory or problem-solving tasks. While the students are getting a chance to exercise their knowledge, the "intelligent" instructional systems that we are considering here attempt to mimic the capabilities of a laboratory instructor. The system works on a one-to-one basis with students, carefully diagnosing what they know, how they reason, and what kinds of deficiencies exist in their ability to apply factual knowledge. The system then uses this inferred knowledge of the students together with its knowledge of pedagogy to determine how best to advance their learning.

Although we are still a long way from attaining this goal, we have developed an organization for intelligent instructional systems (described in Brown, 1977) that appears fruitful. Our methodology for developing this organization (and the theory underlying it) has been to explore parts of the overall organization in *paradigmatic systems*. A paradigmatic system is an easily modified prototype system constructed over a carefully chosen domain of knowledge. This methodology allows experimentation with some aspect of the overall system by simplifying other aspects. We have developed systems for such domains as electronic trouble-shooting—SOPHIE (Brown, Burton, & Bell, 1975; Brown, Rubinstein, & Burton, 1976); arithmetic drill and practice—WEST (Burton & Brown, 1976, 1978); elementary algebra (Brown, Burton, & Bell, 1975); and procedural skills in arithmetic—BUGGY (Brown & Burton, 1978). In addition, systems of similar spirit are being developed by Carr and Goldstein (1977).

One of the major stumbling blocks for an intelligent instructional system is the lack of a natural means of communication between the student and the computer. This chapter addresses the problems of using natural language (English) as the communication language for advanced computer-based instructional systems. The instructional environment places requirements on a natural-language understanding system that exceed the capabilities of all existing systems. These requirements include (a) efficiency; (b) habitability; (c) tutorial capability; and (d) the ability to exist with ambiguity. However, there are major leverage points within the instructional environment that allow these requirements to be met. In the remainder of this section, we will elaborate on these requirements.

A primary requirement for a natural-language processor, in an instructional situation, is *efficiency*. Imagine the following setting: The student is at a terminal actively working on a problem. The student decides that another piece of information is needed to advance the solution, so a query is formulated. Having finished typing the question, the student will wait for the system to give an answer before continuing to work on the solution. During the time it takes the system to understand the query and generate an answer, the student is apt to forget pertinent information and lose interest. Psychological experiments have shown that response delays longer than 2 seconds have serious effects on the performance of complex tasks via terminals (Miller, 1968). In these 2 seconds the system must understand the query; deduce, infer, look up, or calculate the answer; and generate a response. Another adverse effect of poor response time is that more of the student's searching for the answer is done internally (i.e., without using the system). This decreases the amount of information the tutoring system receives and increases the amount of induction that must be performed, making the problem of figuring out what the student is doing much harder (e.g., students will not "show their work" when solving a problem; they will just present the answer).

The second requirement for a natural-language processor is *habitability*. Any natural-language system written in the foreseeable future is not going to be able to understand all of natural language. What a good natural-language interface must do is characterize and understand a usable subset of the language. Watt (1968) defines a "habitable" sublanguage as "one in which its users can express themselves without straying over the language boundaries into unallowed sentences [p. 338]." Very intuitively, for a system to be habitable it must, among other things, allow the user to make local or minor modifications to an accepted sentence and get another accepted sentence. Exactly how much modification constitutes a minor change has never been specified. Some examples may provide more insight into this notion.

1. *Is anything wrong?*
2. *Is there anything wrong?*
3. *Is there something wrong?*
4. *Is there anything wrong with Section 3?*
5. *Does it look to you as if Section 3 could have a problem?*

If a natural-language processor accepts Sentence 1, it should also accept the modifications given in Sentences 2 and 3. Sentence 4 presents a minor syntactic extension that may have major repercussions in the semantics but that should also be accepted. Sentence 5 is an example of a possible paraphrase of Sentence 4 that is beyond the intended notion of habitability. Based on the acceptance of Sentences 1–4, the user has no reason to expect that Sentence 5 will be handled.

Any sub-language that does not maintain a high degree of habitability is apt to be worse than no natural-language capability at all because, in addition to the problem one is seeking information about, the student is faced, sporadically, with the problem of getting the system to understand a query. This second problem can be disastrous both because it occurs seemingly at random and because it is ill-defined.

In an informal experiment to test the habitability of a system, the authors asked a group of four students to write down as many ways as possible of asking a particular question. The original idea was to determine how many of the various paraphrasings would be accepted by the prototype systems we were testing. The students each came up with one phrasing very quickly but had tremendous difficulty thinking of any others, even though three of the first phrasings were different! This experience demonstrates the lack of the student's ability to do "linguistic" problem solving and points out the importance of accepting the student's first phrasing.

An equally important aspect of the habitability problem is multisentence (or dialogue) phenomena. When students use a system that exhibits "intelligence" through its inference capabilities, they quickly start to assume that the system must also be intelligent in its conversational abilities as well. For example, they will frequently delete parts of their statements that they feel are obvious, given the context of the preceding statements. Often they are totally unaware of such deletions and show surprise and/or anger when the system fails to utilize contextual information as clearly as they (subconsciously) do. The use of context manifests itself in the use of such linguistic phenomena as pronominalizations, anaphoric deletions, and ellipses. The following sequence of questions exemplifies these problems:

6. *What is the population of Los Angeles?*
7. *What is it for San Francisco?*
8. *What about San Diego?*

The third requirement for a natural-language processor is that it be *self-tutoring* (i.e., that it should teach the students about its capabilities). As the students use the system, they should begin to feel the range and limitations of the sub-language. When the students use a sentence that the system cannot understand, they should receive feedback that will enable them to determine why it cannot. There are at least two kinds of feedback. The simplest (and most often seen) merely provides some indication of what parts of the sentence caused the problem (e.g., unknown word or phrase). A more useful kind of feedback goes on to provide a response based on those parts of the sentence that did make sense and then indicate (or give examples of) possibly related, acceptable sentences. It may even be advantageous to have the system recognize common unacceptable sentences and in response to them, explain why they are not in the sub-language. (See the fifth section, on experiences with SOPHIE, for further discussion of this point.)

The fourth requirement for a natural-language system is that it be aware of *ambiguity*. Natural language gains a good deal of flexibility and power by not forcing every meaning into a different surface structure. This means that the program that interprets natural language sentences must be aware that more than one interpretation is possible. For example, when asked

9. *Was John believed to have been shot by Fred?*

one of the most potentially disastrous responses is "Yes." The user may not be sure whether Fred did the shooting or the believing or both. More likely, the user, being unaware of any ambiguity, assumes an interpretation that may be different than the system's. If the system's interpretation is different, the user thinks he has received the answer to his query when in fact he has received the answer to a completely independent query. Either of the following is a much better response:

10. *Yes, it is believed that Fred shot John.*
11. *Yes, Fred believes that John was shot.*

The system need not necessarily have tremendous disambiguation skills, but it must be aware that misinterpretations are possible and inform the user of its interpretation. In those cases where the system makes a mistake the results may be annoying but should not be catastrophic.

This chapter presents the development of a technique that we have named *semantic grammars* for building natural-language processors that satisfy the above requirements. The next section presents a dialogue from the "intelligent" CAI system SOPHIE that we used to refine and demonstrate this technique. This dialogue provides concrete examples of the

kinds of linguistic capabilities that can be achieved using semantic grammars. The third section describes semantic grammar as it first evolved in SOPHIE, and points out how it allows semantic information to be used to handle dialogue constructs and to allow the directed ignoring of words in the input. The fourth section discusses the limitations that were encountered in the evolution of semantic grammars in SOPHIE as the range of sentences was increased and how these might be overcome by using a different formalism—augmented transition networks (ATN). This section also reports on the conversion of the SOPHIE semantic grammar to an ATN, and the extensions to the ATN formalism that were necessary to maintain the solutions presented in the previous section. It also includes comparison timings between the two versions of the natural-language processor. The fifth section describes experiences we have had with SOPHIE and presents techniques developed to handle problems in the area of nonunderstood sentences. The sixth section suggests directions for future work.

DIALOGUE FROM SOPHIE

Before delving into the structural aspects and technical details of the semantic grammar technique, we would first like to provide a concrete example of the dialogues it has supported. This section presents an annotated dialogue of a student using the "intelligent" CAI system SOPHIE.[2] SOPHIE was developed to explore the use of artificial intelligence techniques in providing tutorial feedback to students engaged in problem-solving activities. The particular problem-solving activity that SOPHIE is concerned with is the troubleshooting of a malfunctioning piece of electronic equipment. SOPHIE models the piece of equipment and answers the student's requests for measurements and other information to aid in debugging the equipment. More important, throughout the problem-solving session, SOPHIE can evaluate the logical consistency of a student's hypothesis or generate hypotheses that are consistent with the behavior the student has thus far observed.[3] In the dialogue, the student's typing is underlined. Even though the dialogue deals with electronic jargon, the linguistic issues it exemplifies occur in all domains. The

---

[2] The dialogue is intended to demonstrate SOPHIE's linguistic capabilities and, though it touches upon the major features of SOPHIE, it is not meant to exhibit the logical or deductive capabilities of the system.

[3] The reader is encouraged to see Brown and Burton (1975) for further examples and descriptions of SOPHIE's tutorial and inferential capabilities.

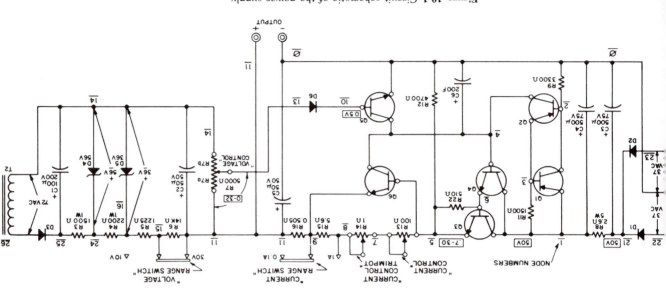

Figure 10.1 Circuit schematic of the power supply.

annotations (below the dialogue) attempt to point out these problems and should be understandable to the non-electronics-oriented reader.

WELCOME TO SOPHIE—A SIMULATED ELECTRONICS LABORATORY.

The circuit (Figure 10.1) is based on the Heathkit IP-28 power supply. The IP-28 is a reasonably sophisticated power supply with both current-limiting and voltage-limiting behavior. These two interrelated feedback loops make troubleshooting this circuit nontrivial.

≫INSERT A FAULT

The student tells SOPHIE to make one of the components in the circuit bad. SOPHIE randomly selects a fault, inserts it into a model of the instrument, and tells the student how the front panel controls are presently set.

THE INSTRUMENT HAS A FAULT AND ITS PRESENT CONTROL SETTINGS ARE:

CC	1.0	CURRENT CONTROL—FROM .0 (MIN CURRENT) TO 1.0
CR	HIGH	CURRENT RANGE SWITCH, HIGH=1 AMP, LOW=.1 AMP
LOAD	1000	LOAD RESISTANCE IN OHMS
VC	1.0	VOLTAGE CONTROL—FROM .0 (MIN VOLTAGE) TO 1.0
VR	HIGH	VOLTAGE RANGE SWITCH, HIGH=30, LOW=10 VOLTS

≫WHAT IS THE OUTPT?
OUTPT ⇒ OUTPUT
THE OUTPUT VOLTAGE IS 1.2 VOLTS.
SOPHIE corrects the student's typing mistake.
Notice that the output was disambiguated as the output voltage.

IF YOU ARE NOT SURE WHETHER A VALUE IS CORRECT, YOU CAN ASK "IS THAT VALUE CORRECT?"
The system points out a feature that the student may not otherwise be aware of. Correct here means what it is in a working instrument.

≫IS THAT RIGHT?
IN A WORKING CIRCUIT THE OUTPUT VOLTAGE IS 30.1 VOLTS.
THAT VALUE IS INCORRECT.
SOPHIE permits reference to previous objects in the dialogue. Here, That refers to the value of the previous measurement.

≫WHAT IS THE VOLTAGE BETWEEN THE CURRENT LIMITING TRANSISTOR
     AND THE CONSTANT CURRENT SOURCE?
THE VOLTAGE AT N4 IS 2.48 VOLTS.
This is an example of some of the complexities that arise in even limited domains. Although the syntax of the sentence is voltage between x and y, it really means voltage at z with respect to ground where z is the point between x and y. The output routines rephrase the input in a simpler form (i.e., between x and y reduces to N4) so that the user knows the system's interpretation and has an easier way of referring to that location.

≫WHAT IS IT BETWEEN THERE AND THE BASE OF Q6?
THE VOLTAGE BETWEEN N4 AND N5 IS 1.28 VOLTS.
Here it refers to the voltage and there refers to N4. Also notice that

≫WHAT IS THE CURRENT THRU THE CC WHEN THE VC IS SET TO 1.0?
WITH THE VOLTAGE CONTROL NOW SET AT 1.0
THE CURRENT THRU THE CURRENT CONTROL IS 30 MILLIAMPS.
    CC and VC are abbreviations. The controls are also "parts" that can be used in measurements.

≫WHAT IS IT WITH IT SET TO .8?
WITH THE VOLTAGE CONTROL NOW SET AT .8
THE CURRENT THRU THE CURRENT CONTROL IS 24 MILLIAMPS.
    Here the system must correctly instantiate two occurrences of it. The referent to the second it could be either CC or VC, since these are both controls.

SEMANTIC GRAMMAR

Introduction

In the first section we described the requirements for a natural-language processor in a learning environment. Briefly, they are efficiency and friendliness over the class of sentences that arise in a dialogue situation. The major leverage points we have that allow us to satisfy these requirements are (a) limited domain; (b) limited activities within that domain; and (c) known conceptualizations of the domain. In other words, we know the problem area, the type of problem the students are trying to solve, and the way they should be thinking about the problem in order to solve it. What we are then faced with is taking advantage of these constraints in order to provide an effective communication channel.

Notice that all of these constraints relate to concepts underlying the student's activities. In SOPHIE, the concepts include voltage, current, parts, transistors, terminals, faults, particular parts, hypotheses, controls, settings of controls, and so on. The dependency relationships between concepts include things such as these: Voltage can be measured at terminals, parts can be faulted, and controls can be set. The student, in formulating a query or statement, is requesting information or stating a belief about one of these relationships (e.g., *What is the voltage at the collector of transistor Q5?* or *I think resistor R9 is open.*)

It occurred to us that the best way to characterize the statements used for this task was in terms of the concepts themselves as opposed to the traditional syntactic structures. The language can be described by a set of grammar rules that characterize, for each concept or relationship, all of the ways of expressing it in terms of other constituent concepts. For example, the concept of a measurement requires a quantity to be measured and something against which to measure it. A measurement is

between has to be treated differently—that is, two nodes are explicit now.

≫IS THERE ANY RIPPLE IN THE VOLTAGE AT THE BASE OF Q4?
I'M SORRY, I DO NOT HANDLE AC CHARACTERISTICS.
    SOPHIE recognizes that the student is moving into an area that it is unable to handle. This is currently done by keyword recognition (e.g., ripple) but points out a technique that should be incorporated in other aspects of the system as well.

≫WHAT IS THE BASE CURRENT OF Q3?
THE BASE CURRENT OF Q3 IS 12 MICROAMPS.
    The following collection of sentences demonstrates the conciseness and flexibility of the dialogue mechanism. After introducing a context in a complete sentence, the student can easily and naturally ask related questions.

≫THRU THE EMITTER?
THE EMITTER CURRENT OF Q3 IS -.26 MILLIAMPS.
    This type of sentence fragment, which we will refer to as an ellipsis, occurs frequently in dialogues. Rather than specifying a complete thought, an ellipsis gives only that piece of the thought that contrasts an earlier thought. Notice that the referent cannot be determined on syntactic grounds (as is possible with the ellipsis "the emitter current"); yet this is the sort of statement a student might make if the last answer had caused a slight shifting of his thinking.

≫Q4
THE EMITTER CURRENT OF Q4 IS -.26 MILLIAMPS.
    In this case, the student is changing his attention to a different transistor. There is ambiguity as to whether he wanted the base current, the emitter current, or both. SOPHIE picks the most recent one and gives its interpretation as a complete sentence.

≫IF C2 WERE LEAKY, WHAT WOULD THE VOLTAGE ACROSS IT BE?
    As this sentence shows, the referent to it can occur earlier in the same sentence.

IS IT OKAY IF I USE 10000 FOR THE LEAKAGE RESISTANCE OF C2?
> YES
IF THE LEAKAGE RESISTANCE OF C2 WERE 10000
UNDER THE PRESENT SETTINGS, THE VOLTAGE ACROSS C2 WOULD BE 26.3 VOLTS.
IN A WORKING CIRCUIT IT IS 28.9 VOLTS.

≫IF Q6 HAS AN OPEN EMITTER AND A SHORTED BAE COLLECTOR JUNCTION WHAT HAPPENS TO THE VOLTAGE BETWEEN ITS BASE AND THE JUNCTION OF THE VOLTAGE LIMITING SECTION AND THE VOLTAGE REFERENCE SOURCE?
BAE ⇒ BASE
VOLTGE ⇒ VOLTAGE
    Several examples of the use of conjunction. Imagine the student's frustration if forced to type this query over because of spelling mistakes.

UNDER THE SETTINGS:
    CC=9, CR=LOW, LOAD=10, VC=1.0, VR=LOW.
THE VOLTAGE BETWEEN N5 AND N13 WOULD BE 8.94 VOLTS.
IN A WORKING CIRCUIT IT IS 9.57 VOLTS.

typically expressed by giving the quantity followed by the thing that specifies where to measure (e.g., *voltage across capacitor C2, current thru diode D1*). These phrasings are captured in this grammar rule (this is not actually a rule from the grammar but is merely intended to be suggestive):

<MEASUREMENT> := <MEASURABLE/QUANTITY> <PREP> <PART>

The concept of a measurement can, in turn, be used as part of other concepts—for example, to request a measurement (*What is the voltage across capacitor C2*) or to check a measurement (*Is the current thru diode D1 correct?*) We call this type of grammar a *semantic grammar* because the relationships it tries to characterize are semantic and conceptual as well as syntactic.

Semantic grammars have two advantages over traditional syntactic grammars. They allow semantic constraints to be used to make predictions during the parsing process, and they provide a useful characterization of those sentences that the system should try to handle. The predictive aspect is important for four reasons:

1. It reduces the number of alternatives that must be checked at a given time.
2. It reduces the amount of syntactic (grammatical) ambiguity.
3. It allows recognition of ellipsed or deleted phrases.
4. It permits the parser to skip words at controlled places in the input (i.e., it enables a reasonable specification of control).

These points will be discussed in detail in a later section. The characterization aspect is important for two reasons:

1. It provides a handle on the problem of constructing a habitable sublanguage. The system knows how to deal with a particular set of tasks over a particular set of objects. The sublanguage can be partitioned by tasks to accept all straightforward ways of expressing those tasks, but does not need to worry about others.

2. It allows a reduction in the number of sentences that must be accepted by the language while still maintaining habitability. There may be syntactic constructs that are used frequently with one concept (task) but seldom with another. For example, relative clauses may be useful in explaining the reasons for performing an experimental test but are an awkward (though possible) way of requesting a measurement. By separating the processing along semantic grounds, one may gain efficiency by not having to accept the awkward phrasing.

Representation of Meaning

Since natural-language communication is the transmission of concepts via phrases, the "meaning" of a phrase is its correspondent in the conceptual space. The entities in SOPHIE's conceptual space are objects, relationships between objects, and procedures for dealing with objects. The meaning of a phrase can be a simple data object (e.g., *current limiting transistor*) or a complex data object (e.g., *C5 open; Voltage at Node 1*).

The meaning of a question is a call to a procedure that knows how to determine the answer. The meaning of a command is a call to a procedure that performs the specified action. (Declarative statements are treated as requests because the pragmatics of the situation imply that the student is asking for verification of his statement. For example, *I think C2 is shorted* is taken to be a request to have the hypothesis *C2 is shorted* critiqued.)

For example, the procedural specialist DOFAULT knows how to fault the circuit and is used to represent the meaning of commands to fault the circuit (e.g., *Open R9; Suppose C2 shorts and R9 opens*). The argument that DOFAULT needs in order to perform its task is an instance of the concept of faults that specifies the particular changes to be made (e.g., *R9 being open*). These same concepts of particular faults also serve as arguments to two other specialists: HYPTEST, which determines the consistency of a fault with respect to the present context (e.g., *Could R9 be open*) and SEEFAULT, which checks the actual status of the circuit (e.g., *Is R9 open?*).

Result of the Parsing

Basing the grammar on conceptual entities allows the semantic interpretation (the determination of the concept underlying a phrase) to proceed in parallel with the parsing. Since each of the nonterminal categories in the grammar is based on a semantic unit, each grammar rule can specify the semantic description of a phrase that it recognizes in much the same way that a syntactic grammar specifies a syntactic description. The construction portion of the rules is procedural. Each rule has the freedom to decide how the semantic descriptions, returned by the constituent items of that rule, are to be put together to form the correct "meaning."

For example, the meaning of the phrase Q5 is the data base object Q5. The meaning of the phrase *the collector of Q5* is (COLLECTOR Q-5), where COLLECTOR is a function that returns the data base item that is the collector of the given transistor.

The rule for <MEASUREMENT> expresses all of the ways that the

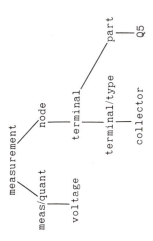

Figure 10.2 Control structure for the <measurement> rule.

student can give a measurable quantity and also supply its required arguments. The structure that results from <MEASUREMENT> is a function call to the function MEASURE that supplies the quantity being measured and other arguments specifying where to measure it. Thus the meaning of the phrase *the voltage at the collector of Q5* is (MEASURE VOLTAGE (COLLECTOR Q5)), which was generated from the control structure (see Figure 10.2).

The grammar rule for <MEASUREMENT> also accepts "meaningless" phrases such as *the power dissipation of Node 4*. In addition, it accepts some meaningful phrases such as *the resistance between Node 3 and Node 14*, which SOPHIE does not calculate. This results from generalizing together concepts that are not treated identically in the surface structure. In this case, *voltage, current, resistance,* and *power dissipation* were generalized to the concept of a measurable quantity. The advantage of allowing the grammar to accept more statements and having the argument checking done by the procedural specialists is that the semantic routines provide the feedback as to why a sentence cannot be interpreted or "understood." It also keeps the grammar from being cluttered with special rules for blocking meaningless phrases. Carried to the limit, the generalization strategy would return the grammar to being "syntactic" again (e.g., all data objects are "noun phrases"). The trick is to leave semantics in the grammar when it is beneficial—to stop extraneous parsings early, or to tighten the range of a referent for an ellipsis or deletion. This is obviously a task-specific trade-off. (Bobrow and Brown [1975] describe an interesting paradigm from which to consider this trade-off.)

The relationship between a phrase and its meaning is usually straightforward. However, it is not limited to simple embedding. Consider the phrases *the base emitter of Q5 shorted* and *the base of Q5 shorted to the emitter*. The thing which is "shorted" in both of these phrases is *the base emitter of Q5*. The rule that recognizes both of these phrases, <PART/FAULT/SPEC>, can handle the first phrase by invoking its constituent concepts of <JUNCTION> (*base emitter of Q5*) and <FAULT/TYPE> (*shorted*) and combine their results. In the second phrase, however, it must construct the proper junction from the separate occurrences of the two terminals involved.

This discussion has been presented as if the concepts were defined a priori by the capabilities of the system. Actually, for the system to remain at all habitable, the concepts are discovered in the interplay between expanding the corpus of sentences the system can handle and adding capabilities to the system. When a particular English construct is difficult to handle, it is probably an indication that the concept it is trying to express has not been recognized properly by the system. In our example *the base of Q5 is shorted to the emitter*, the relationship between the phrase and its meaning is awkward because the present concept of shorting requires a part or a junction. The example is getting at a concept of shorting, in which any two terminals can be shorted together (e.g., *the positive terminal of R9 is shorted to the anode of D6*). This is a viable conceptual view of shorting, but its implementation requires allowing arbitrary changes in the topology of the circuit, which is beyond the efficiency limitations of SOPHIE's simulator. Thus, the system we were working with led us to define the concept in too limited a way.

Use of Semantic Information during Parsing

Prediction

Having described the notion of a semantic grammar, we will now describe the ways in which it allows semantic information to be used in the understanding process. One use of semantic grammars is to predict the possible alternatives that must be checked at a given point. Consider, for example, the phrase *the voltage at xxx*. After the word *at* is reached in the top-down, left-to-right parse, the grammar rule corresponding to the concept *measurement* can predict very specifically the conceptual nature of *xxx*: It must be a phrase that directly or indirectly specifies a location in the circuit. For example, *xxx* could be *the junctions of the current limiting section and the voltage reference source* but cannot be *3 ohms*.

Semantic grammars also have the effect of reducing the amount of grammatical ambiguity. In the phrase *the voltage at xxx*, the prepositional phrase *at xxx* will be associated with the noun *voltage* without considering any alternative parses that associate it somewhere higher in the tree. Predictive information is also used to aid in the determination of referents for pronouns. If the above phrase were *the voltage at it*, the grammar would be able to restrict the class of possible referents to locations.

By taking advantage of the available sentence contexts to predict the semantic class of possible referents, the referent-determination process is greatly simplified. For example:

> 1a. *Set the voltage control to .8?*
> 1b. *What is the current thru R9?*
> 1c. *What is it with it set to .9?*

In 1c, the grammar is able to recognize that the first *it* refers to a measurement that the student would like retaken under slightly different conditions. The grammar can also decide that the second *it* refers to either a potentiometer or to the load resistance (i.e., one of those things that can be set). The referent for the first *it* is the measurement taken in 1b, *the current thru R9*. The referent for the second *it* is *the voltage control*, which is an instance of a potentiometer. The context mechanism that selects the referents will be discussed later.

Simple Deletion

The semantic grammar is also used to recognize simple deletions. The grammar rule for each conceptual entity knows the nature of that entity's constituent concepts. When a rule cannot find a constituent concept, it can either

a. fail (if the missing concept is considered to be obligatory in the surface structure representation) or,

b. hypothesize that a deletion has occurred and continue.

For example, the concept of a TERMINAL has as one of its realizations the constituent concepts of a TERMINAL-TYPE and a PART. When its grammar rule finds only the phrase *the collector*, it uses this information to posit that a part has been deleted (i.e. TERMINAL-TYPE gets instantiated to *the collector* but nothing gets instantiated to PART). The natural-language processor then uses the dependencies between the constituent concepts to determine that the deleted PART must be a TRANSISTOR. The "meaning" of this phrase is then *the collector of some transistor.* **Which** transistor is determined when the meaning is evaluated in the present dialogue context. In particular, the semantic form returned is the function PREF and the classes of possible referents; in our example the form would be (COLLECTOR (PREF (TRANSISTOR))).

Ellipsis

Another use of the semantic grammar allows the processor to recognize elliptic utterances. These are utterances that do not express complete

---

differences between the intended thought and an earlier one.[4] For example, 2b, 2c, and 2d are elliptic utterances.

> 2a. *What is the voltage at Node 5?*
> 2b. *At Node 1?*
> 2c. *And Node 2?*
> 2d. *What about between nodes 7 and 8?*

Ellipses can begin with introductory phrases such as *and* in 2c or *what about* in 2d; however this is not required, as can be seen in 2b. Part of the ellipsis rule is given in Figure 10.3.

```
<ELLIPSIS>      := [<ELLIPSIS/INTRODUCER>] <REQUEST/PIECE> !
                   [<ELLIPSIS/INTRODUCER>] if <PART/FAULT/SPEC>

<REQUEST/PIECE> := [<PREP>] <NODE> !
                   [<PREP>] <PART> !
                   between <NODE> and <NODE> !
                   [<PREP>] <JUNCTION> !
                   etc.
```

Figure 10.3 Ellipsis rule.

The grammar rule identifies which concept or class of concepts is possible from the context available in the elliptic utterance.

Though the parser is usually able to determine the intended concepts from the context available in an elliptic utterance, this is not always the case. Consider the following two sequences of statements.

> 3a. *What is the voltage at Node 5?*
> 3b. *10?*
> 4a. *What is the output voltage if the load is 100?*
> 4b. *10?*

In 3b, *10* refers to Node 10, whereas in 4b it refers to a load of 10. The problem this presents to the parser is that the concepts underlying these two elliptic utterances have nothing in common except their surface realizations. The parser, which operates from conceptual entities, does not have a concept that includes both of these interpretations. One solution would be to have the parser find all parses (concepts) and then choose between them on the basis of context. Unfortunately, this would mean that time is wasted looking for more than one parse for the large percentage of sentences in which it is not necessary to do so. A better solution

---

[4] The standard use of the word *ellipsis* refers to any deletion. Rather than invent a new word, we shall use the restricted meaning here.

would be to allow structure among the concepts, so that the parser would recognize *10* as a member of the concept *number*. Then the routines that find the referent would know that numbers can be either node numbers or values. This type of recognition could profitably be performed by a bottom-up approach to parsing. However, its advantages over the present scheme are not enough to justify the expense incurred by a bottom-up parse to find all possible well-formed constituents. At present, the parser assumes one interpretation, and a message is printed to the student indicating the assumed interpretation. If it is wrong, the student must supply more context in his request. In fact, *10?* is taken as a load specification and if the student meant the node he would have to use *at 10*, *N10*, or *Node 10*. Later we will discuss the mechanism that determines to which complete thought an ellipsis refers.

Using Context to Determine Referents

Pronouns and Deletions

Once the parser has determined the existence and class (or set of classes) of a pronoun or deleted object, the context mechanism is invoked to determine the proper referent. This mechanism has a history of student interactions during the current session that contains, for each interaction, the parse (meaning) of the student's statement and the response calculated by the system. This list provides the range of possible referents and is searched in reverse order to find an object of the proper semantic class (or one of the proper classes). To aid in the search, the context mechanism knows how each of the procedural specialists appearing in a parse uses its arguments. For example, the specialist MEASURE has a first argument that must be a quantity and a second argument that must be a part, a junction, a section, a terminal, or a node. Thus when the context mechanism is looking for a referent that can be either a PART or a JUNCTION, it will look at the second argument of a call to MEASURE but not the first. Using the information about the specialists, the context mechanism looks in the present parse and then in the next most recent parse, etc., until an object from one of the specified classes is found.

The significance of using the specialist to filter the search instead of just keeping a list of previously mentioned objects is that it avoids misinterpretations due to object-concept ambiguity. As an example, consider the following sequence from the sample dialogue in the previous section:

5. *What is the current thru the CC when the VC is 1.0?*
6. *What is it when it is .8?*

Sentence 5 will be recognized by the following rules from the semantic grammar:

```
$1)  <REQUEST> := <SIMPLE/REQUEST> when <SETTING/CHANGE>
$2)  <SIMPLE/REQUEST> := what is <MEASUREMENT>
$3)  <MEASUREMENT> := <MEAS/QUANT> <PREP> <PART>
$4)  <SETTING/CHANGE> := <CONTROL> is <CONTROL/VALUE>
$5)  <CONTROL> := VC
```

with a resulting semantic form of:

```
(RESETCONTROL (STQ VC 1.0)
              (MEASURE CURRENT CC) )
```

RESETCONTROL is a function whose first argument specifies a change to one of the controls and whose second argument consists of a form to be evaluated in the resulting instrument context. STQ is used to change the setting of one of the controls. The first argument to MEASURE gives the quantity to be measured. The second specifies where it is to be measured. To recognize Sentence 6, the application of Rules $2 and $5 are changed. There is an alternative rule for <SIMPLE/REQUEST> that looks for those anaphora (i.e., *that*, *it*, and *one*) that refer to a measurement. These phrases, such as *it*, *that result*, or *the value*, are recognized by the nonterminal <MEASUREMENT/PRONOUN>. The alternative to $2 that would be used to parse (6) is

```
<SIMPLE/REQUEST> := what is <MEASUREMENT/PRONOUN>.
```

The semantics of <MEASUREMENT/PRONOUN> indicate that an entire measurement has been deleted. The alternative to Rule $5,

```
<CONTROL> := it,
```

recognizes *it* as an acceptable way to specify a control. The resulting semantic form for Sentence 6 is

```
(RESETCONTROL (STQ (PREF '(CONTROL)) .8)
              (PREF '(MEASUREMENT) ) )
```

The function PREF searches back through the context of previous semantic forms to find the most recent mention of a member of one of the classes. In the above example, it will find the control VC but not CC because the character imposed on the arguments of MEASURE is that of a "part," not a "control." The presently recognized classes for deletions are PART, TRANSISTOR, FAULT, CONTROL, POT, SWITCH, DIODE, MEASUREMENT, and QUANTITY. (The members of the classes are derived from the semantic network associated with a circuit.)

Referents for Ellipses

If the problem of pronoun resolution is looked upon as finding a previously mentioned object for a currently specified use, then the problem of ellipsis can be thought of as finding a previously mentioned use for a currently specified object. For example,

7. *What is the base current of Q4?*
8. *In Q5?*

The given object is *Q5*, and the earlier function is *base current*. For a given elliptic phrase, the semantic grammar identifies the concept (or class of concepts) involved. In 7, since Q5 is recognized by the nonterminal <TRANSISTOR/SPEC>, the class would be TRANSISTOR. The context mechanism then searches for a specialist in a previous parse that accepted the given class as an argument. When one is found, the new phrase is placed in the proper argument position and the modified parse is used as the meaning of the ellipsis.

Limitations to the Context Mechanism

The method of semantic classification (to determine reference) is very efficient and works well over our domain. It definitely does not solve all the problems of reference. Charniak (1972) has pointed out the substantial problems of reference in a domain as seemingly simple as children's stories. One of his examples demonstrates how much world knowledge may be required to determine a referent: "Janet and Penny went to the store to get presents for Jack. Janet said 'I will get Jack a top.' 'Don't get Jack a top,' said Penny. 'He has a top. He will make you take it back [p. 7]'."

Charniak argues that to understand to which of the two tops "it" refers requires knowing about presents, stores and what they will take back, etc. Even in domains where it may be possible to capture all of the necessary knowledge, classification may still lead to ambiguities. For example, consider the following:

9. *What is the voltage at Node 5 if the load is 100?*
10. *Node 6?*
11. *7?*

In Statement 11 the user means Node 7. In Statement 10, he has reinforced the use of ellipsis as referring to node number. (For example, when Statement 11 is much more awkward.) On the other hand, if Statement 11 had been *1000* or if Statement 10 had been *10?*,

things would be more problematic. When Statement 11 is *1000*, we can infer that the user means a load of 1000 because there is no Node 1000. If Statement 10 had been *10?*, there would be genuine ambiguity slightly favoring the interpretation as a load because that was the last number mentioned. The major limitation of the current technique, which must be overcome in order to tackle significantly more complicated domains, is its inability to return more than one possible referent. It considers each one individually until it finds one that is satisfactory. The amount of work involved in employing a technique that allows comparing referents has not been justified by our experience.

Fuzziness

Having the grammar centered around semantic categories allows the parser to be sloppy about the actual words it finds in the statement. Having a concept in mind, and being willing to ignore words to find it, is the essence of keyword parsing schemes. It is effective in those cases where the words that have been skipped either are redundant or specify gradations of an idea that are not distinguished by the system. For example, in the sentence, *Insert a very hard fault, very* would be ignored; this is effective because the system does not have any further structure over the class of hard faults. In the sentence, *What is the voltage across resistor R8? resistor* can be ignored because it is implied by R8. (The first of these examples could be handled by making *very* a noise word (i.e., deleting it from all sentences). *Resistor*, however, is not a noise word in all cases (e.g., *What is the current through the current sensing resistor?*) and hence cannot be deleted.

One advantage that a procedural encoding of the grammar (discussed later) has over pattern-matching schemes in the implementation of fuzziness is its ability to control exactly where words can be skipped. This provides the ability to blend pattern-matching parsing of those concepts that are amenable to it with the structural parsing required by more complex concepts. The amount of fuzziness—how many, if any, words in a row can be ignored—is controlled in two ways. First, whenever a grammar rule is invoked, the calling rule has the option of limiting the number of words that can be skipped. Second, each rule can decide which of its constituent pieces or words are required and how tightly controlled the search for them should be. In SOPHIE, the normal mode of operation of the parser is tight in the beginning of a sentence, but fuzzier after it has made sense out of something.

Fuzziness has two other advantages worth mentioning briefly. It reduces the size of the dictionary because all known noise words do not have to be included. In those cases where the skipped words are meaningful, the misunderstanding may provide some clues to the user that allow him to restate his query.

Preprocessing

Before a statement is parsed, a preprocessor performs three operations. The first expands abbreviations, deletes known noise words, and canonicalizes similar words to a common form. The second is a cursory spelling correction. The third is a reduction of compound words.

Spelling correction is attempted on any word of the input string that the system does not recognize. The spelling correction algorithm[5] takes the possibly misspelled word and a list of correctly spelled words and determines which, if any, of the correct words is close to the misspelled word (using a metric determined by number of transpositions, doubled letters, dropped letters, etc.). During the initial preprocessing, the list of correct words is very small (approximately a dozen) and is limited to very commonly misspelled words and/or words that are critical to the understanding of a sentence. The list is kept small so that the time spent attempting spelling correction, prior to attempting a parse, is kept to a minimum. Remember that the parser has the ability to ignore words in the input string, so we do not want to spend a lot of time correcting a word that will not be needed in understanding the statement. But notice that certain words can be critical to the correct understanding of a statement. For example, suppose that the phrase *the base emitter current of Q3* were incorrectly typed as *the bse emitter current of Q3*. If *bse* were not recognized as being *base*, the parser would ignore it and misunderstand the phrase as *the emitter current of Q3*, a perfectly acceptable but much different concept.[6] Because of this problem, words like *base*, which if ignored have been found to lead to misunderstandings, are considered critical, and their spelling is corrected before any parse is attempted. Other words that are misspelled are not corrected until the second attempt at spelling correction that is done after a statement fails to parse.

Compound words are single concepts that appear in the surface structure as a fixed series of more than one word. Their reduction is very important to the efficient operation of the parser. For example, in the question, *What is the voltage range switch setting?*, *voltage range switch* is rewritten as the single item *VR*. If not rewritten, *voltage* would be mistaken as the beginning of a measurement (as in *What is the voltage at N4?*) and an attempt would have to be made to parse *range switch setting* as a place to measure voltage. Of course, after this failed, the correct parse could still be found, but reducing compound words helps to avoid search. In addition, the reduction of compound words simplifies the grammar rules by allowing them to work with larger conceptual units. In this sense, the preprocessing can be viewed as a preliminary bottom-up parse that recognizes local, multiword concepts.

Implementation

Once the dependencies between semantic concepts have been expressed in the Backus-Naur Form (BNF), each rule in the grammar is encoded (by hand) as a procedure in the programming language LISP. This encoding process imparts to the grammar a top-down control structure, specifies the order of application of the various alternatives of each rule, and defines the process of pattern matching each rule. The resulting collection of LISP functions constitutes a goal-oriented parser in a fashion similar to SHRDLU (Winograd, 1973), but without the backtracking ability of PROGRAMMER.

As has been argued elsewhere (Winograd, 1973; Woods, 1970), encoding the grammars as procedures—including the notion of process in the grammar—has advantages over using traditional phrase structure grammar representations. Four of these advantages are

1. The ability to collapse common parts of a grammar rule while still maintaining the perspicuity of the grammar
2. The ability to collapse similar rules by passing arguments (as with SENDR)
3. The ease of interfacing other types of knowledge (in SOPHIE, primarily the semantic network) into the parsing process
4. The ability to build and save arbitrary structures during the parsing process. (This ability is sometimes provided by allowing augments on phrase structure rules.)

In addition to the advantages it shares with other procedural representations, the LISP encoding has the computational advantage of being compilable directly into efficient machine code. The LISP implementation is efficient because the notion of process it contains (one process doing recursive descent) is close to that supported by physical machines, whereas those of ATN and PROGRAMMER are nondeterministic and

[5] The spelling correction routines are provided by INTERLISP and were developed by Teitelman for use in the DWIM facility (Teitelman, 1969, 1974).

[6] To minimize the consequences of such misinterpretation, the system always responds with an answer that indicates what question it is answering, rather than just giving the numeric answer.

hence not directly translatable into present architecture. (See Burton [1976] for a description of how it is possible to minimize this mismatch.)

In terms of efficiency, the LISP implementation of the semantic grammar succeeds admirably. The grammar written in the INTERLISP dialect of LISP (Teitelman, 1974) can be block-compiled. Using this technique, the complete parser takes about 5K of storage and parses a typical student statement consisting of 8 to 12 words in around 150 milliseconds!

A NEW FORMALISM—SEMANTIC AUGMENTED TRANSITION NETWORKS

Using the techniques described in the previous section, a natural-language processor capable of supporting the dialogue presented in the second section and requiring less than 200 milliseconds cpu time per question was constructed. In addition, these same techniques were used to build a processor for NLS-SCHOLAR (Grignetti, Gould, Hausmann, Bell, Harris, & Passafiume, 1974; Grignetti, Hausmann, & Gould, 1975) (built by K. Larkin), and an interface to an experimental laboratory for exploring mathematics using attribute blocks (Brown & Burton, 1978). In the construction of these varying systems, the notion of semantic grammar proved to be useful. The LISP implementation, however, was found to be a bit unwieldy. Although expressing the grammar as programs is efficient and allows complete freedom to explore new extensions, the technique is lacking in perspicuity. This lack of perspicuity has three major drawbacks: (a) the difficulty encountered when trying to modify or extend the grammar; (b) the problem of trying to communicate the extent of the grammar to either a user or a colleague; (c) the problem of trying to reimplement the grammar on a machine that does not support LISP. These difficulties have been partially overcome by using a second, parallel representation of the grammar in a specification language similar to the Backus–Naur Form, which is the representation we have been presenting throughout this report. This, however, requires supporting two different representations of the same information and does not really solve problems a or c. The solution to this problem is a better formalism for expressing and thinking about semantic grammars. This section discusses such a formalism.

Augmented Transition Networks (ATN)

Some years ago, Chomsky (1957) introduced the notion that the processes of language generation and language recognition could be viewed in terms of a machine. One of the simplest of such models is the finite state machine. It starts off in its initial state looking at the first symbol, or word, of its input sentence and then moves from state to state as it gobbles up the remaining input symbols. The sentence is **accepted** if the machine stops in one of its final states after having processed the entire input string; otherwise the sentence is **rejected**. A convenient way of representing a finite state machine is as a transition graph, in which the states correspond to the nodes of the graph and the transitions between states correspond to its arcs. Each arc is labeled with a symbol whose appearance in the input can cause the given transition.

In an augmented transition network, the notion of a transition graph has been modified in three ways: (a) the addition of a recursion mechanism that allows the labels on the arcs to be nonterminal symbols that correspond to networks; (b) the addition of arbitrary conditions on the arcs that must be satisfied in order for an arc to be followed; (c) the inclusion of a set of structure-building actions on the arcs, together with a set of named registers for holding partially built structures. (This discussion follows closely a similar discussion in Woods [1970], to which the reader is referred. A reader familiar with the augmented transition network formalism may wish to skip to the section "Advantages to the Augmented Transition Network Formalism.") Figure 10.4 is a specification of a language for representing augmented transition networks. The specification is given in the form of an extended, context-free grammar in which alternative ways of forming a constituent are represented on separate lines and the symbol + is used to indicate arbitrarily repeatable constituents. (+ is used to mean 0 or more occurrences. Though the accepted usage of + is 1 or more, the accepted symbol for 0 or more, *, has not been used to avoid confusion with the use of the symbol * in the augmented transition network formalism.) The nonterminal symbols are lowercase English descriptions enclosed in angle brackets. All other symbols, except +, are terminals. Nonterminals not given in Figure 10.4 have names intended to be self-explanatory.

The first element of each arc is a word indicating the type of arc. For arcs of type CAT, WRD, and PUSH, the arc type together with the second element corresponds to the label on an arc of a state transition graph. The third element is an additional test. A CAT (category) arc can be followed if the current input symbol is a member of the lexical category named on the arc and if the test on the arc is satisfied. A PUSH (network call) arc causes a recursive invocation of a lower level network beginning at the state indicated, if the test is satisfied. The WRD (word) arc can be followed if the current input symbol is the word named on the arc and if the test is satisfied. The TST (test) arc can be followed if the test is

form on the HOLD list to be used at a later place in the computation by a VIR arc. SETF (set feature) provides a means of setting a feature of the constituent being built.

GETR (get register value) is a function whose value is the contents of the named register. LEX (lexical item) is a form whose value is the current input symbol. The asterisk (*) is a form whose value depends on the context of its use:

1. In the actions of a CAT arc, the value of * is the root form of the current input word.
2. In the actions of a PUSH arc, it is the value of the lower computation.
3. In the actions following a VIR arc, the value of it is the constituent removed from the HOLD list.

GETF is a function that determines the value of a specified feature of the indicated form (which is usually *). BUILDQ is a general structure-building form that places the values of the given registers into a specified tree fragment. Specifically, it replaces each occurrence of + in the tree fragment with the contents of one of the registers (the first register replacing the first occurrence of +, the second register the second, etc.). In addition, BUILDQ replaces occurrences of * by the value of the form *. The remaining three forms make a list out of the specified arguments (LIST), append two lists together to make a single list (APPEND), and produce as a value the (unevaluated) arbitrary form (QUOTE).

Advantages of ATN Formalism

The augmented transition network (ATN) formalism was seriously considered at the beginning of the SOPHIE project but rejected as being too slow. In the course of developing the LISP grammar, it became clear that the primary reason for a significant difference in speed between an ATN grammar and a LISP grammar is due to the fact that processing the augmented transition network (ATN) is an interpreted process, whereas LISP is compilable and therefore the time problem could be overcome by building an ATN compiler. During the period of evolution of SOPHIE's grammar, an ATN compiler was constructed (see Burton, 1976). In the next section we will discuss the advantages we hoped to gain by using the ATN formalism.

These advantages fall into three general areas: (a) conciseness; (b) conceptual effectiveness; and (c) available facilities. By conciseness we mean that writing a grammar as an ATN takes fewer characters than LISP. The ATN formalism gains conciseness by not requiring the speci-

```
<transition network> := (<arc set><arc set>+)
<arc set> := (<state> <arc>+)
<arc> := (CAT <category name> <test> <action>+ <term act>)
         (WRD <word> <test> <action>+ <term act>)
         (PUSH <state> <test> <action>+ <term act>)
         (TST <arbitrary label> <test> <action>+ <term act>)
         (POP <form> <test>)
         (VIR <constituent name> <test> <action>+ <term act>)
         (JUMP <state><test><action>+)
<action> := (SETR <register> <form>)
            (SENDR < register><form>)
            (LIFTR <register> <form>)
            (HOLD <constituent name> <form>)
            (SETF <feature> <form>)
            *
            (GETF <form> <feature>)
            (BUILDQ <fragment> <register>+)
            (LIST <form>+)
            (APPEND <form> <form>)
            (QUOTE <arbitrary structure>)
<term act> := (TO <state>)
<form> := (GETR <register>)
          LEX
          *
```

Figure 10.4 A language for representing ATNs.

satisfied (the label is ignored). The VIR arc (virtual arc) can be followed if a constituent of the named type has been placed on the hold list by a previous HOLD action and the constituent satisfies the test. In all of these arcs, the actions are structure-building actions, and the terminal action specifies the state to which control is passed as a result of the transition. After CAT, WRD, and TST arcs, the input is advanced; after VIR and PUSH arcs it is not. The JUMP arc can be followed whenever its test is satisfied, control being passed to the state specified in the second element of the arc without advancing the input. The POP (return from network) arc indicates the conditions under which the state is to be considered a final state and the form of the constituent to be returned.

The actions, forms, and tests on an arc may be arbitrary functions of the register contents. Figure 10.4 presents a useful set that illustrates major features of the ATN. The first three actions specified in Figure 10.4 cause the contents of the indicated register to be set to the value of the indicated form. SETR (set register) causes this to be done at the current level of computation, SENDR (send register) at the next lower level of embedding, so that information can be sent down during a PUSH, and LIFTR (lift register) at the next higher level of computation, so that additional information can be returned to higher levels. The HOLD action places a

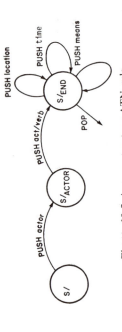

Figure 10.5 A case structure ATN rule.

LISP version of the grammar one could not write loops that are exactly analogous to the ATN (the ATN compiler, after all, produces such code!). However, a rule-oriented formalism does not encourage one to think this way. An alternative rule implementation is

```
<action>:=<actor><action/verb><action1>
<action1>::=<action1><time>
<action1>:=  <action1><location>
<action1>:=  <action1><means>
```

This is easier (shorter) to write but it has the disadvantage of being left-recursive. To implement it, one is forced to write the LISP equivalent of the augmented transition network that creates a difference between the rule representation and the actual implementation. This method also has the disadvantage of introducing the nonterminal <action1> into the grammar.

Another conceptual advantage of the ATN framework is that it encourages the postponing of decisions about a sentence until a differential point is reached, thereby allowing potentially different paths to stay together. In the rule-oriented SOPHIE grammar there are top-level rules for <set>, a command to change one of the control settings, and <modify>, a command to fault the instrument in some way. Sentence 1 is a <set> and Sentence 2 is a <modify>.

1. *Suppose the current control is high.*
2. *Suppose the current control is shorted.*

The two parse paths for these sentences should be the same for the first five words, but they are separated immediately by the rules <set> and <modify>. An ATN encourages structuring the grammar so that the decision between <set> and <modify> is postponed so that the paths remain together. It could be argued that the fact that this example occurred in SOPHIE's grammar is a complaint against top-down parsing or semantic grammars, or just our particular instantiation of a semantic grammar. We suspect the latter but argue that rule representations encourage this type of behavior.

fication of details in the parsing process at the same level required in LISP. Most of these differences stem from the fact that the ATN assumes it has a machine whose operations are designed for parsing, whereas LISP assumes it has a lambda calculus machine. For example, a lambda calculus machine assumes a function has one value. A function call to look for an occurrence at a nonterminal while parsing (in ATN formalism, a PUSH) must return at least two values: the structure of the constituent found, and the place in the input where the parsing stopped. A good deal of complexity is added to the LISP rules in order to maintain the free variable that has to be introduced to return the structure of the constituent. Other examples of unnecessary details include the binding of local variables and the specification of control structure as ANDs and ORs.

The conciseness of the ATN results in a grammar that is easier to change, easier to write and debug, and easier to understand, and hence provide for better communication. We realize that conciseness does not necessarily lead to these results (APL being a counter example in computer languages, mathematics in general being another); however, this is not a problem. The correspondence between the grammar rules in LISP and ATN is very close. The concepts that were expressed as LISP code can be expressed in nearly the same way as ATN but in fewer symbols.

The second area of improvement deals with conceptual effectiveness. Loosely defined, conceptual effectiveness is the degree to which a language encourages one to think about problems in the right way. One example of conceptual effectiveness can be seen by considering the implementation of case-structured rules. (See Bruce [1975] for a discussion of case systems.) In a typical case-structure rule, the verb expresses the function (or relation name) and the subject, and the object and prepositional phrases express the arguments of the function or relation. Let us assume for the purpose of this discussion that we are looking at four different cases (agent, location, means, and time) of the verb GO—*John went to the store by car at 10 o'clock.* In a phrase structure rule-oriented formalism one would be encouraged to write:

```
<statement> :=<actor> <action/verb> <location> <means> <time>
```

Since the last three cases can appear in any order, one must also write five other rules:

```
<statement> :=<actor> <action/verb> <location> <time> <means>
:
```

In an ATN one is inclined toward a graph (see Figure 10.5) that expresses more clearly the case structure of the rule. There is no reason why in the

grammar continues to be semantic in nature, we call the resulting grammar a *semantic ATN*.

Figure 10.6 presents the graphic ATN representation of semantic grammar nonterminal, which recognizes the straightforward way of expressing a terminal of a part in the circuit—the base of Q5, the anode of it, the collector. It also shows a simple example of how the recognition of anaphoric deletions can be captured in ATN formalism. By the state TERMINAL/TYPE, both the determiner and the terminal type—base, anode—have been found. The first arc that leaves TERMINAL/TYPE accepts the preposition that begins the specification of the part. The second arc (JUMP arc) corresponds to hypothesizing that the specification of the part has been deleted, as in *The base is open.* The action on the arc builds a place-holding form that identifies the deletion and specifies (from information associated with the terminal type that was found) the classes of objects that can fill the deletion. The method for determining the referent of the deletion remains the same as described in the third section.

The SOPHIE semantic ATN is compiled using the general ATN compiling system described in Burton (1976). The SOPHIE grammar provides the compiling system with a good contrast to the LUNAR grammar (Woods, Kaplan & Nash-Webber, 1972) (that was used as a test during development of the compiler), since it does not use many of the potential features. In addition, a bench mark, of sorts, was available from the LISP implementation of the grammar that could be used to determine the computational cost of using the ATN formalism.

There were two modifications made to the compiling system to improve its efficiency for the SOPHIE application. In the SOPHIE grammar, a large number of the arcs check for the occurrence of particular words. When there is more than one arc leaving a state, the ATN formalism requires that all of these arcs be tried, even if more than one of these is a WRD (word) arc and an earlier WRD arc has succeeded. This is especially costly, since the taking of an arc requires the creation of a configuration (data structure) to try the remaining arcs. In those cases when the grammar writer knows that none of the other arcs can succeed, this should be avoided. As a solution to this problem, the GROUP arc type was added. The GROUP arc allows a set of contiguous arcs to be designated as

Figure 10.6 A semantic ATN that recognizes deletion.

Another conceptual aid provided by ATNs is their method of handling ambiguity. Our LISP implementation uses a recursive descent technique (which can alternatively be viewed as allowing only one process). This requires that any decision between two choices be made correctly because there is no way to try out the other choice **after** the decision is made. At choice points, a rule can, of course, "look ahead" and gain information on which to base the decision, similar to the "wait-and-see" strategy used by Marcus (1975), but there is no way to back up and remake a decision once it has returned.

The effects of this can be most easily seen by considering the lexical aspects of the parsing. A prepass collapses compound words, expands abbreviations, etc. This allows the grammar to be much simpler because it can look for units like *voltage-control* instead of having to decode the noun phrase *voltage control.* Unfortunately, without the ability to handle ambiguity, this rewriting can be done only on words that have no other possible meaning. So, for example, when the grammar is extended to handle

3. *Does the voltage control the current limiting section?*

the compound *voltage–control* would have to be removed from the prepass rules and included in the grammar. This reduces the amount of bottom-up processing that can be done and results in a slower parse. It also makes compound rules difficult to write because all possible uses of the individual words must be considered to avoid errors. Another example is the use of the letter "C" as an abbreviation. Depending on context, it could possibly mean either current, collector, or capacitor. Without allowing ambiguity in the input, it could not be allowed as an abbreviation unless explicitly recognized by the grammar.

The third general area in which ATNs have an advantage is in the available facilities to deal with complex linguistic phenomena. Though our grammar has not yet expanded to the point of requiring any of the facilities, the availability of such facilities cannot be ignored as an argument favoring one approach over another. A primary example is the general mechanism for dealing with coordination in English described in Woods (1973).

Conversion to Semantic ATN

For the reasons discussed above, the SOPHIE semantic grammar was rewritten in the ATN formalism. We wish to stress here that the rewriting was a process of **changing form** only. The content of the grammar remained the same. Since a large part of the knowledge encoded by the

initions from the semantic network for part names and node names reduces the size of the dictionary and simplifies the operation of changing circuits. In addition, a mechanism called MULTIPLES was developed that permits string substitution within the input. This is similar to the notion of compounding, but differs in that a compound rule creates an alternative lexical item, whereas the multiple rule creates a different lexical item. After the application of a compound rule, there is an additional edge in the input chart; after a multiple rule, the effect is the same as if the user had typed in a different string.

Fuzziness

The one aspect of the LISP implementation that has not been incorporated into the ATN framework is fuzziness, the ability to ignore words in the input. Although we have not worked out the details, the nondeterminism provided by ATNs lends itself to an interesting approach. In a one-process—recursive descent—implementation, the rule that checks for a word must decide (with information passed down from higher rules) whether to try skipping a word, or give up. The critical information that is not available when this decision has to be made is whether or not there is another parse that would use that word. In the ATN, it is possible to suspend a parse and come back to it after all other paths have been tried. Fuzziness could be implemented so that rather than skip a word and continue, it can skip a word and suspend, waiting for the other parses to fail or suspend. The end effect may well be that sentences are allowed to get fuzzier because there is no danger of missing the correct parse.

Comparison of Results

The original motivation for changing to the ATN was its perspicuity. As Winograd (1973) has pointed out, simple grammars are perspicuous in almost any formalism; complex grammars are still complex in any formalism. We found the ATN formalism much easier to think in, write in, and debug. The examples of redundant processing that were presented earlier in this section were discovered while converting to ATN. For a gross comparison on conciseness, the ATN grammar requires 70% fewer characters to express than the LISP version.

The efficiency results were surprising. Table 10.1 gives comparison timings between the LISP version and the ATN compiled version. As can be seen, the ATN version takes less than twice as much time. This was pleasantly counterintuitive, since we expected the LISP version to be much faster because of the amount of hand optimization that had been

mutually exclusive. The form of the GROUP arc is (GROUP arc1 arc2 . . . arcn). The arcs are tried, one at a time, until the conditions on one of the arcs are met. This arc is then taken, and the remaining arcs in the GROUP are forgotten—not tried. If a PUSH arc is included in the GROUP, it will be taken if its test is true, and the remaining arcs will not be tried even if the PUSHed-for constituent is not found. For example, consider the following grammar state:

```
(S/1
    (GROUP (CAT A T (TO S/2))
           (WRD X T (TO S/3))
           (CAT B T (TO S/4))))
```

At most, one of the three arcs will be followed. Without GROUPing them together, it is possible that all three might be followed—if the word X had interpretations as both Category A and Category B.

The GROUP arc also provides an efficient means of encoding optional constituents. The normal method of allowing options in ATN is to provide an arc that accepts the optional constituent and a second arc that jumps to the next state without accepting anything. For example, if in State S/2 the word *very* is optional, the following two arcs would be created:

```
(S/2
    (WRD VERY T (TO REST-OF-S/2))
    (JUMP REST-OF-S/2 T))
```

The inefficiency arises when the word *very* does occur. The first arc is taken, but an alternative configuration that will try the second arc must be created, and possibly later explored. When these arcs are embedded in a GROUP, the alternative will not be created, thus saving time and space. As a result, it will not have to be explored, possibly saving more time. A warning should be included here that the GROUP arc can reject sentences that might otherwise be accepted. In our example, *very* may be needed to get out of the state REST-OF-S/2. In this respect, the GROUP arc is a departure from the original ATN philosophy that arcs should be independent. However, for some applications, the increased efficiency can be critical.

The other change to the compiling system (for the semantic grammar application) dealt with the preprocessing operations. The preprocessing facilities described in the last section included (a) lexical analysis to extract word endings; (b) a substitution mechanism to expand abbreviations, delete noise words, and canonicalize synonyms; (c) dictionary retrieval routines; and (d) a compound word mechanism to collapse multiword phrases. For the SOPHIE application we added the ability to use the INTERLISP spelling correction routines and the ability to derive

EXPERIENCES WITH SOPHIE AND TECHNIQUES FOR HANDLING PROBLEMS

When we began developing a natural-language processor for an instructional environment, we knew it had to be (a) fast; (b) habitable; (c) self-tutoring; and (d) able to deal with ambiguity. The basic conclusion that has arisen from the work presented here is that it is possible to satisfy these constraints. The notion of semantic grammar presented earlier provides a paradigm for organizing the knowledge required in the understanding process that permits efficient parsing. In addition, semantic grammar aids the habitability by providing insights into a useful class of dialogue constructs, and permits efficient handling of such phenomena as pronominalizations and ellipses. The need for a better formalism for expressing semantic grammars led to the use of augmented transition networks. The ability of the ATN-expressed semantic grammar to satisfy the above stated requirements is demonstrated in the natural language front-end for the SOPHIE system.

A point that needs to be stressed is that the SOPHIE system has been (and is being) used by uninitiated students in experiments to determine the pedagogical effectiveness of its environment. Although much has been learned about the problems of using a natural-language interface, these experiments were not debugging sessions for the natural-language component. The natural-language component has unquestionably reached a state at which it can be conveniently used to facilitate learning about electronics. In this section, we will describe the experiences of students using the natural-language component, and present some ideas on handling erroneous inputs.

Impressions, Experiences, and Observations

As mentioned in the introduction, students are very unskilled at paraphrasing their thoughts. This same inability to perform linguistic paraphrase carried over to the actual interaction with SOPHIE via terminal. Whenever the system did not accept a query, there was a marked delay before the student tried again. Sometimes the student would abandon a line of questioning completely. At the same time, data collected over many sessions indicated that there was no standard—canonical—way to phrase a question. Table 10.2 provides some examples of the range of phrasings used by students to ask for the voltage at a node. As Table 10.2 shows, students are likely to conceive of their questions in many ways and to express each of these conceptions in any of several phrasings. Yet other experiences indicate that they lack the ability to

done while encoding the grammar rules. In presenting the comparison timing, it should be mentioned that there are three differences between the two systems that tended to favor the ATN version. (The exact extent to which each of these differences contributed is difficult to gather statistics on because of the INTERLISP block compiler that gains efficiency by hiding internal workings. The exact contribution of each could certainly be determined but was not deemed worth the effort.) One difference is the lack of fuzziness in the ATN version. The LISP version spent time testing words other than the current word, looking ahead to see whether it was possible to skip this word, which was not done in the ATN version. The second is the creation of categories for words during the preprocessing in the ATN version that reduced the amount of time spent accessing the semantic net and hence reduced the time required to perform a category membership test in the ATN system. The third is the simplification of the grammar and increase in the amount of bottom-up processing that could be done because of the ambiguity allowed in the input chart. In our estimation, the lack of fuzziness is the only difference that may have had a significant effect, and this can be included explicitly in the ATN in places where it is critical, by using TST arcs and suspend actions, without a noticeable increase in processing time. In conclusion, we are very pleased with the results of the compiled semntantic ATN and feel that the ATN compiler makes the ATN formalism computationally efficient enough to be used in real systems.

TABLE 10.1
Comparison of ATN versus LISP Implementation

Times (in seconds) are "prepass" + "parsing."

1. *What is the output voltage?*
   LISP − .024 + .018 = .042
   ATN − .048 + .033 = .081
2. *What is the voltage between there and the base of Q6?*
   LISP − .038 + .039 = .077
   ATN − .090 + .046 = .136
3. *Q5?*
   LISP − .010 + .046 = .056
   ATN − .013 + .060 = .073
4. *What is the output voltage when the voltage control is set to .5?*
   LISP − .045 + .038 = .083
   ATN − .096 + .048 = .144
5. *If Q6 has an open emitter and a shorted base collector junction, what happens to the voltage between its base and the junction of the voltage limiting section and the voltage reference source?*
   LISP − .206 + .188 = .394
   ATN − .259 + .090 = .349

intelligent system should also act intelligently when it fails. The first step toward having a system fail intelligently is the identification of possible areas of error. In student's use of the SOPHIE system, we have found the following types of errors to be common:

1. Spelling errors and mistypings—*Shortt the CE og Q3 and opwn its base; What is the vbe Q5?*
2. Inadvertent omissions—*What is the BE of Q5?* (The user left out the quantity to measure. Note that in other domains this is a well-formed question.)
3. Slight misconceptions that are predictable—*What is the output of transistor Q3?* (the output of a transistor is not defined); *What is the current thru Node 1?* (nodes are places where voltage is measured and may have numerous wires associated with them); *What is R9?* (R9 is a resistor); *Is Q5 conducting?* (The laboratory section of SOPHIE gives information that is directly available from a real lab such as currents and voltages.)
4. Gross misconceptions whose underlying meaning is well beyond designed system capabilities—*Make the output voltage 30 volts; Turn on the power supply and tell me how the unit functions; What time is it?*

In the remainder of this section, we will discuss the solutions used in the SOPHIE system to provide feedback.

The use of a spelling correction algorithm (borrowed from INTER-LISP) has proven to be a satisfactory solution to typos and misspellings. During one student's session, spelling correction was required on, and resulted in proper understanding of, 10% of the questions. The major failings of the INTERLISP algorithm are the restriction on the size of the target set of correct words (time increases linearly with the number of words) and its failure to correct run-on words. (The time required to determine whether a word may be two—possibly misspelled—words run together increases very quickly with the length of the word and the number of possibly correct words. With no context to restrict the possible list of words, the computation involved is prohibitive.) A potential solution to both shortcomings would be to use the context of the parser to reduce the possibilities when it reaches the unknown word. Because of the nature of the grammar, this would allow semantic context as well as syntactic context to be used.

Of course, the use of any spelling correction procedure has some dangers. A word that is spelled correctly but that the system does not know may be changed through spelling correction to a word the system does know. For example, if the system does not know the word *top* but

TABLE 10.2
Sample Student Inputs

The following are some of the input lines typed by students with the intent of discovering the voltage at a node in the circuit.

What is the voltage at node 1?
What is the voltage at the base of Q5?
How much voltage at N10?
And what is the voltage at N1?
N9?
V at the neg side of C6?
V11 is?
What is the voltage from the base of transistor Q5 to ground?
What V at N16?
Coll. of Q5?
Node 16 Voltage?
What is the voltage at Pin 1?
Output?

convert easily to another conceptualization or phrasing. Since the nonacceptance of questions creates a major interruption in the student's thought process, the acceptance of many different paraphrases is critical to maintaining flow in the student's problem solving.

Another interesting phenomenon that occurred during sessions was the change in the linguistic behavior of the students as they used the system. Initially, queries were stated as complete English questions, generally stated in templates that we had given them. If they needed to ask something that did not exactly fit one of their templates, they would try a minor variant. As they became more familiar with the mode of interaction, they began to use abbreviations, to leave out parts of their questions, and, in general, to assume that the system was following their interaction. After 5 hours of experience with the system, almost all of one student's queries contained abbreviations and one in six depended on the context established by previous statements.

Feedback—When the Grammar Fails

From our experiences with students using SOPHIE, we have been impressed with the importance of providing feedback to unacceptable inputs—doing something constructive when the system does not understand an input. Though it may appear that in a completely habitable system all inputs would be understood, no system has ever attained this goal, and none will in the foreseeable future. To be natural to a naive user, an

does know *stop*, a user's command to *top everything* can be disastrously misunderstood. For this reason, words like *stop* are not spelling-corrected.

Our solution to predictable misconceptions is to recognize them and give error messages that are directed at correcting the misconception. We are currently using two different methods of recognition. One is to loosen up the grammar so that it accepts plausible but meaningless sentences. This technique provides the procedural specialists called by the plausible parse enough context to make relevant comments. For example, the concept of current through a node is accepted by the grammar even though it is meaningless. The specialist that performs measurements must then check its arguments and provide feedback if necessary:

> WHAT IS THE CURRENT THRU NODE 4?

The current thru a node is not meaningful since by Kirchoff's law the sum of the currents thru any node is zero. Currents can be measured thru parts (e.g., CURRENT THRU C6) or terminals (e.g., CURRENT THRU THE COLLECTOR OF Q2).

Notice that the response to the question presents some examples of how to measure the currents along wires that lead into the mentioned node. Examples of questions that will be accepted and are relevant to the student's needs are among the best possible feedback.

The second method of recognizing common misconceptions is to "key" feedback off single words or groups of words. In the following examples, the keys are *or* and *turned on*. Notice that the response presents a general characterization of the violated limitations as well as suggestions for alternative lines of attack.

> COULD Q1 OR Q2 BE SHORTED?

I can handle only one question, hypothesis, etc. at a time. The fact that you say OR indicates that you may be trying to express two concepts in the same sentence. Maybe you can break your statement into two or more simple ones.

> IS THE CURRENT LIMITING TRANSISTOR TURNED ON?

The laboratory section of SOPHIE is designed to provide the same elementary measurements that would be available in a real lab. If you want to determine the state of a transistor, measure the pertinent currents and voltages.

These methods of coping with errors have proved to be very helpful. However, they require that all of the misconceptions be predicted and programmed for in advance. This limitation makes them inapplicable to novel situations.

The remaining severe problems a user has stem from omissions and major misconceptions. After a simple omission, the user may not see that

he has left anything out and may conclude that the system does not know that concept or phrasing of that concept. For example, when the user types *What is the VBE of Q5?* instead of *What is the VBE of Q5?*, he may decide that it is unacceptable because the system does not allow *VBE* as an abbreviation of *base emitter voltage*. For conceptual errors, the user may waste a lot of time and energy attempting several rephrasings of his query, none of which can be understood because the system does not know the concept the user is trying to express. For example, no matter how it is phrased, the system will not understand *Make the output voltage 30 volts* because measurements cannot be directly changed; only controls and specifications of parts can be changed.

The feedback necessary to correct both of these classes of errors must identify any concepts in the statement that are understood and suggest the range of things that can be done to–with these concepts. This may help the user see an omission or may suggest alternative conceptualizations that get at the same information (for example, to change the output voltage indirectly by changing one of the controls) or at least provide enough information for the user to decide when to quit.

FUTURE DIRECTIONS

Further Research Areas

The SOPHIE semantic grammar system is designed for a particular context–trouble-shooting—within a particular domain—electronics. It represents the compilation of those pieces of knowledge that are general (linguistic) together with specific domain-dependent knowledge. In its present form, it is unclear which knowledge belongs to which area. The development of semantic grammars for other applications and extensions to the semantic grammar mechanism to include other understood linguistic phenomena will clarify this distinction.

Although the work presented in this chapter has dealt mostly with one area of application, the notion of semantic grammar as a method of integrating knowledge into the parsing process has wider applicability. Two alternative applications of the technique have been completed. One deals with simple sentences in the domain of attribute blocks (Brown & Burton, 1978). Though the sub-language accepted in the attribute-blocks environment is very simple, it is noteworthy that within the semantic grammar paradigm, a simple grammar was quickly developed that greatly improved the flexibility of the input language. The other completed application deals with questions about the editing system NLS (Grignetti *et al.*,

1975). In this application, most questions dealt with editing commands and their arguments, and fit nicely into the case-frame notion mentioned in the fourth section. The case-frame use of semantic grammar is being considered for, and may have its greatest impact on, command languages. Command languages are typically case-centered around the command name that requires additional arguments (its cases). The combination of the semantic classification provided by the semantic grammar and the representation of case rules permitted by ATNs should go a long way toward reducing the rigidity of complex command languages such as those required for message-processing systems. The combination should also be a good representation for natural-language systems in domains where it is possible to develop a strong underlying conceptual space, such as management information systems (Malhotra, 1975).

Conclusions

In the course of this chapter, we have described the evolution of a natural-language processor capable of using complex linguistic knowledge. The guiding strand has been the utilization of semantic information to produce efficient natural-language processors. There were several highlights that represent noteworthy points in the spectrum of useful natural language systems. The procedural encoding technique with fuzziness (third section) allows simple natural-language input to be accepted without introducing the complexity of a new formalism. Encoding the rules as procedures allows flexible control of the fuzziness, and the semantic nature of the rules provides the correct places to take advantage of the flexibility. As the language covered by the system becomes more complex, the additional burden of a grammar formalism will more than pay for itself in terms of ease of development and reduction in complexity. The augmented transition network (ATN) compiling system allows for the consideration of the ATN formalism by reducing its run-time cost, making it comparable to a direct procedural encoding. The natural language front end now used by SOPHIE is constructed by compiling a semantic ATN. As the linguistic complexity of the language accepted by the system increases, the need for more syntactic knowledge in the grammar becomes greater. Unfortunately, this often works at cross-purposes with the semantic character of the grammar. It would be nice to have a general grammar for English syntax that could be used to preprocess sentences; however, one is not forthcoming. A general solution to the problem of incorporating semantics with the current state of incomplete knowledge of syntax remains an open research problem. In the foreseeable future, any system will have to be an engineering trade-off between complexity and generality on one hand and efficiency and habitability on the other. We have presented several techniques that are viable options in this trade-off.

REFERENCES

Bobrow, R. J., & Brown, J. S. Systematic understanding: Synthesis, analysis, and contingent knowledge in specialized understanding systems. In D. Bobrow & A. Collins (Eds.), *Representation and understanding: Studies in cognitive science.* New York: Academic Press, 1975.

Brown, J. S. Uses of artificial intelligence and advanced computer technology in education. In *Computers and communications.* New York: Academic Press, 1977.

Brown, J. S., & Burton, R. R. Multiple representations of knowledge for tutorial reasoning. In D. Bobrow & A. Collins (Eds.), *Representation and understanding: Studies in cognitive science.* New York: Academic Press, 1975.

Brown, J. S., & Burton, R. R. A paradigmatic example of an artificially intelligent instructional system. *International Journal of Man Machine Studies,* 1978, *10,* 323–340.

Brown, J. S., Burton, R. R., & Bell, A. G. SOPHIE: A step towards a reactive learning environment. *International Journal of Man Machine Studies,* 1975, *7,* 675–696.

Brown, J. S., Rubinstein, R., & Burton, R. R. *Reactive learning environment for computer assisted electronics instruction* (BBN Report No. 3314). Cambridge, Mass., October 1976.

Bruce, B. C. Case systems for natural language. *Artificial Intelligence,* December 1975, *5,* 327–360.

Burton, R. R. *Semantic grammar: An engineering technique for constructing natural language understanding systems* (BBN Report No. 3453, ICAI Report No. 3). Cambridge, Mass.: Bolt Beranek and Newman Inc., December 1976.

Burton, R. R., & Brown, J. S. A tutoring and student modelling paradigm for gaming environments. *Proceedings for the Symposium on Computer Science and Education,* February 1976,

Burton, R. R., & Brown, J. S. An investigation of computer coaching for informal learning activities. *International Journal of Man Machine Studies,* in press.

Carr, B., & Goldstein, I. *Overlays: A theory of modelling for computer aided instruction* (AI Memo 406). Cambridge: Massachusetts Institute of Technology, February 1977.

Charniak, E. *Toward a model of children's story comprehension* (MIT–TR–266). Cambridge: Artificial Intelligence Laboratory, Massachusetts Institute of Technology, 1972.

Chomsky, N. *Syntactic structures.* The Hague: Mouton and Co., 1957.

Grignetti, M. C., Gould, L., Hausmann, C. L., Bell, A. G., Harris, G., & Passafiume, J. *Mixed-initiative tutorial system to aid users of the on-line system (NLS)* (BBN Report No. 2969). Cambridge, Mass.: Bolt Beranek and Newman Inc., November 1974.

Grignetti, M. C., Hausmann, C. L., & Gould, L. An intelligent on-line assistant and tutor—NLS-SCHOLAR. *National Computer Conference,* 1975, *44,* 775–781.

Malhotra, A. *Design criteria for a knowledge-based English language system for management: An experimental analysis.* Unpublished doctoral dissertation, Sloan School of Management, Massachusetts Institute of Technology, 1975.

Marcus, M. Diagnosis as a notion of grammar. In R. Schank & B. L. Nash-Webber (Eds.), *Proceedings of a Workshop on Theoretical Issues in Natural Language Processing,* 1975, *1,* 6–10.

Miller, R. B. Response time in man–computer conversational transactions. In *AFIPS Conference Proceedings* (Fall Joint Computer Conference). Washington: Thompson Book Company, 1968.

Teitelman, W. Towards a programming laboratory. In D. Walker (Ed.), *Proceedings of the International Joint Conference on Artificial Intelligence*, May 1969.

Teitelman, W. *INTERLISP reference manual*. Palo Alto, Calif.: Xerox Palo Alto Research Center, 1974.

Watt, W. C. Habitability. *American documentation*, 1968, *19*, 338–351.

Winograd, T. *Understanding natural language*. New York: Academic Press, 1973.

Woods, W. A. Transition network grammars for natural language analysis. *Communications of the ACM*, 1970, *13*, 591–606.

Woods, W. A. An experimental parsing system for transition network grammars. In R. Rustin (Ed.), *Natural language processing*. New York: Algorithmics Press, 1973.

Woods, W. A., Kaplan, R. M., & Nash-Webber, B. *The lunar sciences natural language information system: final report* (BBN Report #2378). Cambridge, Mass.: Bolt, Beranek and Newman, Inc., 1972.

SAM

Richard Cullingford

INTRODUCTION

SAM (Script Applier Mechanism) is a system of computer programs written to investigate how knowledge of context can be used to aid in understanding stories. The basic knowledge source SAM applies is the script. Using scripts of varying degrees of complexity, SAM can read (by the process of script application) not only simple stories, but also newspaper articles referring to domains as diverse as car accidents and state visits. Each of these types of texts involve certain invariant components, such as what can happen, the order in which things happen, and who is involved. This consistency of form and content enables the script-based model of reading to be used.

The reasons for building SAM were both practical and theoretical. First, of course, we had a practical desire for a functioning, complete story understander. At the time when work began on SAM (mid-1975), there were no running programs capable of "intelligently" reading stories, although several theoretical proposals had been made (e.g., Charniak's 1972 "demons" and 1978 "frames" models of story comprehension). Already in existence, however, were a conceptual analyzer, ELI, the English Language Interpreter (Riesbeck and Schank, 1977), and BABEL, a Conceptual Dependency-to-English generator (Goldman, 1975). Both of these programs were incorporated into SAM.

While clearly recognizing that script application is not the whole solution to the problem of story understanding, the resulting program successfully models certain key aspects of human reading. SAM processes stories, in English, from "left-to-right" a sentence at a time, in one pass, making a number of necessary inferences as it goes. It can then show that it has achieved a reasonable depth of comprehension of what it has read, by generating English or other natural language summaries or paraphrases of the story, and by answering questions about it.

Scripts in SAM are collections of *episodes* with *turning-points*. The episodes are collections of events linked into *causal chains*. Each event causes one or more states which in turn cause further events. Turning points are places in a script where several different actions might follow. In a restaurant, for example, one may take a seat or wait to be taken to a seat by an employee. Turning points also include "interference" and "resolution" activities, in which the flow of action departs slightly from the "usual". For example, all the tables may be occupied when someone arrives at a restaurant (an interference in the restaurant script), but a patron may choose to wait until a table becomes available (a resolution).

In dealing with the complicated activities found in newspaper articles, we needed a way of organizing the simple scripts of the Schank and Abelson theory (Schank and Abelson, 1977) so that they could be accessed as needed by the understander. Otherwise, the understander ran the risk of being swamped by the host of potentially relevant scripts it possessed. The entities that organize simple scripts are called *situations*. Each situation gives access to a knowledge domain in a hierarchical manner, from the most important activities to the most detailed (DeJong's 1979 "issue skeletons" embody a similar idea). For example, SAM contains situations for motor-vehicle accidents, state visits, and oil spills. People read each of these types of stories to find radically different kinds of information. In a car accident story, we usually want to find out first whether anyone was killed or hurt, then what the police did, and finally the extent of the property damage. Stories about oil spills, though they also begin with an "accident," lead to a different set of questions: Did any oil escape? If so, how much? What beaches, flora and fauna are threatened by the spill?

The ranking of events within situations is governed by the concept of *instrumentality*. Certain events or actions are performed only as a means to support or implement more important, higher-level activities. Consider, as a simple example, the very common situation known as "taking a trip". Starting a car (a very rigid, simple script) is a precondition for driving it (a somewhat more complex script). Driving a car, in turn, is a possible "instrument" for taking trips of various kinds. The "trips" themselves (very flexible, high level scripts) may involve going to the store, on a vacation or business trip, or (in the case of a Very Important Person) a state visit.

The process of script application involves several kinds of inferences. SAM reads stories in a top-down, predictive manner. Each script provides prestored expectations about what will be read, based upon what has already been seen. We identified the need for three important types of inference: causal-chain completion, role instantiation, and role merging. Causal-chain completion refers to the process of inferring the intervening events which must have taken place between two events explicitly mentioned in a story, in a manner which maintains both *causal* and *situational* continuity. Role instantiation refers to the assignment of specific references to the variables in a script, while role merging is recognizing when multiple references refer to the same specific role filler. The following example will illustrate these three different types of inferences:

John walked into a subway station. He went to the express platform.

Causal-chain completion inferences enable us to fill in all the events which must have occurred which are not mentioned explicitly in the story. Here, our knowledge of what happens in subways tells us that John went through a turnstile (after perhaps having acquired a token from a cashier) before going to the platform. We assume that he used steps or an escalator (i.e., he did not magically fly to the platform), and we never consider that he might have gotten a ticket at a ticket window, as would be the case for a train ride. Role instantiation inferences cause us to associate "John" with the role of "rider" in the subway script, and "create" a turnstile for him to go through. Role merging inferences enable us to assume that the "He" in the second sentence refers to John, because the "he" is doing something that the script *predicts* a rider will do at this point, and the role instantiation inference has already established that John is the rider.

SAM is a prediction-based understander attempting to deal with stories expressed "naturally" in English. One of the things we learned in working with a large variety of stories is the variety of subtle, little noticed inferences that are necessary. These inferences are needed to reconcile expectations from causal chains with the real inputs, which often differ from these expectations in "unimportant" ways. For example, suppose we had the following story:

John entered a movie theater, went over to the ticket counter, and asked for a ticket.

The problem here is to identify that the input "... went over to the ticket counter" in fact validly instantiates the expectation which arises from the causal chain, namely "patron goes to *cashier*." The inference needed to instantiate this expectation is quite simple: Things near to the same thing are near to each other (or transitivity of proximity). SAM combines this inference with scriptal information about the cashier role (i.e., "the cashier stands near the counter") in order to conclude that in fact "(John) went over to the counter" and thus that the expectation has been satisfied.

Scripts, constructed and organized as sketched above, together with the inference processes involved in script application, appear to be necessary components for any understander operating in a predictive manner on realistic story inputs. However, aside from its intrinsic interest as an "understander" of texts of a certain kind, SAM also provides a model of one kind of processing that more general understanders of the future will have to perform.

Input/Output Examples

The following examples of input and output illustrate the level of story understanding SAM achieved. In each case, English input is mapped into a Conceptual Dependency representation by the conceptual analyzer, ELI; and natural language output is created by the generator, BABEL.

Input Text:

JOHN WENT TO A RESTAURANT. HE ORDERED A HOT DOG. THE WAITER SAID THEY DIDN'T HAVE ANY. HE ASKED FOR A HAMBURGER. WHEN THE HAMBURGER CAME, IT WAS BURNT. HE LEFT THE RESTAURANT.

Question-Answering Output:

Q1: DID JOHN SIT DOWN IN THE RESTAURANT?
A1: PROBABLY.

Q2: DID JOHN ORDER A HOT DOG?
A2: YES.

Q3: DID JOHN EAT A HOT DOG?
A3: NO, THE WAITER TOLD JOHN THE MANAGEMENT WAS UNABLE TO GIVE IT TO HIM.

Q4: WHAT DID THE WAITER SERVE JOHN?
A4: THE WAITER SERVED JOHN A HAMBURGER.

Q5: WHY DIDN'T JOHN EAT THE HAMBURGER?
A5: BECAUSE THE HAMBURGER WAS OVERDONE.

Q6: DID JOHN PAY THE CHECK?
A6: NO JOHN WAS ANGRY BECAUSE THE HAMBURGER WAS OVERDONE AND SO HE LEFT THE RESTAURANT.

This story, which was processed by an early version of SAM, contains several examples of the "understanding" power provided by a simple script, "going to a restaurant". In reading this story, SAM has constructed a "trace" or scenario through the story, which contains not only the events that were explicitly mentioned, but also those that reasonably could have been inferred to have happened. An example of such a causal-chain completion inference is to be seen in the answer to Question 1, which asks about an event which usually occurs between a patron's entering a restaurant and his placing an order.

Question 4 also shows SAM's ability to *analyze in context*. The story input "(when) the hamburger came" has been identified as referring to the "serving" event. Note that the role merging inference has identified "the waiter" as the active entity in this event, given that hamburgers obviously cannot move by themselves.

In addition to inferring what happened while reading the story, SAM is also capable of making inferences about events that did not happen. In Question 3, the non-occurrence of the highly expected "eating" event is attributed to an "interfering" condition: the restaurant was out of hot dogs. Similarly, in Questions 5 and 6, SAM infers that the reason for the second non-occurrence of "eating," followed by the customers' refusal to pay the check, is a second "interfering" condition: the hamburger was burnt. (The theory embodied in SAM's question-answering subsystem, QUALM, was developed by Wendy Lehnert, and is described in Lehnert, 1978.)

Input:

Friday evening a car swerved off Route 69. The vehicle struck a tree. The passenger, a New Jersey man, was killed. David Hall, 27, was pronounced dead at the scene by Dr. Dana Blauchard, medical examiner. Frank Miller, 32, of 593 Foxon Rd., the driver, was taken to Milford Hospital by Flanagan Ambulance. He was treated and released. No charges were made. Patrolman Robert Onofrio investigated the accident.

English Summary:

AN AUTOMOBILE HIT A TREE NEAR HIGHWAY 69 FOUR DAYS AGO. DAVID HALL, AGE 27, RESIDENCE IN NEW JERSEY, THE PASSENGER, DIED. FRANK MILLER, AGE 32, RESIDENCE AT 593 FOXON ROAD IN NEW HAVEN, CONNECTICUT, THE DRIVER, WAS SLIGHTLY INJURED. THE POLICE DEPARTMENT DID NOT FILE CHARGES.

Spanish Summary:

UN AUTO CHOCO CONTRA UN ARBOL CERCA DE LA CARRETERA 69 EL VIERNES AL ANOCHECER. DAVID HALL, DE 27 ANOS, QUE VIVIA EN NEW JERSEY, EL PASAGERO, SE MURIO. FRANK MILLER, DE 32 ANOS, QUE VIVIA EN 593 CALLE FOXON EN NEW HAVEN, CONNECTICUT, EL CHOFER, QUEDO UN POCO HERIDO. EL DEPARTAMENTO DE POLICIA NO ACUSO A NADIE.

Question-Answering Output:

Q1: Was anyone killed?
A1: YES, DAVID HALL DIED.

Q2: Was anyone hurt?
A2: YES, FRANK MILLER WAS SLIGHTLY INJURED.

Q3: Why was Miller hurt?
A3: BECAUSE THE AUTOMOBILE HIT THE TREE.

Q4: Did Miller go to the hospital?
A4: YES, HE WAS IN THE MILFORD HOSPITAL.

Q5: How did Miller get to the hospital?
A5: THE FLANAGAN AMBULANCE COMPANY TOOK HIM TO THE MILFORD HOSPITAL.

This story, a simplified version of an actual account from the *New Haven Register*, is processed by SAM using the motor-vehicle-accident situation, which contains simpler scripts for "car crash", "ambulance ride", "hospital treatment", and "police investigation". Since SAM is intended to model an average person's understanding of these knowledge domains, the latter scripts are relatively sketchy by comparison with, say, the restaurant or movie-theater script. Nevertheless, as the summary and question-answering output shows, they give SAM a reasonable level of "understanding".

The basic strategy SAM uses in reading newspaper stories is the same as that used for simpler stories. It attempts to locate the events mentioned in the story in the situation. The structure of the situation then tells SAM how to select a causally connected chain of episodes. For example, SAM must connect the input concerning a crash with the one about a person being taken to the hospital. It uses its knowledge about car accidents and the function of ambulance companies (the ambulance script) to infer the probable events that someone saw the crash and called an ambulance, that the ambulance came to the scene, that the ambulance attendants placed the person on a stretcher, etc. It also makes the crucial connection, never stated in the story, that the person who was taken to the hospital must have been *injured* in the crash. As it fills in these causal relations, it makes inferences about the script roles involved in the events. For example, it asserts that the "vehicle" which struck the tree is the "car" that left the road, and that the "New Jersey man" must be "David Hall".

SAM also has a limited capability to use the time/place setting of a story for inferences about where things are happening and how long they take. For example, the use of locational information in the car crash script leads to the conclusion, expressed in both the English and Spanish summaries, that the crash must have happened "near Route 69". Similarly, the crash must have occurred on the same day as the "swerve", namely Friday evening.

Note that the process of role instantiation may be delayed in certain cases until enough information is provided by the story. For example, the story does not give explicit information about the severity of the injuries to the man who went to the hospital. SAM delays its decision concerning this script "role" until the sentence about "treated and released" is read, at which point it concludes that he must have been "slightly injured".

SAM embodies a theory about the nature and use of the essential contextual component of reading. In the beginning, we looked at simple contexts, starting SAM off with simple, made-up stories about eating in restaurants and riding in subways. None of these stories were particularly interesting for a human listener, even a child. Nevertheless, the techniques developed for making causal connections, handling reference problems, using time-and-place setting, and organizing to English summary or question-answering output. It has also "understood" at least four other stories from each domain, using hand-coded analyses of the text.

Each of the stories processed by SAM is "distinct" in the sense that a slightly different inference process is required by each. In one story, for example, all the role merging inferences were concerned with pronominal references. In another, the merging of multiple references involved matching totally different identifications of the same person (e.g., "a New Jersey man" vs. "David Hall, 27"). More complicated inferences were also studied which involved determining when enough information had been accumulated to justify a role instantiation.

Input events are located in the script by comparing them with *patterns* from the causal chains comprising the scripts. Since the patterns are the Conceptual Dependency units of SAM's scripts, the amount of knowledge SAM possesses can perhaps be best characterized by the number of patterns it uses. The simplest script, "train wreck", contains roughly 40 patterns, while the most complicated, "motor-vehicle accidents", contains more than 100.

SAM runs as a collection of from three to six intercommunicating modules, the number depending on the task. The modules were written in UCILISP and MLISP for a DEC System-10 computer (KA-10 central processing unit, 192K words of main memory). They range in size from about 35K words for the smallest module to 75K words for the largest, ELI. In each module, roughly half the memory was comprised of free space for working storage; the rest was assigned to "permanent" code and data.

Processing time for story understanding varied from about 20 seconds to over a minute of CPU time per input clause, of which more than half was typically consumed by the conceptual analyzer. "Logistical" reasons for the slow rate of understanding include the interpretive processing of the system's code, overhead incurred during communication between modules, and the raw speed limitations of the host computer. Little effort was expended in making SAM as small or as fast as possible.

Issues

SAM was a pioneering effort in story understanding, an attempt to directly confront the messy, but real, problems associated with reading connected texts, as opposed to isolated sentences. It was also the first system which brought enough knowledge to bear on a domain that certain interesting problems in summarization, question-answering and machine translation could be attacked.

The version of SAM which was constructed for reading newspaper articles contains situations describing motor vehicle accidents, plane crashes, train wrecks, oil spills, and state visits. In each of these domains, SAM has processed at least one story, ranging from 2 to 10 input clauses, completely from English text input to English summary or question-answering output. It has also "understood" at least four other stories from each domain, using hand-coded analyses of the text.

The process of designing a script for a new domain is now well-understood, though tedious. SAM's approach to script management appears to be efficient enough to allow reasonable access to any piece of information a script-based system might need. Therefore, SAM and its successors are extensible. Each new script is constructed and applied in the same way as existing ones.

SAM, of course, was never a practical system, being vast, slow, and as is especially the case with multi-module programs, fragile. It is slow, however, because it tries to do the job right by understanding every word it reads at a depth that makes it possible to produce a variety of outputs that a human would find reasonable and appropriate. In a research effort directed at an area as large as text understanding, the only reasonable way to proceed is to design a system which, like SAM, consists of a community of experts, each accessing its own specialized knowledge base, as it tries to contribute to the problem at hand (cf. the "knowledge sources" of the Hearsay-II speech processing system, Erman and Lesser, 1975).

Natural language processing research has advanced to the point where a number of plausible proposals have been made describing the sources of knowledge which are needed for story understanding. To name a few, we have story grammars (Rumelhart, 1975), frame-based knowledge (Minsky, 1975; Charniak, 1972), causal/mechanical knowledge, e.g., "commonsense algorithms" (Rieger, 1975), scripts, plans, goals, and belief systems (Abelson, 1973; Schank and Abelson, 1977). The key research problem in the coming years will be to build a system capable of using these diverse sources of knowledge.

To see what some of the problems might be with such an integrated system, consider the following made-up detective story, which has elements of script-based processing in it:

Spillane strolled into the Cafe Budapest. While the waiter was taking his order, the owner, a notorious Mafia figure, approached them threateningly.

The first sentence and the beginning of the second are clearly accounted for by the restaurant script. However, the restaurant script offers no information about the threatening approach of the owner. It simply explains what he is the owner

conceptual elements which are there explicitly, *avoiding inference as far as possible*. In SAM, we deliberately reserved the task of inferring the things which an input leaves out for the "memory" routines (PP-Memory and the Script Applier), rather than for ELI. This is because making inferences of this type depends on the use of world knowledge, rather than on the superficial semantic information ELI possesses as part of its knowledge of English.

ELI builds only conceptual entities which are present explicitly in the input. It constructs its meaning representations by filling slots in conceptual structures which are usually derived from the surface verb. A particular sentence invoking a conceptual structure will fill in some, but not all, of its slots. As an illustration of conceptual slots which may or may not be filled, consider how ELI would handle the following simple story:

John took the BMT to Manhattan to see a play. At the theatre, he walked over to the ticket counter and asked for a ticket. The usher took it from him and showed him to his seat. The play was so offensive that John decided to leave. The theatre refused to refund his money.

When analyzing the first sentence, the Analyzer would not make any inference about where John came from. Similarly, in parsing "... asked for a ticket," it would not make any assertion about the recipient of the communication, other than the default assumption that this must be some "higher animate". Finally, ELI would not attempt to specify references, pronominal or otherwise. The inferences needed to fill empty slots or to make reference specifications depend on detailed world knowledge, and so are more properly performed by the "memory" routines.

ELI maps the surface text into a conceptualization: a piece of data expressing the "inference-free" meaning of the sentence. From this point on SAM deals directly with the meaning representation. The details of the sentence as it actually appeared in the story are lost. This mode of operation is consistent with our claim that understanding is language-free, in a deep sense. This claim is supported by many psychological experiments on the recall of text (e.g., Bartlett, 1932; Johnson-Laird, 1974; and Kintsch and Monk, 1972) which indicate that the representation of stories in memory is "conceptual" or "propositional". What is remembered are the ideas in a text, not the actual words used. ELI sends its results to PP-Memory, the second module of SAM, which is a memory for Picture Producers (PPs).

Conceptualizations are built out of two ingredients: PPs, and propositions about PPs whose central elements are the primitive ACTs and STATEs of Conceptual Dependency. (Chapter 2 introduces the meaning representation. Conceptual Dependency; for a detailed description of CD, see Schank et al., 1975.) PP-Memory's job is to find the PPs in the conceptualization and assign tokens to them. The tokens are tags or handles for the PPs which will be used by all the

of. Other types of knowledge structures must be employed to account for the owner's unexpected behavior. Scripts are necessary, however, to set the scene, and to indicate what is unusual or unexpected in the story. A theory of integration is clearly needed to control the interplay of knowledge sources such as is needed to understand this story. Such a theory, based on a mechanism called a *hierarchical task manager*, is under development (Cullingford, 1979), but a description of it is well beyond the scope of this book.

AN OVERVIEW OF SAM

SAM is configured as a set of three modules: ELI, which analyzes the text into a meaning representation; PP-MEMORY, which tags and identifies references to Picture Producers (PPs); and APPLIER, which applies scripts.

Control is passed around among the modules of SAM in a co-routine fashion. One program may run for a while, send elsewhere for some information it needs to continue, and eventually regain control. Since SAM is designed to read stories by making heavy use of scripts, the basic job of understanding is performed by the Script Applier. However, script knowledge can be, and is, exploited by the other modules as well.

Transforming the English text of a story into a CD meaning representation is the job of the Analyzer, ELI (English Language Interpreter). This is an extremely complicated program whose operation is described in Riesbeck (1975) and Riesbeck and Schank (1976). Script application works using the language-free output of ELI. Although ELI is an integral part of SAM, we will not discuss it in any detail here. A few comments about its function in the story understander may be helpful, however.

ELI is the only module of SAM that is concerned with linguistic knowledge, and it is the only one that worries about the particular ways that English indicates meaning via the choice of word senses, the order of words, the inflection of words, etc. ELI's job in SAM is to extract from an English sentence only the

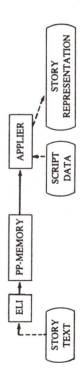

Rectangles represent processes.
Ovals represent stored information
Solid lines represent flow of control.
Dotted lines represent flow of information.

FIG. 5.1. SAM understanding phase.

by the Script Applier, the module which knows about contexts and what can be a role in a context.

When PP-Memory is finished processing ELI's output, it sends the result to the Script Applier. This program has three fundamental problems to solve as it processes a new conceptualization: (1) locating a new input in its database of scripts; (2) setting up predictions about likely inputs to follow; and (3) instantiating the appropriate segment of the script up to the point referred to by the input. Of these three problems, the first one, which we call the *script-management problem*, is the most important. To solve this problem, we had to answer questions such as: Which pieces of SAM's episodic knowledge are relevant at any given point in processing? When should a context be removed, and what should take its place?

The Script Applier controls the comprehension process by consulting its collection of scripts. Each script has several important parts. First, there are the script's characteristic event-chains, or episodes. Since an event in a script may be realized in the world in many ways, the events in script episodes are *patterns*. These are data structures containing constant parts which are expected to appear exactly in an input, and variable parts which define a range of alternative inputs.

A special set of patterns is found in the script "preconditions", or those global facts which SAM assumes to be true when a script is entered for the first time, unless it reads something to the contrary. When the restaurant script is activated, for example, the Script Applier will assert that the restaurant patron is hungry and has money to pay for the meal. If the text has indicated that the patron does not have any money (if, for example, he left his wallet at home), the violation of the precondition will trigger a prediction that the patron will have trouble when it comes time to pay the bill.

An important part of each script is the information which is always in active memory. This includes static data such as an initial list of those patterns which activate the script, how related episodes are combined into chunks or "scenes", time- and place-setting data for the script, and how other, simpler scripts may be used as units in the main script.

The Script Applier's control structure is sketched in Fig. 5.2. The three main procedures are a Pattern-Matcher, a Predictor, and an Instantiator. All the procedures run under an Executive, and all have access to script data. The Pattern-Matcher consists of a routine which sets up desired script contexts one at a time, the Matcher proper, and a set of auxiliary inference processes. The Predictor adds and removes event-patterns based on the pattern currently active and what has gone before.

An "active" script in SAM defines a context which consists of:

1. A list of patterns which predicts what inputs will be seen at a given point in a story.
2. A binding list which links the tokens for PPs produced by PP-Memory with script variables.

other parts of SAM. This module also supplies tokens for roles which the Script Applier has encountered in the course of instantiating a script path, but which were not mentioned in the input. In the above story, the Applier would tell PP-Memory to create a token for the cashier who is implicitly introduced by the conceptualization for "... asked for a ticket."

A PP in an ELI conceptualization may refer either to something SAM has seen before or something "new". Therefore, PP-Memory has to deal with the problem of *reference*: is a new PP in a conceptualization an instance of one already seen, a reference to a "permanent" token known to the system, or a pointer to someone, something, someplace, etc., not seen before? The data structures possessed by PP-Memory encode "time-invariant" facts about PPs such as the "conceptual class" they belong to (human, physical object, organization, etc.), what roles they have in different script contexts, and certain assertions about them which are true in any context. For example, the PP "chair" denotes a "physical object" which people sit on in a variety of contexts. It is realized as "chair" in a restaurant environment, and as "seat" in the bus or subway environment (since it presumably can't be moved). Attached to "chair" in a real human memory would be additional things such as its "visual image" (perhaps the chair at the person's desk), and facts such as "a chair usually has legs, a seat and a back." SAM's memory for PPs does not have much in the way of the latter kinds of information because we frankly don't yet know how to represent images and quantified assertions very well. What it does have is data about how PPs are used in script contexts. PP-Memory is a memory for scriptal roles and props.

At any point in understanding, then, SAM has a list of tokens already identified, and a set of new tokens from the current conceptualization. Some of the new tokens correspond to pronouns in the surface sentence, thus confronting us with the well-known problem of pronominal reference (e.g., in the above story, the word "he" is used to refer to John several times). A more difficult reference problem is created by the occurrence of "it" in "the usher took it from him...". Here, recourse to detailed world knowledge from the theater script about the duties of ushers is needed to enable the correct assignment of "it" to the "ticket" John presumably got from the cashier. In each of these cases, the reference problem is solved by the Script Applier.

Another class of tokens refers to well-known people and things in the world. These are called "permanent" tokens. Examples of permanent tokens in this story are "the BMT" and "Manhattan". Although permanent tokens are identified as such immediately by PP-Memory, they may have differing script roles in different stories. "Chairman Mao", for example, might be the head of state who extended the invitation in a "visiting-dignitary" story, or the deceased VIP in a "state-burial" story. As in the case of pronominal reference, therefore, PP-references of this kind can only be settled by detailed examination of context: the PP with its associated conceptualization, and what has been read before. The PP reference problem is always solved cooperatively in SAM, by PP-Memory and

primary features used in Rolefit are: (1) the conceptual "class" the object belongs to, e.g., human, animate, physical object, organization, etc., and (2) any indicator of the function the PP might have. If the PP is a person, for example, Rolefit would look for an occupation, title or associated script.

If the variable is an "old" one, there already exists a PP-token which has to be compared to the new one. The comparison is carried out by a procedure called Rolemerge. This looks at the conceptual class and function of the input, as before, then checks secondary features of the input PP and the previous one (e.g., residence, age, etc.) looking for contradictions. The Rolemerge process is SAM's method of doing reference specification.

A form of pattern-directed function invocation (Hewitt, 1970) is used to check on special features of the input which SAM may be interested in at any given point. Suppose, for example, the system is reading a story about a car accident and comes to a description of injuries. When the pattern in the script for "someone was hurt" is matched, the Script Applier automatically calls a function to check to see how hurt the person was, i.e., was the person "slightly hurt," "seriously injured" or even "dead". The result of this function call would be to modify predictions about future inputs, e.g., how long the subsequent stay in a hospital is likely to be.

Once an input has been located in a script, the instantiator links it up with what has gone before in that script, and then checks on the effect this may have on other active scripts. If a script is being referenced for the first time, the Applier checks on the script Preconditions to see whether a script is being entered normally, or whether some unusual events are to be expected in the new context because of a previous event. If more than one script is active, the Applier may be able to update the story representation on the basis of the static information that is always available for the scripts. For example, the bus script contains the information that this script is "sequential" with the train script. That is, if the bus script is active when the train script is first invoked, the instantiation of the bus script must be completed before the train script is started. On the other hand, the train script contains the information that a reference to the restaurant script context via "dining car" in an existing train script context defines a "parallel-nested" relationship. Inputs to follow may refer to either script, but the restaurant script should be completed before the train script.

Many transactions between component scripts are handled by the more complex scripts which define the "global" context of the story. For example, taking a bus, train, plane, etc., are known to be "instrumental" means of reaching or leaving the place where the "goal" activity of a trip takes place. The global trip script may be explicitly introduced, as in "John went to Miami on a business trip", or implicitly referenced by one of its instruments, as in "John took a train to Miami." Script situations, as these global scripts are called, provide the most important machinery for the solution of what we have called the script-management problem.

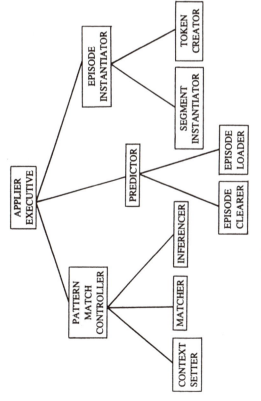

FIG. 5.2. Script applier control structure.

3. A record of the script scenes which are currently active.
4. A list of scriptal inferences—events which have happened which interfere with the normal flow of activity in the script—which are currently outstanding.
5. A script-global "strength" indicator which SAM uses to flag how strongly it "believes" in its inferences.

The Script Applier's basic cycle is to call in these script contexts one at a time, and attempt to locate an input in the context invoked. Candidate scripts are brought into active memory in the following order: first are those script contexts which were explicitly referred to by the input or which were indirectly accessed via a PP or sub-conceptualization in the input; next are the currently active scripts; last are the scripts the system possesses but which have not been invoked.

The Applier uses its Pattern Matcher to decide which script is being referenced by an input. The matching process has two distinct phases. First the "backbone" of the pattern, i.e., the ACTs, STATEs and other constants, is matched against the backbone of the input. If the input backbone is of the right type, then the features of the PPs appearing in the input are checked against the features of the corresponding script variables.

Script variables referred to by an input may either be ones which were previously bound, or ones which have not been accessed. The feature-checking process is slightly different in each case. If the script variable is a "new" one, a process called Rolefit determines whether the candidate PP can be an instance of the variable. Since script variables are really defined by *function*, the two

When the linking process has been completed, SAM updates its predictions about the context, based on the new input and what has gone before, by merging the specific incremental predictions associated with the pattern that was matched with the script global search list. The updated context is then stored, and the next round of processing is started with a call to ELI. After the whole text has been absorbed, the Script Applier constructs a representation of the story that is used by all the postprocessing routines. The representation is a network of causally connected conceptualizations: both those which were explicitly accessed by an input, and those which could be inferred to have happened. "Header" information is also provided which the summarizing and question-answering modules use to get at the important events in the network, the global structure of the story in terms of the scripts which were referred to, and the details of the script role bindings.

SAM's summary and paraphrase methods are discussed in Schank et al. (1975) and Schank and Abelson (1977). Briefly, these routines access the story representation and pick out the "interesting" events recorded there. Since the CD structures SAM deals with internally are interlingual, output can be generated in any language which incorporates the requisite world knowledge. As a machine translation system, SAM can express summaries or paraphrases in Mandarin Chinese and Spanish, or simulate "simultaneous translation" of an English story into Chinese (Stutzman, 1976). The generators used by SAM are modifications of Goldman's BABEL program (Goldman, 1975).

The summary/paraphrase task is one of choosing what it seems appropriate to say. Even if we have the means for expressing any conceivable conceptualization memory may have access to, there is the prior problem of deciding which ones are the best response in a given situation. That is, the summary/paraphrase process has to answer these two questions: (1) which of the conceptualizations marked by the Script Applier as being important are "interesting" enough to be expressed? and (2) what time- or place-setting information should be included to formulate the result into a connected whole?

The ability to answer questions about a story that has been read is in many ways the most crucial test of whether the story has really been understood. The theory underlying SAM's question-answering (Q/A) capability is provided by Lehnert's QUALM, discussed in detail in Lehnert (1978).

AN ANNOTATED EXAMPLE

This section presents some excerpts from the processing log SAM kept as it read a three-line story about a state visit of the Premier of Albania to China.

Our sample story is understood by SAM as referring to the VIP-visit script situation, which has component scripts for travelling, parades, banquets, etc. The first output is from the understanding phase of SAM. Then a summary for

the story is expressed in English and Spanish. Finally, SAM answers several questions about the story.

The text of the story is as follows:

Sunday morning Enver Hoxha, the Premier of Albania, and Mrs. Hoxha arrived in Peking at the invitation of Communist China. The Albanian party was welcomed at Peking Airport by Foreign Minister Huang. Chairman Hua and Mr. Hoxha discussed economic relations between China and Albania for three hours.

Though superficially quite simple, this story contains very real problems of analysis, inference and generation, as will be indicated below. Although the log contains output from every module of SAM, the emphasis will be on the interactions of the "deep-memory" modules, viz., PP-Memory and the Script Applier, rather than on the internal workings of the other modules. The Conceptual Analyzer, in particular, carries a large processing load in SAM. Except for the most complex stories, it uses the most CPU time of all the routines. However, the log will contain only the sentences input to it and the LISP CD representations it computes.

The log from which these excerpts were taken was made under a DEC System-10 utility program called OPSER, which has facilities for starting up and controlling several jobs, and sending any output from the jobs to a single terminal. Lines beginning with a "!" are OPSER messages indicating the module from which succeeding lines of output came. PARSER is the Conceptual Analyzer, TOK is PP-Memory, and APPLY is the Script Applier. SAM starts up with the Script Applier in control:

```
!(APPLY)
SCRIPT APPLIER MECHANISM... VERSION 4.1.... 12 JULY 1976
PROCESSING NEWSPAPER TEXT (TEXT . V3)
AVAILABLE SCRIPTS:
($TRAINWRECK $VIPVIST $VEHACCIDENT)
GETTING NEW INPUT
```

The version of the Script Applier shown here processes newspaper stories about train wrecks, state visits and motor-vehicle accidents. It contains special procedures for handling lead sentences, making predictions from what it finds in them, and taking care of the reference problems that the complicated noun groups found in these stories often cause.

PARSER gets control and analyzes the first sentence. The conceptualization for "arrived" says that a group consisting of Premier and Mrs. Hoxha PTRANSed themselves into the city of Peking, and that the arrival happened in some temporal relation to an invitation by Communist China. (PTRANS is the

CD action primitive for events which contain a change in physical location. The MODE specifier on the conceptualization indicates that the PTRANS ceased ("arrived" vs. "went") in Peking.)

Next TOK replaces references to PPs in the conceptualization with tokens which name the property-list structures that the memory modules use. If the PP is a "permanent token", a well-known person or place in the world, TOK also copies the information from the permanent token onto the new token created for this story. "Enver Hoxha", "Peking", and "Albania" are examples of permanent tokens.

!(PARSER)
Sunday morning Enver Hoxha, the Premier of Albania, and Mrs. Hoxha arrived in Peking at the invitation of Communist China.

CONCEPT: GN1
((ACTOR TMP32 <=> (*PTRANS*) OBJECT TMP32
    TO (*INSIDE* PART (#POLITY POLTYPE (*MUNIC*)
                          POLNAME (PEKING)))
    FROM (NIL) INST (NIL))
MODE (MOD1) TIME (TIME2))

MOD1 = (*TF*)

TIM2 = ((WHEN TMP7)(DAYPART MORNING)(WEEKDAY SUNDAY))

TMP7 = ((<=>($INVITATION INVITER (#POLITY POLTYPE (*NATION*)
                                   POLNAME (COMMUNIST CHINA))
        INVITEE (NIL)
        INVITOBJ (NIL))))

TMP32 = (#GROUP MEMBER (#PERSON GENDER (*FEM*)
                          LASTNAME (HOXHA))
              MEMBER (#PERSON GENDER (*MASC*)
                          FIRSTNAME (ENVER) LASTNAME (HOXHA)
                          TITLE (PREMIER)
                          POLITY (#POLITY POLNAME (ALBANIA)
                                          POLTYPE (*NATION*))
                          REF (DEF)))

!(TOK)
top level PARSER atom is: GN1

processing PP:
(#GROUP MEMBER TMP24 MEMBER TMP28)
creating new token: GROUP0

processing PP:
(#PERSON GENDER TMP25 LASTNAME TMP26)
creating new token: HUM0

processing PP:
(#PERSON GENDER TMP11 FIRSTNAME TMP12 LASTNAME TMP13 TITLE TMP19
   POLITY TMP20 REF TMP23)
creating new token: HUM1

processing PP:
(#POLITY POLNAME TMP21 POLTYPE TMP22)
creating new token: POLIT0

processing PP:
(#POLITY POLTYPE TMP59 POLNAME TMP60)
creating new token: POLIT1

processing PP:
(#POLITY POLTYPE TMP74 POLNAME TMP75)
creating new token: POLIT2

PERMANENT TOKEN IDENTIFIED:
POLIT2 IS !POLI101
PERMANENT TOKEN IDENTIFIED:
POLIT1 IS !POLI100
PERMANENT TOKEN IDENTIFIED:
POLIT0 IS !POLI103
PERMANENT TOKEN IDENTIFIED:
HUM1 IS !HUM100

top level TOK atom for GN1 is MEM0

!(APPLY)
NEW INPUT: MEM0

At this point, the Script Applier has received the conceptualization with tokens added, representing the meaning of the first sentence of the story. It is important to note what the PARSER and TOK have done, and what they did not do. The PARSER has not attempted any inferences about where the Hoxhas came from, or how they got to Peking, although world knowledge suggests that they probably flew from their homeland, Albania, to China. Furthermore, though we know that invitations characteristically precede the invited person's actually going somewhere, PARSER has suggested only that there is some temporal relation between the inviting and arriving events. The surface string or input does not directly state who was invited or what the reason for the invitation was, so the PARSER leaves the corresponding slots in the conceptualization empty.

TOK has provided tokens for the PPs appearing in the conceptualization, e.g., the Premier and his wife. It has also recognized that the Premier, Peking, Albania and China are permanent tokens. Like PARSER, however, TOK does not have the knowledge required to infer that the group that arrived is the one that was invited, so it leaves this slot alone. Finally, TOK has not been able to suggest a possible script that the PPs in this conceptualization may be participating in. This is because people, cities and nations are associated with so many contexts that it is impossible to make a processing suggestion.

APPLY searches first for the imbedded "invitation".

!(APPLY)
FINDING IMBEDDED CDS: (MEM6)

SEARCHING FOR MEM6 IN SCRIPT $TRAINWRECK
SEARCHING FOR MEM6 IN SCRIPT $VIPVISIT

LOCATED AT VAR1
BOUND SCRIPT VARIABLE: &INVGSTATE TO POLIT2
TRACK $VIP1 of $VIPVISIT ACTIVATED

SETTING PARSER WORD-SENSES FOR $VIPVISIT

APPLY searches for the input in the trainwreck script and fails. Invitation is found in the VIP-visit script. The pattern found also says that China fills the role of the state which extended the invitation.

Now the system is primed to read more about events from the VIP-visit script domain. APPLY was able to identify the nature of the invitation from the fact that a nation, China, was doing the inviting, rather than a private citizen. Since SAM now assumes that it knows which context is active, it biases the Analyzer to check first on words and phrases which are appropriate for the state-visit context. APPLY now looks for the "arrival" that was mentioned in the input:

SEARCHING FOR MEM0 IN SCRIPT $VIPVISIT

PATTERN BACKBONE MATCHED AT VAR3
VARIABLE BINDING CONTRADICTION IN (&PTRORG . GROUP0)
TRYING INFERENCE TYPE CONVEY ON VAR3
PATTERN BACKBONE MATCHED ON DERIVED PATTERN:
((ACTOR &INVDGRP <=> (*PTRANS*) OBJECT &INVDGRP TO
          (*INSIDE* PART &INITDEST)))
SUCCESSFUL MATCH ON DERIVED PATTERN

LOCATED AT VAR3
BOUND SCRIPT VARIABLE:
  &INITDEST TO POLIT1
  &INVDGRP TO GROUP0

GETTING NEW INPUT

Now that the first sentence has been read, a number of predictions about what will come next have been made, and some of the script's variables have been identified. The pattern-match on the "arrival" event contains a typical example of the auxiliary inferencing processes SAM uses to reconcile small differences between an input and a pattern which encodes a specific expectation about what will be read. One of the predictions which is active when the top-level conceptualization is accessed is for a journey by the invited person, specifically, a pattern for an organization such as an airline company or a passenger shipping line to move this person, or a group containing this person, to the country making

the invitation. What SAM gets instead is a conceptualization in which a VIP party moves itself there. In this circumstance, SAM infers that the VIPs were moved by an organization which wasn't mentioned. If this pattern were instantiated for inclusion in the story representation at this time, APPLY would assume that an airline was, in fact, the organization that did the moving.

SAM now starts on the second sentence of the story. PARSER interprets this as a "state welcome" since it is the VIP-visit script which is active:

!(PARSER)
The Albanian party was welcomed at Peking Airport by Foreign Minister Huang.
CONCEPT: GN7
((<=> ($VIPWELCOME WELCOMER (#PERSON TITLE (FOREIGN MINISTER)
                                  LASTNAME (HUANG))
                   WELCOMEE TMP55))
TIME (TIM3) MODE (MOD7))
TMP55 = (#GROUP RESIDENCE (#POLITY POLTYPE (*NATION*
                                    POLNAME (ALBANIA))
                   REF (DEF))
TIM3 = ((WHEN TMP72))
TMP72 = ((ACTOR TMP55 IS (*LOC* VAL (*PROX*
                   PART (#LOCALE LOCTYPE (*AIRPORT*
                                    LOCNAME (PEKING)))))))

As in the first sentence, the top-level conceptualization for "welcomed" is related to another conceptualization by a temporal link. The modifying conceptualization states that "the Albanian party" (a group pronoun) was in the proximity of "Peking Airport". After TOK has processed PARSER's output, APPLY looks for the latter event:

!(APPLY)
SEARCHING FOR MEM15 IN SCRIPT $VIPVISIT

TRYING INFERENCE TYPE IMRES ON VAR4
PATTERN BACKBONE MATCHED ON DERIVED PATTERN:
((ACTOR &INVDGRP IS (*LOC* VAL (*PROX* PART &PTRTERM))))

SUCCESSFUL MATCH ON DERIVED PATTERN
LOCATED AT VAR4

ROLE INSTANTIATED: &PTRORG

!(TOK)
creating new token: ORGO

!(APPLY)
GOT TOKEN ORGO FOR &PTRORG
BOUND SCRIPT VARIABLE:
  &PTRTERM TO LOC0

This sequence illustrates a typical interaction between APPLY and TOK in the process of inferencing during pattern-matching. APPLY is looking for a pattern where the VIP group comes to the arrival point (e.g., an airport), while the story talks about their already being "at Peking Airport". Thus SAM must make the inference that because the group is already at the airport, they must have arrived there previously. Also, because an airport has been mentioned, APPLY now knows the identity of the transporting organization. It calls TOK to obtain a token of the right type, and binds it to the appropriate script variable.

Now APPLY searches for the "welcoming" event:

```
SEARCHING FOR MEM11 IN SCRIPT $VIPVISIT
PATTERN BACKBONE MATCHED AT WEL4
CHECKING GROUPS: (GROUP1 GROUP0)
POSSIBLE REFERENCE FOUND: GROUP1 IS GROUP0
LOCATED AT WEL4

MERGING TOKENS ((GROUP1 . GROUP0))
```

Here we see the first case of a reference that needs to be filled in. When TOK identified the Hoxhas as permanent tokens, it copied the information it had about these individuals onto the tokens created for them in this story. Additionally, the Hoxha family group was marked as having the same residence as its members, Albania. The group for "the Albanian party" is merged with the original group on this basis. Since SAM keeps only one token around for each script variable, it tells TOK to copy any new information available from the second token it made for the Hoxhas onto the first, and throw the second one away.

This TOK does, and SAM starts on the final sentence of the story:

```
!(PARSER)
Chairman Hua and Mr. Hoxha discussed economic relations between China and Albania for
three hours.

CONCEPT: GN13
((ACTOR TMP171 <=> (*MTRANS*)
MOBJECT (*CONCEPTS* REGARDING
(#CONTRACT
TYPE (*ECONOMY*)
PARTY (#GROUP MEMBER (#POLITY POLTYPE    (*NATION*)
POLNAME (ALBANIA))
MEMBER (#POLITY POLTYPE (*NATION*)
POLNAME (CHINA)))))
INST ((ACTOR TMP171 <=> (*SPEAK*)))
FROM (*CP* PART TMP171) TO (*CP* PART TMP171))
TIME (TIM7) MODE (MOD3))
TMP171 = (#GROUP MEMBER (#PERSON GENDER (*MASC*)
LASTNAME (HOXHA))
MEMBER (#PERSON TITLE (CHAIRMAN)
LASTNAME (HUA)))
```

PARSER interprets this event as a dual-MTRANS involving a group consisting of Hoxha and Hua, about an "economic contract" (agreement of some sort) between the countries of Albania and China. After TOK has finished, APPLY searches for the event in $VIPVISIT:

```
!(APPLY)
SEARCHING FOR MEM20 IN SCRIPT $VIPVISIT
PATTERN BACKBONE MATCHED AT TALK2

LOCATED AT TALK2

BOUND SCRIPT VARIABLE:
&INVITOBJ TO CNTRCT0
&GRP1 T8 GROUP2
```

Now all three sentences have been recognized within the VIP-visit script. The final conceptualization about an economic agreement has realized one of the main conceptualizations (Maincons) of the script, since this is a possible reason for the state visit. Other possible reasons, not instantiated in this story, include the signing of a treaty or the issuance of an official communique. APPLY is prepared at this point to hear about other official ceremonies, or about the VIPs leaving Peking for home.

There are no more story inputs, so APPLY builds a memory representation for the story:

```
BUILDING STORY REPRESENTATION FOR (TEXT .V3)

MAKING STORY SEGMENT FOR SUBSCENE $VARRIVE1 IN $VIPVISIT
MAKING STORY SEGMENT FOR SUBSCENE $VWELCOME1 IN $VIPVISIT
MAKING STORY SEGMENT FOR SUBSCENE $VTALK1 IN $VIPVISIT

BINDING SCRIPT VARIABLE &MTGPLC TO POLIT1

EVENT GRAPH:
((EVNT1 EVNT2 EVNT3 EVNT4)
(EVNT5 EVNT6 EVNT7)
(EVNT8 EVNT9))
```

This story has instantiated three episodes from the VIP-visit script: (1) an episode in which a VIP group travels to Peking; (2) an official-greeting episode, acted out, in this case, at Peking Airport; and (3) an instance of the "official talks" episode. APPLY uses the script-variable bindings it has accumulated during the recognition part of the run to instantiate the events in these episodes. Along the way, it has made inferences about variables which the story did not explicitly mention. For example, the place where Hua and Hoxha met for their talks was not explicitly stated, so APPLY assumes it was in the city where the Hoxha party arrived. The result of the instantiation process is the "event graph" of instantiated, interconnected episodes. The event graph, the details of the script variable bindings, and other information about the story are stored in permanent memory.

At a later time, this information is loaded by the summary postprocessor of SAM, which selects events of interest and passes them to a Generator for expression. In the output shown below, ENGLSH is the English generator, and SPANSH is the Spanish generator. (The summarizer SAM uses was programmed by Jerry DeJong. The Spanish output was obtained from a modification of Goldman's BABEL, programmed by Jaime G. Carbonell.)

```
!(ENGLSH)

CONSTRUCTING SUMMARY FROM STORY (TEXT . V3)

PREMIER ENVER HOXHA, THE ALBANIA GOVERNMENT HEAD, AND
CHAIRMAN HUA KUO-FENG, THE CHINA GOVERNMENT HEAD, DISCUSSED
ALBANIA/COMMUNIST-CHINA ECONOMIC AFFAIRS IN PEKING, CHINA
TWO DAYS AGO.
```

For this simple story, the summarizer has chosen to express only the script Maincon. The Maincon has been augmented by setting information provided by the Script Applier. For example, APPLY has inferred that the official discussions took place in Peking, China. The information that TOK had as part of its knowledge of the permanent tokens "Enver Hoxha" and "Chairman Hua" has been reflected in the summary by the additional information about their names and occupations that ENGLSH has been instructed to express.

Now the Spanish generator expresses the summarizer output:

```
!(SPANSH)

CONSTRUCTING SUMMARY FROM STORY (TEXT . V3)

EL JEFE DEL GOBIERNO DE CHINA, HUA, Y EL PRIMER MINISTRO
DE ALBANIA, HOXHA, DISCUTIERON UN TRATADO SOBRE ASUNTOS
ECONOMICOS EN PEKING.
```

Finally, SAM answers some questions about the story it has read. In the Q/A configuration of SAM, PARSER, TOK and ENGLSH are the Analyzer, PP-Memory and English Generator, as before. QA is the question-answering module. The details of the Q/A strategies incorporated in SAM can be found in Lehnert (1978).

PARSER analyzes the first question:

```
!(PARSER)
Who went to China?
```

```
CONCEPT: GN1002
((ACTOR TMP8 <=> (*PTRANS*) OBJECT TMP8
    TO (*PROX* PART (#POLITY POLTYPE (*NATION*)
                     POLNAME (CHINA)))

    FROM (NIL) INST (NIL))
    MODE (MOD0) TIME (TIM2))

TMP8 = (*?*)

!(TOK)
top level PARSER atom is: GN1002

processing PP:
(#POLITY POLTYPE TMP39 POLNAME TMP40)
creating new token: POLIT101

top level TOK atom for GN1002 is MEM101
```

PARSER interprets this as a question, marked by (*?*), about the ACTOR of a PTRANS which ended up in the vicinity of China. TOK assigns a token to China in the usual way. Then QA gets control:

```
!(QA)
NEXT QUESTION:
((ACTOR (*?*) <=> (*PTRANS*) OBJECT (*?*)
    TO (*PROX* PART POLIT101)))

(QUESTION TYPE IS CONCCOMP)
(SEARCHING $VIPVISIT-SCRIPT STRUCTURE)
(FOUND AT SCRIPT STRUCTURE LEVEL)

THE ANSWER IS:
(GROUP0)

!(ENGLSH)
PREMIER ENVER HOXHA AND MRS. HOXHA
```

QA takes the conceptual question, identifies it as a query about a role in a conceptualization, and searches the story representation for an answer. It finds the needed role-filler, Premier Hoxha and his wife, and instructs ENGLSH to express this answer.

The answer to the question "Who went to China?" depends, as is usually the case, on an inference. First of all, the story does not explicitly say that anyone went to China, only that an official party arrived in Peking. The answer depends on the causal-chain inference that an arrival in the capital of a country (or anywhere else in the country) must be preceded by entering that country. The Script Applier, as part of its world knowledge about official visits, built this information into the top level of the story representation. Why the top level? The VIP-visit script is a special case of the trip script. People, especially VIPs, are always taking trips, using standard means of transportation (that is, scripts whose Maincons are based on a PTRANS) to get to and from the places they want to visit. The VIP-visit script has the general structure of a trip. Therefore, the Script Applier keeps a record of the "going" part of the trip, which the question-answering module accesses to find the answer to the question "Who went to China?"

```
!(PARSER)
How did they get to China?

CONCEPT: GN1008
((ACTOR TMP103 <=> (*PTRANS*) OBJECT TMP103
  TO (*PROX* PART (#POLITY POLTYPE (*NATION*)
                          POLNAME (CHINA)))
  FROM (NIL) INST (TIM5))

MODE (MOD1) TIME (TIM5))

TMP103 = (#GROUP MEMBER (#PERSON) REF (DEF))

!(QA)
NEXT QUESTION:
((ACTOR GROUP101 <=> (*PTRANS*) OBJECT GROUP101
  TO (*PROX* PART POLIT102) INST (*?*)))

(QUESTION TYPE IS INSTPROC)
(SEARCHING $VIPVISIT-SCRIPT STRUCTURE)

THE ANSWER IS:
((ACTOR ORGO <=> (*PTRANS*) OBJECT GROUP0
  TO (*PROX* PART POLIT2)))

!(ENGLSH)
MRS. HOXHA AND PREMIER ENVER HOXHA FLEW TO COMMUNIST-CHINA
```

The answer to the question "How did they get to China?" depends on three crucial inferences that the Script Applier has made. First, "they" must be recognized as the Hoxha party. This is a reference problem which TOK and QA solve by using the same methods that the Script Applier used to determine the reference for "the Albanian party" in the story input. Secondly, "China" was recognized as "Communist China" by the Script Applier, rather than "Nationalist China", on the basis of its knowledge of where "Peking" is. Finally, the instrumental means that enabled the Hoxhas to get to China was determined by a role-instantiation inference that the Script Applier made when the phrase "... welcomed at Peking Airport" was read. As in the answer to "Who went to China?", the answer to "How did they get there?" is stored in the story representation as the instrument of the conceptualization which summarizes the "going" part of the State-Visit Trip.

```
!(PARSER)
Why did Enver Hoxha go to China?

CONCEPT: GN1015
((CON (*?*) LEADTO
  ((ACTOR TMP160 <=> (*PTRANS*) OBJECT TMP160
    TO (*PROX* PART
        (#POLITY POLTYPE (*NATION*)
                 POLNAME (CHINA)))
    FROM (NIL) INST (NIL))
  MODE (MOD2) TIME (TIM6))) MODE (NIL))

TMP160 = (#PERSON GENDER (*MASC*) FIRSTNAME (ENVER)
                                  LASTNAME (HOXHA))

!(QA)
NEXT QUESTION:
((CON (*?*) LEADTO
  ((ACTOR HUM102 <=> (*PTRANS*) OBJECT HUM102
    TO (*PROX* PART POLIT103)))))

(QUESTION TYPE IS CAUSANT)
(SEARCHING $VIPVISIT-SCRIPT STRUCTURE)

THE ANSWER IS:
(BECAUSE ((CON ((ACTOR GROUP2 <=> (*MTRANS*)
   INST ((ACTOR GROUP2 <=> (*SPEAK*)))
   MOBJECT (*CONCEPTS* REGARDING CNTRCTO)
   FROM (*CP* PART GROUP2)) TIME (TIME10))
   IS (*GOAL* PART (GROUP2))) TIME (TIME10)))

!(ENGLSH)
BECAUSE CHAIRMAN HUA KUO-FENG AND MR. ENVER HOXHA WANTED TO DIS-
CUSS CHINA/ALBANIA ECONOMIC AFFAIRS.
```

This concludes our sample computer run of SAM on a newspaper story. Let's highlight once more some of the important inference processes which actually came into play as SAM read this story.

As the first sentence is processed, a procedure called Rolefit checks to see that at least one member of the group that arrived is a Very Important Person. This is done to establish that this event fits into VIP-visit script rather than some other script, such as the tourist script. An allied process, Rolemerge, is used in the second sentence to determine that "the Albanian party" is the same group as the one mentioned in the first sentence, namely Premier and Mrs. Hoxha. Note that in the second sentence, a special sense of "welcome" is used which typically involves bands, speeches, etc. This sense of "welcome" is itself a script imbedded in the VIP-visit script, and is analyzed as such by SAM within the state-visit context.

Other inferences which SAM makes can be seen in the outputs produced for the story. The need for time- and place-setting information can be seen in the summary, which asserts that the meeting between Hua and Hoxha occurred in

Peking on the same day as the arrival, even though the story does not explicitly say this. (SAM inserts the phrase "two days ago" because it is arranged, by convention, to be reading newspaper articles on Tuesday.) The answer to "Who went to China?" depends on a causal-chain inference, that going to Peking must be preceded by entering the country that Peking is part of. Finally, a role-instantiation inference is required in answering the question "How did they get to China?", which assumes that visiting VIPs who are greeted at airports were transported by plane. This is a typical useful, but only "probably" true, natural inference that story understanders make all the time.

THE PROGRAM ITSELF

Script Structure

This section describes some of the important features of script structure. We will return to the subway script as an illustration.

What does a "standard" trip on the subway look like (in New York, for example)? A patron enters the station and goes to a turnstile. Next, the patron puts a token in, passes through, and goes to the appropriate platform. Eventually, the train comes. The patron enters and finds a seat. After a number of stops, the destination is reached, the patron leaves the train and exits from the station.

This stereotyped sequence of events is the "backbone" of the subway script, $SUBWAY, as understood and used by millions of commuters in New York, and, with minor variations, in other cities as well. In each case, what we have is an organization (the subway company or Authority) providing a certain kind of transportation to a member of the public in return for money. In the fundamental subway script, there is a cast of characters ("roles"); the objects they use while going about their business ("props"); and the places ("settings") where the script's activities happen. The roles, props and settings of a script taken together make up the script *variables*, which are matched up against the real-world people, places and things that a story contains. (Upper case names preceded by "$" indicate a script, and names preceded by "&" indicate a role from a script. Thus, DRIVER would be the "driver" role from the bus script, $BUS.)

Below is a list of the roles of the subway script:

&PATGRP   a group of subway riders
&CASHIER   the cashier
&CONDUCTOR   the conductor
&DRIVER   the person controlling the train
&SUBORG   the subway organization

Picture Producers (PPs) which fill script roles must belong to one of the "primitive", higher-animate PP-classes of Conceptual Dependency. For example, the

patron role in $SUBWAY must be filled by a PP of the class "person" or "group", since we want to be able to accept both "John Smith" and "Mr. and Mrs. Smith" as role fillers. The subway company providing the service, for example, "the BMT", must belong to the class "organization".

The settings of a script are the places where the script's events happen. Settings belong to the PP-class "locale". In $SUBWAY, the three most important settings are the originating station, the inside of the car the patron selects, and the destination station.

The props of a script are associated either with the script's roles or its settings. Examples of the former are small objects, such as tokens and coins (PP-class "money"), which people handle and carry around. The latter props have the function of "furniture" in a setting. For example, the cashier's booth and the turnstile are furniture in the subway concourse; seats and bubble gum machines are furniture on a platform. (These PPs have the class "physical object".) A special prop in $SUBWAY is the train itself. This is an example of a "structured" physical object whose parts, the cars, are important locations for script activity in their own right. The props of $SUBWAY include:

&TOKEN   a token
&FARE   money paid for a token
&TURNSTILE   a turnstile
&PLATSEAT   a seat on the platform
&SUBWAY   the train itself
&SUBWAYCAR   one of the cars
&CARSEAT   a seat on the car
&STRAP   a strap for the patron to grasp
&EXITGATE   the gate leading from the platform at the destination station

The most important components of $SUBWAY are its events, involving the roles, props and settings. An example is the patron's giving money to the cashier at the cashier's cage. The events in all of SAM's scripts are based on a single CD ACT or STATE primitive, with appropriate script variables filling the slots in the conceptual structure. The event described above would look like:

$$((ACTOR \ \&PATGRP <=> (*ATRANS*)$$
$$OBJECT \ \&FARE \ TO \ \&CASHIER))$$

This uses the CD action primitive ATRANS, which signals an abstract transfer of possession or control.

Several things need to be emphasized about events in scripts. First of all, they are *language-free*. The CD representation of an event provides a canonical form into which SAM's Analyzer maps the many surface strings or inputs which are conceptually "equivalent". We would use the same form whether the sentence were "John gave 50 cents to the cashier," "The cashier got 50 cents from

John," or "50 cents was received from John by the cashier." The use of CD representation thus cuts down tremendously on the size of the script, since only the conceptual content of sentences need be considered. It also reduces the amount of processing SAM needs to do, since the needed inferences can be tied directly to the conceptual events, rather than having to be duplicated for each "equivalent" surface string.

Another point about script events is that they contain both "constant" parts (e.g., ACTOR and *ATRANS* in the example given above) and "variable" parts (e.g., &PATGRP and &FARE). Each event, therefore, is really a *pattern*—a data structure designed to match an arbitrary range of real-world events. For example, any member of the public can ride on the subway, so the corresponding slot in the script's events cannot be fixed but must accept any person or group that comes along in a story. In the "paying the cashier in the subway" activity, we need a way to specify the things which are always true. For example, this event has a person handing over an amount of money to another person who is an agent of the subway organization. We also have to provide for things which can vary in small details. The fare may be expressed as "fifty cents" or a "half dollar", "John" may pay the cashier, or "John and Mary" may pay.

In one common form of pattern matching, a script role is compared with a person or organization mentioned in a story. The following is a definition of a typical person as it would exist in property-list format in PP-Memory:

"Dr. Marcus Welby, 53, of 45 Orchard St., New York"

HUM0:

    CLASS (#PERSON)
    TITLE (DOCTOR)
    OCCUPATION (*MD*)
    (PERSNAME (MARCUS)
    SURNAME (WELBY)
    AGE (53)
    GENDER (*MASC*)
    RESIDENCE (LOC0)

LOC0:

    CLASS (#LOCALE)
    LOCTYPE (*ADDRESS*)
    STREETNUMBER (45)
    STREETNAME (ORCHARD STREET)
    POLITY (POL0)

POL0:

    CLASS (#POLITY)
    POLTYPE (*MUNIC*)
    POLNAME (NEW YORK)

(We're assuming that "Marcus Welby" is a permanent token known to PP-Memory. This is the basis for the specification of "medical-doctor" under the OCCUPATION property. Similarly, "New York" is known to be a city.)

Suppose that Marcus Welby is taking a ride on the subway. At some point, the token HUM0 might be matched up against the script variable for the patron role, &PATGRP. This script variable has the following property-list definition:

&PATGRP:

    CLASS (#PERSON #GROUP)
    DUMMY T
    SFUNCTION (*NONE*)

This means that the atom &PATGRP is a dummy variable to be bound to PPs belonging to either the PP-class "person" or "group". Since Welby is a person, so far so good. The property SFUNCTION states that a PP which can fill this role in the script must not have some other function in the script (i.e., a subway patron can not be the same person as the subway train driver). Indicators of the functions people can have are to be found on the OCCUPATION and FUNCTION properties of the corresponding token. Here, the occupation *MD* is not one which is internal to $SUBWAY, so again the PP checks out. If, however, the PP were "Marcus Welby, the driver", the token would contain a FUNCTION (*DRIVER*) flag, and the possible role of Welby as the "driver" of the subway would prevent the acceptance of the PP as an instance of the patron role.

This simple example of the relation between a script variable and the real PPs that may instantiate it illustrates two basic facts about roles and props in scripts. First is the observation that they are "abstract" or "generalized". It doesn't matter that Welby is a masculine adult, since all kinds of people ride on subways. This leads to a second fact, namely, that script variables are really defined by *function*. Concentrating on what people do and what objects are for (this might be called an "episodic" approach), rather than on the details of their structure as bundles of features representing various abstract classes (a "semantic" approach) makes psychological sense. When asked what a waiter is, for example, people invariably reply on some functional basis such as "a person who takes orders in a restaurant and brings people their food."

The basic idea in defining a pattern is to include only the minimum amount of information needed to uniquely identify the event. Consider, for example, the pattern for:

"Patron enters station"

    ((ACTOR &PATGRP <=> (*PTRANS*)
    OBJECT &PATGRP
    TO (*INSIDE* PART &STATION1)))

This pattern would be matched by the conceptualizations corresponding to inputs such as:

(a) John and Mary went into a subway station.
(b) John walked into a subway station.
(c) John strolled out of a restaurant up the street into a subway station.
(d) John went into the BMT.

Example (a) would instantiate the pattern because, as we explained above, John and Mary form a group undistinguished by function. In example (b), the pattern would consider the fact that John "walked" to the subway as insignificant; it would create the same conceptualization if John had "sauntered", "rambled", "ran", or even "come in on a skateboard". In (c), where John came from is of no interest to $SUBWAY, although in this case, it would constitute a signal to $RESTAURANT (presumably active at this point) that this script should be closed before $SUBWAY is opened. Finally, (d) would instantiate the pattern because PP-Memory would contain a permanent token for "BMT", which is marked as a subway organization.

An important class of patterns which will serve to illustrate all of them is that of *headers* of scripts. A script header is a collection of patterns for those events which will "invoke" or "initiate" a script. Each header has a set of predictions about what should happen next in a particular context; these patterns (and thus these predictions) are the only ones present in active memory if the script has not been accessed by the conceptualizations read so far.

The basic rule in defining a script header is that a complete event is needed to bring the script into play. That is, in order for a script to be instantiated, a conceptualization must be recognized rather than just because "a restaurant" is mentioned. For example, $RESTAURANT should not be invoked just because "a restaurant" is mentioned. This is not to say that script-related information should be completely suppressed, because it may be useful in later stages of understanding. For example, in "I met a truck driver in a diner", remembering the role the person had in $TRUCK may be crucial to understanding what he might say or do later.

Conceptualizations can be produced not only by surface clauses, but also by certain kinds of prepositional phrases. Such phrases can act as complete thoughts by modifying the time- or place-setting of the main event. Consider the following sentence:

Mary was killed in an accident.

The above sentence can be paraphrased roughly as "When there was an accident, Mary was killed." The top-level event of Mary's being killed is placed into some temporal relation to the "accident". Thus just the prepositional phrase "in an

accident" is sufficient to create a conceptualization which can invoke the entire accident script.

Script headers come in four varieties, which are ranked on the basis of how strongly they predict that the associated context will be instantiated. The first type is called a *precondition header* (PH) because it triggers a script on the basis of a main script precondition being mentioned in the text. (A precondition is an important global condition which SAM assumes to be true when a script is activated, unless the text says otherwise.) As an example, the sentence "John was hungry" is a PH for $RESTAURANT because it is an enabling condition for the main conceptualization (INGEST food) of the script. A story understander having access to both scripts and plans would make the prediction (a relatively weak one, to be sure) that $RESTAURANT would come up because this is known to be a common means (i.e., a plan) of getting fed. A related PH would be an actual statement of the goal that the script is normally assumed to achieve, or one from which that goal could easily be inferred. In "John wanted to eat a hamburger" or "John wanted some Italian food", the inference chain to the script precondition is relatively straightforward. Patterns for PH's are explicitly stored in the script, since SAM does not have the ability to use plans.

A second type of header, which makes stronger predictions than a PH about the associated context, is the *instrumental header* (IH). An IH commonly comes up in inputs which refer to two or more scripts, at least one of which can be interpreted as an "instrument" for the others. For example, in "John took the subway to the restaurant", both $SUBWAY and $RESTAURANT would be predicted, since subsequent inputs about either make perfectly good sense. Here, the reference to $RESTAURANT is anticipatory, and $SUBWAY is a recognized instrumental means of reaching locales in which more important script goals can be expected to be accomplished.

The notion of a time-place setting for a script leads to the third and most strongly predictive type of header, the *locale header* (LH). Many organizations have a "residence" or "place of business" in which they characteristically carry on their activities. They may have distinctively designed ornaments or buildings (e.g., a pawn shop's sign, a barber's pole, or McDonald's Golden Arches) which signal their script to the world. When an understander reads that an actor is in the proximity of the residence, or, better yet, inside the residence, its expectations about the occurrence of the script are correspondingly reinforced. Examples of LH's are "John went to the soccer field" and "John went into the Museum of Modern Art."

The final type of header is a flat assertion that the script occurred. Examples include:

There was a car accident.
An earthquake struck.
John went on vacation.
Mary went sailing.

Such a *direct header* (DH) is the top-level pattern in a script. DHs are always the first patterns to be checked in a context, since they have the maximum predictive power. They are always checked, since sentences (especially from newspaper stories) may use them to fill in a role or other attribute of the script. Consider, for example, phrases such as "a two-car crash", "a violent hurricane", "a three-day state visit."

Here are the headers of the subway script:

SBIN1:   [Direct Header]
((<=> ($SUBWAY MAIN &PATGRP PTRORG &SUBORG
                        ORIG &ORIG DEST &DEST)))

SBIN2:   [Locale Header]
((ACTOR &PATGRP <=> (*PTRANS*
            OBJECT &PATGRP
            TO (*INSIDE* PART &STATION1))))

SBIN3:   [Instrumental Header]
((ACTOR &SUBORG <=> (*PTRANS*
            OBJECT &PATGRP
            TO (*PROX* PART &DEST)))

SBIN4:   [Precondition Header]
((CON ((ACTOR &PATGRP <=> (*PTRANS*
            OBJECT &PATGRP
            TO (*PROX* PART &DEST)))
            IS (*GOAL* PART &PATGRP)))

The DH is intended to handle conceptualizations corresponding to inputs such as "John took a subway ride to Coney Island." The LH takes care of sentences such as "John walked into the Boro Hall subway station." The IH will handle conceptualizations such as "The IRT took John to Shea Stadium." Finally, the PH would match conceptualizations for sentences such as "John wanted to go downtown."

Activities in scripts are stereotyped. Events follow one another in one of a small set of recognized ways. On entering the subway, for example, the patron may either proceed directly to the turnstile, or stop to buy a token. A chain of event-patterns describing one of these well-understood activities is called an *episode*. "Buying a token" is an episode consisting of the events: "enter the station", "see the cashier's cage", "go to it", "ask for a token", "be told the fare", and "pay the fare". Note that the script demands that the fare be paid *before* the token is handed over. This is how this episode is always structured in the subway script, although the actions can be reversed in other scripts, such as when a person is buying an ice cream cone.

Every episode has a main conceptualization, or Maincon, which is the goal, or point, of the episode. The episodes (marked with "E") and Maincons (marked with "M") of $SUBWAY are shown in Figure 5.3.

In Fig. 5.3, the branching of paths at (1) leads to the subsequent episodes E2 and E3, which describe alternative ways of arranging to get through the turnstile. A branch of this type is called a *turning point*. The "loops" at points (2) and (3) are for the *cyclic* episodes E5 and E7, that is, for episodes which may happen several times in succession. At (2), several trains may arrive before the one the patron wants, and so the patron must continue to wait.

One could make a single episode out of all the events from entering the subway to leaving the destination station. If we did this, however, we would clearly be ignoring important facts about the structure of $SUBWAY. Some parts of the subway ride are more important, more central to the situation, than others. Getting a token, for example, is an important activity in $SUBWAY because without one a patron can't get through the turnstile to get his ride. Taking a seat on the platform, on the other hand, is not so important because it doesn't really have any effect on whether the patron can get on the train. Another fact is that sometimes different ways to do the same thing may be available. Having a token before the ride, asking for one at the counter, or showing the cashier a special

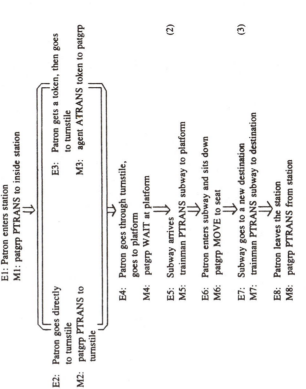

E1: Patron enters station
M1: patgrp PTRANS to inside station

E2: Patron goes directly to turnstile
M2: patgrp PTRANS to turnstile

E3: Patron gets a token, then goes to turnstile
M3: agent ATRANS token to patgrp

E4: Patron goes through turnstile, goes to platform
M4: patgrp WAIT at platform

E5: Subway arrives
M5: trainman PTRANS subway to platform

E6: Patron enters subway and sits down
M6: patgrp MOVE to seat

E7: Subway goes to a new destination
M7: trainman PTRANS subway to destination

E8: Patron leaves the station
M8: patgrp PTRANS from station

FIG. 5.3.   Episodes of the Subway script.

fill in any known tokens. Thus after analysis, the first sentence of the above story looks like this:

"John Smith decided to go to a museum."

GN0:

((ACTOR GN1 <=> (*MBUILD*) to (*CP* PART GN1)
                                    MOBJECT GN2))

GN2:

((ACTOR GN1 <=> (*PTRANS*) OBJECT GN1
                                    TO (*PROX* PART GN3)))

GN1:

(#PERSON PERSNAME (JOHN) SURNAME (SMITH))

GN3:

(#ORGANIZATION ORGOCC ($MUSEUM) REF (INDEF))

PP-Memory replaces the list structures (#PERSON . . .) and (#OR-GANIZATION . . .) with tokens having the appropriate properties:

"John Smith"   HUM0:

                CLASS (#PERSON)
                PERSNAME (JOHN)
                SURNAME (SMITH)

"a museum"   ORGO:

                CLASS (#ORGANIZATION)
                ORGOCC (MUSEUM)
                REF (INDEF)

Then, PP-Memory attempts to identify the tokens just created with tokens already present in its memory: "permanent" tokens for well-known PPs which are always around; and tokens created in the course of reading the story thus far. Assuming that "John Smith" is not a special person known to SAM, PP-Memory can't identify either PP at this point. The REF (INDEF) marker is left by the Analyzer to tell PP-Memory not to look for a referent for the PP among existing entities.

Next, PP-Memory flags the museum script ($MUSEUM) as a suggested script to be tested by the Script Applier. The tokenized conceptualization is then passed to the Script Applier. The Script Applier decomposes the conceptualization into sub-conceptualizations containing only a single CD ACT or STATE. The result of this process is a list of simple conceptualizations which preserve the temporal or causal ordering between events.

pass are all possible ways of procuring a ride. In this case, we have a set of episodes which seem to go together.

The activities of a script which always have to occur for us to recognize that the script has in fact been instantiated are called its *scenes*. The scenes of $SUBWAY are:

$SUBWAYENTER   enter the station and wait at the platform
$SUBWAYRIDE   enter the train and ride to destination
$SUBWAYEXIT   leave the station at destination

"Entering", including buying and using a token, is a scene of the subway script because it is necessary to procure a ride. "Riding" is a scene because this is the transporting activity that the script is all about. "Leaving" is a scene because we can't be sure that the ride is over until the patron exits from the station (he might otherwise just be transferring between subway lines). Each scene of a script is defined by a set of episodes which (1) describes the different ways in which the important activity of the scene can happen, and (2) describes other, less important, actions, such as sitting down on the platform, which can be interlinked with the main episodes, but which don't contribute directly to their accomplishment. The use of "$" before scene names is meant to suggest that each scene (and each component episode) shares some of the features of the script it belongs to.

Applying Scripts

The Script Applier attempts to understand a story by introducing the "largest", most inclusive script it possesses which is initiated by the first conceptualization in the story. As each input conceptualization is recognized in the script, predictions are made by the Script Applier about future inputs. This cycle continues until the system receives an input which does not refer to a predicted event. At this point, it again brings in the largest script which the input initiates, matches roles and props across the script interfaces, checks the preconditions, if any, for the new script, and starts matching inputs in the new context.

As an illustration of the Script Applier's cycle of pattern-matching, instantiation, and prediction, consider SAM's processing of this simple story:

John Smith decided to go to a museum. The subway took Smith to Manhattan. He strolled up Fifth Avenue and entered the Metropolitan Museum. He gave the cashier fifty cents. He looked at some sculpture. Then he looked at some paintings. Later he went home.

The first step in understanding a story is to internalize a conceptualization that the Analyzer has produced. This means that SAM will give the conceptualization the internal labels (such as "GN" below) which are used by memory, and will

Initially, the record of the script contexts contains only the headers for the scripts in the system, and the variables keeping track of the active contexts are null. When the Script Applier receives the tokenized conceptualization for the first sentence of the museum story above, it will look at the museum script, $MUSEUM, because of PP-Memory's suggestion. Because this is the first input, the high-priority search queue of scripts is simply a list of suggested scripts which so far contains only $MUSEUM.

The input is matched successively against the headers. The input matches a Precondition Header of $MUSEUM ("main actor decides/wants to go to a museum"), and $MUSEUM is activated. More predictions from the script are loaded, and $MUSEUM is added to the list of active scripts and the script search list. It is also marked as being the most recent script accessed by an input.

In addition, the setting of the museum script has the property that other scripts can take place there. These scripts (e.g., $BATHROOM and $RESTAURANT) are added to the search list. Next, the Analyzer's handling of lexical and phrasal information is changed. For example, ELI is given special definitions of museum-related words such as "exhibit" and "painting".

Finally, the information that $MUSEUM is usually imbedded in a trip situation is used. $TRIP is a higher level trip script situation which consists of a sequential arrangement of three sub-scripts: $GOTRIP, $GOALTRIP, and $RE-TURNTRIP, or travelling to some destination, doing whatever is the goal or point of the trip, and returning home again. $MUSEUM is an appropriate part of the "goal" segment of $TRIP (i.e., MUSEUM is a part of $GOALTRIP which in turn is a part of $TRIP). Because $TRIP is a script situation, it therefore ranks above $MUSEUM in the hierarchy of scripts, and so it takes control of processing.

The current story representation is the variable !STORY. SAM has now set !STORY to $TRIP, which is the most global script currently active, and has added $TRIP to the active script list. The goal-segment ($GOALTRIP) of $TRIP is set to $MUSEUM. Since $MUSEUM was initiated by a precondition header ("desired"), we may hear about the going-segment of $TRIP, $GOTRIP. At this point, SAM has the patterns ready for $GOTRIP as well as for $MUSEUM. $GOTRIP is set to a list of scripts which are appropriate for moving people around, i.e., scripts involving persons and organizations whose Maincons contain a PTRANS. "John Smith" is assigned the role of main actor in both $MUSEUM and $TRIP.

At this point, a number of processing structures have been partially built. At the top level, the story is assumed to be a $TRIP. $TRIP is currently in the go-segment. The go-segment is as yet unspecified, but is expected to be instantiated by a sequential connection among PTRANS-scripts. The goal-segment is expected to consist of a sequential instantiation of $MUSEUM and, perhaps, some other scripts which are appropriate "goal" activities of a trip. The return-segment will also be a sequential arrangement chosen from among the PTRANS-scripts. Finally, the instantiation of $MUSEUM may contain instantia-

Simple conceptualization-patterns are needed to calculate causal-chain results of connections. For example, the causal result of a PTRANS is a change in the location of the OBJECT PTRANSed. Common sentences in any language clump simple conceptualizations together in arbitrarily complex ways. Consider, for example, the CD structure built by the Analyzer for the following sentence:

Mary Jones died Tuesday of head injuries received in a car accident on Sunday.

((CON GN1 LEADTO GN2))

GN1: ((ACTOR GN5 TOWARD (*PSTATE* VAL (*NEGVAL*))
     REL GN3))

GN2: ((ACTOR GN6 TOWARD (*HEALTH* VAL (−10))) TIME (TIM2))
TIM2: ((WEEKDAY TUESDAY))

GN3: ((CON GN4 LEADTO GN1))

GN4: ((<=> ($VEHACCIDENT VEHICLE GN7)) TIME (TIM4))
TIM4: ((WEEKDAY SUNDAY))

GN5: (#BODYPART TYPE (*HEAD*))
GN6: (#PERSON PERSNAME (MARY) SURNAME (JONES) GENDER (*FEM*))
GN7: (#PHYSOBJ TYPE (*CAR*))

This conceptualization basically says that a negative change in the physical state of a bodypart (belonging, by inference, to Mary Jones) caused a terminal change in her state of health, and that the physical change was caused by $VEHACCI-DENT. The process of decomposition would produce the ordered list of simple conceptualizations: "There was a car accident", "A head injury occurred", and "Mary Jones died." In a story containing the above sentence, SAM would try to locate each unit event in the indicated order. Putting the simple conceptualizations into "narrative order" takes advantage of the natural causal/temporal order of the script. Each new conceptualization is expected to be found on the basis of predictions set up by earlier inputs.

In the course of understanding a story, the Script Applier maintains data structures which describe the state of each script present in the system. This information forms a script context which, if the script is active, is updated whenever a new conceptualization is found to fit within the context. Each script context is defined by: the list of patterns from that script which are currently in memory; an association-list of tokens bound to script variables; the name of the last pattern matched in the script; the list of script episodes currently in memory; the header for this incarnation of the script; and a script-global inference-strength indicator which the Applier uses to flag how probable its inferences appear to be.

The most important data structure is the story representation structed by the Script Applier for the current text. This structure provides access to the final record of the story, from the most general information about the story to the most specific.

tions of $BATHROOM and $RESTAURANT as well. Thus the global story representation, !STORY, has the following property-list structure:

```
!STORY:  (SEQ SCLAB1)

SCLAB1:  (SEQ SCLAB2 SCLAB3 SCLAB4)
    scriptname: $TRIP
    scriptseg: $GOTRIP

SCLAB2:  (SEQ)
    scriptname: $GOTRIP
    scriptq: ($BUS $SUBWAY $TRAIN $DRIVE $WALK)

SCLAB3: (SEQ SCLAB5)
    scriptname: $GOALTRIP
    scriptq: ($MUSEUM $RESTAURANT $MOVIE $THEATER
              $VARIETYSTORE)

SCLAB4: (SEQ)
    scriptname: $RETURNTRIP
    scriptq: ($BUS $SUBWAY $TRAIN $DRIVE $WALK)

SCLAB5:
    scriptname: $MUSEUM
    scriptq: ($BATHROOM $RESTAURANT)
```

This method of introducing $TRIP partly "hides" the activities appropriate to $MUSEUM. The active script list is currently ($TRIP $GOTRIP $MUSEUM). Since the global search list which guides the selection of contexts is built up from the active-script global, the patterns appropriate for $TRIP will be looked at first, then those for $GOTRIP, and finally those for $MUSEUM. The script search list thus has this structure:

```
$TRIP
$BUS $SUBWAY $TRAIN $DRIVE
$MUSEUM
      $BATHROOM $RESTAURANT
```

The pattern for the precondition header matching the conceptualization underlying the first sentence of the story is:

```
((ACTOR &MGRP <=> (*MBUILD*) TO (*CP* PART &MGRP)
    MOBJECT
      ((ACTOR &MGRP <=> (*PTRANS*)
         OBJECT &MGRP
         TO (*PROX* PART &MORG)))))

EXPLICIT (&MORG)
```

The variable &MGRP is the main actor of $MUSEUM, that is, a group of people (perhaps only one) who don't have a function in $MUSEUM and who will perform as the "public" in this script. &MORG is a variable standing for the museum organization, the "actor" providing this service to the public. The property EXPLICIT on the pattern indicates that the museum organization must explicitly appear in the input conceptualization. This avoids a spurious match on an input such as "John decided to go."

The first phase of matching consists of a comparison of the "constant" parts of the conceptualization with the constant parts of the pattern.

The full form of the conceptualization for the first sentence of the story, after PP-Memory has finished with it, is:

"John Smith decided to go to a museum."

```
MEM1:
   ((ACTOR HUM1 <=> (*MBUILD*)
                  TO (*CP* PART HUM1)
                  FROM (NIL)
                  INST (NIL)
                  MOBJECT MEM2)
                  TIME (TIM1) MODE (NIL) MANNER (NIL))

TIM1: ((BEFORE *NOW* X))
MEM2:
   ((ACTOR HUM1 <=> (*PTRANS*) OBJECT HUM1
                  TO (*PROX* PART ORG1)
                  FROM (NIL)
                  INST (NIL))
                  TIME (TIM2) MODE (NIL) MANNER (NIL))

TIM2: ((VAL GN0))

HUM1: "John Smith"

ORG1: "a museum"
```

Note that many "slots", such as the INSTrument of the PTRANS (how John went), have been left unfilled (NIL), because the sentence did not explicitly refer to them.

The basic rules in the backbone match are: (1) "literal" roles and fillers specified by the pattern must appear in the input; (2) extra roles and fillers in the input are ignored; (3) a dummy must be matched against the same conceptual cluster each time it appears in the pattern; and (4) an empty filler slot in the input matches anything, unless the pattern, using the EXPLICIT property, demands that the filler be explicitly present.

Applier resorts to a form of pattern-directed function invocation, to examine the input and the association-list of tentative variable bindings for applicability. In a state-visit context, for example, there is a header pattern looking for the arrival of a VIP. If a group of people actually arrived, this pattern would call a function to search among the members of the group to see if one of them qualifies as a VIP. This is the only way to distinguish $VIPVISIT from other manifestations of the trip situation, such as $VACATION or $BUSINESSTRIP. A characteristic of functions invoked at match time is that they have no real side-effects. If the match fails, all is as before.

The process of fitting new PPs to script variables bound to PPs from previous conceptualizations is called Rolemerge. Note that Rolemerge can, in fact, be implemented in two different places in SAM: in PP-Memory or in the Script Applier itself. The primary reference processor, however, is the Script Applier, since this module may have to act as a "backstop" for PP-Memory in cases where too little information is available in the PPs alone to make the decision. The Applier can make the needed reference in these latter cases because it has additional information from the predicted pattern that was matched.

When the Analyzer reads a definite reference such as "he" or "the man", it produces a PP with the note (REF (DEF)) attached. This is the signal to do a Rolemerge. For example, "he" is mapped into (#PERSON GENDER (*MASC*) REF (DEF)).

This processing note is first seen by PP-memory, which looks for the referent among the tokens already in existence, those created during the processing of the current conceptualization, or in its collection of permanent tokens. If the PP is a permanent token, PP-Memory makes the connection and turns off the processing suggestion. The Script Applier then searches for the PP as though the reference were indefinite. Suppose, for example, the second sentence of our story referred to "the BMT", rather than to "the subway". The PP for BMT will match the predicted subway PP.

Each time a pattern is matched, the "window" on the associated script must be moved to conform with the script's expectations about what will happen next. The prediction process has two distinct phases: (1) clearing patterns from active memory which refer to events which occurred before the presently matched pattern; and (2) bringing in episodes containing the patterns predicted by the present one. The removal of unneeded patterns is accomplished by consulting the permanent memory structures for the script to determine which scenes currently in memory precede the currently active scene.

In the above story, $TRIP is active after the first sentence is read. $TRIP is a linear sequence of going-, goal- and returning-segments, with appropriate events filling the segments. The "conceptual" structure of the story is:

$TRIP

$GOTRIP $GOALTRIP $RETURNTRIP
$SUBWAY $MUSEUM $SUBWAY

Since the pattern does not contain instrumentals, and doesn't care where John is deciding to leave FROM, these roles are not examined. Since the OBJECT to be PTRANSed is the same as the ACTOR of both the PTRANS and the MBUILD, we avoid a spurious match on a sentence such as "John decided to throw a ball at the museum." Finally, because of the EXPLICIT marker on &MORG, the backbone match will fail if the corresponding slot is (NIL). This would abort the match if the sentence were "John decided to go."

The result of a successful backbone match is a list of bindings of candidate PPs to script variables. The next step in the matching process is checking that the candidates can in fact be instances of the variables. The general process of fitting variables to PPs is called Rolefit. When a variable has been previously bound to a token by Rolefit, the fitting process must be augmented by checks to be sure that the new PP can be an instance of both the variable *and* the old token. This process is the manifestation in SAM of Reference Specification, and is called Rolemerge.

Rolefit in this example involves an intersection of the conceptual class markers of PP and token, and a check that the *function* specified by the variable can be performed by the PP. &MGRP can either be a person or a group, since we want the script to handle cases such as "John and Mary went to a museum." "Museum" matches the class specified for &MORG exactly. The point of this initial check on PP-class is to find out quickly if the candidate PP obviously cannot fill the specified role.

The checking of function is also facilitated by the existence of the PP-classes. One feature of each class is that the indicators of function it may contain are to some extent unique to the class. For people, a title or occupation marker strongly suggests the function the person will have in a context. For organizations, the associated script (and the sub- and super-scripts it points to) is the main indicator of function. Physical objects, however, often have a function in more than one script. A car, for example, can figure as a "vehicle" in a driving situation, or as the "object of sale" in a car-showroom situation. A input reference to "a car" maps into a conceptual structure of the form (#STRUCTURE TYPE (*CAR*)), where the reference to *CAR* is a shorthand for the cluster of functions and other information that PP-Memory possesses about cars in general:

```
*CAR*: CLASS (#STRUCTURE
           SCRIPTROLES ((&VEHICLE1 . $DRIVE)
                        (&SALE-OBJ . $AUTOSHOWROOM))
```

Picture Producers fit into scripts on the basis of function. Because of this, a simple comparison of features may not be sufficient to determine whether a PP can be an instance of a variable. This is the case, for example, with the "obstruction" role in $VEHACCIDENT, and the role "group of visiting dignitaries" in $VIPVISIT. When faced with complex functions such as these, the Script

The processing of this story will involve, at various points, predictions from its component scripts: $SUBWAY and $MUSEUM. But there are predictions from situations, over and above what the component scripts provide. The $TRIP situation, for example, predicts that only certain scripts will be used in each of its segments. For example, it initially prescribes that only personal and organizational PTRANS scripts will be referenced. You have to get to the place where something "important" is happening before you can participate in it. Furthermore, a text can refer to a trip in general without filling in too many details. Consider, for example, what it means to "take a train trip", "go on vacation", or "return from Miami".

In SAM, when a story is read with the aid of a situation, its predictions are the first to be looked at. After the first sentence of the story is processed, the $GOTRIP segment of $TRIP is active.

When a predicted pattern has accepted the current input, the input has been "recognized" within the script, and a causal chain is constructed which connects the last input to the new one. This chain contains events which can be plausibly inferred to have happened given the inputs that were read. The Script Applier builds up causal chains by examining the episode structure stored in permanent memory for the active script. Suppose, for example, we read:

Smith went into the BMT. He took the train downtown.

The first sentence instantiates an event from the entering scene, $SUB-WAYENTER of $SUBWAY, and activates the script. The second sentence realizes the Maincon of $SUBWAY, which is part of $SUBWAYRIDE. If the episodes are in the same scene, then the Applier searches the causal successors of the earlier event, remaining on the main paths of the episodes, until the later event is found. While looking at any given main path event, the Applier also checks immediate inferences (forward or backward) from it.

If the original events are in different scenes, the Applier connects the earlier event to a "default" Exitcon from the earlier scene, connects the later event to a default Entrycon for the later scene, and connects the two scenes with the default paths for the scenes in between. Since $SUBWAYENTER and $SUBWAYRIDE are adjacent scenes, only the Exitcon and Entrycon are needed.

The mainpath connection between events that is built is a list of uninstantiated patterns. The Applier takes this list and replaces the occurrences of script variables in the patterns with the PP-tokens bound to them. For example, in the pattern for "patron goes to cashier":

$$((ACTOR\ \&PATGRP <=> (*PTRANS*)\ OBJECT\ \&PATGRP$$
$$TO\ (*PROX*\ PART\ \&CASHIER)))$$

the variable &PATGRP would be replaced by the token for Smith (e.g., HUM0). The above pattern contains a variable, &CASHIER, which is not bound to a PP,

because the role was not mentioned. When this happens, we have a need for a Role-Instantiation inference, in which the Applier asks PP-Memory for a token having properties which are appropriate, in default, for this role. At the time $SUBWAY was activated, PP-Memory was informed about the properties of all the variables having a place in the script. It uses this information to supply the Instantiator with a token for "cashier" in which the PP's place in the script is recorded under the SROLES property:

HUM1:
    CLASS (#PERSON)
    SROLES (($SUBWAY . &CASHIER))

With this token supplied, the realized form of the pattern is:

$$((ACTOR\ HUM0 <=> (*PTRANS*)\ OBJECT\ HUM0$$
$$TO\ (*PROX*\ PART\ HUM1))\ TIME\ (TIME5))$$

where TIME5 defines an appropriate temporal relation between this conceptualization and the other events in the causal chain.

When the second sentence of the story is read, $SUBWAY is activated under control of the $GOTRIP segment of $TRIP. This means that the bindings for "person(s) taking trip", "conveyance", and "destination" are copied from $GOTRIP to $SUBWAY, and various parts of $SUBWAY up to the point referred to by this conceptualization instantiation of $SUBWAY are realized. The instantiation of $SUBWAY up to the point referred to by this conceptualization has several parts. First, the preconditions of $SUBWAY are realized. For example, the Script Applier assumes that Smith has a token to get through the turnstile, and wants to go somewhere on the subway. The "main character" is "Smith", and the "destination" is "a museum", which both already exist, so only "a token" has to be created by PP-Memory. Next, the Script Applier constructs a causal chain from the default Entrycon to the Maincon (which the second sentence instantiates), obtaining tokens from PP-Memory for "cashier", "turnstile", "platform", etc., as it goes. The first part of the third sentence instantiates an Exitcon from $SUBWAY, so a path consisting of the default episodes of $SUBWAYRIDE and $SUBWAYEXIT is constructed, and $SUB-WAY is closed.

The conceptualization for the second part of this sentence ("... he entered the Metropolitan Museum.") activates $MUSEUM using the locale header. At this point the situation moves into the goal-segment, $GOALTRIP, because this is the goal activity that was predicted at the beginning of the story. The specification of the reference for "he" in this clause is made on the basis that the main character in a change of location which is part of a trip is required to be the same as the global main character, &TRPGRP. Activation of $MUSEUM results in the prediction of a possible "admission" event, in which a member of the public pays to get into a museum. This pattern matches the next sentence from the story: "He gave the cashier fifty cents." Now that the main character is inside the museum, the script predicts museum episodes. One of the most important of these is the "cyclic" episode in which the patron goes to an exhibit of some sort, and studies the things on display there. The Maincon of this episode matches the conceptualizations for the next two sentences, where each instance of matching predicts another possible instantiation of the episode.

The last sentence of the story fails to match the outstanding predictions in either $GOALTRIP or $MUSEUM. It does, however, fit the prediction associated with the returning-segment of $TRIP. This pattern has as one of its roles the conveyance that the main character used to get back to where he started from. The conveyance is not mentioned in the last sentence, so $RETURNTRIP assumes that the conveyance that was instantiated in $GOTRIP (the subway) is the one that Smith used to get home.

A CONCEPTUAL THEORY OF QUESTION ANSWERING

Wendy G. Lehnert
Department of Computer Science
Yale University
New Haven, Ct. 06520

ABSTRACT

A theory of Q/A has been proposed from the perspective of natural language processing that relies on ideas in conceptual information processing and theories of human memory organization. This theory of Q/A has been implemented in a computer program, QUALM. QUALM is currently used by two story understanding systems (SAM and PAM) to complete a natural language processing system that reads stories and answers questions about what was read.

Keywords: natural language processing, computational question answering, conceptual information

1. INTRODUCTION

If a computer is going to answer questions in a manner which is natural for human interaction, the computer must have knowledge of how people ask questions and what kinds of answers are expected in return. A competent question answering system must be based on a theory of human question answering that describes:

(1) what it means to understand a question
(2) how context affects understanding
(3) what kind of responses are appropriate
(4) how to extract answers from memory

A theory of conceptual question answering has been developed which addresses these four problems [Lehnert '77]. This theory has been implemented in a computer program (QUALM) which runs in conjunction with two story understanding systems, SAM [Cullingford '77] and PAM [Wilensky '76], enabling these systems to answer questions about the stories they read.

The theory of question answering proposed by QUALM is a theory of natural language processing. This distinguishes QUALM from many other question answering systems which are oriented towards information retrieval. Many systems which attempt to answer questions phrased in natural language have been designed in two pieces: (1) a memory retrieval system, and (2) a natural language interface. Very often the interface problem is considered secondary to the retrieval system and the two subsystems are designed as if they were

----

This work was supported in part by the Advanced Research Projects Agency of the Department of Defense and monitored under the Office of Naval Research under contract N00014-75-C-1111.

theoretically independent of each other [Shortliffe '74, Woods '72].

The theory behind QUALM extends theories of memory processing which originated with the study of parsing [Riesbeck & Schank '77] and generation [Goldman '75]. Conceptual Dependency [Schank '75] has proven to be a strong representational system for the task of question answering. Parsing and generation strategies based on Conceptual Dependency were naturally adopted for question answering without significant alterations. This approach to question answering which utilizes existing theories of natural language processing constitutes a major departure from the information retrieval viewpoint where natural language is considered to be merely a "front end" for a question answering system.

In order to understand questions, QUALM must interface with a conceptual analysis program that parses an English question into its Conceptual Dependency representation [Schank '75]. In SAM and PAM, QUALM interfaces with a parser designed by Christopher Riesbeck [Riesbeck & Schank '76]. In order to produce answers in English, QUALM also needs a generator that can translate Conceptual Dependency representations into English. The generator used by SAM and PAM is based on a generator designed by Neil Goldman [Goldman '75]. All of the processing specific to answering questions occurs on a conceptual level that is language independent. If QUALM interfaced with a Russian parser and a Chinese generator, it would be able to understand questions stated in Russian and produce answers to these questions in Chinese. No changes in QUALM are required to accommodate different languages since the question answering processes are independent of language.

2. CONCEPTUAL CATEGORIES FOR QUESTIONS

When QUALM initially receives a question from the parser, the question is represented as a Conceptual Dependency conceptualization. This conceptualization must then be categorized into one of thirteen possible Conceptual Categories. The Conceptual Categories for questions are:

(1) Causal Antecedent (7) Instrumental/Procedural
(2) Goal Orientation   (8) Concept Completion
(3) Enablement   (9) Expectational
(4) Causal Consequent (10) Judgemental
(5) Verification   (11) Quantification
(6) Disjunctive   (12) Feature Specification
           (13) Request

The conceptual parse of a question represents a very literal or naive understanding of the question. Conceptual Categorization constitutes a higher level of interpretation which is designed to determine exactly what the questioner really means. For example, if a stranger walks up to John on the street and asks:

Q1: Do you have a light?

John would parse this question into a conceptualization equivalent to asking:

Q2: Do you have in your immediate possession an object capable of producing a flame?

If John does not interpret the question any further than this, he could answer:

A1: Yes, I just got a new lighter yesterday.

and then walk away. This sort of response indicates that John did not have a complete understanding of the question. He understood it on a preliminary level, but he did not understand it in terms of what the questioner had intended. His misinterpretation can be explained as faulty Conceptual Categorization. What John understood to be an inquiry deserving a yes or no answer, should have been understood as a request deserving a performative action. The person asking Q1 didn't just want to know if John had a light; he wanted John to offer him a light (flame). In terms of Conceptual Categories, we would say that the question should have been interpreted as a Functional Request rather than a Verification Inquiry.

If a question is not categorized correctly, it will be impossible to produce an appropriate response.

RIGHT: Q3: How could John take the exam?
         (an Enablement question)
         A3a: He crammed the night before.
         (an Enablement answer)

WRONG: Q3: How could John take the exam?
         (an Enablement question)
         A3b: He took it with a pen.
         (Instrumental/Procedural answer)

Q3 is asking about the enabling conditions for taking an exam. In order to take an exam, one has to be prepared for it, presumably be a student, and so forth. Q3 suggests that the questioner does not believe John satisfied some necessary enabling condition. An appropriate answer to Q3 will address this questioned enablement (He crammed the night before, or he bribed an administrator). A3b does not address the Enablement conditions at all. A3b answers the question on a much lower level of instrumentality, indicating that the question was understood to be an Instrumental/Procedural question instead of an Enablement question.

RIGHT: Q4: How did John die?
         (Causal Antecedent question)
         A4: He caught the swine flu.
         (a Causal Antecedent answer)

WRONG: Q4: How did John die?
         (Causal Antecedent question)
         A4b: Well, first he was alive.
         (an Enablement answer)

This time A4b indicates that Q4 was understood to be an Enablement question. A necessary enablement for dying is being alive. But Q4 should not have been interpreted to be asking about the enabling conditions for dying. Q4 is more reasonably understood to be asking about the cause of John's death: Was it an accident? Was he ill? Did he kill himself?

RIGHT: Q5: How did John get to Spain?
         (Instrumental/Procedural question)
         A5a: He went by plane.
         (Instrumental/Procedural answer)

WRONG: Q5: How did John get to Spain?
         (Instrumental/Procedural question)
         A5b: He wanted to see Madrid.
         (a Causal Antecedent Answer)

An appropriate answer to Q5 would specify the transportational means which was instrumental to John's getting to Spain (he took a cruise, he flew, etc.) But A5b tells us what caused John to go to Spain. A5b answers a Causal Antecedent question instead of an Instrumental/Procedural question.

When Q3–5 are represented in Conceptual Dependency, it is easy to see which Conceptual Category should be assigned to these questions. In QUALM, parsed conceptualizations are run through a discrimination net which assigns a Conceptual Category to each question. But Conceptual Categorization does not constitute complete understanding of a question. Each conceptual question is subject to further interpretive processing before a memory search for an answer can begin.

3. INFERENTIAL ANALYSIS

Complete understanding of a question often involves inferences in addition to Conceptual Categorization. When interpretation of a question does not include analysis by inference, answers may be produced which are technically correct, but completely useless. Suppose John is mixing cake batter and he asks his wife:

Q6: Now what haven't I added?
A6: A pound of dog hair and an air filter.

She's probably right; he probably didn't add a pound of dog hair and an oil filter. But her answer is inappropriate because John was "obviously" asking for what he hadn't added that he should have added. The intent of this question is obvious only when an interpretive inference mechanism can be invoked to supply an implicit constraint. There is an entire class of questions that require the same type of inferential analysis:

Q7: Who isn't here?
    (Who isn't here who should be here?)
Q8: What did I forget to buy?
    (What didn't I buy that I should have?)

In each of these questions, an inference must be made that specifies appropriate constraints for potential answers. When Q7 is asked by a professor upon entering his class, appropriate answers refer to members of the class. When Q8 is asked in the context of shopping for a dinner party, appropriate answers refer to those things that are needed for dinner.

The Universal Set Inference, a general inference mechanism, is needed for questions of this class. This mechanism examines the context of a question and determines appropriate constraining factors. But before this mechanism can be invoked, some process must be responsible for recognizing which questions require this particular inference mechanism. The Universal Set Inference should not be summoned for questions like:

Q9: Who is coming to your party?
Q10: Isn't this the book you wanted?

The successful application of an interpretive inference mechanism relies on the ability to know when that mechanism is needed. This is one way Conceptual Categorization is exploited. One of the thirteen Conceptual Categories is the class of Concept Completion questions. These correspond roughly to fill-in-the-blank questions. During the interpretation of a question, the Universal Set Inference is applied if and only if:

(1) the question is categorized as a Concept Completion question, and
(2) the conceptual question has MODE = NEG

Q6-8 each satisfy these requirements. While the lexical statement of Q8 does not appear to be negated, the conceptual representation for Q8 is equivalent to asking "What didn't I remember to buy?" which is encoded as an MTRANS with negative MODE. Q9 is a Concept Completion question but it fails to meet the criteria because it has a non-negative MODE. Q10 fails because it is a Verification question instead of a Concept Completion question.

A useful system of categorization will provide simple test criteria for inference mechanisms of the sort just described. Different questions require different processing. A strong categorization system can recognize which processes are required for a given question and dictate subsequent processing accordingly.

4. CONTEXT-SENSITIVE INTERPRETATION

In the last section we claimed that one general inference mechanism, the Universal Set Inference, could be invoked to establish appropriate constraints on Concept Completion questions with MODE = NEG. This inference mechanism relies on the context in which questions are asked.

Q7: Who isn't here?

requires contextual information that implicitly specifies who should be here. If this question is asked by a professor in a class, it means "Which of my students aren't here?" If it is asked by a host at a party, it means "Who isn't here who was invited?" Without contextual information, it is impossible to know what implicit constraints are appropriate.

Specific constraints on questions can be derived from whatever scripts [Schank & Abelson '77] are actively operating in a given context. When a script is active, its script-defined roles and role instantiations [Cullingford '77] delineate the universal set these questions implicitly reference.

The Universal Set Inference

Question Category: Concept Completion
Question Criteria: MODE value = NEG
Contextual Criteria: there is an active script

If these test criteria are satisfied, interpretive constraints are imposed by those roles defined in the active script(s).

question	scriptal context	constraining roles
Who isn't here?	party	guests
What didn't I add?	cooking	ingredients
Who hasn't bid?	bridge game	bridge players

Many questions must be understood in terms of their surrounding context. It is therefore crucial to be able to characterize contextual information in terms of general knowledge structures (Schank & Abelson '77) so that general interpretive inference mechanisms can be designed which are sensitive to context without being context-specific. That is, a contextually sensitive processing mechanism should be applicable in different contexts. A theory of question answering that needs to propose a new set of processing strategies for each new context encountered is not much of a theory.

5. CONTENT SPECIFICATION

Once a question has been sufficiently understood, retrieval processes can begin to look for an answer. The first part of the retrieval process decides how much of an answer is needed. Consider the following story:

John went to a restaurant and the hostess gave him a menu. When he ordered a hot dog the waitress said they didn't have any. So John ordered a hamburger instead. But when the hamburger came, it was so burnt that John left.

If asked:

Q14: Did John eat a hot dog?

There are many possible answers. When SAM reads this story, SAM can answer Q14 three different ways:

A14a: No.
A14b: No, the waitress told John they didn't have any hot dogs.
A14c: No, the waitress told John they didn't have any hot dogs and so John ordered a hamburger.

These answers are all different in terms of the amount of information they convey. In fact, answers can vary not only in terms of their relative content, but in terms of the kind of content they communicate. For example, if Q14 had been answered "Yes," in the context of our story where John didn't eat a hot dog, then the content of this answer would be described as wrong.

The decision-making processes that determine what kind of an answer should be returned are part of Content Specification. Content Specification takes into account the Conceptual Category of each question and intentionality factors that describe the "attitudinal" mode of the entire system in order to determine how a question should be answered. A system of descriptive instructions are produced by Content Specification to instruct and guide memory retrieval processes as they look for an answer.

The primary challenge involved in Content Specification is precisely how these instructions to memory retrieval are formalized. It is not enough to say "give a minimally correct answer," or "bring in everything you can find that's relevant." The instructions generated by Content Specification must tell the retrieval heuristics exactly how to produce a minimally correct answer and exactly what has to be done to do to come up with everything that's relevant.

One type of Content Specification mechanism that guides retrieval heuristics are Elaboration Options. Each Elaboration Option has four parts: an Intentionality Threshold, a Question Criterion, an Initial Answer Criterion, and Elaboration Instructions. Intentionality refers to variables within the system that are set with suggestively-named values like "talkative," "cooperative," "minimally responsive," etc. The Intentionality Threshold specifies what sort of Intentionality must be assigned to the system in order for an Elaboration Option to be attached to the question. The Question Criterion describes what Conceptual Category must be assigned to the question in order for it to receive the Elaboration Option. If either the Intentionality of the system or the Conceptual Category of the question fail to meet the specifications of the Intentionality Threshold and the Question Criterion, then the Elaboration Option is not used. The Answer Criterion specifies the type of conceptual answer which the memory search must initially return in order for the Elaboration Option to be executed. And the Elaboration Instructions specify exactly how an elaboration is to be extracted from memory and integrated into the conceptual answer.

To see exactly how an Elaboration Option works, we will discuss one of the simpler Elaboration Options that has been implemented in QUALM. Consider the following story:

John went to New York by bus. On the bus he talked to an old lady. When he left the bus, he thanked the driver. He took the subway to Leone's. On the subway his pocket was picked. He got off the train and entered Leone's. He had some lasagna. When the check came, he discovered he couldn't pay. The management told him he would have to wash dishes. When he left, he caught a bus to New Haven.

After reading this story SAM answers:

Q15: Did John go to New York?
A15: Yes, John went to New York by bus.
Q16: Did John eat?
A16: Yes, John ate lasagna.
Q17: Did someone pick John's pocket?
A17: Yes, a thief picked John's pocket.
Q18: Did John pay the check?
A18: Yes, John paid the bill.

These are answers SAM gives when it has a talkative Intentionality. If SAM were running with a less than talkative Intentionality, each of these questions would have been answered with a simple "Yes." The longer answers (A15-18) are the result of the Verification Option. This is a very simple Elaboration Option which is defined as follows:

The Verification Option

Intentionality Threshold: Talkative
Question Category: Verification
Answer Criterion: initial answer is Yes
Elaboration Instructions:

final conceptual answer is "Yes, *X*" where *X* is the conceptualization found in the story representation that matches the question concept.

The retrieval heuristics for a Verification question search the story representation for a conceptualization matching the conceptual question. If it finds a match, the initial answer is Yes. A conceptualization from the story representation doesn't have to correspond to the question concept exactly in order to match it; it may contain more information than the question concept. This is why A15-17 appear to volunteer information. A15 tells how John went to New York, A16 says what John ate, and A17 asserts who stole John's wallet.

6. FINDING AN ANSWER

Retrieval heuristics vary for each Conceptual Category of questions. A number of interesting problems arise in designing processes that extract information from memory. We will briefly outline three such problems which reflect the scope and depth of the difficulties involved.

6.1 Integrative Memory Processing

Expectational questions are interesting because they cannot be answered on the basis of a story representation alone. Expectational questions correspond roughly to why-not questions. These questions require "integrative" memory processing. The term integration is very often used in the context of adding new information to memory. A single unit of information is "integrated" into a larger memory structure. But in the context of retrieving information from memory, an integrative process is one which combines information from different sources to produce new information.

After reading the burnt-hamburger story, SAM answers:

    Q19: Why didn't John eat a hot dog?
    A19: Because the waitress told John they
         didn't have any hot dogs.
    Q20: Why didn't John eat the hamburger?
    A20: Because the hamburger was burnt.

These questions are answered by an integrative process that combines the story representation with predictive mechanisms in order to reconstruct expectations that were alive at some time during the understanding process. When John ordered a hot dog we had an expectation that he would eat a hot dog until we heard there were none. When John ordered a hamburger we expected him to eat a hamburger until we heard that the hamburger was burnt and John just left. Expectational questions ask about expectations which were aroused at some point during the understanding process and then subsequently violated by an unexpected turn of events. Had we asked "Why didn't John swim across the lake?" the question would seem unreasonable since we never had any expectations about John going swimming or crossing a lake.

The theories of memory representation implemented in SAM and PAM adhere to the premise that a story representation should encode information about things that happened in the story. This includes inferences about things that probably occurred (but weren't explicitly mentioned) as well as conceptualizations for events that were explicitly described in the input story. But Expectational questions ask about things that didn't happen. To answer an Expectational question, we must use the same predictive processes used during story understanding to reconstruct failed expectations which were alive at some time during understanding. The reconstruction of failed expectations is achieved by an integrative

memory process called ghost path generation.

The generation of ghost paths cannot be fully understood without a fundamental understanding of script application [see Cullingford '77]. But some sense of what goes on should be apparent from the following diagram. In this diagram, the chain of events in the center corresponds very roughly to information in the story representation that SAM generated at the time it read the burnt-hamburger story. The two chains on either side correspond to the two ghost paths needed to answer Q19 and Q20.

```
                    John enters
                    restaurant

                    John is seated

                    John gets a menu
                    from the hostess

          ┌──────── John orders a
          │         hotdog
          ↓
waitress     (I1)┌─ waitress tells ┐
serves           │  him no         │
a hotdog         └ ── ── ── ── ── ─┘

┌ ── ── ──┐  (R1) John orders a
│John eats│        hamburger
│the hotdog│
└ ── ── ──┘       waitress serves
                  the hamburger ──────┐
John gets                             │
a check                               ↓
             (I2)┌hamburger ┐    ┌─ John eats ──┐
John pays        │is burnt  │    │  the hamburger│
                 └ ── ── ── ┘    └ ── ── ── ── ─┘
John leaves      John gets         John gets
                 angry             a check

             (R2) John leaves      John pays

                                   John leaves
```

6.2 Answer Selection

While Expectational questions are interesting because they cannot be answered on the basis of a story representation alone, there are many questions that do not need information outside of the story representation which are still difficult to answer. Causal Antecedent questions are complicated in this respect. A Causal Antecedent question is one which asks for the reason behind an event. After reading the Leone's story, consider the following answers:

    Q21: Why did John wash dishes?
    A21a: Because he couldn't pay the check.
    A21b: Because he had no money.
    A21c: Because he had been pickpocketed on the
          subway.

SAM answers Q21 "Because he had no money." But is this the best answer of the three? What factors determine the superiority of one answer over another?

Effective answer selection entails making assumptions about what the questioner knows. Anyone who asks Q21 can be assumed to know that John washed dishes. If we go on to assume that the questioner knows two more things: (1) John washed dishes in a restaurant, and (2) washing dishes in a restaurant is classically what happens when someone eats and then can't pay, then the questioner can infer: (3) John couldn't pay the check. If the questioner can figure out for himself that John couldn't pay the check then A21a does not tell him anything he doesn't know to begin with. A good answer must take into account what the questioner does and doesn't know, and address the knowledge state of the questioner by telling him something new.

A21b is a weak answer for the same reasons that A21a was weak. If someone knows that John couldn't pay a check, they can reasonably infer that John didn't have (enough) money. Both inferences:

1) John couldn't pay the check.
2) John didn't have any money.

can be made by the questioner on the basis of general world knowledge and knowing that John washed dishes in a restaurant. But there is no way the questioner can infer that John was pickpocketed on the subway without additional knowledge of the story. Therefore A21c is the best answer to Q21 as long as we assume the questioner has knowledge about the world and can make inferences on the basis of that knowledge.

If we assumed that the questioner knew nothing about restaurants, A21a would be the best answer. If we assumed that the questioner knew about restaurants but didn't understand about paying for things, A21b would be the best answer. It is impossible to judge various answers to a question without knowing (or assuming) something about the person being addressed.

6.3 Conceptual Organization of Knowledge

When people answer questions, their answers sometimes tell us something about the form and organization of conceptual information in human memory. For example, consider the following story:

John was sitting in a dining car. When the train jerked, the soup spilled.

Suppose we ask:

Q22: Where was the soup?

This is a specification question that can be answered a number of ways. Two common answers are:

A22a: In a bowl.
A22b: On the table.

A much less natural answer would be:

A22c: On a plate.

A22c seems to be very odd answer which conjures up an image of a soup puddle on a plate. This is not the scene most people envision when hearing the story. Most people imagine the soup in a bowl on a plate on a table.

The acceptable and unacceptable answers to Q22 tell us something about human memory organization. It never occurs to people to answer "On a plate." Furthermore, when this answer is given it provokes a wrong image of soup resting directly on a plate. But "On the table," is a natural answer. Why is it that "On a plate," is a bad answer but "On the table," is perfectly reasonable? The soup does not rest directly on the table any more than it rests directly on a plate. Why is it acceptable in one case but not the other? This phenomenon must be accounted for in terms of memory organization.

When people hear this story they assume a causality between the train jerking and the soup spilling. (If asked "Why did the soup spill?" people will answer "Because the train moved.") This causality relies on the fact that the soup is physically connected to the train in some way. This physical connection can only be recognized by constructing a path of physical objects between the soup and the train. This path of connections must be accessed in order to answer Q22. If a path is constructed the same way people build one, it will be easy to retrieve answers to Q22 that seem natural. If the path is built differently, we may end up with an answer like A22c.

Suppose we construct a path like the following:

A BAD PATH: soup (inside-of)
               bowl (on-top-of)
               plate (on-top-of)
               tablecloth (on-top-of)
               table (on-top-of)
               floor (inside-of)
               dining car (part-of)
               train

With this memory representation it is not clear how we can extract the answers A22a and A22b without also getting answers like "On a plate," or "On a tablecloth." There is nothing in this memory representation that tells us where the good answers are. What we need is a memory representation that makes it easy to find a bowl and a table but hard to retrieve a plate.

A BETTER PATH: soup (inside-of)
                  bowl (part-of)
                  placesetting (part-of)
                  tablesetting (on-top-of)
                  table (part-of)
                  dining area (part-of)
                  dining car (part-of)
                  train

This path suggests a very simple retrieval heuristic to produce the answers A22a and A22b: trace the path looking for objects which are connected by either "inside-of" or "on-top-of" links.

The closer a memory representation is to human memory organization, the easier it will be to produce answers that make sense to people. A system of memory representation for physical objects has been proposed [Lehnert '77] which is designed to facilitate inference and retrieval problems of the sort just described. Conceptual descriptions of objects in this system are based on decompositions into a set of seven object primitives in much the same way that Conceptual Dependency [Schank '75] describes actions by decomposing them into a set of primitive acts.

7. CONCLUSIONS

The overall question answering process can be intuitively approached in two stages: understanding the question (interpretation) and finding an answer (memory retrieval). Each of these stages is likewise divided into two parts:

INTERPRETATION:
    [1] Conceptual Categorization
    [2] Inferential Analysis

MEMORY RETRIEVAL:
    [3] Content Specification
    [4] Searching Heuristics

[1] Conceptual Categorization guides the subsequent processing by dictating which specific inference mechanisms, elaboration options, and retrieval heuristics should be invoked in the course of answering a question.

[2] Inferential Analysis is responsible for understanding what the questioner really meant when a question should not be taken literally.

[3] Content Specification determines how much of an answer should be returned in terms of detail and elaborations.

[4] Searching Heuristics do the actual digging in order to extract an answer from memory.

All of the processes within these four phases are specific to question answering per se and are language-independent, operating within a conceptual representation system.

QUALM represents a theory of question answering which is motivated by theories of natural language processing. Within the context of story understanding, QUALM has provided a concrete criterion for judging the strengths and weaknesses of story representations generated by SAM and PAM. If a system understands a story, it should be able to answer questions about that story in the same way that people do. Although the computer implementation of QUALM is currently limited to the application of answering questions about stories, the theoretical model [Lehnert '77] goes beyond this particular context. As a theoretical model QUALM is intended to describe general question answering, where question answering in its most general form is viewed as a verbal communication device between people.

While many of QUALM's question answering techniques are designed for answering questions about stories, QUALM is not limited to stories about a specific content domain. QUALM is applicable to any story that can be understood in terms of scripts and plans [Schank & Abelson '77]. This limitation is not content-specific; it is dependent on the general knowledge structures that are used in text understanding. When new scripts and plans are added to the knowledge base for SAM and PAM, questions can be answered about stories using this new knowledge without any additional alterations to QUALM.

BIBLIOGRAPHY

Cullingford, R. E. (1977) Organizing World Knowledge for Story Understanding by Computer. (thesis) Department of Engineering and Applied Science. Yale University, New Haven, Ct.

Goldman, N. (1975). Conceptual generation. In R. C. Schank, ed: Conceptual Information Processing. North Holland Amsterdam.

Lehnert, W. (1977). The Process of Question Answering. (thesis) Research Report #88. Department of Computer Science, Yale University, New Haven, Ct.

Riesbeck, C. and Schank, R. (1976). Comprehension by Computer: Expectation-Based Analysis of Sentences in Context. Research Report #78. Department of Computer Science, Yale University, New Haven, Ct.

Schank, R. C. (1975). Conceptual Information Processing. North Holland, Amsterdam.

Schank, R. C. and Abelson, R. P. (1977). Scripts, Plans, Goals and Understanding. Lawrence Erlbaum Associates. Hillsdale, N.J.

Shortliffe, E.H. (1974). MYCIN: A Rule-Based Computer Program for Advising Physicians Regarding Anti-Microbial Therapy Selection. (thesis) Stanford Artificial Intelligence Laboratory Memo-AIM251. Stanford University, Stanford, CA.

Wilensky, R. (1976). Using Plans to Understand Natural Language. Proceedings of the Annual Conference of the Association for Computing Machinery. Houston, Texas.

Woods, W.A., Kaplan, R.M., Nash-Webber, B. (1972). The Lunar Sciences Natural Language Information System: Final Report. BBN Report No. 2378, Bolt, Beraneck and Newman, Inc. Cambridge, Mass.

INDEX